Jon Belserak 0121 415-4881 (W)
~~07867 838 758 (m)~~
Univ. of Birmingham 07920-263-702
Elmfield House
ordered during Christmas break Dec 2003

Hebrew Bible / Old Testament
The History of Its Interpretation

Volume I/2

V&R

Hebrew Bible / Old Testament
The History of Its Interpretation

Edited by
Magne Sæbø

VOLUME I
From the Beginnings to the Middle Ages
(Until 1300)

Göttingen · Vandenhoeck & Ruprecht · 2000

Hebrew Bible / Old Testament
The History of Its Interpretation

VOLUME I

From the Beginnings to the Middle Ages
(Until 1300)

In Co-operation with
Chris Brekelmans and Menahem Haran

Edited by
Magne Sæbø

PART 2

The Middle Ages

Göttingen · Vandenhoeck & Ruprecht · 2000

Die Deutsche Bibliothek – CIP-Einheitsaufnahme

Hebrew Bible, Old Testament:
the history of its interpretation /
ed. by Magne Sæbø. –
Göttingen: Vandenhoeck und Ruprecht

Vol. 1. From the beginnings to the Middle Ages (until 1300) /
in co-operation with Chris Brekelmans and Menahem Haran.
Pt. 2. The Middle Ages. – 2000
ISBN 3-525-53507-4

Financially supported by the
Förderungs- und Beihilfefond Wissenschaft der VG WORT, Munich
and by the Norwegian Research Council, Oslo

Manufactured by Hubert & Co., Göttingen

Contents

Supplement to Chapter Five

Ben Sira and the Wisdom of Solomon: Their Interpretative Significance

Preface

The first volume of the project *Hebrew Bible / Old Testament: the History of Its Interpretation*, entitled *"From the Beginnings to the Middle Ages"*, was planned as just one volume, not only for formal reasons, but even more on 'inner' objective grounds. For volume I was intended to comprise, as indicated by its title, the first main part of the scriptural history of interpretation, which in spite of inner tensions and many differences exhibits a remarkable ideological consistency, and after which the Renaissance, in various ways, heralded something new and different. In order to keep the original unity of the first volume, at least to some extent, its continuous counting of 37 chapters and its tripartite division have been retained – the present part volume on the Middle Ages constituting its main part C.

In fact, the need for a division of volume I into two part volumes became soon obvious, not to say required; for the rich and variegated material of scriptural interpretation from the Middle Ages, on the Christian as well as on the Jewish side, made it imperative to give more attention and space to this epoch, that so often has been neglected and, due to different forms of prejudice, has been depreciated as "the Dark Ages". It would indeed represent a most positive side effect if the present volume might contribute to a diminishing of prejudice regarding the Middle Ages and to a fostering of an adequate recognition of its richness in exegetical reflection, insight and practice; and, also, even the transition to the Renaissance may in this way be less radical and complicated.

Furthermore, as was stated in general terms in the Preface to the first part volume, that there is a "need for a comprehensive research history in the field, written anew in the light of the current status in biblical as well as in historical disciplines", this, not least, is a burning question as regards the Middle Ages. For in this field, the historians for quite some time have discussed extensively an accurate determination of the term, limitation and content of the so-called 'Middle Ages'. Some aspects of these tangled problems need to be dealt with also on this occasion; that will be done briefly in the introductory chapter.

It belongs to the international and interconfessional character of the HBOT Project that it is written by scholars representing different scholarly milieux and traditions. This state of affairs has its merits, but at the same time it includes some risk of fragmentation, which was discussed in the Prolegomenon of the first part volume (cf. HBOT I/1, p. 24); and also it may involve some risk of overlapping, when different authors are treating items that are closely related to each other or even comment on the same subject. Although cases of apparent overlapping have been avoided, the point at issue, nevertheless, has been handled with tolerance, for it may be regarded as positive when a matter, in a stereo-like way, is treated by different authors from various angles and viewpoints. Finally, on questions of style and transcription, particularly with regard to Hebrew names and to technical terms a standardization has been aimed at, but at the same time one will find, to some degree, minor deviations among the individual authors.

A Project of this kind cannot exist and be pursued without many relations of dependence and support, for which I have the pleasure of expressing my deep gratitude. Once again, I should like to pay tribute to the Co-Editors of the First Volume, especially Professor Haran who so generously has helped at some critical points of the road. I also wish to thank Professor Dr. Drs. h.c. Otto Kaiser, of Marburg, for valuable help. Once again, my deepfelt thanks go to Dr. Arndt Ruprecht and Reinhilde Ruprecht, PhD, for their unabated support and to the staff of *Vandenhoeck & Ruprecht* for taking such good care of the Project. Also this time, I am deeply indebted to *Förderungs- und Beihilfefonds Wissenschaft der VG Wort*, of Munich, that has granted a considerable financial support, and so also to the *Norwegian Research Council*, as well as to the *Norwegian Academy of Science and Letters* and to the *Fridtjof Nansens Fond*, of Oslo, for their financial support of the editorial work, and in this respect, also to my own Faculty, *The Norwegian Lutheran School of Theology*, and its Director Finn Olav Myhre, for all practical support of the Project, even after my retirement. Finally, I should like to express my very best thanks to HBOT's linguistic consultants, first cand. theol. Richard Lee Blucher, of Oslo, and now especially Professor Ronald E. Clements, of Cambridge, for their required and invaluable help; and I also thank stud. theol. Eskil Helgerud Andersen for his helpful work on the Indexes.

Last but not least, the present volume of HBOT would have been nothing without its authors. I feel deeply obliged for their respective essays which not only represent actual surveys but also new research, whereby they have contributed positively to the progress of biblical and historical scholarship.

Oslo, in March 2000 Magne Sæbø

C.

Christian and Jewish Interpretation of the Hebrew Bible / Old Testament in the Middle Ages

Chapter Twenty-three

The Problem of Periodization of 'the Middle Ages' Some Introductory Remarks

By Magne Sæbø, Oslo

General works: D. Abulafia et al. (eds.), *The New Cambridge Medieval History* I–VII (Cambridge: Cambridge UP 1995–); J. B. Bury / H. M. Gwatkin / J. P. Whitney (eds.), *The Cambridge Medieval History* I–VIII (London: Cambridge UP 1911–36); C. Andresen, *Geschichte des Christentums,* I. *Von den Anfängen bis zur Hochscholastik* (ThW 6; Stuttgart: W. Kohlhammer 1975); idem / A. M. Ritter, *Geschichte des Christentums* I/2: *Frühmittelalter – Hochmittelalter* (ThW 6,1; Stuttgart: W. Kohlhammer 1995); C. Andresen / A. M. Ritter / K. Wessel / E. Mühlenberg / M. A. Schmidt, *Die Lehrentwicklung im Rahmen der Katholizität* (HDTG 1; Göttingen: Vandenhoeck & Ruprecht 1982); A. Angenendt, *Das Frühmittelalter. Die abendländische Christenheit von 400 bis 900* (Stuttgart / Berlin / Köln 1990); M. Banniard, *Genèse culturelle de l'Europe – V^e^- VIIIe siècle* (Paris 1989); G. von Below, *Über historische Periodisierungen* (Berlin 1925); H. Boockmann, *Die Gegenwart des Mittelalters* (Berlin: Siedler 1988); Chr. Dawson, *The Making of Europe* (London 1932); *Dictionary of the Middle Ages* [DMA], 1–13 (New York: Scribner 1982–89); C. F. Delzell (ed.), *The Future of History: Essays in the Vanderbilt University Centennial Symposium* (Nashville, TN: Vanderbilt Univ. Press 1977); L. Diestel, *Geschichte des Alten Testamentes in der christlichen Kirche* (Jena 1869; repr. Leipzig 1981); O. Engels, "Geschichte / Geschichtsschreibung / Geschichtsphilosophie, VI. Von Augustin bis zum Humanismus", TRE 12 (1984) 608–30; F. W. Farrar, *History of Interpretation* (1886; repr. Grand Rapids 1961; 1979); R. Fossier (ed.), *The Cambridge Illustrated History of the Middle Ages* (orig. *Le Moyen Age*) I–III (Cambridge: Cambridge UP; I. 350–950; tr. J. Sondheimer; 1989; II. 950–1250; tr. S. Airlie / R. Marsack; 1997; III. 1250–1520; tr. S. Hanbury Tenison; 1986); H. Fuhrmann, *Einladung ins Mittelalter* (München: C. H. Beck [4]1989); F. Graus, *Lebendige Vergangenheit. Überlieferung im Mittelalter und in den Vorstellungen vom Mittelalter* (Köln / Wien 1975); R. S. Hoyt, *Europe in the Middle Ages* (New York / Burlingame: Harcourt, Brace & World 1957); O. Köhler, "Abendland (*Occident, Europa*)", TRE 1 (1977) 17–42; W. Lammers (ed.), *Geschichtsdenken und Geschichtsbild im Mittelalter* (WdF 21; Darmstadt: Wiss. Buchgesellschaft 1965); *Lexikon des Mittelalters* [LM], 1–10 (München: Artemis, 1980–99); G. W. H. Lampe (ed.), *The West from the Fathers to the Reformation* (CHB 2; 1969, repr. 1980); P. Lehmann, *Vom Mittelalter und von der lateinischen Literatur des Mittelalters* (Quellen und Untersuchungen zur lateinischen Philologie des Mittelalters V/1; München 1914); A. de Libera, *La philosophie médiévale* (Paris: PUF 1995); J. Marenbon, *Early Medieval Philosophy: an Introduction* (London: Routledge & Kegan Paul 1983); idem, *Late Medieval Philosophy: an Introduction* (2nd ed.; London: Routledge 1993); M. Nordberg, *Den dynamiska medeltiden* (Stockholm: Tidens Förlag 1984); R. Pernoud, *Pour en finir avec le Moyen Age* (Paris 1977); E. Pitz, "Mittelalter", LM 6 (1993) 684–87; H. Graf Reventlow, *Epochen der Bibelauslegung,* II. *Von der Spätantike bis zum ausgehenden Mittelalter* (München: Beck 1994); P. Riché / G. Lobrichon (eds.), *Le Moyen Age et la Bible* (BTT 4; Paris: Beauchesne 1984); K. Schäferdiek, "Mittelalter", TRE 23 (1994) 110–21; R. Schönberger / B. Kible (eds.), *Repertorium edierter Texte des Mittelalters aus dem Bereich der Philosophie und angrenzender Gebiete* (Berlin: Akademie-Verlag 1994); C. Sirat, *A History of Jewish Philosophy in the Middle Ages* (Cambridge: Cambridge UP [1985] repr. 1995); O. E. Strasser, "Les périodes et les époques de l'Histoire de l'Eglise", *RHPR* 30 (1950) 290–304; H. Zimmermann, *Das Mittelalter* I–II (Stuttgart 1975/1979; esp. "Das Mittelalter als Problem", I, 1–14).

Bibliographies: R. Stadelmann, "Grundformen der Mittelalterauffassung von Herder bis Ranke", *Deutsche Vierteljahrschrift für Literaturwissenschaft und Geistesgeschichte* 9 (1931) 45–88;

K. F. Stroheker, "Um die Grenze zwischen Antike und abendländischem Mittelalter", *Saec.* 1 (1950) 433–65.

Special studies: K. Arnold, "Das 'finstere' Mittelalter. Zur Genese und Phänomenologie eines Fehlurteils", *Saec.* 32 (1981) 287–300; H. Aubin, "Die Frage nach der Scheide zwischen Altertum und Mittelalter", *HZ* 172 (1951) 245–63 (also in Hübinger [ed.], Zur Frage der Periodengrenze [1969] 93–113); P. Dinzelbacher, "Mittelalterliche Kirchengeschichte", EKL 3 (1992) 472–84; idem, "Mittelalterliche Kultur", EKL 3 (1992) 484–96; D. Gerhard, "Periodization in European History", *AHR* 61 (1955/56) 900–13; E. Göller, *Die Periodisierung der Kirchengeschichte und die epochale Stellung des Mittelalters zwischen dem christlichen Altertum und der Neuzeit* (Freiburg / Br.: Guenther Verlag 1919; repr. in: Libelli 263; Darmstadt: Wiss. Buchgesellschaft 1969, 7–73); O. Halecki, *The Limits and Divisions of European History* (London / New York: Sheed & Ward 1950); H. Heimpel, "Über die Epochen der mittelalterlichen Geschichte", in: idem, *Der Mensch in seiner Gegenwart* (Göttingen ^{2}1957) 42–66, 198–200; K. Heussi, *Altertum, Mittelalter und Neuzeit in der Kirchengeschichte. Ein Beitrag zum Problem der historischen Periodisierung* (Tübingen: Mohr 1921; repr. in: Libelli 263; Darmstadt: Wiss. Buchgesellschaft 1969, 74–146); P. E. Hübinger (ed.), *Kulturbruch oder Kulturkontinuität im Übergang von der Antike zum Mittelalter* (WdF 201; Darmstadt: Wiss. Buchgesellschaft 1968); idem (ed.), *Zur Frage der Periodengrenze zwischen Altertum und Mittelalter* (WdF 51; Darmstadt: Wiss. Buchgesellschaft 1969); J. Huizinga, "Zur Geschichte des Begriffs Mittelalter", in: idem, *Geschichte und Kultur* (Stuttgart 1954); H.-D. Kahl, "Was bedeutet 'Mittelalter'?", *Saec.* 40 (1989) 15–38; A. Klempt, *Die Säkularisierung der universalhistorischen Auffassung. Zum Wandel des Geschichtsdenkens im 16. und 17. Jahrhundert* (Göttinger Bausteine zur Geschichtswissenschaft 31; Göttingen 1960); J. Knape, "Die Problematik unseres Geschichtsbegriffs fürs Mittelalter", *GRM* NS 38 (1988) 15–34; U. Köpf, "Kirchengeschichte und Geographie. Möglichkeiten und Grenzen einer historischen Geographie des Christentums", *ZTK* 77 (1980) 42–68; idem, "A European View of the Problems of Dividing Church History into Periods. The Inclusion of the 'Third World' in the Presentation of the History of the Church", *Towards a History of the Church in the Third World* (Papers and Report of a Consultation on *The Issue of Periodisation*, ed L. Vischer; Bern 1985) 87–109; Th. E. Mommsen, "Petrarch's Conception of the 'Dark Ages'", *Spec.* 17 (1942) 226–42 (also in: idem, *Medieval and Renaissance Studies*, Ithaca, NY 1959, 106–29); K. Müller, "Die Grenze zwischen Altertum und Mittelalter in der Kirche", PrJ 60 (1887) 257–78; U. Neddermeyer, *Das Mittelalter in der deutschen Historiographie vom 15. bis zum 18. Jahrhundert. Geschichtsgliederung und Epochenverständnis in der frühen Neuzeit* (Phil. Diss. Univ. Köln; Kölner historische Abhandlungen 34; Köln / Wien: Böhlau Verlag 1988); L. I. Newmann, *Jewish Influence on Christian Reform Movements* (New York 1925); J. H. J. van der Pot, *De periodisering der geschiedenis. Een overzicht der theorieën* ('s-Gravenhaage 1951), esp. 113–23; G. Salomon, *Das Mittelalter als Ideal der Romantik* (München 1922); E. Sanford, "The Twelfth Century – Renaissance or Proto-Renaissance", *Spec.* 26 (1951) 635–42; P. Schaeffer, "The Emergence of the Concept 'Medieval' in Central European Humanism", *Sixteenth Century Journal* 7 (1973) 19–30; C. Schmid, *Die Mittelalterrezeption des 18. Jahrhunderts zwischen Aufklärung und Romantik* (EHS, R. 1: Deutsche Literatur und Germanistik 278; Frankfurt / M.: Peter Lang 1979); R. Schönberger, *Was ist Scholastik?* (Philosophie und Religion 2; Hildesheim: Bernward 1991); K. Schubert, "Das Judentum in der Umwelt des christlichen Mittelalters", *Kairos* 17 (1975) 161–217; S. Skalweit, *Der Beginn der Neuzeit. Epochengrenze und Epochenbegriff* (EdF 178; Darmstadt: Wiss. Buchgesellschaft 1982); L. W. Spitz, "Periodization in History: Renaissance and Reformation", in Delzell (ed.), The Future of History (1977) 189–218; R. E. Sullivan, "The Middle Ages in the Western Tradition: Some Considerations", in: B. K. Lackner / K. R. Philip (eds.), *Essays on Medieval Civilisation* (Austin / London: University of Texas Press 1978) 3–31; J. Voss, *Das Mittelalter im historischen Denken Frankreichs. Untersuchungen zur Geschichte des Mittelalterbegriffs und der Mittelalterbewertung von der zweiten Hälfte des 16. bis zur Mitte des 19. Jahrhunderts* (Veröffentlichungen des Historischen Instituts der Universität Mannheim 3; München 1972); L. Varga, *Das Schlagwort vom "finsteren" Mittelalter* (Veröffentlichungen des Seminars für Wirtschafts- und Kulturgeschichte 8; Baden / Wien 1932; repr. Aalen 1978).

When moving from Antiquity, which was the subject of the first part volume (HBOT I/1) to the subsequent epoch of history, the so-called 'Middle Ages', that is the special field of the present part volume, one is confronted with a most delicate historiographical problem: for what really does the term 'Middle Ages' mean, and still more difficult: what period of time does it more exactly comprise? In the present context, where the epoch as a whole is under discussion, it will not only be most appropriate but simply necessary to make some introductory reflections on this problem of modern historiography.

The conventional term 'Middle Ages' seems *prima facie* to be quite simple, meaning literally the time 'in the middle' of some other periods; indicated is the period between Antiquity and the New or 'Modern' Time. However, the meaning and use of the term are not as obvious or 'simple' as it at first may seem; for, as far as modern historical research is concerned, the term 'Middle Ages' appears to be a highly problematic one, not least from a methodological point of view.

Problematic is this term not only because of the indicated *tripartition* of history, especially when seen in a wider and universal perspective,[1] but also with regard to the way in which this historical division generally has been carried through. When it comes to a more exact determination of the 'Middle Ages', an approach of this kind will have a bearing on several complex problems. In the first instance, it raises questions of an adequate chronological delimitation of its beginning and end as a specific historical epoch as well as of complicated socio-political, cultural and ideological descriptions of its 'content' or inner structure, in other words, what may constitute this epoch as unique in comparison with the preceding and the following epoch. The 'simple' terminology, then, involves many and manifold problems, among which even the problem of *periodization*, both on a chronological and a structural level, is of a basic character and function. In an introductory discussion of this particular problem it may be appropriate to focus briefly on the (1) terminological, (2) chronological, and (3) ideological and theological aspects of the 'Middle Ages'.

1. The commonly used *term 'Middle Ages'* – similarly *Mittelalter* in German and *Moyen Age* in French – that indicates a specific historical epoch in 'the middle' of History, is not very old but it has roots in older traditions. Therefore, it may be meaningful to differentiate between the use of the term as a term of periodization and the idea of some historical 'middle period'.[2]

The first use of 'Middle Ages' as a term of historical periodization has generally been associated with a three volume handbook in World History by Christoph Cellarius (Keller; 1638–1707), of Weimar and Halle; his three volumes were related to a tripartite scheme of history, i. e. Antiquity (*Historia antiqua*, 1685) – Middle Ages (*Historia medii aevi*, 1688) – New Time (*Historia nova*, 1696).[3] But he was not the first one to use this scheme of periodization

[1] Cf. Köpf, Kirchengeschichte und Geographie (1980); idem, A European View (1985).

[2] See esp. Huizinga, Zur Geschichte des Begriffs Mittelalter (1954); Kahl, Was bedeutet 'Mittelalter'? (1989). Diestel, Geschichte (1869/1981) 244, spoke of the Middle Ages as *"die mittlere Zeit"*.

[3] Later his handbook of History was entitled *Historia universalis in antiquam et medii aevi ac novam divisa* (Jena 1704–08). See esp. van der Pot, De periodisering der geschiedenis (1951); cf. Göller, Periodisierung (1919/1969) 8–11/14–17; Heussi, Altertum, Mittelalter und Neuzeit (1921/1969); Halecki, Limits and Divisions (1950); Schäferdiek, Mittelalter (1994) 113; Hübinger, Zur Frage der Periodengrenze (1969) vii.

of history, for some years earlier GEORG HORN (1620–1670), of Leiden, had already made use of it, although within a framework of a different kind.[4] It seems likely, though, that it was the handbook of CELLARIUS that had the greater influence on the historiography to come.

The main thing, however, was the fact that a historical periodization of this kind appeared for the first time in the seventeenth century and, notably, found its specific form in the later part of the century.[5] Even though a historical handbook had given the term its most effective start its rise can scarcely be explained on practical or pedagogical grounds alone; its general acceptance may have had deeper reasons and presuppositions. On this occasion, with the focus on the history of scriptural interpretation, it may be appropriate to point to two different, but also related, circumstances.

First, to begin with the latest and possibly most specific one, there was a 'modern' condition, fostered by the approaching and developing Enlightenment, namely, the enhancing secularization of history and historiography.[6] In the course of time, History lost its biblical and theological basis and was no longer regarded as some sort of *Heilsgeschichte*;[7] nor was it, comparably to still other religiously related partitions of History, divided into two main parts any more, i.e., the pagan times before Christ and the times after Christ, the era of the Church.[8] The universal History was, moreover, to incorporate Church History, for which the new state of affairs generated new problems, as in particular K. HEUSSI has pointed out.[9]

Second, the new historiographical use of the term 'Middle Ages' had old roots in Humanism, that is to say in the idea of *medium aevum*, a 'middle era', which leads back to an early time of the Renaissance. In this way Humanism provided an ideological bridge from the Renaissance to the new historical terminology that was worked out in the course of the seventeenth century. However, when early Italian humanists, like Petrarch,[10] as well as later humanists spoke of a *medium tempus* – or in similar forms of this expression – the term was not related to History in a strict sense, not to say historiography, but it was used in a literary and linguistic sense – as also the well-known humanistic device *ad fontes* was used in a literary, not in a historical sense. It was not least with regard to the use and standard of Latin as practised by the Church in the preceding centuries compared with the classic use of it in Antiquity that the

---

[4] *Arca Noae sive historia imperiorum et regnorum a condito orbe ad nostra tempora* (Leiden 1666). Cf. Voss, Das Mittelalter (1972) 56 f.

[5] Schäferdiek, Mittelalter (1994) 112, goes even back to 1601, when the historian H. Canisius edited a collection of documents, *Antiquae lectiones*, whose content was described as *antiqua documenta ad historiam mediae aetatis illustrandam*, including documents from the third to the sixteenth century.

[6] Cf. Klempt, Die Säkularisierung der universalhistorischen Auffassung (1960).

[7] See esp. Fuhrmann, Einladung ins Mittelalter (1989) 17 f.

[8] Cf. Hoyt, Europe (1957)

[9] See Heussi, Altertum, Mittelalter und Neuzeit (1921) 2–8/(1969) 80–86; he is in principle critical to the tripartition of the Church History, Part II, 34–68/112–46. Cf. also Gerhard, Periodization (1955/56) 901–03; Hoyt, Europe (1957) 1–3; Spitz, Periodization (1977) 190–92.

[10] Cf. Mommsen, Petrarch's Conception of the 'Dark Ages' (1942/1959).

'middle age' was looked upon as an inferior period, or, as "a period of decline".[11]

Although the idea and term of a 'middle age' for a long time was not used in a historiographical sense, it nevertheless expressed a historical perspective: over the 'time in between', one looked back at the time of Antiquity, like a cultural Golden Age, in comparison with which the *medium aevum* was regarded not only as an inferior period but was characterized in a still more negative way when the period was called *saeculum obscurum*, the 'Dark Ages'.[12]

The term 'Middle Ages', then, was from the beginning not just a neutrally dividing term of time but also, in a clearly negative manner, a characterizing term, coined at a distance by humanists who most consciously regarding their own time evaluated the 'time in between' against the background of Antiquity's classic culture. The negative expression was carried on and even reinforced by many Protestants for whom the 'Dark Ages', against the background of the New Testament and the Church Fathers, mirrored the negative sides of the Catholic Church, whereas in the time of Enlightenment – for representatives like VOLTAIRE and D. HUME – the 'Middle Ages' first of all embodied ignorance.[13] Although estimated in the time of Romanticism,[14] the negative characteristics of the Middle Ages have been carried on, up to the present time; *mirabile dictu*, also FARRAR used the term 'Dark Ages'.[15] But slowly, new and increased insights into the creativity and richness of the Middle Ages seem to bring about a more positive – and adequate – portrayal of these central centuries.

2. The question that has been asked by many, especially in recent research, relates to the limits of the period in question: when did the 'Middle Ages' really begin and when did it end? To be sure, when the definition of the *term* 'Middle Ages' turns out to be a rather intricate question, as was shown above, the *chronological delimitation* of the assumed epoch seems to be an even more controversial matter. Scholars have been far from any consensus in this respect, while the historical discussion continues; correspondingly, the concrete descriptions of the chronological limits of the 'Middle Ages' differ considerably – and, in general, may be met with some reservation. Also here, the old saying: *quot homines, tot sententiae* reminds one of required prudence.[16]

For CELLARIUS the 'Middle Ages' comprised the long period from the times

---

[11] Schäferdiek, Mittelalter (1994) 110–12; Gerhard, Periodization (1955/56) 901.

[12] See esp. Varga, Das Schlagwort vom 'finsteren' Mittelalter (1932/1978); Arnold, Das "finstere" Mittelalter (1981).

[13] Cf. Arnold, ibid. 290–91.

[14] See esp. Salomon, Das Mittelalter als Ideal der Romantik (1922); Schmid, Die Mittelalterrezeption des 18. Jahrhunderts (1979); cf. Arnold, Das "finstere" Mittelalter (1981) 289.

[15] Cf. Farrar, History (1886/1979) 245.

[16] Cf. Hoyt, Europe (1957) 1: the term of 'Middle Ages' "is purely conventional, because historians cannot agree when the Middle Ages began and ended, or else they are agreed that the beginning and end of the period cannot be assigned to specific dates"; cf. also Gerhard, Periodization (1 955/56) 900: "The historian knows that any division of time into definite periods is artificial. Recent experience has taught him that even in the midst of upheavals and utter destruction there is no complete break with the past".

of Constantine the Great to the capture of Constantinople by the Turks,[17] i. e., from about 313 (as far as the *Decree of Milan* is included) to 1453, in other words, it covered more than a millenium. However, it may be neither possible nor necessary to discuss the potential reasons for such a broad delimitation of the 'Middle Ages'; it is remarkable, though, that this very long span of time was not unusual, up to the present time.[18] On this occasion, it may suffice to make some brief remarks on the beginning, the question of a possible inner division, and the end of the epoch.

In current historical scholarship, it is the *beginning* of the 'Middle Ages', its limit 'in front', that has been the prime subject of many historical studies; and as far as the 'front limit' is concerned it is mainly the important – but difficult – transition from *late* Antiquity to the early 'Middle Ages' that has been brought into focus.[19] As for this transition two related points – among others – have attracted the attention of scholars. First, there was a shift of scene. Although *Imperium Romanum* had its distant *limes* in countries like Britannia and Germany, its 'home scene' for centuries was around *mare nostrum*, it was the Mediterranean world, which also included peoples of North Africa and the Near East. It may be contended that with the gradual fall of the glorious Roman Empire also Antiquity came to an end as a specific epoch – but not in its long and influential *Wirkungsgeschichte*. "During the early Middle Ages the unity of the Mediterranean world was permantly broken: the sea which had been the center of a civilization, a channel of communication, now became a frontier to be crossed for commerce or for war."[20] After the *sacco di Roma* in 410, through increasing attacks by migrating peoples from the North and with still other elements of a most complex historical process of transition, something quite new entered the stage during the following centuries. For, secondly, in this politically and culturally new and different situation the formation of *Europe* took place;[21] remarkably, Charlemagne has been called "the Father of Europe". At the same time, as the Eastern parts of the Mediterranean world for various reasons had receded into the background, whereas the Arabs made continued progress, also a specific *Western* civilization was now developing.[22] Though being a rich heir of the Mediterranean world, Europe moved its main points of influence and administration from the

[17] The full title of the second volume was: *Historia medii aevi a temporibus Constantini magni ad Constantinopolim a Turcis captam deducta*; cf. Schäferdiek, Mittelalter (1994) 113.

[18] Cf. Fuhrmann, Einladung ins Mittelalter (1989) 16f. Fossier, Cambridge History of the Middle Ages I–III (1986–97), covers the period from 350 to 1520.

[19] See esp. the collections of studies edited by Hübinger, Kulturbruch oder Kulturkontinuität (1968), and Zur Frage der Periodengrenze zwischen Altertum und Mittelalter (1969); cf. also Müller, Die Grenze zwischen Altertum und Mittelalter (1887); Aubin, Die Frage nach der Scheide zwischen Altertum und Mittelalter (1951/1969).

[20] So Hoyt, Europe (1957) 5; cf. also Kahl, Was bedeutet 'Mittelalter'? (1989) 19.

[21] Cf. Schäferdiek, Mittelalter (1994) 114f: "Als Phase der europäischen Geschichte ist das Mittelalter die Zeit der Heranbildung der geschichtlichen Eigengestalt Europas ... in seiner kulturellen Einheit und nationalen Vielfalt".

[22] See esp. Köhler, Abendland (1977); cf. Aubin, Die Scheide zwischen Altertum und Mittelalter (1969) 110f; Gerhard, Periodization (1955/56) 905; Kahl, Was bedeutet 'Mittelalter'? (1989) 16–17, 32ff; also A. Grabois, in the next chapter of this volume.

South to the Northwest, to Ireland and Britain, to France and Germany, beyond the old *limes* of the Roman Empire. With this radical shift of scene and the growth of a new Europe there was also a radical "shift of paradigms",[23] that makes it meaningful to speak of a new historical epoch.

Also within the 'Middle Ages', it is customary to make a tripartite division of Early, High and Late Middle Ages. The division, however, is not only highly relative but it may be of less importance as well.[24] In recent historical research, it seems to be of primary significance to focus upon the longer inner developments, tensions and divers transitions as exhibited by the new nations and kingdoms, like, for example, the establishing of political, social and financial systems, within the framework of mainly agrarian societies, the tension of ecclesiastical and political authorities or the special relationship between Christians, Jews and Muslims in Spain, and the development of cultural and ecclesiastical institutions, like the monasteries and the different orders. In the present context of a history of scriptural interpretation, it lays near at hand to mention the development of education and the school system.[25] In all, the 'Middle Ages' presents itself as a rich and dynamic epoch.[26]

As for the question of the *end* of this epoch, it is – like the question of its beginning – to an essential degree open to discussion; a borderline between the so-called 'Late Middle Ages' and the Renaissance is hard, if ever possible, to draw. Sometimes, the 'Late Middle Ages' is extended to the sixteenth century; on the other hand, the question has been raised whether it is appropriate to speak of a Renaissance or 'Proto-Renaissance' already in the twelfth century;[27] recently, there seems to be some tendency to push Renaissance as long as possible back into the Middle Ages.[28]

When the present volume of the HBOT Project, except for chapters on the Syrian Churches and on the Medieval Jewish-Christian disputations, ends with the Victorines of Paris and the great Masters of the thirteenth century,[29] it is mainly for two reasons.

(a) As the first part volume, dealing with Antiquity, was concluded with an essay on Augustine, whose creative and synthetical work seems to 'crown' the traditions of theological reflection and exegetical practice of the Old Church, a corresponding ending of the second part volume is intended with essays on the great theologians and exegetes of the 'High Middle Ages'; and similarly it may be said of the contemporary Jewish exegesis, especially as it was performed by Rashi in the school of literal Jewish exegesis in Northern France.[30]

---

[23] Th. S. Kuhn, *The Structure of Scientific Revolution* (Chicago 1962) x, 43–51.

[24] Cf. Heussi, Altertum, Mittelalter und Neuzeit (1921/1969) 55 f/133 f: "bei der Gliederung des Stoffes würde es sich um *Klassifikation*, nicht um *Partition* handeln, also nicht um eigentliche historische Perioden".

[25] See on this chap. 27 of the present volume: "The Institutional Framework of Christian Exegesis in the Middle Ages", by U. Köpf.

[26] Cf. Nordberg, Den dynamiska medeltiden (1984).

[27] See esp. Sanford, The Twelfth Century – Renaissance or Proto-Renaissance (1951).

[28] Cf. Hoyt, Europe (1957) 4–5.

[29] Chap. 34, by R. Berndt, and chap. 35, by K. Froehlich.

[30] See chap. 32, by A. Grossman; cf. chap. 31 and 33 for the rich and significant Jewish exegesis in Spain, and also elsewhere.

(b) Since there seems to be a "shift of paradigms" also in the Renaissance in relation to the 'Middle Ages', similar to a characteristic of the transition from Antiquity to the 'Early Middle Ages', and here as early as in the fourteenth century,[31] it may be regarded as most reasonable and appropriate that this phenomenon is ensured sufficient space and given adequate treatment in the next volume (HBOT II), especially as regards the early part of the Renaissance.[32]

3. The question of a *structural determination* of the 'Middle Ages', finally, is in some way dependent on the two aspects treated above, or, rather vice versa: both the term and the delimitation of the 'Middle Ages' are dependent on how the epoch is described on its own terms, in other words, on the basis of its 'inner' idiosyncratic structure,[33] of which some few but characteristic elements may be indicated here.

The discussion of the two other aspects above may have shown that the 'Middle Ages' was a most complex and dynamic epoch. Just to mention, again, there were, among many characteristics, divers tensions and competing interests. Significant in this respect, was the particular state of affairs that the new national states, in comparison with the centralistic Roman Empire, represented a clear national *particularism*, a phenomenon that also might be exposed in other ways.[34] However, counter to the particularism of varying kind, there were also unifying factors, a *universalism*; and the recognition of this Janus-faced character of the 'Middle Ages' may be a salient point for the understanding of its 'content' and structure.

Whereas the national and other particularistic tendencies were mainly on the political and social level, the unifying factors may first of all be found on the cultural – in spite of all cultural amalgation[35] – and, not least, on the religious and ecclesiastical level.

Above, we noted the humanists' negative and condescending judgment of the Latin of the 'Middle Ages', namely, its inferior standard as compared with the classical Latin of Antiquity. However, the function of Latin as the one common and shared language, across all national languages, had a culturally and even socially unifying effect.[36]

Latin was the language of the Church and of the schools that were mainly in the service of the Church, without which Latin would not have had its great unifying function. It is generally recognized and accepted that on many levels in the national societies as well as in the community of a growing and developing Europe as a whole, the Church was more than any other institution *the*

---

[31] See what was said of Petrarch, above (and n. 10).

[32] There have been some problems, and hesitation, where to place Nicholas of Lyra (ca. 1270–1349) in this project, but in the end the treatment of his important exegetical work was reserved for the early Renaissance of the next volume – and this alone may demonstrate the problems of periodization at the transition from 'Late Middle Ages' to the Renaissance.

[33] Cf. Heussi, Altertum, Mittelalter und Neuzeit (1921/1969) 55f/133f. (and see n. 24 above).

[34] Cf. Aubin, Die Scheide zwischen Altertum und Mittelalter (1969) 112–13; Kahl, Was bedeutet 'Mittelalter'? (1989) 19–21, 32–33; Schäferdiek, Mittelalter (1994) 119–20.

[35] Cf. Hoyt, Europe (1957) 5–6

[36] Cf. Kahl, ibid. 31–32.

unifying element in the new Europe.[37] It had the same services in all countries and nations, with different traditions; it had the same system of a variety of orders and monasteries spread around; it had its various schools and its teaching as well as its preaching and social work everywhere; and it had the same theological doctrines for all regions. It may be said that after the fall of the Roman Empire, the Church, to some degree, continued the Empire's unifying and even centralistic function, among the nations of Medieval Europe.

Last but not least, in the context of the present history of scriptural interpretation, it also may be appropriate to point to the basic unifying significance that the one Bible represented, both in the reading and its interpretation. In this respect, with regard to the Hebrew Bible, some Christian theologians and exegetes reached out their hands to Jewish colleagues.

In *conclusion*, it may be said that the problematic term 'Middle Ages', and even its conventional sub-divisions, may be retained as practical terms of periodization, but with required critical reservation. This concession, in spite of all criticism, is not given just because the term 'Middle Ages' is a relatively old and well established term of periodization, but – with all its shortcomings – because it nevertheless has functioned as a reasonable means of historical division and periodization; so it is hard to find a functional alternative. As for the chronological delimitation of the epoch, a narrow description of its limits seems to be more commendable than the usual broad one.

But also in this way, the 'Middle Ages' terminology has its limitation, first of all in a broader context.[38] One of its weak points, although at the same time a strong point of its uniqueness, is the fact that the 'Middle Ages' is so strongly related to Europe. Outside of Europe this terminology looses some of its significance; but, on the other hand, the 'Middle Ages' was the cradle of Europe; later this rich heir of Antiquity had to find its place in the 'world'.

---

[37] See, among many others, Kahl, ibid. 37–38, who asks and states (37): "Läßt sich unter den Entwicklungen, die zur Konstituierung von 'Mittelalter' beitragen, eine Rangfolge festlegen? Am wichtigsten dürfte jeweils die Christianisierung sein", whereby he also includes the missionary work of the Church.

[38] Cf. Köpf (see n. 1 above).

Chapter Twenty-four

Political and Cultural Changes from the Fifth to the Eleventh Century

By Aryeh Grabois, Haifa

Sources: I. Alfasi, *Halakhoth* (Canons) 1–6 (ed. Vilna; 1804–1808); H. Batsgen (ed.), *Libri Carolini* (Hannover 1924); A. Boretius / V. Krause (eds.), *Capitularia Regum Francorum* 1–2 (Hannover 1883–1889); Ennodius, *Panegyricus dictus clementissimo regi Theodorico*, CSEL 6 (ed. Hartel); E. Friedberg (ed.), *Corpus Juris Civilis* (Leipzig 1905); Gregorius Turonensis Episcopus (Gregory of Tours), *Historia Francorum* 1–2 (ed. R. Latouche; Paris 1963); Hananel bar Hushiel, *Migdal Hananel* (Hananel's Tower) (ed. A. Berliner; Berlin 1876); idem, *Perush ʿal ha-Talmud* (Commentary on the Talmud) 1–2 (ed. Vilna; 1906–1912); P. Jaffe / S. Loewenfeld (eds.), *Regesta Pontificum Romanorum* 1–2 (Jena 1888); Jordanes, *Getica*, MGH. AA 5 (ed. Th. Mommsen); B. N. Lewin (ed.), *Iggereth Sharira Gaon* (The Epistle of Sharira Gaon) (Haifax 1921); J.-B. Mansi (ed.), *Concilia* 1–32 (Rome 1763–1790); C. Mirbt (ed.), *Quellen zur Geschichte des Papsttums und römischen Katholizismus* (Tübingen 1901); Nissim bar Jacob, *Mafteah le-Man'ulei ha-Talmud* (A Key to the Locks of the Talmud) (ed. Vienna; 1847); Jacob Tam, *Sefer Hayashar* (The Book of the Just) (ed. E. Rosenthal; Berlin 1898); Prosper Tiro, *Chronicon*, MGH. AA 1 (ed. Th. Mommsen); Yehiel bar Nathan, *'Arukh* 1–6 (ed. A. Kohut; repr. New York 1965).

General works: F. Altheim / R. Stiehl (eds.), *Die Araber in der alten Welt* 1–2 (Berlin 1964–1969); S. W. Baron, *The Jewish Community* (Philadelphia 1943); idem, *A Social and Religious History of the Jews* 1–16 (Philadelphia 1951–61) [abbr.: Baron, SRH]; N. H. Baynes, *Byzantine Studies and Other Essays* (London 1955); O. Bertolini, "I papi e le missioni fino alla meta del secolo VIII", SSAM 14 (1967) 327–363; B. Bischoff, "Die Hofbiliothek unter Ludwig dem Frommen", *Medieval Learning and Literature* (Essays Presented to R. W. Hunt; Oxford 1976) 3–22; R. Blachère, *Histoire de la littérature arabe* 1–3 (Paris 1952–1966); B. Blumenkranz, *Die Judenpredigt Augustins* (Basel 1946; Paris [2]1973); R. Boutruche, *Seigneurie et féodalité* 1–2 (Paris 1968); M. Chambers, *The Fall of Rome* (New York 1963); H. Corbin, *Histoire de la philosophie islamique* (Paris 1964); C. Courtois, *Les Vandales et l'Afrique* (Paris 1955); R. Dévréesse, "Arabes 'perses' et Arabes 'romains'. Lakhmides et Ghassanides", *VivPen* 2 (1942) 263–307; S. Dill, *Roman Society in the Last Century of the Western Empire* (London 1898); R. Doehaerd, *Le Haut Moyen Age occidental: Economies et sociétés* (Paris 1971); L. Duchesne, *Les premiers temps de l'Etat pontifical* (Paris 1908); R. Dussaud, *La pénétration des arabes en Syrie avant l'Islam* (Paris 1955); E. Ennen, *Frühgeschichte der europäischen Stadt* (Bonn [2]1978); W. Ensslin, *Theoderic der Grosse* (Munich [2]1959); L. Finkelstein, *Jewish Self-Government in the Middle Ages* (Philadelphia 1924); R. Folz, *Le couronnement impérial de Charlemagne* (Paris 1964); idem (ed.), *De l'Antiquité au monde médiéval* (Paris 1972); D. Gardel, "Ilm al-Kalam", Encyclopaedia of Islam, NE IV (Leiden 1971) 1141–1150; A. Grabois, "Ecoles et structures sociales des communautés juives dans l'Occident aux IXe–XIIe siècles", SSAM 26 (1980), 937–962; idem, "Charlemagne, Rome, and Jerusalem", RBPH 59 (1981) 792–809; A. Guillou, "L'Empire romain d'Orient aux Ve et VIe siècles", in: R. Folz (ed.), *De l'Antiquité au monde médiéval* (1972) 134–54; M. Gysseling, "La genèse de la frontière linguistique dans le Nord de la Gaule", *RNord* 44 (1962) 5–37; A. H. M. Jones, *The Later Roman Empire, 284–602*, 1–4 (Oxford 1964); idem, *Constantine and the Conversion of Europe* (London 1967); S. Katz, *The Jews in the Visigothic and Frankish Kingdoms of Spain and Gaul* (Cambridge, MA 1937); idem, *The Decline of Rome and the Rise of Mediaeval Europe* (Ithaca 1968); M. L. W. Laistner, *The Intellectual Heritage of the Early Middle Ages* (Ithaca 1957); idem, *Thought and Letters in Western Europe, 500–900* (Ithaca 1959); J. Leclercq,

"L'Ecriture sainte dans la hagiographie monastique du haut Moyen Age", SSAM 10 (1963) 103–128; P. Lehmann, "Der Einfluss der Bibel auf frühmittelalterliche Geschichtsschreiber", SSAM 10 (1963) 129–140; E. Lévi-Provençal, *Histoire de l'Espagne musulmane* 1–4 (Paris 1944–1955); F. Lot, *La fin du monde antique et le début du Moyen Age* (Paris 1927; rééd. M. Rouche; Paris 1986); idem, *L'art militaire au Moyen Age en Europe et dans le Proche Orient* 1–2 (Paris 1946); A. S. McGrade, "Two Fifth-Century Conceptions of Papal Primacy", *Studies in Medieval and Renaissance History*, 7 (1969) 5–45; F. McCraw Donner, *The Early Muslim Conquests* (Princeton 1981); R. McKitterick, "Charles the Bald (823-877) and his Library: the Patronage of Learning", *EHR* 95 (1980) 28–47; idem, *The Carolingians and the Written Word* (Cambridge 1989); K. F. Morrison, *The Two Kingdoms* (Princeton 1964); Ch. Oman, *The Art of War in the Middle Ages* 1–2 (London 1924); F. Prinz, *Frühes Mönchtum im Frankenreich* (Munich 1965); P. Riché, *Education et culture dans l'Occident barbare, VIe–VIIIe siècles* (Paris 1962; rééd. 1990); idem, "Les bibliothèques de trois aristocrates laïcs carolingiens", *MA* 68 (1963) 87–104; idem, *Les Carolingiens. Une famille qui fit l'Europe* (Paris 1983); A. Saltman, "Rabanus Maurus and the Pseudo-Hieronymian, *Quaestiones Hebraice in Libros Regum et Paralipomenon*", *HTR* 66 (1973) 43–75; Th. Schieffer (ed.), *Europa im Wandel von der Antike zum Mittelalter* (Stuttgart 1976); M. Simon, "*Verus Israel*", in: idem, *Christianisme antique et son contexte religieux* (Tübingen 1981); D. Sourdel, "L'Empire abbaside de 750 à 945", in: R. Folz (ed.), *De l'Antiquité au monde médiéval* (1972) 414–51; R. W. Southern, *Islam and the West in the Middle Ages* (Cambridge, MA 1963); J. Stengers, *La formation de la frontière linguistique en Belgique* (Bruxelles 1959); R. A. Sullivan, "The Papacy and Missionary Activity in the Early Middle Ages", *MS* 17 (1955) 46–106; H. Z. Taubes, "The Arukh of Jehiel b. Nathan of Rome", in *Scritti in Memoria di Sally Meyer (1875–1953)* (Jerusalem 1955) 126–41; H. Terrasse, *Islam de l'Espagne* (Paris 1958); G. Tessier, *Le baptême de Clovis* (Paris 1964); E. A. Thompson, *A History of Attila and the Huns* (Oxford 1948); G. Vismara, "Romani e Goti di fronte al diritto nel regno Ostrogoto", SSAM 3 (1955) 409–462; F. W. Walbank, *The Decline of the Roman Empire in the West* (London 1946); J. M. Wallace-Hadrill, "Rome and the Early English Church", SSAM 7 (1960) 519–548; idem, *The Long-Haired Kings* (London 1962); idem, "A Carolingian Renaissance Prince: Emperor Charles the Bald", PBA (London 1978) 155–184; W. Montgomery Watt, *Muhammad in Mecca, Muhammad in Medina* (London 1958); idem, "Shiism under the Ummayads", *JRAS* (1960) 158–172; K. F. Werner, "*Missus, marchio, comes.* Entre l'administration centrale et l'administration locale de l'Empire carolingien", in: W. Paravicini (ed.), *Histoire comparée de l'administration* (Beihefte der Francia 9; 1980) 191–239; L. White, *Medieval Technology and Social Change* (Oxford 1962). – Further, see n. 66 below.

Special abbreviation: Baron, SRH = S. W. Baron, *A Social and Religious History of the Jews* (see above).

The Medieval society and its culture were deeply influenced by the Bible, to the point that Latin terms, like *scripturae* and *bibliotheca*, changed their broader meanings and were used as qualifications for the biblical books; for example, the term *Scripturae*, in this particular meaning, passed to vernacular languages and hence the Scriptures became synonyms to the term Bible. However, in contrast to classical Antiquity, when the Hebrew Bible / Old Testament was exclusively related to Judaism, the new monotheistic religions, Christianity and Islam, considered themselves as heirs of the Book. While already in its formative period in late Antiquity, Christianity adopted the Old Testament as an integral part of its Sacred Scriptures, Islam had adapted oral fragments to its needs and finally included them in the text of the *Koran*. This process of adoption and adaptation, parallel to the important changes which occurred in the world of Judaism, evolved from the Palestinian and "Babylonian" centres to the extension of these schools of learning and of knowledge throughout the various communities of the Jewish Diaspora. They call for a study of the background conditions, connected with political and cultural changes which occurred in the Early Middle Ages.[1]

It is widely accepted by historians that the phenomena which signified the political and social evolution of the last century of Antiquity and the first centuries of the Middle Ages should be characterised as a "break-up of unity". This is particularly seen as a result of the fall of the Roman Empire, which had created the political unity of the Mediterranean world, and of the disintegration of its Hellenistic-Roman society, which symbolized its syncretic civilization.[2] But while there is no reason to contest the accepted definitions of the nature of political changes, nor to connect them with the fate of social structures, the cultural and religious aspects of these revolutionary changes could hardly be qualified as "break-up of unity". Neither the evolution of post-biblical Judaism, nor the rise and spread of Christianity and Islam, correspond to such a definition. In this respect, the term 'proliferation' seems to be a more correct qualification of the historical process, which led to the creation of a new unity, characterized by each of these religious entities, with their proper cultural attributes.

1. The Decline of the Roman Empire and Its Successors

Contemporary research emphasizes that the decline of the Roman Empire had been a long-term historical process, which began in the second century CE, and was largely a consequence of its internal crises. In this respect, Hadrian's difficulties in repressing Bar-Kokhba's revolt in Judaea, together with the abandonment of Dacia and Mesopotamia by the imperial government, may be considered as the turning point in the Empire's history and therefore marked the beginning of the process of decline.[3] The demographic crisis had a particular impact on the Roman stock of population, and it was followed by an assimilatory evolution, which favoured the rise of provincial societies and also had an important impact on the decay of Roman-Latin culture. Different attempts to redress the situation, began with Caracala's edict of 212, who granted Roman citizenship to the inhabitants of the Empire, inspired by an urgent need to recruit them in the army. This was followed by measures taken by Diocletian and Constantine in the first quarter of the fourth century, which were conservative and aimed at returning to the 'old age' of the Augustan Empire. They

---

[1] The bibliography concerning the period discussed in the present survey is very abundant; for a general view, the synthesis by Lot, La fin du monde antique (1927), opened in its time new perspectives. Even though during the last sixty years many important studies have been published, Lot's work still remains a stimulating study; see its annotated reedition by M. Rouche (Paris 1986). On the other hand, Th. Schieffer, Europa im Wandel von der Antike zum Mittelalter (1976) represents newer trends of historical research.

[2] The reasons for the fall of Rome and of the break-up of the Mediterranean unity are a characteristic topic of historical controversy. In his Fall of Rome (1963), Chambers gathered excerpts from the main theses of this controversy, as well as the various aspects discussed by historians in their studies.

[3] See Katz, The Decline of Rome (1968) 5–24.

were ineffective and proved the incapacity of the giant Empire to reform itself radically.[4] Moreover, Caracala's reform reinforced centrifugal elements, opening the way to anarchy, because the new stock of soldiers proved to be primarily loyal to their own generals.

Parallel to this political and institutional evolution, the social body lost its coherence and unity during the third and fourth centuries; while, due to the cultural Roman and Hellenistic syncretism, the structures and the institutions developed in the classical period appear not to have changed. Oriental cults and provincial elements became dominant in both the civil society and in the army. It resulted with the emergence of particularist trends that, in the long term of the process, radically transformed the Greco-Roman society, mainly in the Western parts of the Empire. The differences between Italians, Africans, Gallo-Romans, and Ibero-Romans were patent and they contributed to deepen the gaps between these groups.[5] The freed slaves who, from the third century on, gained with their liberty the Roman citizenship and were enrolled in the army, led to the emergence of an additional factor of transformation, by the penetration of the Christian element within these military and civil structures. This process, an outcome of the spread of primitive Christianity among the slaves and the humble elements of society, reached its peak at the eve of the Constantinean period, when the Christians became the major part of the imperial army. It was Constantine's merit to be the first Emperor who became aware of the new reality; through his famous edict of Milan (313), he won the support and the loyalty of the Christian soldiers. Thus, he was able to overcome his rivals in the struggle for power and to become the sole Emperor, as significally stated: *in hoc signo vinces.*[6] Accordingly, the social revolutionary change resulted in the fourth century with the christianization of the Roman Empire. The new Empire, established by Constantine and reorganized by Theodosius towards the end of the same century, represented an entirely different society and culture, where the Scriptures, first the Septuagint and the *Vetus* Latin texts, and finally the *Vulgata*, replaced the classical tradition and its books.

These internal crises and the transfer, in the fourth century, of the imperial government to Constantinople, which was followed by the emigration of an important part of the military leadership and aristocracy from the Western provinces and their settlement in the new capital and its surroundings, favoured the penetration of Germanic tribes beyond the *limes* of the Danube and Rhine. This penetration, either in the form of a peaceful immigration of tribes that were recognized as "allies" of the Empire and were supposed to serve in the army, or bearing the character of violent invasions, such as those of the Goths in the Balkans, constituted a catalyst in the process of the Empire's disintegration. The impact of this external factor, even though an impor-

---

[4] The failure of the attempts to reform the Empire was meticulously discussed by Walbank, The Decline of the Roman Empire (1946); his study is a thoughtful analysis of the main problems related to the decline.

[5] See Laistner, Thought and Letters (1959) 15–53.

[6] See the excellent study by Jones, Constantine and the Conversion of Europe (1967).

tant one, was secondary however to the effects of the internal crises, which led Roman society to the point of inability to find appropriate means to overcome its difficulties. The spectacular victory of the Goths at Adrianople in 378, which has been interpreted by some modern historians as one of the symbolical events marking the turning point from Antiquity to the Middle Ages,[7] compelled the Roman authorities to react in order to assure the defense, and even the survival of the Empire. A consequence of these reflections on the fate of the Old Empire, was Emperor Theodosius' decision finally to divide the Roman Empire between his two sons, in 395. However, it is important to remark that, despite the continuous use of an archaic terminology, the Goths' victory was achieved over a weakened society, and over an inferior Legion, manned mainly by 'barbarians'.

Thus the division of 395 was in no way the beginning of the fifth-century decline of the Empire, but a turning point in a longer-term process of decay. In the immediate present, it gave advantage to the new "Eastern Roman Empire", where the political and social structures were less affected by the crisis, and the thriving economy raised substantial revenue for the government. Accordingly, Emperor Arcadius and his successors were able to undertake the necessary steps for a recovery, based upon a well organized bureaucracy, and to build up the entity destined to become the Byzantine Empire. Based on the paramount influence of the Greek-Christian element, which became dominant in the Eastern Empire, the government of Constantinople recovered the Balkans from the Goths and succeeded in establishing the unity of the Eastern Mediterranean area, which lasted until the seventh century.[8] Moreover, even after the rise of Islam and the Muslim conquests of its Middle Eastern and North African provinces, the structures of the Byzantine Empire, combining the political and administrative institutions with the religious and social elements, were still viable during most of the Medieval millenium.

On the other hand, the Western Roman Empire was already disintegrating at the beginning of the fifth century, and unable to replace its decayed political and social structures. With some minor exceptions in various areas of Italy, Gaul, and North Africa, the Germanic federates became the dominant element in the army and reached positions of command. This brought them into alliances with aristocratic families, among them even the imperial dynasty. Moreover, the government and the army were unable to resist the new processes of infiltration and invasions by the Germanic tribes. While Britain was evacuated, the famous *limes* of the Danube and the Rhine collapsed. The Visigoths invaded Italy and, after having sacked Rome in 410, settled in Southern Gaul and in the major part of Spain, where they established a powerful kingdom. The Vandals, who passed the Rhine westwards in 406, invaded southern Spain, named Andalusia after them, and finally conquered North Africa in 430; their kingdom was the sole Germanic realm adapted to the maritime civilization. It became a maritime power, which controlled the West Mediterra-

[7] The basic works on this field are the classical discussions by Oman, The Art of War (1924), and by Lot, L'art militaire (1946).

[8] See the detailed presentation by Jones, The Later Roman Empire (1964).

nean traffic. Their repeated attacks on the Italian shores gained them the false reputation of cruelty, to the point that their name gave rise to the current expression of 'vandalism'.[9] Moreover, as a result of the emigration of the Roman aristocracy to the new imperial centre in the East, mainly in Constantinople, many of the estates (*villae*) of the Western provinces became deserted in the fifth century. Thus, various Germanic chieftains, accompanied by the fighters attached to their families and by their servants, settled peacefully in these estates. They became the demographic basis of the new realms, founded in the aftermath of the 'barbarians migrations'. Accordingly, already during the fifth century, this combined process of invasion, infiltration and settlement led to a radical change in the lands of the Western Roman Empire, both political and demographic. In this last field, two main ethnic elements divided the large territory of the Western Empire; thus, Italy, Southern Gaul and Spain were the countries with a dominant "Romanic" element, although this Gallo-Roman population still remained the majority in some areas of Northern Gaul. These were the various Wallonies or Valois, which preserved the tradition of these Romanized inhabitants.[10] On the other hand, Northern and Eastern Gaul, and the lands between the Danube and the Alps acquired a Germanic character, both by the settlement of Germanic tribes and by the assimilation of the local elements and their Germanization.

Due to these conditions, the ancient Roman provinces of Gaul were gradually lost to the Empire. While already in 406 the Burgundians did establish an independent realm in the South-Eastern parts of Gaul, the areas west of the Rhône and south of the Loire rivers became a part of the kingdom of the Visigoths, who established in 420 their capital at Toulouse. On the other hand, in the North-Eastern parts of the country, the former province of *Gallia Belgica*, was settled by the Franks, who established some petty realms in the area. By the middle of the fifth century, only a small part of Gaul still remained under a nominal Roman authority, ruled by generals who, in collaboration with the surviving Gallo-Roman aristocracy, attempted to pursue a semblance of the imperial government.[11] Their victory over the Huns of Attila near Châlons in 452, was the last military achievement of the Roman Empire. However, this triumph was reached by a coalition of these remnants of Gallo-Romans and Germanic tribes, especially the Franks, led by one of their kings, Merovech, who gave his name to the merovingian dynasty, then based at Tournai. While this victory allowed the Roman administration to maintain its authority in Central and North-Western Gaul (i. e. the "state" of Syagrius), the real beneficiaries were the Franks who, as the main allies of the Empire, became the most important factor in this area. Moreover, the descendents of Merovech, kings of Tournai, enjoyed an increased prestige in the aftermath of the victory, which enabled them gradually to impose their authority over the other kings

[9] Courtois, Les Vandales et l'Afrique (1955) is the best study on the Vandals.

[10] Among many excellent studies on this topic, see those by STENGERS and by GYSSELING, though they are limited to Belgium and Northern Gaul.

[11] Despite its date, Dill, Roman Society (1898), remains the most authoritative study on this topic.

of this big tribal confederation of the Franks. Once this process was complete and the Franks were united under the rule of Clovis, the grand son of Merovech, they turned to an expansionist policy. Clovis's victory at Soissons, in 485, resulted in the conquest of the last Roman enclave in Gaul and the establishment of the most powerful Germanic kingdom in Western Europe. However, this military achievement was pursued by a peaceful process of settlement, which created the condition of peaceful co-habitation between the pagan and rural Franks and the Christian urbanized Gallo-Romans.[12]

In contrast to the evolution of these political and social changes in Gaul, Spain and North Africa, Italy, which was destined to be the centre of the Western Empire, experienced a long period of anarchy after the departure of the Visigoths. The Emperors were dependent on the recruitment of small Germanic tribes to the army and were compelled to appoint their chieftains to commanding positions. Although nominally these chieftains became "Roman citizens" and most of them even romanized their names, they did not change their manners and were thus designated by the Latin sources as 'barbarians'. This difference of manners prevented their integration within the Italo-Roman stock of population. Moreover, tribal feuds and chieftains' rivalries increased the state of anarchy, to the point that Italy became a target of further invasions and attacks, like the maritime plunders by the Vandals, from their North African kingdom.[13] Although the imperial documents were still formulated in the traditional style, that retained claims to the exercise of full power and sovereignty by the Emperors, as for example the letter of Emperor Valentinian III to Pope Leo I, this documentary fiction only emphasized the gap between the imperial symbolism and the reality. When Attila and his Huns invaded Italy in 453, neither the military nor political authorities were able to deal with the challenge; in contrast to the initiative which created the successful coalition in Gaul in the previous year, Pope Leo provided the necessary leadership. He went to Florence, where he met the Altayan chief, and bought the Huns' retreat to the former province of Pannonia by "rich presents".[14] The period of anarchy reached its peak in 476, when Odoacer, the chieftain of the Heruls, deposed the last "Roman" Emperor of the West, Romulus Augustulus, the son of a Roman princess and of a 'barbarian' chieftain. Moroever, Odoacer did not lay claim to the imperial title and, by sending the imperial *insignia* to Constantinople, he symbolically abolished the Western Roman Empire.

Thus, the fall of Rome signified the beginning of a new era in Western Europe, even though, as a matter of fact, this specific event was hardly perceived by contemporary observers. During the last fifty years of its formal history the Western Empire was a shadow. Regarding the profound political and social changes that were occurring from the fourth century, but which were still not finished in 476, it was an anachronistic entity. The two main political changes which occurred in Western Europe belong to the next decade; both the conquest of Gaul by the Franks and the establishment of the Ostrogothic kingdom

[12] See Wallace-Hadrill, The Long-Haired Kings (1962).
[13] See Courtois, Les Vandales (1955)
[14] Prosper Tiro, *Chronicon*, 482. See Thompson, A History of Attila (1948).

in Italy by Theodoric the Great were more important events than the deposition of Romulus Augustulus and they had a deeper impact upon the fate of Western Europe. Undoubtedly, the settlement of the Ostrogoths in Italy and the reign of Theodoric had been the major events of the end of the fifth and the beginning of the sixth century. This was not only due to his successful attempt at reuniting Italy, but particularly because of Theodoric's policy of integrating the Roman heritage and administration with the government of his own Germanic kingdom. For these purposes, he appointed Italo-Roman magistrates to senior positions in his government, and employed at his court reputable intellectuals, like the philosopher Boethius. However, this attempt at integration was destined to fail. Most of Theodoric's appointees were dismissed, exiled and even imprisoned, as was Boethius' fate. The gap between the Ostrogothic court of Verona and Rome was never bridged, and the remarks by contemporaries that the failure must have been imputed to the 'Barbarian manners' of the Ostrogoth monarch should be considered as only a partial view.[15] The main reason resided however on the religious level; like their kinsmen, the Visigoths, the Ostrogoths converted to Arian Christianity and, accordingly, were considered as the bitter enemies of the 'Romans', who belonged to the well organized Orthodox-Catholic Church. As such, they considered themselves to be the genuine heirs of the classical tradition and of Roman unity.[16] Such considerations had a tremenduous impact in the period of the creation of the new political and social structures in Western Europe. By comparison, there were no expressions of complaint concerning the behaviour of Clovis after his conversion to Orthodox-Catholic Christianity; his baptism transformed him into a "Roman Christian", despite his 'barbarian' manners, especially regarding his more accultured contemporary, Theodoric.

This failure of integration led to the fall of the Ostrogoth realm after the death of Theodoric (528) and to the active collaboration of the Italians with Justinian's generals. The conquest of Italy by the East Roman Empire, followed by that of the North African realm of the Vandals, in 531–535, seemed for the enlighted spirits of the epoch, to be a step toward the reunification of the Roman Empire, even though, effectively, these countries became remote provinces of the Byzantine Empire, which did not dispose of the necessary means for their defense.[17] Thus, a short time after Justinian's death, the major part of Italy was conquered without difficulties by the Lombards, in 568, while the Byzantine rule in the North African province was made possible, due to the lack of external challenges, until the middle of the seventh century.

In these circumstances, the Church played a growing role in the transmission of the heritage of the Roman legacy in Western Europe. From the middle of the fifth century the Papacy gained a particular authority over Latin Christendom and, unlike the four Patriarchal Sees in the East, the Patriarchs of the

---

[15] For example the views of Jordanes, *Getica,* passim, and of the sixth-century's Ennodius, in his *Panegyricus dictus clementissimo regi Theodorico.* See Ensslin, Theoderich der Grosse (1959).

[16] See the discussion by Vismara, Romani e Goti (1955).

[17] See Guillou, L'Empire romain d'Orient (1972) 134–54, emphasizing his criticism of Justinian's policy.

Western Church, which now constituted the Latin Church, did not share their pre-eminence with any other competitive religious centre. In addition to their spiritual leadership, they also fulfilled a political role. This political ascendance, begun with Leo I's meeting with Attila at Florence, was manifested by the continuous opposition of the Popes to any overwhelming imperial authority over the Church, as it was formulated at the end of the fifth century by the Eastern Roman Emperor Zenon, in his *Henoticon*, which became effective in the Eastern Greek-Orthodox Church. The objections of Pope Gelasius I to the *Henoticon*, pointed to the division of the Government of Christian society, between the imperial secular authority and the spiritual authority of the Church. Formulated as the "Doctrine of the two swords",[18] the Gelasian theory was widely accepted in Western Europe and became a basic principle of Roman Catholicism. However, the revival of the Byzantine Imperial power in the sixth century, manifested by the conquest of Italy, compelled the Popes to recognize a wide imperial authority, either exerced directly from Constantinople during Justinian's reign, or mainly through the Byzantine Exarch of Ravenna. But this authority was merely limited to the confirmation of papal elections, in the form of the imperial decree of *jussio*, i.e. a formal "order" addressed to the elected Pope, instructing him to begin the exercise of his function. Another important manifestation of this authority was the current appointment of a Byzantine duke as the governor of Rome who, among the military and administrative functions, was considered the "protector" of the Popes. Only after the Lombard conquest of the major part of Italy, whose results were the isolation of Ravenna, Pope Gregory the Great reached his virtual independence from the Byzantine sovereignty. He proclaimed in 590 St. Peter's sovereignty over Rome, a step that was subsequently considered as the ground-stone towards the foundation of the Medieval Papal State.[19]

As a consequence of the Ostrogoth and Byzantine failures to reach either a new integration, or the renewal, of Roman unity in the West, the impact of the conquest of Gaul by the Franks constituted the most important development in the process of building new political and social structures in Western Europe. The conversion of Clovis and his Franks to the Roman-Catholic faith was undoubtedly a factor that favoured the process of integration and assimilation between the Germanic conquerors and the Gallo-Roman population. In this respect, the circumstances of the conversion are less important than the fact itself; either it was the result of the influence upon her husband of Clotilde, the catholic wife of Clovis, and of the missionary efforts of St. Rémi, the Bishop of Rheims, who actually baptized Clovis, or a consequence of the king's political considerations. These were the result of his difficult battles against the Alamans and Visigoths, which created a need to rely on the loyalty of the Gallo-Romans. From either cause the conversion was a revolutionary event, and a precedent for further conversions. Accordingly, ecclesiastical sources describe it as a miraculous story, particularly Gregory of Tours, who compiled his

---

18 Mirbt, Qellen (1901) 67–68. See McGrade, Two fifth-century Conceptions of Papal Primacy (1969).

19 The best study remains that by Duchesne, Les premiers temps (1908).

chronicle at the end of the sixth century. This legendary account of Clovis' conversion was adapted in line with the vision of Constantine, at the eve of the battle of Milan, in 312, witnessing to the contemporaries' awareness of its paramount importance. Accordingly, Gregory of Tours described how the Frankish monarch sought the help of the "God of the Christians", at the eve of his battle of Tolbiac in 496, against the Alamans.[20] Certainly, the prompted conversion of the Franks served well both their own interests, and those of the Church, engaged in a bitter struggle against the Aryan Burgundians and Visigoths. Thus, after the victory of Clovis over the Visigoths at Vouillé, in 507, the entire former Gaul was again reunited under the authority of the Merovingian Franks. These enjoyed the loyalty of the Gallo-Roman population, and the collaboration of the administrative structure of the Church in the government of their realm.

Despite the frequent divisions of the kingdom between the members of the Merovingian dynasty, which reflected the implementation of the Germanic patrimonial conception of royalty, the Roman-Catholic Church was the factor of unity of this Kingdom. Moreover, the "Frankish Church" became the channel for the spread of Christian Latin civilization in Western Europe, meaning both the remnants of the classical tradition, and the biblical heritage. This culture was developed in the different episcopal schools, that replaced the ancient public schools of the Roman city, and particularly in the monasteries, which were richly endowed by the kings. The intellectuals of the Early Middle Ages inherited the study of several classical authors, whose works were considered as in conformity with the Christian faith. Some of these intellectuals became distinguished Christian poets, while others dedicated themselves to the study of the Bible, following the model of patristic exegesis. These cultural activities accompanied the process of social integration of the Romanic and Germanic elements, and became the foundation for building the new European society. The monks of the Frankish monasteries were active agents in spreading Christianity in Western Europe, either as a result of personal initiatives, like the conversion of the Irish by St. Patrick, after the achievement of his studies at Auxerre, or serving the interests of the Church and the policy of the Merovingians, in the pagan marches of the Eastern areas conquered by the Franks, such as Franconia and Thuringia.[21] Moreover, their activities served as a model for the conversion of other Germanic tribes, especially in the seventh century, and emphasized the missionary vocation of Roman-Catholic monasticism. These missionaries succeeded in converting the Aryan Visigoths of Spain, the heathen Lombards in Italy, and the Anglo-Saxons in Britain. However, the Anglo-Saxon mission, led by St. Augustine of Canterbury in 601, was the result of Pope Gregory the Great's decision to employ Benedictine monks for missionary tasks. It became the precedent for establishing the Papal missionary policy in the seventh and eighth centuries.[22] Thus, the process of spreading the

---

[20] Gregory of Tours, *Historia Francorum*, I, 119–21; see Tessier, Le baptême de Clovis (1964).

[21] See Prinz, Frühes Mönchtum (1965).

[22] The role of the Papacy as the leading authority of Christian missions from the end of the sixth century was emphasized by several scholars of the last generation. Among them, see Sullivan,

Christian faith in Western and Central Europe, which reached its peak in the eighth century, was finally the result of the combined spiritual leadership of the Papacy, of Frankish military support, and the activity of Anglo-Saxon monks, who undertook the missionary field-work. It also led to an emphasis on the study of the Old Testament, both in order to properly adapt the ideas of the "Holy Land, the Chosen people, and the biblical ideal of sacred Kingship" to the new circumstances, and, in a comparable way, because the legacy of biblical Israel adapted well to the rural mentality of the Germanic societies.

The biblical texts were particularly used by the thinkers of the Church as a source of authority for the development of Christian doctrine, and for its teaching. In the Greek-Orthodox Church, i.e. in the Eastern Roman Empire, the emphasis was put on the New Testament, which served as the main source for theologians like Gregory of Nyssa, John Chrysostom, Moschus of Constantinople (in his *Pratum spirituale*), and Sophronius of Jerusalem.[23] In contrast, the Western Fathers especially stressed the legacy of the Old Testament. They formulated conceptions of a historical evolution, grounded in the sacred history of the Sons of Israel and of the Davidic kingship, and continued in the history of the Christian Roman Empire, as well as in the Christianized Germanic Kingdoms. Already present in the fourth-century works of Orosius, this conception was brought to its perfection by historians of the Early Middle Ages, like Gregory of Tours, in the late sixth century, whose narratives on the rise and development of the Kingdom of the Franks became the "Holy History of the Franks", or Bede the Venerable, in the eighth century, in his "Holy History of the Britons". Accordingly, these authors epitomized the historical books of the Old Testament, and the history of Christian Rome, as preludes to their chronicles. On the other hand, treatises concerning the moral teaching of Christian doctrines and those concerning pastoral care, were modeled on biblical exegesis; in this field the most important contribution was that of Pope Gregory the Great, whose treatise *Moralia in Job* was widely diffused during the entire medieval epoch, and became an example for the new trends of biblical exegesis, as well as of the development of Christian moral thinking.[24] Accordingly, ideas of spiritual reward for pious behaviour, or of the punishment of sins, were based on texts from the Prophets, and were preached by the missionaries, who connected them with the development of ideas concerning a divinely elected nation. Grounded on the biblical legacy of the Covenant between God and Israel, this alliance was conceived as that of Divinity with Christendom, which formed the 'spiritual Israel'. Moreover, the Psalms were widely used in liturgy, and inspired the emergence of Christian liturgical hymns in the sixth century. After the reunification of the Kingdom of the Franks by Clotar II and the celebration of the council of Paris in 615, the pre-

---

The Papacy and Missionary Activity (1955), Bertolini, I papi e le missioni (1967) and, concerning the first "Papal mission", Wallace-Hadrill, Rome and the Early English Church (1960).

[23] See the works of Baynes, reprinted in his Byzantine Studies (1955).

[24] See Laistner, Thought and Letters (1959); he expressed these ideas in his Intellectual Heritage (1957) in a more general frame; on the other hand, see Riché, Education et culture (1962/1990).

cepts of the Old Testament were integrated in the religious and lay legislation of the Franks, who considered themselves as the "elder sons of the Church".[25]

Thus, the decline and fall of the Roman Empire and the rise of its successors in the fifth and the sixth centuries led to the break-up of the political unity of the lands around the Mediterranean Sea. While the Eastern lands were restructured and reunited within the Byzantine Empire, the Western countries, first divided and ruled by chieftains of petty tribal realms, were finally structured within more important and powerful 'barbarian' kingdoms, especially those of the Franks, Visigoths, and Lombards. In the same perspective, the disintegrated Roman-Hellenistic society, which had borne a closely similar character throughout its structures, institutions, and civilization, was fundamentally changed, both in the Eastern Byzantine Empire, and in the West-European kingdoms. Nevertheless, while in the fourth century the spread of Christianity brought about the political and cultural assimilation of the Roman imperial legacy to Christian teaching, the events of the late fifth century, in the aftermath of the fall of the Western Roman Empire, led the leaders of the Church to initiate missionary activity among the Germanic tribes. This was pursued further until the christianization of Scandinavia, in the eleventh century. The results of these ecclesiastical missions consisted in the rise of the conception of 'brotherhood', meaning egality between the Romanic and the Germanic elements, and they led to the creation of a new unity in Western and Central Europe, based on the common Roman Catholic religion and the development of its culture. In the framework of this religious unity, the process of ethnic and social integration between the Romanic and romanized elements, and the Germanic settlers, led to the emergence of new societies. However, while the religious unity signified the rule of one common faith and the adoption of common rites, grounded in the use of Latin as the theological and liturgical language, these new societies developed their own particular identities, in certain cases even within tiny areas, like the county. Hence, a dichotomy developed in the medieval Western world, where 'universalist' ideas, as expressed by a religious and intellectual cultural unity, were continuously confronted and challenged by the 'particularistic' reality of the social order, by the rise of vernacular tongues, and by the development of the popular culture of feudal societies.

2. The Rise of Muslim Civilization

The nomadic tribes of the Arabian deserts had already experienced a long period of relations, mainly through confrontations, with the sedentary population of the "fertile Crescent", i.e., Mesopotamia, Syria, and Palestine, before the rise of Islam in the seventh century. Manifested sometimes by peaceful infiltration and sometimes by large-scale immigration, or by the settlement of refugees, like those Jews who fled Palestine after the destruction of the second

[25] See Leclercq, L'Ecriture sainte dans la hagiographie monastique (1963), and, concerning the impact of the Bible on the writing of history, Lehmann, Der Einfluss der Bibel (1963).

Temple in 70 and settled in Hejjaz, and of Christian anchoretes in the deserts, these relations were characterized by a continuous interaction of the different elements, most of them Semitic. As a result of these contacts, the nomads acquired some cultural traditions of sedentary populations, whether they were hellenized Semites, or exponents of the Jewish, and later, Christian faith. The establishment of a Jewish community in Yatreb (the future *Al-Medinah*) led to the spread of Jewish religious practices among the tribes of Hejjaz, and even to a certain degree of knowledge of the Old Testament, mostly diffused through oral tales.[26]

On the other hand, the penetration of Arabic elements to the countries of the "fertile Crescent" occasionally resulted in the creation of political entities, for example the Kingdom of the Nabateans, which extended over the areas of Southern Transjordan and the Negev. This kingdom, which flourished between the first and the third centuries, controlled the trade routes of balsam and spices, which were exported to the various provinces of the Roman Empire through the port of Ghaza; in the third century, the Nabateans converted to Christianity, and became integrated in the Christian society of Roman Palestine. However, as a consequence of the need to deploy elements of the Roman army in the other parts of the imperial territories, the government of the Eastern Roman Empire adapted the old policy of using *foederati* tribes to the Palestinian *limes* for the defense of its borders. They thereby created a Christian Arabic buffer state, the Ghassanid principality, which was situated in the area between the Jordan and the Northern Arabian desert.[27] This measure proved its relative efficiency as a barrier between the settled "fertile Crescent" and sporadic attempts at nomad infiltrations, until the beginning of the seventh century, when the Ghassanids collapsed under the attacks of the Persians, who conquered Jerusalem in 614. Thus, when the Arabs, united under Muhammad, undertook their invasion in 630, there had no more been an organized defense of the "fertile Crescent's" frontiers.

Muhammad's activity in Mecca, and especially in Medinah, after his forced migration of 622, does not need a new consideration.[28] As the founder of a new monotheistic religion, Islam, he was able to unite under his leadership and religious authority the various Arab tribes who, during a period of eight years, converted to the new faith and prepared their assault on the "fertile Crescent", assault conceived as a Holy War (*Jihad*), destined to spread the faith of Islam. This war was conducted after his death by his old companions of Mecca, who followed him in the Medinah exile and became his immediate successors. Named *Khalifs*, i.e. the Prophet's substitutes, they succeeded during the next twenty years in conquering the entire "fertile Crescent", Egypt and Persia. While the first of these four *Khalifs*, Abu-Bakr, extended Muslim

[26] For Pre-Islamic Arabia, see the studies gathered by Altheim / Stiehl, Die Araber im der alten Welt (1964–1969).

[27] The best study concerning the role of the Ghassanid principality is that by Dévréesse, Arabes 'perses' et Arabes 'romains' (1942). For the process of Arabic penetrations in Syria and Palestine, see Dussaud, La penetration des arabes en Syrie (1955).

[28] Among many excellent studies, see Montgomery Watt, Muhammad in Mecca (1958).

rule over Transjordan, the real conqueror was his successor, Omar Al-Khatib, whose victory of Yarmuk, in 636, over the Byzantine army was decisive. The Muslims crushed on the Yarmuk river the sole military force that was considered capable of defending the Empire's Oriental provinces. Thereafter, they effectively met a weak resistence in their conquests. The animosity of the Oriental Christians to the Byzantine government, as a result of their oppression by the Greek Orthodox hierarchy which accused them of heresy, played a crucial role in favouring the Muslim conquests. These Christians not only adopted a passive attitude in the battles, but even, welcomed the Muslim conquerors as their "liberators".[29]

The expansion of Islam continued after 660 under the leadership of the Ummayad Khalifs, the first Arab dynasty, which established its capital in Damascus. Up to the beginning of the eighth century these conquests extended in the East as far as the banks of the river Indus (704), while in the West, they covered the whole of North Africa and the major part of Spain (711–719), where the kingdom of the Visigoths collapsed. However, the Ummayad domination was fiercely contested by the followers of 'Ali, Muhammad's son-in-law, whose claims to the Caliphate were set aside in favour of Muawiyah, the founder of the Ummayad dynasty. While the rulers of Damascus were able to overcome their adversaries, mainly based in Iraq, this rivalry led to a split in the Muslim world in the second half of the seventh century. The followers of the sons of 'Ali, named the *Shi'ites*, adopted, in addition to their dynastic claims, a series of theological arguments, based on their pretension of practising a "pure Islam". Thereby they emphasized their fundamentalist interpretation of Islamic religion.[30] On the other hand, the Ummayads, who gained the loyalty of the great majority of Muslims, i.e. the *Sunnites*, are considered as the genuine founders of the Islamic theology and of Muslim civilization. In this respect, the Sunnite theologians were influenced by the Jewish and the Christian exegesis of the Old Testament, to which they contributed by their own methods of interpretation, namely the *Qalam.*[31] Accordingly, the ancient Hellenistic schools of Alexandria in Egypt, and of Antioch in Northern Syria, were converted into Muslim centres of philosophical and scientific studies, based on the translation into Arabic of the Greek treatises, especially the writings of Aristotle. These new centres of learning, which expanded in the eighth century to Baghdad and the Iranean centres, and in the ninth to *Al-Andalus*, the Arabic name of Spain, became the basis of the emergence and development of the Muslim 'Golden Age', which lasted until the twelfth century.[32]

It is important to remark that, despite the exclusive use of Arabic, both in theological treatises and in liturgy, and in philosophical and scientifical works, this cultural awakening was the result of the collaboration of a pluralist society of scholars. This included besides Arabs and Arabized elements in the Middle

---

[29] See McGraw Donner, The Early Muslim Conquests (1981), who emphasized the crucial importance of the period between 622–660.

[30] See Montgomery Watt, Shiism under the Ummayads (1960).

[31] See the authoritative article by Gardel, Ilm al-Kalam (1971), and his bibliography.

[32] See Lévi-Provençal, Histoire de l'Espagne musulmane (1949–1955).

East and Spain, Muslim Iranians, Syriac Christians and Copts, as well as Jews. The use of Aristotelian methods in the search for rational grounds of faith and its precepts, characterized the trend of studies of the Muslim Iranian Ibn Sinna, in the eighth century, and of his disciples until the times of the Andalusian philosopher Ibn Rushd (*Averroes*, d. 1198) of Cordova, as well as those of the Jewish Saadiah Gaon in the first half of the tenth century, until the period of Maimonides (d. 1204).[33] As a result of the use of the Arabic language by the Jewish philosophers in the Middle East and in Spain, their books were accessible to Muslim scholars; hence, Muslim theologians became acquainted with the interpretations of biblical texts by Jewish scholars and exegetes.

The Muslim conquests of the seventh and eighth centuries brought about the break-up of the Ancient Roman unity of the Mediterranean region, bringing the long-term evolution begun in the third century to its end. By the eve of the Abbasid revolution (750) and the transfer of the Caliphate's capital to Baghdad, this large area was divided into three main entities: the remnants of the Eastern Roman, i.e. the Byzantine Empire, mainly in the coastal areas of the Balkan peninsula and in Asia Minor; the Germanic realms of Western Europe with the Roman Catholic countries, and the huge Caliphate, stretching from the borders of India, through the Middle East, along the southern Mediterranean, to Spain. However, the rise of the Abbasids led to political divisions within the Caliphate: the Ummayad governors in Spain did not recognize the authority of the *Khalifs* of Baghdad and managed to create and establish their own "Caliphate of Cordova", which flourished in the ninth to the eleventh centuries.[34] Moreover, while having recognized the supreme authority of the Abbasids, the governors of several provinces in the Mediterranean areas attained in the ninth century a large degree of autonomy. They established their own dynasties, like the Idrisids, in Morocco, the Aglabites of Kairuwan, who were the Emirs of Western North Africa and Sicily, and the Tulunids, in Egypt and Palestine, who were the most important rulers of a confused mix of small Emirates. Thus, within the religious unity of the Muslim world, the Caliphate was divided into a multitude of political entities, correspondinq to the kingdoms which emerged in Western and Central Europe in the ninth century from the division of the Carolingian Empire.

However, in contrast to the political disintegration, religion was a factor of unity within the three main entities, which divided the Mediterranean world. The expansion of Christianity in Western and Central Europe led to the religious union of the various societies in the Northern Mediterranean countries, which included Northern Europe; Latin, as the language of liturgy and theology became the ecumenical language of culture of the Roman Catholic world. In a similar way, despite the political split of the Abbasid Caliphate, the area

[33] Blachère, Histoire de la littérature arabe (1952–1966) replaces now the classical work by Brockelmann. For unitarian and centrifugal trends of the Abbasid civilization, see Sourdel, L'Empire abbaside de 750 à 945 (1972). For the philosophy, see Corbin, Histoire de la philosophie islamique (1964).

[34] In addition to Lévi-Provençal, see the convenient survey by Terrasse, Islam de l'Espagne (1958).

represented a religious and cultural unity, based on the common religion of Islam, its Muslim culture, and on Arabic, as the unique learned language of the various Muslim societies. The religious division between Christendom and Islam however had an important impact on the historical evolution of the main components of medieval society. It caused a sharp separation between Muslims and Christians, to the extent that, until the twelfth century, they ignored each other and developed misconceptions concerning the 'other world'; some of them remained isolated until the nineteenth century. These misconceptions, were the result of a religious separation which lasted through many centuries, despite the continuous economic relationships between the various components of the Mediterranean communities.[35]

3. The New Political and Social Order in the Carolingian Era

Technically, the Carolingian revolution may be defined as the achievement of a process of dynastic change, occurring in the Kingdom of the Franks, by the replacing of the weakened and decayed Merovingian Kings by the families of the Pippinide (later called Carolingian) *major domi*, who already held from the middle of the seventh century hereditarily, the real power in the various Frankish realms. Even though, nominally, the traditional divisions of the Merovingian kingship continued to be practiced, the Austrasian *major domus* Pippin II exercised this function in all the four Merovingian Kingdoms and, thus, united the Frankish Kingdom under his rule (689). His son, Charles Martel, became the uncontested master of this state and, finally, his grandson, Pippin III acceded to the royal title in 753. However, besides this dynastic event, the real impact of this revolution was related to the emergence and establishment of a new political and social order, first in the land of the Franks, and later, extending to the whole West-European region. As the greatest landowners in the realm, mainly in the Western Kingdom of Austrasia, where they held an important part of its territory as their family possessions, which were mainly situated between the Rhine and the Somme rivers, the Pippinides became the lords of an impressive mass of warriors who, either voluntarily or compulsorily, were dependent on them and entered their *mundeburdium*. The exercise of this pre-feudal authority enabled them to recruit the most efficient army available in Western Europe during the seventh century, and enabled them to impose their power in the Kingdom, administering the royal landed property.

---

[35] The long debate on the Pirenne theses is beyond the scope of the present essay. While the decline of the Roman cities in Western Europe and the emphasis on the agrarian economy in the new realms of Western Europe resulted in an important diminution of the trade between East and West, there is no evidence that the Muslim conquests led to the cessation of this trade, following the political and religious division of the Mediterranean world. Ships continued to sail, connecting in the eighth century Christian and Muslims harbors and, according to accounts of pilgrims to the Holy Land, there were no difficulties in finding vessels ready to sail. For the Mediterranean trade in the seventh to the ninth century, see Doehaerd, Le Haut Moyen Age occidental (1971) 273–281. Nevertheless, tendencies of ignoring each other resulted in misconceptions concerning the 'other world'; see Southern, Islam and the West (1963).

Thus they had the power to increase the number of their *antrustiones* (an earlier term for vassals). Despite a bitter family war after the death of Pippin II (714), which lasted three years, until Charles Martel seized power, these warriors remained loyal to the Pippinides and did not attempt to change lords or free themselves from their lordship.[36]

The reorganization of the Kingdom by Charles Martel and particularly his victory over the Muslims at the battle of Poitiers (732–733), not only increased his prestige in Christendom, but also led a growing number of warriors to submit to his lordship. Charles' use of mounted cavalry in his wars, which was a consequence of technological changes in Western Europe at the beginning of the eighth century, implied a change in the system of rewarding military service, by giving the warriors larger estates.[37] Practically, Charles Martel rewarded the service of this new type of mounted warrior by administering the estates of the Church; given to these vassals as a benefice for the period of their service, the new system imposed a reinforced dependence of the vassals on their lord, assured them of appropriate revenue needed for their equipment and, formally, did not change the protected status of ecclesiastical property, even though bishops and abbots were no more free to dispose of it. Thus, on the eve of his death (741), Charles Martel enjoyed unlimited power over the Frankish Kingdom and arranged its division between his two sons, Carloman and Pippin "the Short". However, Carloman's conversion to monasticism and his retirement to the Abbey of Monte-Cassino, left Pippin the sole master of the Kingdom. While he brought to completion within the realm the social and military changes initiated by his father, Pippin III strengthened his relations with the Papacy. He pursued his father's protection of the missionaries who were acting in Germany, on behalf of the Papacy, and reinforced the concept of a joint policy aimed at christianizing the pagan tribes East of the Rhine. On the other hand, he also became active in Italian politics, as the ally of Papacy against the Lombards and the remnants of the Byzantine *exarchate* of Ravenna. The right of privilege he issued in 757, recognizing papal sovereignty in Rome and Ravenna, formed the basis for the establishment of "St. Peter's Patrimony", i. e., the foundation of the Papal State, which was destined to last until 1870. This policy brought him the ecclesiastical support he needed for his elevation to the kingship; having deposed the Merovingian monarch, Chilperic III, Pippin did not content himself with a traditional acclamation by his warriors, which was the symbolic 'election' and recognition of kings in the Germanic societies. In addition to this ancient ceremony, he sought ecclesiastical legitimacy, formulated by the papal recognition of his kingship. Moreover, Pope Stephen's journey to Rheims, where he anointed Pippin and his two sons, was not only an innovation in itself, but also carried a particular significance, because it evoked the biblical practice of anointing kings; thus, the Pope played the role of the prophet Samuel and, according to Old Testament precedent, he established in the person of the new Carolingian monarch a 'sacred kingship',

---

[36] See Riché, Carolingiens (1983).

[37] As emphasized by the excellent study by White, Medieval Technology (1962) 1–28.

modeled after the biblical monarchy, where the king was, besides the people, an agent of the Covenant.[38]

Hence, the Carolingian revolution brought about a much more profound transformation than a simple change of dynasty in one of the 'barbarian' realms of Western Europe, even though it had been the most important among them. Due to the ecclesiastical character of the royal anointing and coronation, it laid the ground for the emergence of medieval theocratical monarchy. Instead of the simple title *vir inluster* of the Merovingian kings, the Carolingians and, subsequently, the other medieval monarchs, reigned *Dei gratia* and, accordingly, were considered to represent in their realms the Divine sovereignty. Thus, besides their lay authority, exercised through military command, through the securing of justice to their subjects, and the administration of the realm, they were held responsible for their subjects' behaviour, in collaboration with the clergy.

These theocratical trends were emphasized by Charlemagne, during his long reign (769–814). They clearly appear in the royal and imperial *capitularia* issued after the desastre of Roncevals (787), and defined both the significance of the oath of fealty required to be taken by all his subjects, and the moral and religious duties of the monarch. The same ideas were expressed in Charlemagne's letter addressed to Pope Leo III in 796, where he congratulated him for his election to the Papal See and laid down the grounds of the imperial claims for spiritual authority. The implementation of these theocratic ideas stressed the variety of fields Charlemagne considered as his moral duty to be involved in, beginning with the forceful constraint of the Saxons to convert to the Christian faith, through his ordinances of establishing schools, including the *curriculum* of study, and extended to his involvement in purely theological matters, especially at the Council of Frankfurt in 794. It was thus a natural outcome that the authorship of the *Libri Carolini*, a theological treatise summing up the positions adopted by the hierarchy of the Frankish Church, was attributed to him.[39] Moreover, the mirror of this theocratic royalty was projected over the West-European Christendom, as a result of Charlemagne's imperial coronation in 800.

In this respect, Charlemagne's military achievements, including the conquest of Italy and his coronation at Pavia as "King of the Lombards" in 774, created the appropriate conditions for the revival of the Western Empire. Certainly, neither in geographical terms, nor in its ethno-social structure was Charlemagne's Empire a new version of the ancient Western Roman Empire. Its axis was no longer the Mediterranean, but the Rhine valley and, while the Roman Church evoked its religious unity, the Germanic groups, with their particularist tendencies, were the dominant ethnical element of an Empire that, by and large, included Italy, France, and Germany. These differences between the two empires were perceived by contemporaries. While Pope Leo III hailed the new "Emperor of the Romans", whom he crowned on the basis of alleged

---

[38] See Folz, Le couronnement impérial de Charlemagne (1964) 40–42.

[39] *Admonitio generalis* (789), in Baretius' *Capitularia Regum Francorum*, 53–62; these ideas were developed in 794 in the *Libri Carolini*. See Folz, ibid. 91–120.

rights the Papacy enjoyed through a false document named the "Donation of Constantine", which thereby alluded to a rebirth of the Western Roman Empire, Charlemagne and his counsellors did not hide their reluctance to adopt this title. Most of them preferred Alcuin's idea of an "Empire of the Christians", which should have included the Patriarchates of Rome and Jerusalem.[40] In order to emphasize the difficulties created by these different titles, it should be recalled that the process of the *Renovatio Romani Imperii* under Otto I (962) led to the use of a new title, "The Holy Roman Empire of the Germanic Nation", that fitted better the nature and the idea of this imperial entity. In the aftermath of the imperial coronation of 800 it was even not clear whether the imperial title had been a personal one, bestowed upon Charlemagne alone, or whether it was also to be inherited by his successors. While the first idea was expressed in Charlemagne's capitulary of 806, providing the division of his realms between his three sons, a decision that reflected the implementation of the old Frankish traditions, the second view prevailed after the death of his two elder sons. This led him to bestow his entire heritage, as well as the imperial title on Louis the "Pious", who was crowned in 813 by his father.[41]

However, despite Charlemagne and Louis' efforts to maintain the unity of the Empire, this huge State was unable to resist both external attacks, mainly by Scandinavian "Norman" invaders, and internal anarchy. Lacking any efficient administrative structure that assured the viability of the Byzantine Empire, despite its weakeness and loss of important territories to Muslim and Slav invaders, the Carolingian Empire became, in the ninth century, the victim of feudal centrifugal forces. Thus, already during the reign of Louis the "Pious" it became evident that the empire was to be divided among his sons, on the ground of the new ethno-linguistic realities. The "Verdun Agreement" of 843, concluding the war begun after Louis' death in 840, laid down the grounds of the foundation of three states, France, Germany, and the Imperial Lotharingia, which included Italy; however, Lotharingia was soon divided into a multitude of small realms and principalities. But despite the impact of centrifugal forces towards the disintegration of the Carolingian Empire, the Frankish Church continued to be a factor of unity until the late ninth century.

The activity of the leaders and thinkers of the Frankish Church, among them monks and clerics of different origins, such as Italians, Spaniards, and Irish, was related to the cultural awakening named the "Carolingian Renaissance". Many of them, like Hincmar of Rheims, Jonas of Orleans or Theodulf "the Goth", were concerned with the idea of the Empire and its 'spiritual' unity. Their political thought was influenced by the Augustinean ideal of the City of God, but also by their attempt of implementing the ideas of biblical kingship, as the idealistic mirror of the Carolingian Empire, through the interpretation of the Old Testament. Such attempts resulted with the revival of exegesis, for example in the works of Hrabanus Maurus, Abbot of Fulda and Archbishop of Mainz. Moreover, some of the thinkers connected biblical and post-hellenistic cosmological views into a development of the analogy of the

---

[40] See Grabois, Charlemagne, Rome, and Jerusalem (1981).
[41] See Riché, Carolingiens (1983) 130–45.

'celestial' hierarchy and the actual social order. Expressed, particularly by John Scott Eriugena, in the terms of the Neo-Platonic philosophy, such an analogy tended to legitimize the earthly social order, considered to be the expression of the Divine will; accordingly, the biblical political ideas were connected to the actual social order, and that, despite the ecclesiastical opposition to feudalism.[42]

It is commonly accepted that the Carolingian Renaissance had been a conservative cultural movement, merely tending to the revival of the past, instead of innovating. While this definition is correct in many aspects, such as the revival of the "Seven Liberal Arts", philosophical thought or the writing of history, it had a more original expression concerning the Bible and its study. In this field, the ninth-century *scriptoria* produced more copies than any other anterior period, to the point that the Vulgate became the most widely used book, in the monastic and cathedral libraries, as well as in the private libraries of the Carolingian lay aristocracy. Some of these copies were richly illustrated, creating a visual interpretation of the ideological and political message of the Scriptures.[43] But besides the production of copies and their spread, Carolingian scholars, beginning with Alcuin, in the late eighth century, and across the ninth century, dedicated themselves to the study of the Old Testament and its exegesis. However, since this topic is dealt with in Chap. 28.3–4, it will not be discussed here.

In addition to its political and cultural aspects, the Carolingian revolution signified a radical change in the nature and structure of society, a change whose impact was felt in the next centuries, until the results of the urban revolution led to another long-term evolution, beginning in the twelfth century. Certainly, the rural character of early medieval societies, which emerged and developed in Western Europe from the fifth century on, as a result of the settlement of Germanic people in the countries of the former Western Roman Empire, remained the constant basis of social structure. Either being juridically freemen or belonging to the servile class, the peasants worked the fields and raised cattle. When settled in the estates (*villae*), they were compelled to serve their landlords by working in their holdings and household, and by giving them part of their crops, instead of paying taxes. A characteristic change in the structure of peasant society that occurred in the Carolingian era was the gradual disappearance of slavery, thereby bringing an end to a process begun in late Antiquity. Hence, the term *servi*, used in classical Latin for slaves, changed its meaning, to signify dependent peasants, attached to the estate, i. e. villeins. They were required to fulfil a larger number of working-service days than the free peasants, but on the other hand, they were not expected to serve in the army.[44] However, towards the end of the eighth century, economic rea-

---

[42] See Morrison, The Two Kingdoms (1964), emphasizing Carolingian political and ecclesiological thought, and McKitterick, The Carolingians and the Written Word (1989).

[43] See for example, Riché, Les bibliothèques de trois aristocrates (1963) Bischoff, Die Hofbibliothek unter Ludwig dem Frommen (1976); Wallace-Hadrill, A Carolingian Renaissance Prince (1978); McKitterick, Charles the Bald and his Library (1980).

[44] See Boutruche, Seigneurie et féodalité (1968), I, 65–158.

sons, resulting from the subsistance nature of the agrarian economy, led to the abolition of military service requirements even from free peasants. Only those who possessed a landed property of four *mansi*, which entitled them to the service and revenues from three other peasant families, were still obliged to fulfil military service.

The real revolutionary changes however concerned the landlords and the mounted warriors, the cavalry. During the century that followed the reforms of Charles Martel, the use of the beneficiary system for rewarding the military service of vassals was spread to practically all of the countries under the dominion of the Carolingians. This reached the point that it became a general practice. Moreover, during the reign of Charlemagne, this system was extended to reward administrative service; it was generally accepted that one of the monarch's vassals, upon his appointment to govern a county, should be entitled to be invested with a considerable estate as benefice, the income of which would correspond to the appropriate expenditure, according to his "honor". Accordingly, the feudal system was extended in order to build up an administrative machinery, composed by landlords, who replaced the ancient Roman bureaucracy. Thus, the beneficiary regime became the basis for the rise of a new aristocracy, the corner stone of the new social order, which was composed by tenants of estates. While mounted warriors were considered as the lower *stratum* of this aristocracy, the holders of "honors", which included the different officials who were appointed to administrative and gubernatorial tasks, emerged, already during the reign of Charlemagne, as the new high aristocracy of the Empire. The nucleus of this was composed of members of about forty families, originally of the Austrasian Frankish realm, i. e. descendents of the traditional companions of the Pippinide-Carolingian dynasty. To this *groemium* were joined scions of other distinguished Frankish and Germanic families, as well as Romanic elements. During the ninth century, they became a social class, partly due to the processes of intermarriage and partly to the process of the inheriting of functions and their benefices, which were now named *feuda*. Under the pressure of these clans, the Carolingian monarchs were obliged to bestow "honores", meaning both the function and the land assigned to it, on their sons, with no consideration for their capacities or for royal interests.[45]

However, from the beginning of the ninth century, the trend of confounding the tenures and the lands possessed by the vassals as private proprieties (the *allodia*) became manifest, despite the formal orders of Charlemagne, prohibiting this practice. The appointment by the Emperor of *missi dominici* ("the Envoys of the Lord"), who were sent annually to the various provinces in order to spread imperial ordinances and to enforce on the Emperor's behalf the proper exercise of the local governors and administrators' functions. This was also intended to enforce the distinction between private properties and the benefices rewarding public functions; however, since the *missi* were selected from the same aristocratic families, the effectiveness of accomplishing these duties had

[45] Ibid. 161–97.

been limited, despite the presence of ecclesiastical personalities in these delegations. After the death of Charlemagne in 814 and the emergence of the centrifugal forces that led to the disintegration of the Carolingian Empire, the *missi* ceased to be the faithful representatives of the central government, i.e. the kings. By the middle of the ninth century, this decayed institution disappeared. Hence, the evolution of feudal practices was achieved, and the holders of "honores" practically became the lords of the vassals in the respective counties, duchies or marquisates, including the former royal vassals.[46] These tenants-in-chief exercised in the territories of their lordship the royal prerogatives, i.e. military command, the administration of justice, and receipt of the royal taxes; yet, having no more been controlled by the *missi*, the high aristocracy appropriated these prerogatives and exercised them throughout their own estates and the territories they ruled on behalf of the royal authority. Accordingly, in the second half of the ninth and in the tenth century, they became the effective lords, by hereditary right, of their duchies (in Germany) or counties (in France and Italy), nominally bound to the kings by the oath of homage and fidelity.

4. The Effect of Political, Social and Cultural Upheavals for the Jewish Settlements and Centres of Learning

In late Antiquity, the great majority of Jews lived in the Middle Eastern countries, especially in Mesopotamia and Egypt, though there also were important settlements in Palestine, Syria and Asia Minor. However, from the first century CE on, many Jews settled in the Western provinces of the Roman Empire, where the most important community was that of Rome. These settlements increased with the arrival of prisoners taken in the aftermath of the wars in Judaea, who were brought to serve as slaves in the *castra* of the Roman army. Whether they were voluntary immigrants or descendents of exiles, the Jewish element established in the different settlements and adapted the structures of the Palestinian communities to the new realities.[47] Concentrated around the local synagogue, these communities enjoyed a religious autonomy that gradually became the origin of a communitarian self-government, through small groups of *parnassim* (notables), who were the equivalent of the first-century Palestinian councils of "the seven elders", or "the good men of the town". According to the privilege issued by Emperor Theodosius to the community of Cologne on the Rhine (ca. 390), which represents the most ancient document concerning the imperial policy towards Jewish communities, the leadership that exercised self-government was regarded as a college of dignitaries of the Synagogue.[48] Yet, because the members of this college practically ruled the entire community, these Jewish settlements were regarded by Roman Law as reli-

[46] The study by Werner, Missus, marchio, comes (1980), replaces the various works on the *missi dominici*.

[47] See Baron, Community (1943), chap. I.

[48] *Codex Theodosianus*, XVI.8.4 (ed. Friedberg, *Corpus Juris Civilis*).

gious entities. This nature of Jewish social organization was thereafter inherited by the heirs of Rome, whether they were the Christian or the Muslim realms, created in the fifth to the seventh centuries.

However, the collapse of the Roman Empire in Western Europe was an additional factor in the process of consolidating the autonomy of these communities. The fourth-century emigrations to the East, resulting from the gradual decline of the Western Roman city, left in these towns a reduced number of inhabitants, who constituted the new urban society of the early Middle Ages. Besides an ecclesiastical settlement, destined to become the groemium of the future Christian parishes, this society included some Christian merchants, immigrants from Syria and Palestine, who left their native countries in the aftermath of the Muslim conquests of the middle of the seventh century and settled in different towns of Italy and Gaul where they were known by the name of *Syri*; and there were ancient Jewish communities as well. The rulers of the new Germanic realms showed little interest in urban life and its economy and, accordingly, the townsmen reached a larger degree of freedom within their respective quarters than the peasants. In the absence of the former public authorities, bishops undertook the leadership of the new city, although practically, they used to limit it to the area of the Cathedral and its surroundings. In this area they exercised their authority over the *familia* of the bishopric, which included the clergy, monastic settlements, as well as the laymen employed in their service.[49] As regards the Jewish settlements, the communitarian organization remained the last surviving feature of the ancient urban order. As such, it served as a model for the constitution of the new urban parishes, and also established an autonomous socio-religious entity within the urban settlement.

On the other hand, ecclesiastical councils decreed, from the fifth century on, a series of canons, aimed at segregation between the Christian and Jewish inhabitants. These included the prohibiting of the possession of slaves by Jewish owners, and banned the participation of Jews in common meals in the city.[50] Motivated by a desire to prevent newly converted Christians from being influenced by Jewish religious practices, that might persuade them to abjure their religion and convert to Judaism, these measures reflected, in no less a degree, the impact of the Judeo-Christian theological controversy. The already old christological dispute was enlarged by the inclusion of new issues, among them the debate over *verus Israel*; thus, Christian theologians, such as Origen in the third century, Eusebius of Caesarea in the fourth, or Augustine of Hippo in the fifth, argued that since Jews were obstinate in their refusal to accept the Divinity of Christ and the Gospels, they were denied the divine promise of being the elected people. Accordingly, while the Jews were recognized as the "blood and flesh" descendents of the Sons of Israel, the Christians became the "spiritual", i.e., the real Israel. Having adopted the Old Testament ideas of sin and punishment, Christian theologians emphasized that the Exile of the Jews was the divine punishment inflicted upon them for having denied Christ, stressing however that their repentance, by conversion to Christianity, was the sole

---

[49] See Ennen, Frühgeschichte der europäischen Stadt (1978).

[50] Council of Agde (510) (ed. Mansi, Concilia), 8, 331–32.

way for their salvation.[51] Hence, the anti-Jewish attitude of the Church was expressed not only in theological polemics, but also in a repressive policy, intended to prove to the Christians that the fate of those who denied Christ consisted not only in an abstract damnation, but especially in an effective punishment. On the other hand, in order to bring Jews to repentance, the Church adopted a missionary policy. But in contrast to missionary activity among pagans, efforts at converting the Jews carried with it a series of debates concerning the meaning of the Scriptures, with a particular emphasis on interpretations of the christological messages of the Old Testament. However, since Jews had a good knowledge of the biblical texts, these disputations and preachings generally failed to obtain the desired results. Accordingly, the Church authorities adopted measures of segregation merely as a defensive attitude, attempting to avoid the "nefarious influence of Judaism over the Christian people".[52]

This attitude of principle was effective particularly in Spain. The conversion of the Visigoths to the Roman-Catholic faith at the beginning of the seventh century, followed by the paramount influence of the Spanish Church's hierarchy, had its impact on the process of worsening the status of the Jews in the Visigothic kingdom. The repressive policy, conceived by the leaders of the Spanish church, especially by Isidore of Seville and his brother Julian of Toledo, found its expression through the century in the canons of the Toledo councils, and was implemented by the kings. This policy effectively excluded the Jews from tenure of public offices, as well as from holding landed property. It consequently reduced them to the status of "aliens", which implied the denial of any rights within the kingdom.[53] Hence, the Jews naturally welcomed the Muslim army which invaded Spain in 711 as their liberators from Visigothic oppression. On the other hand, the Jews of the Frankish kingdom and of Italy enjoyed a more liberal attitude from the lay and ecclesiastical authorities, and were able to pursue their economic activities in a framework of tolerance. For example, after the conquest of Languedoc by the Franks in 757, they continued to own estates in the area; a decade later, Pope Stephen III's intervention, exhorting the Archbishop of Narbonne, Aribert, to seek the implementation of ecclesiastical legislation prohibiting Jews from possessing Christian slaves, remained ineffective. In practice, Jewish landlords continued to employ slaves on their estates in the area until the twelfth century.[54]

The Jewish communities of Western Europe continued their process of organization and the establishment of their own institutions until the end of the eighth century. While the majority adapted ancient Palestinian structures and established councils of "elders", some of the communities of Spain, of Languedoc and Italy were governed by an aristocratic leadership of prestigious families. However, the religious government was entrusted to members of the

---

[51] The topic was studied by Simon in his excellent "Verus Israel" (1981).

[52] The principles of this attitude were formulated by Augustine of Hippo in his "Preaching to the Jews"; see Blumenkranz, Die Judenpredigt Augustins (1946/1973).

[53] See Katz, The Jews in the Visigothic and Frankish Kinqdoms (1937).

[54] Jaffe / Loewenfeld, *Regesta Pontificum Romanorum* (1888), I, No. 2389. See Katz, ibid. 157–59.

Beth-Din, the Rabbinical Court, the primary role of which was the rendering of justice, according to talmudic jurisdiction. In contrast to feudal contemporary justice, based on the oral traditions of "common law", the rabbinical jurisprudence implied a knowledge of the texts, i.e. a professional formation. The members of the courts were also the teachers in the community schools, most of them on an elementary level, which were usually located in the synagogues (hence the German-Yiddish name of *Schul* for synagogue). They spread throughout the communities of the Jewish Diaspora. The *curriculum* of these schools included Hebrew for liturgical needs, the study of the Old Testament and of some treatises of the Talmud. However, until the ninth century the Western communities were dependent upon the Mesopotamian centres of learning, both for the interpretation of the Holy Books, and for jurisprudence. Community leaders required the merchants, who were travelling for their trade to the Middle East, to carry their letters containing matters they wanted to consult with the heads of the Mesopotamian *Yeshivoth* (Academies), the *Geonim*. Upon their return, these merchants, who acted as *Shelihim de'Rabbanan* (the Messengers of the Rabbis), carried the *Responsa*.[55]

The Abbasid revolution of 750 affected these links, especially between Spain and Mesopotamia, where the remnants of the Ummayad dynasty maintained their authority. In these circumstances, reputable scholars of the Mesopotamian *Yeshivoth* who, for different reasons, either travelled in the Western Mediterranean, or were exiled due to internal strife, began to settle in different communities. In these they founded schools, disseminating the talmudic studies. While the story of the migration and settlement in Spain of the "Babylonian" scholar Natronay ben Habibay in 771 is mentioned by Sharira Gaon in his authoritative "Letter",[56] the origin of other highly reputed Western schools is legendary. It seems, however, that their founders might have been either Mesopotamian scholars or former students at these *Yeshivoth* who, upon their return home, transmitted to their communities the legacy of Mesopotamian methods of study. The development of these new centres of learning was made easier as a result of an important change in the study of the texts. While until the mid-eighth century, the text of the Talmud was memorized by sages and their students, implementing the principle of the "oral Law", the first written versions of different treatises began to be spread in this period, first in Syria and Egypt, where they were copied and diffused among the schools of the North African and European communities.[57] According to local traditions, the first autonomous schools were founded in Kairuwan (North Africa), as well as in Spain, Italy and Provence and, during the ninth century, they began to develop their original characteristics.

The evolution of these new centres of learning was connected with the revival of the Hebrew language, particularly in Spain, where the activity of grammarians like Menaḥem ben Saruq and Dunash ben Labraṭ developed since the beginning of the tenth century into exegetical activity, by the elucidation of

[55] Baron, Community (1993) s.v.
[56] *Iggereth Sharira Gaon*, 104.
[57] Baron, SRH VI, 109–16.

the literal sense of biblical texts. This trend of exegesis was particular to the *Sefardi* schools, especially of Cordova, where they reached their highest prestige at the beginning of the eleventh century, under the leadership of Samuel *Hannagid* ibn Nagrela. It also developed in Toledo and, subsequently, achieved its perfection in the twelfth century, through the works of Abraham ibn Ezra and David Qimhi. Moreover, as a consequence of the use of logical methods of grammar, it became the basis for philosophical interpretations of the Scriptures. After emerging with the work of the tenth-century Saadiah Gaon, who worked in Baghdad, the philosophical method became characteristic to the work of the *Sefardi* scholars, like Solomon ibn Gabirol (known in the Latin Europe as *Avicebron*) of the eleventh century. It culminated with Maimonides in the second half of the twelfth. However, Maimonides' treatise *Moreh Nevokhim* ("The Guide of the Perplexed") gave rise to a bitter polemic in the Jewish world from the late twelfth to the beginning of the fourteenth century, challenging the very use of philosophical methods for biblical exegesis.[58]

On the other hand, the North African and Italian centres of learning were concerned merely with the study of the talmudic texts and their analytical interpretation. Both in Kairuwan and in the two main Italian schools, of Rome and Lucca, the Sages pursued the traditions of study of the Mesopotamian Academies. In this respect, the school of Kairuwan became, towards the end of the tenth and in the first half of the eleventh century, the most important centre for the analytical study of the Talmud in the Western Mediterranean area. The work of Nissim bar Jacob ibn Shahin, *Mafteah le-man'ulei ha-Talmud*, ("The Key to the Locks of the Talmud"), widely used in most of the North African, Spanish and Italian centres of learning, became the standard manual of this method.[59] It largely inspired scholars to abandon the traditional mnemotechnic method, inherited from the Mesopotamian Academies. Among them, Isaac Alfasi, who had studied at Kairuwan before he returned to his native city of Fes, where he taught until 1075 is the most important; the Almoravid conquest of Morocco compelled him to seek refuge in Andalusia (d. 1107). He wrote the monumental *Halakhoth* ("Canons"), a considerable work of talmudic jurisprudence, which became the most authoritative book in this field, and is generally published with the editions of the Talmud.[60] On the other hand, the commentaries of the Kairuwan scholar Hananel ben Hushiel, in the first half of the eleventh century, opened new perspectives for pietist exegesis;[61] they were widely spread in Italy and in Germany, where they influenced the works of the Sages of the school of Worms. In Italy itself, the ancient school of Rome, which held its traditions of following the Palestinian teachings since the first century CE, acquired its reputation from the ninth century on; in addition to the adoption of the Mesopotamian methods of tal-

[58] Baron, SRH VII, 3–70; cf. in this volume Chap. 31.3, sect. 2 and 5.
[59] Nissim ben Jacob, *Mafteah.*
[60] Alfasi, *Halakhoth.*
[61] The treatises of Hananel bar Hushiel were spread among the schools of the European Jewish communities; on Hananel's influence, see Grabois, Ecoles et structures sociales (1980).

mudic studies, its scholars dedicated themselves to Hebrew lexicology, under the influence of the Sefardi grammarians. The *'Arukh* by Yehiel bar Nathan (ca. 1105) signifies the main achievement in this regard.[62]

The Talmudic school of Lucca, which according to its tradition had been founded by the Mesopotamian scholar Manasses ben Sabetay towards the end of the eighth century, preserved however the learning traditions of the Mesopotamian Academies. Towards the end of the ninth century, one of his descendents, Calonymus, settled in the Rhineland and gained a reputation as the founder of the important *Ashkenazi* centre of studies, at Worms. It seems however that already in the middle of this century a Jewish school had flourished at Mainz where, according to his own testimony, Hrabanus Maurus used to seek for consultants, whose expertise in the Old Testament helped him in his exegetical work.[63] Though their origins are somewhat confused and subject to controversies, these two schools of Mainz and Worms became the most important Jewish centres of learning in the Carolingian and post-Carolingian Europe, where the masters developed the four traditional senses of exegesis, i.e. the *peshat* (literal elucidation), *derash* (homilies), *raz* (allegory), and *sod* (mysticism) which, through their initials PARDES, became the four senses of Jewish biblical exegesis. These schools attracted students from the communities of Germany, Lorraine and Northern France, who customarily spent a number of years there; they usually took notes from their masters' teaching, which included extended quotations from books by various authors, among them the Sages of the Mesopotamian Academies and of the schools of Kairuwan and Italy. These note-books beared the name of *Kuntres*, contracted from the Latin *commentarius*, signifying the main purpose of the curriculum, i.e. comments on the Holy Books.

The Rhenan schools attained a considerable prestige throughout the Jewish world at the beginning of the eleventh century; some of their masters enjoyed a great authority, which may be compared with that of the Mesopotamian *Geonim* of the previous centuries. In this respect, the ordinances of the Moguntine master, Gershom (d. 1031), *Maor ha-Golah* ("the Light of the Exile"), were widely accepted by the European communities, including some of his innovations, such as his decrees instituting monogamy or prohibiting a husband from repudiating his wife without her consent; by this measure, the biblical and talmudic practice of repudiation was transformed into divorce. Gershom's decrees were issued for a period of a "thousand years", and any possible derogations implied a procedure that required the endorsement by Rabbis of the "four countries",[64] a term adapted from the Ottonian late-tenth-century conception of the Empire, as the union of the "four realms" of Germany, Italy, Burgundy, and Lotharingia (or France). The most outstanding student of the

---

[62] Yehiel bar Nathan (ca. 1035–1110), *'Arukh*. See Taubes, The *Arukh* of Jehiel b. Nathan of Rome (1955).

[63] See Saltman, Rabanus Maurus (1973).

[64] Gershom's decrees are included in the second half twelfth-century's treatise of Jacob Tam (*Rabbenu Tam*) of Ramerup, Champagne, *Sefer Hayashar*, passim. See Finkelstein, Jewish Self-Government (1924), chap. II, and Grabois, Ecoles et structures sociales (1980).

school of Worms was Solomon ben Isaac of Troyes, known as *Rashi* (1040–1115) who, upon his return to his native city, undertook the task of commenting on the old Testament and the Talmud. This achievement gained him the reputation of being the most famous exegete in Judaism. The French school founded by Rashi became in the twelfth century the most important Jewish exegetical centre in the Middle Ages.[65]

The process of proliferation of Jewish schools in the Middle East and in the areas of Western Mediterranean and continental Europe concerned mainly the high schools, i.e. the *Yeshivoth* "for adults", since the elementary education, the *Yeshivoth* "for youth", was dispensed in the Jewish settlements wherever communities were established. These new centres of learning reached their reputation in certain cases towards the second half of the tenth century, while others became influential during the eleventh. They reached the point that Western Judaism, either in the *Sefardi* or the *Ashkenazi* tradition, was no longer dependent upon the authoritative interpretations of the Holy Books nor upon *Responsa* issued by the Mesopotamian centres. It is however important to emphasize that, despite this process of proliferation and the differences between the *Sefardi* and North African methods of literal, analytical and philosophical studies, and the Franco-*Ashkenazi* homiletic and juridical interpretations of texts, this pluralism did not affect the textual unity. Thus, the variety of schools and methods was based on the unity of faith, of precepts and religious practices, manifested within the social cohesion of the Jewish community and its institutions, as well as through current consultations between the Sages.[66]

---

65 Baron, SRH VI, 135–39; see also Chap. 32 in this volume.

66 This essay was completed in 1994. The bibliography and the notes reflect the state of research by that time. The author is aware of the important number of books and articles published recently; however, they did not change his views as presented here.

Chapter Twenty-five

Jewish Bible Interpretation in Early Post-Talmudic Times

25.1. The Significance of Hebrew Philology for the Development of a Literal and Historical Jewish Bible Interpretation

By Frederick E. Greenspahn, Denver, CO

General works: S. Baron, *A Social and Religious History of the Jews* 1–16 (2nd ed.; Philadelphia: The Jewish Publication Society of America 1951–1961); W. Bacher, "L'exégèse biblique dans le Zohar", *REJ* 22 (1891) 33–46, 219–29; N. Sarna, "Hebrew and Bible Studies in Medieval Spain", *The Sephardi Heritage* (ed. R. Barnett; London: Vallentine & Mitchell 1971) 323–66.

Special studies: D. Weiss Halivni, *Peshat and Derash, Plain and Applied Meaning in Rabbinic Exegesis* (New York: Oxford UP 1991); R. Loewe, "The 'Plain' Meaning of Scripture in Early Jewish Exegesis", *Papers of the Institute of Jewish Studies* (University College, London) 1 (1964) 140–85.

Jews have been associated with literal interpretations of the Bible since Antiquity. Early Christians, who often sought Jews to explain the Bible to them, spoke of its literal meaning as the *sensus judaicus.*[1] For their part, Jews insisted that Scripture never loses its plain sense (*peshaṭ*).[2] Even for the Song of Songs, which has traditionally been interpreted allegorically by Jews and Christians alike, there have always been at least some Jewish advocates of a more literal reading.[3]

As much as Jews have held to a literal (better: 'straightforward' or 'natural') interpretation of the Bible, that has seldom been the only way they understood it. Indeed, by the Middle Ages Jewish tradition enumerated four separate modes of interpretation, which were linked in the mnemonic word *pardes* (lit. 'orchard'). Alongside the 'straightforward' (*peshaṭ*) understanding which was to become normative, these include the allegorical (*remez*), homiletical (*derash*), and mystical (*sod*) interpretations. Despite the late date at which this acronym emerged, probably under the influence of Christianity's four-fold way,[4] the individual methods themselves are deeply rooted in ancient Jewish tradition.

---

[1] Origen, *In Jesu Nave*, homily 7.5 (PG 12, 860); cf. *Selecta in Exodum* (PG 12, 289).

[2] *B. Shabb.* 63 a.

[3] Cf. A. S. Halkin, "Ibn Aḳnīn's Commentary on the Song of Songs", *Alexander Marx Jubilee Volume* (New York: Jewish Theological Seminary of America 1950; English section), 392, this despite the prohibition of straightforward reading in *b. Sanh.* 101 a.

[4] Bacher, L'exégèse biblique (1891) 37–38; cf. A. Kaminka, "Bibelexegese", *Encyclopedia Judaica* 4 (Berlin: Verlag Eschkol 1929) 633.

Both Midrash and Kabbalah are replete with spiritual, allegorical, and mystical interpretations, some of which made their way into Christianity. Even the view that Scripture is polyvalent can be traced back to the Talmud, which asserts that "each passage has many meanings".[5]

Even in our own time when the *peshaṭ* clearly prevails, Jews continue to interpret the Bible in a variety of ways. Thus, alongside a generation of Jewish biblical scholars who are fully engaged in the contemporary academic study of the Bible, midrashic lore abounds, not only on the more traditional end of the Jewish spectrum, but also among liberals and secularists.[6]

From these observations, it is reasonable to infer that the modern tendency to elevate the straightforward interpretation above other modes of exegesis within Jewish tradition may reflect contemporary more than historical facts. But that does not mean that this distortion is a modern invention so much as that it serves contemporary needs. Indeed, the shift from including the *peshaṭ* alongside other methods to valuing it over them is first found among Jews during the Middle Ages. It is evident, for example, in the choices made by the eleventh century French exegete Rashi from among the divergent views preserved in the tradition from which he drew. In his words: "There are many aggadot, which our Rabbis arranged according to their appropriate places in *Genesis Rabbah* and the other Midrashim, but I have tried to give the Bible's *peshaṭ* and aggadah which explains the words of the Bible in a fitting way".[7]

Although this impulse was at work among French Jewry, it was in the Islamic ambience of medieval Spain that the Jewish commitment to *peshaṭ* reached its apogee.[8] There were, no doubt, many factors which contributed to this development. Among these, the interest in philology – which had both internal and external sources – played a significant role. The reasons for this are not hard to understand. Whereas other approaches, such as the homiletical and mystical ones, rely on the assumption that the text's meaning was inserted into it by God, the philological method presumes that words have correct meanings which the interpreter must discover, using whatever tools are available, including, potentially, other texts and other languages as well as the clues provided by its own context.

It is no accident that this development took place in Muslim Spain. Jewish scholars there drew heavily on the methods of their Arab contemporaries, who ascribed a central role to the philological study of the Koran.[9] But Jews have

---

[5] *B. Sanh.* 34 a, based on Jer 23:29 (cf. *b. Shabb.* 88 b) and *Num. Rab.* 13:15, which states that "there are seventy ways of interpreting the Torah".

[6] Cf. M. GELLMAN, *Does God Have a Big Toe? Stories about Stories in the Bible* (New York: Harper & Row 1989) and D. C. JACOBSON, *Modern Midrash: The Retelling of Traditional Jewish Narratives by Twentieth Century Hebrew Writers* (Albany, NY: State University of New York Press 1987).

[7] At Gen 3:8; cf. his comment at Lam 1:1 and those of his grandson, Samuel ben Meir (Rashbam), in his preface to *Mishpaṭim* and at Gen 37:2. See also GROSSMAN on Rashi (Chap. 32.5 below).

[8] Cf. Abraham ibn Ezra's introduction to his commentary to the Pentateuch, where he contrasts five different approaches to scriptural interpretation. For a survey of biblical studies among Spanish Jewry, see Sarna, Hebrew and Bible Studies (1971) 326–28.

[9] Arab influence is explicitly acknowledged by Ibn Janah (*Sefer Ha-Riqmah*; ed. M. Wilensky; Berlin: Hotsa'at Ha-Akademiya 1925; repr. Jerusalem: Academy for Hebrew Language 1964, 277)

historically resisted ideas and practices which they perceive as alien. It is not, therefore, sufficient to explain such ideas as the result of Muslim influence. Contributing to Jews' philological orientation toward the Bible was their belief in the sanctity of Hebrew which, they thought, God had used to create the world. Proof for this was found in the words *'îš* ('man') and *'iššâ* ('woman'), which were believed to be etymologically related, thereby providing a linguistic reflection of the biblical statement that woman had been created out of man.[10]

The sanctity with which Hebrew was viewed fostered Jewish interest in approaching the Bible linguistically. The earliest stages of this can be found in the Bible itself, which manifests in several places a sensitivity to and interest in the inner workings of language.[11] For example the aetiologies, which are so common in the book of Genesis, seek to trace proper names to some event which took place at that location or in which a particular individual was involved. Thus Isaac was called *Yiṣḥaq* because his mother had laughed (*ṣḥq*) when she first heard that she would bear a son (Gen 21:3,6), and Beersheba acquired its name because it was there that an oath (*šbʿ*) was sworn near the local well (*bĕ'ēr*, Gen 21:22–31). Quite apart from the linguistic merits of such statements, they do demonstrate an interest in understanding the origins of particular words, especially proper nouns. The authors of later books in the Bible must have possessed some degree of philological interest, too, given their occasional efforts to substitute a clearer word or expression for what appeared to be a more obscure term in their earlier source.[12]

These efforts continued into the post-biblical period, when the Rabbis resorted to a variety of techniques to clarify what they regarded as difficult biblical passages. These include gematria and notarikon, which were borrowed from the Graeco-Roman culture in whose midst the Jews were living at the time[13] and are no loncer convincing; other methods, such as seeking foreign cognates or interpreting a word on the basis of its meaning in some other passage, continue in use to the present day.

Paradoxically contributing to Jews' reputation as relatively literal in their interpretation of Scripture was the Christian tenet which distinguished the spirit of Scripture from its letter. This dichotomy originated with Paul, who, not surprisingly, assigned the latter to the Jews, while reserving the former for the emerging Church.[14] Despite the often critical tone with which this distinction

---

and Abraham ibn Ezra (*Sefer Ṣaḥot*; ed. G. H. Lippmann; Fürth: D. Zürndorffer 1839, 12 a); a similar comment can be found in Saadiah's introduction to his *Kitāb 'uṣūl al-shiʿr al-ʿibrāni* (J. Haywood, *Arabic Lexicography and Its History and Its Place in the General History of Lexicography*, Leiden: Brill 1964, 121). Cf. Baron, A Social and Religious History 6 (1958) 243 and 275.

[10] E. g. Judah Halevi, *The Kuzari* (*Kitab al-Khazari*) 2.68; cf. Abraham ibn Ezra's comment at Gen 11:1 and David Qimhi's at Gen 2:20.

[11] So H. Hirschberg, *Literary History of Hebrew Grammarians and Lexicographers* (London: Oxford UP 1926) 5.

[12] Note, for example, how the phrase *mĕpazzēz ûmĕkarkēr* in 2 Sam 6:16 is replaced by *mĕraqqēd ûmĕśaḥēq* in the parallel 1 Chr 15:29.

[13] Cf. F. E. Greenspahn, "Biblical Scholars, Medieval and Modern", *Judaic Perspectives on Ancient Israel* (ed. J. Neusner / B. A. Levine / E. S. Frerichs; Philadelphia: Fortress Press 1987) 250.

[14] 2 Cor 3:6, cf. Rom 2:29. Augustine applies Paul's statement that "the letter kills" to those

was expressed, it also betrays a grudging appreciation and perhaps even envy for the more intimate relationship of Jews with the Bible than that possessed by the Church. This impression was confirmed by the fact that Jews continued to study and write, if not always to speak, in Hebrew, while the Church read the Bible in translation,[15] a fact that would become a source of dispute within Christendom as well. Thus the recurring charge that Jews had corrupted their edition of the Bible[16] can be read, in part, as the defensive posture of a church which was, on some psychological level, all too acutely aware of the hermeneutical distance between its positions and the textual basis on which they were claimed to rest.

Finding themselves at arm's length from their own Bible and committed to understanding it in a way that was anything but self-evident, early Christians made frequent recourse to Jewish scholars who, Christians believed, were better able to explain the text's *literal* meaning, even if they could not recognize its more sublime truth.[17] As Augustine put it: "although [the Jews] took signs of spiritual things for the things themselves, not knowing what they referred to, yet they acted as a matter of course that through this servitude they were pleasing the One God of All whom they did not see".[18] Confronted with this theological challenge – which was often supported by political power – it is no wonder that Jews held fast to a more natural interpretation of the Bible, warn-

---

who mistakenly read figurative passages literally *as the Jews do* (*De doctrina Christiana*, 3.5.9; CCL 32, 82), though a similar point might be made by a Jew like Philo who regarded Scripture's literal meaning as a concession to those who are "altogether dull in their natures" (*De Somniis* 1.40.236–37). Cf. Martin Luther's comment: *Das man die Sprache und Grammatica von ihnen [the Jews] lernet das ist fein und wol gethan. ... Aber unsern glauben und verstand der Schrifft lernen sie nicht. Also sollen wir auch die Sprache vom ihnen lernen, aber iren glauben und verstand von Gott verdampt, meiden* (*Vom Schem hamphoras und vom Geschlecht Christi* [1543], WA 53, 646) and his reference to Christians, *die den Verstand Christi haben on wilchen auch die Kunst der Sprache nichts ist* (introduction to translation of the Pentateuch [1523], WA, *Die Deutsche Bibel*, 8, 30); cf. his remark about the Jews: *quidem sunt Grammaticis sed res non norunt* (lecture on Gen 4:13, WA 42, 218).

[15] This idea can be heard underlying Thomas Jefferson's reference to David Levi's ability to confound Christians by "speaking in the very language of the divine communication while they can only fumble on conflicting and disputed translations" (letter to John Adams, April 18, 1816, in: *The Writings of Thomas Jefferson* 14 [ed. A. A. Lipscomb; Washington, D. C.: The Thomas Jefferson Memorial Association 1903] 471) following his reference to Levi's use of "emendation, transposition, ellipsis, metonomy, and every other fixture of rhetoric; the name of one man is taken for another, one place for another, days and weeks for months and years". These correspond to several of the methods applied in traditional Jewish exegesis; see Greenspahn, Biblical Scholars (1987; n. 13 above) 248–50; see, for example, Jonah ibn Janah, *Sefer ha-Riqmah* (n. 9 above) 104, 199, and 307–33; see also chap. 31.1 below.

[16] E. g., Justin Martyr, *Dialogue with Trypho* 68–73 (PG 6, 631–50), cf. Origen's homily on Jer 16:10 (PG 13, 450–51). Maimonides notes that a similar charge was made by Muslims in his *Epistle to Yemen* (ed. A. S. Halkin; New York: American Association for Jewish Research 1952) 38–39; cf. Koran 2:79 and 4:44–46 as well as 3:78 and 5:15.

[17] In addition to the reference in note 1 above, see Jerome's introductions to Samuel (PL 28, 604) and Job (PL 28, 1140) as well as his *Contra Rufinum* 2.35.530 (PL 23, 478); also Luther's comments on Gen 4:13 and 42:29–34 (WA 42, 218 and 44, 510–11). However, contrast Origen's comment, *Neque magistri, neque doctores in Judaea aliqui remanserunt* (*Homily on Jeremiah* 10.4; PG 13, 362).

[18] *De doctrina Christiana* 3.6.10 (CCL 32, 83); the translation is by D. W. Robertson Jr. (New York: Liberal Arts Press 1958) 84.

ing that biblical passages never lose their straightforward meaning (*'ein miqra' yoṣei' min hapeshaṭ*),[19] albeit without discarding Judaism's longstanding acknowledgement that any particular passage of the Bible can have several different interpretations.

External threats were not the only ones confronting the Jewish community. Much of Jewish mystical teaching rested on a non-literal reading of the Bible; the Zohar is, after all, constructed as a biblical commentary.[20] And the Karaite challenge, which originated in the eighth and ninth centuries, attacked the Rabbis on similar grounds, suggesting that they failed to take the Bible at face value when they supplanted its authority with that of a tradition that lay outside of it. These challenges together forced rabbinic Judaism to defend its own legitimacy from the Bible.

Supporting these converging pressures was the belief that *all* knowledge would be found in the Hebrew Bible so that, in the words of an early Rabbi, one should "turn it and turn it, for everything is in it".[21] Following the model of their second century forebear Akiba, the Rabbis employed the system of Nahum of Gamzu, which holds that there is a reason for every feature of the text, including even spelling and syntactic idiosyncrasies.[22] This led them to focus close attention on every detail of the text in order to determine exactly what it requires. Typically, this approach allowed textual anomalies to become grist for the Rabbis' halakhic mill, as they sought to find in Scripture a theological basis for their own beliefs and practices. The same techniques were also used for non-legal interpretation, yielding classical Midrash which, however distant it may sometimes appear to be from modern biblical studies, rests on a sensitivity to textual details (many of which may appear to be trivial) and concern with apparent anomalies that are the equal of the most pedantic nineteenth century source critics.

In order for such an enterprise to succeed, all those involved need to have confidence in the reliability of the text. This became all the more urgent in the context of Christian and Muslim charges that the Jews' sacred text was corrupt.[23] Addressing these needs was the work of the Masoretes, who examined every conceivable textual anomaly, even as they defined the correct text and, through their system of vowels and accents, sought to ensure that it was accurately read.[24]

---

[19] *B. Shabb.* 63 a. Maimonides asserts that "whoever ... removes the words of the commandments from the literal meaning – such a person is a liar, a wicked person, and a heretic" (*Mishneh Torah, Hilchot Melachim* 11.3 [mss.]); however, RAPHAEL LOEWE warns that *peshaṭ* refers to the 'correct' meaning and should not be confused with what we understand as the 'literal' meaning; hence, he views the talmudic phrase as meaning that students should learn their teacher's interpretation before venturing their own (Loewe, The 'Plain' Meaning of Scripture, 1964, 181–82).

[20] But see Bacher, L'exégèse biblique (1891) 41–46, regarding the Zohar's attitude toward *peshaṭ*.

[21] *M. 'Abot* 5:22.

[22] Contrast the talmudic view that the prophets put God's message into their own words (*b. Sanh.* 89 a, cf. *b. Ḥag.* 13 b).

[23] See note 16 above.

[24] A. DOTAN finds the roots of the study of Hebrew grammar in masoretic enterprise, see his "Min ha-Masorah 'el ha-Diqduq", *Leshonenu* 54 (1989/90) 155–68.

None of this is to suggest that the Rabbis' interpretation of the Bible would satisfy our sensitivities, although modern scholarship can only benefit from paying heed to the issues they address; but for all the reasons enumerated, their approach did entail careful attention to matters of style and substance. In this, they paved the way for a more modern approach, once the need for it became urgent.

Alongside their interest in biblical language, Jews have also attached importance to the events described there. Indeed, how could it have been otherwise, given their belief to be the direct descendants of the ancient Israelites? Deuteronomy's statement that God's covenant was with both "him who is standing here with us this day before the Lord our God and with him who is not here with us this day" was understood to refer to *all* Jews – present and future;[25] in other words, they believed God had literally given the Torah to them, as well as to their ancestors. From this perspective, the Bible is not so much a theological treatise as a kind of 'family history', something Gentile Christianity could not claim.

Besides supporting Jewish concerns with the details of the biblical text, this attitude also piqued their interest in the personalities and events it describes. Contributing to this more historical orientation may also have been the fact that the Rabbis viewed the Bible primarily as a source of halakha (religious law), thus directing their attention towards the Pentateuch, where the laws that were so central to rabbinic teaching were encased in a historical frame that provides the theological basis for God's commandments.[26] By way of contrast, the Church's attention centered largely on the prophets and the Psalms,[27] which are inherently less historical, even apart from the Christian project of applying them to a much later era than that in which they were written.

These factors combined to create within Jewish circles an interest in the historical events described in the Bible, a phenomenon evident in the Rabbis' efforts to identify ambiguous personalities in biblical tradition.[28] The roots for this, too, can be traced back to the Bible itself, where later books sometimes undertake an effort to clarify apparent ambiguities in earlier sources. An obvious example is the book of Chronicles, which identifies the mountain on which Isaac was to be sacrificed as Zion (2 Chr 3:1), an interpretation which can also be discerned in the parallelism of Ps 76:3.[29] Another example of pro-

---

[25] Deut 29:13–14 as interpreted in *b. Shev.* 39 a.

[26] Cf. *Mekilta Baḥodesh* 5 (ed. H. S. Horovitz; Jerusalem: Bamberger & Wahrman 1960) 219; a similar view underlies Rashi's comment at Gen 1:1.

[27] The New Testament quotes from the prophets and Psalms more than twice as often as it does from the Pentateuch; of these citations, roughly one third are from the book of Isaiah and almost another third from the Psalms.

[28] E. g. Chileab (2 Sam 3:3) was identified as Daniel (*b. Ber.* 4 a, cf. 1 Chr 3:1), Amraphel (Gen 14:1) as Nimrod (*b. ʿErub.* 53 a), Malachi (used as a title in Mal 3:1, from which it was inferred to be a name) as either Ezra (*b. Meg.* 15 a and *Tg.* Mal 1:1) or Mordecai (*b. Meg.* 14 a). The prophet Obadiah mentioned in 1 Kgs 18:4 was identified as the author of the book of Obadiah (*b. Sanh.* 39 b), the Jonah mentioned in 2 Kgs 14:2 with the author of the book of Jonah (*b. Yebam.* 98 b), the Zechariah mentioned in Isa 8:2 with the author of the book of Zechariah (*b. Mak.* 24 b), and the Micaiah of 1 Kgs 22:28 apparently with the prophet Micah (1:2).

[29] Note the ambiguity of Gen 22:2, although a similar view may be hinted at in v. 14; indeed

to-historical interpretation can be found in the book of Psalms, where several poems have been given headings that locate them at identifiable points in the life of David.[30] So, too, the tradition, first attested in the Septuagint, that Jeremiah was the author of Lamentations is an early effort to place this biblical work within Israelite history and identify its probable author.[31] This kind of effort to flesh out the history of the biblical period would reach a much fuller form in the later intertestamental and rabbinic periods.

If both the linguistic and the historical approaches to the Bible are rooted deep in the soil of Jewish history, it is nonetheless true that they flowered during the Middle Ages, when several elements of Jewish life, particularly under Islam, converged to give them growing emphasis. Conflicts with both Jewish and non-Jewish rivals drove the Rabbis to the Bible in order to mount their own defense,[32] with the straightforward approach inevitably that which served Jewish purposes best in their confrontation with Christianity. Literalism may not have served them so well in their competition with the anti-rabbinic Karaites, but there too the agenda required that Scripture be interpreted naturally. Finally, the Arabic-speaking milieu in which so many Jews lived provided them with another Semitic language to which Hebrew could be compared as well as the model of another people who prized their language for theological reasons, leading to the growth of schools of philological interpretation.[33] At the same time, Hebrew philology went even further in certain respects than its Muslim counterpart. Particularly conspicuous is Jews' development of a comparative method, which allowed them to draw on the resources of other languages that were related or, at least, believed to be related to Hebrew.[34] This, in turn, was no doubt fueled by diaspora Jewry's familiarity with several languages related to Hebrew, most notably Aramaic (the language of the targumim and much of the Talmud) and Arabic, which gave Jews a rich store of comparative Semitic data. Moreover, the idea of using information relating to one language in order to explain another, which has no parallel in Muslim scholarship, had long been accepted within Jewish tradition, where the Talmud, which is acutely aware of the differences between rabbinic and biblical Hebrew, reports numerous efforts to correlate difficult biblical vocabulary with terms from other languages or Hebrew usage in other periods.[35]

---

the root *r'h* runs through this passage (cf. vv. 4, 8, 13, and *yr'* in v. 12). On a larger scale, see M. FISHBANE, *Biblical Interpretation in Ancient Israel* (Oxford: Clarendon Press 1985); see also his essay above (HBOT I/1, Chap. 1).

[30] F. F. BRUCE, "The Earliest Old Testament Interpretation", OTS 17 (1972) 37–52; cf. the song ascribed to David in 1 Chr 16:7–30, which is composed of sections from various Psalms, including 96:1–13, 105:1–15, and 106:47.

[31] Cf. *b. B. Bat.* 15 a.

[32] The most extensive challenge can be seen in the work of the ninth century heretic Hivi al-Balkhi, whose arguments are laid out systematically by J. ROSENTHAL, "Ḥiwi al-Balkhi", *JQR* NS 38 (1947/48) 317–42. A list of passages subject to heretical interpretations is listed in *b. Sanh.* 38 b.; cf. *Gen. Rab.* 8:9 and *Exod. Rab.* 29:1.

[33] Baron, A Social and Religious History 6 (1958) 275.

[34] This was a reasonable response to the widely held view that the Bible preserved only a fraction of ancient Hebrew's original breadth, as stated in Judah ibn Tibbon's introduction to *Sefer ha-Riqmah* by Jonah ibn Janah (ed. M. Wilensky) 4.

[35] *B. ʿAbod. Zar.* 58 b, *b. Ḥul.* 137 b, and *b. Qidd.* 2 b; cf. *b. Shabb.* 36 a and *Pesikta Rabbati* 3:2.

In this context, it bears remembering that the Judaism which emerged from the medieval melting pot was not monolithic – hardly so in a community which could burn the writings of Maimonides and, shortly thereafter, so enthusiastically place much of its confidence in a figure like Shabbatai Zvi, or even his predecessor Isaac Luria. Nonetheless, at least one of the strains of Judaism which flowered during this period used philology as an exegetical tool to achieve a straightforward treatment of Scripture.

To be sure, this approach would in time be submerged by the rising power of Kabbalah, the emergence of non-intellectual approaches to Judaism in parts of Eastern Europe, the despair which followed the Inquisition, and a turn to the Talmud as the main locus for Jewish study.[36] But it did not die. On the one hand, it was transmitted to the Christian world, where a resurgence of interest in the Bible was underway, nourished by the forces unleashed by the Renaissance and the Reformation.[37] This movement honored Antiquity and elevated the Bible which, it was thought, any plowboy could understand.

Many of the figures involved in these movements had studied the Bible with Jews such as Elijah Levita and Obadiah Sforno, who provided a conduit for the methods and conclusions of their earlier co-religionists into the Protestant-inspired development of modern biblical studies during the seventeenth and eighteenth centuries.[38] At the same time, commitment to the *peshaṭ* lay largely dormant within the Jewish community, which directed much of its attention to rabbinic texts. However, Jewish biblical scholarship would rise again in the nineteenth and, especially, the twentieth centuries, when a resurgence of interest in the Bible in both America and Israel gave rise to a generation of Jewish scholars wedded to history and philology. That this occurred in a benign and pluralistic setting, where Jewish tradition had come to be cherished in a culture that was both curious about the Bible and respectful of Jews' closeness to it, need not be accidental. Nor is the rise of a new generation of Jews who proudly sought to reclaim a tradition they could trace back for centuries.[39] Still, however much this development is a product of modern circumstances, it nonetheless marks the reemergence of a tendency with deep roots in the Jewish tradition, a return to reading Scripture naturally and to focusing on its straightforward meaning.

See F. E. Greenspahn, "How Modern are Modern Biblical Studies?", *Minḥah le-Naḥum. Biblical and Other Studies Presented to Nahum M. Sarna in Honor of his Seventieth Birthday* (ed. M. Brettler / M. Fishbane; Sheffield: Sheffield Academic Press 1993) 168, n. 1.

[36] F. Talmage, "Keep Your Sons From Scripture: The Bible in Medieval Jewish Scholarship and Spirituality", *Understanding Scripture. Explorations of Jewish and Christian Traditions of Interpretation* (ed. C. Thoma / M. Wyschogrod; Mahwah, NJ: Paulist Press 1987) 84–85.

[37] Cf. J. Friedman, *The Most Ancient Testimony. Sixteenth Century Christian-Hebraica in the Age of Renaissance Nostalgia* (Athens, OH: Ohio UP 1983).

[38] Cf. J. L. Kugel, "Biblical Studies and Jewish Studies", *Association for Jewish Studies Newsletter* 36 (1986) 22–23; J. D. Levenson, "The Hebrew Bible, the Old Testament, and Historical Criticism", *The Future of Biblical Studies: The Hebrew Scriptures* (ed. R. E. Friedman / H. G. M. Williamson; Decatur, GA: Scholars Press 1987) 28–47.

[39] Cf. S. D. Sperling, *Students of the Covenant. A History of Jewish Biblical Scholarship in North America* (Atlanta: Scholars Press 1952) 115–35.

25.2. The Interpretative Value of the Massoretic Punctuation

By E. J. Revell, Toronto

Sources: The Old Testament Diligently Revised according to the Massorah and the Early Editions with the Various Readings from MSS and the Ancient Versions by C. D. Ginsburg (London: British and Foreign Bible Society 1926; repr. as תורה נביאים וכתובים מהדורת כ. ד. גינצבורג [ירושלים: מקור 1970]); G. E. Weil, P. Rivière et M. Serfaty, *Concordance de la cantilation du pentateuque et des cinq megillot* (Documentation de la Bible 1; Paris: Éditions du C. N. R. S. 1978); idem, *Concordance de la cantilation des premiers prophètes: Josué, Juges, Samuel, et Rois* (Documentation de la Bible 2; Paris: Éditions du C. N. R. S. 1982).

Early sources describing the accents are referred to in Dotan, Vocalisation and Accentuation, and Yeivin, Introduction; their use by the commentators is surveyed in Ackermann, Das hermeneutische Element, and Kogut, המקרא בין טעמים לפרשנות as listed below.

General works: A. Ackermann, *Das hermeneutische Element der biblischen Accentuation* (Berlin: S. Calvary 1893); I. Adler, "Histoire de la musique réligieuse juive", Encyclopédie des musiques sacrées (Paris: Éditions Labergerie 1968) I, 469–93; M. Aronoff, "Orthography and Linguistic Theory: The Syntactic Basis of the Masoretic Hebrew Punctuation", *Language* 61 (1985) 28–72; S. Avinun, אספקטים תחביריים, לוגיים וסמנטיים של חלוקת פסוקים לפי טעמי המקרא, *Leshonenu* 53 (1988/89) 157–92; M. Breuer, פיסוק טעמים שבמקרא [ירושלם: ההסתדרות הציונית 1958]; idem, טעמי המקרא בכ״א ספרים ובספרי אמ״ת [ירושלים: הוצאת מכללה 1982]; idem, כתר ארם צובה והנוסח המקובל של המקרא [ירושלים: מוסד הרב קוק 1977]; D. Cohen / D. Weil, הביצוע המקורי של טעמי המקרא הטברניים: מחקר בגישה דדוקטיבית על סמך חוקים בסיסיים בביצוע קולי־התפקיד התחבירי, *Leshonenu* 53 (1988/89) 7–30; A. Dotan, ספר דקדוקי הטעמים לר׳ אהרן בן משה בן אשר [ירושלים: האקדמיה ללשון העברית 1967]; idem, "Vocalisation and Accentuation", Sect. 5 of his art. 'Masorah' EJ 16 (1971) 1433–71, bibliography 1481–82; B. E. Dresher, "The Prosodic Basis of the Tiberian Hebrew System of Accents", *Language* 70 (1994) 1–52; I. Eldar, תורת הקריאה במקרא, *Tarbiz* 54 (1985) 225–43; A. Herzog, "Masoretic Accents (Musical Rendition)", EJ 11 (1971) 1098–1111; S. Kogut, המקרא בין טעמים לפרשנות – בחינת לשונית ועניינית של זיקות ומחלוקות בין פרשנות הטעמים לפרשנות המסורתית [ירושלים: מאגנס 1994]; M. Lavian, טעמים ומשמעותם במקרא [ירושלים: דפוס א.ב. 1978–1985]; S. J. Lieberman, "Towards a Graphemics of the Tiberian Bible", *Linguistics and Biblical Hebrew* (ed. W. R. Bodine; Winona Lake: Eisenbrauns 1992) 255–78; E. J. Revell, *Biblical Texts with Palestinian Pointing and their Accents* (Masoretic Studies 4; Missoula: Scholars Press 1977); E. Shereshevski, "The Accents in Rashi's Commentary" *JQR* 62 (1971/72) 277–87; D. M. Weil, *The Masoretic Chant of the Bible* (Jerusalem: Rubin Mass 1995); W. Wickes, *A Treatise on the Accentuation of the Three so-called Poetical Books of the Old Testament, Psalms, Proverbs, and Job* (Oxford: Clarendon Press 1881); idem, *A Treatise on the Accentuation of the Twenty-One so-called Prose Books of the Old Testament* (Oxford: Clarendon Press 1887); idem, *Two Treatises on the Accentuation of the Old Testament* [The above two works reprinted, with a prolegomenon by A. Dotan] (New York: KTAV 1970); I. Yeivin, מבוא למסורה הטברנית [ירושלם: אקדמון 1976]; idem, *Introduction to the Tiberian Masorah* [A translation of the above with additions] (Masoretic Studies 5; Missoula: Scholars Press 1980); idem, כתר ארם צובה: ניקודו וטעמיו [כתבי מפעל המקרא של האוניברסיטה העברית ג׳; ירושלים: מאגנס 1969].

The term 'Massoretic punctuation' refers to the signs commonly called 'accents' in English, which are used in codices and printed texts of the Hebrew Bible.

The use of these signs is based on the verses, the short units into which the biblical text is divided. In grammatical terms, a verse may consist of a single clause, of several clauses, or it may consist of a part of a clause, as is the case with the three-word verses into which the list of names in Neh 10:3–8 is divided. The verse division is conditioned in a general way by syntax, but also by content, longer verses being characteristic of narrative passages, where the language is relatively easy to understand, and its message relatively unimportant. A systematic study of the basis of the verse division, however, has yet to be made.

Units similar to the biblical verses are marked in a few ancient texts. The example closest to biblical Hebrew is that of the inscription of Mesha, King of Moab (mentioned in 2 Kgs 3:4). Possibly, then, the verse division may reflect some feature characteristic of public reading or speech in the language of ancient Israel and the surrounding nations. The traditional division of poetic passages is reflected in the earliest known manuscripts of the Septuagint, and in the Hebrew manuscripts from Qumran. Verse-like divisions in prose passages are marked in one or two early manuscripts of the Greek translation, but this is not usual; the marking of such divisions in Hebrew texts became customary only with the development of the accent signs.[1]

Before the marking of verse divisions in texts was customary, these divisions were maintained orally in the reading tradition. They are recognized in some passages of the Talmud, such as those dealing with the way the text is to be read in the synagogue. The Greek translation shows a certain amount of difference from the verse division of the received Hebrew text, but this feature has not been studied. Differences within the Hebrew tradition are reflected in the phenomenon known as *pisqah be'emṣaʿ pasuq*.[2] Talmudic comments also occasionally reflect differences from the received division. Manuscripts which mark verse divisions show that, from the ninth century on, the tradition is fixed; any variation from the received verse division is most probably accidental.

The accents subdivide the verses. Subdivisions of the same sort are marked in the earliest known Septuagint manuscript, but the accent signs themselves are known only from the Hebrew codices of the ninth century and later.[3] Sys-

---

[1] The divisions in the inscription of Mesha text are described in A. Niccacci, "The Stele of Mesha and the Bible", *Orientalia* 63 (1994) 226–48, at pp. 231–36. Information on the divisions marked in Greek prose texts is given by E. Tov, in: *The Greek Minor Prophets Scroll from Naḥal Ḥever* (DJD VIII; Oxford: Clarendon 1990) 9–12. For the division of poetic passages, see Deuteronomy 32 in F. Dunand, *Papyrus grecs bibliques (Papyrus F. Inv. 266)* (Le Caire: Imprimerie de l'Institut Français d'archéologie orientale 1966), and in 4QpalaeoDeut[r].

[2] A paragraph division within a verse. Some Qumran MSS which show paragraphing generally consistent with the massoretic *pisqot*, as 4QpalaeoExod[m], occasionally mark such a division within a massoretic verse. *Pisqot* are described in Yeivin, Introduction (1980) #74–5; for a full study see J. M. Oesch, *Petucha und Setuma: Untersuchungen zu einer überlieferten Gliederung im hebräischen Text des Alten Testaments* (OBO 27; Freiburg: Universitätsverlag / Göttingen: Vandenhoeck & Ruprecht 1979). The significance of the phenomenon of *Pisqah be'emṣaʿ pasuq* is discussed by R. Kasher, 'פיסקא באמצע פסוק' בזיקתה לחלוקת המקרא לפסוקים לאור כתבי־יד עבריים לספר שמואל, Textus XII (1985) לב–נה.

[3] The interrelation of accents and *shewa* vowels suggests that the MT accent system was already in use quite early in the first millennium. See A. Dotan, לתולדות התהוותה של מערכת הטעמים

tems of marking vowels and accents arose independently in different parts of the Jewish world; three systems of signs are recognized (each of which shows some variant forms), called the Tiberian (that of the received text), the Babylonian and the Palestinian. The Babylonian system differs from the Tiberian to some extent in the way the verse is subdivided. The Palestinian system is less precisely marked than the Tiberian, but rarely conflicts with it in more than minor matters, and so seems to represent the same basic tradition.[4] Variations within the Tiberian system persisted until the text was printed, but can scarcely ever be said to be of any significance for interpretation. The Tiberian accentuation of the three 'poetical books' (Psalms, Proverbs, and Job) differs from that used in the rest of the text (the '21 books').[5] This survey is concerned with the Tiberian system used in the 21 books, which is described in the works of M. Breuer, W. Wickes, and I. Yeivin listed in the Bibliography.

In medieval texts, the accents are designated by words referring to melody, as Arabic *laḥn*, Hebrew נגינה, or to meaning, as Hebrew טעם, as in the treatise of the famous massorete Aharon ben Mosheh ben Asher (Dotan, ספר דקדוקי הטעמים 1967). Terms of both types are used in the Talmud (*b. Meg.* 3a, 32a), but the precise referents of the words in question are uncertain. Elan Dresher argues persuasively that the system of accents originated in a transcription of the prosodic patterns of the traditional liturgical reading (Prosodic Basis, 1994). However, there is no doubt that the chants used in medieval and later times had ancient roots; melodies were no doubt used from early times to give prominence to significant prosodic features. The basic purpose of the liturgical reading was to present the text to the congregation in a way that enhanced their understanding of it. Weil finds, through his reconstruction, that musical and logico-syntactical features were harmoniously integrated through the original performance (Masoretic Chant, 1995, 291). The units into which the text was divided by the prosodico-musical patterns were units of sense; the accent signs which represent these patterns can be understood as punctuation.[6] The following survey is concerned with this aspect of the signs.

In the Tiberian tradition represented in the received text, each word is marked with an accent, or with the hyphen-like *maqqef*.[7] Accents are of two types: conjunctive, showing that the word so marked is joined to what follows,

[מחקרים בלשון ב-ג], (1987) 355–63. The system of performance represented must date from the second Temple period according to Weil, Masoretic Chant, 301–18. For the use of spaces in a Greek text corresponding closely to the massoretic disjunctives, see E. J. Revell, "The Oldest Evidence for the Hebrew Accent System", *BJRL* 54 (1971/72) 214–22.

4 The Babylonian system is described in A. Spanier, *Die massoretischen Akzente: Eine Darlegung des Systems nebst Beiträgen zum Verständnis ihrer Entwicklung* (Berlin: Akademie Verlag 1927), the Palestinian in Revell, Biblical Texts (1977).

5 The signs used in 'the 3 books', and the details of their use, differ from those in 'the 21' to some extent, but the general principles of use are the same. The same is true of the Palestinian system, but not of the Babylonian.

6 Thus Dresher finds it almost unnecessary to consider music as affecting the deployment of the signs (Prosodic Basis, 1994, 47–48), as do other scholars mainly concerned with their syntactic value, as J. D. Price, *The Syntax of the Masoretic Accents in the Hebrew Bible* (Lewiston: E. Mellen 1990) 13–15. On musical aspects of the accentuation generally, see Adler, Histoire I (1968), 469–93; Herzog, Masoretic Accents (1971).

7 Words joined with *maqqef* form a unit chanted to the melody represented by the accent on

and disjunctive, showing that it is separated. The different conjunctive accents are generally regarded as equivalent in joining power.[8] They were not marked in the Babylonian system (save in later manuscripts, where the Tiberian signs were used). A set of signs was developed in the Palestinian system, but fewer were used than in the Tiberian, and most Palestinian manuscripts either do not mark conjunctives, or use a single sign corresponding to any Tiberian conjunctive or *maqqef*.

Each disjunctive accent marks the end of a prosodic phrase, which may consist of a single word, or of several joined by conjunctives. The disjunctive accents form a hierarchy, so that the disjunctive chosen to mark each phrase shows the relation of that phrase to those which precede and follow. Thus the accentuation of a verse shows how the words in it relate to each other. The relationship so marked is most easily described as a series of dichotomies: each verse is divided into two parts, each of which is itself divided into two, and so on. The result is similar to the 'immediate constituent' form of analysis used by some linguists, as is shown by the following example (Ruth 1:1):[9]

ויהי בימי שפט השפטים ויהי רעב בארץ
וילך איש מבית לחם יהודה לגור בשדי מואב הוא ואשתו ושני בניו

1	*revia*	It happened ‖
2–3	*pashṭa-zaqef*	in the days of ǀ the judging of the judges |||
4–5	*tifḥa-atnaḥ*	that there was a famine ǀ in the land ||||
6–7	*geresh-revia*	and a man went ǀ from Bethlehem Judah ‖
8–9	*pashṭa-zaqef*	to stay ǀ in the fields of Moab |||
10–11	*tifḥa-silluq*	he and his wife ǀ and his two sons

As this example shows, the punctuational value of each accent is relative, not absolute. Thus in #2–3, the accent *pashṭa* divides a prepositional phrase; in #8–9, the same accent separates an infinitive from a prepositional modifier, a much more important division in terms of grammar. The punctuational value of an accent depends on its position in the hierarchy, and on the length and structure of the verse over which the hierarchy of accents is deployed. The essential basis for the understanding of the accents as punctuation is, therefore, knowledge of the hierarchy, and this is the concern of the early handbooks, as well as more recent descriptions listed above. The implications of each accent for what is to come form an important aspect of the information provided by adequate knowledge of the hierarchy. A traditional descriptive analysis of the use of the written signs allows only limited possibilities of prediction. Thus *pashṭa* implies a following *zaqef*, and so a unit of text suitable to carry it, but

---

the last. Besides its primary accent, a word may bear secondary signs relating to minor details of the chant.

[8] However ACKERMANN states that the first of two successive conjunctives represents the closer relationship, see Das hermeneutische Element (1893) 79, #29.

[9] Literal translation is offered to demonstrate the system to those not familiar with Hebrew, but imitation of Hebrew word order is rarely necessary. A vertical line shows that the Hebrew equivalent of the preceding word has a disjunctive. Additional vertical lines denote a higher position in the hierarchy. For treatment of the accentuation as syntactic analysis, see Aronoff, Orthography and Linguistic Theory (1985) 28–72; Weil, Masoretic Chant (1995) 26–46.

zaqef may be followed by another *zaqef* unit, or by *tifḥa* followed by *atnaḥ* or *silluq*.[10] In *Masoretic Chant*, Weil restates the traditional description of the system in structuralist terms. He is thereby able to show that the implications of the written signs (and so of the musical tropes they represent) for what is to come are in fact, quite specific.

The example from Ruth 1:1 demonstrates a second important point. The basis for the division of the text by the accents is not grammatical structure. In grammatical terms, the main division in any clause is that between subject and predicate. In #6, however, the subject and the head of the predicate form one of the six accent phrases into which the clause is divided. Ruth 1:3 is composed of two clauses, each made up of a verb followed by a three word subject. The main verse division separates the two clauses, but, in each of those, the first phrase is formed by the verb and the first word of the subject (which is its head).[11] Again, in the second half of Ruth 1:5, the main division separates verb + subject from modifiers of the verb. Divisions marked by major disjunctive accents rarely conflict with syntactic structure in this way, but they are clearly not intended to mark it. The accentuation divides the verse into units of content, just as the verses themselves are units of content, and not grammatically defined. The syntactic structure is not the essence of the content, it is the support used to present it.[12]

The use of the accent signs as indicated above can be described in a series of 'rules'.[13] Two closely related words are typically joined, but, in a group of three, the first has a disjunctive if the third is dependent on the second. Thus in phrases #2–3 in Ruth 1:1 there is a disjunctive on "In the days of", while "the judging of the judges" is treated as a unit to which the preceding word is added, precisely reflecting what was called 'hierarchical structure' in immediate constituent analysis. The same principle accounts for the division of the two subjects in Ruth 1:3: "Elimelek | husband of Naomi" and "She | and her two sons". A phrase separated from the word to which it is most closely related is typically preceded by the strongest disjunctive in the unit, so that *zaqef*, the strongest divider in the clause composed of phrases #6–11 in Ruth 1:1, is used after phrase 9, before the extraposed subject, which is immediately related to "a man" in phrase 6. This arrangement has the effect of presenting the basic structure of the clause as a unit. In addition, it isolates the extraposed subject, treating it as a unit of weight equal to that of the basic clause, and so draws at-

---

[10] The possibility of prediction on the basis of the written signs is used in the Palestinian 'shorthand' manuscripts, which do not mark those disjunctives which can be securely predicted. See Revell, Biblical Texts (1977) 67–74.

[11] Phrases of equal length are thus formed. The subdivision of verses may occasionally have been motivated by a desire to produce units of equal size (see below), but this is certainly not usual.

[12] That is, the first question to be asked of accentuation is not how it relates to syntax, but what is the significance of the division for the presentation of the content, as illustrated by the examples in Breuer, טעמי המקרא (1982), chap. 15. It is a mistake to assume that the meaning of a clause must necessarily be presented to those familiar with the language through analysis of its syntax as such.

[13] Ackermann, Das hermeneutische Element (1893) 74–82; Yeivin, Introduction (1980) #202–206; Breuer, טעמי המקרא (1982), chap. 15.

tention to it, as is appropriate for the importance to the narrative of the details which it presents.

It is certainly one of the main purposes of the accentuation to draw attention to significant items in the text. This is achieved by maintaining the unity of, and by isolating, significant groups of words, as just suggested. The particular accents used for the purpose are, in themselves, of no importance. A clear example occurs in Gen 22:10

וישלח אברהם את ידו ויקח את המאכלת לשחט את בנו
"Abraham put out | his hand || and took | the knife ||| to slaughter | his son".

The main division here falls within the second clause, and thus conflicts with the syntactic structure. However, this division presents the description of the action and the statement of its purpose as separate units of content. The words indicating Abraham's dreadful intention are presented in isolation, and so gain the maximum impact. This is an unusually striking example of the common tendency to subordinate introductory clauses to the material they introduce. This is most noticeable in the fact that a clause introducing speech often has a lesser disjunctive than the first unit of the speech it introduces, as in Gen 44:21

ותאמר אל עבדיך הורדהו אלי ואשימה עיני עליו
"And you said | to your servants || bring him down | to me ||| and let me set my eye | on him".

The first clause of the speech is more closely joined to the preceding introductory clause than to what follows. The second clause in the speech, thus isolated, receives greater attention than it would if the main division preceded the first. Joseph's desire to see Benjamin, which is significant in terms of the narrative, is thus given prominence.

The failure to separate an introductory clause sharply from the speech it introduces is usually presented as a feature in which the Hebrew language differed from Greek or English. S. Avinun shows that a short speech is typically separated from its introduction, as in Gen 44:25

ויאמר אבינו שבו שברו־לנו מעט אכל
"Our father | said || return | buy us a little food".

However, length is not the determining factor. In 1 Chr 14:10

ויאמר לו יהוה עלה ונתתים בידך
"God said to him | 'Go up || and I will give them | into your hand'"

the speech is certainly short, but it is not separated from the introduction, but divided in the usual way, with the effect of drawing attention to the promise in the last clause, as in the speech with similar content in Judg 7:9. Where the main division of the unit follows the introduction, as in Gen 44:25, the possibility of drawing attention to the final clause of the speech is avoided. The buying of food, after all, is not of major interest in the narrative at that point. Similar arguments can be made for the other cases of this type presented by

Avinun. Other examples in which a division within the speech could easily have been used occur in Gen 3:12; 15:7, 8; 18:3, 17, etc.[14]

The principle that the accents demarcate significant units of content, and refer only indirectly to the syntax used to convey them, can elucidate most questions of accentuation. Breuer notes a number of cases in which a disjunctive dividing a three-word nominal clause separates two words in a construct chain, rather than, as expected, marking the division between subject and predicate, as in זאת תורת הצרעת "This is the law | of leprosy" (Lev 14:57).[15] There are eight similar cases with 'law' as head of the construct chain. Related usage can be seen in other structures, as in Lev 7:37; 14:54. Breuer notes similar usage with demonstratives in other contexts, but this, too, is not a reflection of a standard feature of the language. The expected division is shown in וזאת תורת האדם אדני יהוה "This | is the law of man ‖ O Lord" (2 Sam 7:19), זאת פאת־ים "This | is the side of the west" (Ezek 47:20), and other examples. The unexpected division presents the crucial information 'This is the law' as a unit, and also draws attention to the following word or words which define the area in which the law applies. It is thus readily intelligible as a presentation of the significant units of content. Where the referents of the words do not require treatment in this way, or are unsuitable for it, such clauses are divided as expected, between subject and predicate.

In the same way, accent variation, such as that recorded in Ginsburg, The Old Testament Diligently Revised (1926), typically follows the standard patterns, and represents nothing more than a slight difference of emphasis. For example, the received text divides Gen 37:31

ויקחו את כתנת יוסף וישחטו שעיר עזים ויטבלו את הכתנת בדם

"They took | Joseph's tunic ‖| and they slaughtered | a goat ‖ and they dipped the tunic | in the blood".

The main division logically separates the initial clause from the two interrelated clauses which follow it. A few manuscripts place the main division after 'goat', giving prominence to the dipping of the tunic (with intent to deceive their father). Such variation can be called incorrect, but only in terms of a particular tradition. Where accentuation appears incorrect in more general terms, it is usually the expectation that the accents mark syntax which is at fault.

Because the accentuation is concerned with content, not with structure, it is impossible to provide completely objective guidelines to the understanding of it. Consequently, where the accentuation does not correspond to some translation or interpretation known from ancient sources, any statement on its motivation is necessarily somewhat speculative. However, even where its motiva-

---

[14] See Avinun, אספקטים של חלוקת פסוקים (1989). Where more than one introductory verb is used (as in Gen 14:19), or where a single verb is followed by לאמר 'saying' (as Gen 1:22), a major disjunctive usually is used to separate the introduction from the speech. For comments on the separation of introduction from speech by the biblical accents as compared to English or Greek, see Wickes, Twenty-one Books (1887) 35; G. Engberg, "Greek Ekphonetic Neumes and Masoretic Accents", *Studies in Eastern Chant* 1 (1966) 41.

[15] Breuer, פיסוק טעמים (1958) 156. Further problems of this sort are discussed by Breuer in מקראות שאין להם הכרע, *Leshonenu* 58 (1994/95) 189–99.

tion is obscure, a traditional accentuation is not likely to have resulted from error. It may well reflect an interpretation which is no longer felt to represent the simple meaning of the text which the accents typically represent. A clear example of such a process of change is known from the words אֲרַמִּי אֹבֵד אָבִי in Deut 26:5. Targum Onqelos and Rashi understood the passage to mean "An Aramaean was trying to destroy my father". They treated the second word as a verb (as did the LXX, but with a different understanding of the passage). Rashbam and Ibn Ezra understood the passage to mean "A wandering Aramaean was my father" (as do most later scholars), taking the word as an attributive. The accentuation, which marks a disjunctive on 'Aramaean', the first of the three words, reflects the former view. That is, the accentuation is 'wrong' for the interpretation now usual, but it represents the interpretation accepted by the massoretic scholars, and so is the correct accentuation in the tradition.

A similar process of change is likely enough to have occurred in other cases where the motivation of the accentuation is obscure. סֶמֶל הַקִּנְאָה הַזֶּה (Ezek 8:5) can be offered as an illustration. The first word is a masculine noun, the second a feminine one. The two, which form a bound (construct) phrase, are followed by a masculine demonstrative: "image of (ms) the jealousy (fs) this one (ms)". A disjunctive is used on the first of the three words, as if the demonstrative applied to the feminine noun, instead of to the masculine one, as syntax requires. There is a parallel in סֶמֶל הַקִּנְאָה הַמַּקְנֶה (Ezek 8:3), which shows the same structure save that the third word is an attributive participle, not a demonstrative. Again there is a disjunctive on the first word, and this is enough to show it unlikely that the accentuation in either case is accidental. Speculation suggests that the words הקנאה המקנה in Ezek 8:3 were taken together, and understood as "jealousy which provokes jealousy", an allusion to Deut 32:21. The similar phrase in Ezek 8:5 was then understood as a reference to this. This suggestion assumes that the requirements of concord were ignored, but the treatment of feminine nouns as masculine is not particularly uncommon in the Bible (cf. Rashi on Gen 8:11).[16]

Such speculation is intended only to make the point that it is anachronistic to evaluate the accentuation with the criteria of modern scholarship. The ancient scholars had an excellent knowledge of the language, but they did not always understand its words in the same way that we do, whether because they lacked some fragment of knowledge now available, or because they were differently predisposed.[17] The medieval Jewish commentators stated the principle that interpretation should be consistent with accentuation, but, on occasion, they tacitly ignored it, as in Deut 26:5. Modern scholars naturally follow the

---

[16] The relationship between the accentuation and interpretation of the text presented in various early and medieval sources is surveyed in Kogut, המקרא בין טעמים לפרשנות (1994).

[17] That is, they may have tended to categorize forms differently from moderns. If the argument in E.J. Revell, "*'Obed* (Deut 26:5) and the Function of the Participle in MT", *Sefarad* 48 (1988) 197–205, on this point is justified, the use of a disjunctive on ארמי in Deut 26:5 is not an example of rejection of the simple meaning through preference for midrashic interpretation, as is sometimes suggested, but of a natural tendency to treat the participle as a verb where it was not clearly other, a tendency which did not persist in later times. One aspect of the argument referred to is now supported by I. Ben David, חילוף שווא/צירי בבינוני, *Leshonenu* 57 (1992/93) 103–07.

same course. However, the fact that interpretation other than that suggested by the accentuation is now preferable in some contexts does not show that the traditional accentuation was wrong in the context for which it was designed. The accentuation of any passage in one particular way was not a legal requirement, but a matter of custom. The written signs were a late development. It is presumably possible that a scribal error could dominate both the written tradition and the tradition of oral presentation (probably more authoritative, at least until the ben Asher text achieved its pre-eminent position), but it would require a very surprising chain of development. The massoretic accentuation of any passage reflects the interpretation of that passage favoured by the massoretic scholars. Where its motivation is obscure, the obscurity must be accepted, since our information on these scholars is not adequate to enable us to correct it.

It is possible that the accentuation was conditioned by other factors, such as the desire to facilitate the chant by providing units of similar length. This might account for the position of the main verse division in Gen 7:13 (but cf. the different division of another compound subject representing the same group in Gen 8:18), or the division of the first half of Num 24:22. Prosodic factors no doubt affected the placing of accents in other ways, as they certainly did the choice of accent. However, such factors are likely to be relevant only where there was no need to use the accents to give prominence to particular units of content. There are also other ways in which the accents are held to convey meaning. The accent sign typically marks the position of the main word stress, and so can distinguish words identical except for stress position. Since prosodic factors can affect stress position, the possibilities are limited, but Rashi occasionally comments on a case of this sort, as in Gen 46:26–27. Accents are also credited with symbolic value, with adding some descriptive content to the word they mark. Thus the use of *shalshelet* on 'he refused', the first word in Gen 39:8, is said in one source to indicate repeated refusal. Such views are usually related only to rare accents, but a comprehensive system has recently been published.[18] Few scholars approach the text in this way, but it is only an advanced form of the very general view that the massoretic accents provide the text with much more than simple punctuation.

The massoretic accentuation is, then, the culmination of a long development, which may have its roots in the spoken form of 'classical' Hebrew. Evidence of this development appears sporadically from the time of the earliest biblical manuscripts on. There is no direct evidence for the use of the system we are familiar with before the appearance of manuscripts with vowel and accent signs in the ninth century, but there is good reason to believe that that system had by then been in use a long time. There was evidently a good deal of variation before the ninth century, including, perhaps, some variation in the boundaries of the verses which the accents subdivide. After that time variation diminished progressively, and typically affects only minor features. The accents divide the verses into units of content, and mark the relationship of these

---

[18] See Lavian, טעמים ומשמעותם (1978). For the comment on *shalshelet* see Wickes, Twenty-One Books (1887) 85 n. 4.

units to each other. The early commentators, such as Saadiah, show relatively little interest in this function of the accents. Rashi was the first major commentator to make much reference to them, but, since he also valued the older interpretations, which ignored the accents, he quite often fails to attend to them. Later commentators valued the accents increasingly as a guide to interpretation, an attitude which spread to some Christian scholars in the Renaissance. This interest led to increasingly detailed description of the system, culminating in the elaboration of the detailed rules for the understanding of the hermeneutic value of the accents in the second half of the nineteenth century. Since that time, interest in the accents appears generally to have diminished as interest in the use of extra-biblical material as a basis for interpretation has grown. Nevertheless, for students of the Massoretic Text in the context for which it was produced, the accents rank with the letters and the vowel signs as one of the three bases of the holy tongue (as medieval scholars put it) on which the pillars of the Bible are built: essential to its understanding.

25.3. The Geonim of Babylonia as Biblical Exegetes

By Robert Brody, Jerusalem

Bibliography: Sh. Abramson, *Topics in Geonic Literature* (Jerusalem: Mossad Harav Kook 1974; Hebr.); S. Assaf, *The Geonic Period and its Literature* (Jerusalem: Mossad Harav Kook 1955; Hebr.; repr. 1967); W. Bacher, "Le commentaire de Samuel ben Hofni sur le Pentateuque", *REJ* 15 (1887) 277–88, 16 (1888) 106–23; H. Ben-Shammai, "New Findings in a Forgotten Manuscript: Samuel b. Hofni's Commentary on *Ha'azinu* and Saʿadya's 'Commentary on the Ten Songs'" (Hebr.), *Qiryat Sefer* 61 (1986) 313–32; idem, "Saadya's Introduction to Isaiah as an Introduction to the Books of the Prophets" (Hebr.), *Tarbiz* 60 (1991) 371–404; R. Brody, *The Geonim of Babylonia and the Shaping of Medieval Jewish Culture* (New Haven: Yale 1998); I. Davidson / S. Assaf / B. I. Joel, *Siddur R. Saadja Gaon. Kitāb Ǵamiʿ Aṣ-Ṣalawāt Wat-Tasābīh* (Jerusalem: Mekize Nirdamim 1941; repr. 1970; Arab. and Hebr.); J. Derenbourg / H. Derenbourg / M. Lambert, *Saadia ben Joseph al-Fayyûmî. Œuvres complètes* I–V (Paris: E. Leroux 1893–1899; repr. Hildesheim: G. Olms 1979; Arab., Hebr. and French); R. Drory, *The Emergence of Jewish-Arabic Literary Contacts at the Beginning of the Tenth Century* (Literature, Meaning, Culture 17; Tel-Aviv: The Porter Institute for Poetics & Semiotics, Tel-Aviv University 1988; Hebr.); R. Ecker, *Die Arabische Job-Übersetzung des Gaon Saadja ben Joseph al-Fajjûmî* (Munich: Kösel-Verlag 1962); L. Ginzberg, *Geonica* I–II (Texts and Studies 1–2; New York: Jewish Theological Seminary of America 1909; repr. 1968); L. E. Goodman, *The Book of Theodicy. Translation and Commentary on the Book of Job by Saadiah ben Joseph al-Fayyūmī* (YJS 25; New Haven: Yale 1988); A. Greenbaum, *The Biblical Commentary of Rav Samuel ben Hofni Gaon. Accordind* [sic] *to Geniza Manuscripts* (Jerusalem: Mossad Harav Kook 1978; Arab. and Hebr.); idem, "The Commentary of R. Samuel b. Hofni on the Pericope *Ha'azinu*" (Hebr.), *Sinai* 100 (1987) 273–90; Ts. Groner, "A List of Hai Gaon's Responsa" (Hebr.), *Alei Sefer* 13 (1986) 1–123; A. S. Halkin, *Josephi b. Judah b. Jacob Ibn ʿAknin, Divulgatio Mysteriorum Luminumque Apparentia. Commentario in Canticum Canticorum* (Jerusalem: Mekize Nirdamim 1964; Arab. and Hebr.); M.-R. Hayoun, *L'exégèse philosophique dans le judaïsme médiéval* (TSMJ 7; Tübingen: Mohr 1992); H. Malter, *Saadia Gaon. His Life and Works* (The Morris Loeb Series 1; Philadelphia: Jewish Publication Society 1921; repr. 1942); J. Mann, "The Responsa of the Babylonian Geonim as a Source of Jewish History", *JQR* NS 7 (1917) 457–90; idem, "A Fihrist of Saʿadya's Works", *JQR* NS 11 (1921) 423–28; J. Musafia, *Geonic Responsa* (Lyck: Mekize Nirdamim 1864; repr. Jerusalem 1967; Hebr.); J. Qafiḥ, *The Commentaries of Rabbi Saadia Gaon on the Torah* (Jerusalem: Mossad Harav Kook 1963; Hebr.); idem, *Psalms with the Translation and Commentary of Rabbi Saadia ben Joseph Fayyumi of Blessed Memory* (New York: American Academy for Jewish Research 1966; Arab. and Hebr.); idem, *Job with the Translation and Commentary of Rabbi Saadia ben Joseph Fayyumi of Blessed Memory* (Jerusalem: Committee for the Publication of the Works of R. Saadiah Gaon 1973; Arab. and Hebr.); idem, *Proverbs with the Translation and Commentary of Rabbi Saadia ben Joseph Fayyumi of Blessed Memory* (Jerusalem: Committee for the Publication of the Works of R. Saadiah Gaon 1976; Arab. and Hebr.); idem, *Daniel with the Translation and Commentary of Rabbi Saadia ben Joseph Fayyumi of Blessed Memory* (Jerusalem: Committee for the Publication of the Works of R. Saadiah Gaon 1981; Arab. and Hebr.); Y. Ratzaby, "Six New Fragments of the Commentary of R. Saadiah on the Torah" (Hebr.), *Sinai* 96 (1984) 1–17; idem, *Saadya's Translation and Commentary on Isaiah* (Kiriat Ono: Mkhon Moshe 1993; Arab. and Hebr.); S. Rosenblatt, *Saadia Gaon: The Book of Beliefs and Opinions* (YJS 1; New Haven: Yale 1948; repr. 1958 [Arabic original: S. Landauer, *Kitâb al-Amânât wa'l-Iʿtiqâdât von Saʿadja b. Jûsuf al-Fajjûmî* (Leiden: Brill 1880)]); U. Simon, *Four Approaches to the Book of Psalms. From Saadiah Gaon to Abraham Ibn Ezra* (Albany: SUNY 1991 [Hebrew original: Ramat Gan: Bar-Ilan 1982]); D. Sklare, *Samuel b. Ḥofni Gaon and His Cultural World. Texts and Studies*

(EJM 18; Leiden: Brill 1996); M. SOKOLOW, "Did R. Samuel b. Hofni Complete his Torah-Commentary?" (Hebr.), *Alei Sefer* 8 (1980) 137–39; idem, "Saadiah Gaon's Prolegomenon to Psalms", *PAAJR* 51 (1984) 131–74; H.A. WOLFSON, *Repercussions of the Kalam in Jewish Philosophy* (Cambridge, MA / London: Harvard 1979); M. ZUCKER, *Rav Saadya Gaon's Translation of the Torah. Exegesis, Halakha and Polemics in R. Saadya's Translation of the Torah. Texts and Studies* (Michael Higger Memorial Publications 3; New York: Philip Feldheim 1959; Hebr.); idem, *Saadya's Commentary on Genesis* (New York: Jewish Theological Seminary of America 1984; Arab. and Hebr.).

1. Introduction

The term Gaon (pl. Geonim) designates the head of one of the central talmudic academies which flourished in medieval Babylonia during a period stretching approximately from the middle of the sixth to the middle of the eleventh century CE.[1] The two major academies were named after the cities of Sura and Pumbeditha where they had begun, although by the end of the period both had relocated to Baghdad, the capital of the Abbasid empire and one of the most important cultural and intellectual centers of the time.

Throughout the earlier part of the geonic period, the literary activity of the Geonim was restricted to a single genre: the *responsum.*[2] One of the major responsibilities of the Gaon was to respond (in the name of, and with the cooperation of, the scholars of his academy) to questions addressed to him by correspondents living in a widespread Jewish diaspora.[3] The overwhelming majority of these questions (or at least of those which survive) are devoted to the areas of talmudic exegesis and Jewish law (*halakhah*). Questions concerning biblical exegesis are to be found already in the earliest period from which significant numbers of responsa have survived (the middle of the eighth century CE), but these are few and far between.[4] Although the choice of topics was dictated by the questioners and not by the respondents, it is probably the case that biblical study played a minor role in advanced Jewish education in the geonic milieu; in any event, the material surviving from this early period is hardly sufficient to permit the reconstruction of exegetical themes or approaches.

In this as in so many other matters relating to the geonic period, the crucial turning-point is the tenure of Saadiah ben Joseph as Gaon of Sura (928–942 CE). Saadiah's upbringing was extraordinary for a Babylonian Gaon: born in the village of Dilaz in Upper Egypt, he had spent a number of years in Pales-

---

[1] There are some differences of opinion concerning these limits, especially with regard to the beginning of the period, but these are irrelevant for our purposes. For surveys of the period and its literature see Ginzberg, Geonica (1909/1968); Assaf, The Geonic Period (1955/1967); Brody, Geonim of Babylonia (1998).

[2] Several works of a different sort (e.g., *She'iltot* and *Halakhot Gedolot*) were produced in the Babylonian sphere during this period, but their authors were almost certainly not Geonim.

[3] For general accounts of the responsa literature see Ginzberg, Geonica I (1909/1968) 182–205; Assaf, The Geonic Period (1955/1967) 211–20; for a survey of the countries to which responsa were sent see Mann, Responsa.

[4] See Musafia 17a–19a (section 45): of the 42 responsa abstracted here, two deal purely with biblical issues and three others are devoted in large measure to biblical topics, but reflect talmudic concerns as well.

tine before emigrating to Babylonia. His appointment to the office of Gaon, despite his undistinguished family and unconventional background, and despite early suspicions (which were later to prove well-founded) that his assertive personality would lead to conflicts with the exilarch (the political head of the Babylonian Jewish community), was made possible by the conjunction of his unusual abilities and the leadership crisis which had afflicted the academy of Sura prior to his arrival.[5] Saadiah, profoundly affected by his prolonged exposure to the multi-faceted intellectual life of Palestinian Jewry, introduced far-reaching innovations into the intellectual and literary activities of the Babylonian Jewish elite. In terms of intellectual content, this meant the intensive cultivation of numerous disciplines which had previously received little if any attention in the Babylonian curriculum, traditionally dominated by the study of the Babylonian Talmud and its jurisprudential application; prominent among these were biblical exegesis and related disciplines, such as Hebrew grammar and lexicography. On the literary front, Saadiah's major innovation was the writing of monographic works in Judeo-Arabic on a wide range of subjects – both traditional ones such as topics of *halakhah*, and innovative ones such as philosophy.

Prominent among Saadiah's monographic writings are translations of, and commentaries on, biblical books. In this – as in others of his literary innovations – Saadiah's lead was followed by some later Geonim: in the case of biblical exegesis, these were Aaron Sarjado, Gaon of Pumbeditha in the mid-tenth century, and Samuel ben Hofni, Gaon of Sura at the end of the tenth and beginning of the eleventh centuries. Other Geonim, including such leading figures as Hai ben Sherira Gaon (head of the Pumbeditha academy in the first half of the eleventh century, and son-in-law of Samuel ben Hofni), followed the traditional pattern in this respect, writing on biblical topics only in the context of responsa. Despite evidence of his interest in biblical exegesis (including an account of his consultation with the Nestorian Catholicos [Patriarch] concerning a difficult verse in Psalms), there is very little documentation of Hai's approach.[6] This article will therefore concentrate on the exegetical writings of the three Geonim mentioned previously, and in particular (since none of Aaron Sarjado's commentaries have yet been published) on the commentaries of Saadiah and Samuel, of which large portions have been published, although much additional material still remains in manuscript.

---

[5] Malter, Saadia Gaon (1921/1942) 25–123, although badly outdated with regard to specific details, conveys a good sense of the situation and the historical background.

[6] For the source of this story, which has been cited by numerous scholars (worth noting is Greenbaum, Biblical Commentary [1978] 316–17, n. 34), see Halkin, Divulgatio Mysteriorum (1964) 494 (Hebr. translation: ibid. 495). For Hai's responsa on biblical topics see Groner, List (1986) 58.

2. The Scope of Geonic Exegesis

In addition to numerous interpretations of biblical verses scattered throughout his other writings – especially his philosophical *magnum opus*, the *Book of Beliefs and Opinions* – Saadiah wrote a number of works devoted exclusively to biblical interpretation. These include a translation of the entire Pentateuch, and a commentary on at least half of it (see below), and works combining translation and commentary on a number of additional books, including Isaiah, Proverbs, Psalms, Job and Daniel.[7] Saadiah assigned special titles to (his commentaries on) the various biblical books, in accordance with what he perceived to be their central themes: The commentary on Isaiah is entitled "The Book of Striving for Improvement in Worship", that on Job "The Book of Theodicy", that on Proverbs "The Book of the Search for Wisdom", and that on Psalms "The Book of Praise".[8] In this context we may draw attention to Saadiah's surprising characterization of the book of Psalms as a collection of prophecies rather than a group of prayers of human authorship. This position, the defense of which required considerable exegetical gymnastics, is probably rooted in the attempt of early Karaite authorities to de-legitimize the Rabbanite liturgy; they claimed that the inspired book of Psalms represented the only acceptable text for liturgical use, while Saadiah argued that it was ludicrous and unacceptable to address God in the same words which He had addressed to humankind.[9] The commentary on the Pentateuch was called *Kitāb al-Azhar*, probably to be translated "The Book of Splendor (or Radiance)".[10] These works, like Saadiah's monographs on other subjects – and their Islamic models – have fairly elaborate introductions, which provide an overview of the biblical book in question, and sometimes – as in the introduction to the commentary on the Pentateuch – contain extensive methodological discussions. In this respect, too, Saadiah served as a model for Samuel ben Hofni.

Samuel translated – independently of Saadiah's earlier translation! – and commented on at least three books of the Pentateuch (see below).[11] The characteristic form of the translation/commentaries of these authors comprises alternating sections: a group of verses is first translated into Arabic, and then discussed at greater or lesser length. These works are known generically by the Arabic term *tafsīr* ('explication'), which may be applied to either a translation or a commentary.

---

[7] See the Bibliography under Derenbourg, Qafiḥ, Ratzaby and Zucker. Commentaries on other books of the Bible have been attributed to Saadiah with varying degrees of conviction and plausibility; see e.g. Malter, Saadia Gaon (1921/1942) 316–27.

[8] See Malter, ibid. 317–21; Ben-Shammai, Introduction (1991) 372–76. Ben-Shammai argues convincingly, against Qafiḥ and others, that Saadiah meant these titles to refer to the biblical books themselves (ibid. 373 and n. 10).

[9] On the centrality of polemic in Saadiah's œuvre see below, p. 85 and nn. 42–43. Cf. also Simon, Four Approaches (1991) 1–57 [especially 5–11]; Sokolow, Prolegomenon (1984).

[10] Malter, Saadia Gaon (1921/1942) 316 (pace Qafiḥ, Commentaries [1963], Introduction 6, who would translate "Book of Blossoms").

[11] See also: Bacher, Commentaire (1887) 279–83; Greenbaum, Biblical Commentary (1978) 442–43.

Two vexed questions with regard to the work of the various Geonim on the Pentateuch must be mentioned here. The first concerns the relationship between Saadiah's commentary and his translation, which was transmitted as a separate work in Arabic-speaking Jewish communities. Saadiah, in the foreword to his translation, describes the relationship between these two works in the following terms:[12]

> I only wrote this book because some petitioners asked me to isolate the simple meaning of the Torah text in a separate work, containing nothing of the discussions of language ... nor of the questions of the heretics, nor of their refutation; nor of the 'branches' of the rational commandments or the mode of performance of the non-rational ones; but extracting the matters of the Torah text alone. And I saw that what I had been requested to do would be advantageous, in order that the audience might hear the matters of the Torah ... briefly, and the labor of someone seeking a particular story would not be protracted because of the admixture of demonstrations of every aspect, which would be burdensome. [And if] he later wants to investigate the legislation of the rational commandments and the mode of performance of the non-rational ones, and the refutation of the claims of those who attack the biblical stories, let him seek it in the other book (i.e., the commentary) ... And when I saw this I wrote this book, the *tafsīr* of the simple meaning of the Torah text alone, clarified by knowledge of the intellect and the tradition; and when I was able to add a word or a letter which would make the desired intention clear ... I did so.

The question is: Did Saadiah simply extract the portions of translation from the compound framework in which they had originally been included, or did he produce a revised translation, to be read separately from the commentary? Scholarly opinion is divided on this question: there are certainly differences between the separate translation and that embedded within the commentary as transmitted, but these might be attributable to scribal errors or emendations. On the whole it seems more likely that Saadiah did prepare a revised translation, adhering more closely to the literal meaning of the biblical text than he did in the context of the commentary, where he could explain at length his reasons for deviating from the literal meaning. In fact it might be said that Saadiah's commentary is actually, to a large extent, an annotated translation, with numerous passages beginning: "I translated X because the word Y has Z meanings in Hebrew ..." – one instance among many of Saadiah's and Samuel's penchant for enumeration. One example of this phenomenon concerns the Tree of Life in Genesis 2–3: in his commentary Saadiah translates this as "The Tree of Health (or Well-Being)", supplying philological arguments in support of this rendering, while his separate translation follows the simple sense of the text.[13]

Another outstanding question, which has implications for the previous question as well, and which has occasioned frequent and sometimes acrimonious scholarly discussion, concerns the scope of the pentateuchal commentaries of each of the three Geonim mentioned above. A twelfth-century author, Joseph ben Jacob *Rosh Ha-Seder*, states that he was inspired to write a commentary on the *Hafṭarot* after studying "the threefold commentary on the Torah: from Bereshit to *Wayeṣe* and from Exodus to Numbers by Rabbi Saadiah Gaon;

---

[12] Derenbourg et al., Œuvres (1893) 4 (with Hebr. translation).

[13] Abramson, Topics (1974) 40–43. Cf. Zucker, Commentary (1984) 78 (Hebr. transl. 296).

from *Wayeṣe* to Exodus and from Numbers until *Shofeṭim* by Rabbi Samuel ben Hofni; and from *Shofeṭim* until the end of the Torah by Rabbi Aaron ben Sarjado".[14] On the face of it, this would seem to imply that it required the combined efforts of all three Geonim to produce a commentary covering the entire Pentateuch: Saadiah commented on the first half of Genesis and on the books of Exodus and Leviticus in their entirety; Aaron on the second half of Deuteronomy; and Samuel on those portions not treated by his predecessors: the second half of Genesis, the first half of Deuteronomy, and the entire book of Numbers. This picture finds support in various early booklists, especially a list (*fihrist*) of works by Saadiah compiled by his sons; the vast majority of citations in later literature also conform to this picture. On the other hand, it is possible that someone in the eleventh or twelfth century had put together a "threefold commentary" comprising selected portions of commentaries by the three Geonim and excluding others; some support for this hypothesis may be found in occasional citations from commentaries of Saadiah or Samuel on portions of the Torah outside the framework suggested above.[15] However, it has been argued that these Geonim may have commented on selected pericopes, either at the request of correspondents or on their own initiative, in addition to their commentaries on entire books or half-books; final resolution of this question must await the publication of additional manuscript material.[16]

It may be appropriate at this point to describe briefly some of the difficulties connected with the publication of this material. Many works of geonic exegesis, including all three Pentateuchal commentaries as well as Saadiah's commentary on Isaiah, suffered a fate common to most early Judeo-Arabic literature: as the intellectual centers of world Jewry moved westwards, to Christian lands, in the course of the Middle Ages, works written in Arabic (with the exception of a minority which were translated into Hebrew) became inaccessible to leading scholars. Only a few works of the early period were transmitted by Arabic-speaking Jewish communities (primarily the Yemenites); the remainder are known today – aside from occasional citations in the works of later authors who were able to consult these works in the original – only from fragmentary remains found in the famous Genizah (repository) of Fostat (Old Cairo). This was located in the attic of the eleventh-century Ben Ezra synagogue, and served for the disposal of unwanted writings, especially those considered sacred. Not surprisingly, in view of the high cost of producing manuscripts, literary works were almost never disposed of in this manner until they had reached a state of severe dilapidation. The fragments deposited in the

---

[14] Mann, Fihrist (1921) 426–27 and nn. 9–10 (misunderstood by Malter, ibid. 427–28); Greenbaum, Biblical Commentary (1978) 424, n. 409.

[15] The evidence of cross-references must be evaluated cautiously, bearing in mind differences between references to completed commentaries and to those planned for the future, and between references to actual commentaries and those to discussions of a given passage, which may have been incorporated in other contexts. Cf. Greenbaum, Biblical Commentary (1978), Introduction 31.

[16] See Greenbaum, ibid. 24–33; idem, Commentary on Ha'azinu (1987) 275–76; Sokolow, Torah-Commentary (1980); Zucker, Commentary (1984), Introduction 11–12 and n. 7; Ben-Shammai, New Findings (1986); Sklare, Samuel b. Ḥofni (1996) 12–15.

Genizah, therefore, are mostly isolated pages or bifolia, and often seriously damaged as well; in addition, almost all lack titles or other unambiguous indications of authorship. This means that the reconstruction of literary works known only from the Genizah resembles the solution of a particularly complex series of jigsaw puzzles, and in some cases identifications will remain uncertain despite the best efforts of scholars. Since the style of the various biblical commentaries of the Geonim is relatively uniform, and probably served as a model for later authors as well, definite identification depends to a large extent on external evidence such as that provided by citations in later writings or by cross-references to other works by the same author, and such evidence is not always forthcoming.[17]

3. Exegetical Principles

The methodological guidelines which the Geonim laid down in the introductions to their commentaries are of particular importance for an appreciation of their methods and aspirations as biblical exegetes. Perhaps the clearest exposition of the philosophical and hermeneutic underpinnings of this school of exegesis is to be found in Saadiah's introduction to the commentary on the Pentateuch:[18]

> Now that I have finished explaining these three types of knowledge, which are necessary for the commentator on the Torah, I see fit to preface (a description of) the method by which one should expound the Torah and the other books of the Prophets. I say: Since these three sorts of knowledge are the foundations, and since every speech includes perforce both unambiguous and ambiguous (expressions – *muḥkam* and *mutašābih*) ... the exegete must consider all words which are in accordance with the prior dictates of reason and the later dictates of tradition as unambiguous words, and all those words which are in conflict with one of these two as ambiguous words. To explain further: A reasonable person must always understand the Torah according to the simple meaning of its words, i.e., that which is well-known and widespread among the speakers of the language – since the purpose of every book is to convey its meaning perfectly to the reader's heart – except for those places in which sense perception or intellectual perception contradicts the well-known understanding of an expression, [or] where the well-known understanding of an expression contradicts another, unequivocal, verse, or a tradition. But if the exegete sees that retaining the simple meaning of an expression will require him to believe one of these four things which I have mentioned, let him know that this expression is not to be understood according to its simple meaning, but contains one or more metaphors (*majāz*);[19] and when he knows which type of metaphor is involved, in order to bring the word to its unambiguous (equivalent, *muḥkam*), this Scripture will be brought into accord with the senses and the intellect, with other verses and with tradition.

This programmatic statement is followed by a series of illustrations, one for each of the four types of contradiction to be resolved by the exegete: The expression אם כל חי which describes Eve in Gen 3:20 cannot be interpreted lit-

[17] As witness the recent debate concerning the attribution of fragments of a commentary on Numbers: Ratzaby, New Fragments (1984); Greenbaum, Commentary on Ha'azinu (1987).

[18] Zucker, Commentary (1984) 17–18 (Hebr. translation: ibid. 191; the reader should be aware of the fact that Zucker's translations frequently deviate considerably from the original).

[19] I adopt this 'literal' translation (see Zucker, Commentary [1984], Introduction 43) for the sake of convenience, although the semantic range of *majāz* is much wider (ibid. 43–46; Ben-Shammai, Introduction [1991] 380–82).

erally as "the mother of all living things", for to do so would be to contradict the evidence of our senses, which inform us that lions, oxen etc. are not born of human mothers; we must assume that the verse contains another word which is suppressed in its surface structure, and translate: "the mother of all speaking living things", i.e., of all humans. The statement (Deut 4:24) that God is "a consuming fire" must be interpreted metaphorically, since (philosophical) reason establishes that fire is contingent and mutable, while God is not. Mal 3:10 must be interpreted so as not to contradict Deut 6:16, which is considered to be unambiguous. The prohibition (Exod 23:19; 34:26; Deut 14:21) to "seethe a kid in its mother's milk" must be interpreted more broadly, in keeping with rabbinic tradition, to prohibit consumption of any mixture of meat and milk, "since the tradition was transmitted by eyewitnesses (of Moses' behavior)".[20]

Parallels for these categories of circumstances which call for non-literal interpretation may be found without difficulty in the commentaries of Samuel ben Hofni. As an instance of non-literal interpretation required by what might be described as the evidence of the senses, we may cite Samuel's comments on Gen 41:54, in which he points out that it is implausible to understand the reference to a famine in "all the lands" literally, or to imagine that the denizens of the entire world came to Egypt to seek food (Gen 41:57), "for the distant lands of the East and those at the ends of the West are not dependent on the produce of Egypt ..."; all the references in this passage are to be understood as referring exclusively to "the lands of the people of Egypt and the cities of Syria and their environs".[21] As an example of philosophically motivated interpretation we may mention his commentary on Num 11:19–20: "Not one day shall you eat, nor two ... but a month ...". Arguing that it is inconceivable that God should brag of His generosity in the manner of misers (despite the continuation of verse 20!), he proposes a novel interpretation of these verses as an explicit threat: those most deserving of punishment will die after a single day of eating meat, those slightly less deserving of punishment will enjoy two days of meat-eating before suffering their fate, etc.[22] In Gen 48:8, "Israel saw" is to be interpreted as "became aware – by their voices or some other trait", in order to avoid contradiction with verse 10 of the same chapter, which states that Israel was unable to see, "and because of this I translated it 'knowledge' rather than 'sight', so that there should be no contradiction between the two statements".[23] Finally, the reference in 1 Sam 31:12 to the cremation of the bodies

[20] Zucker, ibid. 17–18 (Hebr. translation: ibid. 191; cf. ibid. 78, with Hebr. translation ibid. 296), with parallels in Rosenblatt, Beliefs and Opinions (1948/1958) 265–67, and elsewhere (cf. Ben-Shammai, Introduction [1991] 379, with bibliography in n. 38). Only in the last case cited does the *Book of Beliefs and Opinions* offer a different example: the "forty stripes" of Deut 25:3 are actually 39, in accordance with rabbinic tradition, while 40 is a round number; Saadiah supports this assertion by noting that the "forty years" of Num 14:34 should be understood as referring in fact to thirty-nine years, "since the first year of Israel's sojourn in the wilderness did not enter into this punishment".

[21] Greenbaum, ibid. 156–59 (including Hebr. translation).

[22] Greenbaum, ibid. 445 (Hebr. translation: ibid. 444).

[23] Greenbaum, ibid. 325 (Hebr. translation: ibid. 324). Note that Saadiah translated literally in this instance, presumably accepting the interpretation offered by most commentators, that Israel's vision was impaired but he was not completely blind.

of Saul and his sons is not to be understood literally, since such behavior would not have been in keeping with Jewish law; rather, this must refer to the custom of burning goods in honor of deceased kings.[24]

In Saadiah's introduction, the categorization of cases in which the text is to be interpreted non-literally is followed by a list of linguistic and stylistic phenomena to be borne in mind by the commentator; similar lists are contained in Samuel's introductions to the various portions of his commentary. In the fragments of Saadiah's list which have survived, we find such phenomena as a single verb governing two clauses, asyndetic constructions and others in which 'missing' words are to be supplied by the reader, and the substitution of one consonant for another.[25] In a similar list, which has survived almost intact, Samuel requires of the commentator extensive linguistic expertise, which he describes under 22 headings, e.g., "the fourth sort, that he should know all the nouns, whether common or rare, found in Scripture, such as the stones of the breastplate ... the eighth sort, that he should know the past which is expressed as the future, such as 'they will make a calf in Horeb' (Ps 106:19) ... the tenth sort, that he should know the plural which is expressed as singular, such as 'and Israel encamped' (Exod 19:2) ...".[26]

Most of Saadiah's literary innovations are deeply rooted in contemporary Islamic culture, and his work in the field of biblical exegesis is no exception: as demonstrated especially by ZUCKER, both the broad outlines of the philological program pursued by the Geonim (including such linchpins of their system as the *muḥkam/mutašābih* dichotomy adumbrated in the Koran itself), and many of its specific techniques for analyzing linguistic and stylistic phenomena, have close parallels in the literature of koranic exegesis.[27] The philosophical positions of Saadiah and Samuel ben Hofni, which play a leading role in shaping their biblical exegesis, also place these authors well within the framework of contemporary Islamic philosophical thought.[28]

4. Theological and Polemical Dimensions

The philosophical training and sensitivities of the geonic authors find expression in numerous contexts. For instance, Samuel paraphrases accepted philosophical opinions in his discussions of topics such as the nature of beauty or the interpretation of dreams.[29] The theory of the "four elements" was so well es-

---

[24] Greenbaum, ibid. 315 (Hebr. translation: ibid. 314). This example is actually more extreme, in that the Gaon avoids attributing non-halakhic behavior to biblical characters; see inf. 83–84.

[25] Zucker, Commentary (1984) 19–20 (Hebr. translation: ibid. 192–95).

[26] Ibid. 448.

[27] See Zucker, Translation (1959) 229–36; idem, Commentary (1984), Introduction 35–69; and in general Drory, Contacts (1988).

[28] With regard to Saadiah this is a commonplace; see e.g. the works listed by Malter, Saadia Gaon (1921/1942) 376–80, and for two recent treatments: Wolfson, Repercussions (1979); Goodman, Saadia on Job (1988) 31–56; with regard to Samuel see Sklare, Samuel b. Ḥofni (1996).

[29] Greenbaum, Biblical Commentary (1978) 88–89 and n. 50*, 104–07 and n. 35, and see ibid., Introduction 87–90.

tablished in Saadiah's mind that he found it necessary to explain why the biblical account of creation makes no explicit mention of the creation of fire.[30] Ingenious interpretations of biblical verses, designed to avoid such philosophically objectionable elements as anthropomorphism or mythic motifs, are to be found fairly frequently. We shall mention a few examples of verses from elsewhere in the Bible which Saadiah cites and interprets in the course of his commentary on a single chapter, Genesis 1. Ps 104:26 is interpreted to mean that Leviathan was created to play in the ocean (taking בו to refer to the ocean).[31] When God is said in Gen 2:15 to have taken Adam and placed him in the Garden of Eden, this was "not (done by) coercion, because He has no (direct) entry to the actions of speaking creature (i.e., human beings), but by command".[32] And the 'speaking' attributed to Balaam's ass in Numbers 22 is taken to refer to "a voice which was created in proximity to the ass, and which Balaam heard as if it had passed her tongue".[33]

The Geonim find it necessary to explain the indispensability of the Bible in philosophical terms, both globally and locally. Saadiah explains that the Torah comprises three major components, which complement each other in achieving the central aim of motivating the reader to obey the Divine commands:[34]

> ... For it is a book which teaches the service of God, and the essence of the service of God is performance of the commandments. And we have found that the best preparation [for] human acceptance of the commandments is threefold: commandment, (notification of) reward, and (examples for) consideration. Commandment: "Do" and "Do not". (Notification of) reward: exposition of the consequences of actions which we have been commanded or prohibited to do. (Examples for) consideration: accounts of people who kept the commandments and flourished, and those who ignored them and perished ... And because the All-Wise knew that we should derive the greatest benefit from the conjunction of these three types, He made them the pillars of His Torah.

In keeping with this approach, Saadiah proceeds to discuss the benefits to be obtained from other sorts of material contained in the Torah, including genealogies and accounts of journeys, "for it is inconceivable that the Torah contains worthless things".[35] In his commentary on the account of creation, he reiterates several times (even commenting himself on the repetition) a fourfold explanation of the significance of this account. Its purposes are: (1) To move us to worship the Creator, (2) To prevent us from worshipping His creatures, (3) To engender belief in the biblical accounts of miracles involving His creatures, (4) To foster obedience to those commandments connected with these creatures.[36]

---

[30] Zucker, Commentary (1984) 29 (Hebr. translation: ibid. 215).

[31] Zucker, ibid. 242 (in Hebr. translation; the transcription of the corresponding manuscript page is mistakenly omitted on p. 43), and see n. 178 ad loc.

[32] Zucker, ibid. 50 (Hebr. translation: ibid. 251).

[33] Zucker, ibid. Saadiah was attacked for this interpretation; cf. ibid. 251, n. 257.

[34] Zucker, ibid. 7–8 (Hebr. translation: ibid. 171–72).

[35] Zucker, ibid. 9 (Hebr. translation: ibid. 175).

[36] Zucker, ibid. 32, 35, 40–41, 46, 50 (the corresponding Hebr. translations: ibid. 221, 225–26, 236–37, 246, 251).

A related concern is the desire to justify the actions of the forefathers, so that they may serve as fitting models of behavior. The Geonim seem much less willing than the talmudic Rabbis to criticize the actions of biblical figures, and more determined to attempt to justify their behavior.[37] For instance, Samuel refuses to interpret Num 11:22 as indicating that Moses questioned God's omnipotence; in lieu of this he offers two interpretations: Either Moses means to say that the rebels will never be satisfied, even if they are offered all the meat in the world; or else he means that since God had said (in v. 20) that "it will be loathsome to you", all the meat in the world would not suffice to benefit them.[38]

Linguistic arguments of one sort or another frequently serve to resolve theological difficulties, as indicated in the passage from Saadiah's introduction cited earlier: "... If the exegete sees that retaining the simple meaning of an expression will require him to believe one of these four things, let him know that this expression is not to be understood according to its simple meaning, but contains one or more metaphors;[39] and when he knows which type of metaphor is involved, in order to bring the word to its meaning, Scripture will be in accord with the senses and the intellect ...". A clear example of theologically motivated lexicographical (and syntactical) discussion may be found in Saadiah's commentary on Gen 6:6 (וינחם ה׳ כי־עשה את־האדם בארץ ויתעצב אל־לבו). Saadiah justifies his translation of the verb וינחם as 'warned' by distinguishing seven different meanings which he attributes to this root,[40] and adds that in keeping with this interpretation, "he was saddened to his heart" should be taken as referring to (Every)man. However, this explanation is followed by an alternative one, in which the words are interpreted according to their obvious sense, and the theological difficulties presented by the verse are resolved by philosophical arguments.

But linguistic observations, almost invariably documented by reference to other biblical verses, comprise a major component of the geonic commentaries, and are not employed exclusively – and perhaps not even primarily – in the pursuit of theological or philosophical objectives. We may mention, as one instance among many, Samuel's comment on Gen 41:56, in which he argues that פני הארץ means "the wealthy and notables of the land", buttressing this interpretation by reference to Job 22:8.[41] The reader will recall that the linguistic aspect is one of three which Saadiah singled out in characterizing his commentary – or more precisely, in noting what has been omitted from this commen-

---

[37] The motivation for this is probably partly polemical (cf. inf. 85 f. and n. 47) and partly philosophical, reflecting a reluctance to attribute human frailties to heroic figures.

[38] Greenbaum, Biblical Commentary (1978) 447 (Hebr. translation: ibid. 446).

[39] See n. 19 above.

[40] Saadiah's analysis in this instance is fraught with grammatical difficulties, some of which derive from confusion of distinct roots (the discoveries of Hayyuj being still a thing of the future), and others from the joint treatment of various forms of a single root. Cf. Zucker, Commentary (1984) 100–01; Hebr. translation: ibid. 333–35.

[41] In this instance (as noted by Greenbaum, Biblical Commentary [1978] 167, n. 230), the basic interpretation, without the supporting verse, is to be found in *Gen. Rab.* 91:5 (ed. Theodor / Albeck, pp. 1120–21). For the linguistic techniques of the Geonim see especially Bacher, Commentaire (1888) 106–10; Zucker, Translation (1959) 237–66.

tary in his translation: "... a separate work containing nothing of the discussions of language ... nor of the questions of the heretics, nor of their refutation; nor of the 'branches' of the rational commandments or the mode of performance of the non-rational ones". Let us now turn to the remaining two elements emphasized by the Gaon: the polemical aspect and what might be termed "the rabbinic connection".

Polemics occupy a central place in the œuvre of Saadiah. He saw himself as the spokesman of Rabbanite Judaism, more especially in its Babylonian variety, and devoted a number of works specifically to polemics – whether directed against heretics who rejected the authority of the Bible, against Karaites who accepted the Bible but rejected the authority of rabbinic tradition, or against opponents within the Rabbanite camp, including the Palestinian Gaon Aaron [?] ben Meir, and the exilarch David ben Zakkai.[42] But polemical comments, whether implicit or explicit, are also scattered in great profusion throughout Saadiah's writings on other subjects, and are particularly prominent in his biblical commentaries, and especially – for obvious reasons – those on the Pentateuch.[43] One striking passage, in the commentary on Gen 1:14–19, deals at some length with nine or ten different calendrical systems which Saadiah rejects in favor of the traditional Rabbanite calendar; several proponents of these competing systems are named, while others remain anonymous.[44] In the context of his commentary on Gen 1:26, Saadiah notes that the verse is used by Christians as an argument for the Trinitarian doctrine, because of the plural form of the verb נעשה ("Let us make"); he interprets this as an instance of the 'royal we', and goes on to argue at some length that since the Christians agree that various expressions in this passage are not to be taken literally, they cannot legitimately insist on a literal interpretation of this particular verb.[45] A possible case of veiled polemic, this time against Islam, is to be found in Saadiah's discussion of the ʿAqedah (the Binding of Isaac, Gen 22): One of the reasons for this trial, according to Saadiah, is "lest anyone think that Ishmael showed greater submission to God than did Isaac, since he was circumcised at the age of 13, when he understood pain and could have refused, whereas Isaac was circumcised at the age of eight days, when he did not understand pain and was unable to refuse".[46]

The polemical dimension is less pronounced, but not altogether lacking, in Samuel's commentary. We find a number of brief passages devoted to refuting attacks of unnamed opponents on the veracity or plausibility of the biblical account or on the behavior of biblical heroes, as well as a refutation of an argu-

---

[42] See e.g. Malter, Saadia Gaon (1921/1942) 260–71, 380–94; a good deal of additional material has been published since Malter wrote.

[43] See Malter, ibid. 262; Zucker, Commentary (1984), Introduction 17; for some examples in other works: Qafiḥ, Proverbs (1976) 38 and n. 8; Davidson et al., Siddur (1941/1970) 10.

[44] The groups discussed include 'Zadokites', 'Boethusians', 'Badarites', and the disciples of Benjamin (al-Nihawandi) and Tiflisi; cf. Zucker, Commentary (1984) 41–42 (Hebr. translation: ibid. 236–37; and see ibid. 436–47). For other discussions of this subject by Saadiah see Malter, Saadia Gaon (1921/1942) 168–71, 351–53.

[45] Zucker, Commentary (1984) 50–51 (Hebr. translation: ibid. 252); cf. Rosenblatt, Beliefs and Opinions (1948/1958) 107–08.

[46] Zucker, ibid. 140 (Hebr. translation: ibid. 400); cf. EJ, s. v. Ishmael.

ment adduced in favor of a non-Rabbanite calendar.[47] It is interesting to note in this context that Samuel criticizes "the Christian translator" (Septuagint = Peshitta) of Gen 47:31, for reading מטה as *maṭṭēh* ('staff') rather than the masoretic *miṭṭâ* ('bed').[48]

5. The Relationship between Talmudic and Geonic Exegesis

The attitude of the Geonim to rabbinic tradition is a complex one. It unquestionably retained their complete allegiance with regard to matters of law in the broadest possible sense (*halakhah*); and one notable component of their commentaries, as emphasized by Saadiah, is the incorporation of legal material, including quotations from talmudic sources and occasional references to post-talmudic developments.[49] This is particularly noteworthy in view of the fact that practically all of the geonic commentaries published to date are devoted to non-legal portions of the Bible, so that the legal discussions in question have been introduced into a narrative context. One reason for this is undoubtedly the desire on the part of the Geonim to emphasize the connection between rabbinic tradition and the Bible, as part of their struggle against Karaism. But there are other reasons as well; we may cite in this connection Samuel's commentary on Gen 41:49, where he remarks: "We saw fit to dwell at length here on hoarding, because it is relevant to the story and most of the grain merchants in our time do hoard".[50]

The status of rabbinic statements on non-legal matters is much more complicated. The Geonim accepted numerous rabbinic traditions of an *aggadic* nature as authoritative and based their commentaries on them, whether explicitly or implicitly. For instance, Samuel's account of biblical chronology depends explicitly on that of *Seder ʿOlam Rabba.*[51] On the other hand, both Saadiah and Samuel feel free to reject rabbinic statements of a non-legal nature, and sometimes use surprisingly harsh language to describe these rejected opinions.[52] It seems clear that they considered many (perhaps most) aggadic comments to represent individual interpretations rather than authoritative traditions,[53] although it is difficult to define the criteria which guided them in differentiating between these two categories, aside from a subjective assessment of the extent to which they represent serious attempts at exegesis rather than fanciful

---

[47] Greenbaum, Biblical Commentary (1978) 47, 153, 445 (corresponding Hebr. translations: ibid. 46, 152, 444); see ibid., Introduction 91–92; Bacher, Commentaire (1887) 287–88.

[48] See Greenbaum, ibid. 316–17 and n. 34.

[49] See Greenbaum, ibid. 65–75; Zucker, ibid. 13–18; and cf. Bacher, Commentaire (1888) 112, 119–20. For an example of post-talmudic legal development see Zucker, ibid. 149 (Hebr. translation: ibid. 412).

[50] Greenbaum, ibid. 153 (Hebr. translation: ibid. 152).

[51] See Greenbaum, ibid. 42–43, 46–47, 70–71, 88–89, 98–101, 188–91 and n. 306; and cf. ibid. 172–73, 198–99 and nn. 336–37.

[52] With regard to Samuel see n. 54 below; with respect to Saadiah see Zucker, ibid. 267 n. 323, 276 n. 380, 286 n. 422, 300 n. 505, and especially 349–50 n. 77.

[53] This is in keeping with geonic attitudes to Aggadah generally; see Assaf, The Geonic Period (1955/1967) 244 (no. 66); Sklare, Samuel b. Ḥofni (1996) 41–48.

homiletics. The most explicit methodological statement on this point which I have found is contained in a fragment of Samuel's introduction to his commentary on the second half of Genesis, published by ZUCKER:[54]

> The eighth matter: that whatever belongs to the eight categories of the commandments – valid, invalid, forbidden, permitted, unclean, clean, guilty or innocent – he should explain with precision and clarity, without deviation, according to Scripture and the tradition alone. The ninth matter: that whatever is established by an explicit verse or clarified by Scripture or established by rational demonstration, he should state unreservedly and decisively; but of those interpretations (*tafāsir*, pl. of *tafsīr*) which the Sages call *midrashot* and *aggadot* ... in matters other than the commandments, with which he embellishes his discourse, he should say "It may be" or "It is proper".

Geonic exegesis in general may be characterized as more disciplined and less fanciful than earlier rabbinic exegesis, and more concerned with a close, systematic reading of the biblical text, in which attention is devoted both to the smallest textual units and to the integrity of larger narratives. Some differences in this area between the Geonim are, however, worth noting. Saadiah seems to have retained something of the homiletical mentality of the talmudic Rabbis; this finds expression both in interpretations which attribute significance to minor variations in spelling, and in the willingness to offer a number of interpretations for a single verse, of which one is said to be the simple or literal meaning of the text, while the others are obviously and admittedly homiletical in nature.[55] Samuel appears to focus more closely on straightforward interpretations; when he offers multiple interpretations, these are presented as alternatives, only one of which is presumed to be true.[56] Although Samuel's commentary contains numerous passages of a homiletical or hortatory nature, these do not purport to derive their message from textual clues such as variant spellings or 'superfluous' words, but rather from the thrust of the biblical account as a whole, and especially from the actions of exemplary figures such as the Patriarchs and Jacob's sons.[57] On the other hand, Samuel is fond of introducing lengthy digressions having only a tenuous connection with the biblical text on which he is commenting, a practice for which he was roundly criticized by Abraham ibn Ezra.[58] For instance, the account of Jacob's departure from Beersheba in Gen 28:10 occasions a disquisition on journeys and their purposes, including a survey of those mentioned throughout the Bible; while the account of Joseph's storing up grain in preparation for the famine in Egypt provides the opportunity for a lengthy discussion of factors to be considered in grain storage, ending: "And the masters of agriculture have mentioned many things

[54] Zucker, ibid. 448; and cf. Greenbaum, Biblical Commentary (1978) 521 (discussed by Sklare, ibid.).

[55] See, with regard to homiletic interpretations, Zucker, Commentary (1984), Introduction 15–16; for some examples see ibid. 53, 127, 134–35 (corresponding Hebr. translations: 258, 381–82, 393); for examples of multiple interpretations see ibid. 107, 118, 144 (Hebr. translations: 345–46, 366, 403–04).

[56] See Greenbaum, ibid. 136–37, 140–43, 324–25, 332–33, 336–39. But the difference is perhaps one of degree, cf. ibid. 80–81 and Zucker, Commentary (1984), Introduction 51.

[57] See Greenbaum, ibid. 44–45, 64–65, 90–93, 156–57, 182–83, 242–45, 284–85, and cf. ibid. 310–13.

[58] Greenbaum, ibid. 2–6 (Ibn Ezra's criticism: ibid. 3, n. 5).

of this sort which I do not see fit to mention, but I have no doubt that Joseph took care for the grain of Egypt and guarded it in such fashion or in even more effective ways".[59]

The pioneering work of the Geonim exercised considerable influence on succeeding generations of Jewish biblical exegetes, both Rabbanites and Karaites. This influence is especially prominent in the works of authors who wrote in Arabic, including Judah ibn Balaam and Abraham Maimonides, and in the linguistic and lexicographical writings of Jonah ibn Janah. European authors writing in Hebrew, however, also made extensive use of geonic exegesis; this influence is probably most noticeable in the works of Abraham ibn Ezra. A number of geonic interpretations were incorporated in late *midrashic* works, especially those written in Arabic. The *Midrash Ha-Gadol*, a Yemenite compilation written in Hebrew, also contains a very rich vein of geonic exegesis.[60] In a broader sense, the work of the Geonim provided a precedent for the writing of systematic biblical commentaries in a form essentially different from that of classical rabbinic midrash, and doubtless provided inspiration and a sense of legitimacy to numerous commentators who had no direct access to their works.

---

[59] Greenbaum, ibid. 153 (Hebr. translation: ibid. 152); cf. Bacher, Commentaire (1887) 283–88.

[60] See Greenbaum, Biblical Commentary (1978), Introduction 34–50; Zucker, Commentary (1984), Introduction 25–33.

25.4. Medieval Jewish Biblical Exegesis in Northern Africa

By Frederick E. Greenspahn, Denver, CO

Sources: D. Becker, *Ha-Risāla shel Yehudah ben Qoraysh* (Tel Aviv: Tel Aviv University 1984); Joseph ben Judah ibn ʿAqnin, *Hitgallut ha-Sodot ve-Hofaʿat ha-Meʾorot: Peirush Shir ha-Shirim* (trans. and ed. Abraham S. Halkin; Jerusalem: Meqize Nirdamim 1964); S. Y. L. Rapaport, *Toledot Gedolei Yisrael* 2 (Warsaw: ha-Sefirah, from *Bikkurei Ha-Ittim* 12 [1913] 34–55), 45–74.

Bibliograpy: A. Altmann / S. M. Stern, *Isaac Israeli, A Neoplatonic Philosopher of the Early Tenth Century* (Oxford: Oxford UP 1958); *Migdal Chananel* (Leipzig: J. C. Hinrich / Berlin: H. Itzkowski 1876).

General works: S. Baron, *A Social and Religious History of the Jews* 1–16 (2nd ed.; Philadelphia: Jewish Publication Society of America, 1952–61); A. Chouraqui, *Between East and West, A History of the Jews of North Africa* (Philadelphia: Jewish Publication Society of America 1968); H. Z. Hirschberg, *A History of the Jews in North Africa* (Leiden: E. J. Brill 1974).

Jews have lived in the Maghreb, that part of Northern Africa which lies to the west of Egypt (and Libya), since Antiquity. According to Josephus, Jews were stationed in Cyrene in the third pre-Christian century.[1] Some time later, the Talmud designates several ancient Rabbis as Carthaginians, presumably on account of their place of origin.[2] The third century Babylonian amora Rav (Abba Arika) observed that "Israel and its Father in heaven are known from Tyre to Carthage",[3] and by the early part of the fifth century, Augustine had encountered Jewish biblical scholars there.[4]

It was not, however, until the ninth century, when the region fell under Muslim control, that the Jewish communities flowered, leaving an impact which was to affect the history of Jewish learning for centuries. These centers continued to thrive until Jews were prohibited from living in certain key cities by the Almohides, who, according to Abraham ibn Daud, "wiped out every remnant of Jews from Tangiers to al-Mahdiya".[5]

In the interim, there flourished an active Jewish life, making the region a center for Jewish productivity alongside the better known communities of Babylonia and Egypt. The extent of this cultural achievement can be measured by the statement of Pirkoi ben Baboi, who noted early in the ninth century: "We have heard that the Lord has favored you and established houses of study in

---

1 *Contra Apion* 2.44 (LCL 186, pp. 308–11), cf. *Antiquities* 14.7.7/§ 115.

2 *J. Ber.* 4:3 (8a), *j. Dem.* 5:2 (24c), *j. Shabb.* 15:2 (15c), *j. Qidd.* 27b, *b. Ber.* 29a, *b. Ketub.* 27b, *b. B. Qam.* 114b.

3 *B. Menaḥ.* 110a.

4 Epistle 71 (PL 33, 242–45).

5 Abraham ibn Daud, *Sefer Ha-Qabbalah* (ed. G. D. Cohen; Philadelphia: The Jewish Publication Society of America 1967) 96 (Hebrew p. 70).

all the cities of Tunisia and in all the places of Spain".[6] In a similar spirit, an anonymous tenth century Hebrew commentary to the book of Chronicles, possibly written by a student of the great Saadiah Gaon, speaks of the region's students of Bible and Mishnah as "great scholars" (*ḥakamim gedolim*).[7] However, not everyone was so impressed. An admirer of Maimonides put into his master's mouth a warning that his son should "be cautious, especially of the people living in places between Tunis and Alexandria ... for to my mind they are the most ignorant of all, although they hold to their faith".[8]

One indicator of the contribution these centers made to Jewish biblical studies is the number of important scholars who had lived there, even though their works of lasting importance were produced elsewhere. Maimonides is not the only such Jewish figure to have lived in Fez. As his name attests, Isaac Alfasi (1003–1103), the author of an important halakhic epitome of the Babylonian Talmud, was born in that city. More important for our purposes are the famous grammarians Dunash ben Labraṭ, who was born in Fez and studied in Baghdad,[9] and Judah Hayyuj, both of whom composed their most lasting works in Spain.[10] Moshe ha-Sefardi, who spent his most productive years in Jerusalem, was apparently born in Warghla, whither he sent his book explaining difficult biblical words;[11] and David ben Abraham al-Fasi, whose name also testifies to an association with Fez, composed one of the earliest Hebrew dictionaries based an word roots after he had moved to Palestine.[12]

Much of this activity took place in the city of Kairouan. Located in what is today Morocco, its ancient name derives from the Persian word for 'caravan'. By the year 1000 it was home to two prominent rabbinic academies, associated with Jacob ben Nissim ben Josiah and Hushiel ben Elhanan respectively. The importance of these institutions can be gauged by the fact that the latter's origins had already reached legendary dimensions.[13] So important was this city

---

[6] Cf. B. M. Lewin, "Mi-Seridei ha-Genizah", *Tarbiz* 2 (1931) 396.

[7] R. Kirchheim, *Ein Commentar zur Chronik aus dem 10ten Jahrhundert* (Frankfurt/M: Brünne's Druckerei 1874) 18 (at 1 Chr 4:18).

[8] L. D. Stitskin, *Letters of Maimonides* (New York: Yeshiva University Press 1977) 158. Y. Shilat suggests that this pseudonymous letter was composed for polemical purposes after Maimonides had died, cf. his *'Iggerot ha-Rambam* (Jerusalem: Maaliyot 1987) 698.

[9] H. Hirschfeld, *Literary History of Hebrew Grammarians and Lexicographers* (London: Oxford 1926) 26; the reverse is stated in Hirschberg, A History of the Jews in North Africa (1974) 310. According to Moses ibn Ezra, he had studied in Fez (*Sefer Shirat Yisrael*, ed. Ben Zion Halpern; Lipsiae: Abraham Yosef Steibel 1924, 64); Abraham ibn Ezra also identifies him with Fez (*Mozney Leshon Ha-Qodesh*, Ophibeck: Segalspitz 1791, 2 a). See next section, 25.5.

[10] *Sefer Teshuvot Dunash ben Labrat ʿim Hakraʿot Rabeinu Yaʿaqov Tam* (ed. H. Filipowski; London: H. Filipowski 1855) is an attack on the errors of Menahem ibn Saruq; Judah Hayyuj, *Two Treatises on Verbs Containing Feeble and Double Letters* (ed. J. W. Nutt; London: Asher & Co 1870) and *The Weak and Geminative Verbs in Hebrew* (ed. M. Jastrow; Leiden: E. J. Brill 1897). See further chaps. 25.5 and 31.1 below.

[11] Hirschberg, A History of the Jews in North Africa (1974) 160.

[12] Cf. Solomon Skoss, *The Hebrew-Arabic Dictionary of the Bible known as Kitāb Jāmiʿ al-Alfāẓ (Agrōn) of David ben Abraham Al-Fāsī, the Karaite* (New Haven: Yale UP 1936–1945); the relevant biographical information is collected on pp. xxxv–xlix.

[13] The credibility of the tradition surrounding R. Hushiel's arrival in Kairouan was undermined by the contents of a letter found in the Cairo Genizah; see S. Schechter, "A Letter of Chushiel", *JQR* OS 11 (1899) 643–50.

that ibn Daud could assert that after the death of Nissim and Hananel (ca. 1065) Jewish learning in Africa ceased.[14] However, this was not the only center of Jewish learning in North Africa. As has already been implied, Fez, located east of Kairouan and south of the Strait of Gibraltar, also had its share of scholars, and smaller centers could be found at Tahart (the modern Algerian Tiaret) and Ceuta.

Most of the works produced at Kairouan had to do with rabbinic tradition. From these, it is clear that the community was in close contact with prominent academies in both Palestine[15] and Babylonia. Indeed, local authorities sometimes addressed the same inquiry to scholars at different centers, such as Sura and Pumpeditha.[16] It was in response to one such query that the Babylonian gaon Sherira ben Hanina traced the history of rabbinic literature in his famous letter.[17] The success of the Jewish community at Kairouan and its close connections with eastern rabbinic authorities made it an important cultural bridge between those centers of Jewish learning and the growing Jewish population of Spain.

Although the primary contribution of Kairouan Jewry lay in the field of halakha, they also produced a significant, if less extensive body of material in the area of biblical studies. This is hardly surprising, given the number of biblical scholars already mentioned who shared a connection to that city, even if their most important work was produced elsewhere. Further evidence can be drawn from the accomplishments of still other scholars who remained at Kairouan, whatever their origins.

The most prominent figure to emerge from this community was Isaac ben Solomon, also known as Abu Yaʿaqub al-ʾIsraeli, whose life bridged the end of the ninth and the early part of the tenth centuries. Although born in Egypt, it was in Kairouan that Israeli studied medicine under the Muslim physician Isha ibn Amran and became a prominent fiqure, serving as physician to the last of the Aghlabid and the first of the Fatimid rulers. Although Maimonides dismissed him as "only a physician", his philosophical treatises played an important role in bringing Neo-Platonism into the realm of Jewish thought.[18] Although we have no biblical scholarship from Israeli's pen, he is credited by Abraham ibn Ezra with having written a two volume commentary on the first chapter of Genesis.[19] In addition, Dunash (Adonim) ibn Tamim reports that Israeli tried to emulate the Tiberian pronunciation of Hebrew.[20]

---

[14] *Sefer Ha-Qabbalah* (ed. Cohen, 1967), 78 (Hebrew p. 58).

[15] Cf. H. Z. Hirschberg, "*Ha-Qesharim beyn Yehudey ha-Magrev u-vein ʾereṣ-Yisrael bi-Tequfat ha-Geʾonim*", *ʾEreṣ Yisraʾel* 5 (1959) 213–19.

[16] Ibid. 214.

[17] The text can be found in A. Neubauer, *Medieval Jewish Chronicles and Chronological Notes* 1 (Oxford: Clarendon Press 1887) 3–46; it is translated in S. Freehof, *A Treasury of Responsa* (New York: Ktav 1973) 6–12.

[18] Altmann / Stern, Isaac Israeli (1958). Maimonides' comment is contained in a letter to Samuel ibn Tibbon (Shilat, *ʾIggerot ha-Rambam*, 1987, 552).

[19] Abraham ibn Ezra's introduction to his commentary on the Pentateuch (beginning), where he comments that Isaac could not write more *merov devarim.*

[20] Commentary to *Sefer Yeṣirah* (ed. M. Grossberg; London: Rabbinowicz 1902) 22.

Dunash ibn Tamim, who lived in the first half of the tenth century, was himself a native of Kairouan and a student of Isaac Israeli – ibn Ezra's references to him as "the Babylonian" and the "easterner"[21] may refer to his family's roots. His medical training permitted him to follow in his mentor's footsteps, becoming personal physician to the Fatimid caliph. A remark in his commentary to the mystical *Sefer Yeṣirah* suggests that he may have joined Isaac Israeli in correcting an error in the work of Saadiah Gaon.[22] Elsewhere, he challenges Saadiah's view that *bĕlîmâ* (Job 26:7) is a single word.[23] According to Saadiah ibn Danan (fifteenth century), there was an Arabic tradition that Dunash had temporarily converted to Islam;[24] however, there is no confirmation for this relatively late report, which is generally dismissed, in large part on account of the approval with which ibn Tamim's work is cited by other Jewish scholars.

Virtually all our knowledge of Ibn Tamim's work relating to the Bible comes from allusions in the writings of others. For example, Abraham ibn Ezra mentions a work written in Hebrew and in Arabic, and Moses ibn Ezra describes a treatise devoted to the relationship between those two languages.[25] The latter also provides close to twenty citations from Ibn Tamim's exegesis. Others are found in the writings of Tanhum Jerushalmi, Judah ibn Balʿam, Abū Ibrāhīm Iṣḥaq ibn Barun, and Shemuel ha-Nagid, as well as an anonymous commentary to Ps 77:18.[26]

Elsewhere, Abraham ibn Ezra denigrates Ibn Tamim's interpretations of Gen 38:9 (that *šiḥēt ʾarṣâ* refers to unnatural sexual behavior) and Ecclesiastes 12:5 (that *ʾabîyônâ* is a diminutive form).[27] Collectively, these suggest that Ibn Tamim's work was for the most part lexicographically oriented. However, we know that his interests extended into phonology as well as possibly calculus and astronomy. In addition, Abraham Abulafia mentions a commentary on the *Sefer Yeṣirah.*[28]

By far the most important biblical scholar to have worked in Northern Africa was Judah ben Qoraysh. The details of his biography are sparse. Although he seems to have come from Tahart during the first half of the tenth century, he apparently spent some time in Fez, perhaps after Tahart was destroyed in 908.[29] Although he is sometimes thought to have been a Karaite, Ben Qo-

---

[21] At Gen 38:9, Qoh 12:5, and Abraham ibn Ezra, *Mozney Leshon ha-Qodesh* 1 b.

[22] Commentary to *Sefer Yeṣirah* (ed. M. Grossberg, 1902) 17.

[23] Ibid. 24.

[24] Z. Hirsch Edelman, *Ḥemdah Genuzah* (Königsberg: Gruber Euphrat 1856) 16 a.

[25] Abraham ibn Ezra, *Mozney Leshon Ha-Qodesh* 1 b, and Moshe ibn Ezra, *Shirat Yisrael* 54. Cf. Hirschberg, A History of the Jews in North Africa (1974) 306. A fragment of just such a work was found at the Cairo Genizah; see W. Bacher, "Aus einem alten Werke hebräisch-arabischer Sprachvergleichung", *ZDMG* 61 (1907) 700–04.

[26] The references are listed in nn. 32, 33, and 69 of P. Wechter, *Ibn Barūn's Arabic Works on Hebrew Grammar and Lexicography* (Philadelphia: The Dropsie College for Hebrew and Cognate Learning 1964) 129–30, 134–35, and 158. See also chap. 31.1 below.

[27] Ibn Ezra's commentary ad loc.

[28] Cited by A. Jellinek in *Bet ha-Midrasch* 3 (3rd ed.; Jerusalem: Wahrmann Books 1967) xliii; cf. G. Vajda, "Le commentaire kairovanais sur le 'Livre de la Creation'", *REJ* 107 (1946/47) 109.

[29] Cf. Baron, A Social and Religious History 7 (1958) 225, n. 17. The fact that he is mentioned *alongside* the scholars of Kairouan in an anonymous medieval commentary to Chronicles (Kirch-

raysh's use of the Mishna and Gemara make such an identification unlikely.[30] On the basis of available evidence, scholars have speculated that he may also have written a grammar, a dictionary, and commentaries to Deuteronomy and perhaps Chronicles, none of which is extant. What has survived is his *Risāla* (lit. 'epistle').[31] This work is known by a variety of names. Abraham ibn Ezra calls it *Sefer ha-Yaḥas* (Book of Relations) and *Sefer 'Av ve-'Em* (Book of Father and Mother) after the opening entries of its third section.[32] Elsewhere it is identified as *Ha-ʿEgron* and *Sefer Pitronim* (lit. of 'Book of Explanations').[33]

Whatever its title, this document is the oldest known example of comparative linguistics.[34] Written as a letter encouraging the Jewish community of Fez to return to the practice of including an Aramaic translation (*targum*) along with Scripture in worship,[35] it is a polemical defense of the importance of Aramaic. It begins by listing Aramaic cognates for biblical words, but then proceeds to provide cognates from post-biblical (typically mishnaic or talmudic) Hebrew, and then in a third section (which begins with the Hebrew words *'av* and *'em*, accounting for Ibn Ezra's reference) enumerates Arabic analogs to Hebrew terms and usage. There are also occasional comparisons to Greek, Latin, and even Berber, the speakers of which were sometimes thought to have had Canaanite roots.[36] In addition, several entries deal with sound changes within Hebrew itself, while others have to do with grammatical similarities among these various languages.[37]

The impact of this work reached well beyond its stated purpose of encouraging reading of the Targum. Cited by numerous medieval Jewish scholars, it ranks with Saadiah Gaon's *Ha-ʿEgron* as one at the earliest works devoted to biblical Hebrew.

Although the model of Arabic philology undoubtedly provided an impetus for this, Arab grammarians had no interest in comparing their lanuage to others. However, the circumstances of Jewish life virtually guaranteed knowledge of at least three distinct Semitic languages (biblical Hebrew, rabbinic Aramaic, and spoken Arabic), thereby facilitating the kinds of comparison Judah ben Qoraysh was to draw. Moreover, similar comparisons had been

---

heim, Ein Commentar zur Chronik (1874), at 1 Chr 3:17; 6:16; 8:7) weakens the position of those who think he lived there.

30 J. Mann, "*Ha-Hayah R. Yehudah ben Qoreish Noṭeh le-Qara'ut?*" *Tarbiz* 6 (1934) 66–68.

31 Ed. D. Becker (Tel Aviv: Tel Aviv University 1984).

32 Abraham ibn Ezra, *Mozney Leshon Ha-Qodesh*, 1 b.

33 Menahem ibn Saruq, *Maḥberet Menahem* (ed. H. Filipowski) 12 s.v. *'bḥ*, and G. Margoliouth, "Isaac ben Samuel's Commentary on the Second Book of Samuel", *JQR* OS 10 (1898) 400 (folio 42 a at 2 Sam 2:23). See also the next section, 25.5.

34 According to Moses ibn Ezra, Dunash ibn Tamim also pointed out lexicographic (but not grammatical) similarities between Hebrew, Syrian, and Arabic (*Shirat Yisrael*, ed. B. Z. Halpern, 54).

35 For the legal basis of this practice, see *b. Ber.* 8 a.

36 E. g., Procopius, *History of the Wars*, book 4 ("The Vandalic War") 10. 15–21 (LCL pp. 288–289); cf. A. Chouraqui, Between East and West (1968) 3.

37 According to Abraham ibn Ezra, Ibn Qoraysh derived some Hebrew words from single letter roots (*Śafah Berurah*, ed. G. H. Lippman; Fürth: D. J. Zürndorffer 1839, 25 b).

made during the rabbinic period, providing a kind of legitimacy for this approach.[38]

Although the works of Isaac Israeli, Dunash ibn Tamim, and Judah ben Qoraysh are the best known of North African Jewry's contribution to biblical studies, there is ample evidence that they were not alone, even if our knowledge of other scholars is largely limited to titles or brief descriptions. For example, in the early part of the eleventh century, Rabbi Hushiel's son Hananel, whom Abraham ibn Ezra described as one of the greatest teachers in the Arab world,[39] wrote not only an important commentary on the Talmud, but also commentaries on the Pentateuch and Ezekiel.[40] Judging from the excerpts of these works cited by other writers,[41] his comments seem to have been largely aggadic, often straying into discussions of themes suggested by something in the passage on which he was writing. From what can be pieced together, we can perceive his interest in justifying the apparent misbehavior of several biblical figures.[42] He was also willing to differ with rabbinic tradition.[43] Of particular importance to him was the threat of Karaism, to which he responded by defending rabbinic tradition and justifying the Bible, as in his interpretation of Gen 18:18, which he uses to support the equality of the written and the oral law. In this regard, his approach is reminiscent of Saadiah's three-fold principles – reason, text, and tradition.[44]

A list found among the documents of the Cairo Genizah suggests that Jacob ben Nissim ben Josiah ibn Shaḥūn (d. 1006/7), the co-author of the query that occasioned Sherira's famous responsum on the origins of the Mishna, also wrote a commentary on at least parts of Genesis.[45] Another commentary on that book, if not the entire Pentateuch, is credited to Nissim ben R. Yaakov, and there is reason to believe that the commentary to the book of Daniel printed under the name of Saadiah Gaon in many 'rabbinic Bibles' actually emanated from North Africa. One edition of Ibn Ezra's commentary to Esther also cites the interpretation of "one of the African sages" for the word *haṣṣār* at Esth 7:4.[46]

Finally, and strikingly separate from the kinds of exegesis typical of North

---

[38] Cf. F. E. Greenspahn, "How Modern are Modern Biblical Studies?", *Minḥah le-Nahum. Biblical and Other Studies Presented to Nahum M. Sarna in Honor of his 70th Birthday* (ed. M. Brettler / M. Fishbane; Sheffield: Sheffield Academic Press 1993) 168 f.

[39] Cited in W. Bacher, *Abraham ibn Esras Einleitung zu seinem Pentateuch Commentar* (Vienna: Karl Gerolds Sohn 1876) 37.

[40] Collected in *Migdal Chananel* (1876); see also Rapaport, *Toledot Gedolei Yisrael* 2 (1913) 45–74. Cf. M. Barol, *Menachem ben Simon aus Posquières und sein Kommentar zu Jeremia und Ezechiel* (Berlin: Adolf Alkalay & Sohn 1907) 29, 51–52.

[41] See *Migdal Chananel*, xxii–xxvi.

[42] Cf. Bacher, Abraham ibn Esra's Einleitung (1876) 39–40.

[43] *Migdal Chananel*, xxii, where Gen 31:43 is interpreted differently than in *b. Yebam.* 62 b and where other comments are also collected.

[44] See his comment at Exod 21:23; cf. Bacher, Abraham ibn Esra's Einleitung (1876) 37–40.

[45] J. Mann, "Listes de livres provenant de la Gueniza", *REJ* 72 (1921) 164; Hirschberg, A History of the Jews in North Africa (1974) 316. Cf. citations in Rapaport, *Toledot Gedolei Yisrael* 2 (1913) 97–98 (n. 22), Ibn Ezra at Exod 34:6, cf. Tosafot at *b. Roš. Haš.* 17 b which cites *Megillat Setarim.*

[46] J. Zedner, *Commentari in librum Esther* … (2d ed.; Berolini: Adolf Cohen Verlag 1873) 29.

African Jewry, is an allegorical commentary to the Song of Songs called *The Disclosure of the Secrets and the Manifestation of the Lights* (*Inkishāf āl-Asrār wa-Ẓhūr al-Anwār*), which was written by Joseph ben Judah ibn ʿAqnin, who probably lived in Fez near the end of the twelfth century.[47] Drawing on Arab thinkers and writers, the author, who is probably to be distinguished from a similarly named pupil of Maimonides, wrote what he claimed to be the first complete philosophical commentary to the Song of Songs. Following in the spirit of the talmudic dictum that Song of Songs, alone among the books of the Bible, is *not* to be interpreted literally (*b. Sanh.* 101 a), he explains it as an allegorical description of the love between the Active Intellect (i.e. God) and the individual soul.

In sum, although North Africa was not the foremost center of Jewish biblical scholarship, nor was the Bible the primary focus of what study did take place there, significant works were, nonetheless, produced in this field. Indeed, a philological approach to understanding the Bible, based on comparative linguistics, flowered among North African Jews. While the roots of this method reach back to rabbinic times, it was nurtured by the Arabic milieu in which these Jews lived, which provided both a model for linguistic study as well as the linguistic material that made it so productive. At the same time, there is little evidence that North African biblical interpretation reached much beyond the lexicographic level in the way that it did in Spain, although there is no denying the fact that the seeds for the remarkable developments in biblical study which took place on the Iberian peninsula were often brought there by Jews from North Africa.[48] Still, isolated examples of a more philosophical (Isaac Israeli) and theological (Ibn Aqnin) approach can also be found.

---

[47] Published with a Hebrew translation by A. S. Halkin as *Hitgallut Ha-Sodot ve-Hofaʿat ha-Me'orot: Peirush Shir ha-Shirim* (Jerusalem: Meqize Nirdamim 1964).

[48] N. M. Sarna, "Hebrew and Bible Studies in Medieval Spain", *The Sephardi Heritage* (ed. R. D. Barnett; London: Vallentine & Mitchell 1971) 323–66.

25.5. Early Hebraists in Spain: Menaḥem ben Saruq and Dunash ben Labraṭ

By ANGEL SÁENZ-BADILLOS, Madrid

Sources: Maḥberet Měnaḥem (ed. H. Filipowski; London / Edinburgh 1854); *Sefer Těšubot Dunaš ben Labraṭ* (ed. H. Filipowski; London / Edinburgh 1855); *Sefer Těšubot. Těšubot Talmide Měnaḥem ben Ya'ăqob ben Saruq. Těšubot Talmid Dunaš ha-Lewi ben Labraṭ* (ed. S. G. Stern; Wien 1870); *Sefer Těšubot Dunaš ha-Lewi ben Labraṭ 'al Rabbi Se'adyah Ga'on* (ed. R. Schröter; Breslau 1866); *Las Těšubot de Dunaš ben Labraṭ* (Edición crítica y traducción española por A. Sáenz-Badillos; Granada 1980); *Měnaḥem ben Saruq, Maḥberet* (Edición crítica por A. Sáenz-Badillos; Granada 1986); *Těšubot de los Discípulos de Měnaḥem contra Dunaš ben Labraṭ* (Edición del texto y traducción castellana por Santiaga Benavente Robles, revisada y completada por A. Sáenz-Badillos; Granada 1986); *Těšubot de Yěhudi ben Šešet* (ed. E. Varela; Granada 1981).

Bibliography: A. SÁENZ-BADILLOS, "La hermenéutica bíblica de Dunaš ben Labraṭ", *Simposio Bíblico Español (Salamanca 1982)* (Madrid 1984) 697–706; idem, "Los 'hapax legomena' bíblicos en Menaḥem ben Saruq", *Salvación en la Palabra. Homenaje al Prof. A. Díez Macho* (Madrid 1986) 783–809; idem, "La filología hispanohebrea del siglo X como exegesis", *Miscelánea de Estudios Árabes y Hebraicos* 36,2 (1987) 7–28; C. DEL VALLE RODRÍGUEZ, "La exégesis bíblica de Menaḥem ben Saruq", *Revista Catalana de Teología* 2 (1977) 485–99.

General works: W. BACHER, "Die Bibelexegese vom Anfange des 10. bis zum Ende des 15. Jahrhunderts", J. WINTER / A. WÜNSCHE, *Die jüdische Literatur* 2 (Trier 1894) 239–339; A. SÁENZ-BADILLOS / J. TARGARONA, *Gramáticos Hebreos de al-Andalus (Siglos X–XII). Filología y Biblia* (Córdoba 1988); idem, *Los judíos de Sefarad ante la Biblia. La interpretación de la Biblia en el Medievo* (Córdoba 1996); N. M. SARNA, "Hebrew and Bible Studies in Medieval Spain", *The Sephardi Heritage* I (London 1971) 323–66; U. SIMON, "La escuela hispanojudía de exégesis bíblica", *Morešet Sěfarad* (ed. H. Beinart; Jerusalem 1992) 120–42.

1. Introduction

The beginnings of Jewish exegesis in Medieval Spain should be understood against the background of the favourable conditions of life enjoyed by the Jewish community under the Muslim Caliphate, and the integration of the Jewish intellectual leaders in the cultural life of their Islamic neighbours. Spanish Jews were conscious of the progress made by Arab grammarians in the knowledge of their own language. As has long been recognized this was one of the causes that moved Jewish scholars to work with comparable enthusiasm for the study of the sacred language as the main instrument for their approach to the Bible.[1] At the same time they did not forget their own traditions, remaining faithful to their past and their religion. Without renouncing the cultural atmosphere of the time, they accepted the new tendencies developed

[1] See the classical study of W. BACHER, "Die hebräische Sprachwissenschaft (vom 10. bis zum 16. Jahrhundert)", in: Winter / Wünsche, Die jüdische Literatur 2 (1894) 136 ff.

among the Jews in the Orient and in North Africa, integrating them in their own synthesis.

Starting from principles similar to those developed by Islamic philologists, and in the way already opened both by Karaite interpreters and by Saadiah Gaon, Andalusians turned to the Scriptures combining exegesis with the systematic study of the language of the Bible. Instead of continuing the trends of the rabbinical derashic exegesis, they sought to understand the biblical text by analyzing its grammatical aspects down to the smallest details, and by defining the precise meaning of every word that appears in Scripture. This kind of literal, philological interpretation of the Bible can be seen as a new type of *peshat* very different from the traditional *derash*, which, however, was never directly refuted.

Some scholars think that before the epoch of the first exegetical grammarians, there existed in al-Andalus a number of early exegetes who wrote in Arabic, but whose works have been lost. It seems indeed very likely, and it is possible that some of the general references to 'the commentators' found in the first known exegetes frequently allude to such scholars.[2]

In any case, by the middle of the tenth century the study of the biblical Hebrew language emerged in Cordoba under the Caliphs with unexpected strength. Ḥasday ben Shapruṭ, the Jewish minister of the muslim Caliph ʿAbd al-Raḥmān the Third, charged his secretary, Menaḥem ben Saruq, with a "work on the holy language", which he elaborated faithfully and without rest until the first Hebrew-Hebrew dictionary of biblical 'ground forms', the *Maḥberet*, was ready. It did not represent an absolutely new phenomenon, since in several Jewish centres of the Arabic world the tendency had already arisen to study the language of the Bible with the same interest, and many times with the same methods, as employed by the Arabs in their interpretation of the Koran. Menaḥem however did a rather original work, creating his own terminology in Hebrew, developing his own conception of the holy tongue and trying to elucidate the meaning of the whole vocabulary of the Bible based on his own linguistic principles.

In the following pages, besides Menaḥem's *Maḥberet*,[3] we shall deal with the replies to that work written by Dunash ben Labraṭ, a student of Saadiah born in Fez ca. 925, and established in Cordoba. These replies were entitled *Teshuḇot ʿal Menaḥem* and represented 180 answers directed against his Dictionary, which was seen as a danger for uncultivated people, being able to destroy at one and the same time Jewish religion and "the most beautiful of the languages".[4] We shall also deal with the answers formulated by their respective disciples, who continued the debate.[5] In addition, we shall take into account the *Criticisms against Saadiah*, attributed by many scholars to the same Dunash.[6]

---

[2] Cf. Simon, La escuela hispanojudía (1992) 120ff.
[3] Quoted according to my edition (Granada 1986) as *M*.
[4] Quoted according to my edition (Granada 1980) as *D*.
[5] Quoted according to S. Benavente's and E. Varela's editions as *TTM* and *TYŠ* respectively.
[6] We quote R. Schröter's edition as *S*.

The *Sitz im Leben* of this philological and exegetical activity must be sought in the practice of interpretation and commentary of the Scriptures which has been in all times of primary importance for any Jewish community, and in the teaching of younger students.

2. The Philological and Exegetical Work of Menaḥem and Dunash

During the tenth century, Menaḥem, Dunash and their disciples were not practising exegesis in the conventional, expected meaning of the word: they did not write continuous commentaries on the biblical books, nor fix any hermeneutical principles; they did not pay attention to the literary or historical problems of the biblical text. But the whole material discussed in their lexicographical and grammatical works was taken from the Bible, their lexica were thought of as a help for the reading of the Bible, and their warm debates were centred on the sense of biblical passages; all their efforts were directed towards a better comprehension of the plain meaning of the biblical text. They were of course deeply rooted in the ancient Jewish exegetical tradition, but at the same time they tried to go in a substantially new direction, profiting from a knowledge of the language. Many of the problems that repeatedly engaged Saadiah, such as the correspondence between faith and reason, or the internal coherence of the biblical books, did not come to the fore in the works of these grammarians. In contrast with Saadiah and other previous exegetes, they rejected the tendency to explain difficult passages as metaphorical or allegorical. They simply tried to understand the meaning of every word of the biblical text, discussing its most immediate and obvious sense according to its grammatical structure. In al-Andalus, philological studies represented in their true nature an exclusively literal interpretation of Scripture.

In comparison with the richness of meanings which would be detected by the exegetes of the eleventh century, or with other later trends that evolved in the coming centuries among the Jewish exegetes of Spain and Europe, such as introducing philosophic, mystic or allegorical elements in the interpretation of the biblical text, Menaḥem, Dunash and the other philologists of the tenth century could seem too simple and unsophisticated. They were nevertheless establishing the foundations of a true understanding of the text of the Bible and of most of the many-sided exegesis that characterizes the Jewish-Spanish school of the eleventh and twelfth centuries.

It would not be exaggerated to define Menaḥem's *Maḥberet* as an 'exegetical dictionary', especially if we take into consideration the large number of cases where he tries to clarify unusual or doubtful meanings of many biblical passages. One of the names employed by Menaḥem's disciples for their master's work, *Sefer pitronim*, 'Book of Interpretations' (*TTM* 11*, 13, etc.), could point in that direction. Menaḥem sought to analyse and classify more than 12 000 biblical passages around their 'foundations', sometimes putting together sentences with similar meaning, and sometimes clarifying precisely the sense of a particular passage or term. Many strange words or *hapax legomena* deserved a particular explanation. He devoted a good deal of attention to determining the structure and radicals of every word of the biblical text, trying to classify them according to the meaning – a procedure which had obvious exegetical consequences. A large part of Menaḥem's excursus in the *Maḥberet* also had a directly exegetical character. In sum, he undertook a true philogical interpretation of the whole Bible and the responses of Dunash or their disciples dealt exclusively with problems connected with the interpretation of the biblical text.

The grammatical and lexical study of the language of the Bible was for the first Spanish-Hebrew philologists, Menaḥem ben Saruq and Dunash ben Labraṭ, a passionate question, that gave rise to one of the hottest debates that took place in the Middle Ages. From our perspective, it is not easy to understand that the meaning of a word or its appropriate grammatical classification could give rise to such vicious attacks and scornful abuses. But it was not a mere question of words: upon that discussion depended the whole Jewish conception of God and his relation to the world, the way of understanding the moral obligations of mankind, and confirmation of rabbinic tradition over against sectarian views. Therefore, it could not be just a cold and objective science. On the contrary, as Dunash observes, questions in this field have far-reaching implications of a religious and theological nature, both at the theoretical level, for faith, and in practical life, the *halakhah.* As a consequence of this, the first requirement, in his opinion, for approaching this field should be the fear of God. For him, exegesis and theology can never be in contradiction. The first reply to Menaḥem deals extensively with an important theological problem:

> It is an open reprehension, which tries to burn the heart / of that who has brought ruin to the hearts of the creatures,/ destroying fear of God and saying that God sees / how sin is done in order to damage the righteous ones (Lam 3:36)./ But God does not share anything with the man who does evil,/ and who can choose good and evil (*D* 18*, 23).

In Dunash' opinion, Menaḥem's interpretation of the passage has theological consequences that are totally unacceptable; it is necessary to seek an explanation of the passage which is at the same time both linguistically possible and theologically sound. In this case, as Menaḥem's disciples state, it is but an apparent dissension, since the true meaning of their master's words includes nothing which could be considered as unorthodox (*TTM* 16*f, 22ff). In other cases, however, Dunash criticizes interpretations of his adversary which can be considered as near to the Karaites.[7]

In the works of the tenth century Andalusian grammarians, Menaḥem ben Saruq, Dunash ben Labraṭ, and their disciples, different approaches to Bible exegesis can be discerned, with clear peculiarities. Their attitude to the past was not the same: Menaḥem quotes by name only Saadiah and Judah ibn Quraysh, and he mostly dissents from their points of view, as he usually does in respect of other earlier commentators. In his replies, Dunash is much more re-

[7] For instance, *u-mālaq* (Lev 5:8) does not mean "to slaughter", as Menaḥem asserts according the Karaite *halakhah*, but "to wring off", as it is interpreted by the Rabbanites (*D* 97*, 106). I agree in substance with N. Allony's opinion, which sees in Dunash' *Teshuvot* an answer to the possible philo-karaite theories of Menaḥem. See "Hašqafot qĕra'iyot ba-'Maḥberet' Menaḥem wĕ-ha-millim ha-bodĕdot bĕ-ʿerek 'glb'", *'Oṣar Yehude Sĕfarad* 5 (1962) 21–54, and "Haqdamat Dunaš li-tšuḇotaw lĕ-'Maḥberet' Mĕnaḥem", *BethM* 22 (1965) 45–63.

spectful of those masters, and also with regard to the masorah or the Targum. Nevertheless, these philologists share common attitudes which in some cases may have their roots in the spiritual atmosphere of the epoch and in their more or less loose dependency upon the immediate forerunners in the Orient or in North Africa, and in other cases are characteristic of their own approach. For these scholars philology was not an aim in itself, as it would be some years later for «the father of all grammarians», Judah Hayyuj: it was an instrument for an adequate comprehension of the Bible, the only correct way of interpreting the Scriptures. It was the first literal exegesis which truly deserved such a name.

3. Hermeneutical Attitude

Tenth century philologists in Cordoba, in spite of their discrepancies, share several common principles in their approach to the Scriptures:

a) The point of departure for all of them had to be a reliable text of the Hebrew Bible. For Menaḥem, this holy text is sufficient in itself, it does not need any human external help in being comprehensible, so we must be concerned exclusively with obtaining a correct reading of the manuscripts. He even discusses a text-critical problem: the 'Sefardic' reading *yifqod*, in third person, as opposed to the 'Tiberian' one *'efqod*, in first person (Isa 27:3). The first reading means that God protects his vineyard, his people, and hinders that 'any' of his enemies may 'hurt it'; the second one means that God himself can punish his vineyard. Menaḥem finds meaningful the reading *yifqod*, but taking into account the differences in the manuscripts, he does not decide which is the true one: "only God knows which is the correct reading" (*M* 33*).

Dunash, no less than his adversary, tries to take as a starting point a text that is as trustworthy as possible, 'corrected codices', which contain the precise reading and the exact spelling (*D* 78*, 87). And for Menaḥem's disciples too it is important to employ the best texts, "the Tiberian manuscripts corrected according to the divine Torah", or "the correct old codices, from Sefardic or Tiberian origin" (*TTM* 24*, 35; 36*, 57).

b) Menaḥem and Dunash reject what they consider mistakes or grammatical imprecisions of earlier Bible commentators, trying to clarify precisely their own points of view on biblical usages. Their whole philological activity is orientated towards ensuring the exact comprehension of the smallest details included in the text. The whole discussion about the components of the ground forms, the classification of their meanings, the nature of nominal or verbal schemes, the correct vocalization and accentuation, or even about the identification of *realia*, should be understood against that background.

c) The main purpose of both is to be faithful to the literal meaning of the text, but that does not mean overlooking the fact that the Scriptures use metaphors and comparisons that should be understood as such. Dunash for instance recognizes the metaphorical sense of "God is my rock and my fortress" (Ps 18:3, *D* 33*, 41), as well as the use of "he-goats" (Isa 14:9) referring to kings and princes of the people (*D* 39*, 47); he is aware of the comparison *'ên*

Yaʿăqob (Deut 33:28), employed in the sense of "the root of Jacob", from which the waters, that is to say, the sons of Israel, originate, etc. (*D* 102*, 112); he recognizes that the kings may be compared with birds which fly quickly from far away (*D* 53*, 62).

However, when Menaḥem's disciples comment on Ps 63:2 and see in it an allusion to the future situation of Israel in exile, they are severely criticized by Yehudi ben Sheshet, who considers that they have left the direct and literal meaning of the text, taking it as a kind of *mashal* or parable (*TYŠ* 22*f, 47 f).

d) No less than other previous exegetes, Menaḥem and Dunash are concerned by the presence of anthropomorphisms and anthropopathisms in Scripture. Menaḥem asks himself if in Isa 38:17 it is actually said about God "thou hast cast all my sins behind thy back (*gēweka*)", and he answers:

> If we derive it from the root *gewiyyāh*, 'body', the commentator can say that the Torah speaks in the language of human beings. And intelligent men will understand that it is not right to attribute to our God a figure or form or body, but the Torah enlarges the meanings and interpretations, multiplying the figurative expressions according to the knowledge of men and the capacity of their understanding, in order that they may comprehend. Had the Torah spoken according to the power of His high wonders, they would not be able to understand, because He is above their science (*M* 101*f).

In a similar way, Dunash explains the meaning of *wa-yištômēm*, "was astonished" (Isa 59:16): "God, whose Name be exalted, rises over cares and fears, beyond the patience and the sorrow of the heart"; and he justifies it also with the traditional words "the Torah speaks in the language of human beings", that is, it searches for expressions that everybody may understand "in order that they may listen according to their faculties and that they comprehend in the measure of their science" (*D* 46*f, 55).

At the same time, there are deep differences among these philologists in their approach to the biblical text:

a) The philological study of the Scriptures renounces certain methods of interpretation used in rabbinical exegesis, but for Dunash "the thirteen rules by which most of the precepts, laws, norms and instructions are governed and measured" are a complement to the science of the language necessary for the interpretation of the Bible (*D* 15*, 20). He quotes also the traditional translation of the Targum many times; Menaḥem quotes it too, but he does not feel rooted to the same degree in rabbinical tradition.

b) They clearly disagree in trying to determine the consequences of total respect for the biblical text and its understanding in the rabbinical and masoretic traditions. Menaḥem and his disciples limit themselves to the text that they have received without accepting any kind of changes; many times, they do not admit even those proposed by the masoretes or by still earlier interpreters. Dunash, after enumerating in his «Introduction» many requisites for the philological study of the text, includes among them the fundamental principles of the masorah and the corrections of the Sopherim (*D* 15*, 19 f).

In spite of being full of respect for the vocalization and accentuation of the text fixed by the Tiberian masters, very often Menaḥem does not accept the small modifications of the biblical text which had been traditionally integrated in the Jewish reading of the Scriptures, such as the *ketiv / qere*. His disciples, who seem to be more traditional on this point, try to prove that in such cases, the *qere* has the meaning which is convenient to the context, but the *ketiv* has its own independent meaning, and they hold that Menaḥem has the right of referring to the latter, without showing ignorance of, or contempt for, the traditional reading.[8]

The attitude of Dunash and his disciple Ibn Sheshet is quite different. In several replies, Dunash criticizes his adversary for not having taken into consideration the observations of the Sopherim and the Masoretes, in *qere / ketiv* cases,[9] that may have a remarkable influence upon the *halakhah*. Menaḥem understands three passages in the negative sense, according to the written word, *lōʾ*, but the masorah says precisely that all the three should be read with *waw*, *lô*, as positive statements, and for Dunash the consequence is that his adversary "permits what is not allowed, and prohibits what is allowed".[10] The case is similar in other words in which the *ʾalef* should not be read,[11] or "those that come first but ought to come later".[12] These and other elementary principles of the Masorah are enumerated in the prose Introduction to the *Teshuvot ʿal Menaḥem* as part of the essential, indispensable knowledge of the philologist. It seems a clear recrimination against Menaḥem, who has not taken those masoretic observations into account, even if they are necessary for the interpretation of many passages of the Bible.

c) Menaḥem shows a strong opposition to other modifications introduced in the text by many of his predecessors: changing one letter to another or inverting the order of the radicals of a word. These are two well known methods of interpretation used by earlier interpreters in very difficult cases, especially in the *hapax legomena*, when they found no other way of explaining the text. Many scholars who employed those methods before or during the tenth century thought that similar changes of consonants had taken place in some passages of Scripture.

Even if this way of exegesis seems to us strange and scientifically difficult to justify, the authority of Gaon Saadiah gave it strong support. Some biblical usages in his opinion could justify these methods, and he used them when he was not able to explain a passage without any modification, although limiting himself to similar consonants.[13]

The scholar of Kairawan Judah ibn Quraysh (first half of the tenth century), employed these methods with relative frequency, which merited an angry rebuke by Menaḥem (*M* 19*f). Even the well-known Karaite David ben Abraham al-Fāsī knew and used the permutation without ideological restrictions.[14]

---

[8] *M* 227*; *D* 21*, 26; *TTM* 33*, 51 ff; *TYŠ* 30*, 65.

[9] *D* 21*, 26; 58*, 69, etc.

[10] Exod 21:8, Lev 11:21 and Lev 25:30, *D* 21*, 26

[11] Such as *pāʾrûr* in Joel 2:6, *D* 57*, 67; 82*, 92.

[12] E. g. *tôlaʿat šānî* in Exod 28:6 in contrast with Lev 14:6, *D* 122*f, 139 f.

[13] M. Pereṣ, "Yissum ha-ʾemṣaʿy ʾḥilluf ʾotiyyotʾ be-feruše Raḇ Sĕʿadyah Gaʾon", *Tarbiz* 52 (1983) 515–52. In his doctoral thesis presented in Bar-Ilan University (1978), *The Philological Exegesis of R. Jehuda ibn Balʿam* (Hebr.), he studies the methods of the change or inversion of letters in a more fundamental way.

[14] S. L. Skoss, "A Chapter on Permutation in Hebrew from David ben Abraham Al-Fasi's Dictionary, ʾJamiʿ al-alfazʾ", *JQR* 22 (1932/33) 1–43.

Menaḥem accepts the permutation of *'alef*, *hē*, *waw* or *yod*, and, in some few cases, that of *śin* and *samek*.[15] But in general terms, as we have already noted, he is radically against these methods, and many times shows his opposition to the changes introduced by earlier interpreters.

> There are words in the Torah wich lack any counterpart which would permit recognition of their roots, or understanding of their structure; only the context and the order of occurrence offers a guide to their meaning. When interpreters saw this, and were unable to discern the ground forms of the words or their basic root letters so as to discern their meaning, they altered them by changing letters. They thereby altered the language in an unacceptable way (*M* 19*).

When he thinks that two words with the disputed consonants referred to have the same meaning, he does not speak of 'permutation' or 'metathesis', but he introduces the particle *kemô*, establishing a comparison between them. He is strongly against those interpreters who dare to replace one word for another (*M* 96*). He has good rational reasons: "What is the use of interpretation if one can take out, add, change or alter the order?" (*M* 19*f). By this means we would arbitrarily change the meaning of the Scriptures, "their ravines would be plains".[16] It is not the correct method for solving the difficulties of the Hebrew language, since those problems derive from the fact that the holy language, due to the history of the people, is not fully preserved. We are not allowed to fill these gaps with our imagination. Menaḥem is of all medieval commentators, the champion of opposition to such methods. No less than the Karaites, he demands full respect and fidelity to the text and to its grammatical form.

His adversary Dunash speaks less clearly against the use of these methods, and takes it as read that *'alef* and *hē* can be interchanged all over Scripture (*D* 78*, 87 f) like *yod* and *waw* (*D* 50*f, 59; 112*, 123 f). Nevertheless he uses permutation in a very restricted way and does not reply to Menaḥem when he expresses his opposition to Ibn Quraysh.[17] In the *Teshuvot ʿal Seʿadyah* it is stated that "there are words which allow changes in their letters", as *ke<u>b</u>eś* and *keśe<u>b</u>*; for that reason, it seems right to interpret *we-yaḥregû* (Ps 18:46) as *we-yaḥgerû*, "they limp" (*S* 27).

The great grammarian Jonah ibn Janah, in the eleventh century, contributed with success to the acceptance of these methods by medieval Jewish exegesis, writing a whole chapter on each matter, and employing them almost without restriction.[18]

d) Neither Menaḥem nor his disciples willingly accept other external aids, alien to the text of the Scriptures, such as comparison with related languages. In their opinion, the explanation of the meaning of the text should emerge from the passage itself when it is analysed from a philological point of view. For them, it is the context, the vocalization, the intended parallelism of the sentences, that help us to clarify the meaning of the difficult passages in Scrip-

---

[15] See however *M* 96*.

[16] *M* 33*. Cf. 95*ff, 104*ff, 135*.

[17] In some cases, without mentioning the "permutation", he emphasizes that there are many words in the Scriptures written with *śin* and with *same<u>k</u>* with similar meanings: *D* 119*f, 136 f.

[18] *Sefer ha-riqmah* I (ed. Wilensky/Tene; Jerusalem 1964) 352 ff.

ture, including the *hapax legomena.* We do not need to seek in other languages a solution of the problems of the 'holy tongue'.

As a consequence of his ideological attitude, Menaḥem systematically avoids the comparative linguistic approach developed by his forerunners. He does not use Arabic at all, and he even makes a very restricted usage of mishnaic Hebrew, which in his opinion is to be clearly differentiated from biblical Hebrew. In some cases he uses biblical and targumic Aramaic in the explanation of a few roots or unclear passages, and he is apparently not against this last possibility. However we are not sure about his point of view on this matter, since it could be more a recourse to an argument of tradition and authority than a true philological comparative approach. The only solid principle for him is that the holy language should be understood by itself.

Menaḥem's disciples comment: "What do Hebrew and Aramaic have in common? If we say in the case of every word without similarities that there is something that resembles it in Aramaic or Arabic, all those languages would be the same, without differences, and we would learn that part of the Hebrew language which disappeared. That is not possible" (*TTM* 54*f, 88). In general terms, for Menaḥem and his disciples, the 'holy tongue' must be sufficient of itself.

The contrast with Dunash and his disciple's attitude is very clear. These continue the comparative methods initiated by Saadiah and other grammarians in North Africa, and they defend the possibility of comparing the roots of those languages, especially in the case of homophony, in spite of the phonetic changes of some consonants which seem to separate one tongue from the other. Dunash, knowing Menaḥem's reluctance to accept it, asks himself in his adversary's name: "why should we compare Hebrew and the Arabic language?". The answer is significant enough: first of all, he tries to convince his rival of resorting to the Arabic language in many cases, without recognizing it; secondly, he presents more than 160 Hebrew words which have the same meaning as their homophones in Arabic (with the necessary changes of spelling), in order to prove "that the two languages are similar" (*D* 88*ff, 98 ff).

The same can be said of comparison with mishnaic Hebrew, especially in the *hapax legomena*, following Saadiah's usage,[19] and with Aramaic.[20] Dunash, in search of a confirmation or basis for his own interpretations, frequently refers to the Targumim, as traditional interpretations of the Bible, accepting linguistic comparisons in many instances.

The differences of approach between Menaḥem's and Dunash' schools are based both on the linguistic perspective, of defending the proximity of the languages and the possibility of a comparative study, as well as on theological grounds: Dunash relies more on the traditional rabbinic interpretation, while Menaḥem underlines the uniqueness and excellency of the *sola scriptura*, whose divine language cannot be compared with other human works.

---

[19] See for instance *D* 55*f, 65; 78*, 87; 82*, 92.
[20] *D* 116*f., 132, etc.

4. Philological Exegesis

The application of the linguistic analysis of the text to the interpretation of the Scriptures is a common characteristic of tenth century grammarians. Their first interest is the determination of the permanent elements in the root and the right classification of the words; the root is seen more as a logical or mathematical combination of consonants than as a historical unit with form and meaning. Etymologically different but homophonically similar roots were put together, divided in different sections according to their meaning. As the principle of triliteralism was not yet known by Jewish grammarians in its application to the 'weak' verbs, it is not unusual to find merged in a 'biliteral' root different 'weak' triliteral verbs. This is one of the major limitations of tenth century philology.

a) The identification of a letter as 'radical' or 'servile' (additional), especially at the beginning of the words, is many times the first task of the interpreter of the text, and it constitutes one of the most debated themes among grammarians of the period. The inclusion of a consonant in the root or its recognition as an additional element may decisively change the understanding of a passage. For instance, Menaḥem interprets *beśārîm* (Prov 19:10) as the plural of *bāśār*, 'flesh', and reads the verse: "It is not convenient for the slave to have rule over creatures" (*M* 92*); Dunash understands *be-śārîm*, "over princes", and justifies it on the basis of the context (*D* 23*, 29). The Targum, Rashi, Abraham ibn Ezra, as well as many other modern commentators support Dunash, but Menaḥem's opinion cannot be rejected from a grammatical point of view.

The Sefardic master surpasses most of the earlier interpreters thanks to his linguistic knowledge. Discussing the term *nādôn* (2 Sam 19:10), he proves that both occurrences of *nun*, the first and the final one, cannot be additional; the second *nun* belongs to the root, and it cannot be considered as related to *nādad*, 'to be errant', but to *mādôn*, 'dispute' (*M* 128*).

The author of the *Teshuvot ʿal Seʿadyah* states that it is not correct to relate *temaggenekkā* (Prov 4:9) to the substantive *māgēn*, 'shield', since the *mem* of this last word is not a radical letter; with the aid of several texts, he proves that *māgan* and *gānan* differ both in the inflection and in the meaning ('to give' against 'to protect': *S* 54). In the case of *rodēm* (Ps 68:28), he does not agree with the interpretation 'their leader', as if it was of a *lamed-hē* verb, since according to its scheme it must be of the triradical root *rdm* (*S* 56).

In the same way, disputing an Aramaic text of Daniel, Dunash thinks that *benas û-qeṣaf śaggîʾ* (Dan 2:12) is not to be taken as a verb of the root *bns*, 'became enraged' as Menaḥem proposes (*M* 86*), but as a substantive, *nas*, 'rage' preceded by the particle *be-* (*D* 23*, 28).[21]

Menaḥem was probably wrong when he compared *kîdôdê ʾēš* (Job 41:11), "fire flames", with *ba-dûd* (1 Sam 2:14), "in the pot", seeing the *kaf* as additional; his disciples reply, nevertheless, to Dunash that the comparative parti-

[21] See the continuation of this debate in *TTM* 35*, 54; *TYŠ* 28*, 60.

cle allows a good explanation of the passage.[22] The meaning of the text can change radically as well if, for instance, the initial *lamed* of *lešaddî* (Ps 32:4) is additional, as Menaḥem thinks, or if it is a part of the radical, as Dunash says, meaning 'moist'; in the first case, it would be derived from *šādad*, 'to devastate', or perhaps related to *šad*, 'breast'.[23]

b) Menaḥem and Dunash employ paraphrase as the usual way of explaining the text, substituting unclear or difficult words with other terms or expressions which can be better understood. They agree in theory that the exegete should respect every word of the biblical text, without adding unnecessary terms, which do not contribute to the understanding of the passage (*M* 45*f, *D* 103*, 113). It is not allowed to remove a single word from the text.[24]

Nevertheless, they have no difficulties in recognizing that there are unnecessary repetitions in the biblical text, which could have been omitted (*M* 138*). They are aware too of the epenthetic value of some particles which "fall in the interpretation", i.e., that are not strictly necessary for the meaning of the text, and could be eliminated. According to Dunash, such is the case of the *waw* in *û-be-ṣôq ha-ʿittîm* (Dan 9:25), and even clearer, of the *hē* in *be-ha-šāmayîm* (Ps 36:6).[25] The literal exegesis of the tenth century was not as minute as, for instance, that of the Akiba school many centuries earlier.

In the addition of some particles or words in order to make a verse comprehensible, Menaḥem appears much more inflexible than Dunash, even if he sees a possible ellipsis in some passages: Scripture says *hāyû ben Šāʾûl* (2 Sam 4:2), instead of *le-ben Šāʾûl*, etc. (*M* 137*). Dunash states that "we have many passages in the Scriptures which cannot be interpreted other than by adding one, two, or even more words" (*D* 73*, 83). He refers, above all, to the cases where subjects, complements, particles, relatives and so on are implicit. And he tries to convince Menaḥem that he himself does the same many times.[26] Nevertheless, in most cases Menaḥem is strictly literal, while Dunash seems much freer.

In some cases, Dunash thinks that the interpreter is justified in replacing one particle for another, as in Prov 25:22, where *ʿal rōšô* ought to be understood as *mē-ʿal rōšô* or *min-rōšô* (*D* 86*, 96). He reminds his adversary that he does the same in similar cases, e.g., interpreting *ʾet* as *min* (*M* 70*).

Disputing about *la-bālāh niʾûfîm* (Ezek 23:43), Dunash holds that we must add the particle *be-*, as in many other verses (*D* 29*, 36). And in *ke-keḇeś ʾallûf* (Jer 11:19), Dunash estimates, with other earlier authors, that the copulative *waw* should be added: *we-ʾallûf*, distinguishing two different animals in the verse. Menaḥem and his disciples do not see the need of this addition, which modifies the meaning of the passage.[27] In other verses, Dunash thinks that it is

---

[22] *M* 123*, root *dwd*; *D* 26*, 32; *TTM* 49*, 78; *TYŠ* 15*, 29.

[23] *M* 361*; *D* 26*, 33; *TTM* 48*, 76; *TYŠ* 15*, 29.

[24] When Dunash discusses the meaning of *baʿălê ʾăsuppôt* (Qoh 12:11), he blames Menaḥem for having taken out the first of those words, thereby giving a wrong interpretation to the verse (*D* 67*, 75).

[25] *D* 23*, 28; 111*, 122; 112*, 124.

[26] In the interpretation of Jer 18:14 Dunash rejects the addition of *ʾādām*, 'man' introduced by Menaḥem, as unnecessary. *M* 158*; *D* 103*f., 113.

[27] *M* 45*; *D* 68*f, 77; *TTM* 42*, 67.

necessary to add the particle *kî*, *harbeh*, 'more', before a comparative *mem*, the verb *hāyāh*, etc.[28]

c) The interpretation of the text may require the division of a word into two or more words. This is a principle accepted by all grammarians of the time, but its application to concrete cases is not obvious. Even Menaḥem, who is against the introduction of changes of any kind in the text, accepts "that there are words in the Hebrew language which can be divided into two", and gives a list of samples of such words, most of them with pronominal suffixes that can be written separately with the help of a particle, but he refuses to admit the tendency of previous interpreters to extend the category of divisible words to many other cases, such as *talpiyyôt* (Cant 4:4), *belî-māh* (Job 26:7), *'er'ellām* (Isa 33:7), etc., as if composite nouns were usual in Hebrew (*M* 60*ff). Dunash subscribes to the same principle when he analyses *we-naggîdennû* (Jer 20:10), bringing a few examples of suffixed verbs, but he does not agree in practical cases with his adversary: *tiśśa'ēnî* (Job 30:22) cannot be divided into two in the same way as *netattānî* (Josh 15:19), equivalent to *natattā lî*, "you have given to me".[29]

Similar reasons move Dunash to blame his rival when Menaḥem joins two words in one, as in *'almût* (Ps 9:1), interpreted as 'melodies', where the manuscripts and most interpreters read *'al mût*, "on the death of".[30]

d) Both Menaḥem and Dunash agree that it is possible for one biblical word "to be used instead of two" ("double function or double duty particles").[31] For Menaḥem a particle does not need to be repeated in the second part of a sentence.[32] Dunash agrees with him in some cases, but not in others,[33] and he thinks that the rule cannot be applied to every case without previous analysis.

e) The grammatical analysis of the text is of utmost importance for its correct interpretation, e.g., the possibility of a double plural in the Bible can have remarkable exegetical consequences: Menaḥem puts *hārôt ha-gil'ād* (Amos 1:13) in the same section as *hārîm*, 'mountains', but Dunash thinks that it is the plural of *hārāh*, 'pregnant women'.[34]

In Ps 80,16 Dunash holds the opinion that *we-kannāh* cannot be an imperative, but a substantive, 'vineyard'.[35] He insists that we must carefully distinguish verbs and nouns that have the same form: *ṣiyyāh* (Job 24:19) can be understood as the noun 'dryness', or the verb 'it dried' (*D* 93*f, 102).

We should not confuse words with similar meaning but which have different stress on the last or the penultimate syllable, according to the context (*D* 114*, 126). The position of the accent may often decide what is the real form of a

[28] So, e.g., *mi-zônāh*, Ezek 16:41, must be understood as *mi-heyôt zônāh*, "from being a prostitute". See *D* 74*, 82 f; 77*, 86; 112*, 123.

[29] *D* 75*, 84 f.; 118*, 134 f.

[30] *M* 282*; *D* 28*, 34 f.

[31] *M* 139*; *D* 69*, 78.

[32] According to him, in Job 32:9 the negation of the first part, *lo' rabbîm yeḥkāmû*, is to be extended in the second part too, *û-zeqēnîm yāḇînû mišpāṭ*.

[33] So, e.g., in Exod 12:9, where it would introduce a new prohibition.

[34] *M* 142*; *D* 54*, 63; *TTM* 45*, 72; *TYŠ* 15*, 30.

[35] *M* 217*; *D* 92*, 101.

word as well as its root: if *láhag* (Qoh 12:12) has the accent on the penultimate, it cannot be an infinitive with the particle *le-*, but a triradical noun (*D* 96*, 105). The vocalization and the accent together help to distinguish the segolate noun *réḥem* (Job 24:20) and the *pi'el* infinitive *raḥēm* (Jer 31:20) (*D* 53*f, 63). Even the *dagesh* can change the structure and the meaning of a word. Thanks to it we can distinguish the verbally derived noun *pe'ullāh* and the passive participle *pe'ûlāh*, as Menaḥem points out (*M* 51*). According to the author of the *Teshuvot 'al Se'adyah*, *'ămātāh*, "her female slave" (Exod 2:5) is clearly distinct from *'ammāh*, 'elbow'. *Minnîm* (Ps 150:4), a musical instrument, cannot be the same as *minîm*, 'species', in spite of Saadiah's opinion (*S* 1, 128).

Reduplication can cause some problems to the interpreters, but they should know that it is a phenomenon which follows fixed rules, and that it is never arbitrary. Dunash notes that there is no reduplication in *meḥuspās* (Exod 16:14), since triradical verbs duplicate at least two consonants; Menaḥem ought to include it among the roots with four radicals. We must be careful about wrong reduplications: *salsillôt* (Jer 6:9) cannot be derived from *sal*, 'basket'; *galgallîm* does not come from *gal*, 'wave' (*D* 37*, 44 f). True reduplication is to be found exclusively in the biliteral verbs (*D* 87*, 97; 45*, 54 f). The real effect of the reduplication in words such as *'ădamdām* (Lev 13:49) can be disputed: does it strengthen the intensity of the colour, as Saadiah seems to state, or is it employed to point out a weakening in the colour? (*S* 35).

It is important to recognize the change of meaning produced by the use of a verb with a concrete particle: the verb *'ānāh* in *qal* with the particle *be-* means, as Dunash says, 'to witness', while the *pi'el* of the same root, without particle, means 'to humiliate'. Menaḥem's disciples state that this is not always the case, and that, as their master says, in Hos 5:5, *'ānāh be-* means 'to humiliate'.[36]

f) It is usual in tenth century exegesis to explain the meaning of a verse by referring to the context. The interpreter's perspicacity and good sense can be a good aid to this, but it is at the same time a dangerous method, especially if it is used in the most difficult cases, the *hapax legomena*, where it can carry a good dose of subjectivity. When Menaḥem's disciples, for instance, try to decide if *qāret* (Prov 8:3) means 'city', as their master says, or 'roof', as Dunash maintains, they do not find any other way than to prove that the first opinion is more likely according to the context, thereby reducing their rival's hypothesis to absurdity; in this case, they find some parallel texts which can also be taken into consideration.[37] If the context is always a very important help for Menaḥem, it may also be employed by Dunash for interpreting the meaning of Psalm 42 (*D* 45*f, 54).

Sometimes it is not the near context, but other passages of the biblical books that can throw light on a concrete verse: Isa 64:1, according to Dunash, can be understood with the help of Exod 9:23 ff, Deut 4:34, etc., based on the view of the whole Scripture as a unit in the best rabbinical tradition (*D* 72*f, 80 ff).

g) Menaḥem refers many times to parallelism as an aid to the understanding of the text. He has recognized the phenomenon in the Bible, and expresses it

---

36 *M* 285*; *D* 101*, 111; *TTM* 40*, 63; *TYŠ* 19*, 39.
37 *M* 332*; *D* 25*, 31; *TTM* 43*, 69.

in the following way: "the first half of the verse informs us about the second half; it would be enough with that first half, but there is a repetition and the same meaning appears twice in the same verse" (*M* 17*). The principle is accepted by most grammarians; for Dunash, the strict correspondence between two similar verses in two Psalms (Ps 39:7 and 82:5) can be the best way for understanding their meaning (*D* 109*, 120).

h) Daily observation and common sense are also required for the correct interpretation of the Scriptures. Dunash, disputing the meaning of *nidbākîn* (Ezra 6:4), asks his rival "how could one build a house with three walls" (*D* 25*, 31). In his reply about *me'îrôt* (Isa 27:11), he states that it cannot mean 'to collect', but 'to burn', since "neither in the city nor in the house of the verse are there selected fruits that women could pick, but only dry branches like the thistles of the desert" (*D* 67*, 75). And according to his interpretation, based on observation, "the dead fly ruins the perfumist's oil when it swells up in it" (*D* 73*, 82). Trying to stop the debate on the meaning of a passage, he reminds us that fig-trees have no flowers (*D* 108*, 118).

i) One of the most acute problems for the grammarians and interpreters at that time is that of the *hapax legomena.* Words that appear only once in the Bible are especially difficult to understand. Many earlier exegetes, from the time of Saadiah, had paid especial attention to those words, trying to decipher their meaning by means of a comparison with mishnaic Hebrew or with other Semitic languages, and referring to the context.

Menaḥem is deeply interested in the theme, and elaborates a long list of almost one hundred *hapax*;[38] we could add to the list about fifty more cases which are included as such in the Dictionary. In comparison with previous studies about the same matter, such as those of Saadiah, Ibn Quraysh or the *She'elot 'atiqot*, Menaḥem's results are very different, and in many cases he does not agree with these forerunners. One of the most notable differences is that while most authors usually quote mishnaic texts which could be related to the *hapax*, Menaḥem generally tries to understand the words exclusively from the context, and he mentions mishnaic Hebrew and Aramaic on very few occasions. It is one more proof of *his tendency to allow Scripture to explain itself.* Nevertheless, his attitude is not the only representative one of the spiritual atmosphere of the epoch. Dunash' approach to the *hapax*, as well as to other matters, coincides largely with that of earlier grammarians and also with the main eleventh century representatives.

[38] See the root *glb*, *M* 106*.

25.6 Karaite Exegesis

By DANIEL FRANK, Columbus, OH
(The Ohio State University)

Primary sources: Relatively few Karaite Bible commentaries have been published; printed editions have been noted below. The vast majority of Karaite texts, especially those in Judeo-Arabic, remain in manuscript. There are particularly rich collections of Karaitica in the Russian National Library (formerly the Firkovich collections) and the Institute of Oriental Studies (both St. Petersburg), the British Library (London), the Bodleian Library (Oxford), The Jewish Theological Seminary of America (New York), the Bibliothèque Nationale (Paris), and the Bibliotheek der Rijksuniversiteit te Leiden.

Bibliographies: Z. ANKORI, *Karaites in Byzantium* (1959; see below); D. J. LASKER, "Karaites: Developments 1970–1988", *EncJud Yearbook* (1989) 366–67; D. FRANK, "The Study of Medieval Karaism 1959–1989", *Bulletin of Judaeo-Greek Studies* 6 (1990) 15–23; idem, "The Study of Medieval Karaism, 1989–1999", *Raphael Loewe Festschrift* (Cambridge: Cambridge UP; in press); N. SCHUR, *History of the Karaites* (BEATAJ 29; Frankfurt/M: Peter Lang 1992); idem, *The Karaite Encyclopedia* (BEATAJ 38; Frankfurt/M: Peter Lang 1995). A comprehensive bibliography of Karaitica is being prepared by B. D. WALFISH. A revised version of S. POZNANSKI's unpublished bio-bibliographic encyclopedia of Karaite authors is being prepared under the direction of H. BEN-SHAMMAI.

General works: Z. ANKORI, *Karaites in Byzantium: the Formative Years, 970–1100* (New York: Columbia UP 1959); S. W. BARON, *A Social and Religious History of the Jews* 5 (New York / London: Columbia UP ^{2}1957) 209–85; B. CHIESA / W. LOCKWOOD, *Ya'qûb al-Qirqisânî on Jewish Sects and Christianity: A Translation of "Kitâb al-Anwâr", Book I, with two introductory essays* (Judentum und Umwelt 10, Frankfurt/M: Peter Lang 1984); J. E. HELLER / L. NEMOY, "Karaites", EncJud 10, 761–85; J. MANN, *Texts and Studies in Jewish History and Literature* II. *Karaitica* (Philadelphia: JPSA 1935); L. NEMOY, *Karaite Anthology: Excerpts from the Early Literature* (New Haven / London: Yale UP 1952); idem, "Karaites", EncRel 8, 254–59; N. WIEDER, *The Judean Scrolls and Karaism* (London: East and West Library 1962); YA'QÛB AL-QIRQISÂNÎ, *Kitâb al-Anwâr wa'l-Marâqib* 1–5 (ed. L. Nemoy; New York: Alexander Kohut Memorial Foundation 1939–43; cited by volume and page; references to Chiesa / Lockwood translation of Treatise I in parentheses).

1. Introduction: Karaism and Scripturalism

The Karaites (Heb. *qara'im, benei miqra'*), Judaism's oldest surviving sect, derive their name from the Hebrew word for Scripture and their identity from its interpretation. Denying the authority of the rabbinic tradition, they originally sought to ground their laws and beliefs directly in the Bible. During the ninth century, the sect emerged in the Islamic East where its ideology was shaped by the surrounding religious and intellectual milieu. Quite possibly, the first Karaites found inspiration in the writings of earlier sectarians such as the Sadducees, although no conclusive evidence for such direct links has yet been discovered. During its earliest phase, the sect was self-consciously scripturalist, insofar as this was possible. With the gradual establishment of an exegetical consensus, however, both a communal identity and a Karaite tradition were formed. Ultimately, there were (and continue to be) concessions even to Rabbanite tradition. All the same, Karaites always professed great fidelity to the biblical text, consistently justifiying their practices and beliefs on scriptural grounds. Not surprisingly, their attacks on the rabbinic tradition elicited harsh responses from leading Rabbanite authorities. Polemics between the two groups centered upon questions of legal interpretation. At the same time, the Karaites' rationalistic, philologically-oriented approach to the Bible bears strong affinities to the contextual or *peshat* reading advocated by many leading Rabbanites. Alternately diverging and converging, Karaite and Rabbanite modes of exegesis have influenced each other significantly.

2. Origins in the East (ca. 750–950)

2.1. Anan ben David

Sources: A. Harkavy, *Aus den ältesten Karäischen Gesetzbüchern* (Studien und Mitteilungen VIII; St. Petersburg 1903); S. Schechter, *Documents of Jewish Sectaries* II (Cambridge 1910).

Studies: H. Ben-Shammai, "The Karaite Exegetes and their Rabbanite Environment" (Heb.), *Proceedings of the Ninth World Congress of Jewish Studies: Panel Sessions: Bible Studies and Ancient Near East* (Jerusalem: World Union of Jewish Studies 1988) 43–58; idem, "The Karaite Controversy: Scripture and Tradition in Early Karaism", *Religionsgespräche im Mittelalter* (ed. B. Lewis / F. Niewöhner; Wolfenbütteler Mittelalter-Studien 4, Wiesbaden: Otto Harrassowitz 1992) 11–26; idem, "Between Ananites and Karaites: Observations on Early Medieval Jewish Sectarianism", *Studies in Muslim-Jewish Relations* 1 (1993) 19–29; L. Nemoy, "Anan b. David", EncJud 2, 919–22; idem, Anthology (1952), 3–20; S. Poznanski, "Anan et ses écrits", *REJ* 44 (1902) 161–87; 45 (1902) 50–69.

Anan b. David (Iraq, mid-eighth c.) is usually connected with the origins of Karaism. For reasons that remain obscure, he came to reject the rabbinic tradition, deriving a new, independent halakhah directly from Scripture. Well-versed in the literature of the Rabbis, Anan composed a code in Aramaic and employed rabbinic hermeneutics that depended to a great degree on analogy between words and phrases (Heb. *gezerah shavah*, *heggesh*). To take one example, where the Rabbanites permitted pre-existing fires to continuing burning in Jewish homes on the sabbath, Anan prohibited fire altogether by drawing an analogy between the words *teva'aru* ("you shall [not] kindle", Exod 35:3) and *ta'aśu* ("you shall [not] perform", Exod 20:10), which both begin with the letter *tav.*[1] This decision, lacking any contextual rationale, may hardly be deemed "scripturalist"; it points, rather, to the promotion of alternative *midreshei halakhah.* The strictness of this particular law also typifies Anan's halakhic outlook; he may be regarded as the founder of a rival legal school (Arab. *madhhab*) rather than a true sect.[2] Certainly, some early Rabbanites regarded him in this light.[3] His followers, on the other hand – the Ananites – constituted one of several Jewish sects that flourished in the Islamic East under the Abbasid Caliphate.

---

[1] Harkavy, Karäischen Gesetzbüchern (1903) 69f; Nemoy, Anthology (1952) 17–18; Poznanski, Anan (1902) 174–76.

[2] Ben-Shammai, The Karaite Controversy (1992) 20.

[3] So, e.g., Natronai Gaon (ninth c.); see Ben-Shammai, ibid. 18.

The Karaites emerged in the same period, either as an offshoot of the Ananites or as an independent scripturalist group.[4] Apparently, the two sects coalesced during the tenth and eleventh centuries. Karaite writings from this period refer frequently to Ananite positions. Although these are often rejected, Anan was still regarded as "the first to reveal the whole truth about the laws".[5] A slogan is frequently attributed to Anan both in Karaite sources and the modern scholarly literature: "Search well in Scripture, but do not rely upon my opinion" (*happisu be-orayta shappir ve-al tishʿanu ʿal daʿati*).[6] Whatever the phrase's origin, the first clause certainly encapsulates the scripturalist ideal that would define the Karaite approach to the Bible during the tenth and eleventh centuries.

2.2. *Daniel al-Qûmisî*

Sources: Daniel al-Qûmisî: *Pitron Sheneim ʿAsar* (*Commentarius in Librum Duodecim Prophetarum*; ed. I. D. Markon; Jerusalem: Mekize Nirdamim 1957); J. Mann, "A Tract by an Early Karaite Settler in Jerusalem", *JQR* NS 12 (1921/22) 257–98; A. Marmorstein, "Fragments du commentaire de Daniel al-Kumisi sur les Psaumes", *JA*, IIème série 7 (1916) 177–237; idem, "*Śeridim mi-pitronei ha-qara'i daniel al-qumisi*", *Hazofeh: Quartalis Hebraica (Budapest)* 8 (1924) 44–60, 321–37; 9 (1925/26) 129–45.

Studies: Ankori, Karaites in Byzantium (1959), index, s. v. "Daniel al-Kumisi"; H. Ben-Shammai, "Fragments of Daniel al-Qumisi's Commentary on the Book of Daniel as a Historical Source", *Hen* 13 (1991) 259–82; idem, "Return to the Scriptures in Ancient and Medieval Jewish Sectarianism and in Early Islam", *Les Retours aux écritures: fondamentalismes présents et passés* (É. Patlagean / A. Le Boulluec; Louvain / Paris: Peeters 1993, 319–39); Mann, Texts and Studies, II (1935) 8–18; L. Marwick, "Daniel al-Qûmisî and the Pitrôn Shenem ʿAsar", *Studies in Bibliography and Booklore* 5 (1961) 42–61; Nemoy, Anthology (1952) 34–39; idem, "The Pseudo-Qûmisîan Sermon to the Karaites", *PAAJR* 43 (1976) 49–105; Wieder, Judean Scrolls (1962) 265–69.

The key figure in early Karaite history was Daniel al-Qûmisî (or al-Dâmaghânî), who originally admired Anan but later despised his teachings. Al-Qûmisî was the first Karaite to polemicize explicitly against Rabbanite Judaism and to advocate real scripturalism.[7] For ideological reasons, he emigrated to Jerusalem from his native Tabaristan (northern Iran) during the last quarter of the ninth century. Renouncing the sinfulness of Diaspora Judaism which he blamed upon a corrupt rabbinic leadership, he preached a theology of return – to Scripture, to an austere life-style, and to the Holy City. Convinced that the End of Days was near, he advocated a program of mourning practices, study, and prayer in order to hasten the coming of the Messiah.[8] While he was

[4] An important early figure was Benjamin b. Moses al-Nahâwandî (ninth c.). Portions of his code (written in Hebrew) have been preserved; see Nemoy, Anthology (1952) 21–29, and idem, EncJud 12, 86.

[5] Yaʿqûb Al-Qirqisânî, *Kitâb al-Anwâr*, vol. 1, p. 13, lines 3–4 (Chiesa / Lockwood, 103). Cf. Salmon b. Jeroham, comment on Ps 69:1 (ed. Marwick, p. 89, lines 3–6). On the connections between the two groups see esp. Ben-Shammai, Between Ananites and Karaites (1993).

[6] The genuineness of the dictum – particularly the second phrase – has been questioned; see Ben-Shammai, ibid. 27, n. 34.

[7] Ben-Shammai, The Karaite Controversy (1992) 23–24; idem, Return to the Scriptures (1993) 328–30.

[8] Mann, Tract (1921/22); partial translation in Nemoy, Anthology (1952) 34–39, full transla-

not much cited by later authors, his philological and prognostic approach to Scripture influenced the Karaite *Avelei Ẓion* ("Mourners for Zion") of tenth-century Jerusalem.[9] Our main sources for his teachings are writings ascribed to him and references in Yaʿqûb al-Qirqisânî's *Kitâb al-Anwâr wa'l-Marâqib.*

Al-Qûmisî is the earliest Jewish exegete whose works have survived. Though he was a prolific author, only his commentary on Minor Prophets (*Pitron Sheneim ʿAsar*) has been preserved virtually intact.[10] Composed in Hebrew, these are not Midrashim but true commentaries. While al-Qûmisî refers (anonymously) to other scholars, he projects a clear authorial voice and provides unambiguous interpretations.[11] He proceeds verse by verse, frequently glossing the text in Arabic and offering clear, concise explanations.[12] Most strikingly, he applies *pesher*-type exegesis to the biblical prophecies, referring many of them to his own time. Al-Qûmisî likely derived this type of "prognostic" exegesis from ancient sectarian writings that circulated in the Middle Ages; we will discuss its importance to the Mourners for Zion below.

Al-Qirqisânî (ca. 935 CE; see below) states that al-Qûmisî advocated speculation and research in religious matters, constantly rethinking his positions and even instructing his disciples to correct copies of his works accordingly. At the same time, he was apparently "dissatisfied with reason, disowning it and frequently criticizing its practitioners in his books".[13] Al-Qûmisî likely drew a distinction between the rationalistic, philological interpretation of Scripture (which was desirable) and studying the speculative works of gentiles (which could be dangerous).[14] His disdain for Anan probably derived from the latter's unrestrained use of analogy in deriving new laws, an approach that scarcely seemed to differ from rabbinic modes of exegesis.

Al-Qûmisî attacks rabbinic Judaism for devising a man-made tradition which he brands *miṣvat anashim melummadah.*[15] He also rejects the rabbinic notion that Scripture possesses multiple meanings, arguing:

---

tion / re-edition by Nemoy, Pseudo-Qûmisîan Sermon (1976). Though cautious about ascribing the work to Daniel, Nemoy acknowledges that it "palpably belongs to a very early period of Karaite history" (50).

9 On the names by which the community styled itself, see below, 3.1.

10 Daniel al-Qûmisî, *Pitron* (1957). Al-Qûmisî's authorship has been disputed by Marwick, Daniel al-Qûmisî and the Pitrôn (1961), but his arguments have been convincingly rebutted by Wieder, Judean Scrolls (1962), 265–69.

11 See, e.g., his explicit rejection of an interpretation, *Pitron*, p. 41, lines 1–2 (Jonah 1:1): "Some people said ... but this is not the case". For other indications of an authorial voice see, e.g., *Pitron*, p. 57, n. 23 (Zeph 2:5): "... which I explained in the Book of Nahum", and p. 62 (Zech 1:8): "I would almost suggest ..." (*ki-me'aṭ daʿati*).

12 For Arabic glosses, see, e.g.: *Pitron*, p. 26, nn. 5, 28 (Joel 1:4,7); p. 36, n. 7 (Amos 6:3); p. 40, nn. 8,9 (Obad 14); p. 42, n. 16 (Jonah 4:10); p. 44, n. 1 (Mic 2:3). Occasional Persian glosses reflect Daniel's place of origin; see, e.g., *Pitron*, p. 60 (Hag 1:6).

13 Al-Qirqisânî, *Kitâb al-Anwâr*, vol. 1, pp. 4–5 (Chiesa / Lockwood 94); see also p. 58 (Chiesa / Lockwood 151). Al-Qirqisânî also states that al-Qûmisî was the last to establish a school of thought (or sect, Ar. *madhhab*), compose a book, and gain a following; see ibid., p. 14, lines 8–10 (Chiesa / Lockwood 104).

14 See the Arabic text ascribed to al-Qûmisî in M. Zucker, *Rav Saadya Gaon's Translation of the Torah* (Heb.) (New York: Philipp Feldheim 1959), 176–78, esp. 177, lines 2–6.

15 On the Karaite use of the phrase (deriving from Isa 29:13) see Wieder, Judean Scrolls and Karaism (1962) 259–63.

> Every word in the Bible has but one (true) interpretation (*pitron*), not two. But since people do not know (Scripture's true) meanings, some will interpret it in one way and others in another until the coming of the Teacher of Righteousness (*moreh ṣedeq*).[16]

The task of the honest interpreter is to discover the *one* correct interpretation of every biblical verse through the exercise of reason.[17] While uncertainties are inevitable, the Teacher of Righteousness will arrive at the End of Days to clarify all ambiguities. This appeal to the Teacher, whom al-Qûmisî identifies elsewhere with Elijah, is strongly reminiscent of Qumran *pesher.*[18] And the designation of Elijah as the final arbiter at the End of Days is familiar from rabbinic sources. Where al-Qûmisî parts company with his contemporaries, however, is in denying the possibility of multiple, conflicting traditions.

2.3. Polemics between Saadiah Gaon and Karaite Scholars

Sources: SAADIAH GAON: B. M. Lewin, "*Eśśa' Meshali*", *Qoveṣ Rav Se'adya Gaon* (ed. J. L. Fishman [Maimon]; Jerusalem 1943) 481–678; *Saadya's Commentary on Genesis* (ed. M. Zucker; New York: Jewish Theological Seminary of America 1984); SALMON B. JEROHAM: *The Book of the Wars of the Lord* (ed. I. Davidson; New York 1934).

Studies: A. HARKAVY, "Fragments of anti-Karaite writings of Saadiah in the Imperial Public Library at St. Petersburg", *JQR* 13 (1901) 655–68; H. HIRSCHFELD, "The Arabic Portion of the Cairo Genizah at Cambridge", *JQR* OS 18 (1906) 113–20, 600–20; 19 (1907) 136–61; H. MALTER, *Saadia Gaon: His Life and Works* (New York 1926) 260–67, 380–84; Nemoy, Anthology (1952) 69–82; S. POZNANSKI, "The Anti-Karaite Writings of Saadiah Gaon", *JQR* OS 10 (1897–98) 238–76; idem, "The Karaite Literary Opponents of Saadiah Gaon in the Tenth Century", *JQR* OS 18 (1905–06) 209–50; repr. in *The Karaite Literary Opponents of Saadiah Gaon* (London 1908); M. ZUCKER, "Against Whom Did Se'adya Ga'on Write the Polemical Poem 'Essa Meshali'?" (Heb.), *Tarbiz* 27 (1957) 61–82; idem, "Comments on 'Essa Meshali' of R. Se'adya Gaon" (Heb.), *Tarbiz* 33 (1963) 40–57.

The Karaite attacks on the rabbinic tradition led them to criticize the great Rabbanite institutions of the day: the Exilarchate, the Gaonate, and the Academies, together with the literary instruments of geonic authority, the Mishnah and Talmud. The polemic between the Karaites and Rabbanites reached its climax in the harsh exchanges between the greatest of the Babylonian Geonim, Saadiah b. Joseph (882–942), and several sectarian scholars. The Gaon's views are attested in his polemical poem, *Eśśa Meshali* ("I take up my parable"), fragments of Judeo-Arabic tracts, and lengthy citations in the works of his opponents. The Karaite position is abundantly documented in the works of such scholars as Ya'qûb al-Qirqisânî, Salmon b. Jeroham, and Japheth b. Eli.[19]

---

[16] Comment on Ps 74:6; see Marmorstein, Seridim (1924) p. 336, lines 16–17 = idem, Fragments (1916) 196.

[17] As for the Rabbanite notion that the Torah can be interpreted in forty-nine ways, cf. W. BACHER, *Die exegetische Terminologie der Jüdischen Traditionsliteratur.* II. *Die Bibel- und traditionsexegetische Terminologie der Amoräer* 2 (Leibzig 1905) 157, s. v. *panim.*

[18] For the identification of Elijah with the Teacher of Righteousness see *Pitron*, p. 29 (Joel 2:23). On the Teacher see generally Wieder, Judean Scrolls (1962) 86–87, and J. Murphy-O'Connor, ABD VI, 340–41.

[19] See Poznanski, The Anti-Karaite Writings of Saadiah Gaon (1897/98); idem, The Karaite Literary Opponents of Saadiah Gaon in the Tenth Century (1905/06); H. Hirschfeld, The Arabic

In Saadiah's view, the Rabbis did not produce a new body of halakhah; rather, they codified and set down an Oral Law which had existed since Moses' day. This Oral Law, he maintains, is essential to any proper understanding of the Law, particularly of the ceremonial commandments. Only tradition can provide knowledge of the "revealed" laws and their details, argues the Gaon in the introduction to his commentary on Genesis.[20] Thus, the Bible does not indicate the required number of fringes to be worn (Num 15:38), the dimensions of the booths in which Jews are to dwell (Lev 23:42), the nature of the labor prohibited on the sabbath (Exod 20:10), or even the order of prayer. These laws are all mandated by the tradition that preserves the practices of Moses and the Children of Israel who received the Sinaitic revelation. In rebutting Saadiah's arguments, Salmon maintains that the details of some commandments were not prescribed precisely because they were left to the individual's discretion. Other laws can be derived directly from the Bible by rational means. Al-Qirqisânî adds that the Rabbanites are inconsistent: although they wear fringes, they omit the blue cord mandated by Scripture; although their tradition prohibits certain activities on the sabbath, it permits others in direct violation of the biblical text. Both Karaites insist that the Bible contains liturgical instruction and specific prayers (e.g. Dan 6:11; 9:3 ff).[21]

There is an irony here. While the sectarians had originally attacked the Rabbis' derivation of new laws from the Bible by means of certain hermeneutic principles, they in turn developed their own body of exegetical rules.[22] For their part, many Rabbanites – following the lead of Saadiah Gaon – came to downplay the role of *midrash halakhah*, insisting instead on the wholesale acceptance of the Oral Law.[23] And though the Karaites continued to deny the binding authority of the rabbinic tradition, they inevitably came to accept the force of their own received teachings which they dubbed *sevel ha-yerushah* ("the burden of the inheritance").[24] The two groups would soon differ far more sharply over the authority of their respective legal traditions than over the methods by which their laws were derived from the Bible.

Saadiah and his Karaite adversaries lived in an Islamic environment, and Arabic culture permeated their works. While they composed some Hebrew verse (e.g. *Eśśa' Meshali* and *The Wars of the Lord)*, they wrote all their prose in Arabic. Familiar with contemporary Islamic and Christian writings, they developed genres that were new to the Jewish literary tradition: dictionaries, grammars, codes, and theological treatises. Aimed at a sophisticated Jewish audience that was losing interest in traditional Hebrew and Aramaic texts, the

Portion of the Cairo Genizah (1906/07); A. Harkavy, Fragments of anti-Karaite writings of Saadiah (1901).

[20] He advances seven arguments; see *Commentary on Genesis*, 13–15 (Arab.), 180–84 (Heb.); J. M. Harris, *How Do We Know This? Midrash and the Fragmentation of Modern Judaism* (Albany, NY: SUNY Press 1995) 76–77.

[21] Salmon, *Wars of the Lord*, 47 (Nemoy, Anthology [1952] 80–82); al-Qirqisânî, *Kitâb al-Anwâr*, vol. 1, pp. 124–25, 128–32.

[22] Some of these are identical with rabbinic hermeneutical principles; see al-Qirqisânî, *Kitâb al-Anwâr*, vol. 2, pp. 343–470, transl. G. Vajda, *REJ* 108 (1948) 63–91 and 120 (1961) 211–57.

[23] Harris, How Do We Know This (1995), chap. 4.

[24] N. Wieder, "Three Terms for Tradition", *JQR* 49 (1958/59) 108–21.

new works fully exploited Arabic rhetorical models, stylistic devices, and technical terminology.[25]

This enterprise gave birth to the first true Jewish commentaries on the Bible. Unlike Midrashim, these works project clear authorial voices and offer systematic interpretations. They include programmatic introductions (Arab. *muqaddimât, ṣudûr*), complete Arabic translations of the biblical text, and embedded excursuses on a wide variety of topics. Rationalistically- and philologically-inclined, the authors also delineate a scriptural book's principal themes and seek to define its central message. Saadiah Gaon was unquestionably the first to produce this type of commentary on a large scale, but the tenth-century Karaite exegetes in Iraq and Jerusalem far surpassed him in the volume, if not the quality, of their compositions.

2.4. Al-Qirqisânî

Sources: Yaʿqûb al-Qirqisânî: Kitâb al-Anwâr wa'l-Marâqib (1939–43); Chiesa, "A New Fragment of Al-Qirqisânî's Kitâb al-Riyâḍ" (see below); B. Chiesa / W. Lockwood, "Al-Qirqisani's Newly-found Commentary on the Pentateuch" (see below); H. Hirschfeld, Qirqisani Studies (1918) (see below).

Studies: H. Ben-Shammai, "The Doctrines of Religious Thought of Abû Yûsuf Yaʿqûb al-Qirqisânî and Yefet ben ʿElî" 1–2 (Heb.) (Hebrew University Ph. D. dissertation, 1977); B. Chiesa / W. Lockwood, Yaʿqûb al-Qirqisânî on Jewish Sects and Christianity (1984); B. Chiesa, "Dai 'Principi dell'esegesi biblica' di Qirqisani", *JQR* 73 (1982/83) 124–37; idem, "A New Fragment of Al-Qirqisânî's Kitâb al-Riyâḍ", *JQR* 78 (1987/88) 175–85; idem, *Creazione e caduta dell'uomo nell'esegesi giudeo-araba medievale* (Brescia: Paideia Editrice 1989); B. Chiesa / W. Lockwood, "Al-Qirqisānī's Newly-found Commentary on the Pentateuch: the Commentary on Gen. 12", *Hen* 14 (1992) 153–80; P. B. Fenton, "'À l'image de Dieu': l'interpretation de Genèse I, 26 selon quelques exégètes qaraïtes du moyen âge", *Hen* 15 (1993) 271–90; H. Hirschfeld, *Qirqisani Studies* (London 1918) 39–59; L. Nemoy, "Al-Qirqisânî's Account of the Jewish Sects and Christianity", HUCA 7 (1930) 317–97; idem, Anthology (1952) 42–53; idem, "Kirkisani, Jacob al-", EncJud 10, 1047–48; C. Sirat, *A History of Jewish Philosophy in the Middle Ages* (Cambridge: Cambridge UP, 1990), 38–53; G. Vajda, "Études sur Qirqisânî", *REJ* 106 (1940–45) 87–123; 107 (1946/47) 52–98; 108 (1948) 63–91; 120 (1961) 211–57; 122 (1963) 7–74; idem, "Du prologue de Qirqisânî à son commentaire sur la Genèse", *In Memoriam Paul Kahle* (ed. M. Black / G. Fohrer; Berlin: de Gruyter 1968) 222–31.

Yaʿqûb al-Qirqisânî was the leading Karaite scholar in the first half of the tenth century. Only a small part of the many works that he composed in his native Iraq have survived: his code, *The Book of Lights and Watchtowers* (*Kitâb al-anwâr wa'l-marâqib*); portions of his *Book of Gardens and Parks* (*Kitâb al-riyâḍ wa'l-ḥadâ'iq*), a commentary on the non-legal portions of the Pentateuch; and fragments of a separate commentary on Genesis (*Tafsîr bereishit*).[26]

[25] See R. Drory, *The Emergence of Hebrew-Arabic Literary Contacts at the Beginning of the Tenth Century* (Heb.) (Tel-Aviv: Hakibbutz Hameuchad 1988).

[26] Al-Qirqisânî, *Kitâb al-Anwâr.* For translated sections see: Nemoy, Anthology (1952) 42–53; idem, Al-Qirqisânî's Account (1930); Chiesa / Lockwood, Yaʿqûb al-Qirqisânî on Jewish Sects and Christianity (1984); and Vajda, Études sur Qirqisânî (1940–63). The commentaries remain largely unedited and unpublished. Ben-Shammai, The Doctrines (1977) includes extensive excerpts and analyses. See also Chiesa, A New Fragment (1987/88); idem, Creazione e caduta (1989); Chiesa / Lockwood, Newly-found Commentary (1992).

Like Saadiah, Al-Qirqisânî wrote in Arabic, the *lingua franca* of the Islamic East, whose rich technical vocabulary admirably suited his needs. He regarded his code and commentaries as part of a single exegetical project, encompassing the legal and narrative sections of Scripture. His rationalism and broad learning are apparent throughout his *œuvre.* He cites both Jewish (Rabbanite and Karaite) and non-Jewish authorities and applies secular knowledge to the resolution of religious and exegetical problems.[27]

Carefully structured, *Kitâb al-Anwâr* includes a lengthy methodological discussion in which Qirqisânî sets forth the sources of legal authority, the manner in which the Bible presents legislation, and the various modes of legal reasoning. Both Karaites and Ananites, he explains, derive their knowledge of the law from three sources: Scripture, analogy, and consensus. While the ancient Rabbis accepted these legal roots, their modern successors deny the validity of analogy since they find that many of their practices are undermined when they are subjected to critical reasoning.[28] Qirqisânî's affirmation of analogy (*qiyâs*) as a means of constructive legislation leads him to consider the hermeneutics of classical rabbinic halakhah, the so-called Thirteen Principles of Rabbi Ishmael enunciated at the beginning of the Sifra to Leviticus.[29] Examining each of the principles in turn, he accepts some – e.g. *qal va-ḥomer* or reasoning *a fortiori* – while rejecting others (e.g. *gezerah shavah*, inference from similar phrases). Though he does not reject several of these rules *per se*, he objects to their application by the Rabbanites.[30] As a general rule, he asserts that all precepts should be understood according to their plain sense unless this would express something manifestly false or would imply a contradiction:

> This principle applies not only to the precepts but also to all biblical texts, including narratives (*akhbâr*) and others. We have already provided certain explanations of this matter. In effect, were it permissible to attribute a hidden (*bâṭin*) meaning to certain precepts – different from the plain sense – without there being any necessity of doing so, we would have grounds for doing this with *all* the commandments and they would become invalid, their true meaning becoming unknown, since the hidden meaning (*al-bâṭin*), i.e. the figurative interpretation (*al-ta'wîl*), might be extended in any direction, developing according to the wishes of each interpreter. This would obviously be the ultimate perversion; there is no need to elaborate upon it.[31]

At best, allegorization is a last resort. At worst, it represents a threat to the community whose very existence depends upon a unified understanding of Scripture. For Karaites this means seeking a "plain sense" (*ẓâhir*) in both legal and non-legal contexts. As an example of unacceptable figurative interpretation, Qirqisânî singles out Anan's exegesis of the commandment, "You shall not boil a kid in its mother's milk".[32] Relating the injunction to the preceding clause in Exod 23:19 and 34:26 ("the first of the first fruits of your ground

---

[27] See Sirat, A History of Jewish Philosophy (1990).

[28] *Kitâb al-Anwâr*, vol. 2, p. 343; see Vajda, Études, III (1948) 63.

[29] He refers to them as the thirteen "gates" or "categories". On the principles of Rabbi Ishmael see R. Kasher, "The Interpretation of Scripture in Rabbinic Literature", *Miqra* (CRINT II/1; ed. M. J. Mulder; Assen: Van Gorcum / Philadelphia: Fortress Press 1988) 584–86.

[30] Vajda, Études, III (1948) 73–74.

[31] *Kitâb al-Anwâr*, vol. 2, pp. 385–86; see Vajda, Études, III (1948) 74–75.

[32] *Kitâb al-Anwâr*, vol. 2, p. 386; see Vajda, Études, III (1948) 75.

you shall bring into the house of the Lord your God"), Anan takes the phrase as an injunction against delaying the bringing of the first fruits to the Temple by leaving them to ripen in the ground. Qirqisânî points to the third verse (Deut 14:21), arguing that its context ("You shall not eat anything that dies of itself ...") will admit only a literal interpretation, viz. a prohibition of eating flesh. Now, since the expression *per se* is perfectly intelligible without allegorization, there is no reason for doing so and it must be taken literally in all three instances.[33]

The introduction to his *Book of Gardens and Parks* also contains important programmatic statements explaining al-Qirqisânî's motivations, exegetical aims, and methods.[34] Arguing that revealed truths can only be ascertained by reason, he points to Solomon as a model religious philosopher and cites numerous verses as mandates for speculation. Isa 41:20, e.g., supports the inference of a Creator from the observation of His creation – the standard argument by analogy in Islamic theology. And Ps 19:8–10 assures us of the Law's intrinsic rationality, truth, and clarity, hallmarks of its perfection. Having demonstrated the need for religious speculation, al-Qirqisânî sets forth thirty-seven exegetical premises; these include:[35] (1) that Moses wrote the Pentateuch; (2) that Scripture must be interpreted literally, except where this would entail contradiction[36]; (3) that the Hebrew language is primordial; (4) that anthropomorphism is a means of accommodation ("Scripture speaks in human language")[37]; (5) that the Bible clearly labels all false statements as such; (6) that biblical dialogue may be recorded either in the original language (e.g. Aramaic) or in Hebrew translation; (7) that the details of a given narrative may be furnished from several biblical accounts; (8) that biblical style admits both prolixity and brevity; and (9) that events are not always presented in chronological order.[38]

Al-Qirqisânî's openness to contemporary speculative trends obviously influenced his exegesis. In his Commentary on Genesis 1, for example, he describes the world in terms of bodies, accidents, and substances and posits four principal, created elements – earth, air, water, and fire – from which the rest of the world was fashioned. He refers the biblical "heavens" (*shamayim*) to the

[33] For Qirqisânî's criticism of rabbinic exegesis, see *Kitâb al-Anwâr*, vol. 5, 1213. On Exod 23:19 etc. cf. the extended discussion, ibid., pp. 1226–27; for a discussion and translation see L. Nemoy, "Al-Qirqisânî: 'Thou Shalt Not Seethe a Kid in Its Mother's Milk'", *"Open Thou Mine Eyes ...": Essays on Aggadah and Judaica Presented to Rabbi William G. Braude* (ed. H.J. Blumberg et al.; Hoboken, NJ: KTAV, 1992) 219–27. Cf. Zucker, *Rav Saadya Gaon's Translation* (1959) 161.

[34] Text: Hirschfeld, Qirqisani Studies (1918), 39–59 (mis-titled *Tafsîr Bereishit*). Partial translations with textual notes: Nemoy, Anthology (1952) 53–68; Vajda, Du prologue de Qirqisânî (1968); and Chiesa, Dai 'Principi dell'esegesi biblica' di Qirqisânî (1982/83).

[35] The text breaks off in the middle of the twenty-fourth.

[36] Cf. Saadya Gaon, *The Book of Beliefs and Opinions* 7.2 (transl. S. Rosenblatt; New Haven / London: Yale UP 1948) 265–67.

[37] Al-Qirqisânî cites the rabbinic dictum *dibberah torah ki-leshon benei adam* (*b. Ber.* 31 b). On its significance in rabbinic literature see Kasher, Interpretation (1988) 588–89.

[38] Cf. the rabbinic *ein muqdam u-me'uḥar ba-torah* (*b Pes.* 6 b); on its significance in rabbinic literature see Kasher, ibid. 590–91. For Qirqisânî's application of the rule, see his commentary to Gen 12:4 in Chiesa / Lockwood, Newly-found Commentary (1992) 173.

philosophers' spheres. And he employs the well-known argument from design in demonstrating the createdness of the world.[39] He also consulted at least one Christian priest on exegetical matters.[40] The Iraqi environment in which al-Qirqisânî lived clearly fostered such scholarly exchanges; the main stage of Karaite activity was, however, shifting westward.

3. The Jerusalem School (ca. 950–1099)

3.1. The Mourners for Zion (ca. 950–1000)

Sources: JAPHETH B. ELI: Sagit Butbul / Sarah Stroumsa, "Commentary on Genesis 1:1–5", Judaeo-Arabic Manuscripts in the Firkovitch Collections: Yefet ben ʿEli al-Basri, Commentary on Genesis (see below); M. SOKOLOW, "The Commentary of Yefet Ben Ali on Deuteronomy XXXII" (Yeshivah University Ph. D. Dissertation 1974); *The Arabic Commentary of Yefet Ben ʿAli the Karaite on the Book of Hosea* (ed. P. Birnbaum; Philadelphia: Dropsie College 1942); *Jefeth ben Ali's Arabic Commentary on Nahum* (ed. H. Hirschfeld; London 1911); O. LIVNE-KAFRI, "The Commentary on Habakkuk (Chapters 1,3) by the Karaite Yefeth b. ʿEli al-Basri" (Heb.), *Sefunot* NS 6 [21] (1993) 73–113; *Rabbi Yapheth Ben Heli Bassorensis Karaïtae in Librum Psalmorum Commentarii arabici* (ed. J. J. L. Bargès; Paris 1846; introduction and commentary on Psalms 1 and 2); *Kitâb al-zubûr: Libri Psalmorum David regis et prophetae versio a R. Japheth ben Heli Bassorensi Karaita, auctore decimi seculi* (ed. J. J. L. Bargès; Paris 1861; Arab. translation only); *Der Commentar des Karäers Jephet Ben ʿAli Halevi zu den Proverbien* (ed. I. Günzig; Krakau 1898; chaps. 1–3); *Rabbi Yapheth Abou Aly ... in Canticum Canticorum Commentarium Arabicum* (ed. J. J. L. Bargès; Paris 1884); *Der Commentar des Karäers Jephet ben ʿAli zum Buche Ruth* (ed. N. Schorstein; Berlin 1903); R. M. BLAND, "The Arabic Commentary of Yephet ben ʿAli on the Book of Ecclesiastes, Chapters 1–6" (University of California, Berkeley Ph. D. dissertation 1966); *A Commentary on the Book of Daniel by Jephet ibn ʿAli the Karaite* (ed. D. S. Margoliouth; Oxford 1889). – SALMON B. JEROHAM: *The Arabic Commentary of Salmon ben Yeruḥam the Karaite on the Book of Psalms, Chapters 42–72* (ed. L. Marwick; Philadelphia 1956); *Le Commentaire des Psaumes par le Qaraïte Salmon ben Yeruḥam, Psaumes 1–10* (ed. and trans. J. Alobaidi; Bern: Peter Lang 1996); M. RIESE, "The Arabic Commentary of Solomon Ben Yeruḥam the Karaite on Ecclesiastes" (Heb.) (Yeshiva University Ph. D. dissertation, New York 1973); *The Book of the Wars of the Lord* (ed. I. Davidson; New York 1934).

Studies: E. BATAT / H. BEN-SHAMMAI / S. BUTBUL / S. STROUMSA, *Judaeo-Arabic Manuscripts in the Firkovitch Collections: Yefet ben ʿEli al-Basri, Commentary on Genesis. A Sample Catalogue. Texts and Studies* (Jerusalem: Center for the Study of Judaeo-Arabic Culture and Literature / Ben-Zvi Institute 2000); H. BEN-SHAMMAI, "The Karaites", *The History of Jerusalem: The Early Muslim Period, 638–1099* (ed. J. Prawer / H. Ben-Shammai; Jerusalem: Yad Izhak Ben-Zvi / New York: New York UP 1996) 201–24; idem, "The Doctrines of Religious Thought of Abû Yûsuf Yaʿqûb al-Qirqisânî and Yefet ben ʿElî" 1–2 (Heb.) (Hebrew University Ph. D. dissertation, 1977); idem, "Edition and Versions in Yephet b. Ali's Bible Commentary" (Heb.), *Alei Sefer* 2 (1976) 17–32; idem, "The Attitude of Some Early Karaites Toward Islam", *Studies in Medieval Jewish History and Literature* 2 (ed. I. Twersky; Cambridge, MA: Harvard UP 1984) 3–40; idem, "Poetic Works and Lamentations of Qaraite 'Mourners of Zion' – Structure and Contents", *Kenesset Ezra: Literature and Life in the Synagogue, Studies Presented to Ezra Fleischer* (Heb.) (ed. S. Elizur et al.; Jerusalem 1994) 191–234; P. BIRNBAUM, "Yefet ben Ali and his Influence on Biblical Exegesis", *JQR* NS 32 (1941/42) 51–70, 159–74, 257–71; Y. ERDER, "The Negation of the Exile in the Messianic

---

[39] See Ben-Shammai, The Doctrines (1977), vol. 1, chap. 5 for a full discussion.

[40] Nemoy, Anthology (1952) 43. The impact of Christian writings upon Jewish exegetes writing in Arabic requires further study; for now see Chiesa, Creazione e caduta dell'uomo (1989), and S. STROUMSA, "The Impact of Syriac Tradition on Early Judaeo-Arabic Bible Exegesis", *ARAM* 3 (1991) 83–96.

Doctrine of the Karaite Mourners of Zion", HUCA 68 (1997) 109–40; idem, "The Attitude of the Karaite, Yefet ben Eli, to Islam in Light of his Interpretation of Psalms 14 and 53" (Heb.), *Michael* 14 (1997) 29–49; D. Frank, "The *Shoshanim* of Tenth-Century Jerusalem: Karaite Exegesis, Prayer, and Communal Identity", *The Jews of Medieval Islam: Community, Society, and Identity* (ed. D. Frank; Leiden: E.J. Brill 1995) 199–245; idem, "Karaite Commentaries on the Song of Songs from Tenth-Century Jerusalem", *With Reverence for the Word: Medieval Scriptural Exegesis in Judaism, Christianity, and Islam* (ed. Jane Dammen McAuliffe et al.; Oxford: Oxford UP; in press); M. Gil, *A History of Palestine, 634–1099* (Cambridge: Cambridge UP 1992); L. Marwick, "Studies in Salmon ben Yeruḥam", *JQR* NS 34 (1943/44) 313–20, 475–80; L. Nemoy, "The Epistle of Sahl ben Masliah", *PAAJR* 38/39 (1970/71) 145–77; M. Polliack, "Medieval Karaite Views on Translating the Hebrew Bible into Arabic", *JJS* 47 (1996) 64–84; M. Polliack, *The Karaite Tradition of Arabic Bible Translation: A Linguistic and Exegetical Study of Karaite Translations of the Pentateuch from the Tenth to the Eleventh Centuries* (Leiden: E.J. Brill 1997); J. Shunary, "Salmon Ben Yeruham's Commentary on the Book of Psalms", *JQR* NS 73 (1982) 155–75; U. Simon, "The Karaite Approach: The Psalms as Mandatory Prophetic Prayers", *Four Approaches to the Book of Psalms: From Saadiah Gaon to Abraham Ibn Ezra* (Albany: State University of New York Press 1991) 59–111; G. Tamani, "La Tradizione delle opere di Yefet b. Ali", *Bulletin d'Études Karaïtes* 1 (1983) 27–76; G. Vajda, *Deux commentaires karaïtes sur l'Ecclésiaste* (Leiden: E.J. Brill 1971); idem, "The Opinions of the Karaite R. Yafeth b. Ali on the Destruction of the World in the End of Days" (Heb.), *American Academy for Jewish Research Jubilee Volume* (Jerusalem: AAJR 1980) 85–95; idem, "Quelques Aggadôt Critiquées par Yefet ben ʿEli", *Studies in Judaica, Karaitica, and Islamica Presented to Leon Nemoy* (ed. S. R. Brunswick et al.; Ramat-Gan: Bar-Ilan UP 1982) 155–62; N. Wieder, The Judean Scrolls and Karaism (1962).

During the second half of the tenth century, Jerusalem emerged as the Karaites' spiritual and intellectual center.[41] Since al-Qûmisî's time, Mourners for Zion had settled in the Holy City; now, as the community became firmly established, Karaite scholarly activity flourished. Seeking to persuade Rabbanites and encourage their co-sectarians, leading figures like Salmon b. Jeroham, Japheth b. Eli, David b. Abraham al-Fâsî, Sahl b. Masliaḥ and David b. Boaz produced a large body of Judeo-Arabic literature – including commentaries, codes, and grammatical works – most of it exegetical in nature.[42] Their Bible commentaries are complex and multi-tiered, embodying substantial prefaces, complete Arabic translations of the scriptural text, and verse-by-verse explications.[43] Much of this corpus is extant in manuscript, awaiting publication and analysis.

Active around the middle of the tenth-century, Salmon b. Jeroham is chiefly remembered for his poetic Hebrew polemic, *The Wars of the Lord*, directed

[41] See Gil, A History of Palestine (1992), 777–820; Ben-Shammai, The Karaites (1996); Erder, The Negation of the Exile (1997).

[42] Salmon and Japheth will be discussed below. On David al-Fâsî see *The Hebrew-Arabic Dictionary of the Bible known as "Kitâb Jâmiʿ al-Alfâẓ" (Agrôn) of David ben Abraham al-Fâsî the Karaite* 1–2 (ed. S. L. Skoss; Yale Oriental Series – Researches 20–21; New Haven 1936–45) and L. Marwick, "A First Fragment from David b. Abraham al-Fasi's Commentary on Psalms", *Studies in Bibliography and Booklore* 6–7 (1962–65) 53–72. On Sahl see: Nemoy, The Epistle of Sahl ben Masliah (1970/71); idem, "Sahl ben Maẓli'aḥ ha-Kohen Abu al-Surri", EncJud, *Decennial Book* 1973–82 (Jerusalem 1983) 542–43; and M. Sokolow, "Kidnapping in Karaite Law according to the Commentary of Sahl ben Masliah", *JQR* 73 (1982) 176–88. On David b. Boaz, see EncJud 5, 1349.

[43] Karaite Bible translations diverge markedly from Saadiah's classicizing style, often tending towards a slavish literalism. On their singular character, see Polliack, Medieval Karaite Views (1996), and idem, Karaite Tradition of Bible Translation (1997).

against Saadiah Gaon. But he also wrote commentaries on the Psalms, Song of Songs, Lamentations, and Ecclesiastes.[44] Internal references would seem to indicate, remarkably, that the first three were composed during 955–56 CE.[45] In choosing which books he would explicate, he seems to have been guided by specific communal needs. Rather than attempting a commentary on the entire Bible or even the Pentateuch, he selected books that held special significance for the Avelei Zion: the Psalms and Lamentations provided the community's main liturgical texts; the Song of Songs and Daniel were both regarded as prognostic works containing information concerning the imminent End of Days; Ecclesiastes and Proverbs furnished theological and ethical guidance.

Salmon was more a compiler than an original exegete. While he mentions the efforts of earlier anonymous commentators disparagingly, he operates within an established tradition. The Introduction to his commentary on Psalms is devoted to justifying the Karaites' choice of the Psalter as their main prayer book over the Rabbanite *siddur* championed by Saadiah. Against Saadiah, he argues that David was not the actual author of every Psalm but rather that he compiled the Psalter; Moses (Ps 90), Solomon (Pss 72, 127), Jeduthun and Asaph (Ps 77), and the sons of Korah (Ps 44) all composed prayers via inspiration. For the Mourners, the Psalms were prophetic compositions intended by their ancient authors not only for the Temple service but also as prayers for future generations, i.e. for the period of Exile which they now experienced.[46] Salmon's work, therefore, is really a liturgical commentary for contemporary worshipers.[47] The commentary on Lamentations goes even further: it apparently embodies the community's liturgy of mourning and includes Hebrew dirges and litanies.[48] All the same, Salmon's works do betray a distinctive authorial voice, advancing criticisms of earlier scholars and suggesting preferred interpretations. They also feature extensive homilies on biblical passages that are not the immediate subjects of discussion.[49]

---

[44] All extant. *Com. Psalms*: the partial editions of Marwick and Alobaidi; Shunary, Salmon Ben Yeruḥam's Commentary on the Book of Psalms (1982); G. Vajda, "Le Psaume VIII commenté par Salmon b. Yerûḥîm", *Essays on the Occasion of the Seventieth Anniversary of the Dropsie University*, (Philadelphia: Dropsie University Press 1979) 441–48; and idem, "La péricope du Serviteur souffrant interprétée par le Karaïte Salmôn ben Yerûḥîm", *De la Tôrah au Messie: études d'exégèse et d'herméneutique bibliques offertes à Henri Cazelles* (ed. M. Carrez / J. Doré / P. Grelot; Paris: Desclée 1981) 557–65. *Com. Lamentations*: the edition of Feuerstein; Marwick, Studies (1943/44); Ben-Shammai, Poetic Works and Lamentations (1994). *Com. Ecclesiastes*: the edition of Riese; Vajda, Deux commentaires (1971). The commentary on Song of Songs is extant in St. Petersburg, RNL ms. Evr-Arab I. 1406 and several extensive fragments; see Frank, Karaite Commentaries on the Song of Songs from Tenth-Century Jerusalem. Salmon's commentaries on the books of Esther, Job, Proverbs, Daniel, and Isaiah have apparently not survived.

[45] See S. Poznanski, "Karaite Miscellanies", *JQR* OS. 8 (1896) 688, nn. 2–4, and Marwick, Studies (1943/44), 319, nn. 20 and 21.

[46] Shunary, Salmon Ben Yeruḥam's Commentary on the Book of Psalms (1982) and Simon, The Karaite Approach (1991).

[47] Japheth ben Eli's commentary on the Psalter had much the same function; see Simon, "The Karaite Approach" (1991) and Frank, The *Shoshanim* (1995).

[48] Ben-Shammai, Poetic Works and Lamentations (1994).

[49] See, e. g., the homily on Isaiah 52–53 in Comm. Ps 72, discussed by Vajda, La péricope du Serviteur souffrant (1981) and the homily on Isaiah 5 embedded in the Introduction to Comm. Song of Songs, RNL ms. Evr-Arab I. 1406, fols. 8 a–11 b.

Japheth b. Eli (Abu ʾl-Ḥasan b. ʿAlî al-Baṣrî, active ca. 960–1000) was the first Jew to write commentaries on the entire Bible.[50] His works are far more systematic than Salmon's in both form and content. His introductions are usually methodical examinations of a biblical book's central themes, aims, and authorship. The commentaries feature complete translations of the text and word-by-word (or phrase-by-phrase) explications of each verse, indicating alternative interpretations. Occasionally Japheth offers grammatical observations.[51] Like Saadiah, he displays a fondness for categorization and enumeration. In discussing revelation, for example, he elaborates eight purposes for prophetic missions and six degrees of prophecy.[52] He is also sensitive to literary questions. In treating the Solomonic books he addresses the problem of generic classification, distinguishing between various types of song (*shir*) and parable (*mashal*).[53] He discerns different types of scriptural discourse and perceives the larger textual units that constitute a biblical book; in his comments on Exod 1:1 and Deut 1:1, for example, he precisely delineates each book's main sections.[54] In his commentary on the Psalms, he explains how the biblical editor arranged the Psalter and seeks the thematic connection between each Psalm and its predecessor.[55] Japheth's discussions frequently become short essays and his commentaries on certain books, e.g. Ecclesiastes and Job, are virtual monographs on specific subjects.

A special feature of Salmon's and Japheth's commentaries is the prognostic exegesis through which they referred biblical prophecies to the recent past, the present, and the immediate future.[56] They applied this approach not only to the prophetic books and Daniel but also to biblical songs, notably the Psalter and Song of Songs, as well as such passages as Genesis 49, Exodus 15, the oracles of Balaam in Numbers 23–24, Deuteronomy 32–33, Judges 5, and 1 Samuel 2. For tenth-century Karaites in Jerusalem, therefore, the Bible predicted current events and described contemporary institutions. Thus, in the Kenite of Num 24:21 they saw a reference to the Fatimid dynasty that had emerged in North Africa, and in the profanation of the Temple and removal of the contin-

---

[50] For a survey of mss. in Western European libraries see Tamani, La Tradizione (1983). There are several hundred additional mss. and fragments in the RNL, St. Petersburg (formerly Firkovich collections); see now Batat et al., *Judaeo-Arabic Manuscripts* (2000).

[51] On Japheth's grammatical comments see S. Munk, "Notice sur Abou'l-Walîd Merwân ibn-Djanâḥ et sur quelques autres grammairiens hébreux du Xe et du XIe siècle", *JA*, 4ème série, 15 (1850) 297–337, and Birnbaum, Commentary on Hosea (1942), xxxvi-xxxvii.

[52] According to Comm. Hosea (ed. Birnbaum, 1–3), the purposes of prophetic missions are: (1) to communicate laws; (2) to perform miracles; (3) to encourage repentance; (4) to intercede through prayer; (5) to proclaim future events; (6) to recount the deeds of the past; (7) to compose books for later generations; and (8) to offer consolation for the Exile. The six degrees of prophecy are enumerated in various contexts, e.g. Com. Num 12:6–7 (B.L. ms. 2474, fols. 52b–53b) and Com. Isa 1:1 (RNL ms. Evr. I. 568, 6a–7a); see C. Sirat, *Les Théories des visions surnaturelles dans la pensée juive du moyen-âge* (Leiden: E. J. Brill 1969) 47–57, and Ben-Shammai, The Doctrines (1977) 1, 267–78; 2, 173–74.

[53] Comm. Song of Songs 1:1 (ed. Bargès) iii–iv; Comm. Prov. 1:1 (ed. Günzig) vi–vii.

[54] Exodus: RNL ms. Evr-Arab I. 0121, fols. 5b–6b; Deuteronomy: RNL ms. Evr-Arab I. 0114, fols. 1b–3a. According to Japheth, Exodus comprises five units and Deuteronomy six.

[55] Simon, The Karaite Approach (1991), esp. 88–93.

[56] On these terms, see Wieder's studies noted below.

ual burnt offering (Dan 11:31) they found an allusion to the Carmathian raid on the sanctuary in Mecca and the suspension of the *ḥajj*.[57] Similarly, the ephah and the leaden weight of Zechariah 5 represented the Mishnah and the Talmud, and the two women (vv. 9–11), the Babylonian Academies.[58]

What lent this type of exegesis its force were the emblematic appellations that the Karaites found in certain biblical names, words, and phrases. Like the Rabbanites, they identified Ishmael and Kedar with Islam, Edom and Seir with Christianity.[59] But they isolated and applied to themselves a set of biblical code-names, e.g. *maskil* ("Teacher"), *shoshanim* ("Lilies"), *temimei derekh* ("The Perfect of Way"), *shavei peshaʿ* ("The Penitent"), and *she'erit yiśra'el* ("Remnant of Israel").[60] Once the "lily among thorns" in Cant 2:2 was taken as an allusion to the Jerusalem Karaites, the "lilies" in the superscriptions to Psalms 44, 69, and 80 had to be understood in the same fashion. This, in turn, colored the interpretation of these Psalms as a whole:

> The phrase "Concerning the lilies" (Ps 69:1) indicates that this prayer for salvation (was composed) on account of the righteous who are compared to lilies in Cant 2:2. They have also been compared to flowers, a vineyard, and a fig tree (Cant 2:12–13) as well as to many other plants and fruits, each of which has its own special significance which we will mention, God willing, in our commentary on the Song of Songs.[61]

The name by which the Jerusalem Karaites are best known, "Mourners for Zion", derives similarly from Isa 61:3. By means of these appellations they defined themselves as the watchmen upon the walls of Jerusalem (Isa 62:6), who were to pursue an ascetic life of mourning, prayer, and Bible study.

3.2. The Scholastic Phase (Eleventh Century)

Sources: ʿAli ben Suleiman: *The Arabic Commentary of ʿAli Ben Suleiman the Karaite on the Book of Genesis* (ed. S. L. Skoss; Philadelphia: Dropsie College for Hebrew and Cognate Learning 1928. – Jacob ben Reuben: *Sefer ha-ʿOsher* (with Aaron b. Joseph, *Mivḥar Yesharim*; Gozlow 1834). – Judah Hadassi: *Sefer Eshkol ha-Kofer* (Gozlow 1836).

---

[57] Japheth b. Eli, Comm. Num 24:21 (Ben-Shammai, Edition and Versions [1976] 30); Comm. Dan 11:31 (ed. Margoliouth [1889], vi, 67 [Eng.], 127 [Arab.]). The Carmathians took Mecca in 929. Cf. the reservations expressed by A. Schenker, "Die Geburtswehen der messianischen Zeit nach Japhet ben Eli", *Bulletin d'Études Karaïtes* 2 (1989) 39–48.

[58] Japheth b. Eli, Comm. Zech 5:9–11 (B. L. Ms. Or. 2401, fol. 172b); see Poznanski, Anan et ses écrits (1902), 184–85. Daniel al-Qûmisî maintains that the ephah refers to the law-court in which the Babylonian Jewish leaders administer justice corruptly, and the woman (v. 7) to the Exilarch; see his commentary ad loc. (ed. Markon, 66).

[59] Ben-Shammai, Attitude (1984) 8–23; Erder, Attitude (1997).

[60] There are strong affinities between the prognostic exegesis and epithets employed by the Karaites and the pesher of the ancient Dead Sea sectarians. See Wieder, The Judean Scrolls and Karaism (1962); idem, "The Dead Sea Scrolls Type of Biblical Exegesis among the Karaites", *Between East and West: Essays dedicated to the Memory of Bela Horovitz* (ed. A. Altmann; London: East and West Library 1958) 75–106; and idem, "The Qumran Sectaries and the Karaites", *JQR* NS 47 (1956/57) 97–113, 269–92. Cf. A. Paul, *Écrits de Qumran et sectes juives aux premiers siècles de l'Islam: Recherches sur l'origine du Qaraïsme* (Paris 1969) and note the apposite remarks of Ben-Shammai, The Karaite Controversy (1992) 12, and Return to the Scriptures (1993) 321.

[61] Salmon b. Jeroham, Comm. Ps 69:1 (ed. Marwick, 97). In his commentary on Song of Songs 2:12–13 (ed. Bargès, 31–34 [Arab.]), Japheth b. Eli discusses the significance of these words as epithets for the Jerusalem Karaites; see Frank, Karaite Commentaries on the Song of Songs from Tenth-Century Jerusalem.

Studies: Ankori, Karaites in Byzantium (1959); idem, "The Correspondence of Tobias ben Moses the Karaite of Constantinople", *Essays on Jewish Life and Thought Presented in Honor of Salo Wittmayer Baron* (New York 1959) 1–38; W. BACHER, "Le Grammairien anonyme de Jérusalem et son livre", *REJ* 30 (1895) 232–56; D. BECKER, "The 'Ways' of the Hebrew Verb according to the Karaite Grammarians Abu-Al-Faraj Harun and the Author of the Me'or Haʿayin" (Heb.), *Te'udah* 7 (1991) 249–79; H. BEN-SHAMMAI, "Yeshuah Ben Yehudah – A Characterization of a Karaite Scholar of Jerusalem in the Eleventh Century" (Heb.), *Peʿamim* 32 (1987) 3–20; idem, "*Sefer Ha-Mitzvoth* of the Karaite Levi ben Yefet" (Heb.), *Shenaton Ha-Mishpat Ha-Ivri* 11–12 (1984–86): 99–133; G. KHAN, "ʿAbû al-Faraj Hârûn and the Early Karaite Grammatical Tradition" *JJS* 50 (1997) 314–34; A. MAMAN, "Karaites and Mishnaic Hebrew: Quotations and Usage" (Heb.), *Leshonenu* 55 (1991) 221–68; idem, "Medieval Grammatical Thought: Karaites vs. Rabbanites" (Heb.), *Language Studies* 7 (1995) 79–96; G. MARGOLIOUTH, "The Arabic Writings of Abu'l-Faraj Furkan Ibn Assad", *JQR* OS 11 (1898/99) 187–215; S. POZNANSKI, "Aboul-Faradj Haroun ben al-Faradj: Le grammairien de Jérusalem et son Mouschtamil", *REJ* 33 (1896): 24–39, 197–218; M. SCHREINER, *Studien über Jeschuʿa ben Jehuda* (Berlin 1900); D. SKLARE, "Yûsuf al-Baṣîr: Theological Aspects of His Halakhic Works", *The Jews of Medieval Islam: Community, Society, and Identity* (ed. D. Frank; Leiden: E. J. Brill 1995, 249–70); D. SKLARE / H. BEN-SHAMMAI, *Judaeo-Arabic Manuscripts in the Firkovitch Collections: The Works of Yusuf al-Baṣir. A Sample Catalogue. Texts and Studies* (Heb.) (Jerusalem: Center for the Study of Judaeo-Arabic Culture and Literature / Ben-Zvi Institute 1997); O. TIROSH-BECKER, "Preliminary Studies in Rabbinic Quotations Embedded in the Pentateuch Commentaries of the Karaite Scholar Yeshuʿa Ben-Yehuda" (Heb.), *Massorot* 5–6 (1991) 313–40; idem, "A Linguistic Study of Mishnaic Quotations Embedded in Yeshuʿa Ben Yehuda's Commentary on Leviticus" (Heb.), *Massorot* 7 (1993): 145–86; G. VAJDA, *Al-Kitâb al-Muḥtawî de Yûsuf al-Baṣîr* (Leiden: E. J. Brill 1985).

3.2.1. Joseph ben Noah

Towards the end of the tenth century, Joseph b. Noah (Abû Yaʿqûb Yûsuf b. Nûḥ) founded an academy in Jerusalem, giving the community a further institutional framework.[62] According to a fifteenth-century chronicle, his disciples included Abu 'l-Faraj Hârûn, Levi b. Japheth b. Eli, and Yûsuf al-Baṣîr (Joseph b. Abraham) – who would all become leading scholars.[63] Joseph wrote both an extensive commentary on the Pentateuch and a shorter set of grammatical notes. The former has been preserved in an abridgement by Abu 'l-Faraj Hârûn; this, in turn, was epitomized by ʿAlî ben Suleimân at the beginning of the twelfth century.[64] While it is impossible to ascertain the precise form of Joseph's original work, the style and content of the abridgement suggest that it followed the models established by his contemporaries Japheth and Sahl.

---

[62] On Joseph b. Noah and Abu 'l-Faraj Hârûn see The Arabic Commentary of ʿAli ben Suleimân (1928) 4–27; Khan, ʿAbû al-Faraj Hârûn (1997); and Maman, Medieval Grammatical Thought (1995).

[63] See G. MARGOLIOUTH, "Ibn al-Hiti's Arabic Chronicle of Karaite Doctors", *JQR* OS 9 (1896/97) 429–43, esp. 433–34, 438–40. Levi b. Japheth (Abû Saʿîd) wrote brief exegetical notes on the Bible but was better known for his code; see Ben-Shammai, Sefer Ha-Mitzvoth (1984–86) and Frank, The Shoshanim (1995) 207–08. Yûsuf al-Baṣîr was renowned as a theologian and jurist; see Vajda, Al-Kitâb al-Muḥtawî (1985), Sklare, Yûsuf al-Baṣîr (1995), and Sklare / Ben-Shammai, Judaeo-Arabic Manuscripts in the Firkovitch Collections (1997).

[64] A fragment of Joseph's grammatical notes is preserved in St. Petersburg RNL ms. Evr-Arab I. 2723. For Abu 'l-Faraj's abridgement of Joseph's commentary, see ms. Evr-Arab I. 1754; ʿAli b. Suleimân's epitome was edited by Skoss, The Arabic Commentary of ʿAli Ben Suleiman (1928).

3.2.2. *Abu 'l-Faraj Hârûn*

Joseph's own expertise in philology likely influenced Abu ʾl-Faraj who would achieve renown as a grammarian, even eliciting the admiration of Abraham Ibn Ezra a century later.[65] His grammar, *al-Mushtamil* ("The Comprehensive Work on the Roots and Sections of the Hebrew Language"; ca. 1026 CE), was one of the earliest attempts to provide a systematic description of the Hebrew language. Like his predecessor David b. Abraham, Abu ʾl-Faraj subscribed to a theory of biliteral roots. He also elaborated a theory of "ways" according to which paradigms are derived from certain base forms (imperative, perfect, etc.) that can be generated from artificial mnemonic "signs".[66] In addition to the grammatical topics treated (e.g. the nature of the infinitive, gender and number, pronominal suffixes) the *Mushtamil* includes lexicographic, stylistic, and syntactic discussions. Like several of his contemporaries, the author regularly drew upon Arabic and Aramaic in order to elucidate Hebrew expressions; he also discusses morphological similarities between the three languages. Abu ʾl-Faraj succeeded Joseph as head of the Academy. Together with Yûsuf al-Baṣîr and Levi b. Japheth he taught the most important Karaite exegete of the eleventh century, Yeshuʿah b. Judah.

3.2.3. *Yeshuʿah ben Judah (Abu 'l Faraj Hârûn Ibn al-Asad)*

The foremost Karaite scholar of his day and an important communal leader, Yeshuʿah was a prolific author. In addition to several halakhic works, he composed a Long Commentary on the Pentateuch, a Short Commentary (including a complete Arabic translation), and *Bereishit Rabbah*, an exegetical treatment of theological issues in the opening chapters of Genesis.[67] His writings, like those of Yûsuf al-Baṣîr, are scholastic in character. Infused with Muʿtazilite kalam, they also feature closely-argued treatments of legal problems. Yeshuʿah was learned in Rabbanite literature and cites classic rabbinic sources *in extenso*. In his Longer Commentary on Leviticus, for example, we find entire passages reproduced from the Mishnah and Sifra. This attitude is consonant with his scholastic style of citation and refutation, and he does not hesitate to adopt certain rabbinic arguments he finds compelling.[68]

---

[65] Bacher, Le grammairien anonyme (1895); Poznanski, Aboul-Faradj Haroun (1896); The Arabic Commentary of ʿAli ben Suleimân (1928), 11–27.

[66] Becker, The 'Ways' of the Hebrew Verb (1991). Abu ʾl-Faraj maintained that the imperative was the primary base form; see Khan, ʿAbû al-Faraj Hârûn (1997).

[67] Schreiner, Studien über Jeschua ben Jehuda (1900); Margoliouth, The Arabic Writings of Abu'l-Faraj Furkan Ibd Assad (1898/99); Poznanski, The Karaite Literary Opponents of Saadiah Gaon (1907) 65–72; Mann, Texts and Studies (1935) 34–40; Ben-Shammai, Yeshuah Ben Yehudah (1987). The Long Commentary was truly monumental in size; a fifty-folio fragment (BL Or. 2494, fols. 31–80) covers only Lev 11:37–44!

[68] These citations, incidentally, provide important textual and linguistic evidence for rabbinic literature in eleventh-century Palestine; see Maman, Karaites and Mishnaic Hebrew (1991); Tirosh-Becker, Preliminary Studies (1991), and idem, A Linguistic Study (1993).

3.2.4. The Byzantine "Literary Project"

During the mid-eleventh century, Byzantine Jews arrived in Jerusalem to study at the Karaite academy. Literate in Hebrew and speaking Greek, these sectarians transcribed, translated, and epitomized the teachings of their eastern masters, transforming an enormous Arabic library into a substantial Hebrew corpus.[69] Predating the efforts of the famous Provençal translators (the Ibn Tibbons and Cimhis) by over a century, these renderings employ an awkward, artificial language and are replete with Greek glosses. Nevertheless, they were valuable in transmitting Jerusalem scholarship to a new, Byzantine readership. The most important of these scholars was Tobias b. Moses, who studied with Yûsuf al-Baṣîr and translated his theological writings. He compiled an enormous commentary on Leviticus, *Oṣar Neḥmad*, of which the single extant volume (Oxford Bod. ms. Opp. fol. 26) treats Leviticus 1–10 in some three hundred folios.[70] Somewhat later, Jacob b. Reuben produced a terse Hebrew epitome of Japheth b. Eli and David b. Boaz's commentaries, entitled *Sefer ha-ʿOsher*.[71] Finally, in the mid-twelfth century, Judah Hadassi composed his encyclopedic *Eshkol ha-Kofer*, a repository for virtually all earlier Karaite learning.[72] Neither original nor lucid, these works were only partially successful in preserving and promoting Karaism. But with the extinction of the Jerusalem community and the emergence of a new sectarian center in Byzantium, they would offer some access to the Karaite heritage.[73]

4. The Later Byzantine Phase

Sources: Aaron ben Elijah: *Sefer ʿEṣ Ḥayyim* (ed. F. Delitzsch; Leipzig 1841; Gozlow 1847); Aaron ben Elijah: *Sefer ha-Miṣvot ha-Gadol Gan ʿEden* (Gozlow 1864); Aaron ben Elijah: *Sefer Keter Torah* (Gozlow 1866; repr. Ramleh, Israel 1972). Aaron ben Joseph: *Sefer ha-Mivḥar* (Gozlow 1835); Aaron ben Joseph: *Mivḥar Yesharim* (Gozlow 1834). Elijah Bashyatchi: *Adderet Eliyahu* (Odessa 1870; repr. Israel 1966). Judah Gibbor: *Minḥat Yehudah*, in *Siddur ha-Tefillot ke-Minhag ha-Yehudim ha-Qara'im* 1–3 (Vilna 1890; repr. Ramleh, Israel 1961/62, vol. 1; 342–93).

Studies: Ankori, Karaites in Byzantium (1959); idem, "Elijah Bashyachi: An Inquiry Into His Traditions Concerning the Beginnings of Karaism in Byzantium" (Heb.), *Tarbiz* 25 (1955/56) 44–65, 183–201; J.-C. Attias, *Le Commentaire biblique: Mordekhai Komtino ou l'herméneutique du dialogue* (Paris: Cerf 1991); D. Frank, "Abraham Ibn Ezra and the Bible Commentaries of the Karaites Aaron ben Joseph and Aaron ben Elijah", *Abraham Ibn Ezra and His Age: Proceedings of*

[69] Ankori, Karaites in Byzantium (1959) 415–51.

[70] Ankori, The Correspondence of Tobias ben Moses (1959), and idem, Karaites in Byzantium (1959) 418–38 and index, s. v. "Tobias b. Moses."

[71] Ibid., index, s. v. "Jacob b. Reuben". Partially published with Aaron b. Joseph, Mivḥar Yesharim (1834).

[72] Ankori, Karaites in Byzantium (1959) index, s. v. "Yehudah Hadassi"; H. H. Ben-Sasson, "Hadassi, Judah (ha-Avel) ben Elijah", EncJud 7, 1046–47; W. Bacher, "Jehuda Hadassis Hermeneutik und Grammatik", *MGWJ* 40 (1896) 14–32, 68–84, 109–26; D. J. Lasker, "The Philosophy of Judah Hadassi the Karaite" (Heb.), *Shlomo Pines Jubilee Volume*, Pt. I (= *Jerusalem Studies in Jewish Thought* 7; ed. M. Idel et al.; Jerusalem: The Hebrew University 1988) 477–92.

[73] On the final years of the Jerusalem community see Ben-Shammai, The Karaites (1996) 221–22.

the International Symposium (ed. F. Díaz Esteban; Madrid: Asociación Española de Orientalistas 1990) 99–107; idem, "The Religious Philosophy of the Karaite Aaron ben Elijah: The Problem of Divine Justice" (Harvard University Ph. D. dissertation, 1991); I. Husik, "Aaron ben Elijah of Nicomedia", *A History of Mediaeval Jewish Philosophy* (Philadelphia: JPSA 1940) 362–87; D. J. Lasker, "Maimonides' Influence on Karaite Theories of Prophecy and Law", *Maimonidean Studies* 1 (1990) 99–115; idem, "Aaron ben Joseph and the Transformation of Karaite Thought", *Torah and Wisdom: Torah ve-Ḥokhmah: Studies in Jewish Philosophy, Kabbalah, and Halacha: Essays in Honor of Arthur Hyman* (ed. Ruth Link-Salinger; New York: Shengold 1992) 121–28; P. E. Miller, "At the Twilight of Byzantine Karaism: The Anachronism of Judah Gibbor" (New York University Ph. D. dissertation, 1984).

During the thirteenth-fifteenth centuries, Byzantine Karaites struggled to maintain their scholarly tradition, while producing new works that corresponded in form and content to the most popular Rabbanite texts. As the writings of Abraham Ibn Ezra (d. ca. 1165) and Moses Maimonides (d. 1204) were disseminated throughout the Mediterranean basin, these sectarians encountered new exegetical styles, novel philosophical systems, and a fresh form of Hebrew. The rationalistic, philological approach of Ibn Ezra naturally appealed to them. His harsh, anti-Karaite pronouncements were mitigated by his frequent citation of Karaite authorities (notably Japheth and Yeshuʿah) and his predilection for *peshat*.[74] The lucid Hebrew of Sefardic Rabbanites was also much easier to read than the awkward language of the eleventh-twelfth century Byzantine sectarians. But since the later scholars retained a loyalty to their spiritual and intellectual ancestors, they produced highly eclectic works.

The two Karaite exegetes active in this period were Aaron b. Joseph, "the Elder" and Aaron b. Elijah of Nicomedia, "the Younger".[75] Aaron b. Joseph's works include a commentary on the Pentateuch (*Sefer ha-Mivḥar* = *ShM*), commentaries on the Former Prophets, Isaiah, Psalms (*Mivḥar Yesharim*) and Job (lost), and a Hebrew grammar (*Kelil Yofi*).[76] Aaron b. Elijah produced a trilogy: *Sefer ʿEṣ Ḥayyim* ("The Tree of Life", a Karaite *Guide of the Perplexed*, 1346 CE); *Sefer Gan ʿEden* ("The Garden of Eden", a code, 1354 CE); and *Sefer Keter Torah* (= *KT*, "The Crown of the Torah", a commentary on the Pentateuch, 1362 CE).

Rabbanite influence on both authors is manifest in frequent citations, many of them anonymous. Rashi, Ibn Janah, Ibn Ezra, Maimonides, Nahmanides, and David Cimhi are all cited by name. Ibn Ezra's impress is immediately apparent in the introductions to *ShM* and *KT*. In rhymed prose, Aaron b. Elijah even presents a four-part classification of interpretive approaches (Scripturalist vs. Traditionalist Jews, with literalists and allegorists in each camp). Like Ibn Ezra, he rejects them all in favor of a "fifth way", grounded in sound philol-

---

[74] On the attitude of Andalusian Rabbanites to Karaism see D. J. Lasker, "Karaism in Twelfth-Century Spain", *Journal of Jewish Thought and Philosophy* 1 (1992) 179–95.

[75] Frank, Abraham Ibn Ezra and the Karaite Exegetes (1990); idem, The Religious Philosophy of the Karaite Aaron ben Elijah (1991); Lasker, Maimonides' Influence on Karaite Theories of Prophecy and Law (1990); and idem, Aaron ben Joseph and the Transformation of Karaite Thought (1992).

[76] The commentary on Psalms remains in manuscript. Aaron b. Joseph also arranged the standard Karaite prayerbook; see P. S. Goldberg, *Karaite Liturgy and Its Relation to Synagogue Worship* (Manchester 1957), 2–5.

ogy.[77] Both Karaite commentaries are "Andalusian" in style: grammatical, rationalist solutions are preferred, "since the *peshat* is the main thing" (*ShM*, fol. 10 a, line 21). While both exegetes include some *derash* (gleaned, e. g., from Rashi), they generally reject aggadic interpretations – sometimes through recourse to Ibn Ezra's criticisms.[78]

Philosophical discussions figure prominently. At Gen 18:21, for example, Aaron b. Joseph attacks Ibn Ezra (without naming him) for asserting that God's knowledge extends only to universals, not particulars, and that His knowledge of human events is therefore deficient. Aaron b. Elijah dismisses this reading of Ibn Ezra and offers an astrological explanation for his cryptic words.[79] Aaron b. Elijah's other works also reflect his deep interest in speculation and exegesis. In *ʿEṣ Ḥayyim*, ch. 90, for example, he analyzes Job in detail and criticizes earlier Karaite and Rabbanite interpretations.[80] And in *Gan ʿEden* he exhaustively reviews the Rabbanite and Karaite positions on every major halakhic issue, evaluating the exegetical validity of each view vis-à-vis the biblical texts upon which it is based.

Halakhic subjects apart, the contextual approach of the two Aarons was virtually identical with the Spanish Rabbanites' quest for *peshat*. Sharing interpretive ideals and a respect for Andalusian learning, Karaites and Rabbanites in fifteenth-century Byzantium studied sacred and scientific texts together.[81] Sectarian scholars, such as Elijah Bashyatchi (d. 1490), accounted for this affinity by suggesting that Ibn Ezra had been Japheth b. Eli's disciple: when the Andalusian attacked the Karaites, he was dissimulating out of fear – his real sympathies were sectarian![82] The intellectual rapprochement in Byzantium was so strong that some Karaites even indulged in philosophical allegory and Kabbalah; true scripturalism had been dead for half a millennium.[83] What lived on, however, was the Karaite intellectual and literary heritage, a profound commitment to "searching well in Scripture".

---

[77] The Introduction then concludes with a clear statement of the three main points of dispute between Karaites and Rabbanites: the Oral Law's existence; the need for Tradition; and the permissibility of rabbinic legislation; see *KT* I, 3 b–4 b.

[78] For Aaron b. Joseph's attitude towards *derash*, see *ShM* I, 10 a. He follows Ibn Ezra in rejecting, e. g., the aggadah concerning Jochebed cited by Rashi *ad* Gen 46:15; see *ShM*, I, 64 a. For Aaron b. Elijah's (anonymous) citation of a homiletic interpretation given by Rashi see, e. g., *KT* I, 38 b on Gen 9:7. Elsewhere, he peremptorily dismisses aggadic suggestions; see, e. g., *KT* I, 44 a on Gen 14:13 ("The *derash* (on this point) is useless").

[79] Ibn Ezra's statement likely derives from Avicenna, and Aaron b. Joseph's critique follows Nahmanides; see *ShM* I, 42 a and *KT* I, 50 b–51 a and Frank, Ibn Ezra and the Karaite Exegetes (1990) 104–06.

[80] Frank, The Religious Philosophy (1991) cxi–cxxi, 151–79; Husik, Aaron ben Elijah (1940), 377–79.

[81] One Rabbanite in particular, Mordechai Comtino, had many sectarian disciples; see Attias, Le Commentaire biblique (1991), chs. 2–3.

[82] Ankori, Elijah Bashyachi (1955/56), 60–65, 196–98. Elijah b. Baruch Yerushalmi develops this subject in his treatise *ʿAsarah Ma'amarot* ("Ten Articles on the Differences Between the Rabbanites and the Karaites"); see Oxford Bod. ms. Opp. Add. 4 to, 121, fols. 170 b–71 a.

[83] E. g. Judah Gibbor; see Miller, At the Twilight of Byzantine Karaism (1984). See also P. B. Fenton, "De quelques attitudes qaraïtes envers la Qabbale", *REJ* 142 (1983) 5–19.

25.7. Clearing *Peshat* and *Derash*

By Stephen Garfinkel, New York

Bibliography: Sh. Carmy, "Biblical Exegesis: Jewish Views", EncRel 2, 136–42; R. P. Carroll (ed.), *Text as Pretext: Essays in Honour of Robert Davidson* (JSOTSup 138; Sheffield: Sheffield Academic Press 1992); J. J. Collins, "Is a Critical Biblical Theology Possible?", W. H. Propp / B. Halpern / D. N. Freedman (eds.), *The Hebrew Bible and Its Interpreters* (Biblical and Judaic Studies from The University of California, San Diego, 1; Winona Lake, IN: Eisenbrauns 1990) 1–17; A. Cooper, "Reading the Bible Critically and Otherwise", R. E. Friedman / H. G. M. Williamson (eds.), *The Future of Biblical Studies: The Hebrew Scriptures* (Atlanta: Scholars Press 1987) 61–79; F. W. Danker, "Biblical Exegesis: Christian Views", EncRel 2, 142–52; M. Fishbane, *Biblical Interpretation in Ancient Israel* (Oxford: Clarendon Press 1985); I. Frankel, *Peshaṭ (Plain Exegesis) in Talmudic and Midrashic Literature* (Toronto: La Salle Press 1956); E. S. Frerichs, "Introduction: The Jewish School of Biblical Studies", J. Neusner / B. A. Levine / E. S. Frerichs (eds.), *Judaic Perspectives on Ancient Israel* (Philadelphia: Fortress Press 1987) 1–6; K. Froehlich, *Biblical Interpretation in the Early Church* (Sources of Early Christian Thought; Philadelphia: Fortress Press 1984); S. Garfinkel, "Applied *Peshat*: Historical-Critical Method and Religious Meaning", *JANES* 22 (1993) 19–28; B. Gelles, *Peshat and Derash in the Exegesis of Rashi* (Leiden: Brill 1981); W. A. Graham, "Scripture", EncRel 13, 133–45; R. M. Grant / D. Tracy, *A Short History of the Interpretation of the Bible* (Philadelphia: Fortress Press 1963; ^{2}1984); F. E. Greenspahn, "Biblical Scholars, Medieval and Modern", J. Neusner / B. A. Levine / E. S. Frerichs (eds.), *Judaic Perspectives on Ancient Israel* (Philadelphia: Fortress Press 1987) 245–58; E. L. Greenstein, "Medieval Bible Commentaries", B. W. Holtz (ed.), *Back to the Sources* (New York: Summit 1984) 213–59; A. H. J. Gunneweg, *Sola Scriptura: Beiträge zu Exegese und Hermeneutik des Alten Testaments* (zum 60. Geburtstag herausgegeben von P. Höffken; Göttingen: Vandenhoeck & Ruprecht 1983); D. W. Halivni, *Peshat and Derash: Plain and Applied Meaning in Rabbinic Exegesis* (New York / Oxford: Oxford UP 1991); W. W. Hallo, "The Concept of Canonicity in Cuneiform and Biblical Literature: A Comparative Appraisal", K. L. Younger, jr. / W. W. Hallo / B. F. Batto (eds.), *The Biblical Canon in Comparative Perspective* (Scripture in Context 4; Ancient Near Eastern Texts and Studies II; Lewiston / Queenston / Lampeter: Mellen 1991) 1–19; M. Haran, "Midrashic and Literal Exegesis and the Critical Method in Biblical Research", S. Japhet (ed.), *Studies in Bible* (ScrHier 31; Jerusalem: The Magnes Press 1986) 19–48; S. Kamin, *Rashi's Exegetical Categorization in Respect to the Distinction between Peshat and Derash* [Heb.] (Jerusalem: The Magnes Press 1986); J. L. Kugel, "Early Interpretation: The Common Background of Late[r] Forms of Biblical Exegesis", J. L. Kugel / R. A. Greer (eds.), *Early Biblical Interpretation* (Philadelphia: The Westminster Press 1986); idem, "The Bible in the University", W. H. Propp / B. Halpern / D. N. Freedman (eds.), *The Hebrew Bible and Its Interpreters* (Biblical and Judaic Studies from The University of California, San Diego, 1; Winona Lake, IN: Eisenbrauns 1990) 143–65; J. D. Levenson, "The Hebrew Bible, The Old Testament, and Historical Criticism", R. E. Friedman / H. G. M. Williamson (eds.), *The Future of Biblical Studies: The Hebrew Scriptures* (Atlanta: Scholars Press 1987) 19–59; M. I. Lockshin, "Tradition or Context: Two Exegetes Struggle with Peshat", J. Neusner / E. S. Frerichs / N. M. Sarna (eds.), *From Ancient Israel to Modern Judaism: Intellect in Quest of Understanding* (Essays in Honor of Marvin Fox 2; Brown Judaica Series 173; Atlanta: Scholars Press 1989); R. Lowe, "The 'Plain' Meaning of Scripture in Early Jewish Exegesis", J. G. Weiss (ed.), *Papers of the Institute of Jewish Studies in London* 1 (Jerusalem: Magnes Press 1964) 140–85; idem, "Jewish Exegesis", DBI 346–354; G. F. Moore, "The Definition of the Jewish Canon and the Repudiation of the Christian Scriptures", *Essays in Modern Theology and Related Subjects Gathered and Published as a Testimonial to Charles Augustus Briggs on the Completion of his*

Seventieth Year (New York: Charles Scribner's Sons 1911) 99–125; J. G. RECHTIEN, "The Structural Significance of *Sola Scriptura*", *Centerpoint* 2/1 (1976) 7–19; G. W. SAVRAN, *Telling and Retelling: Quotation in Biblical Narrative* (Bloomington / Indianapolis: Indiana UP 1988); B. J. SCHWARTZ, "On *Peshat* and *Derash*, Bible Criticism, and Theology", *Prooftexts* 14 (1994) 71–88; U. SIMON, "The Religious Significance of the *Peshat*", *Tradition* 23/2 (1988) 41–63; W. C. SMITH, "The Study of Religion and the Study of the Bible", *JAAR* 39 (1971) 131–40; B. UFFENHEIMER / H. GRAF REVENTLOW (eds.), *Creative Biblical Exegesis: Christian and Jewish Hermeneutics through the Centuries* (JSOTSup 59; Sheffield: Sheffield Academic Press 1988); G. VERMES, *Scripture and Tradition in Judaism: Haggadic Studies* (SPB 4; Leiden: Brill 1961); idem, *Post-Biblical Jewish Studies* (SJLA 8; Leiden: Brill 1975).

For the entire duration of its history, the very nature of sacred Scripture has made it vulnerable to exegesis. The inescapable reality is that from the time of its canonization, Scripture has been and is susceptible to interpretation; in the words of PFEIFFER: "Every sentence in the OT was profane literature before it became canonical sacred scripture".[1] Conversely, however, from that point on even the once-profane sentence becomes canon, serving as fertile and legitimate ground for interpretation.

Some scholars contend that exegesis, the interpretive process, might have begun even earlier than the completion of canonization.[2] The ongoing debate is whether 'internal' exegesis is more accurately to be included in the developmental stage of the canon – as KUGEL calls this stage "the Bible-in-the-making"[3] – or in a separate interpretative stage, after the canon had been closed. Without entering directly into the fray, our citation of the following popular example appears to endorse *both* sides of the controversy.

Exod 12:9 commands the Israelites: "Do not eat any of it [the Passover lamb sacrifice] raw, or boiled / cooked [*bšl*] in any way with water, but rather roasted over fire, its head with its legs and entrails". Deut 16:7, however, requires that "You shall boil / cook [*bšl*] it and eat it in the place where the Lord your God shall choose". One attempt to reconcile the two evidently incompatible verses is to translate *bšl* in the second verse as 'roast'.[4] Nonetheless, this ignores the fact that however the verb is translated, one verse prohibits performing the action (of *biššûl*) while the other requires it! Another method of reconciliation, however, may already be found in 2 Chr 35:13, which declares: "They cooked ('boiled' [*bšl*]) the Passover lamb in fire, as prescribed, while

[1] R. PFEIFFER, "Canon of the OT", IDB 1, 498–520; 499. See also Chap. 2.2 above (J. BARTON, "The Significance of a Fixed Canon of the Hebrew Bible", HBOT I/1, 67–83).

[2] While (Rabbi) Samuel ben Meir (Rashbam) already provided examples of this phenomenon in his twelfth-century commentary on the Pentateuch, the topic has been treated in a more systematic and analytic manner in M. WEISS, *The Bible from Within: The Method of Total Interpretation* (Jerusalem 1984); A. SHINAN / Y. ZAKOVITCH, "Midrash on Scripture and Midrash Within Scripture", S. JAPHET (ed.), *Studies in the Bible 1986* (Jerusalem 1986) 257–277; M. FISHBANE, *The Garments of Torah: Essays in Biblical Hermeneutics* (Bloomington / Indianapolis 1989) 3–18; cf. also his essay in Chap. 1 above ("Inner-Biblical Exegesis", HBOT I/1, 33–48) as well as the aftermath in Chap. 7 by J. HARRIS ("From Inner-Biblical Interpretation to Early Rabbinic Exegesis", HBOT I/1, 256–269). One aspect of internal exegesis often neglected in this regard is treated in Savran, Telling and Retelling (1988).

[3] J. Kugel, Early Interpretation (1986) 57.

[4] This appears, e. g., in the translation of the Koren Publishers (Jerusalem 1969).

the sacred offerings they cooked in pots, cauldrons, and pans, and conveyed them quickly to all the people". By using the disputed verb ([*bšl*]) in an unknown, if not impossible, manner – one cannot actually "boil in fire" – and additionally by announcing that this was done "as prescribed", the Chronicler has created a new canonical text while also having interpreted the other two verses at the same time. The process, therefore, is part of the developmental stage of canon and simultaneously part of the interpretive stage.

Therefore, we are justified in refining a sentence from the opening paragraph of this section: From *at least* the time of its canonization, Scripture has been and is susceptible to interpretation. As a religious document and a foundational text of communities of faith, it is the function and need of Scripture be interpreted. In medieval exegetical parlance, the text cries out for exegesis.

Even – or perhaps especially – early rabbinic sages recognized and appreciated the fact that once canonized, the biblical text demanded to be interpreted. In answer to the question "What is Torah?" the Talmud exclaims that Torah, itself, is nothing other than "exegesis of Torah".[5] This arresting statement reflects an awareness that any serious reading of the biblical text cannot proceed unconsciously. Reading the Book must be undertaken methodically, whether the method employed be one of *peshat* or of *derash*. To be certain that the two are clearly delineated, however, we pause momentarily to identify the key elements of each.

First we refute a widely-held notion that *peshat* should be understood as the 'straightforward', 'obvious' or even 'literal' meaning of a text.[6] Such terminology misleads the reader and creates confusion rather than clarity. The literal rendering of an idiom or of a hendiadys, for example, would almost certainly not represent its *peshat*. Nor should *peshat* be deprived of the richness which a metaphor, seldom 'literal', provides. The literal fallacy was understood already in talmudic times, as in the pronouncement that "one who translates a verse literally (lit., "according to its form") is a misrepresenter ...".[7]

Instead of equating *peshat* exegesis with literality, a more useful taxonomy affirms that *peshat* interpretations acknowledge the historical, linguistic, and literary contexts of a phrase, verse, or pericope.[8] *Derash*, by contrast, seeks acontextual interpretations; it ignores and overrides the constraints of contexts. It often serves functions which are primarily other than an examination

---

[5] *Qidd.* 49 a–b. This text is also cited in the important article by Lowe, The 'Plain' Meaning of Scripture (1964) 183, n. 200. The idea that "Torah is exegesis of Torah" is to some extent an interesting parallel to that of *sola scriptura*, or that of *Scriptura sui ipsius interpres* (see HBOT I/1, 464, 481, 556, 560). The relationship among these concepts warrants separate study.

[6] The description of *peshat* as "what we all sense a text really means" is too elusive to be a useful definition; see M. Lockshin's review of D. W. Halivni's work Peshat and Derash (1991) in *Hebrew Studies* 33 (1992) 126.

[7] *Qidd.* 49 a. Frankel cites this text and assesses the practice even more stridently. He calls the offender a "liar"; see his Peshaṭ (Plain Exegesis) (1956) 88.

[8] This is explained and demonstrated by Greenstein, Medieval Bible Commentaries (1984) 213–59, esp. 217–23. More recently, in his challenging review of Halivni's work, Peshat and Derash, B. Schwartz has raised the issue of how broad or narrow the *peshat* context might be, *Prooftexts* 14 (1994) 74.

of the biblical text, using the text as a pretext for other purposes, ritual or moralistic.[9]

Does the appreciation of contextual analysis extend to an epoch as early as the talmudic era? According to MENAHEM HARAN, such a foundation developed only at a much later time: "the critical study of the Bible ... is, then, a novel manifestation and it would be vain to look for its first sparks in the statements of talmudic or medieval sages".[10] However, a nascent appreciation of *peshat* as a worthwhile exegetical enterprise does seems to be discernible in – or at least capable of extrapolation from – sporadic talmudic sources and techniques.[11] How consistent and self-conscious even this embryonic stage was, however, awaits further exploration.

Canonicity provided the text with its foundational status within the faith community, although the relationship between a community and its canon(s) is complex. A community defines (and occasionally refines) its canon; no less, however, the canon defines a community.[12] Canonicity compels the community to devote immediate and constant attention to the sacred texts. Such attention is what we have been calling interpretation or exegesis. It has been applied by the scholars and commentators surveyed in the previous sections of this volume and by astute lay readers, as well.

Every exegete forms part of an unending hermeneutic enterprise. Sometimes the endeavor is designed to make sense of the ancient text on its own terms; sometimes the goal is to provide renewed applicability for an old text in danger of irrelevance or insignificance. Yet the insistent power of canon is stronger than the prospect of oblivion, and so the text is renewed, revived as it were, by each generation. These two exegetical foci – examining the text on its own terms or appropriating it for changing times – define the two basic interpretive methods, *peshat* and *derash*, and distinguish between them. This differentiation is central to classifying all exegetical procedures, which fall into one part of the dichotomy or the other.

The two-fold split is not gainsaid even though classic Jewish exegesis knows of a four-fold division, *peshat*, *derash*, *remez* ('hint'), and *sod* ('secret'). In practice, the last three categories are actually little more than varied applications of acontextual exegesis. For the purposes of this section, therefore, they should be classified together, as *derash* in contradistinction to contextual ana-

[9] G. VERMES differentiates between applied and pure *midrash* (exegesis) in his Post-Biblical Jewish Studies (1975) 63–91. See also Carroll, Text as Pretext (1992).

[10] Haran, Midrashic and Literal Exegesis (1986) 31.

[11] The talmudic statement that a biblical verse never "leaves the hands of the *peshat*" is well-known (*Šabb.* 63 a; *Yebam.* 11 b; *Yebam.* 24 a), although we leave unresolved whether that rabbinic maxim is to be given credence as an active hermeneutic force, even as a minority view, or was merely an empty slogan. Nor should one neglect the well-known story (*Šabb.* 31 a) in which a heathen asked Shammai "How many Torahs [*tôrôt*] do you have?". Shammai's answer, "Two – the Written Torah and the Oral Torah", is often deprecated in comparison with Hillel's response to the heathen. As a result, unfortunately, the hermeneutic implications are ignored.

Other exegetical traits appear to mimic *peshat* characteristics, but should not be claimed to constitute a systematic concept of *peshat*. See, e.g., the use of a formulaic expression like "the word [x] means nothing other than [y]", or the technique of deriving meaning from juxtaposed pericopae.

[12] See BARTON, Chap. 2.2, above.

lysis, *peshat.* Similarly, medieval Church exegesis also exhibited a four-part pattern: the letter (visible and surface data, sometimes considered the 'historical' information); allegory (presenting the hidden or theological meaning); moral sense or tropology (embodying practical guidance); and anagogy or eschatology (for the contemplative life). This division, too, seems to have derived from an earlier dichotomy.[13]

Recognition of the fundamental dichotomy between *peshat* and *derash* should not be disguised by the multiplicity of terms used to describe and analyze the basic distinction between the two. One encounters widespread terminological variety scattered throughout the scholarly literature, including designations such as, but not limited to, the following: *sensus litteralis* or *sensus plenior*; text or tradition; tradition or context; historical or propagandistic exegesis; scripture or tradition; what the text meant or what the text means. Nomenclature notwithstanding, however, the two modes of interpretation are discrete.

The preferred exegetical methods varied in part according to the conditions, temperament, and intellectual climate of a given region and era. But beyond such generalizations, each of the exegetes described in the pages above as well as each yet to be examined in the forthcoming sections developed a personal style and approach within the broader scholastic tendencies. Some rely more heavily on analyses that reflect the *peshat* method; others employ techniques of a more midrashic leaning. Most exegetes, however, did not rely on either exclusively, but blended some elements of each sort. Commentators today, too, may favor a more historical-critical approach or one oriented more toward *midrash.* Their commentaries and exegetical writings may vary by intended audience, purpose, or time. The most important element in preserving the integrity of an interpretation is not *which* approach is selected or applied, for surely each approach has its benefits, but rather that the exegete be cognizant of the method employed at a given time.

Ironically, the need to retain the distinctiveness between *peshat* and *derash* as separate exegetical methods does not necessarily preclude the use of one in the service of the other. With judicious application, an exegete using a *peshat* orientation may, nonetheless, be directed by a *derash* interpretation to discern a textual nuance that would otherwise have been overlooked. For instance, rabbinic literature, with its predilection for close reading, might draw the exegete's attention to an unusual semantic usage or syntactic oddity. Gen 21:14 speaks of Abraham providing bread and a skin of water for Hagar and Ishmael when they were sent away. Reacting to the awkward positioning of the phrase "and the child", a rabbinic comment suggests that Ishmael (too) needed to be carried on Hagar's shoulder because of a fever (caused by Sarah).[14]

---

[13] DANKER cites the sixteenth-century jingle, noting its much earlier antecedents, in which Augustine summarized the four approaches; see his Biblical Exegesis (1987) 145. Cf. also HBOT I/1, 701–30, as well as Indexes / Topics, s.v. 'exegesis', 'hermeneutics', 'interpretation', and 'meaning'; further Grant / Tracy, A Short History of the Interpretation (1984) 85–86; and Froehlich, Biblical Interpretation in the Early Church (1984).

[14] *Gen. Rab.* 53:13, also cited by Rashi, ad loc., thus also explaining why the water ran out (v. 15).

Although that response does not reflect a *peshat* exegesis, it does focus the reader's attention on the textual difficulty. Thus, NAHUM SARNA comments that only the bread and water container were placed on Hagar's shoulder since "Ishmael, who is now at least sixteen years old, could hardly have been carried by his mother".[15]

This direction of mutual benefit between *peshat* and *derash* – that the latter can redirect or focus one's attention for exegesis, even by means of the former – is often admitted. The converse, however, is still largely unrealized, although studies with this interest are beginning to appear. One such recent attempt outlines measures for using *peshat*, or historical-critical study, in the service of providing 'renewed applicability' or even 'religious meaning' of the text.[16] Such cross-fertilization, however, must not blur the lines between *peshat* and *derash*.

The rudimentary point of the present, albeit brief, section may still need to be stated explicitly. It serves as one of the theses underlying the previous sections of this volume and provides a framework for the material which follows. Simply stated, *peshat* and *derash* may each enrich the reader's understanding of the biblical text. Neither is the only lens, or the 'correct' lens, through which to read. Neither should even be viewed as an inherently 'preferred' technique, except as reflecting the inclinations of author and audience. Both approaches, *peshat* and *derash*, can provide profound insights into the text, and both should be employed in developing as full an understanding of the scriptural text as possible.

The two techniques have been and remain endless sources of knowledge and wisdom. They function properly as parallel strands in the activity of biblical exegesis.

---

[15] N. SARNA, *The JPS Torah Commentary: Genesis* (Philadelphia: The Jewish Publication Society 1989) 147.

[16] See Garfinkel, Applied *Peshat* (1993); also see Simon, The Religious Significance of the *Peshat* (1988). Other related studies include Collins, Is a Critical Biblical Theology Possible? (1990); Cooper, Reading the Bible Critically and Otherwise (1987); Levenson, The Hebrew Bible, The Old Testament, and Historical Criticism (1987); and Uffenheimer / Reventlow (eds.), Creative Biblical Exegesis (1988)

Chapter Twenty-six

Gregory the Great: a Figure of Tradition and Transition in Church Exegesis

By Stephan Ch. Kessler, Freiburg/Br.

Sources: The critical edition of the works of Gregory the Great (beside the reprint of the Maurinian edition in PL 75–79) is published in various series: *Moralia in Iob* (abbr. *Mor*): CCL 143. 143 A. 143 B (ed. M. Adriaen); *Mor* 1–2: SC 32 bis (ed. R. Gillet); *Mor* 11–16: SC 212. 221 (ed. A. Bocognano). *Registrum Epistularum* (*Ep*): CCL 140. 140 A (ed. D. Norberg); *Ep* 1–2: SC 370. 371 (ed. P. Minard). *Regula pastoralis* (*Rpast*): SC 381. 382 (ed. B. Judic / F. Rommel / Ch. Morel). *Homiliae in Evangelia XL* (*HEv*): FontC 28. 1/2 (ed. M. Fiedrowicz). *Dialogorum libri IV. De miraculis patrum italicorum* (*Dial*): SC 251. 260. 265 (ed. A. de Vogüé). *Homiliae in Hiezechielem Prophetam XXII* (*HEz*): CCL 142 (ed. M. Adriaen). *Expositio in Canticum Canticorum* (*In Cant*): CCL 144, 3–46 (ed. P. Verbraken); SC 314 (ed. R. Bélanger). *In Librum Primum Regum* (*In I Rg*): CCL 144, 49–614 (ed. P. Verbraken); *In I Rg* 1, 1–2, 28: SC 351 (ed. A. de Vogüé); 2, 29–3, 37: SC 391 (ed. Ch. Vuillaume); Grégoire le Grand / Pierre de Cava 3, 38–4, 78: SC 432 (ed. A. de Vogüé). A Latin-Italian edition of the works of Gregory the Great is being published: Opere di Gregorio Magno (Bibliotheca Gregorii Magni, ed. P. Siniscalco et al.; Roma: Città Nuova 1992 ff).

Bibliographies: A. Vernet / A.-M. Genevois, *La Bible au moyen age. Bibliographie* (Paris 1989); R. Godding, *Bibliografia di Gregorio Magno 1890–1989* (Opere di Gregorio Magno, complementi 1; Roma: Città Nuova 1990).

General works: R. Manselli, "Gregorio Magno e la Bibbia", *Settimane di studio del centro italiano di studi sull'alto medioevo* 10 (1963) 67–101; D. Hofmann, *Die geistige Auslegung der Schrift bei Gregor dem Großen* (Münsterschwarzacher Studien 6; Münsterschwarzach: Vier-Türme-Verlag 1968); C. Dagens, *Saint Grégoire le Grand. Culture et expérience chrétiennes* (Paris: Études Augustiniennes 1977); J. Richards, *Consul of God. The Life and Times of Gregory the Great* (London 1980; German transl.: *Gregor der Große*, Graz: Verlag Styria 1983); R. A. Markus, *From Augustine to Gregory the Great. History and Christianity in Late Antiquity* (London: Variorum Reprints 1983); idem, "Gregor I.", TRE 14 (1985) 135–45; *Grégoire le Grand. Colloques internationaux du Centre National de la Recherche Scientifique 1982* (ed. J. Fontaine / R. Gillet / S. Pellistrandi; Paris: Éditions du CNRS 1986); C. E. Straw, *Gregory the Great. Perfection in Imperfection* (Transformation of the classical heritage 14; Berkeley: University of California Press 1988); *Gregorio Magno e il suo tempo* (XIX Incontro di studiosi dell'antichità cristiana in collaborazione con l'École Française de Rome 1990; SEAug 33. 34; Roma 1991); S. Müller, *"Fervorem discamus amoris". Das Hohelied und seine Auslegung bei Gregor dem Großen* (Dissertationen, Theologische Reihe 46; St. Ottilien: EOS 1991); M. Fiedrowicz, *Das Kirchenverständnis Gregors des Großen. Eine Untersuchung seiner exegetischen und homiletischen Werke* (RQ Suppl. 50; Freiburg: Herder 1995); *Gregory the Great. A Symposium* (ed. J. C. Cavandini; Notre Dame: University of Notre Dame Press 1995); S. C. Kessler, *Gregor der Große als Exeget. Zur theologischen Interpretation der Ezechielhomilien* (Innsbrucker Theologische Studien 43; Innsbruck: Tyrolia 1995); P. Riché, *Petite vie de saint Grégoire le Grand* (Paris: Desclée de Brouwer 1995; German translation: *Gregor der Große. Leben und Werk* [München: Neue Stadt 1996]); S. C. Kessler, "Die Exegese Gregors des Großen am Beispiel der 'Homiliae in Ezechielem'", StPatr 30 (1997) 49–53; R. A. Markus, *Gregory the Great and his world* (Cambridge: Cambridge UP 1997); M. Schambeck, *Contemplatio als Missio. Zu einem Schlüsselphänomen bei Gregor dem Großen* (Studien zur systematischen und spirituellen Theologie 25; Würzburg:

Echter 1999); S. C. KESSLER, "Gregor der Große und seine Theorie der Exegese: Die 'Epistula ad Leandrum'", *L'esegesi dei Padri Latini dalle origini a Gregorio Magno* (SEAug; Roma: Institutum Patristicum Augustinanum 2000) [in print].

1. General and Biographical Remarks

Through his exegetical writings Gregory the Great became a prominent biblical theologian during the transition from patristic times to the Middle Ages. As interpreter of the Bible he mainly concentrated on the exegesis of passages and figures from the Old Testament and became as biblical theologian one of the most important mediators of patristic exegesis in relation to the following centuries. Regarding the constant stream of influence exerted by the exegetical writings of Gregory on the biblical culture of the Middle Ages HENRI DE LUBAC could speak of this period as "the Gregorian age".[1] The Reformation and the Age of Enlightenment with their new historical approach and critical exegesis regarded the allegorical exegesis of Gregory as second-class interpretation of the Bible. His way of dealing with the Scriptures was unwarranted considered as pre-critical, un-systematic and depending purely on the Augustinian pattern.

Research in the field of the history of exegesis in recent years has brought to view rather new insights: Despite the undeniably great influence of Augustine's thought on his writings, Gregory modifies especially in his biblical commentaries the exegetical practice of Late Antiquity by going back to the Origenist tradition.[2] Thus the first pope from a monastic background became the founder of a new and independent Bible-theology on the eve of the Middle Ages with a special emphasis on the interpretation of passages from the Old Testament and determined by the characteristics of tradition and transition.

On the grounds of his exegetical work Gregory exerted perhaps the most significant single influence upon the medieval system of Christian interpretation with different senses adumbrated in the writings of Origen and Augustine. Gregory followed Augustine's view in many fields; but his version lacked the deeply pondered theoretical foundations Augustine had laid for them. In the view of Gregory the world had changed so that it had become a Christian world in its old age (*mundus senescens*). Consequently, the interpretation of the Scriptures had altered as well.[3] In this way, the exegesis of Gregory represents one of the central keys to an adequate understanding of the culture and mentality of the Middle Ages.[4]

---

[1] H. DE LUBAC coined the expression of "l'âge grégorien" (*Exégèse médiévale. Les quatre sens de l'écriture* 1/1; Paris 1959, 537–48); R. WASSELYNCK, "L'influence de l'exégèse de S. Grégoire le Grand sur les commentaires bibliques médiévaux", *RTAM* 32 (1965) 157–204.

[2] Hofmann, Auslegung (1968) 73; V. RECCHIA, "La memoria di Agostino nella esegesi biblica di Gregorio Magno", *Aug* 25 (1985) 405–34; Kessler, Gregor (1995) 175–90.

[3] Straw, Gregory (1988) 49 f; Markus, Gregory (1997) 47–50.

[4] Manselli, Bibbia (1963) 70; *The reception of the Fathers in the West. From the Carolingians to the Maurists* (ed. I. Backus; 2 volumes; Leiden: Brill 1997).

Gregory was born in Rome around 540. His family was of senatorial rank and handsomely rich with estates in Sicily in addition to the palace on the Caelian hill and properties in the neighbourhood of Rome. Due to the restoration of Byzantine power in Italy after the war against the Goths Gregory spent the important years of his formation in a time of relative peace. He received the best education available in sixth century Rome with special emphasis on grammar and rhetoric, and he probably had legal training as well which qualified him for a career in public service and later as a theologian. In 573 Gregory reached the summit of his public career being Prefect of the City (*praefectus urbi*), the highest civil dignitary in Rome. In 574 he sold the patrimony in Sicily and resigned from public life. He experienced his conversion (*conversio*) to monastic life and, as a simple monk, he spent his happiest years in the monastery working on the exposition of biblical scriptures. But this contemplative tranquillity was short-lived, for in 579 he was called to serve the Church as papal legate (*apocrisarius*) to Constantinople, where he must have learned at least some Greek.[5] He returned to Rome in the middle of the next decade and performed the duties of a deacon while living in his monastic community and writing biblical commentaries. But again he could stay only for a little while at the "tranquil shores of prayer", because he was elected pope in 590. As bishop of Rome Gregory "was tossed about on the seas of secular affairs", yet he found the time for the exposition of the Sacred Scriptures through homilies. Of great significance for the development of Western Christianity was his missionary activity: By sending missionaries to the Frankish and English Churches Gregory established a model of a European Church, no longer confined to the Mediterranean world as the natural milieu of Christendom. In the person and work of Gregory the ideal of ancient Roman traditions and of Christian loyalty became fused together: as the last Roman on Peter's chair he was characterised as consul of God (*consul Dei*). He held office until his death on 12th March 604.[6]

The Bible stands at the very centre of Gregory's activities as monk and as bishop of Rome. In particular the books of the Old Testament are a main source of inspiration for his writings. Gregory's legacy in the interpretation of Scripture comes down to posterity in his commentaries and his homilies: The huge commentary on the Book of Job, the interpretation of some verses from the Song of Songs as well as his 40 Homilies on the Gospel passages from the liturgy, and on the Prophet Ezekiel. The commentary on 1 Kings long attributed to Gregory is now regarded as the work of an Italian medieval abbot. Other exegetical works on the Heptateuch, the Proverbs and on biblical prophets, which are mentioned in a letter of the pope, seem to be lost (*Ep* 12.6 [CCL 140A, 975]).

2. The Role of the Bible in the Non-Exegetical Scriptures of Gregory

Even the works not expressly exegetical in a large proportion of the instances read like a biblical commentary, because they breathe the imagery of the Bible and are imbued with a profound biblical orchestration. In his declining world Gregory found an entire culture in the Bible, since it was for him an inexhaustible source of knowledge and final authority for the committed

---

5 Kessler, Gregor (1995) 158–66; G.J.M. Bartelink, "Pope Gregory the Great's knowledge of Greek", Gregory the Great. A Symposium (1995) 117–36.

6 Regarding historical and biographical dates: E. Caspar, *Geschichte des Papsttums* 2 (Tübingen: Mohr 1933), 306–514; Richards, Consul (1980); R. Gillet, "Grégoire le Grand", DHGE 21 (1986) 1387–1420; Riché, Grégoire (1995); Markus, Gregory (1997).

Christian life. For example, the enormous number of letters written by Gregory during his pontificate dealing with questions of church-administration, pastoral counselling and spiritual advice use the Bible as practical guide for the every-day life of his correspondents.[7]

Biblical scriptures are a "letter of God to his creature" writes Gregory to Theodore, the physician of the Emperor: "What else are the Sacred Scriptures if not a letter of the omnipotent God to his creature?" (*Ep* 5.46 [CCL 140, 339]). If it would be a letter of the Emperor – Gregory assumes – Theodore would not rest until he understood its message. Therefore he should read and meditate each day on the letter written for his salvation by the Emperor of heaven. The collection of the letters shows that Gregory as a pastorally minded man does not look on the Bible from a theoretic point of view: From the Scripture texts he goes immediately to ordinary life.

The importance of the Bible for Gregory is also shown in the *Regula Pastoralis* where the newly elected pope at the beginning of his pontificate draws his ideal of men in secular and in spiritual power: "rector" and "preacher".[8] Their main task consists in ruling over the lives and souls of the faithful ones. In order to get acquainted with this "*ars artium*" of governing the souls it is their first obligation to muse on the "divine laws" (*Rpast* 1.1 [SC 381, 128]; 2.11 [252–56]). The rector or preacher has to make the Bible speak through his words and his life in all the ways it is designed to do, and to make himself a suitable interpreter of its message. Therefore Gregory postulates interpreting the bars in the golden rings of the ark (Exod 25:12–15) that men in wordly or spiritual power should "meditate diligently and every day on the precepts of the sacred word" because the bars shall be put through the four golden rings, which are the four books of the holy Gospels; for it is evidently necessary that they who devote themselves to the office of preaching should never depart from the occupation of sacred reading (*RPast* 2.11 [SC 381, 252–54]).

The last non-exegetical work – in the strict sense of the word – are the four books of the *Dialogorum libri quatuor de miraculis patrum italicorum*, a hagiographical collection of miracle-stories, written by Gregory during the early years of his pontificate. At first sight it seems that the scriptures of the Bible in this work on "the life and the miracles of the Italian fathers" do not play the same role which is granted to them in the other works of Gregory. From an exegetical point of view, the Dialogues seem so different from the rest of the corpus of Gregorian texts that the authenticity of this work has been disputed.[9]

The initial conversation of the author with his dialogue-partner, the deacon Peter, gives the answer to the different structure of this work: there are pedagogical and pastoral reasons which lead the author to a different use of the

---

[7] G. Rapisarda Lo Menzo, "L'Écriture Sainte comme guide de la vie quotidienne dans la correspondance de Grégoire le Grand", Grégoire le Grand (1986) 215–25.

[8] G. Cremascoli, "La Bibbia nella Regola Pastorale di San Gregorio Magno", *Vetera Christianorum* 6 (1969) 47–70; B. Judic, "La Bible miroir des pasteurs dans la *Règle pastorale* de Grégoire le Grand", BTT 2 (1985) 455–73.

[9] F. Clark, *The Pseudo-Gregorian Dialogues* (Studies in the History of Christian Thought 37.38; Leiden: Brill 1987); against the theories of Clark: P. Meyvaert, "The enigma of Gregory the Great's Dialogues. A response to Francis Clark", *JEH* 39 (1988) 335–81; A. De Vogüé, "Les Dialogues, Œuvre authentique et publiée de Grégoire lui-même", *Gregorio Magno e il suo tempo* (SEAug 34; Roma: Institutum Patristicum Augustinianum 1991) 27–40.

Bible. Gregory states that there are some people more inspired by examples of holy lives than by preaching the Scriptures (*Dial* 1, prol. 9 [SC 260, 16]). Instead of exposing biblical passages in his Dialogues Gregory interprets the life and deeds of contemporary holy men. He regards the miracles of his days as the continuation of the history of salvation and applies the same exegetical method to these miracle-stories as in his biblical works. The same God who spoke and acted in the two Testaments of the Bible is now at work in the lives of these Italian saints of the sixth century. Therefore, telling the life of a saint of this world means a more popular kind of pastoral exegesis for those Christians not able to read and meditate on the Bible.

Despite the non-biblical contents in the legendary work of the Dialogues again the Bible and especially personalities from the Old Testament play a central role. Biblical patterns are the key for the correct understanding of the structure of the miracle-stories.[10] Gregory tells the remarkable stories of holy men performing miracles according to biblical concepts. The heroes of the Dialogues are shaped according to the prototypes of biblical personalities: Benedict, the central figure of the second book, acts like Moses, Elisha, Elijah and David (*Dial* 2. 8. 8 [SC 260, 164–66]). In the view of Gregory the secular world has become an allegory which has to be interpreted like the Holy Scriptures. The Dialogues adapt in a narrative form the exegetical method known in the explicit biblical writings and therefore can be regarded as an authentic work of Gregory.

3. Gregory's Exegetical Work

The same pastoral intention as in the Dialogues can be found in Gregory's biblical work of the forty *Homiliae in Evangelia* where also examples play an important role. This collection of sermons on New Testament passages of the liturgical readings is an attempt at a popular interpretation of the Gospels during the eucharistic celebration. The pope's homiletic interpretation of these New Testament passages are full of Old Testament quotations and allusions.[11] As in the view of Gregory both the Old and the New Testament reflect the one mystery of the salvation in Christ and they elucidate each other (*HEv* 1. 11. 5 [FontC 28. 1, 188–90]; 2. 25. 3 [FontC 28. 2, 450–52]). Therefore words and examples from the Old Testament enrich and deepen the understanding of the Gospel. The Bible as a whole and in particular the Old Testament with its great figures of faith is the basis of Gregory's theological approach to his moral teaching and his view of the world. The nearly 300 Old Testament quotations in Gregory's sermons on the Gospel accomplish different functions with-

---

[10] S. C. Kessler, "Das Rätsel der Dialoge Gregors des Großen: Fälschung oder Bearbeitung?", *ThPh* 65 (1990) 566–78; 576 f.

[11] L. Giordano, "L'antico testamento nelle Omelie sui Vangeli di Gregorio Magno", Annali di storia dell'esegesi 2 (1985) 257–62; idem, "La metaphora nelle Omelie sui Vangeli di Gregorio Magno", Annali di storia dell'esegesi 8 (1991) 599–613.

in his homiletic interpretation: The Vulgate version of Ps 67:5 serves as testimony for the resurrection of Christ after the fall of the passion: "*Iter facite ei, qui ascendit super occasum*" (*HEv* 1.17.2 [FontC 28.1, 268]). Beyond the proof of the truth of the Gospel the allegorical interpretation of the Old Testament passages leads to the spiritual understanding of the New Testament (*HEv* 1.17.8–12 [FontC 28.1, 278–88]). Eventually the moral interpretation of the Gospel is often based on events or examples from the Old Testament. In this sense Bileam (Num 23:10) serves as example for the moral interpretation of Luke 8:8 (*HEv* 1.15.2 [FontC 28.1, 244]). The diversity of the Old Testament is important for Gregory's biblical and exegetical practice interpreting Scripture with the help of Scripture.

The pope's first exegetical work in the proper sense of the word on the Old Testament which has come down to our times is a commentary on the book of Job: *Moralia in Iob.* This enormous work containing 35 books is a verse-by-verse exegesis of the book of Job and is the revision of biblical deliberations originally delivered as monastic lectures to an audience of like-minded friends during Gregory's time as papal representative at the court of Constantinople between 579–585/6. In the years after his return to Rome, but before his election to the papacy, Gregory was occupied with rearranging these oral lectures as a biblical commentary in book-form.[12] What interested Gregory in expounding the book of Job was what it says about the committed Christian life: Conversion, culminating in the life of contemplation, is the objective of his understanding of the Bible. The main theme of Gregory's commentary on Job is given through the discussion of the ordeals suffered by the righteous. The problem of evil and suffering is conveyed at the literal level of the book of Job, and the pope – despite lengthy disgressions – always returns to this crucial quest. The whole commentary on the biblical book of Job has the intention to give through the exegetical explanations a full compendium of theology as Gregory conceived it. The *Moralia* is the attempt to be *a Christian encyclopedia not in a logical but in a biblical form.*

The programmatic letter of dedication of the *Moralia* to his friend Leander of Sevilla is one of the most important sources for the understanding of Gregory's exegetical method since it gives the theoretic outline of his way of dealing with the Scriptures and of his concept of exegesis. The basis of all exegesis for Gregory lies in the classical distinction of different senses that are hidden in the Sacred Scriptures by divine providence. Therefore all Scripture according to Gregory has to be interpreted three-fold (*Mor*, ep. dedic. 3 [CCL 143, 4]).[13] This hermeneutical concept of biblical texts with different senses is based on the fundamental distinction between 'letter' and 'spirit' which is to be found in the Bible itself and was diversified over the centuries of biblical interpretation. Gregory proves to be a loyal heir to this history of exegesis.

The interpreter's main task according to Gregory consists in creating an equilibrium while exposing the text between the outward 'letter' and the 'inner'

---

[12] *Ep* 1.41 (CCL 140, 49) shows that the revision of the *Moralia* must have been completed by 591 whereas the final publication took until 595 (*Ep* 5.53; CCL 140, 348).

[13] G. Penco, "La dottrina dei sensi spirituali in S. Gregorio", *Ben.* 17 (1970) 170–201.

spirit.[14] The plan for the commentary on Job perfectly comprises the idea of a correct balance between the inward and the outward in exegesis, as it is said about Job who in all his external ordeals is an example of a balanced and even tempered mood (*constantia mentis*). Gregory recognizes the need to keep an equilibrium between straining for an inward and spiritual interpretation, on the one hand, and forcing a historical interpretation of the letter, on the other. There is always a weighing of the reading of the biblical text between literalness and allegorical mysticism.

From the tradition of Christian exegesis – especially Origen – Gregory inherited the three-fold form of exegesis: Every page of the Bible reflects three senses which the exegete has to recognize and to explain (*tripliciter indagamus*). According to this exegetical triad the first step in dealing with the Scriptures is the *literal* understanding of the text (*verba historiae*). Thereafter the same passage should be interpreted in its *allegorical* meaning (*allegoriarum sensus*), and then at a third level the text should be applied to the moral practice of a Christian life (*Mor*, ep. dedic. 1 [CCL 143, 2]). Gregory compares this way of exegesis metaphorically with the construction of a mental edifice as a spiritual stronghold:

> One should know, that we shall run quickly through some passages with a historical exposition; some we shall examine by means of allegory for their typical sense; others again we shall discuss by means of allegory only for their moral bearing; some, finally, we shall investigate thoroughly in all three ways. In the first place we lay the foundations of the history; then we raise in spirit a mental edifice as a stronghold of faith by the typical meaning, and finally through the decoration of the moral interpretation we put, as it were by paint, colour on the building (*Mor*, ep. dedic. 3 [CCL 143, 4]).

This outline in theory of the exposition of Job makes clear that according to the Gregorian approach to the Bible there are always three different senses in each passage. Gregory makes a distinction between a literal or historical sense, and an allegorical sense, which may be either moral or typical. The literal interpretation of the historical facts is the undisputed basis of all exegesis.[15] Gregory takes a special concern for the letter of Scripture and for history: "Who sometimes ignores accepting the words of the history according to the letter, hides himself from the light of truth" (*Mor*, ep. dedic. 4 [CCL 143, 5]). Upon the historical facts of the text the interpreter has to construct the spiritual edifice as a stronghold of faith by typological allegorization. The allegory with its spiritual interpretation finally leads to the goal of all exegesis: contemplative ascent and Christian morality. The exploration and explanation of these three senses form the theoretical structure of Gregory's exegesis.[16]

But this order of exegesis (*ordo exegeticus*) with the historical, allegorical and moral-mystical interpretation exists only in the theory of the introductory parts of the *Moralia*. The exegetical practice of Gregory looks very different:

---

[14] P. Aubin, "Intériorité et extériorité dans les Moralia in Job de saint Grégoire le Grand", *RSR* 62 (1974) 117–66.

[15] P. Catry, "Epreuves du juste et mystère de Dieu. Le commentaire littéral du Livre du Job par saint Grégoire le Grand", *REAug* 18 (1972) 124–44 = idem, *Paroles de Dieu, amour et Esprit-Saint chez saint Grégoire le Grand* (Vie Monastique 17; Bégrolles en Mauge 1984) 38–58.

[16] *Mor* 3.27.56 (CCL 143, 150); 6.5.6 (CCL 143, 288).

beginning already with the fourth book of the *Moralia* the original triad of senses is no more recognizable.[17] Only a few passages of his Bible commentaries show that the author applies the proposal in the letter of dedication. Despite his emphasis on the literal understanding as basis in his *Moralia* Gregory passes quickly over the literal-historical sense and goes immediately to the allegorical and mystical interpretation. Starting with book five of the *Moralia* Gregory comments on the biblical text of Job in a solely allegorical and mystical way. Exegesis for Gregory in practice turns out to be merely two-fold, despite his strong emphasis of three senses. The pope follows the Pauline pattern of *littera* and *spiritus* (2 Cor 3:6).[18] The Bible has two aspects: on the one hand, the literal and historical meaning which according to Gregory has to be the beginning and the foundation of all exegetical investigation and, on the other hand, the spiritual sense whose discovery is the proper aim of all work with the Bible. This, indeed, is the fundamental dichotomy and the distinction variously stated in Gregory's exegetical works between carnal and spiritual, literal and allegorical, historical and typical, outer and inner understanding.

Allegorical interpretation of the biblical texts for Gregory becomes a synonym for spiritual exegesis under a dual aspect: biblical typology and moral tropology. It is impossible to discern these two stages of Gregory's spiritual interpretation. In his sight they melt into the one spiritual sense that should lead towards the morality of a Christian life and the heights of contemplation. Allegory in the view of Gregory as a pastorally minded churchman implicitly means a moral interpretation aiming at the practice of faith.

Gregory explains the book of Job because in the life and teachings of this biblical figure he discovers an inspiring example of the *ordo praedicatorum*. In addition to this he feels a close relationship and a very personal identification with the enduring righteous one of the Bible. Through his own sufferings Gregory believes he understands Job better than others: "*Et fortasse hoc divinae providentiae consilium fuit, ut percussum Iob percussus exponerem, et flagellati mentem melius per flagella sentirem*" (*Mor*, ep. dedic. 5 [CCL 143, 6]). In his exegesis Job is stylized as the ideal man who bears all the sufferings God sends (*flagella Dei*) and, despite the vicissitudes of life, is always calm and steadfast in mind (*constantia mentis*). One should learn to suffer adversity and prosperity as Job did, both loving and fearing God in the ups and downs of life.[19] The suffering righteous one in the *Moralia* is interpreted at first as a typos of Jesus Christ who also had to bear tribulations. Since Christ is head and body of the Church Job can also signify the community of the Church (*Mor* 1.24.33 [CCL 143, 43]).

The twenty-two *Homiliae in Ezechielem Prophetam* are not a full commentary to the biblical book although Gregory intended to give a full interpreta-

---

[17] The last lines of *Mor* 3.37.70 (CCL 143, 157) announce that the threefold exegesis is coming to an end.

[18] For Gregory's use of the vers, cf. e.g. *Mor* 11.16.25 (CCL 143A, 601); 18.39.60 (CCL 143A, 926); *In Cant* 4 (CCL 144, 5).

[19] C. E. Straw, "'Adversitas' et 'Prosperitas': une illustration du motif structurel de la complémentarité", Grégoire le Grand. Colloques (1986) 277–88.

tion similar to his exegesis of Job. These homilies on the prophet explain the call narrative and the initial vision of God of the first chapters (Ezek 1:1–4:3 = book 1). The state of siege of the city of Rome through the Langobards between 593/94 caused an interruption of these homiletic explanations. But the spiritually interested audience of clerics and monks encouraged Gregory to resume his exegesis of Ezekiel. Despite the political difficulites he started again with his homilies – most probably delivered at the matins-services in the Basilica of the Lateran. For the last decade of homilies he chose the concluding vision of the new temple (Ezek 40–48 = book 2). The text of Ezekiel who lived in exile and witnessed the destruction of Jerusalem and the temple described for Gregory and his audience the actual political situation they had to go through. As the people of Israel was without hope of return from exile in the days of Ezekiel Gregory sees the condition of Rome as hopeless. The pope identifies himself and his task with the situation and the role of prophet: As Ezekiel was the watchman for Israel (Ezek 3:17) Gregory sees himself now as the guardian (*speculator*) of Rome and of the Church (*HEz* 1.11.4–6 [CCL 142, 170–72]). This way of personal identification with the biblical figures is the reason for his very personal approach in the exegetical writings on Holy Scripture.[20] Gregory develops a special exegetical technique to identify with the biblical personalities, preferably taken from the Old Testament, and to discover in them models for his ascetic ideal of a monastic and pastoral life, living and working in the world and at the same time striving for the heights of contemplation.[21]

It seems that the difficulties in understanding Ezekiel and the darkness of his visions were of special interest to Gregory as exegetical preacher and author. He describes the visions as "*magnis obscuritatibus clausum*" (*HEz* 1.9.1 [CCL 142, 123]) and the architecture of the new temple in the final vision as so complicated and covered by impenetrable fog that intellectual understanding can hardly recognize anything in the vision (*HEz* 2, praef. [CCL 142, 205]). The "*obscuritas*" of the Bible is another characteristic sign of Gregory's theology of Scripture. Gregory overcomes the hidden aspects of the Bible through personal identification with the figures of the text. Through the technique of spiritual interpretation he surmounts the difficulties of understanding the text.

The enigmatic visions of Ezekiel give to the author the chance to show that the literal meaning of the Bible only exists for the sake of a higher spiritual interpretation. Not all parts of Scripture have a literal meaning. The dimensions of the temple-building described in Ezek 41:1 for example have according to Gregory no lasting significance. He determines that it is impossible that the architecture could have any durability according to a literal understanding: "*iux-*

---

[20] D. Wyrwa, "Der persönliche Zugang in der Bibelauslegung Gregors des Großen", *Sola Scriptura. Das reformatorische Schriftprinzip in der säkularen Welt*, (ed. H. H. Schmid / J. Mehlhausen; Gütersloh 1991) 262–78.

[21] Old Testament figures as models of Christian life in the *HEz*: Joseph in Egypt (*HEz* 2.9.19 [CCL 142, 373 f]); Moses (*HEz* 1.7.11–13 [CCL 142, 90 f]); 2.3.21 [CCL 142, 252–54]); Aaron (*HEz* 1.7.12 [CCL 142, 91]); Samuel (*HEz* 1.7.12 [CCL 142, 91]); Elijah (*HEz* 2.2.3 [CCL 142, 226 f]); David (*HEz* 1.7.14 [CCL 142, 92]); Job (*HEz* 1.9.14 f [CCL 142, 130 f] 2.7.20 [CCL 142, 332–34]).

ta litteram accipi nullatenus potest" (*HEz* 2.1.3 [CCL 142, 208]). There is, Gregory says, evidence for this in the biblical text itself: Ezekiel (Ezek 40:2) speaks of a "*quasi aedificium*". The new temple is only described "as if" it were a building and therefore the text must be interpreted in an allegorical sense. Since the origin of the Bible lies in God there can be no contradiction in the Holy Scriptures and therefore this passage must be understood and interpreted in a spiritual way. Apparent contradictions result in the wrong understanding of the Scriptures. It is the task of the exegete to discern the two sides of Scripture: inside and outside. For "the book of the Holy Scripture is written allegorically inside and historically outside. Inside for spiritual understanding, outside in the simple literal sense" (*HEz* 1.9.30 [CCL 142, 139]; cf. Hieronymus, *In Ezechielem* 1.29 [CCL 75, 31]).

The pattern of "exterior words" and "interior insight" is also the *Leitmotiv* of Gregory's interpretation of the Song of Songs. Most probably the *Expositio in Canticis Canticorum* belongs to the series of homiletic interpretations of Old Testament scriptures in the first half of Gregory's pontificate. The interpretation shows his growing interest in the world of contemplation since the text of the Song of Songs was traditionally regarded as a book on contemplation. After a lengthy introduction with exegetical remarks he interprets the biblical text only up to Cant 1:8 but it seems that this fragment is the complete text because everything is said.[22] In Jewish exegesis, as well as in the interpretation of the Early Church, this biblical book of love-songs is regarded as a text which has no significance in its literal meaning but only an allegorical one. In the Song of Songs God descends to the language of human love in order to inflame and to exalt man to the divine love (*In Cant* 3 [CCL 144, 4]). Therefore allegorical interpretation is the appropriate and only way to explain these verses of the Bible. Gregory compares the technique of allegory to a fitting mechanism or pulley (*quandam machinam*) which raises up the souls who are far from God through sin (*In Cant* 2 [CCL 144, 3]). The love-relationship of the Song of Songs describes – according to Gregory who follows in this the exegetical tradition of Origen – the love of Christ for his Church or for the single soul of a faithful Christian. Perfection of the Church and of the single soul is the aim of the exegesis of the Song of Songs. The prevailing ecclesiological dimension of Gregory's exegesis finds its expression in the interpretation of the passage where the king introduces the bride into his chamber. For Gregory this "*cubiculum*" signifies the Church which is similar to a royal house where one enters through faith (*In Cant* 26 [CCL 144, 27 f]).

The authenticity of the six books *In Librum Primum Regum* as the last exegetical work traditionally attributed Gregory was disputed for a long time. Recent research by A. de Vogüé led to the assumption that the commentary on I Kings, which has been generally regarded as a work of Gregory, was in fact composed by a twelfth-century abbot, Peter of Cava-Venosa.[23] Yet it seems

---

[22] Müller, Hohelied (1991) 234.

[23] A. de Vogüé, "L'auteur du Commentaire des Rois attribué à Grégoire: un moine de Cava?", *RBén* 106 (1996) 319–31; idem, *Commentaire sur le Premier Livre des Rois* (SC 432; Paris 1998) 9–28; 9 f.

that authentic material from Gregory was used because there are unmistakably Gregorian traits.[24] The work is a commentary on the biblical text of 1 Samuel up to the anointing of David as king (1 Sam 1:1–16:13). In contrast to the authentic writings the commentary *In Primum Regum* extends the classical exegetical theory of three senses into "*multipliciter exposita*" (*In I Rg*, prologus 3.5 [CCL 144, 51; SC 351, 150]). Similar to the *Moralia in Job*, in most cases a two-fold spiritual interpretation to each passage is given: typological and moral or merely spiritual. According to the typological sense Samuel's father Elkana (1 Sam 1:1 f) represents Christ and his two wives represent the Church (Hannah) and the Synagogue (Pennena). In the moral reading of the same passage Elkana stands for the man who has rejected the world and his wives signify the life of contemplation and action (*In I Rg* 1.1–8 [CCL 144, 55–60; SC 162–84]). It is also important for the interpreter of the Sacred Scriptures to avoid misinterpretations, such as the Jews and the heretics fall into by not reading the words before them correctly.[25] The prophet Habakkuk, for example, says according to the Vulgate-version: "I shall rejoice in Jesus my God" (Hab 3:18: *In I Rg* 1.88 [CCL 144, 104; SC 351, 348]). Here according to the exegesis of *In Primum Regum* Jesus is explicitly called God. But the Jews await a saviour whom they do not believe to be God. This is at least in part because their exegesis is confined to the literal sense and they do not see spiritual truths. In this biblical commentary on the Book of Kings the Church and its structure are more explicitly in focus, especially in its moral interpretation, whereas Gregory in his authentic commentaries mainly dealt with themes like the priesthood and monasticism.

4. Conclusion

The exegesis of Gregory the Great at the dawn of the Middle Ages belongs in the main stream of the traditional Christian Bible-interpretation handed down by the fathers of the Church. In the view of Gregory there is an inseparable unity between the two testaments of the Bible. Therefore according to the traditional concept of the "*concordantia testamentorum*" each passage of the Old Testament can be interpreted in a New Testament sense. Gregory points out that under the letter of the Old Testament the New Testament is hidden through allegory: "*in Testamenti veteris littera Testamentum novum latuit per allegoriam*" (*HEz* 1.6.12 [CCL 142, 73]). The unity of the Bible as a whole provides the reason for the considerable Old Testament orchestration of all the works of this monk and bishop of Rome. Gregory expounds his theory of the essential unity of the Bible in the exegesis of Ezekiel's vision of the wheel in

[24] F. Clark, "Authorship of the commentary 'In 1 Regum': Implications of A. de Vogüé's discovery", *RBén* 108 (1998) 61–79; 69 f.

[25] According to Gregory the Jews merely understand the Bible in letter, the Christian readers of the Bible understand it by the lifegiving spirit (*Mor* 18.39.60 [CCL 143 A, 927]). Regarding the hermenutical consequences cf. R. A. Markus, "The Jew as a hermeneutic device: The inner life of a Gregorian topos", Gregory the Great. A Symposion (1995) 1–15.

the wheel (Ezek 1:15f). The two wheels represent the two testaments of the Bible. The Old Testament is the "prophecy" of the New Testament and the New Testament is the "exposition" of the Old Testament (*HEz* 1.6.15 [CCL 142, 76]). The aim of the Bible as a whole rests in the proclamation of Christ. The Old Testament announces Christ who is to be born as a man whereas the New Testament tells about Jesus who is to come at the end of time (*HEz* 2.4.14 [CCL 142, 268]). Besides the christological interpretation especially of Old Testament passages Gregory develops a second branch of an ecclesiological reading in accordance with his theory that "Christ and the Church are one person".[26] Just as every person and every event of the Old Testament can be interpreted as a typos of Christ, in the same way the same things can be understood as a symbol of the Church. *The Church is the predominant hermeneutical place for reading and interpreting the scriptures of the Bible.*

Gregory also has a dynamic concept of Scripture. In his sight the Bible has different grades or levels according to the mental and spiritual capacity of the reader or hearer of the word. The wheels of God's throne seen by Ezekiel in his vision are described as touching the ground and leading upwards at the same time (Ezek 1:21). Correspondingly the Bible gives simple words to those on the ground of an active life and leads with the same words to the heights of contemplation those who are spiritually mature (*HEz* 1.7.16 [CCL 142, 93]). This dynamic understanding of the word of God finds in Gregory its expression in the idea of a growing understanding of the Bible: "*divina eloquia cum legente crescunt*".[27] Reading the divine Scriptures leads into a process of spiritual growth which is always appropriate to the situation of the reader.[28] The Scripture feeds the life of the spirit at every level. It accomodates itself to the capacitiy of the intellect seeking to understand it: "You have progressed to the active life, it walks with you. You have arrived to an unchanging constancy of spirit, it stands with you. You have come by God's grace to the contemplative life, it flies with you" (*HEz* 1.7.16 [CCL 142, 93]). The Scriptures contain riches to exercise the learned and to encourage the weak; they are at the same time "a deep and a shallow river, where a lamb can walk and an elephant swim" (*Mor*, ep. dedic. 4 [CCL 143, 6]).

Exegesis for Gregory always means an actualisation and an identifying *lecture existentielle* of the divine words.[29] Interpreting the Bible for him is far more than a mere technical application of the theory of different senses. The place to read and to interpret the Sacred Scriptures is the Church. Only there does the word of God come to its fulfilment. At the end of the age of Antiquity

---

[26] M. Doucet, "'Christus et ecclesia est una persona'. Note sur un principe d'exégèse spirituelle chez saint Grégoire le Grand", in: *Collectanea Cisterciensia* 46 (1984) 37–58.

[27] *HEz* 1.7.8 (CCL 142, 87); cf. *Moralia in Iob* 20.1.1 (CCL 143A, 1003) and John Cassian, *Conlationes* 14.11 (CSEL 13, 411).

[28] P. C. Bori, "Circolarità e sviluppo nell'interpretazione spirituale: 'Divina eloquia cum legente crescunt'", Annali di storia dell'esegesi 3 (1986) 263–74.

[29] B. Studer, "Die patristische Exegese, eine Aktualisierung der Heiligen Schrift. Zur hermeneutischen Problematik der frühchristlichen Bibelauslegungen", *Mysterium Caritatis. Studien zur Exegese und Trinitätstheologie in der Alten Kirche* (Studia Anselmiana 127; Roma: Pontificio Ateneo S. Anselmo 1999) 97–127.

the first pope with a monastic background develops an original way of interpreting the Bible which was to have a major influence on the exegesis of the following centuries that Gregory rightly can be called "father of medieval Bible-exegesis".[30] By going back to the Origenist tradition he modified the Augustinian way of dealing with the Bible and as such Gregory the Great proves to be a figure both of tradition and transition in Church exegesis.

[30] H. Graf Reventlow, *Epochen der Bibelauslegung* 2 (München: Beck 1994) 105–114; 114.

Chapter Twenty-seven

The Institutional Framework of Christian Exegesis in the Middle Ages*

By Ulrich Köpf, Tübingen

General sources: *Sacrorum conciliorum nova et amplissima collectio* 1–53 (ed. J. D. Mansi; Firenze 1759–1827; repr.; quoted: Mansi); *Conciliorum Oecumenicorum Decreta* (ed. J. Alberigo / J. A. Dossetti / P.-P. Joannou / C. Leonardi / P. Prodi; Bologna ³1973; quoted: COD).

General literature: F. Stegmüller, *Repertorium biblicum medii aevi* 1–9 (Madrid 1940–1977).

Special abbreviations:

Canivez	=	*Statuta capitulorum gen. Ordinis Cisterciensis* (see Sect. 2, Sources);
COD	=	*Conciliorum Oecumenicorum Decreta* (see above and general Abbreviations);
CUP	=	*Chartularium Universitatis Parisiensis* (see Sect. 3, Sources);
Fournier	=	*Les statuts et privilèges des universités françaises* (see Sect. 3, Sources)
Mansi	=	*Sacrorum conciliorum ... collectio* (see above);
Opuscula	=	*Die Opuscula des hl. Franziskus von Assisi* (see Sect. 3, Sources);
RB	=	*Regula Benedicti* (see Sect. 2, Sources);
Statuta antiqua	=	*Statuta antiqua Universitatis Oxoniensis* (see Sect. 3, Sources).

1. Preliminary Notes

In the history of medieval learning and education and therefore in the history of medieval theology, too, we have to distinguish two periods.

A comparatively great variety of Christian educational institutions existed before 1200. Ecclesiastical synods and authorities – like responsible sovereigns – made repeated efforts to realize certain aims and conceptions of education. Especially Charlemagne and his son Louis the Pious are distinguished by reformatory measures in the fields of education and ecclesiastical life. But reality for the most part remained behind such postulates and programs. Most of all, there was lacking a comprehensive concept and an effective attempt to unify the different forms and institutions of higher education and scholarly work. From late Antiquity until the end of the twelfth century, the most important institutions of theological scholarship and erudition were on the one hand the monastery and on the other hand the school for the secular clergy, both institutions being equipped with *scriptoria* and libraries. A third, intermediate position between monastery and school for the clergy was occupied by the chapters of regular canons under the rule of St. Augustine, which had flourished from

* Dedicated to the memory of my daughter, stud. theol. et phil. Eva Köpf, born 19 May 1973, died 1 February 1995.

the second half of the eleventh century. After the beginning of the twelfth century, this position was occupied by the Premonstratensian canons as well. Concerning their form of life, these communities displayed similarities with monastic life. However, due to their pastoral tasks they were more closely associated with the secular clergy and its conception of education.[1] They did not create an independent third kind of theology. We will therefore confine our discussion on the following pages to the two main institutions of education and scholarship. The development of the monastery and the school for the secular clergy culminated in the twelfth century – an age of outstanding cultural variety. Two different types of theology came to existence in these institutions: *monastic theology* and *scholastic theology*.

At the transition from the twelfth to the thirteenth century, a turning point in the history of the occidental institutions of education and in the history of Christian scholarship was initiated by the formation of the universities at Paris and Oxford, the two first full universities containing a theological faculty. These universities were not created by a foundation act. On the contrary, they came into existence by a fusion of diverse already existing schools and teachers (*magistri*). These newly created institutions were acknowledged and endowed with privileges by ecclesiastical and secular authories. Especially the university of Paris in its organization and its statutes became the most important model for subsequent foundations of universities all over Europe by the pope or the emperor, by bishops, cities or sovereigns.

This basic change of the institutional framework had drastic consequences for instruction and erudition in all fields:

1. It caused the development of unified teaching and work methods in all different disciplines.
2. It promoted a concentration of capacities and means which led to an increasing success and a spreading of erudition.
3. At the same time, it caused a certain monotony of methods and results.

A relatively homogeneous practice in Western theology can therefore be observed from the beginnings of Paris university until the humanism of the fifteenth century in spite of all the differences that constituted and divided philosophical and theological schools at the same time. Exposed to the competition with the faculties of theology, the function of the traditional educational institutions for the clergy was reduced to the task of providing the clergy with elementary knowledge. The importance of the old monasteries as institutions of theological learning and erudition was reduced since the thirteenth century. Then, Benedictines as well as Cistercians went to the universities, where they obtained their own chairs and founded colleges for their students. However, in the older monastic communities in the fourteenth century the interest in erudition slackened. In 1335, the Cistercian pope Benedict XII had to tighten up the instructions for the study of theology by Benedictines and Cistercians.[2]

---

[1] Cf. e.g. Anselm of Havelberg, *Epistola ad Ecbertum abbatem Huysborgensem contra eos qui importune contendunt, monasticum ordinem digniorem esse in Ecclesia quam canonicum* (PL 188, 1119–40).

[2] Canivez 3, 410–36.

Only in the reformatory thought of the fifteenth century and in humanism did the studies of the monks revive.

2. Theological Education before the Universities

Sources: Regula Benedicti (*Benedicti Regula*, ed. R. Hanslik; CSEL 75; Wien 1960; *La règle de saint Benoît*, ed. A. de Vogüé / J. Neufville; SC 181–183; Paris 1972; quoted: RB); *Statuta capitulorum generalium Ordinis Cisterciensis ab anno 1116 ad annum 1786* 1–8 (ed. J.-M. Canivez; BRHE 9–14B; Leuven 1933–1941; quoted: Canivez).

Literature: H. Graham, *The Early Irish Monastic Schools* (Dublin 1923); G. Paré / A. Brunet / P. Tremblay, *La Renaissance du XIIe siècle. Les écoles et l'enseignement* (Publications de l'Institut d'études médiévales d'Ottawa 3; Paris / Ottawa 1933); Ph. Delhaye, "L'organisation scolaire au XIIe siècle", Traditio 5 (1947) 211–68 (repr. in: idem, *Enseignement et morale au XIIe siècle*, Fribourg / Paris 1988, 1–58); J. de Ghellinck, *Le mouvement théologique du XIIe siècle* (Bruges ²1948; repr. Bruxelles 1969); J. Leclercq, *L'amour des lettres et le désir de Dieu. Initiation aux auteurs monastiques du moyen âge* (Paris 1957); *Los monjes y los estudios* (Poblet 1963); F. Weissengruber, "Monastische Profanbildung in der Zeit von Augustinus bis Benedikt", RÖHM 10 (1966/67) 12–42, slightly modified repr. in: *Mönchtum und Gesellschaft im Frühmittelalter* (ed. F. Prinz; WdF 312; Darmstadt 1976) 386–429; D. Illmer, *Formen der Erziehung und Wissensvermittlung im frühen Mittelalter. Quellenstudien zur Frage der Kontinuität des abendländischen Erziehungswesens* (MBM 7; München 1971); *La scuola nell'occidente latino dell'alto medioevo*, I–II (Settimane di studio del Centro Italiano di Studi sull'alto medioevo 19,1–2; Spoleto 1972); P. Riché, *Les écoles et l'enseignement dans l'Occident chrétien de la fin du Ve siècle au milieu du XIe siècle* (Paris 1979); idem, *Instruction et vie religieuse dans le Haut Moyen Âge* (London 1981); *Renaissance and Renewal in the Twelfth Century* (ed. R. L. Benson / G. Constable; Cambridge, MA 1982); *Schulen und Studium im sozialen Wandel des hohen und späten Mittelalters* (ed. J. Fried; Vorträge und Forschungen 30; Sigmaringen 1986); J. J. Contreni, *Carolingian Learning, Masters and Manuscripts* (London 1992); U. Köpf, "Monastische Theologie im 15. Jahrhundert", Rottenburger Jahrbuch für Kirchengeschichte 11 (1992) 117–35; idem, "Monastische und scholastische Theologie", in: *Bernhard von Clairvaux und der Beginn der Moderne* (ed. D. R. Bauer / G. Fuchs; Innsbruck / Wien 1996) 96–135.

2.1. Monastic Erudition

2.1.1. The Variety of Early Medieval Monasticism

In the early Middle Ages, monasteries were the most important site of religious and theological education and scholarship. Early Christianity had not created any new, specifically Christian institution of education. On the contrary, the Christians attended the existing schools and finally came to occupy the antique institutions of learning. It was in monastic communities that the first Christian schools came into existence. Spiritual life in a religion with a Holy Scripture needs alphabetization to a high degree. Even if education may have been based extensively on oral teaching and on learning by heart, the teachers needed at least a minimum of higher education.

Unlike Eastern monasticism, which – formed by the Regulae of St. Basil of Caesarea – had a relatively uniform character, Western monasticism of the early Middle Ages presents a great variety of forms of life. The most important types are (1) Irish monasticism which was distinguished by an especially strict asceticism. Irish monasticism influenced the continent directly by its missionary activities, which were inspired by the idea of the ascetic *peregrinatio*, and indirectly via the Anglo-Saxon mission. This way, Irish monasticism became blended with the continental forms of monastic life (Irish-Frankish monasticism). In the late Carolingian age, it was completely swept away by (2) Benedictine monasticism. Refering to older traditions and utilizing the *Regula Magistri*, St. Benedict of Nursia had written a rule for coenobites. St. Benedict's rule was established as obligatory for the Frankish kingdom by the legislation of Charlemagne and Louis the Pious, and by cooperation of Benedict of Aniane. That way, St. Benedict's rule became the prevailing monastic rule in the Occident for four centuries. In addition to that, there existed (3) the model of the clerical monastery which was initially established by bishop Eusebius of Vercelli and spread in North Africa by Augustine. The *Regula Augustini* offered an alternative to the monastic tradition which was used in the vehemently reinforced efforts to establish a *vita canonica* in communities of clergymen during the eleventh century.

2.1.2. Concept and Reality of Monastic Education

The combination of educational influence and monastic life is an old monastic notion.[3] Already St. Basil of Caesarea called the monastery "the school of the commandments of God".[4] John Cassian, who made crucial impulses from Eastern monasticism available to the Occident, speaks repeatedly about the *scolae* of the *coenobia*.[5] Referring to this old monastic tradition, the introduction to the *Regula Magistri* ends with the request for a *schola* for the service of the Lord.[6] This request was taken over literally by St. Benedict.[7] The idea of the *schola*, however, can be found in Irish monasticism as well: e. g. it is reported that St. Fintan (Munnu) had attended the school of St. Columba (Columkille).[8]

In older scientific literature, *schola* for a long time was translated simply by "school" and was in this way connected with corresponding modern conceptions, or at least associated with anachronistic medieval forms of teaching. Modern research, however, has demonstrated that the idea of a well organized form of education in monasteries modernizes and actualizes in an incongruous

---

[3] Cf. B. Steidle, "Dominici schola servitii. Zum Verständnis des Prologes der Regel St. Benedikts", in: idem, *Beiträge zum alten Mönchtum und zur Benediktusregel* (ed. U. Engelmann; Sigmaringen 1986) 206–15.

[4] *Reg. fus. tract.* 2.1 (PG 31, 908 C): τὸ διδασκαλεῖον τῶν ἐντολῶν τοῦ θεοῦ.

[5] *Conlationes* 3.1.2; 18.16.15; 19.2.4; 19.11.1 (CSEL 12; SC 42. 54. 64).

[6] *Regula Magistri*, Thema (*La règle du maître* 1; ed. A. de Vogüé; SC 105; Paris 1964, 326).

[7] RB Prol. 45: *Constituenda est ergo nobis dominici scola servitii.*

[8] *Vita prior S. Fintani* 5 (*Vitae Sanctorum Hiberniae*, ed. W. W. Heist; Subsidia Hagiographica 28; Brüssel 1965, 199): *venit Fintanus ad scolam sancti Columbe Kylle [...] et ibi legit apud Collumbam divinam scripturam.* Another version is given by Ch. Plummer, *Vitae Sanctorum Hiberniae* 2 (Oxford 1910) 228: *venit beatus Munnu ad scolam sancti Columbe, qui tunc erat magister in loco qui dicitur scotice Ceall Mor Dhithraimh [...]. Et ibi sanctus Munnu legit apud virum sapientem Columbam.* Cf. also *Vita S. Dagaei* c. 5 (Heist 390). – Cf. A. Lorcin, "La vie scolaire dans les monastères d'Irlande aux Ve–VIIe siècles", *RMAL* 1 (1945) 221–36.

way what in monastic literature is meant by *schola*.[9] *Schola* in the meaning applied to this term in late Antiquity and the early Middle Ages does not refer to a school which is organized in classes and formed by a curriculum. Instead, it refers to a notion that has much in common with *universitas* which later on became so important: an association of persons, who lived together in a monastic or other kind of community which was at the same time the site of their working. In that sense, already Tertullian can call the church *schola Christi*.[10] *Schola* is the term for a community with distinctive duties like the *schola* of the *notarii*, or of the *defensores ecclesiae* or, especially well known, the *schola cantorum*. Apart from that, *schola* describes the form of life of all members of a community of this kind. Applied to monasticism, it means the life and learning, above all the practice of the discipline in the monastic community. Strictly speaking, *schola* describes the relation between the disciples and their teacher, in fact, the circle of disciples formed around a teacher. These relations are always very personal, not really fixed by organization.[11] Nevertheless, it is beyond doubt that there were regular schools in some monasteries at least for some time. As long as monasteries admitted *pueri oblati* they were obliged to take care of their education.[12] The *schola interior* was the institution designated for the supply of monastic personnel by oblates and novices. Apart from that, there may also have existed a *schola exterior* in some monasteries at times which was responsible for persons coming from outside the monastery (clergymen, laymen, especially noblemen).[13] But these schools could provide only a primary education for the most part (reading, writing, *computus*, and the like).

On the other hand, there had been for a long time considerable reservations against learning and teaching in monasticism. Great scruples concerning secular knowledge and the reading of profane literature were rather common as can be seen in the famous audition of Jerome.[14] In Western monasticism, Gregory the Great's account on the retreat of St. Benedict of Nursia from his studies in Rome served as a model.[15] Over and over again, Jerome's remark is quoted that the monk's duty is not teaching but mourning.[16] This famous sen-

---

[9] Cf. Illmer, Formen der Erziehung (1971).

[10] *Scorpiace* 12.1 (CChr. SL 2, 1092, 6).

[11] It is reported about the instructions of Saint Finnian, the abbot of Clonard: *apud sanctum Fortkernum psalmos ympnosque cum aliis ecclesiasticis officiis didiscit* (*Vita Finniani abbatis de Cluain Iraird* 2, Heist [cf. note 8] 96), about his own teaching: *Fama enim bonorum operum eius ex diversis terre partibus viros illustres, partim ad scripturam sacram addiscendam, partim ad ecclesiasticam institutionem percipiendam, quasi ad totius sapientie admirabile sacrarium attraxit* (c. 19, ibid. 101). Among Finnian's many famous pupils, there was also Columba of Hy (Iona), of whom is reported: *Finnianum igitur episcopum, sapientie luce clarissimum, ad discenda scripturarum misteria adivit* (*Vita S. Columbae* 3, ibid. 366).

[12] Oblation is suggested in RB 59. Benedict expects, that boys would be present at the monastery at all times (*pueri:* RB 30.1; 39.10; 63.9; 63.18; *infantes:* 31.9; 37.1; 45.3). It is indispensible to care for their education.

[13] Cf. U. Berlière, "Écoles claustrales au moyen âge" (Académie royale de Belgique. Bulletins de la Classe des lettres; 1921) 530–72.

[14] Jerome, *Ep.* 22.30 (CSEL 54, 189–91).

[15] Gregory the Great, *Dialogi* 2, Prol. (ed. U. Moricca; Roma 1924, 71 f).

[16] Jerome, *Contra Vigilantium* 15 (PL 23, 367 A): *Monachus autem non doctoris habet, sed plangentis officium: qui vel se, vel mundum lugeat, et Domini pavidus praestoletur adventum.*

tence is mentioned e.g. in the twelfth century by Bernard of Clairvaux[17] or Hugh of St. Victor.[18] The tasks of secular clergymen (preaching and teaching) and of monks (praying) are clearly distinguished; however, it is admitted and accepted that monks often assume genuine clerical functions.[19] Monastic rigorists and reformers like Petrus Damiani welcome the lack of schools in monasteries.[20] Consequently they demand the right to abstain from the admission of oblates.[21] The reservations against regular teaching by monks increased continuously and finally led to the almost complete removal of the school from the monastery in the twelfth century. This means, however, neither the renounciation of scholarship and theological learning nor of theological teaching. However, monastic education takes place not so much in fixed forms of instruction but in personal communication between teacher and disciple.[22] Monastic studies consist not so much of a formally organized acquisition of knowledge as rather of an individual effort to understand and apply the Holy Scripture. In this sense, the *schola dominici servitii* becomes the personal practice of service to God. The true teacher in the monastery – representing Christ – is the abbot who instructs his convent by his example and his words.[23] For the religious and theological education of the monks as well as for the history of monastic exegesis, the preaching of important abbots plays a central role. Certainly the most outstanding example of such spiritual and theological instruction in the twelfth century is represented by the series of sermons given by Bernard of Clairvaux: 17 *sermones* of the year 1139 on Psalm 90 (91) *Qui habitat in adiutorio altissimi*, and 86 *sermones* of the years 1135–1153 on *Cantica Canticorum* 1:1–3:1.[24]

2.1.3. The Monastery as Framework of Monastic Erudition

In *Vivarium* Cassiodorus had created a virtual monastery for learned monks, and in his *Institutiones* he had given instruction for the study of the Bible based on an extensive knowledge of the *artes liberales*. Medieval monasticism did not

---

[17] *Sermo super Cantica Canticorum* 64.3 (S. Bernardi *Opera* 2, ed. J. Leclercq / C. H. Talbot / H. M. Rochais; Roma 1958, 168, 3f): *scimus monachi officium non docere esse, sed lugere*; *Ep.* 89.2 (ibid., 7, 236, 3f).

[18] *Didascalicon* 5.8 (PL 176, 796D): *Non est tuum docere, sed plangere.*

[19] Cf. Anselm of Laon, *Ep. ad H. Abbatem S. Laurentii Leodiensis* (PL 162, 1590BC): *Clerici electi sunt ad praedicandum et ad docendos subditos, monachi vero ad orandum; quia clerici propter distractiones officii et negotiorum jugiter orationi vacare non poterant. Tamen causa necessitatis, ex praecepto episcopi, saepe monachi assumunt officium praedicandi et docendi.*

[20] *Opusc.* XXXVI *De divina omnipotentia*, 16 (PL 145, 621): *Hoc ibi non mediocriter placuit quod ibi scholas puerorum, qui saepe rigorem sanctitatis enervant, non inveni.*

[21] Ulrich of Cluny to William of Hirsau (PL 149, 637B): *ego autem certus sum illam te radicem funditus exstirpasse, ex qua sola praecipue omnia sunt monasteria destructa, quae destructa sunt vel in Teutonica vel in Romana lingua.*

[22] Cf. e.g. Beda's account on Englishmen who travelled to Ireland for the sake of *lectio divina* and ascetism: *Et quidam quidem mox se monasticae conuersationi fideliter mancipauerunt; alii magis circueundo per cellas magistrorum lectioni operam dare gaudebant* (*Hist. eccl.* 3.27; ed. G. Spitzbart; Darmstadt 1982; 1, 298).

[23] RB 2.2; 2.6; 2.11f; 5.6.

[24] S. Bernardi *Opera* [cf. note 17], 1/2 (1957/58); 4 (1966) 381–492.

simply take up his suggestions. The culture of the medieval monks should rather be understood from their true aims: asceticism and service to God without complete neglect of their own subsistence. Worship by means of the word affords a certain degree of education and thus promotes education whereas the freedom of intellectual activities is limited by a strengthened inclination to asceticism or an emphatic care for the subsistence. However, this observation can only point out certain tendencies, as a comparison between continental and Irish monasticism will show: Although ascetism was renounced and manual labor reduced in continental monasticism (especially by the Cluniacensians), it did not always take care of intellectual life, whereas Irish monasticism combined strictest asceticism with outstanding scholarship.[25]

On the Continent, monasteries under the *Regula Benedicti* offered an ideal frame for theological studies. The monastery's separation (*claustrum*) from the world (*saeculum*) and the monastic *stabilitas in congregatione* (RB 4.78) guaranteed the free space necessary for scholarly work. The monastic day is divided first and foremost by the *horae*. Between the divine services, intervals are designed not only for sleep and repose, meals and manual labor, but for individual reading, for study, and meditation, too. The prayers of the *horae* contain especially biblical texts, first of all the Psalter, moreover post biblical texts like the *Ambrosianum* (RB 9.4). For the *Vigiliae* expositions of the Scripture are used, too (*expositiones*, RB 9.8). Apart from the worship, common readings in the community before the *Completorium* (RB 42.3) and above all during the meals (RB 38) are scheduled. There is also enough time for individual reading (RB 48.1: *lectio divina* apart from the *labor manuum* as a means against idleness). A special function is carried out by the reading on Sundays (RB 48.22) and during Lent: In the beginning of the *Quadragesima* every monk receives a book which he is supposed to read from cover to cover (RB 48.15f). The importance of reading is also evident from the fact that it is one of the central services to the guests of the monastery – like the prayer (*oratio*) and the entertainment (*humanitas*, RB 53.9).

For the common as well as for the personal reading the following books are mentioned in addition to the Holy Scripture: the rule of Benedict (RB 66.8) and the rule of Basil (RB 73.5), the works of John Cassian and the biographies of the desert fathers: *Collationes, Instituta*, and *Vitae Patrum* (RB 42; 73). In the course of the Middle Ages, the *lectio divina* and the study of patristic works were supplemented by the reading of medieval authors, as is shown by the monastic libraries. An important part in private studies at all times is played by the commentaries of the Bible. Especially important for monastic devotion in the Middle Ages were also hagiographic literature and the increasingly sophisticated shaping of worship which was closely connected with the increasing number of saints' days.

An essential part of monastic (as of all medieval) learning consists in learning by heart. The rule of Benedict demands that a part of the readings must be

---

[25] J. Ryan, *Irish Monasticism* (Dublin ^{2}1972; repr.) 378: "To the Irish mind an illiterate monk was a contradiction in terms".

recited from memory.[26] On the other hand, also learning by heart supposes a correct tradition of the texts. This requires - even in a culture that is still based on oral communication - the possession of books (above all the Holy Scripture, commentaries to the Scripture, liturgical books). The more extensive the literature and the more complicated the liturgy becomes, the more the ability of reading and writing is required. As shown above, St. Benedict already assumes the existence of a monastic library used by the monks.[27] Indeed, each medieval monastery is likely to have possessed a library - in many cases of a very limited size - which had its place in a bookcase, in the sacristy, or even in a separate room. Hence the proverb: *"Claustrum sine armario quasi castrum sine armamentario"*.[28] On the contrary, not every monastery was equipped with its own *scriptorium*; but many monasteries had outstanding and productive *scriptoria* which provided not only their own libraries with manuscripts but had, in fact, the function of publishing houses. These important places for the production of books were in most cases at the same time centres of scholarship. In the early Middle Ages Irish monasteries excelled at first: Armagh, Bangor, Kildare, Clonmacnois, Clonard, and others.[29] While at the same time scholarly monasteries like Canterbury, Wearmouth and Jarrow, Ripon and others were founded by the English church that depended on Rome, Irish monks transplanted their scholarship to Scotland (Iona a. o.), England (Lindisfarne a. o.) and to the continent (Bobbio a. o.). Apart from the monastery of Tours founded by Bishop Martin, the following monasteries were especially prominent in the early Middle Ages: St. Gallen, Reichenau, Würzburg, Fulda, Corbie, Fleury, Reims. Whereas until the eleventh century the Benedictines dominated monastic publishing, new forces took part in the production of books during the twelfth century. Although they put more emphasis on manual labor,[30] the Cistercians took care of their libraries as well.[31] The Carthusians who were obliged to absolute silence did read and write intensively.[32] Likewise, the new orders founded since the beginning of the thirteenth century possessed big libraries: the Dominicans according to the aim of their founda-

---

[26] RB 9. 10: *lectio [...] ex corde recitanda;* 10. 2: *memoriter dicatur;* 12. 4: *ex corde;* 13. 11: *memoriter recitanda.*

[27] Even if *bibliotheca* (RB 48. 15) should refer to the Holy Scripture.

[28] Cf. H. Silvestre, "A propos du dicton 'Claustrum sine armario, quasi castrum sine armamentario'", *MS* 26 (1964) 351–53.

[29] K. Hughes, "The Distribution of Irish Scriptoria and Centres of Learning from 730 to 1111", in: N. K. Chadwick / K. Hughes / C. Brooke / K. Jackson, *Studies in the Early British Church* (Cambridge 1958) 243–72.

[30] Cf. e. g. *Exordium Cistercii, Capitula et Summa Cartae Caritatis* 15.2 (*Les plus anciens textes de Cîteaux*, ed. J. de la Croix Bouton / J. B. van Damme; Cîteaux. SD 2; Achel 1974, 123).

[31] Cf. T. Hümpfner, "Archivum et bibliotheca Cistercii et quatuor primarum filiarum eius", *ASOC* 2 (1946) 119–45; A. Wilmart, "L'ancienne bibliothèque de Clairvaux", Mémoires de la Société Académique d'Agriculture, des Sciences, Arts et Belles-Lettres du Département de l'Aube 54 (1917) 125–90, repr. in: *COCR* 11 (1949) 101–27; 301–19; C. Oursel, "La Bible de Saint Étienne Harding et le scriptorium de Cîteaux (1109–vers 1134)", *Cîteaux* 10 (1959) 34–43.

[32] Cf. Guigo I, *Consuetudines Cartusiae* 28.3 (Guiges Ier, *Coutumes de Chartreuse*, ed. par un Chartreux; SC 313; Paris 1984, 224): *Libros quippe tanquam sempiternum animarum nostrarum cibum cautissime custodiri et studiosissime volumus fieri, ut quia ore non possumus, dei verbum manibus predicemus.*

tion,[33] the Franciscans, on the contrary, against the original intention of their founder, but following the Dominicans example and often excelling them.[34] Influenced by the monastic reforms of the fifteenth century, monastic possession and production of books revived. Benedictine reformatory congregations, the Augustinian canons of Windesheim, and the newly founded community of the Brethren of the Common Life devoted themselves intensively to the production and the care of books.

2.2. Urban Clerical Schools

Already in late Antiquity, the *curia episcopalis* became a centre of Christian scholarship. Bishops themselves were often important scholars and became the teachers of their clergy - especially if they lived together with the clergy in an ascetic community following the example of St. Augustine. Many bishops were monks, in particular during late Antiquity and in the early Middle Ages. Monastic influences therefore early penetrated the life at the *curia episcopalis* and the education of the junior clergymen. Episcopal churches possessed libraries even in the Early Church. In late Antiquity, synods again and again demanded the providing of clerical education. Thus, the second synod of Vaison (529) decided that parish schools for the education of clergymen should be established at all parish churches.[35] The second synod of Toledo (531) decided that every bishop should educate young men for the clerical profession.[36] The bishop was the true teacher of his clergy even if he delegated the educational work for the most part to a clergyman of his charge. The Second Council of Nicaea (787) demanded from the bishop that he had to know the complete Psalter thoroughly (by heart) in order to be able to examine the Psalm praying of his clergy.[37] Charlemagne pursued the project of improving the education of the clergy, especially of the bishops, with great energy. He tried to reach this aim by introducing an examination as the condition for ordination, as well as by visitation, and by application of canonical laws.[38] As the essential instru-

---

[33] On Dominican care for books: Humbertus de Romanis, *De officiis ordinis* 13 *De officio librarii* (B. Humberti de Romanis *Opera de vita regulari* 2; ed. J. J. Berthier; Turin 1956, 263–66). Cf. A. Walz, "Vom Buchwesen im Predigerorden bis zum Jahre 1280", in: *Aus der Geisteswelt des Mittelalters* (Ed. A. Lang / J. Lechner / M. Schmaus 1; BGPhMA. Suppl 3/1; Münster 1935) 111–27; S. Axters, "Boekenbezit en boekengebruik bij de Dominikanen in de dertiende eeuw", in: *Studia mediaevalia in honorem … R. J. Martin* (Brügge 1948) 475–97.

[34] G. Abate, "Manoscritti e biblioteche francescane del medio evo", in: *Il libro e le biblioteche* (Atti del Primo Congresso Bibliologico Francescano Internazionale 20–27 Febbraio 1949, 2; Bibliotheca Pontificii Athenaei Antoniani 6; Roma 1950) 77–126. Already in the second half of the 13th century, a comprehensive catalogue was written containing more than 180 Franciscan monastic libraries in England and Scotland (W. R. Jones, "Franciscan Education and Monastic Libraries: Some Documents", *Traditio* 30 [1974] 435–45).

[35] C. 1 (Mansi 8, 726).

[36] C. 1 (*Concilia Galliae A. 511–A. 695*; ed. C. de Clercq; CChr. SL 148A; Turnhout 1963) 78.

[37] Can. 2 (COD 139 f): παντῶς τὸν ψαλτῆρα γινώσκειν.

[38] *Admonitio generalis* 789 (no. 22), c. 72 f (MGH. Cap 1, 52–62; here: 59 f); *Capitula de examinandis ecclesiasticis* 802 (no. 38), c. 1 f (ibid. 109–11; here: 109 f); *Capitulare missorum* 803 (no. 40), c. 2 (ibid. 114–16; here: 115).

ment for achieving an extensive education, he advanced the establishment of schools.[39] In his reformatory efforts he was assisted mainly by Alcuin, the most important scholar of his age. Alcuin had been teacher at the cathedral school of York. From 781 he was chancellor of the Frankish king and head of the Carolingian academy, and from 796 until his death in 804 he was abbot of St. Martin of Tours. However, the Carolingian reform of education could improve the level of education only to a limited extent. Again and again possibilities of education were lost, a decreasing level of education was complained about at synods, and new instructions for the education system were issued. In 1078, for example, Gregory VII demanded anew the establishment of cathedral schools by all the bishops.[40] In 1179 the Third Lateran Council decided that the teachers who were responsible for the instruction of the clergy and of other disciples at every cathedral should get a prebend for subsistence.[41] The Fourth Lateran Council renewed this instruction in 1215 and extended it to other schools whose resources rendered the subsistence of a teacher possible. It demanded theological learning for the clergy of each cathedral.[42] However, further development of the cathedral school as an institution of theological work was limited by competition with the theological faculties of the university.

In spite of the fundamental and constantly repeated demands for the establishment of cathedral schools, it is not likely that in the Middle Ages each cathedral possessed an institution of this kind. Even where cathedral schools are attested, they flourished in most cases only for a limited time. In the eighth century the cathedral school of York, from which Alcuin emerged, played an eminent part. In the eleventh century the school of Tournai excelled. In the beginning of the twelfth century Laon under Anselm was a centre of theological studies but lost its importance soon after Anselm's death (1117). The school of Chartres, which was the site of the work of great theologians in the eleventh century, became in the first half of the twelfth century a centre of outstanding studies on diverse fields (*artes liberales*, canon law and theology). Other important cathedral schools were located at Reims, Angers and Bourges, Canterbury and Durham, Toledo, Bamberg, Magdeburg, Cologne and at other sees. In Italy, on the other hand, cathedral schools were neglected at times. In the course of the twelfth century, Paris became the prominent place for Western theology.

From an observation of the development of single schools or the biography of a teacher like Peter Abelard it becomes quite clear that the reputation, the frequentation, even the existence of a cathedral school first of all depended on the teacher (*magister*) or the head of the school (*magister scholarum, scholasticus*). Thus, it becomes obvious that 'school' here, too, is not so much a durable,

---

39 *Admonitio generalis* 789 (no. 22), c. 72 (ibid. 60).

40 Concilium Romanum V (Mansi 20,509).

41 Can. 18 (COD 220).

42 Const. 11: *Sane metropolitana ecclesia theologum nihilominus habeat, qui sacerdotes et alios in sacra pagina doceat et in his praesertim informet, quae ad curam animarum spectare noscuntur* (COD 240).

well organized institution of education but rather the personal relationship between a teacher and his disciple. When Peter Abelard changed the site of his activities during the course of his eventful career as a teacher several times, his disciples followed him each time. In this relationship the attachment to the teacher as a person was stronger than the attachment to the site of the school.[43] The teachers at cathedral schools were mostly members of the cathedral chapter, in the twelfth century often dignitaries. Many of them later became bishops, archbishops, and cardinals: for example, Peter Lombard became bishop of Paris, Peter Cantor bishop of Tournai, Stephan Langton archbishop of Canterbury and cardinal.[44]

Education at cathedral and canonical schools had much in common with education in the monasteries. This is due to the fact that the way of life of the secular clergy was influenced by the monastic form of life. Continuous efforts were made to obligate the clergy of chapters and even of cathedrals to lead a *vita canonica* according to the rule of St. Augustine. The aims and the subject matters of learning therefore often resembled their counterparts at the other institution concerning their reference to life: Like in the monastery, the Psalter constituted the centre of the religious and theological education in cathedral and canonical schools. As the monasteries – although under different personal arrangements – all cathedral schools and chapters possessed libraries and many of them were equipped with schools for writing manuscripts.[45]

In other respects, however, the theological studies in those schools, especially in the cathedral school, were different from the theology in the monastery. Basically, the reflections of the monk were concentrated on themes important within the monastery: on the monastic community and – as its heart – on individual religious life and individual salvation. The monk's strong separation from the world (*saeculum*) included the renounciation of activities both in the world and on behalf of worldly matters. Accordingly, monastic theology was concentrated on the situation of the monk that nevertheless reflects very common and fundamental experiences of the Christian. The education of the secular clergy was different. Its tasks and its form of life were of an apostolic (pastoral) character. A model whose essence can be traced back to Augustine and which was common from the twelfth century, having been classically formulated by William of Auxerre, distinguishes fundamentally between three functions of reason (*ratio*) in theology. From that concept three main activities of the secular clergy may be derived: 1. the increase and strengthening of faith in believers (dogmatics), 2. the defence of the faith against its enemies (apolo-

---

[43] Cf. Peter Abelard, *Historia calamitatum* (ed. J. Monfrin; [2]1962) 64, 45–47: *ut [...] ad scolarum regimen adolescentulus aspirarem;* 64, 50. 52 f.: *scolas nostras a se removere conatus [...] nostrarum preparationem scolarum prepediret;* 64, 58: *Ab hoc autem scolarum nostrarum tirocinio;* 66, 117 f.: *ego Melidunum reversus scolas ibi nostras sicut antea constitui;* 66, 129–31: *extra civitatem in monte Sancte Genovefe scolarum nostrarum castra posui.*

[44] Cf. the exemplaric study by J. W. Baldwin, "Masters at Paris from 1179–1215", in: *Renaissance and Renewal in the Twelfth Century* (ed. R. L. Benson / G. Constable; Cambridge, MA 1982) 138–72.

[45] Cf. e. g. B. Bischoff, *Die südostdeutschen Schreibschulen und Bibliotheken in der Karolingerzeit* I. *Die bayrischen Diözesen* (Wiesbaden [3]1974).

getics, polemics), 3. the advancement of the untutored and those weak ones in faith (didactics, catechization).[46] These tasks were required of the secular clergy at all times. The ability to fulfil them supposes an education that is open to the problems of the world and enables the secular clergy to a high degree to carry on dialogue and discussion. The practice of scholastic theology is formed by such conditions as distinguished from monastic theology.[47]

Already in the early Middle Ages the beginnings of this type of theology can be found, a theology formed by its reference to schools. A completely developed form, however, does not exist until the occurrence of early scholastic theology in the twelfth century. It is distinguished above all by two new characteristics:

First, by the elaboration of a systematic arrangement of the whole theological tradition which is in the Middle Ages (leaving aside the Holy Scripture) seldom available in the complete original versions but in excerpts and anthologies. The theologians of the twelfth century, however, are not satisfied with an arbitrary collection of biblical and patristic sentences but try to organize this material systematically. In this effort, they may refer to former attempts of systematization: first and foremost to Augustine's *Enchiridion*, Gennadius' of Marseille *Liber sive definitio ecclesiasticorum dogmatum* and Fulgentius' of Ruspe *Liber de fide ad Petrum.*[48] Nevertheless, a definite systematization of the manifold and diffuse material was achieved only in the *Sentences* and *Summae* of the twelfth century. For example, Peter Abelard and his disciples arranged the material under the three key words: *fides – caritas – sacramentum* (dogmatics – ethics – doctrine of the sacraments), whereas Peter Lombard displayed his Sentences divided into four books and in a way arranged as it were according to a salvation-historic (*heilsgeschichtliches*) proceeding from trinity unto eschatology.

Second, another innovation concerns the theological method. According to John of Salisbury, teaching in the twelfth century consists of *lectio, doctrina* and *meditatio.*[49] The subject matter of theological work is the tradition, i.e. first of all the Holy Scripture, and moreover the materials gathered from Christian and philosophical literature. In addition to the bare commenting of these texts in *glossae*, there arose an increasing want of a discussion focusing on problems: the *quaestio*. Already in the Early Church the method of question and answer concerning theological themes had been usual.[50] In the twelfth century, however, it was taken up in a new way in connection with the efforts for a systematic arrangement of the material. In this discussion, the Biblical-Christian and the philosophical tradition turned out to be so incompatible that

---

[46] *Summa aurea* 1 Prol. (ed. J. Ribaillier, 1; SpicBon 16; Paris / Grottaferrata 1980, 15 f).

[47] On the two types of monastic and scolastic theology cf. Köpf, Monastische Theologie im 15. Jahrhundert (1992); idem, Monastische und scholastische Theologie (1996).

[48] Cf. A. Grillmeier, "Vom Symbolum zur Summa", in: *Kirche und Überlieferung* (ed. J. Betz / H. Fries; Freiburg / Basel / Wien 1960) 119–69; H. Cloes, "La systematisation théologique pendant la première moitié du XIIe siècle", *ETL* 34 (1958) 277–329.

[49] *Metalogicon* 1.23 f. (ed. J. B. Hall; CChr. CM 98; Turnhout 1991, 50–55).

[50] Cf. G. Bardy, "La littérature patristique des 'quaestiones et responsiones' sur l'écriture sainte", *RB* 41 (1932) 210–36; 341–69; 515–37; 42 (1933) 14–30; 211–29; 328–52.

it was necessary to look for possiblities of reconciliation between these contradictory positions. The most impressive demonstration of these contradictions is presented by Abelard's work *Sic et non*, in which arguments *pro* and *contra* from the tradition are adduced for each subject. In the age of enormously increasing dialectics (logic), a solution of the contradictions with the aid of the concepts and methods of that science suggested itself. It seemed reasonable to treat each theme as a question in whose discussion the contradictory traditions were introduced as arguments *pro* and *contra*.[51] For considering the arguments and balancing them against one another, the dialectics had prepared instruments which had been improved continuously since the twelfth century. The *quaestio* soon became part of the treatment of texts, especially of the interpretation of biblical books. For example, Robert of Melun (d. 1167), who was teaching in Melun since about 1142, composed his *Quaestiones de divina pagina* and *Quaestiones de epistolis Pauli*. In the thirteenth century the *quaestio* had already become the most important instrument of philosophical as well as of theological study. Then, the *quaestio* was refined and standardized as an element of teaching (*disputatio*) and as a form of literary argumentation, as an indispensable means of solving problems even in the interpretation of the Scripture.

2.3. Other Sites of Christian Education

In comparison with the two types of centres of clerical and religious education and erudition described above, the secular institutions of scholarship are less important for exegesis. Secular institutions in the early and high Middle Ages basically consisted of the sovereign's court with the court chapel, the chancellery and the court school, the *scriptorium* and the library. In the late Middle Ages, moreover, the urban school of the citizens came into existence. The importance of these secular institutions for theology and especially for exegesis is, however, limited, although important theologians taught at these institutions.

The court of Charlemagne turned into a centre of learning that became very influential for the occidental education system. At this place, the most important scholars of the Frankish empire worked, and here a regular court school and an extensive court library existed.[52] These institutions formed the conditions necessary for the great and comprehensive enterprise of the Carolingian reform of the education system.[53] For the renewal of biblical studies Charle-

---

[51] Peter Abelard, *Sic et non*, Prol. (PL 178, 1349A): *placet [...] diversa sanctorum Patrum dicta colligere, quando nostrae occurrerint memoriae aliqua ex dissonantia, quam habere videntur, quaestionem contrahentia;* Gilbertus Porreta, *Expositio in Boethii libros de Trinitate* (ed. N. M. Haring, in: *Nine Mediaeval Thinkers*, ed. J. R. O'Donnell; STPIMS 1; Toronto 1955) 37: *Hic commemorandum est quod ex affirmatione et ejus contradictoria negatione quaestio constat. Non tamen omnis contradictio quaestio est. [...] Cujus vero utraque pars argumenta veritatis habere videtur, quaestio est.*

[52] Cf. *Karl der Große. Lebenswerk und Nachleben* (ed. W. Braunfels), II. *Das geistige Leben* (ed. B. Bischoff; Düsseldorf ^{2}1966), here 28–41: F. Brunhölzl, "Der Bildungsauftrag der Hofschule"; 42–62: B. Bischoff, "Die Hofbibliothek Karls des Großen".

[53] J. Fleckenstein, *Die Bildungsreform Karls des Großen als Verwirklichung der norma rectitudinis* (Bigge-Ruhr 1953).

magne's care for the biblical text was fundamental. This care is testified by laws and edicts and perhaps even more effectively by Alcuin's revision of the Vulgate.[54] Under these circumstances, the necessity arose to take care of antique literature as well, and of those disciplines which served the exegesis of the Holy Scripture.[55] Other sovereigns' courts could scarcely reach the Carolingian court's level. Otto the Great did not maintain a court school, but he carefully furthered the cathedral schools of the empire.[56]

3. Theological Education and Learning at Universities

Sources: H. Denifle, "Die Constitutionen des Prediger-Ordens vom Jahre 1228", *ALKGMA* 1 (1885) 165–227; idem, "Die Constitutionen des Predigerordens in der Redaction des Raimund von Peñafort", *ALKGMA* 5 (1889) 530–64; *Chartularium Universitatis Parisiensis* 1–4 (ed. H. Denifle / Ae. Chatelain; Paris 1889–1897; quoted: CUP); *Les statuts et privilèges des universités françaises depuis leur fondation jusqu'en 1789* (ed. M. Fournier; 1. *Moyen-Âge*; Paris 1890; quoted: Fournier); *Statuta antiqua Universitatis Oxoniensis* (ed. S. Gibson; Oxford 1931; quoted: Statuta antiqua); *I più antichi statuti della Facoltà teologica dell' Università di Bologna* (ed. F. Ehrle; Universitatis Bononiensis Monumenta 1; Bologna 1932); R. Creytens, "Les Constitutions des Frères Prêcheurs dans la rédaction de s. Raymond de Peñafort (1241)", *AFP* 18 (1948) 5–68; A. H. Thomas, *De oudste constituties van de Dominicanen* (BRHE 42; Leuven 1965); K. Esser, *Die Opuscula des hl. Franziskus von Assisi. Neue textkritische Edition* (besorgt v. E. Grau; SpicBon 13; Grottaferrata ^{2}1989; quoted: Opuscula).

Literature: H. Denifle, *Die Entstehung der Universitäten des Mittelalters bis 1400* ⟨I⟩ (Berlin 1885; repr. Graz 1956); P. Glorieux, *Répertoire des maîtres en théologie de Paris au XIIIe siècle* 1–2 (EPhM 17–18; Paris 1933); V. Doucet, "Maîtres franciscains de Paris. Supplément au "Répertoire des maîtres en théologie de Paris au XIIIe siècle" de M. le Chan. P. Glorieux", *AFH* 27 (1934) 531–64; H. Rashdall, *The Universities of Europe in the Middle Ages* (New ed. by F. M. Powicke / A. B. Emden; Oxford 1936; repr. Oxford 1988); P. Glorieux, Art. "Sentences (Commentaires sur les)", DTC 14 (1940) 1860–84; W. A. Hinnebusch, *The History of the Dominican Order* 1–2 (New York 1966/73); J. Moorman, *A History of The Franciscan Order from its origins to the year 1517* (Oxford 1968; repr. Chicago 1988); P. Glorieux, "L'enseignement au moyen âge. Techniques et méthodes en usage à la Faculté de Théologie de Paris, au XIIIe siècle", *AHDL* 43 (1968) 69–186; J. Verger, *Les universités au Moyen Age* (Collection SUP - L'historien 14; Paris 1973); U. Köpf, *Die Anfänge der theologischen Wissenschaftstheorie im 13. Jahrhundert* (BHT 49; Tübingen 1974); K. Rückbrod, *Universität und Kollegium, Baugeschichte und Bautyp* (Darmstadt 1977); D. Berg, *Armut und Wissenschaft. Beiträge zur Geschichte des Studienwesens der Bettelorden im 13. Jahrhundert* (GuG 15; Düsseldorf 1977); *Le scuole degli ordini mendicanti (secoli XIII–XIV)* (Convegni del Centro di Studi sulla spiritualità medievale 17; Todi 1978); *The Universities in the Late Middle Ages* (ed. J. Ijsewijn / J. Paquet; Mediaevalia Lovaniensia 1, 6 = Université Catholique de Louvain. Publications de l'Institut d'études médiévales 2, 2; Louvain 1978); *Les genres littéraires dans les sources théologiques et philosophiques médiévales* (Université Catholique de Louvain. Publications de l'Institut d'études médiévales 2, 5; Louvain-la-neuve 1982); *The History of the University of Oxford* (Gen. ed. T. H. Aston; I. *The Early Oxford Schools;* ed. J. I. Catto; Oxford 1984); L. Pellegrini, *Università - Ordini mendicanti. Incontro di due istituzioni medioevali* (Pescara 1984); B. C. Bazàn / G. Fransen / D. Jacquart / J. W. Wippel, *Les questions disputées et les questions quodlibétiques dans les facultés de théologie, de droit et de médecine* (TSMAO 44–45; Turnhout 1985); *Schulen und Studium*

[54] B. Fischer, "Bibeltext und Bibelreform unter Karl dem Großen", in: Karl der Große, II (cf. note 52) 156–216.

[55] Cf. especially the *Epistola de litteris colendis* to abbot Baugulf of Fulda, between 780 and 800 (no. 29: MGH. Cap 1, 78 f).

[56] J. Fleckenstein, "Königshof und Bischofsschule unter Otto dem Großen", in: idem, *Ordnungen und formende Kräfte des Mittelalters* (Göttingen 1989) 168–92.

im sozialen Wandel des hohen und späten Mittelalters (ed. J. Fried; Vorträge und Forschungen 30; Sigmaringen 1986); O. WEIJERS, *Terminologie des universités au XIIIe siècle* (Lessico Intellettuale Europeo 39; Roma 1987); W. J. COURTENAY, *Schools and Scholars in Fourteenth-Century England* (Princeton, NJ 1987); D. NEBBIAI-DALLA GUARDA, *I documenti per la storia delle biblioteche medievali* (secoli IX–XV) (Roma 1992); *A History of the University in Europe*, I. *Universities in the Middle Ages* (ed. H. de Ridder-Symoens; Cambridge etc. 1992).

3.1. The First Universities

At the turn of the twelfth to the thirteenth century the first university with a theological faculty came to existence in Paris. Unlike later universities, it was not founded by a papal, episcopal, urban or princely act of foundation but by the voluntary fusion of different schools that had already existed in Paris: the cathedral school of Notre Dame and some private schools for the *artes liberales*, for law, and medicine. These schools were situated on the Isle in the Seine. Their teachers had obtained their *licentia docendi* from the chancellor of the cathedral.[57] To be sure, the private law schools of Bologna had united to an university some years before (about 1180–1190). The result of this fusion was, by the way, maintained not by the teachers but by the students. This university, however, was dominated by jurisprudence and never had a faculty of theology before 1360.[58] In Paris, on the other hand, for the first time a higher school existed with the four classical faculties of the arts, theology, law, and medicine. The first royal privilege was issued by king Philip II Augustus in 1200;[59] the first preserved statutes date from 1215.[60] But only in the course of the thirteenth century did the university of Paris assume that shape which, in the following centuries, laid the pattern of so many university foundations. It was not much later than in Paris that in the small but strategically important town of Oxford the first university in England came into existence. Like the university of Paris, it developed from already existing schools of the *artes liberales*, the civil and canon law, theology, and perhaps medicine, too. Here, however, a cathedral school did not exist because Oxford did not have a see. Rudiments of a corporational organization can be discovered at the beginning of the thirteenth century: in 1201 a *magister scholarum Oxoniae* is mentioned for the first time. After the return of teachers and students who had emigrated from Oxford in 1209, a chancellor is mentioned for the first time in 1214 and soon after (about 1216) a university which, however, was not acknowledged as a corporate body before 1231. Meanwhile, a new university was founded in 1209 in Cambridge by the *magistri* and students who had emigrated from Oxford. This new university soon consisted of four faculties as well.[61] Similarly, the university of Toulouse, which resulted from the strike of Paris university in

---

[57] On the contrary, monastic schools and schools of regulated chapters (Ste. Geneviève, St. Germain des Prés, St. Victor and others) kept aloof from the fusion.

[58] I più antichi statuti (1932).

[59] CUP 1, 59–61 no. 1.

[60] CUP 1, 78–80 no. 20.

[61] R. W. SOUTHERN, "From Schools to University", in: History of the University of Oxford 1 (1984) 1–36; M. B. HACKETT, "The University as a Corporate Body", ibid. 37–95.

1229, possessed a theological faculty from the beginning which, however, never really flourished.[62] Otherwise, theology was excluded from the majority of universities until the second half of the fourteenth century.[63] Up to the fourteenth century, Paris and Oxford remained the centres of scholastic theology. During the Middle Ages, the theological faculty of Paris occupied the first place, being favoured by the popes at least during the thirteenth century. The prohibition against teaching and studying *ius civile* in Paris, pronounced by Honorius III in 1219, was also intended to support theological studies.[64] In the second quarter of the thirteenth century, the theological faculties of the universities were confronted with rivals, i.e. new institutions of theological education, which were maintained by a new kind of religious person: the mendicant orders.

3.2. Masters and Students at the Theological Faculty

3.2.1. Secular Clergy and Monks

For the most part, those teachers and students who at Paris and Oxford formed a corporation called 'university', a *universitas magistrorum et scholarium*, belonged to the secular clergy. They were in any case *saeculares*, not monks (*religiosi*).[65] This points also to the fact that in the course of the twelfth century the cathedral schools took over the leading role in theological education. Until 1228, at the faculty of theology in Paris teachers were exclusively secular clergymen, and this group continued to constitute the majority (until 1218: 8 chairs, from that time onward 12, from which three were lost to the new orders after 1229, from 1275/77: 11).[66]

In the meantime, however, also in the older monasticism which lived according to the rule of Benedict, the implications of the innovation in the field of higher education were comprehended. Benedictines and Cistercians tried to participate in university studies.[67] Already in 1224, Clairvaux possessed a house near St. Germain des Prés.[68] In the early fourth decade of the thirteenth century, Stephan of Lexington, from 1229 abbot of the Cistercian abbey Sa-

---

[62] Cf. the circular letter of the *Universitas magistrorum et scholarium Tholose studium in nova radice statuentium* from 1229/30 in Fournier 1 (1890) 439 f.

[63] Denifle, Entstehung der Universitäten (1885) 27; ibid. 703: "Von den 46 Hochschulen, die bis 1400 in Aufnahme gekommen sind, war bei der Gründung von ungefähr 28, d.i. nahezu bei zwei Drittheilen, der Unterricht in der Theologie ausgeschlossen".

[64] Bull *Super speculam:* CUP 1, 90–93 no. 32.

[65] From the twelfth century onwards, definitively after universities had come into existence, intellectuals were distinguished from uneducated persons *(laici)* as *clerici.* Thereby the meaning of the two terms changed from the original meaning that had referred to ecclesiastical *ordines.* Cf. Weijers, Terminologie (1987) 183–85. In the second half of the twelfth century, Petrus Cantor distinguishes: *Clericorum duo sunt genera [...]: quidam ecclesiastici, quidam scolastici.* (*Summa Abel,* quoted by J. W. Baldwin, *Masters, Princes and Merchants. The Social Views of Peter the Chanter and His Circle* II; Princeton 1970, 51 n. 57).

[66] Glorieux, Répertoire (1933) 1, 227 f and folded pages.

[67] R. Schneider, "Studium und Zisterzienserorden", in: Schulen und Studium (1986) 321–50.

[68] G. Müller, "Gründung des St. Bernhardkollegiums zu Paris", Cistercienser-Chronik 20 (1908) 1–14, 38–50; here: 1.

vigny, complained about a neglect of studies in his order.[69] When Cistercians who studied in Paris changed from their own to the new religious orders,[70] Stephan, who became abbot of Clairvaux in 1243, founded the first college of the Cistercian order, St. Bernard's College, in the years 1244/45.[71] The general chapter of the year 1245 decided moreover that all abbeys - or at least one in each province - should maintain a *studium theologiae*. At the same time the *studium* established at Paris should be retained - both *studia*, however, without obligations for individual monks.[72] In 1254, Innocent IV endowed the Cistercians with the privilege of teaching theology regularly after their graduation.[73] Two years later, abbot Guy de l'Aumône received the first chair of his order.[74] The Cistercians soon were followed by the Cluniacense monks. Under abbot Theobald, the abbey of Fleury established a college at Paris in 1258,[75] in 1259 Galdericus of Cluny is attested as first Benedictine Professor,[76] and during the years 1260/62, the Collège de Cluny was founded.[77] In the second half of the thirteenth century, communities of regulated canons occupied two more chairs of theology: First, the Ordo Vallis Scholarium (Val des Écoliers), which was confirmed in 1219, had a chair occupied by Magister Evrardus in 1259;[78] second, the abbey of Mont-Saint-Éloi near Arras had a chair occupied by Étienne du Fermont in 1272/73.[79] The Premonstratensians did not hold a chair of their own, but had their own college from 1255.[80] The Carthusians, on the contrary, provided neither masters, nor did they send friars as students to the university; but again and again, academic theologians joined their order.[81]

3.2.2. The New Orders

The theology of Paris university in the thirteenth century was not so much influenced by the theologians from the secular clergy, and least of all by Benedictines, Cistercians, and the other monks mentioned above, as by members of

---

[69] Letter to abbot John III of Pontigny in: *Registrum epistolarum Stephani de Lexinton* (ed. B. Griesser), *ASOC* 2 (1946) 1–118; here: 116–18.

[70] Cf. the demands of the general chapter of 1242 to prevent these conversions: Canivez 2, 253 no. 42.

[71] Approbated by Innocent IV on January 5: CUP 1, 175 f no. 133. On September 4 in 1245, Innocent asked the abbots of the order to support the studies that have begun at Paris: CUP 1, 183 f no. 146.

[72] Canivez 2, 289 f no. 3 f.

[73] CUP 1, 251 no. 227.

[74] P. Michaud-Quantin, "Guy de l'Aumône, premier maître cistercien de l'Université de Paris", *ASOC* 15 (1959) 194–219.

[75] H. Denifle, "Das erste Studienhaus der Benedictiner an der Universität Paris", *ALKGMA* 1 (1885) 570–83.

[76] In a letter of Alexander IV: CUP 1, 389 no. 340.

[77] Cf. the decisions of the general chapters at Cluny in 1260: CUP 1, 410 f no. 361, and in 1261: ibid. 418 f no. 370.

[78] Mentioned for the first time CUP 1, 389 no. 340.

[79] Glorieux, Répertoire (1933) 2, 284 f and 1, 228/29 (folded page).

[80] CUP 1, 290 f no. 254.

[81] Generally, D. Mertens, "Kartäuser-Professoren", in: *Die Kartäuser in Österreich* 3 (ACar 83; Salzburg 1981) 75–87.

the newly founded mendicant orders: first of all by the Dominicans and Franciscans, and later on to a lesser degree by Augustinian friars and Carmelites, too.

The orders of Dominicans and Franciscans had their beginnings at approximately the same time in the deep religious crisis of the high Middle Ages. Both orders were a reply to the religous demand for a life according to the life of Christ in poverty, simplicity and penitence, that arosed in the twelfth century. Their different organizations and their different attitudes towards studies (different at least in the beginnings) can be traced back to the different characters and aims of their founders. In their attitude towards erudition, we can recognize diverse influences. They owe the demand of the *lectio divina* to the older monastic tradition. Because they were in opposition to the Cathars, Waldenses, Poor Catholics etc., they had to be in competition with their schools,[82] too. The mendicants began to participate in scholarly theological studies at the university of Paris. It was a most momentous occurrence that the orders of the Dominicans and Franciscans with their centralized and mobile organization, living near to the people and closely connected with the citizens, came into existence just when the university was born. For that reason, the new communities became the representatives not only of new religious ideas but also of new developments in theology and in scholarship in general. In addition to their activities at the theological faculties, they established - especially in towns without university - their own religious studies (*studia generalia*), but they always aspired to integrate their studies into existing or newly founded universities.

Dominicus of Caleruega in Castile (about 1175–1221), a member of the cathedral chapter of Osma, was travelling from 1203 to 1206 together with his bishop Diego in the south of France, when he felt called to perform the tasks of converting pagans and convicting heretics. In the south of the county of Toulouse, he preached against the Cathars, and in 1215 founded a community of preaching clergymen who were to live according to the rule of Augustine and the observance of Prémontré. In 1216 Honorius III confirmed the new community which he acknowledged as Fratres Ordinis Praedicatorum in 1218, and in 1220 he required the order to observe strict poverty. Their self-chosen task was an apostolic life of preaching and ministry among Catholics, heretics, and pagans. This aim, however, required a thorough education which was mainly guided by care for the trusted souls.[83] Whereas in the Middle Ages no learning was required to obtain ordination, the activity as preacher required studies of theology.[84] Therefore, the Ordo Praedicatorum was connected with

---

[82] Cf. C. Thouzellier, *Catharisme et Valdéisme en Languedoc à la fin du XIIe et au début du XIIIe siècle* (Marseille ^{3}1982) 221–23. Already about the year 1215, the Cathars sent their rising generation from Italy to Paris in order to study (A. Borst, *Die Katharer* [SMGH 1; Stuttgart 1953] 107).

[83] *Constitutiones* of Raimundus of Peñafort, Prol. (Denifle, Constitutionen [1889] 534; Creytens, Constitutions [1948] 29): *cum ordo noster specialiter ob predicationem et animarum salutem ab initio noscatur institutus fuisse, et studium nostrum ad hoc debeat principaliter intendere, ut proximorum animabus possimus utiles esse.*

[84] *Constitutiones fratrum predicatorum* 1228, dist. 2 c. 31 (Denifle, Constitutionen [1885] 223; Thomas, Constituties [1965] 363 f).

theological studies from the outset. Already in 1217, Dominicus sent seven of his fellows to Paris to study. In 1218 (definitively in 1221), they got the previous hospital St. Jacques as their first – and during the whole Middle Ages most important – college for a study in the order. The first one to teach there was the founder of the college, the secular clergyman John of Barastre, dean of St. Quentin, who occupied one of the theological chairs until about 1225/26.[85] His successor on the chair at St. Jacques was the secular clergyman John of St. Giles.[86] In 1229, during the university strike when many masters had left Paris, he arranged that Roland of Cremona, who had entered the order as *magister regens artium* in Bologna already in 1219, got the *licentia* and the first chair of the Dominicans in Paris. The Dominicans got a second chair when John of St. Giles himself entered the order in 1230. These two chairs remained reserved for the Dominican friars. Already the *Constitutiones* of the order from 1228 had laid down that the superiors of the provinces should delegate qualified friars to study,[87] and that no convent should be founded without a *doctor* as a member.[88] At first, it was decided that from each province three friars should be sent to Paris to study.[89] This number not being sufficient for the rapidly growing order, it was decided to establish four new *studia generalia* in the provinces of Provence (Montpellier), Lombardy (Bologna), Germany (Cologne),[90] and England (Oxford) already in the middle of the thirteenth century. If possible, the *studia* of the order were incorporated into already existing or newly founded universities. In Oxford, where Dominicans were present from 1224, they got a theological chair even before 1234, when the famous *magister regens* Robert Bacon (d. 1248) entered the order.[91] How highly studies were esteemed compared to prayer by the Dominicans, can be seen from the demand that the *officium* should be prayed only so long that the *studium* would not be impeded by it.[92] Raimund of Peñaforte, the third *magister generalis* of the order, formed the version of the *Constitutiones* (1238–1240) which was to be valid for the following centuries. In this version the same high evaluation of the studies is kept as in the eldest version.[93] Finally, the fifth *magister generalis*, Humbert de Romanis (1254–1263) developed the studies in the Dominican order by his writings which essentially and theologically improved on them.[94]

---

[85] Glorieux, Répertoire (1933) 1, 274. In medieval sources, he is called only John of St. Albans or John, Dean of St. Quentin. Cf. Hinnebusch, History (1973) 2, 73 n. 112.

[86] Ibid. 52 f.

[87] Dist. 2 c. 16 (Denifle, Constitutionen [1885] 218; Thomas, Constituties [1965] 353).

[88] Dist. 2 c. 23 (Denifle ibid. 221; Thomas ibid. 358).

[89] Dist. 2 c. 36, probably added between 1229 and 1236 (only ed. by Denifle, ibid. 226).

[90] On the *studium generale* at Cologne founded in 1248, a comprehensive account by E. Meuthen, *Kölner Universitätsgeschichte* 1. *Die alte Universität* (Köln / Wien 1988) 42–48.

[91] B. Smalley, "Robert Bacon and the Early Dominican School at Oxford", THS 4th Ser. 30 (1948) 1–19.

[92] Dist. 1 c. 4; dist. 2 c. 29 (Denifle, Constitutionen [1885] 197, 223; Thomas, Constituties [1965] 316, 362).

[93] Cf. e. g. the demand to found no convent without a *doctor*: dist. 2 c. 1 (Denifle, Constitutionen [1889] 549; Creytens, Constitutions [1948] 48), or the paragraph *De studentibus*: dist. 2 c. 14 (Denifle ibid. 562–64; Creytens ibid. 65–67).

[94] Cf. especially his *Expositio regulae B. Augustini* c. 143 *De utilitate studii in ordine Praedicato-*

Soon after the Dominicans, the Friars Minor obtained their first chair. The founder of their community, Francis of Assisi (1181/82–1226), had been reserved against studies. As a merchant's son, he had been educated for the profession of his father. He had not received a learned education, and even after his conversion, he never did aspire to erudition. His ideal of *humilitas* and *simplicitas* was contradictory to any aspiration to a knowledge that is overbearing before God and over other men.[95] As for himself and his first companions, he stressed ignorance.[96] His first companions, indeed, mainly (with the exception of only few friars: Bernard of Quintavalle and Peter Cathanii) did not belong to the educated classes. His ideal of poverty (*paupertas*) was contradictory to the possession of books with the exception of liturgical texts.[97] But in spite of all personal simplicity and modesty, and in spite of his demands of the community, St. Francis did not set forth hostility to education and erudition as far as it served the church. He was different from the reformatory movements of his age by his esteem for the ministry which he often expressed.[98] In his opinion, knowledge and the possession of books have their value not in themselves, but only with regard to their purpose. Whereas the clergymen in the community who pray the *divinum officium* may have the necessary liturgic books, and the literate laymen may possess a Psalter, the illiterates are not allowed to own books.[99] Francis expresses reverence for all theologians because they mediate spirit and life.[100] He approves of the theological teaching of Anthony of Padua inasmuch as he thereby does not extinguish the spirit of prayer and devotion contained in the rule.[101] He is able to praise the *regina sapientia* as sister of the *sancta pura simplicitas*.[102] By this comparison, however, he does not mean the knowledge acquired in this world; because "the pure holy wisdom destroys all the wisdom of this world and all the wisdom of the body".[103] On the contrary, he contrasts the understanding directed by the Holy Spirit with the bare knowledge of the letter.[104] From such sayings could be built a bridge to scholarship soon after the death of Francis in spite of all reservations against the activities of schools and universities. The bull of Pope Gregory IX *Quo elongati* (1230) marks the accomplishment of this step; theological studies

---

rum (*Opera de vita regulari* [cf. note 33] 1, 433–35); *Expositio super constitutiones fratrum praedicatorum* c. 8 *De utilitate studii in nostro ordine* (ibid. 2, 28–31).

95 *Epistola ad fideles* II 45 (Opuscula 210): *Non debemus secundum carnem esse sapientes et prudentes, sed magis debemus esse simplices, humiles et puri. Regula non bullata* 17.15 (ibid. 392): *Et studet ad humilitatem et patientiam et puram et simplicem et veram pacem spiritus.*

96 *Epistola toti ordini missa* 39 (ibid. 262): *quia ignorans sum et idiota; Test.* 19 (ibid. 440): *Et eramus idiotae et subditi omnibus.* Cf. OKTAVIAN SCHMUCKI (VON RIEDEN), "'Ignorans sum et idiota'. Das Ausmaß der schulischen Bildung des hl. Franziskus von Assisi", in: *Studia historico-ecclesiastica. Festgabe für Prof. Luchesius G. Spätling* (ed. I. Vásquez; Rom 1977) 283–310.

97 *Regula non bullata* 3.7–9; 8.3 (ibid. 380, 384).

98 Cf. e.g. *Testamentum* 6f, where priesthood is evaluated even higher than *sapientia* (ibid. 438).

99 *Regula non bullata* 3.3–8 (ibid. 378f).

100 *Regula non bullata* 3.3–8 (ibid. 378f).

101 *Epistola ad s. Antonium* 2 (ibid. 153).

102 *Salutatio virtutum* 1 (ibid. 427).

103 *Salutatio virtutum* 10 (ibid. 428).

104 *Admonitiones* 7 (ibid. 110).

by the Friars Minor are already considered as a matter of course.[105] The active participation in teaching theology at the university of Paris was inevitable. If the new community wished to be active in the Church, it could prevent an opening to theological erudition as little as it could prevent clericalization. There is no doubt that in this development the model of the Dominican order played an important part. The Friars Minor obtained the first theological chair at Paris university due to the fact that the secular clergyman Alexander of Hales (c. 1185–1245, from about 1220/25 *magister theologiae*) entered the Franciscan order probably in 1236 and may have retained the chair until his death.[106] In this case, it is likely that from 1238–1245 a second Franciscan chair existed, occupied by John of Rupella. From 1224, Franciscans were in Oxford, too. For eighteen years (1229–1247) secular masters directed their studies, a prominent figure among them being the great scholar Robert Grosseteste (1229/30 until his appointment as bishop of Lincoln).[107] The first Franciscan to become professor of theology in Oxford was Adam Marsh (de Marisco) in 1247, who was a member of the order already in 1232/33.[108]

Obviously, both new orders were very attractive to many students and masters. It is true that at first original scholarly impulses did not come from them. But the religious ideals they embodied – ideals of an evangelical life in absolute poverty in accordance with a strictly organized form of life and with the aim of apostolic preaching – as well as the accompanying spirituality, could win many intellectuals for them. On the other hand, the masters who had entered the mendicant orders soon proved to be very attractive to the students. Although the mendicants were received in a friendly way during the first years of their appearance by the secular clergy, and although they were admitted to the staff of the university without problems, their teaching as well as their activities in preaching and ministerial work were increasingly considered as inconvenient competition by the secular clergymen of Paris from about the middle of the thirteenth century. The most important and most attractive theological masters of the age were mendicants: Alexander of Hales, John of Rupella, Odo Rigaldi, Hugh of St. Cher, Albertus Magnus. Friction between mendicants and their colleagues of the secular clergy was inevitable.[109] In 1252, the theologians passed a statute according to which each community of religious people were to have only one chair and only one *scola*.[110] This regulation caused particular concern among the Dominicans, and they obstinately and ef-

---

[105] *Bullarium Franciscanum* (ed. J. H. Sbaralea 1, Roma 1759; repr. S. Maria degli Angeli 1983) 68–70, here: 69[b].

[106] Generally concerning Alexander's *vita*: Alexander de Hales, *Glossa in quatuor libros Sententiarum Petri Lombardi* (ed. PP. Collegii S. Bonaventurae, I; BFSMA 12; Quaracchi 1951), Prolegomena 7*–75*, especially 64*–74*.

[107] R. W. Southern, *Robert Grosseteste. The Growth of an English Mind in Medieval Europe* (Oxford 1986).

[108] A. G. Little, "The Franciscan School at Oxford in the thirteenth century", *AFH* 19 (1926) 803–74.

[109] Cf. M.-M. Dufeil, *Guillaume de Saint-Amour et la polémique universitaire parisienne 1250–1259* (Paris 1972). An informative chronological survey is given by P. Glorieux, "Le conflit de 1252–1257 à la lumière du Mémoire de Guillaume de Saint-Amour", *RTAM* 24 (1957) 364–72.

[110] CUP 1, 226 f no. 200.

fectively resisted the abrogation of one of their two chairs. On later occasions, the controversy deepened. It took place in lectures, sermons, and public meetings as well as in polemical pamphlets. As one of the consequences of the mendicant controversy, the Dominican Thomas Aquinas as well as the Fransciscan Bonaventure were not admitted to the professorate although they had already been graduated to *magistri theologiae* by their colleages. In June 1256, an agreement of sorts was achieved between the contending factions.[111] However, only when the main opponent of the mendicants, William of St. Amour, was excluded from Paris university in 1257, did their situation improve visibly.[112] Only then were Thomas and Bonaventure accepted by their colleagues. The conflict, however, continued under the leadership of Gerard of Abbeville until the eighth decade of the thirteenth century and was ended by the decree *Religionum diversitatem* at the Second Council of Lyon in 1274.[113] But on another level, the controversy about the mendicants dragged on far into the fourteenth century.[114] Nevertheless, the mendicants emerged invigorated from the vehement conflicts with the Paris secular clergy. In spite of their quantitative inferiority, they were dominant during the thirteenth and fourteenth century, and only in the fifteenth century were they pushed back again by the secular clergy which held an important place especially at the German universities that were founded, beginning in the second half of the fourteenth century.

During the first controversy about the mendicants at Paris, the Ordo Eremitarum S. Augustini came into existence by a fusion of several Italian hermit communities which lived according to the rule of St. Augustine, and was approved by Pope Alexander IV in 1256. Already at the end of the year 1259 the new order settled in Paris.[115] But it did not obtain its own theological chair until 1285. The first holder of this chair (1285–1291) was a disciple of Thomas Aquinas, Aegidius Romanus, elected general of the order in 1295.[116] – The Carmelites as the fourth mendicant order did not obtain a chair in the theological faculty until 1295. The hermits from Mount Carmel seem to have founded their first house in Europe in the year 1235. A few years later, they moved to Europe entirely, where they obtained a mitigated rule from Innocent IV in 1247 and soon developed into a mendicant order. Already at the end of the 1240s they settled at Cambridge, in 1256 at Oxford, and a few years later at Paris where they established a house in 1260.[117] About 1270, their first students are attested, and in 1295 Gerard of Bologna was the first member of the order to obtain a chair.[118]

---

[111] Cf. CUP 1, 319–26 no. 280–82.

[112] On August 9 in 1257 pope Alexander IV has withdrawn from him *omnem docendi ac predicandi [...] facultatem* (CUP 1, 362 no. 314).

[113] The decrete: COD 326 f. Cf. also B. Roberg, *Das Zweite Konzil von Lyon [1274]* (Konziliengeschichte, ed. W. Brandmüller, Reihe A; Paderborn / München / Wien / Zürich 1990) 330–43.

[114] Cf. Y. M.-J. Congar, "Aspects ecclésiologiques de la querelle entre mendiants et séculiers dans la seconde moitié du XIIIe siècle et le début du XIVe", *AHDL* 36 (1961) 35–151.

[115] CUP 1, 405 f no. 358.

[116] Glorieux, Répertoire (1933) 2, 293–308.

[117] CUP 1, 409 f no. 360.

[118] Glorieux, Répertoire (1933) 2, 336 f.

3.3. The Institutions of Theological Studies[119]

3.3.1. The Educational Work and Its Literary Outcome

At the end of the twelfth century, Peter Cantor in a sentence, that later on was often quoted, describes the task of the theologian as *lectio, disputatio*, and *praedicatio*.[120] Here both main forms of teaching at the medieval university are mentioned, the two forms which generated two elementary forms of literature.

At the core of all medieval university teaching is the lecture. It is so fundamental that *legere* can clearly have the meaning of 'teach' as it is expressed for instance in the formulation *licentia legendi*.[121] *Lectio*, strictly speaking, is the regular lecture. Its basis in all faculties are texts prescribed by the authorities, texts which are read and discussed chapter for chapter and word for word. The free exposition of one's own thoughts without relation to a basic text, however, is unknown – at least in university teaching. The two basic texts for the theologian are the Bible and, from the middle of the thirteenth century, the Sentences of Peter Lombard. The Paris statutes from the second half of the fourteenth century require that each student of theology has to bring these texts to the lectures.[122] In an age, however, when books were rare and precious, it could not be expected that all students were able to buy the books needed for study at the bookseller's (*stationarius, venditor librorum*).[123] It was possible to borrow books with a correct (corrected and approved) text (in layers as well: *peciae*) in order to copy them or have them copied.[124] But the lecture gave the students the opportunity to obtain basic works plus an interpretation just by taking notes. The literary result of the lecture is the commentary (*glossa, commentarius, expositio*).[125]

The second main form of university teaching is the disputation (*disputatio*). It is derived from the method of the *quaestio* that was developed in the twelfth century in connection with the *lectio*: questions of the interpreted text are treated by detaching from the wording and by concentrating on the substantial problem. At the beginnings of Paris university, the disputation existed in an elaborated form and soon became a central component of teaching at all facul-

[119] A concise summary is rendered difficult by the fact that, on the one hand, the preserved official sources provide only very defective information, on the other hand, the conditions and the terminology of the diverse universities are quite different from one another and varied in the course of the years. On the following pages a standardized structure will be given that corresponds to the organization of Paris university. Cf. on the conditions in the thirteenth century Glorieux, Enseignement (1968); on the terminology in the thirteenth century Weijers, Terminologie (1987).

[120] *Verbum abbreviatum* 1 (PL 205, 25AB): *In tribus igitur consistit exercitium sacrae scripturae: circa lectionem, disputationem et praedicationem. [...] Lectio autem est quasi fundamentum et substratorium sequentium [...] Disputatio quasi paries est in hoc exercitio et aedificio [...] Praedicatio vero, cui subserviunt priora, quasi tectum est tegens fideles [...].*

[121] Weijers, Terminologie (1987) 292.

[122] *Statuta Facultatis theologiae* 14f: CUP 2, 698, no. 1189.

[123] Cf. K.W. Humphreys, *The Book Provisions of the Mediaeval Friars* (Studies in the History of Libraries and Librarianship 1 = Safaho Monographs 2; Amsterdam 1964).

[124] Cf. e.g. Guiard's de Laon remark: *Pauperes enim scolares manu sua propria sibi vel aliis scribunt* (in C.H. Haskins, *Studies in Mediaeval Culture* [Oxford 1929] 63 A. 12).

[125] Comprehensive literature on the genre of theological commentary is lacking.

ties. The details of its performance and its terminology, however, changed in the course of time and were different from university to university. Nevertheless, certain characteristics can be pointed out. The *disputatio* is not a free discussion in the modern sense but an exactly regulated and formalized procedure. Apart from the private disputation (*disputatio privata, in scholis propriis*) which only unites the master and his disciples, two kinds of public disputation (*disputatio publica*) can be distinguished:

1. The *disputatio ordinaria*[126] is a regular form of magistral teaching which takes place weekly or every other week, or even more rarely. It is devoted to a certain theme or range of themes which is always the same during a part of the term. Subject and time of this disputation are determined by the master actually responsible. The disputation's procedure is exactly regulated: In the beginning, the thesis is formulated which is to be discussed. Then, arguments *pro* and *contra* are gathered. In the following steps a solution is proposed, and those arguments are answered which are not acknowledged in the solution. The master presides over the discussion and formulates the problem or the thesis; the *opponens*, a *baccalareus*, delivers the arguments *pro* and *contra*; a *respondens* who is likewise a student makes a preliminary reply; finally, as a rule in a second session, the master makes a definitive reply (*determinatio*), in which he mostly summarizes the previous development of the *disputatio*, utters his personal solution of the problem and refutes the arguments which contradict his thesis.

2. A special form is the *disputatio de quolibet*[127] which seems to have come into existence in about 1230 during the university strike at the Parisian faculty of theology. Its procedure corresponds to the *disputatio ordinaria* from which it differs in the following ways:

a) This *disputatio* can treat *de quolibet*. It is not restrained to a previously fixed or a conventional range of themes but can deal with any conceivable problem. Therefore, the *disputatio de quolibet* deals even in a conspicuous manner with actual questions. Moreover, to the question put first further questions may be linked which are related to the first question's subject matter in any way. In that manner, frequently in a *disputatio de quolibet* twenty, thirty or more questions are asked. Therefore, it is far less uniform with regard to its contents than the *disputatio ordinaria*.

b) In this *disputatio* the questions may be put not only by the leading master, but by each person present: by other masters, by students, even by educated people who are not members of the university. This results in a wider spectrum of themes than in the *disputatio ordinaria*.

---

[126] B. C. Bazàn, "La *quaestio disputata*" in: Les genres littéraires (1982) 31–49; idem, "Les questions disputées, principalement dans les facultés de théologie", in: Bazàn et al., Les questions (1985) 13–149; cf. also G. Fransen, "Les questions disputées dans les facultés de droit", ibid., 223–77; D. Jacquart, "La question disputée dans les facultés de médecine", ibid. 279–315.

[127] P. Glorieux, *La littérature quodlibétique de 1260 à 1320*, 1–2 (BiblThom 5. 21; Le Saulchoir Kain 1925 / Paris 1935); J. F. Wippel, "The Quodlibetal Question as a distinctive literary genre", in: Les genres littéraires (1982) 67–84; idem, "Quodlibetal questions chiefly in theology faculties", in: Bazàn et al., Les questions (1985) 151–222.

c) The variety of questions treated and of themes demands a much greater effort and a more careful preparation of the solution than in the *disputatio ordinaria.* Much more so than in the *disputatio ordinaria,* it is expected in the *disputatio de quolibet* that the *determinatio* is carefully elaborated, rich in ideas, and persuasive. Particular attention must be payed to a thoroughly considered arrangement of the diverse questions and subjects. An important instrument in this process is the logical method of the *divisio.* Thus the *determinatio* demands the master's complete faculties.

d) Accordingly, the *disputatio de quolibet* is carried out with special solemnity. Because the whole faculty and even auditors from outside are present, and because it needs much preparation, the *disputatio de quolibet* is celebrated only during well established, strictly limited periods (mostly in the Advent season and before Easter, at many universities only once a year).

As a rule, both kinds of disputations were taken down by assistants. The master needed such records (*reportationes*) already for the elaboration of his *determinatio.* On the basis of all the *reportationes,* he could later on write a text of the disputation for publishing.[128] The two kinds of disputations had their literary outcome in the two literary genres of the *quaestio disputata* and the *quaestio de quolibet* (also: *quaestio quodlibetalis* or *quodlibetum*). In addition, the *quaestio* which was removed from the exposition of texts in the course of the twelfth century and had become an independent form, thus by way of the disputation found its way back into the *lectio.* Anyway, the use of the *quaestio* was indispensable for the lecture on the Sentences. But in lectures on biblical books, too, individual problems were discussed increasingly in *quaestiones* that expanded more and more. Due to the fact that the biblical lecture offered the only opportunity to the master to express his theological opinions in a coherent train of thoughts, he made use of it in order to discuss dogmatic and ethical themes in the form of *quaestiones* with reference to certain biblical passages. That way, also exegetic questions were often treated thoroughly. But on the whole, the logical treatment of problems that sometimes were connected only loosely with the text, supplies and replaces the bare interpretation of the text to an increasing extent. Apart from the use of the *quaestio,* scholastic practises which were developed in the *disputatio* (*definitio, divisio,* argumentation *pro* and *contra,* syllogism etc.) became part of the exegesis.

In addition to these two characteristic forms of university teaching, the religious speech is an equally important part of the master's obligations.[129] It is not characteristic for the university but continues the preaching of the secular clergy and the monastic preaching of the twelfth century within a new framework and by new means. However, preaching at the university without doubt underwent a rapid development under the influence of the mendicants who were devoted to preaching. On the other hand, masters of theology not only

---

[128] P. Glorieux, "Le Quodlibet et ses procédés rédactionnels", Divus Thomas (Piacenza) 42 (1939) 61–93.

[129] Survey in J. B. Schneyer, *Geschichte der katholischen Predigt* (Freiburg 1969) 132–54; idem, *Repertorium der lateinischen Sermones des Mittelalters* 1–11 (BGPhMA 43, 1–11; Münster 1969–1990), especially 6, 1975, 7–259: *Sermones Universitatum.*

preached at the university but also outside of it, at synods, in convents, and to the people. Already in the middle of the thirteenth century, a scholastic but popular form of preaching came into use. The sermon in its original conception (*praedicatio, sermo*) came first. Apart from that, a second preaching which took place in the evening (*collatio*) was known at the university. The *collatio* mostly referred to and continued the sermon of the morning but could be designed totally independent of it as well. In addition, like the exegesis the preaching took over elements of the scholastic *disputatio.*

But the term *collatio,* connected with the monastic tradition since the Early Church, in theological teaching had other connotations, too.[130] Among the mendicants, it meant a formal but less ceremonial discussion between students under supervision of the master, a kind of repetition and an exercise in disputing.[131] This form of discussion training was propagated beyond the mendicant orders into the secular clergy, and the colleges,[132] and beyond Paris to other universities even in the thirteenth century.[133] Furthermore, *collatio* in later sources means "a part of academic addresses".[134] Finally, the term is used as well for discourses by persons who were not members of the university or which were held before a larger auditory, for instance the discourses which Bonaventure, the general minister of the Franciscans, repeatedly gave at Paris after resigning his chair.[135]

3.3.2. The Theologian's Academic Career

The goal of the studies at each of the four traditional faculties is the graduation, i.e. the acquisition of an academic degree. This degree has no immediate importance for a professional activity outside the university. The ordination of a priest, for example, supposes by no means a degree, not even a study of theology, in the Middle Ages. The graduation first of all is relevant for an academic career. It is always connected to the qualification to teach at a certain level. The aim of the education at university, therefore, is the *licentia docendi,* i.e. the authorization for autonomous teaching. As a rule, it is conferred by an

[130] On the term *collatio* cf. S. CLASEN, "Collectanea zum Studien- und Buchwesen des Mittelalters. (Mit besonderer Berücksichtigung der Kölner Universität und der Mendikantenstudien)", *AGPh* 42 (1960) 159–206, 247–71; here: 172f; J. HAMESSE, "'Collatio' et 'Reportatio': Deux vocables spécifiques de la vie intellectuelle au moyen âge", in: *Actes du colloque 'Terminologie de la vie intellectuelle au moyen âge'* Leyde / La Haye 20–21 septembre 1985 (ed. O. Weijers; CIVICIMA – Études sur le vocabulaire intellectuel du moyen âge 1; Turnhout 1988) 78–87.

[131] Weijers 372ff. The matter is disposed of already in the statutes of the Dominican Order in 1228: dist. 2 c. 29 (Denifle, Constitutionen [1885] 223; Thomas, Constituties [1965] 362; partially in CUP 1, 113 no. 57). In the statutes for the study from the year 1259 it is decided: *Item, quod fiant repetitiones de questionibus et collationes de questionibus semel in septimana, ubi hoc commode poterit observari* (CUP 1, 385f, here: 386).

[132] It was, for example, developed into the 'Sorbonique' (*[disputatio] Sorbonica*) at the Collège de Sorbonne in the fourteenth century: CUP 2, 554–56 no. 1096.

[133] On Oxford, cf. J. I. CATTO, "Citizens, Scholars and Masters", in: History of the University of Oxford 1 (1984) 151–92, here: 188f.

[134] Clasen, Collectanea [cf. note 130], 173.

[135] *Collationes de decem praeceptis* (1267), *Collationes de donis Spiritus Sancti* (1268), *Collationes in Hexaemeron* (1273). Cf. Glorieux, Enseignement (1968) 122.

ecclesiastical authority, in most cases by the bishop (archbishop) or by his chancellor. In the earliest universities – Bologna, Paris, and Oxford – the licence originally was confined to the site where it had been conferred; but later this restriction was abandoned. The first university to get the privilege to confer an unlimited licence to teach (*libera potestas ubique regendi*) was the university of Toulouse in 1233.[136]

In the medieval university, there are as a matter of principle two steps of graduation and hence two degrees.

First, there is the degree of the *baccalareus.*[137] He continues his studies at the faculty where he graduated but, at the same time, has to work as an assistant teacher.

Second, there is the degree of the *magister* or *doctor.* He has finished his studies and possesses the unlimited authority to teach in his discipline. His title differs depending on the university, faculty, and epoque; *doctor* is more usual in the higher faculties than in the faculty of arts. When the graduate gets a regular professorship (*cathedra magistralis,* chair),[138] he is called *magister* or *doctor (actu) regens.*[139]

Each step in the academic career presupposes certain achievements. The act of being awarded a degree consisted of solemnities that included the swearing of an oath.[140] As a rule, the condition for being admitted to the study of theology (as to the study of law or of medicine) is a study at the faculty of arts that was completed by the graduation.[141] While the *magister artium* begins the study of theology as a plain *auditor,* he is teaching regularly as a master at the faculty of arts. During his studies, the student always works under the supervision and instruction of an appointed master.[142] After he, for the most part passively, has participated in lectures and other forms of teaching for some years,[143] the student of theology graduates as *baccalareus* and gets the charge of teaching theology within certain limits besides his studies as an *auditor.*

---

[136] Bull of pope Gregory IX, April 30, 1233 (Fournier 1, 441[b]): *Et ut quicumque magister ibi examinatus et approbatus fuerit in qualibet facultate, ubique sine alia examinacione regendi liberam habeat potestati.* (*Regere* here means: *legere, docere*).

[137] The spelling differs; on variations cf. Weijers, Terminologie (1987) 178–80.

[138] It is said: *cathedram magistralem ascendere* (e.g. CUP 1, 85 no. 27 from 1218), *magistralem cathedram adipisci, ad cathedram proficere (provehi)* (e.g. CUP 1, 253 no. 230). Cf. Weijers, Terminologie (1987) 119–21.

[139] Weijers, Terminologie (1987) 294. Cf. the definition of a statute of the artists' faculty from 1275: *Per actu regentem intelligimus eum qui legit qualibet die legibili in scolis in habitu et hora debita [...]* (CUP 1, 530–32 no. 461; here: 531).

[140] The forms of the Parisian oaths until ca. 1350 are collected in CUP 2, 672–686 no. 1185. On this matter, cf. P. Kibre, "Academic Oaths at the University of Paris in the Middle Ages", in: *Essays in Medieval Life and Thought. Presented in Honor of Austin Patterson Evans* (ed. J. H. Mundy / R. W. Emery / B. N. Nelson; New York 1965) 123–37.

[141] Exceptions are possible especially among the mendicants, if the *artes liberales* have been completed in a study of the order.

[142] The first Parisian statutes of Robert of Sorbon from 1215 decide concerning the theologians: *Nullus sit scolaris Parisius, qui certum magistrum non habeat* (CUP 1, 78–80 no. 20; here: 79).

[143] The duration of different parts of the studies is regulated differently at the diverse faculties of differing universities in differing times. The statutes of Robert of Sorbon say on the study of theology: *Circa statum theologorum statuimus, quod nullus Parisius legat citra tricesimum quintum etatis sue annum, et nisi studuerit per octo annos ad minus, et libros fideliter et in scolis audierit, et quinque*

The baccalaureate consists of two steps. In the beginning of his teaching, the theologian is *baccalareus biblicus* or *cursor*. The attribute *biblicus* means that he has to give lectures on the Holy Scripture for one, later on for two years. Originally, one of his lectures had to deal with a book from the Old and another lecture with a book from the New Testament. Later on, the lecturer could choose to give both lectures on two books of the Old or of the New Testament. The name *cursor* refers to the fact that the interpreted text may be read only *cursorie* (*ad cursum*),[144] which means that the text is to be read relatively hastily and scantily, putting emphasis on the literal meaning, and without investigating a deeper sense *(sensus spiritualis)*, further with the help of the main glosses but without the discussion of difficult questions.[145] The aim of this lecture is to provide the students with an elementary knowledge of the biblical text in its literal sense. As distinguished from the *baccalarei biblici* of the secular clergy, those of the mendicants and the Cistercians gave lectures on all books of the Bible during two years.[146] Relatively few records are preserved from the biblical lectures of the *cursores*, corresponding to their inferior importance.

The second step of the baccalaureate is that of the *baccalareus sententiarius*. In his lectures, he has to comment on the four *Libri Sententiarum* of Peter Lombard within two years.[147] This most successful of all collections of *sententiae* in the twelfth century was used for the first time by Alexander of Hales, still a secular clergyman, as a basis of his lectures. This procedure became exemplary during the 1240s in Paris,[148] and a little later at Oxford.[149] Within a few decades, despite some resistance (especially in the Franciscan convent of Oxford[150]), the Sentences of the Lombard became the textual basis of the only systematic lecture of the medieval theologians. Whereas, at first, masters introduced the Sentences into the theological teaching, the sentence lectures soon became a fixed duty of the *baccalareus*.

According to their importance, the statutes required a careful preparation for these lectures. Whoever read on the Sentences was prohibited from using the expositions of other scholars, so that he was obliged to give his own interpretation. By the lecture on the Sentences, the future professor of theology had the opportunity to work independently through the whole dogmatic and

---

annis audiat theologiam, antequam privatas lectiones legat publice [...] (CUP 1,78–80 no. 20; here: 79). The detailed Oxford statutes before 1350 demand among other things: *magistri arcium antequam septem annos theologiam [...], laudabiliter audiendo quam opponendo et respondendo, compleuerint, lecturam libri sentenciarum agredi non presumant.* (Statuta antiqua [1931] 48).

[144] Weijers, Terminologie (1987) 329–35.

[145] Cf. e.g. Statuta antiqua (1931) 50: *Ne autem lecture varie confundantur, et ut expedicius in lectura Biblie procedatur, statutum est ut Bibliam biblice seu cursorie legentes questiones non dicant nisi tantummodo literales.*

[146] *Regulae speciales pro qualibet facultate*, after 1335, c. 11 (CUP 2,691–697 no. 1188; here: 692).

[147] Shortened to one year after the middle of the fourteenth century at some places.

[148] Cf. Alexander of Hales, Glossa [cf. note 106], Prolegomena 65* f.

[149] On Oxford, cf. J. I. Catto, "Theology and theologians 1220–1320", in: History of the University of Oxford 1 (1984) 473, 489.

[150] Köpf, Wissenschaftstheorie (1974) 32 f.

ethic tradition.[151] Details may be omitted here. But it should be mentioned that in the systematic discussion of theological problems innumerable biblical quotations (*auctoritates*) were referred to. Consequently, the lecture on the Sentences is an exposition of countless biblical passages in a systematic arrangement, including many considerations and statements which are fundamental for the exegesis. Generally, this lecture is begun by a discussion of the principles of theology (a sketch of the theory of theology as a discipline like philosophy and the other disciplines of the university). Frequently, the principles of biblical hermeneutics are discussed in it as well.[152] The lecture on the Sentences has its literary outcome in the Commentary on the Sentences which is preserved from all important theologians, sometimes even in two or more versions.[153] The *Summa*, on the contrary, that was created during the twelfth century as a literary form of organizing the theological material, is no longer the immediate result of teaching in the thirteenth century but a private work[154] for which, however, records from the teaching can be utilized.[155]

Whoever has finished with the lecture on the Sentences (from the fourteenth century: whoever is beginning to lecture on the third book of the Sentences) obtained the title of a *baccalareus formatus*. Before he is admitted to the acquisition of the *licentia* he has to be active at the faculty for some more years.[156] During this time, he prepares for autonomous teaching as a master by participation in lectures and academic ceremonies, by preaching, giving *collationes*, and first and foremost by cooperating in disputations (*respondere*). The culmination and conclusion of his career as a theologian is the graduation as *magister* (*doctor*).[157] It consists of two parts: At first the candidate acquires full authority to teach (*licentia [docendi]*). Its necessary requirements are that he has passed the test in cursory reading on the Bible and in lecturing on the Sentences.[158] The actual examination before the imparting of the *licentia* consists in a disputation on the treatment of some *quaestiones* which is submitted by the candidate. Thereafter, the *magistri regentes* account for the scholarly and moral qualities of the candidate (*depositio magistrorum*).[159] The *licentia* includes the right to dispute within the faculty of theology, to give lectures, to

---

[151] Hence the interdiction to deliver a lecture from another person's manuscript: *Statuta facultatis theologiae* (about the middle of the thirteenth century), c. 36 (CUP 2, 697–704 no. 1189; here: 700).

[152] Köpf, Wissenschaftstheorie (1974).

[153] F. Stegmüller, *Repertorium commentariorum in Sententias Petri Lombardi*, 1–2 (Würzburg 1947); V. Doucet, "Commentaires sur les Sentences. Supplément au Répertoire de M. Frédéric Stegmüller", *AFH* 47 (1954) 88–170, 400–427; S. Wlodek, "Commentaires sur les Sentences. Supplément au Répertoire de F. Stegmüller", *BPhM* 5 (1963) 144–46; 6 (1964) 100–04; 7 (1965) 91–95.

[154] E. g. Thomas Aquinas, *Summa contra gentiles; Summa theologiae.*

[155] E. g. Henry of Ghent, *Summa quaestionum ordinariarum.*

[156] At Oxford before 1350 two years (Statuta antiqua [1931] 50); at Paris three to five years (*Regulae speciales*, after 1235, c. 13: CUP 2, 692; *Statuta facultatis theologiae*, at the middle of the thirteenth century, c. 39: CUP 2, 700).

[157] Cf. Weijers, Terminologie (1987) 385–424.

[158] Cf. for Paris: CUP 1, 226, taken up again 281; for Oxford: Statuta antiqua (1931) 49,15–22.

[159] Bazàn, Questions disputées (1985) 111.

preach, and to perform all activities of a master.[160] The second part of the act, the actual graduation as *magister* (*doctor*), consists of the most solemn ceremonies in academic life, which have different forms at different universities. Their forms change in the course of time: at first the *vesperiae*, a strictly formalized solemn disputation on the eve of the ceremony, afterwards the introduction into the circle of the masters by another disputation (*inceptio, principium, [disputatio in] aula* or the like), at last the beginning of independent teaching by the resumption of the *principium* begun at the *inceptio* (therefore: *resumpta*), i.e. the inaugural lecture at the beginning of regular teaching as a master.

Not only the *inceptio* of the master but each advancement in the academic career is connected with solemn acts. Apart from the examination and the oath, inaugural lectures are prescribed at the beginning of each new step in teaching. Already the *baccalareus biblicus* has to deliver an *introitus* (*principium*) at the beginning of each of his two cursus. An *introitus* is a general introduction to the Holy Scripture (*Commendatio S. Scripturae*) referring to a biblical *motto*. It is often connected with statements about the biblical books but without biblical *quaestio*.[161] Similarly, the *baccalareus sententiarius* has to introduce the lecture about each of the four Sentence Books by *principia*. They commence with biblical *motti* as well; their method corresponds to the method used in the *principia* of the *baccalarei biblici*. Finally, the newly admitted master, too, has to give an inaugural lecture on his text that is likewise a *commendatio S. Scripturae*. All these lectures are connected with one another within a genre of literary introductions (*introitus, accessus ad auctores* and the like) which were in use from the early Middle Ages referring to antique patterns. They are structured according to different points of view; in the thirteenth century, the Aristotelian scheme of the four *causae* (*materialis, formalis, efficiens, finalis*) is added to the elder series of aspects. Many of these inaugural lectures are preserved, partly handed down as isolated pieces, partly used for the introductions of commentaries on the Sentences and on the Bible.[162]

In summary: The master is the member of the teaching staff who is authorized to teach on a full range of subjects. Apart from his care for the students, their examination, and different administrative functions at the university, he has three main tasks:

1. the independent performance and direction of the disputation, the formulation of the theme and the finding of a solution. An outstanding part is played at the theological faculty of the Paris university by the *disputatio de quolibet*.

2. the lecture: Its regular subject matter from the second half of the thirteenth century is the Holy Scripture.[163] The master has free choice of the bibli-

---

[160] *De modo licenciandi in theologia* c. 24 (CUP 2, 683 no. 1185): *[Cancellarius] auctoritate Dei omnipotentis et apostolorum Petri et Pauli et sedis apostolice dat eis licenciam disputandi, legendi et predicandi et omnes actus exercendi in theologica facultate qui ad magistrum pertinent [...].*

[161] Cf. the Bolognese statutes, Rubr. 6 (I più antichi statuti [1932] 21, 11–15).

[162] Köpf, Wissenschaftstheorie (1974) 46, 74 f and other passages.

[163] In the beginnings of theological faculties the *Historia Scholastica* of Peter Comestor was probably occasionally used not only as an aid in lectures but as their basis. Cf. the Oxford statutes from 1253 (Statuta antiqua [1931] 49): *nullus [...] incipiat in theologia [...] nisi legerit aliquem librum de canone Biblie uel librum sentenciarum uel historiarum.* The lectures on the Sentences were

cal books on which he comments; but some focal points were developed: Genesis, the Prophets (especially Isaiah), the Psalter; Matthew, John, the Epistles. The lecture of the master differs from the biblical lecture of the cursor by its completeness of detail and its profoundness. There are no directions on the time which is at disposal for individual books. The master can expand his lectures to any extent. He can deepen the exposition of the literal sense not only by allegorical interpretation but by inserting *quaestiones* about problems without limits. That way, the exegesis of the master quite often becomes a presentation of his theology.

3. The preaching (*sermo, collatio*) is in addition to both kinds of teaching the third main duty of the master. Its theme is taken from the Holy Scripture. The preaching, too, like the commentary of the Bible, is influenced by scholastic forms of thinking and writing.

4. Retrospective View: The Bible in the Medieval System of Education

The central position of the Old Testament in monastic erudition can be detected clearly from the description of the monastic form of life. For the monk, the most important book in the Holy Scripture is the Psalter, the basic text of his daily prayer which, according to the rule of Benedict, has to be prayed completely during one week beginning with Sunday (RB 18.23). Moreover, for the monk the Psalter is the embodiment of biblical religious instruction. The knowledge of its wording and the understanding of its content is therefore the central aim of learning in monastic education. The daily occupation with the Psalter results in an intense monastic exegesis as well as a language impregnated by quotations from the Psalms. But for the clergy, too, the Psalter has central importance as a prayer book and as an instruction for the religous life. Therefore, the Psalter plays an outstanding part in the cathedral school as well. In addition, monks and clergymen are familiar with the whole Bible due to liturgy and *lectio divina.* They show great familiarity especially with the Gospels and the Epistles of the New Testament, as well as with the text of the Prophets, and are interested in their exposition. While in monasteries the commentary and the exposition are firmly established as part of the sermon too, at cathedral schools it is also common to study biblical texts and problems in *quaestiones* by the means of logic.

The survey of the career and the teaching of the university theologian demonstrated that the Bible played the central part at the theological faculty.

1. Problems of introduction, dispositions and general interpretations of the Holy Scripture as well as of individual books are explained mainly in the academic *principia* of the *baccalareus biblicus* and the master, but also ventilated in *quaestiones* of disputations, sentence commentaries and Bible commentaries.

---

given by a master only in the beginnings; later on they were exclusively the duty of the *baccalarei.* Cf. also P. Glorieux, Art. Sentences (1940), especially 1865.

2. Whole biblical books are interpreted in lectures. The cursory presentation of the content of biblical books is the task of the *baccalarei biblici*; its careful and often long lasting commentary is the duty of the masters.

3. Many problems which are connected with the biblical text are discussed in the disputations, in commentaries of the masters, and in a systematic context in sentence commentaries.

4. *Sermones* and *collationes* always have a biblical theme. Thus, likewise, they give the opportunity for an exposition of individual biblical passages.

Chapter Twenty-eight

Aspects of Old Testament Interpretation in the Church from the Seventh to the Tenth Century

By Claudio Leonardi, Florence

Bibliography: B. Bischoff, "Wendepunkte in der Geschichte der lateinischen Exegese im Frühmittelalter", *SacEr* 6 (1954), 189–251; repr. in idem, *Mittelalterliche Studien* I (Stuttgart 1986) 205–73; B. Bischoff / M. Lapidge, *Biblical Commentaries from the Canterbury School of Theodore and Hadrian* (Cambridge 1994); J. Black, "De Civitate Dei and the Commentaries of Gregory the Great, Isidore, Bede, and Hrabanus Maurus on the Book of Samuel", *Augustinian Studies* 15 (1984) 114–27; idem, "Isidore, Bede and Hrabanus Maurus on the Book of Samuel", *Old English Newsletters* 16 (1983); F. Brunhölzl, *Geschichte der lateinischen Literatur des Mittelalters* I (München 1975; French tr. *Histoire de la littérature latine du Moyen Age*, I/2; Turnhout 1991); Silvia Cantelli Berarducci, *Angelomo e la scuola esegetica di Luxeuil* (Spoleto 1990); eadem, "L'esegesi al tempo di Ludovico il Pio e Carlo il Calvo", *Giovanni Scoto nel suo tempo* (Spoleto 1989); eadem, "L'esegesi della Rinascita carolingia", in: G. Cremascoli / C. Leonardi (eds.), *La Bibbia nel Medio Evo* (Bologna 1996) 167–98; M. Cappuyns, *Jean Scot Erigène. Sa vie, son œuvre, sa pensée* (Louvain 1933); J. Châtillon, "Recherches sur les sources et l'influence des *Quaestiones* in Vetus Testamentum d'Isidore de Séville", *Mélanges A. Robert* (Paris 1957) 533–47; J. J. Contreni, "The Biblical Glosses of Haimo of Auxerre and John Scottus Eriugena", *Spec.* 51 (1976) 797–813; idem, "Carolingian Biblical Studies", *Carolingian Essays. Andrew W. Mellon Lectures in Early Christian Studies* (ed. Uta-Renate Blumenthal; Washington, DC 1983) 71–98; G. Cremascoli, "Tradizione esegetica e teologia nell'Alto Medioevo", *L'Italia tra Tardo Antico e Alto Medioevo* II (Roma 1981) 713–29; G. Cremascoli / C. Leonardi (eds.), *La Bibbia nel Medioevo* (Bologna 1996;) J. Fleckenstein, *Die Bildungsreform Karls des Grossen als Verwircklichung der norma rectitudinis* (Bigge 1951); J. Fontaine, "Fins et moyens de l'enseignement ecclésiastique dans l'Espagne wisigothique", *La scuola nell'Occidente latino dell'Alto Medioevo* (Spoleto 1972) 145–202; idem, "Grammaire sacré et grammaire profane: Isidore de Séville devant l'exégèse biblique", in: idem, *Tradition et actualité chez Isidore de Séville* (London 1998) 311–29; idem, *Isidore de Séville et la culture classique dans l'Espagne wisigothique* 1–2 (Paris 1959) 3 (Paris 1983); idem, "Isidore de Séville, pédagogue et théoricien de l'exégèse", *Stimuli. Exegese und ihre Hermeneutik in Antike und Christentum. Festschrift für Ernst Dassmann* (Münster i. W. 1996); Beatrice Gigli, *Le Quaestiones in vetus Testamentum di Isidoro di Siviglia* (diss. pro ms.; Firenze 1993); *Glossae divinae historiae. The Biblical Glosses of John Scottus Eriugena* (ed. John J. Contreni / Pádraig P. Ó Néill; Firenze 1997); M. Gorman, "Bede's VIII Quaestiones and Carolingian Biblical Scholarship", *RBén* 109 (1999); idem, "A Carolingian Epitome of St. Augustine's De Genesi ad litteram", *REAug* 29 (1983) 7–30; idem, "The Commentary on Genesis of Claudius of Turin and Biblical Studies under Louis the Pious", *Spec.* 72 (1997) 279–329; idem, "The Commentary on Kings of Claudius of Turin and its Two Printed Editions", *Filologia mediolatina* 4 (1997) 99–131; idem, "The Commentary on the Pentateuch Attributed to Bede in PL 91. 189–394", *RBén* 106 (1996) 61–108; idem, "The Encyclopedic Commentary on Genesis Prepared for Charlemagne by Wigbod", *RAug* 17 (1982) 173–201; idem, "From Isidore to Claudius of Turin: the Works of Ambrose on Genesis in the Early Middle Ages", *REAug* 45 (1999) 121–38; idem, "An Unedited Fragment of an Irish Epitome of St. Augustine's De Genesi ad litteram", *REAug* 28 (1982) 76–85; idem, "The Visigothic Commentary on Genesis in MS Autun 27 (S. 29)", *REAug* 29 (1996) 167–277; idem, "Wigbod and Biblical Studies under Charlemagne", *RBén* 107 (1997) 40–76; idem, "Wigbod and the Lectiones on the Hexateuch attributed to Bede in Paris lat. 2342", *RBén* 38 (1995) 310–47; J. B. Hablitzel, *Hrabanus Maurus. Ein Beitrag zur*

Geschichte der mittelalterlichen Exegese (Freiburg i.B. 1906); idem, "Paschasius Radbertus und Hrabanus Maurus", *Studien und Mitteilungen zur Geschichte des Benediktinerordens* 57 (1939) 113–16; W. Hartmann, "Die karolingische Reform und die Bibel", *Annuarium historiae Conciliorum. Internationale Zeitschrift für Konziliengeschichtsforschung* 18 (1986) 58–74; D. Iogna-Prat, "L'œuvre d'Haymon d'Auxerre", *L'école carolingienne d'Auxerre, De Muretach à Remi 830–908* (Paris 1991) 157–79; Giuliana Italiani, *La tradizione esegetica nel commentario ai Re di Claudio di Torino* (Firenze 1979); Jean Scot, *Commentaire sur l'Evangile de Jean* (ed. E. Jeauneau; Paris 1980); idem, *Homélie sur le Prologue de Jean* (ed. E. Jeauneau; Paris 1969); C. Jenkins, "Bede as Exegete and Theologian", in: A. Hamilton Thompson (ed.), *Bede. His Life, Times, and Writings* (Oxford 1935) 152–200; C. Leonardi, "L'esegesi altomedievale: da Cassiodoro ad Autperto (secoli VI–VIII)", G. Cremascoli / C. Leonardi (eds.), *La Bibbia nel Medio Evo* (Bologna 1996) 149–65; idem, "La spiritualità di Ambrogio Autperto", *Studi medievali* 9 (1968) 1–131; idem, "Il Venerabile Beda e la cultura del secolo VIII", *I problemi dell'Occidente latino del secolo VIII* (Spoleto 1973) 603–58; E. A. Matter, "The Lamentations Commentaries of Rabanus Maurus and Paschasius Radbertus", *Traditio* 38 (1982) 137–63; idem, "The Pseudo-Alcuinian De Septem Sigillis. An Early Latin Apocalypse Exegesis", *Traditio* 37 (1980) 3–37; R. E. McNally, *The Bible in the Early Middle Ages* (Westminster, MD 1959); idem, "The Pseudo-Isidorian 'De Vetere et Novo Testamento Quaestiones'", *Traditio* 19 (1963); idem, "The 'Tres Linguae Sacrae' in Early Irish Bible Exegesis", *TS* 19 (1958) 395–403; W. Neuss, *Die Apokalypse des hl. Johannes in der altspanischen und altchristlichen Bibelillustrationen (Das Problem der Beatus-Handschriften)* I–II (Münster i.W. 1931); F. Ogara, "Tipología bíblica según S. Isidoro", *Miscellanea Isidoriana. Homenaje a San Isidoro de Sevilla en el XIII centenario de su muerte* (Roma 1936) 135–50; W. Otten, "The Texture of Tradition. The Role of the Church Fathers in Carolingian Theology", *The Reception of the Church Fathers in the West* I (ed. I. Backup; Leiden 1997) 3–50; Sara Passi, *Il commentario ai Vangeli attribuito a Vigbodo* (diss. pro ms.; Firenze 1996); R. D. Ray, "Bede, the Exegete, as Historian", *Famulus Christi. Essays in Commemoration of the Thirteenth Centenary of the Birth of the Venerable Bede* (London 1976) 125–40; H. Reinelt, "Hrabanus Maurus als Exeget", *Hrabanus Maurus und seine Schule* (ed. W. Böhme; Fulda 1980) 64–76; E. Riggenbach, *Die ältesten lateinischen Kommentare zum Hebräerbrief* (Leipzig 1907); A. Saltman, *Pseudo-Jerome, Quaestiones on the Book of Samuel* (Leiden 1975); M. Simonetti, "De mirabilibus Sacrae Scripturae, un trattato irlandese sui miracoli della Sacra Scrittura", *Romano Barbarica* 3 (1979) 225–51; idem, "La tecnica esegetica di Beda nel commento a 1 Samuele", *Romano Barbarica* 5 (1983) 75–100; Maria Novella Todaro, *Il commentario di Rabano Mauro a Geremia* (diss. pro ms.; Firenze 1997); M. Zarb, "Sancti Isidori cultus erga Sacras Litteras", *Miscellanea Isidoriana. Homenaje a San Isidoro de Sevilla en el XIII centenario de su muerte* (Roma 1936) 91–134.

1. Isidore of Seville

Isidore was born in Seville in ca. 570. His father Severianus belonged to a Hispano-Roman family of the lesser nobility, and came from Carthagena, the city on the Southern coast founded by Hannibal in the third century BCE, that the Visigoths had conquered and looted, as Isidore himself recalls in the *Etymologiae* (XV.I.67): "a Gothis subversa atque in desolationem redacta est". At Carthagena were born Isidore's brothers and sisters, Leander, Fulgentius and Florentina. Severianus had left Carthagena around the middle of the century and had died soon after Isidore was born, so that it was his brother Leander, who became bishop of Seville in 596, who brought him up. At his death, in 600, Isidore succeeded him in the episcopate. Leander's political and cultural activity was continued and greatly developed by Isidore, in the tradition inaugurated in the sixth century by Boethius and Cassiodorus in particular. With the two brothers, and particularly the younger, the cultural interest had its focus in the Bible as well as in a set of notions typical of a pagan tradition having their starting-point and centre in grammar.[1]

Indeed, the Spanish situation, with the Visigoths enjoying political supremacy, largely resembled that of Boethius and Cassiodorus in Italy, under the Ostrogoths. While the situation changed in Italy, as shown by the work of Pope Gregory I (590–604), in Spain a cultural state of affairs still persisted in which pagan culture flourished alongside a Christian one; in Italy now, after the Lombard occupation, such a culture no longer seemed possible; Gregory I experienced a culture by now exclusively ecclesiastical, without any link with the school system and concerned first and foremost with the spiritual formation of the clergy and the faithful.

For Isidore, on the other hand, it was possible to think of, and to operate in, a culture setting grammar as the foundation of education, even though such education was mainly directed towards the clergy. Cassiodorus, after the conquest of Italy by Justinian, had imagined an élite school for monks, almost outside the lay world; now Isidore conceived a school for ecclesiastics who would be committed by now, after king Recared's (580–601) conversion, to create a unified kingdom by means of the Visigoths' integration into the Romano-Christian tradition. Of this integration Isidore was the champion.[2]

Grammar was seen by Isidore as the fundamental science for learning. With etymology as its capital instrument (in Isidore's view), it enabled him to create as vast an encyclopedia as the *Etymologiae*, written between 620 and his death in 636. This work represented the *summa* of Christian and human learning interpreted on the basis of the *etymon*, disclosing the original truth of every word and therefore of every thing. In Isidore, grammar becomes an instrument of culture by way of its linguistic element. It was such an instrument which enabled him to think of a synthesis of the whole Christian heritage, of an all-encompassing theology in which the concrete demands of a school might be met.

For an episcopal school biblical information was in itself of primary importance.[3] Therefore, besides many other works, Isidore also wrote biblical commentaries, which clearly look like compilations: Isidore really wanted to use them to create a *summa* of the Patristic Tradition to bring it to bear on his own political aim: to create a cultural élite capable of shaping the *Hispania* (for which he would also write the celebrated *Laus Spaniae*). His exegetical works are the following: the *De ortu et obitu Patrum*, written at the beginning of the seventh century; the *Allegoriae quaedam sacrae Scripturae*, datable to 612–615; the *Proemia in libros veteris ac novi Testamenti*, reworked over almost two decades until 615, and finally the *Quaestiones in vetus Testamentum* or *Mysticorum expositiones sacramentorum*, written in the last few years of his life (approximately between 624 and 636).

The first two commentaries deal with the main characters of the Old and New Testament: in *De obitu Patrum* (PL 83, 129–156), one finds an historical

---

[1] Cf. J. Fontaine, Isidore de Séville et la culture (1959/1983); idem, Isidore de Séville pédagogue (1996) 423–34.

[2] Cf. J. Fontaine, Fins et moyens (1972); idem, Grammaire sacré (1998).

[3] Cf. C. Leonardi, L'esegesi altomedievale (1996) 160–61.

synopsis of their life, in the *Allegoriae* (PL 83, 97–130) Isidore gives an allegorical interpretation of them, i.e. an explanation of the doctrine hidden in their story. In the former case, Isidore clearly employed a literal exegesis, in the latter an allegorical one, focusing on a selection of biblical characters which was to a great extent always the same. He felt the need for school teaching to be brief and clear, as he pointed out in the preface to the *Allegoriae*: "Quaedam notissima nomina Legis Evangeliorumque ... breviter deflorata contraxi celeriter, ut plana atque aperta lectoribus redderem" (PL 83, 97–98). The typological interpretative key applied to the Old Testament is of the classical kind, Origenian and Augustinian: the Old is a figure of the New Testament, the characters of the Old are a figure of Christ. The same exegetical criterion may be noticed in the *Proemia* (PL 83, 155–180), in which for all the books of the Bible (Old and New Testament) a short summary is given. With such a trilogy, Isidore seems to have supplied a simple and clear handbook on the characters and stories of the Christian Bible from Genesis to the Apocalypse.[4]

More important and significant, besides these three small treatises, is the vast work of his full maturity. The title indicates Isidore's intention of composing a work unveiling the truth of the *sacramenta*, of the mysteries, contained in the Old Testament, so that they may become clear to Christians: therefore the *Mysticorum expositiones sacramentorum* (PL 83, 207–424) form a work of doctrine and doctrinal clarification, later called *Quaestiones in Vetus Testamentum* to show their exegetical nature in an immediate and practical manner.[5]

The Old Testament is exclusively read in the *Quaestiones* according to the allegorical interpretation, also because Isidore must have written a similar work according to the literal interpretation, as indeed he claims himself in the opening lines: "quia iam pridem iuxta litteram a nobis sermo totus contextus est, necesse est ut praecedente historiae fundamento allegoricus sensus sequatur" (PL 83, 208 B). The work containing this reading according to the letter of the Old Testament has not been discovered until now, but it would correspond to the plan already implemented with the pair consisting of the *De obitu Patrum* and the *Allegoriae*.

The *Quaestiones* do not cover the whole of the Old Testament, but only the books from Genesis to Kings. Isidore's commentary, as in the other exegetical works of his, is clear and brief, but this time, he shows at least a tendency to carry it out verse by verse. He constructed his exegesis by means of a wide selection of his sources, as he himself states: he has summarised "in unam formam compendio brevitatis" the precious writings of the Fathers, so that the reader "non nostra leget sed veterum releget", and he repeats: "quod ego enim loquor, illi dicunt, et vox mea ipsorum est lingua". And he immediately lists his sources: Origen, Marius Victorinus, Ambrose, Jerome, Augustine, Fulgentius, John Cassian and his own contemporary Pope Gregory (PL 83, 207, 209 A).[6] This is a case in which his own commentary is denied originality and its value

[4] Cf. Ogara, Tipología bíblica (1936); Zarb, Sancti Isidori cultus (1936).
[5] Cf. Châtillon, Recherches (1957).
[6] Cf. Gigli, Le Quaestiones (1993); Gorman, The Commentary on the Pentateuch (1996) 299–302.

is attributed to the sources: the Latin Fathers alone, up to Gregory, which had corresponded with Isidore's brother Leander, and to Origen, read in the Latin translation by Rufinus. We thus face the issue of Isidore's originality. If one analyses the sources used to explain the individual verses, one realises that he mostly resorted to the method of a sharp reduction of the sources set side by side, regardless of the times of composition and of the exegetical modes. And this he was able to do because he had a clear objective in mind, guiding his choice, the composition of connecting parts and most probably also his own personal interpretations.

Isidore's originality lies in his full reduction of the Old to the New Testament. Allegory is used by him to read every Old Testament passage and to discover in it the proclamation of Christ's own message and / or of his Church. He avoided theological discussions and spiritual or mystical implications. I would argue that in seventh-century Spain, in a multi-ethnic Romano-Germanic society as it was now, just recently converted to a single religion, Catholicism, in a society, moreover, in which one had to restore scholastic institutions and restructure them, gaining an understanding of the Old Testament represented a major difficulty for teachers and pupils, for bishops and clergy. The letter of the New Testament, on the other hand, was much more immediately clear to the old and to the new faithful. Isidore paid therefore particular attention, with the *Quaestiones*, to the Old Testament, and attempted to refer it entirely to the New.

His aim was to make of the *Quaestiones* a reference manual, easy enough for whoever came across any Old Testament quotation. And he constructed it with great skill: driven by the concern to be, as in the other exegetical works, brief and clear, using his favourite instruments, etymology, and grammar, seen as a science of linguistic precision. Within this rather rigid scheme, he developed a straightforward theology, meaning to instruct his readers with the minimum of doctrine concerning Christ and his Church. The doctrinal interest could but lean on Augustine's work[7], whereas for the allegorical interpretation he had to use above all Origen. A complete study of the *Quaestiones* has not yet been carried out. But one may already say, to mention but a few examples, that Augustine's *Contra Faustum Manichaeum* was in Isidore's mind in the commentary on Exodus and Leviticus, that Origen's *homiliae* were in that on Exodus and Joshua, that Jerome's ep. 78 is very much exploited in the Commentary on Numbers, while Cassian's *Collationes* feature in that on Deuteronomy.[8]

When one thinks that Isidore had written a work resembling the *Quaestiones* devoted to the literal explanation, one may see how his hermeneutic interest was related to the understanding of the text (by grammar and etymology) and to a doctrinal reflection. A trace of this interest of his is also found in the chapters he devoted to the Bible in books VI and VII of the *Etymologiae*. This dual and explicit method of constructing his commentary is adjusted by Isidore, uninterested as he was in integrating it into a single method, to the

---

[7] Cf. Black, De Civitate Dei and the Commentaries (1984).
[8] Cf. Gigli (1993).

educational needs of the clergy, at a time in Spain's history in which the clergy itself begins to take on a leading political role.

2. The Venerable Bede

Isidore apparently read the Old Testament in the light of the New, hence his reading was totally typological; but also apparent in him is the need for the Old Testament, and also for a comprehensive commentary on Scripture. Yet, most probably in Visigothic Spain itself, some decades after Isidore, a commentary on Genesis was written in which a literal interpretation prevails; the commentary is found in a manuscript in Visigothic half uncial held in Autun, Bibliothèque Municipale, n. 27.[9]

However, the exegetical standpoints of Isidore and of Spain during his lifetime were soon to prove too broad for the demands of the public and the needs of the school. The Germanic political hegemony had greatly contributed to the making of Medieval Europe, but its strong link with the oral traditions and its albeit partial refusal of written culture had, over approximately two centuries, from the sixth to the eighth, dramatically reduced the space of written exegesis. A number of facts highlights this state of affairs. Indeed, even Isidore's *Quaestiones* must have seemed too rich and broad a commentary, if soon after someone felt the need to make an abridgement of it.[10] This hermeneutic position may indeed be justified on the basis of a fall in the demand for written commentaries: at school one could be content with explanations of single words for each verse or for the main verses: almost a translation into a simpler language.

Too many texts are yet to be studied, or have yet remained anonymous, or have been edited with such philological uncertainty as to make it extremely difficult to afford a clear historical picture. And perhaps too many of these texts have been classified under the heading of Irish exegesis, though undoubtedly many Irish teachers did draw up commentaries.[11] Only a few Old Testament books had been fully commented upon by the Latin exegetical tradition, ensuring that each verse be exhaustively explained: among these the book of Psalms by Cassiodorus, and of Job by Gregory the Great. Very well-known and used were the commentary on the Psalms by Augustine (taken up by Cassiodorus)[12] and that on the Exameron by Ambrose, which on the contrary was less successful.[13] Undoubtedly the Middle Ages, guaranteeing for centuries the central place of the Bible in its culture and education, were faced with as daunting a problem as a comprehensive commentary on the books of the Old and the New Testament.

This problem however did not concern the Irish. As far as Old Testament exegesis is concerned, an abridgement of Gregory the Great's *Moralia in Iob*

---

[9] Cf. Gorman, The Visigothic Commentary (1996).
[10] Cf. Gorman, From Isidore to Claudius (1999) 124–25.
[11] Cf. Bischoff, Wendepunkte (1954/1986).
[12] Cf. Gorman, An United Fragment (1982) 76–85; idem, A Carolingian Epitome (1983) 7–30.
[13] Cf. Gorman (as at n. 10).

was made by an Irishman, Lathcen; to Augustine the Irishman has been attributed a *De mirabilibus sacrae scripturae*,[14] describing and explaining several miracles told in the Bible; anonymous are the *Pauca problemata de aenigmatibus ex tomis canonicis*, "where perhaps the character of such exegetical literature stands out more clearly, i. e. its focus on the explanation of the individual passages, in order to devise a commentary in the form of a string of glosses, in which erudition prevails as a result of scholastic schematism".[15] For this reason the commentaries held to be of the Irish school are written as a question-and-answer set of dialogues between masters and pupils, a set of *quaestiones* and *responsiones.*

In fact, many are the anthologies, the abridgements, the collections of various kinds with second- alongside first-hand material not always classifiable as genuine biblical commentaries. In Visigothic Spain itself, at the end of the seventh century, just before the Arabic conquest, Taio of Zaragoza (651–683) gathered in his *Sententiae* (PL 80, 727–990) a number of patristic texts in which exegetical works occur also; while most noteworthy is the *Antikeimenon* (PL 96, 595–704) of Julian of Toledo (667–698), where the individual biblical passages held to be particularly difficult are explained using the question-and-answer literary format.

In comparison with this production, the work of Bede, called the Venerable (ca. 673–735), marks a distinct progress.[16] A native of Northumbria and later a monk at Wearmouth-Jarrow, he was the representative of a culture formed in a Germanic territory but grown to the full maturity of the written culture. While his masterpiece remains the *Historia ecclesiastica gentis Anglorum*, he also wrote many other historical and hagiographical works, he dealt with various issues, metrical, chronological and cosmological, and he spent a great deal of his time explaining and writing commentaries on the books of the Bible, fully developing the first Anglo-Saxon commentaries of the Canterbury school.[17] Thus in various ways, and more or less comprehensively, he wrote exegesis on the following biblical books: Genesis, Exodus, Kings, Ezra and Nehemiah, Tobit, Proverbs, the Song of Songs, Habakkuk in the Old Testament; and Mark, Luke, the Acts of the Apostles, the Catholic Epistles and the Apocalypse in the New Testament.

This vast exegetical production is an attestation of how the Bible had by now become one of the inevitable interests of early Medieval scholars. The first origins of biblical commentaries from within the schools may also be testified by the form in which they have been transmitted. Bede's one on Genesis was written in three forms: one gets to Genesis 2:3, that is to the six days of Creation and to the concluding seventh (in one book); a second one (in two books) covers the same story but is extended as far as Gensis 3:2 (the beginning of the

---

[14] Cf. Simonetti, De mirabilibus Sacrae Scripturae (1979) 225–51.

[15] Cf. Leonardi (as at n. 3), 162.

[16] Cf. Jenkins, Bede as Exegete and Theologian (1935); Leonardi, Il Venerabile Beda (1973); Ray, Bede, the Exegete, as Historian (1976) 125–40.

[17] Cf. Bischoff / Lapidge, Biblical Commentaries (1994); McNally, The Tres Linguae Sacrae (1958); idem, The Pseudo-Isidorian (1963).

account of the original Fall); the third one, in three books, is the exegesis of Genesis 1:1 to 21:10, that is to the birth of Isaac, and covers then more than half of the whole book.[18] For the four books of Kings (thus according to the Septuagint and the Vulgate) we have a similar thing: Bede wrote a commentary on the first book (also called Samuel I), but only as far as 21:33,[19] and then the *Triginta quaestiones in libros Regum*, a *De templo Salomonis* (in the third book) and finally the *Octo quaestiones*.[20] The commentary on the Acts of the Apostles, just to hint at the New Testament books, is also transmitted in two versions.

Yet, Bede's objective was not only and not quite didactic. In him a hermeneutic intention and an exegetical awareness are clearly manifest. Indeed he not only considered the opportunities offered by the school, but also met the demands of exegesis. Of the Gospels he only commented on Mark and Luke, because those of Matthew and John (the latter the subject-matter of Augustine's *Tractatus*) had been sufficiently explained; and among the epistles he only dealt with the Catholic ones, since the Pauline ones had already been commented upon. But Bede was perfectly aware of having to find a norm for his own exegesis and he found it in the Fathers: he wrote "iuxta traditionem Patrum aeque catholicorum" (*De temporum ratione*, V),[21] and for every commentary not only did he scrupulously indicate his sources in the premises or in the epistola dedicatoria, but he also made it a habit of marking on the margins of his manuscript the sources he used with an abbreviation for each name; these abbreviations have sometimes passed from his own manuscript onto the copies which have come down to us.

It is not feasible to say, however, that Bede wrote his commentaries as a mere compilation of excerpts from the Fathers. Drawing inspiration from Gregory the Great, he actually developed an exegesis of his own taking into account the four-fold interpretation of Scripture, but equally capable of giving the Bible a global, all-encompassing meaning applied verse by verse, even in repetitive terms. And this interpretation has as his centre and address Jesus Christ, more than his Church (as was the case with Gregory), as a concrete congregation of faithful. The integration between the Germanic and the Christian Latin traditions had for the most part already taken place, it had reached a certain degree of maturity; Christianity was taking shape, that is a society having as its own single reference point the Christian values. It is to this society in its formative stages, which for Bede had already got Rome as its centre, that he addressed the *Historia ecclesiastica* and also his biblical commentaries. For him Christ was the leader of the people, but Christ was also the friend of the human heart; his reading of the Old Testament was wholly typological; he made use of allegory in particular, just like Isidore, to disclose the doctrine proclaiming Christ, but more often he perused every verse of the Bible, of the Old and of the New Testament, to discover an affirmation of fullness and sal-

[18] Cf. Gorman, The Commentary on the Pentateuch (1996).
[19] Cf. Simonetti, La tecnica esegetica di Beda (1983).
[20] Cf. Gorman, Bede's VIII Quaestiones (1999).
[21] Cf. Corp. Christ., 123-B, p. 59.

vation, in which he believed and which he intended to communicate as the only pacifying message of the Bible. Such a reading may be defined, at root, spiritual and mystical.

On the fringes of the Carolingian Renaissance, some decades after Bede, operated two exegetes of great worth, of good learning and of great significance: Ambrose Autpert,[22] who died in Southern Italy under the Lombards in 784, and Beatus / Blessed of Liébana,[23] who met his death in the Asturias in 798. They commented on the Apocalypse in different and original terms, but did not directly deal with the Old Testament books.

However in the eighth century we see the beginnings of a new type of exegesis, the first example of which seems to be provided by Wigbod.

3. Biblical Exegesis at the Time of Charlemagne

The innovation in the exegesis of the Carolingian era, from the last decades of eighth to the beginning of the tenth centuries, seems to have been triggered, as was the case for other literary genres and in fact for the whole of the culture of this period, by a political impulse, and precisely the will of Charlemagne (742–814) himself. Undoubtedly Charles, as his kingdom grew gradually larger and stronger, thought it fit that a unified culture be promoted in all his lands.[24] In spite of him being very closely attached to the Germanic traditions and to their oral culture, with him the Germanic world moved most maturely towards a written culture. The Bible became in Charlemagne's own planning an integral part of the school syllabus.[25] It was no longer individual teachers who studied it and taught it, it was a scholastic system which promoted the study of the Bible and consequently exegesis.[26]

A pioneering role at the beginning of the exegetical activity promoted by Charlemagne seems to have been played by Wigbod.[27] We know very little about him. It seems that in 786 he was a member of the king's delegation in England, and that he was at Lorsch and Trier. For certain he wrote a commentary on the Octateuch commissioned to him directly by Charlemagne, as he himself recalls in the poem placed at the beginning of the commentary (PL 96, 1103). His *Quaestiones in Octateuchum* were probably the first case of, and therefore the model for, Carolingian exegesis: a model that would be applied particularly by the first and second generations of scholars and school teachers of the Carolingian era, which may be summed up in the names of Alcuin of York and Hraban Maur.

Wigbod still adopted the *quaestio* technique, based on questions and answers, and commented on the books from Genesis to Ruth by collecting pas-

---

22 Cf. Leonardi, La spiritualità (1968).

23 Cf. Neuss, Die Apokalypse (1931).

24 Cf. Fleckenstein, Die Bildungsreform Karls des Großen (1951).

25 Cf. Hartmann, Die karolingische Reform (1986).

26 See a list of Commentaries in McNally, The Bible (1959); cf. Cantelli Berarducci, L'esegesi della Rinascita (1996) 167–98; Contreni, Carolingian (1983) 71–98.

27 Cf. Gorman, The Encyclopedic Commentary (1982); idem, Wigbod and the Lectiones on the Hexateuch (1995); idem, Wigbod and Biblical Studies (1997).

sages from previous commentaries, transcribing them verbatim, and taking care that every verse be commented upon; he did not select verses, but systematically commented on them choosing between the sources at his disposal. Wigbod's sources for Genesis are above all Augustine with the *De Genesi ad litteram*, the *Hebraicae Quaestiones* and other short tracts by Jerome for literal exegesis, and Isidore's *Quaestiones* for the allegorical one. In other terms, Wigbod drew inspiration from Isidore's method, but applied it fully to the whole text of one or more biblical books, reducing to a minimum or to nil his own personal written contribution. The choice of sources and their integration within the body of the text thus became the absolute criterion of exegesis. A quotation from the Fathers is not always direct: so, for instance, Wigbod did not know the *De genesi ad litteram* directly, but through anonymous Medieval texts, such as the *Explanatio sex dierum* (PL 93, 207–234) and the *Exhymeron*, an abridgement of Irish origin.[28]

To Wigbod has also been recently attributed, with good reason, a commentary on the four Gospels.[29] He clearly attempted, under Charlemagne's impulse, to embark on a comprehensive commentary on the Bible according to cultural and didactic needs different from those of earlier times. Wigbod's new method was followed and perfected by Alcuin, by Claudius of Turin and above all by Hraban Maur. Alcuin (ca. 734–804) was the main collaborator of Charlemagne's cultural policy. Of Anglo-Saxon origin and an admirer of Bede, he must be credited with the use of Bedian exegesis in its Carolingian offshoots. Among others, Alcuin wrote commentaries on Genesis (PL 100, 515–566), on Ecclesiastes (PL 100, 667–722), on the Song of Songs (PL 100, 641–664), on the Gospel of John and perhaps on the Apocalypse.[30] He sometimes used the *quaestio* methodology, as in his *Interrogationes et responsiones in Genesim* (281 questions), generally abridged or cut down his sources, but in more than one case he freely intervened with additions and glosses; his personal reputation made it possible for his exegetical works (as is the case for the commentary on Genesis) to be very widespread already in the Carolingian period.

More direct followers of Wigbod's method were Claudius of Turin (who died in ca. 827) and Hraban Maur (ca. 776–856). Both of them operated, at least for a period in their life, in close and somehow direct contact with the courts, and as for Wigbod, their commentaries were commissioned by the court circles. The Carolingian power had a vested interest in an ideological justification which at that time could but refer to Christian theology. If this ideology found it necessary to fix its general and genealogical reference point in the Genesis story, it could find in the books of Kings, in the figures of the kings of Israel, from Saul to Solomon, and in David in particular, it could find a direct justification for the potentially absolute power of the Carolingian kings, also inclined to claim a supremacy over the Church.[31]

It is significant that after Wigbod, Claudius, who, before becoming bishop

---

[28] Cf. Gorman, An Unedited Fragment (1982).
[29] Cf. Passi, Il commentario (1996).
[30] Cf. Matter, The Pseudo-Alcuinian De Septem Sigillis (1980) 3–37.
[31] Cf. Hartmann, Die karolingische Reform (1986).

of Turin had been at the court of Aquitaine, commented on Genesis, Leviticus, Numbers, Kings, Joshua, and Ruth, whereas Hraban Maur drew up exegetical texts for the whole of the Octateuch. We are dealing with commentaries which in Bede's tradition indicated on the margins the sources selected, and attempted to explain in an exhaustive manner the individual books of the Bible, the authors resorting to all they know of the exegetical tradition and transcribing it verbatim. That is why we encounter long commentaries, almost exegetical summae, in which the literal, allegorical and sometimes tropological, less frequently anagogical, interpretations follow one another for each verse. They almost belong to the encyclopedias' genre.

Of Claudius of Turin, besides the commentary on the Octateuch (excluding Deuteronomy) one should cite that on Kings for the Old Testament and for the New Testament those on Matthew and the Pauline Epistles.[32] He started to write in approximately 810 and he was the first to use the work on Genesis by Ambrose of Milan,[33] besides Augustine, Isidore and other sources. However, it is Hraban Maur who used Wigbod's methodology most fully.[34] Indeed it is he who conceived the project of preparing systematically comprehensive commentaries on any of the books of the Bible which had not yet been subjected to this type of exegesis; in other words, he intended to construct for each book of the Bible a collection of previous sources, which would be both encyclopedic and arranged according to three or four types of interpretation. It is certainly unusual that, such a short time after Claudius's works, Hraban, should embark again with an extraordinary effort on a commentary on the whole Octateuch and on the books of Kings; and above all it is important that he should be the first in the West to conduct an exegesis of the same type of that created for the Octateuch (PL 107–108) and Kings (PL 109, 9–208), also on the Paralipomena I–II (PL 109, 279–540), on the Book of Wisdom (PL 109, 671–762), Ecclesiastes (PL 109, 763–1126), Lamentations (PL 111, 1181–1272), and on the two books of the Maccabees (PL 109, 1125–1256). But he also commented on Esther, Judith, on the four major prophets, Matthew, and Paul's letters (PL 107, 109–112). It was a unique set for the Carolingian era. What Hraban did not comment upon, had already been covered by those he considered the masters, in actual fact or ideally, and precisely by Alcuin, at whose school at Tours he had been formed, and through Alcuin by the Venerable Bede, who remained one of his privileged sources whenever he was able to use it.

This large set of works for the great part is yet to be studied in detail. For far too long the significance of Carolingian exegesis has been underestimated, on the assumption that it wholly depended on the Fathers and exhibited no originality of its own. On the other hand, over the last few years scholarship has tended to show how Carolingian exegesis marks a decisive moment in the

---

[32] Cf. Italiani, La tradizione esegetica (1979); Gorman, The Commentary on Genesis (1997) 279–329; idem, The Commentary on Kings (1997) 99–131.

[33] Cf. Gorman (as at n. 10), 128–29.

[34] Cf. Hablitzel, Hrabanus Maurus (1906); Reinelt, Hrabanus Maurus (1980); Cantelli Berarducci, L'esegesi della Rinascita (as at n. 26); Black, Isidore, Bede and Hrabanus Maurus (1983).

history of exegesis. First of all it has been observed that the renaissance of studies named after Charlemagne did not happen, as it was long thought, by way of a restoration of pagan writers, but that it happened above all through an extraordinary effort in reading the Bible and the Fathers (almost exclusively the Latin ones, or, as for Origen, in Latin translation). Among the works of the Fathers particular attention was paid to biblical commentaries.

Precisely for this reason the first mark of originality of Carolingian exegesis lies as has been mentioned above in its view of the biblical commentary as a cultural summa, from the Fathers to the *doctores moderni*, as Angelomus of Luxeuil would call the more recent exegetes, most probably Isidore and Bede.[35] The second characteristic aspect of this production lies in its attempt to provide exhaustive commentaries on every biblical book, by recasting and integrating previous commentaries when they did not cover the whole text, or by writing many others from scratch.

The Carolingian school believed therefore that it had to prepare a full and comprehensive (verse by verse) exegetical corpus, at the same time paying respect to, and summarising the Tradition: a true novelty in comparison with seventh- and eighth-century exegesis, and also with Isidore. It is then easy to see how this should be the basis, at least until the beginning of the thirteenth century, for all Western exegesis, and also easy to explain the origins of the *Glossa ordinaria* (and how it was possible to attribute it to Walafrid Strabo). Such a result, which would be attained in the eleventh or twelfth century, is also an offshoot of Carolingian exegesis: it was from the heap of patristic and early Medieval loci (ranging from Gregory the Great to Bede), reinterpreted and synthesised by the Carolingians, that it became possible to compile a set of straightforward glosses for an immediate explanation of the biblical text, as the *Glossa ordinaria* proposed to do and did.

Thus Carolingian exegesis exhibits the great reading and learning ability of the educated who played their role as teachers commenting on the Bible starting from the last decade of the eighth century. A remarkable cultural acceleration must be signalled, affecting not only the centre of the Frankish kingdom but spreading, in but a few decades, over many other centres. For it should be noted that Carolingian exegesis did not simply accomplish a restoration of the Fathers, but of the whole Latin tradition, i. e. of the exegetical and non-exegetical texts produced in the sixth to the eighth centuries, ranging from Gregory the Great and Isidore to Bede and Alcuin himself, very soon used as a source. Thus, to give an example, Hraban Maur used, for his commentary on Genesis, among his sources, Bede's and Alcuin's commentaries, Augustine's *Quaestiones in Heptateuchum*, Jerome's *Hebraicae quaestiones in Genesim*, the abridgement of Gregory made by Paterius, Isidore's *Quaestiones in Vetus Testamentum*.[36] For the commentary on Jeremiah, Hraban used Origen's sermons, various works by Jerome, Gregory the Great and Bede, Augustine's and Cassiodorus' commentary on the Psalms, and some other sources.[37]

---

[35] Cf. MGH, Epist., V, p. 623.

[36] Cf. Cantelli Berarducci (as at n. 26), 174.

[37] Cf. Todaro, Il Commentario (1997).

These last sources testify to a further aspect of the work of Hraban and of Carolingian exegetes more generally. In order to write a commentary on a book of the Bible, they used previous commentaries on the same book; but this was possible only for a few books as a whole, and for many only partially or for very little portions. This would explain why Hraban and other exegetes, from Wigbod onwards, always resorted to not specifically exegetical works (for Jeremiah, as we have seen, Hraban used also the commentaries on the Psalms) and to non-exegetical works; he used, that is, all the works a commentator may have known to complete the exegesis of each verse.

This work was necessary also because medieval exegesis, up to the whole of the ninth century, with only a few exceptions, was Christian. Because of this the exegetes started from the literal interpretation but they were particularly interested in the spiritual interpretation (be it allegorical, moral or eschatological). Such a need was particularly felt for the Old Testament, starting from Gregory the Great and from Isidore onwards (to remain within the chronological confines of the Medieval centuries), according to the typological reading of the Church Fathers. As further studies should confirm, Carolingian exegetes mostly took pains to combine, verse by verse in the biblical text they were commenting on, the literal interpretation with at least a spiritual interpretation, often the moral one, mostly the allegorical one, given that the general outline of the commentary remained typological.

4. From Angelomus of Luxeuil to Remigius of Auxerre

The great accumulation made by the first generation of Carolingian exegetes gradually brought about a change in the structure of their commentaries on the Bible. The first symptom of such a change may perhaps be recorded in Angelomus of Luxeuil. This monastery had been founded by Columbanus at the end of the sixth century; in 821 Ansegisus was abbot and from 833 Drogo of Metz, who belonged to the imperial family. We know that Angelomus had been educated within the monastery, under master Mellinus' guidance, that later perhaps he took his place, and that he had been, at least for some time, at Lothar's court.

He is the author of three commentaries, on Genesis, Kings, and the Song of Songs, approximately between 825 and 855, given that in the preface to the Genesis commentary abbot Drogo is not mentioned (which would support the dating hypothesis) and that in the commentary on the Song of Songs he mentions the death of Lothar's wife, Ermengarda, who died in 851. Angelomus' exegesis, which has recently been studied,[38] is close to that of Claudius of Turin and of Hraban Maur, but equally justified seems to be Franz Brunhölzl's critical conclusion: "Les explications bibliques du moine Angélome de Luxeuil

[38] Cf. Cantelli Berarducci, Angelomo (1990); Gorman (as at n. 10), 130, n. 42 announces on forthcoming article on Angelomus.

(milieu du IXe siècle à la cour de Lothar Ier) sont originales, savantes et vivantes malgré une méthode qui relève de la compilation".[39]

One can actually point to many sources transcribed verbatim by Angelomus according to Wigbod's method, the criterion of selecting interpretations (literal and spiritual) typical of Hraban and others; it should be noted, however, that he took greater liberty even in relation to this alleged scheme ("ecce historiam praelibavimus, sed spiritalem intellectum necesse est ut breviter tandem tangamus"[40]) and that he frequently intervened no longer transcribing, but summarising his sources, perhaps supported by Mellinus' teaching and by his own reflection. His sources must no doubt be considered. For the Genesis commentary Origen's sermons, Augustine's two commentaries (the *Genesis contra Manicheos*, probably through Isidore), Jerome, Paterius' anthology from Gregory the Great, Isidore's *Quaestiones*, Bede's and Alcuin's commentaries. For the Book of Kings he again used Isidore and various partial commentaries by Bede, but also Origen and Paterius, the anonymous *Quaestiones Hebraicae in libros Samuelis* attributed to Jerome, Alcuin and perhaps Hraban. For the Song of Songs, Angelomus based himself on Aponius, Gregory the Great and Isidore, Alcuin and Hraban.[41]

The use of the *Quaestiones Hebraicae in libros Samuelis* reveals Angelomus' interests,[42] inasmuch as it exhibits a precise interest of his in the philological and historical interpretation of the text, a critical attention to what he reads (as may be observed in quite a number of asides, such as this: "Non enim legendum est, ut falso in quibusdam codicibus invenitur: Et transivit vadum Iacob, sed Iaboc").[43] The *Quaestiones in Samuelem* are indeed the work of a learned Jew, datable perhaps to the beginning of the ninth century, and they are one of the few texts of this kind in the Carolingian period. This and other fairly rare texts reveal the care Angelomus took in devising his commentaries. He made use of this care in handling his sources for the literal interpretation for a strongly allegorical one, as was generally the case for the tradition inaugurated by Wigbod, but with a preoccupation of his own to make his thoughts more precise, to propose parallels and supplementary integrations, to look for philological consistency as well as for doctrinal accuracy.

The exegetes of the second half of the century (who have so far received very little scholarly attention and who are mostly still anonymous) followed, in more than one respect, in the steps of the first Carolingian commentators, inasmuch as they also referred to the Tradition, but for them the Tradition did not end with Bede or even with Alcuin, but continued at least to include Hraban. It was Hraban who, with his vast work concerning almost all the biblical corpus, replaced Bede as an immediate reference figure for exegetical work. The reform introduced by Charles generated new energies, even at a local le-

---

39 Cf. Brunhölzl, Geschichte (1975) 563; see the French translation *Histoire de la littérature latine du Moyen Age* I/2 (ed. H. Rochais; Turnhout 1991) 297.
40 Cf. *Enarrationes in libros Regum*, PL 115, 252 A.
41 Cf. Cantelli Berarducci (as at n. 38); eadem (as at n. 26), 183–86.
42 Cf. Saltman, Pseudo-Jerome (1975).
43 Cf. PL 115, 222.

vel, developing to some extent autonomously, outside the unified political framework which has slowly collapsed. It could nevertheless take root within particular forces and traditions, sometimes very significant ones. Regrettably it is not possible to offer a fully qualified picture of this situation, since it has not yet been investigated except for some isolated case studies.

Certainly, personalities and works such as those of Haimo and Remigius of Auxerre deserve full attention. The former, confused for centuries with Haimo of Halberstadt,[44] had been a pupil of a well-known grammar teacher of Irish origin, Murethac (and something of his teaching must have remained also in this way of handling problems). Haimo remained then permanently at Auxerre as a teacher,[45] whereas Remigius, who was younger than him and who would die at the beginning of the tenth century, after receiving his early education at Auxerre, was master in various schools, at St-Amand and in Paris. Many are the exegetical works attributed to them, and it is difficult to claim with some certainty, especially for Remigius, which are their genuine works. To Haimo, as far as the Old Testament is concerned, are attributed at least the commentaries on the Song of Songs and on Isaiah.[46]

Haimo and Remigius shared a number of features, even though each of them had a profile of his own. They shared a need to summarise at least in part their own sources, no longer to accumulate them, and above all to judge them (whatever their own personal opinion), as well as to be able to positively choose or to exclude as inconvenient or as erroneous the opinions of whoever preceded them. Two aspects of their exegetical work are most apparent: (a) the regular occurrence of a discussion in the commentaries, which may originate in the school or in the theological debate which had become, in the middle of the century, more lively and acute; (b) a new appreciation of the text of the Bible, since in the scholarly process of discussion, evaluation and critical selection, the biblical text took on a value similar or equal to that of the sources, from Origen to Hraban. One may perhaps say that with these exegetes and texts we see how for the first time the Bible and Tradition were compared and set on an equal footing, since either was felt as a source of God's revelation to mankind.

Along the same lines may be read the commentaries of two further exegetes of great value, Pascasius Radbertus[47] and John Scotus Eriugena, who had very different biographical and personal profiles, and yet offered much deeper insights than some other Carolingian exegetes. We owe to the former the commentaries on Psalm 47 and on Lamentations for the Old Testament and on Matthew for the New (PL 116–118, 120), and to the latter only three interventions on the Gospel of John (with glosses to the text, with a commentary to the prologue, and a commentary as far as 6:14).[48] John translated works of Gre-

[44] Cf. Riggenbach, Die ältesten lateinischen Kommentare (1907).
[45] Cf. Iogna-Prat, L'œuvre d'Haymon d'Auxerre (1991).
[46] Cf. Cantelli Berarducci, L'esegesi al tempo (1989).
[47] Cf. Hablitzel, Paschasius (1939); Matter, The Lamentations Commentaries (1982); Contreni, The Biblical Glosses (1976) 797–813.
[48] Cf. *Glossae divinae* (1997); Jean Scot, Homélie (1969); idem, Commentaire (1980).

gory of Nyssa, Dionysius pseudo-Areopagite and Maximus the Confessor, and was thus deeply steeped in Greek reflection on the Christian faith.[49] His exegetical works reflect this link. He shows no interest in writing commentaries on the Old Testament (or at least he chose not to), and for the New his attention was reserved to John and to some places in John, both more densely filled with doctrine and more highly mystical.

One may say that with John Carolingian exegesis made a decisive step forward; I mean that, after a period of long decades of erudite preparation, of continual discussion within the school and between schools, of philological and theological debate, it encountered the genius of an exegete-theologian which enabled it to reach the highest point, in the Christian tradition, of what the Bible and biblical exegesis truly mean:[50] the construction of a discourse on the presence of God in man and on the *cumfilietas*, as John calls it, of man with God.

---

[49] Cf. Cappuyns, Jean Scot Erigène (1933); more recently Otten, The Texture of Tradition (1997).

[50] Cf. Cremascoli, Tradizione esegetica (1981) 713–29.

Chapter Twenty-nine

Genres, Forms and Various Methods in Christian Exegesis of the Middle Ages

By Gilbert Dahan, Paris

Sources: It does not seem useful to present here a bibliography of the medieval commentaries quoted or not quoted below. It may be sufficient to mention two inventories and, with their abbreviations, some major collections of texts. *Inventories of texts*: J. B. Schneyer, *Repertorium der lateinischen Sermones des Mittelalters* (Münster / W.: Aschendorff 1969–90); F. Stegmüller, *Repertorium Biblicum medii aevi*, 1–11 (Madrid / Barcelona: CSIC 1950–80); G. de Martel, *Répertoire des textes latins relatifs au livre de Ruth* (Steenbrugge-Dordrecht: 1990). – *Collections of texts*: CCCM; CCL; CSEL; PL.

Bibliographies: K. Reinhardt / H. Santiago-Otero, *Biblioteca Biblica Ibérica Medieval* (Madrid: CSIC 1986); A. Vernet / A.-M. Genevois, *La Bible au Moyen Age. Bibliographie* (Paris: CNRS 1990).

Studies: L'abbaye parisienne de Saint-Victor au Moyen Age (ed. J. Longère; Paris / Turnhout: Brepols 1991); D. L. d'Avray, *The Preaching of the Friars. Sermons diffused from Paris before 1300* (Oxford: Clarendon Press 1985); J. W. Baldwin, *Masters, Princes and Merchants. The Social Views of Peter the Chanter and his Circle* (Princeton: UP 1970); G. Bardy, "La littérature patristique des *Quaestiones et responsiones* sur l'Écriture", *RB* 41 (1932) 210–36, 341–69, 515–37; 42 (1933) 14–30, 211–29, 328–52; P. Barzillay Roberts, *Studies in the Sermons of Stephen Langton* (Toronto: Pontifical Institute of Mediaeval Studies 1968); L.-J. Bataillon, "Les sermons de saint Thomas et la *Catena aurea*", *St. Thomas Aquinas, 1274–1974. Commemorative Studies* (Toronto: Pontifical Institute of Mediaeval Studies 1974) 67–75; idem, "Intermédiaires entre les traités de morale pratique et les sermons: les *distinctiones* bibliques alphabétiques", *Les genres littéraires dans les sources théologiques et philosophiques médiévales. Définition, critique, exploitation* (Louvain-la-Neuve: Univ. cath. de Louvain 1982) 213–26 (repr. in L.-J. Bataillon, *La prédication au XIIIe s.* [1993]); idem, "De la *lectio* à la *praedicatio*: commentaires bibliques et sermons au XIIIe s.", *RSPT* 70 (1986) 559–74 (repr. in *La prédication au XIIIe s.*); idem, *La prédication au XIIIe s. en France et en Italie. Etudes et documents* (Aldershot: Variorum 1993); B. Bazan, "La *quaestio disputata*", *Les genres littéraires dans les sources théologiques et philosophiques médiévales. Définition, critique, exploitation* (Louvain-la-Neuve: Univ. cath. de Louvain 1982) 31–49; idem, "Les questions disputées, principalement dans les facultés de théologie", B. Bazan / J. W. Wippel et al. (eds.), *Les questions disputées et les questions quodlibétiques dans les facultés de théologie, de droit et de médecine* (Turnhout: Brepols 1985) 13–149; G. Beaujouan, "Le symbolisme des nombres à l'époque romane", *CCM* 4 (1961) 159–69; N. Bériou, "Les sermons", J. Berlioz (ed.), *Identifier sources et citations* (Turnhout: Brepols 1994); eadem, *L'avènement des maîtres de la Parole. La prédication à Paris au XIIIe siècle* (Paris: Institut d'études augustiniennes 1998); R. Berndt, "Les interprétations juives dans le Commentaire de l'Heptateuque d'André de Saint-Victor", *RAug* 24 (1990) 199–240; idem, *André de Saint-Victor († 1175). Exégète et théologien* (Paris-Turnhout: Brepols 1991); *La Bibbia nel Medio Evo* (ed. G. Cremascoli / C. Leonardi; Bologna: Edizioni Dehoniane 1996); *The Bible in the Medieval World. Essays in Memory of Beryl Smalley* (ed. K. Walsh / D. Wood; Oxford: B. Blackwell 1985); P.-M. Bogaert, "La Bible latine des origines au moyen âge. Aperçu historique, état des questions", *RTL* 19 (1988) 137–59, 276–314; J. G. Bougerol, *Introduction à l'étude de Saint Bonaventure* (Paris / Tournai: Desclée 1961); idem, "Les sermons dans les *studia* des Mendiants", *Le Scuole degli Ordini Mendicanti* (Todi: Centro di studi sulla spiritualità medievale 1978) 251–80; H. Brinkmann, *Mittelalterliche Hermeneutik* (Tübingen: M. Niemeyer 1980); *The West from the Fathers to the Reformation* (CHB II; ed. G.W.H.Lampe; Cambridge: UP 1969); Ph.Buc, *L'Ambiguïté du Livre. Prince, pouvoir et peuple dans les commentaires de la Bible au Moyen Age* (Paris: Beauchesne 1994); H.Caplan, "The Four Senses of Scriptural Interpretation and the Medieval Theory of Preaching", *Spec.* 4 (1929) 282–90; P.T.Charland, *Artes praedicandi. Contribution à l'histoire de la rhétorique au moyen âge* (Paris: Vrin 1936); J.Châtillon, "La Bible dans les écoles du XIIe siècle", *Le Moyen Age et la Bible* (BTT 4; Paris 1984) 163–97; idem, *Le mouvement canonial au XIIe siècle* (Paris / Turnhout: Brepols 1993; posthum.); M.-D.Chenu, "*Antiqui, moderni.* Notes de lexicographie médiévale", *RSPT* 17 (1928) 82–94; idem, *La théologie comme science au XIIIe siècle* (Paris: Vrin [2]1943); idem, *La théologie au douzième siècle* (Paris: Vrin [2]1966); B.Clausi, "Elementi di ermeneutica monastica nel *De schematibus et tropis* di Beda", *Orpheus* NS 11 (1990) 277–307; M.L.Colish, "*Psalterium Scholasticorum*: Peter Lombard and the Emergence of Scholastic Psalms Exegesis", *Spec.* 67 (1992) 531–48; G.Conticello, "San Tommaso ed i Padri: la *Catena aurea super Ioannem*", *AHDL* 57 (1990) 31–92; G.Dahan, "Guillaume de Flay et son Commentaire du Livre des Juges. Etude et édition", *RAug* 13 (1978) 37–104; idem, "L'article *Iudei* de la *Summa Abel* de Pierre le Chantre", *REAug* 27 (1981) 105–26; idem, "L'exégèse de l'histoire de Caïn et Abel du XIIe au XIVe s. en Occident", *RTAM* 49 (1982) 21–89; 50 (1983) 5–68; idem, "Les interprétations juives dans les commentaires du Pentateuque de Pierre le Chantre", *The Bible in the Medieval World. Essays in Memory of Beryl Smalley* (1985) 131–55; idem, "Exégèse et polémique dans les commentaires de la Genèse d'Etienne Langton", *Les juifs au regard de l'histoire. Mélanges B.Blumenkranz* (ed. G.Dahan; Paris: Picard 1985) 129–48; idem, "Une introduction à l'étude de l'Ecriture au XIIe s.: le Prologue du Commentaire du Pentateuque de Rainaud de Saint-Eloi", *RTAM* 54 (1987) 27–51; idem, "Les figures des juifs et de la Synagogue. L'exemple de Dalila. Fonctions et méthodes de la typologie dans l'exégèse médiévale", *RAug* 23 (1988) 125–50; idem, "Juifs et chrétiens en Occident médiéval. La rencontre autour de la Bible (XIIe–XIVe s.)", *RSyn* 110 (1989) 3–31; idem, *Les intellectuels chrétiens et les juifs au moyen âge* (Paris: Cerf 1990); idem, "L'exégèse de Genèse 1,26 dans les commentaires du XIIe s.", *REAug* 38 (1992) 124–53; idem, "La connaissance de l'hébreu dans les correctoires de la Bible. Notes préliminaires", *RTL* 23 (1992) 178–90; idem, "Arithmologie et exégèse. Un chapitre du *De scripturis* de Hugues de Saint-Victor", *PRIS-MA* 8 (1992) 155–73; idem, "Saint Thomas d'Aquin et la métaphore. Rhétorique et herméneutique", *Medioevo* 18 (1992) 85–117; idem, "Nommer les êtres: exégèse et théorie du langage dans les commentaires médiévaux de Genèse 2, 19–20", *Sprachtheorien in Spätantike und Mittelalter* (ed. S.Ebbesen; Tübingen: G.Narr 1995) 55–74; idem, "L'utilisation de l'exégèse juive dans la lecture des livres prophétiques au XIIIe siècle", *Neue Richtungen in der hoch- und spätmittelalterlichen Bibelexegese* (ed. R.E.Lerner; München: Oldenbourg 1996) 121–38; idem, "L'exégèse d'Antoine de Padoue et les maîtres de l'école biblique-morale (fin XIIe–début XIIIe s.)", *Euphrosyne* 24 (1996) 341–73; idem, "Lexiques hébreu-latin? Les recueils d'interprétations des noms hébraïques", *Les manuscrits des lexiques et glossaires, de l'Antiquité à la fin du moyen âge* (ed. J.Hamesse; Louvain-la-Neuve: FIDEM 1996) 481–526; idem, "La critique textuelle dans les correctoires de la Bible du XIIIe siècle", *Langages et philosophie. Hommage à Jean Jolivet* (ed. A. de Libera / A.Elamrani-Jamal / A.Galonnier; Paris: Vrin 1997) 365–92; idem, "La connaissance de l'exégèse juive par les chrétiens du XIIe au XIVe s.", *Rashi et la culture juive en France du Nord au moyen âge* (ed. G.Dahan / G.Nahon / E.Nicolas; Leuven / Paris: Peeters 1997) 343–59; idem, *L'exégèse chrétienne de la Bible en Occident médiéval, XIIe–XIVe siècle* (Paris: Cerf, 1999); M.-M.Davy, *Les sermons universitaires parisiens de 1230–31. Contribution à l'histoire de la prédication médiévale* (Paris: Vrin 1931); P.Delhaye, "L'organisation scolaire au XIIe s.", *Traditio* 5 (1947) 211–68; L.Delisle, "Les Bibles de Théodulfe", *Bibl. de l'Ecole des Chartes* 40 (1879) 5–47; F.M.Delorme, "Deux leçons d'ouverture de Cours biblique données par Jean de La Rochelle", *La France Franciscaine* 16 (1933) 345–60; H.Denifle, "Die Handschriften der Bibel-Correctorien des 13.Jahrhunderts", *ALKMA* 4 (1888) 264–311, 471–601; idem, "Quel livre servait de base à l'enseignement des maîtres en théologie dans l'Université de Paris?", *RThom* 2 (1894) 149–61; R.Devreesse, "Chaînes exégétiques grecques", DBSup I (1928) 1084–1233; C.Douais, *Essai sur l'organisation des études dans l'ordre des frères prêcheurs au XIIIe et au XIVe s.* (Paris / Toulouse 1884); *L'école carolingienne d'Auxerre, de Murethach à Remi, 830–908* (ed. D.Iogna-Prat / C.Jeudy / G.Lobrichon; Paris: Beauchesne 1990); A.d'Esneval, "La division de la Vulgate latine en chapitres dans l'édition parisienne du XIIIe s.", *RSPT* 62 (1978) 559–68; idem, "Le perfectionnement d'un instrument de travail au début du XIIIe s.: les trois glossaires bibliques d'Etienne Langton", *Culture et travail intellectuel dans l'Occident médiéval* (Paris: CNRS 1981) 164–75; idem, "Les quatre sens de l'Ecriture à l'époque de Pierre le Mangeur et de Hugues de Saint-Cher", *Mediaevalia Christiana. Hommage à Raymonde Foreville* (ed. C. Viola; Paris: Editions universitaires 1989) 355–69; G. R. Evans, "The Place of Peter the Chanter's *De tropis loquendi*", *ACi* 39 (1983) 231–53; eadem, *The Language and Logic of the Bible: The Earlier Middle Ages* (Cambridge: UP 1984); eadem, *The Language and Logic of the Bible: The Road to Reformation* (Cambridge: UP 1985); B. Fischer, *Die Alkuin-Bibel* (Freiburg: Herder 1957); idem, *Lateinische Bibelhandschriften im frühen Mittelalter* (Freiburg: Herder 1985); J. de Ghellinck, "*Pagina* et *Sacra Pagina.* Histoire d'un mot et transformation de l'objet primitivement désigné", *Mélanges Auguste Pelzer* (Louvain: Ed. de l'Institut supérieur de philosophie 1947) 23–59; M. Gibson, "The Twelfth-Century Glossed Bible", StPatr 23 (1989) 232–44 (repr. in *'Artes' and the Bible in the Medieval West*; Aldershot: Variorum 1993); eadem, "The Place of the *Glossa ordinaria* in Medieval Exegesis", *Ad litteram: Authoritative Texts and their Medieval Readers* (ed. K. Emery / M. D. Jordan; Notre Dame 1992) 5–27 (repr. in *'Artes' and the Bible in the Medieval West*); E. Gilson, "Michel Menot et la technique du sermon médiéval", *Les idées et les lettres* (Paris: Vrin 1955) 93–154; idem, "De quelques raisonnements scripturaires usités au moyen âge", *Les idées et les lettres* (Paris: Vrin 1955) 155–69; H. H. Glunz, *History of the Vulgate in England from Alcuin to Roger Bacon* (Cambridge: UP 1933); M. Grabmann, *Die Geschichte der scholastischen Methode* (Freiburg / B.: Herder 1909–11); R. Grégoire, *Bruno de Segni, exégète et théologien monastique* (Spoleto: Centro italiano di studi sull'alto medioevo 1965); A. L. Gregory, "Indices of Rubrics and Incipits in the principal Manuscripts of the *Questiones* of Stephen Langton", *AHDL* 5 (1930) 221–66; H. Hailperin, *Rashi and the Christian Scholars* (Pittsburgh: UP 1963); N. Haring, "The lectures of Thierry of Chartres on Boethius' *De Trinitate*", *AHDL* 25 (1958) 113–226; G. Hasenohr, "Un recueil de *distinctiones* bilingue au début du XIVe s.", *Romania* 99 (1978) 47–96, 183–206; R. W. Hunt, "The Introduction to the *Artes* in the XIIth cent.", *Studia Mediaevalia ... R. J. Martin* (Bruges: De Tempel 1948) 84–112 (repr. in: *The History of Grammar in the MA*, ed. G. L. Bursill-Hall; Amsterdam: John Benjamins B. V. 1980); T. Käppeli, "Eine aus frühscholastischen Werken excerptierte Bibelkatene", *Divus Thomas* 9 (1931) 309–19; A. Kleinhans, "Der Studiengang der Professoren der hl. Schrift im 13. und 14. Jahrhundert", *Bib.* 14 (1933) 381–99; idem, "Nicolaus Trivet, o. p., Psalmorum interpres", *Ang.* 20 (1943) 219–36; S. Kuttner, *Repertorium der Kanonistik, 1140–1234*, I. *Prodromus Corporis Glossarum* (Vatican: Biblioteca Apostolica Vaticana 1937); G. Lacombe, *La vie et les œuvres de Prévostin* (Paris: Vrin 1927); idem and B. Smalley, "Studies on the Commentaries of Cardinal Stephen Langton", *AHDL* 5 (1930) 5–220; A. Landgraf, "Die Schriftzitate in der Scholastik um die Wende des 12. zum 13. Jahrhundert", *Bib.* 18 (1937) 74–94; idem, *Introduction à l'histoire de la littérature théologique de la scolastique naissante* (French transl.; Paris: Vrin 1973); H. Lange, *Les données mathématiques des traités du XIIe siècle sur la symbolique des nombres* (Copenhagen: Cahiers de l'Institut du moyen âge grec et latin 1979); J. Leclercq, "Prédicateurs bénédictins aux XIe et XIIe s.", *RMab* 33 (1943) 48–73; idem, "Ecrits monastiques sur la Bible aux XIe–XIIIe s.", *MS* 15 (1953) 95–106; idem, *La spiritualité de Pierre de Celle (1115–1183)* (Paris: Vrin 1946); idem, "From Gregory the Great to Saint Bernard", in the chapter "The exposition and exegesis of Scripture", CHB II (1969) 183–97; idem, *L'amour des lettres et le désir de Dieu. Initiation aux auteurs monastiques du moyen âge* (Paris: Cerf [3]1990); E. Lesne, *Histoire de la propriété ecclésiastique en France*, V. *Les écoles de la fin du VIIIe s. à la fin du XIIe s.* (Lille: Facultés catholiques 1940); L. Light, "Versions et révisions du texte biblique", *Le Moyen Age et la Bible* (BTT 4; 1984) 55–93; G. Lobrichon, "Une nouveauté: les gloses de la Bible", *Le Moyen Age et la Bible* (BTT 4; 1984) 95–114; R. Loewe, "Herbert of Bosham's Commentary on Jerome's Hebrew Psalter", *Bib.* 34 (1953) 44–77, 159–92, 275–98; idem, "The Medieval History of the Latin Vulgate", CHB II (1969) 102–54; J. Longère, *La prédication médiévale* (Paris: Etudes augustiniennes 1983); idem, "La prédication en langue latine", *Le Moyen Age et la Bible* (BTT 4; 1984) 517–35; H. de Lubac, *Exégèse médiévale. Les quatre sens de l'Ecriture* I–IV (Paris: Aubier 1959–64); D. E. Luscombe, *The School of Peter Abelard* (Cambridge: UP 1969); idem, "Peter Comestor", *The Bible in the Medieval World* (1985) 109–29; F. McCulloch, *Medieval Latin and French Bestiaries* (Chapel Hill 1960); M. Magrassi, *Teologia e storia nel pensiero di Ruperto di Deutz* (Rome: Pontificia Universitas Urbaniana 1959); A. Maieru; "Tecniche di insegnamento", *Le scuole degli ordini mendicanti (sec. XIII–XIV)*, (Todi 1978) 305–52 (= idem, *University Training in Medieval Europe* [ET, D. N. Pryds; Leiden: Brill 1994] 1–35); P. Mandonnet, "Chronologie des écrits scripturaires de saint Thomas d'Aquin. 3° Enseignement de la Bible selon l'usage de Paris", *RThom* 34 (1929) 489–519; E. Mangenot, "Correctoires de la Bible", DB II (1899) 1022–26; J. P. P. Martin, "Le texte parisien de la Vulgate", *Le Muséon* 8 (1889) 444–66; 9 (1890) 55–70, 301–16; H. Meyer, *Die*

Zahlenallegorese im Mittelalter. Methode und Gebrauch (München 1975); A. J. MINNIS, *Medieval Theory of Authorship. Scholastic Literary Attitudes in the Later Middle Ages* (Aldershot: Wildwood House 1984); *Le Moyen Age et la Bible* (BTT 4; 1984); F. OHLY, *Hohelied-Studien. Grundzüge einer Geschichte der Hoheliedauslegung des Abendlandes bis zum 1200* (Wiesbaden: E. Steiner 1958); L. PANNIER, *Les lapidaires français du moyen âge* (Paris 1882); G. PARÉ / A. BRUNET / P. TREMBLAY, *La Renaissance du XIIe s. Les écoles et l'enseignement* (Paris / Ottawa: Vrin 1933); V. PERI, "*Correctores immo corruptores.* Un saggio di critica testuale nella Roma del XII sec.", *Italia medioevale e umanistica* 20 (1977) 19–125; E. A. QUAIN, "The Medieval *Accessus ad auctores*", *Traditio* 3 (1945) 215–64; R. QUINTO, "Stefano Langton e i quattro sensi della scrittura", *Medioevo* 15 (1989) 67–109; idem, "Die *Quaestiones* des Stephan Langton über die Gottesfurcht", *Cahiers de l'Institut du moyen âge grec et latin* 62 (1992) 77–165; P. RICHÉ, *Education et culture dans l'Occident barbare, 6e–8e s.* (Paris: Seuil 1962); R. H. and M. A. ROUSE, "Biblical *distinctiones* in the XIIIth century", *AHDL* 41 (1974) 27–37; A. SALTMAN, "Supplementary Notes on the Works of Ralph Niger", *Bar-Ilan Studies in History* (ed. P. Artzi; Ramat-Gan: Bar-Ilan UP 1978) 103–13; idem, "Rabanus Maurus and the Pseudo-Hieronymian *Quaestiones Hebraicae in Libros Regum and Paralipomenon*", *HTR* 66 (1973) 43–75; idem, "Pseudo-Jerome in the Commentary of Andrew of St. Victor on Samuel", *HTR* 67 (1974) 195–253; B. SMALLEY, "Stephen Langton and the four Senses of Scripture", *Spec.* 6 (1931) 60–76; eadem, "The School of Andrew of St. Victor", *RTAM* 11 (1939) 145–67; eadem, "Some Thirteenth-Century Commentaries on the Sapiential Books", *Dominican Studies* 2 (1949) 318–55; 3 (1950) 41–77, 236–74; eadem, "A Commentary on the *Hebraica* by Herbert of Bosham", *RTAM* 18 (1951) 29–65; eadem, "Les commentaires bibliques de l'époque romane: glose ordinaire et gloses périmées", *CCM* 4 (1961) 15–22; eadem, "The Bible in the Medieval Schools", CHB II (1969) 197–220; eadem, "William of Auvergne, John of La Rochelle and St. Thomas Aquinas on the Old Law", *St. Thomas Aquinas, 1274–1974. Commemorative Studies* II (Toronto: Pontifical Institute of Mediaeval Studies 1974) 11–71; eadem, *The Study of the Bible in the Middle Ages* (Oxford: Blackwell [3]1983); eadem, "Glossa ordinaria", TRE XIII (1984) 452–57; C. SPICQ, *Esquisse d'une histoire de l'exégèse latine au moyen âge* (Paris: Vrin 1944); A. STRUBEL, "Allegoria in factis et allegoria in verbis", *Poétique* 23 (1975) 342–57; M. THIEL, *Grundlagen und Gestalt der Hebräischkenntnisse des frühen Mittelalters* (Spoleto: Centro italiano di studi sull'alto medioevo 1973); J. P. TORRELL, *Initiation à saint Thomas d'Aquin* (Paris / Fribourg: Cerf / Editions universitaires 1993); L. VALENTE, "Arts du discours et *sacra pagina* dans le *De tropis loquendi* de Pierre le Chantre", *Histoire, épistémologie, langage* 12/2 (1990) 69–102; J. VERGER, "L'exégèse de l'Université", *Le Moyen Age et la Bible* (BTT 4; 1984) 199–232; J.-L. VERSTREPEN, "Raban Maur et le judaïsme dans son commentaire sur les quatre livres des Rois", *RMab* 68 (1996) 23–55; H. WASSELYNCK, "L'influence de l'exégèse de saint Grégoire le Grand sur les commentaires bibliques médiévaux (7e–12e s.)", *RTAM* 32 (1965) 157–204; Y. ZALUSKA, *L'enluminure et le Scriptorium de Cîteaux au XIIe s.* (Cîteaux: Commentarii Cistercienses 1989).

The purpose of this chapter is to study the forms and methods of Christian exegesis in the Middle Ages. Recent studies on literary or philosophical medieval texts have shown the importance and the relevance of a formal study and have permitted an evaluation of the pertinence of the means of literary analysis, such as the notions of forms and genres, when applied to the written production of the Middle Ages.[1] Apart from some innovative research done by ALASTAIR MINNIS,[2] it does not seem that this approach has been undertaken in the field of biblical commentaries. It is true that we have here a material whose limits are very fluctuant and, as STEGMÜLLER's *Repertorium* shows clearly, very extensive.[3] Furthermore, such a formal analysis may not look so urgent, be-

[1] Cf. H.-R. JAUSS, in *Grundriss der romanischen Literaturen des Mittelalters* I (Heidelberg 1970); French transl.: "Littérature médiévale et théorie des genres", *Poétique* 1 (1970) 79–101; P. ZUMTHOR, *Essai de poétique médiévale* (Paris: Seuil 1972).

[2] Minnis, Medieval Theory of Authorship (1984).

[3] Stegmüller, Repertorium Biblicum (1950–80).

cause in these commentaries we only seek a spiritual teaching or historical data. However, in the following pages, we hope to show that this approach, which allows us to enter the workshop of the exegete, will be enlightening. We shall first give an analysis of the *genres* (in the sense of literary genres). This notion of genres, the application of which still remains vague despite several wide-ranging theoretical studies, will allow us to determine three main categories of commentary, each of them having proper characteristics and a specific place in history: the monastic exegesis, the exegesis of the schools, and the exegesis of the university. Then, we shall try to establish a typology of the forms found in exegesis, distinguishing simple (or elementary) forms from complex ones. Finally, we shall describe, although at a somewhat different level, the methods of medieval exegetes, in spiritual exegesis as well as in literal exegesis, again from a formal point of view. It goes without saying that in this chapter we shall not speak about hermeneutics, although the result of our analysis may lead us toward a more precise characterization of medieval exegesis, including hermeneutical aspects.

Cautious of how the medieval authors perceived their own exegetical processes, we shall mention their most significant texts in regard to our analysis. Immediately, the importance of the *prologue* of the medieval commentaries may be stressed; their structure changed throughout centuries. Due to the fact that these prologues integrated the techniques of the literary analysis of their time (the *accessus*, the scheme of four Aristotelian causes), the authors were compelled to ask the same questions about sacred texts as the profane commentators did about poetical or philosophical texts; those concerning the *modus* (in fact the style), the *genus operis* (the literary genre) and the *materia* (the subject-matter) of the commentated book are here of prime interest. An approach of this kind was stimulated by various elements, also considered as authoritative, even before the study of the actual text of the Bible on which the exegete was to comment: first of all summaries, prologues of St. Jerome, various other prologues (originating from the *Glossa ordinaria*), all of them integrated by the commentator in his interpretative work in the same way as the sacred book that required his care.

1. The Genres

1.1. Monastic Exegesis

In the life of the monk, the Bible is everywhere: the liturgy is woven with its texts and monastic customs require its study.[4] Besides specific times (collation, liturgy), its reading and study were practiced by the individuals in silence. The expression *lectio divina*, sometimes used to designate more generally the monastic exegesis, was at first applied to this physical act of reading Scripture itself (as well as to the text itself). As for the teaching in the monasteries (outside of the elementary teaching of reading, which was based on the Psalms), it was

[4] *Rule* of St. Benedict, §§ 16–18 and 48.

also primarily focussed on the study of the Bible itself.[5] Thus it is not surprising to note that the monks wrote in praise of Scripture and that among biblical commentaries, an important part is made up of monastic works.[6] We can even ask ourselves if a specific monastic exegesis existed, given this proportion. Following Jean Leclercq, we will answer this question positively and attempt to define what is specific to this exegetic genre.[7]

The principal characteristics of monastic exegesis. The monastic texts (notably Benedictine and Cistercian) seem to have a particular quality, not easy to define because there are many of these texts, which we find from the High Middle Ages to the fifteenth century. Obviously, it is not a question of merely giving an historical definition, based on the monastic origin of these texts, for monks also wrote commentaries which we would not class among the texts of monastic exegesis, and non-monastic authors wrote monastic commentaries. Our difficulty is intensified by the absence of fixed structures: the form is free, each writer flavouring the text in his own fashion. The first thing one generally notes is that these monastic commentaries are long and unrestrained. Inspired primarily by personal meditation and not organized teaching, these texts were free of time constraint and, like the songs destined for divine liturgy, they developed freely. Monastic commentaries were made verse by verse and attempted to study each word of the text for all its significations. The commentary of the Pentateuch of Rainaud of St. Eloi (beginning of the twelfth century) is a good example of this amplitude unconstrained by a sense of time: it consists of not less than 296 folios in a big volume.[8] The commentary on Psalm 44 only by Pascase Radbert takes 107 pages in the recent edition of the *Corpus Christianorum.*[9] One of the common procedures of monastic exegesis resulting from this liberty was the free association of ideas, from verses or from words; the consequence is the multitude of digressions, scientific or historic, in varied order.[10] We shall examine the beginning of Rainaud of St. Eloi's commentary on Genesis. He analyzes the word *creauit* in Gen 1:1, studying the difference of sense between *creare* and *facere*; then the word *Deus* is analyzed, even as far as etymology; the same is done for the terms *celum* and *terra*; the process of the creation is examined more broadly with an extract of Bede's *De natura rerum.* This first verse's commentary closes with a remark on the four elements.[11]

---

[5] See Lesne, Histoire de la propriété ecclésiastique V. Les écoles (1940) 640–42; Riché, Education et culture (1962) passim.

[6] For the praise of Scripture, see Peter of Celle, *De afflictione et lectione* (ed. Leclercq, La spiritualité de Pierre de Celle; 1946) 233–34: "Cellam sine lectione infernum reputo sine consolatione, patibulum sine releuamine, carcerem sine lumine … Lectio animae est alimentum, lumen, lucerna, refugium, solatium et condimentum omnium spiritualium saporum". On the quantitative importance of monastic commentaries, see Leclercq, L'amour des lettres et le désir de Dieu (1990) 70–71.

[7] Leclercq, L'amour des lettres (1990) 70–86. See also idem, Écrits monastiques sur la Bible (1953).

[8] MS. Paris, BN lat. 2493. See Dahan, Une introduction à l'étude de l'Écriture au XIIe s. (1987).

[9] Ed. B. Paulus (Turnhout 1991). Rupert of Deutz's commentaries could also be mentioned.

[10] See Leclercq, L'amour des lettres (1990) 76–86, and sect. 3.2.4. below.

[11] MS. Paris, BN lat. 2493, fol. 4 rb–4 vb.

On the other hand, the monastic commentaries were, at least until the twelfth century, frequently "anthological", meaning they were largely composed of patristic or high medieval text fragments. Very often, the origin of these fragments was not indicated and there is no difference in presentation between them and the actual work of the exegete, which can be significant. Going back to the beginning of Rainaud of St. Eloi's Genesis, besides the extract from Bede, *Venerabilis Beda*, his commentary on the first verse seems above all personal, but that on the second verse is composed of extracts from Isidore of Seville's *Sentences* (the first extract is introduced by *ut beatus dicit Isidorus*) and from Gregory the Great's *Moralia in Iob* (his authorship is not noted); broken up and restructured, these fragments were sometimes rewritten. We can look at a similar work in the commentaries of Raban Maur, who, contrary to many others, often carefully identified his sources.[12] It is necessary also to note that the personal contribution of the author in quite a few monastic commentaries is important: we need only think of St. Bernard's *Sermones in Cantica*, which can be considered as a part of this monastic exegesis.

Monastic exegesis may also be characterized by another feature: the importance of *tropology* or moral interpretation. This can be subdivided into general tropology and monastic tropology. The first is found most obviously in the other exegetic genres; however, it seems that its frequency and detailed use are more specific to the monastic commentaries. In this case, the exegesis is more psychological than moral: it is a question of retracing the individual worthy or unworthy soul's itinerary and finding why and how the soul has acted and what are the ways which are open to it. It is not surprising to find moral teachings in these traditional ethical and religious texts, but it is perhaps unexpected to discover that in some authors the moral exegesis can turn to introspection and even – although this term is obviously anachronistic – psychoanalysis. Guibert of Nogent's commentaries and, to a certain degree some texts of Bernard of Clairvaux, furnish us with remarkable examples of this characteristic. Let us look at Guibert of Nogent's commentary on Zech 1:18–19:

> He raises his eyes, when his soul discovers a spiritual vision from the core of the imagination. He sees, when he puts together spiritual realities. He looks at the four horns, when he considers the four passions which dominate human senses. Boethius said of them: *Cast out joy, Cast out fear, Rid yourself of hope and grief.*[13]

We may quote another example in a Cistercian text, the spiritual commentary of William of St. Thierry on the Song of Songs:

> Here is the spiritual meaning. The soul is turned toward God and must marry God's Word; it learns to understand the richness of God's grace and it is permitted to taste how the Lord is gentle; then it is left in the house of its conscience to study, to be chaste in loving obedience, to

[12] See Verstrepen, Raban Maur et le judaïsme.

[13] MS. Paris, BN lat. 17282, fol. 60 vb: "Oculos suos leuat, cum mens spiritualem intuitum ab ymaginationum profundo resuscitat. Videt, cum spiritualibus spiritualia comparat. Quatuor cornua intuetur, dum quatuor passionum potencias perpendit, que humanis sepe sensibus dominantur. De quibus Boecius: *Gaudia pelle, pelle timorem ne dolor assit, spemque fugato* ...". The quotation is Boethius, *The Consolation of Philosophy*, I, m. VII, 25–28 (ed. and transl. S.J. Tester; London / Cambridge: Heinemann / Harvard UP 1973).

be purified from worldy vices and to be glorified by virtue, aspiring to be worthy of being admitted to spiritual grace of Love and to the affect of Virtue, which is the Bridal chamber.[14]

Such monastic exegesis specifically develops a particular tropology, which is linked to the monk's life: it is not a question of analyzing the individual Christian comportment but rather of studying the individual evolution of the monk, in his collective milieu, the monastery. For example, in the case of Pascase Radbert, Psalm 44, which is generally viewed as an *epithalamium*, the commentary of which he addressed to the nuns of Notre-Dame of Soissons, "has for a subject the vigils of the virgins and it is sung in honor of those who are the flowers of the Church and the lilies of paradise".[15] Similarly, in his commentary on the Canticles, Honorius Augustodunensis understands the king's *cellaria* (Cant 1:3; Vulg.) to be the cloisters where the faithful soul rests in the shadow of Christ.[16] Although the frequency of tropology, notably monastic tropology, characterizes monastic exegesis, the other levels of meaning are not ignored; as in all medieval Christian exegesis, allegory is common, but it is necessary to note that, contrary to accepted ideas, the literal sense is not neglected, because it gives a stable foundation for the spiritual exegesis and because of the considerable attention given to the words themselves by monastic authors. Gregory the Great, whose *Moralia in Iob* and *Homelies on Ezechiel* were always a model for monastic exegesis, insisted on the importance of the literal meaning. Thus he affirms in the dedicatory letter of his *Moralia in Iob*, referring to Job 31:16:

Wanting only to see an allegory in these words is to empty all reality from these merciful works. Divine word should stimulate scholars by its mysteries and, often, comfort ordinary people by its clear lessons.[17]

By a comparison with the two other exegetic genres, we can see another characteristic: the university exegesis demonstrates the totality of knowledge, while the exegesis of the schools attempts to develop the dialectic elements and the information given by the arts of the *quadrivium*. In the monastic exegesis, the *trivium*, notably grammar and dialectic, seems more important. Some texts of the High Middle Ages provide methodological models. Cassiodorus' commentary on Psalms, for example, has a particular interest in the analysis of rhetorical tropes identified in the biblical text.[18] One of the problems posed by the ex-

[14] William of St. Thierry, *Commentary on the Song of Songs* (ed. M.-M. Davy; Paris: Vrin 1958) 40: "Sensus autem spiritualis hic est. Conversa ad Deum anima, et Verbo Dei maritanda, primo prevenientis gratie divitias intelligere perdocetur, et permittitur gustare quam suavis est Dominus. Postmodum vero in domum conscientie sue remittitur erudienda, castificanda in obedientia caritatis et perfecte mundanda a vitiis et perornanda virtutibus, ut ad spiritualem gratiam pietatis admitti et affectum virtutum, qui Sponsi thalamus est, digna habeatur".

[15] "Ad uigilias uirginum totus expenditur psalmus et in laude earum decantatur quae uere sunt flores ecclesiarum et lilia paradisi", cit. ed., 4.

[16] This example is quoted by de Lubac, Exégèse médiévale I/2 (1959) 577; in his study on monastic exegesis (ibid. 571–86), he understands it essentially as monastic tropology.

[17] *Moralia in Iob*, epist. dedic. § 4.

[18] Marginal abbreviations indicate the field to which certain passages of the commentary are relevant: GEO for geometry, * for astronomy, AR for arithmetics etc. The rhetorical figures are pointed out by SCHE (*schemata*) and RT (*ars rhetorica*). The list and the explanation of these abbreviations are written in front of the commentary in several manuscripts; cf. ed. M. Adriaen (CCSL 97; Turnhout 1968) 2.

egetes was to know to which measure the word of God could fit into the moulds of human grammar and rhetoric. The opinion that God has nothing to do with human rules was not the most common, even if we can find it in some texts of the eleventh century.[19] On the contrary, it was generally considered that grammar and rhetoric acted as helps for human understanding of divine texts. Thus, the monastic contribution to what we can call a first type of scientific exegesis was important.[20]

The fact that grammar and rhetoric were the object of a particular interest in monastic exegesis did not mean that it excluded other fields of knowledge. The introduction of physical considerations was the consequence of another feature: the link established between the Bible and the natural world. The fact that there was a connection between the exegesis of the words of the Scriptures and the interpretation of the things of the universe[21] explains these digressions into geography, physics, botany, zoology or other disciplines, seen frequently in monastic commentaries, notably those of the twelfth century.[22] We will study later the processes, in dealing with the methods of spiritual exegesis (see 3.2 below). Here it may be observed that bestiaries, lapidaries, diverse collections of allegories and arithmological treatises came from the monastic milieu and were composed with the intention of providing practical guides of spiritual interpretation.

Theoretical texts. Obviously, there is no medieval text that presented itself as a "theory of monastic exegesis". The monk who commented on the Bible saw himself as a Christian exegete and, if he gives any hermeneutical reflection, he did not limit it to the field of monastic thought. However, some texts present such a theory or at least describe some elements of the monastic exegesis. We should, first of all, consider texts of Gregory the Great, scattered throughout his works, which provide a first theoretical basis. These texts were familiar and influential to almost all exegetes during the Middle Ages.[23] This can be said for the works of Cassiodorus as well.[24] We might also cite the *Etymologies*

---

[19] See the texts quoted by Lesne, Les écoles (1940) 647–48, and Chenu, La théologie au douzième siècle (1966) 90, notably the following assertion by Smaragd of St. Mihiel: "Donatum non sequimur, quia fortiorem in divinis scripturis auctoritatem tenemus", "We do not follow Donatus [the most authoritative in the field of grammar], because we have a stronger authority in the divine Scriptures".

[20] See Chenu, La théologie comme science au XIIIe s. (1943) 16–17; Leclercq, L'amour des lettres (1990) 71.

[21] See especially Strubel, Allegoria in factis et allegoria in verbis (1975); Brinkmann, Mittelalterliche Hermeneutik (1980) 52–153.

[22] Most of the commentaries on the beginning of Genesis give room to discussions of subjects pertaining to cosmology or zoology (Angelom of Luxeuil, Rémi of Auxerre, Arnaud of Bonneval, Honorius Augustodunensis etc.).

[23] On Gregory's exegesis, see the important contribution of B. de Vregille, "Ecriture sainte et vie spirituelle", *Dictionnaire de Spiritualité* IV (Paris: Beauchesne 1960) 169–76. On his influence: de Lubac, Exégèse médiévale I/2 (1959) 467–98, 537–48; Wasselynck, L'influence de l'exégèse de saint Grégoire le Grand (1965) 157–204. See also chap. 26 above.

[24] The first part of the *Institutiones*, "De institutione divinarum litterarum", is a manual of exegesis, which expounds particularly the rules of Tichonius, according to St. Augustine; the second part, "De artibus ac disciplinis liberalium artium", is an account of liberal arts, considered by Cassiodorus as necessary for Bible exegesis (ed. R. A. B. Mynors; Oxford 1937); see the conspicious notice of M. Cappuyns, *Dictionnaire d'histoire et de géographie ecclésiastiques* XI (Paris: Letouzey et Ané 1949) 1349–1408.

of Isidore of Seville, who was not a monk, but whose widespread works strongly influenced the monastic exegesis of the High Middle Ages.[25] Later Bede's treatise *De schematibus et tropis sacrae scripturae* presented a catalogue of rhetorical figures illustrated with biblical verses. For example, for the syllepsis (which "occurs when words which do not agree in number are used together to constitute a simple thought") the quotation is from Psalm 77, *Attendite, populus meus, legem meam*, "Give [in the plural] ear, o my people [sing.], to my Law".[26] Evidently, Bede's *De tropis* must have been considered as a useful repertory to these exegetes so eager to analyze rhetorical figures. The beginning of book III of Raban Maur's *De clericorum institutione* is really a guide for exegesis, in which the author, after having praised Scripture, presents a typology of the "signs" of biblical language and studies the problems arising from "transfers of meaning".[27] Moving on to the twelfth century, we find several prefaces containing interesting hermeneutic reflections. Previously, we paid attention to the reflection by which Rainaud of St. Eloi introduced his commentary on the Pentateuch and which constitutes a valuable guide to the interpretation of the Bible.[28] Guibert of Nogent's *Liber quo ordine sermo fieri debeat* that is usually classed amongst treatises on preaching is in fact an introduction to the *Moralia Geneseos* and contains considerations on the exegesis, notably on the tropology, that this author loved so much.[29] We have already mentioned the name of Peter of Celle; his writings also contained elements of an exegetic theory, particularly his short treatise *De afflictione et lectione*.[30] Rupert of Deutz explains his exegetic principles throughout his works, notably in his *De victoria Verbi Dei*, which comments on some verses throughout the Bible.[31] Other monastic works contain further reflections on the theory of exegesis.

Some significant authors. An exhaustive list will not be given.[32] We may, however, note some significant authors in addition to those already mentioned. The monastic school of St. Germain in Auxerre produced many works during the High Middle Ages; Haymo and Remigius wrote important biblical

---

[25] Book VI of the *Etymologies* is intitled "De libris et officiis ecclesiasticis" but we find only a few remarks on exegesis in a strict sense; but other works of Isidore contain interesting statements on the matter: *Allegoriae sacrae Scripturae* (PL 83, 97–130), *Proemia in libros veteris et novi Testamenti* (PL 83, 155–80), *Liber numerorum in sanctis scripturis occurrentium* (PL 183, 179–200).

[26] It seems that the *De schematibus* constitutes the second book of a treatise, of which the *De arte metrica* would be the first book; cf. *Bedae Opera didascalica* I (ed. C. B. Kendall; CCSL 123A; Turnhout: Brepols 1975) 142–71 (the quoted example is on p. 145; translation in J. M. Miller / M. H. Prosser / Th. W. Benson, *Readings in Medieval Rhetoric*, Bloomington / London: Indiana UP 1973, 99). On this text, see Clausi, Elementi di ermeneutica monastica (1990).

[27] PL 107, 377–93. He also makes use of Augustine's *De doctrina Christiana*.

[28] Dahan, Une introduction à l'étude de l'Écriture (1987).

[29] Ed. R. B. C. Huygens (CCCM 127; Turnhout: Brepols 1993) 47–63.

[30] Leclercq, La spiritualité de Pierre de Celle (1946) 231–39.

[31] See particularly the prologue and the first chapters (ed. R. Haacke; Weimar: H. Böhlaus 1970).

[32] We refer again to the works of Leclercq, particularly to his contribution in CHB II (1969), "From Gregory the Great to Saint Bernard", in the chapter on "The exposition and exegesis of Scripture".

commentaries.[33] Amongst the Benedictines, the rich commentaries of Rupert of Deutz and Bruno of Asti (or of Segni) are remarkable.[34] After St. Bernard the Cistercians cultivated a particular type of exegesis, where the characteristics of monastic exegesis were emphasized and where spiritual considerations were given first priority (William of St. Thierry, Gilbert of Hoyland, Thomas of Perseigne). The commentaries on the Song of Songs have a very particular style.[35]

1.2. The Exegesis of the Schools

The urbanization of twelfth century society had as a consequence the growth of schools in the towns, most commonly attached to cathedral churches. The principal centres, Laon, Chartres, Paris, will be described in the next chapter of this volume. As was the case for the monastic schools, the Bible occupied a fundamental place in the teaching of these urban schools.[36] Because of social, economic and institutional conditions, the exegesis of the Bible underwent a change. In looking at the cases of Laon and, above all, Paris (schools of St. Victor, Ste Geneviève, Notre-Dame), we can speak of an "exegesis of the schools", which has been characterized by some scholars as "pre-scholastic", and which presents some notable features.[37]

The principal characteristics of the exegesis of the schools. Commentaries did not yet have a fixed structure, but they were moving towards an internal organization in accordance with the different levels of interpretation, of which a list of four senses was codified in the twelfth century. The masters of the Paris schools, particularly Stephen Langton, contributed much to what was to become the common exegetic theory – even if this proved not to be the exclusive practice.[38] Let us look for example at Peter the Chanter's commentary on Zechariah: each unit of the commentary consists of a group of verses corresponding to a vision of the Prophet or to another semantic unit. Peter first gives a literal or historical analysis; then he goes to spiritual exegesis, pointed out by the words *mystice*, *allegorice*, *moraliter*; the most interesting passages are those which contain several levels of interpretation. The same can be found in the commentaries of Stephen Langton, at least in those which maintain several levels; for, as it is known, the *reportatores* often have chosen either the literal parts or the moral ones (*moralitates*).[39] In the complete commentaries, we find

[33] Cf. several studies in the collection volume L'école carolingienne d'Auxerre (1990).

[34] See Grégoire, Bruno de Segni, exégète et théologien monastique (1965).

[35] Cf. Ohly, Hohelied-Studien (1958).

[36] On the teaching of Bible in the schools, see Grabmann, Die Geschichte der scholastischen Methode (1909–11); Lesne, Les écoles (1940) 643–76; Paré / Brunet / Tremblay, La Renaissance du XIIe s. (1933) 213–39; Delhaye, L'organisation scolaire au XIIe s. (1947).

[37] On the exegesis of the schools, see Smalley, The Study of the Bible (1983) 83–263; eadem, The Bible in the Medieval Schools, CHB II (1969) 197–220; Châtillon, La Bible dans les écoles du XIIe s., in Le Moyen Age et la Bible (1984) 163–97.

[38] See Smalley, Stephen Langton and the four Senses of Scripture (1931) ; d'Esneval, Les quatre sens de l'Écriture (1989); Quinto, Stefano Langton e i quattro sensi della scrittura (1989).

[39] Lacombe / Smalley, Studies on the Commentaries of Cardinal Stephen Langton (1930).

the same terms as in Peter the Chanter (for the spiritual senses *allegorice*, *mystice*, *moraliter*); as in Peter the Chanter, the levels of exegesis are pointed out by marginal headings.[40]

From this, the commentaries began to have a more organized structure than that found in the monastic exegesis. The commentaries are structured by the division into chapters (using the old systems, previous to Stephen Langton: the chapters were shorter than today);[41] the basic unit could have been a chapter or a group of verses having a thematic or narrative unity. The literal exegesis (explanation of words or historic context) is first given, followed by the spiritual explanation, sometimes divided into different categories; *spiritualiter*, *mystice* are the general terms, and *allegorice*, *moraliter* are the particular terms. In this regard, the commentaries of Andrew of St. Victor, limited to the literal sense, are an exception, even though in other ways they perfectly illustrate the exegesis of the schools. On the other hand, the commentaries are often preceded by prologues, which consider globally the text from the point of view of literary analysis, more systematically than in monastic exegesis, where we also find prologues but in which the goal (general considerations on exegesis, spiritual value of the book) was different. In this respect, the commentaries of Andrew of St. Victor are representative: thus, his prologue on Isaiah contains reflections on what the modern commentator can bring, as well as a eulogy to the prophet. The *Introitus in libros Salomonis* is based on an analysis of the parable as literary device.[42] Concerning again the structure of the commentaries, we should note that St. Jerome's prologues have become an important element and that they are also explained with care; this is often of great interest for stylistic analysis.[43]

Another characteristic element of the exegesis of the schools was that the *gloss* became the basic form, at least for literal interpretation, to the detriment of the running commentary (that we find again in the spiritual or mystic parts). From this, the exegesis of the schools seems shorter and more concentrated than the monastic one. The *notes* on historical books of Hugh of St. Victor, the commentaries of Andrew, of Peter the Chanter and, above all, of Stephen Langton illustrate this characteristic. The following passage from the commentary of Andrew of St. Victor on chapter 21 of Proverbs shows this technique:

> *Cogitationes robustorum abundantia* (21:5). *Cogitationes robustorum* ad hoc fiunt ut omnibus bonis abundent. *Lingua mendacii* (21:6) ut falsa laudatione et testificatione et huiusmodi. *Detrahent* (21:7) ad mortem. *Iudicium* (ibid.) rectum. *Aliena* (21:8) a bono. *In sinu* (21:14) occultum. *Gigantum* (21:16) qui solis uiribus innitebantur.[44]

---

[40] For example, see our edition of the commentary on Gen 4:1–17 in: L'exégèse de l'histoire de Caïn et Abel (1983) 17–24.

[41] It seems that the chapter-division in use today goes back to Stephen Langton; see Landgraf, Die Schriftzitate in der Scholastik (1937); d'Esneval, La division de la Vulgate latine en chapitres (1978).

[42] Prologue on Isaiah, ed. Smalley, The Study of the Bible (1983) 377–80; *Introitus* (ed. R. Berndt, *Andreae … Expositiones historicas in libros Salomonis*; CCCM 53 B; Turnhout: Brepols 1991) 3–5.

[43] For example, Peter the Chanter, *Glossae super Genesim* (ed. [of the prologues and chap. 1–3] A. Sylwan; AUG; Göteborg 1992) 2–17.

[44] Ed. Berndt 68: "*Cogitationes robustorum abundantia* (21:5). *Cogitationes robustorum* ad hoc

The importance of *textual remarks* seems also typical of the exegesis of the schools. Grammatical considerations in monastic exegesis sometimes led the authors to compare the different versions of the biblical text. This is more systematic for the urban masters of the twelfth century: these textual explorations, even going back to St. Jerome (notably for Genesis and the Prophets), which cite the Hebrew text, the Septuagint, or the Old Latin used by the Fathers, give a scientific aspect to this exegesis. The role of the Victorines in this regard is significant, particularly that of Andrew, who produced a rich material integrating the remarks of St. Jerome and enlarged it considerably. Here are two examples. On Ezek 1:10, Andrew of St. Victor compares several Latin manuscripts with the original Hebrew text:

> What we find in some manuscripts *facies aquile desuper ipsorum iiii*, is not in the corrected manuscripts of the Latins nor in the *hebraica veritas*.[45]

On Zech 5:2 (the vision of the flying book), Peter the Chanter goes back to the text of the Septuagint (i.e. one Old Latin):

> *Ego uideo uolumen* [I see a book]. The Septuagint: a flying scythe, i.e. the judiciary sentence of God, which cuts the sins of everyone.[46]

The exegesis of the schools is further characterized by the enlargement of the sources. The *Glossa* later called *ordinaria* was influential in this evolution.[47] Elaborated during the first half of the twelfth century, in Laon and then in Paris (we wonder today to what degree the Victorines contributed), the *Glossa* was at the crossroads of monastic exegesis, in which it took on an anthological aspect, and of the exegesis of the schools, of which it had the systematic aspect and the relative brevity. To the corpus of texts given by the *Glossa*, the masters of the schools added many authors: some Greek Fathers, who became more familiar in the twelfth century (Pseudo-Dionysius, Gregory of Nazianzus, Gregory of Nyssa – Origen and John Chrysostom or the texts attributed to him, for a long time better known, enjoyed a revival), as well as Jewish interpretations different from those found in the works of the Fathers and already quoted by certain authors of the High Middle Ages (Isidore of Seville, Remigius of Auxerre) and by the *Glossa*, also later authors like Hugh of St. Victor, Bernard of Clairvaux (for the Song of Songs) or Ralph of Flay (for Leviticus); the *moderni* were referred to more and more as *auctoritates*.[48] The work of one

---

fiunt ut omnibus bonis abundent. *Lingua mendacii* (21:6) ut falsa laudatione et testificatione et huiusmodi. *Detrahent* (21:7) ad mortem. *Iudicium* (ibid.) rectum. *Aliena* (21:8) a bono. *In sinu* (21:14) occultum. *Gigantum* (21:16) qui solis uiribus innitebantur".

[45] "Quod in quibusdam codicibus scriptum invenitur *facies aquile desuper ipsorum iiii*, nec emendatiora latinorum habent exemplaria nec in hebraica ueritate legitur" (ed. M. A. Signer; CCCM 53E; Turnhout: Brepols 1991) 15. Cf. Berndt, André de Saint-Victor (1991) 228–32.

[46] "*Ego uideo uolumen.* Septuaginta: *falcem uolantem*, id est iuditiariam Dei sententiam, que cunctorum delicta succidit", MS. Paris BN lat. 16793, fol. 139 va.

[47] See the numerous studies of B. Smalley, summarized in her article "Glossa ordinaria" (1984), and in this volume (Chap. 30), G. R. Evans, "Masters and Disciples: Aspects of Christian Interpretation of the Old Testament in the XIth and XIIth centuries".

[48] On the knowledge of Greek authors in the XIIth century, see Chenu, La théologie au XIIe s. (1966) 274–308; de Lubac, Exégèse médiévale I/1 (1959) 221–304 (Origen). For Jewish interpretations, see below 3.1.3. For the role of the *moderni*, see Chenu, op. cit., 351–65 ("Authentica et magistralia") and idem, Antiqui, moderni (1928).

of these masters of the Parisian schools, Peter Comestor's *Historia scholastica*, was quickly commentated on and glossed by contemporaries, one of them being Stephen Langton.[49]

Finally, there was a widening of perspectives in the masters of the twelfth century: the sciences of the *trivium* (including dialectics) and of the *quadrivium* were used more frequently. Certainly, it was an old idea, and, after St. Augustine (in the *De doctrina Christiana*), monastic authors of the High Middle Ages had used it and, as may be seen, had already made digressions on physical science. In this regard, the novelty of the exegesis of the schools was that information taken from the *artes* no longer served the spiritual considerations but was better used for the literal explanation of elements of the biblical texts. We find this clearly expressed in the theoretical works of Hugh of St. Victor, the *Didascalicon* and the *De scripturis*, commented upon below.

On the other hand, the exegesis of the schools sometimes brought theological developments. The majority of the masters, even though remaining *magistri in sacra pagina* ("biblical teachers"), contributed considerably to the formation of theological science by compiling collections of sentences (Anselm of Laon, Robert of Melun, Peter Lombard, Peter of Poitiers, Stephen Langton) as well as by elaborating theological *quaestiones* in their commentaries, even combining collections of *quaestiones* on biblical books (Robert of Melun) or having them separate (Stephen Langton).[50] It is not surprising then to note that the most commentated books were the beginning of Genesis, the Psalms and the Pauline Epistles. The commentary on the Hexaemeron of Peter Abelard, the commentaries of Gilbert de la Porrée (Psalms, Epistles), and those of Geroch of Reichersberg and Stephen Langton are examples of theological exegesis.[51]

Theoretical texts. Theoretical reflection on the exegesis of the Bible developed in the schools and several of their texts contain hermeneutical thoughts, in which we see many of the characteristics described above. Among the Victorines, Hugh of St. Victor wrote two important works: first, the *Didascalicon* or *De studio legendi* which constitutes an introduction or a preparation for the study of the Bible, and which underlines the importance of literal exegesis and defines the role of the *artes*;[52] second, the *De scripturis et scriptoribus sacris*, a true hermeneutical manual which affirms the importance of the literal level as well as that of the spiritual sense and tries to create objective criteria for spiritual interpretation.[53] The prefaces of Andrew of St. Victor contain numerous

---

[49] See Stegmüller, Repertorium biblicum V, n° 7710–30 (*Expositio litteralis*) and 7731–43 (*Expositio moralis*).

[50] See the informations given by Landgraf, Introduction à l'histoire de la littérature théologique (1973).

[51] In separate theological questions, there is an extensive use of Scripture (cf. Gregory, Indices of Rubrics and Incipits in the Questiones of Stephen Langton [1930]; Quinto, Die *Quaestiones* des Stephan Langton über die Gottesfurcht [1992]); in the biblical commentaries, however, the theological subjects are generally not discussed; see Dahan, L'exégèse de Genèse 1, 26 (1992).

[52] Ed. C. H. Buttimer (Washington 1939); see also the English trans. by J. Taylor (New York: Columbia UP 1961), and the French transl. by M. Lemoine, *Hugues de St-Victor. L'Art de lire. Didascalicon* (Paris: Cerf 1991).

[53] PL 175, 9–28. See the summary of our lectures in *École pratique des hautes études. Section des sciences religieuses, Annuaire* 100 (1991/92) 377–78.

methodological indications for a literal study of the Bible (the *littera* being understood as a complex ensemble encompassing the textual study, literary analysis and historical investigation). In spite of certain outdated claims, some important pages of the introduction of Robert of Melun's *Sententiae* must be considered as representative of the exegesis of the schools; he not only described contemporary exegetical practices but also neatly formulated rules and methods, in terms similar to those of the Victorines.[54] Amongst the considerations of the masters at the end of the twelfth century, Peter the Chanter's *De tropis loquendi* constitutes on the one hand an updating of Bede's opuscule enriched by the knowledge acquired during the century, and represents on the other hand a work with different hermeneutical perspectives resulting from the role of dialectics and from a kind of philosophical thought.[55] More formally, Stephen Langton's prefaces also offer new elements in exegetic theory.[56]

The representative authors. The masters of the scholastic exegesis may be classified by schools.[57] The importance of the Laon masters is well known, notably Anselm and Ralph, as well as their real or assumed disciples (William of Champeaux, Hugh of Rouen). Anselm's teaching was criticized by Peter Abelard (he commented on the beginning of Genesis), who in turn established a school (and his students commentated on the Pauline Epistles).[58] Founded by William of Champeaux, the school of St. Victor evolved rapidly under Hugh; his disciples developed the hermeneutical program which he traced: Andrew specialized in literal interpretation, and Richard in spiritual interpretation (but without rejecting the literal level).[59] The masters of Chartres were little interested in Bible commentary, even if their lectures were in part dedicated to this; we have only the commentaries on the beginning of Genesis by Thierry of Chartres and Clarembald of Arras.[60] Further, the Porretans, namely Gilbert de la Porrée (who commentated on the Psalms and on the Pauline Epistles) and his disciples (who commentated on the New Testament). Peter Lombard (who commentated on the Psalms and on the Pauline Epistles) and Peter of Poitiers (*Allegoriae super tabernaculum*, *Distinctiones super Psalterium*) are also

---

[54] *Œuvres de Robert de Melun*, III/1 *Sententie* (ed. R. M. Martin; Louvain: Univ. cath. 1947) 159–97.

[55] See Evans, The Place of Peter the Chanter's *De tropis loquendi* (1983); Valente, Arts du discours et *sacra pagina* (1990).

[56] Cf. Smalley, Stephen Langton and the four Senses of Scripture (1931).

[57] See Landgraf, Introduction à l'histoire de la littérature théologique (1973) (not only on the exegesis), and the study of G. R. Evans in this volume (Chap. 30), where the bibliography is given.

[58] See Luscombe, The School of Peter Abelard (1969). Several texts have been edited by A. Landgraf: *Comment. Cantabrigiensis in Epistolas Pauli e schola P. Abaelardi* (Notre Dame, in: UP 1937–45); *Commentarius Porretanus in Primam Epistolam ad Corinthios* (City of Vatican 1945).

[59] The bibliography is abundant; see the recent collection book L'abbaye parisienne de Saint-Victor au Moyen Age (1991), the studies of J. Châtillon collected in a postumous volume, Le mouvement canonial au XIIe siècle (1993), and the essay by R. Berndt in this volume (Chap. 34).

[60] Thierry of Chartres, *Tractatus de sex dierum operibus* (ed. N. M. Häring, *Commentaries on Boethius by Thierry of Chartres and his School*; Toronto: Pontifical Institute of Mediaeval Studies 1971, 553–75); Clarembald of Arras, *Tractatulus super librum Genesis* (ed. N. M. Häring, *Life and Works of Clarembald of Arras*; Toronto: Pontifical Institute of Mediaeval Studies 1965, 225–49).

representative of the exegesis of the schools.[61] The Parisian Masters at the end of the twelfth century have been regrouped under the name of "biblical moral school":[62] we have already named the principals, Peter Comestor ("the Eater"), Peter the Chanter and Stephen Langton. The *Historia scholastica* of the former is not presented in the form of a commentary but it does hold an important position in the story of the exegesis; it brought together all the previous tools of the schools and became the basic text for the teaching and study of the Bible. It was translated into many languages and was commentated from the thirteenth century.[63] To the same trend we can add the *Aurora* of Peter Riga, which is a versified presentation of Scripture and, like the work of Peter Comestor, assimilates the improvements of the exegesis of the twelfth century, while staying attached to traditional methods of spiritual interpretation.[64] It may be observed that the masters of the biblical moral school aspired to comment on the whole of Scripture: did they want to replace the *Glossa ordinaria* by another enriched running gloss? It seems that they partially succeeded: besides the *Historia scholastica*, which was popular, the commentary of Peter the Chanter and that of Stephen Langton were considered as standard for the next two or three generations, at least in the Parisian schools and until the *Postilla* of Hugh of St. Cher.

Inasmuch as the monastic exegesis did not end with the twelfth century, the same can be said of the exegesis of the schools, after the creation of the universities. The most important commentary of the thirteenth century (by its impact), the *Postilla* of Hugh of St. Cher, pertains more to the genre of exegesis of the schools than to that of university exegesis, which grew during his lifetime. It may also be asked if the *Postilla* of Nicholas of Lyra, that replaced the *Glossa ordinaria* and the commentary of Hugh of St. Cher from the fourteenth century, was not yet a part of the exegesis of the schools; for it has its principal characteristics: like brevity (despite some developments), separation of the levels of exegesis, or frequent recourse to Jewish interpretations, while certain significant traits of the university exegesis are absent.

1.3. The Exegesis of the University

During the thirteenth century, the growth of the towns and the development of educational institutions continued. The birth of the universities had as consequence a profound modification of the structures of knowledge in Christian society. The mendicant orders, growing at the same time, soon played a major role in the university, in Paris as well as in Oxford. Further, they created their own structures of teaching, the *studia*, which had, at the highest levels, the

---

[61] See the recent study of Colish, *Psalterium Scholasticorum*: Peter Lombard and the Emergence of Scholastic Psalms Exegesis (1992).

[62] The expression has been coined by Grabmann, Die Geschichte der scholastischen Methode (1901–11), and taken up by Smalley, The Study of the Bible (1983). On these masters, see Baldwin, Masters, Princes and Merchants (1970).

[63] See the recent study of Luscombe, Peter Comestor (1985).

[64] *Aurora. Petri Rigae Biblia versificata* (ed. P.E. Beichner; Notre-Dame, IN: UP 1965).

same characteristics as those of the teaching of the universities.[65] Despite the importance given to the *Sentences* of Peter Lombard, the Bible was again the fundamental text in the teaching at the theological faculties at two levels. At the elementary one, the students heard lectures on the whole Bible (which was read *cursorie*), limited to textual and literal questions and to a mere mention of the principal spiritual themes; this reading was done by the "biblical bachelor". The second approach, at the end of the *cursus*, consisted in lectures by the masters in theology: it was a detailed study of one biblical book, explaining all its aspects.[66] The consequence of this university study was that the sacred text was not considered as before. Surely, its sanctity was not questioned, but it was taken also as a matter of study, and, as required in the program of a *cursus*, it was investigated with all the tools used for the analysis of any human text. Now these tools were considerably renovated with, on the one hand, the introduction of the texts of Aristotle and of the Arabic and Greek commentators at the Faculty of Arts, and, on the other hand, at the Faculty of Theology, the development of the techniques of analysis of Peter Lombard's *Sentences*. All these techniques were transposed in the study of the Bible, giving to the exegesis of the university a very characteristic aspect.[67]

The separation of pagina sacra *and* theologia. Before describing the major features, it will be convenient to sketch the evolution of the theology which permitted the development of this kind of exegesis. Until the years 1235–40, the words *sacra pagina* and *theologia* were quite equivalent:[68] theology had its roots in the study of the Bible, even more, it existed only as biblical exegesis. Even if works like those of St. Anselm and Abelard had laid the foundation of autonomous thinking, even if in scholarly circles during the twelfth century more and more structured collections of sentences and theological questions were elaborated, it was always the exegetical effort, starting from the scriptural data (with the mediation of the patristic works) that permitted the labor of the theologian. The importance of Peter Lombard's *Sentences* led to a reflection on the essential differences between this text and the biblical texts, both constituting *theologia* or *pagina sacra*.

This reflection was intensified through an analysis of the language of these texts: around 1240, several theologians formulated a distinction between biblical and theological language. The language of the Bible was defined as *non-scientific*, because of its frequent use of metaphor and symbols; the language of theology was defined as *scientific*, i. e. univocal and rigorous. A distinction was made between theology and biblical exegesis, and therefore theology was constituted as a true science. It is possible to look at this evolution in the prologues

---

[65] On the study of the Bible in the *studia*, see Douais, Essai sur l'organisation des études dans l'ordre des frères prêcheurs (1884) 113–25, 270–82; Maieru, Tecniche di insegnamento (1978).

[66] The historians do not agree on this point; see Denifle, Quel livre servait de base à l'enseignement des maîtres en théologie (1894); Mandonnet, Chronologie des écrits scripturaires de saint Thomas d'Aquin (1929); Kleinhans, Der Studiengang der Professoren der hl. Schrift (1933).

[67] The works on the university exegesis are too rare; besides Spicq, Esquisse d'une histoire de l'exégèse latine au moyen âge (1944), and Smalley, The Study of the Bible (1983) 264–355, see Verger, L'exégèse de l'Université (1985).

[68] See de Ghellinck, *Pagina* et *Sacra Pagina*. Histoire d'un mot (1947).

of the *Sentences* commentaries, from Alexander of Hales to St. Thomas Aquinas, in whose works it reached its completion.[69] If in fact this separation was more significant for the theological science that could thereby be developed for itself, did it also have major consequences for the exegesis of the Bible? Of course, yes, and the most important consequence was that it also became a science (I mean by this word a structured knowledge possessing its own techniques), and even an autonomous science, able to put a distance between itself (using a scientific language as theology did) and its object (the biblical text, with a total assumption of its symbolic and metaphorical aspects). From an institutional point of view, the exegesis of the Bible became a matter of teaching; it could then welcome the tools utilized in other textual studies (Aristotle, classical texts, the *Sentences*). This does not mean that theological thinking was eliminated from exegesis: on the contrary, it constituted an important element in the lectures of the masters, but it was delimited and distinguished from the other parts of the commentary.

Major characteristics of the university exegesis. For all the above reasons, the university exegesis seems to be easier to characterize than the monastic one or even that of the schools. First of all, the commentaries are very *strongly structured.* The basis is the *lectio* whose length depends on the length of the lesson itself; it can cover one chapter of the Bible (according to the new chapter divisions) or only a part of a chapter. The *lectio* itself is rigorously constructed and it is composed in principle of the following three elements:

(a) the *divisio.* This is the division of the commentated text (the first *lectio* gives the division of the whole biblical book) and the subdivision from the beginning ("this book consists of two parts; the first consists of three parts; then the first part is subdivided in ..."). We find these important divisions at the beginning of each *lectio*; not only is the chapter so divided, but also, in some commentaries, each verse. This is not merely a question of a gratuitous or purely formal exercise. On the one hand, the grouping in broad compass inspired a general reading of the considered text; on the other hand, the study of micro-structures refined the analysis and drew attention to all the details of the text. These divisions were not standardized; each author proposed his own system, thus providing his own emphasis.

(b) the *expositio.* This is the explanation verse by verse or even word by word, limiting itself to textual and literal difficulties. The form is close to the running gloss but the commentary is not anthological. The fragments extracted from the Fathers and other sources were integrated into the writing of the author, and therefore we generally find in the *expositio* elements of philosophy and other disciplines; these can become developed *excursus.*

(c) *dubia* or *quaestiones.* After the *expositio*, the end of the *lectio* considered doctrinal problems. The structure of the *dubia* is a simple one: the problem is

[69] The question *De modo tradendi* (or *exponendi*) *sacram Scripturam* allows us to follow this evolution; see Chenu, La théologie comme science au XIIIe s. (1943); Minnis, Medieval Theory of Authorship (1984) 118–45; and the summary of our lectures in *Ecole pratique des hautes études. Section des sciences religieuses, Annuaire* 101 (1992/93) 311–13.

formulated, then the solution is given. The *quaestiones* have a more complex structure, which can be that of the so-called scholastic *quaestiones* (see below).

As in the exegesis of the schools, the commentary was preceded by a prologue, most often constituting an overall literary analysis of the biblical book and leading to the spiritual sense. From the mid-thirteenth century on, the prologue itself was rigorously structured and it started from a scriptural citation (not from the commentated book). This verse was divided according to the techniques described above. We can look at the proemium of St. Bonaventure's commentary on Ecclesiastes: it contains two sections, the first is based on a theme provided by a verse of the Psalms (Ps 39 [40]:5) *Beatus vir cuius est nomen Domini spes eius, et non respexit in vanitates et insanias falsas.* Bonaventure examines the notions of beatitude and vanity. Beatitude is described from two viewpoints: the love of celestial realities (analysed according to four *rationes*), and the distrust of earthly things (also according to four *rationes*). Four types of vanity are distinguished as well as the four ways in which wordly man is seduced by these vanities. There is a short transition bringing us back to the subject of the three books attributed to Solomon. The second section more precisely introduces the study of Ecclesiastes, using the schema of the four Aristotelian causes (*finis* = goal, *materia* = subject, *forma* or *modus agendi* = literary form, *causa efficiens* = author). Each of these causes is examined under the *quaestio* form (e. g. for *finis*: two arguments *pro*, two arguments *contra*, and the conclusion of the master).[70]

Linked to this rigid structure, a stylistic feature typical of the university commentaries may be mentioned: they formally present a systematic aspect, each part being subjected to a determined rhythm. The above mentioned analysis of St. Bonaventure's text also offers an example of this feature.

Of course, it has to be observed that many late thirteenth and fourteenth century commentaries that were not products of university teaching (or from a *studium*) had the same structure. However, it is right to consider them also to be a part of the genre of university exegesis.

A second major characteristic of the university exegesis is its *scientific aspect* (besides the above-mentioned qualification) which appears in several elements. The textual study is generally more developed here than in the exegesis of the schools. It profited from the expertise of the Victorines and furthered it (Andrew was again the authority in this respect). From the second half of the thirteenth century, the commentators willingly used the *correctoria*, products of the same university backround and of the same scientific exigence. These *correctoria* permitted the knowledge of different versions of the biblical text and the comparison of the Vulgate text with the Hebrew and the Greek.[71] Furthermore, the literal exegesis was enlarged once more in the directions initiated by the Victorines in the previous century: doctrinal considerations and the use of the sciences.[72] Even so, the spiritual exegesis sought to base itself on objective criteria and to reject any arbitrary steps.

---

70 Bonaventura, *Opera omnia* VI (Quaracchi 1893) 3–8.

71 See below 3.1.1.

72 Smalley, Some Thirteenth-Century Commentaries on the Sapiential Books (1949/50).

The third characteristic proceeds from the previous one: *the growth of the available sources.* More frequently than in the twelfth century some *moderni* were considered as *auctoritates*: Andrew of St. Victor was cited by name, the name of Bernard of Clairvaux appeared often, and the works of St. Thomas Aquinas became authoritative in fourteenth century exegesis; thus, Dominic Grima took care to cite St. Thomas at the end of each *lectio* in his commentaries on the Pentateuch.[73] Jewish interpretations continued to appear, sometimes as primary sources; Rabbi Moyses (Maimonides) was occasionally cited.[74] But the most impressive was the introduction of Aristotle and his Arab commentators, not only in the *excursus* of philosophy or physics, but also with regard to moral or metaphysical problems.[75]

Theoretical texts. There were numerous reflections on the exegesis in the university milieu. As for the preceding genres, however, the authors did not define a specific university exegesis but gave rules concerning more general Christian exegesis. Here again, the prologues provide important elements; their methodical aspect emphasizes the hermeneutic analysis. But the university created a new form, in which a theoretic reflection developed: the *principia* that the biblical bachelor and then the beginning master had to deliver in the inaugural lesson. The *principia* made a division of the sacred books and / or a praise of Scripture. We have several of these inaugural lessons (Jean of La Rochelle, Albert the Great, Thomas Aquinas, Peter of John Olieu and others). In other university exercises, the masters could also present a theory of exegesis: for example, among the quodlibetal disputations, we have a very important question on hermeneutics by St. Thomas Aquinas.[76] An inventory of these texts has yet to be made.

Significant authors. The university commentaries are numerous: besides the university texts, we have those of the Dominican or Franciscan *studia*, which present the same features.[77] Briefly and schematically some names may be listed. Amongst the secular masters: John Halgrin of Abbeville († 1237), commentator on the Octateuch, on the Psalms and on the Song of Songs; Odo of Châteauroux († 1273), who wrote *introitus* on almost all the books of the Bible; Nicolas of Tournai; Henri of Gand († 1293), to whom is attributed an interesting commentary on the *Hexaemeron.* Amongst the Dominicans: Guerric of St-Quentin († 1245), commentator on the Prophets and on the Hagiographers; Albert the Great; Thomas Aquinas; William of Alton († c. 1265), who commentated on nearly all of the Old Testament but whose authorship is sometimes doubtful; Nicholas of Gorran († 1295), who also commentated on a large part of the Bible; Dominic Grima († c. 1347); Meister Eckhart

[73] Cf. MS. Paris, BN lat. 365, fol. 1: "In fine autem summe litteralis cuiuslibet lectionis, sensum misticum ubi differt a litterali et maxime moralem perstringam. Et tandem super textum ad minus duas mouebo questiones et pro earum determinacione remittam ad aliquod operum Doctoris communis, scilicet fratris Thome de Aquino nostri ordinis".

[74] See Smalley, William of Auvergne, John of La Rochelle and St. Thomas Aquinas on the Old Law (1974); Dahan, Les intellectuels chrétiens et les juifs au moyen âge (1990) 320–21.

[75] Smalley, The Study of the Bible (1983) 292–328.

[76] Thomas Aquinas, Quodl. VII, q. 6.

[77] See Verger, L'exégèse de l'Université (1985).

(† 1329), whose commentaries (Genesis, Exodus, Ecclesiasticus) have many of the characteristics of the university genre. Amongst the Franciscans: Robert Grosseteste; Bonaventure; Roger Bacon, who does not seem to have written commentaries but whose reflections on contemporary exegesis are very valuable; William of Middleton († 1257), who commentated on the Pentateuch, Sapiential Books, the Minor Prophets and Job; Alexander of Alexandria († 1314), commentator on Job, Isaiah, John and the Epistle to the Romans; Thomas Docking († after 1269), who commentated on Deuteronomy, Isaiah and the Epistles. We must add here the commentaries of Peter of John Olieu (Olivi) († 1298); even though he was not a master of theology (he did however teach in the *studium* of Narbonne), his commentaries (Genesis, the Prophets, Job, the Psalms, the New Testament) belong to the university genre; his postils on the Apocalypse, however, are of a different type. The *Postilla* of Nicholas of Lyra, on the whole Bible, had considerable influence from the fourteenth to the sixteenth century, becoming the standard commentary on the Bible. But it presents only certain aspects of the university genre.

2. The Forms

After having described the three genres of medieval exegesis, we will undertake the study of its forms and attempt to make a provisional typology. Genres and forms are not always linked: if some forms seem to be connected to a given genre (the scholastic *quaestio* is linked to university exegesis – but the simple *quaestio* was found also in the commentaries of the schools and even in monastic exegesis), other forms, like the running gloss, are present in the three genres. The scholastic *lectio* is found only in university exegesis (it will not be necessary to give another description here). The homily poses a particular problem: to what degree does it constitute an exegetic form (and not a form pertaining only to preaching)? In any case, it will be considered here as an exegetical form, because it has carried the major themes of medieval exegesis and presents a rich material for the historian of biblical exegesis; it is not restricted to one of the three genres defined above. Furthermore, we shall use the simple form / complex form opposition, borrowed from the analysis of literary forms; it is useful and it allows us to distinguish elementary structures (like that of the gloss) from much more elaborated constructions (like that of the scholastic *quaestio*). We shall, however, take it more as a tool which will be useful for a clearer typology, than as an analytic instrument according to which a classification would have been arbitrarily set.

2.1. The Exegetical Chains

We shall begin with a rather uncommon form in the medieval exegesis in the West and which is not easy to define: the exegetical chain (*catena*), which was in turn frequent in Greek exegesis.[78] To our knowledge, only two texts from

[78] See the works of Devreesse, particularly his article Chaînes exégétiques grecques (1928).

the Latin Middle Ages bear this form. The better known is St. Thomas Aquinas' *Catena aurea* written between 1263 and 1268, at the request of pope Urban IV. Drawing from 57 Greek authors and 22 Latin authors, it fits into the context of the controversy with the Greeks.[79] It seems that the title of *catena* has been given to this work in the fourteenth century: Aquinas designated it as *expositio continua* on the Gospels. According to a recent historian of St. Thomas Aquinas, it is "a great collection of exegetical quotations from the Fathers, arranged into a running explanation, verse by verse, of the four Gospels".[80] However, the part of the author is not small: besides the choice and the layout of the fragments and the fact that he had inspired new translations of Greek texts unknown before in Western countries, St. Thomas added some notes, as we can see from his own words:

> From several doctors I have compiled a running explanation of this Gospel, adding however a few things to the words of recognized authors, most of them from the Glosses; in order that they could be discerned from the other texts, I have entitled them *Glossae*.[81]

The passages indicated by the word *Glossa* are short glosses; further research will show if they are additions of St. Thomas or fragments of recent authors, drawn from the *Glossa ordinaria* or from later texts such as the commentaries of Peter the Chanter or Hugh of St. Cher. For example, here is the *catena* on Matt 2:10–11:

> [2:10] Eusebius, *Hist. eccl.*; Hieronymus; Dionysius, *De cael. hier.*; Chrysostomus, *Super Matth. (op. imperf.)*; Hieronymus; Remigius; Chrysostomus, *Super Matth. (op. imperf.)*; Remigius; Beda; [2:11] Glossa; Iosephus, *Ant. iud.*; Augustinus, *de Cons. Evang.*; Glossa; Chrysostomus, *In Matth.* (hom. 9); Augustinus, *de Cons. Evang.*; Hilarius, *In Matth.*; Rabanus; Glossa; Hieronymus; Chrysostomus, *Super Matth. (op. imperf.)*; Augustinus, *de Cons. Evang.*[82]

The other chain we referred to is wholly different: it is an anonymous compilation, from the beginning of the thirteenth century, as it seems; some manuscripts and two printings of the sixteenth century contain it; we have made use of the MS. Paris, Bibl. Mazarine 179. George Lacombe described this "curious work" in these words: "It is a marquetry of bits taken from the glosses of the preceding 200 years. Like certain contemporary compilers, the author was kind enough to cite his authorities in the margin".[83] Only *moderni* are quoted (and named): for example, in the *catena* on Gen 4:1–17 (fol. 4 v°), we note the following names: Bruno (of Segni), Bernard (of Clairvaux), Aelred (of Rievaulx), Stephanus (Stephen Langton), Gilebertus (Gilbert of Hoyland?), Peter

---

[79] See Bataillon, Les sermons de saint Thomas et la *Catena aurea* (1974); Conticello, San Tommaso ed i Padri (1990).

[80] Cf. Torrell, Initiation à saint Thomas d'Aquin (1993) 494–95 (see also 200–06): the *Catena aurea* "se présente comme un vaste recueil de citations exégétiques des Pères, agencé en exposition continue, verset par verset, de la totalité des quatre évangiles".

[81] *In Catenam super Matthaei Evangelio* epist. dedicatoria: "Ex diversis Doctorum libris praedicti Evangelii expositionem continuam compilavi, pauca quidem certorum Auctorum verbis, ut plurimum ex Glossis, adiiciens, quae, ut ab eorum dictis possent discerni, sub Glossae titulo praenotavi" (ed. A. Guarienti; Rome / Turin: Marietti 1953) 4.

[82] Ibid. 42–44.

[83] Lacombe, Studies on the Commentaries of Cardinal Stephen Langton (1930) 133, indicates three other manuscripts and two XVIth century printings (we have not been able to consult them). See also Käppeli, Eine aus frühscholastischen Werken excerptierte Bibelkatene (1931).

of Ravenna (?).[84] As we can see by the room given to Cistercians authors, it is rather a spiritual work.

Is it right to distinguish these exegetical chains from other forms which are similar to them, as the "anthological commentary" and the gloss? Two features seem specific to the *catena*: first, it is a running commentary (and thus it differs from the gloss, in which the explanation is fragmentated and which makes a choice in the commentated verses); then, the author of the *catena* is merely a compiler, who never gives his own sentences (from this aspect, the *catena* differs from the gloss as well as from the anthological commentary). Even if we take in account the *glossae* of St. Thomas' *Catena aurea*, it seems that this remark remains true.

2.2. Anthological Commentaries

With this designation, we mean works composed to a great extent of fragments of the Fathers (and of *moderni*); the writing is continuous and often the role of the author is important (thus, they differ from the glosses). It is the basic form of medieval exegesis, monastic as well as that composed in the schools. Is it, strictly speaking, really a specific form? The length of such commentaries is variable (those written in monastic milieux being longer than those of the schools), but their structure, though not rigid, is rather homogenous: the commentary is made verse by verse (or by fragment of verse), it is running (not as the gloss), and the patristic fragments are integrated in the author's writing (it differs from the exegetical chain where the fragments are juxtaposed and not linked). Most of the time, patristic or "modern" texts are not identified nor delimited (but we have seen that Raban Maur noted the name of his authorities).

Another specific element is that the author is not merely a compiler: besides his editorial labor, he often gives his own interpretation. It will not be useful to analyze examples of this form, which is the most common in medieval exegesis. The commentaries of Rupert of Deutz or that of Ralph of Flay on Leviticus can give a good idea of its structure.

2.3. The Running Gloss

It would be proper first to distinguish the gloss as a simple form: it is a short explanation on one or a few words of the biblical text, which can be lexicographic, literary (identification of rhetorical figures), historical or even theological (on a point of dogma or a spiritual consideration). In most of the cases, it is written between the lines of the commentated text (*glossa interlinearis*) or in its margins (*glossa marginalis*). The interlinear gloss is given above the explained word; the marginal gloss begins with a lemma, i.e. the first words of the commentated verse. As the late Beryl Smalley has well shown, the ques-

[84] See Dahan, L'exégèse de l'histoire de Caïn et Abel (1982) 46–48.

tions of make-up are important.[85] The place of the gloss depends on its length: between the lines when it is short, in the margin when it is longer. Some scholars have tried to differentiate interlinear and marginal glosses according to the content: interlinear glosses would be on the literal level, marginal ones on the spiritual level.[86] It seems that this view is wrong and that only the length determines the place of the gloss. It is true, however, that interlinear glosses, because of the little space in which they must be written, often give only synonyms or they clarify understatements; but we find also allegorical or typological explanations, or even moral considerations.[87]

We give here some examples of glosses; first, interlinear glosses and among them lexicographic ones:[88]

– Gen 6:4: Giants ⟨great by their body, glorious by their strength, tough by their behavior⟩;
– Exod 7:1: Aaron your brother shall be your prophet ⟨your interpreter⟩.

Some glosses give historical or archaeological precisions:

– Hos 1:2: The land ⟨of Juda or more precisely of Samaria and Israel, i.e. the ten tribes who had gone afar from the Lord when these words were spoken⟩;
– Hos 3:2: a *khomer* of barley ⟨thirty measures⟩ ... half a *khomer* of barley ⟨.xv. measures⟩.

We also find allegorical interpretations:

– Exod 7:20: Raising his stick ⟨the Cross⟩ he struck the water of the river ⟨the dogmas of the philosophers⟩;
– Exod 27:14: Three columns ⟨because of faith, hope and charity⟩.

It is also remarkable that the glosses often give the "interpretation" of proper names, as in the following example:

– Hos 1:1: ... to Oseah ⟨Saviour⟩ son of Beeri ⟨of my well⟩ in the days of Ozias ⟨strength of Lord⟩, Iotham ⟨the Lord's consummation⟩ ...

We will quote only two (shorter) marginal glosses taken from the Gloss on the Psalms; the first one contains a literal explanation:

– Ps 15:1: The title] Cass[iodorus]. This title is taken from the Gospel, not from the Old Testament. The title's meaning, i.e. victory and reign, applies to Christ, which is the subject of the Psalm.

The other is a spiritual one:

– Ps 15:2: Augustinus. Christ speaks here as a man, whose royal title emanated from his Passion *Ihesus Nazarenus Rex Iudeorum.*[89]

It may be observed that the form of the gloss is not specific to Christian Bible exegesis: it is often used in Jewish commentaries as well as in profane exegesis

---

85 Les commentaires bibliques de l'époque romane: glose ordinaire et gloses périmées (1961). See also Gibson, The Place of the *Glossa ordinaria* in Medieval Exegesis (1992).

86 Or, within the literal sense itself, interlinear glosses would pertain to the strictly speaking *littera* (synonyms, questions of grammar) and marginal glosses to *sensus* or *sententia.* Cf. Paré / Brunet / Tremblay, La Renaissance du XIIe s. (1933) 118.

87 On the glosses, see the bibliography of Smalley, and Lobrichon, Une nouveauté: les gloses de la Bible (1985); Gibson, The Twelfth-Century Glossed Bible (1989).

88 We make use of the edition of Antwerpen 1634, *Biblia sacra cum Glossa* (etc.).

89 "Augustinus. Christus secundum hominem hic loquitur, de quo titulus regalis in passione eminuit *Ihesus Nazarenus Rex Iudeorum.*"

of classical (glosses on Ovid, on Martianus Capella), philosophical (on Aristotle) and, above all, juridical texts (it seems that the *Glossa ordinaria* on Roman Law had given the model for the biblical one).[90]

We call "running (or continuous) gloss" a commentary that is wholly composed of the above described glosses. Running glosses are also anthological: their sources are the Fathers or the authors of the Middle Ages; they are often identified. During the twelfth century, a standard running gloss was compiled, at Laon and Paris. Later, it was designated as the *Glossa ordinaria*, but the exegetes of the thirteenth and fourteenth century, who frequently quoted from it, called it the *Glossa interlinearis* or only the *Glossa* (generally the *Glossa marginalis*). Numerous glossed texts can be found before the elaboration of the *Glossa ordinaria*: they were not fixed commentaries. The choice of the authorities and of the commentated words was not always the same, and the changing make-up of the manuscripts clearly indicates that the compilers were free in their choice. The elaboration of a standard gloss constituted an important step in the history of medieval exegesis: a reference tool was at the disposal of the commentators, which easily gave them numerous sources. They made a large use of it, from the second half of the twelfth century. It is understandable that this tool, created in the context of the schools, had a quick success in this milieu of urban schools. If the running commentary was again an anthological form, the part of the authors must be emphasized: it was more consistant in later texts (e.g. the gloss on Psalms by Peter Lombard) than in those which were compiled at Laon, at the beginning of the twelfth century.[91]

The completion of the *Glossa ordinaria* did not mean the end of this form: the *Postilla* of Hugh of St. Cher had still the form of a running gloss. In some ways, the same can be said of Nicholas of Lyra's *Postilla*: the form was that of the gloss, but the part of the author was much more important, not only because he quoted very numerous Jewish interpretations not found before in Latin exegesis, but also because of his frequent personal reflections.

2.4. Distinctiones

At the end of the twelfth century, the first collections of *distinctiones* were written: intended for spiritual exegesis, they were often in the form of dictionaries of words taken from the Bible; for each word, the verses containing this word were given, classified according to the different spiritual or theological senses.[92] The first known collection is probably Peter the Chanter's *Summa Abel* (so called from its first entry). The most significant collections are those of Alan of Lille,[93] Maurice of Provins, Nicholas of Biard, Nicholas of Gorran,

[90] See Smalley, The Study of the Bible (1983) 52–55 (note of H. Kantorowicz); Kuttner, Repertorium der Kanonistik (1937).

[91] See the studies referred to at nn. 85 and 87.

[92] On the *distinctiones* see R. H. and M. A. Rouse, Biblical *distinctiones* in the XIIIth century (1974); Hasenohr, Un recueil de *distinctiones* bilingue (1978) espec. 47–54; Bataillon, Intermédiaires entre les traités de morale pratique et les sermons: les *distinctiones* bibliques alphabétiques (1982).

[93] His collection is printed under the title *Distinctiones dictionum theologicalium* in PL 210.

Peter of Capua and Arnold Royard.[94] As an example, here is the beginning of the *distinctio* "aura" ("breath") of Alan of Lille:

> *Aura*, breath in proper sense. It signifies a light judicial sentence, as in Genesis [3:8]: *As the Lord walked in the garden for the breath in the afternoon*, in order to judge Adam lightly. *Breath* also means the Holy Spirit's Scripture, which is mild and not terrifying, as in Job [4:16]: *I have heard a voice like that of a light breath. Breath* signifies adulation, as in Isaiah [57:13]: *The wind of the enemies carries away our days, and the breath lifts them up.* It is very convenient that breath signifies adulation, because, as the breath separates the grain from the straw, so adulation separates light men from serious, inconstant men from firm.[95]

The *distinctiones* always have a schematic presentation. The explanation of the spiritual or theological meaning, preceding the biblical verse, can be more or less developed. It is not a concordance; the list of the occurrences is not exhaustive; the purpose is only spiritual.

The *distinctiones* are not only a tool for the exegete or the preacher but they also constitute a form of exegesis; in the beginning of the thirteenth century, there were several commentaries on the Psalms which were presented as *distinctiones.* The commentator found in the biblical text some words which could give a *distinctio* and the commentary then had a very schematic form. Here is the commentary on Psalm 129 [130] of Prevostin of Cremona (we have added the scriptural references):

> *From the depth I have cried* (Ps 129:1 [130:1]). The sinner cries:
> – from his heart, when he consents to sin and when he rejoices knowingly of it. So: *They meditated and cried injust words* (Ps 72:8 [73:8]);
> – from his mouth. So: *They cried their sins like Sodom and did not hide themselves* (cf. Isa 3:9);
> – from his work. So: *As I was mute, my bones were worn out, while I cried all day* (Ps 31:3 [32:3]);
> – from his habit. So: *The cry of the Sodomites came to me* (cf. Gen 18:20).
> *Till the night* (Ps 129:6 [130:6]). Death is compared to night:
> – as for extinction of light. So: *The lamp of the impious is extinguished* (Prov 24:20);
> – as for the obscurity. So in Solomon: *The life of the impious is obscure* (Prov 4:19);
> – as for the succession: as night succeeds day, so death succeeds life. So: *The wise and the foolish both die* (Eccl 2:16).[96]

---

[94] In an appendice to the study cit. n. 92, Father Bataillon has published the text of the *distinctiones* "Iuramentum" of Maurice of Provins and "De iuramento" from *Summa de abstinentia* attributed to Nicholas de Biard. See also our study L'article *Iudei* de la *Summa Abel* de Pierre le Chantre (1981).

[95] PL 210, 714: "Aura proprie. Dicitur sententia iudiciaria leuis, unde in Gen.: *Dum deambularet Dominus in paradiso ad auram post meridiem* [Gen 3:8], ut scilicet leuiter iudicaret Adam. Dicitur Spiritus sancti scriptura, quae mulcet, non terret; unde in Iob: *Vocem quasi aurae leuis audiui* [Job 4:16]. Dicitur adulatio, unde in Isaia: *Dies nostros aufert ventus hostium, tollet aura* [Isa 57:13]. Eleganter adulatio aura dicitur, quia, sicut aura separat grana a paleis, sic adulatio separat a grauibus leues, a firmis instabiles".

[96] MS. Paris, BN lat. 454, fol. 66 v. "*De profundis clamavi.* Clamat peccator:
– corde dum consentit et delectatur scienter in peccato. Unde: *Cogitauerunt et locuti sunt nequitiam* [Ps 72:8];
– ore. Unde: *Predicauerunt sicut sodoma peccatum suum nec absconderunt* [cf. Isa 3:9];
– opere. Unde: *Quoniam tacui inueterauerunt ossa mea, dum clamarem tota die* [Ps 31:3];
– consuetudine. Unde: *Clamor sodomorum uenit ad me* [cf. Gen 18:20].
Usque ad noctem [Ps 129:6]. Mors comparatur nocti
– propter luminis extinctionem. Unde: *Lucerna impii extinguitur* [Prov 24:20];
– propter obscuritatem. Unde Salomon: *Vita impii tenebrosa* [cf. Prov 4:19];
– propter successionem, quia sicut nox diei, sic et mors uite succedit. Unde: *Eque moritur doctus et indoctus* [Eccl 2:16]"

Amongst the other commentaries presented as *distinctiones*, we can also mention the *Distinctiones in Psalmos* of Michel of Corbeil and the *Distinctiones in Psalterium*, extracted from the commentary of Peter of Poitiers.[97] We need a complete list of this type of commentary, but it seems that it was uncommon and used only at the beginning at the thirteenth century.

2.5. *The* questio

It is a simple form, the evolution of which was important. We find early (Fathers, High Middle Ages) commentaries entirely composed of *questiones*; the schools and university commentaries often contained *questiones*, but the exposition by *questio* was only one element among others. We can define this form as the exposition of a scriptural problem (textual, literary, historical or theological) arising from the text itself; the minimal schema has the dual aspect of question / answer.

The history of this form is rich. It is already found in patristic exegesis, Greek and then Latin. Gustave Bardy sketched its history until the beginning of the twelfth century.[98] Among Latin works we can mention the *Quaestiones veteris et novi Testamenti* of Ambrosiaster (ps. Augustine), several works of St. Augustine (notably the *Quaestiones in Heptateuchum*) and the first book of Eucher of Lyon's *Instructiones.* In the High Middle Ages we have works of Isidore of Sevilla, the Venerable Bede, Alcuin and Claudius of Turin.[99] As G. Bardy noted, the form of these questions, as well as their length, is varied: it can be only the simple formulation of the question followed by a short answer, or a more complex development, with an argumentation. On the other hand, this exchange of questions and answers may be only a pedagogical device as in Alcuin's *Quaestiones.*[100] Moreover, the word *questio* in a title may only mean that the commentary scrutinizes the difficulties of a given biblical book, without making use of the *questio* form. It is the case, for example, in Jerome's *Hebraicae quaestiones in Genesim* or Isidore's *Quaestiones in Vetus Testamentum.*

The 'question' arises generally from a contradiction in the commentated text (internal contradiction or between this text and another one) or from an anomaly in this text. Let us take an example from a patristic text, the *Instructiones* of Eucher, bishop of Lyons in 434, the first book of which is composed of "rather difficult questions of the Old and the New Testament"; the example is taken from the chapter on the Psalms:

> *Interrogation*: As God does not take care of the beasts, as it is said of the oxes [I Cor 9:9], how can the Psalm [Ps 35:7] say: *And thou wilt preserve men and beasts, o Lord? Response*: He has called men those who have the intelligence, beasts those who are deprived of it; he says that the

[97] See Lacombe, La vie et les œuvres de Prévostin (1927) 105–30.

[98] Bardy, La littérature patristique des *Quaestiones et responsiones* (1932/33).

[99] Isidore of Sevilla, *De Veteri et Novo Testamento quaestiones* (PL 83, 201–08); The Venerable Bede, *Quaestiones 30 in libros Regum* (PL 91, 715–36); Claudius of Turin, *Quaestiones super libros Regum* (PL 104, 809–11).

[100] Alcuin, *Interrogationes et responsiones in Genesim* (PL 100, 515–66).

former will be preserved due to their present behavior, the latter due to their future conversion.[101]

In the twelfth century, the form of the *questio* changed: its structure became more complex. On the one hand, the dialectic argumentation gave it a more systematic form; on the other hand, it often opposed *auctoritates*. Peter Abelard (*Sic et non*) and Gilbert de la Porrée were probably at the origin of this evolution.[102] Robert of Melun wrote commentaries that only consisted of *quaestiones* (*Questiones de divina pagina*, *Questiones de epistolis sancti Pauli*). It may be observed however that his *Questiones de divina pagina* are not always centred on scriptural texts but also on patristic and canonical quotations or even on theoretical problems; we are near the genre of the collections of sentences. His *questiones* have often an elementary, dual structure: *Queritur* (it is asked) ... *solutio* (solution). Sometimes, a *nota* gives an alternative solution. Some questions have a more complex structure; for example, the q. 94 which is articulated as follows:

Queritur utrum inter infideles coniugium sit (It is asked if the marriage between unbelievers is legal).
Quod auctoritates velle videntur (Some authorities seem to give a positive answer: John Chrysostom, Augustine, Ambrose, Gregory).
E contra Ambrosius (but Ambrose says no).
Solutio. Non fuit ante coniugium sed forma coniugii (first solution: it is not a legal marriage but only the form of such a marriage).
Sed opponitur (opposition to this opinion).
Solutio (Robert's own answer).[103]

Besides Robert of Melun, the *questio* in the twelfth century was generally an element of the commentary (often, an anthological one) which developed a theological argument. So in Thierry of Chartres' commentary on Hexaemeron, on Gen 1:1:

It is asked how some words of the saints do agree: this one *He who lives in the eternity has created the universe together*, and this one *The Lord worked for six days* etc. But you must know that the first authority is to be understood as referring to the primordial matter; the second concerns the distinction of the forms, which is studied according to natural sciences.[104]

The commentaries of Peter the Chanter and Stephen Langton also contain this type of question.

In the thirteenth century, in the university, the *questio* again became more

---

[101] "*Interrogatio*: Cum de iumentis, sicut *de bubus cura non sit Deo* [I Cor 9:9], quo modo psalmus [Ps 35:7] ait: *Et iumenta saluabis, Domine*? *Responsio*: Homines appellauit rationes capaces, iumenta rationis expertes; saluandos uero confirmat illos per praesentem conuersationem, hos per futuram conuersionem", ed. C. Wotke (CSEL 31; Wien 1894) 91.

[102] On the twelfth century evolution, see *Œuvres de Robert de Melun*, I, *Questiones de divina pagina* (ed. R. M. Martin; Louvain: Univ. cath. 1932) XXXIV–XLVI.

[103] Cit. ed. 48–49.

[104] "Queritur autem quomodo inter se dicta sanctorum concordant: hoc scilicet *qui uiuit in eternum creauit omnia simul* et illud *sex diebus operatus est dominus* etc. Sed sciendum est quod prior auctoritas de primordiali materia intelligenda est: sequens autem de distinctione formarum, de qua deinceps secundum phisicam tranctandum est", *Tractatus de sex dierum operibus* (ed. N. M. Häring, *Commentaries on Boethius by Thierry of Chartres and his School*; Toronto: Pontifical Institute of Mediaeval Studies 1971) 557.

complex. The so-called scholastic question was in the final phase of its development as follows:

- question (*queritur an*, *utrum*);
- answer *sic / non* (*videtur quod sic / non*), argued by some authorities;
- answer *non / sic*, argued by some authorities;
- the answer of the master (*respondeo*);
- solution of the arguments given in the answer contrary to that of the master.

The question was a fundamental technique in university teaching: it became a solemn exercise (disputed question, quodlibetal question).[105] Obviously, it was not specific to scriptural exegesis. Some biblical university commentaries included 'scholastic' questions: we recall that it was a part of the *lectio* and that the *dubia*, by which the *lectio* ended, were often in fact *questiones.* Amongst the commentators who had recourse to the form of the *questio*, we can mention Albert the Great, Bonaventure, Thomas Aquinas, Nicholas of Gorran, Dominic Grima and most of the university authors at the end of the thirteenth century and in the fourteenth. As an example, the structure of a *questio* in the commentary of St. Thomas on Isaiah (Isa 8:3) may be analyzed; this commentary presents several simple questions, but this one is more complex:[106]

> Contra hoc quidam multipliciter obiciunt quod non possit ad litteram intelligi 1° quia ... 2° quia ... 3° quia ... 4° quia ... et ideo uolunt quod intelligatur ...
> Hec expositio [of some *quidam*] non est tante auctoritatis ...
> Unde secundum hoc potest responderi ad obiectiones prius factas, ad primam ... ad secundam ... ad tertiam ... ad quartam ...[107]

2.6. *The Homily*

Preaching is a fundamental source for our knowledge of medieval exegesis. In view of the listeners, the exegesis of the preacher could be on a popular level (in the *sermones ad populum*) and in the vernacular (but the report of which was written in Latin), or on a scholarly level (*sermones ad monachos, ad clericos, ad scholares*).[108] Are we right in seeing it as an exegetical form? A distinction must be made between the sermon and the homily: the sermon, even if it has a verse of Scripture as *thema* (and this occurs most often), is not really an exegetical work; the homily, oral commentary of a passage of the Bible, may be rightly considered as an exegetical form. The medieval authors did not make

---

[105] See Bazan, La *quaestio disputata* (1982) 31–49; idem, Les questions disputées, principalement dans les facultés de théologie (1985) 13–149.

[106] Here is the structure of some simpler questions in the same commentary (reference to the Leonine edition): on Isa 1:2: sed uidetur inconueniens / sed dicendum est (p. 10); Isa 1:13: sed obicitur de hoc quod dicit Glosa / Et dicendum quod (p. 14); Isa 2:2: sed uidetur quod / ad quod dicendum quod (p. 20) etc.

[107] Leonine ed., 60–61.

[108] On preaching, see Longère, La prédication médiévale (1983); d'Avray, The Preaching of the Friars (1985); Bataillon, La prédication au XIIIe s. en France et en Italie (1993); Bériou, Les sermons (1994).

this distinction; for them the homily was merely the preaching on the Gospel or the Epistle of the day (it is an exegetical form, but we cannot analyze it on this occasion). However, if we accept the definition of the homily as "a running commentary of a biblical text delivered before an audience", it is possible to comprehend in this form numerous sermons on texts of the Old Testament, such as the sermons of the Cistercians on the Song of Songs (St. Bernard, Gilbert of Hoyland).[109]

The sermon, strictly speaking, became a very structured form from the thirteenth century.[110] Although the form of the homily remained freer, it also changed at the same time. Earlier, it was only an oral commentary (as we can see it in some written reports), with a rather diffuse framework, depending on the succession of the biblical verses; then in the thirteenth century it was influenced by the techniques described in the *artes praedicandi* (manuals of preaching).

The ancient model of the homilies on Old Testament texts was Gregory the Great's *Homilies on Ezekiel.* We find this form in the three genres of medieval exegesis. In monastic exegesis, William of Flay, Guerric of Igny, Odo of Canterbury and the Cistercians on the Canticles are good examples.[111] In the exegesis of the schools we find some sermons of the Victorines, of the masters of the "biblical moral school" (notably of Peter Comestor and Stephen Langton), as well as of St. Antony of Padua.[112] In the university exegesis, we can mention some sermons of Odo of Châteauroux, Bonaventure, Albert the Great and other masters.[113]

It is appropriate to mention here the *collationes*, arisen, as it seems, from an old monastic tradition renewed by the mendicant orders in the thirteenth century. It was a preaching delivered in the evening at the convent.[114] The subject of these collations could vary; some of them had a connection with Bible exegesis: the best known are those of Bonaventure, *De decem praeceptis* and *In Hexaemeron*, of which we possess written records.[115] Reading them we can see, however, that these collations are very different from the traditional ho-

[109] The links (especially direct links: sermons inserted in commentaries and *vice versa*) between preaching and exegesis are examined by Bataillon, De la *lectio* à la *praedicatio* (1986). He quotes particularly as a "series of homelies on a single biblical book" the *Sermones in Psalterium* of Philip the Chancelor.

[110] It must be referred to the classical study of Gilson, Michel Menot et la technique du sermon médiéval (1955). See also Caplan, The Four Senses of Scriptural Interpretation and the Medieval Theory of Preaching (1929); Davy, Les sermons universitaires parisiens de 1230–31 (1931); Charland, Artes praedicandi (1936). Schneyer, Repertorium der lateinischen Sermones des Mittelalters (1969–90), has given an invaluable inventory.

[111] See Leclercq, Prédicateurs bénédictins aux XIe et XIIe s. (1943); Ch. de Clecq / R. Macken (eds.), *The Latin Sermons of Odo of Canterbury* (Brussel: Paleis der Academiën 1983; especially the sermons *de vita christiana*).

[112] See J. Châtillon (ed.), *Galteri a Sancto Victore et quorumdam aliorum sermones XXXVI* (CCCM 30; Turnhout: Brepols 1975); Barzillay Roberts, Studies in the Sermons of Stephen Langton (1968).

[113] See Longère, La prédication en langue latine (1985); Bougerol, Les sermons dans les *studia* des Mendiants (1978).

[114] See Davy, Les sermons universitaires parisiens (1931) 26–27.

[115] See Bougerol, Introduction à l'étude de S. Bonaventure (1961) 178–88.

milies: the structure of running commentary has been abandoned; we are near the *lectio* (but the *collatio* has not its rigorous organization) and the university sermon. If we take the case of the *Collationes in Hexaemeron*, we may see that the first three of them have a verse of Ecclesiasticus (Sir 15:5) for *thema* (the same verse for the three) and that *collationes* XI, XII and XXII have also a *thema* which is not a verse of Genesis (in any case, however, there is a link between the Hexaemeron and these verses); all the other *collationes* are built on a verse of the beginning of Genesis:

– coll. IV–VII, Gen 1:4; coll. VIII–X, Gen 1:8; coll. XIII, Gen 1:9–10; coll. XIV, Gen 1:11; coll. XV–XIX, Gen 1:12; coll. XX, Gen 1:14–19; coll. XXI–XXIII, Gen 1:16.[116]

We can give as an example the analysis of the *collatio* XIV, on Gen 1:11: *Germinet terra herbam virentem et facientem semen.* The introduction sets out an argument taken from the verse: the germination designates the sacramental figures of Scripture. The first part shows how the three essential qualities of the germination suggest the properties of the mysteries of Scripture, which are analyzed with rigour. The second part sets forth the twelve principal mysteries in the time (before the Law, under the Law, at the time of prophecy, from Christ to the end). As may be seen, the reflection on the exegesis is deeply linked with theological themes: both come from the biblical text. We are not far from the type of development found in the university commentary.

To close this typology of the forms of medieval exegesis, we may quote a frequently mentioned passage of Peter the Chanter. He said that three things constituted the study of Scripture: the lecture (*lectio*), the dispute, and the preaching.[117] This tripartite division, which in fact goes beyond Bible exegesis, indicates all the duties of the master, but it can easily help to classify the exegetical forms: to *lectio* pertain running commentaries (anthological as well as continued glosses), to *disputatio* pertains the *quaestio*, and to *praedicatio* the homily.

3. Methods

We shall not enter here into the field of hermeneutics, as it will be treated in other chapters of this volume. Here our purpose is to describe the actual methods of Christian exegesis in use in the Middle Ages. We can look at the bi-partition (literal exegesis / spiritual exegesis) present in numerous medieval authors, to which could be reduced the more complex lists of three or more senses.[118] We shall make use of the above mentioned theoretical works and ex-

---

116 St. Bonaventura, *Opera omnia* V (ed. Quaracchi; 1891) 329–449.

117 *Verbum abbreviatum* (PL 205, 25): "In tribus consistit exercitium sacrae Scripturae: circa lectionem, disputationem et praedicationem".

118 It is truly a bi-partition which appears in the chapter 3 of Hugh of St. Victor's *De scripturis* (PL 175, 11–12), in spite of what is said in the beginning of the chapter: "Secundum triplicem intelligentiam exponitur sacrum eloquium" ("The Scripture is explained according to a triple understanding"); in fact, the development of the chapter shows the opposition between historical and allegorical (spiritual) senses. We find the same feature in Thomas Aquinas' Quodl. VII, quest. 6, a. 2

amine the methods proper to literal exegesis, then those proper to spiritual exegesis. We shall not give an exhaustive report of the various exegetical techniques but only describe cursorily the best characteristic and the most identifiable of them.

3.1. *The Methods of Literal Exegesis*

First of all it must be remembered that by literal exegesis (*littera* or *historia*), notably from the twelfth century, a complex totality is meant. Its three components were perfectly defined by Hugh of St. Victor: the strictly speaking *littera* (textual and grammatical study), the *sensus* (literary and historical study), and the *sententia* (theological study).[119] Some specific techniques pertain to the literal exegesis (but there is no strict correspondence with these three elements).

3.1.1. *Textual Study*

During the Middle Ages, the exigence of a well established text was formulated several times.[120] At the time of Charlemagne, Alcuin and Theodulf revised the text of the Bible; the latter referred to the Hebrew text of the Old Testament, perhaps with the assistance of a (converted?) Jew.[121] Alcuin's recension was the most widespread; it became the basis of the so-called "Parisian text" (university text of the thirteenth century) and, later on, of the Clementine recension at the end of sixteenth century, which was considered to be the authoritative text in the Catholic Church until 1960.[122] In the twelfth century this concern for a good biblical text caused an important work of collation of Latin manuscripts, first by Stephen Harding, abbot of Cîteaux, then by another Cistercian, at Rome, Nicholas Maniacoria.[123] In the thirteenth century the Parisian text was carefully studied several times, particularly by Dominicans (Hugh of St. Cher, Thibaud of Sézanne, the group of St. Jacques in Paris) and by Franciscans (William of Mara). This study led to the elaboration of the *correctoria Biblie*, of which we possess more than ten texts.[124] They consist of

("Utrum debeant distingui quatuor sensus sacrae Scripturae"), who establishes the four traditional senses on the opposition *sensus historicus sive litteralis / sensus spiritualis.*

[119] See Hugh of St. Victor, *Didascalicon* III, 8 (ed. C. H. Buttimer, 58): "Littera est congrua ordinatio dictionum, quod etiam constructionem uocamus. Sensus est facilis quaedam et aperta significatio, quam littera prima fronte praefert. Sententia est profundior intelligentia, quae nisi expositione uel interpretatione non inuenitur".

[120] On the revision of the Bible in the Middle Ages, see the comprehensive studies of Loewe, The Medieval History of the Latin Vulgate (1969); Light, Versions et révisions du texte biblique (1984); Bogaert, La Bible latine des origines au moyen âge (1988).

[121] See Fischer, Die Alkuin-Bibel (1957); idem, Lateinische Bibelhandschriften im frühen Mittelalter (1985); Delisle, Les Bibles de Théodulfe (1879).

[122] On the Parisian text, see Martin, Le texte parisien de la Vulgate (1889/90); Glunz, History of the Vulgate in England (1933) 259–93.

[123] On Stephen Harding, see Zaluska, L'enluminure et le Scriptorium de Cîteaux (1989) 63–111. On Nicholas Maniacoria, see Peri, *Correctores immo corruptores.* Un saggio di critica testuale (1977).

[124] Denifle, Die Handschriften der Bibel-Correctorien (1888) 264–311, 471–601; Mangenot, Correctoires de la Bible (1899); Dahan, La connaissance de l'hébreu dans les correctoires de la Bible (1992).

notes on verses considered as corrupted or for which the manuscripts presented various readings; the "correctors" confronted the Hebrew and Greek original texts, the Old Latin versions, ancient and recent manuscripts of Jerome's translation (Vulgate). Two examples of these critical notes may be given here; they are extracted from the *correctorium* of the Franciscan William of Mara (de la Mare), who was, as it seems, a good hebraist and hellenist:

– [On I Sam 9:20] Item f.[125] Nonne tibi et domui patris tui. Anti[qui] non interponunt *omni* nec etiam septuaginta, quare presumo quod non fuit in antiquis hebreis.
– [On I Sam 10:17] Item f. Anti[qui] secundum heb[reum] et grecum "ad Dominum in maspha" sine th uel t finali.[126]

Critical efforts of this kind are observable in exegetical works, from the Carolingian commentaries onwards, but especially from the twelfth century. Andrew of St. Victor was careful of the divergences in the Latin manuscripts and gave numerous comparisons with the Hebrew text.[127] As examples, some notes from his commentary on Numbers may be quoted:

– Num 21:18: *In datore legis.* This is not in the Hebrew text.
– Num 24:15: *Cuius est obturatus oculus.* In the Hebrew and in Origen's translation, we have: "Cuius reuelatus est oculus".
– Num 24:16: *Qui cadens apertos habet oculos.* The Hebrew is clearer: "Qui ponens (id est collocans se in lecto) apertos habet oculos".[128]

Andrew's notes were taken up by his disciples, the masters of the "biblical moral school", and by many exegetes in the thirteenth century, who sometimes indicated that they came from Andrew.[129] Similarly, the *correctoria* were used in the commentaries: when we found in them comparisons between the different versions of the commentated verse or reports of various readings, they often were borrowed from these *correctoria.* We may, for example, quote an observation of Peter of John Olieu, on Amos 2:13, which occurred already in several *correctoria* (Hugh of St. Cher, St. Jacques, William of Mara):

Ecce ego stridebo subter vos. Hebrei habent *subter,* sed nostri libri antiqui habent *super,* quod maiorem oppressionem designat.[130]

3.1.2. Literary Analysis

The analysis of rhetorical figures is long-standing: we have noted that Cassiodorus regularly pointed out in the margins those present in Psalms. Bede proposed a systematization in his *De tropis et schematibus.* Medieval authors continued this tradition: the revival of Latin rhetoric in the twelfth century and the

---

125 Before the verse-division used today (which goes back to the XVIth century), there was a system based on the letters A to G for the internal divisions of the chapters: the reference to the chapter is given at the first occurrence concerning the chapter.
126 MS. Vatican lat. 3466, fol. 32 v.
127 Cf. Berndt, André de Saint-Victor (1991) 159–63.
128 *Andreae de Sancto Victore Opera,* I. *Expositio super Heptateuchum* (ed. Ch. Lohr / R. Berndt; CCCM 53; Turnhout: Brepols 1986) 190–91.
129 See Smalley, The School of Andrew of St. Victor (1939); Dahan, Exégèse et polémique dans les commentaires de la Genèse d'Etienne Langton (1985) 133–36.
130 MS. Paris, BN lat. 507, fol. 7 va.

refinement of the doctrine in the *Artes poetriae* gave it a new vigor and a greater technical scope, as we can see in the *De tropis loquendi* of Peter the Chanter. In the commentaries themselves, cursory remarks on these figures were rather frequent, notably in the twelfth and thirteenth century. Here again, Andrew of St. Victor played a stimulating role, but it was a rather common device. We shall give two examples from Andrew's commentary on Genesis. Andrew makes the following remark on the words *cete grandia*, "great whales" (Gen 1:21): "The whales are called great *per epitheton* (an epithet of nature), as 'a dark crow' or 'the profound sea'". Similarly, on Gen 4:15, where God directly speaks to Cain, Andrew identified a rhetorical figure: "But anyone who will kill Cain, i.e. you: *aposiopesis*".[131] We can also cite Peter the Chanter, who notes "irony" in Gen 3:21;[132] but this type of occurrence is very frequent in the twelfth and thirteenth century.

At this time a technique of general analysis of the commentated books developed; it was influenced by the methods used for profane texts. It is found especially in the prologues of the commentaries, in which some authors used the schemas of the *accessus ad auctores* and posed questions about the inspired texts which were common in the study of classical texts.[133] Richard W. Hunt defined "three main types of schema": type A: *persona, locus, tempus*; type B: *vita auctoris, titulus operis, qualitas, intentio, numerus et ordo librorum, explanatio*; type C: *intentio, utilitas, ordo (modus agendi), nomen auctoris, titulus, ad quam partem philosophiae.* We do not regularly find all of these categories, but the presence of some of them permit us to define the type of *accessus* used in the considered prologue. It is sometimes said that Abelard was the first author to make use of an *accessus*-schema in a biblical commentary.[134] His *Expositio in Hexaemeron* contains a study of *materia* and *intentio*; in his commentary on the Epistle to the Romans, he analyzed successively *intentio, materia* and *modus tractandi.*[135] The prologues of the commentaries on Psalms often made use of *accessus*-schemas, as is the case in Gilbert de la Porrée's commentary where we find the following parts: *materia, modus, finis, titulus, genus prophetie, nomen libri, numerus psalmorum.*[136] Geroch of Reichersberg also treated *materia, intentio, modus tractandi, titulus libri*; and Peter Lombard's commentary has: *materia, intentio, modus tractandi, ordo.*[137] The *accessus* schema was still in use in the thirteenth century, in spite of the concurrence of different

[131] Ed. Berndt / Lohr, 18, 42.

[132] "*Ecce Adam factus est quasi unus ex nobis.* Ironia est, quasi voluit esse ut Deus, sed modo in evidenti est quod non est" (ed. A. Sylwan) 78.

[133] See Quain, The Medieval *accessus ad auctores* (1945); Hunt, The Introduction to the *Artes* in the XIIth century (1948). On the *accessus* in the biblical commentaries, cf. Minnis, Medieval Theory of Authorship (1984) 40–58.

[134] Minnis, 41, picks out schemas of *accessus* in works attributed to authors prior to Abelard (Bruno the Carthusian, Comment. on Psalms: *intentio, titulus, modus agendi*; Anselm of Laon, Comment. on the Song of Songs: *intentio, nomen libri, materia, modus agendi, finis* etc.), which are perhaps later.

[135] PL 178, 732–33 et 783; cf. Haring, The lectures of Thierry of Chartres on Boethius' *De Trinitate* (1958) 120.

[136] MS. Paris, BN lat. 12004, fol. 1. Cf. Hunt, The Introduction to the *Artes* (1948) 128.

[137] See Haring, The lectures of Thierry of Chartres (1958) 117–22, who gives other examples.

types of prologues. The commentary on Isaiah by St. Thomas Aquinas made use conjointly of two schemas of *accessus*: the first considers *actor*, *actoris minister*, *modus*, and the second *ratio explanationis*, *utilitas explanationis*, *materia explanationis*.[138] Together with the points concerning the authorship of the biblical books, the most interesting questions seem to be those which tend to identify the literary genre of the biblical text (*modus agendi*).

In the second half of the thirteenth century, the prologues adopted the Aristotelian schema of the four causes, giving thus a new form to literary analysis. We find examples of it in the prologues of St. Bonaventure's commentaries. In his commentary on Ecclesiastes, he considers the four causes of this book: its aim, *finis* (the distrust of the world), its subject matter, *materia* (the vanity), its style or form, *forma*, *de modo agendi*, and its efficient cause, *causa efficiens* (Solomon).[139]

Further, the question of the type of language used in the commentated book also preoccupied the exegetes and gave rise to analyses of great interest.[140] This is notably the case in the university *principia* or *introitus*, which had to classify the books of the Bible (not always in accordance with the traditional classifications) and which were sometimes based on stylistic criteria. In this respect, John of La Rochelle proposed two divisions of the Old Testament: the first classifies the books of the Law, taken in the larger sense, in observance of the Commandments (the Pentateuch), examples (the Historical Books) and admonitions (Sapiential Books); the second, that integrates the Prophetic Books, takes into account the *doctrina credendorum, operandorum et orationum*, i.e. the dogmas, morals and the prayers.[141]

3.1.3. Jewish Interpretations

The use of Jewish interpretations for enriching the literal study is ancient; we often find it in Origen and Jerome. The Christian commentator thought to have answers from the Jews to questions concerning the text itself and especially its archaeology. The fact that the Jews were considered by medieval thinkers as Christ's contemporaries, observing Mosaic laws in the same manner as in the time of Christ, caused the exegetes to expect from them precise explanations of the rites prescribed in the Old Testament.[142]

Jerome was the source of most of the Jewish interpretations reported in the commentaries of the High Middle Ages; generally infrequent, they appear more often in the texts of Raban Maur, Remigius of Auxerre and Angelom of Luxeuil. In the Carolingian period, a supplementary source of Jewish interpretations was added: the *Quaestiones* on the books of Samuel, Kings and Chronicles, written by a converted Jew in the beginning of the ninth century;

138 *Opera omnia* XXVIII (ed. Leonine; Rome 1974) 1.

139 *Opera omnia* VI (Quaracchi; 1893) 5–8.

140 We must also note that the introductions to the commentaries on the *Sentences* contained reflections on the language of Scripture, on which classifications of biblical books were sometimes based; see Minnis, Medieval Theory of Authorship (1984) 118–59.

141 Delorme, Deux leçons d'ouverture de Cours biblique (1933) 352–53.

142 See Dahan, Les intellectuels chrétiens et les juifs au moyen âge (1990) 289–307.

they were soon attributed to St. Jerome and, because of this prestigious authorship, became widespread.[143] Jewish interpretations appeared in the *Glossa ordinaria*, which thus served as a link between Jerome (and the Carolingian authors) and the later commentators. In the twelfth century, however, the use of Jewish interpretations had an important development when the Victorines (Hugh, Andrew) gathered new interpretations from Parisian Jews and integrated them into their commentaries.[144] This development was followed by the masters of the "biblical-moral school", who made use of Jerome, the *Glossa* and the Victorines, but also gave in turn newer Jewish interpretations.[145] Herbert of Bosham, a disciple of Andrew of St. Victor, had a certain knowledge of Hebrew, in contrast to his predecessors; this allowed him to enrich his commentary on the Psalms (one of the rare medieval commentaries on the *Iuxta Hebraeos* psalter) by the use of numerous Jewish glosses.[146] In the thirteenth century, the proportion of new Jewish interpretations was smaller but the reference to the *Hebrei* remained constant (through intermediate sources) as may be seen in Hugh of St. Cher or Albert the Great, whose commentaries are rich in Jewish interpretations.[147] In the second half of the thirteenth century, the knowledge of Hebrew by some Christian authors was a novelty. It allowed them a direct use of Jewish sources: the documents gathered in the polemical works of Raymond Martin (*Capistrum Iudeorum*, *Pugio fidei*) were used by the exegetes. But above all, in the beginning of the fourteenth century, Nicholas of Lyra in his *Postilla* on the whole of the Bible made a frequent use of Jewish sources for the Old Testament books, especially of Rashi (Solomon of Troyes), whose name appears in an abridged form (Rab. Sal. or Ra. Sa.), as well as of the midrashic commentaries.[148] In turn, Nicholas of Lyra's *Postilla* was useful to numerous commentators. Also the slightly later commentary on the Psalms of Nicholas Trivet may be mentioned; this text also reflects a certain knowledge of Hebrew.[149]

The references to Jewish interpretations were often identified: the expression *Hebrei dicunt* ("The Hebrews say") introduced an admitted interpretation, whereas *Iudei fabulantur* or *sompniantur* ("The Jews fantasize" or "are dreaming") indicated a rejected interpretation. Further, the formula *Hebreus meus* indicated the consultation of a living Jew, but the terms *Hebreus* or *Heb-*

---

143 *Pseudo-Jerome. Quaestiones on the Book of Samuel* (ed. A. Saltman; Leiden: Brill 1975); A. Saltman, Rabanus Maurus and the Pseudo-Hieronymian *Quaestiones Hebraicae in Libros Regum* (1973).

144 Smalley, The Study of the Bible (1983), passim; Berndt, Les interprétations juives dans le Commentaire de l'Heptateuque d'André de Saint-Victor (1990); Dahan, Juifs et chrétiens en Occident médiéval (1989).

145 Dahan, Les interprétations juives dans les commentaires du Pentateuque de Pierre le Chantre (1985).

146 Smalley, A Commentary on the *Hebraica* by Herbert of Bosham (1951); Loewe, Herbert of Bosham's Commentary on Jerome's Hebrew Psalter (1953).

147 Dahan, L'utilisation de l'exégèse juive dans la lecture des livres prophétiques (1996); idem, La connaissance de l'exégèse juive par les chrétiens du XIIe au XIVe s. (1997).

148 See Hailperin, Rashi and the Christian Scholars (1963).

149 Kleinhans, Nicolaus Trivet, o. p., Psalmorum interpres (1943).

rei alone often referred to the Hebrew text of the Bible or to Jerome's translation, regularly called *Hebraica veritas.*

The Christian exegetes were primarily looking for clarifications on the *littera* by addressing themselves to their Jewish neighbours. It must be noted, however, that their informants were probably not the scholars who transformed Jewish exegesis, notably in Northern France (Rashi, Rashbam, Joseph Qara), and, separating the literal exegesis (*peshat*) from the spiritual one that made use of the myth (*agada*) as an explicative system (*derash, midrash*), emphasized the former. The informants of the Victorines and of their successors did not distinguish between the different levels of scriptural sense and often transmitted midrashic interpretations that the Christian scholars took as literal exegesis. This contributes to explain the dismissal of some Jewish interpretations, expressed by *Iudei fabulantur.*[150]

Other aspects of literal analysis, such as historical, archaeological and theological study, are not specific exegetical methods; hence we will not examine them here.

3.2. Methods of Spiritual Analysis

Like literal exegesis, spiritual exegesis represents a complex body, which was often described by medieval authors; its main components were allegorical interpretation and tropology, to which the anagogy was sometimes added. One of the major contributions of the twelfth century exegesis (Victorine, notably) was its attempt to define methods of spiritual analysis and to show that it was not a wild fantasy but that it had to rely on precise methods, as rigorous as those of the literal analysis. When presenting them, we will start from the well-known distinction, of Augustinian origin, between names and objects. Spiritual exegesis was based in large part on the fact that it is characteristic of the biblical texts that they have a meaning both on the level of their words and on the level of the things.[151]

3.2.1. The Words Signify

We are here in the system common to all human texts: words signify. However, the exegetes went beyond the obvious signification of the words of Scripture and found in their etymology or their "interpretation" the foundations of spiritual interpretation. In its medieval connotation, *etymology* did not mean what it does today: it was not a question of looking for the ancient origin of the word and its original meaning (which is the goal itself of the "interpretation"),

[150] Dahan, Les intellectuels chrétiens (1990) 289–307.

[151] For example, see Hugh of St. Victor, *De scripturis,* 14: "Philosophus in aliis scripturis solam vocum novit significationem; sed in sacra pagina excellentior valde est rerum significatio quam vocum" (PL 175, 20); Robert of Melun, *Sententie* I, Ia, 6: "Est autem, ut dictum est, sacre scripture significatio bipartita: una videlicet vocum, altera rerum" (ed. R. M. Martin, 170). – On the processes of spiritual analysis, see the stimulating study of Gilson, De quelques raisonnements scripturaires usités au moyen âge (1955).

but to unravel, in a phonetic approximation which can seem to be like a game, the essence of the thing. In reference to Adam's naming of things (Gen 2:19–20), Rupert of Deutz furnished the following reflection:

> Adam considered the natures [of the animals] and created various words derived from their diverse qualities; for example, the Latins call a horse *caballus*, from *cavere*, "to dig", because the horse digs the ground with its shoe; the ass, *asinus*, from *assidere*, "to be seated near"; the pig, *porcus*, as in *sporcus*, because it is dirty ...[152]

Interpretation applied especially to proper names and looked for the first signification of them. Jerome provided a collection of *Interpretationes nominum hebraicorum*, classed by biblical books. Before the twelfth century a collection based on the interpretations of Jerome was in circulation, but this time it was organized in alphabetical order.[153] This list was modified, enriched, and refined, resulting in a collection frequently used in the thirteenth century, known by its incipit *Aaz apprehendens*, owing perhaps to Stephen Langton.[154] Many other lists appeared in the thirteenth and fourteenth centuries; that of Ralph Niger, incidentally a little diffused, written in collaboration with a converted Jew, was very different from the others and gave many new interpretations.[155] Some lexicons integrated elements coming from the etymological research and from these interpretations; the most widespread was the *Summa Britonis* by William the Breton, who also wrote a shorter *Brito metricus*.[156]

Etymologies and interpretations provided starting points for spiritual considerations which were a part of allegory as well as tropology or anagogy. As examples, two types of spiritual interpretations may be cited. The first in Peter the Chanter's commentary on Zechariah, is relatively simple: Peter used the "interpretations" of a series of proper names as the basis for his allegory:

> [Zech 6:9] Allegorical meaning. Oldai means "intercession of the Lord", Tobia "the good of the Lord", Ydaia "who is recognized by the Lord", Hen "grace", Helem "dream". Those who have been captured by vices come back to Jerusalem, i.e. the Church, where they offer the gold of divine wisdom and the silver of divine word.[157]

The second type of use of *interpretationes* was more complex: William of Flay referred constantly to them in writing his often tropological commentary on Judges. Thus, regarding the first verse, the name of the 'Canaanite' underwent this development:

---

[152] *De sancta Trinitate. Genesis* (CCCM 21; ed. R. Haacke; Turnhout: Brepols 1971) 227–28. Some considerations in Dahan, Nommer les êtres: exégèse et théorie du langage dans les commentaires médiévaux de Genèse 2, 19–20 (1996).

[153] See Thiel, Grundlagen und Gestalt der Hebräischkenntnisse (1973); Dahan, Les intellectuels chrétiens (1990) 244–48.

[154] D'Esneval, Le perfectionnement d'un instrument de travail ... les trois glossaires bibliques d'Etienne Langton (1981).

[155] Saltman, Supplementary Notes on the Works of Ralph Niger (1978).

[156] *Summa Britonis* (ed. L.W. / B.A. Daly; Padova: Editrice Antenore 1975); *Brito Metricus* (ed. L.W. Daly; Philadelphia: Univ. of Pennsylvania Press 1968).

[157] MS. Paris, BN lat. 16793, fol. 140 rb: "[Zech 6:9] Allegorice Oldai 'deprecatio Domini', Tobia 'bonus Domini', Ydaia 'notus Domini', Hen 'gratia', Helem 'sompnium'. Hii sunt qui prius capti a uitiis reuertuntur in Ierusalem, ecclesiam, ubi offerunt aurum diuine sapientie et argentum diuini eloquii ...".

> Canaanite is interpreted as 'merchant'. Thus it signifies the devil, whose merchandise is mortal pleasures, which he displays to the approaching miserable and praises their sweetness through his chatting; then he sells them to the careless for a transitory happiness and is paid back with their souls for an everlasting damnation.[158]

3.2.2. Things Signify

The major characteristic of holy Scripture for the medieval scholars was that things, as well as words, have a signification. The things designated in sacred text lead to another reality, which can be Christ and the Church (allegory), the interior life of man (tropology) or the superior world which transcends history (anagogy). In his *De scripturis*, Hugh of St. Victor established the categories of these *res* which lead to *res secundae*: objects, persons, numbers, places, time, gestures; he always gave examples.[159] Here is one for *time*:

> Time has a signification. For example, Jesus was staying at the gate of Solomon and it was winter. Mention is made of winter so that by the quality of time the quality of the spirits is designated, that is the torpor and the unbelief of the Jews.[160]

Tools permitting deciphering of second significations were established from the twelfth century. We find them in the above-mentioned collections of *distinctiones*, but also in more specific works as collections of allegories, amongst which we will mention that of Garnier of Langres, the *De bestiis* wrongly attributed to Hugh of St. Victor or certain parts of Richard of St. Victor's *Liber exceptionum*.[161] In this same category, we have specialized lexicons such as treatises of arithmology, bestiaries, lapidaries and works on the signification of plants.[162]

---

[158] "Chananeus interpretatur 'negociator'. Significat autem istic diabolum, cuius sunt merces mortifere libidines, quas miseris affectantibus ostentat, quarum suauitatem multipli suggestione iactat; tum incautis eas uendit ad transitoriam iocunditatem et eorum animas in precio accipit in eternam dampnationem" (ed. Dahan, Guillaume de Flay et son Commentaire du Livre des Juges; 1978) 69.

[159] *De scripturis*, 14 (PL 175, 20–21). See also Robert of Melun, *Sententie*, I, Ia, c. 6 (ed. R. M. Martin) 176–79; Pierre of Poitiers, *Allegoriae super Tabernaculum Moysi* (ed. Ph. S. Moore / J. A. Corbett; Notre Dame, in: UP 1938) 100–01.

[160] PL 175, 23.

[161] Garnier of Langres (or of Rochefort), *Allegoriae Scripturarum* (PL 112, 849–1088; among Raban Maur's works); ps. Hugh, *De bestiis et aliis rebus quae in Scripturis leguntur* (PL 177, 14–164); Richard of St. Victor, *Liber exceptionum* (ed. J. Châtillon; Paris: Vrin 1958). See Chenu, La théologie au XIIe s. (1966) 159–209.

[162] The are only a few comprehensive studies on these categories of texts; for example, Pannier, Les lapidaires français du moyen âge (1882); McCulloch, Medieval Latin and French Bestiaries (1960). Treatises on arithmology have been more studied: cf. Beaujouan, Le symbolisme des nombres à l'époque romane (1961); Meyer, Die Zahlenallegorese im Mittelalter (1975); Lange, Les données mathématiques des traités du XIIe siècle sur la symbolique des nombres (1979; H. Lange has also published the treatises of Odon of Morimond, Geoffroy of Auxerre and Thibaud of Langres). For an example of use of these considerations in biblical exegesis, see Dahan, Arithmologie et exégèse. Un chapitre du *De scripturis* de Hugues de Saint-Victor (1992).

3.2.3. Analysis of the translatio

From the twelfth century, the transition from the literal sense to the spiritual sense became the object of profound consideration. In spite of the elaboration of the previously described techniques, the transition from the *littera* to the spiritual sense posed a very delicate analytical problem. The notion of *translatio*, transfer of meaning, played an important role in this analysis. Raban Maur was already proposing, in the third book of his *De clericorum institutione* a reflection on the *translatio*, inspired by Augustine's *De doctrina Christiana*. He noted that the misunderstanding of certain scriptural passages had two sources: ambiguous signs and transferred signs (*signa translata*). He defined these: "Signs are called transferred when the things themselves that we mean by words, are used to signify something else". He gave as an example the ox, which designates properly the animal, but with transferred sense the Evangelist Mark. The exegete's goal was to clarify ambiguous terms and to determine the presence of *translata ignota*.[163] This reflection developed through the twelfth century, particularly in Hugh of St. Victor's *De scripturis*. Raban and Hugh, by determining where there was a transfer of meaning, where we therefore must pass on to spiritual exegesis, established a typology that produced the categories mentioned above. In the thirteenth century the frequent recourse to the connected notions of symbols, allegory and above all metaphors, with a more extensive use of Pseudo-Dionysian texts, permitted the refinement of this analysis.[164] The commentaries on the prophetic books (and their prologues) aimed to distinguish stylistic devices (that pertain to the *littera*) from passages requiring spiritual interpretation.[165]

3.2.4. Analysis by Concordance

This is an ancient and traditional method of Christian exegesis. More frequent in monastic exegesis, it is also present in the two other genres. Jean Leclercq gave a very precise description of this method that we can summarize.[166] By the meditation or the "rumination" on the text, the exegete seeks to "attach himself to the sentence which he recites, by weighing all the words, to arrive at complete understanding". Reminiscence plays a major role in this meditation: a phonetic or semantic analogy brings together the words. But this may be still broader: "It is possible by this method to find spontaneousloy a text or a word which perfectly fits to the situation described in a given text and explains each of its words".

This process was frequent in medieval exegesis; and we find it also in Jewish exegesis. The aim was to *explain the Bible through the Bible* and thus, by analogies or oppositions, to draw the meaning of a word or of a verse from another

163 *De cler. instit.* III, 8–15 (PL 107, 384–92).
164 Dahan, Saint Thomas d'Aquin et la métaphore. Rhétorique et herméneutique (1992).
165 See the considerations by St. Thomas Aquinas, Quodl. VII, q. 6.
166 Leclercq, L'amour des lettres (1990) 72–75. See also Gilson, De quelques raisonnements scripturaires (1955) 156–59.

word or verse. By this device, it is possible to understand the mechanism of a part of allegorical or typological exegesis, when an Old Testament text is explained by a text of New Testament: for example, in the story of Samson, when the hero is described as very tired (Judg 16:16), *defecit anima eius et ad mortem usque lassata est* ("his soul failed and was tired to death"), the words *ad mortem usque* remind us of the verse of Matthew where Christ on the cross said *tristis est anima mea usque ad mortem* ("my soul is sad to death") and thus allow a typological interpretation of Samson as a figure of Jesus.[167] But the exegetes also made use of this process in bringing together verses of the Old Testament only.

Trying to explain how the transition from the letter to the spiritual meaning was done and examining the methods of allegory, we are on the borders of hermeneutics, whereas our task was merely to examine the forms and methods of Christian exegesis in the Middle Ages. However, this analysis of the genres, the forms and various methods may at the same time have shown how the medieval commentaries are rich and interesting also from this formal point of view.[168]

[167] See the text of Osbern of Gloucester published in an appendice of Dahan, Les figures des juifs et de la Synagogue (1988) 147.

[168] I would like to thank Iona Dahan and Kate Forlenza for their help in the translation of this text that was completed in 1994. I am very grateful to Richard Lee Blucher and Ronald E. Clements for their careful revision.

Chapter Thirty

Masters and Disciples: Aspects of Christian Interpretation of the Old Testament in the Eleventh and Twelfth Centuries

By G. R. Evans, Cambridge

Bibliography: M. R. Arduini, "'Rerum mutabilitas': Welt, Zeit, Menschenbild und 'Corpus Ecclesiae' – Christianitas bei Honorius von Regensburg (Augustodunensis)", *RTAM* 52 (1985) 78–108; J. W. Baldwin, *Masters, Princes and Merchants* 1–2 (Princeton 1970); U. Berlière, "L'exercice du ministère paroissal par les moines dans le haut moyen âge", *RBén* 39 (1927) 246–50; E. Bertola, "Le critiche di Abelardo ad Anselmo di Laon ed a Guglielmo di Champeaux", *RFNS* 52 (1960) 495–522; F. Bliemetzrieder, "L'œuvre d'Anselme de Laon et la littérature théologique contemporaine", *RTAM* 5 (1933) 275–91; idem, "L'œuvre d'Anselme de Laon et la littérature théologique contemporaine. I Honorius d'Autun et II Hughes de Rouen", *RTAM* 5 (1933); 6 (1936) 261–83; 7 (1935) 235–62; B. Blumenkrantz / J. Châtillon, "De la polémique anti-juive à la catéchèse chrétienne", *RTAM* 23 (1956) 40–60; F. Châtillon, "Recherches critiques sur les différents personnages nommés Manegold", *RMAL* 9 (1953) 153–70; G. Dahan, "L'exégèse de l'histoire de Caïn et Abel du xiie au xive siècle en Occident", *RTAM* 49 (1982) 21–90; idem, "L'exégèse de l'histoire de Caïn et Abel du xiie au xive siècle en Occident", *RTAM* 50 (1983) 5–68; idem, "Une introduction à l'étude de l'Écriture au xiie siècle: le prologue du Commentaire du Pentateuque de Rainaud de Saint-Éloi", *RTAM* 54 (1987) 27–52; E. Eitlinger, *Der Sogennante Anonymus Mellicensis de Scriptoribus Ecclesiasticis* (Karlsruhe 1896); I. A. Endres, *Honorius Augustodunensis* (Kempten–Munich 1906); G. R. Evans, *The Logic and Language of the Bible* 1–2 (Cambridge 1983/84); J. Fischer, "Die Hebräischen Bibelzitate des Scholastikers Odo", *Bib.* (1934) 50–93; V. I. J. Flint, "The true author of the Salonii Commentarii in parabolas Salomonis et in Ecclesiasten", *RTAM* 37 (1970) 174–86; idem, "Some notes on the early twelfth century commentaries on the Psalms", *RTAM* 37 (1971) 80–85; idem, "The 'School of Laon': a reconsideration", *RTAM* 43 (1976) 89–110; J. de Ghellinck, "The Sentences of Anselm of Laon and their Place in the Codification of Theology during the XII Century", *ITQ* 6 (1911) 427–28; idem, *Le mouvement théologique du xiie siècle* (Brugge [2]1948); N. Golb, "New Light on the persecution of French Jews at the time of the First Crusade", *PAAJR* 34 (1966) 1–45; J. Gross, "Die Ur- und Erbsündenlehre der Schule von Laon", *ZKG* 76 (1965) 12–40; T. Gregory, *Anima Mundi: la filosofia di Guglielmo di Conches e la scuola di Chartres* (Florence 1955); G. S. Gutjahr, *Petrus Cantor, sein Leben und seine Schriften* (Graz 1899); R. W. Hunt, "The Disputation of Peter of Cornwall against Symon the Jew", *Studies in Mediaeval History Presented to F. M. Powicke* (Oxford 1948) 143–56; R. Javelet, *Image et ressemblance au douzième siècle* (Paris 1967); A. Landgraf, *Écrits théologiques de l'école d'Abélard* (SSL 14; Louvain 1934) 61–289; idem, *Introducción a la historia de la literatura teólogica de la escolástica incipiente* (Barcelona 1956); J. Leclercq, "Le commentaire du Cantique des Cantiques attribué à Anselme de Laon", *RTAM* 16 (1949) 29–39; G. I. Lieftinck, "Psalterium Hebraicum from St. Augustine's Canterbury", *Transactions of the Cambridge Bibliographical Society* 2 (1954–58) 97–104; R. Loewe, "Herbert of Bosham's Commentary on Jerome's Hebrew psalter", *Bib.* 34 (1953) 44–77, 159–92, 275–98; idem, "The mediaeval Christian Hebraists of England", TJHSE 17 (1953) 225–49; O. Lottin, "Manegold de Lautenbach, source d'Anselme de Laon", *RTAM* 14 (1947) 218–23; idem, *Psychologie et morale aux xiie et xiiie siècles* V (Gembloux 1959); D. Luscombe, *The school of Peter Abelard: the influence of Abelard's thought in the early scholastic period* (Cambridge 1970); M. Reeves, *The influence of prophecy in the later Middle Ages* (Oxford 1969); M. Signer, "Exégèse et enseignement: les commentaires de Joseph ben Simeon Kara", *AJu* 18 (1982) 60–63; H. Silvestre, "A propos de la Lettre d'Anselme de Laon à Heribrand de Saint-Laurent", *RTAM* 28 (1961) 5–25; idem, "Marginalia au t. V (1959) de *Psychologie et morale aux xiie et xiiie siècles* de dom Lottin", *RTAM* 52 (1985) 209–16; B. Smalley, "Gilbertus Universalis, Bishop of London (1128–34)", *RTAM* 7 (1935) 235–62; idem, "A commentary on the Hebraica", *RTAM* 18 (1951) 29–65; idem, *The Study of the Bible in the Middle Ages* (Oxford ³1983); R. W. Southern, *St. Anselm and his Biographer* (Cambridge 1963); T. M. Tomasic, "William of St. Thierry on the Myth of the Fall. A Phenomenology of Animus and Anima", *RTAM* 46 (1979) 5–52; H. Weisweiler, *Das Schrifttum der Schule Anselms von Laon und Wilhelms von Champeaux in deutschen Bibliotheken*, BGPhMA 33 (1936/37) 92–93; W. Wetherbee, *Platonism and Poetry in the Twelfth Century* (Princeton 1972); A. Wilmart, "Le commentaire sur le prophète Nahum attribué à Julien de Tolède", *Bulletin de Littérature Ecclésiastique de Toulouse* vii–viii (1922) 235–79; idem, "Un commentaire des psaumes restitué à Anselme de Laon", *RTAM* 8 (1936) 341–43.

1. The Axis of Paris: Laon

One cannot convincingly speak of 'schools of exegesis' in the eleventh and twelfth centuries because the institutional framework of studies was still in its infancy, and pupils were likely to hear many masters and to draw from each for their own use if they became teaching masters themselves. V. I. J. Flint has outlined difficulties in the case of 'the school of Laon'.[1] The attempt of D. Luscombe to reconstruct the 'school' of Peter Abelard reveals similar problems even in the next generation.[2] The best one can do is to point to the work of a number of pioneers and suggest ways in which they may have influenced others. The cathedral schools and their satellites provided a degree of continuity and stability, so that in this sense of the term 'school' one can find a focus of exegetical endeavour. But monastic scholars worked in parallel with those teaching in the cathedral schools, and although there was a nascent tendency for the monastic tradition to keep to the pace of *lectio divina* while the cathedral schools strove to cover the text more brisky, it would be artificial to look for any hard and fast distinction of content or methodology. H. Weisweiler pointed out that a good deal of the early manuscript evidence for the 'Laon' material came from monastic libraries.[3]

A high proportion of the prominent Old Testament exegetes of the late eleventh and early twelfth centuries were associated, at least for a time, with the cathedral schools of Paris and Laon, although there was, in this peripatetic period of scholarship, a good deal of moving about. Peter Abelard was not the only scholar to be associated with both schools.

[1] Flint, The 'School of Laon' (1976) 89–110.
[2] Luscombe, The School of Peter Abelard (1970).
[3] Weisweiler, Das Schrifttum der Schule Anselms von Laon (1936/37) 92–93.

1.1. *The Cathedral School at Laon*

The cathedral school at Laon flourished at the end of the eleventh century and the beginning of the twelfth.[4] V. I. J. FLINT seeks to make a distinction between the school *at* Laon, whose existence, as run by the brothers Anselm and Ralph, is unassailable, and a school *of* Laon.[5] Anselm seems to have been largely responsible for creating the school at Laon. He was teaching there before 1100. Ralph was important chiefly as author of parts of the *glossa ordinaria*, with his brother and Gilbert the Universal. Gilbert the Universal, who can be placed at Auxerre at least from about 1110–20, seems also to have had some connection with Nevers, where it is not impossible that he was invited to reestablish the cathedral school as he probably did at Auxerre. There is also some possibility that he may have been a canon of Lyons.[6] Gilbert seems to have been responsible for the glosses on the Pentateuch, the major prophets and Lamentations, while Anselm was the main author of those on the Psalms. Ralph may have produced that on the minor prophets.[7]

The influence of the school was considerable through the *gloss* itself,[8] and also through personal contacts and the spread of its ideas, or at least its work on ideas which had wide common currency. The collections of *sententiae* associated with the school present difficulties of attribution because there was clearly a good deal of such 'common doctrine' abroad. It is not without significance that the manuscripts in which the 'sentence-collections', linked by LOTTIN and others with Laon, survive are very widespread throughout Europe, and, as FLINT puts it, "in an appallingly tangled state".[9] This is, in itself, an indication of the live interest in such items much more extensively than at Laon.

The *Sententiae divinae paginae* may represent Anselm's own theological teaching. The *Sententiae Anselmi* (MS Gonville and Caius College, Cambridge, 151), FLINT suggests, may be based on Ralph's teaching.[10] Writings of about the same period, which came to be ascribed to "Master Manegold",[11] contain similar sentiments. Manegold seems to have commented on the Psalms, the Song of Songs, Isaiah and Matthew and possibly the Apocalypse.[12] These are evidence of at least a broad similarity of approach to exegesis. FLINT suggests that the comparatively limited range of subject-matter these *sententiae* cover, and their tendency to recur to certain topics again and again, is best seen as an indication that they are drawn from exegesis on the same familiar groups of biblical books, with which indeed they can readily be

---

[4] Landgraf, Introducción a la historia de la literatura teólogica de la escolástica incipiente (1956).

[5] Flint, The 'School of Laon' (1976) 90.

[6] Smalley, Gilbertus Universalis (1935) 236–37.

[7] On all this, see Smalley, The Study of the Bible (1983) 60 ff.

[8] On the *glossa ordinaria*, see Chap. 29 above.

[9] Flint, The 'School of Laon' (1976) 94.

[10] Flint, ibid., 92.

[11] Possibly Mangold of Lautenbach, but it is impossible to be sure. See Châtillon, Recherches critiques (1953) 153–70.

[12] Eitlinger, Anonymus Mellicensis (1896) 91. See, too, Flint, Some notes (1971) 80–85.

linked: the Pauline Epistles (92 of Lottin's 128 'Anselm' sentences), Genesis (38), the Psalms (6), Matthew (5), the Song of Songs (3), Luke and John (2).[13] That does not in itself show that the exegesis in question was truly the work of a Laon 'school', but it does give it a certain coherence.

Anselm of Canterbury was almost certainly influenced in the framing of the arguments in his *Cur Deus Homo* by the need to take a stand on an issue which we know to have been currently under discussion at Laon. Anselm argues that the Devil had no rights in fallen humanity and that there was therefore no question of God's having to ransom man from Satan.[14] Guibert of Nogent, whose own *Liber quo ordine sermo fieri debeat* prefaces a commentary on Genesis, was himself an acquaintance of Anselm of Canterbury.[15] Peter Abelard heard Anselm of Laon lecture and was himself stimulated to give lectures on Ezekiel to show that he could do better. So the circle of contacts with the school of Laon and its study of Old Testament matters can be drawn widely.

The contemporary handling of the story of Cain and Abel exemplifies very well the degree to which this Old Testament commentary material is common property, copied and recopied. Literal interpretations stress that Cain is the father of civilisation, because he is the farmer and Abel the shepherd. In the twelfth century this raises acutely the question whether agriculture is thus condemned, and of the opposition between nature and culture.[16] The mark of Cain was also an object of some curiosity.[17] Cain could be seen as representing the Jews, and in that case his 'mark' or sign is circumcision and the keeping of the Law. This notion was borrowed from Augustine's *Contra Faustum* by Isidore and Rabanus Maurus and finds its way by these routes into twelfth century thinking. There is also an association of Cain with Antichrist, so that the sign of a horn is on the forehead.[18] Raynaud de Saint-Éloi and Rupert of Deutz, to whom we shall come in a moment, favour this idea.

Cain and Abel were susceptible of a tropological explanation. Guibert of Nogent sees Abel as the inner man and Cain as the outer man. There were allegories, too,[19] with Cain and Abel as the two cities, or Cain once more representing the Jews.[20]

---

[13] Flint, The 'School of Laon' (1976) 94–95; see also nn. 72–74 below.

[14] See Southern, St. Anselm and his Biographer (1963), on this theory and its currency at Laon.

[15] Guibert speaks in his *De Vita Sua* (ed. G. Bourgin; Paris 1906) of the way Anselm taught him at Fly how the inner man of his soul (*interior homo*) should live.

[16] Dahan, L'exégèse de l'histoire de Cain et Abel (1982) 59.

[17] Andrew of St. Victor says that he was *vagus et instabilis, et timidus et tremorem membrorum sustinens.* Hugh of St. Victor, Rupert of Deutz and Peter Lombard agree. Cf. Dahan, L'exégèse de l'histoire de Cain et Abel (1982) 65 ff; and see PL 175. 44 for Hugh.

[18] Cf. Dahan, L'exégèse de l'histoire de Cain et Abel (1982) 44, on the Jewish sources of this notion.

[19] Stephen Langton takes the theme "allegorically, mystically and morally" and stresses, from Jerome, some of the meanings of the names. Cain is interpreted 'possession' or 'acquisition' and Abel 'grief', he notes. See Dahan, ibid., 18. Cf. Jerome, Heb. Nom. (CChr. SL 72) 63.

[20] Dahan, ibid., 77.

1.2. Paris

At Paris in the late eleventh and twelfth centuries there were two great 'institutional' foci of biblical studies: the cathedral school of Notre Dame and the school of the house of regular canons at St. Victor (treated below by R. Berndt, Chapter 34). There was also a floating population of masters and students who set up more evanescent teaching communities.

William of Champeaux, born about 1070, was able to hear the lectures of Manegold [of Lautenbach?] at Paris and those of Anselm at Laon. He thus forms one of the links between Paris and Laon.[21] He himself was a teaching master at Notre Dame in Paris in 1103, but was - Abelard says - driven thence to found the house of canons at St. Victor in 1108. He became bishop of Châlons-sur-Marne in 1113 and died in 1121. His own biblical work helped perhaps to provide an arena in which a series of major Parisian scholars of the next generation were able to push the *studium Sacrae Scripturae* forward.

As already indicated, there is another question of importance; it is instructive that William of Champeaux gave his energies to the house of canons at St. Victor. The schools for canons were both proto-universities and proto-theological colleges. They were concerned not only to educate in academic theology, but, in part, to improve the level of education of pastoral clergy for practical purposes. Here the role of the regular canons, Victorine and Augustinian, in the early twelfth century was highly important. Their work should discourage us from making an antithesis between 'speculative' and 'pastoral' theology and from trying to locate the study of the Old Testament at this date in either camp separately.

Peter Abelard is another of the links between Paris and Laon. He got a taste of Old Testament exegesis when he went first to hear and then to challenge Anselm at Laon.[22] It is well-known that he announced that he himself could do better, and that he would lecture on Ezekiel to prove it. He did so the next day. These lectures do not survive,[23] but even without detailed evidence of content we can say that the choice of Ezekiel is significant. Ezekiel's vision was widely-held to be especially difficult to interpret and Abelard was deliberately choosing a task which would be seen to be highly challenging, and which would therefore, if he could succeed in it, do a good deal to establish his reputation as a theologian.

Peter Abelard had pupils and disciples and a diffusive influence, which leaves its traces in a number of surviving works touching on the Old Testament. The *Ysagoge in Theologiam*, completed about 1146, survives only in MS Trinity College, Cambridge, B. XIV. 33.[24] It was clearly designed among other things as a text to be used in polemic against the Jews, and gives citations from Scripture in Hebrew (first) as well as in Latin. It is evidently not by Abelard,

---

[21] See Gross, Die Ur- und Erbsündenlehre (1965) 12–40.

[22] As he describes in his *Historia Calamitatum* (ed. J. Monfrin; Paris 1959).

[23] *Dialogus* (ed. R. Thomas; Stuttgart 1970).

[24] See Landgraf, Écrits théologiques de l'école d'Abélard (1934) 61–289, introduction, on the versions elsewhere and on the plan of the work.

but it certainly borrows from his writings, as well as from other contemporary sources. In the second book, which deals with redemption, Jewish objections are raised and dealt with, along lines familiar in Abelard's work. This is a contribution of some importance to the popular literature of Christian-Jewish apologetic in this period.[25]

Robert of Melun, an Englishman who became Bishop of Hereford at the end of his life (d. 1167), taught for much of his life at Paris. He was in some respects a successor of Peter Abelard, and his work illustrates well how the Paris-Laon axis had its influence in the next generation. He was already a noted teacher in the 1130s, when John of Salisbury heard him on the trivium.[26] He worked with Peter Lombard in the opposition to Gilbert of Poitiers in Paris in 1147. In about the 1150s, he produced both *sententiae* and *quaestiones* which survived, and which show strong Abelardian influence in places. Robert lacked Abelard's flair. He is much more pedestrian. But he caught from Abelard an interest in presenting evidences to Christian truth from the Old Testament with the intention that they should influence the Jews towards conversion. He makes use of Abelard's collection of Old Testament texts supporting the doctrine of the Trinity.[27] Robert is also sensitive to the contemporary debate about the relative positions of Christians and Jews in the providential plan. "The Jews were first, because they were converted first, and because the Lord came to them in his own person and preached to them in his own person. The gentiles were last in calling and conversion. After the Passion of Christ, the Apostles also preached to the Jews; but they resisted their preaching".[28]

We can trace the network of connections further, into another generation. Other cathedral schools bred and attracted masters who had links with either or both Paris and Laon. Simon of Tournai came from a cathedral city whose school had had a high preeminence in the late eleventh century. It had seemed "a second Athens" to the chronicler Herman. The school at the abbey of St. Martin, Tournai, took over leadership from its foundation in 1092. Walter of Mortagne opened a school at Laon about 1120, and Hugh of Tournai followed him there, though he retired to Tournai to be prior of St. Martin's.

Simon of Tournai appears to have settled in Paris first as student and then master. He is the author of a series of *disputationes* in which questions arising in the course of lecturing on the sacred text were separately considered. A number of these disputations concern Old Testament passages. As an example, disputation X asks whether Adam's immortality, which he had before he sinned, was a natural thing, that is something which was part of his nature; or a free gift of God. The conclusion is that sin did not deprive him of what was natural to him, but wounded him in his nature.[29] Disputation XXIII asks whether Abraham's merits were enough to save him. He went down to hell

---

25 Cf. Fischer, Die Hebräischen Bibelzitate des Scholastikers Odo (1934) 50–93.

26 *Metalogicon* (ed. C. C. J. Webb; Oxford 1929) II. 10.

27 This is noted by Luscombe, The School of Peter Abelard (1970) 285. Luscombe gives references from Martin's edition of Robert and adds others.

28 Robert of Melun, *Quaestiones (Theologice) de Epistolis Pauli* (ed. R. Martin; 18; 1938) 283.

29 Simon of Tournai, *Disputationes* (ed. J. Warichez; 12; 1932) 40 ff.

with his merits. No one can be saved except by Christ's death, and Christ had not yet died. We who live after the death of Christ are saved by grace, not by our own merits. Abraham's case is like having enough food for dinner, but not having set the table nor put the wine upon it.[30] Ought Abraham to have wanted to sacrifice his son? It is implied though not stated that he should have wanted it, until the instruction was revoked, because he believed that it was what God wanted.[31] Was Abraham deceived into thinking his son must be sacrified? If so, was this in some way a 'good' error?[32]

Peter Comestor, another Paris master (d. circa 1169), seems to have been a pupil of Peter Lombard.[33] Peter Comestor wrote a *De Sacramentis* in which he addresses a central question of the twelfth century: what is the relationship of the sacraments of the Old Testament and the New? Augustine was important here. His view that those of the Old Testament promise and signify and those of the New give salvation (*dant salutem*)[34] is fundamental to Peter's case. Peter argues that among the sacraments of the Old Testament that of circumcision then provided the remedy against original and actual sin which baptism now provides, but that it did not confer grace. In the time of Abraham, before circumcision was initiated, the remedy for sin was sacrifice. When parents understood their sacrifice spiritually, their infants were freed from their sins by those sacrifices made on their behalf by their parents. After circumcision was instituted, a problem arises in the case of women. It is argued that these are freed from sin by faith and good works, and if they are infants, by the faith and good works of their parents. Children who died uncircumcised perished then as unbaptised children do now, as Bede says.[35] Circumcision was changed to baptism because baptism is *utilius et perfectius.* That must be so because grace is given in baptism in addition to what is given by circumcision.[36] This fundamental distinction is reiterated in another *De Sacramentis* of the mid-twelfth century, by Master Simon. He points out that circumcision does not open the kingdom of heaven as baptism does; for baptism purges of sin through the shedding of Christ's blood.[37] In both texts there is a strong sense of importance that the Old Testament should be seen to point forward to the New. Master Simon notes that the *purgationes* of the Old Testament performed with water are a witness to baptism.[38] Peter the Chanter and Stephen Langton, who left the school in 1206 and so takes us into the thirteenth century, wrote glosses[39] to cover the Old and New Testaments.

Further, the continuance of the interdependence of monastic and 'school'

---

[30] Simon of Tournai, ibid., 75 ff.

[31] Simon of Tournai, ibid., 151 ff, Disputation LII.

[32] Simon of Tournai, ibid., 271 ff, Disputation XCIV.

[33] See Baldwin, Masters, Princes and Merchants (1970); see too Pierre le Mangeur, *De sacramentis* (ed. R. M. Martin; SSL 17; 1937) xxv*–xxvi*. See Chap. 35.3 below.

[34] *Enarrationes in Psalmos* 73.2 (PL 36.931; CChr. SL 39; 1956; 1005–06).

[35] *Homilia 10 in Circumcisione Domini*, PL 94.54.

[36] *Master Simon et al De sacramentis* (ed. R. Martin; SSL 17; 1937) 9*–12*.

[37] *Master Simon et al De sacramentis*, ibid., 83.

[38] *Master Simon et al De sacramentis*, ibid.

[39] Gutjahr, Petrus Cantor (Graz 1899) 54, lists Peter the Chanter's glosses by initia. MS Peterhouse, Cambridge, contains Stephen Langton's notes on the Octateuch and on historical books of

exegesis of the Old Testament at Paris may be demonstrated. Prior of the house of Saint-Éloi in Paris in the first half of the twelfth century, Raynaud was the author of a commentary on the Pentateuch.[40] He explains that he intends to take the five books of Moses "which seem to be carnally written" and deal with them *allegorico sensu ... ad spiritalem intelligentiam Novi Testamenti.*[41] He refers to the Hebrew, but often from Jerome's *Hebrew Questions.* Raynaud distinguishes twelve kinds of Law: *lex carnis; lex Dei; lex maledicti; lex pedagogi; lex litterae; lex naturae; lex peccati; lex psalmi; lex prophetiae; lex iustitiae; lex intelligentiae; lex mistica scientia scripturarum.*[42] The theme of the law was topical because this was also a period when there was growing interest in legal texts. Ivo of Chartres is the author of a *Panormia* and other collections in which attempts were made before Gratian to bring order to the mass of sentences and 'decretals' and other statements of legal principles which had come down somewhat haphazardly from the Roman and Carolingian periods. It was a constant course of difficulty to the compilers that theology and the law partly overlap; sin and crime pose different problems of definition; a priest is both a pastor and a judge of his penitents; *iustitia* is both 'justice' and 'righteousness'; the Old Testament is severe and the New merciful; Christ is both advocate and judge, in defiance of the rules of natural justice, and so on.

Raynaud de Saint-Éloi says with Isidore that the Old Testament is so-called because it was brought to an end by the New (*cessavit veniente novo*).[43] He attempts also a comprehensive account of the Cain and Abel story. Abel is a shepherd of sheep and so he specially signifies Christ and generally the pastors of souls who yearn inwardly over those who suffer. God approves of them as they contemplate him. Cain's fault was not in the gifts he offered but in the spirit in which he offered them. These two sons of Adam are allegorically the Jews and the Christians, the Christians the younger by birth. Cain's horn is compared with the horns of Moses, which are like the two arms of the cross and also signify the Two Testaments. Learned Jews say that Cain had the sign of circumcision written by God on his forehead so that he would not be killed.[44]

Guibert of Nogent, another monastic scholar whose connection with members of this circle has already been noted, wrote a *Moralia in Genesim* and tropological interpretations of Hosea, Amos and Jeremiah.[45] Hugh, Archbishop of Rouen had earlier been abbot of Reading. He, too, is an example of the intimate connection between monastic and cathedral school study in the Laon circle. He studied at Laon and became the author of *Dialogi* and *Questiones theo-*

the Old Testament. Trinity College, Cambridge, B. II. 26 contains Langton on The Twelve Prophets.

[40] Dahan, Une introduction à l'étude de l'Écriture (1987) 27–52.

[41] Dahan, ibid., 42 ff, in edition of the Prologue.

[42] Dahan, ibid., 48.

[43] Isidore of Seville, *Etymologiae* VI. 1 ff. (ed. W. M. Lindsay; Oxford 1909); Dahan, Une introduction à l'étude de l'Écriture (1987) 44, in edition of the Prologue.

[44] Text edited in Dahan, L'exégèse de l'histoire de Cain et Abel (1983) 5–68, 7–11.

[45] PL 156. See, too, Guibert de Nogent, *Quo ordine sermo fieri debeat* (ed. R. B. C. Huygens; CChr. CM cxxvii; 1993).

logicae in seven books, which use some Old Testament material, and of a treatise on the Hexaemeron.[46]

Central to the shared endeavour of monastic and cathedral schools in the pastoral application of Old Testament exegesis was its homiletic character. As indicated, Guibert of Nogent wrote a handbook on preaching, the *Liber quo ordine sermo fieri debeat.* The twelfth century produced an important body of preaching on the Song of Songs. Bernard of Clairvaux remained a monastic scholar, but was much involved in controversy in the schools, especially in Paris. He began a fashion here, with the series he began in the 1130s, which eventually ran to eighty-six sermons.[47] These, whether delivered or not as sermons, were certainly polished for wider publication by Bernard himself.[48] He was able to use them as pegs on which to hang disquisitions on a number of topical matters. For example, Evervin of Steinfeld wrote in the mid-1140s to ask Bernard to refute the teachings of heretics in Cologne.[49] The text "catch us the little foxes that destroy our vines" (Cant 2:15) proved a convenient anchor-point. In a similar way, Bernard was able to use the sermons to refute errors of Gilbert of Poitiers. But his principal purpose was to develop the motifs of the symbolism of the relationship of Christ and the Church and that of Christ and the soul which had been discovered by Origen and other earlier Christian exegetes within the Song of Songs.

Bernard had his imitators in the exposition of the Song of Songs. Gilbert of Hoyland continued the series Bernard left unfinished.[50] William of St. Thierry, Bernard's biographer, and the friend who first drew to his attention the "errors" of Peter Abelard, was attracted like Bernard to the lessons to be drawn from the Song of Songs about the living of the contemplative life. He did research on the book to equip himself for his task, drawing together excerpts from Gregory the Great[51] and from Ambrose.[52] William's commentary is chiefly tropological, and concerned with the relations of Christ and the soul.[53]

So, alongside the *Glossa ordinaria* with its schema of commentary, run homilies which comment on Scripture, as the Fathers preferred to do, as a means of applied teaching for those striving to understand the faith and live the Christian life. These were novel in some respects in the eleventh and twelfth centuries. For the first time, it was not usual simply to read the existing homilies of Augustine and Gregory the Great, but to compose new ones.

The 'Laon' sentence-collections show a preoccupation with questions of

---

[46] Bliemetzrieder, L'œuvre d'Anselme de Laon (1933–36).

[47] On the sequence and dates of the writing, see J. Leclercq, Introduction to the translation of Bernard's Sermons in the Cistercian Fathers series, vol. 4 (Kalamazoo / London / Oxford 1980).

[48] *Letter* 153.2 (PL 182.313) to Bernard of Portes, *Opera Omnia* (ed. J. Leclercq; vol. 7; Rome 1974), 359–60. On the question whether they were preached in the form we have them, see J. Leclercq in the introduction to the translation of Bernard's Sermons in the Cistercian Fathers series, vol. 2 (Kalamazoo / London / Oxford 1976).

[49] *Letter* 472.1 (PL 182.677).

[50] PL 184 and *Sermones in Canticum Salomonis* (tr. L. G. Braceland; Cistercian Fathers 14, 20, 26; Kalamazoo 1978–79).

[51] PL 180.441–74.

[52] PL 15.1947–2060.

[53] Text and translation (ed. J.-M. Déchanet / M. Dumentier; Paris 1962).

sin,[54] and with pastorally-important questions such as baptism and marriage, virtues and vices. There are also recurring discussions of theory and practicalities with an Old Testament or Jewish connection – sentences on Mosaic Law, on usury, on the need to avoid fraternising with Jews because that may be a stumbling-block to the faithful, on circumcision, validity of Jewish marriages.[55] FLINT argues convincingly that the physical make-up of the earliest manuscripts indicates that they may have been used for pastoral purposes. They are frequently accompanied by the Creed, prayer, sermons, treatises on morals and on ecclesiastical offices and vestments. The manuscripts are mostly small, portable volumes. She suggests that the preoccupation with Genesis, the Psalms, the Gospels and the Pauline Epistles can be explained in this way, as arising naturally in such an essentially pastoral context. FLINT's case is that these collections sprang primarily from the world outside the schools.[56]

The late eleventh and very early twelfth centuries were a period when a few masters were seeking their way to a methodology in exegesis. Anselm of Bec and Canterbury wrote three little treatises to help "introduce" beginners to the study of Holy Scripture. In these he concentrates on showing them how ideas adumbrated by Augustine might now be developed in the light of advancing knowledge of logic. The techniques have to do with the behaviour of language and the special pecularities of behaviour of biblical language. Others seem to have been interested in the relation between speculative theology and the *studium Sacrae Scripturae* which was to remain a bone of contention throughout the Middle Ages and beyond. Scripture is not systematic. Nevertheless, it gives rise to questions and suggests answers on various points of theological interest. It was clearly desirable for these to be made conveniently accessible, and for opinions contributed by the Fathers and by modern masters to be grouped with them.

It is at this period that the fundamental structure of the future *summa* was laid down, with its treatment of issues in a logical order, beginning with the nature of God himself and of the Trinity, continuing with creation, the Fall, Incarnation and redemption and going on to ecclesiology and the Last Things. Such a structure in an inchoate form is already visible in the ordering of the 'Laon' sentence-collections.

By the later twelfth century, masters in the cathedral schools were incontrovertibly preparing students in a business-like way. Increasingly, a syllabus had to be covered. But the earlier developments pointing that way were already noticeable in the earlier twelfth century. A number of teaching aids for the study of the Bible were evolving during the last decades of the twelfth century. Stephen Langton and others constructed 'concordances' of parallel texts as they glossed.[57] Alan of Lille made something closer to a dictionary of biblical terms.[58] His purpose was to provide a help for preachers as well as lecturers. A

[54] Gross (1965) 12–40.
[55] Flint, The 'School of Laon' (1976) 106.
[56] Flint, ibid., 97–100; 106.
[57] Smalley, The Study of the Bible (1983) 241.
[58] PL 210.

given term, occurring in the text on which a sermon was to be preached, could thus be collated with examples of the same term occurring in other biblical contexts and with a variety of senses, and material for a sermon thus conveniently assembled. The *distinctio* is a genre with earlier antecedents, but in the late twelfth century it was developed so as to set out the material in the form of a schema.[59]

2. Anselm of Laon

It may be looked in more detail at the work of the master who seems to deserve a central place in this web of Old Testament exegesis. The life of Anselm of Laon[60] remains largely obscure. Nothing is known for certain about his education.[61] We do not know whether he studied or taught at Paris or elsewhere. His name is associated almost exclusively, and over thirty years, with the cathedral school at Laon.[62] From 1115 until his death in 1117 he was archdeacon there, although it is impossible to be sure that he was still teaching until the end. It has been thought to be Anselm's vision to produce a gloss on the whole Bible. Peter the Chanter, nearly a century later, suggests that the administrative load he carried made it impossible.[63]

It is by no means certain that the commentary on the Song of Songs attributed to Anselm of Laon is his; there is also doubt about the commentary on Genesis.[64] There seems, however, to be no doubt about his contributions to Old Testament parts of what was to become the *Glossa ordinaria*, notably on the Psalms.[65]

Anselm left continuous commentary on Scripture and *sententiae*, or opinions on points raised in connection with Scripture. Anselm's continuing importance lies in large part in his contemporary fame. He drew to him as students or rivals individuals of whom we later hear a good deal in their own right – Peter Abelard, William of Champeaux, Guibert de Nogent, Gilbert of Poitiers, Hugh of Amiens.

Anselm as a teacher at Laon is a real enough figure, indeed one unusually vi-

---

59 Cf. Smalley, The Study of the Bible (1983) 246 ff.

60 On Anselm of Laon, see G. Lefèvre, *De Anselmo Laudunensi scholastico* (*1050–1117*) (Evreux 1895); de Ghellinck, The Sentences of Anselm of Laon (1911) 427–28; A. Wilmart, Un commentaire des Psaumes (1936) 341–43; de Ghellinck, Le mouvement théologique (1948); Lottin, Psychologie et morale (1959); Silvestre, Marginalia (1985) 209–16; Bertola, Le critiche di Abelardo ad Anselmo di Laon ed a Guglielmo di Champeaux (1960) 495–522.

61 It has been held that he was a pupil of the greater Anselm at Bec, and also that he studied at Paris. A. Wilmart notes that there is no reason to think so. A. Wilmart, Un commentaire des Psaumes (1936) 341, n. 58.

62 Master Manegold commented on Isaiah, the Psalms, the Song of Songs, but he was probably never at Laon. See Lottin, Manegold de Lautenbach (1947) 218–23; idem, Psychologie et morale (1959) 146–53.

63 Smalley, The Study of the Bible (1983) 50.

64 PL 162. 1187–1228, see Leclercq, Le commentaire du Cantique des Cantiques (1949) 29–39. See, too, Flint, The "School of Laon" (1976) 91.

65 Flint, Some notes (1971) 80–85.

vid to us thanks to Peter Abelard's account of his own contact with him. Abelard describes him in his *Historia Calamitatum* as "venerable, a name which he acquired more from old age than from wit or reputation". If a person who did not know something asked him a question, he gave him a yet more uncertain answer. He sounded impressive but there was little content to what he had to say. When he lit a fire he filled his house with smoke. To those who saw it from a distance, his tree seemed full of leaves, but when one came close one could see the bare branches.[66] Abelard of course saw him with the eyes of an able and arrogant young man, impatient with what he saw as the out-dated methods. But through the mockery we can glimpse something of the towering figure Anselm seemed to be in his heyday.

Anselm made a name in controversy too. He is apparently the author of a letter to Abbot Heribrand of St. Laurence of Liège about Rupert of Deutz.[67] Its context must almost certainly be the confrontation which was at its height in the early twelfth century over the pastoral ministry of monks.[68] Monks anxious to assert their right to pastoral ministry were, it seems, collecting or utilising the 'sentence' material generated by Anselm and others. In the controversy Rupert of Deutz aligned himself with Heribrand against Anselm of Laon and William of Champeaux. Rupert of Deutz – later abbot of Deutz, but at that time monk of Liège – who argued for the pastoral responsibilities of monks, set out on one occasion riding on a donkey to meet Anselm of Laon in a confrontation.[69] Anselm was also ready with practical advice. Guibert of Nogent says that when Anselm was asked whether a robber should be punished or paid to say where the stolen goods were, he answered that he should be bribed.[70]

Anselm was, as mentioned above, the author or possible author of a series of *sententiae*, or opinions on disputed questions (the forerunners of later pedagogic forms in the schools), which survived in *florilegium* collections. These are comparatively unspeculative in their contents.[71] Of the *Sentences* identified by Lottin as Anselm's, thirty-eight come from the exegesis of Genesis, six from the Psalms, three from the Song of Songs.[72] The most notable of these for Anselm's work is the *Liber Pancrisis* (in MS Troyes 425, f. 95 ra–148 rb, and in British Museum, MS Harley 3098; a less full collection survived, with authorial attributions, in MS Avranches 19). There Anselm's opinions are included amongst the views of Augustine, Jerome, Gregory the Great, and along with those of some contemporaries (*moderni magistri*)[73] of Anselm: Ivo of Chartres, William of Champeaux and Anselm's brother Ralph. The close cor-

---

[66] Abelard, *Historia Calamitatum* (ed. J. Monfrin; Paris 1959) 68.

[67] PL 162. 1587–92, see Lottin, Psychologie et morale (1959) 175–76, with corrections. On the evidence that this was addressed to Heribrand, see Silvestre, A propos de la Lettre d'Anselme de Laon à Heribrand de Saint-Laurent (1961) 5–25.

[68] Berlière, L'exercice du ministère paroissal par les moines (1927) 246–50.

[69] *In Regulam Sancti Benedicti*, PL 170. 482–83.

[70] Guibert of Nogent, *De Vita Sua* (ed. G. Bourgin; Paris 1907) III, xv; 207.

[71] Flint, The 'School of Laon' (1976) 97.

[72] Flint, ibid., 94–95. See above p. 240 and n. 13.

[73] MS Troyes 425, f. 95 ra.

respondence of the order of the sentences in these collections and the consistency of attribution, make it possible to identify with some confidence a number of genuine sentences of Anselm. Other collections preserve texts which are likely or possible to be his.[74]

Among the genuine sentences are a number dealing with Old Testament themes. The fundamental questions concern the status of the Old Testament itself, and the value of the Law in the Christian era. A Testament, Anselm reminds, contains precept and promise. The Old Testament is seen as offering promises of temporal things, the New Testament promises of heavenly things (53, p. 50). As for the Law Anselm reviews a number of contemporary opinions, at some length. Some believed the Law to be given as a means of teaching humanity, others that it was a sign; others thought "that sin might abound", and the elect be distinguished from the damned (113, p. 89). He argues that it convicts of sin but that God's promise is to be obtained by those who recognise its weakness and their own and trust to grace (9, p. 21). He also thought that Old Testament figures could be saved by their faith, that God would act in the way he subsequently did (118, p. 96).

Anselm considered it important that the first tablet given to Moses had on it the three commandments pertaining to God himself, with the second containing the seven which pertain to men and which include a promise if they are kept (12, p. 23; 181, p. 128). Law has three aspects: precept, sacrament, and promise. In Old Testament 'sacraments' the sign existed without the thing signified (as in the miracles of the Red Sea, the manna, and in circumcision). The 'sacramental' aspect of the Old Testament is emptied out into the New, where the *res sacramenti* accompanies the sign, as cleansing from sin in baptism. The precepts of the Old Law are not all superseded. Some of them were *naturalia*, as the love of God and one's neighbour, and these remain (51, p. 48). This distinction between 'natural' and 'written' or positive Law is also made in another sentence (49, p. 48).

There is, further, discussion of justification under the Old Law (118, p. 96). The principle approved is that no one could be justified unless he was spiritually a man of the New Testament. On the festivals of the Old Law, Anselm is asked why there are not feast-days for the saints, such as Abraham. He knows that the Greeks celebrate such feasts. There is in fact a feast for John the Baptist (95, p. 80).

The next group of topics concerns the creation. The question whether God made everything at once is raised (101, p. 84). The text of Genesis describes how one thing was made after another, over six days, but it was being argued by contemporaries that the substance of all things could still have been made at once. For Anselm of Laon the chief interest in the sphere of the creation is in Adam. We do not yet find the sophisticated speculative and theological discussions of a generation or so later on the relationship between the Genesis account of the beginning of the world and that of Plato. So Anselm asks about the creation and fall of man. He says that God made man by Word and will

[74] See Lottin's introductions to his editions of these texts. The references which follow are to Lottin, Psychologie et morale (1959).

alone, and not through an angel, as some say (*ut quidam volunt*). He made him in his own image, that is, rational and wise (*rationalis et sapiens*). This is seen only in Christ. The 'likeness' (*similitudo*) is another matter. This is found in the soul, for in our bodies we can grow and diminish and die, and that is not like God (29, p. 30). Alternatively, Gen 1:26 can be interpreted as indicating that the 'image' of God is destroyed in us because it meant imitating God in meekness and humility, justice and mercy, obedience unto death, loving good and hating evil. The likeness remains, for that lies in our possession of a soul (30, pp. 30–31).

Anselm argues that Adam was created for obedience, and without concupiscence. Before he sinned he was in a 'real' (*realis*) not merely an allegorical paradise, Anselm insists. He had the capacity to suffer and die or not to suffer and die (38, p. 36). His mortality was natural, his immortality a condition (*conditio*) (41, p. 37). Had he been able to remain in Paradise after he sinned to eat of the tree of life and the others, he would not have felt hunger or thirst or grown old or died (Gen 3:22) (39, p. 37). His fault, it is argued, lays in his presumption in going against the Creator's prohibition. There was nothing poisonous in the forbidden fruit (179, p. 127). When he disobeyed concupiscence ran riot in him (24, p. 26). The effect was to bring corruption to his body (28, p. 29). His soul was affected by becoming subject to the tug of the body's sensuality (28, p. 29).

A number of sentences have survived on original sin (43, pp. 38 ff). These are perhaps not strictly inspired by Old Testament exegesis. They discuss themes we know to have been currently popular – especially that of the mode of tranmission of the sin of Adam to his progeny, on which Anselm hoped to live long enough to write.

A further distinction is made between the condition of man after the Fall and before the Flood, and their state after the Flood. Afterwards mankind's pride was humbled by shortening human lives and making them weaker and less wise (180, p. 128).

Of continuing interest was the fate of the *patres* who had died before Christ. It is Anselm's view that they were not punished, because they had lived justly as far as is possible for human beings, but that they could not win heaven by their own merits and they lived before Christ (50, p. 48).

Comparison of Christ with Adam was often made (55, p. 52; 142, p. 109; 183, p. 128). A chief concern was to stress that Christ was a second Adam, setting an example for those who came after, but a contrasting one. Adam spent as long being happy in Paradise as Christ spent on the Cross bearing the penalty of death for the redemption of the human race.

There were questions about the prophets. Prophecy is defined as divine inspiration which tells how things will happen either through actions (examples are given, such as Noah's Ark or Abraham's sacrifice) or through words, and in a reliable manner. It is a gift of the Holy Spirit (164, p. 121). Where did Balaam get the power to curse? The answer must be that he somehow had God's permission, as devils may have to tempt God's people (84, p. 72).

It remains difficult to be sure what the educational purposes of these *sententiae* were, or what their genre was. Peter Abelard gives a clue in his *Historia*

Calamitatum[75] that they may have been brief treatments of the theological issues which arose during the course of sequential commentary. He himself does the same thing in his Commentary on Romans. His *sententiae* there are often lengthy. Certainly by the time we get to Simon of Tournai these discussions are beginning to turn into separate *disputationes*. Topics appear to have been held over for discussion, so as to give time for them separately from the cursory lectures. It may be that the compilers of these sentence-collections already perceived the usefulness of drawing together the more explicitly theological and speculative material. SMALLEY thinks that the glosses which survive often seem to have been collected by students from lectures as they were actually given, even before a formal system of *reportatio* developed.[76] On the other hand, the putative line of development which makes these proto-*disputationes* is not without objections. In some respects they were more like the magisterial resolutions of a later age. Anselm of Laon himself saw them, it seems, as settled 'opinions' arrived at by mature learning, and not as discussions.[77]

There has been considerable debate about the way the compilations might have been made. Anselm of Laon himself did not encourage pirating.[78] There is no evidence that a system of *reportatio*, or official reporting at the wish of a master, was yet in use.[79] The muddle of the surviving manuscripts does not suggest that Anselm himself had a hand in their making, or that he himself circulated them in any way. R. SILVAIN classifies the products of 'Laon' into 'model' texts, isolated texts and compilations, giving the *Summa Sententiarum* a special place.[80]

3. Exegesis in the Schools of Chartres and Other Cathedrals

The artificiality of trying to distinguish sharply between the work of Paris and that of Laon extends to the attempt to characterize the work of other cathedral schools separately. The scholars associated with Chartres, Gilbert of Poitiers, Thierry of Chartres, Clarembald, have other links too, Gilbert with Paris, Clarembald with Arras.

The Old Testament account in Genesis was of course a prime source for the discussion of creation, and this seems to have been a favourite topic at Chartres.[81] But it was not an exclusive preoccupation of Chartrian scholars. Robert of Melun wrote on creation in his *Sententiae*, with two special emphases which

---

[75] See n. 66 above and Lottin, ibid., 178–83.

[76] On the making of notes and later of *reportationes*, see Smalley, The Study of the Bible (1983) 201 ff.

[77] Lottin, ibid., 175–76.

[78] Abelard, *Historia Calamitatum*, 69.

[79] This is R. SILVAIN's suggestion; cf. "La tradition des Sentences d'Anselme de Laon" *AHDL* 16 (1948) 1–52; 17–19.

[80] Silvain, ibid., 3–4.

[81] Wetherbee, Platonism and Poetry (1972); Gregory, Anima Mundi (1955); Javelet, Image et ressemblance (1967); Tomasic, William of St. Thierry on the Myth of the Fall (1979) 5–52; Thierry of Chartres, *Commentaries on Boethius* (ed. N. M. Häring; STPIMS 20; Toronto 1971); *The Life and Works of Clarembald of Arras* (ed. N. M. Häring; STPIMS 10; Toronto 1974).

reflect philosophical awareness. He insists that God created everything at once, with no delay between the *conditio* and the *formatio* and *dispositio.*[82] He also considers Plato's account in the *Timaeus* and tries to argue that Plato in fact did think that God created as well as forming and disposing the *elementa.*[83] Robert, further, looked at the work of the six days. He preferred the traditional 'six ages' motif. He gave the first age to the period from Adam to Noah, the second to the period from Noah to Abraham, then Abraham to David, David to the Babylonian exile, Babylon to Christ, with the sixth age beginning with Christ.[84]

Honorius of Autun presents himself in his *De luminaribus ecclesiae sive de scriptoribus ecclesiasticis* as *Augustodunensis ecclesiae presbyter et scholasticus.* That may mean that he was running the cathedral school at Autun in the first quarter of the twelfth century.[85] But he has also been associated with Regensburg.

Honorius says that he wrote twenty-three works.[86] Among them is a long commentary on the Song of Songs in which he used substantial pieces of a commentary which derives from Laon.[87] His *Elucidarium* is a *summa* of Christian theology in the form of a dialogue. He includes in it several 'Old Testament' questions. He asks, for example, why the world was created and how. The latter can be answered from the Psalms: "He spoke and all things were made" (Ps 33:9). Was this by the sound of the words? God speaks by the Word, that is the Son; that is why the Psalm says: "You have made everything in wisdom" (Ps 104:24). Did God create bit by bit or all at once? He created everything at once, as Ecclesiasticus says (Sir 18:1). What does it mean when it says: "evening and morning" (Gen 1:5, 8)? The evening refers to the end of one stage of the work of creation, the morning to the beginning of a stage yet to be completed.[88]

Mixed in with these close questionings of the text of Scripture are speculative elements drawn from ancient philosophy and contemporary discussion, but wherever Scripture gives a clear indication it is used. Another example is: why does it say that after sin they saw they were naked (Gen 3:7)? The reason is that after they had sinned they began to burn with desire for one another. This is notably the case for the issues of moral theology, to which Honorius turns in Book II. It is written: "You have hated nothing which you have made" (Wis 11:25). So how can it be said that God loves the good and hates the wicked? Deceivers provoke God's wrath (Job 36:13). "There is no peace for the wicked" (Isa 48:22). "The just shall fear nothing" (Prov 28:1).

---

82 *Sententiae* (ed. R. Martin SSL 21; 1947) 214–15.

83 *Sententiae* (ed. R. Martin) 210.

84 *Sententiae,* I. xvii (ed. R. Martin) 202. How is a prophecy to be explained when it may refer to any point in the future? Hugh of St. Victor is able to allow for the possibility that a given prophecy in Joel could refer to the siege by the Assyrians under Senacherib, or to the coming of Christ. Cf. Smalley, The Study of the Bible (1983) 101.

85 Bliemetzrieder, L'œuvre d'Anselme de Laon (1933) 275–91. See, too, Arduini, "Rerum mutabilitas" (1985) 78–108. Endres, Honorius Augustodunensis (1906) disagrees.

86 Bliemetzrieder, ibid., 276.

87 Flint, The true author of the Salonii Commentarii (1970) 174–86; PL 162. 1187–1228.

88 PL 172. 112–13.

Rupert of Deutz taught for a time at Liège and Siegburg. About 1120 he became abbot of Deutz near Cologne. He became the author of a series of works, including the monumental *De Trinitate et Operibus Eius.* He may have intended these to form a contrast to the teaching-style and content of Anselm of Laon and other contemporaries, by giving them something of the slow, reflective pace proper to *lectio divina.* The great achievement of *De Trinitate* is to set the whole of the Old and New Testament in order in the context of the divine providential plan as directed by each of the Persons of the Trinity in turn. The work of Father, Son and Holy Spirit is, however, indivisible, and it is to the glory of God as both one and three that Rupert's work is directed.[89]

The Old Testament contains a good deal of history, and writers of history in the earlier Middle Ages commonly began with it as standing in continuity with the events of their own more recent times. This encouraged the discovery of patterns in history. The work of Rupert of Deutz is an important example of this. He organised his vast commentary on Scripture within the framework of the "age of the Father", the "age of the Son", and the "age of the Holy Spirit". Throughout the text of the Old Testament part of the work he looks to the New and beyond. This *De Trinitate et Operibus Eius* had its sequels, notably in the work of Joachim of Fiore.[90] Rupert of Deutz also wrote on the Song of Songs. He lists the six 'songs' of the Old Testament,[91] after which the Song of Songs comes as the seventh and last.[92]

A New Testament writer citing the Old Testament sometimes quotes from the Old Testament giving a textual reading of a sense which differs from that of the Hebrew original. This raised with irresistible practicality for the scholars the question of the reliability of the text. But work on this came comparatively late in our story. Emendation of the text was a concern of Hugh of St. Victor and also of Andrew of St. Victor, Peter Lombard, Peter Comestor and Peter the Chanter. But Stephen Langton seems to have gone about it systematically. He made lists of variant readings and compares them with Jerome and other sources. When the thirteenth century tidying up of the text was achieved Langton was often cited in the *correctoria.* But his instinct was not simply to achieve a correct reading. He liked to collect examples of textual variants so that he could provide a spiritual interpretation of one of them.[93] Peter the Chanter and Peter Comestor testify to the growing need for a coherent system of chapter divisions. Stephen Langton seems to have taken this further than most, or at least was believed by later historians to have done so. However, the evidence from his own work is inconclusive.[94]

---

89 Prologus, *De Trinitate et Operibus Eius* (ed. H. Haacke, CChr. CM 21; 1971).

90 Reeves, The influence of prophecy (1969).

91 Exod 15:1–19; Deut 32:1–43; I Kgs 2:1–10; Isa 12:1–6; Isa 38:10–20; Hab 3:2–19. This, he explains, is the song of God's great kindness, the song of his love, when he descended upon the Virgin Mary and became man. Here history provides the securest possible foundation for the mystical interpretation.

92 *Commentaria in Canticum Canticorum* (ed. H. Haacke; CChr. CM 26; 1974) 7–8.

93 Smalley, The Study of the Bible (1983) 219 ff.

94 Smalley, ibid., 222 ff.

4. The Impact of Christian Contact with Jewish Exegetes

4.1. Knowledge of Hebrew

Christian contact with Jews was important in the early twelfth century.[95] At this time, the Jewish society of Northern France fostered some great Bible scholars, like Solomon ben Isaac, or Rashi of Troyes, and Joseph ben Simeon Kara.[96] Rashi (1040–1105) enlarged the range of modes of exegesis available to Jewish scholars. Hitherto they had been largely confined to the *halachic* method (which was roughly equivalent to the tropological or moral in Christian exegesis in its concentration on drawing lessons for the right living of life), and the *aggadic* or midrashic method. Here much material of an illustrative kind might be introduced by way of stories and allegory. Rashi focused upon a literal interpretation, with a good deal of reflection on the grammatical structure of the text. He had his disciples. Joseph Kara (d. ca. 1130) sought – though unsuccessfully – to eliminate all midrashic elements. Samuel ben Meir, or Rashbam, Eliezer of Beaugency and Joseph Bekhor Shor of Orleans pressed the literal approach further.[97]

Hugh of St. Victor consulted Jews on the Hebrew text and he included transliterations of certain Hebrew words. Stephen Harding had led the way here.[98] To judge from his use of explanations which do not appear to have a Christian source and which he himself refers to "the Jews", he also tried to follow the exegetical methods of the Hebrew tradition where it seemed appropriate to him.[99] This had been attempted by Sigebert of Gembloux before him.

Together with the acquiring of some knowledge of Hebrew[100] by certain twelfth century Christian scholars went a curiosity about the way Jewish writers of the Old Testament did things, which were of direct interest to the particular scholars we have been considering. It is, comments Robert of Melun, "the Hebrew way" to give a book a title from its first part. Thus Genesis is called after 'beginning'. "We do often that too in speaking of the Psalms. So we are accustomed to say that *beatus vir* is the first Psalm".[101] In Andrew of St. Victor there are many comparisons in *Hebreo. Nonne si bene egeris recipies* (Gen 4:7) gets the comment, *in hebreo pro 'recipies' 'dimittetur tibi', delictum scilicet.*[102]

---

[95] See Golb, New Light on the persecution of French Jews (1966) 1–45.

[96] Signer, Exégèse et enseignement (1982) 60–3. See also Chap. 32 below (A. Grossman).

[97] Smalley, The Study of the Bible (1983) 151.

[98] Smalley, ibid., 102–3.

[99] Examples are given by Smalley, ibid., 103.

[100] Smalley, The Study of the Bible (1983) chap. 4; idem, A commentary on the Hebraica (1951) 29–65; R. Loewe, 'Herbert of Bosham's Commentary on Jerome's Hebrew psalter', *Bibl.* 34 (1953); idem, The mediaeval Christian Hebraists of England (1953); Hunt, The Disputation of Peter of Cornwall against Symon the Jew (1948); Lieftinck, Psalterium Hebraicum from St. Augustine's Canterbury (1954–58); Blumenkrantz / Châtillon, De la polémique anti-juive à la catéchèse chrétienne (1956).

[101] *Sententiae* (ed. R. Martin; 1947) 183.

[102] Dahan, L'exégèse de l'histoire de Cain et Abel (1983) 13.

Hugh of St. Victor discussed also the translation of the Old Testament from the Hebrew into Greek, in terms which cover the question of the authoritativeness of translation too. He lists translations by Aquila the Jew, Symmachus and Theodotion; also the Old Latin; and translations by Origen, rendered by Eusebius and Pamphilus. Jerome comes last and he is rightly preferred because he keeps more faithfully to the text (*verborum tenacior est*) and he is clearer (*perspicuitate sententiae clarior*). The Septuagint, Hugh explains, was done by a team in which each member was an *interpres* "through the Holy Spirit". So no part of it is less reliable than the rest. But he knows that Jerome queries this.[103]

It is a cardinal principle of the exegesis of these authors that Old Testament language is seen to be figurative of the New, and Old Testament persons and events to be themselves significant of things and persons which were to be described in the New Testament. The whole issue of what is 'proper' and what is 'transferred' in signification is raised by Robert of Melun in his *Sententiae*, together with the issue of the relationship of signification by things and signification by words (*res* and *vox*) on which Augustine had given a substantial lead in his *De doctrina Christiana*.[104] Robert of Melun explains, for example, that Abraham's willingness to sacrifice his son signifies the Father's willingness to sacrifice his own Son. That is an instance of the way a person can signify. He also gives examples of signifying by times, places and so on.[105] In both these areas twelfth century scholars had made important technical advances.[106]

Hugh understood the senses of Scripture as rising one above another like the floors of a building. He made the astute point that the literal sense is like a rough foundation, in which the stones are not cut neatly. The higher, spiritual senses, fit into, as well as onto, that foundation, because their stones are cut exactly to key into it. To master the historical sense the student should read Genesis, Exodus, Joshua, Judges, Kings, Chronicles, the Gospels and Acts. As he does so, he should learn the events, the persons, the times and the places mentioned.[107] When he starts to learn allegory, the student ought to begin with the New Testament, Matthew's and John's Gospels, the Epistles, especially those of St. Paul, the Apocalypse. When he has learned what is foreshadowed in the Old Testament, he can then read the Old Testament itself with understanding, the Hexaemeron, the Law, Isaiah, Ezekiel's opening and conclusion, Job, the Song of Songs, the Psalms.[108]

Hugh himself unaffectedly uses the *accessus*[109] as the most natural means of introducing each book of the Bible on which he comments. With its sequence of asking who is the *auctor*, and what is his *intentio* in writing, as well as what branch of study the subject falls into. This encourages the focussing of attention on the Bible's human authors. In Genesis, for example, Moses can be said to be "a historiographer, setting out history from the beginning of the world

[103] PL 176.780, IV. 5.
[104] *Sententiae* (ed. R. Martin) 170.
[105] Ibid., 177.
[106] See Evans, The Logic and Language of the Bible (1984).
[107] VI. iii. 799–802.
[108] VI. vi. 805–06.
[109] On the *accessus*, see R. B. C. Huygens, *Accessus ad Auctores* (Leiden 1970).

to the death of Jacob". It also makes it possible to select particular points of importance in a given book. Among other things, Moses intends to stress God's work as creator in writing Genesis.[110]

Simon of Tournai further asks whether the teaching of the Law was necessarily in that form for the sake of the simple ones. They could not grasp the spiritual sense. But the literal sense kills. Nevertheless, they could venerate the letter which contais the spiritual understanding, and by that alone were able to be saved. Just as now someone may say the Lord's Prayer without having enough education to understand it, but be saved by the devoutness with which he does it. It is not understanding but respecting the spiritual which counts.[111]

The concept of 'two testaments' and the relation of the Old to the New were discussed frequently by these scholars. Is it fitting (*conveniens*) for the Old Testament to precede the New? asks Robert of Melun. Certainly it is fitting for the figure which signifies to precede the truth which is signified.[112] The Old Testament is therefore not to be despised in comparison with the New Testament, but revered the more. It is a true witness to the New.[113]

The relationship of Old Testament to New in terms of Law and Grace or Law and Gospel is a frequent preoccupation of these authors, as was clear in the case of Anselm of Laon. Simon of Tournai asks in one of his disputations whether the yoke of the Law is heavier than that of the Gospel, since the Gospel constrains hand and mind, while the Law constrains only the hand. He argues that the yoke of the Law was heavier for three reasons: because there was so much to observe; because the Law is so lengthy and detailed; because of the severity of the penalties.[114]

Robert of Melun asks in his *Quaestiones de Divina Pagina* whether the faith of men under the Law is the same as that of those under Grace. Augustine says that times change but the faith remains the same.[115] But he also says that they believed Christ was to come, and we believe that he has come. So there is a difference in faith, says Robert. Moreover, the Jews believe that Christ is to come, so it can be argued that Abraham's faith is in fact the same as that of the Jews today. That cannot be so. Robert argues that they have merely an opinion, and Abraham a certainty.[116]

Is the Law to be held to within the Gospel? Yes, says Robert of Melun. Both confirm our faith and so both must be held by the faithful. Yet what is it to hold a law but to obey its precepts? There are problems here. Christ came as a light to put away darkness and the Law is the shadow (*umbra*) of the Gospel.

---

[110] PL 175. 33.

[111] Simon of Tournai, *Disputationes* (ed. J. Warichez, SSL 12; 1932) 254 ff, Disputation LXXXIX.

[112] *Sententiae* I. i (ed. R. Martin) 159.

[113] *Sententiae* I. ii (ed. R. Martin) 160. Cf. Augustine, *Retractationes* 1. 22, cited by Robert, ibid.

[114] Simon of Tournai, *Disputationes* (ed. J. Warichez, SSL 12; 1932) 120 ff, Disputation XLI.

[115] Tracts on John 45, PL 35. 1722.

[116] Robert of Melun, *Quaestiones de Divina Pagina* (ed. R. Martin, SSL 13; 1932) 46, Question 91.

How can the shadow bear witness to the reality? And if the Gospel is not sufficient without the Law, the *doctrina Christi perfecta non est.*[117]

Within the ambit of the scholars working at Laon and their acquaintances came an interest in the conversion of Jews. We know that lively discussions took place between Jews and Christians. Gilbert Crispin's *Dialogue*[118] testifies to that, as does Abelard's later *Dialogus.* Anselm's *Cur Deus homo* perhaps took its beginnings partly from this debate too. The focus of interest theologically speaking was upon the question of the incarnation. But there was also a good deal of talk about the role of Scripture as giving authority for the Christian interpretation of events, and especially of the Old Testament, which Jews as well as Christians must accept.

The most detailed account of the part exegesis played in bringing about conversions is given by a former Jew himself. Hermannus Judaeus describes how he was eventually won over when he was persuaded that the Jews' tendency to keep to the literal sense only left them on the surface. The figurative interpretations were more beautiful and richer. It was put to him that the Jews were like brute beasts, content with the outer husk, while the Christians, like rational men, nourished themselves on the sweet inner kernel.[119]

4.2. The Victorines at Paris

The first of these is Hugh of St. Victor. Hugh of St. Victor came to St. Victor about 1118, probably from the Netherlands.[120] He was teaching in Paris from about 1125 and died in 1141. Hugh of St. Victor[121] was first a pedagogue and only to a modest degree a researching scholar. Hugh himself wrote 'little notes' (*notulae*) on the Octateuch,[122] concentrating on literal meaning, homilies on part of Ecclesiastes, an exposition of Lamentations, some notes on the Psalms, Joel, Abdias.[123] These belong to a variety of genres of twelfth century biblical works. The homilies would have been preached to the brothers, as were the two treatises Hugh wrote on Noah's Ark.[124] The commentaries seem to have been meant for study by reading. The *notulae* occur in the manuscripts in two series and their ordering seems untidy. Perhaps they were preserved in an early form of *reportatio*, by pupils keeping notes from Hugh's lectures. Unfortunately they do not tell us enough to enable us to guess how Hugh set about the teaching in detail.[125] But we have other clues.

His great achievement was to reduce to a modest compass material from Au-

---

117 *Sententie* I. 3. (ed. R. Martin, SSL 21; 1947) 162.

118 Gilbert Crispin, *Opera Omnia* (ed. A. Abulafia / G. R. Evans; London 1986).

119 Hermannus Judaeus, *De Conversione Sua* (ed. G. Niemeyer; Weimar 1963) 73–74.

120 See J. Taylor, The origin and early life of Hugh of St. Victor (Notre Dame 1957). See further the discussion of the Victorines at Paris in Chap. 34 of this volume (R. Berndt).

121 ca. 1096–1141.

122 PL 175. 29–114.

123 It is possible that a surviving commentary on Nahum is also his; see Wilmart, Le Commentaire sur le prophète Nahum (1922).

124 PL 176.

125 Smalley, The Study of the Bible (1983) 99.

gustine and elsewhere on exegesis, so that his students could absorb it easily. In his *Didascalicon* he intended to provide a practical introduction to methods and purposes of study for his pupils. He stresses the importance of the slow, meditative reading of the *lectio divina* of the cloister as much preferable to the hasty skimming of a text with the glosses favoured in the schools.[126]

The student will need a grounding in the liberal arts and then he must learn to read Scripture in each of its senses. Hugh relays Augustine's opinions about the usefulness of the rules of Tichonius the Donatist. But his own assumption is that the fourfold system popularised by Gregory the Great is the most appropriate for modern use. Hugh had a innovatory approach to the relationship between the literal and the other senses in giving a higher place to the literal than had recently been usual.

Hugh also made use of something close to the *summula* method of the lawyer Bulgarus (fl. ca. 1115–65). This involved summarising at the beginning the main contents of what is to follow. So Hugh approaches Leviticus by summarizing the chief kinds of sacrifice it prescribes, together with the persons who are to offer the sacrifices and the times when they are to do it.[127]

Hugh of St. Victor's *De sacramentis* is divided into two parts, the *opus creationis*, running historically from the beginning of the world to the Incarnation, and the *opus restaurationis*, which tells the story from that point. He thus gives a substantial place in his *summa* to Old Testament matters.

Hugh of St. Victor used the motif of Noah's Ark as a starting-point and framework, first for a morality and then for a mystical interpretation (PL 176). In *De Arca Noe Morali* he describes how he and the brothers were discussing the living of a good life, and that gave him the idea of writing the two books. The device is somewhat like that of the art of memory, where *loci* are used as pigeon-holes for ideas. The structure of the ark, its measurements, its windows and door, prompt reflections. In the *De Arca Noe Mystica*, for example, the soul can go out of the windows and door in contemplation.[128]

Andrew of Wigmore was almost certainly an actual pupil of Hugh's. He had written his own commentary on the Octateuch by 1147. He was then made abbot of Wigmore in Herefordshire in England. This did not prove a success, and Andrew returned after a few years to Paris. On the death of the abbot chosen in his place, the canons begged him to return, and in the early 1160s, he did so. He seems then to have stayed and to have ceased to maintain active contact with the teaching at Paris. His exegetical work concentrates on the detailed exposition of particularly interesting passages. He was not interested in spiritual or figurative explanations. His taste was for the literal and his ambition was to add something to what the Fathers had said. He tried to do it through sheer learning, especially in the classical authors and in the rules of grammar. He turned to Josephus a good deal, and to living Jewish scholars for help on literal renderings. He was able to do real pioneering work in expounding the Prophets in the literal sense, for, apart from Jerome, none of the

[126] V. vii. 796.
[127] Smalley, The Study of the Bible (1983) 99.
[128] PL 176. 617–20.

Fathers he can have read had done so. He was also able to take an entirely fresh look at the problem of the creation narratives. He argues that Moses framed them as he did for simple people, because mention of the Trinity and of angels would have confused them and tempted them into polytheism. Another commonly-expressed difficulty is how Moses, who was not there, can have known the creation story. Perhaps, Andrew suggests, it was a direct revelation to him by the Spirit? Or perhaps an oral tradition existed, preserved through the generations and found out by Moses by his own investigation? His approach to these issues and to the classic question whether God created everything in six days or simul, all at once, as Ecclesiasticus 18:1 has it, is to look to Moses' purposes as an author. He approaches the prophets in a similar way.[129]

Richard of St. Victor (d. 1173) was probably a Scot by origin. He was a disciple though not a pupil of Hugh, who died in 1141 before he arrived at St. Victor. Richard was himself a teacher there in the 1150s. His own strongest interest was in the spiritual or mystical interpretation of Scripture. He made notes on the Psalms, a commentary on the Song of Songs and wrote a monograph on the dream which Daniel interpreted. His *Benjamin Minor* (*The Twelve Patriarchs*) and *Benjamin Major* (*The Mystical Ark*) take Jacob's family and the tabernacle respectively, to form a framework within which to expound on contemplation. In the first treatise he explains the preparation of mind and body for contemplation by learning to achieve inner peace. Jacob is taken to represent the rational soul. His wives, Rachel and Leah are reason and feeling (including desire in the will). Rachel seeks truth, Leah virtue. Rachel's handmaid Bala signifies imagination, linking reason to sense-perception through the forming of images. Leah's handmaid Zelpha links feeling with the world through the five senses. Here Richard is clearly drawing in the tradition which made Leah and Rachel types of the active and the contemplative life, but he develops the possibilities of the notion in new ways.

In the *Benjamin Major*, he discusses the six varieties of contemplation and the ways in which they can attain their objects, making use of a wide variety of Old Testament material.

He wrote literal exposition too: on the Temple, making a serious attempt with diagrams to show how the dimensions given could produce a building which would stand up. He composed a study of the visions of Ezekiel and a chronology of the kings of Israel and Judah, on which he consulted Jewish advisers.[130]

An anonymous letter, which seems to have been written by an author who knew Hugh of St. Victor's teaching and wanted to clarify some points for a friend, recommends the beginner working on his own to read the whole Bible several times, looking for the historical or literal sense. He should make a note of passages which cannot be taken literally. When he reads the Law, Joshua, Judges, Kings, Chronicles, he can get help from Josephus or Egesippus. When

[129] Smalley, The Study of the Bible (1983) 112–95, on Andrew of St. Victor.

[130] These are all noted by Smalley, ibid., 106–07. See, too, Richard of St. Victor, The Classics of Western Spirituality (tr. Grover A. Zinn; New York / London 1979).

he reads the Prophets he can make notes of which prophecies have been fulfilled already and which still await literal fulfilment. Then he can read the rest of the history book of the Old Testament and go on to Proverbs, Wisdom, Ecclesiasticus and Ecclesiastes. When he comes lastly to the Psalms, Job and the Song of Songs he will see that these have no historical meaning and he can begin to understand how to interpret allegorically by reading them as speaking of Christ and the Church.[131]

[131] *Epistola anonymi ad Hugonem amicum* (ed. Martène / Durand; Thesaurus Novus Anecdotorum i. 487–88).

Chapter Thirty-one

The Flourishing Era of Jewish Exegesis in Spain

31.1. The Linguistic School: Judah Ḥayyūj, Jonah ibn Janāḥ, Moses ibn Chiquitilla and Judah ibn Balʿam

By Aharon Maman, Jerusalem

Sources: Judah Ḥayyūj: S. Abramson, "Sefer Al-Tajnis le-R. Judah Ibn Balʿam", in: S. Lieberman / S. Abramson / E. Y. Kutscher / S. Esh (eds.), *Henoch Yalon Jubilee Volume on the occasion of his seventy-fifth birthday* (Jerusalem 1963) 51–149; *Tajnis* was reedited in Abramson, Shlosha Sefarim, 1976, 7–88, but his introduction was not reprinted); idem, "Min Kitāb Al-Nutaf le-R. Judah Ḥayyuj li-Shmuel beth", *Leshonenu* 42 (1978) 203–36, 43 (1979) 29–51; N. Allony (ed.), "qetaʿ ḥadash mi-sefer ha-qorḥah le-R. Judah Ḥayyūj", *BetM* (1963) 96–110 [repr. in: Allony, Missifrei, 1970, 1–15]; I. Eldar, "Qetaʿ min Kitāb Al-Nutaf le-R. Judah Ḥayyūj li-Trei-ʿAsar", *Leshonenu* 43 (1979) 259–54; 44 (1980) 240; A. E. Harkavy, "Un quatrième ouvrage de Juda Hayyoudj", *REJ* 31 (1895) 288-89; M. Jastrow (ed.), *The Weak and Geminative Verbs in Hebrew by Abu Zakariyya Yaḥya Ibn Dawud of Fez Known as Ḥayyuğ* (Leiden 1897); P. Kokowtzow, *Noviye Materiali dlya kharakteristiki Yehudi Khayudja, Samuila Nagida i nekotorikh drugikh predstaviteley evreiskoy filologicheskoy nauki v-x, xi i xii vieki* [= *K istorii srednevekovoy yevreyskoy filologii i yevreysko-arabskoy literaturi* II] (Peterbourg 1916, the Hebrew material was reprinted in Allony, Missifrei, 1970, 1–58, 193–204); J. W. Nutt (ed. & tr.), *Two treatises on verbs containing feeble and double letters by R. Yehuda Hayug of Fez, translated into Hebrew from the original Arabic by R. Moses Gikatilia of Cordova; to which is added the Treatise on punctuation by the same author tr. by Aben Ezra, ed. from Bodleian mss. with an English translation* (London and Berlin 1870); idem (ed.), *Kitāb Al-Tanqīt* ('The Book of Vocalization'), in: Nutt, Verbs, 1870 [between the Hebrew and the English parts, i. e. between p. 132 Hebrew and p. 146 English] (London 1870).

Ibn Janāḥ: W. Bacher (ed.), *Sepher Haschoraschim, Wurzelwoerterbuch der hebraeischen Sprache von Abulwalīd Merwan Ibn Ganāḥ (R. Jona). Aus dem Arabischen ins Hebraeische uebersetzt von Jehuda Ibn Tibbon* (Berlin 1896); J. et H. Derenbourg, *Opuscules et traités d'Abou'l-Walid Merwān Ibn Janāḥ* (Paris 1880); idem (ed.), *Le livre des parterres fleuris – Grammaire hébraïque d'Abou'l-walid Merwān Ibn Djanāḥ* [abbr. Luma'] (Paris 1886); A. Neubauer, *The Book of Hebrew Roots by Abu'l-Walid Marwan Ibn Janāḥ, Called Rabbi Jonah* (Oxford 1875); M. Wilensky / D. Téné, *Sefer ha-Riqmah (Kitāb al-Lumaʿ) le-R. Jonah Ibn Janāḥ be-targumo ha-ʿivri shel R. Judah Ibn Tibbon* (ed. by M. Willensky; Berlin 1929; sec. ed. by D. Téné; Jerusalem 1964).

Judah ibn Balʿam: S. Abramson (ed.), *Shlosha Sefarim shel Harav Judah Ibn Balʿam* (Jerusalem 1976); N. Allony, "Sheloshah qetaʿim ḥadashim me-ḥibburei Ibn Balʿam", *BetM* 9 (1964) 87–122; J. Derenbourg (ed.), *Gloses d'Abou Zachariya Ben Bilam sur Isaïe* (Paris 1892) (repr. from *REJ* 17–23 [1889–1892]); M. Goshen-Gottstein (ed. and tr.), "heʿteq perush 'al sefer Yehushuaʿ lerabi Yehudah ben rabi Shemuel ibn Balʿam misefat 'aravit (mitokh ketab yad Peterbourg" [abbr. Joshua], in: Beth-Gad, sefer ʿasara (1952) 31–37; idem (ed. and tr.), "heʿteq perush sefer Shoftim lerabi Yehudah ben rabi Shemuel ibn Balʿam misefat 'aravit" [abbr. Judges], in: Beth-Gad, sefer ʿasara (1952) 38–45; idem (ed. and tr.), "perush ʿal sefer Yirmeyah lerabi Yehudah ben rabi Shemuel ibn Balʿam" [abbr. Jeremiah], in: Beth-Gad, sefer ʿasara (1952) 45–47; idem, *R. Judah Ibn Balʿam's Commentary on Isaiah: The Arabic Original according to MS Firkovitch (Ebr-arab I 1377), with the assistance of Maʿaravi Perez* [abbr. Isaiah] (Ramat Gan: Bar-Ilan University Press 1992); J. Israelsohn (ed.), "Arabischer Kommentar zum Buche Jeremia von Jehuda ibn Balʿam", in: D.V. Guenzburg / I. Markon (eds.), *Festschrift zu Ehren des Dr. A. Harkavy* (St Petersbourg 1908), II [The Hebrew part] 273–308; M. Perez, "Qetaʿ mi-perush R. Judah ibn Balʿam le-sefer Neḥemya", *Leshonenu* 55 (1991) 315–22; idem, *Commentary on Numbers & Deuteronomy [from Kitāb al-Tarǧīḥ] by Jehuda b. Shmuel Ibn Balʿam* (Master Thesis in Hebrew; Bar-Ilan University, Ramat Gan 1970); S. Poznanski (ed.), "perush ʿal sefer Yehoshuaʿ lerabbi Yehudah ben Balʿam" [abbr. Joshua], in: A. Freimann / M. Hildesheimer (eds.), *Festschrift zum Siebziegsten Geburtstage A. Berliners* (Frankfurt/M 1903; the Hebrew part) 91–107; idem (ed.), *Judah Ibn Balʿam, perush ʿal sefer Shoftim* [abbr. Judges] (Frankfurt/M 1906); idem (ed.), "The Arabic Commentary of Abu Zakariya Yahya (Judah ben Samuel) Ibn Balʿam on the Twelve Minor Prophets", *JQR* NS 15 (1924/25) 1–53 (separate outprint; Philadelphia 1924); idem, "Mitteilungen aus handschriftlichen Bibel-Commentaren, I. Aus Jehuda Ibn Balʿam's Commentar zu II Samuel", *ZHB* 1 (1896/97) 96–99; M. Steinschneider, "Ein Unbekanntes Werk von Jehuda ibn Balam", *MGWJ* (1885) 287–89.

Ibn Chiquitilla: W. Bacher (ed.), "Arabische Uebersetzung und Arabischer Kommentar zum Buche Hiob von Mose ibn Chiquitilla", in D.V. Guenzburg / I. Markon (eds.), *Festschrift zu Ehren des Dr. A. Harkavy* (St Petersbourg 1908), I [The Hebrew part] 221–72; N. Allony, "Qetaʿim mi-perushei R. Moshe Hakohen Gikatila", *Sinai* 24 (1949) 138–47; A.E. Harkavy, "Un fragment du Livre des masculins et féminins de Moïse ibn Gikatilla", *REJ* 31 (1895) 288–89; M. Perez, "Another Fragment of the Commentary of R. Moshe ibn Giqatila to Psalms", *ʿAlei Sefer* 18 (Ramat Gan: Bar-Ilan University Press 1996) 49–57 (Heb.); idem, "Qetaʿ Genizah mi-perush R. Moshe ibn Gikatila li-Thillim (Ps. 9–10)", *Sinai* 106 (1990) 12–22; idem, "Qetaʿ 'aḥer mi-perush R. Moshe ibn Gikatila li-Thillim (Ps. 51:7–21; 52:1–6; 60:2–7)", *Sinai* 108 (1991) 32–44; idem, "Qetaʿ ḥadash mi-perush Moshe ibn Gikatila li-Thillim (Ps. 55:19–23; 56:3; 58:4–10)", *Sinai* 107 (1991) 1–11; S. Poznanski, *Moses b. Samuel Hakkohen ibn Chiquitilla nebst den Fragmenten seiner Schriften* (Leipzig 1895); idem, "Aus Mose ibn Chiquitilla's arabischem Psalmkommentar", *ZA* 26 (1912) 38–60.

Others: A. Sáenz-Badillos, *Teshubot de Dunash ben Labrat* (Granada 1980); idem, *Menaḥem Ben Saruq, Maḥberet* (Granada 1986); H. J. Beth-Gad (ed.), *Sefer ʿasara me'orot hagedolim uferusham ʿal hatora* (Johannesburg 1952); J. Finkel, "Perush R. Moses b. Samuel ibn Chiquitilla 'al Tehillim - ha-mizmorim 3, 4, 8", *Ḥoreb* [A Semi-Annual Journal devoted to Research in Jewish History and Literature] III (1936) 153–62.

General works: N. Allony (ed.), *Missifrei ha-balshanut haʿivrit bi-ymei ha-benayim* (Jerusalem 1970); W. Bacher (ed.), *Version Arabe du livre de Job. Œuvres Complètes de R. Saadia Ben Iosef Al-Fayyoumi* 5 (Paris 1893); – Judah Ḥayyūj: S. Abramson, "Peraqim she-nogʿim le-Rav Judah Ḥayyūj ul-Rav Jonah Ibn Janāḥ", *Leshonenu* 43 (1979) 260–64. – Ibn Janāḥ: W. Bacher, *Die hebraeisch-neuhebraeische und hebraeisch-aramaeische Sprachvergleichung des Abulwalid Marwan ibn Ganāḥ* (Wien 1885); idem, *Die hebraeisch-arabischen Sprachvergleichungen des Abulwalid Merwan ibn Ganāḥ* (Wien 1884); idem, *Aus der Schrifterklaerung des Abulwalid Merwan ibn Ganāḥ* [= Jahresbericht der Landes-Rabbinerschule in Budapest fuer das Schuljahr 1888–89] (Budapest 1889); idem, "Die Wortvertauschung im Kitāb al-Luma des Abulwalid", *MGWJ* 55 (1911) 233–40; D. Herzog, "Die 'Wortvertauschungen' im Kitāb al-Luma des Abulwalid Merwan Ibn Ganāḥ und in den Schriften A. Ibn Esra's", *MGWJ* 53 (1909) 709–19; 54 (1910) 82–102; S. Munk, "Notice sur Abou'l-walid Merwan ibn Djana'h et sur quelques autres grammairiens Hébreux au Xe et XIe siècle", *JA* XV (1850) 297–337, XVI (1851) 5–50; 201–47; 353–427 (separate printout: Paris 1851). – Judah ibn Balʿam: W. Bacher, "Jehuda Ibn Balaams Jesaja Commentar", *ZAW* 13 (1893) 129–55 [review of Derenbourg, *Ibn Balʿam*]; S. Fuchs, *Studien ueber Abou Zakaria Jachja (R. Jehuda) Ibn Balʿam* (Berlin 1893; review: S. Poznanski, *MGWJ* 38 [1894] 381–84); A. Maman, "Goshen's Judah Ibn Balʿam's Commentary on Isaiah" [review of Goshen-Gottstein, Isaiah] *JQR* 86 (1996) 468–76; M. Perez, *The Philological Exegesis of R. Jehuda Ibn Balʿam: Methodological and Typological Studies on his Commentary on Isaiah as Compared with R. Saadia's Tafsir* (Dissertation., Bar-Ilan University; Ramat-Gan 1978); idem, "Ha-tippul be-millim jeḥida'iyot be-shorshan be-perushei R. Judah Ibn Balʿam", *Leshonenu* 45 (1981) 213–32. — Others: E. ben Yehuda, *A Complete Dictionary of Ancient and Modern Hebrew* (Jerusalem 1911–1959); J. Derenbourg (ed.), *Œuvres Complètes de R. Saadia ben Iosef Al-Fayyoumi* I. *Version Arabe du Pentateuque* (Paris 1893); A. Harkavy, "Miscellen", *ZHB* 5 (1901) 95; M. Held, "'od zugot millim maqbilot ba-miqra uv-kitvei ugarit", *Leshonenu* 18 (1953); A. Maman, *The Comparison of the Hebrew Lexicon with Arabic and Aramaic in the Linguistic Literature of the Jews from Rav Saadia Gaon (10th cent.) to Ibn Barun (12th cent.)* (Jerusalem 1984); idem, "The Contribution of Aramaic and Arabic to the Medieval Philological Exegesis of the Bible", Am Vasefer [Organ of Brit Ivrit Olamit] 7 (Jerusalem 1992) 25–37 (Heb.); J. Muilenburg, "The linguistic and rhetorical usages of the particle כי in the Old Testament", HUCA 32 (1961) 135–60; N. Netzer, *Mishnaic Hebrew in the Works of Medieval Hebrew Grammarians (During the Period of Original Creativity: Saadia Gaon – Ibn Balʿam)* (Raman Gan: Bar-Ilan University 1983); A. Neubauer, "Notice sur la lexicographie hébraïque avec des remarques sur quelques grammairiens postérieurs à Ibn Djana'h", *JA* 13–20 (1861/62) (Separate printout: Paris 1863); M. Perez, "'Substitution' of one Word for another as an exegetical Method used by Medieval Scholars", *Studies in Bible and Exegesis* II (1986) 207–28; S. Poznanski, "Les ouvrages linguistiques de Samuel Hannaguid", *REJ* 57/58 (1909) 253–67; idem, "Hebraeisch-arabische Sprachvergleichungen bei Jehuda Ibn Balʿam", *ZDMG* 70 (1916) 447–76; A. S. Rabinovitz (ed.), *Perush le-Kitvei ha-Qodesh me'et Avi ha-Medaqdeqim veha-Parshanim R. Jonah ha-Sefaradi Ibn Janāḥ* (Tel-Aviv 1926); N. M. Sarna, "Hebrew and Bible Studies in Medieval Spain", in: R. D. Barnett (ed.), *The Sephardi Heritage – Essays in the History and Cultural Contribution of the Jews of Spain and Portugal* (London 1971) 323–66; U. Simon, *arbaʿ guishot lesefer tehillim meRasag ʿad Rabaʿ* (Ramat Gan 1982) 99–104; idem, "Ibn Ezra's Harsh Language and Biting Humour – Real Denunciation or Hispanic Mannerism?", *Teʿuda* 8, *Studies in the works of Abraham Ibn Ezra* (Tel Aviv University 1992) 111–20; S. L. Skoss, *The Hebrew-Arabic Dictionary of the Bible known as Kitāb Jāmiʿ Al-Alfāẓ (Agron) of David ben Abraham Al-Fāsi the karaite (Tenth century)* I–II (New Haven 1936, 1945); M. Steinschneider, *Die Arabische Literatur der Juden* (Frankfurt/M 1902); D. Téné, "The Earliest Comparisons of Hebrew with Aramaic and Arabic", in: K. Koerner (ed.), *Progress in Linguistic Historiography* (Studies in the History of Linguistics 20, Amsterdam Studies in the Theory and History of Linguistic Science III; Amsterdam 1980) 355–77; idem, "hashva'at ha-leshonot viydiʿat ha-lashon be-'ezor ha-dibbur ha-ʿaravi ba-me'ot ha-yod veha-yod-'aleph la-minyan ha-mqubbal", in: M. Bar-Asher et al. (eds.), *Hebrew Language Studies Presented to Professor Zeev Ben-Hayyim* (Jerusalem 1983) 237–87; idem, "Linguistic Literature, Hebrew", EncJud 16 (1971) 1352–90; M. Wilensky, *Meḥqarim be-Lashon ub-Sifrut* (Jerusalem 1978) 35–39 [previously in *Monatsschrift* 90 (1928) 99].

1. Judah Ḥayyūj

Judah Ḥayyūj from Fez, Morocco, who lived and worked in Cordova, Spain, in the last third of the tenth cent. CE, constitutes a turning point in the development of Hebrew linguistics and biblical exegesis. Ḥayyūj is the founder of the triliteral theory in the Hebrew verb – including verbs with weak radicals, א, ו, י or final ה, as well as initial נ, and geminates. The change towards the concept of a Hebrew root has influenced the analysis and understanding of the biblical lexicon with regard to its etymology, morphology and semantics.[1]

Ḥayyūj wrote four books, three on grammar[2] and one on biblical exegesis, *Kitāb Al-Nutaf*,[3] in which he realized his grammatical approach. His grammatical works have survived in full, but only parts of *Nutaf* are still in existence,

[1] Téné, Linguistic (1971); Sarna, Hebrew and Bible Studies (1976) 337–38.

[2] Jastrow, Verbs (1897); Nutt, Tanqit (1870).

[3] Henceforth: *Nutaf*, "The Book of Plucked Feathers", i. e. Selected Exegetical Notes, referred to by A. ibn Ezra (12th cent. CE) as *Sefer ha-Qorḥah*, "The Book of Baldness", and later on as *Sefer ha-Roqḥah*, "The Book of Jam", by a mistaken metathesis.

some of which have been published.[4] *Nutaf* covered only the books of the prophets and comprised eight chapters, corresponding to the number of the former and latter books of the prophets. This is clearly learned from Ḥayyūj's introduction to *Nutaf*, at the very beginning of his commentary on Joshua, and at the end of his commentary on Malachi. The extant portions of *Nutaf* contain parts of the commentary on Joshua,[5] Judges,[6] 2 Samuel,[7] 1 Kings, Isaiah, Jeremiah, Ezekiel[8] and Minor Prophets.[9]

Ḥayyūj explains only difficult and rare words and forms, for grammar or etymology, but not common words or regular forms. Seldom does he deal also with general questions, such as the importance of accentuation in exegesis. *Nutaf* is so grammatical in character that a great linguist and biblical exegete, Tanḥum Hayrushalmi (13th cent. CE), made the mistake of regarding it as merely a supplement to what Ḥayyūj had left out in his three grammatical works, organized in the order of the biblical text.[10] A statistical breakdown provides some idea of the nature of *Nutaf*: the remnants of the commentary on Malachi contain six items on grammar, one on lexicon and only two comments on the content.

1.1. Triliterality of the Hebrew Root

The most outstanding characteristic of Ḥayyūj's exegesis is his linguistic understanding of universal triliterality in the Hebrew verb and in the majority of the nouns.[11] This characteristic is true also of the other exegetes discussed here, and it separates them from their predecessors. The primitive understanding of the root before Ḥayyūj artificially brought together entry-words that were far apart and created forced semantic relationships. As an example, the first section of root ב-ך in *Maḥberet Menaḥem,*[12] which uses the old morphological system, contains these verses: *מבכי* נהרות חבש (Job 28:11); *נבכי* ים (Job 38:16); עמק *הבכא* (Ps 84:7) *נבוכו* עדרי בקר (Joel 1:18) and *ויתאבכו* גאות עשן (Isa 9:17). Menaḥem explained all of them from the meaning of 'movement'. Following his approach, Menaḥem viewed these five words as derived from the same root ב-ך; he therefore forced all of them to fit into one single meaning, 'movement'. But from Ḥayyūj onward they have been regarded as three

---

[4] Harkavy, Un quatrième ouvrage (1895) 288–89, discovered them in the library of St. Petersburg; Kokowtzow, Noviye (1916); Allony, Qorḥah (1963); Abramson, Nutaf (1978); Abramson, Peraqim (1979); Eldar, Nutaf (1979). Some additional parts of *Nutaf* were recently found in the National Library of Russia, and they will be published by N. Bassel.

[5] Edited by Allony.

[6] Edited by Allony and Abramson.

[7] Edited by Kokowtzow, and cf. especially the reconstruction by Abramson.

[8] Edited by Kokowtzow.

[9] Edited by Eldar.

[10] See the excerpt from Tanḥum's inroduction to his commentary on the Pentateuch, presented by Harkavy, Un quatrième ouvrage (1895) 288; Abramson, Nutaf (1978) 201.

[11] Téné, Linguistic (1971).

[12] Sáenz-Badillos, Maḥberet (1986).

separate roots א-ב-ך, ב-ו-ך, (ב-כ-א) ב-כ-י, each with its own meaning – e.g. א-ב-ך explained by Ibn Janāḥ,[13] 'pick up, go up or evaporate'.

A second example: In the first section of root כ-ס Menaḥem includes והרמת *מכס* (Num 31:28), *מכסת* נפשות (Exod 12:4), *תכסו* על השה (ibid.), ליום *הכסה* יבא ביתו (Prov 16:11), *בכסה* ליום חגנו (Ps 81:4), לא יהיה לך *בכיסך* אבן ואבן (Deut 25:13), *כיס* אחד יהיה לכלנו (Prov 1:14), אבני *כיס* (Prov 16:11) and even ה' מנת חלקי *וכוסי* (Ps 16:5) and הצילני מאויבי ה' אליך *כסיתי* (ibid. 143:9), all in one and the same entry with the same basic meaning of 'counting, calculating, dividing into portions, measuring or weighing'.[14] Ḥayyūj and his successors, however, no longer associated the words מכסה, תכסו, הכסה, בכסה, כיס, מכס and כוס with one meaning and certainly not with a single root. Even words that, according to Ḥayyūj and modern scholars, have some semantic relationships – such as בלותי (Gen 18:12), יבול (Ps 1:3) and נבל תבל (Exod 18:18), which were regarded by the ancients as variations of the same root[15] – were regarded by Ḥayyūj and his successors as different roots.

1.2. Characteristics of the Philological Exegesis

Ḥayyūj emphasized the grammatical and etymological analysis, since the main purpose of his approach was to establish the precise etymology of every root and to remove any confusion that had existed prior to him. In fact, the primary difference between Ḥayyūj's exegetical approach and that of his predecessors consists of the grammatical analysis of the word and its meaning. It is for this reason that Ḥayyūj is concerned with the mistakes of his predecessors and makes efforts to eliminate them, e.g. in *מטי* גר (Mal 3:5) he says that the basic form is *מנטי** since it is derived from נ-ט-ה; that the construct plural form is *מטי* גר, whereas the absolute form is *מטים* like *והמטים* עקלקלותם (Ps 125:5); but *ומטים* להרג (Prov 24:11) is not from this paradigm "as thought some of those who do not know the language...".[16]

Aside from the morphological analysis, Ḥayyūj explains sometimes in *Nutaf* the punctuation or the place of the tone, particularly in unusual cases, and as far as the discussed words have close forms, like a shortened form compared to the full one; for instance, וַיְהִי, dealt with at the beginning of *Nutaf*, is explained as a shortened form from the assumed full equivalent וַיִּהְיֶה and from the pausal form וַיֶּהִי (with segol). Sometimes he comments on superfluous letters, e.g. the final yod in מלאתי משפט (Isa 1:21), רבתי עם (Lam 1:1), and

13 Neubauer, Hebrew Roots (1875).

14 Sáenz-Badillos, Maḥberet s.v.

15 E.g. the eighth section of the entry ב-ל in the Maḥberet; and so for many entries there, e.g. root ד-ף, which includes קול עלה *נדף* (Lev 26:36), *להדף* את כל אויביך (Deut 6:19); and root ה-ם, which includes *המו* גוים (Ps 46:7), *נהם* ככפיר (Prov 19:12), and *תהומות* (Ex 15:5). Many more exemples can be seen in Alfāsi (Skoss, Hebrew-Arabic Dictionary).

16 In fact, a semantic and etymological confusion of the roots נ-ט-ה and מ-ו-ט existed prior to Ḥayyūj, examples being David b. Abraham Alfāsi and Menaḥem b. Saruq. See Eldar, Nutaf (1979) 257 and n. 2.

מדושתי ובן גרני (Isa 21:10), and on missing letters, as in למרות (Isa 3:8) standing for להמרות, or מורט (Isa 18:2) for ממורט.[17]

Ḥayyūj also comments on syntax, including word order (*taqdīm wa-ta'khīr*). In his commentary on Judg 7:15, Ḥayyūj presented a list of verses where a word should be transposed, e.g. אכלו וישתחוו כל דשני ארץ (Ps 22:30) should be אכלו כל דשני ארץ וישתחוו and בשנה הרביעית בחדש זיו הוא החדש השני למלך שלמה (1 Kgs 6:1) really means בשנה הרביעית למלך שלמה בחדש זיו הוא החדש השני; also ויהי ממחרת החדש השני (1 Sam 20:27) should be ויהי ממחרת השני מהחדש; and ונחתה קשת נחושה זרועותי (Ps 18:35) means זרועותי נחתה קשת נחושה. There are times where he assumed an ellipsis, e.g. הוי אנחם מצרי (Isa 1:24) means מרעת צרי ומנקמתם. Sometimes he gives the syntax of a word, e.g. עמנואל (Isa 8:8),[18] which is, in his view, either a predicate or a vocative. He also deals with verbs that may govern two objects, with asyndetic sentences, and the like.

Since he also founded the paradigm of conjugations, as accepted to this day (along with the notion of verb groups), let us examine one example, which is morphologically ambiguous. In the parable of Yotam, in Judg 9:9, the verb החדלתי (את דשני) is viewed by Ibn Janāḥ[19] as conjugated in hif'il with a missing questional *he*. However, Ḥayyūj explained it as "*Am I lacking* oil", which implies that we have here a qal conjugation form with questional *he* ה-חדלתי. It appears that he understood the use of the tense *qatal* in חדלתי a participle or an adjective, as it is in the verses ה' אלהי גדלת מאד (Ps 104:1) ("You are great, mighty"), מה רבו מעשיך (Ps 104:24) ("How many are your deeds!"), and many others.

Occasionally in his explanations he followed in the footsteps of the Targum, such as הכרתי והפלתי (2 Sam 8:18) which are "those who shoot with a rainbow".[20] At times he resorted to the Masorah comments, in particular in questions of Qere and Ketib, which amazingly he regarded as two living linguistic traditions that the Masoretes sought to preserve.[21]

The philological exegesis started with Saadiah Gaon, three generations before Ḥayyūj, but Ḥayyūj brought it to a peak and shaped it into a scientific system. He strove to reach the simple meaning of the text. His explanations are very brief, excursuses being rare, and philosophical or theological discussions are completely missing. Ḥayyūj's style is not polemic. Unlike Saadiah, he would not enter into a polemic against the Trinity in Christianity, nor would he argue with Islam. In all these ways Ḥayyūj established a standard for his successors.

---

[17] He also offered an alternative analysis.
[18] Allony, Missifrei (1970) 17.
[19] Neubauer, Hebrew Roots (1875) 211.
[20] Abramson, Nutaf (1978) 29–30.
[21] See, for instance, his commentary on 2 Sam 3:25; 11:24; 12:31 (Abramson, Nutaf (1978) 29–30); 1 Kgs 12:33; 16:25,

1.3. Ḥayyūj's Successors

Ḥayyūj's theory of the triliterality of the Hebrew root and his linguistic approach were accepted with excitement by Hebrew grammarians and exegetes in his time and after, with the exception of three types of writers: (a) those who lived so far from Spain as to be unable to hear of them, such as R. Hai Gaon (Babylonia, 939–1038) – whose dictionary *Kitāb al-Ḥāwī* still follows the old grammatical system;[22] (b) those who were unable to read Ḥayyūj's works in their original Arabic,[23] such as Rashi (1040–1105) in France; and (c) those who were aware of Ḥayyūj's theory but preferred to stick to their own tradition, such as the Karaite Abū-l-Farāj Hārun, who lived and worked in Jerusalem in the first half of the eleventh cent. CE and was the author of the magnum opus *אלכתאב אלמשתמל עלי אלאצול ואלפצול פי אללגה אלעבראניה*, completed in 1026,[24] as well as his anonymous epigone, the author of מאור עין at the end of the eleventh cent. With these exceptions, Ḥayyūj's theory was accepted throughout the world of linguistics; and before long, after Ḥayyūj's and Ibn Janāḥ's works had been translated into Hebrew, they were accepted also in Ashkenaz, as in *Sefer ha-Shoham* of R. Moses b. ha-Nesi'ah in England, and became fundamental in linguistics and exegesis, as they still are.

2. Jonah ibn Janāḥ

The first to develop and to realize in full Ḥayyūj's system of Hebrew linguistics was the Spaniard Jonah ibn Janāḥ (first half of the 11th cent. CE), the greatest Hebrew grammarian and lexicographer after Ḥayyūj.[25]

---

[22] Unless one assumes that R. Hai wrote his *Kitāb al-Ḥāwī* before Ḥayyūj formulated and published his new system, in which case, R. Hai should not be included in the list.

[23] In the course of time, Ḥayyūj's grammatical works were translated into Hebrew, first by Moses ibn Chiquitilla and later by Abraham ibn Ezra.

[24] Cf. W. Bacher, "Le grammairien anonyme de Jérusalem", *REJ* 30 (1895) 232–56; S. Poznanski, "Aboul-Faradj Haroun Ben Al-Faradj le grammairian de Jérusalem et son Moushchamil", *REJ* 33 (1896) 24–39, 197–218; idem, "Nouveaux Renseignements sur Aboul-Faradj Haroun Ben Al-Faradj et ses ouvrages", *REJ* 55 (1908) 42–69; H. Hirschfeld, *Arabic Chrestomathy in Hebrew Characters* (London 1892) 54–60; idem, "An Unknown Grammatical Work by Abūl-Faraj Harūn", *JQR* NS 13 (1922/23) 1–7; A. Maman, "Medieval Grammatical Thought: Karaites vs. Rabbanites", *Language Studies* 7 (Jerusalem 1995) 79–96 (Heb.); idem, "The ʿAmal Theory in the Grammatical thought of Abū-l-Faraj Harūn", *Massorot* 9–11 (1997) 263–74 (Heb.); and his anonymous epigone, the author of *Me'or ʿAyin,* cf. M. Zislin'(ed.), *Me'or ʿAyin* (Moscow 1990; Heb. and Russian).

[25] Had *Kitāb al-'Istighnā'* ('Book of Amplitude') of Samuel ha-Nagid (Kokowtzow, Noviye, 205–24 [Hebrew part]; Poznanski, Hannaguid, and Téné, Lingiustic) not been almost completely lost one might have judged Ha-Nagid to be a greater lexicographer. A. ibn Ezra praised this dictionary in his book *Moznei leshon ha-qodesh, Libra linguae sacrae* (ed. W. Heidenheim; Offenbach 1791) 2b; see also Sarna, Hebrew and Bible Studies (1971) 339.

2.1. His Philological Work

Ibn Janāḥ wrote books that were complementary to the works of Ḥayyūj: *Kitāb al-Mustalḥaq* and other lesser works (Dérenbourg, *Opuscules*, 1880). Later he wrote an exhaustive grammar and lexicon on biblical Hebrew, *Kitāb al-Tanqīḥ*,[26] where he gave a full description of biblical Hebrew. These works, along with those of Ḥayyūj, had a decisive influence[27] on his successors, to the extent that one can say they were merely his epigones. Many of their works were based on the books of Ibn Janāḥ, including some of Judah ibn Balʿam and Moses Chiquitilla, who lived and worked in Spain one generation after Ibn Janāḥ.

As opposed to the other three scholars discussed here, Ibn Janāḥ focused on the linguistic literary genre and did not dedicate a separate work to exegesis. Nevertheless, in his grammar and dictionary he explained many verses and even entire sections and topics of biblical exegesis, much as the early geonim wrote on exegesis indirectly in their responsa and other halakhic works.[28] *Mustalḥaq*, his first work, already contained exegetical excursuses. In various places in his dictionary Ibn Janāḥ does not confine himself to simply explaining the entry-word itself, rather he explains the entire biblical context in which it occurs, and in this regard it is an obvious exegetical tool. Beyond this, in his introduction to *Sefer ha-Riqmah* he says explicitly that understanding language is crucial for understanding the Bible, and this understanding is a precondition for keeping commandments.[29] All Ḥayyūj's grammatical and exegetical characteristics are found also in the works of Ibn Janāḥ and even more so, for his dictionary contains most of the biblical entry-words.[30] Ibn Janāḥ did not know *Nutaf*[31] and was not able to respond to Ḥayyūj's commentaries, except for those implied by the grammatical analyses in his other books.

The majority of the final twenty-one chapters of *Sefer ha-Riqmah* (XXVI–XLVI) deals with exegetical tools – such as additional letters or words for emphasis, including the emphatic ל (XXVI); the plural of plural or the unnecessary plural (e.g. לאחותיכם, Hos 2:3); the emphatic repetition of a word or constructional repetition; the use of a word in the meaning of another (XXVIII), including various types of metaphor and metonymy, synecdoche, synesthesia and others; masculine in place of feminine, based on the content and not on the language; attraction; substitution of one verbal form for an-

[26] Dérenbourg, Lumaʿ (Heb. version: Wilensky / Téné, Riqmah); and Neubauer, Hebrew Roots (1875); (Heb. version: Bacher, Shorashim).

[27] Because of the loss of Ha-Nagid's *Kitāb al-'Istighnā'* one is unable to estimate the extent of his influence.

[28] See Robert Brody, "The Geonim of Babylonia as Biblical Exegetes", Chap. 25.3 above.

[29] In Simon's opinion (Ibn Ezra [1992] 115) the Spanish exegetes viewed philology and theology as two interdependent disciplines, for a proper philology prevents mistakes in the field of faith, and vice versa.

[30] Ibn Janāḥ did not explain the entry-words appearing in Ḥayyūj's grammatical lexicons, but rather referred to Ḥayyūj's works and to his Mustalḥaq. Other entries were left unexplained, because they were "known".

[31] Abramson, Nutaf (1978) 229–30; Eldar, Nutaf (1979) 258, n. 6.

other, such as the infinitive form instead of a finite verb; use of an adjective instead of a verb (e.g. Eccl 1:8: כל הדברים *יגעים* means כל הדברים *מייגעים*), and other substitutions,[32] including one proper name for another (e.g. יעקב in place of אהרן or מיכל in place of מירב); ellipsis; word order; and many more.

These remarks are not emendations to the biblical text, as might be imagined, rather they are explanations and clarifications of legitimate usages in biblical Hebrew in the way of *taqdīr* ('estimation'), even if they are not based on *qiyās* ('syllogism'). For instance, *וזה* הדבר אשר מל יהושע (Jos 5:4) means *ואלה האנשים* and אם זרחה השמש עליו (Exod 22:2) is explained as אם עין העדים נפלה עליו, following the Targum אם עינא דסהדיא נפלת עלוהי ("If the eye of the witnesses saw him"). אסרו *חג* בעבותים (Ps 118:27) really means הכבשים אשר נשחטים *בחג* ("the sheep slaughtered on the holiday"). It is self-evident that all of these are not emendations; therefore his other exegetical techniques also are not emendations, but rather comments, even if they entail letter changes, metathesis, or other oddities that oppose the *qiyās* or the ordinary usage. Bacher[33] dealt with the methods of Ibn Janāḥ's exegesis, and in order to give Ibn Janāḥ's words the nature of a continuous commentary to the Bible, he collected about four hundred verses on which Ibn Janāḥ had commented in his grammars or in his dictionary and arranged them according to their occurrence in the Bible. This figure does not include the verses that Bacher presented in the theoretical part of his book.[34] In his introduction, Bacher expressed the wish that all the exegetical comments of Ibn Janāḥ be collected and organized as one flowing commentary. Rabinovitz (*Perush*, 1926) attempted to realize this wish; he collected about 1,500 verses commented on by Ibn Janāḥ and organized them in the biblical order, but his work received sharp criticism from Wilensky (*Meḥqarim,* 1978). Therefore this task still remains to be done.[35]

Aside from the radical change in exegesis that resulted from Ḥayyūj's revolution in understanding the Hebrew root, Ibn Janāḥ rejected the *derash* approach, which had been common in the traditional exegesis; for example, previous commentators suggested viewing within מנלם (Job 15:29) an acronym of מן + לם. This is Jonathan's translation, and it is Rashi's first suggestion, as well as that of exegetes who followed in their footsteps – from Nahmanides

---

[32] Herzog, Wortvertauschungen (1909/10); Bacher, Wortvertauschung (1911); Perez, Substitution (1896) 207–23, 215–17.

[33] Schrifterklaerung (1889) 92–111.

[34] Where Bacher describes in detail Ibn Janāḥ's methods of exegesis, e.g. ellipsis (1–11), paronomasia (11–15), word order (15–19), rhetoric (30–41), synonymy (49–56), parallelisms (72–81). See also Sarna, Hebrew and Bible Studies (1971) 347.

[35] Not all of Ibn Janāḥ's exegetical methods were accepted by his successors. A. ibn Ezra, for instance, opposed the technique of substituting one word for another and the interchange of letters and transposition. See, for instance, his commentary on Gen 20:2; Exod 19:12; Dan 1:1. This topic is generally discussed by Herzog, ibid.; Bacher, Wortvertauschung (1911); idem, Schrifterklaerung (1889) 28–29; Perez, Substitution (1986); Simon, Ibn Ezra (1992) 111 ff, and A. Sáenz-Badillos, "Some basic Concepts in the Linguistic System of Abraham Ibn ʿEzra", in M. Bar-Asher (ed.), *Studies in Hebrew and Jewish Language, Presented to Shelomo Morag* (Jerusalem 1996), *125–*149, esp. par. 3. See also L. Charlap, *Innovation and Tradition in Rabbi Abraham Ibn-Ezra's Grammar according to his Grammatical Writings and to his Bible Exegesis* (Ph. D. thesis, Bar-Ilan University; Ramat-Gan 1995) 268.

until the Vilna Gaon up to the modern exegetes. But acronyms are a clear example of the *derash* approach. The pursuers of the *peshat* preferred to see מנלם as one word. Saadiah had explained it as מלם ("their speech") "ornamented" (*mufakhkham*) by נ,[36] acceptable on account of his approach in both Hebrew and Aramaic morphology. Alfāsi derived it from the root נ-ל and explained it as 'property', based on a similar sounding Arabic word, מנאלהם. Ibn Janāh[37] derived it from נ-ל-ה meaning 'completing / completeness', and Ibn Ezra and many others followed him in this.[38]

2.2. The Comparison with Rabbinic Hebrew

Ibn Janāḥ based his exegesis also on comparisons of the biblical vocabulary with the rabbinic Hebrew vocabulary. Neubauer (Notice, 1861/62, 231 ff.) was the first to deal with this subject; later, Bacher (Sprachvergleichung, 1885) gathered many of these comparisons; more recently, this material was comprehensively collected by Netzer (Mishnaic Hebrew, 1983, 176–304). Ibn Janāḥ's predecessors, like Saadiah, Ibn Quraysh and Alfāsi also used this technique, and occasionally Ibn Janāḥ adopted their view, e.g. יכרסמנה (Ps 80:14) was compared by Saadiah in *Sab'īn Lafẓa* with[39] קרסמוה. By adopting this practice, Ibn Janāḥ expressed his opposition to the acronym *ימלא כרסו ממנה* suggested by Alfāsi and Menaḥem and already rejected by Dunash.[40] But Ibn Janāḥ turned the method of comparison into a well-founded and systematic tool in biblical exegesis and compared 303 entries.[41] Most of his comparisons were original and all were instructive; for, after all, Ibn Janāḥ never resorted to trivial comparisons, just as in his dictionary he never defined 'known' words. Among his comparisons one can find וישאם (2 Sam 5:21) meaning "he burned them", based on the comparison with משיאין משואות (lighting bonfires).[42] With this comparison he removed any concern that the reader would understand וישאם, referring to the act of King David and his men with the Philistine idols after the war in Baal-Peratsim, in its standard meaning, "he took them". Anyone who understood it that way would likely attribute to David and his men, a sin against the word of God because the Torah warns against idolatry in many places, among them פסילי אלהיהם תשרפון באש (Deut 7:25) ("burn their idols in fire"). With this explanation Ibn Janāḥ resolved also the textual difference between 2 Samuel and its parallel in 1 Chr 14:12, ויאמר דוד וישרפו באש ("and David commended and they burned them"), and also provided a basis for the Aramaic Targum.

---

36 Bacher, Job (1908) 51.
37 Mustalḥaq 157.
38 Maman, Contribution (1993) 31–32, and nn. 39–51.
39 *Pe'a* 2:7; Netzer, Mishnaic Hebrew (1983) 269.
40 Sáenz-Badillos, Teshubot (1980) *55.
41 Netzer, ibid. 299.
42 *Roš Haš.* 2:3; Netzer, ibid. 253.

2.3. *Ibn Janāḥ and the Opinions of the Sages*

In the introduction to *Kitāb al-Tanqīḥ*, Ibn Janāḥ states that his exegetical innovations are not popular among his critics because he "opposes the opinions of our Rabbis", but he claims in response that "they did not pay attention to the words of our Rabbis, of blessed memory: אין מקרא יוצא מידי פשוטו (*b. Šabb.* 63a) ("a verse does not leave its simple meaning"); and they also said פשטיה דקרא לחוד והלכה לחוד (*b. Yebam.* 24a) ("a verse's simple meaning is independent of halakhah") because one expression may have two or more correct meanings, as our Rabbis said: מקרא אחד יוצא לכמה טעמים ("one verse can have many meanings")".[43] In the eyes of Ibn Janāḥ, there is no doubt as to the authority of the Rabbis, of their traditional exegesis, and he never feels that he is arguing with them, but only adding to them. There are even cases where he expresses his opinion and then withdraws it in light of the Rabbis' opinion. Ibn Janāḥ refrains from *peshat* explanations only when they would directly contradict a law established by the Rabbis.[44]

But at times his comment appears to contradict the Rabbis regarding the law, as in the case of a "pierced-ear" Hebrew slave. The Torah says that this slave should work for his master *לעולם* (Exod 21:6), meaning literally 'forever'; but as is known, the Rabbis rather explained this word as "until the Jubilee" (*b. Qidd.* 15a). Ibn Janāḥ shockingly explained it as "for the entire life of the servant or of the master".[45] However, halakhic scholars have attempted to resolve the conflict between the *peshat* and the *derash*, regarding the halakhah and its development.[46]

2.4. *The Comparison with Aramaic and Arabic*

A decisive contribution of Ibn Janāḥ to the philological exegesis of the Bible is based on his systematic and in-depth comparisons with Aramaic and Arabic.[47] The comparison with Arabic intensified the self-confidence of the "pursuers of *peshat*" among the medieval commentators in their ability to arrive at the exegetical truth, which in their eyes, was absolute and unique. Just as the contribution of the Semitic languages to the philological exegesis of the Bible, dis-

---

[43] Wilensky / Téné, Riqmah (1929) XVIII–XIX.

[44] For example, Bacher, Shorashim (1896) 51–52; Maman, Contribution (1992) 36, and n. 59.

[45] Bacher, Shorashim 372.

[46] See, for instance, D. Henschke, "אין מקרא יוצא מידי פשוטו", *Hamma'yan* 17 (Tammuz 1977), C, 7–19; D, 52–69; and generally: E. E. Urbach, *The Halakhah – Its Sources and Development* (1986), esp. chapter 7: Interpretation as the source of Halakhah (93–108), and chapter 8: Laws and supports (102–24). As against Ibn Janāḥ, David Qimhi simply defined ועבדו לעולם in his dictionary (entry ע-ל-ם) "up to the Jubilee", even without attributing his explanation to the Rabbis. Cf. Rabbi Davidis Kimchi, *Radicum Liber sive Hebraeum Bibliorum Lexicon* (ed. J. Biesenthal et F. Lebrecht; Berolini 1847).

[47] Neubauer, Notice (1861/62) 231 ff; Bacher, Sprachvergleichungen (1884); Bacher, Sprachvergleichung (1885); Sarna, Hebrew and Bible Studies (1971) 344; Téné, hashva'at (1983); Téné, Comparison (1980); Maman, Comparison (1984).

covered in the recent generations, is great and strong, so also was the contribution of Arabic and Aramaic some thousand years ago, in spite of all differences that result from the different personalities involved in the field, at different times and places. That is to say, Arabic and Aramaic in their time were instrumental just as Akkadian and Ugaritic have been in the modern period. The main contribution to biblical philology, then as now, is in the area of decoding and explaining esoteric expressions and *hapax legomena* whose meaning was obscure.

The fact that Arabic was a living language was accorded a great importance in biblical commentaries in the Middle Ages. An important part of the biblical lexicon suffered from lack of a verified tradition of meaning, because Hebrew ceased to be a spoken language in the second century CE. This rupture in the continuity of speech resulted in the meaning of a large part of Hebrew *realia* terms being forgotten. Moses ibn Chiquitilla expressed this quite well in his introduction to his translation of Ḥayyūj's works.[48] For example, one knows about the indecisiveness of early and late scholars regarding the nature of כינור and שכוי[49] and other biblical nouns of flora and fauna and other *realia* terms.[50] Nevertheless the exegete or the lexicographer was required to cope with the meaning of every term in the Bible, even if no unequivocal tradition had survived. The encounter with Arabic, which has served continuously for hundreds of years as a living language, provided a solution to this problem to a certain degree. For instance, the word מלתחה (2 Kgs 10:22) is a *hapax* and also is not attested in post-biblical Hebrew. Where there was no traditional explanation or usage, the earlier Rabbis were indecisive as to its meaning. Ibn Janāḥ found the meaning of this word by comparing it with Arabic, with the mediation of Aramaic. He says: "Probably this is a name for a utensil where clothes are put, as the Targum says קמטריא; now קמטר in Arabic is a box".[51]

A quite sophisticated tripartite pattern is used here, which combines the comparison of a biblical word with words from Targumic Aramaic and Arabic. The Hebrew word in itself, here מלתחה, is semantically obscure, for the reason mentioned above. Yet it has a translationally equivalent Aramaic in the Targum, which *a priori* served as an exegetical tool, here קמטריא. But Aramaic too ceased to be spoken among the majority of the Jews during the seventh century CE, so that many Aramaic *realia* terms, that were current in the time of the writing of the Targum, became obscure. Ibn Janāḥ found a solution by means of the third element, namely the Arabic קמטר, which is a cognate of the Aramaic קמטר. The referent of the Arabic word is known because of the daily continuous use of Arabic. Its cognate relationship to the Aramaic קמטרא makes the Aramaic clear, and this in turn explains the Hebrew, since they are translational synonyms (קמטרא / מלתחה). This is a triple thread, through which the Hebrew term is interwoven with its Aramaic and Arabic equivalents to obtain a meaning. Ibn Janāḥ used this pattern in many comparisons. It ap-

48 Nutt, Verbs (1880) 1.
49 See e. g. Ben Yehudah, Dictionary 7562.
50 See e.g. Ibn Ezra's comment on Dan 2:3.
51 Neubauer, Hebrew Roots (1875) 360; Bacher, Shorashim (1896) 250.

pears that the fourth of the 22 rules of R. Samuel b. Ḥofni, that the exegete has to be an expert in linguistics and to know all the nouns, both frequent and rare, including *realia* terms, was finally realized through comparative philology.

Ḥayyūj's comparative philology is scanty, but this appears to be incidental, since he was not interested in lexical explanations; rather he compared grammatical items, such as מה נדברנו עליך (Mal 3:13), on which he commented that נדברנו means "conversation in Arabic, that is people speak to one another, which is not equal to דברנו ("we spoke")".[52] What Ḥayyūj compares here is the *nif'al* conjugation and the Arabic VIth conjugation *tafā'ala*, both used here for reciprocity.

Most of the authorities who worked in the Arabic-speaking area, including Ḥayyūj's predecessors,[53] made comparisons with Arabic, and all did so with Aramaic. Judah ibn Quraysh even made the comparisons systematic in his book *Risālah.* But Ibn Janāḥ succeeded in deepening the investigation in this field. Not only did he establish the meaning of many rare words and *hapax legomena* by virtual comparison, he even uncovered rare and unique meanings in words that were commonplace. For example, the particle כי occurs 4, 475 times in the Bible, and its meanings were well established from the time of the Talmud (*b. Roš Haš.* 3a). Yet Ibn Janāḥ, as a result of his deep inquiries into comparative philology, succeeded in uncovering in it a unique meaning, applied in only two occurrences in the Bible, one in the verse שויתי ה׳ לנגדי תמיד כי מימיני בל אמוט (Ps 16:8). Early and late commentators explained it as "causal כי" and considered the second half of the verse as a reasoning for the first half, in spite of the logical difficulty posed by this explanation. They were therefore forced to distort the simple meaning of the text and to view it as an ellipsis. Ibn Janāḥ discovered that כי is used here in the same sense as Arab. *kay*, 'so that, therefore',[54] i.e. "I have put the Lord in front of me, *so that* I will not fall down at my right hand". To him this is so clear that he states it laconically and one hardly catches it among his comprehensive discussion of the various meanings of this particle. It is probably for this reason that the many exegetes, translators and linguists who intensively used his dictionary did not pay attention to this wonderful explanation. This is the case with A. ibn Ezra, Maimonides, Qimhi and others, and also with the English translations of the Bible that follow the Septuagint or other Jewish traditions.[55] Even MUILENBURG who devoted a comprehensive article to the rhetorical usages of this particle, was not aware of Ibn Janāḥ's suggestion.[56] It is typical that MUILENBURG referred to the occurrence of *ky* in Akkadian, Ugaritic, Moabite and Elephantine Aramaic, but said nothing about its appearence in Arabic. That is how Ibn Janāḥ's astute explanation fell into oblivion.

Here is another example from the field of comparative phraseology: In ex-

---

[52] Eldar, Nutaf (1979) 258 and n. 9.
[53] For example, Saadiah, Samuel b. Ḥofni and David b. Abraham Alfāsi.
[54] Bacher, Shorashim (1896) 219; Neubauer, Hebrew Roots (1875) 317.
[55] Maman, Contribution (1992) 27–31.
[56] The linguistic and rhetorical usages (1961) 148 and n. 3.

plaining the verb ל-ק-ח in the phrase ויקח קרח (Num 16:1), every possible meaning of the verb was utilized in the midrashic traditional exegesis, all assuming an ellipsis: לקח בדברים (i.e. seduced);[57] "he disputed, as if he *took* and separated himself from the community" (*Qorah* V, 43b); לקח מקח רע לעצמו ('he *took*, i.e. made, a bad deal'),[58] לקח עצה ('he *took* advice'). The Targums and many exegetes followed the Midrash, and even modern commentators are indecisive as to the linguistic problem posed by this expression.[59] Ibn Janāḥ explained the use of this verb in an original manner. He systematically examined the various meanings of ל-ק-ח in different phrases, in light of its Arabic equivalent *'-kh-ḏ*, and found that when the Arabic verb is followed by another verb in the imperfect it takes the meaning of 'to begin to do'. Ibn Janāḥ assigned this very meaning to the expression under discussion. Therefore לקח here does not govern an object as in other constructions but rather is an aspectual verb. That is, ויקח קורח ... ודתן ... ויקומו, having the construction ויקח ויקומו, means: Qorah and his party 'began to rise up, to rebel' against Moses. This interpretation was not absorbed in the commentaries of Ibn Janāḥ' successors, probably because of Judah ibn Tibbon's vague translation and A. ibn Ezra's obscure quotation.

The 342 comparisons with Arabic and Aramaic made by Ibn Janāḥ are original. They are not to be found in the works of his predecessors, and they do not include simple comparisons of basic words, but rather unique comparisons that flow from a deep insight. These comparisons reveal how much that was hidden from his predecessors was revealed to him, especially unique meanings in common words.

Many of the ancient suggestions are accepted to this day. One can even find a modern philologist making a comparison, without noticing that he was anticipated by medieval scholars. HELD sums up the modern suggestions for *אמרתי אפאיהם* (Deut 32:26) and finally decides in favour of the opinion of A. SCHULTENS, who compared this word to the Arab. פא"י the meaning 'cutting down / destruction'. HELD did not notice that this suggestion was made some one thousand years ago by Ibn Janāḥ,[60] even though in many other cases HELD praised the medieval scholars for anticipating, in their brilliant suggestions, the modern scholars.

The fact that philological exegesis is common to the four scholars under discussion does not mean that they agree in all cases. In some instances they disagree on the grammatical, etymological or semantic analysis of a word. For example, התקוששו וקושו (Zeph 2:1), is explained by Ḥayyūj 'comparing / paralleling' like הקישו זה לזה rabbinic Hebrew.[61] In contrast, Ibn Janāḥ suggested two etymological derivations and three explanations: one form קושי ,'diffi-

---

[57] Tanḥuma (ed. Buber), *Qorah* II, 43a.

[58] *B. Sanh.* 109b; *Yalqut Shim'oni* 750 (ed. Warsaw 1838) 500.

[59] For example, ARNOLD B. EHRLICH, *Randglossen zur hebraeischen Bibel: Textkritisches, Sprachliches und Sachliches* II (Leipzig 1909) 168; (*Mikra ki-Pheschuto [Die Schrift nach ihrem Wortlaut]: Scholien und kritische Bemerkungen zu den heiligen Schriften der Hebraeer* [New York 1899; ^{2}1969] 269).

[60] Neubauer, Hebrew Roots (1875) 560.

[61] Allony, Nutaf (1963) 15.

culty';[62] one based on the Targum אתכנשו, 'gathering', derived from מקושש עצים (Num 15:32); and a third derivation from קשיש, 'old, wise' – therefore התקוששו means 'be aware / behave wisely like an old sage'.[63] Even though Ibn Janāḥ disagreed with Ḥayyūj in several matters, he comprehensively implemented his theory throughout the Bible.

3. Moses Chiquitilla

Moses Chiquitilla was born in Cordova but lived and worked mainly in Saragossa, in the second half of the eleventh century CE. He was not only an exegete but also a grammarian and a poet.[64] Ibn Ezra characterized him as "one of the great commentators".[65] He translated into Hebrew the two large books of Ḥayyūj on grammar. Then he wrote grammatical books of his own, among them a book on the use of gender in Hebrew nouns.[66]

Chiquitilla's commentary on the Bible was almost entirely lost. Only small parts of it survived, mainly in quotations in the works of his contemporaries and successors. Some of these quotations were collected by L. Dukes (Frankfurt 1844) and W. Bacher (Budapest 1881). However only Poznanski[67] exhausted the material in a monograph where he collected all of the 156 quotations.[68] A minuscule part of Chiquitilla's commentary survived in manuscript, and from these remnants one can learn that he undoubtedly wrote commentaries to the Pentateuch, Isaiah, the Minor Prophets, Psalms, Job and Daniel,[69] of which the commentary on three Psalms (3, 4, 8) were published.[70] Recently other fragments from the Psalms were published[71] and the rest of the remnants from Chiquitilla's commentary to Psalms are under preparation for

---

62 Neubauer, ibid. 633.

63 Ibid. 649.

64 See S. Poznanski (review of), "Catalogue of Hebrew and Samaritan Manuscripts in the British Museum, by G. Margoliouth, Part I, London 1899", *REJ* 41 (1900) 303 and n. 1. See also Sarna, Hebrew and Bible Studies (1971) 339–40.

65 Ibn Ezra, *Moznei leshon ha-qodesh* (Heidenheim's edition; Offenbach 1791) 5b, 13b; Simon, arbaʿ guishot (1892) 96; Perez, Psalm 9 (1990).

66 The remnants of which were discovered in 1895 by A. E. Harkavy among the manuscripts of the Firkovitsch II collection (see A. E. Harkavy, *Ḥadashim gam yeshanim* 2 (1886) 11; 7 (1895/96) 18; repr. in Jerusalem 1970, 23, 126) and published by Kokowzow, Noviye (1916; 66–59 in the Hebrew-Arabic part and 195–200 in the Russion part).

67 Moses ibn Chiquitilla (1895) 93–120, and his notes on 123–84.

68 Simon, arbaʿ guishot (1982) 99.

69 Poznanski, Moses ibn Chiquitilla (1895) 7–20; Finkel, Perush (1936) 153; Perez, Psalm 9 (1990) 12, n. 3. The authorship of the anonymous commentary on Job, published by Bacher, Hiob (1908), is still under dispute. Bacher attributed it to Chiquitilla; Poznanski (Chiquitilla, 15 and n. 3) opposed at first this view but later (Poznanski, Psalmkommentar, 1912, 41) reconsidered the matter and supported Bacher, probably due to Bacher's new reasonings (*REJ* 31, 310). However Finkel (ibid. 1936, 154) revised the question and came to the conclusion that the commentary under discussion was written by a later eclectic author who used materials from Chiquitilla's (lost) commentary. Cf also Perez, Introduction 30.

70 Poznanski, *ZA* 26 (1912) 38–60, published Psalm 8; Finkel published all three of the psalms and translated them into Hebrew (Perush, 1936, 155–62).

71 Perez, Psalm 4–5 (1966); idem, Psalm 51 (1991); idem, Psalm 55 (1991).

publication. ALLONY (Gikatila, 1949) published some additional fragments, but PEREZ (Psalm 9, 1990, 13) cast doubt on their authorship. POZNANSKI (Psalmkommentar) who studied Chiquitilla's commentary on the 84 psalms preserved in manuscript[72] overpraised Chiquitilla characterizing him as "one of the most important monuments of the Spanish exegesis in its Golden Age".[73] As to the method of exegesis, Chiquitilla also based it on the philological approach.[74] According to KOKOWTZOW[75] the linguistic work of Chiquitilla and his young contemporary Judah ibn Balʿam was limited to sorting the rich linguistic material collected by Ibn Janāḥ and Samuel ha-Nagid. Chiquitilla himself explicitly declared Ibn Janāḥ to be the undisputed authority in all questions of grammar and in fact he influenced him greatly.[76] In spite of this, KOKOWTZOW's assessment is exaggerated, for though Ibn Janāḥ's influence on both Chiquitilla and Ibn Balʿam was immense, they showed a high degree of independence. However, it is difficult to determine to what degree Chiquitilla was original in the cases not derived from Ibn Janāḥ, for one cannot reconstruct the extent to which he owed his data to Samuel ha-Nagid (ibid. 162).

Chiquitilla was not content with analyzing forms and meanings but engaged in the content of every Psalm in its entirety and even gave his opinion on general issues. POZNANSKI dedicated a whole chapter of his monograph to Chiquitilla's method of exegesis,[77] where he dealt with Chiquitilla's view of prophecy. More recently, SIMON[78] wrote an important chapter on Chiquitilla's unique understanding of Psalms, according to which his exegesis is largely based on rationalism, expressed in various aspects: Chiquitilla tends to minimize the deviation of miracles from the laws of nature, to assign prophecies to historical events that have already taken place and not to the messianic era, and to use Christian commentaries.[79] In POZNANSKI's view,[80] Chiquitilla's main innovation in his commentary on Psalms was that he clearly postponed the writing of many Psalms to the exilic period. In a comment on Psalm 51, he assigned the last two verses to a Babylonian writer.[81] He also took the linguistic liberty of interpreting headings like לדוד ('to David') as referring either to the author or to the addressee in honour of whom the Psalm was written, as against Saadiah who believed that the entire Book of Psalms was written by King David.[82] Consequently, Chiquitilla regards the Psalms not as prophecies, but rather as prayers not necessarily written with the aid of the Holy Spirit.[83] Also he was

---

[72] II Firkovitsch Collection, ms. 3583 f. 285.
[73] Poznanski, Psalmkommentar (1912) 58.
[74] Cf. Poznanski, ibid. 34–37.
[75] Noviye (1916) 195 in the Russian part.
[76] Cf. Kokowtzow, Novize (1916) 200, n. 1; Poznanski, Chiquitilla (1895) 26 and Perez, Introduction, I, VII, XI–X.
[77] Poznanski, Chiquitilla, chapter II, 26–38: Ibn Chiquitilla als Bibelexeget.
[78] Simon, arbaʿ guishot (1982) 96–119.
[79] Poznanski, Psalmkommentar (1912) 59; Finkel, Perush (1936) 158; 162 and n. 64; Simon, ibid. 97.
[80] Psalmkommentar (1912) 176.
[81] Ibid. 32; Simon, ibid. 105.
[82] Simon, ibid. 107.
[83] Ibid. 110–11.

the first to assign the chapters 40 ff. in Isaiah to a second prophet. According to a quotation from his commentary on Isaiah 41, "The first Restorations are meant to the second Temple period, not the messianic era". Of Ps 106:47 he declared the author to be from Babylonia. SIMON[84] believes that he rationalized Elia's miracle in reviving the son of the widow in such a way that the son did not really die but rather stopped breathing and fell into a coma for a while. In taking all these stands, he infuriated Ibn Balʿam.[85]

4. JUDAH IBN BALʿAM

Ibn Balʿam lived and worked in the second half of the eleventh century CE, first in Toledo and later in Seville. He authored books on grammar, halakhah and biblical commentary, which have come down to us almost in their entirety, some having even been edited (SARNA, 340).

He entitled his commentary on the Pentateuch *Kitāb Al-Tarjīḥ* ('The Book of Decision').[86] His commentaries on Genesis, Exodus and Leviticus have survived in part, and on Numbers and Deuteronomy in full. Small fragments of his commentary on Genesis have been published;[87] but of his commentary on Exodus only a quotation by another exegete has been published.[88] POZNANSKI published a few excerpts from Ibn Balʿam's commentary on Leviticus.[89] FUCHS in his monograph on Ibn Balʿam published many excerpts from his commentaries on Numbers and Deuteronomy, and PEREZ has edited the entire commentary on Numbers.[90]

Ibn Balʿam entitled his commentary on the prophets and the hagiographa *Nuqat al-Miqra* ('Glosses to the Scripture'), but not all of it has survived.[91] POZNANSKI edited the commentaries on Joshua, Judges and the Minor Prophets, ALLONY (Ibn Balʿam, 1964, 113 f.), edited part of the introduction to the commentary on Joshua, DERENBOURG published the commentary on Isaiah;[92] ISRAELSOHN (Arabischer Kommentar, 1908) edited the commentary on Jeremiah, POZNANSKI (Mitteilungen, 1896) described the commentary on 2 Samuel, and ABRAMSON reconstructed this commentary on the basis of excerpts quoted by R. Isaac b. Samuel ha-Sepharadi,[93] and PEREZ published a fragment from the commentary on Nehemiah (Nehemya, 1991). The Institute for the History of Jewish Bible Research founded by the late M. Goshen-Gottstein, and

---

84 Ibid. 97, n. 9.

85 According to SARNA (Hebrew and Bible Studies, 1971, 340), Chiquitilla in Ps 8:1 expressed anti-Karaite opinions.

86 Steinschneider, Arabische Literatur (1902) 141.

87 Poznanski, The Arabic Commentary (1924) 2, n. 7, and 4, n. 10; Abramson, Tajnīs (1963) 54; and Allony, Ibn Balʿam (1964) 117–22. Poznanski published part of Ibn Balʿam's introduction to the Pentateuch, and Allony republished it in its entirety.

88 See Steinschneider, Ibn Balam (1885) 288; B. HALPER, "A volume of the book of Precepts by Ḥefeṣ B. Yaṣliaḥ", *JQR* NS 5 (1914) 74–76, and Abramson, Tajnīs (1963) 64, n. 8.

89 ZHB IV (1900) 17–22.

90 Perez, Commentary (1970); see also small fragments and quotations in A. E. HARKAVY, *Ḥadashim gam yeshanim* 7 (1895/96) 18–22; 10 (1896) 24 (repr. in Jerusalem 1970, 126–130).

91 Steinschneider, Arabische Literatur (1902) 343. Cf. on the one hand, Poznanski, The Arabic Commentary (1924) 3; 10, n. 23, and on the other hand, Abramson, Tajnīs (1963) 55 and nn. 6–17; Allony, Ibn Balʿam (1964) 114.

92 Part of the R. Hai Gaon responsa quoted in Ibn Balʿam's commentary on Isa 38:5 has been published by S. POZNANSKI, "Das Responsum Hai's über die Flucht Jonas", *MGWJ* 44 (1900) 548–49

93 See Abramson, Nutaf (1978) 236.

now directed by U. Simon, is in the process of preparing a new critical edition of all the surviving portions of Ibn Bal'am's commentary; in 1992 the Institute published a new edition of *R. Judah Ibn Bal'am's Commentary on Isaiah.*[94]

These editors and scholars focused on one or another aspect of Ibn Bal'am's commentaries. DERENBOURG emphasized in his introduction to *Isaiah* Ibn Bal'am's criticism of his predecessors. BACHER strove to reveal Ibn Bal'am's sources and the degree of their influence on him and also described Ibn Bal'am's linguistic exegetical method, like punctuation, ellipsis, comparative philology. FUCHS in his monograph focused on the historical background of the period prior to Ibn Bal'am, on the flourishing of the study of Hebrew linguistics following Ḥayyūj, on many details of Ibn Bal'am's life and work, and on his criticism of his predecessors. All of these scholars[95] have noted that Ibn Bal'am's commentary is selective, i.e. he does not explain every word, not even every difficult word, and he omits verses and sometimes entire chapters. For instance, in Deuteronomy he skipped chapter 19 and in Isaiah he skipped chapters 12 and 39. Hence he deliberately selected the words to be discussed.[96] But these scholars have not revealed his motives. Perez[97] succeeded in pointing out Ibn Bal'am's special tendency to comment on words or expressions whenever he had good reason to reject the explanations of his predecessors, or when he suspected that other readers or exegetes might understand them in a hypothetical and incorrect way.[98] He selected words whose derivational etymology is unequivocal. For instance he derived זרו (Isa 1:6) from ז-ו-ר, meaning 'squeezing', in order to exclude the hypothetical derivation from ז-ר-ה meaning 'scattering'. He also chose words whose roots can be explained in different ways, e.g. he explained נצורה (Isa 1:8) as derived from the meaning 'destruction' in order to exclude the hypothetical relationship to נצרים ('shoots / offsprings'). Ibn Balᶜam took a stand whenever polysemy or homonymy were involved and in considering rare words or meanings, either to reject a previous explanation or to prevent a future hypothetical one. KOKOWTZOW (Noviye, 195, 201 and elsewhere) decided that Ibn Balᶜam was an epigone of Ibn Janāḥ and that his contribution was limited to partial completions of what Ibn Janāḥ had omitted but he contributed nothing in methodology. Other scholars too have noted Ibn Balᶜam's dependency on Ibn Janāḥ.[99] In fact several remarks of Ibn Balᶜam himself indicate that he systematically examined the works of Ibn Janāḥ so that he could complete anything omitted by him.[100] However, even though he depended on his predecessors, Ibn Balᶜam exhibited independence in his ability to choose from alternative explanations of his predecessors, to correct the text (Isa 5:5: משוכתו; 16:8: תעו, and the like), to criticize his predecessors on the basis of severe grammatical or syntactical analysis, etymology

---

[94] Goshen-Gottstein, Isaiah (1992); Maman, Ibn Balᶜam (1996).
[95] Dérenbourg, Gloses (1892); Bacher, Jesaja Commentar (1893); Fuchs, Studien (1894) 1–10; cf. also Poznanski, Joshua (1903) 93 and Abramson, Tajnīs (1963) 56.
[96] Perez, The Philological Exegesis (1978), Introduction XI–XII.
[97] Perez, ibid. 241 ff.
[98] Perez, ibid., Hebrew Abstract II.
[99] For example, Poznanski, Joshua (1903) 93.
[100] Maman, Ibn Balᶜam (1996) 468–69.

and semantics, and on the basis of accordance with the widespread meaning, of the written form (the Ketib) as opposed to the one to be read (the Qere), of comparative philology, of logic and of human experience. If the context required deviation from these principles, he tried to limit this deviation. In his commentaries on Joshua and Judges he analyzed many words grammatically,[101] repeating again and again the Arabic term *naḥwuhu* ('its grammar analysis / formation', i.e. of the word under discussion), which is almost totally missing from the commentaries on Isaiah, Jeremiah and the Minor Prophets.

As is appropriate for a commentary that centers on the philological *peshat,* many entries contain only a grammatical discussion.[102] In other places Ibn Balʿam expands beyond what is necessary to an understanding of the verse under discussion, extending to excursive monographs, e.g. on the meanings of initial ה (Num 15:15), on the syntactical accord between subject and predicate (Num 24:7), and on the comparison of Hebrew with Arabic (Isa 59:13). But there are cases where he also discusses general matters of content, such as the procedure for the transmission of the commandments to Moses (Num 9:8; 15:32), defence of the Patriarchs (Num 11:22 and elsewhere), theology (Num 22:9, Isa 6:10 and elsewhere), philosophy (Isa 8:19 and elsewhere), *realia* (Num 21:6 and elsewhere), history (Isa 13:12 and elsewhere), geography (Isa 7:25 and elsewhere), the order of prophecies (Isa 6:1; 7:1), the historicization of the Restoration prophecies (Isa 60:12), the types of impurities and the laws relating to them (Num 5:2), the gifts to the priests (Num 18:8–32), the contradictions between various passages in the Bible (Deut 2:29), and the survival of the soul after death (Isa 8:19). In his commentary on Isaiah 38, where we are told of the addition of 15 years to the life of King Hezekiah, Ibn Balʿam used a long excerpt from a response of R. Hai Gaon on the question of God's change of will which involves the question of human free will and the relationship of this freedom to the omniscience of God.[103] The discussion of such topics is more frequent in Ibn Balʿam's commentary on the Pentateuch and as a result it is much longer than his commentary on the prophets and the hagiographa.

As noted earlier, Ibn Balʿam took a stand vis-a-vis his predecessors, and he especially argued with Chiquitilla and disagreed with Ibn Janāḥ. For instance, he rejected Chiquitilla's opinion that מבליגיתי (Jer 8:18) is a compound word made up of מה and בליגיתי, and while discussing כנלתך (Isa 33:1), he rejected Chiquitilla's argument that this word contains a superfluous נ and should have been כלות, the infinitive form from *כלה* ה׳ את חמתו (Lam 4:11). According to Ibn Balʿam, this explanation is afflicted with excess and deficiency: (1) one does not add נ in Hebrew without significance; (2) contrary to the usage, the particle כ has been omitted, even though it is essential to the meaning, for the first part of the verse has כהתמך, using כ. Ibn Balʿam himself explained it as a

[101] Poznanski, Joshua (1903) 93.
[102] See, for instance, Isa 5:30; 6:12; 7:3–4; 14:10; 16:7–10; 19:13; 22:19; 23:3, 11; 28:16, 22; 51:1–2, and many more.
[103] Bacher, Jesaja Commentar (1893) 136; Goshen-Gottstein, Isaiah (1992) 167–171.

contracted infinitive form derived from כהנלתך, cast in the pattern of הרבות or הפנות (1 Sam 10:9). He also explained the *dagesh* in the נ, whose nature was unclear to Ibn Janāḥ, in phonetic terms: it is meant to prevent the נ from being assimilated with ל, since they are both phonetically articulated in the same organ. Finally, he related the word to ולא יטה לארץ *מנלם* (Job 15:29) and explained both from the meaning 'completion', based on the parallelism with כהתמך. As to the formation of מנלם, he compared it to the pattern of מכרם (Num 20:19).[104]

Generally speaking, Ibn Balʿam's originality is revealed wherever he opposes his predecessors. He lectured on his method in the introduction to his commentary on prophets, where he says that he intends to comment on the difficult words in three ways: by translating them into Arabic; by relating them to cognate words in the Bible; and, when such words do not exist, by relating them to their equivalents in post-biblical Hebrew, Aramaic or Arabic[105] and by analyzing their morphology and syntax.[106]

In his commentary Ibn Balʿam used all the philological knowledge available in his time, as for phenomena like vocal change, consonant change, metathesis, syntactical ellipsis, and word order. He was learned and sharp-witted not only in the Bible but also in post-biblical literature, in updated linguistics and exegesis, as well as in Arabic literature, as testified by his references to such literature. He had no hesitation in rejecting classical rabbinic biblical interpretation or in supporting one rabbinic interpretation over another (e.g. Isa 6:1; 11:8; 28:25). Similarly he did not hesitate to disagree with leading medieval Rabbis.[107] According to one of his principles, whenever the *peshat* contradicts the halakhah, he supports the halakhah, using the *ta'wīl* to determine the context (e.g. Deut 4:24; Josh 7:25). Actually his commentary to the Pentateuch is full of quotations from rabbinic literature and gaonic verdicts.

A serious problem that Ibn Balʿam encountered was the deciphering of terms of biblical *realia*. As we have seen, Ibn Janāḥ had already made a great effort to decipher some of them and even visited artisans in Spain to examine their tools, assuming that they were identical to those of the biblical epoch. Ibn Balʿam followed Ibn Janāḥ's example (e.g. Isa 3:20, 21; 28:25: כסמת). But sometimes he refuted others' identifications, even if he did not offer his own suggestions; it was preferable, he felt, to leave a word unexplained rather than to make a baseless suggestion. Ibn Balʿam said that he was unable to identify the jewels and ornaments in Isa 3:18–21. So he left the terms נטיפות, רעלות, לחשים, צעדות, פארים, and חריטים unexplained; so also for כומז (Num 31:50).[108] This tendency is not confined to *realia*. Sometimes he refutes all of the suggested interpretations, without providing any alternative (e.g. בעים, Isa 11:15). Ibn Balʿam also made efforts to identify geographical names: for instance, חבור identified with the river כ'אבור in Khurasan and נהר גוזן with the

[104] Kokowtzow, Noviye (1916) 201; Bacher, Jesaja Commentar (1893) 137.
[105] Allony, Ibn Balʿam (1964) 113–14; Maman, Comparison (1984) 15, 2.
[106] Maman, Ibn Balʿam (1996) 473.
[107] Maman, ibid. 474.
[108] Perez, Ha-tippul (1981) 27, 218; Maman, Comparison (1984) 5.3.2.10.

river near the town גנזה, the capital of Khurasan in Ibn Balʿam's time (Isa 7:25). He also identified כתים with Cyprus (Isa 23:1).

He believed that his commentary was capable of extricating the reader from the different and confusing exegeses that he would encounter and from the many varied grammatical, syntactical and lexical analyses – which is why he entitled his commentaries *The Book of Decision* and *The Book of Precision*. His main contribution resides not in techniques but rather in his initiative, his daring and his lack of partiality towards his sources and towards the earlier authorities, except regarding the halakhah.[109] But outside the scope of halakhah he does not hesitate to disagree with the Rabbis, as in the case of שעירים (Lev 17:7) and הכרתי והפלתי (2 Sam 8:12), or with the Targums, as with Pseudo-Jonathan to מחרצנים ועד זג (Num 6:4), and even more so with the gaonites, the exegetes and the linguists who were close to his time, such as Saadiah (e.g. שורק; שם: Isa 5:2), Ḥayyūj (e.g. ונקיצנה: Isa 7:6; הגה: Is 27:8), Ibn Janāḥ (e.g. מישור: Jer 21:13; ובדמשק: Amos 3:12) and Chiquitilla (e.g. כפה: Isa 9:13; חרוץ: Isa 28:27).

109 See for instance in מחרצנים ועד זג (Num 6:4) and many other places (Perez, The Philological Exegesis (1978) 291 ff).

31.2. The Aesthetic Exegesis of Moses ibn Ezra

By Mordechai Cohen, New York

Sources: *Works by Moses ibn Ezra*: (A) *Kitāb al-Muḥāḍara wa-'l-Muḏākara* [abbr. K], in following editions: A. Halkin (*Sefer ha-ʿIyyunim we-ha-Diyyunim* [Jerusalem 1975], ed. critically Arab. text, with modern Heb. tr.); B. Halper (*Shirat Yisrael* [Leipzig 1924]; looser Heb. tr.); M. Abumalhan Mas (ed. Arab. text with Spanish tr.; Madrid 1985). – (B) *Maqālat al-Ḥadīqa fī Maʿna 'l-Majāz wa-'l-Ḥaqīqa* [abbr. M] (Jerusalem Hebrew National Library MS 5701; formerly Sassoon MS 412); partial medieval Hebrew translation, *ʿArugat ha-Bosem* [abbr. A], published in: *Zion* 2 (1849) 117–23, 134–37, 157–60, 175, and in: *Litteraturblatt des Orients* 10 (1849) 747–48; P. Fenton (ed. critically Arab. and medieval Heb. text, with modern Heb. tr.; Jerusalem, forthcoming); Arabic passage on music in: *Hebrew Writings Concerning Music* (ed. I. Adler; Munich 1975) 159–64; republ. with Eng. tr. by A. Shiloah, "The Musical Passage in Ibn Ezra's *Book of the Garden*", *Yuval*: *Studies of the Jewish Music Research Centre* 4 (1982) 211–24; repr. in: *The Dimension of Music in Islamic and Jewish Culture* (London 1993), chap. IV; Arabic passage on commandments, with modern Heb. tr., published by A. Halkin, "Moses Ibn Ezra's Conception of the Commandments" [Heb.], *Arabic and Islamic Studies* II (ed. J. Mansour; Ramat-Gan 1978) 26–40. – (C) Fragmentary exegetical note published by W. Bacher, "Ein unbekanntes Werk Moses Ibn Esras", *MGWJ* 51 (1907) 343–49.

General works: M. Abumalham, "Reflexión acerca de los métodos de Moše ibn ʿEzra", *Sef.* 46/1–2 (1986) 17–26; A. Berlin, *Biblical Poetry Through Medieval Jewish Eyes* (Bloomington 1991); R. Brann, *The Compunctious Poet: Cultural Ambiguity and Hebrew Poetry in Muslim Spain* (Baltimore 1991); V. Cantarino, *Arabic Poetics in the Golden Age* (Leiden 1975); M. Cohen, "'The Best of Poetry …': Literary Approaches to the Bible in the Spanish *Peshat* Tradition", *Torah U-Madda Journal* 6 (1995/6) 15–57; idem, "Moses Ibn Ezra vs. Maimonides: Argument for a Poetic Definition of Metaphor (*Istiʿāra*)", (2000); idem, *Three Approaches to Biblical Metaphor: Radak and His Predecessors, Abraham Ibn Ezra and Maimonides* (forthcoming); J. Dana, *Poetics of Mediaeval Hebrew Literature According to Moshe Ibn Ezra* [Hebrew] (Jerusalem 1982); R. Drory, "Literary Models and Where to Find Them: On Arabic Literary Models in Medieval Jewish Literature", *Poetics Today* 14:2 (1993) 277–302; P. Fenton, *Philosophie et exégèse dans le Jardin de la métaphore de Moïse Ibn ʿEzra* (Leiden 1997); W. Heinrichs, "On the Genesis of the *Ḥaqīqa-Majāz* Dichotomy", *StIsl* 59 (1984) 111–40; idem, "*Isti ʿārah* and *Badiʿ* and Their Terminological Relationship in Early Islamic Literary Criticism", *Zeitschrift für Geschichte der Arabisch Islamischen Wissenschaften* 1 (1984) 180–211; J. Kugel, *The Idea of Biblical Poetry* (New Haven 1981); Y. Mashiah, "The Terminology of Hebrew Prosody and Rhetoric with Special Reference to Arabic origins" (unpublished Ph. D. Dissertation, Columbia Univ.; New York 1972); D. Pagis, *Secular Poetry and Poetic Theory: Moses Ibn Ezra and His Contemporaries* [Hebrew] (Jerusalem 1970); R. Scheindlin, "Rabbi Moshe Ibn Ezra on the Legitimacy of Poetry", *MeH* 7 (1976) 101–15; A. Schippers, "Symmetry and Repetition as a Stylistic Ideal in Andalusian Poetry: Moses Ibn Ezra and Figures of Speech in the Arabic Tradition", *Amsterdam Middle Eastern Studies* (ed. M. Woidich; Wiesbaden 1990); idem, *Spanish Hebrew Poetry and the Arabic Literary Tradition* (Leiden 1994); U. Simon, *Four Approaches to The Book of Psalms* (tr. from Hebrew, L. Schramm; New York 1991); S. Stern, *Aristotle on the World State* (Columbia, SC 1968); M. Zohari, "*R. Moshe Ibn Ezra ke-Ḥoqer ha-Miqra*", *BetM* 6 (1961) 32–38.

1. Introduction

Moses ibn Ezra (ca. 1055–1138), a celebrated Hebrew poet, pioneered an original exegetical approach within the vibrant Andalusian tradition. A wide range of interests, colored by his poetic perspective, converge in his exegesis. Following predecessors such as Saadiah and Ibn Janah, he exploited the philosophical and linguistic advances fostered by his Arabic environment to interpret the biblical text. But he did more than merely ride these profound intellectual tides; hoisting his sails to harness the powerful winds of Arabic poetics, Ibn Ezra opened a new horizon by expounding Scripture's literary beauty in an aesthetic exegesis unparalleled in the medieval tradition.

Born in Granada in Andalusia (i.e., Muslim Spain), Ibn Ezra studied under Isaac ibn Ghiyāth, a noted Hebrew poet, exegete, jurist and philosopher. Expert in biblical exegesis, philosophy and rabbinics, Ibn Ezra achieved greatest renown as a poet, inspiring disciples such as Judah Halevi. Revering the Arabic literary tradition, he adhered to its conventions in his Hebrew poetry and used Arabic poetics as a yardstick to gauge the Bible's literary beauty. Ibn Ezra's life changed dramatically around 1090, when he was forced to emigrate to Christian Spain by the Almoravid Berber conquest of Granada. Always longing for the rich Andalusian culture he had once enjoyed, Ibn Ezra never felt comfortable in his new home, where his philosophical bent and certainly his literary notions were viewed as foreign. In his old age, attempting to perpetuate, or perhaps to defend, the learning of his youth, Ibn Ezra wrote his two extant expository works, both in Judeo-Arabic: (1) *Maqālat al-Ḥadīqa fi Maʿna al-Majāz wa-ʾl-Ḥaqīqa* ([abbr. M]; *The Treatise of the Garden on Figurative and Literal Language)*, translated into Hebrew in the twelfth century as *ʿArugat ha-Bosem* ([abbr. A]; *Garden of Spices*), and (2) *Kitāb al-Muḥāḍara wa-ʾl-Muḏākara* ([abbr. K]; *The Book of Discussion and Conversation).*[1]

In *Maqālat al-Ḥadīqa* Ibn Ezra develops a system for interpreting biblical figurative language. In the first section he establishes exegetical principles, which he applies to outline Scripture's perspective on philosophical issues such as God's unity and unknowability, creation, man's nature and the commandments. In the second section he defines the literal and figurative meanings of biblical words associated with the human body. The *Maqāla* typifies – and draws heavily upon – Andalusian Jewish scholarship; but *Kitāb al-Muḥāḍara*, a treatise on poetics, is practically unique in Jewish tradition[2] and draws on Arabic learning. The *Kitāb* was supposedly written for an individual seeking guidance in composing "Hebrew poetry according to Arabic principles"

[1] On the extant MSS of these works, see Fenton, Jardin (1997) 32–33, 38–52. Ibn Ezra may have written other works, including biblical commentaries, that are no longer extant (Fenton, Jardin [1997] 27–28). *ʿArugat ha-Bosem* was apparently translated by Judah al-Ḥarizi in Provence, although the matter is subject to debate (Fenton, Jardin [1997] 52–56). Ibn Ezra's exegesis in the *Maqāla* is analyzed at length by Fenton, Jardin (1997), but scholarship on the *Kitāb* focuses on its historical, literary and cultural aspects; see Drory, Literary Contacts (1993); Scheindlin, Legitimacy (1976); Brann, Compunctious Poet (1991), chap. 3.

[2] Two exceptions can be mentioned. (A) A fragment of a work from Saadiah's circle, which uses Arabic categories to classify biblical literature, is edited, translated and analyzed in *Ha'egron: Kitāb ʾusūl al-shir al-ʿibrānī by Rav Seʿadya Gaʾon* (ed. N. Allony; Jerusalem 1969) 79–82, 386–89; see also E. Fleischer, The Proverbs of Saʿid ben Bābshād [Hebrew] (Jerusalem 1990) 12–17. Parallels to *Kitāb al-Muḥāḍara* raise the possibility that Ibn Ezra used this work (Allony, 112–113). (B) The only other known medieval work on Hebrew poetics is by Elʿazar ben Yaʿakov ha-Bavli, a thirteenth century poet in Baghdad. In the extant fragment of this work (being edited by Y. Yahalom in Jerusalem) he defines and illustrates twenty-five poetic techniques. Elʿazar ha-Bavli knew of Ibn Ezra and cites his poetry, but works with a separate tradition of poetics; see S. Abramson, "A Book of Poetry by Rabbi Elʿazar bar Yaaqob of Babylonia" [Hebrew], *P'raqim* 1 (1967/8) 9–28.

(K 5 b); but this evidently fictitious device thinly veils the work's true aim: to defend the poetic outlook which Ibn Ezra's new milieu viewed suspiciously. The first half of the *Kitāb* surveys Hebrew literature from biblical to medieval times and asserts the superiority of Arabic-style Andalusian Hebrew poetry. Hoping to have sparked interest in a discipline less than popular in Christian Spain, Ibn Ezra offers a practical guide for writing poetry in the second half of the *Kitāb* by illustrating twenty Arabic poetic techniques, for which he finds precedents in Scripture. In so doing, he creates an aesthetic exegesis by using Arabic poetics to outline the Bible's literary features.

Although he left no actual biblical commentaries,[3] Ibn Ezra forms an important link in the exegetical tradition. Apart from formulating a unique aesthetic exegesis, he sheds light on broad trends in the unfolding Andalusian tradition. His linguistic exegesis in the *Maqāla* and review of Hebrew scholarship in the *Kitāb* provide a 'snapshot' revealing the relative impact of exegetes such as Saadiah, Ibn Janah, Ibn Chiquitilla and Ibn Balʿam before they were eclipsed by Abraham ibn Ezra (Moses' younger contemporary, but not a relative) and David Qimhi. The *Maqāla*, bearing the imprint of Saadiah, Ibn Gabirol, Isaac Israeli and Baḥya ibn Paquda, reflects the rationalist currents of Ibn Ezra's time; it also influenced later authors[4] and perhaps served as a model for Maimonides' *Guide of the Perplexed*.[5] And Ibn Ezra's poetic outlook, which emerges even in the *Maqāla*, reveals the literary underpinnings of Andalusian *peshat* exegesis. In the subsequent sections of this essay, we delineate Ibn Ezra's work in the conventional domains of the *peshat* tradition, his unique poetic analysis of Scripture and impact on subsequent scholarship.

2. In the Rationalist Tradition

2.1. Ibn Ezra's Sources

Ibn Ezra exploits a wide variety of sources to elucidate Scripture. In addition to Jewish literature, he draws upon Arabic learning, including literary criticism, poetry, koranic exegesis and philosophy, which, by his time, included translated ancient Greek works. The merit of harnessing Arabic and Greek learning to advance biblical scholarship was recognized in Andalusia and would be applied a generation later by Maimonides; but a more conservative attitude prevailed in Christian Spain. Countering anticipated criticism from

---

[3] On possible lost commentaries, see above, n. 1. Numerous biblical allusions in Ibn Ezra's poetry indirectly reflect exegesis; see A. Mirsky, "*Ko'aḥ ha-Miqra be-Shir Sefarad*", *Sinai* 73 (1973) 19–23; notes in *Moshe Ibn Ezra: Shirei ha-Ḥol* (ed. D. Pagis; Jerusalem 1977) vol. III and *The Collected Liturgical Poetry: Moshe Ibn Ezra* (ed. S. Bernstein; Tel-Aviv 1957). This potential source requires further study, but it appears that while Ibn Ezra devises some original readings, he usually adopts views current in eleventh century Andalusia, especially those of Saadiah and Ibn Janah.

[4] These include exegetes, philosophers and kabbalists; see Fenton, Jardin (1997) 196–234, 380–88.

[5] See S. Pines, "*Sefer ʿArugat ha-Bosem: ha-Qeṭaʿim mi -Tokh Sefer Meqor Ḥayyim*", *Tarbiẓ* 27 (1958) 218 n; S. Klein-Braslavy, *King Solomon and Philosophical Esotericism in the Thought of Maimonides* [Hebrew] (Jerusalem 1996) 49–50; Cohen, Three Approaches (forthcoming), chap. 4.

"contemporary jurists" who insisted on interpreting Scripture using only rabbinic tradition, he adduces earlier authorities, Saadiah and Hai, who freely drew upon Koran and Christian exegesis to elucidate Scripture (K 119 b–120 a).[6] He argues further that Scripture affirms Greek mastery of philosophy and science as well as Arabic talent in language and literary expression, whereas the Jewish people, gifted with prophecy, fathom the divine will, embodied in *halakha* (i. e., Jewish law; K 19 a–22 b).[7] Demonstrating that these branches are linked in a universal tree of knowledge, he punctuates his writings with bundles of Greek, Arabic and Hebrew sources expressing common ideas.[8]

Apart from polemical considerations, it was critical for Ibn Ezra himself to reconcile Greek and Arabic learning with rabbinic tradition, which he adhered to ardently. He regularly draws upon rabbinic literature and regards Saadiah, a champion of rabbinic Judaism, as his model of scientific biblical study. He condemns the Karaite schism and its motto, attributed to ʿAnan, "examine Scripture diligently and do not rely upon my view", which created religious and exegetical anarchy (M 63). Yet this hardly prevented Ibn Ezra from offering novel readings. The Rabbis, for example, take Ps 30:1, "A Psalm of David. A Song for the Dedication of the *House*", to refer to the Holy Temple, a view adopted by "the commentators" of Ibn Ezra's day.[9] But since David did not build the Temple, Ibn Ezra, aiming for greater historicity, argues that "the house" refers to David's cedar palace (2 Sam 5:11; M 199).[10]

Ibn Ezra knew that his scientific methods depart from rabbinic hermeneutics. Having rejected ʿAnan's principle of autonomy which would have relieved this tension, Ibn Ezra, like other rabbinite *peshat* exegetes, strikes a balance between rabbinic authority and his innovative exegesis. To preclude divergence

---

[6] Judah b. Barzilai of Barcelona, e. g., criticizes "Bible scholars ... ignorant of Talmud ... [and] the oral Torah, which is the interpretation and key to the written Torah" (*Commentar zum Sefer Jezira* [ed. S. Halberstam; Berlin 1885; photo repr. Jerusalem 1970] 5). The precedent of Saadiah and Hai was invoked earlier by Ibn Janah (*Sefer ha-Riqma* [ed. M. Wilensky; Jerusalem ²1964] 17) and later by Joseph ibn Aqnin (*Hitgallut ha-Sodot we-Hofaʿat ha-Meʾorot: Perush Shir ha-Shirim* [ed. A. Halkin; Jerusalem 1964] 490–95; Eng. tr., A. Halkin, "Ibn ʿAḳnin's Commentary on the Song of Songs", *Alexander Marx Jubilee Volume* [ed. S. Lieberman; New York 1950] 406).

[7] Simon, Four Approaches (1991) 172–73. Ibn Ezra cites Gen 9:27 ("May God beautify Yephet [i. e., Greece]") and Isa 42:11 ("The inhabitants of Qedar [i. e., Arabia] ... shall sing and cry out ..."). In citing Gen 9:27, he follows *b. Meg.* 9 b; but the Talmud seems to use the verse to praise Greek language (Rashi, ad loc.), a virtue Ibn Ezra assigns to Arabic; he thus applies it to Greek philosophy.

[8] He cites, e. g., Proverbs, Aristotle, Koran and medieval Arabic sources on the fleeting nature of material accomplishments (K 53 b–54 a); Aristotle's "Golden Mean" is supported from biblical, rabbinic, Koranic and medieval Arabic sources (K 103 a). Most strikingly, Ibn Ezra cites Socrates and Aristotle, in addition to biblical and rabbinic sources, on critical theological tenets such as God's incorporeality and unknowability (below, nn. 22, 23), and the nature of messianic times (below, n. 30).

[9] See *Mek. Shirata* chap. 1; Saadiah (Ps 30:1) and Moses ibn Chiquitilla (cited by Abraham ibn Ezra, ad loc., who himself sides with Moses ibn Ezra).

[10] He manifests a similar historical sense in diverging from the talmudic view, based on Gen 26:5, "He kept ... My commandments, laws and teachings", that Abraham fulfilled the commandments later given at Sinai (*b. Yoma* 28 b). Ibn Ezra, adopting a view current in the rationalist tradition, instead takes this verse to mean that Abraham adhered to the "ways of God", i. e., self-evident ethical precepts and fulfilled God's explicit commands to him, as recorded in Scripture (M 58–59; Halkin, Commandments [1978] 31, 34–35; Fenton, Jardin [1997] 134–36).

from normative Judaism, he accepts rabbinic legal (*halakhic*) exegesis implicitly; for example, he follows a tenuous talmudic reading in taking Ps 150:6, "May all that breathes (*kol ha-neshama*) praise the Lord", to be a directive to recite a benediction on spices (M 184).[11] Nor is he care-free in rejecting nonlegal rabbinic exegesis; he often defends his divergence from a rabbinic source by reading it homiletically (as *derash*)[12] or figuratively,[13] or by citing an earlier medieval rabbinic authority, such as Saadiah or Hai.[14]

2.2. Linguistic Exegesis

Ibn Ezra's conviction that foreign disciplines precipitated decisive advances beyond rabbinic learning is especially evident in his assertion that the greatest breakthroughs in the scholarship of biblical Hebrew are attributable to Arabic influence:

> When the Arabs conquered the Andalusian peninsula ... our exiles there ... learned ... their tongue, excelled in their language ... and became accustomed to their inflections ... to the point that God revealed to them the secret of the Hebrew language and its grammar (K 29b).

Though he credits Saadiah as a pioneer in this field, Ibn Ezra deems Hayyuj, who more fully exploits Arabic linguistics, to be the true father of Hebrew scholarship (K 30a–b). But the primary source of his linguistics is Ibn Janah, whose views he often prefers over those of the Rabbis and Saadiah.[15] Apart

---

[11] *B. Ber.* 43b, taking *neshama* as "spirit", yielding "Praise the Lord for that which the spirit, but not the body, savors [i.e., spices]", hardly the plain sense (cf. Saadiah and Abraham ibn Ezra, who interpret literally). See also M 231; Fenton, Jardin (1997) 330. Rejecting another literal reading in accord with *b. Qidd.* 21b, Ibn Ezra (M 56) interprets Exod 21:6, "He shall remain his slave *le-ʿolam* (lit. forever)", as limited servitude, taking *le-ʿolam* as "until the Jubilee year". Yet this reading (adopted by Saadiah and Abraham ibn Ezra; cf. Rashbam, who interprets literally) does not prove submission to talmudic authority, since it conforms with Lev 25:40 ("... only until the Jubilee year") and thus coincides with Ibn Ezra's *peshat* method, which requires reconciling biblical contradictions (below, sec. 2.3).

[12] See, e.g., K 152b (Judg 9:13; *b. Ber.* 35a). This appears to be his view of rabbinic *gemaṭria* (numerology), which he grants a measure of credibility by classifying as *išāra* (allusion, one of the twenty Arabic ornaments [below, n. 55]), although he also calls it "harmless foolishness and useless wisdom" (K 123a; cf. Abraham ibn Ezra's harsher attitude on Gen 14:14; short comm. on Exod 1:7). The strategy of taking rabbinic readings as homilies rather than genuine exegesis appears in Judah Halevi (*Kuzari* 3.73) and Maimonides (*Guide* 3.43); see M. Saperstein, *Decoding the Rabbis* (Cambridge, MA 1980) 9–11.

[13] See, e.g., below, n. 27. This strategy is common among Spanish rationalists; see Abraham ibn Ezra, intro. to Pentateuch ("Fourth Approach") and Lamentations; Maimonides, intro. to *Pereq Ḥeleq, Mishnah ʿim Perush ha-Rambam: Neziqin* (ed. J. Qāfiḥ; Jerusalem 1965) 202; Saperstein, Decoding the Rabbis (1980) 11–14; Klein-Braslavy, Solomon (1996) 101.

[14] See, e.g., below, n. 25 (Saadiah); see also K 26a (Hai).

[15] Halkin, *Kitāb* (1975) passim; Fenton, Jardin (1997) 377–80. Ibn Ezra sometimes rejects Ibn Janah's views, e.g., his aesthetic judgement regarding "repetition of the ... same idea [in different] words" (below, n. 61). He more firmly rejects the 'substitution' principle ("[Scripture uses a word with the meaning of another"; *Riqma*, chap. 27), arguing that it undermines exegetical integrity ("if it were completely valid, no narrative would remain reliable nor would any commandment endure"; K 134b). This is not unique in the Spanish tradition; see M. Pereẓ, "*Ḥilluf millah be-zulatah ke-middah parshanit eẓel hakhme yeme ha-benayyim*", *Iyyune Miqra U-farshanut* II (ed. U. Simon; Ramat Gan 1986) 207–28.

from reflecting the influence of this "absolute authority on Hebrew" (K 74 a) in eleventh century Spain, this preference reveals Ibn Ezra's belief in the continuous progress of Hebrew scholarship.

Manifesting the spirit of comparative linguistics, Ibn Ezra recommends the work of his friend, Isaac ibn Barun, *The Book of Comparison Between the Hebrew and Arabic Languages* (K 22 a),[16] and his own linguistic exegesis relies heavily on Arabic and Aramaic cognates. He exploits his knowledge of Arabic as a living language by adducing its idiomatic expressions, metaphorical usages and grammatical anomalies to illuminate biblical locutions.[17] Further assuming – perhaps overstating – a shared Hebrew-Arabic cultural heritage, Ibn Ezra cites verses of Arabic poetry to offer novel biblical readings. Job 29:20, קשתי בידי תחליף, for example, was rendered "My bow *is ever new* in my hand" by the "majority of great exegetes" in his time.[18] But Ibn Ezra, based on mishnaic use of the verb חלף for trees growing foliage *(m. ʿAbod. Zar.* 3:4), invokes the Arabic topos of a stick sprouting in the hands of a blessed man and reads this verse as an imaginative depiction of dead wood reviving in Job's hand, yielding "My bow sprouts leaves in my hand" (K 138 b).[19]

2.3. Philosophical Exegesis

Walking another path well trodden in Andalusian scholarship, Ibn Ezra aims to harmonize Scripture and human reason. In the first section of the *Maqāla*, he devises an epistemology to establish the accuracy of scientific knowledge and formulates a corresponding exegetical method, asserting that a verse contradicting (1) sense perception, (2) rational or received truth, (3) deductive reasoning or (4) another biblical verse must be reinterpreted (M 28–29). To implement this method, he uses the Arabic *majāz-ḥaqīqa* dichotomy: *ḥaqīqa* (lit. truth; Heb., *'emet*) is the label he applies to literal, accurate language (*muḥkam*), which conforms with reason and need not be reinterpreted; but if a phrase contradicts reason, it must convey a meaning other that its literal sense and is *majāz* (lit. metaphor; Heb., *haʿavara*), i. e. non-literal language (M 27–28).[20] Exod 24:10, "They *saw* the God of Israel" is thus *majāz* since God is invisible; but Exod 33:20, "Man cannot see Me and live", is *ḥaqīqa* (M 44). The

---

16 See P. WECHTER, *Ibn Barun's Arabic Works on Hebrew Grammar and Lexicography* (Philadelphia 1964) 4–6.

17 See Fenton, Jardin (1997) 341–74.

18 See Saadiah, ad loc.; Ibn Janah, *Shorashim*, s. v. חלף.

19 The image of a miraculously sprouting stick is biblical (Num 17:23), but one sprouting in a man's hand is specifically Arabic. For other examples in which Ibn Ezra cites Arabic poetry to elucidate Scripture, see below, n. 83 (Job 31:24); M 171–172 (Ps 77:5); Schippers, Spanish Hebrew Poetry (1994) 37–39.

20 This can be traced to Saadiah and his school; see *Beliefs and Opinions* 7.1 and *Saadya's Commentary on Genesis* (ed. and tr., M. Zucker; New York 1984) 17–18 (Arab.), 190–92 (Heb.). For the range of Ibn Ezra's Jewish and Arabic sources in applying the *majāz-ḥaqīqa* dichotomy, see Fenton, Jardin (1997) 243–98. Although some scholars render *majāz* as "metaphor," Ibn Ezra, following medieval usage, applies it to a wide range of non-literal language; see Heinrichs, Genesis (1984); Ḥ. BEN-SHAMMAI, "Saadya's Introduction to Isaiah" [Hebrew], *Tarbiẓ* 60 (1991) 380–82. We therefore avoid translating *majāz* as "metaphor" (which should be reserved for the technical term *istiʿāra*; below, sec. 3.3).

term *ḥaqīqa* is also used in a second sense, to denote the "true meaning" of a *majāz* expression; for example, "killing" is the *ḥaqīqa* of the biblical idiom "spilling blood" (*dam shafakh*; M 138).

According to Ibn Ezra, the exegete's task is to "strip away" the "husks" of Scripture's imprecise *majāz* and "(re)clothe" the "true idea" (Arab. *al-maʿna al-ḥaqīqi*; Heb. *ha-ʿinyan ha-ʾamiti*) in more accurate language (M 46; A 137),[21] an operation especially crucial with respect to concrete biblical depictions of God. For example, verses that speak of God dwelling in heaven, such as Qoh 5:1 and Ps 2:4, must be classified as *majāz*, since God lacks material form and cannot be located in a physical universe (M 42; A 135).[22] Despite their imprecision, such depictions are meaningful; Scripture, for example, speaks of God "dwelling in the heavens" because they illuminate and surround the world, indicating that He is the spiritual luminary that 'encompasses' the universe (M 42–43; A 135). More fundamentally, Ibn Ezra argues that *majāz*, even graphic anthropomorphism, is a worthy medium for describing God and that insistence on exact language is unreasonable, since God's essence is unknowable and hence, indescribable (M 46; A 137).[23] This tolerance for anthropomorphism diverges from the more severe attitude of philosophers such as Saadiah and Maimonides, and conforms, instead, with Ibn Ezra's poetic outlook, which encourages vivid metaphorical depiction, despite its inexactness.[24]

Asserting that human reason intuitively discerns *majāz* from *ḥaqīqa*, Ibn Ezra assumes that no tradition is required to apply the exegetical method stemming from this dichotomy (M 28–29). This frees him from the bonds of rabbinic exegesis[25] and enables him to interpret Scripture using Greek and Arabic philosophy. He invokes pythagorean mathematical theories to explicate biblical references to God's unity, neo-Platonic and Muʿtazilite doctrines to interpret biblical names and attributes of God, Kalam for the biblical account of creation, and Plato's psychology for man's nature and the biblical terms, *nefesh* (soul) and *ru'aḥ* (spirit).[26] Hardly an iconoclast in this respect, Ibn Ezra

[21] Fenton, Jardin (1997) 118 observes that this passage is adapted from Baḥya ibn Paquda.

[22] Ibn Ezra cites Aristotle and Socrates for this theological principle. In *ʿArugat ha-Bosem* (but not the Arabic MS), 1 Kgs 8:27, "Even the heavens ... cannot contain You", a verse regarded as *ḥaqīqa*, is also cited.

[23] He cites Neh 9:5, "May Your glorious name be blessed, exalted though it is above all blessing and praise"; but the doctrine of 'negative attributes', attributed to Aristotle (M 34–36; A 122), may have also influenced him (Fenton, Jardin [1997] 94–101).

[24] See sec. 3.2 below. Ibn Ezra's tolerant attitude can also be traced to the more moderate philosophical stance of Baḥya ibn Paquda, *Duties of the Heart* 1.10 (echoed in Judah Halevi, *Kuzari* 4.3–5). See Fenton, Jardin (1997) 290–92; S. Rawidowicz, "Baʿayat ha-Hagshama le-Rasag we-la-Rambam", *Hebrew Studies in Jewish Thought* (Jerusalem 1969) 182–88.

[25] Ibn Ezra thus follows a tradition of the Bible scholars described by Baḥya ibn Paquda (*Duties of the Heart* 3.4) who interpret Scripture "in its plain sense, without [rabbinic] tradition" and devote their efforts to distinguishing between *majāz* and *ḥaqīqa*, especially in connection with anthropomorphism. Indeed, Ibn Ezra does not hesitate to note his disagreements with the Rabbis. E.g., after citing the literal rabbinic reading of Exod 10:21, "Darkness could be felt" ("it was as thick as a dinar"; *Exod. Rab.* 14:1), he argues that since darkness is a lack of light, not a substance (for which he cites Saadiah, *Beliefs and Opinions*, 1.3), this phrase must be hyperbole (*'īgāl*; 1951; M 263–64).

[26] Fenton, Jardin (1997) 83–93, 94–125, 125–34, 174–84.

simply follows rationalist rabbinic predecessors who had already introduced Greek and Arabic philosophy into Jewish learning. Moreover, he maintains that his interpretations express the essence of rabbinic thought, and where rabbinic literature seems to indicate otherwise he argues for a *majāz* reading. For example, rabbinic anthropomorphic depictions of God were adduced by Muslims and Karaites alike as evidence that the Rabbis, unschooled in philosophy, believed that God is corporeal. But Ibn Ezra argues that such depictions, just as those in Scripture, were never meant literally (M 46; A 137).[27]

Despite its centrality in his thinking, Ibn Ezra cautions against over-applying *majāz* readings. Implicitly criticizing Christian exegesis, he rejects any allegorical reading of the Pentateuchal commandments (K 148 a).[28] He is less decisive on supernatural eschatological prophecies, which were routinely reinterpreted by medieval Jewish rationalists. As a believer in nature's permanence, Ibn Ezra regards Isa 65:17, "I am creating a new heaven and a new earth", for example, as *majāz* (K 140 b); yet he cautions against radically revising the traditional view of "the end of days", insisting that

> passages depicting the awaited [messianic] kingdom ... are neither allegory nor hyperbole ... [rather] all of the miracles are true in their plain sense ... and one who interprets [otherwise] is not a believer in Jewish tradition (K 139 a).

The anonymous heretical view is that of Moses ibn Chiquitilla, who rejects the literal sense of such passages and their application to messianic times.[29] Elsewhere, Ibn Ezra reveals mixed feelings about Ibn Chiquitilla, "a foremost scholar ... and a great writer and poet, although some madness was within him, which diminished his great stature" (K 36 a). On the eschatological prophecies, Ibn Ezra sides with Ibn Chiquitilla's antagonist, Judah ibn Balʿam, referring to his work (no longer extant) on biblical miracles (K 139 a). Marshalling support from another sphere, Ibn Ezra cites Aristotle's prediction of an ideal future world republic, which he equates with the traditional view of "the eagerly awaited [messianic] prophetic assurances" (K 139 b).[30]

3. A Poetic Perspective

3.1. The Arabic Model

While sailing the currents of the rationalist tradition in his *Maqāla*, Ibn Ezra sets an independent course in the *Kitāb*, a work that reveals a different facet of his thinking. The *Maqāla* is devoted to biblical exegesis; the *Kitāb*, a hand-

---

[27] Fenton, Jardin (1997) 288–89.

[28] Abraham ibn Ezra explicitly refers to this as a Christian tendency in both recensions of his introduction to the Pentateuch.

[29] Simon, Four Approaches (1991) 113–15; idem, "Ibn Ezra Between Medievalism and Modernism: The Case of Isaiah XL–LXVI", VTSup 36 (1985) 259–61. His non-eschatological reading of Isa 11:6–7 ("The wolf shall dwell with the lamb ..."), e.g., is cited by Maimonides, *Treatise on Resurrection* (ed. and tr. Y. Shilat; Jerusalem 1987) 329 (Arab.), 359 (Heb.) and Abraham ibn Ezra on Isa 11:1.

[30] See Stern, Aristotle (1968) 1–10, 78–80.

book for writing Arabic style Hebrew poetry, deals with Scripture tangentially. Whereas the *Maqāla* aims to wrest Scripture's meaning from its poetic exterior, it is the stylistic aspect that engages Ibn Ezra's interest in the *Kitāb*. Two distinct objectives vis à vis Scripture emerge in the *Kitāb* itself. Ibn Ezra's stated aim is to establish the Bible's aesthetic merit in the face of the imposing beauty of Arabic poetry, which he achieves by 'tracing' Arabic literary conventions to Scripture. Yet his findings also serve to justify the adoption of Arabic poetics by Andalusian Hebrew poets, who viewed their work as an extension of biblical literary tradition.[31] In pursuing these interests, Ibn Ezra formulates an aesthetic exegesis by using Arabic poetics as a prism to reveal Scripture's poetic qualities.[32] This analysis was revolutionary in Jewish tradition; but just as Ibn Ezra attributed the dramatic advance of Hebrew scholarship to Arabic linguistics, he believed that Arabic poetics could unlock the secrets of biblical literary style.[33]

Novelty was not the most controversial aspect of the *Kitāb*. In adopting the Arabic model, Hebrew poets implicitly conceded its aesthetic superiority over biblical style, a display of *ʿarabiyya* (Arabism) that many viewed as a threat to Jewish cultural identity.[34] In treating Arabic poetics as a definitive literary yardstick, using it even to evaluate Scripture, Ibn Ezra renders the same verdict explicitly. Asserting that Andalusian Hebrew poetry owes its excellence to Arabic influence (K 28 b), he advises poets to avoid biblical style where it conflicts with Arabic conventions (K 86 b; 117 b–118 a).[35] Though debated even in Andalusia, Ibn Ezra's views emerge from the same rationalist outlook that valued the achievements of other cultures and prompted Saadiah to utilize Greek philosophy and Hayyuj to use Arabic linguistics. Indeed, Ibn Ezra's aesthetic exegesis yields profound results particularly because of its 'foreign' gauge. Other medieval authors vaguely assert the Bible's literary excellence, often in response to similar Arab claims about the Koran,[36] but Ibn Ezra, resisting

[31] Scheindlin, Legitimacy (1976) 109–10; Brann, Compunctious Poet (1991) 81–82. Ironically, even in this respect Ibn Ezra parallels Arabic tradition, since Arab poets also sought Koranic precedents for these techniques to justify using them (Brann, loc. cit.; Cantarino, Arabic Poetics [1975] 18; Heinrichs, Istiʿārah [1984] 188–89).

[32] An aesthetic bent also emerges in the *Maqāla* (see Fenton, Jardin [1997] 301–04, 332–41) but is subordinated to the interpretive focus of that work and does not match the systematic, comprehensive literary analysis of the *Kitāb*.

[33] The *Kitāb* draws extensively upon Arabic experts on poetry such as Ibn al-Muʿtazz (d. 908), Qudāma Ibn Jaʿfar (d. 932), al-Ḥātimi (d. 998) and Ibn Rašīq (d. 1065); for full analysis of Ibn Ezra's Arabic sources, see Dana, Poetics (1982).

[34] See Brann, Compunctious Poet (1991) 14–16, 30–33, 69–70.

[35] See below, n. 61. This does not imply that the Bible had been superseded as a religious text; Ibn Ezra simply argues that its stylistic exterior (not its content) is less than perfect; see Cohen, Best of Poetry (1995/6) 38–39. Scheindlin, Legitimacy (1976) 114, argues that Ibn Ezra defends Arabic-style Hebrew poetry in part by viewing poetic style as "a relatively unimportant phenomenon, hardly more than a craft", which makes Arabic poetry superior to Scripture only in a minor respect. Early Christian writers such as Gregory the Great (d. 604) and Isodore of Seville (d. 636) similarly admit that the eloquence of secular poetry may surpass that of Scripture, which transcends other literature by virtue of its inner wisdom (G. E. von Grunebaum, *A Tenth-Century Document of Arabic Literary Theory and Criticism* [Chicago 1950] xv; see also Kugel, Idea [1981] 159–72).

[36] E. g. Judah Halevi and Samuel ibn Tibbon; see Berlin, Biblical Poetry (1991) 62–64, 88–89; Cohen, Best of Poetry (1995/6) 23–25.

dogmatic prejudice, uses the scientific tools of his day to define Scripture's artistry empirically.

3.2. Literary Theory

Medieval Arabic poetics focused primarily on formal features, a perspective Ibn Ezra embraces, devoting almost half of his *Kitāb* to twenty poetic 'ornaments', i.e., rhetorical embellishments known collectively as 'the *badīʿ*' (lit. new [style]).[37] Adhering to Arabic theory, Ibn Ezra views these as decoration for ideas that could be expressed more directly and precisely in plain language. Although literal language *(muḥkam)* is most precise, he concedes, the "cloak of metaphor" (*ṯawb al -istiʿāra*), a principal ornament (see below), adds elegance that makes the former seem "naked" by contrast (K 118 b). On this basis, he justifies the maxim of medieval poets, "the best of poetry is its most false" (Arab. *aṭyab aš-šiʿr akḏabuhu*; Heb. *meiṭav ha-shir kezabo*; K 62 a), a target of those who accused poetry of deceit in a tradition dating to Plato. Admitting that a poem devoid of 'falsehood', i.e., hyperbole, fanciful metaphors and other ornaments, "would not be a poem", Ibn Ezra argues that this characterizes the poem's external 'garb' alone, not its true content (K 62 b).[38]

The value Ibn Ezra attributes to poetic form *per se* depends on his overall aesthetic theory, expressed in a section on music in the *Maqāla*. The "ancient [Greek] philosophers", he records, explain how music "stir[s] up the noble forces of the soul" and awakens man's aesthetic sensibilities, a capacity recognized by Scripture, which assigns to music a central role in the temple service and prophecy.[39] Speaking of poetry (which he compares with visual art [K 64 a]) in similar terms, he suggests that it, too, stimulates man's aesthetic sense: its rhythm, meter, sound-plays, imagery and other ornaments cause it to be "most strongly fastened to the ears and most closely attached to [man's] nature" and penetrate his heart like "engraving in a stone" (K 14 b–15 a; 76 b).[40]

The form-content dichotomy underlies Ibn Ezra's conception of language, which is comprised of a given idea *(maʿna)* conveyed by specific wording (*lafẓ*). He conceives the latter as an incidental "husk" and the former as its "kernel" or "essence":

> The husk is ... perceived by the ear, much as the other senses with respect to what they perceive; but [sense] perception is not understanding ... which occurs only in the heart ... [when] the

---

[37] On the formalism of Arabic poetics, see G. E. von Grunebaum, "The Aesthetic Foundation of Arabic Literature", *Comparative Literature* IV (1952) 326–29; repr. in *Themes in Medieval Arabic Literature* (London 1981); see also below, n. 41. On the *badīʿ* and the techniques it included, see von Grunebaum, Tenth-Century Document (1950) 116–17. On the Arabic sources of Ibn Ezra's list of twenty ornaments, see Schippers, Symmetry (1990) 172.

[38] See Brann, Compunctious Poet (1991) 72, 191; Scheindlin, Legitimacy (1976) 107–08. On the parallel discussion in the Arabic tradition, see Cantarino, Arabic Poetics (1975) 27–40.

[39] Shiloah, Musical Passage (1982) 218–20 (Arab.), 221–24 (Eng.). Ibn Ezra cites 1 Chr 25:1–5 to demonstrate that the Psalms were set to music in the temple and 2 Kgs 3:15 to indicate that music inspires prophecy.

[40] For other medieval authors who compare music and poetry; see Berlin, Biblical Poetry (1991) 44–46; 89–99.

idea is received by the intellect ... The [biblical] sage [says], "Incline your ear and listen to the words of the wise/ Direct your heart to my wisdom" (Prov 22:17) ... He specifies the ear for hearing ... the husk ... and the heart for [understanding] the essence, i.e., the idea (K 77 b).[41]

Arguing that the "husk" is virtually extraneous to the "essence" it contains, Ibn Ezra asserts that each biblical prophet would independently formulate the words of his prophecy, "though different from the wording he heard [from God]; but what does not change is the idea" (K 77 b).[42] Appearing elsewhere in the Spanish tradition, this claim acquires special meaning for Ibn Ezra since it implies that while the content of prophecy is divine, its literary form is the work of the prophets. Further indicating that the prophet was responsible for the aesthetic dimension that would intensify the emotive force of his divine message, Ibn Ezra equates the biblical word *nāḇī* (prophet) with Arabic *šāʿir* (poet), taking both to signify the craft of conveying ideas in the most beautiful and fitting language (K 12 b–14 a).[43] In viewing biblical prophets as literary artists, Ibn Ezra reduces the distance between them and medieval Hebrew poets, providing a conceptual framework for his analysis of Scripture in terms of the human science of poetics.

The axiom that poetry consists of ideas literarily adorned, applied to Scripture, invites the interpretive method of the *Maqāla*, which "strips away" the "husks" of the Bible's "false", though beautiful, *majāz* to reveal its "true idea" (above, sec. 2.3). This exegetical corollary of Arabic poetics reveals the ideology of the *peshat* tradition, which typically identifies aesthetic features only to argue that their interpretation is unnecessary.[44] In the *Maqāla*, Ibn Ezra speaks the language of that tradition, but in the *Kitāb* he instead describes how the Bible 'clothes' ideas in poetic ornaments and celebrates its 'false' artistic exterior as a guide for Hebrew poets.

Manifesting his aesthetic concerns, Ibn Ezra warns that a precise translation of Scripture may forfeit its literary elegance, as he illustrates with an anecdote intended to disprove the Koran's supposed aesthetic superiority:

In my youth, in my hometown, a Muslim scholar ... asked me to recite the Ten Commandments in Arabic. I understood his intention, to demonstrate the paucity of its rhetoric. I therefore asked him to recite the opening of his Koran in Latin ... but when he set out to translate it into that language its words became ugly and its beauty tarnished. He understood my intention and released me from his request (K 24 a).

He instead favors a free translation possessing its own rhetorical refinement, and cites the work of Hafṣ al-Qūṭi, a ninth century Christian who translated Scripture into versified Arabic (K 23 b).[45]

---

41 On the Arabic *lafẓ-maʿna* distinction, see Cantarino, Arabic Poetics (1975) 46–51; J. Sadan, "Maiden's Hair and Starry Skies", *Studies in Medieval Arabic and Hebrew Poetics* (ed. S. Somekh; Leiden 1991) 58–67. Borrowing other common metaphors for this distinction, Ibn Ezra (K 77 b) portrays the wording as a "vessel" that holds the idea and as a "body" that houses the "soul" (i.e., the idea); compare Abraham ibn Ezra, long comm. on Exod 20:1; chap. 33.2 of this volume (U. Simon).

42 Compare Abraham ibn Ezra, *Sefer Sefat Yeter* § 84; see also Kugel, Idea (1981) 184–85.

43 See Scheindlin, Legitimacy (1976) 111.

44 Cohen, Best of Poetry (1995/6) 16–19, 25–33; see also chap. 33.2 of this volume (U. Simon).

45 See M. Urvoy, *Le Psautier Mozarabe de Hafs le Goth, édition et traduction* (Toulouse 1994).

Ibn Ezra's admission that poetic form in general tends to be 'false' enables him to adopt a sanguine attitude towards the erotic literal sense of the Song of Songs, a controversial matter in his time. Defending erotic medieval Hebrew poetry, he writes:

> The love and passion ... [depicted by] the poets of our people are not repugnant since this is found in the Holy Writings, even though the hidden meaning of that work is different from the obvious meaning of the words (K 143 a).

Following rabbinic tradition, he takes the Song allegorically as a portrait of divine, rather than human, love. Yet he recognizes the literary charm of its external sense, which, while 'false', beautifully clothes the Song's true 'inner content' and is thus an artistic model worthy of emulation.[46]

3.3. Defining Biblical Poetics

Ibn Ezra begins his poetic analysis of Scripture by classifying it within the spectrum of Arabic literary genres. Adopting the Arabic judgement that poetry (*šiʿr*), i.e., rhymed, metrical verse (*naẓm*; lit. string of pearls; K 14 a–15 a), is artistically superior to prose (*naṯr*; lit. scattering; K 10 a),[47] he ponders whether "metrical verse was known to our Israelite nation in [ancient times]" (K 5 a). Citing the biblical evidence, he concludes:

> We have found nothing in [Scripture] departing from prose (*manṯūr*) save these three books: Psalms, Job and Proverbs. And these ... employ neither meter nor rhyme in the manner of the Arabs, but are only like *rajaz* compositions (K 24 b).

Though written in verse (i.e., stichographically rather than continuously), these books are not 'poetic' in the Arabic sense; and even the comparison to *rajaz*, the lowest Arabic poetic form, is inexact, since *rajaz* is normally rhymed.[48]

Echoes of alternatives to this harsh verdict can be heard in the *Kitāb*. Ibn Ezra cites an unnamed scholar[49] who believed that 1 Kgs 5:12, "[Solomon]'s

---

Reflecting the tenuous balance between accuracy and elegance, Ibn Ezra lauds al-Qūṭi's loose translation of Ps 55:22 but notes the "many errors in the remainder [of his work]" (K 128 a); see A. Schippers, "Medieval Opinions on the Difficulty of Translating the Psalms", *Give Ear to My Words, Psalms and other Poetry in and Around the Hebrew Bible: Essays in Honour of Professor V. A. van Uchelen* (ed. J. Dyk; Amsterdam 1996) 219–26.

[46] See Pagis, Secular Poetry (1970) 273; idem, "*À propos de l'amour intelectuel dans les œuvres de Moïse Ibn Ezra*", *REJ* 126 (1976) 191–96; Brann, Compunctious Poet (1991) 78. Ibn Ezra's attitude is echoed by Joseph ibn ʿAqnin, who argues that the Song's poetic beauty is intended to captivate readers; see Ibn Aqnin, *Perush Shir ha-Shirim* (1964) 2; Eng. tr. in Halkin, Ibn ʿAḳnin's Commentary (1950) 407.

[47] See Cantarino, Arabic Poetics (1975) 41–45.

[48] Ibn Ezra cites three rhymed verses in Job (28:16; 33:17; 21:4) but recognizes that they do not reflect a pattern, commenting that "sometimes by chance in some of the[se] books there is something by way of *rajaz*" (K 25 a). A similar list, Job 28:16, 21:4 and Isa 49:1, appears in the fragment on poetics from Saadiah's school (Allony, Haʾegron [1969] 112; above, n. 2). If this was Ibn Ezra's source, he may have substituted Job 33:17 for Isa 49:1 because he did not regard Isaiah as a poetic book (Berlin, Biblical Poetry [1991] 81).

[49] Probably a reference to his teacher, Isaac ibn Ghiyāth (Simon, Four Approaches [1991] 271).

poetry (*shir*) was one thousand and five", refers to lost poetry of the higher *qaṣīda* form, but he himself is skeptical that these differed from existing biblical 'poetry' (25 a–b). Other authors pointed to biblical passages explicitly labeled *shir(a)*, the medieval Hebrew term for "poetry" (phonetically similar to Arabic *šiʿr*),[50] but Ibn Ezra is more cautious:

[Aside from the three poetic books,] some biblical *shirot* depart from prose: "Then Moses uttered this *shira* ..." (Exod 15:1 ff) "Give ear, O heavens ..." (Deut 32:1 ff), "David uttered the words of this *shira* ..." (2 Sam 22:1 ff). I say *some* of the *shirot* because prose [texts] also are called *shira*, e.g., the Song of Songs (*shir ha-shirim*), the Song (*shira*) of the Well (Num 21:17–18) and others (K 25 a).

Applying empirical criteria, he concludes that the biblical term *shir(a)*, unlike the medieval term, does not signify 'poetry'.

Faced with the Bible's lack of prosody, Ibn Ezra upholds its poetic merit by devising an aesthetic exegesis based on the *badiʿ*. Aristotle had enumerated eight techniques "through which poetry is refined and embellished ... [e.g.,] beauty of the similes and quality of the metaphors"; but it was the Arabs that "explored them meticulously and divided into many more [categories]" (K 76 a–b).[51] Accordingly, Ibn Ezra takes his definitions and examples of the ornaments from Arabic works on poetics. Yet he also labors to find biblical examples, as he explains in introducing the twenty ornaments comprising the *badiʿ*:

For each ... I cite an example from Arabic verse and juxtapose with it what I find in the Holy Scriptures, lest ... it be said that the Arabic language is unique in these embellishments ... and that our language is devoid of them (K 116 b).[52]

Wary of anachronism, Ibn Ezra admits that his biblical 'examples' merely resemble, but are not conscious applications of, the *badiʿ* (K 116 b), although at times he implies that biblical authors intuitively employed the very techniques that would later be defined by Arabic poetics.

To resolve this ambiguity, we must divide the *badiʿ* into three groups based on Ibn Ezra's programmatic preface. Most of the ornaments are uniquely Arabic conventions and lead him to either (1) follow his stated procedure, citing Arabic examples followed by biblical quasi-examples, or (2) admit being unable to find the latter. But in one subset of the *badiʿ*, which includes universal techniques such as those identified by Aristotle, (3) the biblical examples precede and even eclipse the Arabic ones, indicating that they are genuinely represented in Scripture.[53] Below we analyze seven ornaments that reflect this distinction; the first four, stemming from Arabic verse forms, exemplify the first group, the last three exemplify the third:[54]

---

[50] See Berlin, Biblical Poetry (1991) 33–34.

[51] For possible Aristotelian influence on Arabic poetics, adumbrated here by Ibn Ezra, see G. J. H. van Gelder, *Beyond the Line* (Leiden 1982) 4–5; Cantarino, Arabic Poetics (1975) 66, 71–72.

[52] See Brann, Compunctious Poet (1991) 82. This echoes an actual claim raised by Arab poets; see S. A. Bonebakker, "Aspects of the History of Literary Rhetoric and Poetics in Arabic Literature", *Viator: Medieval and Renaissance Studies* 1 (1970) 75–95.

[53] Dana, Poetics (1982) 117–18, 125, 152, 161, 177.

[54] The unique Arabic literary outlook, even towards universal techniques, complicates translat-

i. *Ḥašw bayt li-qāmat wazn* (padding a verse to support the meter)
ii. *Taqsīm* (specification)
iii. *Tardīd* (reiteration, anaphora)
iv. *Muṭābaqa* (antithesis)

The remaining eight ornaments of the first group are: *išāra* (allusion), *muqābala* (correspondence), *tashīm* (distribution), *tatbī'*, (ellipsis), *tablīg* (excess), *istiṯnā'* (reservation), *i'tirāḍ* (parenthetical clause) and *taṣdīr* (inclusio).[55] The four not found in Scripture are: *tatmīm* (completion), *ḥusn al-ibtidā'* (grace of the opening), *taḫalluṣ* (transition) and *istiṭrāḍ* (digression).[56]

v. *Isti'āra* (metaphor)
vi. *Tašbīh* (simile, comparison)
vii. *Maṯal* (allegory, parable)[57]

The other two 'universal' ornaments are: *mujānasa* (paronomasia, word play) and *guluww* (hyperbole).[58]

i. *Ḥašw bayt li-qāmat wazn* (padding a verse to support the meter) is based on the premise that strict meter is required "for a poem to be a poem" (K 135 b), a principle that Ibn Ezra admits is foreign to the Bible. Yet he claims that

> in Scripture there is something resembling it, for example, "I shall provide you with shepherds after my own heart / And they shall pasture you with knowledge and skill" (Jer 3:15); now once it says "after my own heart" the intention is complete; [the next phrase] is a delightful [poetic] addition (K 135 b).[59]

Associating it with the Arabic "padding" technique, Ibn Ezra suggests that this "delightful addition" creates some sort of metrical structure, without actually adhering to a strict Arabic meter. The features of this biblical quasi-meter, left undefined here, emerge in connection with ornaments that dictate specific verse forms, such as *taqsīm, tardīd* and *muṭābaqa.*

Before turning to these ornaments individually, we should note that Ibn Ezra uses them to offer a novel analysis of biblical verse structure. The Andalusian *peshat* school devised the rule that Scripture "permits repetition of the ... same idea if the words are changed" in order to avoid over-exegesis typical

---

ing these literary terms; for analysis and other possible translations, see Mashiah, Terminology (1972); Dana, Poetics (1982).

[55] On *išāra*, see above, n. 12; on *tashīm, taṣdir* and *muqābala*, see notes below.

[56] Though it does not illuminate biblical poetics, this group confirms Ibn Ezra's objectivity by revealing his willingness to concede the Bible's lack of poetic refinement. Manifesting an atypical tone, however, he writes that *ḥusn al-ibtidā'* (i. e., opening a poem with a digression from the main topic) does not occur in Scripture, "since the Holy Scriptures are so exalted and holy ... [that] every opening [in them] ... is noble and exalted" (K 141). The idea that holiness produces poetic elegance normally provided by the *badī'.* (suited to more dogmatic medieval authors [above, n. 36]) occurs nowhere else in the *Kitāb.* For attempts to explain why Ibn Ezra adopts this approach particularly towards *ḥusn al-ibtidā'*, see Mashiah, Hebrew Prosody (1972) 181–84; Van Gelder, Beyond the Line (Leiden 1982) 140–42.

[57] *Maṯal* appears separately, following the twenty ornaments; see Dana, Poetics (1982) 175–78.

[58] On *mujānasa* and *guluww*, see notes below.

[59] It is surprising that his single biblical example is from Jeremiah, a book he does not consider poetic (above). He may intend to show that even biblical prose manifests the *badī'.*

of the Rabbis, who labor to discern between synonymous phrases (K 87 a).[60] "An eminent scholar of language", i.e., Ibn Janah (*Riqma* 303), rendered the corollary aesthetic judgement that repetition is "elegant and beautiful style" (*fasāḥa wa-balāga*; K 87 a). But Ibn Ezra could not accept this, since Arabic theory regarded redundancy as a fault and favored brevity (K 88 a, 92 a).[61] On one level, he concedes that biblical authors adhered to a non-Arabic standard, which he advises poets of his day to avoid, saying that "inasmuch as we follow the Arabs especially closely in poetry, it is necessary for us to follow them to the degree that we can" (K 86 b). Yet he attempts to harmonize Scripture with Arabic theory by invoking techniques such as *taqsīm* and *tardīd*, which themselves necessitate redundancy, to demonstrate that the Arabic aversion towards repetition is not absolute and may be suspended in favor of other poetic values.

ii. *Taqsīm* (specification) involves symmetrical, parallel versets in which "the poet clarifies that with which he began and does not leave [out] from it any item required by the topic" (K 127 a).[62] Although an idea could be stated in a succinct general formulation, *taqsīm* implies the superiority of a series of vividly specific balanced versets. Assessing an Arabic verse laden with seemingly redundant details, Ibn Ezra says: "not one extra letter enters among its descriptions and similes" (K 127 b), a judgement he applies to biblical verses such as "Her rulers judge for bribes / Her priests rule for a fee / And her prophets divine for money" (Mic 3:11). Though the idea of corruption could be expressed in a single verset, Micah augments the rhetorical effect of his rebuke by specifying three types of illicit payments in three balanced versets (K 127 b).[63]

iii. *Tardīd* (reiteration, anaphora) entails "the poet's affixing a word to [the beginning of] the first hemistich (*bayt*) and then he repeats the very same [word] at [the beginning of] the second hemistich (*miṣra*)" (K 129 b). Applying the two-hemistich Arabic verse form to Scripture, Ibn Ezra finds a number of biblical examples, including "Your right hand, O Lord, glorious in power / *Your right hand* shatters the foe" (Exod 15:6) and "Ascribe to the Lord, O divine beings / *Ascribe to the Lord* glory and might" (Ps 29:1; K 130 a).[64] Hinting at the redundancy

---

[60] E.g., Ibn Ezra cites an unnamed exegete who argued that in Isa 43:7, "I have created, formed and made him", the word "created" refers to conception, "formed" to formation of limbs and veins, and "made" to growth of skin; but he considers this "[overly] detailed analysis ... [since] the intent is [simply] emphasis" (K 87 a). The rule that Scripture "repeats ideas in different words", was embraced by later *peshat* exegetes, especially Abraham ibn Ezra and Radak; see Kugel, Idea (1981) 176–80 and chaps. 33.2 (U. Simon) and 33.3 (M. Cohen) of this volume.

[61] Perhaps this is why he resists the otherwise persuasive exegetical rule of repetition. E.g., citing a view that "Your land", "birthplace" and "father's home" (Gen 12:1) are synonymous, he argues instead that the first phrase refers to Abraham's "country" (Mesopotamia), the second his "city of birth", the third his "neighborhood" (K 89 a); see Kugel, Idea (1981) 180. Interestingly, a similar tendency emerges in Joseph Qimhi, a less poetically inclined author, who formulates the exegetical rule: "wherever you can find a sound explanation, do not invoke [the rule of] repetition (*kefel*)" (comm. on Prov 14:13); see chap. 33.3 of this volume (M. Cohen), sec. 1.3.

[62] See Schippers, Symmetry (1990) 165–66.

[63] *Tashīm* (distribution) is a similar ornament which also involves a series of symmetrical versets; e.g., "Dull that people's mind / Stop its ears / And seal its eyes" (Isa 6:10; K 129 a–b; see Schippers, Symmetry [1990] 168).

[64] Ibn Ezra's French contemporary, Rashbam, also notes this pattern, but, lacking a poetic framework, he could neither analyze its aesthetic function nor relate it to other stylistic patterns (see Rashbam on Gen 49:22; Exod 15:6; see also S. Japhet / R. Salters, *The Commentary of R. Samuel Ben Meir* Rashbam *on Qohelet* [Jerusalem 1985] 52).

this technique requires, he comments: "now this does not ruin [the verse]; but rather increases its beauty" (K 129 b),[65] since it produces a poetically symmetrical verse.[66]

iv. *Muṭābaqa* (antithesis) involves two contrasting ideas in metrically equivalent verse halves (K 124 b–125 a). Substituting a simple two-hemistich verse structure for strict Arabic meter, Ibn Ezra asserts that "in Hebrew [Scripture] it is abundant, e.g., ... 'Let every valley be raised / And every hill and mount be made low' (Isa 40:4) ... and a beautiful antithesis is 'A hot-tempered man provokes quarrel / But a patient man calms strife' (Prov 15:18)". Although it does not entail repetition, *muṭābaqa*, like the previous two ornaments, creates a symmetrical verse form, as Ibn Ezra indicates in his praise of Ps 90:6, "In the morning it sprouts and grows / In the evening it withers and dries up", on which he comments: "each word in the first part parallels each word in the second and contrasts with it" (K 125 b).[67]

Beyond providing the key for reconciling Scriptural repetition with Arabic theory, the four aforementioned techniques lead Ibn Ezra to a new understanding of biblical verse structure. Instead of viewing repetition *per se* as elegant, he identifies it as a byproduct of a more basic artistic value, namely poetic balance. Discerning a 'meter' in the two- and three-stich parallel verse structure, he demonstrates that biblical authors aimed for rhythmic symmetry, not simply repetition, within poetic lines. *Muṭābaqa* achieves symmetry through semantic contrast; *taqsīm* through semantic equivalence; *tardīd* through phonetic repetition; *ḥašw bayt li-qāmat wazn* implies the basic need for poetic balance.[68] Breaking out of the medieval preoccupation with repetition, Ibn Ezra discovers a more basic structural feature of biblical verse, foreshadowing the concept of 'parallelism' that was introduced by Robert Lowth in the eighteenth century and is now recognized as the central principle of biblical verse structure.[69]

---

[65] These words are unclear in the MS; see Halkin, Kitāb (1975) 248 (reading adopted here) and Dana, Poetics (1982) 285; cf. Halper, Shirat Yisrael (1924) 175; Schippers, Symmetry (1990) 169.

[66] Repetition also creates a symmetrical structure in *taṣdīr* (inclusio), in which "the poet opens with a word at the beginning of the verse and [uses] the very same word at the end and thus beautifies the verse" (K 130 a), e.g., "Of their mothers they ask 'Where is bread ...' as their life runs out in the bosom of their mothers" (Lam 2:12; K 130 b). In contrast with *tardīd* and *taṣdīr*, repetition of phonemes without regard to structure features in *mujānasa* (paronomasia, word play), defined simply as a "coincidence of wording (*lafẓ*) but difference of meaning (*maʿna*)" (K 125 b). Unrelated to Arabic verse forms, *mujānasa*, one of the genuinely 'biblical' ornaments, is illustrated with forty-one biblical examples, such as "In Bet-leʿafra / strew dust (*ʿafar*) ..." (Mic 1:10) and "The houses of Akhziv are / [like] a spring that fails (*akhzav*)" (Mic 1:14; K 125 b).

[67] *Muqābala* (correspondence; K 127 b–128 a) is a similar ornament that entails parallel versets, each of which manifests an internal antithesis (Dana, Poetics [1982] 132–35); e.g., "You sowed much but brought in little / Ate but are not satisfied / Drank but are not sated / Clothe yourselves but are not warmed" (Hag 1:6; K 129 a).

[68] This also applies to the ornaments cited in notes above: *muqābala* and *tashīm* achieve balance through semantic equivalence; *taṣdīr* through phonetic repetition. On symmetry as an ideal for Ibn Ezra and Arabic poets, see Schippers, Symmetry (1990).

[69] Ibn Ezra's examples of *taqsīm, muṭābaqa* and *tardīd*, resemble what is now known, respectively, as 'synonymous', 'antithetical' and 'staircase parallelism'. (Berlin, Biblical Poetry [1991] 76, claims that *muṭābaqa is* not 'antithetical parallelism' since it does not require opposition of entire versets; yet the examples Ibn Ezra considers archetypal, e.g., Ps 90:6, do meet this criterion.) Ibn Ezra cannot take full credit for discovering parallelism, for although he discerns its various forms, he does not attribute them to a single structural principle as Lowth does. On the history of scholarship relating to parallelism, see Kugel, Idea (1991).

Unlike the specifically Arabic ornaments which led Ibn Ezra to unique discoveries about biblical style, the universal ones were recognized by other Andalusian exegetes.[70] Still, Ibn Ezra provides a unique poetic perspective, as his analysis of biblical figurative language illustrates. The Andalusian school, as reflected in the *Maqāla* (above, sec. 2.3), classified figurative language as *majāz*, viewed it as a barrier hiding Scripture's true meaning and devised a method to 'decode' it. In the *Kitāb*, Ibn Ezra instead analyzes figurative language as a means of creating poetic imagery and enhancing Scripture's beauty. Other exegetes, interested in Scripture's meaning, rarely differentiated among various types of figurative language; Ibn Ezra, focusing on poetic technique, defines three, *isti'āra, tašbīh* and *maṯal*.[71]

v. *Isti'āra* (metaphor, lit. borrowing) is defined by Ibn Ezra, following Arabic poetic tradition and the literal sense of this technical term, as 'imaginary ascription', i. e., "'borrowing' an object from its original 'owner' who possesses it in our real world and giving it on loan to one who does not".[72] He illustrates this in discussing a verse by Ibn Gabirol, "The night wore armor of darkness / And thunder pierced it with a spear of lightening":

> He lent (*fa-sta'āra*) "armor" to the darkness of night, "a spear" to the flash of lightening, its quality being "pierced it". These are all from among the implements of warfare (K 121 a).

Picturing the night as a soldier in battle, the poet imaginatively ascribes armor to the darkness and a piercing spear to lightening. Hardly a mere linguistic anomaly, metaphor thus conceived releases the imagination from the confines of empirical reality to yield brilliantly vivid, fanciful poetic scenes.[73]

Ibn Ezra holds the aesthetic value of metaphor to be self-evident: "if you examine it thoroughly ... its superiority becomes apparent" (K 120 a).[74] Reflecting the centrality of metaphor in medieval Arabic and Hebrew literature, he argues further that it is indispensable for elegant writing, whether prose or poetry (K 118 b–119 a). Hardly gratuitous, this claim is intended to counter un-

---

[70] In addition to metaphor, simile and allegory (below), his predecessors observed biblical hyperbole (*guluww*; below, n. 75) and paronomasia (*mujānasa*; above, n. 66; see Ibn Janah, *Riqma*, 23; Judah ibn Bal'am, *Kitāb at-Tajnīs*, mentioned by Ibn Ezra [K 126 b]).

[71] By contrast, Saadiah and Ibn Janah use the terms *isti'āra, tašbīh, maṯal* and *majāz* almost interchangeably, following medieval Arabic convention (Heinrichs, Genesis [1984] 122); Abraham ibn Ezra and Radak use the single term *mashal* to denote metaphor, simile and allegory (see Cohen, Three Approaches [forthcoming], chap. 1).

[72] W. Heinrichs, *The Hand of the Northwind* (Wiesbaden 1977) 9; see following note.

[73] Western tradition generally follows Aristotle's notion of metaphor as a name transfer, e. g., calling a brave man a "lion", which does amount to little more than a linguistic anomaly; see P. Ricœur, *The Rule of Metaphor* (tr. R. Czerny; Toronto 1975) 3, 13–24. But as Heinrichs, Hand (1977) 10, observes, the Arabic poetic definition of *isti'āra* "does not refer to words or names (it does not turn the proper use of the word into a figurative use), but to objects (it turns real objects into imaginary ones)". Maimonides (*Treatise on Logic*, chap. 13) does, in fact, use al-Fārābī's Aristotelian model of metaphor (M. Türker, "Musa b. Maymun'un Makāla fī Ṣinā'at al-Manṭiḳ'i", *Publications of the Faculty of Letters, Istanbul University, Review of the Institute of Islamic Studies*, 3/1–2 [1956–60] 58–59, n. 17); but Ibn Ezra (K 120 a) borrows the definition of the literary critic Ibn al-Mu'tazz, which reflects 'imaginary ascription'; see Heinrichs, Hand (1977) 1–11, 33–34; Cohen, Argument (2000); cf. Pagis, Poetry and Theory (1970) 56; Dana, Poetics (1982) 115.

[74] See also citation from K 118 b (above, sec. 3.2).

named, but evidently influential, authors who eschewed metaphor in favor of precise literal language (K 118 b–119 a).[75] Concerned lest this enthusiasm for metaphor be perceived as submission to *ʿarabiyya*, Ibn Ezra champions its inherent virtue by observing that "in Scripture it is abundant",[76] and he even suggests that Arab poets followed this sacred precedent (K 119 a). To demonstrate his assertion about Scripture and illustrate the workings of metaphor, he cites forty biblical examples, including "the *dew* of your youth" (Ps 110:3), "the *wings* of dawn" (Ps 139:9), and "*fruit* of their thoughts" (Jer 6:19; K 119 a).[77]

vi. *Tašbīh* (simile, comparison) juxtaposes dissimilar objects or ideas for comparison, with or without the comparative particle, *kaf*.[78] Ibn Ezra cites examples of both: "*As* the coldness of snow at harvest time / is a trusty messenger to those who send him" (Prov 25:13) and "An open city without walls *is* a man whose passion is without restraint" (Prov 25:28; K 134 b). Revealing the aesthetic criteria by which he evaluates simile, Ibn Ezra notes that Song 4:3, "As a scarlet thread are your lips", "combines three similarities to the lip: softness, color and delicateness" and adds that "if the Song of Songs would boast to Ecclesiastes on the basis of this verse, it would be justified" (K 134 b).[79] An effective simile, like a fine painting, highlights the features of its subject sharply and vividly.[80]

Ever concerned with verse structure, Ibn Ezra seeks poetic balance in biblical similes. The ivory white tone in the first verset of Lam 4:7, "Her Nazirites were purer than snow, whiter than milk", he observes, is offset by the rosy tint of the second, "Their limbs were ruddier than corals, their form like sapphire", thus avoiding a portrait of pale, ugly young men. Lauding this colorful balance, he regards this verse as "one of the wondrous similes of the Hebrews" (K 134 b).[81] Ibn Ezra's passion for poetic balance sometimes compels him to take an unusual exegetical stance, e.g., on Job 31:24, "Did I put my reliance on gold / Or regard *silver* (*ketem*) as my bulwark?". In biblical Hebrew, *ketem* usually means 'gold', but here Ibn Ezra takes it to mean 'silver' to conform with

[75] The origin of the objection to metaphor is unclear. Rationalists were disturbed by its imprecision (Dana, Poetics [1982] 116), but far-fetched metaphors were also attacked in Arabic tradition on poetic grounds (Heinrichs, Istiʿārah [1984] 188–89). Ibn Ezra's discussion of *guluww* (hyperbole) manifests similar tensions: "the ancient [Rabbis] ... call it vain language" (*leshon habai; b. Ḥul* 90 b), a disparaging designation that highlights its imprecision and invites 'translating' it into literal language, as Ibn Ezra does in the *Maqāla*. But in the *Kitāb* he observes its rhetorical qualities and, pointing to its ubiquity in Scripture, argues that "the aim [of the biblical prophets] would not have been realized without it" (K 137 b).

[76] Much as he justifies erotic love poetry based on its occurrence in the Song of Songs (above, n. 46).

[77] Applying his analysis of Ibn Gabirol's verse, Ibn Ezra would say, e.g., that "the morning lent dew to youth". The genitive construction ('A of B'), a feature of all forty of his biblical examples, best illustrates imaginary ascription (i.e., that 'C lent A to B'); see Heinrichs, Hand (1977) 8; Cohen, Argument (2000).

[78] This differs from modern usage, in which simile requires the comparative particle, "like" or "as".

[79] On the textual uncertainty here, see Dana, Poetics (1982) 151.

[80] Dana, Poetics (1982) 150–51.

[81] Dana, Poetics (1982) 150.

the imagery of 31:26, "If I ever saw the sun[82] shining / The moon ... in full glory"; 'sun' corresponds to 'gold', 'moon' to *ketem*, which thus means 'silver' (K 135 a–b).[83]

vii. *Maṯal* (allegory, parable) is a tale "with a hidden interpretation other than the one apparent from its words"[84] and, like simile and metaphor, is based on a comparison (*tašbīh*) between a real subject and an image (K 146 a–b).[85] Unlike the technical terms *isti'āra* and *tašbīh*, for which biblical Hebrew has no equivalents, Ibn Ezra takes the biblical word *mashal* as a technical term equivalent to Arabic *maṯal*, which immediately enables him to identify this technique in Scripture. Securing a working definition of allegory from passages explicitly labeled as *mashal*, e.g., Ezek 17:2 ff (the eagle allegory), he also identifies and analyzes "*meshalim* in the prophetic writings not labeled as *meshalim*, such as 'My beloved had a vineyard ...' (Isa 5:1 ff)" (K 148 b–150 a). Citing a common medieval doctrine, Ibn Ezra records that "the ancient [Greek] philosophers" used allegory to hide their esoteric wisdom from the uneducated masses (K 146 b).[86] Recognizing, though, that this motive hardly suits the biblical prophets, who addressed all classes of people, he argues that they employed allegory "since knowledge of the senses [evoked by a 'tangible' tale] is more immediate and easier for the masses than intellectual knowledge" (K 148 a).[87] Since poetic imagery concretizes abstract concepts, allegory is an effective medium for communicating spiritual ideals.

4. Legacy

Ibn Ezra was the product of a multi-cultural age that came to a close soon after his death. Continued Almohide advances sent Jewish scholars into exile, and the Christian *reconquista* later eradicated Arabic culture from the Iberian peninsula, forcing Andalusian scholarship to transplant in Christian Spain and Provence. The *Maqāla*, translated into Hebrew, influenced subsequent Jewish scholarship, but the *Kitāb* did not survive this cultural transition and remained

[82] Like Saadiah, he takes *'or* to mean 'sun', in order to parallel *yareaḥ* (moon) in the second half of the verse.

[83] He takes 'sun' and 'moon' as metaphors for 'gold' and 'silver', citing, for support, a verse by Mutanabbi ("I have not said to the moon you are silver; Nor have I said to the sun you are gold") and his own Hebrew verse ("Could a man profit by selling the gold of the sun with the silver of the moon?"); see Schippers, Spanish Hebrew Poetry (1994) 37–38. This illustrates a novel, but tenuous, reading based on an Arabic topos (above, n. 19).

[84] This definition appears in the *Kitāb* juxtaposed with the biblical term *ḥida* (riddle) but evidently applies to *maṯal* as well, since "both are from one stream and closely related" (K 146 b).

[85] Ibn Ezra also discusses fables, proverbs, riddles, etc., in this chapter; like other Arab theorists (see *Encyclopedia of Islam*², s. v. *maṯal*), he evidently defines *maṯal* more broadly than 'allegory' in the Western sense; see Dana, Poetics (1982) 177.

[86] This notion also appears in Maimonides, who may have seen Ibn Ezra's comment; see Klein-Braslavy, King Solomon (1996) 28, 49–50.

[87] Saadiah offers this explanation in his introduction to Proverbs (Qāfiḥ ed.), 13. It is also cited by the eleventh century Arab literary critic, Abd-al-qāhir al-Jurjāni; see *Asrār al-Balāgha: The Mysteries of Eloquence* (ed. H. Ritter; Istanbul 1954) 15, 108.

untranslated until modern times.[88] It is an irony of history that Ibn Ezra's less exceptional work outlasted his more original and profound one, but the reasons for this are evident. The *Maqāla* blended into the rationalist *peshat* tradition, which survived its original Muslim milieu because it had already reached maturity by the twelfth century, its foreign components having been assimilated into Jewish tradition by authorities such as Saadiah, Hayyuj, Ibn Janah and Maimonides. But the *Kitāb* could flourish only in a culture that cherished Arabic poetry, and if Ibn Ezra anticipated objections to this aesthetic yardstick in his time, the *reconquista* would certainly render it irrelevant. The very thought of evaluating Scripture's literary quality became suspect in Christian Spain and sparked sharp criticism from the author of the *Zohar* (III. 152 a), who argues that if the literary standard were valid, one could replace the Holy Torah with a more beautiful, and thus superior, human work.[89]

If controversy once dimmed the *Kitāb*'s luster, the work shines again today as the most substantial medieval analysis of biblical poetics, a discipline that would resurface in the Renaissance[90] and evolve into a principal field of modern biblical scholarship.[91] To be sure, the modern perspective reveals flaws in Ibn Ezra's methods. Apart from the fact that he overstates the shared Arabic and biblical literary tradition, which at times yields tenuous readings, the horizon defined by the *badiʿ* limits his literary range. Ibn Ezra's focus on ornaments occurring within a single verse precludes analysis of larger literary units.[92] Moreover, adhering to the formalism of Arabic theory, he never explains how Scripture's poetic style enriches its meaning, a crucial question in modern theory, which views form and content are integrally related.[93] These shortcomings were thc price Ibn Ezra paid to harness the winds of Arabic poetics and develop, perhaps ahead of its time, a meaningful aesthetic exegesis, charting a course for more sophisticated attempts powered by newer methodologies.

---

[88] On the *Maqāla's* influence, see above, n. 4. The *Kitāb* was available for about two centuries; it is quoted, e. g., by Isaac ibn Latif (thirteenth century) and Judah ben Saadiah (fourteenth century), both of Toledo (Stern, Aristotle [1968] 80–84). For an isolated sixteenth century citation, see Fenton, Jardin (1997) 32.

[89] See Cohen, Best of Poetry (1995/6) 24–25.

[90] Some later medieval Jewish authors address literary issues briefly (see Berlin, Biblical Poetry [1991] 87–133), as do Jerome, Augustine and other early Christian authors (see Kugel, Idea [1981] 149–70). On the resurgence of biblical poetics, reflected, for example, in the writings of Azariah de Rossi and Robert Lowth, see Kugel, Idea (1981) 200–86; Berlin, Biblical Poetry (1991) 133–71.

[91] The convergence of Bible scholarship and literary criticism has produced numerous studies in recent decades, as reflected, e. g., in R. Alter / F. Kermode (eds.), *The Literary Guide to the Bible* (Cambridge, MA 1987). For an overview of the application of modern literary methods to Scripture, with bibliography, see M. Weiss, *The Bible from Within* (Jerusalem 1984) 1–46.

[92] Pagis, Secular Poetry (1970) 32–33. On the 'molecularity' of Arabic poetics, see Van Gelder, Beyond the Line (1982) 1–23.

[93] *Princeton Encyclopedia of Poetry and Poetics* (Princeton 1974), s. v. "New Criticism"; Pagis, Secular Poetry (1970) 40–46; Brann, Compunctious Poet (1991) 72; Weiss, Bible from Within (1984) 37.

31.3. The Philosophical Exegesis

By Sara Klein-Braslavy, Tel Aviv

Sources: Abraham ibn Ezra: *The Interpretations of the Tôra of Rabènu Abraham ibn Ezra* (ed. A. Weiser; Jerusalem: Mosad Harav Kook 1976; Hebr.: ***פירושי התורה לרבינו אברהם אבן עזרא*** [עורך: א. וייזר, ירושלים : מוסד הרב קוק 1976]). – Bahya ben Joseph ibn Pakuda: *Al-Hidâya 'ila farâ'id al-qulûb* (ed. A. S. Yehuda; Leiden 1912); *The Book of Direction to the Duties of the Heart* (tr. M. Mansoor; London 1973); *Seper Tôrat Hôvôt ha-Levavôt* (Arab. and Hebr.; ed. and tr. Y. Kafiḥ; Jerusalem 1973). – Judah Halevi: *Kitâb al-radd wa-'l-dalîl fi 'l-dîn 'l-dhalîl 'Al-Kitâb al-Khazarî*) (ed. D. H. Baneth, prepared for publication by H. Ben-Shammai; Jerusalem 1977); *Das Buch al-Chazari des abu-l-Ḥassan Jehuda Hallewi* (ed. D. Kassel; Leipzig 1869). – Moses Maimonides: *Mishnah with the Commentary of Rabènu Moses ben Maimon* (Arab. and Hebr.; ed. and tr. Y. Kafiḥ; Jerusalem: Mosad Harav Kook 1963–68; Hebr.: ***משנה עם פירוש רבינו משה בן מיימון*** (מקור ותרגום [תרגם י״ד קאפח, ירושלים: מוסד הרב קוק 1963–1968]); *The Code* (Jerusalem: Môsad Harav Kook 1975; Hebr.: (משה בן מיימון *משנה תורה*, [ירושלים: מוסד הרב קוק 1975]); *Dalâlat al-Ḥâ'irîn* (ed. S. Munk / I. Joel; Jerusalem 1930/31); *The Guide of the Perplexed* (tr. S. Pines; Chicago: Chicago UP 1963). – Solomon ibn Gabirol: *Kitâb Iṣlâḥ 'l-Aẖlâq* (ed. S. Weis; New York 1901); *Seper Tiqqûn Middôṭ han-Nepeš* (tr. Judah ibn Tibbon; Tel Aviv: Maḥbarôṭ le-Siprût 1951); *Seper Tiqqûn Middôṭ han-Nepeš* (tr. N. Baron; Tel Aviv: Maḥbarôṭ le-SiPrût 1951).

General works: A. Altmann, "The Ladder of Ascension", *Studies in Religious Philosophy and Mysticism* (London: Routledge and Kegan 1969) 41–72; W. Bacher, *Die Bibelexegese der jüdischen Religionsphilosophen des Mittelalters vor Maimûni* (Strassburg 1892); idem, *Die Bibelexegese Maimunis* (Strassburg 1897); W. J. Bekkum, "Deutung und Bedeutung in der hebräischen Exegese", *Frankfurter Judaistische Beiträge* 23 (1996) 1–13; B. L. V. Berman, "Maimonides on the Fall of Man", *AJS Review* 5 (1980) 1–15; D. Burell, "Maimonides, Aquinas and Gersonides on Providence and Evile", *RelSt* 20 (1984) 335–51; J. P. Cohen, "Figurative Language, Philosophy and Religious Belief: An Essay on Some Themes in Maimonides' The Guide of the Perplexed", *Studies in Jewish Philosophy* (ed. N. Samuelson; Lanhem, MD: University Press of America [1987] 367–96); J. I. Dienstag, "Biblical Exegesis of Maimonides in Jewish Scholarship", *Samuel L. Mirsky Memorial Volume* (ed. G. Appel and others; New York 1970) 151–90; S. Feldman, "The Binding of Isaac: A Test-Case of Divine Foreknowledge", *Divine Omniscience and Omnipotence in Medieval Philosophy* (ed. T. Rudavsky; Dordrecht: D. Reidel 1985) 105–33; Jul. Guttmann, "Zu Gabirols allegorischer Deutung der Erzählung vom Paradies", *MGWJ* 89 (1936) 180–84; M. Greenberg, "Bible Interpretation as Exhibited in the first Book of Maimonides' Code", *The Judeo-Christian Tradition and the U. S. Constitution* (1989) 29–56; M. W. Z. Harvey, "Maimonides' Interpretation of Genesis 3,22", *Daat* 12 (1984) 15–21 [in Hebr.]; idem, "Maimonides and Aquinas on Interpreting the Bible", *PAAJR* 55 (1988) 59–77; idem, "How to Begin to Study the *Guide of the Perplexed*, I, 1", *Daat* 21 (1988) 5–20 [in Hebr.]; S. Harvey, "Maimonides e l'interpretazione filosofica della Bibblia", *La lettera ebraica della Scritture* (1995) 221–35; I. Heinemann, "Die wissenschaftliche Allegoristik des Jüdischen Mittelalters", HUCA 23 (1950–51) 611–43; A. Hyman, "Maimonides on religious language", *Studies in Jewish Philosophy* (ed. N. Samuelson; Lanhem, MD: University Press of America 1987) 351–65; H. Kasher, "Job's Image in the *Guide of the Perplexed*", *Daat* 15 (1985) 81–87 [in Hebr.]; eadem, "Maimonides' Interpretation of the Story of the Divine Revelation in the Cleft of the Rock", *Daat* 35 (1995) 29–66 [in Hebr.]; A. D. Kaufmann, "Die Theologie des Bachja ibn Pakuda", *Gesammelte Schriften von David Kaufmann* II (ed. Brann; Frankfurt a/M 1910) 1–98; idem, "Salomon ibn Gabirols philosophische Allegorese", *Studien über Salomon ibn Gabirol* (Budapest 1899) 63–79; S. Klein-Braslavy, "The Creation of the World and Maimonides' Interpretation of Gen. ch. 1–5", *Maimonides and Philosophy* (ed. S. Pines / Y. Yovel; Dordrecht: Nijhoff 1986) 65–78; eadem, *Maimonides' Interpretation of the Story of Creation* (sec. ed.; Jerusalem: Rubin Mass 1978; in Hebr.); eadem, *Maimonides' Interpretation of the Adam Stories in Genesis – a Study in Maimonides' Anthropology* (Jerusalem: Rubin Mass 1986; in Hebr.); eadem, "Maimonides' Interpretation of Jacob's Dream of the Ladder", *Annual of Bar-Ilan University – Studies in Judaica and Humanities* 22–23 (1987) 329–49 [in Heb.] ; eadem "King Solomon and Metaphysical

Esotericism according to Maimonides", *Maimonidean Studies* 1 (1990) 57–86; eadem, *King Solomon and Philosophical Esotericism in the Thought of Maimonides* (Jerusalem: The Magnes Press, The Hebrew University of Jerusalem 1996; in Heb.); L. S. KRAVITZ, "Maimonides and Job – An Inquiry as to the Method of the Moreh", HUCA 28 (1967) 149–58; J. LEVINGER, "Maimonides' exegesis of the Book of Job", *Creative Biblical Exegesis* (Sheffield 1988) 81–88; A. MELAMMED, "⟨Let not the wise man glory in his wisdom⟩ Philosophical Interpretations to Jer 9, 22–23 in Jewish Medieval and Renaissance Thought", *Jerusalem Studies in Jewish Thought* 4 (1985) 31–82 [in Hebr.]; S. MUNK, "Ibn Gabirol, ses écrits et sa philosophie", *Mélanges de philosophie juive et arabe* (Paris: Librairie philosophique J. Vrin 1955) 166–67; D. NOVAK, "Maimonides' Theory of Religious Language", *Law and Theology* (New York 1976) 28–37; A. NURIEL, "⟨The Torah Speaks in the Language of Human Beings⟩ in the *Guide of the Perplexed*", *Religion and Language* (ed. M. Hallamish / A. Kasher; Tel Aviv: University Publishing Projects 1981) 97–103 [in Hebr.]; idem, "The Concept of Satan in the *Guide of the Perplexed*", *Jerusalem Studies in Jewish Thought* 5 (1986) 83–91 [in Hebr.]; idem, "Maimonides on parables not explicitly identified as such", *Daat* 25 (1990) 85–91 [in Hebr.]; S. RAWIDOWICZ, "On Interpretation", *PAAJR* 26 (1957) 83–126; idem, "The Problem of Anthropomorphism According to Saadia and Maimonides", *Iyyunim Bemahashevet Yisrael – Hebrew Studies in Jewish Tought* 1 (ed. B. C. I. Ravid; Jerusalem: Rubin Mass 1969) 171–233 [in Heb.]; S. ROSENBERG, "On the Interpretation of the Tora in the *Guide of the Perplexed*", *Jerusalem Studies in Jewish Thought* 1 (1981) 85–157 [in Hebr.]; E. ROSENTHAL, "Medieval Jewish Exegesis: its Character and Significance", *JSS* 9 (1964); J. SCHLANGER, "Salomon ibn Gabirol, sa vie, son œuvre – Exégèse biblique", *La philosophie de Salomon ibn Gabirol, étude d'un néoplatonisme* (Leiden: E. J. Brill 1968) 13–15; K. STEIN, "Exegesis, Maimonides and Literary Criticism", *Modern Language Notes* 88 (1973) 1134–54; G. VAJDA, *La théologie ascétique de Bahya ibn Paquda* (Paris 1947); A. WOHLMAN, *Maimonide et Thomas d'Aquin: Un dialogue impossible* (Fribourg 1995); M. YAFFE, "Providence in Medieval Aristotelianism: Moses Maimonides and Thomas Aquinas on the Book of Job", *Hebrew Studies* 20–21 (1979/80) 62–74.

1. Introduction

During the eleventh and twelfth centuries the Jews of Spain lived in an Arab cultural environment and were influenced by it. Through it they encountered Muslim theology, together with Muslim ascetic literature, Greek and Hellenistic philosophy translated into Arabic, and Arabic philosophy. In philosophy, they became familiar with the writings of both the neo-Platonic and the Aristotelian streams. The encounter with these streams of thought also led those Jewish philosophers who lived in Spain during this period to interpret Scripture under the influence of the ideas they absorbed from them.

The Arabic environment likewise influenced the language of writing of the Jewish philosophers. As both the language of cultural discourse and the spoken language of the Jews during that period was Arabic, the Spanish Jewish philosophers wrote their works in that language.[1] However, as they were addressing themselves to Jews rather than to the Arabic environment, this was written in Hebrew characters. When interpreting Scripture in these works, the words or verses under discussion are quoted in the original Hebrew, while the exegesis is conducted in Arabic, including at times a translation of words or phrases from the Hebrew text – itself an act of interpretation.

The interest of the Jewish philosophers is primarily theological and philo-

[1] With the exception of Maimonides, whose central halakhic work, *Mishneh Torah*, which contains a theoretical section, *Seper ham-Mada'*, was written in Hebrew.

sophic, biblical exegesis being secondary to these interests. Hence, they do not write running contextual interpretations of the biblical books. Rather, their interpretations of words, expressions, isolated verses, passages, or even entire chapters of the Bible are incorporated within their philosophical and theological discussions.

2. Solomon ibn Gabirol

The first biblical exegete among the Jewish philosophers of Spain was *Solomon ibn Gabirol* (ca. 1021/22–1058). Ibn Gabirol is known in several respects: as a major poet, who wrote both sacred and secular poetry, including the famous *Keter Malkûṯ* ("the Crown of the Kingdom"); as the author of a philosophic work in the neo-Platonic spirit, written originally in Arabic but which survived in its entirety only in its Latin version, *Fons Vitae*, selections from which by Shem Tov Falquera are extant in Hebrew translation; and as the author of the first Jewish ethical work written in Spain, *Kitâb Iṣlâḥ ʾl-Aḫlâq* (*Sep̄er Tiqqûn Middôṯ han-Nep̄eš*). In addition, he composed Bible commentaries, fragments of which are cited by R. Abraham ibn Ezra in his own commentaries.

The passages from Ibn Gabirol's commentaries cited by Ibn Ezra do not contain any formulation of a theory of biblical exegesis, but it is clear from them that Ibn Gabirol's central tendency was to harmonize between philosophy and the biblical text by interpreting these texts as neo-Platonic philosophical allegory.

The exegeses cited by Ibn Ezra are concise, partial, truncated and enigmatic. Thus, at times they may be understood in a number of different ways and require exegetic completion by the reader, primarily on the basis of knowledge of Ibn Gabirol's philosophy in *Fons Vitae.* It is not clear whether this was Ibn Gabirol's original manner of writing, or was simply the way in which his words were cited by Ibn Ezra.

The richest and most important interpretation cited by Ibn Ezra is the exegesis of the story of the Garden of Eden. From what is given of this interpretation by Ibn Ezra, it would appear that Ibn Gabirol did not interpret it as a historical event, but as a trans-temporal philosophical allegory whose subject is "the secret of the soul". His interpretation of this narrative focuses primarily upon the key nouns therein, each one of which is given a philosophical meaning. For example: 'Eden' is the supernal world, the 'river' is the general matter of the world, and the 'four streams' that split off from it are the four elements. The protagonists of the Eden story are the various powers of the soul of neo-Platonic psychology. 'Adam' is the rational soul, 'Eve' the animal soul, while the 'serpent' is the appetitive soul. Ibn Gabirol justifies only some of the meanings that he attributes to the nouns in the Eden story, making use here of the conventional methods of rabbinic Midrash. One such method is the etymological interpretation of words. For example, the name 'Eve' (Heb. *ḥawâh*) is derived from 'life' (*ḥayâh*), indicating that she is the animal soul. The Serpent is the appetitive soul. Here, Ibn Gabirol incorporates another method used by the Rabbis – the interpretation of a verse or a word from a verse by means of another biblical verse, explaining the word *naḥaš* (serpent) as derived from "such a man as I can surely divine" (*naḥēš yenaḥēš*, Gen 44:15).

The brief interpretation of Jacob's dream of the ladder, cited by Ibn Ezra in the name of Ibn Gabirol, is similar in nature to his interpretation of the Eden story. Here too, Ibn Gabirol identifies central nouns found in the description of the dream with philosophical concepts, this time without making any attempt to justify this interpretation in a philological manner or by means of the 'biblical lexicon': "And R. Solomon the Spaniard said that the ladder alludes to the supernal soul, and the angels of God are the thoughts of wisdom". It seems reasonable to accept here Munk's interpretation, according to which the ladder is the intellective soul while the angels are the thoughts of this soul, at times relating to a more spiritual subject and at times to a bodily or more lowly subject.[2]

An allusion to a philosophic exegesis of the Creation narrative by Ibn Gabirol is given in his name by Ibn Ezra in his interpretation of Isa 43:7: "Every one that is called by My name, and whom I have created for My glory, I have formed him, yea, I have made him". Ibn Ezra notes that Ibn Gabirol remarked here, "for this is the secret of the world". It would appear that Ibn Gabirol specifically interpreted the verbs in this verse, which he saw as the key to understanding the Creation story.

In three places in his commentary to the Torah (on Gen 3:1; in the 'new approach' to Gen 1:3; and on Num 22:28), Abraham ibn Ezra also mentions Ibn Gabirol as one who opposed the literalistic interpretation of the supernatural phenomenon of the serpent's speech in the Garden of Eden narrative. In support of this, Ibn Gabirol invoked a logical argument, based upon the biblical text and upon experience. According to the biblical text, the serpent was not punished by being stricken dumb. This being so, had he been able to speak then he would also be able to speak today – which is not the case. Ibn Gabirol does not present here a philosophical exegesis, but only attempts to neutralize the supernatural dimension of the story and thereby harmonize between it and logical, and not necessarily philosophical, thought.

There is barely an echo of any religious belief in his philosophic work (apart from *creatio ex nihilo*), nor is even one biblical verse mentioned or interpreted therein. On the other hand, his ethical work, *Kitâb Iṣlâḥ 'l-Aḫlâq* (*Sep̄er Tiqqûn Middôṯ han-Nep̄eš*) contains many biblical verses, most of which are cited without any elaboration in order to show that there is agreement between the ideas he brought – at times philosophical opinions – and the Bible. In some isolated cases, he does provide an interpretation of isolated verses, or even interprets several consecutive verses from the same chapter in their context.

His most interesting exegeses are found in the introduction to his ethical book, where they are brought to support the structure of his discussion of ethical qualities. Referring, for example, to Qoh 9:11:

I returned, and saw under the sun, that the race is not to the swift, nor the battle to the strong,

[2] Munk, Ibn Gabirol (1955) 166.

neither yet bread to the wise, nor yet riches to men of understanding, nor yet favour to men of skill; but time and chance happeneth to them all –

Solomon alludes the verse to the five senses. Thereafter he explains the methodological principle of this interpretation, in his exegesis to Ps 37:1–23. He argues that there are two kinds of verse in the Bible: verses that are to be understood literally, and verses that only allude to their subject. Qoh 9:11 is divided into five units of meaning, each one alluding to one of the senses, in the following order: smell, hearing, taste, feeling, and sight. As, according to his interpretation, the verse is not written literally, but allusively, he does not deal with the meaning of its words, but only attempts to understand to what they allude; for example: "not to heros is the battle" alludes, in line with his interpretation, to the sense of hearing. He explains: "for war takes place through hearing, with din and tumult".

According to the exegesis of Ibn Gabirol, Ps 37:1–23 presents all twenty qualities of the soul which he discusses in his book. Here he provides a running commentary of each verse of the chapter, in order to prove this exegetical claim.

3. Baḥya ben Joseph ibn Paquda

Baḥya ben Joseph ibn Paquda (ca. 1100) is known in the history of medieval Jewish thought as the author of the book of religious behavior that has been of the greatest importance and influence since the Middle Ages until modern times – *Al-Hidâya 'ila farâ'id al-qulûb* ("The Duties of the Heart"). Baḥya is not concerned with the confrontation between religion and philosophy. Rather, his book is intended to guide the believing Jew in the true service of God, which is an inner spiritual service. Although *The Duties of the Heart* is not devoted to biblical exegesis, Baḥya deals there not only with the interpretation of biblical words and verses, but also with the theory of biblical exegesis.

From remarks concerning biblical exegesis scattered throughout the book,[3] it would seem that he distinguishes among several exegetical approaches. They are also ranked according to the level of man's progress in understanding of the biblical text:[4] (1) study of the linguistic aspect of the Bible, the morphology of language; (2) study of the lexical aspect of the biblical text – the interpretation of difficult words and distinction among different kinds of nouns, particularly the distinction between a regular noun and a derivative noun; (3) understanding the meaning of the biblical text. This is an almost literal form of exegesis of text, and it is not based upon the rabbinic exegetical tradition. On this level, one already finds the beginning of a theological interpretation of the biblical text: a distinction is drawn there between those biblical words which are

[3] Cf. Introduction (17, 41–42); 3.4 (148–51); 8.3 (367–69). All quotations are taken from the edition of Y. Kafiḥ; the page numbers are in brackets.
[4] Cf. 3.4.

to be understood literally, and those whose meaning is derivative or which are of equivocal meaning. The discussion of the corporeality of God is based upon this distinction. Finally, (4) understanding the esoteric level of the biblical text. Here, evidently under the influence of Muslim ascetic literature, which may be seen throughout his book, Baḥya distinguishes between the literal interpretation (Arab. *ẓahir*) and that based upon the 'inner' or hidden dimension (Arab. *baṭin*) of the biblical text. In this one finds Baḥya's exegetical and theological innovation in the history of Jewish thought. On the hidden level, we find *The Duties of the Heart* – which is the central subject of this work.[5] The biblical text 'alludes' to this level, which is only subject to understanding by "those who have intellect and understanding".[6]

The most striking thing in Baḥya's use of the biblical text is his citation of verses as prooftexts for his arguments, using the formula "as it is written", "as Scripture says", or "as is said". Baḥya inherited this method from the Talmudic Sages, who thereby strengthened the continuity and unity of the Jewish tradition. In Baḥya, it is also used to demonstrate that the opinions which he presents, including those taken from the Arabic environment – the Kalam, neo-Platonism, and the Muslim ascetic texts – appear in the Jewish tradition and are not alien to it. Only rarely does he also interpret the verse which he cites as a prooftext.

The interpretation of the divine attributes given by Baḥya in his biblical exegesis is especially worth noting. He argues that those attributes corporealizing God have two meanings. The one is the literal interpretation, intended for the average person. The Bible has an educational goal: to impress upon the soul of the average person the knowledge of the existence of God, which is a precondition for His worship. To that end, the Bible adapts itself to the understanding of the average person, utilizing corporeal expressions for Him.[7] This is necessary in order for the average man to know of the existence of God. Baḥya relies here upon the rule of the Sages, "the Torah speaks in the language of human beings" (*b. Ber.* 31b, and numerous parallels in the Babylonian Talmud). According to his interpretation, this rule explains the presence of corporeal images of God in the Bible. But whereas the Rabbis used this rule in the exegesis of texts bearing implications for Jewish law (halakhah), Baḥya, like the Geonim before him, applies it to the biblical terms that corporealize God. Baḥya is the first of the medieval Jewish philosophers to understand this rule in this way.[8] Although Baḥya agrees with the Sages that "the Torah speaks in the language of human beings", he also refers to the adaptation of the Bible to the manner of speech of the masses of people, in this case the emphasis is upon the adjustment of Scripture to the understanding of the average person, rather than to his manner of speech.

Baḥya claims, secondly, that the same corporealizing attributes may also be

---

[5] Introduction (41).
[6] Cf. 1.10 (79–80).
[7] Allusions to this idea also appear among the pure brothers. See Kaufmann, Die Theologie des Bachja (1910) 76, n. 1.
[8] Cf. Bacher, Bibelexegese (1892) 72, n. 1.

given a non-literal, spiritual interpretation. "The enlightened, wise and understanding man" knows how to strip the corporealizing words "of their shells" and to attain gradually a spiritual understanding of God, in accordance with his power of understanding. In addressing the enlightened person, the Torah makes use of a special method, a 'hint', which the enlightened man apprehends and according to which he understands the matter.[9]

In explaining the attributes of action, Baḥya anticipates Maimonides in the exegesis of Exod 34:6–7: "The Lord, the Lord, God, merciful and gracious, long-suffering, and abundant in goodness and truth; keeping mercy unto the thousandth generation", etc. as referring to "God's ways in relation to the created beings" – that is God's attributes of action, and not to the qualities of God.

Another subject appearing in Baḥya's biblical exegesis is the World to Come. Baḥya, like R. Saadiah Gaon before him, is aware that the Bible does not explicitly discuss reward and punishment in the next world, nor survival of the soul; he was also evidently aware that this subject was one that appeared in the polemics of Christianity against Judaism. In several places in his book, he hence deals with proofs that the belief in the survival of the soul and in the World to Come do indeed appear in Scripture. In the 'Gate of Service', Chapter 4, and in 'The Gate of the Unity of Action', Chapter 5, Baḥya enumerates a series of verses, without interpreting them, which in his opinion allude to the belief in the World to Come. One of these verses, Zech 3:7, "then I will give thee free access among these that stand by", is interpreted in the Fourth Gate, 'The Gate of Trust', Ch. 4. He argues there that it is impossible to understand this verse except as applying to a situation in which the soul survives after death and thus constitutes a proof of the faith in the World to Come.

In addition, one finds in Baḥya, as in Ibn Gabirol, a number of allegorical interpretations of biblical verses, which are understood as prooftexts for his ideas.[10] In his allegorical interpretations of verses from the Ecclesiastes,[11] he dissects each 'parable' into the individual units of meaning comprising it, explaining why each such unit ought to be given the particular allegorical meaning he ascribes to it. For example, in his interpretation of Qoh 9:14–15, "there was a little city, and few men within it",[12] which he sees as a metaphor for the subjugation of the human impulse to the intellect, he explains: "He described man as a 'little city', because he is a microcosmos" (p. 249). In his interpretation of the verse, "Now there was found in it a man poor and wise" (v. 15), he uses, like Ibn Gabirol before him, yet another exegetical technique, which as mentioned was very widely used by the rabbinic Sages: the interpretation of one biblical verse by means of another biblical verse. Here he interprets the verse by means of another portion of the same verse, and by part of another

[9] Baḥya holds that the Torah alludes to other spiritual matters as well, such as the World to Come and the hidden wisdom, because they are difficult to anderstand and intended only for the enlightened, for whom such hints are sufficient to understand; cf. 1.10 (798).

[10] Qoh 12:11, in 2. Introduction (97) and a number of parables concerning the Evil Impulse: Qoh 9:14–15 (5.5) 2 Sam 12:4; Ps 1:1 (8.3 [354–55]).

[11] See above, n. 10.

[12] 5.5 (249–50).

verse further on in the same chapter: "That is to say: the Intellect, which he described as an unfortunate person because of the small number of those following it and assisting it, as is said of him, 'yet no man remembered that same poor man' (v. 15), and it says, 'the poor man's wisdom is despised' (v. 16)" (ibid.).

4. Judah Halevi

Judah Halevi (Toledo, 1075 – Egypt / Palestine, 1141) is known as one of the greatest Jewish poets of the Middle Ages and as the author of the *Book of the Khazars* (*Al-Kitâb al-Khazarî*), commonly known as the *Kuzari*, a theological-philosophical treatise of an apologetic-polemical nature. The *Kuzari* was written as a defense of the Jewish religion against philosophy, the other monotheistic religions, and Karaism.

Unlike Baḥya, Halevi hardly deals at all with the theory of biblical exegesis. According to his teaching, revelation belongs to a unique realm of its own, which it is impossible to base upon philosophy and whose contents cannot be proven by means of the intellect. This being the case, he does not engage in philosophical exegesis of Scripture so as to harmonize between it and philosophy, as was done by Maimonides after him.[13] His biblical interpretations are primarily historical-philosophical and theological. Their central subjects are the nature of the Jewish people as a chosen people, the place and importance of the Land of Israel, exegesis of the prophetic visions, and interpretation of the attributes of God and His names.

According to his theory, the Jewish people are "the chosen[14] among all human beings" by virtue of being the people of prophecy, a people that has a direct connection with God. Halevi interprets the biblical stories concerning the history of mankind from Adam through the twelve sons of Jacob as a history of the 'chosenness' or 'election'. Parallel to this, Halevi argues that the Land of Israel has a special religious status: only there is prophecy of the 'chosen' possible; hence, one who is 'chosen' needs to live there in order to attain prophecy. He establishes this feature of the land of Israel, among other things, by the interpretation of the biblical stories concerning the relationship between the chosen individuals of the people of Israel and the Land.

Halevi takes special interest in the interpretation of prophetic visions. According to his interpretation, these are extra-mental concrete realities which were created by God and apprehended through prophetic experience. Prophetic visions are a unique religious phenomenon, which cannot be based upon rational concepts. Hence, Halevi does not see them as 'parables' requiring interpretation in order to determine their 'true meaning'. On the basis of this fundamental approach, Halevi interprets various phenomena mentioned in Scripture, such as: "the pillar of cloud", "the consuming fire", "thick cloud and mist", "fire", "radiance" (*Kuzari* 2.7), "the glory of the Lord", "the Lord", as

[13] Nevertheless, in *Kuzari* 5.2 he mentions, in the name of others, a philosophical exegesis of the first verses of the account of the Creation in Genesis.

[14] Halevi here uses a term taken from the Shiite lexicon, *safwa*.

well as the verse, "And the Lord descended on Mount Sinai" (*Kuzari* 2.4), "fire and cloud and image and picture", "the angels seen by Isaiah, Ezekiel, Daniel, and Ezekiel's vision of the Chariot" (*Kuzari* 4.3). In his view, these phenomena are "fine spiritual matter" (2.4) or "a refined body" (2.3) created by God, whose ontological status is an intermediate stage between the pure spirituality of God and the corporeality of the physical world which we are able to perceive by means of our senses. This matter is embodied in spiritual form at the will of God, by means of "the spark of divine light" (2.7). Elsewhere, he interprets part of these phenomena as physical forms which were created by God at His will for a particular prophet at a particular moment.

One of the foci of Halevi's biblical exegesis, like that of Baḥya, is the doctrine of the deity. Here, Halevi is interested in removing any anthropomorphic perception of God, building a doctrine of attributes according to which one may ascribe to God attributes of action, attributes of relation, and negative attributes, but no essential attributes. He goes on to explain the nature of the concrete qualities ascribed to God by the Bible on the basis of this doctrine of attributes; for example, "merciful and gracious" (Exod 34:6), "a jealous and avenging God" (Nah 1:2), are attributes of God's actions; "High and Lofty One" (Isa 57:15) are attributes which man ascribes to God out of his admiration of Him, while "living" is a negative attribute, meaning that God is not dead, but also that He is not alive in the same sense in which human beings are alive. To these terms, which conform to the Aristotelian god, he adds other attributes based upon the perception of God as acting wilfully: "forming", "creating", and "alone doing great wonders" (Ps 136:4).

Halevi displays particular interest in interpretations for the names of God. These interpretations also reflect an explicitly theological tendency. He interprets the Ineffable Name, YHWH, and the names *'elôhîm*, *qâdôš* (Isa 6:3), *'ehyeh* (Exod 3:14) and *'adônây*. Halevi sees the Tetragrammaton, YHWH, as the 'personal' name of the Divine. This name is used to identify the specific God who appears in revelation. The name *'ehyeh* is likewise connected with revelation, according to his interpretation: *'ehyeh* is the God who reveals Himself to the people of Israel when they seek Him. The name *'elôhîm* is the name for the philosophical God, whom one reaches by means of rational proof; its meaning is 'ruler' and 'judge'. As opposed to YHWH, which is the personal name of God, *'elôhîm* is a generic name, a term used for a group of different powers, different from one another, which are the causes of motion in the world and rule those things therein.

Like Baḥya before him, Halevi also utilizes the rule: "the Torah speaks in the language of man", which he applies to the doctrine of the deity. Halevi interprets only one subject in the Bible by its means – those verses which seemingly indicate that God needs to be reminded of something or to have His attention drawn to something (Num 10:9–10; Lev 23:24). He argues that we find here an example of the rule: "the Torah speaks in the language of man"; that is, that the Torah speaks in the manner generally known to human beings, according to the understanding of the masses. Therefore, things are formulated as if one were speaking of the remembrance of the people of Israel before

God. In fact, these verses teach the idea that when the deeds and intention will be perfect, they will merit recompense from God.

One also finds in Halevi one allegorical interpretation, namely, the exegesis of Cant 5:2–4. Whereas in Jewish medieval philosophy the Song of Songs is commonly interpreted as a parable for the human soul, Halevi sees these verses as a historical parable relating to the Jewish people in Exile during the Second Temple period.

A number of Halevi's biblical interpretations bear a polemical character. Halevi interprets one of the central passages in the biblical Jewish-Christian polemic, the words of Isaiah to the "Servant of the Lord" (Isa 52:13; 53:1–4), in a manner that rejects the Christian interpretation of these words. According to his exegesis, the "Servant of the Lord" in Isa 52:13 is the Jewish people itself, not Jesus. Isa 53:1–4 depicts the suffering of the Jewish people in Exile. The people of Israel, and not Jesus, suffer on behalf of mankind, and will thereafter redeem it. The Jewish people as a whole has a messianic task; its function in human history is to bring about the connection between God and the world.[15]

5. Moses ben Maimon / Maimonides (Rambam)

R. Moses ben Maimon (Lat. Maimonides, acronym: Rambam; Cordoba, 1135/38 - Fostat, 1204) is known as both the greatest Jewish philosopher and the greatest Jewish jurist (halakhist) of the Middle Ages. Similar to Baḥya and Halevi before him, Maimonides did not write a systematic commentary of any of the biblical books or any part thereof. His biblical exegeses appear within his halakhic works, in his epistles, and in his philosophic-theological work, *The Guide of the Perplexed* (*Dalâlat al-Ḥâ'irîn*).

Particularly in his halakhic works, but also in the *Guide*, Maimonides, like Baḥya, utilizes the biblical text as a prooftext for the ideas that he articulates or for the practical instructions that he gives to the reader. These prooftexts are frequently invoked without any commentary; their interpretation is left to be inferred by the reader from the fact of their use in support of a particular opinion or instruction. Less frequently, he also interprets these prooftexts. However, unlike Baḥya, Maimonides does not suffice with bringing biblical prooftexts for his opinions. Rather, biblical exegesis occupies a central place in his writings, primarily in the *Guide of the Perplexed.*

Whereas Baḥya and Halevi, as well as Maimonides in his halakhic works and his epistles, only incorporate biblical interpretations within their theological discussions, Maimonides represents the exegesis of the Bible – specifically, the interpretation of equivocal terms according to their logical classification, and the interpretation of parables in the Bible – as the purpose of his theological-philosophical work, the *Guide of the Perplexed.*[16] This goal is not ex-

[15] *Kuzari* 2.34–44; 4.22–23.

[16] Interpretations of the Bible also appear in those sections of Maimonides' halakhic writings that deal with matters of faith and belief: the *Commentary on the Mishnah*, the *Mishneh Torah* [abbr. MT] (the Code).

pressed in the structure of the book. The majority of the chapters dealing with the interpretation of equivocal terms appearing in the Bible are concentrated at the beginning of the book; thereafter, Maimonides proceeds to deal with theological-philosophical subjects. His interpretations of textual units, consisting of a verse, a paragraph, or even a chapter, as well as the interpretation of equivocal terms, are scattered within these discussions throughout the various chapters of the book, and are not presented in any systematic manner.

The Guide of the Perplexed is meant to answer a challenge presented by the period in which Maimonides lived – namely, the confrontation between religion and philosophy. According to the Introduction, the book is intended for the reader who is, on the one hand, a believing religious person, who observes the commandments and accepts the Bible as a sacred and authoritative text, not only in the realm of religious-ethical behavior, but also in that of beliefs and opinions. On the other hand, he is an intellectual who is well acquainted with the philosophy of the Aristotelian tradition that was widespread in his day (primarily that of a Alfarabi and Avicenna) and accepts them as true. Such a person finds inconsistency and even contradiction between the literal understanding of Biblical texts and Aristotelian philosophy, and for this reason is 'perplexed'. Maimonides' goal is to free this individual from his 'perplexity' by means of a reinterpretation of Scripture which will demonstrate that the truth of philosophy and that of the biblical text are in fact harmonious. Maimonides thus engages in philosophical exegesis of the Bible, by means of which he shows that the inner significance of the biblical text is none other than that of Aristotelian physics and metaphysics.

The attempt to harmonize between religion and philosophy by means of biblical exegesis acquires a specific coloration in Maimonides. Maimonides adopts the idea of philosophic esotericism, particularly in the version of this idea promulgated by Avicenna. He argues that the philosophic contents, especially metaphysical ideas, ought to be concealed from the broader public, because knowledge of philosophy is liable to damage their religious faith. He identifies this esotericism with tannaitic and amoraitic esotericism – namely, the requirement not to expound publicly the *Maʿaśeh Berēšît* ('Account of the Beginning') and *Maʿaśeh Merkâbâ* ('Account of the Chariot') – explaining that 'Account of the Beginning' refers to Aristotelian physics, while 'Account of the Chariot' corresponds to Aristotelian metaphysics. Since this philosophic esotericism is embodied in legal instructions of the Sages, Maimonides is himself required to obey it, and needs to conceal his philosophic opinions from the masses, primarily in metaphysical matters, as well as part of his philosophical interpretation of Scripture. The Sages not only prohibited the public dissemination of the 'Account of the Beginning' and 'Account of the Chariot', but also stated that one may only transmit the contents of the 'Account of the Chariot' in "chapter headings" – that is, by means of allusion – to those individuals who are deserving to receive them, to one who is "wise and understands by himself". In *Guide of the Perplexed*, Maimonides uses a method whereby he simultaneously hides and reveals a part of his biblical exegesis: hiding it from the broad masses, and revealing it to one who is capable of understanding matters by himself. This being the case, he does not always give a full and clear interpretation of words, verses or entire biblical passages, but only alludes to their meaning. Moreover, at times he also uses another method: the scattering of allusions among a number of different chapters of the *Guide*. The reader is then required to complete these interpretations by himself: to understand the hints that Maimonides gives to certain interpretations, and to combine these with one another. Thus, at times Maimonides' Bible interpretations themselves require interpretation.

What makes Maimonides' approach to biblical exegesis unique is that he not only deals with the interpretation of the Bible in practice, but that he also presents, particularly in his Introduction to the *Guide*, the exegetical theory underlying his biblical exegesis. This theory deals with the language of the biblical text and its literary form, justifying his claim that the inner meaning of the biblical text is philosophical and his theory concerning the literary form of the biblical text.

In his Introduction to the *Guide*, Maimonides explicitly mentions two components of the biblical text that require interpretation: individual words or 'terms', and textual units consisting of a verse or a number of consecutive verses, which he designates as 'parable'. In the chapters on prophecy, he also speaks of a number of forms of expression that are characteristic of the prophets: "figurative uses, exaggerations and hyperbole".

In practice, the *Guide of the Perplexed* contains two different theories concerning equivocal 'terms'. The first theory, which he presents in the Introduction to the work, is the theory of homonyms taken from the literature of Aristotelian logic, which he knew through the writings of al-Farabi. He applies this to the Bible, arguing that a number of different kinds of homonymal nouns appear in the Bible: completely equivocal terms, derivative terms, conventional terms, amphibolous terms, and equivocal terms used in a general and particular sense. In order properly to understand the biblical text and to avoid error in its interpretation, it is necessary to discern that there are in fact words there that are of multiple meaning, to recognize the nature of their multiplicity of meaning, to know their various significances, and to apply them in a proper manner in the proper context.

The second theory argues that the Bible contains equivocal words whose second meaning is to be determined on the basis of their etymology (in fact, frequently on the basis of their imagined etymology), or by changing the order of their letters. This theory is presented by Maimonides at the beginning of his interpretation of the story of the Creation and of the story of the Garden of Eden (end of *Guide* 2.29), and in the chapters on prophecy (*Guide* 2.43).

According to Maimonides' teaching, the 'parables' are verses or passages that have two levels of meaning: a revealed level (Arab. *ẓahir*) and a hidden level (Arab. *baṭin*). In the Introduction to the *Guide*, he distinguishes between two basic types of parable: (1) parables which are no more than a complex of terms, each one of which has its own meaning. In order to understand their hidden level, it is necessary to interpret each of the equivocal terms which comprise it on the basis of the semantic axis of the parable, and to combine them together. In this kind of parable, each word is of importance, because it contributes to the understanding of its general meaning; (2) parables constructed around one central image, not all of whose words are significant on the hidden level. Some of them appear simply to adorn the parable, while others are intended to create a deliberate obscurity on the level of the parable, so as to conceal its true meaning from the reader for whom the hidden level is not intended. In order to understand them, it is therefore sufficient to interpret their central image and a number of key words conducted with them, and there is no need to attempt to interpret all of the words therein.

In the chapters on prophecy in *Guide* 2.43, Maimonides presents a further classification of parables: (1) "Parables whose purpose it is to imitate certain notions"; (2) parables "whose purpose it is to point to what is called to the attention by the term designating the thing seen because of that term's derivation or because of an equivocality of terms"; (3) parables using "certain terms whose letters are identical with those of another term; solely the order of the letters is changed; and between the two terms there is in no way an etymological connection or a community of meaning" (Pines, 392).

In this classification, we find that there are in practice two central kinds of prophetic parables. The first type is group (1), in which the significance of the 'parable' is alluded to by means of the object seen in the prophetic vision or in the prophetic dream. Its appearance and qualities indicate the significance which it wishes to convey. The second type of prophetic parable is composed of groups (2) and (3). Here, the significance of the parables is rooted, not in the objects seen in the prophetic vision, but in the names of those objects; the visual serves as an intermediary for the verbal. One must relate to these dreams as linguistic phenomena, rather than as systems of sensory images requiring interpretation.

In addition to the parables, in the chapters on prophecy (*Guide* 2.47) Maimonides discusses three further literary forms used by the prophets, far less widely found than the parables, which also require interpretation: hyperbole, exaggeration and derivative uses. The common denominator of all three is that in a literal reading the text appears to be saying something absurd. The problem that occupies Maimonides in their interpretation is not the harmony between philosophy and revealed religion, but the harmony between the biblical text and logic.

Maimonides justifies his exegetical theory in a number of ways. Like Baḥya and Judah Halevi, Maimonides utilizes, in his halakhic writings, in his epistles, and in the *Guide of the Perplexed*, the rabbinic dictum that "the Torah speaks in the language of human beings", which he applies to corporealizing expressions of God in the Bible. "The Torah speaks in language of human beings" means, in his understanding, that the Torah speaks according to the understanding and apprehension of the multitude. According to his epistemology, the apprehension of the multitude is characterized by the imaginative faculty, whereas the philosopher apprehends things in an intellectual way. He also cites a psychological reason for corporealization: the ordinary person understands God through comparison to himself, and therefore thinks that He is corporeal and possesses the same perfections as human beings. Like Baḥya, Maimonides believes that corporealization of God in the Bible serves an educational function. However, whereas Baḥya thought that the corporeal expressions for God in the Bible were simply intended to bring the average person to faith in the existence of God, Maimonides claimed that they were also intended to lead him to faith in the perfection of God. In order to convey the concept of God's perfection to the average person, the Torah attributes to God that which would constitute perfection in man.[17] Whereas Baḥya justified by means of this expression the very existence of corporealizing terms in the Bible, Maimonides understood this rule primarily as justifying the non-corporealizing interpretation of nouns, primarily derivative nouns, spoken by God in the Bible.[18] Similarly, Maimonides utilizes another rule of the Sages in order to justify his claim that the Torah contains hyperbolic expressions which cannot be understood literally: "[The Sages] have given an explanation by saying, 'The Torah speaks in exaggerated language' (*b. Ḥul.* 90 b; *b. Tamid* 28 a) – that is, hyperbole".[19]

He bases his claim that there are parables in the Bible which are to be interpreted on the basis of the etymology of their key words upon the Scripture itself – the prophecy of Jeremiah (Jer 1:11–12) – "I see a rod of an almond-tree", and that of Amos (Amos 8:1–2), who saw a basket of "summer fruit" in his prophetic vision. What is unique about these two prophecies is that the visions seen therein are interpreted within the prophecies themselves on the basis of the etymology of the central word therein: 'almond' (*šâqēd*) in Jeremiah and 'summer fruit' (*qayîṣ*) in Amos. Maimonides is thus able to infer that the exegetical principle of the interpretation of words in the prophetic parables on the basis of etymology is found in the Bible itself.

His double claim – that the literary form of the 'parable' is found in the Bible, and that the true meaning of the 'parable' is a philosophic one, to be found on its esoteric level – is justified by Maimonides, among other things, by the psychology of prophecy. According to his teaching, prophecy is an intellectual emanation overflowing from the Active Intellect to the rational faculty of the prophet, from whence it acts upon his imaginative faculty, in which the intelligible concepts are embodied in sensory images. It follows from this that the significance of the prophetic parables is rational, identical to Aristotelian philosophy, which is the fruit of intellectual thought. Thus, in order to understand them, one needs to interpret the sensory images which compose them in an intellectual way.

The claim that the esoteric level of the parables consists of Aristotelian philosophy is justified by him through a variation of a tradition that was widespread in Jewish and Arabic philosophy of the Middle Ages, according to which philosophy had originally been the legacy of the people of Israel, but was lost during the Exile (*Guide* 1.71).

As we have seen in the Introduction to the *Guide of the Perplexed*, the purpose of the book is to interpret equivocal terms of the logical type and biblical parables. Maimonides devotes 42 chapters of the *Guide* to this lexicon of equi-

---

[17] *Guide* 1.26, 29, 33, 46, 47, 53, 59; 3.13; *MT*, *Yesodê hat-Tôrâh* 1.9, 12; Introduction to *Heleq*, 3rd sect.; *Iggeret Tehiyat ham-Metim* (letter on Resurrection).

[18] In the *Guide* 1.59, he understands this rule in a manner more similar to Baḥya.

[19] *Guide* 2.47.

vocal terms, most of them concentrated in the first half of the first part of the work. This lexicon serves, first and foremost, the goal of removing the corporealization of God in the Bible. This being so, the predominant structure in these chapters is the following: (1) presentation of an equivocal term or terms at the beginning of the chapter; (2) listing of the various meanings of this term or terms. Alongside each meaning, Maimonides cites biblical verses from which one may understand the meaning he points out, through the context of that same verse or passage to which it belongs. By this, he confirms the existence of each meaning by means of Scripture itself, and establishes a 'biblical lexicon'. (3) Finally, Maimonides explains which of the significances of the term in question may be applied to sentences in which God is either the subject or object. His exegetical assumption here is that God is not corporeal, so that there is an obligation to choose, among those existing meanings of the terms noted in the beginning of the chapter, those which will not lead to His corporealization. At this stage, he also brings examples of the biblical use of these terms in their non-corporeal sense, thereby providing an interpretation for some concrete verses in which they appear.

Within the framework of the lexicographical chapters of the *Guide*, Maimonides interprets, not only biblical verses that refer to God, but also biblical verses dealing with other subjects, such as 'the Account of the Beginning', 'the Account of the Chariot', and his doctrine of prophecy. In this way, his lexicon serves further exegetical goals of the *Guide* – the interpretation of verses connected to subjects that are "secrets of Torah". In his interpretation of those terms that are to be understood on the basis of their etymology, more specifically on the basis of their imagined etymology, as well as through the interpretation of names by means of switching letters, Maimonides uses an accepted Jewish exegetical method: the interpretation of terms by means of etymology appears in the Bible and in rabbinic Midrashim, while the interpretation of words through the switching of letters is also found in rabbinic literature.[20] In practice, only infrequently does Maimonides interpret terms by means of etymology or by switching letters, and even then only in order to interpret texts which involve a particular exegetical difficulty.

In the Introduction to the *Guide of the Perplexed*, Maimonides claims that most of the parables in Scripture belong to the second type mentioned above, those constructed around one central image. As an example of a parable of this type, he cites Prov 7:6–21, built around the central image of "a married harlot", which he identifies with matter. According to this interpretation, the parable of the "married harlot" is a warning against following one's corporeal nature, which is the source of man's bodily desires. Nevertheless, most of the parables interpreted in the *Guide* are closer to the parable of the first type mentioned above: namely, a parable built upon a series of equivocal words. In the Introduction to the *Guide*, Maimonides cites as an example of such a parable the dream of Jacob's ladder in Gen 28:12–13, which he divides into seven units of meaning. In *Guide* 1.15, this parable is interpreted as being concerned

[20] As we have noted, he claims that he learns the interpretation of names on the basis of their etymology from the biblical text.

with the structure of the physical world, which devolves from God and descends to the element of earth in the sublunar world, or to the four elements of which all things in the sublunar world are composed, man's graduated cognition of the ladder of nature, a cognition which ultimately brings him to apprehension of the eternal God who is beyond the highest sphere, and the prophet, who is also the ideal political leader, who knows nature and guides human society through imitation of God's actions in the world.

Maimonides here utilizes his biblical lexicon in interpreting the equivocal terms 'stand' (*niṣab*), 'descend' (*yârad*), 'ascend' (*ʿâlâh*), and 'angel' (*mal'âkh*), but also in interpreting terms that do not appear in his biblical lexicon: 'earth' (*'ereṣ*) and 'heaven' (*šâmayîm*), which according to his exegesis allude to terms from Aristotelian physics. He only alludes to the meaning of 'ladder' (*sullâm*).

Parallel to, and simultaneously with, the exegesis of parables by means of the interpretation of their central image or the equivocal words which constitute them, Maimonides uses an additional method of interpreting biblical parables: interpreting the Bible by means of its rabbinic Midrash. The assumption underlying this usage is that the Sages are the authoritative exegetes of the biblical text, and therefore one should rely upon their interpretations to assist its understanding.

The use of Midrash in order to interpret a biblical parable stands out particularly in two of Maimonides' interpretations of Jacob's dream of the ladder,[21] in his exegesis of the account of the Creation and of the Garden of Eden, and in his interpretation of the figure of the 'Satan' in the frame story of the book of Job.

One may speak of at least four basic types of biblical exegesis by means of Midrash in Maimonides. The first is that of biblical interpretation based upon aggadic expansions found in the Midrash; that is: upon elements added to the biblical text by the Midrash in order to interpret it, in which there are found the additional explanations by the Rabbis of the biblical text. For example, in his exegesis of the story of the Garden of Eden, we find an exegesis of a biblical parable by means of a Midrash, in which Maimonides also saw a 'parable'. In order to understand this interpretation, Maimonides first needs to interpret the rabbinic Midrash, and thereafter interpret the biblical text by its means. Maimonides states that the figures of Adam, Eve and the Serpent in the biblical account are none other than the components of man, primarily those of the human soul: Eve is either the body and the animal soul of man, or his animal soul alone; Adam is the intellect; while the serpent is the appetitive faculty of the soul. In order to explain man's attraction towards physical appetites, it is important for Maimonides to introduce another figure into the biblical story. Here he relies upon a Midrash from *Pirqê de-Rabbi 'Eliʿezer*, Ch. 13, which introduces another protagonist into the story – the demon Samael, who 'rode' upon the 'serpent'. This Midrash makes it possible for him to allude to an interpretation according to which the serpent ridden by Samael is identified with the appetitive faculty of man, which is ruled by the imaginative faculty. It fol-

---

[21] In *Yesodê hat-Tôrâh* 3.7; *Guide* 2.10.

lows from this that the sin of the Garden of Eden consisted in following irrational appetites.

Yet another, second, form of biblical exegesis based upon Midrash is the citing of a midrashic interpretation which is understood literally. In that case, the exegetical act essentially consists in the choice of this particular Midrash among the various Midrashim which interpret the text, and its use as a proof-text for the interpretation of the biblical text.

A third type of midrashic-related biblical exegesis is the interpretation of the Bible by means of an implicit Midrash. In this case, Maimonides does not actually cite the Midrash, but one can see that he derives his basic exegetical idea from a midrashic interpretation of the text. A clear example of an interpretation of this type is found in another interpretation of Jacob's dream of a ladder, found in the Introduction to the *Guide* and in *Guide* 1.15. The division of this biblical text into seven units of significance, and its interpretation as speaking about a prophet who is a political leader, is implicitly based upon *Gen. R.* 68:12. This Midrash likewise divides the dream of the ladder into seven units of meaning, drawing a numerological equation (*gematria*) between 'Sinai' and 'ladder' (סלם equivalent to סיני) seeing the dream of the ladder as a dream of the ascension of Moses and Aaron to Mount Sinai.

A fourth type of biblical interpretation based upon Midrash is one in which the biblical exegesis occurs by means of a Midrash which serves as an allusion to its exegesis. Maimonides does not complete the exegesis, but expects the reader who "understands by himself" to do this for himself. An example of an interpretation of this kind is that of the figure of 'Satan' in the frame story of Job. Maimonides alludes to its meaning by referring to a Midrash in *b. B. Bat* 16 a which interprets this figure, and by a number of comments concerning the direction in which it is to be interpreted.

As we already have seen, Maimonides deals also with the interpretation of certain biblical texts which he sees as 'parables' – that is, as texts which have two levels of meaning: a revealed level and a hidden level, and whose true meaning is to be found on the hidden level. He devotes several chapters or portions of chapters in the *Guide of the Perplexed* to such interpretations. *Guide* 2.30, for example, deals with the exegesis of the Creation narrative, which Maimonides sees as a parable whose true subject is Aristotelian physics. The account of the Creation is hence not cosmogony, but cosmology – that is, a description of the structure of the physical world. *Guide* 1.2 and 2.30 contain exegesis of the stories of the creation of man and of the Garden of Eden (Genesis 1–3). The stories of the creation of man, the Garden of Eden, and the sons of Adam (Genesis 4–5) are to be understood as philosophical anthropology rather than as historical accounts. Adam and Eve are not two individual human beings, but the two basic components of the substance 'man' – matter and form. The protagonists of the Eden narrative are thus the faculties of the human soul and intellect. *Guide* 1.54 deals with the exegesis of the revelation of God to Moses in the cleft of the rock in Exodus 33–34. According to Maimonides' interpretation, these chapters are concerned with the doctrine of the divine attributes. In *Guide* 2.22–23, Maimonides engages in exegesis of the frame story of the book of Job and of the main part of the book. For him, the book of Job is a parable dealing with divine Providence and the problem of the source of evil.

Guide 3.1–7 engages in exegesis of Ezekiel's vision of the chariot. This exegesis is conducted by means of hints, and is rather obscure. In general terms, he interprets Ezekiel's vision of the chariot as an apprehension of the structure of the world of spheres, the primary matter and the four elements of the lower world, and the apprehension of the separate intellect.

In addition to his interpretation of equivocal terms of the logical type, equivocal terms that are to be understood on the basis of etymology, parables, exaggerations, hyperboles, and derivative terms, Maimonides engages in the exegesis of other subjects in the Bible. Like R. Judah Halevi before him, Maimonides addresses himself to the problem of divine names in the Bible. Like Halevi, Maimonides claims that the name YHWH is God's unique name. Indeed, for Maimonides this is the only divine name that indicates His essence. All other names are interpreted by him as describing various attributes of God derived from his actions in the world. He interprets the name "I will be" (*'ehyeh*), following the teaching of Avicenna, as indicating God as 'necessary existence' – a concept of God that may be attained by philosophical means, through proof of the existence of God. *'Elôhim* (generally translated as 'God') is interpreted as denoting God as judge, but not as ruler (*Guide* 1.2, 61; 2.6, 30).

Maimonides pays special attention, both in his halakhic writings and in the *Guide of the Perplexed*, to the interpretation of the phenomenon of biblical prophecy, to the historical images of the prophets mentioned in the Bible, and to the manner of their prophecy. His concern is to give meaning to the Bible within the framework of his theological-philosophical teachings and on their basis. He deals with the question as to whether one is to see certain biblical figures as prophets, arguing that Hagar, Manoah, Laban and Abimelekh were not at all prophets. Those who were prophets prophesied, according to his interpretation, on different degrees of prophecy, which he presents in *Guide* 2.45. The true prophets prophesied on degrees 3–11 of prophecy. In describing these degrees, Maimonides notes the degree of various actual prophecies in the Bible according to his classification.

King Solomon and the books attributed to him according to Jewish tradition – Proverbs, Ecclesiastes, and the Song of Songs – occupy a special place in the biblical exegesis of Maimonides. Maimonides sees Solomon as an esoteric metaphysician, who on the one hand warns against publicly disseminating knowledge of the 'Account of the Chariot', and on the other hand, as the 'sage', who guides those who are capable towards attaining the final perfection. According to his interpretation, the Book of Proverbs is concerned with physics and with anthropology (the parable of the "married harlot" is commented in *Guide* 3.8 and in the Introduction to the *Guide*, referring to Prov 7:6–21 and Prov 6:26 respectively) and hence with the 'Account of the Beginning'. However, its uniqueness lies in the fact that it also deals with theoretical aspects of biblical exegesis. According to Maimonides' exegesis, Prov 25:11, "A word fitly spoken is like apples of gold in settings of silver", is a parable of the perfect biblical parable.

This survey has shown that, even though Maimonides did not write running commentaries to the Bible, one finds in his writings a biblical exegesis unusually rich in exegetical ideas, dealing with many and varied aspects both of the exegetical theory of the biblical text and of its actual interpretation, on the basis of a philosophical-semantic axis. Maimonides' exegesis of the Bible had a profound influence upon all of the philosophical Bible exegesis which followed him. All subsequent medieval Jewish philosophical biblical exegesis carries his stamp. It is impossible to understand and to evaluate the history of philosophical Bible exegesis among the Jews in the Middle Ages after Maimonides without familiarity with his exegesis.

CHAPTER THIRTY-TWO

The School of Literal Jewish Exegesis in Northern France

By AVRAHAM GROSSMAN, Jerusalem

Sources: MENAHEM B. HELBO: S. A. POZNANSKI, "Interpretations of R. Menahem b. Helbo to the Holy Scriptures" (Heb.), *Sepher ha-Yôbhel le-Nahum Sokolow* (Warsaw 1904) 389–439. – RASHI: A. BERLINER (ed.), *Commentary on the Pentateuch*, Reggio di Calabria 1475, also based on first editions and manuscripts (Frankfurt/M 1905); *Commentary on Former and Latter Prophets and Hagiographa, Miqra'ôt Gedôlôt* (Venice 1524–26); Y. FLORSHEIM, *Rashi on the Bible in his Commentary on the Talmud* I–III (Jerusalem 1981–89); M. LEHMANN (ed.), *Commentary on Exodus, Leviticus, Numbers*, based on a Yemenite MS (New York 1982); A. J. LEVY (ed.), *Rashi's Commentary on Ezekiel 40–48* (Philadelphia 1931); I. MAARSEN (ed.), *Minor Prophets* (Amsterdam 1930); *Isaiah* (Jerusalem 1933); *Psalms* (Jerusalem 1936); I. M. ROSENTHAL (ed.), "Commentary on the Song of Songs" (Heb.), *Sepher ha-Yôbhel le-Sh. K. Mirsky* (New York 1958) 130–88. – JOSEPH KARA: M. M. AHREND (ed.), *Perûsh Rabbi Yôseph Qara le-Sepher Iyyôbh* (Jerusalem 1988); A. BERLINER, *Plêtat Sôferîm* (Breslau 1872) 12–25 [Fragments of the commentary to various passages in the Pentateuch]; S. BUBER (ed.), [*Commentary on Lamentations*] (Breslau 1900); [*Commentary on Former Prophets and Isaiah*], *Mikra'ot Gedolot 'Haketer'* (ed. M. Cohen; Ramat-Gan 1992–96); *Commentary on Latter Prophets, Miqra'ôt Gedôlôt* (Lublin 1897–99); B. EINSTEIN (ed.), *R. Josef Kara und sein Kommentar zu Kohelet* (Berlin 1886) 6–60; S. EPPENSTEIN (ed.), [*Commentary on Micah*], *Birkat Abraham* (*Sepher ha-Yôbhel ... A. Berliner*; ed. A. FREIMANN; Berlin 1903) 17–26; idem (ed.), *Perushê Rabbi Yôseph Qara li-Nebhî'îm Rîshônîm* (Jerusalem 1972); H. Y. A. GAD (ed.), [*Commentary on Esther, Ruth and Lamentations*] Appendix to Commentary of Joseph Bekhor Shor on Deuteronomy (Benê Beraq 1959); idem, *Hamishâ Me'ôrôt ha-Gedôlîm* (Johannesburg 1953) 7–37 [Fragments of the commentary to various passages in the Pentateuch]; A. HUEBSCH-JAFFE (ed.), [*Fragments from Commentary to the Five Scrolls*] (Prague 1866); A. KRISTIANPOLLER, "Gleanings from Rabbi Joseph Kara's Commentary on Isaiah" (Heb.), *Sepher ha-Yôbhel ... S. Krauss* (Jerusalem 1937) 110–16; A. L. SCHLOSSBERG (ed.), *Commentary on Jeremiah* (Paris 1881); Y. TEOMIM-FRAENKEL (ed.), *Commentary on Hosea* (Breslau 1861). – RASHBAM: S. JAPHET / R. B. SALTERS, *The Commentary of R. Samuel b. Meir on Qoheleth* (Jerusalem 1985); D. ROSIN (ed.), *Perûsh ha-Tôrâ asher katav Rashbam ...* (Breslau 1882). – JOSEPH BEKHOR SHOR: H. Y. A. GAD (ed.), [*Commentary on Genesis and Exodus*] (Jerusalem 1956); [*Commentary on Leviticus*] (London 1960); [*Commentary on Deuteronomy*] (Benê Beraq 1959). – ELIEZER OF BEAUGENCY: J. W. NUTT (ed.), *Commentary on Isaiah of Eliézer de Beaugency* (Oxford 1897); S. POZNANSKI (ed.), *Perûsh al Yehezkel u-Terê ʿAsar le-Rabbi Eliʿezer mi-Belganzi* (Warsaw 1913).

General works: M. M. AHREND, *Le commentaire sur Job de Rabbi Yoseph Qara* (Hildesheim 1978); idem, "Rashi's Method in Explaining Words" (Heb.), *Sepher Rashi* (ed. Z. A. Steinfeld; Ramat-Gan 1993); Y. AVINERI, *Hêkhal Rashi* (Jerusalem 1979); I. BAER, "Rashi and the Historical Reality of His Time" (Heb.), *Sepher Rashi* (ed. Y. L. Maimon; Jerusalem 1956); M. BANITT, "Les Poterim", *REJ* 125 (1966) 21–33; idem, *Rashi Interpreter of the Biblical Letter* (Tel-Aviv 1985); A. BERLINER, "On the History of Rashi's Commentaries" (Heb.), *Ketabhîm Nibhharîm* II (Jerusalem 1949) 179–226; idem, *Pelêtat Sopherîm* (Breslau 1872); B. BLUMENKRANZ, *Les auteurs chrétiens latins du moyen âge sur les Juifs et le Judaïsme* (Paris 1963); G. BRIN, *Mehqarîm be-Perûshô shel R. Yôseph Qara* (Tel-Aviv 1990); M. CATANE, "Le monde intellectuel de Rashi", *Les Juifs au regard de l'histoire. Mélanges en l'honneur de Bernhard Blumenkranz* (ed. G. Dahan; Paris 1985) 63–85; G. DAHAN, *Les intellectuels chrétiens et les Juifs au moyen âge* (Paris 1990); A. DARMESTETER /

D. S. Blondheim, *Les glosses françaises dans les commentaires talmudiques de Raschi* I–II (Paris 1929–37); H. Englander, "Grammatical Elements and Terminology in Rashi", HUCA 14 (1939) 387–429; E. Eppenstein, "Recherches sur les comparaisons de l'Hébreu avec l'Arabe chez les exégètes du Nord de la France", *REJ* 47 (1903) 47–56; idem, "Studien über Joseph ben Simeon Kara als Exeget", Jahrbuch für jüdische Geschichte und Literatur 4 (1906) 238–68; A. Freimann, "Manuscript Supercommentaries on Rashi's Commentary of the Pentateuch", *Rashi Anniversary Volume* (New York 1941) 73–114; A. Geiger, *Parschandatha; die nordfranzösische Exegetenschule* (Leipzig 1855); B. Gelles, *Peshat and Derash in the Exegesis of Rashi* (Leiden 1981); A. Grabois, "The Hebraica Veritas and Jewish-Christian Intellectual Relations in the Twelfth Century", *Spec.* 50 (1975) 613–34; M. Greenberg, "The Relationship between Rashi's and Rashbam's Commentaries on the Torah" (Heb.), *Sepher I. A. Seeligmann* (ed. Y. Zakovich / A. Rofe; II; Jerusalem 1983) 565–66; A. Gross, "Rashi and the Tradition of Studying the Written Torah in Spain" (Heb.), *Sepher Rashi* (ed. Z. A. Steinfeld; Ramat-Gan 1993) 27–55; H. Gross, *Gallia Judaica* (Amsterdam ²1969); A. Grossman, "From the 'Italian Geniza' – Fragments of R. Joseph Kara's Commentary on the Torah" (Heb.), *Pe'amîm* 52 (1992) 16–36; idem, *Hakhmê Ashkenaz ha-Rîshônîm* (Jerusalem ²1989); idem, *Hakhmê Sarephat ha-Rîshônîm*, 2nd ed. (Jerusalem 1996); idem, "The Jewish-Christian Debate and Jewish Bible Exegesis in France in the 12th Century" (Heb.), *Zion* 51 (1986) 29–60; C. H. Haskins, *The Renaissance of the 12th Century* (London 1927); H. Hailperin, *Rashi and the Christian Scholars* (Pittsburgh 1963); S. Japhet, "The Commentary of Hizqûnî on the Torah – the Nature of the Composition and its Purpose" (Heb.), *Sepher ha-Yôbhel la-Rabh Mordecai Breuer* (ed. M. Bar-Asher; I; Jerusalem 1992) 91–111; S. Kamin, *Rashi – Peshûtô shel Miqra û-Midrashô shel Miqra* (Jerusalem 1986); N. Leibowitz / M. Ahrend, *Perûsh Rashi la-Tôrâ – 'Iyyûnîm be-Shittatô*, I–II (Tel-Aviv 1990); E. M. Lipschuetz, *R. Shelomo Yishaqî* (Warsaw 1912); M. Littmann, *Joseph b. Simeon Kara als Schrifterklärer* (Breslau 1887); F. Lotter, "Das Prinzip der 'Hebraica Veritas' und die heilsgeschichtliche Rolle Israels bei den frühen Zisterziensern", *Bibel in jüdischer und christlicher Tradition. Festschrift für Johann Maier* (Frankfurt/M 1993) 479–517; A. Marx, "The Life and Work of Rashi", *Rashi Anniversary Volume, American Academy for Jewish Research* (New York 1941) 9–30; E. Z. Melammed, *Mephareshê ha-Miqra, Darkhêhem we-Shittôtêhem* I–II (Jerusalem 1978); Y. Nebho, *Ha-Parshanût ha-Sarephatît* (Kephar Hasîdîm [Israel] 1994); A. K. Offenberg, "The Earliest Printed Editions of Rashi's Commentary of the Pentateuch", *Rashi 1040–1990* (ed. G. Sed-Rajna; Paris 1993) 493–506; A. Ovadiah, "Rashi's Commentary on the Torah and its Commentators" (Heb.), *Sepher Rashi* (ed. Y. L. Maimon; Jerusalem 1956) 543–669; S. A. Poznanski, *Mabho 'al Hakhmê Sarephat Mephareshê ha-Miqra* (Jerusalem ²1965); Y. Rahman, *Aggadat Rashi* (Tel-Aviv 1991); P. Riché, *Ecoles et enseignement dans le Haut Moyen Age* (Paris 1979); I. Rosenthal, "The Anti-Christian Polemic in Rashi on the Bible" (Heb.), *Rashi, his Teaching and Personality* (ed. S. Federbusch; New York 1958) 45–59; D. Rosin, *R. Samuel b. Meir als Schrifterklärer* (Jahresbericht des jüdisch-theologischen Seminars; Breslau 1880); A. Saltman, "Alexander Nequam – His Commentary on the Song of Songs and Jewish Exegesis" (Heb.), *Sepher ha-Zikkarôn le-Sarâ Kamîn* (ed. S. Japhet; Jerusalem 1994) 421–52; M. Z. Segal, *Parshanût ha-Miqra* (Jerusalem 1971); Y. Shapira, "Commentators on Rashi's Commentary on the Torah" (Heb.), *Bissarôn* 1 (1950) 426–27; E. Shereshevsky, *Rashi: The Man and his World* (New York 1982); M. A. Signer, "The Anti-Jewish Polemic of Andreas of Saint-Victor" (Heb.), *Sepher ha-Zikkarôn le-Sarâ Kamîn* (ed. S. Japhet; Jerusalem 1994) 412–20; B. Smalley, *The Study of the Bible in the Middle Ages* (Oxford 1952); I. Sonne, "Text Criticism of Rashi's Commentary on the Torah" (Heb.), HUCA 15 (1940) 37–56; E. Talmage, "Christian Exegesis in the Middle Ages and its Interrelationship with Jewish Exegesis" (Heb.), *Parshanût ha-Miqra ha-Yehûdît: Pirqê Mabhô* (ed. M. Greenberg; Jerusalem 1983) 101–12; I. Ta-Shma, "The Library of the French Sages", *Sepher Rashi* (ed. G. Sed-Rajna; Paris 1993) 535–40; E. Touitou, "Rashbam's Exegetical Method on the Background of the Historical Reality of His Time" (Heb.), *Sepher ha-Yôbhel le-E. Z. Melammed* (ed. Y. D. Gilat et al.; Ramat-Gan 1982) 48–74; idem, "On Rashbam's Method in his Commentary on the Torah" (Heb.), *Tarbiz* 48 (1979) 248–73; E. E. Urbach, *Ba'alê ha-Tôsaphôt* (Jerusalem ⁴1980); W. J. Van Bekkum, "Hebrew Grammatical Tradition in the Exegesis of Rashi", *Rashi 1040–1990* (ed. G. Sed-Rajna; Paris 1993) 427–36; D. Weiss Halivni, *Peshat and Derash* (New York 1991); E. Yassif, "Rashi Legends and Medieval Popular Culture", *Rashi 1040–1990* (ed. G. Sed-Rajna; Paris 1993) 483–92; L. Zunz, "Salomon ben Isaac, genannt Raschi", *Zeitschrift für Wissenschaft des Judentums* I (Berlin 1822) 277–384; M. Zohari, *Midreshê Halakhâ ve-Aggadâ be-Perûshaw shel Rashi* I–XVI (Jerusalem 1994).

1. Introduction: The Revolution in Eleventh Century France

The second half of the eleventh century witnessed a dramatic change in the field of Jewish Bible exegesis in Northern France. The change was twofold: a sudden increase in exegetical activity, and a new predilection for the plain, literal interpretation of the text (*peshat*). Anonymous commentators, whom Rashi refers to as *pôterîm*, had been active in the first half of the eleventh century, listing French translations of difficult words in the biblical text. By the middle of the century, however, R. Menahem b. Helbo was writing systematic commentaries on many books of the Prophets and the Hagiographa. In the last quarter of the century, Rashi, the greatest master of medieval exegesis, wrote his commentary on the Bible, which occupies a central position in his literary output. Some of his closest disciples were already writing their own commentaries while Rashi was still alive; their creativity reached a peak in the first half of the twelfth century. Though much of their work has been lost, it was clearly quite comprehensive and extensive. In view of this great surge of exegetical activity, spread over two generations, as against the almost total silence of North-French scholars in the first half of the eleventh century and the dearth of biblical commentaries by German scholars in that century, it may not be inappropriate to speak of a veritable revolution.

The revolution was not confined within the walls of the academy or the study house. We know from the sources that disciples continued their masters' literary work, also applying the new method in their teaching activities. A new school had thus taken shape; it not only considered the literal interpretation to be a legitimate exposition of the biblical text but also advocated the methodological separation of *peshat*, the plain meaning, from *derash*, homiletical exposition, these being two distinct approaches to the text. Whereas *derash* had been the principal, if not only, method of exposition in previous generations, it was now displaced by the *peshat*.

As an indication of the intensity of the 'new movement', we might mention that at least ten commentaries on the book of Job were written in French-Jewish society alone between the years 1070–1170 (some of these are still in manuscript).

At the centre of the movement, for four generations, stood seven scholars. The greatest and most famous was Rashi, but the others also had a significant part to play in the development of the school of literal exegesis. Listed approximately in order of their birth dates, the seven were: Menahem ben Helbo (1015–1085), Solomon ben Isaac, or Rashi (1040–1105), Joseph Kara (1050–1130), Shemaiah (1060–1130), Samuel ben Meir, or Rashbam (1080–1160), Eliezer of Beaugency (fl. mid 12th century) and Joseph ben Isaac Bekhor Shor (fl. third quarter of 12th century). In parallel, dozens of other scholars applied themselves to biblical exegesis, including some of the more important Tosafists.

The revolution was in fact a gradual process. The first harbinger of change was Menahem b. Helbo, who devoted much attention to *peshat* but also frequently used the method of *derash* as well. Rashi progressed further toward *pe-*

shat. By the end of the eleventh century and the beginning of the twelfth, Samuel b. Meir (Rashbam) and Joseph Kara had made literal interpretation the central goal of their work. Not content with Rashi's magnificent commentary, written shortly before, they sometimes explicitly opposed their illustrious predecessor, usually without mentioning his name. Rashi's commentary did not satisfy them. Rashbam, Rashi's grandson, writes of "*peshatôt* [= plain interpretations] being innovated every day" (commentary to Gen 37:2); that is to say, every day, new expositions of biblical verses, based on the method of *peshat,* were being proposed. The school of literal exegesis was still active in the second half of the twelfth century, as represented, in particular, by Eliezer of Beaugency, Joseph Bekhor Shor and the disciples of Joseph Kara. However, the school fell into decline as suddenly as it had risen. After blooming for a little more than one hundred years, it was already withering by the end of the twelfth century.

These rapid and large-scale changes raise four central questions:

(1) What were the historical reasons for the great boom in literary creativity in the late eleventh and twelfth centuries?

(2) Was the considerable increase in literal exegesis a real revolution, or can one discern traces of the method in earlier generations, in Germany or in France?

(3) Why was literal exegesis of the Bible placed at the centre of literary activity?

(4) Why did the school decline so quickly, fading away within four generations?

The scholars who have discussed these questions fall, essentially, into two groups: those scholars who view the emergence of the French school of literal exegesis as an internal development, and those who link it with developments in the (Christian) host society and culture. Among the prominent representatives of the first group one counts M. Z. Segal and E. M. Lipschuetz. In Segal's view, the Jew's constant study and exposition of the Talmud produced a parallel interest in biblical exegesis:

> Since the Talmud and the Bible were, for them, simply two sides of one Torah, they therefore carried over the method of studying the Talmud to the study of the Bible. To understand the Bible, they used the same means they had used in understanding the Talmud, that is, explaining the words according to the dictates of language, and explaining the content according to the needs of context and in accordance with plain logic (Segal, Parshanut [1971] 62).

Lipschuetz, for his part, held that the 'new' method of literal interpretation was actually an ancient one, commonly used in oral study among Jews since the Second Temple period but never committed to writing. Now, in eleventh-century France, its potential was finally realized.

Both of these hypotheses are questionable. German-Jewish scholars had been deeply involved in interpreting the Talmud as much as two generations before Rashi, and the same was true of R. Hananel, a North-African scholar. Nevertheless, neither in Germany nor in North Africa, at the time, do we find any creativity in the area of literally oriented biblical exegesis, as we do in France. If there were indeed some connection with exposition of the Talmud, such literal exposition of the Bible should have flourished in particular in the academies of Mainz and Worms. Neither can we accept LIPSCHUETZ's attempt to trace the method back to the way the Bible was studied centuries before in the Land of Israel. If true, it would imply that the method had disappeared without trace for centuries. Moreover, LIPSCHUETZ's theory does not explain why the school of literal exegesis emerged in France – and nowhere else – in the second half of the eleventh century.

A radically different idea was proposed by IZHAK F. BAER, one of the most important historians of medieval Jewry. The main reason for the appearance of the new method, he suggested, should be sought in relations with contemporary Christian society. Developments within Christian theology and scholastic philosophy brought about an intensification of literary polemics between Judaism and Christianity, which reached a peak in the mid-twelfth century. In BAER's view, Rashi wrote many of his commentaries not just to explain the Bible but also as a contribution to anti-Christian polemics, to educate and encourage his fellow Jews in those times of stress. His intention was, through his biblical exegesis, to reinforce his contemporaries' faith in the principles of Judaism and in future redemption, at a time of persecution and weakness. Since the Jews of Germany and France had not yet learned how to write prose literature dealing with questions of faith, ethics and religious dispute, Rashi found in biblical exegesis a suitable means to that end.

There is indeed a close connection between the French school of literal exegesis and the religious differences between Jews and Christians – a point to which I shall return later in this study.

A similar explanation was recently proposed by ELEAZAR TOUITOU. He suggested that, besides the element of Jewish-Christian polemics, the cultural renaissance of the twelfth century was also a crucial factor in the development of the French school. I agree with him in principle, but to my mind there is a third, highly important factor to be considered as well – the influence of Spanish-Jewish biblical exegesis upon French scholars; this point, too, will be discussed later.

2. Biblical Exegesis in Germany and Northern France before Rashi

The study and interpretation of the Bible in the Jewish communities of Italy, Germany and France date back to Antiquity. It is obvious from rabbinical responsa and correspondence that the Rabbis were well versed in the Bible. Thus, R. Meshullam b. Kalonymus, the greatest scholar of Northern Italy in the second half of the tenth century, possessed a thorough knowledge of the Bible. His commentary on Tractate Abot of the Mishnah is written in a Hebrew replete with biblical expressions and idioms. Moreover, in the course of explaining various points in the Mishnah he also comments on biblical expressions or passages, sometimes with considerable originality. The early scholars of Northern France also made much use of biblical language in their literary output. However, this pre-eleventh century exegesis was mostly based on the homiletical method. Even so, one already finds Rashi's teachers, in their Talmud commentaries, explaining various biblical expressions according to their plain meanings, with regard to both words and contexts. Some of their interpretations show amazing originality. Thus, for example, R. Isaac Halevi, one of Rashi's teachers, argues that the 'striped tunic' made by Jacob for Joseph was not a specially made piece of clothing but an ornamental piece of cloth wound *around Joseph's arm* to indicate that he was considered the firstborn, the chosen son. Another pre-Rashi scholar (in Germany) who wrote biblical exegesis was Meir b. Isaac, but the surviving fragments of his work have yet to be published.

It would not be true, therefore, to claim that the interest in biblical exegesis was something completely new in German and French Jewry. One basic element of the new method, the central role of the linguistic aspect, was not unknown in Germany when Rashi was studying there, in the sixties of the eleventh century. Nevertheless, at that stage it was represented by only a few, isolated, instances. The first real evidence of the imminent change was the work of Menahem b. Helbo, who lived in Germany or France. We know that he studied under the scholars of Provence in the middle of the eleventh century. While studying in Provence he apparently came into close contact with the philological and exegetical work of the early Hebrew grammarians who had been active in Spain. At one point in his commentaries he seems to be echoing Menahem b. Saruq. It is plausible that Menahem b. Helbo's acquaintance with the work of the Spanish scholars was partly responsible for the new approach already discernible in his exegesis. The fact that two other scholars then active in France, Joseph Tov Elem (Bonfils) and Elijah b. Menahem, were familiar with Spanish-Jewish culture and influenced by it,[1] supports our assumption with regard to Menahem b. Helbo. We may conclude, therefore, that not only in Germany, but also in Provence and Northern France, there was a movement among Jews toward studying the language of the Bible; this was a first step in preparation for the real revolution that came one generation later.[2]

3. Reasons for the Rise of Literal Exegesis

The revolution in biblical exegesis that began in the second half of the eleventh century may probably be attributed to the combined influence of three main factors: (1) the influence of Spanish-Jewish culture; (2) the twelfth-century renaissance in Europe; (3) Jewish-Christian polemics.

The first reason has not hitherto received adequate attention, but it is of great importance, being wholly consistent with the gradual disengagement of the Jews of Northern France from the cultural heritage of German Jewry.

---

[1] For a detailed discussion of this subject see Grossman, Hakhmê Sarephat (1996) 77–79, 98–102.

[2] These sources were cited in Grossman, ibid. 344–45.

3.1. *Influence of Spanish-Jewish Culture*

The Jewish grammarians in Spain, who frequently dealt with scriptural interpretation, had considerable influence on Rashi and his disciples. As a rule, there was a close link between the Jewish centres in France and in Spain, as early as the first half of the eleventh century. Two of the most prominent scholars of France at that time, Joseph Bonfils and Elijah b. Menahem, were influenced by *paytanim* (liturgical poets) then active in Spain. They adopted the style of the Spanish poets and may in fact have been personally acquainted with them.

This acquaintance was highly influential for the development of biblical exegesis in Northern France. French-Jewish scholars, influenced by the cultural renaissance of twelfth-century Europe and in need of new ways to respond to Christian interpretations of the Bible, were willing to embrace new methods; however, they were in need of new tools, particularly in the area of philology. At that particular time, there was no more suitable source of new methods and tools than Jewish Spain. The three factors were, therefore, intimately bound up with one another.

Rashi frequently uses the work of the linguists Menahem b. Saruq and Dunash b. Labrat, who were active before his time in Spain. But since he sometimes does so without explicit reference, one cannot evaluate their impact on Rashi's commentaries on the exclusive basis of the number of times he mentions them – which he does fairly frequently. Rashi's awareness of the importance of Arabic for explaining biblical Hebrew words is also largely due to the influence of Spanish scholars. Rashi's student and colleague, Joseph Kara, was considerably influenced by Dunash b. Labrat, not only in content but also in style. Kara's rational approach, clearly evident in his frequent discussion of the reasons for the commandments and his tendency to find natural explanations for miracles, is also typical of the Spanish exegetes. Another disciple of Rashi, Shemaiah, explicitly mentions a scriptural interpretation that he had received from 'a Spaniard'. Rashi's grandson Rashbam was similarly inclined; he, too, expressed his admiration on several occasions for accurate texts of Bibles copied in Spain, on which basis he corrected the texts then available in France.

It is inconceivable that the French scholars could have been so conversant with the linguistic research of Spanish-Jewish scholars without being influenced by their approach to scriptural interpretation. The association with Spanish exegesis of the Bible is most evident in the work of Joseph Bekhor Shor, in the second half of the twelfth century. Some of the most characteristic features of his commentaries, which will be pointed out below, may be traced to commentators active in Spain before and during his lifetime. He also quotes a Spanish scholar (otherwise unknown) named Obadiah b. Samuel.

The readiness of North-French scholars to draw on the cultural heritage of Spanish Jewry in biblical exegesis was consistent with the receptivity of French scholars in general to influence from other Jewish centres. The French Jews were indeed more open in this respect than any other Jewish community in

Europe. They also borrowed copiously from the Jewish cultures of Germany, Provence, Italy and Byzantium, unchecked by psychological factors of the type that prevented German Jews, too proud of their magnificent historical heritage, from responding to Spanish-Jewish influences in the eleventh century. The Jews of France had no difficulty in linking their cultural heritage with that of other centres, expanding and modifying it, taking up new modes of spiritual creativity with new forms of content.[3]

3.2. The Twelfth-Century Renaissance

In the middle of the eleventh century, Europe experienced a major awakening, reaching its peak in the twelfth century, which has been called 'the twelfth-century renaissance'. There was a resurgence of activity in several areas of the cultural, spiritual and social life of Christian Europe, particularly in Northern France. Distinguished itinerant teachers, wandering from college to college and from town to town, played a crucial role in these developments.

The cultural renaissance in general; the great war of ideas between faith and rationalism; the question of scriptural authority and interpretation; the students who flocked to hear great teachers and were encouraged to take an active part in the spiritual disputations then in progress – all these events and issues had striking parallels in French-Jewish society. Similarities can also be discerned in literary activity, such as interest in grammar, critical – if only in part – study of the Bible, a quest for the literal meaning of Scripture, a desire for accurate texts, a more rational approach to the reasons for the commandments, efforts to commit the traditions and practices of great teachers to writing; and so on. Although there was no question of direct influence, it is typical of such spiritual movements that they leave their imprint on people and create a common cultural contact, laying the foundations for cultural and spiritual creativity in each respective society. Literal interpretation of the Bible, now espoused by both Jews and Christians, must be seen in the context of the rationalism typical of the twelfth-century renaissance. There was a new confidence in the power of human reason, as scholars distanced themselves, to some extent, from legends and folk tales.

One of the most overt instances of contact between Jewish scholars and Christian savants in France was the school of biblical exegesis that developed during the twelfth century in the Monastery of St. Victor. Founded by William of Champeaux, the school flourished under the leadership of Hugh, Richard and Andrew in the years 1120–1175. These scholars were influenced by their Jewish contemporaries, particularly in regard to their insistence on literal interpretation of Scripture; they in fact refer explicitly to their close contacts with Jewish Bible commentators. Nevertheless, attempts to explain the emergence of the French-Jewish school of literal exegesis as due to the foundation of the school of St. Victor are mistaken. The chronology is at variance with

[3] For a detailed discussion of the issue see Grossman, ibid. 539–71.

such an interpretation: the Jewish school reached its fullest literary expression at least one generation earlier. Thus, for example, Hugh was born around 1097 and died in 1141. At the time of his birth, Joseph Kara, whom we have already mentioned as a major representative of the French-Jewish school of literary exposition, had already written some of his commentaries. Rashbam's commentaries, one of the greatest achievements of the school, were written while Hugh was still in his youth.

Hugh made use of Jewish traditions. According to Andrew, Hugh learned the literal meaning of the Pentateuch from the Jews. He used to compare Jewish exegetical traditions with Christian interpretations. Richard, who died in 1173, also mentioned having consulted with Jews. Of the three, it was Andrew (d. 1175) who maintained the closest contacts with Jewish scholars. He, too, declared that it was Jewish scholars who had taught him the plain meaning of the biblical text. He also noted that, for lack of money, he had been unable to buy Hebrew manuscripts of commentaries to the Bible.[4]

The close cultural contacts between Jews and Christians at that time should not surprise us. Economic ties between Jews and Christians, coupled with contacts in many other areas, could not but produce cultural relations as well. This was true in Germany and, in particular, in France. Jews employed non-Jewish servants in their homes, and day-to-day encounters with members of the majority society were quite common. It was only natural that such contacts could create intimate relations and friendships. Rashi, in fact, admonishing a Jew who, he believed, had mistreated his wife, describes some Christians' good relations with their wives as an example to be emulated.

3.3. Jewish-Christian Polemics

The debate between Judaism and Christianity in Europe was making its literary mark as early as the ninth century, *inter alia*, in the works of Agobard and his disciple Amulo. Polemical tracts were an important genre of Jewish literature in the twelfth and thirteenth centuries, attesting to the important place of Jewish-Christian polemics in the cultural activity of Jews and of the senior levels of the Christian clergy.

Jewish-Christian polemics left a deep imprint on Jewish Bible exegesis in France in the period under discussion. They influenced not only the content of various interpretations offered in response to christological interpretations, but also some of the most characteristic features of the new exegetical school and its emphasis on the plain meaning of the text. Jewish exegetes did not normally state the anti-christological thrust of their comments in so many words, but in actual fact they were frequently motivated by the desire to reject the

[4] On Jewish-Christian contacts in the area of biblical exegesis see mainly Smalley, Study of the Bible (1952); Grabois, Hebraica Veritas (1974); R. Berndt, "L'influence de Rashi sur l'exégèse d'André de Saint-Victor", *Rashi Studies* (ed. Z. A. Steinfeld; Jerusalem 1993) vii–xiv; Dahan, Intellectuels chrétiens (1990). On the school of St. Victor in particular see Chap. 34 below, by R. Berndt.

ideological message that the opposing camp claimed to find in the biblical text; we shall return to this below in our discussion of the individual commentators.

Jewish leaders of the time were greatly concerned lest the intense Christian polemical efforts influence the Jews. We cannot go into this weighty issue in any detail here, merely mentioning a few salient points.[5]

The most powerful argument with which Jewish scholars had to deal, and the most dangerous, was the question of the length of the exile and the lowly status of Jews among the other nations. How could Judaism, which claimed to be the true, superior faith, explain its wretched condition? Why had the first exile, from the destruction of the First Temple to the Edict of Cyrus, lasted only a short time, while the present exile was already into its second thousand years? The fact that many French and German Jews were converting to Christianity, whether owing to economic and social pressure or because of Christian propaganda, intensified the leaders' fears.

The main fear of Jewish Bible commentators was that their adherence to the old, homiletical style of exegesis, the technique of *derash*, would help Christian propaganda and its liking for allegorical interpretation. On the other hand, once the Jewish exegetes began to place more emphasis on the literal meaning of the text, Christians argued that the Jews were thereby losing the underlying spiritual meaning of the Bible. Contemporary Christian literature reiterates time and time again that the Jewish understanding of Scripture was 'bovine' (*bovinus intellectus*), because it dealt only with the plain meaning of the words and did not try to penetrate beneath the surface. For example, Alexander Nequam (1157–1217) claimed that the Jews were like swine which, when sparkling pearls are spread on the ground before them, trample them rudely into the ground without realizing their great value. The Jewish commentators, with their reliance on the plain meaning of the text (*litterator hebreus*), are incorrigibly superficial. They are the real successors of Abraham's servants, tarrying with the ass at the foot of Mount Moriah while Isaac was being bound; they are incapable of understanding the true meaning of the Bible. While the Christians are enjoying the luscious meat of the pomegranate, the Jews are merely chewing its rind.[6] On the other hand, adherence to the literal meaning of the text could also place obstacles in the way of Christian symbolic interpretations and cause difficulties for Christian scholars in their bitter religious dispute with the Jews.

As stated, most Bible commentators in France disguised the polemical thrust of their commentaries, probably in order to make their message more convincing, as polemical statements are generally considered less reliable. Nevertheless, this element is clearly detectable in all seven commentators mentioned above, including Rashi; we shall return to this later when dealing with each one individually. Any reader of Rashi's commentaries on Psalms and the Song of Songs, or those of Joseph Kara on Isaiah and the Minor Prophets, who does not notice the strong association with Jewish-Christian polemics is losing one of the most distinctive elements in these works.

---

[5] For a detailed discussion see Grossman, Hakhmê Sarephat (1996) 475–506.

[6] Saltman, Alexander Nequam.

We will now survey the activities of the above-mentioned Bible commentators, only then going on to discuss such questions as the scope and degree of their influence, as well as the reasons for the rapid decline of the new exegetical school toward the end of the twelfth century.

4. Menahem ben Helbo

Menahem ben Helbo lived approximately in the years 1015–1085. He was given the title of '*qara*', meaning a person who studied the Bible (Heb. *miqra*) extensively and taught it in public. There are several reports of his role as a teacher. Although his precise birthplace is unknown, it is clear that he lived in Provence for some time and studied under Provençal scholars. His Bible commentaries include translations (*le'azim*) into German and French, as is common in other commentaries of the time, including that of Rashi. Menahem presumably spent time in Germany and Northern France.

Most of Menahem b. Helbo's teachings are now lost. The scant remnants have survived mainly through the works of his nephew Joseph Kara, who studied under him. These remnants indicate that he wrote commentaries on all the books of the Prophets and the Hagiographa, as well as on liturgical poetry. A few dozen fragments of his commentaries were collected and published by S. A. Poznanski. Today there exist a few further commentaries in manuscript.

R. Menahem b. Helbo's approach to biblical exegesis shows seven characteristic features:

(1) He always aims to explain the plain meaning of the text, although he frequently draws on rabbinic Midrash as a basis for his interpretations.

(2) His comments are generally short, limited to explaining the text and its content. Only rarely does he discuss ideas; grammar also receives little attention.

(3) He is aware of the intimate connection between Hebrew and Arabic and occasionally relies on it. In this respect he was most probably influenced by the Spanish-Jewish linguists and exegetes. He presumably learned of the importance of Arabic for biblical exegesis during his stay in Provence.

(4) Menahem frequently uses foreign words in his commentaries, mostly, as already stated, in French and a few in German.

(5) He tries to find links between different passages, a technique that was developed and expanded by his nephew R. Joseph Kara and by Rashbam. Menahem b. Helbo may well have pioneered this technique, which became standard among French scholars in the next two generations.

(6) On two occasions his comments may be linked with the contemporary Jewish-Christian debate. It is readily seen that he was deeply affected by the sorry situation of the Jewish people in his time.

(7) R. Menahem received exegetical traditions from various other scholars, both Provençal and others with whom he came into contact. This eclecticism is

an indication of his intellectual curiosity. A similar approach is evident in the work of Joseph Kara and Shemaiah, both of whom are eager to find exegetical traditions originating with Jewish scholars from various centres. To some extent, Rashi shows the same proclivity. These scholars travelled to various centres in their search for new exegetical traditions. This intense interest is more typical of the Jewish centre in France than of any other contemporaneous centre of European Jewry.

Although the surviving fragments of Menahem's commentaries are insufficient for a full account of his literary opus, they indicate that he had considerable influence on later scholars in Northern France. He may be regarded as one of the trailblazers of the new exegetical methods, which were to develop further in the next generation.

5. Solomon Yishaqi / Rashi (1040–1105)

Solomon Yishaqi (or Solomon ben Isaac), generally known by the acronym Rashi (= **R**abbi **Sh**elomo Yishaqi), was one of the most important Jewish Bible commentators of all time, and the most famous and influential of all. As a young man, Rashi studied in the academies of Mainz and Worms in Germany, spending some ten years there. In Germany he also studied the Bible, particularly under R. Jacob ben Yakar. Rashi showed an independent mind when still young. In spite of his extreme modesty, he was firm and forceful in arguments with his teachers and colleagues on points of biblical and talmudic exegesis, always placing truth at the top of his scale of values. Thus, for example, MS Vat. 318 preserves the testimony of one of his disciples about a major emendation Rashi made in an ancient prayer, traditionally recited in his community of Troyes, in which he claimed to have found an incorrect version.

Rashi always sought the underlying roots of any subject with which he was concerned, drawing conclusions on the sole basis of reason. He refused to be bound by traditions and customs of unknown origin – a trait attesting to the great receptivity characteristic of him and his school. For him, as for his disciples, the quest for truth was the exclusive criterion. Accordingly, he was always ready to admit error and reconsider his opinion, at times even encouraging his pupils to disagree with him. One frequently finds in his biblical commentaries such expressions as "I do not know what that is supposed to teach us", "I do not know the meaning", and the like.

The receptive attitude that Rashi inculcated in his academy was in part typical of the German academies where he had studied. He maintained close relationships with his disciples, who transmitted and recorded many reports of his actions, practices and views. They even report on such matters as his food, his behavior while bathing and his practice in prayer and at the table. The picture emerging from these reports is one of intimacy and deep friendship between Rashi and his disciples. Parallels may be found in contemporary Christian society, where we know of similarly close relationships between certain renowned teachers and their pupils, and students at Christian seminaries also wrote down their masters' actions.[7] Rashi's close bonds with his disciples affected the method of study in his school, encouraging his students freely to exercise their creativity in scriptural interpretation as well.

Rashi's character is clearly reflected in his Bible commentaries, both in content and in style.[8]

5.1. Text of Rashi's Commentaries

Rashi apparently wrote commentaries on all books of the Bible, but the commentaries ascribed to him on the books of Ezra, Nehemiah, Chronicles and the end of Job (from 40:25) are not his, as they differ in style and method of exegesis from his other commentaries, and occasionally refer to authors known to have lived later than Rashi. Some of his comments to passages at the end of Job have been preserved in manuscript, from which it is clear that Rashi wrote a commentary on the whole book but the last part has been lost. This supports the thesis that Rashi wrote commentaries on all the books of the Bible, though it is not conclusive proof. The commentaries ascribed to him in the printed editions of Ezra and Nehemiah may be based on his own work, having been reworked and expanded by disciples. The phenomenon of interpolations in Rashi's commentary is also known from his commentaries on other books, and it directly concerns one of the major problems in any discussion of Rashi's Bible commentaries: the text. The Bible commentaries, both in the printed editions and in manuscript, also contain comments by his disciples, in particular Shemaiah, Joseph Kara and Rashbam, some added by Rashi himself, as a supplementary or even alternative explanation, others written by disciples in the margins of his manuscript commentaries and interpolated by copyists into the main text.

Because of the copyists' interpolations and the great popularity of Rashi's commentaries in various centres, there are several different versions of the text. Attempts have indeed been made by various scholars to arrive at a reliable text, on the basis of first editions and manuscripts, but these have had only partial success.[9]

The question of the text of Rashi's commentary on the Pentateuch is of particular interest. Any examination of the text of that commentary in the different manuscripts reveals the great quantity of interpolations. Some even identify the interpolator by name; we know, for example, that many interpolations were made by R. Joseph Kara. In time the names of these scholars were dropped and the added text became part of the basic text of Rashi's commentary.

No other work of a medieval Jewish scholar arouses such doubts and argu-

---

[7] On pupils at Christian seminaries who recorded their mentors' teachings see B. Toelken, "The Folklore of the Academe", *The Study of American Folklore. An Introduction* (ed. J. H. Brunvand; New York / London 1966) 502–28.

[8] See Grossman, Hakhmê Sarephat (1996) 160–66, and references cited there in the notes.

[9] For the main editions, see the bibliography at the beginning of this chapter.

ments in respect of its text, mainly because different editions were written within Rashi's own lifetime. He himself revised and corrected his Bible commentaries, as he testifies in one of his responsa, and his closest pupil, Shemaiah, made further emendations, some in accordance with the master's own request, some based on exegetical traditions that Shemaiah heard from other scholars shortly after Rashi's death. There is no question, therefore, of an *Urtext*, as there were already alternative versions in Rashi's lifetime. However, the most significant interpolations were made over the next two or three generations. The commentary was already widely circulated in the twelfth–thirteenth centuries. Scholars who studied it and teachers who taught it jotted down various notes in the margins of their copies, some of which were later inserted into the text by copyists. Another cause of confusion is the structure of the commentary, most of which consists of extracts from rabbinic *midrashim*. Scholars and copyists emended the *midrashim*, copying them out in full, abbreviating them or even omitting well-known passages and adding others that seemed of relevance. Such emendations also crept into the body of the commentary as time went on.

Eleazar Touitou is of the opinion that much of the printed edition of Rashi's commentary is not his. Grossman, however, believes that the proportion of extraneous material is smaller, not exceeding ten percent.

An important tool in the determination of the original text of Rashi's commentary on the Pentateuch is MS Leipzig 1, written in the thirteenth century.[10] The text of this manuscript probably corresponds more closely than any other available version to what Rashi himself wrote, though it too contains late additions and copyists' errors. The margins of the Pentateuch commentary in this manuscript contain numerous glosses by his disciple Shemaiah.[11]

A. Berliner may be credited with an important attempt to publish a reliable text of the commentary on the Pentateuch. He examined more than one hundred manuscripts and many printed editions and added references to Rashi's sources, as well as other important comments. Nevertheless, even the Berliner edition is incomplete, and several important manuscripts were not available to him.

5.2. Relation between Plain and Homiletical Meaning in Rashi's Commentaries

The central problem facing Rashi was the relationship between the plain meaning, the *peshat*, and the homiletical, the *derash* – and that is indeed the question that has received most attention in the scholarly discussions of Rashi's commentaries on the Bible. Several books have been written on the subject in the last twenty years, not to speak of dozens of articles. Rashi's commentary

[10] For a detailed discussion of MS Leipzig 1 and its great importance in text criticism of Rashi's commentary to the Pentateuch, see Grossman, Hakhmê Sarephat (1996) 184–93.

[11] Berliner published some sixty marginal glosses from this manuscript, which are extremely hard to decipher. I have been able to decipher about 200 further glosses. See Grossman, ibid. 184–93.

on the Pentateuch is largely culled from rabbinic literature; only about one quarter is original, dealing mainly with linguistic questions. The situation is different with regard to the Prophets and the Hagiographa, where Rashi's original comments are more abundant and he deals more frequently with content and with historical or literary issues. Some scholars have suggested that his choice of *midrashim* was not guided by interpretive considerations and that the commentary is essentially just an anthology of midrashic material; however, this thesis is untenable. After all, Rashi himself reveals, in his comment on Gen 3:8, that the choice was by no means random but quite purposeful: "There are many *midreshê aggadah* ... As for me, I am only concerned with the plain meaning of the Scriptures and with such *aggadah* as explains the biblical passages in a fitting manner". Similar comments may be found elsewhere as well.

On the basis of Rashi's comments elsewhere, the meaning of the phrase *dabhar dabhûr ʿal ofnaw*, here translated as "in a fitting manner", seems to comprise two main elements: to explain the text in accordance with the rules of grammar and the syntactical context. This is also stated explicitly in a responsum, written in connection with that statement (MS Parma 655), that he sent his disciple Shemaiah.[12]

Rashi did not always conform to his self-imposed criterion. He sometimes cites *midrashim* quite remote from the plain meaning, whether linguistically or contextually. It seems clear, therefore, that he did not consider all the *midrashim* he quoted to be in accord with the literal meaning of the text.

The term 'the plain [or: literal] meaning of the text' (Heb. *peshûtô shel miqra*) appears, in a variety of combinations, more than forty times in the commentary to Genesis alone, whereas the Talmud uses it only a few times. In other words, a term of marginal significance in the Talmud took centre stage in Rashi's usage, reflecting its paramount importance in his interpretive approach.[13]

Even the selection of *midrashim* that Rashi included in his commentary represents a considerable and significant exegetical effort. He chose only a small number of the many *midrashim* at his disposal, doing so after careful examination and deliberation, as we know from his own remarks on various occasions.

In order to characterize the criteria that guided Rashi in his choice of rabbinic *midrashim*, we must consider several central questions: Were his criteria purely interpretive, or also esthetic and ideological? Did Rashi cite *midrashim* even when the language of the text did not require them, say in order to create a fitting literary frame or with some didactic purpose in mind? Why, though generally content with a single *midrash*, did he sometimes quote two or more? And is the order in which he cites *midrashim* of any significance?

It hardly seems likely that Rashi was guided by interpretive considerations

---

[12] Quoted in Grossman, ibid. 197.

[13] There is a comprehensive literature on the relationship between *peshat* and *derash* in Rashi's commentaries. The major studies are cited above in the bibliography. See, in particular, Kamin, Rashi; Gelles, Peshat and Derash; Melammed, Mephareshê ha-Miqra; Weiss Halivni, Peshat and Derash; and Ahrend, Le-Darko shel Rashi.

alone: more probably, the choice also reflects his world of ideas and his didactic ideals. Only thus can we explain his occasional use of *midrashim* so remote from the plain meaning of the text that they could not possibly be intended to resolve some interpretive difficulty, and from the occasional presentation of two explanations when there is no interpretive motive for so doing. To illustrate, we cite one example, from Rashi's comments regarding the enslavement of the Children of Israel in Egypt. Rashi describes Pharaoh as an evil, hypocritical and cruel person, eager to harm the Israelites as much as possible while pretending to be an honest, righteous person. Rashi selects several *midrashim* to that effect, ignoring others that paint a less negative picture. He was presumably guided by his understanding of the history of the Jews in exile, and by his desire to demonstrate how rulers could exploit the Jews and then treat them ungratefully and cruelly. In the same vein, he also selected *midrashim* describing Divine Providence and God's protection of his people.

Why did Rashi make such extensive use of *midrashim*, despite the fact that he attributed importance to the literal meaning? One explanation might be that, out of his great appreciation and love for the Bible, he felt the need to supply various details about which the biblical text itself is relatively silent: protagonists' motives, identification of characters, missing elements in the plot and in legal material, and so on. In the quest for these missing details, Rashi resorted to rabbinic sources, which he saw as the sequel to the Written Torah, an ancient tradition kept alive by the Sages.

Rashi was concerned with the question of the relationship between *peshat* and *derash* to the end of his life. His grandson Rashbam states that Rashi, in his last years, told him that, had the time been available, he would have provided different explanations, "according to the plain meanings (Heb. *peshatôt*) that are discovered every day".[14]

Once Rashi had selected a suitable *midrash*, he was faced with the problem of its wording. Very frequently, he reworked the text as formulated by the Sages, omitting part of the talmudic argument, adding and omitting words and sometimes even changing the wording. At times, it seems, he did so in order to adapt the *midrash* to his own world view. Rashi created a stylistic continuum, and his commentary reads like a fully formed creation, by no means a patchwork. At the same time, such elements as variety, richness, idiom, etc. are all mobilized in the service of his interpretive goals.

In the legal parts of the Pentateuch, Rashi's commentary is almost completely identical with the halakhic Midrash, though here, too, he tried to follow the rules he had imposed upon himself throughout his work, both in the selection of *midrashim* and in their style and mode of presentation. In these legal passages, too, Rashi saw his major task as interpretive. He carefully chooses a small part of the legal material relating to each topic, sometimes explicitly stating that the halakhic *midrashim* are at variance with the plain meaning of the text and will therefore not be quoted. In a few cases his explanation of the text actually conflicts with the accepted halakhic ruling.

[14] Rashbam on Gen 37:1.

5.3. *Language and Grammar*

Rashi attached much importance to linguistic and grammatical questions, and these are quite prominent in his commentaries. He was strongly influenced in this area by the Hebrew linguists of tenth-century Spain, particularly Menahem b. Saruq and Dunash ben Labrat. Nevertheless, he did not always agree with their views, sometimes opposing them, and in some cases his achievements were superior.[15]

Rashi's proficiency in Hebrew grammar was considerable, and he strongly influenced later commentators in France. Scattered throughout his commentaries are numerous important rules of linguistic usage and distinctions between the different nuances of synonyms. He made much use of mishnaic Hebrew. On occasion he distinguishes between biblical and mishnaic Hebrew, among other things explaining approximately one hundred and twenty biblical words in terms of their equivalents in rabbinic Hebrew. Ninety of these words were not mentioned by earlier scholars. At times he points to these equivalences even without support from the language of the Bible itself, and was indeed criticized for so doing by Rashbam, who argued that biblical and mishnaic Hebrew should be treated as separate, unrelated entities, neither having any implications for the other.

Rashi explains some one thousand words in the Bible by giving their translations in the French of his time. Some of these French words, known as *leʿazim* in Hebrew, are not known from medieval French literature, Rashi's commentary being the sole source preserving them. Many *leʿazim* have been distorted by copyists' and printers' errors. Occasionally, Rashi cited words in languages other than French – German and Slavonic, though some of these seem to be late additions, not from Rashi's own hand.

Rashi's French *leʿazim* were carefully investigated by A. Darmesteter, who realized their great importance for the reconstruction of Old French and researched them thoroughly. He examined the variations of the *leʿazim* in the different manuscripts of Rashi's commentary, selecting the best readings and reconstructing the original French spelling. All in all, he covered more than three thousand words preserved in Rashi's commentaries to the Bible and the Talmud, laying the foundations for all further studies of Rashi's *leʿazim*. Darmesteter's work was continued by D. S. Blondheim, who examined many additional manuscripts, studied the special features of the Old French used by Rashi and described the various manuscripts and printed editions in the long introduction to his *magnum opus*. Important contributions to the understanding of Rashi's *leʿazim* were made more recently by M. Banitt and M. Catane.[16]

---

[15] On Rashi's attitude to the Hebrew grammarians of Spain see, in particular, Melammed, Mephareshê ha-Miqra (1978) 1:398–402. In addition to explicit references to Menahem b. Saruq, Rashi frequently cites him without mentioning his name. See further Chap. 25.5 above (by A. Sáenz-Badillos).

[16] See Darmesteter / Blondheim, Glosses françaises (1929–37); Banitt, Poterim (1966); idem, Rashi (1985); Catane, Monde intellectuel (1985).

Modern scholarship has devoted much attention to the linguistic elements in Rashi's writings, mainly in the areas of grammar and lexicography. His method of explaining words has been discussed by various authors. One of the major works in this field is the comprehensive dictionary of Rashi's language in the Bible and the Talmud, by Y. AVINERI (the second part of *Hêkhal Rashi*), which collects the word definitions and explications scattered through Rashi's writings. Rashi had no knowledge of earlier works of the genre, such as Saadiah Gaon's *Sepher ha-Agrôn*, Jonah ibn Janah's *Sepher ha-Shorashim* and Nathan b. Jehiel's *Sepher ha-ʿArûkh*; he was influenced by Menahem b. Saruq's *Mahberet* and, according to BANITT, by a French translation of the Bible on which he based his definitions of biblical words. However, M. AHREND has questioned this conclusion, as Rashi only seldom refers explicitly to the earlier *pôterîm*, and in fact no glossaries predating Rashi have survived. The existing documentation of complete vernacular translations of the Bible (known in Hebrew as *laʿaz ha-ʿôlam*), is mostly from the thirteenth century.[17] W. J. VAN BEKKUM recently published a survey of the literature on Rashi's linguistic activity.[18]

Rashi frequently refers to the cantillation accents of the Masoretic Text, which he considered highly significant: "Had I not seen a *zaqef gadôl* accent marked on the word 'faces' [indicating a pause at that word] I would not have known how to explain it" (Ezek 1:11). At other times, however, he does not hesitate to offer an interpretation clashing with the traditional cantillation.

The Aramaic targums were among Rashi's most important sources. His commentary to the Pentateuch makes abundant use of Targum Onqelos; he studies its reading of the text, explains it, suggests support for it and even lays down rules for studying the Targum. But here, again, he does not hesitate to reject the targumic reading of the text when necessary. In his commentaries to the Prophets and the Hagiographa he often draws on Targum Jonathan.[19]

Rashi sometimes seeks connections between different verses or passages of the Bible, attempting to explain their juxtaposition or particular order, but he did not treat the subject systematically. Seemingly superfluous details were intended, in his view, to clarify events mentioned elsewhere in the Bible. However, he resorts to this technique only infrequently, though his disciples in France made more use of it in their biblical exegesis.

5.4. Philosophy and Mysticism

Rashi did not concern himself with philosophical questions, as philosophy had not yet reached French and German Jewry at that time. Nevertheless, traces of rationalism may already be discerned in France toward the end of Rashi's life, e.g., in Joseph Kara's commentaries. The problem of harmonizing rationalism with the biblical world, which troubled masters of scriptural interpretation in

[17] See Banitt, Rashi (1985) 68–69.
[18] Van Bekkum, Grammatical Tradition (1993).
[19] See Poznanski, Mabhô (1965) 17–18.

Spain, as well as Joseph Kara, Rashbam and later also R. Joseph Bekhor Shor in France, receives little attention in Rashi's writings, only its first signs being discernible there. For the same reason, he only rarely treats such issues as the reasons for the commandments, ethical evaluation of the Patriarchs' actions, the structure of the books of the Bible and the contradictions among them, and so on. Neither does he discuss the relationship between miracles and the laws of nature. One topic that did occupy him more frequently was the chronology of biblical events.

A most interesting question, almost ignored in the scholarly literature, is Rashi's attitude to Jewish mysticism. According to the traditions of Hasîdê Ashkenaz, some of France's greatest scholars were well versed in esoteric lore. There is no explicit evidence in Rashi's commentaries that he was familiar with mystical literature, although various later scholars claimed to have found strong links between Rashi and mysticism. However, workers in this field have overlooked the books used by Rashi's disciple Shemaiah, as reflected in his commentaries to liturgical poetry, some of which were written during Rashi's lifetime. It is clear, therefore, that these sources were available to Rashi. The same is true in regard to Rashi's use of the literature of *Merkabhah* mysticism, as written works of this genre were already known in his time in various Jewish centres and could well have been on Rashi's bookshelf. This question is currently a topic of scholarly debate and still remains open. It is clear, however, that Rashi used the mystical work *Sepher Yezîrah*; he was also acquainted with the book *Hakkemoni* and perhaps with the homiletical work *Ôtiyyôt de-R. Aqîba.*[20]

5.5. *Jewish-Christian Polemics*

Rashi makes scant reference in his commentaries to contemporary problems; the few known instances are rather unclear and there is little agreement on their meaning. There is nevertheless little doubt that the events of his time left their mark on his biblical exegesis. One of the most obvious indications of this is his introduction to the commentary on the Song of Songs, where he explains the book as also relating to the Diaspora in his time and embodying God's pledge to redeem his people.

Jewish-Christian polemic, however, made a considerable imprint on Rashi's commentaries to the Bible, particularly in the books of Psalms and Isaiah. Thus, he explains various passages mentioning unnamed enemies of Israel as referring to 'Esau', 'Edom' or 'Rome', that is, Christianity. Many of these polemical comments were later omitted or altered by censorship, being preserved only in manuscript, and have therefore not received their proper place in the scholarly literature.

Occasionally, one finds explicit statements in the commentaries that the explanation is meant as a response to *mînîm* (lit. 'heretics') or *hôleqîm* (lit. 'schismatics'), that is, Christians. However, these remarks appear only in some ver-

---

[20] On Rashi's library see Melammed, Mephareshê ha-Miqra (1978) 1:395–98.

sions of the texts, and not in the most reliable manuscripts, implying that these are late additions and not from Rashi's own hand. Here are two examples. (i) Commenting on Isa 9:5, "He has been named 'Wonderful Counsellor, Mighty God, Everlasting Father, Prince of Peace'", the text reads: "Who shall be so named? – the king who accepts the dominion of the Holy One, blessed be He, upon himself, to fear Him ...". An addition to the text continues: "This is an answer to the others. But the true explanation is that 'Prince of Peace' is also one of God's names". (ii) The comments on the next verse, "... now and evermore" (ibid. v. 6), explicitly rebut the Christian claim that this passage foretells the birth of Jesus Christ.

The interpolation of these additions probably attests to the high esteem in which Rashi's commentary was held. There are many places in which Rashi, indirectly and by allusion, takes issue with christological interpretations, without explicitly saying so, and it is not always easy to detect the polemical intent. One such example occurs in the commentary to Zech 9:9:

> "Rejoice greatly, Fair Zion; raise a shout, Fair Jerusalem! Lo, your king is coming to you. He is victorious, triumphant, yet humble, riding on an ass, on a donkey foaled by a she-ass" – This cannot be interpreted save in regard to the Messianic King, of whom it is said "His rule shall extend from sea to sea", and we have found no such ruler of Israel in the time of the Second Temple.

The words used here – "this cannot be interpreted ..." – are pointless unless construed as a response to the familiar Christian propaganda according to which this verse foretells the advent of Jesus.

The place of the Jewish-Christian polemic in Rashi's commentary is even more conspicuous in the manuscript version of his commentary to Psalms. More than one half of the chapters are linked in some way to the debate with Christianity – mostly by allusion, though on two occasions the association is made explicit. In fact, he places such an interpretation on many psalms whose literal meaning has nothing to do with any religious debate. Thus, King David's frequent complaints against his persecutors are explained as referring to Christianity ('Esau', 'Edom'). Rashi does so even with regard to psalms describing the beauty of creation and the greatness of the Creator. This trend is no accident. Rashi wrote his commentary to Psalms after the devastation and slaughter wrought during the First Crusade, in 1096, and it should be seen as a reaction to those events.[21]

5.6. Realia, Historical Background and Literary Elements

Rashi was extremely attentive to realia. Suffice it to look into his commentary on the making of the Tabernacle to realize his concern for such matters. In this respect, Joseph Kara and Shemaiah show a similar concern. In Kara's case we

---

[21] See A. GROSSMAN, "Rashi's Commentary on Psalms and the Jewish-Christian Polemic" (Heb.), *Sepher ha-Yobhel le-Moshe Ahrend* (Jerusalem 1996) 59–74, where I suggested the plausible thesis that Rashi's polemical use of the book of Psalms might derive from the central role of that book in both Jewish and Christian liturgy.

cannot state with confidence that this was due to Rashi's influence, but it is almost certain that Shemaiah followed in his master's footsteps. Rashi added sketches to clarify difficult passages in his commentaries to both Pentateuch and Talmud. Among other things, he drew a map of Palestine, which has been preserved in several manuscripts.[22] Some of his drawings have been omitted by copyists and printers. Rashi frequently draws on the realia of his own times, with which he was quite familiar. He deals in detail with a variety of different areas, such as minting of coins, glass manufacture, stone engraving, military strategy, nature, bird hunting, cultivation of plants, animal husbandry, and the like. Thanks to this information scholars have been able to rely on Rashi's commentary in studies of contemporary life.

Rashi sometimes attempts to identify geographical sites mentioned in the Bible. Such attempts are mentioned in many places. The effort he invested in that respect is particularly obvious in Josh 15, but, with no precise tools and knowledge, he was sometimes forced to engage in guesswork.

In his commentaries on the books of Prophets and Hagiographa, Rashi sometimes bases his explanation of the text on the historical background of the prophets' times. A striking example of this attitude is his commentary to the book of Isaiah. Although he of course lacked the tools now at our disposal to study the history of the period, he aptly explains most of the prophecies in Chapters 1–39 on the background of the rise of Assyria, its extensive conquests and Sennacherib's defeat at the gates of Jerusalem. On occasion, he puts such an interpretation on prophecies which at first sight have nothing to do with those events. In this aspect of his commentary he surpasses many of his Spanish contemporaries and, at times, some modern commentators.

Rashi is less cognizant of literary questions than his colleague Joseph Kara, who frequently discussed that aspect of the biblical text. Nevertheless, he does touch upon the subject at times, in a variety of ways.

5.7. Scriptural Interpretation in Rashi's Commentary to the Talmud

Rashi explains hundreds of words and phrases from the Bible in his commentary on the Talmud. These explanations raise certain difficulties, as they sometimes differ from those of the same words in his commentary on the Bible.

The first scholar to deal with this problem was A. H. Weiss. He suggested that, commenting on the Bible, Rashi interpreted the biblical text in accordance with the context. In his commentary to the Talmud, however, he had to explain the same biblical phrase or verse in the context of the talmudic discussion, that is to say, as they were understood by the Sages of the Talmud on that particular occasion. Weiss himself, however, admitted that his solution resolved most but not all of the contradictions:

---

[22] I reproduced this map, which appears in MSS Leipzig 1 and Munich 5, in my article "R. Shemaiah's Glosses and the Reading of Rashi's Commentary on the Torah" (Heb.), *Tarbiz* 60 (1991) 67–98.

> Indeed, one thing should be noted in this connection, and it is to our mind significant. And that is: where we have found innumerable times in his commentary that he explains words and phrases in his commentary to the Talmud and contradicts what he himself wrote in the commentary to the Bible, and we do not know which [explanation] is the right one in his eyes, this or that, or perhaps both together depending on the changing context and position ... While in his commentary to the Bible he explains as he sees fit in his interpretation, taking no note of what the sages of the Talmud explained for that passage ... And now, that is the rule that we should observe, only through it are most of the contradictions between his commentary to the Talmud and his commentary to the Bible resolved.

The topic has recently been taken up by Y. Florsheim,[23] in his three volumes of Rashi's explanations of biblical texts culled from the Talmud. In the introduction to the first volume (texts from the Pentateuch) he points out the importance of these sources for the study of Rashi's commentaries as a whole, and notes that Weiss's solution is insufficient to explain away all the differences between the commentaries to the Bible and the Talmud. The subject, he writes, is important not only because of the contradictory explanations, but also because of passages that receive more detailed explanations and, even more, explanations of verses or phrases which received no treatment in Rashi's commentary to the Bible. It is interesting that these explanations are not always required by the context, that is, the talmudic discussion, so that only by combining Rashi's comments in the Bible commentary with those in his commentary to the Talmud does one obtain a full commentary to the Bible.[24] As of the time of writing, no fully satisfactory explanation of these differences has been proposed.

5.8. Emendations and Additions

Rashi did not consider his Bible commentaries as a complete, finalized work. As we have already stated, he was constantly correcting and adding, whether on the basis of his own reflection, discussions with colleagues and pupils or new sources he had received. This approach once more exemplifies his quest for the truth and the unceasing efforts he was willing to make to that end.

The evidence of additions and emendations has been preserved in various places. The most impressive piece of evidence now available is Rashi's commentary to the Pentateuch in MS Leipzig 1, which has survived together with Shemaiah's glosses on the commentary. Shemaiah prefaces his glosses with some such phrase as "My master explains ...", "Heard from my master", or just "My master". In two places he states that the glosses were added on Rashi's explicit request: "My master instructed me to emend ...". There are nearly fifty glosses in MS Leipzig 1 that may be ascribed to Rashi himself.

Rashi's glosses are of different types. They include explanations, linguistic comments, discussions of realia (borders of the Promised Land) and brief quotations from rabbinic *midrashim*. Shemaiah sometimes refers in his glosses to

[23] Florsheim, Rashi on the Bible (1981–89).
[24] A discussion may also be found in Melammed, Mephareshê ha-Miqra (1978) 1:439–41.

Rashi's thoughts and actions. On one occasion we find Rashi criticizing other commentators' interpretations.

Rashi also corrected and completed his commentary to the books of the Prophets. A letter he wrote to the community of Auxerre explicitly mentions his corrections to the commentary on Ezekiel: "In any case, I erred in that explanation ... And thus I explained at the end of the matter, and my words contradicted each other, and now I have dealt with it together with our brother Shemaiah and corrected it" (Rashi, *Responsa*, no. 10). Similarly, in his commentary to Isaiah one readily detects glosses and additions. Many of them are prefaced by the words "And it may also be explained ..."; they include interpretations that Rashi received from R. Joseph Kara.

Rashi's commentary to Psalms also contains additions and corrections; this tendency toward constant correction and revision was, therefore, typical of all his Bible commentaries. It is clear from what he and Shemaiah write that he took great pains in the wording of his commentaries, in an attempt to achieve the greatest possible accuracy. It follows that his remark to his grandson Rashbam, already quoted above, that if he could he would have written the commentary to the Pentateuch differently, because of "*peshatôt* [= literal interpretations] being innovated every day", was no empty metaphor, but an apt characterization of his entire approach.

Did Rashi write different editions of his Bible commentaries, or did he content himself with emendations and glosses? It would appear that the latter is correct. There is no evidence of different editions in the modern sense of the term, that is, different layers of interpretation. Moreover, Rashi's commentary increased in circulation mainly after some of these revisions had been made. This is indicated by the fact that many of the glosses, of which Shemaiah explicitly states that they were written on Rashi's express request (as stated in MS Leipzig 1), may be found in numerous manuscripts of Rashi's commentaries, such as MSS Munich 5, Vienna 23 and St. Petersburg Evr. I 11, all of which are early and excellent manuscripts. It is true that medieval Jewish scholars use the word 'editions' of Rashi; but they also used that term in reference to corrections and *variae lectionis*.

5.9. The Continuing Importance of Rashi's Commentaries to the Bible

Rashi's commentary to the Bible, in particular, to the Pentateuch, achieved great popularity. His commentary to the Pentateuch became the standard commentary of its kind; for many centuries it has guided countless Jews in their perusal of the portions of the Torah, and through it they have absorbed rabbinic *midrashim* and the educational values that they embodied. In the past, every Jewish child studying in the traditional elementary school (*heder*) or other educational institution was expected to study the weekly portion with Rashi's commentary. Judah Khalaz, who went from Spain to North Africa in the second half of the fifteenth century, relates that while wandering through the kingdom of Granada he was asked to teach Pentateuch and Rashi, and he notes that "It has become the custom throughout Israel to have the beginners

[= children making their first steps in study] begin with the reading of Rashi". The commentary indeed exerted tremendous influence, not only in the various Ashkenazic communities in the various regions of Europe, but also in Spain and many other centres. Few other works have had such a profound influence on all generations of Jewish culture.

Rashi's commentary to the Bible was the first Hebrew printed book. Numerous supercommentaries have been written – the number exceeds 150. Among the more important writers of such supercommentaries one should mention Elijah Mizrahi, Abraham Bukarat and the Marahal of Prague. Halakhic codes, beginning in the thirteenth century, ruled that a person reading the Pentateuch with Rashi's commentary, instead of Targum Onqelos, was considered to have fulfilled the obligation of reading the weekly portion "twice Hebrew and once the Targum". This ruling endowed Rashi's commentary with a unique sanctity, as the duty of reading the Targum is already mentioned in the Talmud. No less important is Rashi's influence on the development of the French school of literal exegesis.

Christian scholars also took an interest in Rashi's commentaries from the thirteenth century on. Some of them were influenced by it after the dispute over the Talmud in 1240. Particularly worthy of mention is Nicholas of Lyra (1270–1349), one of the most important Christian Bible exegetes of the Middle Ages, who knew Hebrew perfectly and was well acquainted with other Hebrew commentaries to the Bible. Some authorities believe that he was of Jewish descent. In any case, he frequently relies on Rashi, referring to him by name.[25] Rashi's commentary was first translated into foreign languages, including German, Yiddish, English and French, in the seventeenth century.

What was it that made the commentary so popular and influential? Why were other, excellent commentaries, such as that of Abraham ibn Ezra, pushed aside? There is no definitive answer to this question, and one should probably attribute the work's success to a combination of factors. The three most important factors are (i) the character of the commentary, (ii) the historical reality in which the Jewish communities lived from the thirteenth century to the closing years of the Middle Ages, and (iii) Rashi's renown as a commentator on the Talmud.

Two of the characteristic qualities of Rashi's Pentateuch commentary made a major contribution to its tremendous popularity: (1) the pleasing combination of literal and homiletical interpretation (*peshat* and *derash*) and the attractive fleshing out of the terse biblical text by rabbinic interpretation; (2) the concise, lucid language. Completely literal commentaries, like those of Abraham ibn Ezra and Rashbam, were intended for scholarly readers, familiar with Hebrew grammar. The masses sought a commentary that would briefly round

---

[25] On Nicholas of Lyra see S. Eidelberg, "Was Nicholas of Lyre of Jewish Descent?" (Heb.), *Sinai* 64 (1969) 204–06. On his attitude (and that of other Christian exegetes) to Rashi see Hailperin, Rashi (1963). On Christian interest in Rashi after the Paris dispute in 1240 see G. Dahan, "Un dossier latin de textes de Rashi autour de la controverse de 1240", *Rashi Studies* (ed. Z. A. Steinfeld; Jerusalem 1993) xv-xxix. Further literature on the relationship between Christian scholars and Rashi see Grossman, Hakhmê Sarephat (1996) 214 n. 273.

out the picture given in the Bible, lend the text depth and meaning and enrich readers' intellectual and emotional worlds. Nahmanides indeed described his approach in the introduction to his commentary:

> I will comport myself as did the early sages / to appease the minds of the students / weary through exile and trouble, when they read the portion on Sabbaths / and festivals, and to appeal to their hearts with plain interpretations and some pleasant things.

Even if one treats this declaration as an elaborate metaphor, the motif of students "weary through exile and trouble" may surely be taken at face value. This thought was doubly valid in the thirteenth to fifteenth centuries, with the gradual deterioration in the Jewish condition. The decline and degeneration of Spanish Jewry in the fourteenth–fifteenth centuries and the expulsions of Jews from various German cities in the fifteenth century further increased the need for spiritual reinforcement. Commentaries confining themselves to the plain, literal sense of the text, revolving around linguistic interpretation, might attract individuals, scholars and highly educated persons – but not the common people. Such commentaries were considered "dry and devoid of spirit". The carefully selected compilation of rabbinic Midrash embedded in Rashi's commentary, linked up with the language of the Bible, as well as the concise, crystal-clear, readily comprehensible language, were able quite naturally to attract the attention of the masses, enhance their interest in studying the Bible and sometimes also hearten people in times of stress and give some meaning to their sufferings in Exile.

Spanish kabbalists also considered Rashi's commentary a highly significant weapon in their war against philosophy and its representatives. It is no accident that Nahmanides, one of the foremost representatives of the kabbalists in that struggle, described the commentary to the Pentateuch as "the lights of the pure lamp" and avowed that Rashi should be given "pride of place".

Yet another important reason for the popularity of Rashi's Bible commentary was his prestige and authority as the foremost commentator on the Babylonian Talmud. One can hardly divorce the great popularity of his biblical exegesis from the recognition of his immense stature as commentator on the Talmud. The opponents of Jewish philosophy in Provence and Spain – the focus of the anti-Maimonidean controversy in the thirteenth century – presumably took advantage of this situation when they presented Rashi's commentary as the most faithful expression of authentic Jewish tradition. In support of this assumption we cite the fact that rationalist circles in Spain took exception to Rashi's commentary, instead favouring that of Abraham ibn Ezra. Ibn Ezra himself, in the twelfth century, had criticized Rashi for not adhering to the literal meaning of the text. Later Spanish scholars, of the rationalist school, followed suit, disapproving of what they considered Rashi's excessive use of Midrash in his commentary to the Bible. The fourteenth century saw a renewal of interest in Ibn Ezra's commentaries, with a corresponding increase, in some circles, in criticism of Rashi. One book even describes Rashi as having caused the Jews to remain "divested of the plain meanings of the Torah and the Bible" and to reach a state of "blindness and confusion". This bitter criticism is proof in itself of the growing popularity of Rashi in Spain and the degree to which he was studied. His commentary was particularly esteemed among followers of R. Isaac Canpanton, who established a new school of Talmud study in fifteenth-century Spain.

Important evidence of the great respect for Rashi's commentaries in the fifteenth century has survived in writings of the Castilian scholar Judah Khalaz (d. before 1537), already quoted above. He favoured studying Rashi in depth, declaring that Rashi's wisdom was so great that, had he been alive "in the time of the ancients and the early *ge'ônîm*, he would have instructed them in the proper way to understand the verses of the Bible and the Talmud".

It is highly ironical that Rashi himself remained all his life unaware of the great value of his commentaries on the Bible and the Talmud. He certainly did not foresee the great influence that they would have on later generations – this is obvious from letters and responsa he wrote toward the end of his life. Just one generation after his death, the Rabbis of Germany and France were referring to him in the most superlative terms. The greatest German scholar of the time, R. Eliezer b. Nathan, defined him as having "stood the world on a third leg". Esteem for Rashi remained high everywhere in the cultural realm of Ashkenazic and French Jewry, throughout the Middle Ages. Only among the *Hasîdê Ashkenaz*, the pietist circle active in Germany in the late twelfth and first half of the thirteenth centuries, were his commentaries less appreciated. This may be due to their wide-ranging struggle against the heritage of French Jewry, whom they considered to have deviated from the true path of authentic Ashkenazic tradition.

6. Joseph Kara (1050–1125)

Joseph Kara played a crucial part in the development of the North-French school of literal exegesis, of which he was one of the founders and formative figures. The evolution of the school, in its essentials, seems quite clear: the first steps in literal interpretation were taken by Menahem b. Helbo. Rashi developed the trend further, but still gave preference in his commentaries to the homiletical approach, having more recourse to that method than to the literal. Joseph Kara advanced further, both in his adherence to the new method and in his vigorous opposition to its detractors. Rashbam, active a few years later, brought the school to its supreme achievements, but this should by no means obscure the great personal contribution of Joseph Kara.

Joseph's surname 'Kara' (or *qara*) shows that his principal occupation was biblical commentary, and also that he taught Bible (Heb. *miqra*).

R. Joseph Kara was a bold and supremely confident person, who unhesitatingly criticized interpretations that he believed were too remote from the plain meaning of the text. The new school of exegesis had already aroused opposition among French scholars. Joseph Kara's writings contain explicit reactions to these opponents' arguments. Presumably, such opposition was not forthcoming to the previous work of Menahem b. Helbo and Rashi, who still relied heavily on midrashic literature in their interpretation of the biblical text.

Neither did Menahem and Rashi explicitly attack representatives of the old school. It was in the time of Joseph Kara, who explicitly objected to non-literal interpretations, that the controversy over the nature of Bible exegesis became more acrid. Clearly, Joseph Kara's commentaries and his attacks on the opponents of the method required courage and considerable confidence in the legitimacy of his approach.

Kara himself referred to his opposition, sometimes directly, at other times obliquely. He insisted that he was guided exclusively by truth, not by conventions or accepted standards. Elsewhere he wrote that, though aware that "all the experts in Aggadah and Talmud" would reject his interpretation for various reasons, he, being interested solely in the truth, was unwilling to make allowances for their objections. His style of writing also indicates self-confidence and a feeling of leadership; it is no accident that he took an important part in the Jewish-Christian polemics of the times. He is described in polemical literature as one of the main spokesmen. As we shall see below, this aspect of his activities is frequently referred to in his Bible commentaries.

Joseph Kara was a prolific writer, though active only in the field of exegesis, in three connections: interpretation of the Bible, of liturgical poetry (*piyyut*) and of Midrash. Unlike Rashi, Shemaiah, Rashbam and Joseph Bekhor Shor, he was not a halakhist.

He wrote commentaries on the great majority of books of the Bible, perhaps in fact on all of them.[26] In the past it was thought that he had not dealt with some books, but recently discovered manuscripts indicate that he wrote commentaries on these as well. Large parts of his exegetical oeuvre have survived – mainly his commentaries to the books of the Former and Latter Prophets, the twelve Minor Prophets and the five scrolls – but these, too, are mostly rather different from his original commentary. Incontrovertible evidence of the many changes introduced in his texts may be derived from a comparison of his commentary on the books of the Former Prophets as printed in the Lublin edition with the manuscript commentaries to many of these books. It is readily seen that the Lublin edition omitted many passages, while others were added by copyists and editors. His commentaries to liturgical poetry fared similarly. Joseph Kara's exegetical works have suffered considerably from accretions, omissions and redaction, more than the writings of any other North-French commentator on the Bible.

Only at the end of the nineteenth century were Kara's commentaries on some books of the Bible first printed (Lublin edition), but no conclusions may be drawn from this delay as to the value placed on his work in the Middle Ages. In the generations immediately following his own, his Bible commentaries were highly appreciated, only to be gradually supplanted by Rashi's commentaries, particularly from the thirteenth century on, when the school of literal exegesis was largely abandoned.

---

[26] Joseph Kara's numerous commentaries, including those misattributed to him, were described in detail by Poznanski, Mabhô (1965) XXV–XXXI. I dealt at length with new information concerning his commentaries on Isaiah, Psalms and Job in my book, Hakhmê Sarephat (1996) 288 ff; the main points are summarized here.

6.1. Joseph Kara's Commentary on the Pentateuch

Until recently it was believed in scholarly circles that R. Joseph Kara never wrote a commentary on the Pentateuch. More than one hundred comments on individual verses were indeed known from various printed books and manuscripts, but these were generally considered to be glosses on Rashi's commentary. There were two main reasons for the assumption that these comments were not part of a systematic work: (i) the fact that none of the fragments were concerned with larger textual units; (ii) the nature of some of the comments on individual verses. In some of them, Joseph explicitly states that he wrote them while studying Rashi's commentary and as a reaction to the latter – hence they clearly have the nature of glosses and completions.

New sources, recently discovered in Italian archives, testify, however, that R. Joseph Kara did write a commentary on the Pentateuch. Four large fragments, obviously part of an important and comprehensive commentary, have been found.[27]

In recent years, many pages of medieval Hebrew manuscripts have been discovered in Italian archives. We now have more than 4.000 such pages, and the work of search and discovery is still in progress.[28] These were pages torn out of various original works and sold to archives, where they were used to prepare folders, bindings and wrappers. As a result, pages of a single book could – and often were – scatter among different archives.

One of these books, its pages torn out and dispersed in several Italian archives, originally contained Joseph Kara's commentaries on several, if not all, books of the Bible. Only a few leaves of this important book have come to light. The pages are partly torn, some missing the margins, and are therefore particularly difficult to decipher. They are nevertheless of great importance. The most interesting are the remnants of Kara's commentary on the Pentateuch. Three fragments of this commentary were found in the municipal archives of Bologna, and a fourth in that of Imola; all four were torn from the same volume. In these fragments Joseph Kara not only explains the text and its contents, but also describes customs that were current in Germany in his time and devotes special attention to the reasons for the commandments, as we shall see below.

6.2. The Commentary on Psalms

Another book on which, so it was thought in the past, R. Joseph Kara wrote no commentary is the book of Psalms. Two generations ago, Poznanski, surveying the books of the Bible for which Kara did not write a commentary, sta-

---

[27] For a detailed discussion of this issue, including a description of the remains, see Grossman, Hakhmê Sarephat (1996) 291–302.

[28] The fragments are of considerable significance for various issues relating to Jewish culture and society in the Middle Ages, beyond their bearing on Jewish scriptural interpretation. Important work in the discovery of these fragments is currently being done by Mauro Perani of the University of Bologna.

ted categorically: "... But for Psalms and Daniel we have no trace of a commentary by Kara".[29] However, the recently discovered leaves from the Italian archives have apparently preserved some of his comments on Psalms. There is no definite proof that he was indeed the author of these fragments, but the probability that he was is quite high, judging from the style and from parallels between the comments in them and comments in his extant commentaries on other books of the Bible.[30]

The whole commentary seems to be a typical product of the French school of literal exegesis. It concerns itself mainly with questions of language, the historical background of the Psalms and literary features. The author seeks out inner relationships between different parts of specific psalms and between different psalms. He cites rules for understanding the Bible and explaining words, deals frequently with linguistic matters and cites from ancient liturgical poems. He addresses the reader, as it were, personally, in the second person, using the Hebrew word *ummôt* as a technical term designating the gentile nations in general as foes of the people of Israel. These are all features typical of Joseph Kara and common in his commentaries. One also finds in the commentary numerous words and phrases characteristic of Kara and commonly used in his commentaries. A prominent example is the word *pitrônô*, meaning 'its explanation', which also often opens his comments. It occurs dozens of times in the commentary on Psalms, in each and every chapter. On the other hand, it is rarely used by other French scholars.

6.3. Printed Editions and Manuscripts of Kara's Bible Commentaries

There are a great many differences between R. Joseph Kara's commentaries to the Prophets and Hagiographa as preserved in the printed editions, on the one hand, and the manuscripts, on the other. The reader sometimes receives the distinct impression that the commentary could not have been written by a single person. In some cases the commentary is essentially a compilation. New, recently discovered manuscript sources have revealed more about the extent of the changes introduced in Kara's original commentaries. This is particularly true with regard to the already mentioned fragments unearthed in Italian archives, which are from his commentaries to Isaiah, Micah, Hosea, Amos and Job.

It is clear from these fragments, as well as from other commentaries by Joseph Kara, that we do not possess one complete, authentic manuscript of Kara's commentary to the Latter Prophets and Hagiographa. Unfortunately, the Italian archives have not yet produced any pages from his commentaries to the Former Prophets, so we cannot properly evaluate the version published by Eppenstein, based on MS Kirchheim, which seems to be original and authentic.

[29] Poznanski, Mabhô (1965) XXXI.

[30] For a detailed discussion of these fragments and their attribution to Joseph Kara see Grossman, Hakhmê Sarephat (1996) 308–11.

The omissions from Kara's commentaries had a most significant effect, for some of the omitted passages are quite unique and characteristic. Copyists and scribes generally omitted his characteristic phraseology, discussions of linguistics, traditions cited in the name of his uncle Menahem b. Helbo, as well as his own interpretations based on the technique of *peshat*, and remarks extolling his own interpretations as against rabbinic Midrash. Thus, it was midrashic passages and brief commentaries that were preserved, because the copyists usually found them more interesting. An invaluable tool for studying Joseph Kara's original opus was thus lost, and the brilliance of one of our most original exegetes, possessing an individual style and great expressive power, was dimmed.

This loss robbed Joseph Kara of his rightful place as one of the greatest medieval commentators, despite scholars' frequent discussion of his work. Today, thanks to the pages that have surfaced in Italian archives, as well as the preservation of his commentary on Isaiah in MS Lutzki 778, some of this lost glory can be restored.

Kara's commentary on Isaiah is a perfect example of copyists' confusion in their evaluation of his exegesis. For the printed edition of *Miqra'ôt Gedôlôt* (Lublin 1857–1859) they chose as their basic version that of MS Lutzki 777, today in the library of the Jewish Theological Seminary of America, New York. As this version has survived in five other manuscripts, it was considered the best extant version of Joseph Kara's commentary on Isaiah – in particular, as the manuscript in question was quite early – 1268. This assumption, however, was wrong. MS Lutzki 777 and the five similar manuscripts stem from the same branch of transmission, while the commentary preserved in the single MS Lutzki 778 represents an alternative branch which is far superior and much more faithful to the original commentary. It contains historical data of paramount importance, such as anti-Christian polemics and dozens of foreign words, sometimes entire sentences in French, that the copyist of MS Lutzki 777 omitted. One does not have to be an expert to realize the superiority of MS Lutzki 778. The most superficial perusal of the printed commentary on Isaiah immediately detects omissions, sometimes obscuring the whole meaning of the text. In addition, many of Joseph Kara's most characteristic turns of language are missing and his eloquent, lucid and easily flowing presentation is impaired. One of the most obvious omissions occurs in the chapters on 'The Lord's servant', which are explicated in the printed edition only in their first part, whereas the text of MS Lutzki 778 treats the whole unit.[31]

The foreign words in the version of MS Lutzki 778 are also of considerable significance for the study of medieval French and German. They are not only more numerous than the *le'azim* in MS Lutzki 777 but also more reliable.

[31] For the differences between the manuscripts and the superiority of MS Lutzki 778 see Grossman, Hakhmê Sarephat (1996) 308–11. The new edition of *Mikra'ot Gedolot 'Haketer'* (1996) is based on MS Lutzki 778.

6.4. Kara's Approach to the Biblical Text

R. Joseph Kara's primary object in his biblical exegesis was to reveal the *peshat*, the plain meaning of the text, generally in a rational manner. In his own, clearly phrased words:

> But whosoever is ignorant of the plain meaning of the biblical text, preferring the homiletical interpretation, resembles a person who has been washed away by a flowing river, is drowning in the depths of the water and grasps at whatever he can to save himself; while if he heeded the word of the Lord he would investigate the explanation and the plain meaning (commentary to 1 Sam 1:17).

In some of his explanations, mainly in the commentary on Isaiah, after setting out the plain meaning, Kara returns to the beginning of the passage and adds several selected *midrashim.* There are no such passages in his commentaries to the books of the Former Prophets, and it is still unclear why he chose to do so here. Had he reconsidered his original decision to avoid homiletical explications, or was Isaiah perhaps the first book on which he wrote a commentary? In this case the difference cannot be attributed to disciples' glosses. It is quite clear from the style that Joseph Kara himself wrote these homiletical additions. Perhaps he selected a few *midrashim* for further study, alongside and not instead of the literal interpretation; he chose this method in some books of the Latter Prophets, since the world of ideas represented by this type of material was more suitable for prophetic visions than the straightforward, factual text of the books of the Former Prophets.

On the other hand, Kara argues against rabbinic Midrash hundreds of times in his commentary, though without saying so explicitly. Rather, he simply presents an alternative explanation, obliquely indicating that this explanation is to be preferred. This technique is also adopted by Rashbam, and can in fact be detected quite frequently in Rashi's commentary.

Joseph Kara's determination to reveal the literal meaning often brought him into conflict with Rashi's explication of the same text. Occasionally he does so explicitly, but generally he does not mention the clash. As a rule, Kara made frequent use of Rashi's commentaries, referring to them as "the commentaries of our Master Solomon". His deep regard for Rashi is quite obvious, despite his frequent objections to the older master's comments, whether explicit or otherwise.

One prominent, characteristic feature of R. Joseph Kara's exegetical technique is his proposal of rules for understanding the text and language of the Bible. Scattered through his commentaries are dozens of rules, some of which have been discovered only now through the new fragments emerging from the Italian archives. Some of the rules concern linguistic questions, but they are more frequently literary, sometimes revealing Kara's considerable sensitivity to literary matters. In some cases the rules have an educational purpose, probably also aimed polemically against Christianity. For example, he repeatedly states his rule that "Wherever you find rebuke, you will find it accompanied by a fitting [prophecy of] comfort" (commentary to Hos 2:1). In other words, the prophecies of comfort contain motifs similar to those figuring previously in prophecies of destruction, testifying that God has not repudiated his people and breached his covenant; the harsh prophecies of destruction are merely temporary; God will ultimately redeem Israel and compensate them for their suffering.

6.5. Kara's Rational Approach

One of the most important characteristics of Joseph Kara's exegesis is his rational approach. This affects his entire exegetical method, particularly in relation to the reasons for the commandments and the tendency to limit the supernatural element in miracles to some extent.

Menahem b. Helbo and Rashi, who laid the foundations for the French school, did not offer reasons for the commandments, except in a few places where they quoted rabbinic opinion. Until recently it was believed that the first French scholar to address this question was Rashbam, but the new fragments from Joseph Kara's commentaries indicated that he, too, devoted considerable attention to such matters. We cannot state with any confidence that his commentary to the Pentateuch predates that of Rashbam, in which case he would be considered the trailblazer of this aspect of biblical exegesis. Nevertheless, it is clear that he began to write his commentaries when Rashbam was still a child.

A few examples of Kara's method here will suffice. He states, for example, that a slave's ear must be pierced by the door or the doorpost (Exod 21:6) because they are near the public domain, so that passersby will witness the act and learn thereby of the evils of slavery.

Another example concerns the institution of levirate marriage, which requires a widow whose husband has died without offspring to marry the deceased's brother (the levir), as prescribed in Deut 25:5–6. Should the brother refuse to carry out this duty, the widow removes the levir's shoe in a special ceremony, known as *halîzah* (ibid., v. 9). The Bible itself states that the purpose of levirate marriage is to preserve the dead brother's memory. Kara adds that if the levir refuses to marry the widow and undergoes the *halîzah* ceremony, this too, because of its exceptional features, will help to memorialize the deceased. The injunction to call the levir "the family of the unsandaled one" is meant not to shame him but to perpetuate his dead brother's memory.

It is no accident that the commandment to blot out the memory of Amalek (Deut 25:17–19) is effective only after the appointment of a king. The reason is pragmatic: the difficulty of fighting several enemies at once.

Finally, the prohibition of plowing with an ox and an ass together (Deut 22:10) derives from the injunction against cruelty to animals – not physical cruelty, as explained by Abraham ibn Ezra, but mental: the ox is a ruminant, so that the ass, seeing the ox constantly chewing, will think that the ox has been fed while he, the ass, has not, and will therefore be distressed.

This approach to explaining the reasons for the commandments is in good agreement with the emphatically rational conception of all Kara's Bible commentaries. This conception concerns not only his preference for the plain, literal meaning of the text; it also underlies his frequent objections to *midrashim* too remote from the literal meaning, and, in particular, to his explications of biblical miracles. Indeed, his constant effort to explain miracles in as natural a manner as possible is a major characteristic of his exegesis. It was hitherto believed that Joseph Bekhor Shor was the first French commentator to do so (under the influence of the rationally minded Spanish exegetes), and a similar tendency may be detected in Rashbam. It turns out, however, that Joseph Kara preceded both.

A few examples will illustrate this important issue. In the story of the war of Deborah and Barak against Sisera we read, "The stars fought from heaven, from their courses they fought against Sisera" (Judg 5:20). Kara comments that this should not be understand as stating that the stars actually fought Sisera, for "you have never seen the celestial bodies, from the day they were created, changing the laws of the heavens and coming down from the sky to the earth". Joshua's pointing of the javelin in the battle at Ai (Josh 8:18) involves nothing mystical; it was merely a sign to the soldiers to emerge from the ambushing positions and capture the city. When Moses, in battle with Amalek (Exod 17:11), raised his hands to the heavens, the Israelites were victorious for natural reasons – soldiers at war raise a standard or flag to encourage their colleagues and rouse them to action. The act was not a mystical one: Moses' hands simply played the part of a flag. And there are many other examples of this line of thought.

Another typical trait of Kara's biblical exegesis, also born of his rationalism, is his attitude to the redaction of the books of the Bible. He may be viewed in this respect as paving new paths in the French-Jewish scriptural interpretation of those times. Rashi concerns himself very rarely with such matters, relying primarily on rabbinic opinion, unlike Joseph Kara.

6.6. *Manifestations of Religious Polemics in Kara's Commentaries*

No account of R. Joseph Kara's commentaries is complete without note of his deep involvement in the Jewish-Christian polemics of his time, even though the expression of this involvement is generally covert. The influence of the polemic is sometimes obvious in his comments on individual verses or passages, in his explanation of the meaning and date of prophecies of comfort, and in certain conceptual issues, such as the meaning of the Exile and Israel's enslavement to the gentile nations, the Jews' relations with the other nations and the value of the commandments. Paradoxically, the polemical motif is also shown by his readiness at times to depart from the plain meaning and favour more fanciful *midrashim*, in cases where this may serve his polemical purposes. In addition, his involvement moved him to launch bitter attacks on Jewish scholars who, to his mind, were not sufficiently aware of the danger in the argumentation of the Christian camp and therefore proposed interpretations that might serve the Christians in their anti-Jewish propaganda.[32]

---

[32] Thus, Kara objects sharply, in his commentary on 1 Kgs 7:33, to Rashi's interpretation of *Maʿaseh Merkabhah*. Rashi describes the wheels of the Chariot as held together by crossed bars. Joseph Kara, fearful that Christian polemicists might seize on this as proof that God's Chariot was supported by the cross, accused Rashi of misleading "all Israel" in his explanation.

While Rashbam and Joseph Bekhor Shor frequently brought their polemical arguments out into the open, R. Joseph Kara was usually more circumspect, concealing his polemical goal and his motives, which are not always easily revealed. The influence of Jewish-Christian polemics on Kara's Bible commentaries found its literary expression in several ways: in the content of the interpretation, its style, in discussions of conceptual matters, in the emphasis on certain literary features and in the tendency to explain the Patriarchs' actions in as positive a manner as possible.

Some of Joseph Kara's explicit attacks on Christianity were deleted for fear of Christian reactions or because of censorship. Of particular importance is his commentary to Isa 33 (vv. 13–14), which does not appear in the printed editions but has been preserved in MS Vienna 23. Kara argues there that the people of Israel have been condemned to subjugation in exile because Christianity originated in Judaism.

The Bible remained at the centre of Jewish-Christian polemics in the twelfth century too, despite changes in the intervening years with the intrusion of new elements (such as the Talmud).[33] This is not surprising, for both faiths, Jewish and Christian, based themselves on the Bible. The correct interpretation of a particular verse or passage therefore carried with it supreme, binding authority. Christian exegetes tried to find allusions in the Bible to the basic tenets of their religion, in a variety of ways – frequently purely artificial.

In view of this polemical thrust, Joseph Kara had a unique interpretation for the passage describing the messianic king in Zech 9:9:

> Rejoice greatly, Fair Zion; raise a shout, Fair Jerusalem! Lo, your king is coming to you. He is victorious, triumphant, yet humble riding on an ass, on a donkey foaled by a she-ass.

Kara disputes interpretations by other commentators, who understand the phrase "humble, riding on an ass" as referring to the righteous messianic king mentioned in the biblical text. Kara explains the adjective 'humble' as referring to the people of Israel, whom the righteous king will redeem – a rather forced interpretation, quite remote from the plain meaning of the words. Most probably, Kara departed from his usual method and suggested his very artificial explanation in view of Christian claims that the word 'humble' supported their interpretation of the text as referring to Jesus.

Of particular interest is R. Joseph Kara's treatment of passages that refer to Israel's sins. On many occasions he refers, directly or otherwise, to the Christian argument that Israel, having sinned and breached its covenant with God, has been rejected. Thus, he explains the verse "Fallen, not to rise again, is Maiden Israel" (Amos 5:2) as referring only to the Israelites deported by the Assyrian king Shalmaneser in the ninth year of Hosea son of Elah's rule; these exiles, as the Bible states, never returned to their homeland.

One of the most impressive proofs of the influence of the Jewish-Christian

---

[33] See, e.g., A. Funkenstein, "Shifts in the Religious Debate between Jews and Christians in the twelfth Century" (Heb.), *Zion* 33 (1968) 125–44; D. Berger, *The Jewish Christian Debate in the High Middle Ages* (Philadelphia 1969). It should be noted that Christian biblical exegesis of the eleventh and twelfth centuries vigorously continued the anti-Jewish debate.

debate on Joseph Kara's commentaries on Bible and liturgical poetry alike is his attitude to Exile and Redemption. This was the most difficult problem facing the Jews in the Middle Ages. R. Joseph Kara had recourse to numerous verses and biblical passages to explain the long duration and purpose of the Exile. He devoted much attention to the question of the 'rejection of Israel', as well as to the question of the date of the Redemption and the purpose of exile.

One example, preserved in MS Moscow-Ginzburg 615, will suffice, illustrating his choice of a highly non-literal interpretation for a polemical motif, though he does not explicitly state this:

> "He gives food to those who fear Him" [Psalms 111:5] and some say that He has given Israel, who fear Him, as prey to the nations, in order to show the world that they adhere to his fear.

The plain meaning of the text refers to God's care for those who fear Him, whom He supplies with food. The Hebrew text here uses the word *tereph* for food, which also means prey; this enabled Kara to turn the whole meaning of the verse around, explaining that "those who fear Him", that is, Israel, have fallen prey to the nations.

Kara could, of course, have supported many such interpretations by having recourse to the Midrash. However, this does not detract from this evidence of his world of ideas, for there exist other, conflicting *midrashim*, and the mere choice of one or the other may be significant.

6.7. The Relationship between Kara's Bible Exegesis, His Commentaries on Liturgical Poetry and the Heritage of Spain

R. Joseph Kara was the greatest commentator on liturgical poetry (*piyyut*) in the Middle Ages. His considerable influence and widespread renown in that field is comparable to the value placed on Rashi's commentaries on the Bible and the Talmud. From the late twelfth century on, his comments are frequently ascribed to *ha-mepharesh*, "*the* commentator", without further qualification. In medieval commentaries on *piyyut* one finds frequent quotations from "R. Joseph" or "R. Jose", both referring to Joseph Kara. His great fame in the field is no accident, and his commentaries to *piyyutim* should not be viewed as a 'routine' commentary, one of many.

Kara's broad view, his wide-ranging familiarity with rabbinic Midrash, frequent attention to linguistic and literary qualities, his habit of formulating rules to characterize different poets' approaches, his attention to the historical background of the text and his traditions concerning the poets' lives – such qualities made Kara's commentaries on *piyyut* so important and earned them their central position in the exegesis of liturgical poetry.

R. Joseph Kara's commentaries on *piyyutim* made much use of biblical expressions as he understood them. Conversely, in his Bible exegesis he frequently used his own interpretations of *piyyutim*, as did his elder colleague Rashi in his time.[34]

---

[34] For a detailed discussion of Joseph Kara's commentaries on liturgical poetry, including the relationship to his biblical exegesis, see Grossman, Hakhmê Sarephat (1996) 325–40.

Kara was considerably influenced by the Spanish grammarians Menahem b. Saruq and Dunash b. Labrat, particularly by the latter. On the other hand, he unhesitatingly disagreed with Dunash on occasion, despite his admiration for him, though he did so as a disciple offering his master a new idea. Not only the content of the Spanish linguists' writings affected him, but also their style of writing, particularly that of Dunash. The personal style that he used throughout his innovatory comments was also borrowed from Dunash, as was his frequent use of dialectic phraseology. Joseph Kara's Bible commentaries on occasion quote Arabic words, which reached him through the works of the early Spanish-Jewish scholars, either directly or through the agency of his uncle Menahem b. Helbo.

7. Shemaiah (1060–1130)

Shemaiah is surely one of the most important scholars of the French school of literal exegesis, though not an entirely typical representative of that school. He was very close to Rashi and gave him much assistance in literary matters. His literary opus was considerable and highly varied: commentaries on the Bible, the Talmud, the Midrash and liturgical poetry, halakhic monographs, among other things. Most of his works, however, have been lost, and much of what survives is still in manuscript.[35]

In biblical exegesis, Shemaiah was overshadowed by his revered master Rashi. No systematic commentaries to parts of the Bible by Shemaiah have come down to us, nor do we know that such commentaries ever existed. There survive a few fragments of commentaries, but as they are so few in number, we cannot be sure whether they were part of a full, systematic commentary or, as seems more likely, glosses on Rashi's commentary and comments on individual passages.

As part of his commentaries on liturgical poems, R. Shemaiah also interpreted hundreds of biblical expressions, but they do not always reflect his own, independent understanding of them. In most cases he is forced to explain them in keeping with their context in the poem, that is, according to whatever use the poet made of them and in conformity with the poet's interpretation of them. His major activity in the area of Bible exegesis was his assistance to Rashi in editing the Master's commentaries and the writing of glosses to Rashi's commentary on the Pentateuch and the books of the Prophets. Rashi himself refers to his disciple's aid in editing his commentary to the Bible: "At any rate, I erred in that interpretation … and my words contradicted one another. But now I have dealt with it together with our brother Shemaiah and corrected it". Rashi calls Shemaiah "our brother", because of the warm friendship between the two. This particular quotation is from Rashi's commentary on Ezekiel; we

[35] For a detailed account of what is known of Shemaiah's life, literary works and close relationship with Rashi, including his considerable assistance to the latter in his literary work, see Grossman, Hakhmê Sarephat (1996) 347–411.

have evidence that Shemaiah also edited Rashi's commentary on Isaiah, and possibly also on other books of the Bible. Commenting occasionally on Rashi's exegetical method, Shemaiah, as it were, admits us into his master's 'laboratory' and affords us a glimpse of how the commentaries were created and developed.

R. Shemaiah's glosses to Rashi's commentary on the Pentateuch, preserved in MS Leipzig 1, are of great importance. Numerous other glosses were merged with Rashi's commentary and became an integral part of it, without any mention of their author's identity.[36]

Returning to the glosses in MS Leipzig 1, we note that the sixty-one glosses published by BERLINER constitute only about a quarter of Shemaiah's comments and glosses in that manuscript. Indeed, it contains nearly two hundred and fifty glosses attributed to Shemaiah, as well as a few anonymous comments, some or all of which may also be his.

R. Shemaiah's glosses and additions to Rashi's commentary on the Pentateuch may be divided into three categories: (i) corrections and additions by Rashi himself, interpolated at the Master's own initiative; (ii) glosses and comments by Shemaiah himself; (iii) long passages, perhaps also discussions, selected by Shemaiah and juxtaposed with the relevant biblical passages. Shemaiah noted down the first two categories in the margins of a book containing Rashi's commentary on the Pentateuch, which was apparently also copied by Shemaiah himself. Many of his comments were written between the lines of Rashi's commentary. The third category was apparently written on separate folios and then added to the main body of the work.

The glosses attributable to Shemaiah himself, which will mostly concern us here, may be further subdivided into three categories: (i) his corrections to Rashi's commentary; (ii) explanations of biblical passages; (iii) quotations from rabbinic Midrash. In the first category, Shemaiah may correct the wording, compare Rashi's commentaries in different places, propose his own interpretation ("and it seems to me ...", "my view is ...") and sometimes even oppose the Master.

In these glosses, as in all his literary work, Shemaiah frequently touches upon realia: weights and measures, buildings, boundaries and the like. This is one of the characteristic features of his writings, as it is of Joseph Kara's work.

Shemaiah often relied on midrashic literature, being in this respect too a follower of Rashi. Some of his glosses complete or add *midrashim* not quoted in Rashi's commentary. He apparently preferred to cite brief passages which were, as he saw it, in keeping with the literal or obvious meaning of the text. He also at times cited commentaries of other scholars, including some unknown to us from any other source;[37] such quotations are also common in his commentaries to liturgical poetry.

A perusal of Shemaiah's commentaries to *piyyutim* and his glosses on Rashi's biblical exegesis clearly indicate that he, too, was frequently at pains to bring out the literal meaning of the text. Despite his warm regard for rabbinic

---

36 For a discussion of these glosses see Berliner, Rashi's Commentaries (1949) 195–206.
37 Grossman, Hakhmê Sarephat (1996) 187–93, 359–66.

Midrash, he carefully distinguished between the literal meaning and homiletical interpretation of the biblical text. He, too, was a member of the 'new' camp, although he lacked the fanatical devotion to *peshat* that we find in Joseph Kara and Rashbam. He sometimes addresses the question of *peshat* as against *derash*, but much less than in the exegesis of his two colleagues. Only rarely does he openly object to an interpretation cited by Rashi on the ground that it is homiletical, suggesting an alternative explanation based on the plain meaning of the text. Thus, although he sometimes has recourse to the literal meaning in his glosses to Rashi's commentaries and in his other work, and although he in fact laid down certain rules of linguistic usage in the Bible, he cannot be considered a typical representative of the French school of literary exegesis of the late eleventh and early twelfth centuries. Nevertheless, he was considerably influenced by the members of the school. In fact, it would seem that in this respect, too, he emulated Rashi's example, that is, frequent recourse to the literal meaning of the text, coupled with wide use of Aggadah and Midrash. Shemaiah's glosses to Rashi's commentary on the Pentateuch also include many aggadic passages.

A particularly interesting instance is Shemaiah's treatment of the legend that identifies Aaron's grandson Phinehas with the prophet Elijah, in which he implicitly disputes a view that this legend should be taken literally. His own comments clearly show that he belonged to the camp of those explaining rabbinic legend in an allegorical sense; he did not consider such legends the literal meaning of the biblical text.

8. Samuel ben Meir / Rashbam (1080–1160)

8.1. Rashbam's Commentaries

Samuel ben Meir, commonly referred to by the acronym RaShBaM, was Rashi's grandson and pupil. Following in his illustrious grandfather's footsteps, he wrote commentaries to some tractates of the Talmud and was considered one of the greatest Tosafists in Northern France.[38] In many respects he may be seen as having brought the French school of literary exegesis to its peak.

Of Rashbam's commentaries to many books of the Bible, little has survived. His commentary on the Pentateuch exists in only two manuscripts, they too incomplete. This commentary, published in a critical edition by David Rosin in 1881, is his most important work among his commentaries on the Bible. There is also a surviving commentary to the book of Ecclesiastes, but doubts have been expressed as to its authenticity, as there are suspected additions and changes. The same is true of his commentary to the book of Job in MS Lutzki 778, which certainly contains late additions to the original commentary by Rashbam. Still farther from the source is the commentary to the Song of Songs in MS Hamburg Heb. 32, which was published by A. Jellinek in 1855. This

[38] For an account of the man and his literary opus see Urbach, Baʿalê ha-Tôsaphôt (1980) 1:45–59.

commentary has been preserved in other manuscripts, some with superior readings. The proportion of material in this work from the pen of Rashbam himself is still in doubt. Other fragments exist of commentaries to the other scrolls, and a few isolated fragments of commentaries on other books of the Bible.[39]

The most typical characteristic of Rashbam's commentaries is his strenuous effort to explain the literal, plain meaning of the text; this is the primary goal of his Bible exegesis, as he himself declares on several occasions. He decided on this approach at a relatively early age, and when only twenty years old he argued resolutely with Rashi, objecting that some of his interpretations did not conform to the plain meaning. He complains that his predecessors deviated from the *peshat* in their Bible exegesis, thinking it particularly pious to explain the text in keeping with the Midrash. He frequently criticizes Rashi's explanations when they seemed too remote from the literal meaning; his criticism is sometimes phrased in sharp terms. On such occasions he never referred to his polemical purpose, but a comparison of his comment with that of Rashi clearly reveals that his intention was to differ from his grandfather's interpretation.

The truth is that Rashbam's whole commentary on the Pentateuch is intimately connected with Rashi's commentary and in a sense should be considered as complementing it. Rashbam does not explain the entire text, but only 'selected' extracts, and his choice is governed by his close attention to Rashi. When Rashi's interpretation seems to him 'true', that is, in accord with the literal, plain meaning of the text, he offers no comment. He explicitly alludes to this tendency on several occasions, as, for example:

> Let every sensible person know and understand that, although they are of primary importance, I have not come to explain the *halakhôt* ... Some of the *aggadôt* and *halakhôt* can be found in the commentaries of Rabbi Solomon, my maternal grandfather, of blessed memory. My aim is to interpret the literal meaning of Scripture (Exod 21:1).

Another instance is: "As to the pericopes of the Tabernacle, the breastplate and the ephod – if I am brief there, they may be found in the commentaries of Rabbi Solomon, my maternal grandfather, of blessed memory". And in his introductory words to Leviticus he notes: "There are many *halakhôt* in it, and you should study my grandfather's commentaries, for I shall not write at length save in places where the literal meaning of the text has to be determined". Indeed, at the end of his commentary on Exodus he explicitly advises the reader to study his own commentary together with that of Rashi. Clearly, therefore, he considered his own words to complement those of Rashi.

On occasion, Rashbam interprets the text not only against the Midrash but even against Halakhah. Thus, for example, in the account of a Hebrew slave who has chosen to remain with his master, and had his ear pierced, the words "and he shall then remain his slave for life" are interpreted by the Sages to mean "until the Jubilee year", and this is the accepted legal ruling. Rashbam, however, writes: "According to the *peshat* – all the days of his life". And there are numerous other instances. His comments on halakhic passages in the Pen-

[39] Poznanski, Mabhô (1965) XL; Japhet / Salters, Commentary ... on Qoheleth (1985) 17–28.

tateuch are therefore quite brief. A reader studying Rashbam's commentary on the Pentateuch, therefore, must constantly compare it with Rashi's commentary on the same passage. Otherwise one may at times miss the full meaning of Rashbam's interpretation.

Rashi was deeply impressed by his grandson's adherence to the literal meaning of the text, and in his old age amended some of his own interpretations in accordance with Rashbam's suggestions.

Despite his great regard for the *peshat*, Rashbam at times deviates quite considerably from the plain meaning of the text. In discussing the subject of leprous affections (Lev 13:2), he explicitly announces this intention:

> All the chapters of human affections and affections on clothes and on houses ... we gain nothing by considering the literal meaning of the Bible ... On the contrary, rabbinic Midrash ... is then of primary importance.

He will sometimes propose a variety of motives and reasons for the actions of the protagonists of the biblical narrative, thereby expanding the story. Thus, he suggests that Lot was forbidden to look back "because of the distress of his sons-in-law in the city. Moreover, a person who looks back delays along the way. In addition, it was best not to observe the angels and their actions without need" (Gen 19:17). Many other instances might be cited. Rashbam also considered the reasons for the commandments, often offering a rational explanation to that end.

Rashbam laid down several rules in relation to biblical language and narrative. For example, he states that one commonly finds the Bible anticipating, in the sense that it will explain something unnecessary at one point, so that the subsequent material should be better understood. He refers to this rule dozens of times. Another frequent rule is the biblical technique of rendering a general description and only then going on to give details, even if those details are described out of sequence. For example, commenting on Exod 2:15, he states that Moses' arrival in Midian is first described in general terms, "He settled in the land of Midian", and only later does the text go on to give a detailed account of the previous events, describing how he got there. Wherever the text uses the words, "After these things [had come to pass]", Rashbam explains that there is an inner relationship with the previous episode. He also cites rules concerning parallelism in biblical metaphor, and so on.

He is greatly attentive to linguistic matters, frequently relying on the Spanish linguists Menahem b. Saruq and Dunash b. Labrat, though he is not afraid to criticize them. The important role of grammar in his exegetical work is indicated by the fact that he himself wrote a grammar book, named *Sepher Dayaqut.* The book comprises two parts: the first is a treatise on grammar in general, while the second deals with grammatical matters in all books of the Bible – only the first part has survived. This work is clear evidence of the affinity between Rashbam's high regard for grammar and the technique of literal exegesis.[40]

---

[40] See I. Eldar, "The Grammatical Literature of Medieval Ashkenazi Jewry", *Hebrew in Ashkenaz* (ed. L. Glinert; Oxford 1993) 26–45.

Rashbam was very conscientious about his texts, always seeking the most accurate texts possible, including new books arriving from Spain. His own language is lucid and clear, sometimes introducing his own linguistic innovations alongside usages derived from Mishnaic Hebrew. In comparison with Rashi, he does not often cite foreign words (he does so on approximately forty occasions).

The commentary appeals now and again to Targum Onqelos, but much more rarely than Rashi does so. Rashbam also uses the Mishnah, the Talmud and the aggadic and halakhic Midrash much less than Rashi. He commonly disagrees with other scholars, but usually without naming them. He explicitly refers at times to Joseph Kara's commentary, sometimes agreeing with his explanations, sometimes disagreeing. He refers dozens of times to his own interpretations in other places.[41]

Rashbam is unique for his sensitivity to literary form, in this respect also departing from the tradition of homiletical literature. His consideration of literary questions is governed by criteria other than those of the Midrash. This is clearly illustrated by his commentary to the book of Ecclesiastes.[42] The fragments of Rashbam's commentary on the book of Psalms, still extant only in manuscript, point to a more sophisticated literary approach than that of other members of the French school of literal exegesis.

The commentaries on the Pentateuch, Ecclesiastes and the other scrolls do not explain the text verse by verse, but proceed by selected verses; sometimes Rashbam will in fact discuss a whole unit, ignoring its detailed structure. His style of presentation is fluid and lucid. As he goes along, he focuses on salient points as he sees fit, whether discussing linguistic questions or content. He attributes the inner contradictions in the book of Ecclesiastes, among other things, to the author's literary method of using quotations, which actually express other persons' views and not those of the author himself.

Many of Rashbam's explanations are original, sometimes quite surprising. For example, he explains the motif of the 'test' in the story of Abraham's binding of Isaac in the sense of distress rather than 'testing' in the strict meaning of the word. This distress, he declares, was meant to punish Abraham for concluding a covenant with Abimelech, "for the Land of the Philistines is included in the borders of Israel", and so Abraham should not have renounced his claim and made a covenant with Abimelech.

8.2. Rashbam and Jewish-Christian Polemics

Rashbam on several occasions associates his adherence to the plain meaning of the text with Jewish-Christian polemics, writing, for example, "according to the literal meaning of the text and in answer to sectarians" (Lev 11:3), "sectarians" (*mînîm*) being Christians. Or: "That is the main point in the literal mean-

[41] For a detailed discussion see Melammed, Mephareshê ha-Miqra (1978) 1:453–513.

[42] For a detailed account of Rashbam's exegesis of Ecclesiastes see Japhet / Salters, Commentary ... on Qoheleth (1985) 39–44.

ing, and an answer to sectarians" (Exod 3:22), and so on. Several times he explicitly refers to his own personal disputations with Christian scholars, going so far as to claim that on some occasions the Christians were even persuaded by his polemical arguments.

Despite the fact that the actual number of such explicit remarks is small, they constitute important testimony, as it were, one detail attesting to the whole picture. Rashbam's entire exegetical effort and his fanatical concern with the literal meaning are strongly influenced by the religious debate. Indeed, the insistence on explaining the literal meaning of the text was meant, *inter alia*, to hinder efforts on the part of Christian adversaries to offer their christological, allegorical version of the text.

Rashbam's familiarity with Christian exegesis indicates that he took part in the public Jewish-Christian disputations of his time. Christian scholars were acquainted with his work, as demonstrated by Smalley, and traces of his influence may be detected in the writings of Hugh of St. Victor.[43]

Another motif that derives from the religious controversy with the Christians was the tendency, already discernible in Rashbam and even more in the next generation, in the work of Joseph Bekhor Shor and Eliezer of Beaugency, to explain the Patriarch's actions in as positive a manner as possible. He insists, for example, that Abraham was not responsible for his son Ishmael's thirst, but Hagar; Jacob bought the birthright from Esau outright, paying money, and by no means deceiving his brother. And there are other examples. The arguments against which Rashbam is polemicizing were frequently raised in the Christian polemical literature.[44] The most important instance is Rashbam's explanation of why the Children of Israel took silver and gold vessels from the Egyptians. According to him, the verse "Each woman shall borrow from her neighbour" (Exod 3:22) means that the Israelite women were instructed to ask the Egyptian women to make them outright gifts of the vessels; at no time did they so much as hint that they were temporary gifts. It is on this occasion that Rashbam makes the already quoted statement, "That is the main point in the literal meaning, and *an answer to sectarians*". The explanation is palpably forced, clearly motivated mainly by the need to respond to the arguments of Christian disputants.

One finds an even closer affinity with religious polemic in the commentary on the Song of Songs attributed to Rashbam. To my mind, this commentary was written about one generation after Rashbam's life, by a scholar strongly influenced by him but who also borrowed from other authors. The commentator describes the entire Song as a dispute between Israel and the gentile nations. The actual content of the commentary does not differ substantially from that of Rashi's commentary, but while Rashi explicated only a few of the pas-

[43] See Smalley, Study of the Bible (1952) 103–06, 155. On contacts between Jewish and Christian scholars in France around that time see Dahan, Intellectuels chrétiens (1990); cf. also Chap. 34 (by R. Berndt) in this volume.

[44] For this whole issue see D. Berger, "On the Morality of the Patriarchs in Jewish Polemic and Exegesis", *Understanding Scripture* (ed. C. Thoma / M. Wyschogrod; New York 1987) 49–62.

sages relating directly to the controversy, Rashbam went much further and also brought in many other motifs.

8.3. Rashbam and the Twelfth-Century Renaissance

Besides Jewish-Christian polemics, another factor that exerted considerable influence on Rashbam's exegesis was the twelfth-century renaissance. This renaissance brought about a reconsideration, among other things, of the proper relationship between the authority of tradition and that of human reason. The reasons for things and the laws governing their existence were reexamined. Intellectuals took a more objective and discriminating look at nature, including the biblical miracles. Changes also occurred in attitudes to interpretation of the Bible, and there was readiness to take more heed of the literal meaning of the biblical text. This was also the view of Hugh of St. Victor. Rashbam seems to have maintained close contacts with the scholars working in the monastery of St. Victor.

Among the terms that he used, one of the most common is *derekh erez*, that is, literally, 'the way of the world'. It occurs thirteen times in his commentary on the Pentateuch. Indeed, at the very outset of his commentary on Genesis he declares: "Let every sensible person know and understand ... I will interpret the laws according to *the way of the world*". In Mishnaic Hebrew, the expression means proper social norms and manners, as well as worldly matters and human practices. Rashbam apparently added the meaning of 'laws of nature', as is illustrated many times in his commentary on the Pentateuch, in both narrative and legal parts.[45] The influence of the renaissance on Rashbam's exegesis is felt both in the general lines of his commentaries and in the finer details. As a rule, he draws quite frequently on his knowledge and experience of everyday life. He bases explanations on what he had heard "from proper physicians" (Lev 11:3), on what he knew of clerical costume (Exod 28:32), on what he had seen in the harvest season (Deut 32:10), and so on.

9. Eliezer of Beaugency

Eliezer of Beaugency was active around the middle of the twelfth century. His precise dates are not known. He may have been a pupil of Rashbam, one of whose interpretations he quotes in the name of "our Rabbi Samuel". He wrote commentaries on most if not all books of the Bible, but the only ones that have reached us are those on the book of Isaiah (published by J. W. Nutt, Oxford 1879) and on the Minor Prophets (published by S. Poznanski, Warsaw 1913).

Later commentators quote isolated excerpts from his commentaries on the Pentateuch, Jeremiah, Job, Habakkuk, Psalms, Ecclesiastes and Daniel.[46]

---

[45] For a detailed discussion see Touitou, Rashbam (1982).
[46] See Poznanski, Mabhô (1965) CXXX.

Eliezer of Beaugency may be considered the last definite representative of the French school of literal exegesis. His disregard for rabbinic Midrash is unusual, as if he adopted an absolute methodological distinction between the methods of *peshat* and *derash.* His commentaries are based purely on literal interpretation. For this reason he only rarely refers to the difference between the two approaches, as if declaring that his interpretation would have nothing to do with homiletics.

Our knowledge of Eliezer is sparse indeed: we know nothing whatever about his family. A detailed study of his exegetical method was made by Poznanski.[47]

His major sources include the *Book of Josippon*, the liturgical poems of Kallir, Menahem b. Saruq and perhaps also Dunash b. Labrat. He frequently relies on Rashi, though not often mentioning him by name. He also uses the commentaries of Rashbam and Joseph Kara. Some of his comments are identical with those of Abraham ibn Ezra, pointing to some link between the two commentators. Chronologically speaking, Eliezer of Beaugency could have been influenced by Ibn Ezra.

9.1. Eliezer's Exegesis

Eliezer's exegesis is highly independent and original. Although he also relies at times on the work of previous scholars, and refers to "explanations of early scholars" (Ezek 39:13), "first *pôterîm*" (Hos 1:4) and the like, the influence of earlier commentators on his interpretation is less than on his predecessors in the French school of literal exegesis.

The most prominent feature of his commentaries is his technique of interpolating and weaving his own words into those of the text. Rather than explain individual words and phrases, he prefers to create a continuous flow. This quality is particularly obvious in his commentary on the book of Isaiah. There, the reader for a moment thinks he or she is reading the words of the prophet himself, but Eliezer's brief interpolations are highly significant, sometimes altering one's first impression of the text. This exegetical technique had considerable influence on his style. He has neither the brevity of Rashi, the elegance and metaphor of Joseph Kara nor the simplicity of Rashbam. Because of his chosen method – interpolating his explanatory remarks smoothly into the biblical text – he tries to emulate the style of biblical Hebrew, though sometimes he uses the language of the Talmud and the Midrash. He also creates unique linguistic forms, mainly by taking existing verb stems and using them in forms unknown either in the Bible or in the Talmud. Thus, for example, he uses the word *gaôn*, derived from *ge'eh*, 'proud', in the sense of 'proud person' (though this is not the usual meaning of the word in Hebrew). He also uses special and at times artificial expressions as technical terms to explain the language of the Bible and his style of writing.

---

[47] Ibid. CXXV–CLXVI.

Eliezer's commentary is usually brief and concise, though on occasion – for example, in his account of the Temple in the book of Ezekiel – he may write at greater length. His comments are influenced by the context, as he himself notes: "You have no greater rule in the Torah than that the meaning of a passage may be deduced from its context" (Amos 3:12). That is to say, of all factors that help the commentator to explain the text, context is the most important. Accordingly, he uses the expression "the explanation is according to its context" dozens of times, mainly in explaining *hapax legomena*. However, as did Rashi, Eliezer may also admit his inability to explain a passage despite its context.

Like other members of the French school of literal interpretation, R. Eliezer occasionally proposed rules governing one's understanding of the Bible, among other things, rules concerning the properties of the Hebrew language. One example is: "It is the practice of the Bible to liken distress to pregnancy and the act of birth" (Isa 7:14). Elsewhere, he comments that the Bible often likens thought to pregnancy and birth (ibid. 34:11). And there are dozens of other rules.

Grammar receives little attention from this commentator. Like other members of the literal school, he relies on the cantillation signs, but to a lesser degree than the others; on occasion, he suggests explanations that contradict the cantillation signs. On the other hand, he frequently has recourse to the Aramaic targums of the Prophets and the Hagiographa, and he makes copious use of *leʿazim* (foreign words). Many of his *leʿazim* are borrowed from Rashi, but there are numerous ones of his own proposal. Eliezer may have known Latin, though we do not have absolute proof to that effect; on one occasion, he explains a word "in the language of Rome".

Eliezer of Beaugency had a well-developed literary sense and his commentaries also touch on literary questions. For example, he compares Isaiah's reproving prophecy in chap. 1 with Moses' rebuke in Deut 32. It is no accident, he declares that Isaiah calls upon the people to "secure justice for the orphan" and "plead the widow's cause" (v. 17): "For the orphan is not ashamed to plead his cause", but his lack of influence makes it difficult for him to obtain justice; while the widow is ashamed and lacks the self-confidence even to bring her complaint before a court. This is only one of many instances of such sensitivity to variations in wording. Another aspect in which R. Eliezer differs from his colleagues is his attention to the order of the prophecies and the redaction of the biblical books.[48]

Eliezer also shows considerable awareness of historical background. Although one cannot say that he possessed a unique historical view, the mere fact that he considers this aspect is noteworthy. Thus, in the book of Isaiah he identifies various prophecies that speak of Israel's enemies in general as referring to the Assyrians. He explains Isaiah 14 as predicting the return from Babylonian Exile under Cyrus, not the messianic redemption as believed by the

---

[48] For examples see Poznanski, Mabhô (1965) CLI–CLIII, who aptly comments on p. CLI: "Of these matters one finds but little in his successors' writings, but on the other hand they are found in abundance in the work of R. Eliezer".

great majority of medieval Jewish commentators. He also finds allusions to Rome and the Hasmonean period in Isaiah (26) and Zechariah (12).

9.2. Anti-Christian Polemics and the Influence of Rationalism

Like his predecessors in France, R. Eliezer of Beaugency also refers in his commentaries to the debate with Christianity, although only rarely does he explicitly state his opposition to the christological interpretation. Thus, commenting on Isa 9:5, he rejects the christological explanation of the passage, summing up with some vehemence: "But surely there is a lie in their right hand and they have falsified their books ... to apply all the names to the child that will be born". In Ezek 5:4 he explains that the wicked persons to be cast into the fire are "the wicked of Israel ..., such as Jesus and his companions, who misled Israel".

More frequently, R. Eliezer refers obliquely or implicitly to the religious debate, rejecting Christian scholars' use of various biblical verses as proof-texts for their faith.[49] His interpretation of the Vision of Dry Bones in Ezekiel 37 reflects his desire to encourage and comfort his suffering European brethren after the first two crusades:

> This is a great comfort to all those who have died for the unity of [God's] name, even to those who have not been slain, for all their days they have suffered taunts and contempt and are persecuted for not believing in Christianity.

The influence of the twelfth-century renaissance is reflected in R. Eliezer's tendency to explain miracles in natural terms, as did his predecessor Joseph Kara. For example, he argues that the prediction "And the light of the moon shall become like the light of the sun" (Isa 30:26) should be understood only symbolically, as in the phrase "The Jews enjoyed light and gladness" (Esth 8:16). Similarly, he explains that Isaiah's prophecy concerning the creation of "a new heaven and a new earth" (65:17) is not to be taken literally but metaphorically. These are but a few examples.[50]

Eliezer of Beaugency had little influence on his successors. His work is mentioned only rarely by later commentators, even only one generation after him. This scant influence may be associated, most probably, with two factors: (i) the general decline in the standing of the French school of literal exegesis at the close of the twelfth century; (ii) the fact that Eliezer of Beaugency was apparently not a halakhist. Other commentators worked in other areas as well and were generally recognized as gifted scholars; hence their Bible exegesis was more highly valued. French and German Jewry did not treat linguists and literary scholars with the respect they received in Spain.

---

[49] On this issue see Poznanski, Mabhô (1965) CLXII–CLXIII; Grossman, Hakhmê Sarephat (1996) 495–97.

[50] Further examples see Poznanski, Mabhô (1965) CLXIII–CLXIV.

10. Joseph Bekhor Shor (1130–1200)

Joseph ben Isaac was born in Orleans and was also famed for his knowledge of Halakhah and as a Tosafist. The laudatory designation *Bekhor Shor*, 'a firstling bull', is derived from Jacob's blessing of Joseph: "Like a firstling bull in his majesty" (Deut 33:17). Joseph even referred to himself by the title – evidence that it was already accepted during his lifetime. It was in fact applied to other scholars named Joseph.[51]

Joseph Bekhor Shor's most important work was his commentary on the Pentateuch.[52] Brief quotations from a commentary on Psalms have also been preserved. The commentary on the Pentateuch essentially continues the literal method of Bekhor Shor's French predecessors, but he is not a fully typical representative of the school. On the contrary, he may be considered as a last link in a chain of gradual retreat from the extreme literal exegesis represented by Joseph Kara, Rashbam and Eliezer of Beaugency. Although his commentary is concerned mainly with explaining the content of the text, generally in accordance with the literal rather than the homiletical approach, he makes more frequent use of the latter than his predecessors. One of his major contributions to the French school, thanks to which his commentary is still of value today, is his close attention to the supposed motives of various biblical figures. He almost always expands the biblical narrative by examining the characters' possible motives, frequently resorting to psychological arguments. For example, commenting on the fact that Jacob himself immediately proposed that he would work seven years for Rachel's hand, he explains that Jacob, blinded by his great love, was sure that her value was even greater and therefore thought nothing of contracting for seven years. Following the Sages, Bekhor Shor identifies Poti-phera, the father of Joseph's wife Asenath, with Potiphar, Pharaoh's steward, and suggests that Joseph married her out of a natural fear that Pharaoh might depose him, in which case Potiphar / Poti-phera might claim ownership of Joseph as his former, legally purchased slave. Marriage would insure him against such an eventuality. Aaron made the golden calf to keep the people busy; he was afraid that if he refused, the people would appoint a new leader, so that when Moses descended from Mount Sinai a war would ensue between the two leaders. Joseph Bekhor Shor proposes hundreds of similar explanations in his commentaries. Some are quite apt, demonstrating a keen eye for the inner world of the biblical figures; others are more far-fetched.

Another typical feature of R. Joseph's exegesis is his tendency to interpret the biblical text in a realistic light, attempting to understand the real background of the biblical account and explain the causes of events. These causes are usually rationalistic: God instructs Noah to take seven pairs of every clean animal and only two pairs of every unclean one, because the clean animals may

---

[51] For the man and his exegetical writings see Urbach, Baʿalê ha-Tôsaphôt (1980) 1:132–40; Poznanski, Mabhô (1965) LV–LXXIV; G. Walter, *Joseph Bechor Schor, der letzte nordfranzösische Bibelexeget* (Breslau 1890).

[52] Published by Joseph Gad in three volumes: I. Genesis and Exodus (Jerusalem 1957); II. Leviticus and Numbers (London 1960); III. Deuteronomy (Benê Beraq 1959).

be eaten and their number will therefore decrease. Reuben was not with his brothers when they were selling Joseph, it being common practice among shepherds that some eat while the others are tending the sheep. As it was Reuben's turn to be with the sheep when Joseph was sold, he knew nothing of that event. There are many other such explanations. Joseph Bekhor Shor sometimes cites midrashic explanations of the events as well, but rejects them.

Joseph's affinity with the school of literal exegesis is also obvious in his attention to literary matters. He discusses the structure of passages, as well as the relationships between different parts of the texts. Thus, for example, he considers the position of the last two portions of the book of Leviticus (25–26:2; 26:3–27), arguing that they are essentially out of place there, as they were not stated in the Tent of Meeting, like the other parts of Leviticus, but on Mount Sinai. In his opinion, it was the association of these portions with the priests that required their inclusion in the book of Leviticus.

Typically, Joseph Bekhor Shor strives to innovate and suggest original interpretations. Although he frequently has recourse to the commentaries of Rashi, Joseph Kara and Rashbam, whether explicitly or without mentioning names, he no less frequently cites his own explanation. This quest for originality often prompted him to depart from the literal meaning of the text. As a result, as Poznanski remarks, "one finds in his commentary beautiful and wonderfully profound explanations, alongside curious and implausible ones".[53]

Bekhor Shor points out contradictions between different biblical narratives, of the type widely discussed by modern Bible criticism. He resolves such contradictions in a thoroughly original way, remaining faithful to tradition. He never uses the word 'secrets', so common in Ibn Ezra's commentary and hinting at a possibly critical attitude toward traditional explanations. Nevertheless, there is clearly a connection between the two commentators, and for chronological reasons it is obvious that Bekhor Shor was influenced by Ibn Ezra. Possibly, this influence extends to Bekhor Shor's attention to inner contradictions in the Bible, but there is no real proof to that effect. In general, his commentary clearly shows the influence of Spanish-Jewish exegesis. Among other Spanish scholars that he mentions is one "R. Obadiah b. Samuel the Spaniard", who is unknown to us from any other source.

Bekhor Shor endeavored to explain miracles as natural events. Hitherto, scholars have associated this interesting feature with Spanish influence. However, we now know – thanks to the aforementioned archival discoveries in Italy – that Joseph Kara preceded him in this respect, and he may have been the decisive influence on Bekhor Shor. Joseph Bekhor Shor explicitly states his opinion that "God does not change the way of the world". Thus, he explains that Lot's wife became a pillar of salt because, having lagged behind the rest of her family, she shared the fate of the people of Sodom (Gen 19:26). Describing the Tabernacle, Bekhor Shor mentions that the Sages believed that its construction involved miracles, but states that "by the plain meaning of the text" there is no need for such an assumption.

---

[53] Poznanski, Mabhô (1965) LX.

An affinity with rationalism is also obvious in Bekhor Shor's treatment of the reasons for the commandments. He is generally at pains to provide a rational explanation. For example, certain foods, he states, are forbidden because they are injurious to health (Exod 15:26), and he supplies a similar explanation for the laws of impurity and purity. The sacrificial rites also receive a rational explanation: a person, knowing that a serious transgression entails bringing a sacrifice, will take particular care not to repeat it.

We have seen that Joseph Kara also sought rational reasons for the commandments, but Joseph Bekhor Shor outdid him in that respect. The influence of the cultural heritage of Spanish Jewry on Bekhor Shor is also felt in his studious avoidance of anthropomorphism – more than in any other commentator of the French literal school. He repeatedly discusses the subject whenever the text seems to lean in that direction, constantly emphasizing that such turns of speech were adopted "so as to make the text intelligible", or that the Bible "speaks as do men with men". This is a clear indication that there was a certain trend in France or Germany at the time to interpret such personifying passages quite literally, and there is indeed evidence of such a tendency at the end of the twelfth century.

Harshly criticizing the christological interpretation of the Bible for its excessive use of allegory, Joseph Bekhor Shor also attacks Jewish attempts to explain some of the commandments in an allegorical sense: "There are also those of our people whom I have heard expressing doubts about phylacteries and *mezuzzot* and the covering of blood [of slaughtered wild animals] ... Woe to them for the affront to the Torah, for they too will pay the penalty" (Num 12:8). He was probably referring to the appearance of allegorical exegesis toward the end of the twelfth century, in rationalist Spanish-Jewish circles who took up Greek philosophy. It is also not inconceivable that the trend also affected French Jewry, though the sources provide no clear-cut evidence.

Joseph Bekhor Shor clearly differs from Joseph Kara, Rashbam and Eliezer of Beaugency in three main respects: he pays little attention to philological questions, cites rabbinic Midrash relatively frequently and uses the technique of *gematria.*[54] POZNANSKI rightly states that "R. Joseph Bekhor Shor stands on the borderline between the literal commentators of French and the later Tosafists on the Torah".[55] These Tosafists, who began to write commentaries on the Pentateuch at the end of the twelfth century and in particular in the thirteenth century, refer quite often to R. Joseph Bekhor Shor. It was the very fact that he partly disengaged himself from the extreme literal approach of his predecessors that endeared him to the following generations.

In historical perspective, the main value of Bekhor Shor's commentaries lies in his attempts to suggest psychological motives for the actions of biblical figures. In this respect his commentaries are still of value.

---

[54] For examples of his use of *gematria* see Poznanski, Mabhô (1965) LXXIII.

[55] Poznanski, ibidem.

11. The Historical Fate of the School of Literal Exegesis

We have surveyed the work of seven prominent members of the school of literal exegesis that emerged in French Jewry in the eleventh-twelfth centuries. It is evident from the sources that their method influenced many others, both in their approach to Bible study and in the composition of commentaries. Among these scholars one must also count Rashi's grandson Jacob ben Meir, better known as Rabbenu Tam, the greatest of the French Tosafists. Clearly, this was no isolated spiritual trend, confined to a small, scholarly circle, but a movement that, for four or five generations, put down deep roots in the Jewish centre in France.

As we have seen, three main factors influenced the development of the school: (i) the Spanish-Jewish heritage; (ii) the twelfth-century renaissance; and (iii) Jewish-Christian polemics. Of particular interest is the connection between the emergence of the French school of literary exegesis of the Bible and the vigorous development of commentaries on liturgical poetry in the French centre. There was presumably a direct relationship between the two phenomena. In particular, commentators on liturgical poetry automatically interpreted hundreds of biblical expressions and verses.

The considerable attention given to biblical exegesis among the Jews of Northern France should not be considered in isolation from their preoccupation with the exegetical genre as a whole. The French centre applied itself to the interpretation of ancient and sacred texts in general.

The school of literal exegesis did not flourish for long; it disappeared almost as rapidly as it had developed. Its influence outside the borders of medieval France was limited, with the exception of Rashi, who left his imprint even on exegetical literature written in Spain. This limited influence is not surprising. The vigorous exegetical activity of Spanish scholars at the time centred on the philological approach; the needs of Spanish Jews in this area were largely fulfilled by such commentators as Abraham ibn Ezra, the Provençal David Qimhi, and others. Rashi was renowned primarily thanks to his commentary on the Talmud and the support that he provided for the kabbalists and their associates. The kabbalists were then locked in a struggle with the rationalists over the character of Spanish Jewry; preferring traditional methods of exegesis, which revolved around rabbinic Midrash, they found Rashi's approach particularly appropriate.

The influence of the school was not much greater in Germany, where the study of the Prophets and the Hagiographa was less popular. The German pietists known as *Hasidê Ashkenaz*, whose cultural influence pervaded large circles of German-Jewish society at the time, did not consider the work of the French Tosafists worthy of emulation; they do not even refer frequently to Rashi.

It is surprising, however, that even in France the method of literal exegesis experienced a decline at the end of the twelfth century. Independent activity in this field was now concentrated on the Pentateuch and less on interpretation of the books of Prophets and Hagiographa. There were five main symptoms of the decline:

1) Independent exegetical activity was largely replaced by compilatory efforts. Many authors no longer wrote their own works, grappling directly with the biblical text, but preferred to anthologize other people's commentaries.

2) There was a marked decline in linguistic studies of the Bible.

3) Attention again turned to rabbinic Midrash and to homiletical works in general, with less concern for the simple, plain meaning of the text.

4) Interest in numerological techniques (*gematria, nôtarîkôn*) increased.

5) Though some commentators considered the *peshat*, they were more inclined to abstruse, hair-splitting constructions revolving around specific subjects, rather than continuous, systematic commentaries.

Biblical exegesis could now be compared with the usual treatment of talmudic texts, through dialectical discussion – a method that was aptly dubbed '*Tosafot* on the Pentateuch'.[56]

Indubitable evidence that the commentaries of the literal school began to be neglected is the fact that few manuscripts have survived of the work of R. Joseph Kara, Rashbam and other members of the school. Such manuscripts were clearly not in demand. The commentaries were in fact not printed until the Modern Era, almost all of them being overshadowed by Rashi's commentaries.

What were the reasons for this rapid decline? There were apparently two reasons, working together. First, the European 'renaissance' quickly waned and rationalism was abandoned, beginning in the early thirteenth century. Second, the political and social status of the Jews in Europe gradually deteriorated, as evidenced by the anti-Jewish measures of Pope Innocent III at the beginning of the thirteenth century.[57] Interpretation based on *peshat* was well liked by intellectuals but did not endear itself to the masses. It was considered 'dry and lifeless' compared with Rashi's commentaries, which presented many rabbinic *midrashim* in lucid, concise and readily understandable language, much more to the liking of ordinary people.

---

[56] In recent years, Y. Gellis has been collecting and publishing these fragments from printed editions and manuscript. Up to the time of writing, he has published seven volumes (for Genesis and the beginning of Exodus): Y. Gellis, *Sepher Tosaphôt ha-Shalem* (Jerusalem 1982–87).

[57] See, e.g., S. Grayzel, *The Church and the Jews in the XIIIth Century* (rev. ed.; New York 1966).

Chapter Thirty-three

Jewish Exegesis in Spain and Provence, and in the East, in the Twelfth and Thirteenth Centuries

33.1. Isaac ben Samuel Al-Kanzi

By Uriel Simon, Jerusalem

Sources: *Isaac ben Samuel Al-Kanzi's Commentary on the Book of Samuel* (ed. and tr. into Heb. M. Perez; Ramat Gan: Bar-Ilan UP [forthcoming]).

Studies: G. Margoliouth, "Isaac b. Samuel's Commentary on the Book of Samuel", *JQR* OS 10 (1898) 385–403: J. Mann, *Texts and Studies in Jewish History and Literature* 1 (Cincinnati: Hebrew Union College Press 1931) 388–93; U. Simon, "The Contribution of R. Isaac b. Samuel Al-Kanzi to the Spanish School of Biblical Interpretation", *JJS* 34 (1983) 171–78; S. Stauber, "The Commentary on Samuel by R. Isaac ben R. Samuel the Spaniard – Between East and West", in: D. Rappel (ed.), *Studies in Bible and Education Presented to Moshe Arend* (Jerusalem 1996) 159–70 [Heb.].

Rabbi Isaac ben Samuel Al-Kanzi (ca. 1065–1140), talmudic and halakhic scholar, liturgical poet, and biblical commentator, called "the Spaniard" after his (or his father's) birthplace in Andalusia, was a leading religious court judge in Fostat, Egypt. Book lists found in the Cairo Genizah mention his liturgical poems (of which many have survived), his commentary on the talmudic tractate *Ḥullin* (lost), and his commentaries in Arabic on the Former Prophets. Of these last, only a small part survives: part of the commentary on 1 Samuel (MS Firkovitch-St. Petersburg), almost the entire commentary on 2 Samuel (MS British Library), and a substantial number of passages from the commentary on Kings cited in Abraham b. Solomon's *Midrash Al-Ziyani*.

An integral part of the commentary on the Former Prophets is an Arabic rendering of the biblical text. This is not a literary translation intended to be read by itself, but an obviously exegetical version, as indicated by the following three characteristics: each verse is introduced by a Hebrew *incipit*; the Hebrew is rendered word for word, but with the elliptical style filled out explicitly; in doubtful loci, alternative versions are suggested (with no qualms about impeding the flow of the translation).

Al-Kanzi based his commentary on extensive quotations from almost all the exegetical and grammatical authorities in the East and in the West. He quotes by name mainly the Geonim Saadiah (whom he calls "the master of all exegetes") and Samuel b. Hofni, the grammarians Judah Hayyuj (whom he calls "the teacher") and Jonah ibn Janah, the Bible interpreters Moses ibn Chiquitilla and Judah ibn Balʿam, and the lexicographer R. Nathan of Rome. He mentions the great Karaite exegete Japheth ben Ali only once but, as has been demonstrated by TAUBER, he draws from Japheth's (unpublished) commentary on Samuel very heavily: the Arabic translation is practically identical (only the alternative renderings are his own) and forty per cent of the commentary consist of verbatim or paraphrastic quotations from Japheth. Probably the prominent Rabbi could not allow himself to acknowlege openly the extent of his dependence on Karaite scholarship.

In addition, Al-Kanzi incorporated in his commentary a great part of Hayyuj's grammatical glosses on Samuel (otherwise mostly lost) and the entire (extant) commentary on this book by Ibn Balʿam. Usually these passages are cited to provide as a philological basis for his own topical glosses; sometimes, however, he disagrees with his predecessors' interpretations and offers his own instead. He holds steadfastly to the flexible linguistic rules of the Spanish philologists and even expands them. This philological flexibility helps him maintain his threefold loyalty – to the Masoretic text, to accepted beliefs and dogmas, and to the contextual method of exegesis (*peshat*). He makes excessive use of interchanges of letters, deriving the place name Thebez (2 Sam 11:21) from *ʾavaṣ* (= alloy) by means of the reversed substitution alphabet (*atbash*) method (in which alef and tav, bet and shin, etc., interchange); radical lexical substitutions, understanding "all the house of Joseph" (2 Sam 19:20 [MT 19:21]) to mean the house of *Benjamin*; and completion of elliptical phrases – "leaving things unsaid is a very common phenomenon in Hebrew, to the point of [leaving out] three or four words or even more" (comm. on 2 Sam 13:16).

Al-Kanzi relies on letter interchanges as one of the most important ways to bridge between the *ketib* and the *qere*. He frequently suggests that the two alternatives have the same meaning; they are merely phonetic variants, both of which were recorded by the Masoretes as a way of teaching us about the phenomenon of letter interchanges. In his commentary on 2 Sam 12:31, he quotes Hayyuj, who sees the *ketib* – במלכן – as the original text and glosses it as "in the cities of the kingdom". Then Al-Kanzi expresses his own opinion: The *ketib* – במלכן – means "in the brick-making form", just like the *qere* – במלבן – "but the *ketib* teaches us that *kaf* and *bet* may be interchanged". When it is impossible to propose the same meaning for the *ketib* and the *qere*, however, he understands them in different senses and rejects his predecessors' failure to relate to the *ketib*. In his commentary on 1 Sam 18:9, he notes that Hayyuj and Ibn Janah both glossed only the *qere* – עוין – as meaning "looked upon with hostility"; but he also glosses the *ketib* – עון – as a declarative verb meaning "made out to be a sinner", since "it cannot be that the *ketib* is totally devoid of significance". This extreme fidelity to the Masoretes is only relative, though, since he also agrees with Ibn Janah (*Sepher Haššorašim*, s.v. *b.g*) that, in principle, the *qere* reflects the reading of "most of the copyists" and the *ketib* the reading of the minority: "They set down the majority as the *qere* and the minority as the *ketib*" (comm. on 2 Sam 19:41 [AV 19:40]).

His profound talmudic scholarship is reflected in his attitude toward halakhah but not toward aggadah. He endeavors to interpret verses according to the received halakhah: for example, the remarriage of David to Michal after her illegal marriage to Phaltiel son of Laish is explained away by means of the talmudic assertion that Phaltiel never touched her [2 Sam 3:14–16]. Or in his preference of the talmudic rendering of "he [Saul] numbered them בטלאים" (1 Sam 15:4) in the sense of "he enumerated them by means of kids" (derived from *ṭaleh* 'lamb') over Hayyuj's explanation that the enumeration of the troops was in a place called Telaim. Whenever it is not a matter of halakhah, however, he consistently adheres to the contextual method while almost completely ignoring aggadic glosses. In general, he does not conduct a dispute with the aggadists in loci where his interpretation contradicts well-known midrashic readings; nor does he call on them for support when they agree with his understanding. Under this rubric we should note his vigorous rejection of the opinion of "one of the sages" who sought to limit David's culpability in the affair of Bathsheba by asserting that "every soldier who went to war under the House of David wrote out a bill of divorcement for his wife". Al-Kanzi notes that this is a lone opinion (that of R. Jonathan, *b. Shab.* 56 a) and as such is not binding. It should be rejected, in fact, inasmuch as "this is meant to embellish, glorify, and cover up; but God has already disclosed what was hidden by means of His prophet Nathan, and no covering remains!" (comm. on 2 Sam 12:14). The glosses of the Sages are binding on the biblical commentator only when they are either clearly non-homiletical or a reliable "received tradition" – that is, when they are halakhic or historical information (rather than exegetical late opinion), handed down with utter fidelity from generation to generation. In this way, for example, he relies on the "received tradition" in his note on the halakhically problematic verse regarding a non-Aharonic priest, "Also Ira the Jairite was a *kohen* for David" (2 Sam 20:36): "The Sages, their memory for a blessing, passed on the tradition that he was David's teacher, ... and this is [also] what the *targum* [Pseudo-Jonathan] says about him".

Al-Kanzi had before him Saadiah Gaon's long commentary on the Pentateuch, which he seems to have viewed as a model of comprehensive exegesis that deals with the full range of problems – linguistic, thematic, theological, and literary – raised by the narrative text. In his commentary on 2 Sam 21:6, he quotes a long passage from Saadiah's commentary on the weekly portion of *Teṣawweh* (Exod 27:20–30:10) in which Saadiah answers no fewer than nine questions about the Gibeonites. Not only does Al-Kanzi reject a somewhat forced gloss included in this passage, defining it as a homiletic ornament ("what our master Saadiah, his memory for blessing, said about this is by way of reinforcement and embellishment"), he himself is but rarely constrained to offer this kind of far-ranging excursus, typical of geonic exegesis – for example, his survey of the five degrees of proscription that pertain to the Gentiles, compared with the three degrees of punishment that apply to the Israelites (comm. on 1 Sam 15:3).

He often prefaces a short introduction to an episode, to help readers trace the evolution of the plot and attain a deeper understanding of the story. In the body of the commentary he sets himself three objectives: a realistic reconstruction of the historical events, a psychological exposition of the characters' motives, and an ethical-religious appraisal of human deeds and their heavenly deserts. Such a naturalistic view of the exegete's task requires extensive use of auxiliary tools: medieval psychology – for example, he identifies the evil spirit that came over Saul as "melancholia" (excess of black bile), whose symptoms are anxiety, fear, delusions, and evil thoughts, "as happens to one who is ill with epilepsy" (1 Sam 18:10); biblical geography – he was more knowledgeable in this field than were the Spanish commentators because of his residence in Egypt and travels in Palestine and Syria and his reliance on Japheth who wrote in Jerusalem; biblical realia – he tries to find contemporary parallels for biblical musical instruments, articles of dress, foods, and the like, in order to make them more vivid for his readers; and, especially, the art of biblical narrative.

It is his impressive achievements in the systematic clarification of the modes of narrative rhetoric used in the Bible that entitle him to an important place in the history of biblical exegesis, which is his by right until Japheth's share in the development of his literary criteria is explored and defined. When it comes to filling in gaps, he distinguishes between what is explicitly stated, what is reported implicitly, and what is totally omitted, and endeavors to ground his distinctions on general norms derived from a comparison of different biblical stories.

With regard to deviations from strict chronological order, he considers not only why the narrator inverted the order (e.g., because of the narrative technique of interpolating the story of Uriah into the middle of the account of the Ammonite war [comm. on 2 Sam 12:26]), but also precisely where the narrator chose to interrupt the flow of the action and insert a clarifying note (such as the evaluation that "the thing that David had done displeased the Lord" [2 Sam 11:27], which is postponed until after we have been told of David's marriage to Bathsheba), since the unexpected location of the narrator's intrusions is a rhetorical device that requires exegetical attention.

He deals very attentively with the difficult question of the extent to which characters are aware of what is really going on at a given stage in the plot, as against what the reader has already been told by the narrator. Typical of his handling of this subject is his proposal of two alternative motives for Uriah's rejection of David's suggestion that he go home (2 Sam 11:11) – one based on the assumption that Uriah knew what had transpired in his absence, the other on the assumption that he did not. Al-Kanzi decides in favor of the second alternative, reasoning that if Uriah did not open the letter that ordered his death he must not have had any inkling that his life was in danger from the king.

Al-Kanzi's great skill in vivifying the situations described and in identifying with the main characters (for example, the complex description of the relations between Saul and Jonathan in his commentary on 1 Sam 20:30–34) is accompanied by a keen religious and ethical sensitivity and discretion in evaluating the culpability of the protagonists. In order to establish reliable standards he compares analogous situations in widely separated stories: for example, the narrator's silence about Bathsheba's conduct during and after the fateful events, versus Tamar's resistance of Amnon's advances and her public outcry afterwards; or David's public mourning for Amnon versus his private mourning for Absalom.

Nevertheless, some of his literary assumptions suffer from exaggerated rationalism: the idea that there is perfect correspondence, down to most minute details, between a parable and what it refers to, leads him to miss completely the element of disguise in the parable of the poor man's ewe-lamb; the idea that there is an unambiguous link between a metaphor and its tenor engenders his pedantic deciphering of the ideas behind the ten metaphors in the beginning of David's song (2 Sam 22:2–3), which he cites from Saadiah Gaon.

Al-Kanzi's literary analysis is guided and limited by his theological views. The distinction, ascribed to "one of the exegetes", between a prophet-messenger (who cannot possibly commit a grave transgression) and other prophets (who did sin) allows him to boldly accept David's sins exactly as reported, limited only slightly by a pious inclination to minimize the guilt of God's anointed to the extent possible. On the other hand, his absolute confidence that hereditary punishment is utterly unjust (as a matter of Divine justice it is quite inconceivable that the sons of David die on account of their fathers' transgression) forces him to make a significant exegetical effort so that the story, in all its details, can be reconciled with the general moral principle. Despite a number of forced glosses, on the whole his literary analyses benefit from this approach. The commentator's sensitivity to the protagonists' motives is sharpened by his recognition that external theological rationale of the heroes' actions are not enough; one must uncover the internal literary reasons latent in the story.

Al-Kanzi does not draw attention to himself and his original contributions. Perhaps he did not think of himself as an innovator or preferred not to be thought of as such. He does note that his gloss of להקת 'company' (1 Sam 19:20) as a metathesis of קהלת 'congregation' is original with him. On the other hand, he concludes his remarks on David's transgression with the astonishing assertion that this is the opinion of "the majority of the best commentators in their interpretation of this episode" (comm. on 2 Sam 12:14). His steadfast adherence to traditional beliefs is clearly reflected in his inclusion of Agur son of Jakeh (Prov 30:1) and Lemuel (Prov 31:1) in his survey of the five names of Solomon (comm. on 2 Sam 12:24), ignoring Saadiah's suggestion that these are the names of other authors whose sayings were appended to the Book of Proverbs. It comes across even more strongly in his fierce rejection of the rationalistic gloss of R. Samuel ben Hofni, who presents the witch of En-dor (1 Sam 28) as a con artist to whom no supernatural powers should be attributed (he buttressed his case by incorporating into his commentary Moses ben Joseph Kaskil's lengthy polemic against Samuel ben Hofni's view).

Isaac b. Samuel Al-Kanzi is not mentioned by Abraham Ibn Ezra, apparently because his commentaries had not yet reached Spain when Ibn Ezra left that country. Since there is no sign of any influence of Al-Kanzi's contribution to biblical exegesis in the works of Ibn Ezra, the latter's synthesis of the great achievements of the Spanish school lacks an important dimension – the mature literary interpretation developed in Egypt by Al-Kanzi.

33.2. Abraham Ibn Ezra

By Uriel Simon, Jerusalem

Sources: (A) Ibn Ezra's commentaries (in biblical order): *Miqrāʾôt Gedôlôt Meḥōqeqē Yehūdā* 1–5 (commentary on the Pentateuch with a supercommentary by J. L. Krinsky; Piotrkow / Vilna: Zederboim 1907–28); The Second Recension on Genesis (fragment) in: M. Friedlaender, *Essays on the Writings of Abraham Ibn Ezra*, Hebrew section, 1–68 (London: K. J. Truebner 1877); *Ibn Ezra's Commentary on the Pentateuch: Genesis* (transl. into English and ann. by H. N. Strickman / A. M. Silver; New York: Menorah 1988); *The Short Commentary on Exodus* (edition and supercommentary by J. L. Fleischer; Vienna: Menorah 1926); *The Commentary of Abraham Ibn Ezra on the Pentateuch: Leviticus* (transl. into English and ann. by J. F. Shachter; Hoboken, NJ: Ktav 1986); *The Commentary of Ibn Ezra on Isaiah* (ed., transl. into English and ann. by M. Friedlaender; London: Society of Hebrew Literature 1873–77); *Abraham Ibn Ezra's Two Commentaries on the Minor Prophets, An Annotated Critical Edition. 1. Hosea-Joel-Amos* (ed. U. Simon; Ramat Gan: Bar-Ilan UP 1989); *The Commentary of Rabbi Abraham Ibn Ezra on Hosea* (ed. and transl. into English by A. Lipschitz; New York: Sepher-Hermon 1988); the standard commentaries on Psalms, Job, the Five Scrolls, and Daniel are included in various editions of the Rabbinic Bible; "Ibn Ezra's Introduction and Commentary on Psalms 1–2: The First Recension" (fragment, ed. and transl. into English in: U. Simon, *Four Approaches to the Book of Psalms* [see below] 308–30); *Abraham Ibn Ezra's Commentary on Canticles (First Recension)* (ed. H. J. Mathews; Oxford: Clarendon Press 1874); *Abraham Ibn Ezra's Commentary on the Book of Esther (Second Recension)* (ed. J. Zedner; London: David Nutt 1850); *Abraham Ibn Ezra's Short Commentary on Daniel* ([1] ed. H. J. Mathews, in: *Miscellany of Hebrew Literature* 2 (1877) 257–76; [2] ed. and ann. by Aharon Mondshine; M. A. thesis, Bar-Ilan University; Ramat Gan 1977). – (B) Ibn Ezra's other writings: *Kitbē R. Abraham Ibn Ezra* 1–5, reprints of his main grammatical, mathematical, and theological writings (Jerusalem: Makor 1970–72); Abraham ibn Ezra, *Yesod Morah – An Annotated Critical Edition* (eds. J. Cohen / U. Simon; Ramat Gan: Bar Ilan UP 2000) [Heb.]. – (C) Writings of his predecessors mentioned in this article: Saadiah Gaon, *The Book of Beliefs and Opinions* (transl. by S. Rosenblatt; New Haven: Yale UP 1948); *Saadya's Commentary on Genesis* (ed. and transl. into Hebrew by M. Zucker; New York: The Jewish Theological Seminary of America 1984). – Jonah ibn Janah, *Sepher Haššorašim* (i. e. Biblical Lexicon; transl. into Hebrew by Judah Ibn Tibbon; ed. W. Bacher; Berlin: T. H. Ittskovski 1896). – Judah Halevi: *Judah Halevi's Kitab al Khazari* (transl. into English by H. Hirschfeld; new revised edition; London: M. L. Cailingold 1931).

Studies (in chronological order): W. Bacher, *Abraham Ibn Esra's Einleitung zu seinem Pentateuch-Commentar* (Vienna: Karl Gerold's Sohn 1876); M. Friedlaender, *Essays on the Writings of Abraham Ibn Ezra* (London: K. J. Truebner, 1877); M. Steinschneider, "Abraham Ibn Esra", *Supplement zur Zeitschrift für Mathematik und Physik* 25 (1880) 59–128; W. Bacher, *Abraham Ibn Esra als Grammatiker* (Strassburg: K. J. Truebner 1882); D. Rosin, *Die Religionsphilosophie Abraham Ibn Esra's* (printed in installments in:) *MGWJ* 42 (1898) and 43 (1899); J. L. Fleischer, "Rabbi Abraham Ibn Ezra and his Literary Work in England", *Ozar Ha-Chaim* 7 (1931) 69–76, 107–11, 129–33, 160–68, 189–203 [Heb.]; I. M. Millas, "The Work of Abraham Ibn Ezra in Astronomy", *Tarbiz* 9 (1938) 303–22 [Heb.]; P. R. Weiss, "Ibn Ezra and the Karaites on Halacha", *Melilah* 1 (1944) 35–53, 2 (1945) 121–34, 3–4 (1946) 188–203 [Heb.]; L. Prijs, *Die grammatikalische Terminologie des Abraham Ibn Esra* (Basel: Sefer Verlag 1950); J. Reifmann, *Studies in Ibn Ezra's Lore* (coll. and ed. by N. Ben Menachem; Jerusalem: Mossad Harav Kook 1962) [Heb.]; U. Simon, "Ibn Ezra and Kimhi: Two Approaches to the Masoretic Text", *Bar-Ilan Annual* 6 (1968) 191–237 [Heb.]; I. Levin, *Abraham Ibn Ezra: His Life and his Poetry* (Tel Aviv: Ha-Kibbuz Ha-Meuchad 1969) [Heb.]; J. L. Fleischer et al., *R. Abraham Ibn Ezra: Studies in his Life and his Work* (Tel Aviv: Zion 1970) [Heb.]; H. Grieve, *Studien zum jüdischen Neoplatonismus: Die Religionsphilosophie des Abraham Ibn Ezra* (Berlin / New York: Walter de Gruyter 1973); N. Ben Menachem, *Ibn Ezra Studies* (Jerusalem: Mossad Harav Kook 1978) [Hebr.]; A. Lipshitz, *Ibn Ezra Studies* (Jerusalem: Mossad Harav Kook 1982) [Heb.]; Joseph Cohen, *The Philosophical Teaching of Rabbi Abraham Ibn Ezra* (Rishon le-Zion: Shai Publishing House 1996) [Heb.]; U. Simon, "Ibn Ezra between

Medievalism and Modernism: The Case of Isaiah XL–LXVI", VTSup 36 (1985) 257–71; idem, "R. Abraham Ibn Ezra: The Exegete and his Readers", *Proceedings of the Ninth World Congress of Jewish Studies* (Jerusalem: Magnes Press 1988) 23–42 [Heb.]; F. Diaz Esteban (ed.), *Abraham Ibn Ezra and his Age* (Madrid: Asociación Española de Orientalistas 1990); I. Levin (ed.), *Studies in the Works of Abraham Ibn Ezra* (Tel Aviv: Tel Aviv UP 1992) [Heb.]; U. Simon, *Four Approaches to The Book of Psalms: From Saadyah Gaon to Abraham Ibn Ezra* (trans. Lenn J. Schramm; Albany NY: State University of New York Press 1991); I. Twersky / J. M. Harris (eds.), *Rabbi Abraham Ibn Ezra: Studies in the Writings of a Twelfth-Century Jewish Polymath* (Cambridge, MA: Harvard UP 1993); U. Simon, "Who Was the Proponent of Lexical Substitution Whom Ibn Ezra Denounced as a Prater and Madman?" *The Frank Talmage Memorial Volume 1* (ed. B. Walfish; Haifa: Haifa UP 1993) 217–32; idem, "Yizhaki: A Spanish Biblical Commentator Whose 'Book Should be Burned', according to A. Ibn Ezra", *Nahum Sarna Festschrift* (eds. M. Brittler / M. Fishbane; JSOTSup 154, 1993) 300–17; S. Sela, *Astrology and Biblical Exegesis in Abraham Ibn Ezra's Thought* (Ramat Gan: Bar Ilan UP 1999) [Heb.].

Abraham ben Meir ibn Ezra, who was born in Tudela (Navarre) in 1089 and died (apparently in London) in 1164, was a prolific polymath: liturgical and secular poet, philologist and translator, mathematician and philosopher, astronomer and astrologer, and, above all else, a biblical commentator (although, *pace* his popular image, he was neither a talmudic scholar nor a physician).

In 1140, when he was around 50, he was forced to leave Muslim Spain and moved to Italy; for the rest of his life he wandered among the non-Arabophone Jewish communities of Italy, Provence, Northern France, and England. As a consequence of this severance from his original readers he stopped writing in Arabic, and all of his surviving works are in Hebrew. He probably did not write commentaries on every book of the Bible; the earliest (fourteenth century) supercommentators already attest that they did not have commentaries by Ibn Ezra on the Former Prophets, Jeremiah, Ezekiel, Proverbs (the commentary printed as his in Rabbinic Bibles is actually by Moses Kimchi), Ezra and Nehemiah (idem), and Chronicles. On the other hand, two commentaries (complete or fragmentary) survive on seven biblical books – Genesis, Exodus, the Minor Prophets, Psalms, Song of Songs, Esther, and Daniel.

Ibn Ezra summarized his exegetical method, with his characteristic brevity, in the rhymed introduction to his standard commentary on the Pentateuch: "This is *Sēpher hayyāšār*/ by Abraham the poet; / it is bound by cords of grammar/ and approved by the eye of reason; / happy are those who adhere to it". For Ibn Ezra, the word *yāšār* (straight), included in his title, was a synonym for *peshāt* (comm. on Num 22:28). He describes this method as satisfying the dual test of meticulous philology ("the cords of grammar") and strict rational plausibility ("eye of reason"); only this exegetical method can yield the spiritual joy that comes from study of the Torah.

A significant portion of Ibn Ezra's commentary is devoted to precise and multifaceted linguistic clarifications, based on a critical adoption of the major achievements of the Spanish school of Hebrew philology. Particularly conspicuous is his tendency to apply the rules developed by his predecessors with extreme caution and stringency and to limit to a bare minimum the prevalent recourse to exceptions and radical hypotheses (whenever he can do without them he employs the expression: "there is no need"). For example, he rejects out of hand Ibn Janah's system of lexical substitution (that is, the legitimate interchange of similar words), reduces to the minimum his method of consonantal substitution, and even expresses reservations about the prevalent assumption about antonymic homonyms (that is, the possibility that the same word may express two contradictory meanings).

Ibn Ezra demands that the exegetical enterprise be based on rational judgment, on the one hand, and on mastery of all branches of knowledge, on the other: "Reason is the foundation, since the Torah was not given to those who have no knowledge, and the angel [i.e., mediator] between man and God is his intelligence" (introduction to the standard commentary on the Pentateuch, the "Third Way"). He sought rationality not only in the rational commandments but even in the revelational commandments: "Heaven forbid that a single precept might contradict reason" (long comm. on Exod 20:1). Hence the "erudites" are able to explain why eating fruits of the first three years and the flesh of unclean animals is harmful to body and soul (comm. on Lev 19:22). The narrative parts of the Pentateuch, too, must be interpreted in accordance with natural and psychological verisimilitude (comm. on Gen 11:3; Exod 20:1), except for miracles, which are utterly reasonable for one who believes in God's dominion over nature and is confident in the true testimony of Scripture. Miracles do contravene the laws of nature, but they do not contradict either reason (since God is omnipotent) or observation (by the witnesses) (*Sēpher haʿibbūr* 10 a). Accordingly, Ibn Ezra forcefully rejects the tendency to multiply miracles beyond those explicitly recounted in the Bible (long comm. on Dan 1:15), but rejects all doubts about the Noah pericope as the result of idle questions (comm. on Gen 6:20).

The demand for plausibility extends to stylistic plausibility as well, by virtue of the rationalist assumption that Scripture is written in a language similar to "human language"; that is, that it is phrased in language to which the standard rules of syntax and rhetoric apply. The conventional gloss on "I am Esau your firstborn" (which goes back to a midrash and was adopted by Rashi as a way to clear Jacob of lying) – "I am who I am, and Esau is your first-born" – is rejected as "empty words" (comm. on Gen 27:19), since the discrepancy between the text and the interpretative paraphrase is too great to conform to normal rhetoric and syntax. In a similar vein, he refuses to accept a well-known midrash as the true meaning of a verse, "because it is not possible that a *person* would say 'give Reuben's inheritance to Simeon' when he means just the opposite, namely, to give Simeon's inheritance to Reuben" (short comm. on Exod 21:8).

Ibn Ezra vigorously opposes ascribing significance to plene versus defective spelling. He grounds this opposition not only on the absence of any consistent usage in this matter in the various layers of the Bible, from the Pentateuch through Proverbs (introduction to the standard commentary on the Pentateuch, the "Fifth Way"), but also on the empirical fact that in day-to-day life plene and defective spelling have no independent significance (long comm. on Exod 20:1). Because the Bible does not employ supernatural language and its own unique rhetoric ("Heaven forbid that the prophet should express himself in numerology or obscure hints" [short comm. on Exod 1:7]), and because human beings cannot transcend human concepts, it is only natural that the biblical style incorporate many anthropomorphisms: human language necessarily uses metaphors drawn from the human realm to refer to the Divinity that is above man and to nature that is below him (long comm. on Exod 19:20; long comm. on Dan 10:21).

Ibn Ezra's quest for the philological-contextual interpretation, controlled by reason and science, is accompanied by a strong methodological awareness. Relying on the fundamental principle, "let us pursue the text" (long comm. on Exod 9:10), Ibn Ezra rejects midrashic expansions that are not anchored in the biblical text (short comm. on Exod 16:4; long comm. on Exod 7:24). He also feels a duty to vary his terminology to denote the degree of certainty he accords to his proposed interpretations: "but the correct [interpretation] is", "with clear proofs", "perhaps", "in my opinion", "a sort of proof", "this is only a conjecture". Similarly, he frequently offers alternative interpretations when he cannot make an unequivocal decision as to which is better; nor is he afraid to acknowledge his inability to understand some verses – an inability that stems, in part, from our limited knowledge of biblical history (Gen 49:19; Zech 12:11), and our remoteness from the biblical world (Gen 2:11, long comm. on Exod 30:23). Even though he rejects the exegetical validity of most Midrashim (as explained in his two introductions to the Pentateuch, the "Fourth Way"), sometimes he himself finds in the text an additional dimension (literary or conceptual) that he cannot adequately prove from the context; he characterizes this as "a sort of support" (short comm. on Exod 21:1) or as "a sort of homily" (comm. on Deut 16:18).

Ibn Ezra's exegetical method is marked by the fertile tension between belief in the sanctity and truth of the Bible and extreme exegetical freedom. He acknowledges the limited and partial nature of human comprehension and the limits of science (short comm. on Exod 23:20; Isa 40:28) but not the relativity of rational judgment. Hence, when the truth of the Bible contradicts the truth of human reason, the solution must be exegetical. His steadfast adherence to the rationalist assumption that a verse cannot be at variance with knowledge gained from sensory perception or from logical reasoning, just as it cannot contradict another verse, entitles (and obliges) the commentator to make difficult verses correspond to the demands of reason (in this he follows Saadiah Gaon; see *Beliefs and Opinions* 7.1–3). This radical exegetical intervention, which detaches the verse from its primary meaning – by means of metaphorization, allegorization, and other methods of extension – is what Koranic exegesis calls *tawil* and Ibn Ezra calls *tiqqūn* ('correction' or 'adaptation': introduction to the long comm. on Genesis, the "Fourth Way"; long comm. on Exod 6:3). One of its most extreme manifestations is the case of Hosea's marriage, which he insists is a prophetic vision rather than a biographical fact (comm. on Hos 1:1). In view of the risks of arbitrary interpretations, however, and to ward off the danger – whose chief embodiment he saw in Christian exegesis – that *tiqqūn* might be applied to undercut the stories of the Patriarchs, the practical commandments, and messianic promises, he sets (again in the wake of Saadiah) a stringent limit for the commentator: plausible verses must are not to be "corrected". The procedure is permissible only when it is absolutely necessary. At most, one may discover in particularly charged verses a second stratum that supplements rather than replaces the first meaning (introduction to the Pentateuch, the "Third Way"; the allegorical interpretation of the story of the Garden of Eden in the commentary on Gen 3:32).

Another limitation on the exegete's freedom – meant to serve as a shield against the perils of Karaite anarchism – is the belief in the binding validity of talmudic tradition, whose status as revealed Oral Law parallels that of the Written Law. Belief in the truth of the received tradition (*qabbālâ*) – by which he means a reliable tradition that is chiefly halakhic and only secondarily historical and exegetical – and in its harmony with the philological-contextual meaning of the verses was deemed utterly logical: the conspicuous absence of full and comprehensive information about most of the commandments and the disproportion between what is stated explicitly in the Torah and what is only alluded to clearly attest that the Written Law was not meant to stand alone; from the outset it was intended to be rounded out by the Oral Law. Consequently, talmudic halakhah may not be ignored unless it could be divested of its status as "received tradition" because it is a disputed or lone opinion. In Ibn Ezra's opinion, though, the homiletic expositions of the Sages do not belong to the category of the "received tradition", since they are merely the fruit of their efforts to find prooftexts in Scripture to support the received halakhah or provide an underpinning for their own intellectual and spiritual creativity (short comm. on Exod 21:8; *Sāfâ Berūrâ* 5 a–7 a). Thanks to this sharp distinction – between the actual halakhot (which can be traced back to Divine revelation) transmitted by the Sages, on the one hand, and their own expositions, on the other – Ibn Ezra does not have to deal with most Midrashim as binding interpretations ("one who has a heart [i. e., reason] can recognize when they say *derash* and when *peshat*" [*Yesod Môra*ʾ, ch. 6]). This exegetical freedom entails a countervailing exegetical restriction, since his confidence in the perfect correlation between the received tradition and the philological meaning of the text keeps Ibn Ezra from recognizing the legitimacy of any *peshat* interpretation that contradicts halakhah (advanced with no qualms by Rashi, Rashbam, and Nahmanides). Wherever he senses a tension between the accepted halakhah and the text, his intellectual honesty forces him to acknowledge the fact; but his faith requires him to demonstrate that the gap can be closed by means of an alternative philological meaning (long and short commentaries on Exod 13:9 and Lev 21:2).

Just as the talmudic tradition elucidates and complements the Written Law but is not derived from it ("the words of the received tradition are strong and require no reinforcement" [end of the long comm. on Exod 13:9]), so too Scripture should be understood in the light of the sciences and general knowledge; but they need not be based on it ("Here we have evidence that the world is circular rather than square, although there is no need for a verse, since this is known through manifest proofs" [comm. on Isa 40:22]). This recognition that what is known through tradition and what is known through the intellect have separate origins and are independently valid can already be found in Saadiah Gaon (in the introductions to *Beliefs and Opinions* and to his long commentary on the Pentateuch). Ibn Ezra, however, derives from it the far-reaching conclusion that exegetes should reduce to the absolute minimum the projection onto Scripture of both halakhah and science (typical of geonic exegesis). The Torah was given to all Israel, "to be understood by the learned and the unlearned" (long comm. on Exod 20:1); consequently it contains very few allusions to philosophy and the sciences, which must be learned in a fundamental and systematic manner (the two introductions to the Pentateuch, the "First Way"). Because any commentary must be compatible with the nature and goal of the book being glossed, it should include only brief scientific introductions that summarize the knowledge essential for understanding the text ("thus I shall write at length / for I require a firm foundation" [short and long commentaries on Exod 3:15]) or allusions intended for the learned only (long and short commentaries on Exod 25:40; comm. on Job 1:6).

Ibn Ezra fiercely rejects even cautious attempts at conjectural emendation of the text: "there is no need for the words of this prater" [*Ṣāḥōt* 31 a]). In this he shares the fundamental rejection of textual criticism by Ibn Janah (*Sēpher haš-šorašim*, s.v. *ʾ.š.d)* and Judah Halevi (*Kuzari* 3.25–29). He holds that the work of the Masoretes was flawless: "Due to them the Divine Torah and Sacred Books stood in their perfection, without additions or omissions" (*Yesōd Môrāʾ*, ch. 1; compare *Moznayyim* 1 a). Accordingly, he insists that any interpretation respect the punctuational functions of the cantillation signs and the division into verses (and departs from this principle only very rarely); rejects as a "lone view" the tannaitic tradition of the "eighteen emendations of the Scribes"; and deals with differences between *qere* and *ketib*, alternate versions of parallel texts (such as the two versions of the Ten Commandments and of several Psalms), and the discrepancies between Pseudo-Jonathan and the Masoretic text as exegetical problems rather than textual phenomena. Consequently he must rely on various harmonizing solutions put forward by his predecessors: ascribing two names to the same person (*Ṣāḥōt* 71 a; long comm. on Dan 1:1) or the same place (Deut 10:6–7); asserting the thematic and material identity of variant texts (Lev 13:2); and adopting somewhat forced assumptions, such as that 2 Sam 21:8 calls the sons of Merab the "sons of Michal" because they were raised by the latter (Gen 36:2).

His rejection of lower criticism seems to have provided a counterweight for his penchant for higher criticism; in other words, his utter confidence in the accuracy of the text and the reliability of the method provides him with a basis for his extreme exegetical independence and critical approach when it comes to the question of the authorship of the biblical books. He is greatly perturbed by anachronisms; only with great reluctance would he concede that, "through prophecy", people and places might be designated by their later names (comm. on Gen 5:29; Deut 11:30 and 22:8). On the other hand, it is clear to him that elucidating comments – like "the Canaanite was then in the land" (Gen 12:6), "as it is said to this day, in the mount of the Lord it shall be seen" (Gen 22:14), "his bedstead, an iron bedstead, is now in Rabbath of the children of Ammon" (Deut 3:11) – are later additions, just like the last twelve verses of Deuteronomy, which were written by Joshua prophetically (comm. on Deut 1:2, 34:1 and 6). The suggestion by the author of *Sēpher hayyiṣḥāqi* (a Spanish commentator of whom all traces have been lost except for eight glosses cited by Ibn Ezra) that Gen 36:31–36 was written during the reign of King Jehoshaphat of Judah he rejects caustically because of its methodological implausibility – "rightly is his name called Isaac (*Yiṣḥāq*), for all who hear will laugh (*Yiṣḥāq*) at him. ... His book should be burned!" (He attacks Ibn Janah's method of lexical substitution in similar terms, but without mentioning the great grammarian by name [short comm. on Exod 21:8; *Ṣāḥōt* 72 a].) On the other hand, he is much more gentle in his rejection of a similar proposal regarding Num 21:1–3 – "many have said that this section was written by Joshua" – because here the implausibility is only thematic. It should be emphasized that Ibn Ezra's criteria for determining the date of composition of a text are exegetical and literary, not rhetorical and historical. The question that bothers him is, whether it is plausible that Moses and Isaiah wrote such things, and not (as scholars ask today) whether such passages had meaning for their own contemporaries. He cites the specific remark regarding the distant future, "Josiah by name" (1 Kgs 13:2), as an example of a crystal-clear prophecy (introduction to Zechariah). With regard to Daniel's prophecy of the end of days, by contrast, he stresses that the prophet himself did not understand the arcane mysteries spoken to him; but "when the end arrives the learned will understand them" (long comm. on Dan 12:8–9). In fact, it is not rhetorical considerations – the fact that there was no sense or meaning for messages of redemption, return, and the rebuilding of Jerusalem in the days of Hezekiah, or for the proclamation of Cyrus the Mede as the Lord's anointed at a time when the Assyrian Empire still reigned supreme – that lead Ibn Ezra to post-date the prophecies in the second part of the book of Isaiah (carefully veiled hints in his commentary on Isa 40:1). His reasons are distinctly exegetical: the fact that the prophet is described as being present in the Babylonian exile when his consolations are realized (comm. on Isa 49:7); the Babylonian milieu of the present-tense description of the imminent redemption (Isa 55:6); and the exegetical advantage of reading the "servant of the Lord" prophecies as referring to the prophet himself (ibid. 53:12).

On the question of the authorship of the Psalms, discussed in the introductions to his two commentaries on that book, Ibn Ezra adopts the Sages' view that the Psalms were written by divinely inspired prophet-poets, some of whom are identified in the superscriptions. He does not present this view of the "ancients" as binding but as plausible, just as his reservations about the approach of Moses ibn Chiquitilla, who post-dates some Psalms to the Babylonian Exile, relate strictly to the merits of the case without referring to any doctrinal restrictions. In his view, the prayer-psalms of Jonah (2:2–10) and Habakkuk (3:1–19) attest that a prophet's prayer is like a prophecy: it is not necessarily anchored in the circumstances of the prophet's life and may relate to the future ("this psalm expounds the future reward of the righteous" [73:1]) and even be placed in the mouth of the later generation ("this Psalm was written in the voice of the Levite musicians in their exile about Babylonia" [137:1]).

As for the Book of Job, he disputes two talmudic opinions: one that Job is a fictional character, the other that Moses wrote the book. According to Ibn Ezra, Job and his friends were historical figures: Gentile prophets (except, perhaps, for Elihu) who lived before the time of Moses (comm. on Job 1:1) and whose language was not Hebrew, since the difficult language of the book indicates that it is a translation (Job 2:11). Ibn Ezra even distinguishes the speeches of Job and his friends from the narrative frame and the superscriptions of the speeches, which he ascribes to an editor (*Sēpher Haššem*, ch. 8).

Ibn Ezra repeatedly stresses the paucity of our knowledge about the historical and biographical backgrounds of the prophetic books and rejects the use of Midrashim to fill in the gaps; as long as they are not reliable traditions they are not to be drawn on as if they were historical evidence. For example, in the introduction to Joel he writes: "We have no way to know when he lived; on the basis of the *peshat* meaning he is not the son of Samuel" (as a Midrash would have it). He also expresses doubts about the Sages' opinion that Jeremiah was the author of Lamentations (comm. on Lam 3:1) and rejects the midrashic identification of Lamentations with the scroll burned by Jehoiakim (introduction to Lamentations). On the other hand, he is quite certain that Solomon wrote the Song of Songs and Ecclesiastes, since this is explicitly stated in the text. As for the nature of the Song of Songs, he takes a clear traditional stance: it is not to be understood, in keeping with the surface meaning, as an erotic poem (for, he maintains, there was no disagreement among the Sages as to its sanctity); what is more, the application of the allegory to the Jewish people is a binding tradition. Since in 1 Kings we read that the Lord appeared to Solomon twice (3:5–14 and 9:2–9), it should not astonish us that in this book, written through the Holy Spirit, he prophetically sketches out the future of the Jewish people in the time of the First and Second Temples and thereafter until the coming of the Messiah (introductions to his two commentaries on the Song of Songs).

On the awkward issue of the sins of prophets, Ibn Ezra also follows his own way. Rejecting the systematic attempt by Saadiah Gaon, Samuel ben Hofni, the Karaite scholar Japheth ben Ali, and Judah ibn Balʿam to acquit the prophets of all transgressions, especially that of deceit (because it would undermine their credibility as messengers of the Lord), he introduces a principle aimed at reducing to the absolute minimum the doctrinal postulates underlying the discussion. Without mentioning those who adopted his approach before him (such as Isaac ben Samuel Al-Kanzi, who bases himself on "one of the commentators"), he distinguishes between an "emissary of commandments", whom he agrees cannot lie, because the truth of the Torah depends on his absolute trustworthiness, and "prophets of predictions", who might be led by circumstances to deviate from the truth, without this undermining the validity of their prophecy (comm. on Gen 27:19). The first type includes only Moses and Aaron (long comm. on Exod 12:1). He has no doubts that they are innocent of the allegations of deception made in connection with the despoiling of the Egyptians (short comm. on Exod 11:4); moreover, he endeavors to show that even their other transgressions, from Moses' failure to circumcise his son through Aaron's role in the affair of the Golden Calf, were really negligible. When it comes to other prophets, however, he considers himself free to evaluate each individual case on its own merits. In these remarks we can discern his efforts to find, within the confines of the *peshat*, an answer to the contentions of those commentators who attempted to make light of the prophets' transgressions. For example, he rejects the whitewashing of Jacob's deceit (Gen 27:19) and demurs at the attempt to give a favorable sense to Jacob's harsh words about Simeon and Levi by means of a philological interpretation that is not one at all (comm. on Gen 49:6). In a heavily veiled hint (which has fooled even some of his own supercommentators) he acknowledges Reuben's sin with Bilhah (comm. on Gen 35:22). But he clears Abraham of all culpability in connection with the expulsion of Hagar and Ishmael – "the astonishment should be directed at those who are astonished, for Abraham did exactly as the Lord commanded him" (Gen 21:14) – and minimizes Solomon's transgressions – "everything that was said about him in the words of Ahijah (1 Kgs 11:31–33) and Nehemiah (Neh 13:26) was on account of one sin, namely, that he did not keep track of what his wives were doing and they used Solomon's wealth to build high places to their gods" (comm. on Qoh 10:1). Finally, his unexpected adoption as historical fact of the Midrash that defends David's conduct with Bathsheba – "she was not really a married woman" (comm. on Pss 51:2 and 32:1) – attests to the great theological and ethical difficulty in which Ibn Ezra found himself because of the gravity of the sin of adultery.

In Ibn Ezra's commentaries on the poetic chapters of the Bible, the literary and aesthetic dimension is not developed to the extent that might be expected from so great a poet. The custom of the liturgical and secular poets of Spain to indicate the melody to accompany a poem by citing, at its beginning, the opening words of another poem sung to that tune provides the basis for his brilliant conjecture that this is the significance of such opaque superscriptions as על יונת אלם רחקים (comm. on Ps 56:1) or אל תשחת (comm. on Ps 57:1). He does not interpret them as part of the psalms, since their (forgotten) musical significance was their only meaning in these places (see comm. on Ps 7:1 [MT]). Occasionally he comments on poetic ornaments such as *inclusio* ("he ended as he began", comm. on Ps 103:22), antithesis ("saying 'draw nigh' and 'are far' is an elegant manner in poetry" [comm. on Ps 119:150]), paronomasia (comm. on Zeph 2:4; Ps 56:9 [AV 56:8]), palillogy (comm. on Pss 1:1–2; 118:5), and of course parallelism (comm. on Deut 32:2; Ps 29:1–2). In prose he notes that chiasmus is in accordance with "the custom of the holy tongue" (long comm. on Exod 17:7 and 25:22) and that the use of homonyms adds "elegance" (comm. on Gen 3:1; long comm. on Exod 22:5). Not only was he anticipated in almost all of these by Moses Ibn Ezra in his *Book of Studies and Discussions*; these occasional remarks on style are almost always inserted to explain a deviation from the expected mode of expository writing ("do not be astonished that ...") rather than to elucidate the expressive purpose of the stylistic phenomenon. By contrast, remarks that fundamentally deal with the content play a clear exegetical role: on the unity of the subject of a psalm – "most of the commentators understood it as referring to the giving of the Torah ... but they were unable to make the sense cohere" (comm. on Ps 68:2 [AV 68:1] and 104:19); on the thematic continuity of a prophecy – "it is all a single pericope" (comm. on Isa 32:20; see also on Isa 43:8; Hos 2:1 and 14:10); on the antithetical links among the individual elements of a prophecy (comm. on

Hos 2:17, 20, 22; Isa 28:5); and on deviations from chronological order in order to play up the contrasts in a story – "to distinguish the story of Joseph and his master's wife from the story of his brother [Judah]" (comm. on Gen 38:1; see also long comm. on Exod 18:1).

True, such comments are sporadic and unsystematic; but his quest for methodological reliability in this realm, too, finds expression, inter alia, in an examination of the reasonable limits to the use of elliptical language (comm. on Jonah 1:1) and in the assertion that palillogy, as found in prophecy, admonitions, and poetry, is out of place in prose narrative – "but the narrator should not repeat [himself], because this is what happened" (long comm. on Exod 14:19). In this vein he frequently uses the term *ṣāḥōt* (elegance) to indicate the poetic license to play fast and loose with syntax (comm. on Ps 32:9) and standard rhetorical modes (comm. on Ps 118:28; Lev 27:8). Clearly, his aim in this is not to call attention to rhetorical ornaments or clarify the nature of the expression in question, but merely to collapse the underpinnings of homiletic fine points and to bar the path to over-exegesis (short comm. on Exod 19:3).

To guard against the age-old exegetical tradition that all aspects of the text (from "superfluous" words to dotted letters) require a gloss, Ibn Ezra relies on a view of language that was accepted by many of the Jewish and Muslim scholars of Spain: "The words are like bodies, and the meanings like souls. … Hence it is the rule of scholars in every language to preserve the meaning; they do not worry about interchanging words if they have the same meaning" (long comm. on Exod 20:1). The verbal expression is not considered to be an essential part of the meaning, but only one of its garments: "Essentially words are but hints; knowledge of the language has no independent value, but is a vehicle of communication" (short comm. on Exod 23:20). Style, however, is even further removed from the sense; it is no more than an external ornament, pinned onto the garment to make it more attractive. Relying on these assumptions, Ibn Ezra can ignore a host of stylistic phenomena that provide the foundations for glosses he believes remote from the *peshat*; they also enable him to explain to his own satisfaction the significant differences between parallel episodes (from the two reports of Pharaoh's dream through the two versions of the Ten Commandments) by representing them as purely external (*Yesōd Môrā'*, ch. 1). The price of this concept of literary expression as almost exclusively devoted to transmitting information is a notable neglect of fine turns of expression and stylistic niceties inherent in a particular formulation.

His audacious critical hints, and perhaps also his caustic language and polemic temperament, have given Ibn Ezra the image of a radical innovator who conceals the main points of his heterodox opinions behind a veil of traditional declarations of faith. But this picture is mistaken. His sacred poetry allows us to paint his portrait as a genuinely religious personality, steadfast in his allegiance to the Jewish faith and his love of the Jewish people. What is more, his final judgments in most of the fundamental debates of scriptural exegesis reflect a measured and reasoned middle course, motivated by the aspiration to achieve a synthesis of opposing stances. In the four-way polemic presented in his two introductions to the Pentateuch he does not reject the methods of his predecessors outright. Instead, he expresses his reservations about their one-sidedness so that he can incorporate their positive elements into his own multidimensional and balanced method.

Abraham ibn Ezra was eclectic in his philosophical thinking as well as in his exegetical method. His importance in the history of exegesis seems to lie less in his original contributions and more in the standards he established for his critical evaluation of the accomplishments of the Babylonian-Iberian school. His pursuit of the theological, scientific, and exegetical truth was balanced by his commitment to education and his sense of public responsibility. He did not allow himself to give explicit expression to all of his thoughts, lest they undermine the innocent faith of most of his readers. His exile from his Spanish origin and wandering through the Jewish communities of Christian Europe deepened the intellectual and fideistic gap between the commentator and his readership, but he boldly guarded his self-identity and independence: "The Lord alone I fear / And I shall not favor anyone while interpreting the Torah" (the two introductions to the Pentateuch).

33.3. The Qimhi Family

By Mordechai Cohen, New York

Sources: (A) Joseph Qimhi: Citations from Pentateuch Commentary in *Ḥamisha ha-Me'orot ha-Gedolim* (ed. H. Gad; Johanesberg 1952) 39–48; fragments appear in "Joseph Kimchi's Pentateuch-Commentar", *Magazin für Jüdische Geschichte und Literatur* 1 (1874) 21–22; "Ein Sammelwerk in der Bodlejana", *Israelitische Letterbode* 2 (1876/7) 178–80. Proverbs commentary in *The Commentaries on Proverbs of the Kimhi Family* (ed. F. Talmage; Jerusalem 1990) 1–153. Job commentary in *Tiqwat 'Enosh* (ed. Y. Schwartz; Berlin 1868) 151–66; fragment from another MS in S. Eppenstein, "Un fragment du commentaire de Joseph Kimḥi sur Job", *REJ* 37 (1898) 86–102 (for sections still in MS, see Talmage, Proverbs [1990] xiii). *Sefer ha-Zikkaron* (ed. W. Bacher; Berlin 1887). *Sefer ha-Galuy* (ed. H. Mathews; Berlin 1887). *Sefer ha-Berit* (ed. F. Talmage; Jerusalem 1974); Eng. tr., F. Talmage, *The Book of the Covenant of Joseph Kimhi* (Toronto 1972). *Sheqel ha-Qodesh* (ed. and tr. H. Gollancz; London 1919). Fragments of Joseph's Heb. tr. of Baḥya ibn Paquda, *Duties of the Heart* in *Sefer Hovot ha-Levavot* (ed. A. Ẓifroni; Tel-Aviv 1964).

(B) Moses Qimhi: Proverbs commentary in: Talmage, Proverbs (1990) 154–327. *Moses Kimhi: Commentary on the Book of Job* (ed. and tr. H. Basser / B. Walfish; Atlanta 1992). Ezra-Nehemia commentary in Rabbinic Bible (*Miqra'ot Gedolot*). *Mahalakh Shevile ha-Da'at* (Lemberg 1867). *Sekhel Tov* was published a number of times, based on different MSS (see Talmage, Proverbs [1990], xiv), as follows: *Sepher Sechel Tob – Grammatik der hebräischen Sprache* (ed. B. Meyer; Crackow 1894); *Sepher Sechel-Tob – Eine hebräische Grammatik aus dem 13. Jahrhundert* (Karlsruhe 1926); D. Castelli, "Le Sefer Sekhel Tob. Abrégé de grammaire hébraïque de Moïse Qimhi", *REJ* 28 (1894) 101–10; 29 (1894) 212–27; F. J. de Ortueta y Murgoitīo, *Moisés Kimchi y su obra Sekel Tob* (Madrid 1920).

(C) David Qimhi (Radak): *Commentaries*: on Prophets and Chronicles in Rabbinic Bible; other editions and translations listed below. *Perushe Radak li-Bereshit* (ed. A. Ginzburg; Pressburg 1842); *Perushe Rabbi David Kimhi 'al ha-Torah* (Genesis; excerpts from Radak's other writings relevant to remainder of Pentateuch; ed. M. Kamelhar; Jerusalem 1970). *Radak: Petiḥa le-Perush ha-Torah* (ed. A. Golan; Jerusalem 1982). "The Commentary of Rabbi David Kimhi on the Book of Joshua" (ed. N. Goldberg; unpublished Dissertation, Columbia University 1961). *The Commentary of Rabbi David Kimhi on the Book of Judges* (ed. M. Celinker; Toronto 1983). *The Commentary of David Kimhi on Isaiah* (chaps. 1–39; ed. L. Finkelstein; New York 1926). "The Commentary of David Kimhi on Isaiah XL–LXVI" (ed. H. Cohen; unpublished Dissertation, Jewish Theological Seminary 1954). *The Commentary of Rabbi David Kimhi on Hosea* (ed. H. Cohen; New York 1929). "Critical Edition of the Book of Amos" (ed. S. Berkowitz; unpublished Dissertation, Cambridge University 1939). *Der Kommentar des David Qimchi zum Propheten Nahum* (ed. and tr. W. Windfür; Giessen 1927). *Die Kommentare von Raschi, Ibn Ezra, Radaq zu Joel* (Basel 1945). *Perush Radak li-Tehillim* (reprint of first printed edition 1477; Berlin 1938); *Rabbi David Kimhi: Ha-Perush ha-Shalem 'al Tehillim* (ed. A. Darom; Jerusalem 1967); *Radak on The First Book of Psalms, 1–41* (ed. S. Schiller Szinnesy; Cambridge 1883); "The Commentary of Rabbi David Kimhi on Psalms 42–72", ed. S. Esterson, HUCA X (1937/8) 309–443; *The Commentary of Rabbi David Kimhi on The Fifth Book of Psalms, CVII–CL* (ed. J. Bosniak; New York 1951). *The Commentary of Rabbi David Kimhi on Psalms CXX–CL* (tr. J. Baker / E. Nicholson; Cambridge 1973). Proverbs commentary in Talmage, Proverbs (1990) 328–427. Excerpts on Job in Schwartz, *Tiqwat* (1868) 129–45.

D) *Other Works*: *Sefer Mikhlol* (ed. I. Rittenberg; Lyck 1862); *Hebrew Grammar (Michlol) Systematically Presented and Critically Annotated* (ed. and tr. W. Chomsky; New York 1952). *Sefer ha-Shorashim* (ed. J. Biesenthal / F. Lebrecht; Berlin 1847). *Eṭ Sofer* (Lyck 1864). Correspondence with Judah Al-Fakar, *Qoveẓ Teshuvot ha-Rambam we-'Iggerotaw* III (ed. A. Lichtenberg; Leipzig 1859) 1–4.

General studies: S. Abramson, "*Le-Shimush Rav David Kimhi be-Tirgume Sifre Rav Yehuda Hayyuj u-Moreh Nevukhim*", *Qiryat Sefer* 51 (1976) 680–96; idem, *Mipi Ba'ale Leshonot* (Jerusalem 1988); W. Bacher, "Une Version abrégée de la grammaire de Moïse Kimhi", *REJ* 21 (1890)

281–85; idem, "Joseph Kimhi et Abulwalid Ibn Ganah", *REJ* 6 (1882) 208–21; idem, "Remarques sur le Petah Debarai – Grammaire hebraïque anonyme et sur le Sekhel Tob de Moïse Kimhi", *REJ* 29 (1894) 292–97; M. COHEN, "Midrashic Influence on Radak's *Peshaṭ* Exegesis" [Hebrew], *Proceedings of the Eleventh Conference of the World Congress of Jewish Studies, Division A: The Bible and Its World* (Jerusalem 1994) 143–50; idem, 'The Best of Poetry ...': "Literary Approaches to the Bible in the Spanish *Peshat* Tradition", *The Torah U-Madda Journal* 6 (1995/6) 15–57; idem, "Radak vs. Ibn Ezra and Maimonides: A New Approach to *Derekh Mashal* in the Bible" [Hebrew], *Proceedings of the Twelfth World Congress of Jewish Studies, Division A: The Bible and Its World* (Jerusalem 1999) 27–41; idem, *Three Approaches to Biblical Metaphor: Radak and His Predecessors, Abraham ibn Ezra and Maimonides* (forthcoming); S. EPPENSTEIN, "*Meḥqarim ʿal R. Yosef Qimhi*", *Iyyun we-Ḥeqer* (ed. and tr., Z. Bar Meir / H. Leshem; Jerusalem 1984) 134–222; A. GEIGER, "*Maʾamar ʿal R. Yoseph Qimhi*", *Qevuẓat Maʾamarim* (ed. S. Poznanski; Warsaw 1910) 186–220; idem, "*Toledot R. Moshe Qimhi*", *Qevuẓat*, 220–30; idem, "*Toledot ha-Radak*", *Qevuẓat*, 231–53; Y. GIL, "Joseph Kimchi, Bible Commentator" [Hebrew], *BetM* 19 (1974) 265–85; idem, "The Commentaries of Rabbi Joseph Kimchi" [Hebrew], *BetM* 20 (1975) 366–77; A. LIPSHITZ, "Ibn Ezra be-Ferushe Radak u-bi-Sefaraw", *Sinai* 61 (1967) 92–109; idem, "Ibn Ezra in the Writings of Joseph Kimchi", *Ibn Ezra Studies* [Hebrew] (Jerusalem 1982) 1–17; E. MELAMMED, *Perush Radak li-Tehillim, ʾAreshet* 2 (1960) 35–69; idem, *Bible Commentators* [Hebrew] (Jerusalem 1978) 715–932; M. PEREẒ, "*Le-Yaḥaso Shel Radak le-Qabalot Hisṭoriyot Shel Ḥazal*", *Sinai* 92 (1983) 71–85; U. SIMON, "Ibn Ezra and Kimhi: Two Approaches to the Masoretic Text" [Hebrew], *Bar-Ilan Annual* 6 (1968) 191–237; S. STEIN, *Jewish-Christian Disputations in Thirteenth Century Narbonne* (London 1969); R. STEINER, "Meaninglessness, Meaningfulness, and Super-Meaningfulness in Scripture: An Analysis of the Controversy Surrounding Dan 2:12 in the Middle Ages", *JQR* 82 (1992) 431–50; F. TALMAGE, "R. David Kimhi as Polemicist", HUCA 38 (1967) 213–35; idem, "David Kimhi and the Rationalist Tradition", HUCA 39 (1968) 177–218; idem, "David Kimhi and the Rationalist Tradition II: Literary Sources", *Studies in Jewish Bibliography, History, and Literature in Honor of I. Edward Kiev* (ed. C. Berlin; New York 1972) 453–78; idem, *David Kimhi: The Man and the Commentaries* (Cambridge, MA 1975); idem, "Apples of Gold: The Inner Meaning of Sacred Texts in Medieval Judaism", *Jewish Spirituality from the Bible Through the Middle Ages* (ed. Arthur Green; New York 1986) 313–55; I. TWERSKY, "Aspects of the Social and Cultural History of Provençal Jewry", *Journal of World History* 11 (1968) 185–207.

The Qimhi Family

Any family would be proud to produce an eminent biblical exegete; the Qimhi family produced three: Joseph (ca. 1105–70), an emigré from Andalusia (i.e., Muslim Spain) who settled in Narbonne in Christian Provence, and his two sons, Moses (d. ca. 1190) and David (ca. 1160–1235). Together, they formed a channel through which the exegetical streams of the mature Andalusian tradition entered Provençal exegesis. Joseph, aided by his elder son, Moses, began to transplant the scientific *peshat* tradition to Narbonne, where midrashic exegesis was prevalent. But David alone, known as Radak (*Ra*bbi *Da*vid Qimhi), the youngest and brightest star of the Qimhi constellation, would refocus the entire exegetical tradition. Born and educated in Narbonne, this illustrious scion of the Spanish *peshat* tradition was nourished by the midrashic soil of Provence and produced an original exegetical system that integrates elements from both traditions. Radak became remarkably popular in both Jewish and Christian circles; his commentaries have appeared alongside Rashi and Abraham ibn Ezra in the Rabbinic Bible (*Miqraʾot Gedolot*, introduced in the sixteenth century); and he earned for his family the tribute that the rabbinic adage, "There is no Torah without flour (*qemaḥ*)", was adapted poetically as, "There is no Torah without *Qimḥi*".

1. Joseph Qimhi

In his youth in Muslim Spain, Joseph Qimhi absorbed the works of the great Jewish philosophers, linguists and exegetes who had flourished there since the tenth century. Around 1150, he emigrated to Narbonne, a center of talmudic learning, then in the intellectual orbit of Northern France. Unable to read Arabic, Provençal Jewry was unfamiliar with Andalusian scholarship; instead, Joseph found in Narbonne a strong midrashic exegetical tradition in the works of Rashi, Moses ha-Darshan and some anonymous midrashic compilations.[1] This disparity placed Joseph, like other Spanish emigrés in Christian lands such as Judah ibn Tibbon and Abraham ibn Ezra, at a cultural crossroads. Exposing his Hebrew-reading audience to Spanish ethical philosophy, Joseph translated Baḥya ibn Paquda's *Duties of the Heart* and composed *Sheqel ha-Qodesh*, a metrical paraphrase of Solomon ibn Gabirol's ethical anthology, *Choice of Pearls*. Joseph was a translator of philosophy but wrote his own exegetical works to counterbalance the Provençal midrashic tradition. He composed a grammar, *Sefer ha-Zikkaron*, and *Sefer ha-Galuy*, a critique of the linguistic analysis of Jacob Tam, the Northern French talmudist, and Menaḥem ibn Seruq, upon whose antiquated linguistics Tam had relied. Joseph also wrote biblical commentaries; in addition to those extant today on Proverbs and Job, his lost commentaries on the Pentateuch and Prophets are cited by medieval authors, especially Radak.[2] Bringing his Spanish scholarship to bear on a problem unique to his new home, Joseph also wrote *Sefer ha-Berit*, a polemical work defending Jewish faith against Christian critiques.

1.1. Rationalism

Joseph established rationalism, the hallmark of the Andalusian tradition, as a beachhead for promoting the *peshat* method in Provence. To confirm the validity of human reason, he outlines an epistemological system based on Prov 9:1, "Wisdom['s] ... seven pillars", i.e., sources of knowledge: the five senses, true reports and mental perception.[3] He asserts that accurate biblical exegesis, unlike midrashic homiletics, is based on empirical methods, primarily the science of linguistics (*Sefer ha-Galuy*, 3). Rationalism thwarts the Christian adversary in *Sefer ha-Berit*, who argues: "You take ... the Torah literally (*ke-*

---

[1] See Twersky, Aspects (1968). While Rashi's works were popular in Provence, his students, Joseph Qara and Samuel ben Meir were evidently unknown there and are never cited by any of the Qimhi's; see Cohen, Hosea (1929) xxxv.

[2] A commentary on Song of Songs attributed to Joseph in MS Bodl. 63 is probably not his; see Talmage, Man and Commentaries (1975) 197.

[3] Commentary ad loc.; *Sefer ha-Galuy*, 1. Radak (on Ps 119:1) identifies Ibn Gabirol as his father's source.

mashmaʿah), exactly as written, *ped de letra* ... but we take it figuratively (*ʿal derekh mashal*), *figura*" – an attempt to allegorize, and effectively nullify, the laws of the Pentateuch, the heart and soul of Judaism. In response, Joseph makes reason the prism for interpreting Scripture: "The Torah is not entirely literal, nor entirely figurative; [only] that which cannot [reasonably] be interpreted literally, we interpret figuratively", an echo of Saadiah's axiom that a verse must be taken literally unless it contradicts reason.[4]

Applying Saadiah's corollary that verses contradicting reason must be re-interpreted,[5] Joseph introduces another innovative perspective in his new milieu. In Provence, contemporary sources indicate, biblical passages depicting God in human terms were taken literally, an approach fostered by vivid midrashic portrayals of God.[6] Arriving from Spain, where this view was deemed rationally untenable and even heretical, Joseph introduced an exegetical mechanism to undercut it, arguing that biblical anthropomorphisms are "metaphorical (*mashal*), to educate people by letting them imagine God in human form ... [which] does not misguide the wise since they comprehend the truth of the matter" (*Sefer ha-Berit*, 34). Still, by citing its educational value, Joseph avoids Saadiah's radical method of translating anthropomorphic language in a way that eradicates its literal sense. Probably stemming from a less severe strain in the Spanish tradition itself, represented by Baḥya and Judah Halevi, Joseph's moderation may also be a concession to his midrashic Provençal milieu.[7]

1.2. Linguistics

If reason was Joseph Qimhi's guiding star, linguistics was his map, though in midrashic Provence he could not take this for granted. *Sefer ha-Zikkaron* opens with a defense of linguistics that might otherwise have been superfluous: citing the respect accorded to grammar by Arabs and Christians, Joseph argues that Jews must all the more diligently cherish the Holy Tongue. *Sefer ha-Galuy* manifests a yet more polemical tone: "One who does not know Hebrew linguistics thoroughly", Joseph writes, "his interpretation is not credible; his *peshat* is not *peshat*" (p. 4), a conviction that allowed him to challenge Jacob

---

[4] *Sefer ha-Berit*, 37–38; see Radak, Ps 19:10. Saadiah's rule became standard in the Spanish *peshat* tradition. See *Beliefs and Opinions* 7.1 and *Saadya's Commentary on Genesis* (ed. and tr. M. Zucker; New York 1984) 17–18 (Arab.), 190–92 (Heb.); see also Abraham ibn Ezra, introduction to the Pentateuch, standard comm., "third approach" and alternate comm., "fourth approach".

[5] See sources cited in previous note.

[6] See the gloss of Rabad of Posquières (twelfth century) on Maimonides, *Hilkhot Teshuva* 3.7; see also M. Saperstein, *Decoding the Rabbis* (Cambridge, MA 1980) 7–9.

[7] Saadiah's approach, recorded, e.g., by Ibn Ezra on Gen 1:3; 6:6 (alternate commentary), is advanced by Maimonides, who composes a "dictionary" (*Guide of the Perplexed* 1.1–49) to translate anthropomorphic language into more abstract notions and forbade even "the uneducated" to imagine God in corporeal form (*Guide* 1.35,36). For the alterative view, see Baḥya ibn Paquda, *Duties of the Heart* 1.10; Judah Halevi, *Kuzari* 4.3–5. On these two approaches to anthropomorphism, see S. Rawidowicz, "Baʿayat ha-Hagshama le-Rasag we-la-Rambam", *Hebrew Studies in Jewish Thought* (Jerusalem 1969) 182–88; see also, Cohen, Three Approaches (forthcoming), chap. 4.

Tam, the most prominent Northern French talmudist of his day. Reflecting his cultural predicament, Joseph wistfully recalls Hai and Ibn Ghiyāth, Andalusian talmudists who "were intensely involved with Talmud, but also studied grammar", and laments the exclusive study of Talmud advocated by "the Rabbis of France" which fostered ignorance of Hebrew (ibid. 3–4). Joseph records with chagrin that popular midrashic homilies would cause even "great sages of Talmud" to mispronounce the biblical text (ibid. 20; comm. on Prov 2:3).

True to his principles, Joseph's commentaries provide solid grammatical, philological and syntactic analysis. He opens his commentary on Job by identifying the attitude of Job's three friends with the view of "the philosophers" that suffering is a punishment for sin, whereas the correct belief – uttered by God – is that suffering is meant "to demonstrate the forbearance [of the righteous] ... and increase their reward in the world to come". Apart from this brief remark, though, the commentary is noteworthy for a lack of philosophical digression which yields a straightforward textual analysis. The Proverbs commentary, in contrast, reveals a neo-Platonic bent and is punctuated by moralizing aphorisms from rabbinic and medieval sources, especially Joseph's *Sheqel ha-Qodesh.* This skewed distribution of philosophical discussion may reflect a preference for ethics over more theoretical issues like theodicy, which would explain why Joseph translated Baḥya's *Duties of the Heart*, rather than, for example, Saadiah's *Beliefs and Opinions.* Not neglecting his goal of providing a linguistic analysis of Proverbs, he discovered two important stylistic phenomena in that book: parallel versets expressing the same idea and those juxtaposed for contrast, identified as 'synonymous' and 'antithetical' parallelism, respectively, by ROBERT LOWTH in the eighteenth century.[8]

Joseph's philological orientation colors his exegesis. In addition to judiciously employing biblical evidence, he regularly uses Rabbinic Hebrew, Aramaic and Arabic cognates to illuminate difficult biblical locutions.[9] A linguistic bent also leads Joseph to identify formal poetic features of biblical literature. Some anomalous grammatical forms and word choices, he argues, result from a desire to attain poetic elegance through assonance and alliteration.[10] In linguistic matters, Joseph generally traverses a path paved by his Spanish predecessors, especially Jonah ibn Janah, whose views he frequently borrows, albeit with some refinement.[11] Yet he sometimes challenges the prevailing Spanish consensus. For instance, whereas Ibn Janah and Ibn Ezra both maintain that there are superfluous *waw*'s in Scripture that function like the Arabic prefix *fa*, Joseph argues that "every extraneous *waw* points to a missing word resembling the one to which it is attached, e.g., 'Tamar sat and(?) desolate' (2 Sam 13:20), meaning 'Tamar sat *sad* and desolate'".[12]

---

[8] See, e.g., comm. on Prov 10:10; 12:1–4. On LOWTH's categories, see J. KUGEL, *The Idea of Biblical Poetry* (New Haven 1981) 12–15.

[9] See, e.g., citations in Radak, *Shorashim*, s.v., אמם, גנן, and on 1 Kgs 21:5; Zeph 2:1; see also Bacher, Joseph Kimchi (1883); Melammed, Commentators (1978) 743–49.

[10] *Sefer ha-Galuy*, 6; compare Ibn Janah, *Sefer ha-Riqma* (ed. M. Wilensky; Jerusalem ^{2}1964) 23. See also *Sefer ha-Zikkaron*, 13; compare Ibn Ezra, Zeph 2:4.

[11] Bacher, Joseph Kimchi (1883).

[12] *Sefer ha-Galuy*, 6. Cf. Ibn Janah, *Riqma*, 63–66; Ibn Ezra, *Sefer Ẓaḥot* (ed. G. Lipman; Jeru-

Using his linguistically oriented *peshat* method, Joseph most prominently diverges from rabbinic exegesis, which he often dismisses as *derash*. Noting that the Rabbis (*b. B. Bat.* 10 a) take Prov 10:2, "*ẓedaqa* saves from death", to mean that giving charity extends life, Joseph argues that *peshat* requires interpreting this verset in light of the preceding one, yielding, "Ill-gotten wealth is of no avail / but *wealth gathered honestly* saves from death". Joseph also avoids elaborate midrashic strategies for resolving textual difficulties. For instance, on Gen 46:15, "These are the children of Leah, whom she bore to Jacob ... in all thirty-three [who traveled to Egypt]", the Rabbis, responding to the fact that only thirty-two names are listed, maintain that Levi's daughter, Yocheved, born on the journey, was counted but not named (*b. B. Bat.* 123 b). Joseph, as cited later by Radak, adopts Saadiah's simpler solution (ad loc.) that the thirty-three include Jacob.

Identifying a critical theoretical divergence between *peshat* and midrashic exegesis, Joseph demonstrates that in biblical Hebrew "seven" and "ten" are "not precise" (*'eno dawqa*), i.e., they are simply round numbers signifying 'many'. After citing a number of examples to support the 'imprecise' *peshat* method, he adds: "but according to the way of *derash* the[ese numbers] are precise (*dawqa*)", alluding to the rabbinic endeavor to identify the precise number of items – be it seven or ten – referred to in such cases.[13] Penetrating the midrashic mind further, Joseph explains that this 'precise' thinking also motivated the Rabbis to attribute meaning – unnecessarily according to *peshat* – to the exact number of times a word or idea is repeated in a given passage.[14] These critical methodological distinctions later provided the groundwork upon which Joseph's son, David, would build his more comprehensive system for delineating the innovations of the *peshat* method in contrast with the midrashic one.

1.3. Rabbinic Exegesis vs. Rabbinic Traditions

Though Joseph rejects *derash* as a genuine exegetical mode, rabbinic traditions play an important role in his thinking. His knowledge of talmudic and midrashic literature is evident from frequent citations in his writings, among other things, for the purpose of linguistic comparison. On Proverbs, he frequently cites rabbinic moral insights and prescriptions to illuminate biblical ethical philosophy.[15] Rabbinic assumptions about biblical authorship guide Joseph, who does not manifest the critical attitude of Andalusian exegetes like Ibn Chiqui-

salem 1970) 22b, commentary on Gen 22:4; 36:24. The Spanish view is adopted by modern scholars, who refer to this phenomenon as 'pleonastic *waw*'. Joseph's view, on the other hand, which has roots in Menaḥem ibn Seruq, represents a midrashic frame of mind (see below). See Steiner, Meaninglessness (1992) 436–46; Gil, Joseph Kimchi (1974) 274–77.

[13] *Sefer ha-Zikkaron*, 29; see also commentary on Prov 24:16; for the *derash* approach, see, e.g., *b. Shabb.* 32 b. The *peshat* rule (without the contrast to *derash*) is from Ibn Janah, *Riqma*, 318.

[14] Commentary on Prov 24:16. To illustrate the *derash* tendency, Joseph alludes to the talmudic analysis of Judg 5:27, discussed in Radak's commentary ad loc. (see below, sect. 3.2).

[15] See, e.g., Prov 1:21; 3:10; 3:14; 4:26; 11:2; 22:25; 24:23; Radak, *Shorashim*, s.v. ראש.

tilla and Ibn Ezra. Strictly following talmudic opinions (*b. B. Bat.* 15 a), he maintains that Solomon wrote Proverbs, Song of Songs and Ecclesiastes, and that Moses wrote Job.[16]

Manifesting a degree of interpretive spontaneity, Joseph at times violates his own *peshat* rules in formulating a midrash-like interpretation. He occasionally goes to great lengths, for example, to interpret "seven" and "ten" precisely, rather than as round numbers.[17] And on Jer 7:4, as cited by Radak, he cleverly explains the thrice repeated phrase, "the Temple of the Lord":

> The false prophets say that ... God will not destroy his Temple ... and it says three times "the Temple of the Lord" because it had three sections: the Portico (*'ulam*), the Great Hall (*heikhal*) and the Shrine (*devir*), thus interpreted my father. And he explained that the verse, "O land, land, land, [Hear the word of the Lord!]" (Jer 22:29), responds to their words, [as if] the prophet said: the sections of the Temple you speak of are regarded by me as [profane] land, because you sin ... and desecrate the Temple.

Evidently, Joseph assumed that his *peshat* rule (above) – directed at this very type of exegesis – can be suspended in favor of an especially fitting 'precise' reading. He says as much in a programmatic statement, unfortunately buried in his Proverbs commentary. Well aware of the Spanish *peshat* view that Scripture repeats ideas for stylistic purposes,[18] he articulates a counterbalancing principle: "wherever you can find a sound explanation (*perush hagun*), do not invoke [the rule of] 'repetition' (*kefel*)" (Prov 14:13). Joseph's notion of a "sound explanation" is illustrated in a citation by Radak on Isa 61:11, which likens Israel's messianic salvation to "the earth bring[ing] up her growth / and a garden mak[ing] its seed shoot up". Rather than applying the "rule of repetition" to argue that these similar images convey the same idea (as Ibn Ezra seems to do), Joseph creatively examines what is unique to each. Just as "'the earth brings forth her growth' ... without being sown", the messianic redemption will at first develop by itself; but its continued progress, like a carefully tended garden, depends on "that which Israel 'sows' with their righteousness".[19] Joseph's creative "sound explanations" suggest that his stylistic *peshat* rules were intended to avoid forced over-interpretation, but not to preclude midrash-like thinking altogether, a balance that would later engage Radak, who energetically returned to navigate the *peshat-derash* divide.

---

16 Introduction to Proverbs and Job; see also on Prov 25:1; 30:1. On the more critical Andalusian attitude, see below, n. 69. The limits that Joseph places on his exegetical autonomy from the Rabbis are also evident in his approach to 1 Sam 17:55, as cited by Radak, ad loc. That verse raises questions about the literary integrity of the books of Samuel (cf. the critical comment by Joseph Qara ad loc.), which, according to the Rabbis, were written by a single author, Samuel. Implicitly accepting the rabbinic assumption about authorship, he rejects only their exegetical solution to the problem in that verse and instead offers a new one.

17 See commentaries on Prov 6:16–19; 9:1; Job 5:19, 19:3.

18 See below, sect. 3.2.

19 For other examples, see Radak's citations of Joseph's analysis on Gen 49:9; 1 Kgs 14:10; Isa 1:2.

1.4. *Influence*

In resisting the strong midrashic currents of his new home, Joseph Qimhi began to turn the tide of the Provençal exegetical tradition. By transmitting his *peshat* method to students who themselves disseminated his teachings,[20] he created a demand for its continued development on the soil of Provence. Having generated a thirst for *peshat*, he also produced the means for satisfying it in his two foremost students, his sons, Moses and David. A request by a student of Joseph's seeking a *peshat* commentary on Chronicles, for example, prompted Radak's first commentary, which he justifies penning by citing the inadequacy of the midrashic commentaries available in Provence (Chronicles, introduction). Joseph's philological exegesis is cited by Moses and especially by David; and his innovative theory of 'long' and 'short' Hebrew vowels, transmitted by Radak, influenced Hebrew grammarians until modern times.[21] Though Joseph's teachings took root, history was less kind to his writings, which generally circulated for only about century after his death.[22] By the advent of printing late in the fifteenth century, his works – with the exception of *Sefer ha-Berit*[23] – were practically unknown, having been completely overshadowed by those of his progeny. Eminent *peshat* exegetes in their own right, his sons brought to fruition the seeds Joseph had planted.

2. Moses Qimhi

Little is known about Moses Qimhi, who probably arrived in Narbonne with his father and teacher, Joseph. Moses' writings suggest that he took shelter from the midrashic winds of Provence by cloistering himself in the study of grammar and philology, practically to the exclusion of other interests. This may reflect a personal bent as much as the influence of his father, who made linguistics the sword and shield of the *peshat* method. A fellow student of Joseph's, Menaḥem ben Simon of Posquières, who cites Moses frequently in his commentaries on Jeremiah and Ezekiel, manifests a similarly narrow philological method.[24] Menaḥem's works had little impact on the exegetical tradition and were quickly forgotten; but Moses, bearing the Qimhi standard, exerted influence on later biblical scholars. Of his two extant works on biblical Hebrew, *Sekhel Tov* and *Mahalakh Shevilei ha-Daʿat*, the latter was published in

---

[20] See Talmage, Covenant (1972) 9; see also below, n. 24.

[21] See Chomsky, Grammar (1952) xx–xxi.

[22] See Gil, Commentaries (1975).

[23] On early printings of *Sefer ha-Berit*, see Talmage, Covenant (1972) 13. In pondering what caused its relative prominence, we should note that neither Moses nor David wrote their own anti-Christian polemics, which otherwise might have obscured their father's.

[24] See M. Barol, *Menahem ben Simon aus Posquieres und sein Kommentar zu Jeremia und Ezechiel* (Berlin 1907); see also Talmage, Man and Commentaries (1975) 6–7; idem, Proverbs (1991) xiv; U. Simon, "A Disappointing Discovery: The 'Italian Genizah' Fragments of the Commentary on Jeremiah and Ezekiel are not by Ibn Ezra but by Menachem ben Simon" [Hebrew], *Tarbiẓ* 60 (1998) 570–72.

1508, translated into Latin by Sebastian Münster as *Liber Viarum Linguae Sacrae*, and became popular among sixteenth century Christian Hebraists. A third work, *Sefer Taḥboshet*, cited by Radak (*Mikhlol* 63 b) but now lost, evidently dealt with anomalous grammatical forms.

Moses wrote commentaries on Proverbs, Job and Ezra-Nehemia which address philosophical and historical issues when necessary but betray his overriding interest in phonology, morphology, etymology and syntax. Sometimes the biblical text merely provides an excuse for Moses to introduce a grammatical digression. Beyond analysis of individual words, for which he often is indebted to his father, Ibn Janah and Ibn Ezra, he offers innovative syntactic and structural observations. He divides Proverbs into five sections based on stylistic criteria: three demarcated by the heading, "Proverbs of Solomon" (1:1–9:18; 10:1–24:34; 25:1–29:27), a fourth by "The words of Agur" (chap. 30) and a fifth by "The words of Lemuel" (chap. 31). Further subdividing these into units of between two and eleven verses, he demonstrates the logical connection among the verses within each unit. In Job, where alternating speeches automatically structure the text, Moses goes a step further by explaining how the language of each speech responds to that of the previous ones.

In an irony of history, Moses' commentaries circulated widely but were attributed to his illustrious contemporary, Abraham ibn Ezra, a reflection of their quality. Hardly a century after his death, Raymond Martini (Spain, 1220–85) cites the Proverbs commentary in Ibn Ezra's name, a pattern that continued among medieval Jewish authors and inaccurate MS headings. The commentaries on Proverbs (in shortened form) and Ezra-Nehemia have appeared under Ibn Ezra's name in the Rabbinic Bible since the sixteenth century. As for Moses' commentary on Job, it remained in MS until it was printed – in his name – in the nineteenth century.

3. David Qimhi (Radak)

In accord with Qimhi tradition, Radak began his writing career around 1205 with a grammar, *Sefer Mikhlol*, and a dictionary, *Sefer ha-Shorashim*, both of which became definitive, standard works. He continued by writing biblical commentaries on Chronicles, Psalms, Proverbs, Former Prophets, Latter Prophets and Genesis.[25] He composed separate esoteric philosophical commentaries on the 'account of creation' (*maʿaseh bereishit*; Gen 2:7–5:1) and 'account of the Chariot' (*maʿaseh merkavah*; Ezekiel 1).[26] Radak also penned *ʿEṭ Sofer*, a short work on technical textual and grammatical matters. Although Radak wrote no separate polemical work, he refutes christological readings throughout his writings, often drawing upon Joseph's *Sefer ha-Berit*.[27]

---

[25] The commentaries appear to have been written in this order; see Talmage, Man and Commentaries (1975) 59–60; cf. Finkelstein, Isaiah (1926) xix. A commentary on Ruth, printed in Paris by J. Mercer in 1553, is mistakenly attributed to Radak.

[26] The esoteric work on Genesis appears in Finkelstein, Isaiah (1926), the one on Ezekiel in the Rabbinic Bible.

[27] Published separately as "Replies of Radak to the Christians" in *Sefer ha-Niẓaḥon* (Altdorf

Whereas Moses withdrew from the midrashic Provençal milieu by cloistering himself in linguistics, Radak developed a more sanguine attitude that enabled him to return to Joseph's cosmopolitan range of interests and propelled him into the fray between *peshat* and *derash.* Joseph died when Radak was about ten, after which Moses taught him, carefully transmitting their father's legacy.[28] With linguistics as his foundation, young David also absorbed the vast Spanish tradition that had been his father's heritage and kept abreast of its advances since Joseph's time.[29] Abraham ibn Ezra and Maimonides, two twelfth century Spanish emigrés who forever altered the Jewish intellectual landscape, profoundly influenced him.[30] But what truly set Radak apart from his father and brother was his complete confidence in navigating the currents of rabbinic literature. The same cultural crossroads Joseph had traversed now provided a home for his son, Radak, an heir of the Spanish *peshat* tradition comfortable with midrashic exegesis.

Exploiting his multivalent background, Radak takes his raw materials from the two illustrious traditions that converged in twelfth century Provence. He regularly cites Talmud, Midrash, Targum and Rashi alongside his father, Joseph, and a myriad of other Spanish authors.[31] He humbly terms himself "a gatherer after the reapers" (*Mikhlol* 1 a), i.e., an elucidator of predecessors' views rather than an independent thinker. Radak was an educator by profession, by his own testimony spending much of his time "teaching young men Talmud" (*Shorashim*, post-script). His *Mikhlol* and *Shorashim* were intended as textbook versions of the grammar and dictionary of the great linguist, Jonah ibn Janah; and, manifesting the lucidity of a skilled teacher, his paraphrase often clarifies Ibn Ezra's obscure style. But Radak was not merely a teacher, notwithstanding his modest self-portrayal. Using keen analytic skill, he discerned methodological differences among diverse predecessors and integrated their principles to create an original exegetical system.

In his Provençal milieu, Radak saw his work as an extension of the rationalist, linguistic Spanish *peshat* tradition. To be sure, Radak devotes considerable space to *derash*, culled from various rabbinic sources; but he separates it from

1644), republ. in Talmage, *Sefer ha-Berit* (1974). Many of these were removed from the commentaries by Christian censors and Jews fearing censorship. Some minor *halakhic* writings are attributed to Radak; see Talmage, Man and Commentaries (1975) 192–93.

[28] That Radak studied with his father, if only briefly, is indicated by phrases like "thus my father interpreted *for me*" (comm. on Isa 27:4), which are rare among his references to Joseph. Radak regularly refers to Moses as "my teacher, my brother" (see, e.g., Josh 15:8; Judg 5:26).

[29] His family having emigrated from Muslim Spain, Radak knew some Arabic and cites Arabic cognates to illuminate biblical Hebrew. But his ability to read extensive texts, required for the earlier Andalusian scholarship, is debated. See Cohen, Hosea (1929) xix; Abramson, Le-Shimush (1976). By his time, though, many works had been translated into Hebrew; and for untranslated ones he could have consulted his friend, Samuel ibn Tibbon, the great translator (see Talmage, Man and Commentaries [1975] 30).

[30] Joseph barely knew of Maimonides, whose most important works appeared late in the twelfth century. He mentions Ibn Ezra enthusiastically (*Sefer ha-Galuy*, 3) and occasionally borrows his interpretations (as observed caustically by Abarbanel on Hos 4:16 and Amos 9:7). But this exegetical resource arrived late in Joseph's life and does not match Radak's constant use of Ibn Ezra; see Lipshitz, Radak (1967); idem, Joseph Kimchi (1982).

[31] See Cohen, Hosea (1929) xvi–xxvi; see also above, n. 1.

his *peshat* exegesis through formulas like "our Rabbis say", "in the Midrash appears", "there is a *derash*". Often, in fact, he scrutinizes, and sometimes sharply criticizes, these readings.[32] Otherwise accepting rabbinic authority implicitly, Radak viewed much of rabbinic 'exegesis' as mere homiletics, i.e., clever, fanciful readings that provide a diversion from scientific exegesis. Radak implies as much when he states his intention to punctuate his commentaries with "some *derashot* for lovers of *derash*" (introduction to Former Prophets). Yet this accommodation to his audience, and perhaps his own delight in Midrash, actually serves another, more profound function. By juxtaposing *peshat* exegesis with alternative *derash* readings, Radak demonstrates precisely how the two methods diverge, vividly highlighting the skirmishes along the border between them.

Yet Radak goes further than merely outlining or simply refining the Andalusian tradition he inherited; he redraws the interpretive map by incorporating midrashic values into his own *peshat* method. As a Talmud teacher in *derash*-loving Provence, he was stirred by midrashic creativity, depth and inspirational force. Hence, although he rejects many rabbinic readings as *derash*, he subtly absorbs others into his *peshat* exegesis; and at the same time that he champions the Spanish *peshat* method, we can discern midrashic principles in his exegetical thinking. By introducing these elements into his *peshat* system, he transforms the very meaning of *peshat* and the interpretive process itself. Below, we delineate the critical balance which Radak strikes along the *peshat-derash* interface. With (1) rationalism as his center of gravity, he balances (2) scientific linguistics with (3) midrashic sensitivity to nuance, and (4) historical thinking with (5) midrashic passion for religious inspiration.

3.1. Rationalism

Rationalism is the theoretical foundation of Radak's exegetical system. While not an original philosophical or scientific thinker himself, he avidly draws upon Saadiah, Ibn Ezra, Maimonides and other rationalist authors. His purely philosophical exegesis is limited to the esoteric commentaries on Gen 2:7–5:1 and Ezekiel 1, which substantiate Maimonides's view that these sections convey truths of physics and metaphysics. But throughout his writings, Radak regularly addresses philosophical issues, such as providence, miracles, God's nature, and prophecy.[33] Proudly wearing the colors of his rationalist heritage, he also embraces the Maimonidean endeavor to reconcile Scripture with reason, much as Joseph embraced Saadiah's model. Like Maimonides, Radak (Gen 2:1) maintains that the natural order established at creation is immutable and reinterprets passages that indicate otherwise. Following Maimonides (*Hilkhot Melakhim* 12.1), he thus rejects the literal reading of the messianic prophecy, "The wolf shall dwell with the lamb ..." (Isa 11:6).[34]

---

[32] See, e.g., commentaries on Josh 5:14; Judg 16:21; 1Sam 1:9: 2Sam 3:15; 1Kgs 1:1; 2:19; 18:26.

[33] See Talmage, Rationalist (1968); idem, Rationalist II (1972).

[34] Similarly, Radak on Isa 13:10 invokes Maimonides' rule (*Guide* 2.29) that Scripture portrays calamities figuratively as if the heavenly luminaries were extinguished. Radak did not limit

In Radak's day, rationalism was assailed, especially in Provence, as inimical to biblical faith and, in his old age, Radak became embroiled in a controversy over Maimonides' views.[35] This conflict, coupled with Radak's own midrashic side, seems to have tempered his rationalism. Allowing miracles described in Scripture only minimal deviation from the natural order, he nonetheless affirms their supernatural quality. He rejects the view cited by Maimonides (*Guide* 1.42) that the boy "resurrected" by Elijah (1 Kgs 17:17) did not actually die but merely became critically ill and ceased breathing. Yet after stating that "the correct [view] is that he actually died", Radak adds that Elijah "stretched out on the boy three times" to transfer heat to his dead body, to perform the resurrection as naturally as possible.[36] Radak's need to affirm that the boy died perhaps reflects the bitter controversy over Maimonides' views on resurrection early in the thirteenth century. Ibn Ezra (Ps 104:30), who predated the controversies, could cite – without criticism or comment – a view that denies resurrection on scientific grounds. But Radak, in paraphrasing Ibn Ezra, feels compelled to add that this view does not conform with what "we, the progeny of Israel, and those who adhere to our faith", believe, namely, that the "souls will return to the[ir bodies] ... at the time of resurrection".

Radak's moderation also colors his views on anthropomorphism. Despite Maimonides' radical re-interpretation of such portrayals of God, Radak (Jer 14:8) adopts his father's opinion (above, sec. 1.1) that Scripture poetically conjures up a human image of God for educational purposes. Yet out of respect, Radak cites Maimonides on occasion, thereby illustrating the implications of this debate. For example, on Zech 14:4, a depiction of God's "feet (*raglayw*) standing on the Mount of Olives", he records that "Maimonides (*Guide* 1.28), interpreted *raglayw* as 'that which He has caused', like 'He has blessed you *le-ragli*' (Gen 30:30) [i.e.] because of me". To avoid any reference to God's 'feet', Maimonides demonstrated that *regel* (lit. foot) in biblical Hebrew can simply mean "cause".[37] But Radak argues that *regel* here must first be taken literally in an imaginative depiction of God's feet stepping on the Mount of Olives, which refers metaphorically (*derekh mashal*) to the mount splitting miraculously.[38]

Controversies notwithstanding, Radak boldly insists on the point at which his rationalist approach diverges from traditional rabbinic views. On Hos 1:2,

---

himself to Maimonidean strategies for reconciling Scripture with reason. After citing Maimonides' view that Joel 3:4, "the sun shall turn to darkness and the moon into blood" is simply a figure of speech expressing little more than human distress, he cites Ibn Ezra's that it describes an eclipse, a reading that comes closer to the literal sense while preserving the natural order. See also below, n. 38.

[35] See Lichtenberg, *Qobeẓ* (1859); Talmage, Man and Commentaries (1975) 32–39.

[36] See also Radak on 2 Kgs 4:34; Gen 2:21; Josh 5:2.

[37] Following this analysis, *regel* is actually a dead metaphor, i.e., one that no longer evokes its original sense. Maimonides, Radak continues, takes the phrase, "His feet will stand", to mean that "miracles [i.e., 'that which He has caused'] ... then will be apparent [lit. 'will stand'; see *Guide* 1.13]".

[38] See also Radak on Judg 10:16; compare Ibn Ezra, Gen 1:3; 6:6 (alternate commentary). For further analysis of Radak's approach to anthropomorphism in relation to the traditions he inherited, see Cohen, Three Approaches (forthcoming), chap. 4.

for example, he argues – following Ibn Ezra (ad loc.) and Maimonides (*Guide* 2.47) – that Hosea's marriage to a harlot did not occur in reality but was merely a prophetic vision, though he also notes that the Rabbis (*b. Pesaḥ.* 87 a) took the episode literally (*ke-mashmaʿo*). On 1 Kgs 22:19–23, Radak adopts a bolder strategy to avoid a rational dilemma that never distressed the Rabbis. In that passage, the prophet Micaiah, responding to Ahab's false prophets who predicted military success against Aram, describes a vision of God sending a "lying spirit" to mislead the king. Radak rejects the rabbinic view (*b. Sanh.* 89 a) that this scene occurred in heaven, arguing that God could not have sent false prophecy, since "prophecy is true by definition". So disturbed by the alternative, Radak cannot even grant that this scene would have been conveyed in a prophetic vision. Instead, he argues that Micaiah actually fabricated this vivid scene, using poetic dramatization (*divre meliẓa … derekh haẓaʿat devarim*) to frighten and thereby prevail upon Ahab.[39]

3.2. Linguistic and Stylistic Patterns

Rationalism provides a natural context for Radak's scientific analysis of biblical language and style, a realm in which he made his indelible mark. Straightforward linguistic analysis based on sound philology, biblical evidence and cognates in Aramaic, Arabic and Rabbinic Hebrew make up the lion's share of his commentaries. This itself would justify Radak's prominent standing as a biblical interpreter; but he does more to crystallize and advance the rule of *peshat.* With methodological insight, he reveals the theoretical underpinnings of the exegetical principles of his predecessors, Ibn Janah, Ibn Ezra and Maimonides, and integrates them into a comprehensive *peshat* system. Ironically, it may have been Radak's intimate familiarity with rabbinic literature that prompted him to chart the innovations of the *peshat* method, which he often does by citing midrashic readings – supposedly intended for "lovers of *derash*" (above) – alongside his *peshat* exegesis.

Writing in a midrashic milieu, Radak had to justify the innovative *peshat* method, which lacked the traditional authority of rabbinic exegesis. That method, he demonstrates, derives its cogency empirically by identifying patterns of language and style, in contrast with Midrash, which often interprets phrases and words in isolation. Building upon his father's distinction between the "precise" *derash* and "imprecise" *peshat* methodologies (above, sec. 1.2), Radak shows how *derash* tends to interpret words rigidly, leading to exaggerated, dramatic conclusions, whereas the *peshat* method invites greater linguistic flexibility to yield more plausible, if less spectacular, results. For example, on Gen 24:10, "The servant took ten camels … and *all* (*kol*) of his master's wealth *in his hand* (*be-yado*)", he cites the rabbinic view (*Gen. Rab.* 59:11) that the servant carried in his hand a deed representing ownership of Abraham's entire fortune. But Radak observes that *kol* in biblical Hebrew is often used in

[39] Radak's (unnamed) source here is Judah Halevi, *Kuzari* 3.73. For other examples of Radak's rationalist rejection of rabbinic readings, see 1 Sam 28:24; 2 Kgs 2:1; Jer 31:15.

the broader sense of "much" and draws the more modest conclusion that the servant took with him only a *sample* of Abraham's wealth.[40]

By discerning biblical stylistic patterns, Radak also provides support for his rationalist divergence from rabbinic tradition. He records, for example, that the Rabbis (*b. Sanh.* 93 a) "explicated ... literally (*darshu* ... *ke-mashmaʿo*)" a depiction of Joshua the High Priest as a "brand plucked from the fire" (Zech 3:2), i.e., that he was actually cast into a furnace by the King of Babylon and rescued miraculously. But Radak, reluctant to proliferate miracles, takes this verse figuratively, as a reference to Joshua's surviving the harsh Babylonian exile, known from other biblical sources.[41] This *peshat* reading conforms with the wider biblical context, since, as Radak elsewhere (Jer 6:29) observes, the prophets typically use metaphor and rhetoric (*mashal u-meliẓa*) for dramatization.

Revisiting a tendency Joseph labeled "precise" *derash* exegesis, namely the attempt to attribute meaning to redundant language (above, sect. 1.2), Radak illuminates another aspect of the *peshat-derash* divide. More deeply immersed in *derash*, Radak was better equipped to clarify the rabbinic endeavor to attribute meaning to every single word of Scripture, a doctrine recent scholars call 'omnisignificance'.[42] He cites in full a talmudic passage – merely alluded to by Joseph in this connection – which responds to the seven-fold repetition of Sisera's death at Yael's hand: "at her feet he (1) sank, (2) fell, (3) lay outstretched; at her feet he (4) sank, (5) fell; where he (6) sank, there he (7) fell" (Judg 5:27). Attributing significance to each repetitive phrase, the Rabbis (*b. Yebam.* 103 a) deduce that Sisera cohabited with Yael seven times. Though Radak faithfully records *derash*, he is that much more careful to uphold *peshat*. Apart from indicating that the outrageous talmudic reading has no basis in the immediate context, he rejects the very need to interpret such a redundancy, since "the custom of language (*minhag ha-lashon*) is to repeat things in order to stress them". Like metaphorical dramatization, repetition is a stylistic convention employed merely for rhetorical or emphatic effect.[43]

Elsewhere, Radak reduces repetitive language to little more than stylistic flourish, not even indicative of emphasis. For example, on Gen 23:1, "Sarah lived one hundred years and twenty years and seven years", he observes that "it says 'years ...' three times although once would suffice". "There is a *derash*", he continues, "that at one hundred [Sarah] was like a woman of twenty with respect to sin, and at twenty like a woman of seven with respect to

[40] Radak thus implicitly rejects the literal reading of *be-yado*. His analysis of *kol* is from Ibn Janah (*Shorashim*, s.v. כלל) and Ibn Ezra (Gen 41:57; Exod 9:6), although its application to this verse and the contrast with *the derash* is original to Radak.

[41] See Hag 1:1; 1 Chr 5:40–41; 2 Kgs 25:18–21. Radak's *peshat* reading here is taken from Ibn Ezra.

[42] Kugel, Idea (1981) 104–05; see also chap. 33.4 of this volume (Y. Elman), sect. 2.1.

[43] Radak often applies this *peshat* rule, borrowed from Ibn Janah (*Riqma*, 293–95), in contrast with the rabbinic approach; see, e.g., Gen 16:9; Ezek 16:6; *Mikhlol*, 61 a. He sometimes attributes repetitive language to intense emotion, either in prayer or mourning, a more specific explanation still distinct from the *derash* approach; see 2 Sam 19:1; 1 Kgs 18:37; Jer 4:19. Radak also illustrates the *peshat-derash* dichotomy observed by Joseph regarding round numbers; see 1 Sam 1:8; 2:5; Zech 8:23.

beauty". But Radak demonstrates that this type of redundancy is hardly unique in Scripture and sides with "[scholars who] say that this is [simply] literary elegance (*ẓaḥot*) in Hebrew", a reference to Abraham ibn Ezra.[44] He similarly relies on the notion of literary elegance in adhering to Maimonides' view (*Guide*, introduction) that one need not find a deep meaning for every detail of a biblical allegory as the Rabbis do, since this literary genre employs language purely for embellishment (*le-yapot ha-mashal*).[45]

In what would become a hallmark of the Spanish *peshat* tradition and a precursor of the modern notion of 'parallelism', Radak coined the phrase *kefel ʿinyan be-millim shonot* ("repetition of the idea in different words") for the 'seconding' style common in biblical verse.[46] Occasionally he argues that this feature indicates emphasis or adds clarity; but fundamentally he views it simply as the "manner of the [Hebrew] language", i.e. a standard literary technique, not unlike rhyme in English poetry.[47] Radak did not discover this principle; but it was his crisp formula that came to represent it in the exegetical tradition,[48] and he illustrates its innovative nature in contrast with rabbinic exegesis. On Gen 32:8, "And Jacob was greatly frightened and distressed", he cites the Rabbis, who derive meaning from the repetitive language: "'He feared' that he might be killed; 'and he was distressed' that he might have to kill [Esau]" (*Gen. Rab.* 76:2), but himself argues that the repetition merely emphasizes Jacob's "extreme fear".[49]

The *kefel ʿinyan be-millim shonot* rule assumes that distinct biblical formulations (e.g., "he feared" and "he was distressed") can express the same idea, a principle articulated by Ibn Ezra, who undercuts a staple of rabbinic thought by dismissing the discrepancies between the Ten Commandments as recorded in Exodus 20 and Deuteronomy 5.[50] Echoing Ibn Ezra, Radak on Gen 24:39 writes that "the custom of Scripture when it repeats matters, is to preserve the meaning (*ṭaʿam*) but not the words; indeed, this also occurs in the Ten Commandments". Radak invokes this rule on Gen 18:13 to avoid a midrashic explanation for the discrepancy between Sarah's words as recorded in Scripture, "Now that I am withered, am I to have enjoyment – with *my husband so old*?" (v. 12) and as cited by God, "Shall I in truth bear a child, *as old as I am*?" (v. 13). The Rabbis, cited by Rashi, infer from this that one is permitted to lie to preserve family harmony. But Radak argues that the change is insignificant, for "although [God] did not repeat the same words … that she said, He repeated the idea (*ʿinyan*) that she intended to say, for Scripture preserves the meaning but does not preserve the words".[51]

---

[44] On Gen 19:24, Deut 32:7 and Ps 1:3. See also Radak Gen 6:9; Josh 22:22; 2 Kgs 18:39.

[45] Radak, Prov 5:3; see also esoteric commentary on Gen 2:10–14.

[46] See Kugel, Idea (1981) 172–77.

[47] See Radak on Isa 1:2, 1:29, 4:4, 24:1, 26:6; Jer 2:3, 5:28; Ps 6:2.

[48] It is used, e.g., by the nineteenth century rabbinic exegete Malbim (introduction to Isaiah), to reject this axiom of the Spanish *peshat* tradition; see Cohen, Best of Poetry (1995/6) 34–35.

[49] See also Radak on Josh 6:26; Gen 21:1.

[50] Long comm. on Exod 20:1. See chap. 33.2 of this volume (U. Simon); Cohen, Three Approaches (forthcoming), chap. 5.

[51] Radak here clarifies the principle underlying Ibn Ezra's cryptic comment. See Cohen, Three Approaches (forthcoming), chap. 6.

3.3. *Interpreting Linguistic Nuance*

Radak's articulation of the Andalusian *peshat* ideology belies a crosscurrent in his exegesis flowing from a different source. By unleashing his powerful anti-midrashic *peshat* principles, he could have reduced all redundant biblical language and details, the life-blood of rabbinic exegesis, to mere linguistic convention and stylistic ornamentation. Instead, he applies those rules with moderation, bringing a midrash-like strain into his *peshat* exegesis.[52] Though he objected to the extreme doctrine of omnisignificance, he also realized the shortcomings of an exclusive focus on general content at the expense of individual formulations. One might say that Radak reveals a sensitivity to linguistic nuance worthy of a Talmud teacher in *derash*-loving Provence. But if Midrash flooded Radak's Provençal horizon, his father made him thirst for its waters, for it was Joseph who argued, "wherever you can find a sound explanation do not invoke [the rule of] 'repetition' (*kefel*)" (above, sect. 1.3), limiting the anti-midrashic *peshat* principle. Midrash, Joseph Qimhi and the Andalusian tradition would provide the primary colors of Radak's midrashically enriched *peshat* method.

Radak does not hesitate to borrow a midrashic reading that diverges from his anti-midrashic *peshat* principles if, in his view, it conforms with reason and the immediate context. For example, on Gen 29:1, "Jacob lifted his feet and went to the land of the Easterners", he comments:

> Since God reassured him and showed him the great [ladder] vision, he became happy, "lifted his feet" easily and went ... with good heart; for originally he went wearily, as one sadly stealing out of his father's house.

Radak's source is *Gen. Rab.* 70:8, which reacts to the nuanced formulation, "Jacob lifted his feet", in contrast with the more prosaic, "Jacob left Beʾer Sheva ..." (Gen 28:10), fleeing Isaac's house. He might have ignored this subtlety, reasoning that "Scripture preserves the meaning but does not preserve the words"; but instead, he makes the most of it and adopts the midrashic reading, which he supports by showing that a psychological transformation is plausible here.[53] This is quite distinct from Radak's citation of *"derashot* for lovers of *derash"* that serve as a foil for correct, *peshat* interpretations. Radak does not label this reading as *derash*, nor does he even acknowledge its rabbinic origin, indicating that it has been integrated into his own thinking. This Midrash is deployed – cloaked in Radak's paraphrase – for 'lovers of *peshat*'.

Radak's skill in selecting midrashic readings is surpassed by his insight in creating his own. *Gen. Rab.* 84:21 responds to a redundancy in Gen 37:34–35, "Jacob ... mourned for his son [Joseph] many days ... and his father cried for him", by taking "his father" to mean Isaac, *Jacob's father*. Radak cites this as *derash* and could have argued that Scripture "repeats the idea in different words", perhaps to emphasize Jacob's intense mourning (as Rashbam maintains). Instead, he capitalizes on the nuanced repetition:

---

[52] See Cohen, Midrashic Influence (1994).
[53] See also, e.g., Radak on Gen 22:8; 32:7; 34:25; 42:9.

> It says "his father" because [Jacob] showed [Joseph] the love of a father towards a son who served him [faithfully], being at his side constantly ... [but now] whenever [Jacob] needed his help he would remember him and be unable to control his tears.

The Midrash imports Isaac with no contextual basis; Radak sharpens the picture already painted by this verse, distinguishing between Jacob's mourning, a cultural and religious convention, and *the father's crying*, a reflection of deeply personal feelings.[54]

A microcosm of the balance Radak strikes between the Andalusian notion of *peshat* and his own sensitivity to nuance emerges in his treatment of metaphor, allegory and simile, which he refers to collectively as *mashal*.[55] Though he largely relies on the terminology and linguistic theories of Ibn Ezra and Maimonides, he resists their tendency to view these literary techniques as mere linguistic conventions or poetic ornamentation.[56] Instead, he attributes expressive value to the imagery they conjure up and seeks to derive added meaning from it. For example, Ibn Ezra takes Isa 55:1, "Ho, all who are thirsty / Come for water ... / Come buy food ... / Wine and milk", metaphorically, explaining that the meaning (*ṭaʿam*) of "water ... food ... wine and milk" is "Torah wisdom". Limiting himself to stating this equivalence, Ibn Ezra, consistent with his view that "Scripture preserves the meaning (*ha-ṭaʿam*) but not the words", ignores the imaginative value of Isaiah's imagery-laden formulation. Radak pursues a richer exegetical agenda:

> Just as the thirsty desires water, so the wise soul desires Torah and wisdom ... Torah is [also] compared to wine [for] as wine gladdens the heart, so too the words of Torah ... And as milk sustains the suckling child and causes him to grow, the Torah sustains the soul and develops it.

Elsewhere adopting Ibn Ezra's reductive *peshat* rule, Radak avoids applying it here by not simply identifying "Torah and wisdom" as the shared 'meaning' of Isaiah's metaphors. Where imagery is involved, he seeks to attribute meaning to the choice of language; he therefore demonstrates how each of Isaiah's three images evokes another specific property of "Torah and wisdom".[57]

Exploring the associations evoked by imagery, Radak at times opens particularly rich interpretive avenues. For example, on Ezek 36:17, "Israel ... has defiled [their land] ... like the uncleanliness of a menstruous woman their ways are before me", he writes:

---

[54] Sensitivity to nuance became such an integral part of Radak's *peshat* thinking that it required no midrashic impetus. On 2 Sam 12:24, "And David comforted Bathsheba, his wife", he writes: "Now it says 'his wife' since Uriah had died, but earlier it said '[God afflicted the child] born to David by Uriah's wife (2 Sam 12:15), for she was Uriah's wife until he died". The superfluous phrase, "his wife", receives no mention in rabbinic literature, and the reductionist *peshat* rules might have allowed Radak to overlook it. But he instead observes that it contrasts with the earlier formulation and highlights the critical fact that Bathsheba was still Uriah's wife – not David's – until Uriah died.

[55] See Cohen, New Approach (1999); idem, Three Approaches (forthcoming), chap. 3.

[56] Consistent with medieval literary notions, as articulated by Moses ibn Ezra; see chap. 31.2 of this volume (M. Cohen), sect. 3.

[57] Compare also Radak and Ibn Ezra on Gen 49:9, 17; Isa 1:8; 44:4; Joel 4:13; Nah 1:3; 3:4; Ps 78:19. In Genesis 49, comparison with Rashi reveals the impact of Midrash on Radak's thinking.

> Since Israel is – metaphorically – God's wife ... [Scripture] speaks of them metaphorically at the time of their sinfulness as a menstruous woman, whom the husband distances ... So too, God distanced Israel, exiling them to [foreign] lands.

Ezekiel employs a common biblical topos, the marriage of God and Israel, to depict exile as the result of Israel's sinful "defilement". But Radak was not satisfied treating this image as merely a dramatization of what is said literally in vv. 19–20 ("So I poured out my wrath upon them ... [and] scattered them among the nations"). Since marital intimacy returns after purification from menstrual uncleanliness (Leviticus 15), he reasons, this image implies that God "will restore [Israel] once they repent and purify themselves from sin", a prophecy indeed articulated later in this chapter (v. 24). Rather than viewing Ezekiel's metaphor as simply an instance of a general biblical topos, Radak insists on its unique meaning in this context by demonstrating how it simultaneously conveys both alienation and reconciliation, portraying – more powerfully than any literal formulation could – Israel's exile as a temporary setback in an everlasting relationship with God.[58]

That Radak's approach placed him at odds with the extremes of both the midrashic and Spanish traditions is illustrated on Zech 1:8, "I had a vision, and saw a man riding on a red horse", which introduces a prophecy in which an angel foretells God avenging Zion's destruction. Revealing a minimalist orientation, Ibn Ezra insists that "there is no need to explain why [the horse] was red".[59] Alluding to the talmudic reading (*b. Sanh.* 93 a) that prompted his disclaimer, he asserts that "to interpret ... 'red' (*'adom*) as ... 'blood' (*dam*) ... is nothing but homiletics". Reacting, no doubt, to this dismissive attitude, Radak cites the rabbinic reading in full, although he cannot accept it as *peshat* since it is not supported in Zachariah's subsequent prophecy. But his own reading also defies Ibn Ezra's minimalism:

> After [citing] this, *we will attempt to explain what we can* of this vision. "A man" – the Lord's angel ... "Riding on a horse" – to indicate the swiftness of his mission. Perhaps the redness and other colors are meaningful. My father wrote that the "red horse" signifies Nebuchadnezzar, who is called "the head of gold" (Dan 2:38) and gold is red[dish].

Ibn Ezra treated the details of Zachariah's vision as dramatic embellishment, much as Maimonides viewed the 'meaningless' details of a biblical allegory added for literary purposes. Radak applies Maimonides' rule elsewhere (above, sect. 3.2), but attributes meaning to the details of Zachariah's vision in conformity with his prophecy, creating a context-sensitive interpretation that maximizes Scriptural meaning.[60]

The citation of Joseph Qimhi in the preceding example intriguingly suggests that Radak here follows a path blazed by his father. Joseph's Midrash-like 'precise' explanations are, ironically, better illustrated by citations in his son's

---

[58] In this respect, Radak foreshadows a modern view of metaphorical imagery as a unique expressive medium; see M. Weiss, The Bible From Within (Jerusalem 1984) 130–35.

[59] On Ibn Ezra's attempt to keep conjectures to an absolute minimum, expressed in the formula "there is no need (*'en ẓorekh*) ...", see U. Simon, *Four Approaches to the Book of Psalms* (tr. L. Schramm; New York 1991) 180–82.

[60] See also, e.g., Radak on Isa 28:24; Ezek 16:9.

writings than his own extant commentaries, which usually feature straightforward philological exegesis. But the former seems to have sparked his son's creativity. After citing his father on Isa 61:11 (above, sec. 1.3), Radak offers his own strategy to distinguish between the similar images in that verse. That and similar citations point to Joseph as the source of a striking sub-pattern in Radak, namely his avoidance of the *kefel* rule where two poetic images appear in synonymous phrases.[61] His view of imagery as meaning-laden provides sufficient grounds for breaking the *kefel* rule, which he otherwise applies with great consistency.

If the need to offset the reductionist *peshat* approach was integral to the Qimhi legacy, the subjective criterion of a "sound explanation" was a moving target, dependent on intuition rather than strict rules. Though few in number, Joseph's 'precise' readings seem more creative and fanciful – we might say more midrashic – than those of Radak, who cautiously navigates the narrow straits between his father's model and the more sober anti-midrashic *peshat* method. Occasionally, Radak relegates his father's "sound explanation" to the status of *derash*, interesting to cite, but inaccurate. He cites Joseph's 'precise' explanation of the thrice repeated phrase, "the Temple of the Lord" (Jer 7:4; above, sect. 1.3) but notes that "it is the custom of the language to repeat the words in order to emphasize the matter, sometimes with two words, sometimes with three".[62] Elsewhere, though, Radak deems Joseph's method appropriate and does attribute a specific meaning to thrice repeated words.[63]

Radak's sensitivity to nuance is notable from a modern perspective, since literary theory now rejects the medieval separation of formulation (*millim*; "words") from content (*ṭaʿam*, *ʿinyan*; 'meaning'). In fact, the Spanish *peshat* method has been criticized for its failure to address nuances of language, the basis of 'close reading' now prevalent in literary biblical scholarship.[64] Though unaware of modern theory, Radak gives thought to this problem using tools available to him. Though most of his exegesis – statistically speaking – flows from the well-springs of the Spanish *peshat* tradition, Radak signals a change of course by utilizing a different approach in several striking instances, revealing the inadequacy of the stricter *peshat* model. Inspired by his father's creativity, Radak's more flexible, refocused *peshat* method draws upon midrashic thinking to do justice to Scripture's literary subtlety.

---

[61] See, e.g., Radak on Isa 4:2; 49:2; see also Gen 41:6 and Cohen, New Approach (1999) n. 33.

[62] He also records Joseph's midrash-like view that "every extraneous *waw* points to a missing word like the one to which it is attached" (above, n. 12) but agrees with Ibn Ezra, who argues that such *waw*'s are meaningless (*Mikhlol* 44 a). See also Radak, citing his father, on Judg 9:13.

[63] See, e.g., Radak on Isa 6:3; Ezek 21:32.

[64] See Simon, Two Approaches (1968) 204; Weiss, Bible from Within (1984) 37; M. Sternberg, *The Poetics of Biblical Narrative* (Bloomington 1985) 368–74.

3.4. Historical Thinking

Historical thinking was another fertile derivative of the *peshat* tradition that Radak adapted to suit his intellectual bent and Provençal milieu. The Andalusian tradition, confident in its scientific analysis of Scripture, boldly challenged rabbinic assumptions about biblical history and the transmission of the biblical text. Though Radak recognized the opportunities opened by this fresh perspective, his appreciation for rabbinic views propelled him to devise a new mode of historical analysis that incorporates values from both schools. Nominally, Radak accepts the accuracy of rabbinic historical traditions, which he adds to his father's epistemology (above, sect. 1.1) as a cardinal source of knowledge, arguing that the Rabbis possessed data not recorded in Scripture.[65] But to allow for independent analysis, he distinguishes between authoritative ancient traditions (*qabalot*) and conjectures based on rabbinic interpretation (*perush*), which were never meant to be definitive.[66]

Yet Radak finds no surefooted path through the forest of rabbinic literature, which lacks these signposts, forcing him to tread cautiously and hazard his analysis contingent upon the nature of the opposing rabbinic view. On Judg 11:31 he cites his father's novel reading of Jeftaḥ's vow, which contradicts the rabbinic view that Jeftaḥ actually sacrificed his daughter.[67] Joseph's reading, says Radak, is correct according to "the *peshat* of the scriptures" but adds that "if [the rabbinic view] is a historical tradition, we must accept it". This standard disclaimer thinly veils Radak's critical sense, for example, on 2 Sam 14:26, which describes Absalom's immense locks of hair. Challenging the rabbinic view that Absalom was a nazirite, he writes, "This must have been a tradition, since they did not see this in the scriptures". The textual evidence, Radak argues, indicates that "he grew his hair because of its beauty, to satisfy his vanity and make himself attractive".[68]

When Radak invokes his *qabala-perush* distinction, he often cannot avoid circularity. The rabbinic view that Moses wrote Psalm 90, warranted anyhow by the heading "A Prayer of Moses", is deemed a *qabala*; yet the less credible midrashic view that Moses composed Psalms 91–100 is deemed the product of rabbinic conjecture and marginalized as *derash*, to make room for Radak's opinion (introduction to Psalms) that these psalms, lacking attribution, were written by David. Nor does he hesitate to claim, following Ibn Ezra, that the Tower of Babel was intended simply to promote political unity, based on Gen 11:4, "Let us build a city, and a tower … lest we scatter throughout the Earth", whereas the Rabbis accuse the builders of planning to invade heaven and battle the Lord Himself (comm. on Gen 11:1). Deeming the rabbinic view

---

[65] Ps 119:1; see also 1 Chr 4:21.

[66] Introduction to Former Prophets; see Perez̧, *Le-Yaḥaso* (1983). Ibn Ezra (e.g., Gen 22:4; Exod 15:22, longer commentary) strikes a similar compromise; see chap. 33.2 of this volume (U. Simon).

[67] Naḥmanides on Lev 27:29 attributes this reading to Ibn Ezra; but it is not found in his extant writings.

[68] See also Radak on Judg 14:19; 1 Sam 12:2; 2 Kgs 18:17.

unlikely, Radak evidently concluded that it does not reflect an ancient tradition and is open to debate.

A keen historical sense led Radak to confront issues relating to the process of biblical redaction, although he avoided the most radical views of the earlier Spanish tradition.[69] The Talmud (*b. B. Bat.* 15 a) takes Ezra to be the author of Chronicles; but Radak argues that he edited the book using earlier documents (introduction to Chronicles). By considering the historical circumstances in which the biblical text was composed, Radak devises insightful solutions to problems that perplexed the Rabbis. On Ps 3:1, "A psalm (*mizmor*; lit. song) of David while fleeing from Absalom his son", he cites the Rabbi's dilemma: why would David "sing" in his distress? Deeming their elaborate answer *derash*, Radak argues that "according to the way of *peshat* the psalms are called 'songs' because they were sung in the Temple".[70]

Radak's implicit acceptance of the MT's accuracy does not prevent him from probing problems in its transmission. He exploits this very issue to offer a strikingly modern explanation for the variations between the *qere* (reading) and *ketiv* (written text):

> During the first exile the books were lost[71] ... the Torah scholars died, and the men of the Great Synagogue who restored the Torah ... found discrepancies among the manuscripts and accepted the reading of the majority ... Where they could not determine the truth ... they inserted a reading [as the *ketiv*] with the provision that it not be read, or wrote it on the margin [as the *qere*] but omitted it from the main text.[72]

This account of textual confusion in ancient times was, no doubt, bolstered by discrepancies Radak himself found among biblical MSS and targumic readings that reflect a *Vorlage* other than the MT. Boldly confronting this disturbing reality (which Ibn Ezra, for example, largely ignored), he diligently consulted MSS to determine the correct biblical text and wrote a separate work, *Eṭ Sofer*, to insure its preservation.[73] Radak treats vocalization as an integral part of the MT and criticizes predecessors – including his father – whose exegesis di-

[69] Much like his father (above, sect. 1.3). Radak conspicuously avoids the critical opinions in Ibn Ezra's commentaries, e.g., the exilic dating of the second part of Isaiah and selected psalms (in the name of Ibn Chiquitilla; below, n. 88) and hints of post-mosaic interpolations in the Pentateuch (see chap. 33.2 of this volume [U. Simon]). Like his father, Radak never questions the talmudic axiom that Samuel wrote the entire Book of Samuel, although he recognizes the textual problems this assumption creates; see 1 Sam 9:9, 17:55.

[70] See also Radak on Ps 6:1.

[71] Compare Radak's *peshat* suggestion (1 Kgs 5:12) – in contrast to a more elaborate midrashic one – that Solomon's thousands of *meshalim* (parables?) and *shirim* (poems?) have been lost.

[72] Radak, Introduction to Former Prophets. A precedent can be found in Ibn Janah, *Shorashim*, s. v. בג, though Radak makes a comprehensive theory out of that isolated observation. The Talmud (*b. Ned.* 37 b) attributes *qere* and *ketiv* to Mosaic tradition, viewing both as original. While that account is naturally limited to the Pentateuch whereas Radak's is stated only for the Prophets and Hagiographa, his view diverges from the spirit of rabbinic tradition and was later criticized. See Talmage, Rationalist (1968) 215–16; see also Abarbanel, Introduction to Jeremiah.

[73] Radak's MS research is evident, e.g., in *Mikhlol* 46 b, 71 a, 115 a, 164 a; *Shorashim*, s. v. חול, קשב, רקח, and on Judg 6:19; 1 Kgs 7:18; 2 Kgs 17:31; 1 Chr 2:55. See also Cohen, Hosea (1929) xxvii; Talmage, Man and Commentaries (1975) 91–92. Radak notes Targumic divergence from the MT, e.g., on Josh 9:4; Isa 19:18; Jer 17:2; see also Cohen, Hosea (1929) xxix–xxxi. On Ibn Ezra's avoidance of these textual issues, see chap. 33.2 of this volume (U. Simon).

verged from it.[74] On the other hand, Radak does not regard the accent marks (*ṭeʿamim*) or even verse divisions as binding, apparently assuming that they stem from rabbinic exegetical conjecture rather than ancient tradition.[75]

A rich byproduct of Radak's historical thinking is his innovative analysis of prominent biblical personalities, especially in Genesis. Diverging from the Rabbis, who tend to view such figures in mythical terms, attaching momentous religious meaning – often anachronistically – to their actions, Radak's portrait is vividly human, psychologically profound and historically sound. In part, his approach derives from the Spanish reaction against the midrashic perspective. The Talmud paints Abraham as a spectacular paradigm of Jewish faith and observance, who "recognized God at age three" (*b. Ned.* 32 a) and fulfilled all of God's laws that would later be given at Sinai (*b. Yoma* 28 b). Radak deems this *derash* and adopts the more modest Spanish view that Abraham discovered monotheism in middle age and simply fulfilled all that God commanded *him*, as recorded in Genesis.[76]

Beyond simply offsetting midrashic extravagance, Radak provides a glimpse of the demeanor of the forefathers and, viewing them as real people, opens avenues of inquiry overlooked by his predecessors. He wonders why Abimelekh, the Philistine King, was attracted to Sarah at age ninety (Gen 20:2), a question that eluded those whose mythical portrait of Sarah precluded seeing her as a flesh and blood woman.[77] Radak's profile of the forefathers prominently features human weakness. The angel injured Jacob (Gen 32:26), according to Radak, to punish his unjustified apprehension about meeting Esau after God's promise of protection. And in considering Jacob's angry rebuke of Simeon and Levi for their violence towards "the city that defiled their sister" (Gen 34:31), Radak writes in a similar vein that "Jacob, our father was fearful, *as was his custom*; but his sons were courageous men, to avenge the desecration of their honor".[78]

A midrashic tradition may launch Radak's intimate, 'personal' analysis. Scripture relates that Isaac loved his boisterous son, Esau, because "hunting

---

[74] See *Shorashim*, s.v. איש, יחל, בנה; see also Cohen, Hosea (1929) xxviii–xxix. On the origin of the vocalization, however, Radak is unclear; though he posits its Mosaic origin (*Mikhlol* 73 a), he elsewhere speaks of "those who established the vocalization" (*Mikhlol* 54 b). See Simon, Two Approaches (1968) 223.

[75] See Radak on Hos 12:12; Gen 22:4; Josh 13:3; Isa 45:8. See also Cohen, Hosea (1929) xxix; Simon, Two Approaches (1968) 224.

[76] Gen 26:5 ("he kept … my commandments, laws and decrees"), following Ibn Ezra, ad loc. Maimonides, *Hilkhot ʿAvoda Zara* 1.3, relies on the less prominent rabbinic view (*Gen. Rab.* 30:8) that Abraham's faith developed after age forty; Rabad of Posquières (gloss, ad loc.), though, cites the talmudic view (age three) evidently more popular in twelfth century Provence.

[77] Ibn Ezra ignores this question. Perhaps he dismissed the issue as unimportant; or, maybe, the midrashic portrayal was anchored even in his mind, preventing him from considering Sarah's sensual allure. Interestingly, the virulent anti-Jewish eleventh century Muslim Spanish scholar, Ibn Ḥazm, raises this very question (among others) to malign the Hebrew Bible; see his *Kitāb al-Fiṣal fī'l-Milal wa'l-Ahwā' wa'l-Niḥal* (Beirut 1975) I. 135 (I thank my colleague, Dr. Camilla Adang, for this reference). If Ibn Ezra knew this critique, perhaps he deemed it religiously inappropriate to raise himself. Once Radak introduced this cogent question, however, it could no longer be avoided; it thus appears in Nahmanides and Abarbanel, heirs of the Spanish *peshat* tradition.

[78] See also Radak on Gen 37:12.

game was in his mouth" (Gen 25:28). The Rabbis, cited by Rashi, unable to conceive a spiritual man like Isaac impressed by an outdoorsman, explain that Esau "ensnared" his father "with his mouth" by feigning piety. No one in the Spanish tradition, from Saadiah to Ibn Ezra, could seriously consider this interpretation, nor does Radak cite it. Irked by the Rabbis' dilemma, however, he sketches a portrait of Isaac consistent with both his spirituality and the plain sense of this verse:

> Because he was old, and constantly sat at home, Isaac was charmed by Esau, who brought him game and prepared him food every day. Now this was after Isaac had grown old ... his eyes had become weak, and he was home-bound and could no longer manage any matters of the house.

Even Isaac, the great man of spirit, succumbed to old age, blindness and perhaps a degree of senility.

3.5. Religious Inspiration

Radak's intimate, psychologically compelling view of the forefathers entails its own problems. His distinctly un-midrashic approach, lacking the miraculous, pious colors of rabbinic legend, threatens to reduce the titanic figures that fired Jewish religious imagination to unexceptional, uninspiring individuals. As much as the rabbinic passion for spiritual inspiration eclipses Scripture's historical dimension, the drive for scientific accuracy marginalizes its spiritual qualities.[79] Both values attracted Radak: *peshat* powered his exegesis, but he could not forgo the midrashic search for religious meaning. Unwilling to return to the unscientific rabbinic methods, Radak blazed new trails to reach the midrashic goals within the bounds of a *peshat* methodology.

To replace the inspirational luster of Midrash, Radak creates his own system for deriving religious meaning from the forefather narratives. On Gen 14:14, a depiction of Abraham gathering "three hundred and eighteen" men to rescue Lot from mighty kings, he cites the Rabbis (*b. Ned.* 32a) who use *gemaṭria* to deduce that Abraham defeated the kings accompanied only by his lone servant, Eliezer. This dramatizes God's miraculous intervention, matched by Abraham's spectacular courage and faith; but its implausibility ignited the wrath of Ibn Ezra (ad loc.) and blinded him from conceding its religious value. Radak rejects the rabbinic reading but replicates its religious message:

> This story was written in the Torah to indicate the complete, profound faith of Abraham, for with few men he pursued four kings. And to teach that it is proper for a person to place himself in danger [if necessary] to save a relative, as Abraham did (comm. on Gen 14:1).

A plain, honest reading of the narrative – Abraham's pursuit of powerful kings with only three hundred and eighteen men – amply displays his heroic qualities, radiating religious inspiration. Radak's reading lacks midrashic sen-

[79] On this consequence of the *peshat* method, in contrast with Midrash, see U. SIMON, "The Religious Significance of the *Peshat*" (tr. E. Greenstein), *Tradition* 23 (1988) 45–53.

sationalism; but what he loses in glamour he gains in realism, building his religious theme on the sound basis of a scientific reading.[80]

Even disparaging results of Radak's frank evaluation are a source of moral guidance. Asserting (Gen 16:6) that "Sarah acted neither morally, nor piously", in her harsh treatment of Hagar, "for it is improper to ruthlessly punish an underling", Radak explains: "For this reason the story was written in the Torah, to teach people good traits, and discourage bad ones". Riding the wave of the independent-minded Spanish *peshat* tradition, he questions the celebrated matriarch's piety but displays a midrashic touch in deriving a moral lesson from his observation.[81]

Much like his interest in linguistic nuance, Radak's religious sensitivity counters Ibn Ezra's reductionism. According to the Rabbis (*Tanḥuma*, *Toledot* 8) Isaac's blindness (Gen 27:1) resulted from a spiritual cause, the incense of Esau's idolatrous wives. This view, adopted by Rashi and cited by Radak as *derash*, is strongly rejected by Ibn Ezra (on Gen 25:34), who sees no need to seek a special reason for an ordinary human affliction.[82] Radak, at first following Ibn Ezra, attributes Isaac's blindness to old age, much as Jacob lost his sight on his deathbed (Gen 48:10). True, Isaac became blind twenty years before his death; but Radak initially minimizes this difference, saying that "in some, old age comes on faster than in others, according to their nature and behavior". "Or, perhaps", he continues, opening the midrashic line of inquiry Ibn Ezra had sealed off, "the failure of his eyes so early was a 'tribulation of the righteous'". After hazarding a theological explanation, Radak's confidence waxes, producing a more definitive didactic conclusion: "And for this [reason] this story was written, to indicate that God tests the righteous with suffering in this world, according to His wisdom".

In a similar fashion, Radak extracts a religious message from many of the Genesis narratives, using distinctive didactic phraseology such as, "This story was written in the Torah to show ...", "In this story the Torah teaches ...".[83] Others in the Spanish tradition, of course, attributed religious meaning to the Bible; but this endeavor took a more general form and focused on the overall

80 See also Radak on Gen 18:7 (compare *b. B. Meṣ* 86b); 39:7 (compare *b. Yoma* 35b; *b. Soṭa* 36b).

81 See also Radak on Gen 9:20. Nahmanides adopts Radak's analysis on both Gen 16:6 and 9:20 (on v. 26) and was influenced by his tendency to critically evaluate hallowed biblical figures (compare, e.g., Nahmanides on Gen 12:10; Radak ad loc. and v. 12). For an analogous attempt to derive religious meaning from objective *peshat* readings, see Simon, Religious Significance (1988) 56–58.

82 Compare his reaction to the midrashic reading of Zech 8:1, "there is no need to explain why [it] was red" (above, sect. 3.3).

83 See, e.g., Radak on Gen 18:5, 9, 21; 21:15; 24:64; 32:14; see also Melammed, Commentators (1978) 789–92. This tendency, and even Radak's distinctive phraseology, was adopted by Nahmanides, e.g., on Gen 4:17; 9:26; 23:19; 32:4. (The fourteenth century Provençal exegete and philosopher, Levi ben Gershon [Gersonides] brought this endeavor to new heights by systematically deriving a moral lesson [*toʿelet*; lit. benefit, use] from every biblical narrative episode.) Radak's reasons for limiting this pattern to Genesis are unclear; perhaps it reflects his mature thinking (in his final commentary, above, n. 25), or a theological need to attribute religious meaning to the Pentateuch, the word of God Himself (see Radak Ps 19:8). In rare instances he manifests a similar endeavor outside the Pentateuch; see, e.g., Jonah 1:1.

message emerging from larger units.[84] It is not unlikely, then, that Midrash inspired Radak to extrapolate specific religious meaning from individual episodes and narrative details.[85] We should also remember that Joseph Qimhi, in his Proverbs commentary, regularly digresses from his linguistic analysis to provide moral guidance and that he translated ethical works by Baḥya and Ibn Gabirol. Perhaps exposure to this Andalusian ethical stream transmitted by his father made Radak receptive to the religious value of midrashic literature.

In his Prophets and Psalms commentaries, Radak wields another midrashic technique to enhance Scripture's inspirational dimension. He applies biblical prophecies to the awaited messianic salvation and his co-religionists' plight "in this exile", just as King David's enemies, vividly depicted in Psalms, represent Israel's medieval oppressors. David's frightening image, "dogs surround me, a pack of evil ones closes in on me, like lions [maim] my hands and feet" (Ps 22:17), he maintains, describes how "we cannot escape those who devour us, for if we leave the dominion of the Ishamelites [Arabs], we enter the dominion of the uncircumcised [Christians] ... we cannot escape with our feet, nor fight with our hands". Radak reads Israel's suffering into the divine historical plan revealed in Scripture, which culminates in messianic redemption. "All [prophecies of] consolation" in the second part of Isaiah, he writes, "are for the days of Messiah" (40:1), who "will open eyes deprived of light, and rescue prisoners from confinement, from the dungeon those who sit in darkness" (42:7). That verse, he tells his readers, refers to "*your* eyes, blinded in exile by great suffering ... and *you* who are imprisoned in exile, in the dungeon sitting in darkness". Scripture describes the messianic era extensively, Radak explains, "to reassure those who have lost all hope for redemption on account of the length of the [current] exile" (Ps 97:1).

Radak's more modest innovations in this area must be evaluated in light of the traditions he inherited.[86] Both the pattern of rabbinic zeal for relevance at the expense of scientific exegesis and the converse *peshat* trend emerge here in new colors. Midrash typically applies prophecies to the far future; the Andalusian approach, championed by Moses ibn Chiquitilla, to events now buried in ancient history. Though he cogently discovered the meaning of biblical passages in their historical context and indelibly influenced later exegetes, Ibn Chiquitilla represents a high-water-mark that quickly receded, having become controversial even in rationalist Andalusia.[87] In rectifying the scientific deficiencies of midrashic exegesis, he created a religious crisis by depriving medieval Jewry of direct scriptural guidance and messianic dreams. Ibn Ezra already

[84] See, e.g., Maimonides, *Guide* 3.50 (compare intro. to *Pereq Ḥeleq*, *Mishnah ʿim Perush ha-Rambam: Neziqin* [ed. J. Qāfiḥ; Jerusalem 1965] 214–15). An earlier precedent appears in *Saadya's Commentary on Genesis* (ed. and tr. M. Zucker; New York 1984) 7–9 (Arab.), 171–75 (Heb.).

[85] As a rule, Ibn Ezra avoids such analysis, which he may have deemed conjectural (for an exception, see comm. on Gen 23:19). He may have taken religious inspiration from Scripture as a whole, not every detail; see Simon, Four Approaches (1991) 200–03. Yet his Psalms commentary – uncharacteristically – contains a "significant proportion of theological exegeses", i.e., an attempt to derive fundamental religious beliefs from specific passages (ibid., 210–16).

[86] Radak's citations of his father in this regard (e.g., on Isa 52:13; Ps 22:30) suggest influence but are too sparse to conclusively indicate the source of his approach.

[87] See Simon, Four Approaches (1991) 113–15.

signals a decisive retreat from Ibn Chiquitilla's iconoclasm, reviving the traditional approach, albeit sparingly and critically.[88]

Radak, then, did not initiate the trend; but he swung the pendulum closer to its midrashic point of origin. The approach modestly re-introduced by Ibn Ezra fills his horizon, ostensibly applied wherever possible. "This exile" and the messianic redemption, minor themes in Ibn Ezra, grow to huge proportions in Radak, including, for example, much of Isaiah and roughly a third of Psalms, and crowd out Ibn Chiquitilla's radical views, which he never cites.[89] Radak will sometimes apply the midrashic approach over Ibn Ezra's historical objections; for example, the rabbinic equation of Edom with the Roman Empire, rejected by Ibn Ezra, is applied by Radak to relate biblical prophecies to Rome's medieval heirs, Israel's oppressors in "this exile".[90]

In his eagerness to apply Scripture to his own time, Radak admittedly oversteps the bounds of what a modern reader would regard as *peshat.* Still, true to his Spanish heritage, Radak's historical and literary sense do temper his search for religious relevance. When confronted by compelling textual evidence, he adopts a historical reading despite rabbinic attempts to apply a post-biblical one.[91] On the other hand, he sometimes uses scientific tools to further his midrashic goals, citing textual evidence to question the historical reading advanced by his predecessors and argue instead for a messianic reading.[92] He also augments his midrash-like approach with literary explanations to circumvent historical critiques. Outright allegorization grants timelessness at the expense of historicity; Radak on Psalms achieves both by claiming that texts written for one situation were meant to be applied to others. David's prayer in sickness uses "language suitable for any person suffering from disease, as many psalms ... were composed by David to be available for all worshippers" (Ps 6:1). While upholding its original setting, Radak applies this psalm to the remote future: "some say it is said about the exile, for Israel in exile are like sick, afflicted people".[93]

---

88 U. Simon, "Ibn Ezra Between Medievalism and Modernism: The Case of Isaiah XL–LXVI", VTSup 36 (1985) 257–71. On the potential religious paucity of the historical method, see idem, Religious Significance (1988) 52–53.

89 See esp. Radak on Isa 40:1 (cited above) in comparison with Ibn Ezra who cites Ibn Chiquitilla's view. See also Radak on Isa 2:9; 4:2; 11:1 (compare Ibn Ezra), 24:1 (compare Ibn Ezra, v. 14); Joel 3:1. "This exile", in Radak's view, is the subject of Psalms 22, 42, 43, 44, 62, 65, 69, 74, 77, 80, 84; messianic times the subject of Psalms 45–48, 50, 67, 75, 76, 108, 120–134. Radak knew Ibn Chiquitilla's views, if only from citations in Ibn Ezra (compare, e.g., Radak and Ibn Ezra on Ps 51:20), and does cite his less controversial philological exegesis.

90 Compare Ibn Ezra Isa 34:6; Ob 10, Ps 108:1 with Radak Isa 34:1, Ob 1; compare also Ibn Ezra and Radak Ps 42:8. Simon, Four Approaches (1991) 206–10 argues that Ibn Ezra at times (e.g., on Psalm 22) avoided applying biblical passages to medieval times to distance himself from the Karaite method. Interestingly, Radak opts for a historical reading of Psalm 30 and ignores the eschatological reading Ibn Ezra (comm. on v. 1) mentions, albeit as a remote possibility.

91 See Radak on Isa 30:18; 33:24; Ps 2:12; 18:8.

92 See Radak on Zech 10:12; see also 8:12; 11:7 ff.

93 See Radak on Ps 10:1; 38:1; 40:1; 90:1; see also 1 Sam 2:5 (cf. 2:1). Radak's historical and literary insight served him well in his critique of Christological readings, which manifest the exegetical strategies – and deficiencies – of Midrash. The claim that Psalm 87 foretells Jesus' birth, he observes, is inconsistent, since it requires taking some verses literally and others metaphorically in the same context. (This critique, removed from the printed text, appears in Esterson's ed.) Radak

3.6. *Influence*

Radak shines forth as the proud culmination of the Qimhi family, having entered the rarified sphere of classical exegetes that includes Rashi and Ibn Ezra. Unlike Rashi and Ibn Ezra, though, who each represent a single tradition, Radak integrates two: strict scientific Andalusian *peshat* and creative, inspirational Midrash. Pulled by competing interests, he was perforce guided by intuition rather than precise rules in navigating original territory between creative *peshat* and controlled *derash.* Indeed, Radak's choice to allow Spanish *peshat* or midrashic currents to dominate at any given point is not always predictable; yet the constant tension between them makes his exegesis both intellectually stimulating and spiritually satisfying, qualities that no doubt contributed to his wide appeal and influence.

Written in a lucid style that obviated the need for supercommentaries, Radak's works quickly entered the stream of Jewish biblical exegesis and profoundly influenced subsequent biblical scholarship. A generation later in Christian Spain, by then in the orbit of the Northern French talmudists, Nahmanides, situated in the nexus between the indigenous *peshat* tradition and rabbinic exegesis, territory charted by Radak, often drew upon his works.[94] Abarbanel, living three centuries later in a scientific Renaissance milieu, regularly used Radak's linguistic analysis and shows special interest in his historical insights.[95] Radak is cited by contemporary Christian scholars, such as Raymond Martini (Spain, 1220–85) and Bernard Gui (France, 1261–1331), but the cloud of anti-Jewish sentiment prevented any profound influence in the medieval Christian world.[96] By the sixteenth century, however, prominent Christian Hebraists, such as Johannes Reuchlin (Germany, 1455–1522) and Sebastian Münster (Germany, 1489–1552), owed much of their knowledge of biblical Hebrew to Radak; and Christian Bible translators, including the authors of the King James Bible (published 1611), frequently consulted his works.[97] After the advent of printing, Radak's grammar and dictionary were published numerous times, as were his commentaries, many of which appeared

rejects the claim that the "sign [of] a young woman ... to give birth to a son" (Isa 7:14) refers to Jesus, since *ʿalma* in biblical Hebrew does not mean "virgin". Moreover, this "sign", given by Isaiah to reassure Ahaz, would have been useless if it did not bear fruit for hundreds of years. Radak's polemic against Christological messianic readings did not deter him from applying Jewish messianic readings to the very same passages; see, e.g., Mic 5:1; Ps 21:1; 45:18.

[94] See *Kitve Ramban* (ed. C. Chavel; Jerusalem 1964) I. 12; see also above, nn. 77, 81, 83.

[95] See E. Lawee, "On the Threshold of the Renaissance: New Methods and Sensibilities in the Biblical Commentaries of Isaac Abarbanel", *Viator: Medieval and Renaissance Studies* 26 (1995) 289–305.

[96] In fact, medieval Christian citations of Radak's work usually occur in polemical contexts. See J. Cohen, *The Friars and the Jews* (Ithaca 1982) 81, 95, 152.

[97] See L. I. Newman, *Jewish Influence on Christian Reform Movements* (New York 1925) 99–100, 326–27, 542, 622–23. To be sure, hostility towards Radak, motivated especially by his anti-Christian polemics, continued during the Renaissance. His works were denounced by the Mantuan Commission (1581) and even the Christian heretic Michael Servetus (Spain 1509–53), himself profoundly influenced by Radak's exegesis, condemned "the replies ... made by Rabbi Chimchi against the Christians"; see Newman, 327, 540–48.

in the Rabbinic Bible early in the sixteenth century and in subsequent editions until modern times.

Biblical scholarship has changed radically over eight centuries, yet Radak's writings retain their original luster. His linguistic analysis and stylistic observations, based on firm scriptural evidence, extra-biblical cognates and keen intuition retain their cogency to this day. Although Radak had no access to archaeological evidence, some of his historical insights and conjectures are still taken into consideration by modern scholars. Moreover, Radak's ability to interpret the Bible historically without forfeiting its spiritual dimension can still serve as a guiding light for modern readers who look to Scripture for moral and religious inspiration.

33.4. Moses ben Nahman / Nahmanides (Ramban)

By YAAKOV ELMAN, New York

Sources: H. D. CHAVEL, *Perushe Hatora Lerabbenu Moshe ben Nahman (Ramban)*, 1–2 (Jerusalem: Mosad Harav Kuk 1969/70); M. Z. EIZENSTADT (ed.), *Perush Haramban ʿal Hatorah*, I. Bereshit-Vayishlah (New York: 'Zikron Yosef' 1958/59), II. Vayeshev-Vayehi (New York 1959/60).

Studies (on editions of Ramban's Commentary on the Torah): E. GOTTLIEB, "Biqoret ʿal Mahadurat Kitbe Haramban shel Harav H. D. Chavel", *Qiryat Sefer* 40 (1964/65) 1–9; idem, *Meḥqarim Besifrut Haqabbalah* (Tel Aviv: University of Tel Aviv 1976) 88–96, 516–36; K. KAHANA, "Tosafot Haramban Leperusho Latorah", *Hamaʿyan* 9 (1968/69) 25–47; Y. MARSHEN, *Tifʾeret Lemoshe: Hagahot Vetuqqunim Beperush Haramban ʿal Bereshit-Shemot* (Amsterdam 1918/19) (Dutch); idem, *ʿal Vayiqra-Devarim, Hatsofe Lehokmat Yisrael* 7 (Budapest 1922/23) 133–52; M. SABBATO, "ʿAl Nusaḥ Perush Ramban Latorah", *Megadim* 23 (1994/95) 71–81.

1. Biographical and General Remarks

Studies on the historical background: D. BERGER, "Review Essay: The Barcelona Disputation" [on R. Chazan, *Barcelona and Beyond*; see below], *AJS Review* 22 (1995) 379–88; H. H. BEN-SASSON, "Moshe ben Nahman: Ish Besʿivkei Tequfato", *Molad* 1:4 (5728 [1967/68]) 360–66; R. CHAZAN, "The Barcelona 'Disputation' of 1263", *Spec.* LII (1977) 834–42; idem, *Barcelona and Beyond: The Disputation of 1263 and Its Aftermath* (Berkeley: University of California Press 1992); H. D. CHAVEL, *Rabbenu Mose ben Nahman: Toledot Ḥayyav, Zemano Veḥibburav* (Jerusalem: Mosad Harav Kook 5727 [1966/67]); B. Z. KEDAR, "Yehudei Yerushalayim (1178–1267) ve-Ḥeleq ha-Ramban be-Shiqqum Kehilatam", *Peraqim be-Toledot Yerushalayim bi-Ymei ha-Benayyim* (ed. B. Z. Kedar; Jerusalem: Yad Ben Zvi 5739 [1978/79]) 122–36; M. FOX, "Nachmanides on the Status of Aggadot: Perspectives on the Disputation at Barcelona, 1263", *JJS* 40 (1989) 95–109; C. ROTH, "The Disputation at Barcelona (1263)", *HTR* 43/2 (1950) 117–18; B. SEPTIMUS, *Hispano-Jewish Culture in Transition: The Career and Controversies of Ramah* (Cambridge, MA: Harvard UP 1982); Y. SHAHAR, "Ḥotamo shel ha-Ramban", *Peraqim Be-Toledot Yerushalayim Bi-Ymei Ha-Benayyim* (ed. B. Z. Kedar; Jerusalem: Yad Ben Zvi 5739) 137–47; D. J. SILVER, *Maimonidean Criticism and the Maimonidean Controversy* (Leiden: E. J. Brill 1965).

Moses ben Nahman (Lat. Nahmanides, often called by the acronym RaMBaN), was one of the most influential scholars that Spanish Jewry produced, one whose versatility and scope still astonish. He was a penetrating talmudist and legalist, a mystic whose early training in medieval Jewish philosophy nevertheless remained a living influence in his thought, an accomplished courtier and communal leader. Withal, he was a prolific writer, producing some 50 works or more, including talmudic *novellae*, legal and ritual treatises, biblical commentaries, occasional poetry and sermons, and at least one anti-Christian polemic which became a classic, an account of his Barcelona debate with Pablo Christiani in the presence of the royal court of King James I of Catalonia.

Moses ben Nahman, born in Gerona, Catalonia, in 1194, practiced medicine under the name of Bonastrug da Porta; born into the rabbinic and economic elite, he received an excellent education, and was one of the first in Spain to be initiated into the talmudic methods of the tosafists of Northern

France; in addition, he was familiar with the works of the schools of Provence. His disciples included the leading halakhists of the next generation.

His role in public life apparently began in 1232, when he entered the then raging Maimonidist controversy, attempting to find a compromise between the two sides. Even at that early stage in his career, he was consulted by the king on matters affecting the internal life of Catalonia's Jewish community. He may have acted as Chief Rabbi of Catalonia after the death in 1264 of his cousin, R. Jonah Gerondi. It is certain that in the next year he was forced into a debate with the apostate Pablo Christiani in the presence of the king and the leaders of the Dominicans and Franciscans, a disputation he won, receiving 300 dinars from the king. Despite this, he was eventually forced to leave Spain and arrived in Eretz Israel in 1267, where he completed his Pentateuchal commentary and was active in the Jewish communities of Jerusalem and Acre until his death in 1270.

In general, Nahmanides was less an innovator than a remarkable systematizer who adapted and extended methods and insights which he inherited, and combined them within a system of his own devising while putting his own stamp on them. As a Spanish Jew, he was the heir of the Spanish penchant for systematization, but his teacher R. Yehudah b. Yakar enabled him to become a master of the newly devised dialectic developed by Rabbenu Jacob Tam (ca. 1100–71) in Northern France. It was apparently from R. Yehudah that he received his kabbalistic traditions as well.

2. Aspects of Nahmanides' Exegetical Method

General works on rabbinic exegesis: M. Fishbane (ed.), *The Midrashic Imagination: Jewish Exegesis, Thought and History* (Albany: State University of New York Press 1993); D. W. Halivni, *Peshat and Derash: Plain and Applied Meaning in Rabbinic Exegesis* (Oxford: Oxford UP 1991); J. M. Harris, *How Do We Know This: Midrash and the Fragmentation of Modern Judaism* (Albany: State University of New York Press 1995); J. L. Kugel / R. A. Greer, "Interpreters of Scripture", *Early Biblical Interpretation* (Philadelphia: Westminster Press 1986) 52–72; R. Loewe, "The 'Plain' Meaning of Scriptures in Early Jewish Exegesis", *Papers of the Institute of Jewish Studies* I (1964) 140–86; D. Stern, *Parables in Midrash: Narrative and Exegesis in Rabbinic Literature* (Cambridge: Harvard UP 1991).

Special studies on Nahmanides' exegesis: Y. Elman, "It Is No Empty Thing: Nahmanides and the Search for Omnisignificance", *The Torah U-Madda Journal* IV (1993) 1–83; idem, "The Status of Deuteronomy as Revelation: Nahmanides and Abarbanel", *Hazon Nahum: Studies in Jewish Law, Thought and History Presented to Dr. Norman Lamm in Honor of His Seventieth Birthday* (ed. Y. Elman / J. Gurock, 1997; New York: Yeshiva UP 1997) 229–50; A. Funkenstein, "History and Typology: Nachmanides: Reading of the Biblical Narrative", *Perceptions of Jewish History* (Los Angeles: University of California Press 1973) 98–121; Y. Gottlieb, "'Ein Muqdam u-Meʿuhar' be-Ferush Ramban la-Torah", *Tarbiz* 63 (1984) 41–62; M. Idel, "We have No Kabbalistic Tradition on This", *Rabbi Moses Nahmanides (Ramban): Explorations in His Religious and Literary Virtuosity* (ed. I. Twersky; Cambridge: Harvard UP 1983) 51–73; E. Kanarfogel, "On the Assessment of R. Moses ben Nahman (Nahmanides) and His Literary Œuvre", *Jewish Book Annual* 51 (1993/94) 158–72; D. Novak, "Nahmanides' Commentary on the Torah", *The Solomon Goldman Lecture Series* V (1990) 87–104; H. Novetsky, "The Influence of Rabbi Joseph Bechor Shor and Radak on Ramban's Commentary on the Torah" (Master's Thesis, Bernard Revel Graduate School, Yeshiva University 1992); J. Perles, "Über den Geist des Commentars des R. Moses ben Nachman zum Pentateuch und über sein Verhältnis zum Pentateuch-Commentar Raschi's", *MGWJ* 7 (1858) 81–

98, 117–62; idem, "Nachträge über R. Moses ben Nachman", *MGWJ* 9 (1860) 184–95; M. Saperstein, "Jewish Typological Exegesis after Nachmanides", *Jewish Studies Quarterly* 1 (1993/94) 158–70; B. Septimus, "'Open Rebuke and Concealed Love': Nahmanides and the Andalusian Tradition", *Rabbi Moses Nahmanides (Ramban): Explorations in His Religious and Literary Virtuosity* (ed. I. Twersky; Cambridge: Harvard UP 1983) 11–34; idem, "Introduction", *Rabbi Moses Nahmanides (Ramban)* (ed. I. Twersky; 1983) 1–10; E. R. Wolfson, "By Way of Truth: Aspects of Nachmanides' Kabbalistic Hermeneutic", *AJS Review* 14 (1989) 103–78.

As a biblical commentator Nahmanides saw himself as the heir of the Spanish school of Abraham ibn Ezra (1089–1164), with its emphasis on the plain meaning and linguistic understanding, along with the more midrashically oriented commentary of Rashi (1040–1105), who, though stressing the importance of the *peshat* - the plain meaning of the biblical text, included more than a flavoring of rabbinic non-*peshat* teaching, both legal and aggadic, in his commentary. Indeed, Nahmanides' commentary may be considered one of the first great super-commentaries on Rashi; according to one study, he adverts to Rashi in some 38% of his comments in his Pentateuchal exegesis.[1]

A third major acknowledged source, especially in his more philosophical locumbrations is Maimonides (1135–1204). Underpinning all his work is a thorough knowledge of classic rabbinic sources – not only the Babylonian and Palestinian Talmuds, but also the halakhic and aggadic Midrashim, geonic works, as well as such mystical works as *Sefer Ha-Bahir*, which he introduced to a wider audience through the medium of his Pentateuchal commentary.

Despite the close attention to his immediate predecessors of the previous century-and-a-half, he does not hesitate to differ from any of his major sources, classic rabbinic literature excepted, though he treats Rashi and Maimonides, who were also talmudists and legalists, with noticeably greater respect than he does Ibn Ezra.[2]

Formally speaking, Nahmanides' exegetical efforts are mainly to be found in his mystical / midrashic commentary to the Song of Songs, his commentary to Job, which blends a linguistically based plain meaning approach leavened with liberal doses of philosophical and theological discourse, and, above all, his Commentary on the Pentateuch, beyond doubt his *magnum opus* in this area, a work in which both his versatility, insight, and erudition are on display. In it his feeling for structure and theme, historical context, psychological verity, and a balanced theological approach combining both philosophical and mystical foundations – all find their metier. The result is a highly nuanced, often open-ended, multileveled interpretation of the Pentateuch, in which literal meaning, moral and legalistic exegesis, and eschatological and mystical interpretation all find their place.

---

[1] "Le-Darko shel ha-Ramban", *Teʿudah* 3, *Meḥkarim be-Sifrut ha-Talmud, bi-Leshon Ḥazal uve-Farshanut ha-Mikra* (Tel Aviv 1983) 227–33, esp. 228–30.

[2] See Yehudah Cooperman, "Tokhahat Megullah ve-Ahavah Mesutteret", in his collection *Li-Peshuṭo shel Miqra* (Jerusalem 1963/64) 161–86.

2.1. *Omnisignificance*

To one degree or another, most Jewish commentators both before and after Nahmanides' time have followed a program laid out for them by the classic rabbinic midrashic and talmudic texts. That is, they have been concerned with questions of meaning and meaningfulness within their restricted rabbinic sense.

Recently JAMES KUGEL has proposed the term 'omnisignificance' to describe the essential stance of the rabbinic exegesis of Scripture. According to him, 'omnisignificance' constitutes

> the basic assumption underlying all of rabbinic exegesis that the slightest details of the biblical text have a meaning that is both comprehensible and significant. Nothing in the Bible ... ought to be explained as the product of chance, or, for that matter, as an emphatic or rhetorical form, or anything similar, nor ought its reasons to be assigned to the realm of Divine unknowables. Every detail is put there to reach something new and important, and it is capable of being discovered by careful analysis.[3]

If we equate Kugel's "something new and important" with ethical / theological (aggadic) or legal (halakhic) insights, his definition is a restatement of the rabbinic interpretation of Deut 32:47 – "For it is not an empty thing for you, it is your very life, and if [it appears] devoid [of moral or halakhic meaning] – it is you [who have not worked out its moral or legal significance]".[4] Kugel's "meaning that is both comprehensible and significant" thus in rabbinic terms has a sharply limited and highly focused range of admissible interpretation; omnisignificance is restricted to interpretations which give the text a moral or legal dimension.

With relatively few exceptions – Ibn Ezra comes to mind, even those who eschewed the midrashic method in favor of a rationalistic Spanish plain sense interpretive stance were nevertheless concerned with such questions. The tension between the biblical text, and its concern for matters historical, geographical and genealogical, and the rabbinic relegation of such matters to unimportance was constant.

The comment of the mid-third century Palestinian authority, R. Simon b. Lakish's, as recorded in the Babylonian Talmud (*Ḥul.* 60b) demonstrates this tension. "There are verses (*miqra'ot*) which are worthy of being burnt, but they are [after all] essential components of Torah". There follow attempts to tease moral significance from the geographical and historical data recorded in Deut 2:23 and Num 21:26, which are explained as demonstrating how God arranged matters so that Israel could conquer Philistine and Moabite land while still maintaining the oath which Abraham swore to Abimelekh

---

[3] This term has gained some currency through its use by JAMES KUGEL in his *The Idea of Biblical Poetry: Parallelism and Its History* (New Haven / London 1981) 103–04. Most recently, RICHARD STEINER has studied one consequence of the principle at "ground level", and traced its use even among those exegetes most devoted to "pashtanic" (plain sense) readings. See his "Meaninglessness, Meaningfulness, and Super-Meaningfulness in Scripture: An Analysis of the Controversy Surrounding Dan 2:12 in the Middle Ages", *JQR* 82 (1992) 431–50.

[4] *y. Ketub.* 8:11 (32c), based on Deut 32:47.

(Gen 21:23) and the prohibition of "vexing Moab" at Deut 2:9. It is worth quoting the talmudic redactors' response to Deut 2:23, which reports on the geographical location of the Avvites' settlements: "What difference does this make?"

Thus, 'omnisignificance' describes not only a fundamental assumption of the rabbinic view of Scripture, it also serves to guide rabbinic interpretation into certain fairly well-defined channels, and establishes a hierarchy of preference in regard to exegetical alternatives.

Historically, 'omnisignificance' reflects a rabbinic view of Scripture rather than a complete exegetical program. It describes an ideal *which was never actually realized.* Not every feature of Scripture has been interpreted either halakhically or aggadically. Our collections of Midrashim hardly constitute an omnisignificant corpus; not only do they fail to deal with many verses, and even whole biblical chapters, but features which are considered significant – legally or morally – in one context are ignored in others. The rabbinic program or programs do not even attempt to provide a complete commentary, in whatever mode, to any biblical book, chapter, or passage.[5]

Despite the ancient grounding of this concern, Nahmanides was able to translate his sensitivity to matters of structure, proportion and sequence into developing and systematizing sporadic rabbinic insights into novel and enduring omnisignificant approaches to the Pentateuch, and thereby advancing the rabbinic omnisignificant program in ways which would have amazed his predecessors, and, despite his vast prestige, often escaped his successors.

2.2. Structure and Theme

Among the signal characteristics of Nahmanides' Pentateuchal commentary is his sensitivity to structure, and his preference for structural explanations of exegetical cruces. To an immensely greater extent than his predecessors, both Spanish and French, his concern for such matters engendered an ongoing investigation into the Pentateuch's choice, order and arrangement of expositions, incidents and narratives, and into questions of the themes which were expressed by such structures.

Thus, for example, the division of the Pentateuch into *five* books could not be taken for granted, but must be given meaning. It is characteristic of Nahmanides that his search for the meaning of each of these books on its own gave full weight to the content of each, structure played a role as well. Thus, the chronological gap between the end of Genesis (the death of Joseph) and the beginning of Exodus (a resumptive repetition of the descent of the Israelites into Egypt some seventy years *before* Joseph's demise), and that between the end of Exodus (the descent of the divine Presence, which in reality does not occur until Lev 9:23) and the beginning of Leviticus. Thus, for Nahmanides,

[5] The one consistent exception may be Targum, but the relation of this genre in early times to the rabbinic movement is still unclear. In any case, Targum in the strict sense, as represented by Onkelos, seems relatively unconcerned with the omnisignificant ideal.

these two chronological gaps serve to delimit the contents of Exodus in a way which *expresses* the book's essential theme.

The entrance of the Israelites into Egypt is a true "descent", by which they lose the company of the divine Presence, which is only regained with the construction and dedication of the Tabernacle. The heterogenous materials of the book of Exodus – the enslavement, the plagues, the exodus, the theophany at Sinai, followed by the civil and criminal code of the Book of the Covenant, another account of the Sinaitic theophany, the construction of the Tabernacle, interrupted by the idolatrous worship of the Golden Calf, the renewal of the covenant, additional legislation and, finally, the actual construction of the Tabernacle – are subsumed under the thematic heading of "exile and redemption". The loss of the divine Presence represents for Nahmanides, as it did for the Rabbis, the essence of exile, and so the construction of the Tabernacle represents the Israelites' reestablishment of their relationship with God. Thus, the resumptive repetition at the beginning of Exodus, together with the forshadowing of the future descent of the divine Presence at its end, sound the theme of the book as a whole.

In the case of Numbers, however, theme and structure are somewhat at odds. Nahmanides notes another chronological inconnicity at the beginning of Numbers, which is dated to first day of the second month of the second year since the exodus, while Num 9:1 is dated to the first month (see below, 2.4. Sequence). Nahmanides sees these chapters as a sort of appendix to Leviticus, complementing that book's exposition of ritual law with matters dealing with the encampment in the wilderness. The question of why, then, these chapters are placed in Numbers rather than Leviticus becomes urgent, and Nahmanides provides an response of a sort in his introduction to Numbers.

Numbers is devoted, on the whole, to matters which concern the Israelites in the wilderness, rather than providing legislation for future generations. These timely, rather than timeless, rules regarding the encampment therefore fall under this rubric and properly belong in Numbers rather than Leviticus.

Thus, the introductions he composed for three of the books of the Pentateuch (Exodus, Numbers and Deuteronomy) express his view of the purpose of each of them in terms of content and theme. In contrast, however, he also discerned an overarching theme of divine revelation within the last four books of the Pentateuch, coalescing into three great periods – that of the Sinaitic theophany and the giving of the Book of the Covenant, that which took place after the incident of the Golden Calf and the subsequent renewal of the covenant, and the law code revealed in the Tabernacle and encapsulated within Exodus 33–Numeri 31, and the final covenant concluded with the new generation about to enter the land of Canaan, that of Deuteronomy. The subsequent tension was never altogether resolved and the two views of the Pentateuch were not entirely integrated.

2.3. *Patterning*

Closely related to Nahmanides' concern with structure is his sensitivity to recurrent narrative patterns; these are often related to matters of chronology and sequence. For example, in rejecting the midrashic explanation (as adopted by Rashi ad loc. and to be found in *Genesis Rabba* 39:7) of why Terah's death is recorded in Gen 11:32 rather than in its proper chronological place in Genesis 22, he notes that "this is the custom of all recorded [Pentateuchal history] to narrate the life of the father, his begetting a son and [then] dying, and after that to begin [the narrative] regarding the son['s life]" (Gen 11:32).

Again, he rejects Rashi's midrashic explanation for the repetition of the word *ve-hayu* in Exod 4:9, "take some water from the Nile and pour it on the dry ground, and it will become (*ve-hayu*) – the water that you take from the Nile – it will become (*ve-hayu*) blood on the dry ground". According to Rashi ad loc., the repetition of this verb indicates that the water did not turn to blood until it had *hit the dry ground*. In contrast, Nahmanides notes that:

> The meaning is not as the Master gives it, and there is no need for his midrashic comment, for the masters of language [study] have already discovered that it is the custom of many verses to repeat (*likhpol*) words for need (*le-naḥaz*) and for strengthening (*le-ḥizzuq*) or because of the lengthy space (*mitsuʿa arokh*) which comes between them.[6]

Nahmanides offers other examples of this syntactic "resumptive repetition", and cites Lev 27:3; Deut 18:6; Exod 1:15–16; and Gen 46:2 as examples.

Likewise, at times he employs the existence of a small-scale, though not purely syntactic repetitions, in furthering his larger – halakhic-exegetical aims. In his commentary to Num 7:1 he does not explicitly note that the clause "[When] he had anointed and consecrated them" at the end of the verse, may be seen as a resumptive repetition of "he anointed and consecrated it and all its furnishings" at its beginning, but he clearly recognized it as such. He uses the repetition as proof against Ibn Ezra's contention that the consecration was by blood and not oil, since both clauses refer to the same action, the object of which was the Tabernacle in both cases; Ibn Ezra's proof-text requires that we see Lev 8:15, which mentions the blood of the sin-offering in this connection, as a parallel. This may be the intent of Nahmanides' phrase *le-naḥats* ("for [explanatory?] need") in his comments on Exod 4:9, just cited.

Thus, his recognition of narrative and linguistic patterning serve to support a plain-sense reading of the text even against his midrashic and exegetical sources. In particular, his great respect for Rashi never impelled him to withhold his criticism or to soften his rejection of Rashi's interpretation. His commentary is sprinkled with responses such as "it [=his interpretation] is not correct".

---

6 So too in his comments on Gen 6:9. As to the "masters of language study" (*baʿalei ha-lashon*), see Ibn Janah, *Sefer ha-Rikmah* (ed. Wilenski) 296: lines 18 f, and see Chavel ad loc., n. 27.

2.4. *Sequence*

A long-standing consensus counterposes the views of Rashi and Nahmanides as to the degree to which chronology governs the order of Pentateuchal narratives. Like much of medieval exegesis, the roots of this issue lie in the past, in the midrashic / talmudic observation that *ein muqdam u-me'uhar ba-Torah*, "the Torah departs from chronological order".

The *locus classicus* for derivation of the rule is to be found, inevitably, in the Babylonian Talmud, and no justification for the asequentiality is presented. The Talmud's only proof is drawn from an instance which is beyond dispute, the relation of Num 1:1–19 and succeeding passages to 9:1–8. The date of the first is "the first of the second month of the second year" (1:1) of the Exodus era, while the second is dated sometime in "the first month" (9:1) of the same era.[7]

As far as the rule itself goes, no one can deny that this example illustrates the point. It is the conclusion to be drawn from this case that is at issue. Is this typical, or is it the exception that proves the rule, as Nahmanides contends?

Nahmanides and, following him, Don Isaac Abarbanel,[8] reject the hitherto traditional understanding of the talmudic / midrashic view that the Torah often violates strict chronological order, while Rashi and Ibn Ezra accept this rule, extending its application beyond its historic bounds (see below). Moreover, implicit in the consensus-view is the assumption that Rashi and Ibn Ezra represent a plain-sense view of Scripture.[9]

Like most matters of consensus, there is considerable truth to this simplified view of Nahmanides' position. Still, such a view overstates matters and thus overlooks the complexities which such statements mask, remaining satisfied with less than a full account which a more complete analysis of the data allows.

To begin with, Nahmanides and Abarbanel do not reject *in toto* the principle of *ein muqdam.* There are a number of instances in which such rejection is simply impossible, since the framework of the Torah's narrative makes the departure from sequentiality abundantly clear.

Nahmanides argues that the Torah clearly shows its concern with dating and chronology, since it does "inform" us of its departure from sequential order, as in the case of Num 1:1 and 9:1. In essence, he reinterprets the Talmud's proof. Rather than applying to the general principle of asequentiality – *ein muqdam u-me'uhar ba-Torah*, the Talmud's proof applies not to the principle itself, but to a proviso thereof: that the narrative and exposition do not depart from chronological order *unless* the reader is explicitly informed of this, either

---

[7] *Hodesh* here may refer to Rosh Hodesh, the first of the month; see the commentary of R. Joseph Bekhor Shor, ad loc. The talmudic passage ist at *Pesaḥ.* 6b.

[8] On this spelling of the name, see S. Z. Leiman, "Abarbanel and the Censor", *JJS* 19 (1968) 49, n. 1.

[9] On Nahmanides' view of the matter, see EncBibl VIII (Jerusalem 1982) 686–87; E. Z. Melammed, *Mefarshei ha-Mikra*, 434–35, 539–42, 939–40. To Melammed's list of instances in which Rashi claims "*ein mukdam u-me'uhar ba-Torah*" add Gen 6:3; Exod 4:20, and 19:11; to his list of Ibn Ezra's, add Num 16:1 and 16:16.

by means of dates, as in Num 1:1, or by means of chronological data of some other type, such as genealogical data regarding births and deaths, etc. His parade example of the latter is Gen 11:32, where Terah's death is "prematurely" recorded, as can easily be demonstrated in light of the chronological data regarding Abram's birth. If Terah was 70 at Abram's birth (11:26), Abraham was 135 at his death, which therefore should have been recorded in Genesis 22. In his response to Ibn Ezra's claim that this reflect's the Torah's achronological order, Nahmanides suggests the Torah will complete a generational narrative – or, we may add – an exposition, before continuing on to the next generation's history, even at the expense of some chronological inconnicities.

Applying this insight to the text of the entire Torah, Nahmanides thus requires that every narrative be approached with the assumption that the Torah's order reflects the order in which the events recorded took place, when there is no compelling evidence to the contrary. He writes:

> In my opinion, the whole Torah is in order, for in all places in which it postpones [narrating] the earlier [event] it explains [the matter], as for example "God spoke to Moses at Mount Sinai" in this book [= Lev 25:1], [or], for example "On the day Moses completed setting up the Tent" [Num 7:1] in the second book, and similar cases. That is why it states here "after the death", to tell us that this occurred immediately after their death.[10]

Thus, those cases in which the narrative signals its violation of the rule of sequentiality serve as a point of departure for Nahmanides. From these cases he applies his insight to the rest of the Pentateuch, albeit with varying degrees of success. By focusing on these cases, Nahmanides raises the question of when and why these departures take place, a matter to which Rashi does not always attend.

It is important to note that, in taking the position he does, Nahmanides goes counter to his own exegetical tradition on this issue; not only do Rashi and Ibn Ezra assert the contrary, but the thrust of the Talmud's short discussion, especially in light of R. Papa's caveat, seems to support them as well. In the light of all this, his rejection of the rule assumes greater importance.

The dispute between Nahmanides and Abarbanel, on the one side, and Rashi and Ibn Ezra on the other, centers about the question of dating those passages or events whose relation can be determined only by inference. How strained do we allow our reading to become in attempting to interpret the order of narrative as reflecting the historical order?

Furthermore, even when such departures from sequential order are acknowledged, how do we account for them? Or need we account for them at all, or account for all of them? Here, the matter of omnisignificance obtrudes, and this is often the real ground upon which the debate takes place.

For example, the proper interpretation of the dates contained within the self-contained Flood narrative are an issue between Rashi and Nahmanides. Rashi forces each date into the framework demanded by the midrashic state-

---

[10] See his commentary to Lev 16:1; the last sentence means that the following section is displaced, and that its place is really between Lev 10:20 and Lev 11:1. He too seems to have seen this as a programmatic statement, and refers to it in his animadversions against Ibn Ezra at Num 16:1, as the similar wording would indicate.

ment that the Flood lasted a year.[11] To do so, he interprets "the seventh month" of Gen 8:4 as "the seventh month from Kislev, in which the rain ceased".[12] As a consequence, he must add the 150 days during which the floodwaters receded to the forty days of the Flood proper rather than taking the entire 150 day period as *including* the forty days during which the rains fell.

This is problematic, since the date of the beginning of the forty days is the seventeenth day of the second month (2/17), and the end of the 150-day period is thus the seventeenth day of the seventh month (7/17). Nahmanides, assuming months of thirty days each, calculates the 150 days as beginning 2/17, with the start of the Flood, and ending 7/17.[13] Moreover, he notes that in order to sustain his interpretation, Rashi must continually change the dating system in use, taking the date given in 7:11 as referring to start of the Flood, that of 8:4 to the end of the rain, and that of 8:5 (the very next verse!) once again to the start of the Flood.[14]

Nahmanides himself interprets all dates as referring to the same era (= Noah's life, as is evident from 7:11[15]), a procedure more in keeping with the plain meaning of the text.[16]

There is more involved here than the use of a midrash, however, for the positions taken by Rashi and Nahmanides here reflect their sense of narrative time. Since Rashi does not expect sequential order, he is not dismayed when successive dates in the same passage refer to different starting points; Nahmanides is much more concerned in providing a unitary reading of the sequence.

Moreover, Nahmanides' sensitivity to matters of precedence and sequence impelled him to the view that expository prose obeys the same rule of sequentiality as does narrative. Again, and in contrast to Rashi, he insisted that sequentiality *within* a section must be maintained, and an exegete must account for departures from it.[17] Examples of this tendency involve descriptions of rituals which acquire a narrative character, such as Leviticus 16 on the high priest's temple service on Yom Kippur, or the procedure due on the appearance

[11] A solar year; see Rashi to 8:14 s.v. *be-shivʿah.* The source of this opinion is *Mishnah ʿEd.* 2:10 and *Genesis Rabbah* 28:9.

[12] S.v. *ba-ḥodesh ha-sheviʿi.*

[13] See his lengthy comments on 8:4 s.v. *va-tanaḥ ha-teivah.*

[14] See Rashi's (midrashic-style) defense of this procedure in his comments to 8:5.

[15] And not Anno Mundi, as Chavel remarks in his notes to 8:4, unless, of course, Noah was born on Rosh Hashanah. Since the calendar consisted of twelve months of thirty days each and could therefore hardly have been a lunar calendar, or even a lunisolar one similar to the one inaugurated just before the Exodus, identifying this calendar with any of the historical Anno Mundi calendars perpetrates the very anachronism Nahmanides is at pains to disavow.

[16] Nahmanides' justification for doing so is significant: "since Rashi [himself] in other places subjects midrashim to searching examination (*medaqdeq aḥar midreshei ha-haggadot*) and labors to explain the plain meaning of the Scripture, he has permitted us to do so as well, for there are seventy facets to Torah, and there are many conflicting midrashim in the words of the Sages".

[17] See, for example, Nahmanides' trenchant comments regarding (at least by implication) Rashi's understanding of the *Sifra*'s midrashic handling of Lev 14:43–44 in his commentary on 14:43, in which he asserts, i. a., that "it is impossible to cut them [= these verses] with a knife, to move them backward and forward (*lehakdim u-le'aher*) in a matter which is not at all their meaning (*mashmaʿam*)".

of a house fungus in Leviticus 14. But, his attention to matters of sequence is far more pervasive than that. Far more than Rashi, he traces the order of topics within a passage, or the sequence of passages within a greater whole. Among his most characteristic phrases in this endeavor are (*ve*)-*ḥazar ve-amar / u-feresh / u-veʿer / ve-hizkir / ve-tsivvah* and the like, and they appear more than a hundred times in his commentary. In some instances he is most concerned with sequence pure and simple, but most involve some sort of repetition; it is significant, however, that his account of these repetitions nearly always involve some sort of sequence, narrative or expositional.

For example, we may illustrate his concern for sequence pure and simple by pointing to his discussion of the order of laws in the Book of the Covenant (Exodus 21–23), in which he demonstrates that the sequence is not arbitrary.

> The first exposition (*mishpaṭ*) begins with [the topic] of the Hebrew slave, since it involves the matter of freeing the slave in the seventh year, a reminder of the Exodus from Egypt, mentioned in the first Commandment ... And when he completes the exposition (*mishpaṭ*) of this *mitsvah* regarding Hebrew slaves, he begins the exposition (*mishpaṭ*) of "you shall not murder", since it[s prohibition] is the most severe, and [continues] with honor of parents, and stealing, and returns to the exposition (*ḥazar le-mishpaṭ*) of one who strikes [another] non-fatally, and after that to murder of a slave, which is more heinous than killing embryos [as a result of a mistaken blow which leads to miscarriage], and after that to the [injury] of the limbs of Israelites and slaves, and after that to damages to livestock by death – and all the passages are in order and proper intent (*kavvanah*).[18]

As to the second category, where his attention to sequence comes about as a result of the need to account for repetitions of all sorts, see his remarks regarding Pharaoh's double-barrelled accusation of impropriety against Abram in Gen 12:11–13.

> It would seem that the exposition of the verses is that Sarah did not accept upon herself to say so [i.e., to claim sisterhood rather than a marriage-tie with Abraham] ... She remained silent, and did not tell that [she was] his wife, [but] Abraham told of his own that she was his sister, and therefore he was benefitted because of her. And this is [the reason] the verse states "What is this you have done to me? Why did you not tell me that she was your wife?". First he blamed him in not telling Pharaoh that she was his wife when he saw her being taken, and blamed him as well (*ḥazar ve-heʿeshim*) him for saying to the nobles after this that she was his sister. He did not blame the woman at all, for it is not fitting that she contradict her husband ...

It may be noted that the essential purpose of this comment is to account for the fact that Pharaoh did not blame Sarah for the deception; despite this, Nahmanides cannot forbear explaining the sequence of Pharaoh's claims against Abraham.

Nahmanides' keen attention to the matters of order and sequence goes beyond the expositional or narrative progress. Far more than his predecessors, he views the order of elements in all manner of sequences as significant. As a result, he formulated an impressive array of hierarchies to interpret such lists.

He thus employs no fewer than fourteen of these hierarchies: birth order when siblings are listed, either in genealogical contexts or otherwise;[19] order

---

[18] From his comments on 21:2. Such comments are common, though Num 5:5 should be singled out for mention, because it accounts for the incorporation of ritual material within a narrative context.

[19] See his commentary on Num 32:2.

of importance, whether of person, ritual object or other;[20] order of preference or love;[21] order of greater population when clans are listed[22] or otherwise.[23] Likewise, prohibitions and sins will be listed in order of (decreasing or increasing) severity;[24] elements in order of place in the chain of causation;[25] number of people affected;[26] or fearsomeness as perceived by a biblical character.[27] Rules which obtain for the indefinite future (*le-dorot*) precede those which are of temporary validity.[28] Precedence may also indicate initiative,[29] high motivation,[30] or frequency.[31] Finally, as noted above and as a fifteenth category, temporal or narrative sequence may be indicated.[32] In short, sequence almost always has a substantive significance for Nahmanides; it is hardly ever haphazard or mechanical: such is the omnisignificant imperative. While concern for these matters surfaces in midrashic texts, to some extent, they are far more prominent in Nahmanides' commentary.

2.5. *Proportion and Placement*

Nahmanides' sensitivity to structural concerns carries over to another realm; that of proportion. For example, in his comments on Exod 37:8, he enumerates the five-fold appearance of descriptions of the Tabernacle in Exodus 25–30 and 35–40 and ascribes them to the Tabernacle's importance to God (*derekh ḥibbah ve-derekh maʿalah*), explicitly comparing it to Eliezer's re-telling of his journey to Padan Aram in Genesis 24. He quotes the midrashic statement quoted above:

---

[20] See Gen 6:10; 36:12; 46:18–19; Exod 25:1 (the order of the Tabernacle vessels, with the most important first), Lev 23:40 (the citron mentioned first of the "Four Species"); 26:4 (rain is the most crucial of all blessings); Num 1:32 (the tribe of Ephraim before that of Menasseh; see Gen 48:17–20). But compare his discussion of the placement of Japhet as last of the brothers in Gen 6:10; he was the first-born, but second to Shem in rank, and his status as first-born was insufficient to overcome his inferiority to Shem. The result was that Shem was listed first, Ham, the youngest, second, and Japhet brought up the rear. Such is the power of sequentiality!

[21] Deut 28:11.

[22] Gen 46:18–19 or Num 1:32.

[23] Exod 35:22, where those who brought shittim-wood are mentioned after those who donated blue and purple wool, since the former were fewer in number.

[24] Exod 20:3 and Deut 23:5, respectively.

[25] His comments on Lev 26:4 may be interpreted in this way, though in this case its placement may be connected with the importance of rain, but see Deut 2:24, where God's role is adumbrated before the action which He causes is detailed.

[26] See on Lev 16:1, where the sections dealing with the issue of the prevention of the consequences of ritual impurity for the general community of Israel are placed before those which affect only one individual, in this case, Aaron.

[27] Gen 39:8–9, where Potiphar's wife shows greater fear of her husband than of God.

[28] Num 8:4.

[29] Num 14:24.

[30] Gen 17:26.

[31] See Lev 15:54, where he surveys the sequence of sections in Leviticus 13–14, and explains their order in terms of frequency of occurence.

[32] Exod 25:1, Lev 8:30. Of course, birth order and initiative (see Num 14:24) may be considered under this rubric, as may causation.

> The conversation of the servants of the patriarchal households are more pleasing to God than the Torah of their descendants, for the section [detailing] Eliezer['s journey takes] two or three columns [of text] while [the important rule] that the blood of a dead creeping thing causes ritual impurity is derived from one letter.[33]

Nahmanides' keen sense of proportion shows itself in these matters, and he will inquire as to why Scripture devotes more or less attention than he deems proper to one or another matter. In the cases just discussed, his solution, which relates importance to repetition, provides a more global solution, though one not less omnisignificantly oriented. As noted above, for Nahmanides, the number of repetitions a topic receives testifies to that topic's importance.

In discussing the function of Lev 8:1–3 within the complex of sections devoted to Aaron's induction into the priesthood, Nahmanides in his comments to 8:2 refers to the *maʿalah* and *ḥibbah* of Aaron and his sons "before God" – the same words he used in his comment regarding the Tabernacle in Exod 37:1.

The short section then is part of the five-fold series of repetitions, in general and in particular, which Nahmanides mentions in his comments on Exod 37:8. There his enumeration includes: (1) the detailed instructions of Exodus 25–27; (2) the general summation of Exod 31:6–11; (3) "at the time of construction (*bi-sheʿat maʿaseh*) he mentioned them in general terms", to Exod 35:10; (4) a detailed exposition "which is missing in the Torah, but certainly Moses had to tell the skilled craftsmen who carried out the work" what needed to be done in detail at the time the work commenced; and (5) the general summation of the work done in Exod 35:5.[34] In any case, this short section is part of the larger complex which serves to emphasize the importance of this project to God's plan of restoring the spiritual fortunes of the Israelites, which is akin to the duplications of the story of Eliezer's getting a wife for Isaac, a mission which would determine the destiny of the Israelite nation to be, which Nahmanides also mentions in this connection.

Thus, once again, as in the Eliezer narrative, the importance of the matter is in direct proportion to the number of repetitions it warrants.

Importance need not be measured on a cosmic scale. For example, the twelve-fold enumeration of the dedication offerings of the princes, each one identical with the other, is an index of the importance of each prince. Why not, asks Nahmanides, summarize all but the first?

> The correct understanding of this passage is that the Holy One, blessed be He, wished to give honor to those who fear Him. … Behold, the princes all brought this offering upon which they had agreed, on one day, and it is impossible but that one must precede his fellow. … [35] But

---

[33] *Genesis Rabba* 60:8; see Rashi on Gen 24:42 s.v. *va-avo ha-yom.*

[34] As he remarks in his comments on 35:5, "Behold, Moses had to tell the whole congregation [about] all the work which God had commanded him [to have done], in order to inform them of the necessity of bringing large donations, for the [amount of] work [to be done] was great. And therefore he told them: 'the Tabernacle and its tent, and its cover, etc.' – he mentioned all of it *in general terms*".

[35] Since they could not be brought simultaneously, by God's command; see his comments below.

> [God] wished to mention them by name and [give] their offerings in detail, mentioning each one's day separately, and not to mention and honor the first – "this is the offering of Nahshon son of Aminadav" – and then state: "and thus the princes, each one on his day, brought [his offering]", for this would infringe on the honor of the others (*qitstsur bi-khevod ha-aḥerim*).[36]

Thus, the importance of proportion is also related to the rabbinic concern with repetition. Here the impossibility of giving each tribal head his proper due within a twelve-day ceremony impelled a long and repetitious account of the offerings. In contrast to his usual practice, Nahmanides negates the significance priority is usual given by balancing that with the equal treatment accorded each offering. In this case, proportion thus counters sequence.

The role of proportion or repetition in indicating intensity appears in his comments on legal passages as well. In most cases, repetition serves as an alternate means, alongside priority in sequence, of indicating relative importance. A heinous sin will be mentioned before a less heinous one; likewise, a heinous sin will be mentioned more often. Thus, the prohibition, once again, of idolatry in Exod 23:24, prompts this comment: "The Torah repeatedly warns [against idolatry], and even though these verses are redundant (*meyuttarin*), there is no [need] to be concerned with this, because of the severity [of the sin of idolatry]".

Proportion, or repetitiveness, serves other functions which the classic rabbinic system did not necessarily acknowledge. In his comments to Lev 26:8, Nahmanides explains the parallelistic structure of 26:7–8 (ABA'A"B) as occasioned by the need "to give them [= the Israelites] courage and valor to pursue five hundred". The need to encourage and condole provided a rationale for juxtapositions which were otherwise difficult to explain, as in his remarks regarding the placement of the section on drink-offerings in Numeri 15. Since drink-offerings, like the additional festal sacrifices of Numeri 28–29, were to be brought only in the land of Israel, the giving of this section after the debacle of the spies episode, served "to console them and to reassure them (*lehavtiḥam*), since they were discouraged, saying: "Who knows what will be after forty years?" ... And therefore the Holy One, blessed be He, saw fit to console them, for by instructing them regarding the *mitsvot* which depend on [residence] in the land He reassured them that it was revealed before Him that they would come and take possession of it" (Num 15:2).

As noted above, Nahmanides' sense of proportion led him to inquire into either the length at which Scripture dilated on various points, or even into why the passage was included in the Pentateuch altogether. At times the disproportionate amount of attention a particular matter garners in Scripture leads Nahmanides to prefer a typological interpretation for the narrative. Thus, his well-known discussion in his commentary to Gen 27:20, regarding the disputes between Isaac and the Philistines anent the wells Isaac had dug, opens with the inquiry: "Scripture dwells at length in regard to the matter of the wells, [though] there is no [moral] utility nor great honor to Isaac in the plain sense of this narrative ... but there is in this thing a hidden matter, for it comes to in-

---

[36] From his comments on Num 7:2.

form [us] of future matters." Thus, the very narrative of such apparent inconsequentals impells a deeper meaning to the story.[37]

Conversely, his sense of proportion plays a central role in his disagreement with Rashi over the identity of the "king in Israel" mentioned in Gen 36:31, in connection with the "kings of Edom who reigned before a king reigned for the children of Israel". Rashi identifies the king as Saul, and thus categorizes the passage as a prophetic "future history", while Nahmanides identifies this unnamed king with Moses, and thus sees it as history plain and simple. His reason is that "why should prophecy mention these?" In other words, though it is important to list these kings as evidence of the fulfillment of Isaac's blessing to Esau, such an intention is not sufficient reason for providing a prophetic history. Nahmanides's sense of proportion thus provides us with a sort of "Law of Conservation of Prophetic Energy".

In the same vein, Nahmanides will inquire into the reason for the repeating of information already given, as in his comment to Num 10:14, where the list of the tribal princes, already provided in chapter 2, arouses his interest. His quasi-casuistic explanation, that this repetition informs us that they actually led the tribes on their march through the wilderness, and that the same princes remained in office throughout this period, seems to have been unsatisfactory to him, since he prefaces it with a "perhaps".

2.6. Historical Sense

The combination of Nahmanides' sensitivities to sequence and chronology, along with his appreciation of the proportion of space the Pentateuch devotes to matters which, from the rabbinic point of view, were evanescent, led him to a recognition of the historical context of the Pentateuchal narrative. He points out that no detail regarding the production of the golden hooks for the courtyard hangings around the Tabernacle is provided, nor of the rings used to join the wall-boards together – all because they were familiar to the craftsmen of that generation.[38] Nahmanides suggests that the very selection of rules of inheritance to appear in the Pentateuch, in Num 27:6–11, was predicated on the demographic situation of the generation of the wilderness. The very shape of the Pentateuch as a whole is therefore dependant on the demographic, technological, cultural, etc. situation into which it was introduced. This is of course not far from Maimonides' understanding of the purpose of many of the commandments.[39]

---

[37] On Nahmanides' typological interpretations, see Amos Funkenstein, "Parshanuto ha-Tipologit shel ha-Ramban", *Zion* 45 (1979/80) 35–49; a condensed English version appeared in Joseph Dan / Frank Talmage (eds.), *Studies in Jewish Mysticism: Proceedings of Regional Conferences Held at the University of California, Los Angeles, and McGill University in April 1978* (Cambridge, MA 1982) 129–50, and see David Lieber's response on pp. 151–52.

[38] See his comments to Exod 26:24.

[39] In *Guide of the Perplexed*, III. 34–49.

3. Aspects of Nahmanides' Thought

Studies on Nahmanides' thought: D. Berger, "Miracles and the Natural Order in Nahmanides", *Rabbi Moses Nahmanides (Ramban): Explorations in His Religious and Literary Virtuosity* (ed. I. Twersky; Cambridge: Harvard UP 1983) 107–28; H. Hanoch, *Haramban Keḥoqer Umequbbal: Haguto Hatoranit Mitokh Parshanuto Lemitzvot* (2nd ed.; Jerusalem: Makhon Harry Fischel 1978); M. Idel, "R. Moshe ben Nahman – Qabbalah, Halakhah Umanhigut Ruḥanit", *Tarbiz* 64 (1995) 532–80; D. Novak, *The Theology of Nahmanides Systematically Presented* (Atlanta: Scholars Press 1993); B. Safran, "Rabbi Azriel and Nahmanides: Two Views of the Fall of Man", *Rabbi Moses Nahmanides (Ramban)* (ed. I. Twersky; 1983) 75–106; J. Stern, "Nachmanides' Conception of *Taʿamei Mitzvot* and Its Maimonidean Background", *Community and Covenant: New Essays in Jewish Political and Legal Philosophy* (ed. D. Frank; Albany: SUNY Press 1995) 141–72.

3.1. Theological Principles

Nahmanides clearly saw his Pentateuchal commentary as a vehicle for providing theological and legal guidance for laymen whose time for study was limited, but who made it a practice to review the weekly Torah reading with an appropriate commentary. With this pragmatic view in mind we may understand Nahmanides' long excursions on such matters, even when they do not necessarily contribute greatly to the understanding of the verse(s) at hand.

Perhaps the most thoroughgoing and elaborate series of discussions Nahmanides carries on in this manner concerns his understanding of the workings of divine Providence and the question of "hidden miracles" within a natural or essentially occasionalist context (e.g., see his comments at Gen 18:19, Deut 11:13 and Exod 13:16). Indeed, the difference in the thrust of his discussion in his Pentateuchal commentary and that in his commentary on Job, which is more Maimonidean, may perhaps inhere in the audience to which each was directed (or, alternatively, the *change* he perceived in his audience between the time he composed the one and the completion of the Pentateuchal commentary at the end of his life).

Among the many discussions contained in his exegetical works, three stand out: his denial of the appropriateness of the role of natural law to a believing Jew in his long comment on Exod 13:16 ("for no one has a portion in the Torah of Moses our Master until he believes that all our activities and all that happens to us are all miracles [which] have no natural law or 'way of the world' in them"), contrasted to the elaborate scheme which he offers in his comments anent Job 36:7, where he allows for an admixture of natural law and "minor miracles" for an intermediate group of humans who cannot maintain a continuous state of "cleaving" to God; and his comments on Lev 26:11, where he asserts that "all these blessings [of Lev 26:3–13] are all miracles – it is not natural that rains should come and that we will be at peace from enemies ... And though they are hidden miracles by which the world operates, they become known by their constancy".

3.2. Psychological Insights

Because of his openness to varying exegetical approaches, and his keen insight into the vagaries of human nature, his views of biblical characters are often more rounded than those of his predecessors, who relied more on the midrashic principle of attributing wickedness to the wicked, and righteousness to the righteous (*B. Bat.* 119b). Thus, for example, he rejects Rashi's pejorative understanding of Isaac's comment on the disguised Jacob's un-Esau-like speaking style ("the name of Heaven is not common in his mouth") by noting that, in Isaac's view, Esau was indeed a pious person (Gen 27:21). He does not hesitate to condemn Abraham for his duplicity and lack of faith in claiming Sarai as his half-sister without her permission (Gen 12:8). His delicate and nuanced understanding of the difficult relationship between Jacob and his sister-wives, where guilt and blame, jealousy and passion all intertwine is a particularly good example of his technique (see his comments Gen 30:1 and 15), especially when contrasted with his legal views of the permissibility of concubinage in his own time (*JQR* OS V [1892] 116f). His openness to alternate interpretations of the same passage serves him in good stead in this aspect of his commentary; see for example his comments on Gen 30:30.

3.3. Esoteric Interpretations

As Elliot R. Wolfson has remarked, "Perhaps no one figure is more responsible for the legitimization of kabbalah as an authentic esoteric tradition of Judaism than [Nahmanides]".[40] While it has been estimated that only about 8% of Nahmanides' comments include matters of kabbalistic exegesis, he undoubtedly intended the readers of his commentary to become aware of the mystical reading of the Pentateuch. The method he employed was symbolic: "Know that in the true sense Scripture speaks of lower matters and alludes to supernal matters".[41] As Wolfson notes, Nahmanides relates the ten days between Rosh Hashanah and Yom Kippur to the ten *sefirot*, and, more particularly,

> the dynamic of these days involves the unification and balancing of the attributes of mercy and judgement, the masculine and feminine aspects of God: 'Rosh Hashanah is the day of judgment in mercy, and Yom Kippur the day of mercy in judgment'. This kabbalistic truth is alluded to, moreover, by the astrological fact that the sign of this month is Libra, depicted by the scales of balance. Hence, the cosmic phenomenon structurally parallels or mirrors the theosophic reality.[42]

---

[40] See Wolfson, By Way of Truth (1989) 103–78; the quote is from p. 103.
[41] See his comments to Gen 1:5 (ed. Chavel) p. 15.
[42] Wolfson, ibid. 114–15.

33.5. The Post-Maimonidean Schools of Exegesis in the East: Abraham Maimonides, the Pietists, Tanḥûm ha-Yərušalmi and the Yemenite School

By Paul B. Fenton, Paris

Sources: The Maimonides: N. Dana (ed.), *Sefer ha-Maspik le-'Ovdey Hashem* (Ramat-Gan 1989; partial edition and Heb. transl. of the *Kifâya*); P. B. Fenton, *The Treatise of the Pool by Obadyah Maimonides* (London 1981; edition of a pietist text by Abraham's son with a chapter on his exegesis); idem, *Deux traités de mystique juive* (Lagrasse 1987; transl. and study of two pietist texts respectively by Obadyah and David Maimonides); idem (ed.), David Maimonides, *Al-Muršid ilâ t-tafarrud* (*Doctor ad Solitudinem*) (Jerusalem 1987); A. H. Freimann (ed.), *Abraham Maimuni, Responsa* (Jerusalem 1937); S. Rosenblatt (ed.), *The High Ways to Perfection of Abraham Maimonides* 1–2 (New York–Baltimore 1927–38; partial edition and Eng. transl. of the Kifâya); E. Wiesenberg (ed.), *Abraham Maimonides Commentary on Genesis and Exodus* (London 1958). – Abraham he-Ḥasîd: P. B. Fenton, "Some Judaeo-Arabic fragments by Rabbi Abraham he-Ḥasīd, the Jewish Ṣufi", *JSS* 26 (1981) 47–72; idem, "A Mystical Treatise on Prayer and the Spiritual Quest from the Pietist Circle", *Jerusalem Studies in Arabic and Islam* 16 (1993) 137–75; idem, "A Mystical Treatise on Perfection, Providence and Prophecy from the Jewish Ṣufi Circle", in: D. Frank (ed.), *The Jews of Medieval Islam* (Leiden 1995) 301–34. – Ḥanan'el b. Samuel: P. B. Fenton, "A Judaeo-Arabic Commentary on the Hafṭarôt by Ḥanan'êl ben Šemû'el (?), Abraham Maimonides' Father-in-law", *Maimonidean Studies* I (1990) 27–56. – Tanḥûm ha-Yərušalmī: Numerous textual publications of which an exhaustive list can be found in the bibliography contained in H. Shay, *Tanḥum ha-Yerushalmi's Commentary on the Minor Prophets* (Jerusalem 1991; which also has a study on Tanḥum's exegesis). – Zəḵariyah b. Solomon: *Commentary on Canticles*, in: Y. Kafiḥ (ed.), *Ḥameš məgillôt* (Jerusalem 1962); *Commentary on the Hafṭarôt* (ed. L. Nahum; Holon 1950). – Nethanel b. Yeša': A. Kohut, *Light of Shade and Lamp of Wisdom being Hebrew-Arabic Homilies composed by Nathanel ibn Yeshâya* (New York 1892); Y. Kafiḥ (ed.), Nethanel b. Yiša'yah, *Nûr aẓ-Ẓalâm* (Jerusalem 1953). – Manṣûr al-Ḏamârī: A. Kohut, *Notes on a hitherto unknown Exegetical, Theological and Philosophical Commentary to the Pentateuch composed by Aboo Manzur al-Dhamâri* (New York 1892).

Bibliography: G. Cohen, "The Soteriology of Abraham Maimuni", *Proceedings of the AAJR* 35 (1967) 75–98; 36 (1968) 33-56 [republished in: idem, *Studies in the Variety of Rabbinic Cultures;* Philadelphia: JPS 1991, 209–42]; S. Eppenstein, *Abraham, Maimuni: sein Leben und seine Schriften* (Budapest 1914; the first modern account of Abraham's life and works including a study of his exegesis); P. B. Fenton, "More Light on the Judge R. Ḥanan'el b. Samuel", *Tarbiz* 54 (1985) 77–107; idem, "The Literary Legacy of David ben Joshua, last of the Maimonidean Negîdîm", *JQR* 75 (1984) 1–56; idem, "Abraham Maimonides: Founding a Mystical Dynasty", in: M. Idel / M. Ostrow (eds.), *Jewish Mystical Leaders and Leadership in the 13th Century* (New York 1998) 127–54; S. D. Goitein, "Abraham Maimonides and his Pietist Circle", in: A. Altmann (ed.), *Jewish Medieval and Renaissance Studies* (Cambridge, MA 1967) 145–64; account of Abraham's activities based on Genizah documents); I. Goldziher, *Studien über Tanchum Jeruschalmi* (Leipzig 1870); Y. T. Langermann, *Yemenite Midrash, Philosophical Commentaries on the Torah* (New York 1996); R. Margaliot, R. Abraham Maimuni, *Milḥamôt ha-šem* (Jerusalem 1953; with a biographical essay); Y. Kafiḥ, "The Controversy over the Method of Allegorial Exegesis in the Yemen", in: Y. Tobi (ed.), *Le-Rosh Yosef. Texts and Studies in Judaism dedicated to Rabbi Yosef Qâfiḥ* (Jerusalem 1995) 11–67 (Heb.); M. Steinschneider, "Abraham b. Salomo", *Hebräische Bibliographie* 19 (1879) 131–36; 20 (1880) 7–12, 39–42, 61–65; N. Wieder, *Islamic Influences on the Jewish Worship* (London 1948; study of Abraham's ritual innovations).

1. Introduction

Although the period under consideration corresponds to the twilight of Jewish intellectual achievement in the East, nonetheless a number of significant figures arose in the firmament of Jewish letters, whose compositions can still be qualified as creative. In line with the contemporary Encyclopaedist tendency in Arabic literature, Jewish scholars undertook the compilation of comprehensive works in various domains. So too in the area of exegesis, commentators penned vast collections which sought to encompass the achievements of their forerunners in the areas of philology, philosophy, and homiletics. One constant however steadfastly traverses these compilations in their various forms and that is the immense impact of Moses Maimonides' thought. Indeed, all biblical exegesis worthy of note in the post-Maimonidean era, be it of the pietistic or mystico-philosophic or even homiletic type, bore the stamp of the great physician of Fostat. There is hardly a work which does not betray his crucial influence either through approbation or reprobation. As both temporal and spiritual successor to his father Abraham Maimonides is to be considered the very first expositor of this exegetical tendency.

2. Abraham Maimonides

The only son of the celebrated philosopher Moses Maimonides, with whom he studied rabbinics, philosophy and medicine, Abraham Maimonides (1186–1237) was a theologian, a mystical pietist, a physician and a communal leader in his own right.[1] Upon his father's death, Abraham, an outstanding rabbinical authority, assumed the spiritual and temporal leadership of Egyptian Jewry. Taking advantage of this position, he endeavoured to revitalize Eastern Jewry through the propagation of a form of pietism whose ethical concepts and ritual practices were largely inspired by Islamic mysticism. His revivalist programme, which earned him the name of Abraham he-Ḥasīd – the Pious, is set out in his major work – the *Kifâyat al-ʿâbidîn* (*A Complete Guide for Devotees*), a monumental compendium of jurisprudence, ethics and theology. Unfortunately, along with most of his considerable literary legacy, it has survived in an incomplete form. Nonetheless, elements for the investigation of Abraham Maimonide's exegetical methodology can be culled from three different sources. Firstly, from his fully fledged commentary on the Pentateuch; secondly, from the scriptural quotations in his *Kifâya*, and thirdly, to a lesser extent, from his *Responsa*, some of which are replies to queries on difficult biblical passages.[2] However, by dint of its sheer volume, his commentary on the Pentateuch provides both the richest and the most coherent exposition of his exegetical method. We are fortunate in having an autobiographical account of the purpose of

---

[1] Goitein, Abraham Maimonides and his Pietist Circle (1967) 145–64; Fenton, Abraham Maimonides (1998).

[2] Abraham Maimuni, *Responsa*, n°s 9–45.

his commentary which has come down to us in a unique letter, adressed by Abraham Maimonides to a correspondent, R. Isaac b. Israel ibn Šuwayḵ:

> As for the commentary on the Torah of which thou hast heard, it is true that I have begun it, and were I free from the service of the king and other tasks, I would have completed it in a year or two. However I can only write on it in short hours on days far apart for I have not yet finished revising the first composition of which I have said that most of it is complete and finished and (that) the smaller part of it that is left will soon be finished with the help of Heaven. And on this account I have explained in the commentary on the Torah, which I have composed, only close to half the book of Genesis, but I am occupied with it (now) and when I have completed the revision of (my) composition, of which the greater part is (already) complete, I shall endeavor with all my might to complete the commentary on the Torah and also a commentary on the Prophets and the Hagiographa after it, if they will aid me from heaven. But 'the work is long' and the day and the workers are as Rabbi Tryphon put it (*Aboth* 2:15), and 'there are many thoughts in a man's heart but the counsel of the Lord that shall stand' (Prov 19:21). And if the commentary on the (separate) portions (of the Torah) had been copied and revised I would have sent it; but it still requires reviewing and revising as regards its contents, and copying as far as its writing down is concerned, which cannot take place until I have completed the commentary on one of the five books of the Torah. And perhaps that will not be long with the help of the Terrible and Fearful One, so that I may send it to thee if some accident or mishap do not prevent me, for I know not what a day may bear or an hour or a moment.[3]

In point of fact R. Abraham Maimonides completed his commentary on the whole of Genesis and Exodus; at least this is all that has come down to us in a single manuscript also preserved in the Bodleian (Hunt. 116).[4] Besides being acephalous, commencing only with Gen 1:22, this unicum is unfortunately lacking the commentary covering Gen 2:21 until Gen 20:15. The part devoted to Genesis was finished in 1232 and since Abraham Maimonides passed away on the 18th of Kislew 4998 (7th December, 1237), it is unlikely that he terminated the commentary on the whole Penteuch, let alone that he proposed on the Prophets. Though only two biblical books are covered by Abraham's commentary, the latter is relatively voluminous. Indeed E. WIESENBERG's monumental edition running into more than 500 pages, conveys some idea of its extensiveness.

His illustrious father had not been able to realize his ambition of composing a commentary on the Bible[5] and no doubt Abraham cherished the hope of fulfilling that project. Moses Maimonides' philosophical writings had undertaken to establish a proper understanding of the most problematic passages of the Bible, which the son now desired to complete by writing a commentary on the whole of Scripture in a more popular strain. Despite its appealing content and style, the work did not, however, gain universal recognition, probably because it was never translated into Hebrew. Even so, the literary variety of its contents like their volume, is impressive. The present description will necessarily limit itself to general features before discussing particular aspects, such as polemical

---

[3] Ms Pococke 186, A. Neubauer, *Catalogue of the Hebrew Manuscripts in the Bodleian Library* I (Oxford 1886), col. 463, n° 1315. The letter was first published by A. Neubauer in: *Israelitische Letterbode* III, pp. 51–54, and again by S. Rosenblatt, High Ways to Perfection (1927) 124–26.

[4] Neubauer, Cat., col. 55, n° 276. Numerous fragments are to be found in various Genizah collections. Of those that I have identified none relate to the other books of the Pentateuch. Cf. also Fenton, *REJ* 150 (1991) 385–405.

[5] *Commentary on Mishnah, Sanhedrin* 10:1, and *Guide*, Introduction.

elements and, of course, the very original exegesis which developed out of Abraham Maimonides' ethical and religious options.

In addition to Abraham's own personal interpretations, the commentary contains precious quotations from previous authors such as Saadiah Ga'on, from whom he quotes both the short (*basîṭ*) and long (*muttasiʿ*) commentaries, Samuel b. Ḥofnî, and Ḥefeṣ b. Masliaḥ. Naturally Abraham makes considerable use of traditional sources such as the Talmud, Midrash, and Targum. Rashi and certain Spanish authors such as Isaac ibn Ghiyâṯ, Ibn Janāḥ, Abraham ibn Ezra and Jacob ben Eleazar are also cited. Particularly noteworthy are the numerous quotations from the commentaries of both his grandfather Maymûn b. Joseph, and father, Moses Maimonides, which in modern times have aroused much interest. Long prior to the commentary's edition, extracts were published, first by L. Simmons[6] and then S. Eppenstein[7], who also devoted a special chapter of his monography on Abraham Maimonides to the latter's exegesis.[8]

With the exception perhaps of the less original Tanḥûm Yərušalmī, about whom we shall speak presently, Abraham Maimonides was virtually the last of the writers of the Orient, who was still imbued with the spirit of the Golden Age of Andalusian scholars. Though his overall orientation is directed towards the literal meaning of the biblical text, like them he admits philosophical speculation in scriptural interpretation, and adopts an independent attitude towards Aggadah. However, he does not altogether disregard the traditional, homiletic approach and his attitude towards midrashic interpretation displays a certain originality. Indeed in the *Kifâya* he devoted a detailed chapter to the exegetical modalities of the Midrash,[9] and in his Pentateuch commentary he does not hesitate to quote rabbinical explanations, occasionally accompanied with an appreciation such as 'this is a sweet word'. On the other hand, however, he may courageously dismiss an aggadic explanation which he judges superfluous, relying perhaps on his pietist reputation to hold him in good stead against criticism.

His observations are generally terse concentrating on an immediate understanding of the text either through philological or grammatical explanations, semantic reconstructions, known as *taqdîr* in Arabic, or the translation of particular words into Arabic. It is however noteworthy that Abraham also recognizes a certain number of rhetorical categories such as metaphors (*mağâz*) (Gen 31:7), synecdochés (*kinâya*) (Exod 14:2), hyperboles (*mubâlaga*) (Exod 34:7), and similes (*istiʿâra*) (Exod 34:14).

His thrust towards the plain sense of the text is regularly guided by Saadiah

6 *JQR* (1890) 334–69.

7 "Beiträge zur Pentateuchexegese Maimuni's", *MGWJ* (1908) 377 ff; *Festschrift D. Hoffman* (Berlin 1914) 130–42.

8 *Abraham Maimuni, sein Leben und seine Schriften*, ch. II, "Der Kommentar Abraham Maimunis zu Genesis und Exodus", pp. 33–72.

9 A Hebrew translation, entitled *Maʿamar ʿal ha-dêrâšôt*, was published in *Kerem ḥemed* II (1836) 7–16. A current edition is to be found in R. Margaliot (1953) 81–98. Fragments of the Arabic original were published by E. Hurvitz, *Treatise on Talmudic Exegesis by R. Abraham son of Maimonides* (New York 1974).

with whom he sometimes disagrees. However, his explanations, which are often moved by the warmth of his natural humanity, go beyond the sometimes clinical rationalism of the Ga'on. A particular charm pervades the numerous small, ethical remarks strewn throughout the commentary which emanate from the soul of this Hasid. Indeed, as S. D. Goitein has stated:

> His explications of the Bible and the Talmud are so graceful, so lucid, so persuasive that one is almost convinced that his *derâsh* is *peshât*, that his moralistic and pietist interpretation constitutes the literal meaning of the text.[10]

Take for example his explanation for Rebecca's preference for Jacob (Gen 25:28):

> She bore an excessive, natural love. Indeed, a parent may naturally love one child rather than another. This does not signify however that she hated Esau, but rather that her love for Jacob was stronger. To be sure, observe how her concern for Esau was associated with that for Jacob when she declared "Why should I be bereaved of you both in one day?" (Gen 27:45). Her natural love for Jacob was greater since he dwelt within the tents and she was therefore used to his presence, whereas Esau was a "man of the field", to whom she was less habituated.[11]

But Abraham is essentially a pietist and even in his quest for the plain meaning, his naturalness can be tainted with mysticism. Commenting on Jacob's love for Rachel whereby "the seven years seemed unto him but a few days" (Gen 29:20), he objects:

> this verse calls for examination, for ⟨on the contrary⟩, in the eyes of a lover even a short period of time seems long on account of the passion he bears for his beloved. This verse thus shows that despite his love, Jacob was not preoccupied with the state of his animal soul, in which case this period would have seemed endless to him, but his love and thoughts were concerned with the True Beloved (*al-maḥbûb al-ḥaqīqī*),[12] and therefore time passed rapidly.[13]

In keeping with medieval exegesis since Muʿtazilite times, Abraham is particularly sensitive philosophically to anthropomorphic issues. Here is what he has to say concerning the verse: "Thou shalt bow down to no other god; for the Lord, whose name is Jealous, is a *jealous* God" (Exod 34:14):

> This is a metaphor (*istiʿâra*) ⟨expressing⟩ that worship of another ⟨god⟩ is contrary to His Will. "The Torah speaketh in the language of men" (*b. Qidd.* 17b), to wit, a jealous man is covetous of that which is exclusively his and which he shares not with another, as a husband is jealous that his wife be not exposed to another. Now bowing down in worship and other forms of prostration are an exclusive right of God who does not tolerate their being performed in worship to someone other than Him.[14]

On the speculative plane, one of the most interesting aspects of his exegesis is the incorporation into his commentary of the intellectual options dictated by his father's philosophical system. These come into play almost exclusively in the context of prophetic dreams or angelic visions, where Abraham usually adopts the line developed by Maimonides' prophetology. Some of these pas-

---

10 Art. cit. 148–49.
11 Wiesenberg (1958) 67.
12 This Sufi expression refers to God. Abraham uses it also in Gen 21:14.
13 Wiesenberg (1958) 91.
14 Ibid. 481.

sages are qualified by him as mysteries (*sôdôt*).[15] However, in their explication he always maintains a clear language in contrast to the hidden allusions of Abraham ibn Ezra, to whom he has been compared, though there is a significant difference between the two exegetes. Whereas Abraham ibn Ezra's far-fetched attempts to establish a connection between a verse and his speculative explanation often sacrifice the literal meaning of the biblical text, Abraham Maimonides makes a relatively temporate use of philosophy, taking great pains to maintain a middle path between the plain meaning of Scripture and those passages open to philosophical interpretation.

It is noteworthy too that, following his father, Abraham's explications exercise considerable discretion, so as not to fully divulge to the vulgar the esoterical doctrines to which he intimates. For instance, already in his commentary on the first chapter of Genesis, after having drawn attention to the fact that Scripture passes over in silence the creation of angels, he remarks:

> The concealing of the time of their creation, which on all accounts took place during the six days of creation, is a mystery which is hidden from us. I perceive in the fact that Scripture did not disclose the moment of their creation during the six days of creation a hidden reason which I cannot expose except orally to him who is capable of grasping such a subtle mystery (*sôd*). For it is amongst the greatest mysteries of the Account of Creation and the Account of the Divine Chariot.[16]

Numerous other verses appear to contain secrets which are purposely concealed, such as the passages relating to the Divine Name about which he declares: "These are mysteries (*sôdôt*) of which we have a partial perception but whose ultimate meaning eludes us".[17]

Occasionally, Abraham Maimonides' comments resound with a polemical peal, directed against either Islam or Christianity, such as his remarks on Gen 21:10: "He (Ishmael) will not inherit with my son, Isaac":

> It seems to me that ⟨Sarah⟩ hereby alluded through prophetic intuition, that God would ultimately reveal that Ishmael's descendance would have no share with the seed of Isaac in the collective perfection vouchsafed to the descendance of Abraham. He would not completely inherit perfection with Isaac. To be sure, this is in fact so, since Ishmael's seed do not observe the Torah, and, even though they believe ⟨in its truth⟩, they declare it to be abrogated, claiming it was modified and falsified. Moreover, even though they profess the monotheistic creed, they did not do so together with Isaac's descendants, but at the time of the latter's waning. Ishmael therefore did not attain perfection simultaneously with Isaac. Though this interpretation is allusive it is not an implausible.[18]

Gen 49:10 is a *locus classicus* of contention between Christians and Jews, which was no doubt rife even in Abraham Maimonides' day as indicated by his comments on that verse:

> The Christians claim that this verse refers to Jesus since kingship has long since ceased in Israel and our awaited Messiah has not come in contradiction to Jacob's prophecy: "The sceptre shall not depart from Judah until the coming of Shiloh". On the other hand, ⟨they claim⟩ if this pro-

---

[15] He generally employs the Hebrew term *sôdôt* but occasionally also the Arabic *asrâr* (secrets) and *daqâ'iq* (subtleties). Cf. High Ways II (1938) 294.

[16] Ibid. 21.

[17] Ibid. 235.

[18] Ibid. 43.

phecy is applied to Jesus, it is truthful, since the latter was born, arose and was crucified prior to the disappearance of the Kingdom of Israel at the time of the Second Temple.

Abraham Maimonides retorts:

This argument is based on the assumption that 'sceptre' ⟨in this verse⟩ necessarily refers to kingdom as indeed interpreted by certain exegetes and especially Onqelos. ⟨...⟩ I have often observed that they ⟨the Christians⟩ obstinately cling to this proof, the reason being that they have found no similar obscure passage in the Torah wherewith to cling, as they do in the case of other obscure verses in the Prophets and Psalms which they falsify ⟨...⟩. It behoves you to grasp the refutation with which I confronted them, reducing them to silence. We tell them that "the sceptre shall not depart" refers not to kingship, as they maintain, but to the sceptre of power and authority. If they object saying: "nay it refers to kingship", then we reply "if so, that implies that kingship continues amongst the descendence of Judah nor among the Jews until the coming of the awaited Messiah". They then reply: "Yes and so it came to pass, for Jesus indeed appeared at the end of the Second Temple period before the end of the Jewish kingdom and the dissapearance of your state". Then we inquire: "did not the kingship indeed cease between the first and second temples, there being no kingdom either in Judah or elsewhere? Now Jesus only appeared at the close of the Second Temple after kingship had ceased from both temples". Indeed, they most certainly had no king at the outset of the Second Temple period for the appointed king was neither of the house of David nor of the tribe of Judah, as recorded by the historical chronicles.

Since you are thus compelled to admit that "the sceptre shall not depart" when referring to the period between the two temples, implies ⟨not kingship but⟩ authority and leadership, thus we ⟨are at liberty to⟩ interpret this verse as relating to our present exile as a reference to either ⟨the authority of⟩ the Exilarchs or to the officials of Davidic descent, in accordance with the traditional interpretation of the Rabbis. This is an irrefutable rebuttal of their argument, which only vain stubbornness can oppose. This is a marvellous point which is worthwhile remembering.[19]

In Abraham Maimonides' day his native Egypt witnessed a great spread of the Islamic Sufi brotherhoods who constituted an immediate spiritual model for the Jewish population. As mentioned, Abraham did not remain impervious to this *Zeitgeist*, and endeavoured to incorporate into his conception of Jewish ethics and worship Sufi concepts and pratices, which he held in honour and even regarded as being of Jewish origin. Undoubtedly the most original and interesting aspect of Abraham Maimonides' exegesis are those interpretations related to his esoterical doctrine and the particular pietistic path he advocated whose principles he seeks to uncover in the biblical narrative and particularly in the patriarchal past. These doctrines are also referred to as 'secrets', only, upon scrutiny, it becomes clear that these are not the philosophical mysteries to which his father alluded. Their penetration calls for spiritual intuition named *ḏawq* ('taste'), a term which is frequently found in subsequent pietist exegesis.[20] For example, he draws attention to the differences in the formulation of the blessings given by Isaac respectively to Jacob ("God give thee of the dew of Heaven") and Esau ("of the fat places of the earth shall be thy dwelling, and of the dew of heaven from above" (Gen 27:28, 39):

Contemplate how in Esau's blessing "fat places of the earth" takes precedence. This is not by chance for his blessing was also pronounced through the Holy Spririt (*rûaḥ ha-qôdeš*) ⟨...⟩. Not

[19] Ibid. 205.

[20] On this term, see Fenton, R. Abraham he-Hasid, the Jewish Sufi (1981) 64, n. 47, and infra, n. 32.

everyone pays attention to this difference. None can understand its mystery save he who is endowed with spiritual intuition, for whose obtainment the prophet prayed; "Teach me good discernment and knowledge" (Ps 119:66).[21]

Sometimes his pietistic interpretations supersede the traditional rabbinic reading of the text. For instance, Abraham connects the word 'perfect' in the verse: "Jacob was a *perfect* man, dwelling in tents" (Gen 25:27) with the commandment given to Abraham: "walk before me and be *perfect*" (Gen 17:1). Disregarding the rabbinical interpretation which associates this term with bodily perfection, i. e. circumcision, he goes on to say that this is an indication that Jacob followed in his forefather's footsteps with regard to the practice of solitary meditation (*ḫalwa*), devoting himself to spiritual perfection while in his father's abode.[22] Moreover, he states in the *Kifâya* that Jacob was in fact the first devotee to practice meditation in domestic seclusion as well as in the wilderness.[23]

Hence contemporary Sufi practices are projected back into the biblical past, and the Patriarchs are presented as having spent their lives in the wilderness far removed from wordly ambitions in order to practice meditation, as it is stated: "and Isaac went out to meditate in the field" (Gen 29:63) – he withdrew to the desert, says Abraham, in order to practise *ḫalwa.*[24]

Similarly, it was for meditational purposes that the Israelites dwelt in the wilderness for forty years.[25] This practice was perpetuated by the prophets of Israel, such as Elijah, who carried out a spiritual retreat in a cave, while depending for his food on the ravens. Furthermore, such conduct was a perfect illustration of the Sufi virtue of *ittikâl* (trust in God).[26] The latter had also been practised by the patriarch Jacob, who according to Gen 32:11, departed to Haran on foot with nought but his staff.[27] Jacob too carried to perfection the virtue of abstinence since he contented himself with the request for "bread to eat and raiment to don" (Gen 28:20).[28]

A further illustration of how the prophets are credited with Sufi virtues is afforded most strikingly by the statement that the Patriarchs purposely married late – Isaac at the age of forty (Gen 24:1), "for their custom was to delay marriage in order to occupy themselves with achieving spiritual perfection, that which is more important taking precedence".[29] Commenting on 2 Kgs 1:8, Elijah's hairy mantle is even said to refer to the garb of the Sufis.

---

[21] Wiesenberg (1958) 81. Abraham also refers to scriptural mysteries in his *Responsa*, n° 16, 24, 30, 43. He harks back to the blessing of Isaac in an interesting passage in High Ways II (1938) 288–90, where he states that the key to the understanding of the passage lies in the expression "that my *soul* may bless thee" (Gen 27:31), whose implication was only correctly understood by Jacob.

[22] Wiesenberg (1958) 67. On the Sufi practice of *ḫalwa*, see Deux traités (1987) 58–66.

[23] High Ways II (1938) 392.

[24] Ibid. 388 and Wiesenberg, 59.

[25] High Ways II, 392.

[26] Ibid. 393.

[27] Ibid. 94.

[28] Wiesenberg (1958) 89.

[29] A similar interpretation is to be found in High Ways II (1938) 265. Traditional Jewish ethics encourages precocious marriage as opposed to Sufi practice, where celibacy is sometimes advocated. See Deux traités (1987) 68–69.

In order to butress their credibility and encourage their emulation Sufis practices are themselves presented as having been derived from ancient Israelite custom, as we read in the following passage of the *Kifâya*:

> We see the Sufis of Islam also profess the discipline of mortification by combatting sleep. Perhaps such a practice is derived from the statement of David: "I will not give sleep to mine eyes, nor slumber to mine eyelides" (Ps 132:4) and from his statement "At midnight I will rise to give thanks unto Thee" (Ps 119:62).[30]

An extraordinary text from the *Kifâya* throws further light on the virtues of solitary retreat, which can lead to prophetic attainment, referred to here as 'Zion'. It is in fact a systematic interpretation of Ps 84, for which Abraham Maimonides proposes a double interpretation, exoteric and esoteric. The following extracts constitute a fine illustration of his exegetical method. The exoteric level of this Psalm refers to the destruction of the Temple and hope in its rebuilding:

> In the esoteric sense, on the other hand, it refers to the longing for external solitude in the 'temple' and for inward solitude that is attained in it.
>
> "How lovely are Thy tabernacles, O Lord of hosts!" (Ps 84:2) expresses a longing; and his statement: "My soul yearneth, yea, even pineth for the courts of the Lord" (v. 3) explains that what is longed for is solitude in "the courts of the Lord".
>
> Again this statement: "My heart and flesh sing for joy unto the living God" (v. 3) explains that the object of the longing for external solitude is to attain inward solitude of which the fruit is prophetic attainment or what ressembles it, in which the soul, that is attached to the 'heart', is stirred and makes its substratum, which is the flesh and its members, subservient to the love of Him, exalted be He, and the praise of Him. ⟨...⟩.
>
> Then he declared enviable those who were secluded by external solitude in "the house of the Lord" (v. 5) in order to attain inward solitude and what necessarily follows therefrom, wherefore he said: "Happy are they that dwell in Thy house, they are ever praising Thee. Selah." (v. 5).
>
> Then he declared enviable those that have reached spiritual fulfillment and find refuge and strength in Him, exalted be He, having achieved this state by means of the channels of the heart and the paths of meditation in the course of the inward solitude, wherefore he said: "Happy is the man whose strength is in Thee; in whose heart are the highways".
>
> Then he described how profusely the tears stream from their eyes, which overflow with tears like a gushing fountain from which there flows a wady that one crosses over in the same manner as one crosses a wady of water. That is the meaning of his statement "Passing through the valley of weeping they make it a place of springs" (v. 7).
>
> Now this is a circumlocution (*taġâ'ī*) for excessive weeping ⟨...⟩ ⟨resulting⟩ from the intense emotion on achieving what they attained, as the enamoured lover, who, after endeavouring for a number of years to meet his beloved, weeps when he finally meets and is united with her.
>
> "Also blessings does the guide don" (v. 7) refers to God ⟨...⟩ He accepts their praises and 'blessings' wherewith they praise Him. "Does He don" is a metaphor (*isti'âra*) for 'acceptance', like one who puts on the garment of his friend which the latter presents to him. "Guide", because He, exalted be He, is their guide enabling them to utter the words wherewith they praise Him.
>
> Then he said: "They go from strength to strength" (v. 8) ⟨...⟩ which refers to their promotion from a first mystic goal to a second and from a second to a third, until they reach the ultimate worldly goal which is prophetic attainment: "He appeareth before God in Zion" (v. 8).[31]

---

[30] Ibid. 322.
[31] Ibid. 402–04.

3. Pietist Exegesis

Abraham Maimonides was not the only exegete to emerge from the pietist community. As is often the case with religious revivalist movements, the Jewish Sufi circle, gave rise to a rich and variegated literary output, which has partly survived in the Cairo Genizah. Devoted to the reinterpretation of traditional Jewish values in order to bring them into harmony with the principles of pietist doctrine, these writings include not only ethical and theological manuals, which involve a large proportion of exegetical material, but also systematic commentaries on biblical books. Works belonging to this category are easily identifiable insofar as they employ technical terms belonging to the Sufi lexicon. Indeed, many of their explications are introduced by the expression *yuḏâqu* "the meaning can be grasped by *ḏawq*", a term which while recalling the Hebrew *ṭaʿam* ('taste, meaning'), is related to the Sufi concept of 'understanding by spiritual intuition'.[32] Its core is borrowed from Maimonides' allegorical-philosophical approach, amplified by the mystical leanings inspired by pietist doctrine.

Although most of the biblical books are represented in their theological writings, only commentaries on two biblical texts have so far been located, on the Psalms and on the Song of Songs. The former was particularly favoured amongst the pietists who identified with David as the prototype of the *ḥasīd.* Indeed, just as the Arabic word *faqīr* ('poor') was a synonym for Sufi, so the psalmist's evocation of 'pious' and 'humble' invariably meant Jewish Sufi for the pietists. One such commentary on the Psalms was composed by David Maimonides, who will be discussed below. In view of the great importance which Sufism allocates to Divine love, it is not surprising that one of the most mystical commentaries emanating from this circle was written on the Song of Songs, that ancient love-song. We refer to the commentary ascribed to Abraham he-Ḥasid.

3.1. Abû Sulayman Abraham ibn Abi r-Rabīʿa he-Ḥasīd (*d. 1223*)

What little that is known about this remarkable figure is mainly due to details culled from the Genizah and quotations in the works of Abraham Maimonides. He was, it seems, the latter's "spiritual companion (or master) in the Way", and like him was also interested in medicine.[33] He played an important part in the pietists' circle and was responsible for the introduction of some of their liturgical innovations. The surviving fragments of his writings shed new light on the doctrines and hermeneutics of the Egyptian pietist movement. The first is a piece of his commentary on the Song of Songs and informs us of the manner in which the pietists understood this text. The author considers the Song of Solomon as a spiritual manual "leading to the ultimate goal", consisting of an allegorical dialogue between the devotee, intoxicated with divine

[32] Cf. supra, note 20.
[33] Fenton, R. Abraham he-Hasid (1981) 48.

love, and the object of his desire, the beatific vision.[34] Remarkably, the text is thoroughly suffused with Sufi vocabulary.

> Upon beholding the brilliant light (*an-nûr al-bâhir*) and the world of spiritual beings, designated by the word 'bride', he declares (Cant 5:6): "My soul faileth when he spoke". This is an allusion to the soul's agitation at their meeting, as it is said (Dan 10:8) "For my comeliness was altered and no strength remained within me".[35] ⟨...⟩ Whereupon the soul takes delight in this sublime state, despite its disquiet and agitation. But nevertheless, this state does not endure, but it is as the lightening that flasheth then disappeareth,[36] as he says ⟨"I sought him, but found him not"⟩.[37]

Of the quotations adduced by Abraham Maimonides, the most remarkable is a long passage dealing with the Revelation at Sinai in which some of Abraham he-Ḥasīd's prophetological ideas are set forth. Together with further fragments from his pen on a similar theme brought to light in the Genizah, they constitute an extraordinarily subtle piece of pietist exegesis voicing an extremely original doctrine, whose underlying inspiration draws upon Maimonides' *Guide of the Perplexed.* While accepting the latter's reading of Exod 24:2, Abraham skirts the philosophical difficulties raised by the spiritual hierarchy established by Maimonides by reserving the qualification of prophet solely for Moses and substituting the Sufi notion of 'sainthood' (*wilâya*) for that of prophethood in respect of the other persons present at Sinai.[38]

> According to R. Abraham he-Ḥasid's interpretation the first of these two verses: "They beheld the God of Israel" (Exod 24:10) refers to the notion of 'prophethood', whereas the second: "upon the nobles of the children of Israel He laid not His hand" (v. 11) refers to that of 'sainthood' (*wilâya*). This theme is introduced by the verse: "then went up Moses, and Aaron, Nadab, and Abihu, and the seventy elders of Israel" (v. 9), which is followed by the verse: "and they saw (*wa-yir'û*) ⟨the God of Israel⟩" (v. 10). This collective expression includes all of them according to their various levels and degrees in relation to prophethood, just as the intellectual faculty and speech include the whole of humankind despite its hierarchy of individuals, of

---

[34] A similar approach to the Song of Songs is exhibited by David Maimonides in his *Guide to Detachment* (ed. P. Fenton, Jerusalem 1987, 60): "The axis of this book revolves about the stations (*maqâmât*) and the states of the soul when it is wayfaring in the Path of God and it is attaining the ultimate level of the love of God. Because this is a subtle subject and a noble matter, the Sage (i. e. Solomon) produced this in an enigmatic manner ⟨...⟩ in the form of the rapture (*'išq*) of the concupiscent soul for one of the sensual objects of love of the created world". The writer has recently discovered in the St Petersburg manuscript II Firkowitsch Heb.-Arabic I. 3870 an interesting, near complete Judaeo-Arabic commentary on the Song of Songs. In the spirit of the mystical-philosophical tradition, the Song is construed as an amorous dialogue between the soul and Intellect. The latter encourages the soul to free itself from the coils of matter so as to aspire to its intellectual perfection and reach mystical communion (*wusûl*). The hitherto unknown commentary is written in the hand of the scholar and scribe Rabbi David ben Joshua (fl. 1335–1415), the last of the Maimonidean *negidîm*, who may well have been its author. Indeed, the text is replete with the Sufi-type, mystical concepts and terminology which characterizes the *nagîd*'s other works. It is also clear that the author of this text, shortly to be published in *Tarbiz*, had before him Tanḥum Yerushalmī's commentary on the same book (see sect. 4 below).

[35] Cf. Maimonides, *Guide* 2.4, uses this verse to describe the state of ecstasy occasioned by prophetic inspiration.

[36] Cf. *Guide*, Introduction and I, ch. 49, where the selfsame expression is evoked to describe the transient state of inspiration.

[37] Fenton, R. Abraham he-Ḥasīd (1981) 55–56.

[38] On the distinction between these two concepts in mystical Islam, see M. Chodkiewicz, *The Seal of the Saints* (New York 1995). Maimonides (*Guide* 2.33) attributes prophetic perception exclusively to Moses, considering that the Children of Israel did not attein prophecy at Sinai. Abrahm he-Ḥasīd, on the other hand, grants them the quality of sainthood.

whom some have obtained the height of knowledge while others only parts thereof. In the same manner, this assembly saw the God of Israel, each according to the capacity, extent and acumen of his reflection.[39]

Moses' distinction in relation to the rest of the assembly had already been explicitly stated by the verse "and Moses alone shall draw nigh unto the Lord" (Exod 24:2). However, going beyond that statement, though it would have sufficed, the verse again stipulated with regard to the whole assembly that "they did not draw nigh" (ibid.). Now in effect the verse states *yiggâšû*, litt. "they *shall* not draw nigh", alluding to the fact that the 'drawing nigh' experienced by Moses had not been shared by others at that moment and will not be so in the future, in accordance with the verse "there hath not arisen a prophet since in Israel ⟨like unto Moses⟩" (Deut 34:10).[40]

Thereafter the verse repeats that the remainder of Israel, that is the common people, "shall neither ascend with him" (Exod 24:2). Thus while Israel did not ascend, Nadab and Abihu and the seventy elders did, without, however, 'drawing nigh', whereas Moses both ascended and alone drew nigh. However the expression 'they beheld' is applied homonymously, without distinction, to him, Aaron, Nadab, Abihu and the seventy elders together, and applied similarly to Aaron and the rest of the assembly whereas, in fact, this revelation (*mukâšafa*) was divided into three degrees. The first was that of Moses, the second that of Aaron and the third that of Nadab and Abihu and the seventy elders. A fourth degree is that of the 'nobles' who are ⟨to be considered as having occupied the degree of⟩ saints (*awliyâ*). Indeed, in its description of the latter, the verse does not ⟨employ the verb⟩ to 'see' (*ra'âh*) for the "Lord laid not His hand upon them" (v. 11). The meaning here of 'hand' is to be understood according to the expressions which refer to this state such as: "the hand of the Lord was upon Elijah" (1 Kgs 18:46) and "the hand of the Lord was upon me" (Ezek 37:1). The signification is that He did not afford them prophetic inspiration in the manner – to use a simile – that a Majestic King stretches forth His hand to his close companion in order to convey to him that which he does not impart to another. Thus they are to be considered as 'saints' and not 'prophets'.

Thereupon the verse describes the elevation which they attained saying: "And they beheld God" (v. 11). It is possible that this refers to an esoteric, inner unveiling (*mukâšafa*) which is vouchsafed to saints. Thus the description was restricted to the verb *ḥazah* 'behold', unaccompanied by the ⟨direct object⟩ 'the Lord of Israel' as in the case of the preceeding verse (v. 10), but it simply states 'God'.[41] Consequently, the word can be taken either in its literal meaning in the case of such an unveiling, or it can refer to 'other gods', which means that He revealed to them the mysteries of other divine forms, called 'gods', as in the verses: "thou shalt not have other gods" (Exod 20:3), 'Lord of lords' (Deut 10:17) and their realities. They thus discerned the superiority, the greatness and exaltedness of God in relation to them in the manner expressed in the verse: "Now I know that the Lord is greater than all gods" (Exod 18:11).

Then the verse concludes with the expression "and they did eat and drink" (v. 11). The latter either refers back to the 'noble ones' in the sense that hitherto they had been in the same category as other 'eaters and drinkers' and were not distinguished from them in any outstanding detail. They endeavoured to consume the flesh of the burnt-offerings whose blood and fat had been sacrificed previously (v. 5). This is alluded to in the Targum: "they were content with their sacrifices which had been accepted as if they were eating and drinking". Consequently the verse considers them as belonging to the category of "the young men of the children of Israel" (v. 5). Alternatively, 'the noble ones' may actually be identical with 'the young men'. On the other hand, ⟨the latter part of the verse⟩ may in fact refer to both the nobles and the holy assembly according to their various degrees. The verse would then be an allusion to the fact that all of them were in the state of 'rapture' (*ḫalwa*)[42] which occurred in that blessed mountain, while devoting

---

[39] The exegetical principle behind the establishment of this hierarchy was probably inspired by *Guide* 2.32 *in fine*.

[40] Cf. on the sense of Moses' 'drawing nigh' see *Guide* 1.8 and 3.51. See also *Guide* 2.35.

[41] Maimonides, *Guide* 2.43 considers the verbs *ra'ah* and *ḥazah* as synonymous. See also on this particular verse *Guide* 1.5.

[42] On this term, which connotes the spiritual state attending solitary meditation, see our study: "La *hitbodedut* chez les premiers Qabbalistes en orient et chez les soufis", in: R. Goetschel (ed.), *Prière, mystique et judaïsme* (Paris 1987) 133–58.

themselves to God awaiting the attainment of the perfect state of nearness to God and His worship, which they had pursued, each according to his measure. This state was necessarily near to abstention from sustenance and therefore, when this condition came to an end, they partook of food and drink.

As for the verse's connecting their vision to the 'Lord of *Israel*', it is possibly an allusion to the fact that this state of unveiling and spiritual state were ⟨similar to⟩ those of Abraham. To wit, the same Divine attributes, holy worlds and revelations became apparent and were unveiled to them as had been vouchsafed to Jacob, also called Israel, to whom they had been handed down from Isaac and in turn from Abraham. They are referred to in the verses: "and the Lord appeared unto him" (Gen 18:1): "and the Lord appeared unto Abraham" (12:7); and of Jacob it is said: "God Almighty appeared unto me at Luz" (48:3). Moreover, God testified ⟨to Israel⟩ to His having appeared to the Patriarchs in the verse: "And I appeared unto Abraham, Isaac and unto Jacob" (Exod 6:3).

Then the verse made known the quantity and the quality of the unveiling which had been revealed to them: "and there was beneath His feet the like of a paved work of sapphire stone, and the like of the very heaven for clearness" (Exod 24:10). 'Beneath His feet' refers to the sacred, angelic realm which englobes the world of the angels according to their various degrees. Thereafter ⟨the verse stipulates⟩ that this unveiling is likened to the perception of an individual peering through a mirror, for the transparency of sapphire, on account of its subtle substance, allows the perception of other mirrors beyond in perfect clearness.[43]

The meaning of 'work' refers to the effect of transparency in letting through the object perceived to the perceiver. This is an extraordinary simile for, insofar as the beholder remains undetached from his bodily state, it is inconceivable that the unveiling of those spiritual worlds be perceived according to their reality. That inadequacy is likened to ⟨sight⟩ through the medium of that sapphire. It is indeed a vision, albeit unlike the vision of the beholder without an intermediary ... The remainder of his explanation is lacking.[44]

As already observed in the case of Abraham Maimonides, some of Abraham he-Ḥasīd's exegetical remarks draw parallels between Sufi practice and ancient Jewish custom in an endeavour to establish the Jewish origin of these rites. Here is what he says concerning the specifically Sufi practice of carrying out spiritual retreats in dark places, as reported by the author of the *Kifâya*:

Also do the Sufis of Islam practice solitude in dark places and isolate themselves in them until the sensitive part of the soul becomes atrophied so that it is not even able to see the light. This however requires strong inner illumination wherewith the soul would be preoccupied so that it is not to be pained over external darkness. Now Rabbi Abraham he-Ḥasīd, the memory of the righteous be blessed, used to be of the opinion that that – I mean solitude in darkness – was the thing alluded to in the statement of Isaiah: "Who is among you that feareth the Lord, that obeyeth the voice of His servant, who walketh in darkness and hath no light? Let him trust in the name of the Lord and stay upon his God" (Isa 50:10) ⟨...⟩ and David said, in reference to his intimacy with Him, exalted be He, during his solitude in the blackness of night and in the deserts and waterless places: "Yea, though I walk through the valley of darkness, I will fear no evil, for Thou art with me" (Ps 23:4).[45]

Other writings emanating from the pietist circle employ the allegorical method and refer to scriptural mysteries. The author of the mystical *Treatise on Perfection*, who is perhaps identical with R. Abraham he-Ḥasid, also intimates that Scripture is replete with secrets (*sôdôt*). While expounding the verse 'Guard thy foot when thou goest to the house of Lord' (Eccl 4:17), which refers to the precautions which attend spiritual preparation, he specifies that this verse can

[43] Cf. *Guide* 1.28 and 2.26.
[44] Wiesenberg (1958) 376–80.
[45] High Ways II (1938) 418.

be understood exoterically as referring to external cleanliness, such as physical ablutions. However, its real significance is expressed by its inner meaning (*bâṭin*) according to which 'feet' allude to 'the resources of the human condition'. The 'glorious house' in question is, of course, not one made of stone, as it is written: "Where is the house that ye made build me?" (Isa 66:1). 'House' in fact, alludes to 'first gnosis' (*maʿarifa ûlâ*), i.e., recognition of Divine omnipotence pervading all existence, and proximity, which is realized by dint of the practice of ethical virtues. In other words the prophet is saying: "O seeker of proximity to God, waiting upon His Presence, if thine aim is to strive towards His Presence, then safeguard the means by which thou attainest knowledge of Him and reach His Presence ⟨…⟩. Shelter thy deeds from the snares of evil to avoid being diverted from this great and noble aim (1 Sam 2:9)". He then proceeds to highlight the verse's use of the expression 'house of the Lord' (*beyt elohim*) as opposed to the 'house of the Eternal' (*beyt YHWH*). He states that this distinction: "belongs to the secrets which cannot be disclosed in a book, but can only be divulged to an individual who fulfills the conditions laid down by the ⟨Rabbis⟩, to wit that he be wise and understandeth of himself, and then only first principles are entrusted to him" (*b. Ḥag* 13 a). However, having partly raised the veil of secrecy, he resolves to disclose a hint. The perception of the 'house of the Lord' is reached by physical, good deeds, whereas perception of the 'house of the Eternal', the supreme gnosis, requires the assistance of the metaphysical.[46]

In the same writer's *Treatise on Prayer* there occurs an extraordinary passage concerning the pious one's (i.e. the Jewish Sufi) initiatory death prior to his resurrection through gnosis:

> The more love, the more intense the soul's obedience and conversion to its Creator and its passion to please Him. The more intense its conversion and preoccupation with Him and the delight in His recollection (*ḏikr*), the stronger the annihilation of the consciousness of all else (*fanâʿ*) and the emptying of its heart from all beside Him. Thereupon it will be transported to the level of the angels as it is said: "If thou wilt also judge my house and wilt also keep my courts, then I will give thee free access among those that stand" (Zach 3:7).
>
> Know brother, that none can attain to this sublime and elevated level whilst his physical soul has the slightest sway over him. He must have no delight nor desire except in drawing near to his master and the will to please him. His soul will die to the delights and pleasures of the world, as David said: "Precious in the eyes of the Lord is the death of His pious ones" (Ps 116:15). On the other hand it is spoken of the resurrection of the rational soul through knowledge in the verse: "I shall not die" (Ps 118:17).[47]

The notion of *fanâʿ*, which is one of the central tenets of Sufi doctrine, is again read by this same author into the most sacred formula of the Jewish creed, the confession of God's unity:

> It behoves the devotee to meditate on His greatness and to recall (*ḏikr*) his name to the point where love is impressed in his heart by which he turns to Him until he attains the state of unity (*tawḥīd*), that is the annihilation (*fanâʿ*) of humanity and the manifestation of divinity.[48] This is the true unity in which is attained the goal expressed in the verse: "Hear O Israel, the Lord

[46] Fenton, Treatise on Perfection (1995) 317–18.
[47] Fenton, Treatise on Prayer (1993) 163.
[48] This is the Sufi definition of Divine unity, i.e., the intuition of existential Unity through total annihilation of self-consciousness (*fanâʾ*).

our God the Lord is One" (Deut 6:4–5) and the verse: "Thou shalt love the Lord thy God with all thine heart". Whereupon the heart will be filled with light 〈..〉 through the bliss of contemplating the Divine Beauty and Majesty.[49]

3.2. *Ḥanan'el ben Samuel (fl. 1180–1250)*

Unfortunately the exegetical works of R. Ḥanan'el b. Samuel the Judge (ca. 1170–1250), Abraham Maimonides' father-in-law and member of his pietists circle, have come down to us in a very incomplete state. He is thought to have composed a Judaeo-Arabic commentary on the Pentateuch and *Hafṭarôt*.[50] In the preserved fragments, though repeatedly referring to the literal and rational explanations of Saadiah and Ibn Janāḥ, R. Ḥanan'el is seen to practice the allegorical method, coloured with a distinct mystical-philosophical hue which is greatly indebted to Maimonides. The commentator's first aim is to establish a lexicographical understanding of the verse, mainly by way of comparison with other verses and by *taqdīr* (semantic reconstruction). Having established the outer meaning (*ẓâhir*) of certain verses, he then goes on to propound the inner meaning (*bâṭin*), which often refers to a philosophical or spiritual notion. Not infrequently, these have Maimonidean or, indeed, Sufi overtones. As an interesting example which expressly refers to contemporary Sufi practice in Egypt, the following interpretation can be quoted from his commentary on the *Hafṭorah Ki tissâ'*:

And Elijah went up to the top of Carmel, and he bowed himself down upon the earth and put his face between his knees (1 Kgs 18:42).

The verse 'and he bowed himself' signifies he prostrated himself upon the ground in gratitude to God for that which He had wrought for Israel and the destruction of God's enemies, and implore of Him that the rain fall. Similarly it is said of him that assumed his succession Elisha, "and he stretched himself upon him" (2 Kgs 4:34).

Thereafter Elijah seated himself and put his face between his knees, intending thereby to divert his attention from all creation and devote his meditation solely to his present pursuit. The nations (= the Sufis) have taken over this practice from us and adopted, adorning themselves with it (i.e., claim they originated it), whereby they sit in this position for a whole day. They call this practice *tazayyuq*, i.e., the concealing of one's face in the collar, i.e., the hem of one's garment.[51]

3.3. *Obadyah Maimonides (1228–1265)*

Little, too, is known about Obadyah, Abraham Maimonides' son, beyond the fact that he followed the pietist path chartered by his father. His only preserved work, the *Treatise of the Pool*, is an ethico-mystical vade-mecum composed in Judaeo-Arabic, replete with Sufi concepts and expressions. It is also a prime example of pietist exegesis and as such deserves a mention here. His mystical doctrine leans on quite an original method of interpretation not only

---

[49] Treatise on Prayer (1995) 156. The two Sufi notions of Majesty and Beauty correspond to the attributes of awe and mercy. Although the author does not say so expressly, it is possible that he relates the former to the Tetragrammaton and the latter to the Divine Name ELHYM (Elohim).

[50] See Fenton, A Judaeo-Arabic Commentary on the Hafṭarôt (1990).

[51] Ibid. 48–49. See also our study, "La Tête entre les genoux", *RHPR* 72 (1992) 413–26.

of biblical texts but also of rabbinical and midrashic writings. Couched in a very allusive and cursory language, many of his explications are based on some obscure, underlying doctrine, which relies heavily on a highly developed system of symbolism. Obadyah often intentionally conceals what he regards as the deeper meaning of a verse, and is content with merely drawing to it the attention of his readers who are called upon to exercise their intuition to discover its message:

> Know thou that meditatest this treatise that the matter to which we have alluded here cannot be more openly expounded. Thus upon happening on a verse that can be interpreted in several manners, my goal is merely to open the gate and rely upon the disciple's comprehension. If he be endowed with insight and intuition (*ḏawq*) then he will arrive at the true significance through his own ressources.[52]

Obdayah explains that Scripture contains allegories (*alġâz*) (pp. 89, 91, 97), metaphors (*isti'âra*) (p. 90) and wonderful things (pp. 83, 110). He often draws attention to a particular point with expressions such as: "meditate this allegory" (p. 89), "fathom this" (p. 109), "be heedful of this" (p. 110). Obadyah specifies that in the first instance his work is intended for the initiated:

> Know that it is impossible to expound and discuss the subject to which I have hinted and alluded throughout this treatise on account of its extreme abstruseness, the intricacy of its meaning and the remoteness of its essence. Consequently not all men are suited to it nor initially capable of receiving it, except after having acquired certain preliminaries. Hast thou not observed how the Pentateuch and Prophets have expressed these notions in the form of parables in order that they may be comprehended ⟨…⟩ for these questions are at first manifest and then hidden inasmuch as man's grasp of them dependeth upon the measure of his labour and passion.[53]

Seemingly, Obadyah is not interested in the Andalusion philological and grammatical approach to Holy Writ. For him, exegesis is a wholly passionate and intuitive experience involving mnemonic techniques:

> One must read the Scriptures as a 'lover' and a 'seeker' and not as it is read nowadays by the vulgar who consider not what they read but simply recite ⟨the text⟩, as if its sole purpose were in its recital, or in knowledge of the grammatical aspects of its text or in the novel interpretation of a word, explained differently by others. The proper method of scriptural interpretation is to commit its verses to memory, until thy mind is crossed by one of the doctrines to which I have drawn thine attention. Thou wilt happen upon a verse which correspondeth to that doctrine and thou shalt extract therefrom another doctrine, ascending from one doctrine to another until thou beest united with the object of thy quest.[54]

Almost all of Obadyah's exegesis is figurative and in the rare instances when he evokes the literal meaning of a verse, it is often out of key in relation to its context. Indeed, in some instances it is difficult to decode whether a verse is intended to have a hidden meaning or whether it is simply being cited as a literary device in order to embellish the Judaeo-Arabic prose with biblical quotations, as for example when Obadyah says of man's vices that "they hated him and could not speak peacefully unto him" (Gen 37:4).[55]

The author of the *Treatise of the Pool*, like his father, had a marked tendency

---

52 *Treatise of the Pool* (1981) 80.
53 Ibid. 96–97.
54 Ibid. 109.
55 Ibid. 97.

to lend a pietist coloration to the biblical narrative, both from the doctrinal and ritual point of view. He repeatedly insists on the necessity for a meticulous preparation before embarking upon the spiritual path. The following verses, interpreted metaphorically are adduced in support of the imperative character of such preliminaries: "The priests also, that draw near to the Lord, shall purify themselves lest the Lord break forth upon them" (Exod 19:22); "Guard thy foot when thou goest to the house of the Lord" (Eccl 4:17).[56]

Obadyah, too, ascribes Sufi practices to the Patriarchs and Ancient Hebrew prophets. Thus according to him, Jeremiah's ardent prayer: "Oh that I had in the wilderness a lodging place" (Jer 9:2) alludes to his quest for a spiritual retreat (*ḫalwa*).[57] Allegorical interpretations are even lent to the precepts. For instance in the verse: "What man is there that hath built a new house and hath not dedicated it" (Deut 20:5), the word 'house', according to Obadyah, signifies the body, and the word 'dedication' is to be taken in the sense of initiation. Wanting in perfection, the individual is exhorted to turn aside and devote himself to the initiation of his soul.[58]

3.4. *David II Maimonides (fl. 1335–1415)*

The last of the Maimonidean dynasty of *nəgīdīm* recorded by history and also one of the last significant thinkers in the Judaeo-Arabic idiom, David II Maimonides was the author of a vast literary œuvre which included works on philosophy, ethics and exegesis. Indeed, in addition to Arabic commentaries on the *hafṭarôt* and the book of Psalms (*ad-dawqiyyât*),[59] he composed two commentaries on the Torah: (1) an Arabic commentary, *Yəqar ḥoḵmâh* or *ḥemdâh*, of which quotations are extant, and which seems to have been a popular homiletic exposition, individual pericopes of which are referred to by the author as *midrash* so-and-so, and (2) a Hebrew commentary, *Kəlīl ha-yôfī*, known hitherto only through quotations and of which a substantial part was recently discovered by us. This work is most significant insofar as it represents a novel genre in the Eastern school. Somewhat similar in style to Jacob ha-Siqilli's *Talmûd Torah* (completed in Damascus, 1337), it constitutes a blend of philosophy, philology and popular homiletics. Indeed, as such it is a forerunner, and perhaps a literary model of the homiletic genre in later Yemenite literature.

In the introduction to this work, the author provides some interesting information on its purpose – a running commentary in the spirit of Maimonides:

> ⟨Maimonides⟩ did not gather all his pearls unto one place but dispersed them in several chapters of his divine work the *Guide of the Perplexed*, recommending that the content of one chapter be properly compared with another in order to understand its purport. He was followed by noble

[56] Ibid. 80, 116. Abraham Maimonides gives this verse the same interpretation. See High Ways, II (1938) 258, whereas the pietist author (Abraham he-Ḥasîd?) of the mystical Treatise on Prayer (1993) 152, derives this same principle from Amos 4:12.

[57] *Treatise of the Pool* (1981) fol. 25 a.

[58] Ibid. 94–95.

[59] This title is to be connected with the notion of *dawq* discussed *supra*, note 20. Unfortunately these commentaries have not come down to us.

masters who have interpreted the Torah for us in the light of his teachings, such as Rabbi David Qimḥī, Rabbi Moses ben Naḥman, the aforementioned Dayyan Ḥananel our ancestor,[60] Rabbi Ṣadôq the ⟨...⟩,[61] Rabbi Jacob Siqīlī and Rabbi Jacob ⟨Antoli⟩, author of the *Malmad*.

When I considered his words, I understood them partly, whereupon my soul stirred me to undertake this work, to bring upon me the blessing to understand its allegories and parables and explain the subjects of the Torah and certain saying of the Rabbis according to his teachings, each of which is more precious than pure gold and pearls.

Thus, in the words of Rabbi Jacob Siqīlī: "He who meditates these homilies according to their literal meaning, the hair of his flesh stands on end in disgust and he exclaims: "Nought cometh from them, nor from their abundance, nor from their turmoil, neither is there eminency among them" (Ezek 7:11). When, however, he who understands them in an esoteric sense considers them, he finds in them profound mysteries sweeter than honeycomb, marvelous and sublime in divine wisdom and the secret of the electrum. So subtle are they that the philosophers spend their nights and days to attain their understanding, but without avail".

I have already explained certain of their words in the compositions I wrote on Maimonides' work which I entitled *Comments on the Guide of the Perplexed*.[62] To use Rabbi Jacob's expression, "on their basis the individual will be stirred to recognize the marvels of the perfect in knowledge". ⟨...⟩

I have already composed a homiletic commentary on the Torah in the Arabic tongue which I named *Yəqar ḥoḵmâh* compiled from the words of the Ancient and Modern sages. But most of it was intended and written for the vulgar, to deliver sermons each sabbath at the hour of the afternoon prayer. I arranged it for them in mind.[63] At present I deemed fit to compose a commentary on the Pentateuch in the Holy Tongue according to the paucity of my understanding and the weakness of my comprehension, based on the teachings of the *Guide* and on the mysteries of Ibn Ezra, and upon the words of the recent scholars.[64]

In support of his philosophical ideas, David quotes in this work Abraham ibn Ezra as well as his illustrious forbears Moses and Abraham Maimonides, while relying for most of his philological material on David Qimhi. However, it is most interesting to point out that, in strong distinction to the early Yemenite Midrashim, David makes use of kabbalistic sources and, as far as we know, was the very first Oriental author to quote not only the *Bahīr* but also the *Midraš ha-neʿelam*.

In his ethical writings too, he demonstrates much exgetical ingenuity. Continuing the family pietist tradition he uses the allegorical method in his *Muršid, Guide to Detachment*, in order to read into the biblical text doctrines and practices of a Sufi type. Preparation for the spiritual path entails mortification, for fasting predisposes the soul to receive divine favour, as it is written: "It is good for me that I have been afflicted, in order that I might learn they statutes" (Ps 119:71).[65]

On the other hand biblical expressions of nourishment and satiety, allude to spiritual subsistance, as in the verse: "Let the humble eat and be satisfied, let

---

[60] See Fenton, Literary Legacy (1984) 48–49, where we surmised that this is a reference to Hanan'el b. Samuel.

[61] This commentator of a philosophical bent, though mentioned tens of times in the present work, is unidentifiable.

[62] Cf. Fenton, Literary Legacy (1984) 48–49.

[63] This comment constitutes an important element in favour of attributing to this writer the authorship of the Arabic homiletic commentaries on the Pentateuch ascribed to David I Maimonides and known as *Midraš Rabbī Dâwīd ha-nâgīd*. See E. Almagor, *The Manuscripts of David Ha-Nagid's Homilies* (Jerusalem 1995).

[64] Ms. II Firkovic Heb. A 69, fols. 1 a–2 b.

[65] Fenton, *Al-Muršid* (1987) 29.

them praise the Lord that seek after Him; may your heart be quickened forever" (Ps 22:27).[66]

Deut 28:9 has been referred to since talmudic times as a *locus probans* for *imitatio Dei* (cf. *b. Šabb.* 133b). Yet Rabbi David enriches classical exegesis with new dimensions, applying this verse to the mystical doctrine of the Perfect Man enclothed in Divine attributes. At the final stage of the spiritual path, the devotee loses all consciousness of his own individuality and, by virtue of the fundamental symmetry existing between the soul and God, is incapable of discerning between himself and the object of his love, as expressed in the verse: "My soul (= God), I desired you at night" (Isa 26:9). Indeed, this state occurs at night, a time of spiritual awakening when the senses slumber.[67]

4. Late Exegetes in the Oriental School

Subsequent to the pietist school, nearly all biblical exegesis in the oriental world continued to espouse the mystical-philosophical approach in which a relatively significant place is given to Sufi technical terms and notions. This is also the case with the writings of Tanḥum b.Joseph Yərûšalmī (ca. 1220–1291). Known as the 'Ibn Ezra of the East', Tanḥum, as indicated by his name, hailed from Jerusalem, though he was active in Egypt. He is considered to be the last expositor in the Orient of the rational school of exegetes. Though Tanḥum was little more than a compiler, he has enjoyed much attention on the part of Western scholars since his works were acquired quite early by the orientalist libraries of the West. Thus his Judaeo-Arabic commentaries were amongst the first to be known and published. Indeed, studies on Tanḥum's exegesis made their début as early as 1655 when E. Pococke, who brought some of his works back from the East, first referred to his writings in his *Porta Mosis.*

Tanḥum can make little claim to originality for he draws extensively on his predecessors, though he rarely mentions his sources. These include Ibn Ezra, Qimhi as well as Karaite authors. Tanḥum aimed at selecting for his readers the most noteworthy explanations, sometimes bringing several opinions and pointing out the most acceptable. He is invariably guided by the context.

Though he wrote an Arabic commentary on the whole of the Bible entitled *Kitâb al-bayân* (*Book of Explanation*), only the parts dealing with the First Prophets, Jeremiah, Ezekiel, the Minor Prophets, the Five Megillot, Daniel and fragments of the Psalms have been preserved. To these can be added his Arabic translation of the *haftarôt.*

The commentary was preceded by a preliminary discourse entitled *al-Kulliyât* or 'First principles', which is a critical and speculative introduction to Scripture. In this discourse, the author deals, inter alia, with internal contradictions, metaphorical expressions, parables, chronological problems, textual dis-

[66] Ibid. 31.
[67] Ibid. 79–82.

crepancies, and grammatical anomalies. He is also the author of *al-Muršid al-kâfi*, a dictionary of the Mishnah and of Maimonides' *Mišneh Torah*, whose language he compares with biblical Hebrew. In his writings, Tanḥûm reveals an extensive knowledge of Arabic and its grammatical and exegetical terminology. Aware of the similarity between the Semitic languages, he is a partisan of the comparative method in the domain of philology and often adduces lexical elements from the Arabic and Aramaic in his explanations. In the grammatical and philological domain he relies upon the works of Ibn Janāḥ, whom he quotes extensively though he rarely names him. His comparative method is not restricted to dry grammatical and etymological observations, but includes idiomatic expressions, rhetorical devices and similarity of ideas. Of particular significance is the aesthetic appreciation Tanḥum shows for Scripture by his use of numerous rhetorical terms such as figurative speech (*maǧâz*, Shay, 227), metaphor (*isti'âra*, Shay, 161), simile (*tašbīh*, Shay, 225), parable (*tamṯīl*, Shay, 229), synecdoché (*kinâya*, Shay, 89), exaggeration (*mubâlaġa*, Shay, 217), hyperbole (*taġâyī*, Shay, 159), inversion (*taqlīb*, Shay, 213), hysteron proteron (*taqdīm wa-ta'ḫīr*, Shay, 293), and semantic reconstruction (*taqdīr*, Shay, 213), thus continuing the tradition of Hebrew rhetorics initiated by Andalusian exegetes such as Moses ibn Ezra.

Besides his grammatical explanations, Tanḥum contributes a wealth of information culled from his other intellectual interests. He had a wide knowledge of philosophy and apparently had a grasp too of medicine, while geography and mathematics were not strange to him. In speculative matters his master was Maimonides. Following the latter, he often reads into the biblical texts his philosophical views on prophecy, miracles, and the origin of matter.

Interestingly, Tanḥum like Abraham Maimonides refers to these philosophical themes as 'secrets', thus introducing into his exegesis an esoterical dimension, as in the following passage which, following Maimonides, analyses with subtlety the differences between the prophecy of Joshua and that of Moses:

> "And there stood a man over against him with his sword drawn in his hand" (Josh 5:13) – 'drawn' (*šəlûfâh*) means 'remove', its root being to 'draw away' as in the verse: "a man drew off his shoe" (Ruth 4:7) and the term is employed metaphorically in the sens of 'apparition, unveiling' ⟨…⟩.
>
> "Art thou for us, or for our adversaries?". That is art thou a help for us in our victory or that of our enemies. This is an indication that some angels in the supernal world are appointed exclusively over the victory of a specific nation as we shall explain in the case of Daniel's statement: "Michael your prince" (Dan 10:21) and "the prince of Greece" (v. 20), etc. As ⟨the Rabbis⟩ explained in connection with the verse: "and there wrestled a man with him" (Gen 32:26), that it is a reference to the angel appointed over the nation of Esau in the existence of the supernal world.
>
> He replied: "Nay, but I am captain of the Lord's host: I am now come" (v. 14). That is I am a state emanated from the Divine presence in accordance to your temporal predisposition. This was no doubt expressed more highly than the general tone of his discourse which had something natural about it. Therefore Joshua was overcome by his speech and fell before him to the ground ⟨…⟩ and in that state of prophetic inspiration and perception, beseeched him to continue to cast off and strip him of his corporeal state in order to strengthen him with Divine providence. ⟨…⟩ However, he explained that his degree was inferior to that of Moses in respect of his detachment from the physical state, for Moses not only rose above outer bodliness and its coarse faculties but also above the subtle, spiritual faculties to become pure intellect. Therefore

is it stated ⟨in connection with Moses⟩: "put off thy shoes from thy feet" (Exod 3:5) ⟨in the plural⟩, whereas of Joshua it is said: "Put off thy shoe from off thy foot" for his prophecy came about through the intermediary of an angel like other prophets in contrast to Moses' prophecy, which was 'mouth to mouth', without intermediary. This is a great secret which we have dared to ⟨disclose⟩. Understand the allusion in this verse and the following directed to Moses: "for the place whereon thou standest is holy ground" (Exod 3:5) whereas in the case ⟨of Joshua⟩ it is stated: 'holy' (v. 15) without a mention of ground. This is in accordance with the sublime degree of Moses and his purity from any sensual form or image. Understand this.[68]

Although Tanḥum is primarily concerned with the plain meaning of the text, some of his interpretations have a definite mystical strain. Tanḥum does not always make Maimonidean rationalism his measuring-rod. At times he takes a clearly mystical line, and at times he uses Sufi technical terms as in the following passage:

"And Saul sent messengers to take David; and when they saw the company of the prophets prophesying, and Samuel standing as head over them, the spirit of God came upon the messengers of Saul, and they also prophesied" (1 Sam 19:20). With this power belonging to Samuel he drew out their souls and uplifted them from their place to a spiritual degree which was not theirs. The masters of this art call it 'spiritual energy' (*himma nafsâniyya*),[69] which is an influence without intermediary that attains instantaneously that which a proficient seeker cannot reach even after a prolonged period, for he cannot experience such an attraction (*jadhba*).[70] Now this degree is beyond the physical world and can forgo preparation or predisposition. Notice how Elisha was tending to his ox while engaged in ploughing and was devoid of ⟨spiritual⟩ experience. Now when Elijah cast his mantle about him a divine power flowed upon him unawares. Whereupon he declared: "Wait for me until I have bidden farewell to my folk and I shall follow thee". "Let me, I pray thee, kiss my father and my mother, and then I will follow thee" (1 Kgs 19:20), and he replied "Go back; for what have I done to thee?"[71]

Occasionally he even proposes both an esoteric and an exoteric exposition of Scripture, such as his commentary on the following verse, which provides an excellent illustration of his all-round method: "But the Lord is in his holy temple; let all the earth keep silence before Him" (Hab 2:20).

This verse was uttered in contrast to the preceding one in which mention was made of the vainness of idolatrous cult. The latter is ineffective, whereas our Lord is the utmost degree of perfection since His light is in His holy sanctuary and His action reaches unto the furthest limit of created things throughout the universe. Moreover, all beings subsist by virtue of the emanation of His bounty, as if He were, by way of a simile, a voice to which all were listening in order to benefit from the meaning of His discourse. According to this interpretation 'His holy temple' signifies the world of pure simplicity,[72] in whose highest degree God is to be found, who is necessary existence *per se* and from whom issued the existence of every being as it is referred to allegorically in the words "let all the earth keep silence".

---

[68] *Rabbi Tanchum Jeruschalmi arabischer Commentar zum Buche Josua* (ed. Th. Haarbrücker; Berlin 1862) 8–9. See also H. G. von Mutius, *Der Josua-Commentar des Tanchum* (Hildesheim 1983) fols. 8 b–9 a.

[69] This is a Sufi technical term. Cf. Al-Ǧurǧânī, *A Book of Definitions* (ed. G. Flügel; Leipzig 1845) 278: "the turning and directing of the heart with the totality of its spiritual faculties to the Divine presence in order to obtain perfection for oneself or for another".

[70] This too is a Sufi technical term. Cf. ibid. 213: "An individual chosen by God for Himself. He chooses him by the presence of His intimicy, initiating him into the holiness of His Presence and endowing him with all the spiritual stations and degrees without his having to sustain effort or fatigue".

[71] *Commentarium arabicum ad Librorum Samuelis* (ed. Haarbrücker; Leipzig 1844) 33.

[72] Reminiscent of Maimonides' expression in *Guide* 2.1 (ed. Qafiḥ; Jerusalem 1972) 270.

However, according to the exoteric meaning, by 'holy temple', the sanctuary or Jerusalem is meant, and by 'all the earth', the inhabitants of the earth, that is the kingdoms of all the inhabited world. Thus the meaning is that He manifests His light, that His Providence dwells upon Israel and that He wreaks punishment upon their enemies so that all the nations of the earth, as well as their kings, are awed and dumbfounded before Him. The verb *has* 'keep silence' is used here metaphorically to express this awe, though its original sense is 'silence' as in the verse "and Caleb stilled the people" (Num 13:30) – for he who is silent and hearkens is awed by what he hears. Furthermore, this word has an exceptional inflexion for it does not obey the rule either of nouns or verbs and ressembles the Arabic expression *ṣah* (silence!), as explained elsewhere.[73] Moreover, this meaning ⟨of the word *has*⟩ was also adopted by the Targum, who translates "all the idols of the earth are consumed before Him".[74]

His interpretation of the following chapter 'Habakkuk's prayer' is an instructive example of Tanḥum's exegesis of the 'Prayers' and 'Songs' of Holy Writ, to which he generally lends an allegorical meaning, treating them as historical prophecies.

The book of Jonah is deserving of a special mention in this context. Unlike Tanḥum's other commentaries it is a complete allegorical interpretation (*ta'wīl*) of the whole book inspired by neo-Platonic philosophy. The commentator considers Jonah son of Amittai in its literal meaning of 'dove son of Truth', and interprets the name as a symbol for the soul of Divine origin. The latter sinks into the ocean of matter while travelling on the ship, i. e. the body, vessel of the soul, on its journey to Nineveh, from *neweh*, 'abode'.

5. The Yemenite School

Unfortunately present space will not allow for an in-depth study of the Yemenite exegetical school, which, despite its extreme interest, has yet to be undertaken.[75] Indeed, between the fourteenth and fifteenth centuries, Yemen witnessed a considerable flowering of exegetical activity of a particular kind. The works of this period, generally called *midrašīm* and often composed in an eromatic genre, shied away from the philological method of preceding generations and rehabilitated the midrashic style. This movement did not however result in a naïve, literalistic approach to the text, for the authors, under the sway of Maimonides, often had recourse to the philosophical interpretation of Aggadah. Of special interest in this context is the controversy which swept through the Yemenite communities in reaction precisely to the allegorical interpretation of Scripture stirred up, in particular, by an anonymous midrashic commentary on the Pentateuch, *Kitâb al-ḥaqâ'iq*, composed in the second decade of the fourteenth century by an author from Ṣaʿada. The latter, taking his cue from Maimonides, but perhaps also from Muslim Šiʿite exegesis, advocated an extreme form of *ta'wīl*, whereby the whole Torah and its precepts were expounded allegorically. Thus Moses became the Intellect, Aaron the

---

[73] In his commentary on Judg 3:19 (ed. C. Schnurrer; Tübingen 1791) 14.
[74] *Commentary on Habakkuk* (ed. S. Munk; Paris 1845) 44–46; ed. H. Shay; Jerusalem 1992; 221–22 and her Introduction, p. XVIII.
[75] See, meanwhile, Langermann, Yemenite Midrash (1996).

imaginative faculty, the High Priest the Active Intellect, and so forth. The book, which had its defenders, was vilified and banned in no uncertain terms by the Rabbis of Ṣanʿa.

Among the outstanding writers of the homiletic genre was Nethanel b. Yešaʿ, author of *Nûr aẓ-Ẓalâm*, a homiletical exposition of the Pentateuch written in 1339 containing much philosophical material. Yaḥya b. Sulaymân aḏ-Ḏamârî, known in Hebrew as Zeḵaryah ha-Rofe (fl. 1430), authored in an admixture of Hebrew and Arabic two commentaries on the Pentateuch – *Midraš ha-ḥefeṣ* and *Ad-durra al-muntaḫiba*, – largely based on the *Midraš ha-gadôl* with much material from Maimonides' *Guide*. He also wrote a commentary on the *Hafṭarôt*, the Vision of Ezechiel, Isaiah, Esther, as well as a philosophical commentary on Song of Songs. Mention can be made of his contemporary, Manṣûr aḏ-Ḏamârī, known in Hebrew as Ḥôṭer b. Šəlômoh (active 1423), author of *Sirâǧ al-ʿuqûl*, an Arabic homiletical commentary on the Pentateuch drawing on midrashic and philosophical sources. David b. Yešaʿ ha-Lewī, also composed in Arabic a midrashic commentary on the Torah, the *al-Waǧīz al-muġnī* (written between 1484 and 1493), which contains numerous quotes from the *Guide*. Finally, mention should be made of Abraham b. Solomon (fl. 1420), also thought to be of Yemenite extract, author of the Arabic *Midraš aṣ-Ṣiyânī*, which, mainly drawing on Tanḥum and Qimhi, explains the Pentateuch both grammatically and philologically, often entering into allegorical interpretations (*ta'wīl*) inspired by Maimonidean philosophy.

Thus is brought home yet once more the enormous and abiding impact in all subsequent exegesis of Moses Maimonides' thought and hermeneutics, which was no less true in the case of the Yemenites than in that of the other late schools of the Orient.

33.6. Kabbalistic Exegesis

By Moshe Idel, Jerusalem

Bibliography: D. Abrams, "From Germany to Spain: Numerology as a Mystical Technique", *JJS* 47 (1996) 85–101; S. Benin, *The Footprints of God. Divine Accommodation in Jewish and Christian Thought* (Albany: SUNY Press 1993); idem, "The Mutability of an Immutable God: Exegesis and Individual Capacity in the Zohar and Several Christian Sources", *The Age of Zohar* (ed. Joseph Dan; Jerusalem 1989) 67–86; J. Dan, "The Ashkenazi 'Gates of Wisdom'", *Hommage à George Vajda: Etudes d'histoire et de pensée juives* (ed. G. Nahon/Charles Touati; Louvain 1980) 183–89; M. Idel, "Infinities of Torah in Kabbalah", *Midrash and Literature* (ed. G. Hartmann/S. Budick; New Haven: Yale UP 1986) 141–57; idem, *Language, Torah, and Hermeneutics in Abraham Abulafia* (tr. M. Kalus; Albany: SUNY Press 1989); idem, *Kabbalah: New Perspectives* (New Haven/London: Yale UP 1988) 200–49; idem, "Midrashic versus Other Forms of Jewish Hermeneutics", *The Midrashic Imagination* (ed. Michael Fishbane; Albany: SUNY Press 1993) 45–58; idem, "PaRDeS: Some Reflections on Kabbalistic Hermeneutics", *Death, Ecstasy, and Other Worldly Journeys* (ed. J. J. Collins/M. Fishbane; Albany: SUNY Press 1995) 249–64; idem, "The Concept of the Torah in Heikhalot Literature and Its Metamorphoses in Kabbalah", *Jerusalem Studies in Jewish Thought* 1 (1981) 23–84; P. Sandler, "On the Question of *Pardes* and the Fourfold Method" (Heb.), *Sefer Eliahu Auerbach* (Jerusalem 1955) 222–35; G. Scholem, *On the Kabbalah and Its Symbolism* (tr. R. Manheim; New York: Schocken Books 1969); F. Talmage, "Apples of God: The Inner Meaning of Sacred Texts in Medieval Judaism", *Jewish Spirituality* I (ed. Arthur Green; New York: Crossroad 1986) 313–54; A. van der Heide, "*Pardes*: Methodological Reflections on the Theory of Four Senses", *JJS* 34 (1983) 147–59; E. Wolfson, "By Way of Truth: Aspects of Nahmanides' Kabbalistic Hermeneutic", *AJS Review* 14 (1989) 103–78; idem, "The Hermeneutics of Visionary Experience: Revelation and Interpretation in the *Zohar*", *Religion* 18 (1988) 311–45; idem, "Beautiful Maiden Without Eyes: *Peshat* and *Sod* in Zoharic Hermeneutics", *The Midrashic Imagination* (ed. Michael Fishbane; Albany: SUNY Press 1993) 155–203.

1. Kabbalistic Types of Exegesis

In medieval Judaism a strong process of arcanization, namely of understanding of the Jewish canonical texts as replete with secrets, took place. Arcanization is shared by both Jewish mysticism and Jewish philosophy, and it invited the emergence and the development of a long series of exegetical strategies that allow the 'extraction' of a variety of secrets from the canonical writings. Insofar as the Jewish mystical literatures are concerned, there are four main categories of exegetical device:

(a) The monadic understanding of the Hebrew language and implicitly of the Bible; according to this view, which has ancient sources and became, by the intermediary of the kabbalistic material, prevalent in Hasidism, each and every letter was conceived of as a universe in itself. The atomization of the semantic units into letters conceived as designating divine names, the entire system of *sefirot* and the whole alphabet, diminished the importance of the specific sequel of the letters in the Bible, in favor of the immersion of the Kabbalists and, later on, by the Hasidim into the inner world of the letters. It is as if the interpreter was contemplating the text using a microscope.

(b) The hieroglyphic, iconic or ideogrammic understanding of the whole text as the picture of the supernal divine system. This view is closely related to the anthropomorphic view of God in the Heikhalot literature and its metamorphoses in the kabbalistic view of the ten *sefirot* as constituting an anthropomorphic structure. It is as if the exegete was using a telescope in order to see the whole text as one unit. Somewhat related to this hieroglyphic view is the kabbalistic understanding of the white forms of the letters as pointing to a higher reality, in comparison to that symbolized by the black forms of the letter.

(c) A variety of mathematical approaches to the text which consist of methods like *notarikon*, acronym, *gematria*, which deals with the numerical values of the letters of a certain word, the *temurah* or the changes of letters for other letters according to a certain pattern, and *tzerufei 'otiot*, permutations of letters, or other variations of these exegetical techniques.

(d) Last, but not least, the symbolical-narrative exegesis, which transformed the biblical text into a fabric of symbols pointing to the interaction between the divine attributes, or *sefirot*. This is one of the most widespread exegetical techniques, which permeates all the main trends of Kabbalah.

2. Pardes: the Fourfold Kabbalistic Exegesis

Centered on the details of the biblical text more than the Christian mystics, and perhaps more even than the Sufis, the medieval Kabbalah offered a *plethora* of mystical interpretations whose relationship to the already existing corpora of traditional non-mystical interpretations of the Scriptures had yet to be clarified in detail. The major expression of the Kabbalists' attempts to establish an explicit scheme which can explicate the hierarchical relationship between the different types of Jewish exegesis is known by the acronym *PaRDeS*. Originally meaning an orchard, this term is mentioned as part of an ancient rabbinic legend about four sages who entered a state of mystical contemplation of a supernal, and dangerous realm named *Pardes*. As an acronym, it designates however, a fourfold system of exegesis, used mostly in kabbalistic writings. *PaRDeS* stands for *P*[*eshat*], plain sense, *R*[*emez*] or hint, sometimes designating allegorical explanations, *D*[*erash*] or homiletic expositions and finally *S*[*od*] or secret, namely symbolic, interpretations.

There are two main theories attempting to explain the emergence of the *PaRDeS* type of exegesis among the Kabbalists at the end of the thirteenth century: that of W. Bacher who maintained that the Kabbalists adopted and adapted the Christian fourfold theory of interpretation, and the view of P. Sandler, who claims that this exegetical system emerged, as the result of an inner development starting with twelfth century Jewish exegesis. At the beginning, Gershom Scholem adopted the theory of Bacher, though later on he did not reject explicitly the view of Sandler. On the other hand, it is rather difficult simply to accept the Bacher-Scholem thesis because of the simple fact, pointed out already by Sandler, and reiterated by Frank Talmage and van der Heide, that the kabbalistic fourfold method does not correspond in some crucial details to the Christian fourfold method. Though it is always possible that one individual Kabbalist will accept an alien type of exegesis, either Christian or Muslim, it seems to me implausible to assume that several Kabbalists accepted, exactly at the same time and apparently independently, a very similar exegetical method. We must look for a common factor that can explain the concomitant resort of several Jewish authors to these exegetical methods. Can we accept as reasonable the explanation that independent Kabbalists would accept, at roughly the same time, an alien type of exegesis, without having in common more substantial unifying factors? It seems that the obvious fact the Kabbalists, and not the Jewish philosophers, were those who developed such a fourfold method, is highly significant.

The term *PaRDeS* stands in some kabbalistic texts from late thirteenth century for the four methods of exegesis. However, in the period when this exegetical system emerged, it designated methods which were already applied, separately, in different types of Jewish literature. The plain sense was the main subject of the rich exegetical literature produced by the Northern French school of exegetes during the eleventh and twelfth centuries. Homiletical literature, the Midrash, was already a voluminous literature produced between the third century and the early Middle Ages. Since the eleventh century, Jewish philosophers like Solomon ibn Gabirol, Abraham ibn Ezra and Maimonides, had often resorted to allegorical interpretation; its *floruit* can be established in the thirteenth century. Finally, kabbalistic – mainly symbolical-theosophical – interpretations of the Bible and other canonic Jewish writings were already known at the middle of the thirteenth century. The *PaRDeS* fourfold exegetical method incorporated a variety of types of Jewish literature that had been already in existence when the first formulations of this exegetical method were articulated. The latest type of exegetical literature was Kabbalah, and it is no matter of accident that the exponents of this mystical lore were those who first developed the method of *PaRDeS*. There is sufficient evidence to show that some of the Kabbalists who proposed the *PaRDeS* or other systematic exegetical methods underwent a particular spiritual development, before they became Kabbalists. They became acquainted with the three other forms of interpretation before resorting to the various forms of kabbalistic exegesis.

The kabbalistic, onto-hermeneutics of the Torah leads the mystic to the divine world of emanation. The *PaRDeS*-system involves a certain version of *scala mentis ad Deum*; gradually immersing himself into the various aspects of the text, the Kabbalist is, at the same time, fathoming the depths of reality; the Bible became a tool for metaphysical exploration. At the core of this text stands the divinity, or one of its manifestations, and the dynamism of the divine life can be extracted by the explication of the rich secret meanings of the infinite divine text. The hermeneutic enterprise of the Kabbalist brings him, according to the above ontological concord, to an experience of the Divine; exploring the text, the Kabbalist enters another, higher, spiritual domain. A kabbalistic reading of the Torah apparently meant, at least for some of the Jewish mystics, more than a determination of a certain potential meaning of the text; by creating, or extrapolating, this significance, the Kabbalist also experienced it. In other words, some of the important stages of Jewish mysticism envisioned mystical exegesis not only as a manner of extracting novel meanings from a text by propelling some theological or theosophical views into it, but also as a way of encountering deeper levels of reality. In some cases this was perhaps the main purpose of the enterprise. Accordingly the experiential aspects of kabbalistic hermeneutics is a subject that still deserve a detailed study; some of its facets are reminiscent of the modern phenomenological type of reading, which emphasizes the experiential understanding over the analytical 'objective' approach.

In the writings of R. Abraham Abulafia (1240–1291), the founder of the ecstatic Kabbalah, a sevenfold exegetical system was proposed, which combines three non-mystical types of exegesis with allegorical exegesis and, on the top, three numerical forms of exegesis.

3. Kabbalistic Symbolic Exegesis

Symbolic exegesis as cultivated in the theosophical Kabbalah does not supersede the importance of the material reality or of the interpreted text; it only adds a new layer of significance. So, for example, the real city of Jerusalem is holy in itself and also because it represents a higher entity of female nature, in the lower world.

A variety of symbolic systems, which differ from each other both in detail and in principle are found in many of the kabbalistic books. Recurrent as it may be, symbolism is however not ubiquitous in kabbalistic literature. There are whole kabbalistic corpora which are not symbolic, as for example, the ecstatic Kabbalah of Abraham Abulafia and the linguistic Kabbalah of the early Joseph Gikatilla. Nevertheless, the recurrence of symbols in some important kabbalistic corpora has convinced, together with other factors, some of the scholars of Kabbalah to formulate what I would designate a 'pansymbolic' understanding of Kabbalah, namely an assumption that Kabbalah cannot be imagined without the symbolic perception of reality as a whole.

It is in a tense spiritual ambiance, created by the appearance of Maimonides' *Guide of the Perplexed*, which exposed a strongly allegorical approach to the Bible, and the controversies around them, that more comprehensive kabbalistic symbolism had emerged. Its greater vagueness is the result of a more flexible attitude to the exegesis of the texts – a position anchored already in midrashic hermeneutics – and in its establishing a nexus between them and theology that was much more dynamic than the Aristotelian one embraced by Maimonides. Though in part a reaction to his hermeneutics, the kabbalistic view of the symbol is not a complete innovation, but much more an elaboration on fragmentary and obscure *mythologoumena* found in Jewish writings and traditions that preceded the emergence of Kabbalah. The symbolic hermeneutics of the Kabbalists can be better understood as an attempt to counteract the allegorical monosemic code, historically of an alien source, which was conceived as subverting the plain sense of the sacred texts. This seems to be the situation already at the beginning of Kabbalah, and it continued to be a factor in its later development.

The crystallization of the symbolic mode in Kabbalah is, if this explanation is adequate, part of a comprehensive conflict between Aristotelian noetics applied to Scripture, and a growing theosophical system stemming from earlier Jewish sources and neo-Platonic ontology, which invited a different noetics, more neo-Platonic in its propensity, and a more nebulous and polysemic approach to the canonic texts. The most important kabbalistic corpus resorting to symbols, the book of the *Zohar*, composed at the end of the thirteenth century, was described by scholars as a reaction to Maimonides. This general observation is pertinent also insofar as the symbolic hermeneutics is involved. In order to better understand the scriptural nature of the symbolic code, let me introduce some remarks of their nature, resorting to modern semiotics.

In many forms of Kabbalah the symbol may be defined as a word that stands for an absent thing, and in some cases, even for an entity no more existent in this world. The absence is crucial in a system that is exegetical, unlike the symbols as understood in a variety of negative theologies which are concerned more with hidden, though existent, divine realities. The prevalent scholarly views of the symbol in Kabbalah assume that the symbols reflect the hidden divine realities, unknown otherwise. The present theory assumes the opposite: the theosophical system was known to the Kabbalist and he used the sefirotic and sometimes angelic and demonic structures, in order to make sense of the quandaries of the canonic texts. Thus, the very linguistic unit should be understood as a combination of *ratio difficilis* and *ratio facilis*, two categories found in UMBERTO ECO's semiotics. As *ratio facilis* the kabbalistic symbol points to what the Kabbalist believed to be an ontological entity, a divine attribute, whose nature he studied when it was introduced in Kabbalah. However, the fragmentary and obscure nature of the theosophical system invited a more complex situation: the transformation of a biblical word into a symbol for a *sefirah* means not only infusing a certain figurative meaning in that word, but also a transfer of meaning from the word to the imaginary entity on high, and thus we are closer to the concept of *ratio difficilis.* Even more so if the scholarly assumption is that the sefirotic realm is recreated and modified each time someone enriches it by the semiotic process connected to it. In other terms, the more the theosophical system is articulated and the interpretation of the biblical linguistic material is rendered automatic, we face a *ratio facilis*, which brings the kabbalistic symbols closer to philosophical allegory. Historically speaking, kabbalistic symbolism moves from a semiotic phenomenon closer to *ratio difficilis* to one more typical of *ratio facilis.* Indeed, if this suggestion can be corroborated by further research, the widespread opposition between symbol and allegory, which permeates the scholarly treatments of figurative language in Kabbalah, should be transcended by an assumption that the two forms of ratio are describing fluctuations within the kabbalistic semiotics, which better describe what happened in the field. Indeed, if earlier Kabbalah is closer to the *ratio difficilis*, we may speak, using an expression coined by MARTIN BUBER in order to describe Kabbalah *in toto*, of a schematization of the mystery in later Kabbalah, when the semiosis of *ratio facilis* is much more evident.

The kabbalistic resort to a *ratio difficilis* at the beginning of Kabbalah is the result of the absence of a crystallized kabbalistic theosophy on the one hand, and the effort to maintain as strong a role to the plain sense as possible for the

Hebrew original of the Bible on the other. Allegorical exegesis was adopted by thinkers with a propensity toward a conventional theory of language. The *ratio difficilis* confers on language a greater importance, and in the case of many of the Kabbalists who emphasized the vision of Hebrew as a natural or divine language, a symbolic approach was more evident. Language was not a means to convey a message, which is found also in other forms of literature, like medieval philosophy, but also part of the message itself. This is conspicuously the case of R. Joseph Gikatilla, who emphasized the divine nature of Hebrew on one hand, and wrote an influential book on kabbalistic symbolism, *Sefer Sha-ʿarei ʾOrah.* This nexus between symbolic interpretation and the vision of language as non-conventional is part of a broader phenomenon in Jewish mysticism, that of relating the unlimited semiosis to the special nature of Hebrew.

So, for example David, Abraham or any biblical figures, were understood as symbols of the various divine powers, known as *sefirot.* Thus, in order to move from the *signifiant* to the *signifié*, a kabbalist has to rely either on a word, which will point alone toward the higher entity it symbolizes, or upon a concept that emerges from the various contexts of this word. In some cases the concrete entity exists no more, and therefore its significative function as a representative, here below, of the supernal *sefirah* was conceived of as taken over by the word that pointed to it. So, for example, the persona of David the king, who was conceived of as a representative of the last *sefirah*, the kingship, *malkhut*, is no more approachable as an entity here below. Thus, solely the word 'David' is the possible conduit of the meaning which points to the last *sefirah.* However, at least for most of the stages of the development of Kabbalah, the theosophical Kabbalist knew what is the significance of the last *sefirah*, and he determined accordingly the symbolic valence of the biblical word, whose real reference was no more available. In other words, a whole literary universe, mostly a biblical one, compounded of dead persons, destroyed cities, shattered temples or often times no more performed rituals, like the sacrifices for example. These were conceived as once signifying symbolically the supernal theosophical powers and processes, but were now approachable only by means of their linguistic designators, whose valence was determined by the theosophical knowledge of the Kabbalist. Much more than revealing the nature of the deity, the kabbalistic symbols decoded what was conceived as the symbolic meaning of the scriptures.

The theosophical Kabbalists are not to be understood as striving for a comprehensive symbolism of reality, but much more for a comprehensive symbolization of their canonic writings and actions. By and large, outside the canon, there is no need for symbolic valences. Indeed, when dealing with the symbolism of evil, Kabbalists were more creative, inventing demonic names which are hard to be detected in the extant traditions. However, even this modest inventiveness may well be part of our ignorance of the magical and demonic sources which might have inspired the kabbalists.

4. Sexual Polarization as a Kabbalistic Hermeneutical Device

The biblical literature constitutes a fabric of complex crosscurrents, which consist in both efforts at the demythologization of earlier traditions and proposals of another myth, that of the divine will. Demythologization however, was never complete; even when attempts have been made to obliterate the mythical contents of some traditions, vestiges of the mythical imagery are still evident. These vestiges served as starting points for the mythopoeic imagination of the *Zohar*, which created, and sometimes perhaps even recreated, out of the biblical verses and phrases, new myths.

One of the most outstanding characteristics of the kabbalistic exegesis of the Bible is the exploitation of stylistic phenomena of parallelism between the different parts of a verse, in order to introduce a polar reading, which is in many case the polarity between male and female. This approach is related to the comprehensive arcanization of the biblical text, as it implies that mere repetition of synonymous terms would diminish the semantic content of the text. By reading a dual vision into the parallels in the verse, which are synonyms in the biblical style, the *Zohar* creates a drama, often implying a sexual or erotic mythical event occurring in the sefirotic realm. However, central as this exegetical device is for the hermeneutics of the *Zohar*, it is not new with it; it is already found in the early thirtheeth century theosophical Kabbalah, for example R. Ezra of Gerona's *Commentary on the Song of Songs*. The *Zohar* exploits possibilities opened much earlier. Let me give an example of zoharic symbolic exegesis, on Psalm 48:

> "Great is the Lord and highly to be praised, in the city of our God, in the mountain of his holiness." When is the Lord called 'great'? When *Knesset Yisrael* is to be found with Him, as it is written, "In the city of our God is He great". "In the city of our God" means "with the city of our God" ... and we learn that a king without a queen is not a [real] king, and is neither great nor praised. Thus, so long as the male is without a female, all his excellency is removed from him and he is not in the category of Adam, and moreover he is not worthy of being blessed ... "Beautiful for situation, the joy of the whole earth: mount Zion, the side of the North, the city of the great King". The meaning of "Beautiful for situation, the joy of the whole earth" stands for the excellency of their [sexual] intercourse. "Beautiful for situation" [stands] for he Holy, blessed be He, who is the Righteous, [who is] "the joy of the whole earth" and then it is the delight of All, and *Knesset Yisrael* is blessed[1].

Yefe nof (Ps 48:3) which means literally, a 'beautiful view', is understood as a symbol for Divinity, more precisely the ninth *sefirah*, that of *yesod*, that is the male divine power *par excellence*, identified with the *membrum virile*. This limb, which is to be used only in holiness – an imperative recurring often in the *Zohar*, is representative in the zoharic symbolism of the righteous, both the divine, or the ninth *sefirah*, and the human one. This sexual reading has been fostered by the occurrence of the term *masos* in 48:3, translated here as 'joy and delight', which occurs in several texts in the context of the desire of the bridegroom for the bride. Indeed, the reading of *yefe nof* as a bridegroom has been inspired by the Aramaic translation of this verse, where it is written: "Beautiful

---

[1] *Zohar*, III, fol. 5 a.

– like a bridegroom, who is the delight of the inhabitants of the whole earth". The biblical *masos* has been translated as *hedwetah* which is followed by the term *kol*, 'all', a fact that inspired the emergence of the zoharic phrase *hedwetah de-kullah.* The term 'earth', *ha-'aretz*, has been understood by the *Zohar* as a symbol for the last or the tenth *sefirah*, namely *malkhut*, which is synonymous to *Knesset Yisrael*, all of them serving as symbols for the feminine divine manifestation. Also in the case of 48:2 the sexual polarity is involved. This time, the pattern of this interpretation, similar to many other passages in the Kabbalah, involves a differentiation between the meaning of two divine names: the Tetragrammaton YHWH, signifying the Lord – standing for *sefirah* of *tiferet* or the male divine attribute – and *Elohenu*, referring to *malkhut* or the female attribute. However, the novelty here is not to be found in this widespread distinction in Kabbalah; the focus of the exegetical effort is rather on the word 'great', which articulates the relationship between these attributes. Greatness is not an inherent quality of the male, but is acquired through his relation to the female; only by the act of intercourse, as hinted in our discussion, is the quality of 'great' and 'praised' made applicable to the male, whereby he becomes 'man'. The sexualization of the relationship between the divine attributes is a well-known kabbalistic exegetical device, which presupposes a special concern with a duality within the divine world, to be discovered even in those places in the Bible where synonyms were misinterpreted as pointing to different entities. However, beyond the investment of divine names with sexual qualities, common in the Kabbalah, this passage of the *Zohar* adds something more specific: how the greatness and excellency of the male is attained, both in the human and divine realm. The gist of this exegetical endeavor is the appearance of a quality through the establishment of a certain relationship between two entities. The ultimate message of the *Zohar* is not the mere understanding of the condition for perfection; while its symbolism may indeed invite someone to contemplation, his awareness of certain theosophical and anthropological ideas does not change man. In order to attain both his perfection and that of Divinity, he must also act appropriately; otherwise, the very purpose of the exegetical process is not fulfilled. The experiential aspect of apprehending the zoharic exegesis is, therefore, only the first step toward the ultimate goal; understanding is, for the Kabbalist, an inescapable invitation to act, as otherwise the male does not reach the status of 'man', and moreover cannot perform the theurgic activity intended to influence the supernal syzygies. Symbolism is to be viewed as part of an effort toward deepening both the significance of the biblical text and, at the same time, the understanding of human activity. It was understood as theurgical and thus oriented towards the higher world, and not only to the disclosure of a static meaning implemented through certain words.

We may distinguish three distinct steps constituting the inner structure of the zoharic text: (a) 'gnostic' perfection, which stands for the understanding of the theosophical and theurgical significance of the verse; (b) an operative achievement, namely the acquisition of the status of 'man' – i.e., an ongoing way of life together with his wife, just as above two *sefirot* are to be brought together by the kabbalistic way of life; (c) finally, as a perfect man, the Kabbalist induces Divine harmony through the performance of the commandments.

According to the *Zohar* even the fathoming of the depths of the biblical text has an experiential aspect; the second step here, that of becoming a complete 'man', is to be seen, not as the attainment of a static perfection, but as a dynamic activity to be cultivated in relation to the wife. To return to the aforecited passage: the plain sense of Ps 48:2 is apparently simple and obvious – that the Lord is great and, as a separate assertion, that His mountain is located in His holy city. The former is a theological assessment, unconditional and absolute; the latter indicates that the sacred mountain is located geographically in the sacred city. The relationship between God's greatness and the sacredness of the Mountain is not even alluded to; these two theological statements can easily be understood separately, and so there is no intention of describing any peculiar dynamic relationship between God and His city. Even though the biblical conception of the holy city as the city of God is quite explicit, no changing pattern of relationship is implied by this assertion: it is chosen forever. The pattern of relationship is a 'vertical' one; divine holiness, stemming from the supernal world, is imposed upon a material entity, which is metamorphosed thereby into a sacred center. The *Zohar* radically changes this pattern: the 'vertical' relationship is transposed on the divine plan, where it can now be viewed as 'horizontal' – that of two sexually-differentiated entities, which are both divine attributes. In order to determine the relationship between the two parts of the verse, the Hebrew prefix *be*, 'in', is interpreted as meaning 'with'; the dynamics which emerges from the sexualization and the interrelation of the two divine names found in the biblical verse creates the specific quality of kabbalistic exegesis, in comparison with other types of Jewish exegesis. Theosophical Kabbalah alone could put into relief divine attributes, whose affinity with one another gradually turns, at times into semi-myths and at others even into full-fledged myth. The transformation of the vertical relationship into an intradivine polarity does not obliterate the previous vertical understanding of the relation of God to the city. As we have already noted, the corporeal reality is not ignored by the zoharic Kabbalist, but was interpreted so that it will not detract from its substantiality.

5. Kabbalistic Visions of the Text

One of the views characteristic of some of the kabbalistic systems – designated in the following as innovative Kabbalah – is the claim that the Torah, being a divine text, is infinite and thus it is possible to extract from it numberless meanings. This view, whose roots can be detected at the turn of the mid-thirteenth century, was not accepted by the conservative Kabbalists, namely those persons who did not adopt the method of *PaRDeS*. Nevertheless, it is recurrent in the writings of the kabbalistic innovative interpreters. Through the mediation of Christian Kabbalah, this view could have influenced modern theories on the open text.

The central assumption of the kabbalistic understanding of the divine text, namely that it is, like its author, infinite, could be supported better if it were possible to return to the text and reinterpret it mystically time and again. Some of the innovative Kabbalists assumed that it is possible to apply, at the same time, more than one kabbalistic type of interpretation, and implicitly it means that the text was understood to offer a whole range of mystical meanings at the same time. In other words, mystical interpretation is not to be understood as explicating the infinite meanings of the texts as part of an evolving historical process which assumes the accommodation theory of revelation or related types of adaptationist theories. Though indeed the Torah was sometimes described by Kabbalists using theories of accommodation, as it has recently been shown by S. D. Benin, even the lower, mundane manifestation of the Torah was conceived as being pregnant with an infinity of meanings. Regularly, the assumption that the divine message is accommodated to the peculiar period of time, or level of evolution, points to the revelation of one hidden type of meaning implicitly excluding the concomitant existence of other similar types of meanings. In the case of the kabbalistic theory, even in the cases when the theory of accommodation was indeed adopted for one reason or another, this fact did not vitally affect the coexistence of a plurality of symbolic and non-symbolic messages in the same text for the same person. Moreover, the general impression is that innovative Kabbalists, though using sometimes accommodationist formulations, were not eager to acknowledge a lowering of the status of the Torah by attributing to it only one significance which alone will inform the religious life of a particular generation. I would say that Kabbalah preferred the assumption that an infinity of meanings is latent in the *Gestalt* of the divine text, over the view, found in several Christian texts, that the process of interpretation alone is infinite. According to the latter, each and every exegete is able to contribute his view to the exegetical tradition, whereas the text *per se* is only very rarely regarded as infinite in its significances. Indeed it would be much more representative to describe the conception of the Kabbalists regarding the relationship between Torah and man as involving the requirement for the Kabbalist to be assimilated to the Torah rather than vice-versa. It is man that must accommodate himself to the infinite Torah rather than Torah to man. One example will suffice in order to describe the infinity of meanings in the biblical text:

> The worlds change each and every hour, and there is no hour which is similar to another. And whoever contemplates the movement of the planets and stars, and the changes of their position and constellation and how their stand changes in a moment, and whoever is born in this moment will undergo different things from those which happen to one who was born in the preceding moment; hence, one can look and contemplate what is [going on] in the supernal infinite, and numberless worlds ... and so you will understand the changes of the constellation and the position of the worlds, which are the garments of *'Eyn Sof*; these changes are taking place at each and every moment, and in accordance with these changes are the aspects of the sayings of the book of the *Zohar* changing, and all are words of the Living God[2].

---

[2] R. Hayyim Vital, *Sefer 'Etz Hayyim*, I. I. 5, fol. 15 a.

6. The Status of the Interpreter

The arcanization of the text not only encouraged the emergence of complex exegetical systems, but inspired new visions by the kabbalistic exegetes, which explain why and how they were able to offer a large plurality of mystical interpretations. The basic assumption, which emerged in the sixteenth century, is that each soul possesses a special interpretation unique to it alone. So, for example, we learn from an early seventeenth century Kabbalist:

> The issue is that the Torah, "its measure is longer than the hearth, and broader than the sea" [Job 11:9], and just as there is an infinite number of worlds, so is the depth of the Torah infinite. Because in each and every world, the Torah is read in accordance with its [to the respective world's] subtlety and spirituality, namely that there is no end to the degrees of its interpretations. And each and every one of the Tannaites and the Amoraites in this world, understands and interprets the Torah in accordance with the world from which his soul has emanated. This is why some say [so] and others say [otherwise] and the saying of these and these are the words of the Living God. This is why R. Meir apprehended in the Torah something that was not apprehended by someone else, and it was appropriate for him [to interpret this] more than for another sage, because his name was Meir, which means light, and the stored light is good[3].

[3] Jacob Hayyim Tzemah of Jerusalem, *Sefer Meqor Hayyim*, Ms. New York, JTS 2205, fol. 16 b.

Chapter Thirty-four

The School of St. Victor in Paris

By Rainer Berndt, Frankfurt/M

Sources: Hugh of St. Victor: *Opera omnia* (PL 175–77); *Didascalicon-De studio legendi* (ed. C. H. Buttimer; Studies in Medieval and Renaissance Latin 10; Washington 1939); complete critical edition of Hugh's works by the Frankfurt Hugo von Sankt Viktor-Institute within the *Corpus victorinum*: I. *Expositiones in Octateuchum et in libros Regum* (ed. R. Berndt / R. Stammberger; Berlin: Akademie Verlag; [forthcoming]). Richard of St. Victor: *Opera omnia* (PL 196); *Liber exceptionum* (ed. J. Châtillon; Paris 1958). Andrew of St. Victor: *Expositio in Heptateuchum* (ed. C. Lohr / R. Berndt; CChr. CM 53; Turnhout 1986); *Expositio hystorica in librum Regum* (ed. F. A. van Liere; CChr. CM 53A; Turnhout 1996); *Expositiones historicae in libros Salomonis* (ed. R. Berndt; CChr. CM 53B; Turnhout 1991); *Expositio in Ezechielem* (ed. M. A. Signer; CChr. CM 53E; Turnhout 1991); *Expositio super Danielem* (ed. M. Zier; CChr. CM 53F; Turnhout 1990). Thomas Gallus: "Commentaire sur Isaïe de Thomas de Saint-Victor" (ed. by G. Théry, Vie spirituelle. Supplément 47 [1936] 146–62); *Commentaires du Cantique des Cantiques* (texte critique avec introduction, notes et tables par J. Barbet; Paris 1967).

Bibliographies: Hugh: P. Sicard, *Diagrammes médiévaux et exégèse visuelle. Le 'Libellus de formatione arche' de Hugues de Saint-Victor* (Bibliotheca Victorina 4; Turnhout 1993) 273–85. Database of the Hugo von Sankt Viktor-Institute, Frankfurt/Main. Andrew: R. Berndt, *André de Saint-Victor († 1175). Exégète et théologien* (Bibliotheca Victorina 2; Turnhout 1991) 351–81. Richard: M.-A. Aris, *Contemplatio. Philosophische Studien zum Traktat Benjamin Maior des Richard von St. Viktor. Mit einer verbesserten Edition des Textes* (Fuldaer Studien 6; Frankfurt am Main 1996) 134–49. Thomas Gallus: J. Barbet, "Thomas Gallus", DictS 15 (1991) 800–16; K. Ruh, "Thomas Gallus (Vercellensis)", *Deutsche Literatur des Mittelalters. Verfasserlexikon* 9 (1995) 857–61.

General works: *Le Moyen Age et la Bible* (ed. P. Riché / G. Lobrichon; BTT 4; Paris 1984); *L'abbaye parisienne de Saint-Victor au Moyen Age* (Communications présentées au XIIIe Colloque d'Humanisme médiéval de Paris [1986–88] et réunies par J. Longère; Bibliotheca Victorina 1; Turnhout 1991); G. Lobrichon, "Gli usi della Bibbia", *Lo spazio letterario del medioevo. 1. Il medioevo latino*, I, I (ed. by C. Leonardi); idem, "L'esegesi biblica. Storia di un genere letterario (VII–XIII secolo)", *Lo spazio letterario. 1. Il medioevo latino*, I, II (ed. by C. Leonardi); J. W. M. van Zwieten, *The Place and Significance of Literal Exegesis in Hugh of St. Victor* (unpublished thesis; Universiteit van Amsterdam 1992); E. D. English (ed.), *Reading and Wisdom. The 'De doctrina christiana' of Augustine in the Middle Ages* (Notre Dame Conferences in Medieval Studies 6; Notre Dame / London 1995); J. Ehlers, "Das Augustinerchorherrenstift St. Viktor", G. Wieland (ed.), *Aufbruch – Wandel – Erneuerung. Beiträge zur 'Renaissance' des 12. Jahrhunderts* (Stuttgart 1995) 100–22; S. Ebbesen (ed.), *Sprachtheorien in Spätantike und Mittelalter* (Tübingen 1995); R. E. Lerner (ed.), *Neue Richtungen in der hoch- und spätmittelalterlichen Bibelexegese* (Schriften des Historischen Kollegs. Kolloquien 32; München 1996); A. M. Piazzoni, "L'esegesi vittorina", in: G. Cremascoli e C. Leonardi (eds.), *La Bibbia nel Medio Evo* (Bologna 1996) 239–55.

The Canons Regular house of St. Victor, situated on the left bank of the Seine, a short distance from the gates of Paris, went through a rapid growth after being recognized as an abbey in 1113.[1] The reason for this was the initiative of

---

[1] Cf. R.-H. Bautier, "Les origines et les premiers développements de l'abbaye de Saint-Victor

William of Champeaux, founder of the new community, who formerly studied with the brothers Anselm and Raul at Laon and taught afterwards at the Parisian cathedral school of Notre-Dame until 1108.[2] With canons like Hugh, Andrew and Richard the young abbey of St. Victor was able to demonstrate during the two following generations its exegetical capabilities. By their exegetical methods as well as by their specific intellectual profiles the Victorines were pioneering for the twelfth century. Within the thirteenth century among the Victorine community the abbot of San Andrea di Vercelli, Thomas Gallus, is to be considered as an outstanding exegete and commentator of Pseudo-Dionysius.

A noticeable deficiency in our knowledge of Victorine exegesis in particular, and of the twelfth century exegesis in a more general sense, is the difficulty to know exactly which version of the Bible they commented on. Did Hugh, Andrew and Richard refer to the *Glossa ordinaria*, to their biblical text and the sources already identified there? Or did the Victorines use directly Bible manuscripts and did they, consequently, comment on the textual Vulgate-tradition?[3] Or did the commentators, especially Hugh and Richard, but also the abbey's preachers, explain the text of Scripture which they sang and read daily during the liturgical office? These questions cannot be answered with satisfaction, because they are left as research work to the scientific community.[4]

The following presentation refers exclusively to Hugh of St. Victor's authentic scriptural commentaries on the Old Testament, to those of his successors Andrew and Richard and also to explanations of the Victorine Thomas Gallus († 1246). Since the present status of research work is incomplete, we cannot yet distinguish, within the *opera omnia* of Hugh and Richard, between commentaries which are specifically biblical and liturgical commentaries.[5] The re-

de Paris", Longère, L'abbaye parisienne (1991) 23–52. Quite helpful is likewise S. C. Ferruolo, *The Origins of the University. The Schools of Paris and their Critics, 1100–1215* (Stanford 1985) 27–44, 324–28.

[2] Cf. most recently G. Constable, *The Reformation of the Twelfth Century* (Cambridge 1996). Likewise R. Berndt, "Sankt Viktor, Schule von", TRE 30 (1998) 42–46. Cf. moreover Chap. 30 in this volume.

[3] Cf. L. Smith, "What was the Bible in the Twelfth and Thirteenth Centuries?", Lerner, Neue Richtungen (1996) 1–15.

[4] Initial knowledge about the Victorine text of the Vulgate could be obtained while editing the works of Andrew of St. Victor. It then came to light that his exegetical commentaries as well as the Victorine Bible should be considered as excellent sources regarding the biblical textual criticism in Paris during the thirteenth century. But as a whole, research on the Victorine Bible is still waiting to be done. Cf. Berndt, André de Saint-Victor (1991) 108–57.

[5] The progress of editing critically the works of Hugh of St. Victor already shows that he, in various cases, did not comment properly on the Sacred Scripture, but on one or more verses of the Church's liturgical Officium. The *Expositio in Canticum B. Marie*, for instance, is related to the *Magnificat*, but not to the corresponding Gospel text. The *Eulogium sponsi et sponsi* reveals an antiphon to the Feast of the Virgin's Assumption (ms. Paris, Bibl. nat., lat. 14816, f. 256 v), as well as the writing *De assumptione B. Marie* (ms. Paris, Bibl. nat., lat. 14816, f. 250 v–251 r). Also Hugh's *Institutiones in Decalogum* (PL 176, 9–14), *De unione spiritus* (PL 177, 285–89) and *De septem donis* (PL 175, 410–14) are most probably liturgical commentaries. Cf. E. M. Denner, "'Serua secretum, custodi commissum, absconde creditum'. Historisch-systematische Untersuchung der 'Expositio super Canticum Marie' Hugos von St. Viktor", *SacEr* 35 (1995) 133–220. The works of Richard of St. Victor must, in a similar way, be analysed.

ception of the Old Testament in the extensive Victorine sermon-literature[6], as well as within the poetical writings of the Parisian regular canons[7], will be left aside.

1. Hugh of St. Victor

Born in Hamersleben nearby Halberstadt[8], Hugh should have arrived at St. Victor not later than in the year of the abbey's official recognition, that is in 1113, given the amount of works which he wrote up until his death in February 1141. The historiographical documents of the abbey, as well as innumerable manuscripts of his works, call him *magister*. This is not an unusual 'epitheton' for a well-reputed academic teacher, but it points to the fact that Hugh always has been known as the head of the school of Saint Victor.[9]

Hugh's intellectual activities are reflected in an extremely widespread *œuvre* which covers, beyond that, all leading philosophico-theological questions of his time.[10] In general, Sacred Scripture and its reception figures as the point of departure for his thinking and his works.[11] From his early work, the *Didascalicon* (about 1125), until his last work, the *Homilie in Ecclesiasten* (about 1138/40), Hugh is conscious of the particular requirements that the Sacred Scripture asks of its expositors, but also about the pleasure which it is able to grant its readers.[12]

---

[6] While lacking a study in the history of theology and complete editions of sources we have to refer, at the moment, especially to the works of JEAN CHÂTILLON and of JEAN LONGÈRE: Achard de Saint-Victor, *Sermons* (ed. J. Châtillon; Paris 1969); Galteri a Sancto Victore et quorumdam aliorum *sermones ineditos triginta sex* (recensuit J. Châtillon; CChr.CM 30; Turnhout 1975). J. LONGÈRE, *L'Œuvre oratoire des maîtres parisiens* 1–2 (Paris 1975).

[7] The recently published selection of texts by Adam of Saint-Victor, *Quatorze proses mariaux* (Introduction, texte, et traduction par B. Jollès; Paris / Turnhout 1996), instructs in a detailed way, about the poet and composer Adam of St. Victor. Pioneering is still M. FASSLER, *Gothic Song. Victorine Sequences and Augustinian Reform in Twelfth-Century Paris* (Cambridge 1993).

[8] Cf. R. BERNDT, "Hugo von St. Viktor", LTK[3] 5 (1996) 311–12.

[9] Cf. Ferruolo, Origins (1985) 31–32, with more bibliographical material.

[10] At present, the number of writings by Hugh of St. Victor which are to be considered as truly authentic, comprises hardly more texts than those, in-authentic, which have been ascribed to him within the manuscript tradition and within the early modern printings. Cf. J. EHLERS, *Hugo von St. Viktor. Studien zum Geschichtsdenken und zur Geschichtsschreibung des 12. Jahrhunderts* (Wiesbaden 1973), and R. GOY, *Die Überlieferung der Werke Hugos von St. Viktor. Ein Beitrag zur Kommunikationsgeschichte des Mittelalters* (Stuttgart 1976).

[11] Cf. for instance *Miscellanea* I, 75 (PL 177, 510): "Cathedra doctoris sacra Scriptura est, in qua iugiter populo presidere debet et per auctoritatem preceptionis et per exemplum conversationis. Posterior pars cathedre contemplatio est que latet in abscondito, anterior pars predicatio que proponitur in manifesto".

[12] E.g. *In Salomonis Ecclesiasten Homilie, Prefatio* (PL 175, 114–15): "... Omnis Scriptura secundum propriam interpretationem exposita et clarius elucescit et ad intelligendam se faciliorem legentibus pandit accessum. Multi virtutem Scripturarum non intelligentes expositionibus peregrinis decorem ac pulchritudinem earum obnubilant. Et cum occulta reserare debuerint etiam manifesta obscurant. ... Nunc itaque narrationis superficiem ... explanandam suscipimus, ut ea que scripta nunc legitis ... amodo non solum vobis scripta, sed a vobis intellecta gaudeatis".

1.1. Works of Old Testament Exegesis

Hugh of St. Victor identifies the Bible with the Old Testament which is for him plainly *sermo Dei.* In comparison with the Old Testament, the New Testament is complementary in terms of literacy and theology, since the ultimate significance of the Old Testament comes to fruition in the New.[13]

As we have already said, during Hugh's first years of literary activity the *Didascalicon* had been composed, which has in the C. H. Buttimer edition the subtitle *De studio legendi.*[14] At the same time his commentaries to the historical books of the Old Testament, from Pentateuch to Kings, should have also been written. From the corpus of the prophetical writings Hugh commented only on several chapters of the Book of Lamentations (1:1–3:3), but to the sapiential writing of Qoheleth he dedicated with the *In Ecclesiasten Homilie XIX* (1:1–4:8) a large exposition (PL 175, 113–256).[15]

The early modern printed editions of Hugh's works[16] arranged his Psalm exposition among the exegetical writings within the first volume, without becoming aware of the fact, that these Psalm expositions constitute, from the evidence, only a loose coherence. It was J.-P. Migne, who, for the first time, put the often quite short texts together under the title *Adnotationes elucidatoriae in quosdam psalmos David* and printed them as *Liber secundus* of the *Miscellanea* (PL 177, 589–634). But, most probably, originally it should not have been a continuous text because there is, until today, no twelfth century manuscript evidence for such an opinion.[17] These *Notule* or *Expositiones super quosdam Psalmos*, as some manuscripts call them,[18] can be considered as a composition of Psalm commentaries which Hugh pronounced, presumably here and there,

---

[13] E. g. *Miscellanea* I, 160 (PL 177, 558): "Tria sunt in sermone Dei: elementa, exordia et completiones. In elementis expressio vocis, sed intelligentia non est; in exordio sermonis intelligentia est, sed perfecta non est; in completione sermonis perfecta intelligentia est. Figure Veteris Testamenti elementa fuerunt sermonis Dei. Precepta Decalogi exordium fuerunt sermonis Dei, precepta Novi Testamenti completio sunt sermonis Dei ... In Veteri Testamento vox fuit, in Novo intellectus, in vita eterna res. In Veteri Testamento via fuit, in Novo veritas, in eternitate vita".

[14] This edition publishes a precritical text. Because of the 80 manuscripts known at his time, the editor built up his text on the basis of only 30 of them. Above all, however, the critical text corresponds essentially to the text contained in ms. Troyes, Bibl. mun. 301. A new edition is going to be prepared by R. Stammberger within the complete critical edition which is undertaken at the Frankfurt Institute. – I. Illich, *Du lisible au visible: La naissance du texte. Un commentaire du 'Didascalicon' de Hugues de Saint-Victor* (Paris 1991), is an ingenious interpretation, which throws new light on Hugh's question.

[15] The literary form of this work will be established with certitude only as a consequence of the critical edition, because some of the manuscript testimonies (e. g., Oxford, Bodleian Library, Bodl. 345; Paris, Bibl. de l'Arsenal 498; Lisboa, Bibl. nac., Alcobaça LXXIV/242; Troyes, Bibl. mun., 1388) call this text *Tractatus.*

[16] Cf. e. g., the editions of Paris 1526, vol. 1, fol. XXXV vb–LII va, and Rouen 1648, vol. 1, 50–75.

[17] Cf. Goy, Überlieferung (1976) 58–63, who knows 25 witnesses for this work. Although the Frankfurt database of the Hugo von Sankt Viktor-Institut lists meanwhile already 49 manuscripts, nothing changes with respect to the mentioned results.

[18] *Notule super quosdam Psalmos* is the title of the text within ms. Soissons, Bibl. mun., 120; mss. Boulogne, Bibl. mun., 128; Douai, Bibl. mun., 365, as well as Valenciennes, Bibl. mun. 206, call it *Expositiones super quosdam Psalmos.*

during his teaching within the abbey of Saint Victor. Only the critical edition of this work will hopefully be able to provide exact information about composition, manuscript diffusion and the literary form of this fragmentary Hugonian Psalm exegesis.

A considerable number of further Old Testament commentaries can be found among Hugh's authentic *Miscellanea* (PL 177, 469–588);[19] but before they can be retained for a more general presentation of Victorine exegesis, the literary specificity of each of them has to be worked out: exegetical or liturgical commentary, sermon or treatise?

1.2. Methods and Sources

The *Didascalicon* is the first medieval introduction into the sciences which exposes clearly and fully the mutual relationship between the *lectio artium* and the *lectio sacrae Scripturae*. Departing from this, Hugh develops his doctrine of the dual undertaken *lectio sacri eloquii*: the *lectio historica* and *lectio allegorica*. This process ends before the divine mystery, which communicates itself to man as *sacrum eloquium*.

Hugh found the essential sources for his theory of science, evidently, among the ancient rhetoricians and grammarians as well as within the *Bildungstradition* of the *artes*.[20] Moreover, especially Saint Augustine's *De doctrina Christiana* represents the patristic example for the reception of the Sacred Scripture and for the integration of the *ratio* into the theological discourse.[21] Hugh's

---

[19] The following paragraphs belong to this: 2. *De cibo Emmanuelis* (Isa 7) (477–81); 4. *De stulto qui ut luna mutatur* (Sir 27) (481); 26. *De conceptu et partu sapientie* (Prov 8) (491); 29. *Quod Deo nihil inordinatum esse potest* (Isa 13) (491); 37. *Quod creatura non potest bene esse sine creatore* (Qoh 4) (493); 43. *Quod virtus et veritas simul esse volunt* (Wis 7) (494–95); 59–62. *De lectulo et ferculo Salomonis* (Cant 3) (503–04); 69. *De servitute et timore Dei* (Sir 2) (506); 70. *Quod bonus animus sit hortus voluptatis* (Joel 2) (506–07); 76. *Quomodo sapientia vicit malitiam* (Wis 8) (511); 79. *De fuga a vitiis et eorum occasionibus* (Isa 21) (513–16); 89. *De Dei, mulieris et diaboli de mortis incurrenda assertione* (Gen 3) (520); 90. *De penitentia Dei et amore eius in creaturas vario* (Gen 6) (520–21); 91. *Exi de terra tua et de cognitione tua. Sermo ad fratres* (Gen 12) (521–23); 95. *De tribus locis filiorum Israel: Egipto, deserto et terra promissionis* (Ps 113) (524–25); 99. *De gratitudine beneficiorum Dei* (Mic 6) (529–32); 103. *De spiritu Dei et spiritu mundi* (Wis 1) (533–35); 108. *Quomodo se debeat quisque Deo in cibum preparare* (Sir 31) (537); 109. *De fuga Elie a facie Iezabel* (I Kgs 19) (538–39); 111. *De deserto quod est cor hominis* (Cant 3) (539–40); 116. *Favus distillans labia mea* (Cant 4) (643); 117. *De duplici veri Salomonis Christi* (Cant 3) (543); 131. *De dilectore et dilecto duplici* (Cant 1) (549); 142. *De itinere trium dierum et trium noctium* (Exod 3) (551–52); 158. *Melior est iniquitas viri* (Sir 42) (556–58); 159. *De filii Dei generatione eterna* (Ps 2) (558); 181. *Misterium de numero procedentium ad pugnam cum Gedeone* (Judg 7) (579–80).

[20] The authoritative contribution to this question is still L. Giard, "Hugues de Saint-Victor: cartographe du savoir", Longère, L'abbaye parisienne (1991) 253–69. Cf. recently also N. Senger, "Der Ort der 'Kunst' im Didascalicon des Hugo von St. Viktor", *Mittelalterliches Kunsterleben nach Quellen des 11. bis 13. Jahrhunderts* (ed. G. Binding / A. Speer; Stuttgart 1993) 53–75. With respect to the task, already accomplished by Hugh, which is to integrate the *artes mechanice* into the doctrinal building of the *artes liberales*, there can be found some interesting explanations in P. Vallin, "'Mechanica' et 'philosophia' selon Hugues de Saint-Victor", *RHSp* 49 (1973) 257–88.

[21] Cf. M. T. Gibson, "The 'De doctrina christiana' in the School of St. Victor", and E. C. Sweeney, "Hugh of St. Victor: The Augustinian Tradition of Sacred and Secular Reading Revised", English, Reading and Wisdom (1995) 41–47 and 61–83. L. Valente, "Langage et théologie pendant la seconde moitié du XIIe siècle", Ebbesen, Sprachtheorien (1995) 33–54.

original contribution with his early work consists in the fact that he defined the *doctrina* as being composed of *lectio* and *meditatio*, whereby he finally ceased before the objective of the *meditatio*: it would be better to be completely silent than to say something imperfect.[22] The *Didascalicon* is therefore not an introduction to exegesis, but a scientific doctrine which thinks out the theoretical relationship between exegesis and the other intellectual activities and which proceeds as a pedagogical model.[23]

With *De scripturis et scriptoribus sacris* and the *Chronicon* Hugh consecutively achieves a practical introduction to Old Testament exegesis. In the first work, Hugh gives to whoever desires to study Scripture, concrete working tools for the interpretation of texts, according to the Trivium and the doctrine of the four senses of Scripture, in order to build up a kind of *accessus ad Scripturam.*[24] With the *Chronicon*, which had been written in the early thirties of the twelfth century, Hugh presents, according to his own expression the *fundamentum fundamenti* in the field of exegesis, that is to say the *lectio historica* of the whole Sacred Scripture, i.e., a historical *summa.*[25]

Hugh employs this developed spectrum of exegetical methods and working tools in an exemplary manner, when he composes his *Annotatiuncule* to the historical books of the Old Testament, from the Pentateuch until the Books of Kings (PL 175, 29–114).[26] In the foreground of these *Annotatiuncule* is the *expositio historica* of the scriptural text, which is necessary in order to advance to a deeper understanding of the *res geste.*[27] Therefore Hugh also limits himself within this commentary to textual problems, to questions of literary criticism and to semantics. After having treated the usual *accessus*-questions in the chapters 3 and 4 (PL 175, 33–34) before getting specifically to the *Annotatiuncule in Pentateuchum*, the consequences of this procedure for the lemmatization of

---

[22] *Didascalicon* VI. 13 (ed. Buttimer 130): "Et iam ea que ad lectionem pertinent, quanto lucidius et compendiosius potuimus, explicata sunt. De reliqua vero parte doctrine, id est meditatione, aliquid in presenti dicere omitto, quia res tanta speciali tractatu indiget et dignum magis est omnino silere in huiusmodi quam aliquid imperfecte dicere".

[23] M. Carruthers, *The Book of Memory. A Study of Memory in Medieval Culture* (Cambridge 1990) 248: "In many ways, Hugh of St. Victor is a twelfth-century version of Quintilien, not an innovator of technique so much as an admirably clear, practical guide to the best pedagogy of his time."

[24] See for instance *De scripturis et scriptoribus sacris* II (PL 175, 11 C): "In his itaque materiam divinarum Scripturarum considera, ut et in illo de quo tractant et illo modo quo tractant, hoc est in materia et modo ab aliis eas Scripturis distinguere possis"; ibid. III (PL 175, 11 D): "Secundum triplicem intelligentiam exponitur sacrum eloquium." Vgl. A. J. Minnis, *Medieval Theory of Authorship* (London 1984); G. A. Zinn jr., "Hugh of St. Victor's 'De scripturis et scriptoribus sacris' as an 'accessus' treatise for study of the Bible", in: Traditio (1997) 111–34.

[25] *De tribus maximis circumstantiis gestorum* (ed. W. Green, *Spec.* 18 [1943] 491, 11–16): "Sed nos hystoriam nunc in manibus habemus, quasi fundamentum omnis doctrinae primum in memoria collocandum. Sed quia, ut diximus, memoria brevitate gaudet, gesta autem temporum infinita pene sunt, oportet nos ex omnibus brevem quandam summam colligere quasi fundamentum fundamenti, hoc est, primum fundamentum, quam facile possit animus comprehendere et memoria retinere".

[26] Cf. Van Zwieten, Place and Significance (1992) 7–36, 57–94.

[27] *Annotatiuncule in Pentateuchum* III (PL 175, 32 D–33 A): "In hoc autem libro duo precipue attendenda sunt: scilicet veritas rerum gestarum et forma verborum. Quia sicut per veritatem verborum cognoscimus veritatem rerum ita contra, cognita veritate rerum, facilius cognoscimus veritatem verborum. Quia per istam historicam narrationem ad altiorum rerum intelligentiam provehimur".

the scriptural text is, that Hugh divides it mostly into its components. Hugh's '*lemmata*' often consists of one or two words only. The project of literal exegesis seems to draw Hugh, and one generation later, even more, Andrew of St. Victor, to the loss of understanding of the textual unity. Whereas Hugh answers the *accessus*-questions also in the *Homilia I in Ecclesiasten* (PL 175, 115–16), there he lemmatizes the biblical text in the same way as he does in the *Annotatiuncule in Threnos*, but mostly in the scope of whole sentences. The methodical constants, as well as the divergencies between these three scriptural commentaries, might explain themselves sufficiently with the divergent, but specific, intentions of the expositions: while the Hugonian *expositio historica* demands a degree of exegetical craftsmanship, unknown until then, the *Homilie in Ecclesiasten* are below the demands of leading the reader to desire the interiorization of the word;[28] the *Annotatiuncule in Threnos*, finally, use methodically only the threefold form of the senses of Scripture which is largely current within the writings of Hugh.[29]

From a large scale of works of patristic (e. g. Origen, Augustine, Jerome, Isidor of Seville, Bede the Venerable) and early medieval (Rhabanus Maurus, Angelomus, Alcuin, Paschasius Radbertus, Pseudo-Jerome) authors[30] Hugh gets the literal expositions, which he can use in his own *Annotatiuncule in Octateuchum et in libros Regum.* Moreover, he cites also the ancient writers. Since there are not so many commentaries on Ecclesiastes and Lamentations,[31] he could hardly make use of patristic sources for these commentaries of his own (Origen, Gregory the Great, Alcuin, Paschasius Radbertus). It will be reserved to the critical edition of Hugh' s exegetical writings, to provide definite information about Hugh's sources.

1.3. Specificity of Hugh: Exegesis and Theology

A characteristic feature of Hugh's exegesis consists of the fact, that he imputed central importance to the Old Testament: besides commentaries on Old Testament texts, he chose the Old Testament as a point of departure for systematic considerations. His main theological work, *De sacramentis christiane fidei* (PL 176, 173–618), is presented from the very beginning as a systematic work which introduces the whole of Christian doctrine.

It is remarkable that Hugh does not choose as a starting point for his full presentation of theology either the teaching on the sacraments or that on the

---

[28] Cf. *Homilie in Ecclesiasten*, *Prefatio* (PL 175, 115 AB): "… precipue cum ipse auctor hic non tam motibus instruendis uel mysteriis enarrandis intendat, quam in cor humanum ad rerum mundanarum contemptum manifesta rationum veritate atque exhortatione evidenti commoveat".

[29] See for that purpose H. de Lubac, *Exégèse médiévale. Les quatre sens de l'Écriture*, I/1 (Paris 1959) 139–46.

[30] Still helpful remains H. J. Pollitt, "Some considerations on the structure and sources of Hugh of St. Victor's Notes on the Octateuch", *RTAM* 33 (1966) 5–38.

[31] With respect to the Old Testament sapiential / prudential literature see R. Berndt, "Skizze zur Auslegungsgeschichte der Bücher 'Proverbia' und 'Ecclesiastes' in der abendländischen Kirche", *SacEr* 34 (1994) 5–32. With regard to the Carolingian exegesis cf. Chap. 28 in this volume.

Trinity both of which would have been current topics during the whole of the twelfth century.[32] But he starts with the problem of the relationship between Old Testament exegesis and systematic theology; for the prologue of Book I constitutes a theoretical introduction into Holy Scripture (PL 176, 183–86). In this text, Hugh shows that his theological key concepts, *opus conditionis* and *opus restaurationis*, are based on scriptural exegesis and that they are of a theological nature, i.e. a theology of history. To this perspective of a theology of history in *De sacramentis christiane fidei* corresponds the fact, that Book I starts in Part I with the exegesis of the biblical narrative of creation (PL 176, 187–206).[33] Similarly Hugh proceeds in his work *De arca Noe* (PL 176, 617–80), whose biblical reference text obviously is the narrative in Genesis. But instead of the biblical text he used for his lectures about the ark a figurative representation of this biblical building which had been constructed in Saint Victor in Paris itself. In view of the background of the well-known Old Testament text and regarding the illustration in front of him, Hugh had been able to lead his audience to the discovery of the deeper, theological and mystical signification of the ark of Noah for Christian life. In relationship with the *Libellus de formatione arce*, whose destination was, according to Hugh's intention, to take the place of the ark's illustration outside the abbey of Saint Victor, the treatise *De arca Noe* offers to the Victorine Hugh the possibility of developing his ecclesiology, his christology and his soteriology.[34]

The complete work of Hugh of Saint Victor, as we know it nowadays, is recognized, irrespective of individual specific accentuations, exegetical, systematic or spiritual, as being dedicated in its general orientation to the explanation of Sacred Scripture. By this procedure Hugh continues essentially that type of research which he himself had learnt in the writings of figures like Origen,[35] Augustine,[36] Jerome[37] and Gregory the Great. But Hugh receives the heritage of the 'Senses of Scripture' in a creative way by accepting the theological starting point of his time. He receives the patristic triad *historia-allegoria-tropologia* in his Old Testament exegesis,[38] for instance in the commentary to Lamentations and in the *Homilie in Ecclesiasten*. This trilogy, however, inspires him in

[32] With behalf of the historical evolution of theological Summae during the Middle Ages cf. H. Cloes, "La systématisation de la théologie pendant la première moitié du XIIe siècle", *ETL* 34 (1958) 277–329; R. Berndt, "La théologie comme système du monde. Sur l'évolution des sommes théologiques de Hugues de Saint-Victor à saint Thomas d'Aquin", *RSPT* 78 (1994) 555–72; M. Colish, *Peter Lombard*, 2 vols. (Leiden 1996).

[33] Cf. R. Berndt, "Überlegungen zum Verhältnis von Exegese und Theologie in 'De sacramentis christiane fidei' Hugos von St. Viktor", Lerner, Neue Richtungen (1996) 65–78, and idem, "Heilvolle Universal- und Individualgeschichte? Zur Geschichtsdeutung einiger theologischer Summen des 12. und 13. Jahrhunderts", H. Dickerhof (ed.), *Heilsgeschichte oder Geschichte der Menschen?* (Regensburg 2000).

[34] See for that purpose Sicard, Diagrammes médiévaux (1993).

[35] Cf. Chap. 13.3 in HBOT I, 1, 499–542.

[36] Cf. Chap. 21 in HBOT I, 1, 701–30.

[37] Cf. Chap. 19 in HBOT I, 1, 663–81.

[38] See for that extensively de Lubac, Exégèse médiévale, II/2, 287–359. Most recently also Aris, Contemplatio (1996) 38–44; J. Whitman, *Allegory. The Dynamics of an Ancient and Medieval Technique* (Oxford 1987); L. Valente, "Une sémantique particulière: La pluralité des sens dans les Saintes Écritures (XIIe siècle)", Ebbesen, Sprachtheorien (1995) 12–32.

his systematic writings, for instance in the *Sententie de divinitate* and in *De sacramentis christiane fidei*, to a new, biblically conceived theology, which is organized along the path of a history of salvation. During the first half of the twelfth century Hugh did in fact contribute decisively, at the same time as Bernhard of Clairvaux, Peter Abelard and Gilbert Porreta, to what is called the 'mouvement théologique'.[39]

2. Richard of St. Victor

Richard's biography until he joined the abbey of Saint Victor and his early career there are hardly accessible to us with certitude. John of Toulouse, the abbey's historian, designates him as being *scotus*, although we have to understand this 'epitheton' as a less specific indication of origin because it can refer to Ireland as well as Scotland. Certainly he must have entered Saint Victor before 1141, the year of his teacher and model Hugh's death. Many manuscripts call Richard *magister*, which is a testimony to his reputation and an indication of the fact that he had been in charge of teaching in the abbey's school. In contrast to his master Hugh, Richard belonged, however, to the *officiales*[40] of the abbey: already in 1159 he signed a diploma, still being subprior, and after the death of the prior Nanterre in 1162, Richard succeded him in this charge until his death in the year 1173.[41]

2.1. Works of Old Testament Exegesis

Richard reveals himself as a docile pupil and as Hugh's successor, by opening the series of his writings with the *Liber exceptionum*. Among the printed works by Richard in MIGNE's *Patrologia latina* volume 196 there are only a few works which might be considered as exegetical in a narrow sense.[42] As running commentaries, one has to point primarily only to the *Mystice annotationes in Psalmos* (PL 196, 263–402) and to the *Expositio in Cantica canticorum* (PL 196, 405–524). For the rest we know several explanations of single text passages: *Nonnulle allegorie tabernaculi federis* (PL 196, 191–212), *Expositio diffi-*

---

[39] Cf. the exemplary study by J. DE GHELLINCK, *Le mouvement théologique au douzième siècle* (Brugge ²1948). As a model also U. KÖPF, "Monastische und scholastische Theologie", D. R. BAUER / G. FUCHS (eds.), *Bernhard von Clairvaux und der Beginn der Moderne* (Innsbruck / Wien 1996) 96–135, contributes to the new perspective on Bernhard. See by the same author in this volume Chap. 27.

[40] Cf. *Liber ordinis Sancti Victoris Parisiensis* 5–21 (ed. L. Jocqué / L. Milis; CChr. CM 61; Turnhout 1984, 25–94). L. JOCQUÉ, "Les structures de la population claustrale dans l'ordre de Saint-Victor au XIIe siècle. Un essai d'analyse du 'Liber ordinis'", Longère, L'abbaye parisienne (1991) 53–95.

[41] For details and more bibliographical information one can still refer to the article by J. CHÂTILLON, "Richard de Saint-Victor", DictS 13 (1987) 593–654. More recently cf. also M.-A. ARIS, "Richard v. St. Viktor", LM 7 (1995) 825–26.

[42] With regard to chronology cf. Châtillon, Richard (1987); P. CACCIAPUOTI, *'Deus existentia amoris'. Teologia della carità e Teologia della trinità negli scritti di Riccardo di San Vittore († 1173)* (Bibliotheca victorina 9; Turnhout 1998). A differentiated critical interpretation is for the present not possible because of the lack of a complete critical edition.

cultatum suborientium in expositione Tabernaculi federis (PL 196, 211–56),[43] *Expositio cantici Habacuc* (PL 196, 401–04), *In visionem Ezechielis* (PL 196, 527–600); or verses: *Tractatus de meditandis plagis que circa finem mundi euenient* (*In Eccle.* 12:1–7) (PL 196, 201–12), *Quomodo Christus ponitur in signum populorum* (*In Isaiam* 11:10–12) (PL 196, 523–28). Obviously there is one difference with Hugh of Saint Victor: Richard didn't have any interest in the Octateuch and in the Books of Kings, nor in the *expositio historica* of the Old Testament. To this observation corresponds the fact that within Richard's writings the allegorical exegesis of the prophets and the Old Testament Wisdom dominates.

2.2. *Exegetical Methods and Sources*

Richard manifests himself at different times about his conceptions of biblical exegesis and about his methods. For on the one hand he had composed two works, which provides a theoretical foundation for his exegesis (1); on the other hand he explains his exegetical practice in the Prologue of the commentary *In visionem Ezechielis* (2).

(1) The *Liber exceptionum* presents a system of learning which depends by evidence on the *Didascalicon.* Richard writes for beginners in the study of Sacred Scripture, and he knows that his work is a compilation. He does not intend to instruct grammarians or educate the wise. His guide is rather the intellectual interest of his readers who long for deeper knowledge.[44] Richard divides the *Exceptiones* into two parts: the first one leans not only with respect to the subject against the *Didascalicon* (origin of the *artes*, differenciation between literature and Sacred Scripture, geography, world history), but copies *verbaliter* long passages from it; the second part is an allegorico-tropological exposition of the biblical history which still in MIGNE's *Patrologia latina* had been printed as *Allegorie in Vetus et Novum Testamentum* among the works of Hugh (PL 175, 633–924).[45] When Richard had taken over in Part I book 1 of his *Liber exceptionum* the "cartography of sciences"[46] of the *Didascalicon* according to his own intentions, he relies in book 2 likewise largely on Hugh's writings. In order to work out the difference between secular and sacred literature Richard makes use of Hugh's *De scripturis et scriptoribus sacris, De tribus diebus*

---

[43] Cf. now for both these texts A. GRABOÏS, "Richard of St. Victor's 'De Tabernaculo' in its Historical Context", *Medieval Studies. In Honour of Avrom Saltman* (Bar-Ilan Studies in History 4; Ramat-Gan 1995) 135–44.

[44] *Liber exceptionum* I, Prologus (ed. Châtillon 97, 2–10): "Invenies in eo multa ex multis libris collecta, in unam seriem ordinate disposita, sibi prout ratio sensuum postulat coherentia ... dilectionis tue studio satis utilia. Sacrorum namque librorum fertiles agros pervolantes et ex eis potiora queque colligentes, pauca vel nulla simplicitati tue sacre scripture lectionem ingredienti necessaria pretermittimus. Per hec autem que scribimus, nec grammaticos docere, nec sapientes volumus erudire, sed tue petitioni, tuo desiderio volumus satisfacere, tuumque studium in melius adjuvare".

[45] *Liber exceptionum* I, Prologus (ed. Châtillon 97, 16–20): "In prima parte materiam habemus originem artium, situm terrarum, cursum historiarum ab initio usque ad nos decurrentium. In secunda parte materiam habemus sensus allegoriarum et tropologiarum secundum subjacentis lineam historie dispositarum".

[46] Cf. Giard, Hugues de Saint-Victor (1991) 253.

and *De sacramentis christiane fidei.* Only at the end he describes independently the object of Sacred Scripture: while presenting the work of creation, Sacred Scripture attains its true theme, the divine work of redemption. The last will be treated of in the usual manner.[47]

Richard situates his treatise *De Emmanuele* (PL 196, 601–66) within the context of his discussion with Andrew of St. Victor,[48] where he deals with the contemporary inner-Christian polemics about the influence of Jewish exegesis.[49] Although *De Emmanuele* refers primarily to the exegetical difficulties of the pericope Isa 7:7–14, this work is not an exegetical commentary, but rather Richard's treatise in biblical hermeneutics.[50] That is to say, from the very beginning Richard places the discussion on the level of discursiveness: just that exposition of the concerned passage of Isaiah should be permanent whose *rationes* are irrefutable.[51] Therefore Richard looks for the knowledge of the biblical truth less on the way to the *sensus litteralis* of a text; for him, everything is to be decided by the principles of exposition.

While Hugh and Andrew defend a hermeneutic, relative to the text, for which the struggle about the right understanding of Scripture represents the royal way to the knowledge of God and to theology, Richard proceeds to declare with his *De Emmanuele* that he is seeking an interpretation of Scripture beyond the literal text. For with the literal exposition of Scripture he wants to satisfy, primarily, the believer's dedication and to show by which way the prophecy of Isaiah can be related to the incarnation of the Word.[52] The *expositio littere* serves Richard therefore to fortify the Christian faith, but he does not intend to interpret Sacred Scripture, primarily for its own sake and only afterwards to progress in faith.

(2) Considering the exegetical challenge which the vision of Ezechiel represents, Richard, in the Prologue of his commentary (PL 196, 527–28), declares

---

[47] *Liber exceptionum* I. 2. VIII (ed. Châtillon 119, 9–13): "Taliter accedit sacra Scriptura per opus conditionis ad materiam suam, id est ad opus restaurationis. De qua materia tripliciter tractat, sicut supra dictum est, secundum historiam, secundum allegoriam, secundum tropologiam".

[48] *De Emmanuele*, Prologus (PL 196, 601–02): "... An tollendum ergo errorem vel eorum qui iam decepti sunt vel adhuc decipi possunt, statui aliqua scribere et positis obiectionibus obviare".

[49] Cf. latest J. W. M. van Zwieten, "Jewish exegesis within Christian bounds: Richard of St. Victor's De Emmanuele and Victorine hermeneutics", Bijdragen. Tijdschrift voor Philosophie en Theologie 48 (1987) 327–35, as well as Berndt, André de Saint-Victor (1991) 294–301. Cf. M. Awerbuch, *Christlich-jüdische Begegnung im Zeitalter der Frühscholastik* (Abhandlungen zum christlich-jüdischen Dialog 8; München 1980); G. Dahan, *Les intellectuels chrétiens et les juifs au moyen âge. Polémique et relations culturelles entre chrétiens et juifs en occident du XIIe au XIVe siècle* (Paris 1990).

[50] This opinion has been defended already by the late Châtillon, Richard (1987) 608f. See *De Emmanuele* II, Prologus (PL 196, 633): "Exarsit itaque animus meus ad illa que ante iam dixeram adhuc aliquid addere, unde possem eorum etiam infirmitati satisfacere, qui sub hoc erroris contagio videbantur pene usque ad desperationem laborasse".

[51] *De Emmanuele*, Prologus (PL 196, 601–02): "... Vltimo loco libet ex meo addere quantum puto ad refellendas obiectiones posse sufficere"; I. 2 (607C): "Obiciunt multa quibus putant refellere assertionem nostram ... Videamus itaque nunc qualia vel quanti pendanda sunt que nobis cavillatores opponunt".

[52] *De Emmanuele* I. 1 (PL 196, 606 C): "Sufficit mihi hoc loco, si detur in simplicis littere expositione devotioni fidelium satisfacere, et quomodo debeat hec Isaie prophetia ad verbi incarnationem referri potest ostendere".

unmistakably his conception of interpretation of Scripture: In the Old Testament there are necessarily many unintelligible passages,[53] which, beyond doubt, are inexplicable with textual, i.e. literal exegesis exclusively. Therefore it is rationally imperative to find a point of departure for exegesis, which is different from Scripture itself.[54] According to Richard literal exegesis is the foundation of all Old Testament exegesis, but it serves a superior aim.[55]

2.3. *Specificity of Richard: Through Exegesis to Contemplation*

As well as for Hugh also for Richard Christ is the end and the content of every Old Testament interpretation of Scripture. But this destination can be achieved only by means of the authority of the Sacred Scripture, everything else is suspect in Richard's eyes.[56] As long as Christ's teaching concerns only exterior things, or his own identity, man is able to verify this teaching by his own experience. But where the human spirit turns to superior reality, there are witnesses needed. A revelation from above needs witnesses for its verification, by Moses and Elijah for instance, even by the authority of the Sacred Scripture.[57] In the *Beniamin minor* Richard reveals the way in which he conceives the investigation leading from the *sensus litteralis* to the *mystica intelligentia* of the Old Testament. For sure, according to Richard exegesis and mystics are related to one another. With certainty man encounters himself, by exposing Scripture, like in a mirror, but only himself.[58] However, if he wants to ascend to God's contemplation he should recognize, that the words of Scripture say, in reality, God.[59] And if once the mirror would have been turned, it might start

[53] With regard to Gregory the Great's commentary on Ezechiel, Richard explains in his *In visionem Ezechielis* Prologus (PL 196, 528 A): "Certe, idem in eadem Ezechielis expositione dicit, plerumque in sacro eloquio ideo aliquid obscure dicitur, ut dispensante mirabiliter Deo multipliciter exponatur".

[54] *In visionem Ezechielis*, Prologus (PL 196, 528 B): "Multiplex itaque sacre Scripture expositio nunquam respuatur, inquantum rationi consentire vel utilitati deservire videtur. In quantum ergo quisque in hoc gratiam accepit, nemo dubitet cum omni diligentia querere ea que precedentium patrum sagacitas vel ex industria preteriit vel magis necessariorum occupatione implicata explicare non potuit".

[55] *In visionem Ezechielis*, Prologus (PL 196, 527 D/528 A): "Et hoc quidem verum, sed secundum eam acceptionem quam ipse ibi assignavit. Nam si eamdem de qua hoc dicit litteram velimus secundum aliam acceptionem discutere, fortassis etiam iuxta historicum sensum, ex ipsa poterimus congruum intellectum eruere". – Cf. also *Expositio difficultatum suborientium in expositione tabernaculi federis*, Prologus (PL 196, 211 BC).

[56] *De preparatione animi ad contemplationem* 81 (PL 196, 57 C): "Suspecta est mihi omnis veritas quam non confirmat scripturarum auctoritas, nec Christum in sua clarificatione recipio, si non assistant ei Moyses et Elias".

[57] Ibid. (PL 196, 57 CD): "Si Christus docet me de rebus exterioribus vel de intimis meis, facile recipio, utpote in his que comprobare possum proprio experimento. Verum ubi ad alta mens ducitur, ..., ubi de profundis rebus agitur, in tante sublimitatis vertice non recipio Christum sine teste, nec rata poterit esse quamlibet verisimilis revelatio sine attestatione Moysis et Elie, sine scripturarum auctoritate".

[58] Ibid. 72 (PL 196, 51 C): "Precipuum et principale speculum ad videndum Deum, animus rationalis, absque dubio invenit seipsum".

[59] Ibid. (PL 196, 51 D): "Tergat ergo speculum suum, mundet spiritum suum, quisquis sitit videre Deum suum".

gleaming. And this light enlightens man's spirit in order that he can see what is above.[60] Mystical illumination is based therefore, according to Richard, on a corresponding inverted understanding of Scripture, which carries on much further than the *sensus litteralis* does. The truth of Scripture, for Richard, is a gift from above. Nevertheless it is implanted within the text of Scripture which we are called upon to interpret correctly and positively. The contemplation of this biblical truth begins during this life and will be celebrated in the coming eternity.[61]

3. Andrew of St. Victor

Again, about Andrew's biography until he entered the Parisian abbey and about his early years as regular canon, we have no reliable information. His activity becomes historically accessible when he, about 1147/48, had been elected as the first abbot of the recently founded Victorine daughter abbey of Saint-James in Wigmore (Wales). After about six years Andrew had to leave his convent because of unbridgeable difficulties. He spent his exile, until about 1161/62, in his Parisian mother abbey. Then the canons of Wigmore called him back, and Andrew stayed with them until his death in the year 1175. Consequently his teaching – the manuscripts apostrophize him mostly as *magister* – as well as his literary creativity are to be ascribed to the period until his first departure from St. Victor (that is before 1147) and during the exile (from about 1153 until 1162).[62]

3.1. His Works

First of all we have to underline the unique fact that Andrew's works are exclusively exegetical commentaries; moreover, Andrew commented only on books of the Old Testament and almost all of them. During his first literary period until 1147 the commentaries on the Heptateuch and on the Books of Kings must have been composed. During the Parisian exile, from 1153 until 1162, Andrew had written most probably the *expositiones* on Isaiah, Jeremiah, Ezechiel and the Minor Prophets. In a third period – still in Paris, finally in Wigmore – he might have turned over to the Hagiographa. In the understanding of his reception of the *hebraica veritas* Andrew does not only rank the Book of Proverbs and the Ecclesiastes, but also the Book of Daniel to this kind of *ordo* of Old Testament writings.[63]

---

[60] Ibid. (PL 196, 52 A): "Exterso autem speculo et diu diligenter inspecto, incipit ei quedam divini luminis claritas interlucere, et immensus quidam insolite visionis radius oculis eius apparere... Ex huius igitur luminis visione quam admiratur in se, mirum in modum accenditur animus et animatur ad videndum lumen quod est supra se".

[61] *Beniamin maior* I. 1 (ed. Aris [6], 21–22): "Nam veritatis contemplatio in hac vita inchoatur, sed in futura iugi perpetuitate celebratur". Cf. Aris, Contemplatio (1996) 45–64.

[62] A discussion of the details can be found in Berndt, André de Saint-Victor (1991) 17–49.

[63] Cf. Berndt, André de Saint-Victor (1991) 50–88.

3.2. Methods and Sources

In all his works Andrew commented on Jerome's Latin Bible translation, the Vulgate.[64] His choice of the sources and the considerable number of authors used by Andrew, leave us to presume that he always worked on the basis of firsthand biblical manuscripts, and not on the *Glossa* or manuscripts containing Jerome's works. Today we know surely that Andrew's Bible, even the Bible text of the abbey of St. Victor at a whole, constitutes a cardinal point in the medieval history of the Vulgate.[65]

Explicitly Jerome intended by the translation of the Old Testament to enable the Christian to get access to the *hebraica veritas.* Therefore he can be considered as the model of biblical textual criticism within the Church and as the prototype of all translators.[66] This double task – biblical textual criticism and exegesis as translation – had developed after the Carolingian revival during the eighth / ninth centuries and later on, after the "quarrel of the investiture", in a double regard: on the one hand, the exegetes of the twelfth-century schools and the thirteenth-century universities made it to their business to emend the Vulgate's corrupted text according to their resources,[67] on the other hand, the reinforced contacts with the Jews sharpened among the Christians awareness of the fact that the Vulgate was only a translation. Andrew intended, with his exegetical production, to advance in both directions and to contribute to this process by his own.[68]

(1) Andrew's textual criticism consists essentially of two steps: first of all he discusses the value of the different textual variants which he knows from the patristic tradition or of which he gained knowledge through his manuscript study and comparisons; then he decides in favour of one emendated reading;[69] afterwards he re-arranges the biblical text differently from the way he could have known it from the Bibles accessible to him. Andrew undertakes, in general, the new text arrangement with remarkable care. This, he considers, is for him an aid to interpretation with respect to quite difficult exegetical passages.[70] Regarding both procedures Andrew has recourse to information from

---

[64] Cf. Berndt, André de Saint-Victor (1991) 119–57.

[65] Cf. Berndt, André de Saint-Victor (1991) 146–48.

[66] Cf. P. JAY, *L'exégèse de saint Jérôme d'après son 'Commentaire sur Isaïe'* (Paris 1985).

[67] Cf. L. LIGHT, "Versions et révisions du texte biblique", Riché / Lobrichon, Moyen Age et la Bible (1994) 55–93, who offers a survey of the efforts in the field of textual criticism during the Early Middle Ages. Recently J. VAN ENGEN, "Studying Scripture in the Early University", Lerner, Neue Richtungen (1996) 17–38.

[68] Cf. Berndt, André de Saint-Victor (1991) 227–36.

[69] Cf. Berndt, André de Saint-Victor (1991) 149–50, the table of references to the different Bible versions within the *Expositio in Heptateuchum.* Proceeding from the *Instrumenta lexicologica latina*, fasc. 60, 67 and 91 (Turnhout 1991 and 1997), which accompany some of the volumes published until now, the above mentioned table has to be completed. With regard to the Heptateuch, we can identify several of the readings discussed by Andrew, in Bible manuscripts which belonged formerly to the Parisian abbey of St. Victor.

[70] See for instance *In Exodum* 23:15 (ed. Lohr / Berndt 1496–99); *In Isaiam* 9:7 (Hs. Cambridge, Pembroke College, 45, f. 18va); *In Amos* 3:11 (Hs. Salamanca, Biblioteca universitaria, 2061, f. 187va/b). Vgl. Berndt, André de Saint-Victor (1991) 236–42.

the rabbinic tradition, besides Flavius Josephus as well as the *Midrash Rabbah*, and to his Jewish informants.[71]

A characteristic trait of Andrew's choice of the sources consists in the fact that it reflects by evidence his exegetical intention. He is looking for the *hebraica veritas* in the same way as his model Jerome did, and whom Andrew presumes to be in its service through his commentaries. Therefore he questioned the whole Jewish-Christian exegetical tradition, attainable by him, with respect to references which could deliver the desired profile to his works. It is incontestable that Andrew, beyond that, received a considerable amount of new Jewish scriptural interpretations.

The exegetical path which Andrew of St. Victor undertook, i. e. to use philology in the service of a literal explanation of the Old Testament, had been begun before him already by Hugh. Andrew put a special accent on it in order to make Jerome's intended *hebraica veritas* intelligible.

(2) The second and most important aspect of Andrew's textual criticism concerns the problem of the relationship between the original and its translation, between the Hebrew text of the Old Testament and its Latin rendering by Jerome. For Andrew the improving or correcting criticism of a given translation is transformed into the privileged instrument of textual explanation. For sure, from time to time it is possible that Andrew looks for another Latin word only because of semantic developments which had taken place since Jerome.[72] Normally, however, Andrew introduces his new Latin translations by referring to Jewish expositions and so better because made according to the original. On the part of the contemporary rabbinic commentaries the concepts which Andrew received in Latin, act as interpretations. The literal sense of the Old Testament as Andrew worked it out, depends, basically, on a process of translating. So far this method elucidates Richard's reproach to Andrew. For Richard the problem did not consist of whether possibly Christian exegesis might receive contradictory doctrines or not from Jewish exegetes, but the plain fact of the textual reception from a non-Christian context, even in the case of a translation.

As well as his Jewish dialogue partners of Rashi's school,[73] Andrew also turned towards the new possibilities of translation into vernacular languages. Hitherto one could discover in Andrew's works about thirty old-French words which are inserted at times in order to resolve a difficulty caused by the Vulgate, but not by the Hebrew.[74] Nevertheless there has to be taken into account the fact that Rashi's and Andrew's reference languages are not the same.

Explaining by translating: this is a method which originated in the Victorine tradition and to which the rabbinic narratives correspond. Commenting on a

---

[71] Cf. Berndt, André de Saint-Victor (1991) 221–24, and the introductions to the critical editons of Andrew's works.

[72] Formulas like *quasi diceret* or *ac si diceret* introduce normally such purposes.

[73] Cf. for that the research work by M. Banitt, "The La'azim of Rashi and the French Biblical Glossaries", *The World History of the Jewish People* 2 (ed. C. Roth; Tel Aviv 1966) 291–96; *Rashi. Interpreter of the Biblical Letter* (Tel Aviv 1985). Cf. A. Graboïs, "L'exégèse rabbinique", Riché / Lobrichon, Moyen Age et la Bible (1984) 249–50. Within this volume, look especially at Chap. 32.

[74] Cf. Berndt, André de Saint-Victor (1991) 196–201; ed. Signer, *Introduction*, XXV.

text means to recount it so that obscure words are clarified or replaced by other words in order to render the text intelligible and to make its sense apparent.[75]

3.3. *Specificity of Andrew: Exegesis as Theology*

Andrew did not enjoy unlimited recognition among his contemporaries as is shown by the polemic of his brother Richard in his *De Emmanuele.* In what sense was Andrew's interpretation of literal exegesis found to be unacceptable? Which biblical hermeneutic did he really defend by his practice? How did he understand the *eloquium sacrum*, which distinguishes itself from the remaining literature of the world by its subject, the *opus restaurationis*?

During the twelfth century, work in the field of literal exegesis consisted mainly of two steps: the textual analysis of the writing to be explained and enquiry into its doctrinal content.[76] Following the authoritative manual for this purpose, the textual explanation questioned first of all the *superficies littere* and attempted afterwards to attain a deeper understanding of the text, to a *sententia.*[77] In practice Andrew departs from the *Didascalicon*, and so modifies and changes it. Fundamentally he defends the point of view, that the *littera* is not understandable by itself. The commentator has to discuss the various possibilities of signification of the text, and must decide personally which of these he is disposed to accept and to teach. The exegete intervenes on the level of the *littera* by determining its sense.[78] If the commentator tries to deduce a *sententia* of the *littera*, Andrew presumes that the exegete is able to understand the *littera*'s larger context and to formulate it.[79] Within Andrew's works *sententia* signifies the doctrinal exposition of Christian and Jewish authors, the explication given by Scripture itself as well as the consequences which the exegete deduces from this.[80]

Andrew's general and characteristic tendency towards a certain craftsmanship is remarkable in the way in which he employs the hermeneutical vocabulary, taken over from the ancient authors and the Church fathers. The triad *littera*, *sensus* and *sententia* express, specifically and individually, Andrew's idea of the unity of literal exegesis. He prefers to follow the *superficies littere*,

---

[75] Cf. R. Berndt, "La pratique exégétique d'André de Saint-Victor", Longère, L'abbaye parisienne (1991) 286–87; Berndt, André de Saint-Victor (1991) 261–63.

[76] With regard to the practice of Augustinian hermeneutics in Andrew's biblical exegesis cf. recently M. Signer, "From Theory to Practice: The 'doctrina christiana' and the Exegesis of Andrew of St. Victor", English, Reading and Wisdom (1995) 84–98.

[77] See for that *Didascalicon* III (ed. Buttimer 48–69). Cf. H. Brinkmann, *Mittelalterliche Hermeneutik* (Darmstadt 1980) 236.

[78] See *In I Regum* 2:33 (ed. van Liere 634/635): 'Potest simpliciter secundum quod litteram sonare videtur intelligi ...'. – *In Ionam* 3:7 (Hs. Salamanca, *Biblioteca universitaria* 2061, f. 197rab): 'Quidam hanc litteram sic legunt ... vel potius sic secundum hebreos ...'.

[79] See *In Isaiam* 60:4 (Hs. Cambridge, Pembroke College 45, f. 73vb): 'Quam litteram iudei sic exponunt ut dicant... Secundum hanc expositionem etiam ad litteram nostra sic legi translatio potest'.

[80] See for instance *In I Regum* 2:31 (ed. van Liere 620/621): 'Set sequens littera mavult primam quam posuimus sententiam'. Cf. also *In II Regum* 5:6 (ed. van Liere 99/100).

but he insists on preserving the order of the *expositio* to explain, therefore, primarily the *littera.* By this he enlarges considerably the task of the commentator: hence it is incumbent on him to guarantee the conceptual and practical coherence of his exegesis.[81]

One will best become aware of Andrew's originality when one compares his method with that of Hugh of St. Victor. Especially in the *Didascalicon*, but also in the other works, the relation between this literal hermeneutic and his exegesis in accordance with the three or four senses of Scripture is hardly perceptible. In principle the scriptural commentary precedes according to the threefold realization, starting with the *expositio historica. Historia* is for Hugh the sense which is due to things (*res*) primarily because of the words' signification.[82] The term *historia* describes therefore the literal exegesis in its three stages: *littera–sensus–sententia.*

The *expositio historica* of a scriptural text takes place by relating the history of the *opus restaurationis.* This exegesis relates the divine benefits (*res geste Dei*) and is in so far of a historiographic nature. Following Hugh the literal exegesis intends to render intelligible the biblical narrative (*narratio rerum gestarum*), whose language (*voces*) is its literary form.[83] The narrative truth of the story is measured according to its internal coherence and its coincidence with the facts.[84] This relation between *historia* and literal exegesis is varied somewhat by Andrew of St. Victor. By evidence, he employs the term *historia* in a spectrum of signification comparable to that of Hugh; similarly, he intends to write scriptural commentaries which bring out the historical sense of the Bible (*expositiones historice*). But Andrew distinguishes, first of all, the weight of reason and the authority of the exegete while establishing these *expositiones historice.*[85]

For the Victorines the signification of the things (*res*) is far more important than that of the words (*verba*). Nevertheless it proves to be a difficult and delicate task to capture the signification of the words of Scripture. But the exegete has to pay attention so that the *narratio rerum gestarum Dei* does not obscure the biblical text. Its inerrance is attested by Christians and Jews in the same

---

81 Cf. Berndt, André de Saint-Victor (1991) 164–75.

82 Hugo de Sancto Victore, *De scripturis et scriptoribus* III (PL 175, 12 A). Cf. H.-W. Goetz, "Die 'Geschichte' im Wissenschaftssystem des Mittelalters", F.-J. Schmale, *Funktion und Formen mittelalterlicher Geschichtsschreibung. Eine Einführung* (Darmstadt 1985) 202–03; Brinkmann, Hermeneutik (1980) 158. With special reference to the *magistri* of the Parisian University cf. I. Rosier, "'Res significata' et 'modus significandi': Les implications d'une distinction médiévale", Ebbesen, Sprachtheorien (1995) 135–68.

83 See Hugo de Sancto Victore, *Didascalicon* III. 8 (ed. Buttimer 58).

84 See *In Isaiam* 36:1 (Hs. Cambridge, Pembroke College 45, f. 58 vb): 'Hanc hystoriam non ex proposito narrat; sed ut competentius ad prophetias quibus implicata est hystoria explicandas accedat'. *In Danielem* 9:1 (ed. Zier 97, 9/11): 'Quoniam historice veritati et philosophicis assertionibus absque rationabili causa vel auctoritate contrario asserere durum, ne quid aliquid aliud dicam, videtur'.

85 See *Introitus in libros Salomonis* (ed. Berndt 2/8): 'Ad opuscula Salomonis iuxta littere superficies explananda ... ingredientes, quoniam ille in scribendo nos in exponendo potissimum ordinem exequendum esse iudicavimus, a Parabolis igitur ... inchoantes'. *In Genesim* 7:2 (ed. Lohr / Berndt 1488/89): 'Nos vero, qui litteram exponere – non distorquere vel destruere – studemus, hanc litteram sic exponimus ...'.

manner. The role of the commentator, which had been put in the foreground with Andrew's works, is itself indebted to his contacts with the rabbinic schools of his time; because the relation between the Rabbi, the sage in the Jewish tradition, and his Talmud- and Tora-oriented students (within the Northern French exegetical school[86]) may have served Andrew as model for his own work. In a Torah-school on the right bank at Paris Andrew could have taken new exegetes and may have found new inspiration as a result of his self-understanding as a commentator of Scripture. With the example of the Old Testament exegesis of Andrew of St. Victor it became obvious that during the Middle Ages text-oriented exposition of Scripture not only became possible, but had even received a special accentuation. While reformulating the patristic theme *scriptura ipsius interpres* the exegete himself, following Andrew, serves the Church and her Sacred Scripture. He helps its inherent signification to articulate *verbaliter.*[87]

4. Thomas Gallus

About Thomas Gallus, the first abbot of the Victorine foundation San Andrea in Vercelli, on the frontier between Torino and the Piedmont, we know that he was canon of St. Victor, at the latest from 1218 on. Cofounder of the convent San Andrea, the canons named him in 1224 to be their prior, in 1226 they elected him abbot. Involved in a conflict of loyalty between the emperor Frederick II and the pope, Thomas Gallus was removed in 1243 and forced into exile. Only shortly before his death, he was allowed to return to San Andrea, where he died in 1246.[88]

4.1. *His Exegetical Works*

The writings of Thomas Gallus consist mainly in discussion of the works of Pseudo-Dionysius. Most of his numerous commentaries on Dionysius have still not yet been edited critically. In the context of the history of Old Testament exegesis in St. Victor, Thomas has a place on account of his commentaries on the prophet Isaiah and on the Song of Songs. The commentary on Isaiah which Thomas composed already during his stay in the Parisian motherhouse, has to be considered, on the whole, as lost.[89] In part, however,

[86] Cf. for that Awerbuch, Christlich-jüdische Begegnung (1980) 131–63, as well as R. Berndt, "L'influence de Rashi sur l'exégèse d'André de Saint-Victor", Z. A. Steinfeld, *Rashi – Réception en France* (Bar-Ilan 1993) VII–XIV. Recently van Liere, *Introduction*, XXIX–XXXVII, and E. Touitou, "Rashi and his School: The Exegesis on the Halakhic Part of the Pentateuch in the Context of the Judeo-Christian Controversy", Medieval Studies. In Honour of Avrom Saltman (1995) 231–51.

[87] Cf. Berndt, André de Saint-Victor (1991) 164–75.

[88] Beside the already mentioned standard article by J. Barbet in DictS one reads with interest also K. Ruh, Thomas Gallus (1995), and M. Gerwing, "Th. (Gallo) v. Vercelli", LM 8 (1996) 719.

[89] F. Stegmüller, *Repertorium biblicum medii aevi* 5 (Madrid 1955) 8203, refers, nevertheless, to an anonymous commentary on Isaiah in ms. Paris, Bibliothèque nationale de France, lat. 14430, which should probably be ascribed to Thomas Gallus.

it was published some time ago by G. Théry. The three expositions of the Song of Songs, in contrast, have been edited completely.

4.2. Methods and Sources

Beside self-evident, occasional references to Augustine, the writings of Pseudo-Dionysius serve Thomas Gallus as a principal source for his exposition of Scripture. Moreover, the doctrine of the two ways of knowing God (*duplex Dei cognitio*) determines generally Thomas' commentary on the Song of Songs. One form of the knowledge of God is intellectual and is to be obtained through the contemplation of creatures according to the exposition of Ecclesiastes by Hugh of St. Victor.[90] This knowledge is vague and like a reflected image (*cognitio speculativa et enigmatica*); man can acquire it meditating, listening and reading; the pagan philosophers do not acquire anything else.[91] The other form of knowledge of God transcends the former in an uncomparable way (*sapientia superintellectualis*). Thomas explains therefore his interest in the Song of Songs with the theory of this second intellectual procedure, which Pseudo-Dionysius sought to expound in his *Mystical Theology*. Solomon, however, in the Song of Songs, introduces us to the practice of this knowledge.[92] Theory and practice of this supra-intellectual wisdom is for Thomas, in short, the Christian wisdom (*sapientia christianorum*). Looking for her, he expounds the Song of Songs.

At no point does Thomas Gallus express himself in general about the principal methods of exegesis; as little does he declare himself with regard to the doctrine of the various senses of Scripture. Neither does he distinguish between the literal and the allegorical sense. Consequently, he is not interested in the literal sense of Song of Songs, but exclusively with the allegorical-tropological meaning of this biblical text against the background of the pseudo-Dionysian works. The Dionysian teaching functions within Thomas Gallus as a methodological pattern of exegesis.

4.3. Theological Specificity: Knowledge of the Supreme

The dominant problem of both the Old Testament commentaries of the Victorine Thomas is the exposition of the process of how to know God. The soul of man should be on the path (*anima viatoris*) to simple awareness of God in

---

[90] Thomas Gallus, *Troisième Commentaire sur le Cantique des Cantiques*, Prologus (ed. Barbet 107A): "Duplex hic designatur Dei cognitio, una intellectualis que comparatur per considerationem creaturarum in Ecclesiaste, secundum expositionem venerabilis doctoris magistri Hugonis, ...".

[91] Ibid., Prologus (ed. Barbet 107A): "Hec Dei cognitio speculativa est et enigmatica, communiter dicitur et docetur tam meditando quam audiendo, quam legendo. Hanc solam gentiles philosophi attigisse comperiuntur".

[92] Ibid., Prologus (ed. Barbet 107B): "Et, ex doctrina Apostoli, magnus Dionyius Areopagita theoricam huius superintellectualis sapientie scribit, sicut possibile est eam scribi, in libello suo *De mystica theologia*, quem ante annos decem diligenter exposui. In hoc autem libro, Salomon tradit practicam eiusdem mystice theologie, ut patet per totius libri seriem".

silence.[93] As the gift of awareness increases, man so acquires a new capability of intelligence through his sensations.[94] Accordingly faith is on the way; but the experience of burning love illuminates and reinforces the spirit of man, in so far he perceives the essentials of the Trinity in which he already believes.[95]

5. Contacts between the Victorines and Jewish Scholars

The significance of Hieronymian exegesis for the Victorines has already been set out. Hugh's and Andrew's turning towards the biblical text is indebted to Jerome's respect for the *hebraica veritas.* Since the times of the teacher of Bethlehem this positive attitude towards the Jews had, within the Church, led to a long history of encounters and exchanges between Jews and Christians. Jerome's desire for a Bible translation which would respect the Jewish authority concerning the text and its understanding, corresponds as well to his theological vision as to the reality of his life. Similarly the concern for a good exegetical theology had been embodied, in the course of the centuries, both in polemical as also in peaceful contacts between Jews and Christians.[96]

5.1. Knowledge of Hebrew

The twelfth century introduces a period of language studies in the Latin West, but effective results (through the foundation of special language schools) and wideranging efforts (for instance within the scope of mission) were achieved only with the very beginnings of the Mendicant orders.[97]

For Andrew of St. Victor, one essential element while looking for strong contacts with Jewish exegetes, consisted in acquiring the language of his conversational partners. In what measure this happened and how far he advanced with his language studies, is only inadequately shown in the available documents. The present investigation in this field seems to show a sufficient know-

[93] Thomas Gallus, *Commentaire sur Isaïe* (ed. Théry 158, 35–59, 3): "Beata itaque anima experimento edocta dicere potest illud Ysa. 6 a: *Vidi Dominum.* Non dicit 'video'. Puto enim quod anima viatoris dum hoc vidit, non loquitur, *sed fit in celo silentium,* Apoc. 8a, pre nimia visionis occupacione donec hora illa transierit".

[94] Ibid. (ed. Théry 160, 14–16): "Tandem vero inventus est aliquis qui talentum intellectus fideliter multiplicans novam artem super experimentum affectus fundavit".

[95] Ibid. (ed. Théry 160, 21–161, 5): "Sic ergo fides que est in via pertinet ad Cherubym, sicut caritas ad Seraphym et spes ad Thronos et quatuor virtutes cardinales ad secundum hierarchiam. Sepe experiencia estuantis caritatis non mediocriter illuminatur et roboratur mens quatenus articuli Trinitatis prius tenui fide apprehensi, intelligantur ita esse ...".

[96] Cf. besides Dahan, Les intellectuels chrétiens (1990) above all the reference works by H. Schreckenberg, e.g., *Die christlichen Adversus-Judaeos-Texte (11.–13. Jh.). Mit einer Ikonographie des Judenthemas bis zum 4. Laterankonzil* (Frankfurt-M / Bern / New York / Paris ^{2}1991). Recently, the book of R. Moore, *Jews and Christians in the Life and Thought of Hugh of St. Victor* (Philadelphia 1998), investigates thoroughly this theme.

[97] With respect to the Late Middle Ages cf. the recent article by G. Dahan / I. Rosier / L. Valente, "L'arabe, le grec, l'hébreu et les vernaculaires", Ebbesen, Sprachtheorien (1995) 265–321.

ledge of Hebrew which enabled him to work out for himself the exegetical interpretations obtained from his rabbinic teachers.[98]

5.2. New Jewish Sources in the Exegesis of the Victorines

Two main impediments still make the investigation of the sources difficult.

The first difficulty consists in the lack of critical editions not only of the Victorine commentaries themselves, but moreover especially of those of Carolingian writers, such as Alcuin, Remigius of Auxerre and Hrabanus Maurus. In the course of these critical editions we must accord special emphasis on the identification of the Jewish sources of the edited texts so as to be able to distinguish, in each case, between Jerome's contribution and that of the contemporary Rabbis in the knowledge of the *hebraica veritas.* Likewise we need editions of texts of those contemporaries of the above mentioned Victorine authors, who, also, had Jewish dialogue partners and had become aware of the Vulgate's problems of textual criticism, for example, Cistercians like Stephen Harding[99] and Nicolas Maniacoria.[100] In this way the specific contribution of the abbey of Saint Victor to the Jewish-Christian exchange will become more precisely known.

The second difficulty concerns the question which rabbinic text the Victorines have known or actually could have known. Because of the specific oral tradition within the Jewish biblical exegesis we can hardly expect to identify the origin of all the references to Rabbis in Hugh's, Andrew's and also Richard's writings. For certain, a good range of such commentaries by authors of the Northern French rabbinical school has been well conserved.[101] But it is really impossible to reconstruct the teaching which Hugh or Andrew, presumably, might have received at Paris. Nor can we know who were their rabbinic teachers or if they had known, for instance, personally R. Samuel ben Meir (1080–1160).[102] The studies so far of Andrew of St. Victor allow us to confirm the dominant influence of the Northern French exegetical school and to outline it.[103] The interpretations of R. Solomon ben Isaac, Rashi (1040–1105),

---

[98] Cf. Berndt, André de Saint-Victor (1991) 201–13. With regard to Hugh of St. Victor appropriate research work is still waiting to be done.

[99] Cf. for that M. Cauwe, "La Bible d'Étienne Harding. Principes de critique textuelle mis en œuvre aux livres de Samuel", *RBén* 103 (1993) 414–44.

[100] The recent bibliography about Nicolaus Maniacoria limits itself to G. Dahan, "Juifs et chrétiens en occident médiéval. La rencontre autour de la Bible (XIIe–XIVe siècles)", *Revue de synthèse* 110 (1989) 3–31, and B. Munk Olsen, "Les éditions des textes antiques au moyen âge", *The Medieval Text – Editors and Critics. A Symposium* (ed. M. Borch / A. Haarder / J. McGrew; Odense 1990) 83–100.

[101] Cf. R. Anchel, *Les Juifs de France* (Paris 1946) 59–77; B. Blumenkranz, *Auteurs juifs en France médiévale. Leur œuvre imprimée* (Toulouse 1975).

[102] For this topic cf. the study by N. Golb, *Les Juifs de Rouen au Moyen Age. Portrait d'une culture oubliée* (Rouen 1985), who has worked out Rashbam's biography and his career; likewise *The Commentary of R. Samuel ben Meir Rashbam on Qoheleth* (ed. and transl. by S. Japhet and R. B. Salters; Jerusalem / Leiden 1985) 11–14.

[103] Cf. R. Berndt, "Les interprétations juives dans le Commentaire de l'Heptateuque d'André de Saint-Victor", *RAug* 24 (1989) 199–240.

Andrew had received in a large measure in all his commentaries. Andrew cites Rashbam, Rashi's grandson, in his Heptateuch Commentary.[104] Interpretations of Joseph Kara (1050–1125), one of Rashi's pupils, have been discovered in Andrew's exegesis of Ezechiel[105] and they can be found also in his Heptateuch Commentary.[106] Other traces of rabbinical influence in Andrew's exegesis are to be seen in the citations of the Babylonian Talmud, of the *Midrash Rabbah*, the *Chronicle of Megillat Yerahme'el* and of the *Seder ʿOlam.*[107] The reality of the Jewish-Christian exchange within the field of Old Testament exegesis during the twelfth century come to light very clearly in the fact that 72% of those textual explications, which Andrew acknowledged, were introduced for the first time into Christian exegesis.[108]

The Victorines Hugh and Andrew occupy, therefore, a central place within the process of transmission of Jewish-exegetical materials into a Christian cultural milieu. Nevertheless, we should not ignore that at least one other personality of the same century is encountered in the centre of the Jewish-Christian exchange: Peter Comestor, a pupil and friend of the abbey of St. Victor. It is true that the exposition of *Genesis* within the Comestor's main work, the *Historia scholastica*, and the commentary on the Heptateuch by Andrew have in common a considerable number of allusions to Jewish exegesis, which they had taken from the Latin Christian tradition. Peter Comestor's writing contains only a few references to Andrew's newly received material. For his part, Peter Comestor had integrated a lot of interpretations from the Midrash which are lacking in the Victorine writings.[109] The future critical edition of the *Historia scholastica* will show new evidence also with respect to the Jewish-Christian exchange in the field of medieval exegesis.

5.3. Reception of Jewish Exegesis

The rise of the city of Paris from the end of the eleventh century on, constituted an extraordinary fertile ground for the encounters between Jews and Christians and for the exchanges between rabbinic and Christian schools.[110] We know, that the new Parisian foundation of St. Victor had an important part in this movement.[111] The knowledge concerning rabbinical influence upon

---

[104] Cf. Berndt, André de Saint-Victor (1991) 223. See also Chap. 32 in the present volume.

[105] See the *Index auctorum* within the critical edition of the *Expositio in Ezechielem.*

[106] Cf. M. M. Ahrend, *Le Commentaire sur Job de Rabbi Yoséph Qara. Étude des méthodes philologiques et exégétiques* (Hildesheim 1978) 180; Berndt, Pratique exégétique (1991) 279–80.

[107] References to the last mentioned texts can be found in M. Zier, *The Expositio super Danielem of Andrew of St. Victor* (Ph. D., University of Toronto; Toronto 1983; 72*–74*), and the source references of his text edition (Turnhout 1991).

[108] Cf. Berndt, Interprétations juives (1989) 202.

[109] Cf. Berndt, André de Saint-Victor (1991) 329–50. Likewise S. R. Karp, *Peter Comestor's Historia Scholastica: a Study in the Development of literal scriptural Exegesis* (Ph. D., Tulane University 1978).

[110] Cf. R. Chazan, *Medieval Jewry in Northern France* (Baltimore / London 1973) 30–35; R.-H. Bautier, "Paris au temps d'Abélard", J. Jolivet (ed.), *Abélard en son temps* (Paris 1981) 21–77.

[111] B. Smalleys masterpiece and the instructive chapter from de Lubac, Exégèse médiévale, II/1, 287–435, still represent a stimulating reading and offer a lot of information. H. Merchavia, *The*

Hugh and Andrew of St. Victor cannot be restricted, therefore, to a simple investigation of their sources. The historian and the theologian need to know, especially, if there may not have taken place, through this exchange, methodological and / or doctrinal developments on the Christian side.

In Andrew's commentaries the Jewish interpretations act, in general, as argument *ex auctoritate*. It is the basis, for instance, of the major part of the detailed philological information utilised: Andrew prefers the Hebrew explications of words to those in Latin, because Hebrew language is, truly, the *lingua sacra*;[112] he explains biblical narratives by comparing them more with rabbinical than with occidental ways of life.[113] Paradoxically this type of argumentation reinforces, from the methodological point of view, those patterns of interpretation which look beyond the biblical text to be commented on, and which are of a more fundamental nature: reason and the Christian faith. It is evident, that Andrew certainly accepted only those Jewish textual interpretations which are conformable with his theology. Andrew's real exegetical choice among different sources took place long before a firm conception found its way into his commentaries. It had first then been based on the authority of the *hebraica veritas* and obtained, by this route, its proper recognition. Hugh's and Andrew's reception of Jewish exegesis in their respective Bible commentaries corresponds directly with their idea of literal exegesis. Nevertheless, the latter is conditioned by a previous, primary theological perspective.

Accordingly, Andrew of St. Victor is an exception. The historian will discover in him the one who had given priority to the motivating principle of the Glossa ordinaria, that is to say the stressing of exegetical work in the choice of texts. The theologian recognizes in Andrew an expert representative of Jerome's method of exegesis in distinction to the preponderant Augustinian influence. With Andrew's exegetical writings the biblical text which is to be commented on, is set in a different light to produce an exegesis which should serve – according to Richard's conceptions – the development of doctrinal teaching. For sure, it is always Christian faith who inspires such a search. As well as Jerome as the Victorines, they hold that "not knowing Sacred Scripture signifies not to know Christ."[114]

Church versus Talmudic and Midrashic Literature (500–1248) (Jerusalem 1970) [Heb.] 153–64, presents briefly the question. We owe the last overlook to J. Châtillon, "La Bible dans les Écoles du XIIe siècle", Riché / Lobrichon, Moyen Age et la Bible (1984) 163–97.

112 Look for instance on the meaning of such a formula like *idioma est hebreae linguae / locutionis*: *In Genesim* 1:29 (ed. Lohr / Berndt 603/605); *In Exodum* 20:3 (*ibidem* 1275/76); *In Ezechielem* 40:6 (ed. Signer 129/132).

113 See formulas like *consuetudo est Iudaeis*: *In Exodum* 3:5 (ed. Lohr / Berndt 97); oder *sacra Scriptura consueuit*: *In Genesim* 4:15 (ibid. 1278/80).

114 Hieronymus, *Prologus commentarii in Isaiam* (ed. M. Adriaen; CChr.SL 73; Turnhout 1963, 1). Vgl. G. A. Zinn jr., "History and Interpretation: 'Hebrew Truth', Judaism, and the Victorine Exegetical Tradition", *Jews and Christians: Exploring the Past, Present and Future* (ed. J. H. Charlesworth; New York 1990) 100–27, and A. Sapir Abulafia, *Christians and Jews in the Twelfth-Century Renaissance* (London / New York 1995) 94–106.

6. Characteristics and Influence of the Victorine Exegesis

What are the specific features which distinguish the exegesis of the regular canons Hugh, Andrew, and Richard of St. Victor as well as of Thomas Gallus, so that their writings might be considered as representative for exegetical renewal during the twelfth and thirteenth centuries? What influence did they have beyond the thirteenth century?

6.1. Sources of the Victorines

If we desire to understand the exegetical methods of the above mentioned authors and in order to judge their theological importance, we need to be conscious of the milieu within which such writings were composed. Far beyond the patristic tradition, to which the Victorine spirituality had been indebted, undoubtedly new influences are discernible in the exegesis of the *magistri* of the abbey of St. Victor. We already know about the intellectual engagement with which Richard opposed Andrew against certain tendencies in the field of exegesis. Andrew and Richard were contemporaries and therefore pupils of Hugh, to whom the school of St. Victor owes its rise to eminence, if not even its foundation.

It is hardly necessary to mention the one to whom all medieval authors owe their religious impulse and its primary expression. The honorary title *novus Augustinus*, with which Hugh, soon, had been entitled,[115] tells sufficiently the esteem offered to the head of the Victorine school. But this honorary title emphasises also the point of reference, Augustine, the Church father. Concerning the exegesis of the Old Testament the Augustinian influence on the exegetes belonging to the Parisian abbey, is perceptible especially in their hermeneutics. In the succession of Augustine's *De doctrina Christiana* Hugh and Richard, above all, developed the doctrine of the double signification of language. In secular contexts words (*voces*) signify a visible reality (*res*^{1}). The language of Sacred Scripture, on the contrary, has a second level of signification. For though its language points to visible things, it refers also to other, invisible realities, that is to say to mysteries of faith (*res*^{2}).[116] The language of the Old Testament is to be understood, in this sense, allegorically. The exegesis according to the three or four senses of Scripture, which had been inspired by Origen and Augustine, led, during its history, to insist particularly on the development of the second level of signification of these invisible realities. From this point of view one can understand Hugh's polemic against those who disregard the

---

[115] Cf. Thomas Cantimprensis, *Bonum universale de proprietatibus apum* II. 16 (Douai 1597) 174 (cited according to de Ghellinck, Mouvement théologique [^{2}1948] 185).

[116] Hugo de Sancto Victore, *Didascalicon* V. 3 (ed. Buttimer 96); *De scripturis et scriptoribus sacris* XIV (PL 175, 20 D/21 A): '... sed in sacra pagina excellentior valde est rerum significatio quam vocum: quia hanc usus instituit, illam natura dictavit. Hec hominum vox est, illa Dei ad homines'. – Cf. Brinkmann, Hermeneutik (1980) 21–25, and G. Dahan, "Nommer les êtres: exégèse et théories du langage dans les commentaires médiévaux de Genèse 2, 19–20", Ebbesen, Sprachtheorien (1995) 55–74.

literal sense and are not interested in the primary signification of *vox*, but who want to investigate more immediately the allegorical meaning. Yet they denied themselves the only possible way, from the *voces* to the *res.*[117]

One of the most interesting characteristics of the Victorine exegesis is the esteem and appreciation with which the Parisian abbey greet at the same time the teacher of Bethlehem and the teacher of Hippo regius. With the scriptural interpretation of the Victorines Jerome's method of exegesis acquired a new eminence during the twelfth century after being insignificant for a long time.[118] Jerome had undertaken his Bible translation in order that the Latin Church could possess a Sacred Scripture which was based on direct contact with the original version and which could enjoy, therefore, an appropriate authority. Jerome himself, indeed, designated his translation as 'canon hebraice veritatis',[119] but he was not looking for the *hebraica veritas* by itself. Biblical philology constituted, for him, the point of departure for obtaining knowledge of Jewish scriptural interpretation. To look for the literal sense signified for Jerome, to receive the acceptable biblical explications from the Jews so that the Christian investigation of the remaining dimensions of sense of the Old Testament are built on solid foundations.

For his part Hugh does not insist exclusively on the *hebraica veritas*, rather he firmly describes his aim in the *Didascalicon* as spiritual biblical exegesis.[120] The exegesis according to the senses of Scripture, where the literal sense surely takes the first, but not the only, place is given a new importance in Hugh of St. Victor's works. In Hugh and, as we have seen, in Andrew the biblical narrative and the biblical text are treated first of all by the use of a specific argument of authority, that is employing the authority of the *hebraica veritas.* In the background the Christian faith acts as the measure for its reception. Richard does not continue walking completely in Hugh's footsteps. When Richard, in his *Liber exceptionum*, cites the passage of the *Didascalicon* where Hugh exposes his doctrine of the scriptural canon, he integrates himself in Jerome's exegetical tradition. But, Richard seems to prefer the traditional frame of the three scriptural senses for his own exposition of Sacred Scripture, and narrowly seems concerned to look with special attention for the literal sense.[121]

Hugh unified the different intellectual traditions, converging in the Parisian abbey of St. Victor during the first half of the twelfth century in one synthesis. At that time this synthesis was already in the wind and echoed a widespread requirement, at least to judge from the immediate success of the *Didascalicon* and the work called *De scripturis et scriptoribus sacris.* The definitive intellectual elements within the abbey of St. Victor and the methods of teaching, practised

---

[117] Look for instance on the famous text in Hugh, *De scripturis et scriptoribus sacris* V (PL 175, 15 AB) against the 'doctores allegoriarum'. – Cf. de Lubac, Exégèse médiévale, II/2, 287–89; G. R. Evans, *The language and logic of the Bible: The earlier Middle Ages* (Cambridge 1984) 51–56.

[118] Cf. C. Spicq, "Le canon des Livres saints au XIIIe siècle", *RSPT* 30 (1941/42) 424–31; P. Antin, "Jérôme antique et chrétien", *REAug* 16 (1970) 35–45.

[119] Hieronymus, *Epistola* 71.5 (ed. I. Hilberg; CSEL 55; Wien 1912, 6).

[120] Cf. Hugo de Sancto Victore, *Didascalicon* VI. 4 (ed. Buttimer 117–22).

[121] Richardus de Sancto Victore, *Liber exceptionum* I. II. 8–9 (ed. Châtillon 119–20). – Cf. de Lubac, Exégèse médiévale, II/1, 387–89.

by the canons, were linked to a system of knowledge which accomplished three tasks:

- it was able to establish a relationship between the ancient knowledge of the *artes liberales* with the modern knowledge of the *artes mechanice*;
- it assigned to the science of the Divine its own specific place in the world of learning so that the relationships between all areas of knowledge were thereby organized;
- it recommended to the student who wanted to attain wisdom, a precise way showing how to reach his aim.

The order of the scientific disciplines, developed by Hugh, intended to serve these claims. His *Didascalicon* and, one generation later, Richard's *Liber exceptionum*, became, because of their extraordinary popularity, the epistemological schoolbooks *par excellence* during the Middle Ages.[122] By this the school of St. Victor contributed, at the peak of its endeavour, the best possible expression to the logic of knowledge.

6.2. Understanding of the Canon

While Hugh and Richard offered explanations several times in their works concerning the concept of the biblical canon, we only can deduce, in outline, Andrew's teaching on this topic. He left no theoretical treatise concerning the canonical foundations of his scriptural interpretations.

In succession to Jerome, Andrew rejects the Book of Wisdom and Ecclesiasticus which were counted, together with Tobit, Judith and the Books of the Maccabees, among the Apocrypha of the Old Testament. For his part Hugh, as well as Richard, always had rejected as a whole these Old Testament writings.[123] Against the Pauline authenticity of the Epistle to the Hebrews, Andrew repeats, it is true, the doubts of the Church fathers, but he ascribed it neither to Barnabas nor to Clement of Alexandria, as Hugh had done.[124] On the other hand Andrew did not raise the question of the inspiration of Sacred Scripture. He alludes to this merely in his discussions concerning the mission of the prophets. The divine origin of the biblical books and their authority which are confirmed by the Church's exegetical tradition, are for Andrew completely beyond question. Although he presupposes everywhere the inerrancy of Scripture, Andrew defends the opinion, that Sacred Scripture, nevertheless, needs a careful and informed reader and interpreter.[125]

---

[122] Cf. L. Giard, "Logique et système du savoir selon Hugues de Saint-Victor", Thalès 16 (1979/81) 3–32; Chenu, Théologie (^{3}1976) 64–69. 200–209; Châtillon, *Liber exceptionum*, Introduction, 7–96.

[123] Cf. Hugo de Sancto Victore, *Didascalicon* IV. 9 (ed. Buttimer 82–83); Richardus de Sancto Victore, *Liber exceptionum* I. II.9 (ed. Châtillon 120).

[124] See *In III Regum* 8:9 (ed. van Liere 401/405). – Cf. Hugo de Sancto Victore, *Didascalicon* IV. 6 (ed. Buttimer 77).

[125] See *In Ezechielem* 1:10 (ed. Signer 416/419): 'Redeamus ad sacri sermonem eloquii quem nihil in se contrarietatis vel falsitatis habere clarebit, si diligentem et peritum lectorem et explanatorem nactus fuerit'; idem *In Genesim* 7:2 (ed. Lohr / Berndt 1488/89) et 30:35 (2563/2565). Cf. Berndt, André de Saint-Victor (1991) 109–18, and J. Beumer, *Inspiration der Heiligen Schrift* (Freiburg i. Br. 1968).

Hugh accepts Jerome's theory of the canon completely, that is the division of the Old Testament in 22 books, the concept of Apocryphal books, and the doctrine of the *ordines* (*lex-prophete-hagiographi*).[126]

6.3. Lemmatized Commentaries: Related to the Glossa

We are very well informed about the intellectual formation of the first masters of the abbey of St. Victor at the school of Laon. Before he became teacher at the cathedral school of Notre-Dame in Paris, William of Champeaux studied under the direction of Anselm of Laon.[127] At Laon, certainly, he not only learnt the techniques of how to annotate Sacred Scripture. But he could exercise himself, to compile patristic citations or textual passages (*sententie*) in order to explain with their help problematic Bible verses or to answer questions that arose.[128] To gloss the Bible and to form sentence collections: these were at the same time both traditional and new techniques. The *glossator* and the *sententiarius*, both submit to higher authority: the former to the authority of the Divine Word, the latter to the Church fathers.[129] Yet the new developments in this direction of how biblical exegesis is to be conceived and related to systematic theology should not be undervalued. The principle of organisation as well the annotations and sentence collections provides the reason which always governs the choice of texts.[130]

Obviously, the Victorines' teaching had been formed, especially after William of Champeaux's leaving of the abbey, principally by the methods in practice at Laon. This is testified by two complete biblical glosses from the library of St. Victor, the Parisian manuscripts of the Bibliothèque nationale de France, lat. 14398–14410 (end of 12th century),[131] and the Bibliothèque Mazarine, 131–44 (13th century).[132] We know hardly anything at all of the patristic texts or early medieval Bible expositions, which are incorporated into these annotations. Research work has still to be done in order to know if there had been different stages between these Victorine glosses and their relationship to Gil-

---

[126] Cf. R. Berndt, "Gehören die Kirchenväter zur Hl. Schrift? Zur Kanontheorie des Hugo von St. Viktor", JBTh 3 (1988) 191–99.

[127] Cf. J. Châtillon, "Les écoles de Chartres et de Saint-Victor", *La scuola nell'Occidente latino dell'alto medio evo* (Spoleto 1982) 795–839; J. Ehlers, "Hugo von St. Viktor und die Viktoriner", *Mittelalter I* (ed. M. Greschat; Gestalten der Kirchengeschichte 3; Stuttgart-Berlin 1983) 193. See also Chap. 30.2 above (G. R. Evans).

[128] Cf. B. Smalley, "Glossa ordinaria", TRE 13 (1984) 452–57; G. Lobrichon, "Une nouveauté: les gloses de la Bible", Riché / Lobrichon, Moyen Age et la Bible (1984) 95–114; idem, "Gli usi della Bibbia".

[129] In this context the classics such as de Ghellinck, Mouvement théologique (^{2}1948) and Chenu, Théologie (^{3}1976) are still recommendable.

[130] See G. Lobrichon, "Conserver, réformer, transformer le monde? Les manipulations de l'Apocalypse au Moyen Age central", *The Role of the Book in Medieval Culture* (Proceedings of the Oxford International Symposium 26 September–1 October 1982, ed. P. Ganz; 2; Bibliologia 4; Turnhout 1986) 75–94.

[131] Cf. L. Delisle, *Inventaire des manuscrits de l'abbaye de Saint-Victor* (Paris 1869) 12–13.

[132] Cf. *Le Catalogue de la bibliothèque de l'abbaye de Saint-Victor de Paris de 1514 de Claude de Grandrue* (ed. V. Gerz-von Büren / G. Ouy avec R. Hubschmid et C. Regnier; Paris 1983) 3–6. A. Molinier, *Catalogue des manuscrits de la Bibliothèque Mazarine* (Paris 1885).

bert Universalis. Another consequence of the Laonesian influence in St. Victor is to be discerned in the biblical character of the Victorine theology and spirituality. The different Victorine writers had not all been gifted in the same measure with comparable skill, but all of them lived from Sacred Scripture which constituted for them the source of all possible knowledge.

6.4. Influence in the Middle Ages: Relations between Exegesis and Theology

As for the exegesis of Andrew of St. Victor, one can properly ask what type or form of theology this made possible. After the very rough outline of the systematic theology of the twelfth century offered here, some answer to the above question, in regard to Andrew, can be proposed. We have shown that his exegesis was limited to the rhetorical three-step *littera-sensus-sententia*, already well known from Antiquity. Among other exegetes this three-step formula constitutes only one part of a literary exegesis which is thereby integrated into the horizon of the four senses of Scripture. But because Andrew, in practice, had dissociated himself from the latter, the exclusive application of *littera-sensus-sententia* leads towards the separation from the *allegoria.* The logic of the path, which Andrew had undertaken, leads to the type of theology which emerges during the thirteenth century within the world of the universities. But this new, university-based theology could originate only after the Occident had taken account of the Aristotelian concept of science. So, we can say in retrospect that Andrew of St. Victor exhausted the methodological possibilities which were latent in Hugh's *Didascalicon.* By doing so he, indeed, overstretched the understanding and the receptivity of his time, but, nevertheless, he paved the way for the thirteenth century.

In this regard it is appropriate to point to the survival of Peter Lombard's *Sententiae* during the later Middle Ages. Since from the thirties of the thirteenth century onward, the Lombard's *Sententiae* had become t h e university textbook, the history of reception of these *Sententiae* followed a course similar to that of the Bible: Bible commentaries and sentence commentaries became transformed into established subjects for academic exercises of *baccalarii biblici* and *sententiarii.* These had previously been formulating, as *lectores*, their own *doctrina sacra.* Once outlines had been fixed, the young *magistri* at the university could again recommence expounding Scripture.[133]

This is the striking difference between the *sacra doctrina* of the thirteenth century and the systematic projects of the twelfth: We can define the Victorine *doctrina* as divine information, as instruction by the Divine Word, through which mankind could find a way from the creation *via* the *sacrum eloquium*

---

[133] Cf. the instructive contributions by J. VERGER, "L'exégèse, parente pauvre de la théologie scolastique?", and W. J. COURTENAY, "Programs of Study and Genres of Scholastic Theological Production in the Fourteenth Century", *Manuels, programmes de cours et techniques d'enseignement dans les universités médiévales* (Actes du Colloque international de Louvain-la-Neuve [9–11 septembre 1993], édités par J. Hamesse; Louvain-la-Neuve 1994) 31–56, 325–50.

into silence. In comparison, the *sacra doctrina* of university-based reasoning during the following century became organized into discourses.

The Victorine exegesis was received with approval among its contemporaries of the twelfth century, and even among the members of the university of Paris, because it was interested in the personal appropriation of what had already been read in Scripture. All the scientific dedication which we can observe in Hugh's and Andrew's exegetical works served one aim, which is to understand and to seize the Word with all the intellectual and emotional forces which are at man's disposal. Beyond that the Victorine exegesis made clear that the Bible as a book reflects the Creator of the world.[134] No external doctrine is therefore comparable to the personal, contemplative experience of the Word of Scripture since the contemplation of truth educates man to justice.[135] Only in this way could a meeting with the originator of the Word himself become possible.[136]

[134] With regard to the metaphor of nature as book cf. the recent study by F. Ohly, "Zum Buch der Natur", idem, *Ausgewählte und neue Schriften zur Literaturgeschichte und zur Bedeutungsforschung* (Stuttgart / Leipzig 1995) 727–843.

[135] Richardus de Sancto Victore, *Beniamin maior* I. 1 (ed. Aris [6], 22–23): "Per veritatis sane contemplationem homo et eruditur ad iustitiam et consummatur ad gloriam".

[136] Richard de Saint-Victor, *Liber exceptionum* II, Prologus (ed. Châtillon 213, 2–10): "Quicumque sapientie sive scientie studet divine, fructum lectionis proprio magis experimento quam alieno documento cognoscere valet. In ipsa namque legentis animus bonum possidet honeste occupationis, sollertiam meditationis; instantiam invenit orationis, fervorem devotionis, claritatem superne contemplationis. Ibi formatur ad exemplum sancte imitationis, instruitur ad exercitium virtutis, ad exhibitionem boni operis. In ipsa, ..., perducitur ad veram vel ad perfectam veritati cognitionem, ad bonitatis dilectionem".

Chapter Thirty-five

Christian Interpretation of the Old Testament in the High Middle Ages

By Karlfried Froehlich, Princeton, N.J.

Bibliographies: *Bibliographie annuelle du Moyen-Age tardif: Auteurs et textes latins*, Rassemblée à la section latine de l'Institut de Recherche et d'Histoire des Textes (Turnhout: Brepols 1991–); P. Glorieux, *Répertoire des maîtres en théologie de Paris au XIIIe siècle* 1–2 (EPhM 17–18; Paris: Vrin 1933/34); J. B. Schneyer, *Repertorium der lateinischen Sermones des MAs für die Zeit von 1150–1350* (BGPhMA 43:1–10; Münster: Aschendorff 1969–90); F. Stegmüller / N. Reinhardt, *Repertorium Biblicum Medii Aevi* 1–11 (Madrid: Consejo Superior de Investigaciones Cientificas, Instituto Francisco Suarez 1950–80); A. Vernet / A.-M. Genevois, *La Bible au Moyen Age: Bibliographie* (Paris: Editions du CNRS 1989).

General works: *Ad Litteram: Authoritative Texts and Their Medieval Readers* (ed. M. D. Jordan / K. Emery, Jr.; Notre Dame Conferences in Medieval Studies 3; Notre Dame, IN: University of Notre Dame Press 1992); *La Bibbia nell'alto Medioevo* (Settimane di studio del Centro Italiano di Studi sull'Alto Medioevo X; Spoleto: Centro Italiano di Studi sull'Alto Medioevo 1963); *La Bibbia nel Medioevo* (ed. G. Cremascoli / C. Leonardi; Bologna: EDB 1996); *The Bible in the Medieval World: Essays in Memory of Beryl Smalley* (ed. K. Walsh / D. Wood; Studies in Church History, Subsidia 4; Oxford: Published for the Ecclesiastical History Society by Blackwell 1985); Ph. Buc, *L'ambiguité du livre: prince, pouvoir, et peuple dans les commentaires de la Bible au Moyen Age* (Théologie historique 95; Paris: Beauchesne 1994); *The West from the Fathers to the Reformation* (CHB 2; ed. G. W. H. Lampe; Cambridge UP 1969); H. de Lubac, *Exégèse médiévale. Les quatre sens de l'Ecriture*, I–II in 4 vols. (Collection Théologie 41, 42, 59; Paris: Aubier 1959–64); G. R. Evans, *The Language and Logic of the Bible: The Road to Reformation* (Cambridge / New York, NY: Cambridge UP 1985); A. Forest / F. van Steenberghen / M. de Gandillac, *Le mouvement doctrinal du XIe au XIVe siècle* (HE 13; Paris: Bloud & Gay 1956); M. T. Gibson, *The Bible in the Latin West* (The Medieval Book 1; Notre Dame: University of Notre Dame Press 1993); H. Glunz, *History of the Vulgate in England from Alcuin to Roger Bacon* (Cambridge: Cambridge UP 1933); M. Grabmann, *Die Geschichte der scholastischen Methode* 1–2 (Freiburg: Herder 1909–11); J. Hackett, *Medieval Philosophers* (Dictionary of Literary Biography 115; Detroit / London: Gale Research 1992); *Medieval Literary Theory and Criticism c. 1100–c. 1375: The Commentary Tradition* (ed. A. J. Minnis / A. B. Scott; rev. ed.; New York, NY: Oxford UP 1998); A. J. Minnis, *Medieval Theory of Authorship* (2nd ed.; Philadelphia: University of Pennsylvania Press 1988); *Le Moyen Age et la Bible* (BTT 4; ed. P. Riché / G. Lobrichon; Paris: Beauchesne 1984); *Neue Richtungen in der hoch- und spätmittelalterlichen Bibelexegese* (Schriften des Historischen Kollegs, Kolloquien 32; ed. R. Lerner; München: R. Oldenbourg 1996); H. Graf Reventlow, *Epochen der Bibelauslegung* II: *Von der Spätantike bis zum ausgehenden Mittelalter* (München: C. H. Beck 1994); H. Rost, *Die Bibel im Mittelalter. Beiträge zur Geschichte und Bibliographie der Bibel* (Augsburg: M. Seitz 1939); B. Smalley, *The Study of the Bible in the Middle Ages* (3rd rev. ed.; Oxford: Basil Blackwell 1983); eadem, "The Bible in the Medieval Schools" (CHB 2; 1969) 197–220; eadem, *Studies in Medieval Thought and Learning from Abelard to Wyclif* (History Series 6; London: Hambledon Press 1981); C. Spicq, *Esquisse d'une histoire de l'exégèse latine au moyen-âge* (Bibliothèque Thomiste 26; Paris: Vrin 1944).

1. The Old Testament in the Monastery: Bernard of Clairvaux on the Song of Songs

Sources: *Glossa ordinaria*, Pars 22. *In Canticum Canticorum* (ed. Mary Dove; CChrCM 170; Turnhout: Brepols 1997); BERNARD: RBMA 1720–26; Schneyer 1 (1969) 442–57; Commentary on the Song of Songs: PL 183, 785–1198; critical edition: *Sancti Bernardi Opera* 1–2 (ed. J. Leclercq / H. Rochais / C. H. Talbot; Rome: Editiones Cistercienses 1957/58); English tr.: *On the Song of Songs* I–IV (tr. K. Walsh; The Cistercian Fathers Series 4, 7, 31, 40; Spencer, MA / Kalamazoo, MI: Cistercian Publications 1971–80).

Bibliographies: J. BOUTON, *Bibliographie bernardine 1891–1957* (Commission l'histoire de l'Ordre de Citeaux. Etudes et documents 5; Paris: Lethielleux 1958); G. HENDRIX, *Conspectus bibliographicus sancti Bernardi ultimi patrum. 1989–1993* (2nd ed.; RThAM, Suppl. 2; Leuven: Peeters 1995); L. JANAUSCHEK, *Bibliographia Bernardina* [to 1891] (Xenia Bernardina 4; Hildesheim: G. Olms 1959); E. A. MANNING, *Bibliographie Bernardine, 1957–1970* (Documentation cistercienne 6; Rochefort: Abbaye ND de S. Remy 1972); *Repertorium fontium historiae medii aevi* 2 (Rome: Istituto storico italiano per il Medio Evo 1967) 500–05.

Concordance: *Thesaurus Sancti Bernardi Claraevallensis* (CCh Thesaurus Patrum Latinorum; Turnhout: Brepols 1987).

General works: P. DUMONTIER, *Saint Bernard et la Bible* (Bibliothèque de spiritualité medievale; Paris: Desclée de Brouwer 1953); G. R. EVANS, *The Mind of St. Bernard of Clairvaux* (New York, NY: Oxford UP 1983); D. FARKASFALVY, *L'inspiration de l'Ecriture sainte dans la théologie de Saint Bernard* (StAns 53; Rome: Libreria Herder 1964); D. HELLER, *Schriftauslegung und geistliche Erfahrung bei Bernhard von Clairvaux* (Würzburg: Echter 1990); J. LECLERCQ, "Ecrits monastiques sur la Bible du XIe–XIIIe siècles", *MS* 15 (1953) 95–106; E. ANN MATTER, *The Voice of My Beloved. The Song of Songs in Western Medieval Christianity* (Philadelphia PA: University of Pennsylvania Press 1990); D. TURNER, *Eros and Allegory: Medieval Exegesis of the Song of Songs* (Kalamazoo, MI: Cistercian Publications 1995).

By the end of the twelfth century the new context of Bible teaching in the schools as well in the monasteries was fully established, and the forms of the exegetical endeavor had reached a certain level of consolidation. BERYL SMALLEY has described this state of affairs in a substantial chapter of her standard history.[1] The instruction of the masters addressed and reached a much wider group of students than the teaching in the monasteries, and it had a profound impact on Church and society. The phenomenon of peripatetic teachers gathering eager students around them wherever they went had given way to an institutional localization of a wide range of studies including the *artes* and the Bible in the cathedral schools, first and foremost in France: Laon, Reims, Troyes, Chartres, Paris. It was the steady succession of masters in these places that established the reputation of a particular school and determined its attraction for potential scholars. A new factor around the turn of the century was the gradual formation of privileged corporations of masters and students, 'universities', in specific centers of learning. For theological studies, Paris proved to be the most important one. It was joined in the first half of the thirteenth century by Oxford where public teaching had also begun with the arrival of individual masters during the twelfth century, most of them trained in Paris. The range of subjects taught in the schools and early universities, of course, under-

[1] The Study of the Bible in the Middle Ages (1983) 196–263: "Masters of the Sacred Page".

went tremendous expansion during those decades. Since Paris and Oxford developed primarily under ecclesiastical auspices, the *artes* and the theological disciplines rather than law and medicine dominated at these institutions. Even within the theological 'faculties' themselves – the term occurs since 1219 – widely varying interests could be pursued and accommodated. Still, it would be a mistake to assume that biblical teaching took a back seat in the educational ferment of the thirteenth century. Throughout the thirteenth century, theology remained essentially *sacra pagina*; the Bible was the basic textbook for the instruction provided by the masters.[2] The forms of teaching and studying the Bible, however, changed considerably.

Following the example of such monk-scholars as Jerome, Gregory the Great, Bede, and Hrabanus Maurus, the monastic *lectio divina* of previous centuries had combined the study of the Bible as a regular meditative activity with scholarly investigation which used the *artes liberales* as a tool. The goal was the edification of the monastic community and the deepening of individual experience in a liturgical and spiritual life nourished in all its aspects by biblical language and content. In the schools, the accents had to fall differently. The rational investigation of the Bible with the methods employed in the study of classical literature through the disciplines of the *trivium* and *quadrivium* took priority. While the three spiritual senses of the Scriptures were not neglected, the literal sense, and more broadly the literary investigation of the text, assumed a procedural priority which was bound to affect everything: the selection of biblical books to be interpreted, the exegetical procedure, the use of the exegetical tradition, and the resulting literature of biblical interpretation, i.e., the commentaries. The fact that the monastic *lectio divina* had lost its monopoly in biblical interpretation did not mean that it vanished in the monasteries or even diminished in importance as the example of the Cistercian houses shows. On the contrary. *Lectio divina* remained a major part of the religious life even though the results of the new scholastic exegesis were incorporated into the practice, and monastic authors wrote commentaries for wider circulation. Monastic libraries were among the most prominent owners of the commentaries produced in the schools, and monastic scriptoria were one of the primary means of their reproduction and distribution.

In addition, in the monastic homiletic tradition of biblical exegesis a new form of spiritual interpretation made its appearance which, while echoing the pastoral style of Gregory the Great, developed a distinctive profile of its own. One might call it 'affective interpretation' because it has a strong psychological component involving the affects, not just soul and mind, in the anagogy of the contemplative life which was intended to lead the individual to union with God. The goal was not so much the elucidation of the biblical text but its existential application, the self-analysis of the hearer or reader with the help of the text.

---

[2] This point was firmly established by an article of Heinrich Denifle published in 1894: "Quel livre servait de base à l'enseignement des maîtres en théologie de l'université de Paris?", *RThom* 2 (1894) 149–61.

The great master of this new approach was Bernard of Clairvaux.[3] Born in 1090/91 in a family of the French nobility, he entered the new abbey of Cîteaux in 1113 together with a number of relatives and was sent out from there in 1115 as the founding abbot of Clairvaux (Champagne). His frequent involvement in the political and ecclesiastical affairs of his time was the cause of many travels, but Bernard remained deeply attached to his community throughout his life. It is generally agreed that the apex of his literary achievement was the series of Sermons on the Song of Songs on which he worked during the last eighteen years of his life (Advent, 1135, to August, 1153). In the final redaction, the collection numbered eighty-six sermons and covered the biblical text through chapter three, verse one. JEAN LECLERCQ has shown that the existing sermons, while based on Bernard's actual teaching in chapter at the abbey, were the result of a process of dictation, transcription, and revision by the author which was aimed at the production of a literary work.[4]

The Song of Songs was one of the most favorite Old Testament books singled out for sustained attention in the teaching of the monastic schools of the early and high Middle Ages. Commentaries on the Psalms, the Song of Songs, and Genesis far outnumbered the others. A recent list counts more than one hundred pieces of substantial commentation on the Song before 1200.[5] The literal sense was determined by the assumption that Solomon wrote the poem for his Egyptian bride (1 Kgs 3:1). Origen identified it as a dramatic *epithalamion* in the form of a dialogue between bride and bridegroom. He allegorized the individual voices as those of Christ and the Church and the collective ones of their attendants as the choirs of angels and believers.[6] The ecclesiological interpretation was the standard one in the West, especially after Bede had given it his endorsement in his widely read commentary and had explicitly rejected a mariological interpretation of the bride. Precisely the latter option, however, began to make a strong appearance in the commentaries of the twelfth century (Rupert of Deutz; Philip of Harvengt; William of Newburgh; Alan of Lille), probably under the influence of Ambrose who had pictured Mary as the ideal type of the bride-Church, and of the increased Marian devotion of the period with its liturgical expressions in which the lessons for Marian feasts were more and more frequently taken from the Song of Songs.[7] Honorius of Autun's treatise, *Sigillum sanctae Mariae*, written in England,

---

[3] The critical edition of Bernard's works (*Sancti Bernardi Opera*, ed. J. Leclercq / H. Rochais / C. H. Talbot; Rome: Editiones Cistercienses) has been published in eight volumes 1957–76. On Bernard's biblical interpretation, see Dumontier, Saint Bernard et la Bible (1953), and numerous publications by Dom JEAN LECLERCQ (bibliography to 1973 in: *Bernard of Clairvaux. Studies Presented to Dom Jean Leclercq* (CistSS 23; Washington DC: Cistercian Publications 1973) 217–64.

[4] See J. LECLERCQ, "The Making of a Masterpiece", *Bernard of Clairvaux. On the Song of Songs* IV (CiFS 40; Kalamazoo: Cistercian Publications 1980) ix–xxiv.

[5] Matter, The Voice of My Beloved (1990) 203–10.

[6] *Origen, The Song of Songs. Commentary and Homilies* (tr. R. P. Lawson; ACW 26; New York: Newman Press 1957).

[7] See Matter, The Voice of My Beloved (1990) 151–77; F. OHLY, *Hoheliedstudien. Grundzüge einer Geschichte der Hoheliedauslegung des Abendlandes bis um 1200* (Wiesbaden: Franz Steiner Verlag 1958).

comments first on the readings for the Feast of the Assumption and then turns to a Marian interpretation of the entire Song.[8]

Bernard of Clairvaux, although personally a fervent supporter of Marian devotion, did not follow either of these two options but emphasized another interpretive key which had been present as well in the early tradition (Origen; Gregory of Nyssa): the bride as the human soul.[9] This image allowed him to apply the erotic dialogue fully and directly to the intimate yearning of the contemplative soul for union with God, a union which, in the Augustinian tradition, he understood eschatologically as a union of love between God and the resurrected Christian, both body and soul. Bernard's primary aim was not the systematic illumination of the text, but its integration into the "book of experience" (III. 1. 1) with an emphasis on penance, grace, and spiritual progress. "I am not so much interested in expounding words as in imbuing hearts".[10] De Lubac called this affective form of interpretation "mystical tropology", not allegory;[11] in the standard framework of the fourfold sense, allegory referred to the Church, tropology to the soul, anagogy to the "mysteries of the things above". Bernard's approach, closely paralleled in the commentary of his friend and correspondent, William of St. Thierry, dominated the Cistercian commentaries on the Song of Songs throughout the twelfth century: the attempts at completing Bernard's series by Gilbert of Hoyland and John of Ford, Godfrey of Auxerre, Gilbert of Stanford, and Thomas the Cistercian whose encyclopedic compilation adds to the excerpts from Bernard an indiscriminate mass of quotations from all strands of the tradition.

2. The Old Testament in the Schools: Gilbert of Poitiers and Peter Lombard

Sources: *Biblia Latina cum glossa ordinaria: Facsimile reprint of the editio princeps, Adolph Rusch of Strassburg 1480/81* 1–4 (ed. K. Froehlich / M. T. Gibson; Turnhout: Brepols 1992). Gilbert: RBMA 2 (1950) 2511–32; a critical edition of the Psalms commentary is being prepared by T. Gross-Diaz. Peter Lombard: RBMA 4 (1954) 6625–69. 2; 9 (1977) 6625–68; Schneyer 4 (1972) 700–04. PL 191, 55–1296 (the Psalms); B. Smalley / G. Lacombe, "The Lombard's Commentary on Isaias and Other Fragments", *NSchol* 5 (1931) 123–62 (Isaiah).

Bibliographies: A. M. Landgraf, *Introduction a l'histoire de la litterature théologique de la scolastique naissante* (PIEM 22; Montreal / Paris: Vrin 1973); *Magistri Petri Lombardi ... Sententiae in IV Libris Distinctae* I/1 (3rd ed.; SpicBon 4; Grottaferrata: Ed. Collegii S. Bonaventurae Ad Claras Aquas 1971).

General works: M.-D. Chenu, "The Old Testament in Twelfth Century Theology", *Nature, Man, and Society in the Twelfth Century* (ed. and tr. J. Taylor / L. Little; Chicago: University of Chicago Press 1968) 146–61; M. Colish, *Petrus Lombardus* 1–2 (Brill's Studies in Intellectual History 41; Leiden: Brill 1994); G. R. Evans, *Old Arts and New Theology: The Beginnings of Theology as an Academic Discipline* (New York, NY: Oxford UP 1980); T. Gross-Diaz, *The Psalms Com-*

[8] Matter, The Voice of My Beloved (1990) 58, 155–59; V. J. Flint: "The Commentaries of Honorius Augustodunensis on the Song of Songs", *RBén* 84 (1974) 196–211.

[9] Matter, The Voice of My Beloved (1990) 123–50; Ohly, Hoheliedstudien (1958) 135–57.

[10] *Nec studium tam esse mihi ut exponam verba quam ut imbuam corda*, In Cant. Cantic. s. 16 n. 1; *Sancti Bernardi Opera* 1 (1957) 89:1–22.

[11] De Lubac, Exégèse médiévale I/2 (1959) 549–620: chap. ix: "La tropologie mystique".

mentary of Gilbert of Poitiers. From Lectio Divina to the Lecture Room (Brill's Studies in Intellectual History, 68; Leiden: Brill 1996); U. HORST, *Gesetz und Evangelium. Das Alte Testament in der Theologie des Robert von Melun* (VGI NS 13; Paderborn: Schöningh 1971); I. BRADY, "Pierre Lombard", DictS 12:2 (1986) 1604–12; M. ZIER, "Peter Lombard", DMA 9 (1987) 516 f.

Monastic and spiritual expositions of the Song of Songs even outside the Cistercian order continued to value Bernard's affective exegesis, but the tradition of the schools characteristically emphasized the ecclesiological interpretation: Anselm of Laon, the *Glossa ordinaria*, Peter the Chanter, Stephen Langton, William of Auxerre, Hugh of St. Cher. In their introductory discussions of author, subject matter, *modus agendi*, and intention they tried to establish the nature of the book as a literary allegory, seeking to convert it into a teachable text for biblical instruction. Any further investigation of the Song's literal sense was then unnecessary. Allegory had its referent in the life of the Church and therefore yielded "doctrine". The Song of Songs provided plenty of material for the literature of *sententiae* and *distinctiones* which were part of the transformation process of the *scientia scripturarum* into systematic "theology".

The same logic applied to the interpretation of the book of Psalms.[12] Modern research has shown that, along with a continuous stream of monastic commentation, we have Psalms commentaries from many masters of twelfth century schools, although the textual tradition is tangled: Master Manegold (? = Pseudo-Bede), Anselm of Laon (? = Pseudo-Haymo), Letbert of Lille (= Pseudo-Rufinus), Gilbert of Poitiers, Honorius of Autun, Peter Lombard, Peter Comestor, Peter the Chanter, Stephen Langton. Some are polished literary works; others, however, come to us as student *reportationes* only, reflecting actual teaching in the classroom rather than the final word of the master. It seems to have been the common practice of masters to correct and authorize specific *reportationes* for wider circulation. The manuscript evidence is not always conclusive when we ask whether we have the text of the master himself or simply a student copy.

In the Psalms commentaries, the consideration of the original historical sense was overshadowed by the thoroughgoing and total reinterpretation of the Psalter as a Christian book. The two most influential patristic commentators in the West, Augustine and Cassiodorus, had vigorously defended the sole authorship of David for all one hundred and fifty Psalms. Since David was considered a prophet of the messianic era, the Psalms were interpreted as speaking of Christ. Augustine specified: of Christ, head and body, and that meant, of Christ and the Church. Medieval interpreters did not hesitate to call the christological sense the literal though the twelfth century masters still were keenly aware that this literal sense was not the historical, but very close to interpretive allegory. It certainly yielded doctrine in the widest sense of the word, and Psalms commentaries became a major vehicle for the treatment of

[12] On the logic of the Christian Psalter, see A. ROSE, *Les Psaumes, voix du Christ et de l'Eglise* (Paris: Lethielleux 1981); B. FISCHER, *Die Psalmen als Stimme der Kirche. Gesammelte Studien zur christlichen Psalmenfrömmigkeit* (Trier: Paulinus Verlag 1982). On twelfth century Psalms commentaries, see W. HARTMANN, "Psalmenkommentare aus der Zeit der Reform und der Frühscholastik", *Studi Gregoriani* 9 (1972) 313–66.

theological topics. Th. GROSS-DIAZ has recently analyzed Gilbert of Poitiers' Psalms commentary as one of the earliest and most impressive expositions of this type which clearly reflects the milieu of teaching in the schools (RBMA 2511).[13] Expanding a draft written at Laon before 1117 but circulating in the final form not before 1135, the manuscripts demonstrate a new concern for pedagogy directed at a non-monastic audience. The Vulgate text is often added in a second, narrow column near the spine; abbreviations for authors quoted in the text are entered in the margin; the Psalms are numbered; and the commentary is prefaced by a modern *accessus*, a format of introduction borrowed from the manuscripts of classical texts which discusses *materia* (subject matter), *modus* (method of proceeding), *intentio* (purpose), *titulus*, and *utilitas*.[14] This 'information management' reveals that Gilbert treated the Psalms deliberately as literature, not simply as revealed truth. With the tradition, he interpreted their subject matter as *Christus integer caput cum membris*. This was the literal, though not the historical sense. It allowed Gilbert to approach the Psalter as a comprehensive textbook of theology. He did not yet include separate *quaestiones* but discussed doctrinal issues freely in his comments, indicating for each psalm in a mini-accessus its specific location in the economy of salvation. The most intriguing feature of the manuscripts is a system of twelve graphic symbols found in the margins, identifying particular Psalms as belonging to a thematic group of topics such as "on the two natures of Christ"; "on the passion and resurrection"; "on penitence", etc.[15] Gilbert's commentary, GROSS-DIAZ concludes, is an important mile stone on the road from *lectio divina* to the lecture hall.

Equally important for this transition was the Psalms commentary of Peter Lombard whose life and career constitute a unique witness to the great respect which successful teachers at the new schools commanded in the political and ecclesiastical culture of the twelfth century.[16] Born around 1100 in the region of Novara, Peter used to good effect the opportunity to study in France at Reims and Paris where he probably stayed at Saint Victor at the recommendation of Bernard of Clairvaux. As early as 1144, he is mentioned among the renowned teachers of the cathedral school of Notre Dame. In 1145, he was accepted as a member of the chapter, apparently on his scholarly merits alone, and even more surprisingly was elected bishop of Paris in 1159, although he was a foreigner with no high connections in the Capetian establishment. He was consecrated in June, 1159, but died one year later.

Peter Lombard's Psalms commentary (RBMA 6637) is considered to be an early work of his.[17] Herbert of Bosham, who was his student in the late 1150s and prepared a corrected edition at the request of Thomas Becket in 1170/75,

---

[13] Gross-Diaz, The Psalms Commentary of Gilbert of Poitiers (1996).

[14] See E. A. QUAIN, "The Medieval Accessus ad Auctores", *Traditio* 3 (1945) 215–64; Minnis, Medieval Theory of Authorship (1988) 9–72.

[15] Gross-Diaz, The Psalms Commentary (1996) 157–59.

[16] Colish, Petrus Lombardus (1994); L. HÖDL, "Petrus Lombardus", TRE 26 (1996) 296–303.

[17] Colish, Peter Lombard I (1994) 155–88; and "Psalterium Scholasticorum. Peter Lombard and the Emergence of Scholastic Psalms Exegesis", *Spec.* 67 (1992) 531–48. The text of the Lombard's commentary is printed in PL 191, 55–1296.

states that Master Peter had written the commentary as a private exercise in order to clarify for himself the obscurities of Master Anselm's earlier Gloss; he only used it as a basis of class lectures twenty years later in 1158/59. At that time, Peter revised the existing manuscript but was unable to finish the task so that, as Herbert implies, his gloss circulated in versions which had not necessarily been approved by the master.[18] The work enjoyed an immediate and resounding success. Together with the Lombard's commentary on the Pauline Epistles and his *Four Books of Sentences*, it ranks as one of the most frequently copied, used, and quoted exegetical works of the century. IGNATIUS BRADY, the most recent editor of the *Sentences*, has assembled the evidence showing that Peter in fact glossed many other books of the Bible as well, among them Exodus, Isaiah, and the Minor Prophets. Apart from fragments, manuscripts of these glosses have not been located to date.[19]

As the work of a schoolman, Lombard's Psalms commentary parallels many features of Gilbert's earlier work.[20] The Preface presents an extensive *accessus* which covers the same points as Gilbert's, giving them greater precision and further elaboration. Like Gilbert, the Lombard defends the sole authorship of David. He argues that, if the *intentio* of the Psalter is to serve as a guide to Christian doctrine and moral life, then David is the most appropriate author: he was both a prophet of Christ and the Church, and an exemplary sinner who knew of guilt and forgiveness. According to Peter, the Psalter's *materia* is Christ and his body, but further distinctions have to be made: some Psalms speak of Christ's divine nature, others of his humanity. With regard to the Church, some Psalms consider the perfect, some the imperfect, and some the evildoers among its members. Concerning the *modus*, Peter accepts Gilbert's notion of grouping Psalms thematically. It is his expectation that this method might assist in reconstructing the original order which Ezra was unable to restore. The manuscripts present Peter's Gloss in the format of a running commentary, not in that of the *Glossa ordinaria.* But instead of relying on integrated lemmata for text identification, the author gives the full text of each verse or small section first, and then proceeds to an interpretation of words, phrases, and content which draws primarily on quotations from the exegetical tradition. In addition, the Lombard expresses himself here on theological subject matter, drawing in other biblical passages and discussing particular issues or doctrines quite fully while keeping the relation to the Psalm's theme clearly before the reader. His work with the excerpts and summaries from earlier writers is relatively thorough; he tries to assess their accuracy, compares them with the *originalia*,[21] especially in the case of Augustine's *Enarrationes* and Cassiodorus' *Expositio*, attempts to harmonize apparent contradictions, and

---

18 Colish, Peter Lombard I (1994) 23. See also Glunz, History of the Vulgate in England (1933) 219–24; Herbert's remarks are printed on p. 343, lines 58–70.

19 *Magistri Petri Lombardi ... Sententiae in IV Libris Distinctae*, 3rd ed., vol. 2 (SpicBon 5; (1981) 19*–52*. Colish, Peter Lombard II (1994) 27–30.

20 Colish, Peter Lombard I (1994) 170–74; Gross-Diaz, The Psalms Commentary (1996) 146–48.

21 On the medieval use of the term, see M. A. and R. H. ROUSE, *Preachers, Florilegia, and Sermons. Studies on the Manipulus Florum of Thomas of Ireland* (Toronto: PIMS 1979) 36 f.

displays some critical independence in making his decisions. COLISH cites the case of Ps 70 (71):15 f: "Because I am not acquainted with business dealings (*negociaciones*), I will enter into the mighty deeds of the Lord". Anselm of Laon had made the assumption that all merchants are motivated by greed. Peter rejected this opinion. Drawing on Augustine, he submitted that all professions, including business, may be exercised virtuously as well as viciously. COLISH argues that, on the whole, Peter's Psalms commentary is a "rehearsal for the theological teaching" he will be developing in his systematic efforts, especially the *Sentences* which he composed as a class text for a new, topical format of teaching the Bible and which his immediate successors already began to use in their own teaching.[22]

Undoubtedly a major source of Peter Lombard's teaching on the Psalms was the *Glossa ordinaria*. His early private draft was meant to improve on the *Glosa Anselmi*, and his oral teaching later in his career cannot be assumed to have shifted the ground. Using the Laon Gloss as his class text, he followed the practice of Gilbert who through his teaching may well have been the single most important person to have turned the existing earlier glosses, especially on the Psalms and the Pauline Epistles, into the standard textbooks of exegesis in the Paris schools, and who in this way contributed to the universal recognition of a *Glossa ordinaria*.[23] Subsequent generations regarded the *Glossa ordinaria* and Peter Lombard's commentaries as so closely related that the Lombard's work was substituted for the earlier Gloss as the "magna glosatura" in many sets of the standard *Glossa ordinaria* assembled in the late twelfth and early thirteenth century. This perception should not obscure, however, Peter's personal achievement in the exegesis of the Old Testament. It is clear today that, from the middle of the twelfth century on, lectures on the Bible in the schools generally meant lectures on the *glossed* Bible. If they were not simply reciting and dictating what they had before them, the masters were glossing the Gloss, not the plain Bible.[24] We can gauge the immense influence of Peter Lombard's sober biblical interpretation when we consider not only the role played by his *Sentences* in the emerging discipline of "theology", but also the place of his *Magna glosatura* of the Psalms and the Pauline Epistles in the routine of biblical instruction in the schools.

3. Glossing and Preaching: Peter Comestor, Peter the Chanter, Stephen Langton

Sources: PETER COMESTOR: RBMA 4 (1954) 6543–98; Schneyer 4 (1972) 636–51; PL 198, 1054–1722 (Historia Scholastica). PETER THE CHANTER: RBMA 4 (1954) 6445–6531; Schneyer 4 (1972) 628 f; PL 205, 22–554 (Verbum Abbreviatum). STEPHEN LANGTON: RBMA 5 (1955) 7704–7898 (OT); Schneyer 5 (1974) 466–507; G. LACOMBE / B. SMALLEY, *Studies on the Commentaries of Car-*

---

[22] Colish, Peter Lombard I (1994) 178.

[23] This seems to be the implication of Gross-Diaz' chapter on "Gilbert and the Glossa Ordinaria", The Psalms Commentary (1996) 122–48.

[24] This point is emphasized by JOHN VAN ENGEN, "Studying Scripture in the Early University", Neue Richtungen in der hoch- und spätmittelalterlichen Bibelexegese (1994) 17–38; here 22–28.

dinal Stephen Langton (AHDL 5, 1930) 1–220; A. Saltman, *Stephen Langton: Commentary on the Book of Chronicles* (Ramat-Gan: Bar-Ilan UP 1978).

General works: R. Hausherr, "Petrus Cantor, Stephan Langton, Hugo von St. Cher und der Isaias-Prolog der Bible moralisée", *Verbum et signum: Beiträge zur mediävistischen Bedeutungsforschung* 2 (ed. H. Fromm / W. Harms / U. Ruberg; München: W. Fink 1975) 347–64; S. R. Karp, *Peter Comestor's Historia Scholastica: A Study in the Development of Literal Scriptural Exegesis* (Ph. D. Thesis: Tulane University 1978); J. W. Baldwin, *Masters, Princes, and Merchants. The Social Views of Peter the Chanter and His Circle* 1–2 (Princeton, NJ: Princeton UP 1970); R. Quinto, *'Doctor Nominatissimus' Stefano Langton († 1228) e la Tradizione delle sue Opere* (BGPhMA NF 39; Münster: Aschendorff 1994) VIII–XXVI.

This routine is well documented through the work of the three most famous Paris masters at the end of the twelfth century: Peter Comestor, Peter the Chanter, and Stephen Langton. While all three taught at the cathedral school of Notre Dame, they do not form a magisterial succession in the sense of a 'school of thought', but present the standard teaching of two generations in an exemplary way. Grabmann classified the trio as representatives of the "biblical moral school".[25] Smalley objected to the term 'school' but emphasized the continuity with Peter Lombard and the Victorine tradition.[26] One could say that all three scholars in their own ways implemented Hugh of St. Victor's curricular suggestions for the study of the Bible, lifting up the foundational significance of the literal sense of the Old Testament, and applying biblical teaching to the moral and practical issues of contemporary Christian life.

In his *Verbum Abbreviatum*, Peter the Chanter listed the three basic activities of a master in theology: *lectio*, *disputatio*, and *praedicatio*.[27] Using the venerable metaphor of a building, he compared lecturing with laying the foundation, disputing with erecting the walls, and preaching with capping the structure and putting on the roof. Our theologians demonstrate not only the presence of all three activities in their teaching careers, but also their special promise and their problems. *Lectio* in this milieu involved going through glossed texts of specific biblical books, that is, copies of the Vulgate with the *Glossa ordinaria* written between the lines and in the margins.

Peter Comestor, the oldest of our three masters, probably was able to hear Peter Lombard when he came to Paris.[28] He taught at Notre Dame from 1160 to 1178, acting as the school's chancellor since 1168 and residing at St. Victor during his last years. He probably glossed most books of the Old Testament. *Reportationes* are extant of his lectures on the four Gospels (RBMA 6575–78); there is evidence of Peter having glossed Peter Lombard's Psalms commentary (RBMA 6574, 1,3,4). He was also one of the first masters to lecture on the Lombard's *Sentences* as part of his biblical teaching, thus endorsing the topical

---

[25] Grabmann, Die Geschichte der scholastischen Methode 2 (1911) 476–501.

[26] Smalley, Study (1983) 197 f; Châtillon, "La Bible dans les écoles du XIIe siècle", Le Moyen Age et La Bible (1984) 163–97; here 193–97.

[27] *Verbum Abbreviatum* c. 1 (PL 205, 25 AB); cf. Smalley, Study (1983) 208; Baldwin, Masters, Princes, and Merchants (1970) 90–116.

[28] I. Brady, "Peter Manducator and the Oral Teachings of Peter Lombard", *Antonianum* 41 (1966) 454–90. On Peter Comestor, see D. E. Luscombe, "Peter Comestor", The Bible in the Medieval World. Essays in Memory of Beryl Smalley (1985) 109–29; "Petrus Comestor", TRE 26 (1996) 291–93.

approach to biblical materials as appropriate for his students. Of great importance was his *Historia scholastica*, a condensed outline of biblical history from the creation to Christ's ascension which he composed at St. Victor in 1169–73 (RBMA 6543–65).[29] Hugh had expressed the desire for such a *compendium* of the literal sense as a help for beginners. The Comestor showed a keen interest in the *realia* of the biblical narrative, including the geography and archeology of the Holy Land. For confirmation and details he made considerable use of Josephus and pagan historians. Andrew of St. Victor was a major source of his account, and it is possible that references to *Hebrei*, while mostly derived from secondary sources, reflect an interest in Hebrew scholarship dating from his early years at Troyes where a renowned Jewish school was in operation. The *Historia scholastica* enjoyed an immediate success, being hailed by contemporaries as "a highly useful and very welcome work".[30] Stephen Langton glossed it separately, and Innocent III gave it an official nod of approval at the Fourth Lateran Council of 1215. Listening to lectures on the "Histories" became part of a thirteenth century theology student's first year routine. The manuscripts regularly include an expansion covering the story of the Acts of the Apostles, and a "genealogy of Christ" is often added at the beginning. Both pieces were authored by Peter of Poitiers, the Comestor's colleague and successor.

Peter the Chanter taught at Notre Dame from 1170/73 to 1196, acting as *cantor* since 1183.[31] In this capacity, he supervised Church music and the liturgical life at the cathedral. Several of his works were extant at the library of St. Victor in early copies executed at the abbey.[32] Peter's systematic attempt to lecture on the entire Bible is well documented in numerous *reportationes* (RBMA 6454–6531). In the preface to the *Verbum Abbreviatum*, a treasury of moral advice, he criticizes expositions such as those of his colleague, Peter Comestor, as superfluous because they touch externals only, "glosses which speak not from inside the text but around it".[33] His own style is brief, and his interest is concentrated on the text's practical implications, its moral and ecclesiastical usefulness, often leading to casuistic arguments. The beginning sections of his Genesis commentary have been published recently by Agneta Sylwan.[34] The editor points out that this particular text is not a *reportatio* but the author's own redaction. When going through a section, Peter first presents definitions and opinions from the tradition as found in the *Glossa ordinaria*, then discusses the literal meaning and goes on to one of the spiritual senses, introducing his own moral message from time to time. The commentary demonstrates the desparate need of a clear division of the text for this style of biblical survey. Peter

[29] The text printed in PL 198, 1053–1644 is very much in need of being replaced by a modern critical edition.

[30] The quotation is from Robert of Auxerre (1173); see S. R. Daly, "Peter Comestor, Master of Histories", *Spec.* 32 (1957) 62–73; here 67. See also Smalley, Study (1983) 178–80; 214.

[31] On the Chanter, see Baldwin, Masters (1970) and DictS 12 (1986) 1533–38; R. Peppermüller, "Petrus Cantor", TRE 26 (1996) 287–89.

[32] They are today at the Bibliothèque Mazarin; Sylwan (see n. 34 below) xv.

[33] *Verbum Abbreviatum* c. 2 (PL 205, 25 D and 27 b); cf. B. Smalley, *The Gospels in the Schools c. 1100–c. 1280* (London: Hambledon Press 1985) 102–04.

[34] A. Sylwan, *Petrus Cantor. Glossae super Genesim. Prologus et Capitula 1–3* (SGLG 55; Göteborg: Acta Universitatis Gothoburgensis 1992).

uses older systems; for Genesis, these are small sections indicated by Roman numerals in the margin; in some manuscripts chapter divisions in arabic numbers have been added, and his references to Psalms are generally by number.[35] Like the Victorines and Peter Comestor, the Chanter regularly refers to Jewish interpretations. Most of them come from Andrew of St. Victor, the Comestor, Ps.-Jerome, and Maimonides. DAHAN has found a few instances, however, which may be traced to *Midrash Rabba* and Joseph Bekhor Shor directly.[36] A smaller work, *De tropis loquendi* (RBMA 6452f) is also related to Peter's teaching; it discusses grammatical and logical issues raised by biblical texts.[37]

Like Peter the Chanter, Stephen Langton probably glossed the entire Bible during his twenty-five years of teaching at Notre Dame (1180–1206) before moving on to Rome and eventually to the archbishoprick of Canterbury.[38] Most of his commentation is preserved in manuscript in the form of reportations, often in several versions which witness to the master's ongoing attempt to revise and update his notes (RBMA 6454–6531). In the wake of POWICKE's Ford Lectures of 1927, SMALLEY began to sort out the material under the guidance of GEORGES LACOMBE in France, having written her dissertation on Langton's commentary on the Minor Prophets.[39] To date, only the Gloss on Ruth and the Book of Chronicles have found their way into print,[40] but Langton remained a favorite subject of Miss SMALLEY's scholarship. According to her, his teaching seems to have followed closely Hugh of St. Victor's suggested steps of Bible reading: First, the *Historia scholastica* as a survey, then the Gospels for doctrinal orientation, the historical books of the Old Testament, Solomon and Psalms, Pauline Epistles, and finally the prophets.[41] His explanations are lengthy and cumbersome, commenting first on the literal sense at length, then in a separate move more briefly on the moral sense; in the manuscripts, the two parts frequently are separated. They prove that Langton was a conscientious teacher. The needs of simple students were constantly on his mind: he would clarify the exact place and meaning of particular glosses, suggest mnemonic devices to memorize the basics, and draw on the students' knowledge of the *trivium* by raising grammatical, rhetorical, and logical points. Langton did not claim knowledge of Hebrew but, like his colleagues, made use of Jewish exegesis through the same intermediaries. SALTMAN found only

---

[35] Sylwan, Glossae (1992) xxiv–xxx; cf. Smalley, Study (1983) 221 f.

[36] G. DAHAN, "Les interprétations juives dans les commentaires du Pentateuque de Pierre le Chantre", The Bible in the Medieval World (1985) 131–55; Sylwan, Glossae (1992) lxii f.

[37] See F. GIUSBERTI, "A Twelfth-Century Theological Grammar", *Materials for a Study on 12th Century Scholasticism* (Naples, Bibliopolis 1982) 87–109.

[38] Modern Langton studies began with M. POWICKE's Ford Lectures of 1927, *Stephen Langton, Being the Ford Lectures Delivered in the University of Oxford in Hilary Term 1927* (Oxford: Clarendon 1928; repr. NY.: Barnes and Noble 1968). The fullest recent bibliography on Langton is found in Quinto, 'Doctor Nominatissimus' (1994) VIII–XXVI.

[39] The fruit of this collaboration was a monograph-sized article: Lacombe / Smalley, Studies on the Commentaries of Cardinal Stephen Langton (1930) 1–220. On the circumstanes, see R. W. SOUTHERN, "Beryl Smalley and the Bible", The Bible in the Medieval World (1992) 1–16; here 3–5.

[40] Ruth: Lacombe / Smalley (1930) 86–126; Chronicles: Saltman, Stephen Langton: Commentary on the Book of Chronicles (1978).

[41] Smalley, Study (1983) 198.

rare cases of possible contact with original Jewish sources, most likely through converted Jews, but also very little anti-Jewish polemic. On the contrary, many of Langton's comments are similar to those of Western Jewish commentators on Chronicles (Ps.-Rashi; David Cimhi); Jewish and Christian scholars clearly shared the same intellectual atmosphere at that time.[42]

As in the case of Peter the Chanter, Langton's exegetical endeavors produced some new aids to study. Among his works are 211 chapters of *Generalitates* (RBMA 7704) and an alphabetical *Liber interpretationum hebraicorum nominum* (RBMA 7707). Perhaps most importantly, he advanced the urgent task of ordering and subdividing the biblical books for easier reference. Contemporary chroniclers credit him with the "creation" of the standard order and chapter division of the Bible still in use today. Things may not be quite as simple. As the manuscripts show, Langton himself used older divisions in his lectures before 1203, and the 14th century list of the *capitula Cantuarensis archiepiscopi super bibliothecam* in MS Paris Bib. Nat. lat. 14417 (St. Victor 42), fol. 125 f still differs dramatically from the modern counting for Ezra-Nehemia, Tobit, Judith, and Esther. There can be little doubt, however, that with the evolution of the standard "Paris Bible" in the 1230s the chapter division devised by the mature Langton after much trial and error won the day.[43]

The method of the scholastic *lectio* did not escape criticism. In the middle of the twelfth century already, Robert of Melun vigorously attacked the 'glossators' in a famous passage of his Sentences. According to Robert, the preoccupation of the masters with glossing the Bible is entirely misplaced. On the one hand, it detracts from the serious study of the Bible itself and the Fathers by substituting excerpts for the authority of the authentic text; on the other, it leads to superficiality and an obsession with externals at the expense of substantive issues. Understanding the text is the goal of Bible reading, not expertise in dividing and classifying glosses.[44] While the critique was probably directed at Peter Lombard's teaching, it seems to apply even more to the methods of biblical instruction in the schools at the end of the century. In both cases, it was not on target, however. The *Glossa ordinaria* was never meant to replace the study of the Fathers in the original. Ralph Niger, who taught in the 1170s, says in his commentary on the Book of Kings: "We put the sacred expositions of the holy Fathers before our own researches, just as we heard them in the schools, but in brief, that those who read may understand, by reason of this very brevity, that one should go back to the originals for the full knowledge of them".[45] Like Gilbert of Poitiers and Peter Lombard, Stephen Langton did check the excerpts in the Gloss frequently against the full text and remarked on the discrepancies. He was, however, the last great master to give both the introductory and the advanced exegetical lectures. In the thirteenth century,

---

42 Saltman, Stephen Langton (1978) 29–38.

43 Smalley, Study (1983) 221–24. A. d'Esneval, "La division de la Vulgate latine dans l'édition parisienne du XIIIe siècle", *RSPT* 62 (1978) 559–68.

44 *Œuvres de Robert de Melun*, Tom. III/1 *Sententie* (ed. R. M. Martin; SSL 21; Louvain 1947) 4–25; Smalley, Study (1983) 215 f.

45 MS Lincoln 25, f. 6 c, quoted in Smalley, Study (1983) 226.

the surveys became the responsibility of the *baccalarii biblici*, graduate students who read the glossed text *cursorie* for beginning students, while the masters were expected to treat individual biblical books in depth – a practice to which we owe the extensive biblical commentaries of the great scholastic masters.

Robert of Melun's alternative to mere "glossing" was the method of raising substantive questions (*quaestiones*) in the course of exegetical lectures. His own commentary on the Pauline Epistles was full of such content-oriented discussions which circulated independently as *Quaestiones de epistolis Pauli* (RBMA 7466–76).[46] This method echoed Abelard's commentation on Romans, but Peter Lombard also included topical questions in his *magna glosatura* and used them as the organizing principle of his *Sentences*, another form of presenting biblical teaching. The literary remains of our three theologians demonstrate that they too were vitally interested in substantive theological issues arising from their biblical teaching. Peter Comestor lectured on the Lombard's *Sentences*; Peter the Chanter's *Summa de sacramentis* is based on a systematic-practical collection of questions, and Langton left a large corpus of theological *quaestiones* which show that his teaching routine left room for topical discussions, even though the schedule of regular disputations as required exercises was not yet in place.[47]

The most important development, however, was the new role of *preaching* in the emerging theological curriculum.[48] Regular preaching had been part of the monastic routine as Bernard's sermons on the Song of Songs make clear, but not of parish life. Parish priests were expected to administer the sacraments, not to preach sophisticated sermons. This situation changed in the course of the twelfth century. Reform-minded popes and councils insisted on better clerical education. By the 1190s, a tremendous upsurge in actual preaching is in evidence, as is a new interest in, even an enthusiasm for, redefining the place of preaching in the Church. Certain common experiences in the earlier part of the century undoubtedly contributed to this change of mood. Popular preaching had become a more regular phenomenon through the preaching of the Crusades and the activity of charismatic individuals, but especially through popular movements among the laity which the Church tried to exclude as heretical. Some of them, such as the Waldenses, spread as preaching movements; evangelistic preaching was part of their understanding of the call to an apostolic life. The numerous official attempts to stop 'unauthorized' preaching demonstrate, if nothing else, that there was a real hunger abroad for religious oratory, a readiness to listen to impressive preachers. The Church's positive response to this challenge came most powerfully during the pontificate of Innocent III, who organized preaching missions, legislated on regular preaching in parishes by local clergy, and encouraged preachers as well as hearers of sermons by new indulgence policies.

Undoubtedly, the new horizons of systematic and speculative theology con-

---

[46] *Œuvres de Robert de Melun*, tom. II *Questiones [theologice] de epistolis Pauli* (ed. R. M. Martin; SSL 18; Louvain 1938); Smalley, Study (1983) 74.

[47] See the full discussion and catalog in Quinto, Stefano Langton (1994) 91–298.

[48] See the brief survey in Rouse and Rouse, Preachers (1979) 43–64.

tinued to be attractive to masters and students alike, but the masters themselves were more sensitive to the fact that the majority of their students were going to be parish priests, pastors. Not only Peter the Chanter turned to applied theology and thus to pastoral concerns as his main agenda. The new emphasis on preaching was part of this larger re-orientation. All three of our masters preached and provided tools for their students to help with this task. The standard version of the Chanter's *Verbum Abbreviatum* (RBMA 6447–50) was a biblical treatise on virtues and vices for the use of preachers,[49] and his *Summa Abel* (RBMA 6451) inaugurated a new genre of biblical *Distinctiones* which gave to preachers alphabetical or topical lists of biblical terms and their multiple spiritual meanings for use in their sermons.[50] Stephen Langton, in his exegetical lectures, made frequent reference to observations and insights useful for preaching. SALTMAN describes Langton's moral glosses on Chronicles as little more than a loose collection of sermon topics.[51] Peter the Chanter had applied the building metaphor to the activities of a theological *magister*. His explanation clearly indicates the rethinking of the curricular priorities in his circles. For him, preaching, putting on the roof, was the crowning part, the goal, not just a contributing concern, of the master's teaching. Biblical exegesis in the schools now had a purpose in the clear assignment of equipping future pastors for one of their tasks, preaching.

4. Old Testament Interpretation in the Thirteenth Century

Sources: JOACHIM OF FIORE: *Abbot Joachim of Fiore: Liber de concordia Novi ac Veteris Testamenti* (ed. E. R. Daniel; TAPhS 73:8; Philadelphia, PA: American Philosophical Society 1983). HUGH OF ST. CHER: [Dominican Postil, OT]: RBMA 3 (1951) 3631–3716; *Hugonis Cardinalis Opera Onmia in universum Vetus et Novum Testamentum* 1–8 (Venice: Apud Nicolaum Pezzana 1703–54); M. GRABMANN, "Ungedruckte exegetische Schriften von Dominikanertheologen des 13. Jahrhunderts", *Ang.* 20 (1943) 204–18. ROBERT GROSSETESTE: RBMA 5 (1955) 7398–7405, 1; Schneyer 5 (1974) 176–91; R. C. DALES, *Robert Grosseteste: Hexaemeron* (ABMA 4; Oxford UP 1990); English tr.: C. F. J. MARTIN, *Robert Grosseteste: On the Six Days of Creation. A Translation of the Hexaemeron* (ABMA 6 (2); Oxford UP 1996). PETER JOHN OLIVI: RBMA 4 (1954) 6679–6734; Schneyer 4 (1972) 704–06; M. BARTOLI, *La caduta di Gerusalemme: Il commento al Libro delle Lamentazioni di Pietro di Giovanni Olivi* (Istituto Storico Italiano per il Medio Evo: Nuovi studi storici, 12; Rome: Istituto Palazzo Borromini 1991).

General works: L. J. BATAILLON, "De la *lectio* à la *praedicatio*: Commentaire biblique et sermon au XIIIe siècle", *RSPT* 70 (1986) 559–75; D. BERG, *Armut und Wissenschaft: Beiträge zur Geschichte des Studienwesens der Bettelorden im 13. Jahrhundert* (Düsseldorf: Schwann 1977); I. BRADY, "Sacred Scripture in the Early Franciscan School", *La sacra scrittura e i francescani* (Rome / Jerusalem: Pontificium Athenaeum Antonianum; Studium Biblicum Franciscanum 1973); P. MANDONNET, "Dominicains (travaux des) sur les Ecritures", DB (V) 2 (1899) 1463–82; P. GLORIEUX, "L'enseignement au moyen-âge: Techniques et méthodes en usage à la Faculté de théologie de Paris au

[49] PL 205, 21–554. R. TREXLER, *The Christian at Prayer. An Illuminated Prayer Manual Attributed to Peter the Chanter* (MRTS 44; Binghamton, N.Y.: MRTS 1987) distinguishes two books which go under this title, the treatise reproduced in PL 205, and a prayer manual which is preserved in manuscript only.

[50] M. A and R. H. ROUSE, "Biblical Distinctions in the Thirteenth Century", *AHDL* 41 (1975) 23–37.

[51] Saltman, Stephen Langton (1978) 19.

XIIIe siècle", *AHDL* 43 (1968) 65–186; E. GÖSSMANN, *Metaphysik und Heilsgeschichte. Eine theologische Untersuchung der Summa Halensis* (MGI, Sonderband; München: M. Hueber 1964); MANGENOT, "Hugues de St. Cher", DThC 7:1 (1921) 227–36; V. MARCOLINO, *Das Alte Testament in der Heilsgeschichte. Untersuchung zum dogmatischen Verständnis des Alten Testaments als heilsgeschichtlicher Periode nach Alexander von Hales* (BGPhMA NF 2; Münster: Aschendorff 1970); J. J. MCEVOY, *Robert Grosseteste, Exegete Philosopher* (Aldershot UK / Brookfield, VT: Variorum 1994); *Medieval Exegesis of Wisdom Literature: Essays by Beryl Smalley* (ed. R. E. Murphy; Atlanta: Scholars Press 1986); K. B. OSBORNE, *The History of Franciscan Theology* (St. Bonaventure, NY: Franciscan Institute of St. Bonaventure University 1994); *Robert Grosseteste: New Perspectives on His Thought and Scholarship* (ed. J. J. McEvoy; IP 27; Turnhout: Brepols 1995); M. REEVES, *The Influence of Prophecy in the Later Middle Ages. A Study in Joachimism* (1969; new ed.; University of Notre Dame Press 1993); M. A. and R. H. ROUSE, *Preachers, Florilegia, and Sermons. Studies on the Manipulus Florum of Thomas of Ireland* (Toronto: PIMS 1979); *Le scuole degli ordini mendicanti (Secoli XIII–XIV)* (Convegni di Todi 17; Todi: Presso l'Accademia Tudertina 1978); B. SMALLEY, "The Biblical Scholar", *Robert Grosseteste, Scholar and Bishop* (Oxford: Clarendon Press 1956) 70–97; D. C. WEST, *Joachim of Fiore in Christian Thought. Essays on the Influence of the Calabrian Prophet* (New York, NY: B. Franklin 1974).

The importance of the new emphasis on preaching in Church and schools for the exegetical endeavor can hardly be overrated, just as the vivid interest in the literal sense was simply a given at the turn of the century. A hypothesis of D. L. D'AVRAY suggests that "a major function of thirteenth century exegesis was the inculcation of what one might call an ideology of preaching".[52] Of course, the practice of *lectio divina* as the time-honored combination of biblical interpretation and spiritual life continued unbroken in the monasteries, and its earlier fruits, the monastic commentaries, remained standard sources for the new generation of teachers and commentators. Ralph of Flaix' commentary on Leviticus provided the core of the commentation on this book in the schools, just as did Bede on Tobit or Bernard of Clairvaux on the Song of Songs.[53] Monastic writers defended their approach as superior. There was open polemic, not only against dialectic as a method but against the entire educational enterprise of the schools as such. Peter of Celle (died 1183) expressed these apprehensions with clarity: "Oh happy school where Christ himself teaches our hearts through his words, where we assimilate the secret of eternal beatitude without study and *lectio* ..."[54] This is not the voice of a nostalgic conservatism but the programmatic counterposition of a fundamental critique of the rising secular culture of the day. In her book, BERYL SMALLEY spoke of "the spiritual exposition in decline"; the biblical *lectio*, she suggested, was relegated to the role of providing the milk of the intellectual enterprise, while disputation and systematic theology were now considered to be the solid food.[55] In the preface to the third edition of her book (p. xiii), she retracted this assessment, calling this section the "faultiest part" of her treatment and

[52] *The Preaching of the Friars: Sermons Diffused from Paris Before 1300* (Oxford: Clarendon 1985) 187.

[53] On Ralph see B. SMALLEY, "Ralph of Flaix on Leviticus", *RThAM* 35 (1968) 35–82; on the interpretation of Tobit: J. GAMBERONI, *Die Auslegung des Buches Tobias in der griechisch-lateinischen Kirche der Antike und der Christenheit des Westens bis um 1600* (SANT 21; München: Kösel Verlag 1969).

[54] Peter of Celle, *Epistula* 73 (PL 202, 520).

[55] Smalley, Study (1983) 281–92.

admitting that she had underrated the degree of respect which the hermeneutical theory of the fourfold sense continued to enjoy throughout the period. The famous four-line ditty, popularized by the prefaces to Nicholas of Lyra's literal Postill in the fourteenth century, was borrowed from a Dominican textbook of the late thirteenth century which taught the basics of theological methodology to novices: "*Littera gesta docet,/ quid credas allegoria,/ moralis quid agas,/ quo tendas anagogia*".[56] SMALLEY herself had stressed the great interest in *moralitates*, moral applications drawn from biblical teaching, in the early decades of the century. The moral sense or tropology was one of the three spiritual senses, but more importantly, it was the sense indispensable for preaching. Indeed, preaching as the task and goal of exegesis in the schools provides the bridge for understanding the three new factors which must enter any consideration of biblical interpretation in the thirteenth century: The rise of the mendicant orders; the consolidation of the university curriculum; and the effects of the reception of Aristotle.

4.1. Biblical Interpretation in the Mendicant Orders

The first two mendicant orders, Franciscans and Dominicans, arose in the context of the great lay movements of the eleventh and twelfth centuries such as Waldenses and *Humiliati*, who were calling for the restoration of an apostolic life and of the Church's reformist reaction. Biblical teaching was at the heart of the movements. It stood behind their outspoken anti-clericalism as well as their call to voluntary poverty and missionary preaching in following the example of the apostles. Like Bishop Diego of Osma, his mentor, Dominic realized that an adequate response would have to embrace both the biblical basis and the apostolic lifestyle in equal sincerity. His vision of an order whose task it would be to reunite straying sheep with the fold of the Church catholic combined both mendicancy and biblical study as ascetic disciplines in preparation for effective preaching. The fundamental importance of this combination of *studium* and *praedicatio* is clearly visible in the first constitution of his community (1216)[57], a community which Pope Honorius already called an *ordo praedicatorum*. The directions issued by the general chapters since 1220 continue to drive home this point. The brothers were free to read and write in their cells even at night by candlelight in pursuit of their studies.[58] The sole object of these studies was the sacred page. The first chapter of 1220 mandated that the brothers should not study "the books of the pagans and philosophers ... but only the books of theology".[59] A later ordinance lists the basic texts: Peter

[56] The source is the *Rotulus pugillaris* of Augustinus of Dacia; see A. WALZ, "Augustini de Dacia OP 'Rotulus Pugillaris'", *Angelicum* 6 (1929) 256.

[57] A. DUVAL, "L'étude dans la législation religieuse de Saint Dominique", *Mélanges offerts à M.-D. Chenu* (BiblThom 37; Paris: Vrin 1967) 221–47.

[58] A. H. THOMAS, *De Oudste Constituties van de Dominicanen: Voorgeschiedenis, Tekst, Bronnen, Ontstaan en Ontwikkeling (1215–37)* (BRHE 42; Louvain: Bureau de la RHE 1965) 362: 13–18.

[59] Thomas, De Oudste Constituties (1965) 361: 7–11 and note. The injunction was still repeated in 1243 and 1246; see Berg, Armut und Wissenschaft (1977) 61.

Comestor's *Historia scholastica*, Peter Lombard's Sentences, and the Glossed Bible.[60] SMALLEY has called the intellectual life in the Dominican schools a "modernized version of the *lectio divina*", and the parallels to the Victorine mentality are indeed unmistakable.[61] For Dominic, the connection of the order's *studia* with the existing urban schools was vital. As early as 1217 he sent friars to Paris and Bologna, not only in order to study under secular masters, but also to establish communities and recruit academics as members. The premises of St. Jacques in Paris, where they were housed since August, 1218, served as living quarters for a quickly growing Dominican community and soon as the premier *studium generale* of the order as well. Here the required lectors for the provincial and local *studia* were trained in a school with a curricular structure of its own, yet fully integrated into the university both through its students and some of its teachers.[62] The Dominicans acquired their first magisterial chair in the university during the strike of 1229/31 in which they did not participate, the second through the conversion of a secular master who had lectured for them at St. Jacques. In Paris, the history of these two chairs alone makes it clear that tensions were inevitable. On the whole, however, the relationship between mendicant and university education in the thirteenth, fourteenth and fifteenth centuries was nothing short of a symbiosis in which both sides contributed and received. Academically speaking, Paris was as important for the friars as the friars were for Paris.[63] It must not be forgotten that during their first century both institutions, university and mendicant orders, had the strong support of the papacy in the interest of Church reform, a support aimed at the defense of a universal catholic orthodoxy in an age of unprecedented intellectual ferment in the West. Under the protection and encouragement of the popes, the flowering of biblical studies at the universities in the thirteenth century is unthinkable without the mendicants. For one hundred and fifty years after 1220, the production of scholarly biblical commentaries was solidly in their hands, as BERYL SMALLEY has observed.

Different from Dominic, Francis of Assisi was the more immediate heir of the lay movements of the preceding two centuries. His interest in the Bible was nourished by his personal experience, charism, and existential response to the example of Jesus and the apostles, not by study and intellectual curiosity. There is ample evidence that his message of penance, discipleship, and holy simplicity had little room for academic pursuits, book learning, and intellectual sophistication. Yet in practice, Francis accepted everyone into his brotherhood, including academics. He showed a high respect for the clergy and allowed Anthony of Padua, his "bishop", to instruct the brothers in "sacred theology" as long as this study did not "extinguish the Spirit of prayer and de-

---

[60] Thomas, De Oudste Constituties (1965) 361: 12–16.

[61] Smalley, Study (1983) 268.

[62] Berg, Armut und Wissenschaft (1977) 38–40.

[63] d'Avray, Preaching (1985) 136; J. VERGER, "Studia et universités", *Le scuole degli ordini mendicanti (Secoli XIII–XIV)* (Convegni di Todi 17; Todi: Presso l'Accademia Tudertina) 173–203. A list of the succession of mendicant masters from 1229 to 1264 is printed in J. A. WEISHEIPL, "The Life and Works of St. Albert the Great" (below, n. 173) 24.

votion".[64] After his death, the new leadership rapidly clericalized the order. In his *Expositio* of Francis' Rule, Hugh of Dignes suggested in 1242 already that Francis himself endorsed the study of theology among the brothers as necessary preparation for their preaching mission.[65] Under Haymo of Faversham (1240–43), a former Paris master, the order organized its course of study parallel to that of the Dominicans. While in the early days Franciscans, not unlike the Dominicans but far more slowly and reluctantly, were at the receiving end of the educational enterprise in the schools, school theology itself now began to be shaped by them. For the decades between 1230 and 1250, we speak of an "older Franciscan school" as a distinct form of thirteenth century theology.

True to its own charismatic beginnings, however, the order also continued to nourish non-conformist thought and exegesis. In the late part of the century, this "spiritualist" wing defended with equal fervor Francis' strict ethical literalism concerning Christ's and the Apostles' absolute poverty and the contemporary application of the apocalyptic teachings of Abbot Joachim of Fiore (ca. 1135–1202).[66] As a monastic exegete and visionary, Joachim was critical of school theology and its representatives.[67] His three main works, the "Psaltery of Ten Strings", the "Concordia of Old and New Testament", and the "Exposition of the Apocalypse" are not biblical commentaries, but meditations on the spiritual sense of biblical materials fed by the vision of a comprehensive divine plan for all of history which, as he himself says, he received by revelation.[68] According to Abbot Joachim, this plan was most completely spelled out in the New Testament Book of Revelation, but it could also be traced in the *concordantiae*, the typological correspondences between stories and persons of the Old Testament in their literal, historical meaning and those of the New Testament narrative. As prophecy, however, the Apocalypse presented the key not only to the "concordances" of salvation history in the Bible, but also to their continuance in the history of the Church past, present, and future.[69] Following the Augustinian tradition, Joachim developed an elaborate theory of the progress of salvation history which allowed him, e.g., to see the seven-day creation of Genesis reflected in seven stages of Old Testament history.[70] His contemporaries regarded him as a prophet, and the application of his model of three world ages to history's future course bears out this assessment as being his own. The model is trinitarian. It speaks of an age of the Father, an age of the Son, and an age of the Spirit, dominated by (married) laity, (unmarried) priests, and (spiritual) monks respectively. Since the abbot considered the age

---

[64] See the letter to Anthony of 1223/24 in: *Francis and Clare: The Complete Works* (CWS; ed. R. J. Armstrong / I. Brady; New York: Paulist Press 1982) 79.

[65] Berg, Armut (1977) 73 and 176 (notes). See D. Flood, *Hugh of Digne's Rule Commentary* (SpicBon 14; Grottaferrata 1979).

[66] On Joachim and Joachimism, see Reeves, The Influence of Prophecy (1993). See also E. R. Daniel, "Introduction", *Abbot Joachim of Fiore: Liber de Concordia Novi ac Veteris Testamenti* (1983) xi–xxv.

[67] *Tractatus super Quatuor Evangelia di Gioacchino da Fiore* (ed. E. Buonaiuti; FSI Scrittori sec. XII, 67; Rome 1930; repr. Torino: Bottega d'Erasmo 1960) 294: 25–26.

[68] *Expositio in Apocalypsim* (Venice 1527; repr. Frankfurt: Minerva 1964) 39 rb.

[69] Ibid., 89 rab (on Rev 3:11); *Liber de Concordia* (ed. Daniel, 1983) 84.

[70] *Liber de Concordia* (ed. Daniel, 1983) 153 f.

of the Spirit to be close at hand but still in the future, his biblical interpretation had the explosive potential of a reformist apocalypticism which would denounce present ecclesiastical and societal structures in anticipation of a more perfect age. The spiritualist wing of the Franciscan movement proved a fertile ground for the reception of Joachite ideas, even among its academically active supporters.[71]

Peter John Olivi (1247/48–98), one of the most prolific and original exegetes of the late thirteenth century, demonstrates the point. A Paris-trained lector at several *studia* of the Franciscan order, Olivi produced an impressive body of biblical commentary (RBMA 6684–6725).[72] For the Old Testament, the manuscripts preserve commentaries on Genesis, parts of Kings, Job, Ecclesiastes, Canticum, Isaiah, Lamentations, Ezekiel and the Minor Prophets; the explanations of Psalms and Proverbs are incomplete. Only one of these can be consulted in print: the commentary on Lamentations.[73] The recent editor found that Olivi's interpretation was fully in tune with contemporary scholarship. Olivi used the Parisian chapter division, drew heavily on Paschasius Radbertus, and emphasized the literal explanation, even though sections labeled "moral" and "allegorical" were not missing. SMALLEY noted that Olivi quoted Andrew of St. Victor on Kings, Isaiah, Ezekiel, and Ecclesiastes.[74] It is in his references to the historical background of the Book of Lamentations that the Joachite interest in "concordances" appears clearly. According to Olivi, the Fall of Jerusalem in 587 BC corresponds to its Fall in AD 70, but also to the fall of the Christian society at the end of time. Jeremiah and his companions correspond to Christ and his disciples, who in turn reappear in the "evangelical men" of the present, the *ecclesia spiritualis*. The leaders of the people together with the pseudo-prophets correspond to the priests and scribes at Jesus' passion and anticipate the pseudo-monks and hypocritical authorities of the *ecclesia carnalis* which oppose the spiritual men in the last days.[75] The framework of this interpretation is clearly the spiritualist critique of the contemporary Church and society.

The symbiotic relationship between the mendicant orders and the universities took various forms. For the Franciscan involvement in academic studies, the case of Oxford is particularly instructive.[76] Franciscans arrived at Oxford in 1224 and recruited very successfully among young noblemen and students of the arts faculty who then continued to study theology under secular masters at the university. Soon the group moved to a new house of studies but had as yet no lector of its own. In 1228, Robert Grosseteste (ca. 1168–1253), who

[71] Reeves, Influence (1993) 175–228; E. R. DANIEL, "A Re-Examination of the Origins of Franciscan Joachitism", *Spec.* 43 (1968) 671–76.

[72] See FRANZ EHRLE, "Petrus Johannes Olivi, sein Leben und seine Schriften", *ALKMA* 3 (1887) 409–552; here 481–97; on Olivi's life see TRE 25 (1995) 239–42 (WERNER PACKULL), and a number of publications by DAVID BURR, esp. *The Persecution of Peter Olivi* (TAPhS 66:5; Philadelphia: American Philosophical Society 1976).

[73] Bartoli, La caduta di Gerusalemme (1991).

[74] Smalley, Study (1983) 183.

[75] Bartoli, La caduta (1991) xv.

[76] See Berg, Armut (1977) 109 f.

held the equivalent of the chancellorship in the university at that time, began teaching theology at the Franciscan *studium.* There has been considerable scholarly interest in Grosseteste recently.[77] Much admired by English contemporaries such as Roger Bacon, Grosseteste must be regarded as one of the most wide-ranging, original minds of his time. Probably trained in the liberal arts at Hereford, he spent some time in Paris during the interdict of 1208–15 but apparently studied theology "only casually and gradually" later in his life, shortly before his election and during his tenure as bishop of Lincoln in 1235.[78] He obviously was sympathetic to the cause of the mendicants, strongly urging the necessity of Bible study for their apostolic mission. According to SMALLEY, Grosseteste was "old-fashioned" as a biblical interpreter, sharing the convictions of the Victorines and the biblical-moral school. But he incorporated his interest in natural sciences and his philological skills into his exegetical endeavors. As a bishop, he commissioned copies of a Hebrew psalter with a new literal translation written between the lines,[79] but even more importantly, he began to master Greek at that time, a preoccupation which allowed him to draw on the original text of the New Testament as well as the Septuagint and some Greek Fathers for the interpretation of the Old. His Psalms commentary, begun during his years at the Oxford friary in a traditional style, shifted to much fuller notes for Psalms 79–100, utilizing these new tools. The commentary on the Hexaemeron has been edited and translated recently.[80] While presenting a very traditional exposition mixing literal and spiritual interpretations, these worked-up notes of Oxford lectures make use of the Septuagint, supplement the Latin sources by references to Greek Fathers, and draw on Aristotle's *libri naturales* as well as their Arab commentators. This openness for a wide range of sources does not, however, affect Grosseteste's theological convictions; he was not interested in christianizing Aristotle. He acknowledged the irreconcilable difference between a theory of the eternity of matter and the Christian doctrine of a creation *ex nihilo*; on this point, he declared, the philosophers are simply wrong.

Grosseteste's thought about natural science and its relation to biblical teaching is further illumined by an exegetical fragment on Sir 43:1–5 which has been edited under the title, *De operationibus solis.*[81] Its purpose is to show that the

---

[77] See R.W. SOUTHERN, *Robert Grosseteste: The Growth of an English Mind in Medieval Europe* (2nd ed.; Oxford: Oxford UP 1992), and several publications by J.J. MCEVOY, esp. *Robert Grosseteste: New Perspectives on His Thought and Scholarship* (ed. J.J. McEvoy; 1995); also in TRE 14 (1985) 271–74. The basic essay on Grosseteste's biblical writings is Smalley, "The Biblical Scholar", in: *Robert Grosseteste, Scholar and Bishop* (1956) 70–97.

[78] J. GOERING, "When and Where Did Grosseteste Study Theology?", *Robert Grosseteste: New Perspectives* (1995) 17–51.

[79] This so-called "Superscriptio Lincolnensis" is extant in five mss; J.J. MCEVOY, "Editions of Grosseteste Planned and in Progress, and Some Desiderata for the Future", *Robert Grosseteste: New Perspectives* (1995) 395–405; here 400 f. MCEVOY plans to publish an edition which was prepared by RAPHAEL LOEWE.

[80] Dales, Robert Grosseteste: Hexaemeron (1990); Martin, Robert Grosseteste: On the Six Days of Creation (1996).

[81] S.H. THOMSON, "Robert Grosseteste: De operationibus solis", *Medievalia et Humanistica* 11 (1957) 34–43.

literal sense of the passage coincides with scientific knowledge and observation. Scripture already contains all the truth that may be found in nature.[82] Grosseteste's biblical interpretation with its unusual combination of concern for biblical theology and natural science cannot be easily categorized, but it contributed greatly to Oxford's rise and had an enormous impact on the Franciscans there. Thomas of Eccleston, the contemporary chronicler of the Franciscans in England, said of Grosseteste: "Under him, within a very short time, the brothers made incalculable progress both in scholastic discussion and in subtle moralities suitable for preaching".[83]

4.2. The University Curriculum and Its Tools

In Paris, the curriculum for theologians, both mendicants and seculars, was settling into a standard routine which continued to be based on the study of Scripture but also reached out into new subjects.[84] A "scholar" began his studies by listening to lectures on the Bible and the Sentences, disputations, sermons, and solemn university acts. Then, while still following the lectures of the masters, he would take over the surveys as *baccalarius biblicus* or *cursor*, going through the text of the biblical books one at a time, giving literal explanations and noting the important glosses without raising doctrinal issues;[85] there was room for the latter activity during the following two years as *baccalarius sententiarius*. Interpreting the biblical texts more fully was the duty and privilege of the masters who chose one book at a time, often for a period of several years, and alternating between Old and New Testament. They lectured during prime time in the early morning, while the surveys were scheduled in the afternoon. This routine, on the one hand, engendered the large body of thirteenth century commentaries most of which remain unedited; SMALLEY called them "postills".[86] On the other hand, it led to an enormous interest in useful tools for Bible study.

---

[82] See J.J. McEVOY, "The Sun as *res* and *signum*. Grosseteste's Commentary on Ecclesiasticus 43:1–5", *Robert Grosseteste: Exegete and Philosopher* (CS 446; Aldershot: Variorum 1994), I, 44–60.

[83] Quoted by Smalley, The Biblical Scholar (1956) 72.

[84] See Smalley, Study (1983) 216–20; Glorieux, L'enseignement au moyen-âge (1968) 65–186.

[85] The statutes of the theological faculty of Cologne specify: *"Item baccalarei biblici et cursores legendo cursus suos seu Bibliam inter alia ordinate et solide textum exponant et per glosas notabiles declarent, secundum modum cursorie legendi Parisiis observatum"*, see F.J. VON BIANCO, *Die alte Universität Köln* I (Köln 1855), App. V, Tit. 4:38–39. And the Oxford statutes enjoin: *"Ne autem lecture varie confundantur, et ut expedicius in lectura biblie procedatur, statutum est, ut Bibliam biblice seu cursorie legentes questiones non dicant nisi tantummodo literales"*, *Statuta antiqua universitatis Oxoniensis* (ed. S. Gibson; Oxford 1931) no. 50.

[86] Smalley, Study (1983) 270. She argued that the term came into use at that time und remains useful for designating the continuous scholastic commentary in contradistinction to 'glosses'. The derivation of the term is unclear; Smalley cites the traditional etymology, "post illa verba". M.T. GIBSON thinks of the marginal hints in exegetical manuscripts such as N(ota), M(oraliter), Ier(onimus), S(olutio), 'sign-posts' (old French 'postel'), as the possible origin of the name: *The Bible in the Latin West* (The Medieval Book 1; Notre Dame: University of Notre Dame Press 1993) 62. This comes close to F. Pelster's reference to the Italian word 'postilla' meaning 'annotation': "Die Expositio super quatuor evangelia des hl. Thomas von Aquin. Ein Nachtrag und ein Beitrag zur Erklärung des Wortes 'postille'", *Bib.* 5 (1924) 64–72. Pelster lists early occurrences.

John van Engen has criticized Smalley's narrative of the development of biblical interpretation during the twelfth and thirteenth centuries as all too linear, suggesting that there actually were two major cultural shifts during this period: The decades between 1050 and 1200 mark the time when Scripture was transformed into a textbook for instruction and Bible truth was taught as systematic theology; the decades between 1225 and 1275 saw the shift to the application of biblical knowledge to contemporary issues: philosophical, apologetic, moral, pastoral, practical.[87] Richard and Mary Rouse, who have done so much to illumine the history of the instruments of Bible study in the high Middle Ages, have called this period an "age of tools" – tools, they emphasize, not primarily for biblical instruction in the universities, but for the university-trained preachers in the parishes and the mendicant orders.

The *Glossa ordinaria* was the major textbook for the lectures of the biblical bachelors. The Paris statutes of 1366 still insist that, during their first four years, students must bring their own (glossed) Bibles to class, and a list of essential books for a Dominican reference library from the 1260s mentions in the first place *Biblia glosata in toto vel in parte.*[88] The glossed Bible was a standard tool of the preacher as well. The production of Gloss manuscripts seems to have fallen off during the thirteenth century. One reason probably was that similar works became available which, while not intending to replace the *Glosssa ordinaria*, were more directly aimed at the needs of preachers. The most important of these was the Dominican *Postilla in totam Bibliam* which, as recent research has established, was not authored by Hugh of Saint-Cher, but was the result of a genuine team effort at St. Jacques under Hugh's direction.[89] For the literal sense of Old Testament passages the team did draw on Jewish exegesis, often via Andrew of St. Victor but also using other sources, especially Maimonides. It also employed the new chapter numbers and subdivided each chapter into smaller sections designated by the letters A–G. A similar team effort produced the first full verbal concordance to the Latin Bible which was completed at St. Jacques in 1239 at Hugh's initiative and was developed further during the century.[90]

Humbert of Romans' above-mentioned book list names a "plain Bible" as the second required item in a standard Dominican reference library. One-volume portable Bibles begin to appear in the early thirteenth century, and the small pocket Bibles which were produced from ca. 1230 on show signs of their intended use by preachers; many of them include anti-heretical appendices

---

[87] "Studying Scripture in the Early University", *Neue Richtungen* (above, n. 24) 17–38.

[88] *"Primo quod scolares qui noviter incipiunt audire theologiam, primis quatuor annis portant vel portari faciant ad scolas biblici Bibliam, in qua lectiones Biblie diligenter audiant", Chartularium Universitatis Parisiensis* 2 (ed. H. Denifle / A. Châtelain; Paris 1890; repr. Bruxelles: Culture et Civilisation 1964) 1189:698. – The Dominican book list is found in *Humbertus de Romanis: Opera de vita regulari* II (ed. J. J. Berthier; Rome 1888; repr. Milan 1956) 265.

[89] See R. Lerner, "Poverty, Preaching, and Eschatology in the Revelation Commentaries of 'Hugh of St. Cher'", *The Bible in the Medieval World* (above, n. 28) 157–89; here 181–89.

[90] M. A. and R. A. Rouse, "The Verbal Concordance to the Scripture", *Archivum Fratrum Praedicatorum* 44 (1974) 5–30.

and sermon materials.[91] Concern for a reliable text of the Vulgate had been part of the scholarly efforts in the earlier schools. The routine of academic Bible study in the universities demanded even more urgently a standardized text basis. Taking its clue from a passage in Roger Bacon, older Vulgate scholarship assumed that an *exemplar Parisiense*, a normative text, was indeed agreed upon by a commission of Paris masters and officially adopted by the university. The evidence of the surviving manuscripts, however, does not bear out this assumption. It is true that, by the end of the century, one can speak of a fairly uniform type of a "Paris Bible" in use everywhere, but its textual form and its distinctive characteristics such as chapter numbers, a fixed order of biblical books, the presence of a specific series of prologues and of a glossary of Hebrew names occur before 1230 and do not exclude continuing variety.[92] The situation is similar with regard to the so-called *correctoria* of the thirteenth century. We have over thirty manuscripts which offer alternative readings to Vulgate texts, especially in Old Testament books. They were not official lists of mandated corrections and were not meant to lead to an improved standard text but offered choices for preachers and scholars to consider in their interpretation.[93]

Biblical studies did experience an immense evolution during the thirteenth century. By the end of the century, the Vulgate text used by scholars and preachers everywhere showed greater uniformity than ever, even though a multitude of variant readings could be considered. Concordances made the text searchable; glossaries, dictionaries, and collections of *distinctiones* helped to unlock the philological details and the spiritual senses. Obviously, the interpretation of the Old Testament profited by these developments at least as much as that of the New, and the consistent application of scholastic methods of text analysis such as definition, division, raising and solving contradictions, and illustration by examples allowed a much more sophisticated approach to the Bible as a book in the context of an ever widening horizon of intellectual curiosity than was possible in the earlier schools.

4.3. The Impact of the Reception of Aristotle

A major ingredient in this development was the rediscovery of the complete Aristotle.[94] The Stagirite, of course, was not unknown to Christians. But the

[91] LAURA LIGHT, "The New Thirteenth Century Bible and the Challenge of Heresy", *Viator* 18 (1987) 275–88.

[92] L. LIGHT, "Versions et révisions du texte biblique", *Le Moyen-Age et la Bible* (BTT 4; ed. P. Riché/G. Lobrichon; Paris: Beauchesne 1984) 55–93; Bacon's text is quoted here on p. 76, n. 79; eadem: "French Bibles c. 1200–30. A New Look at the Origin of the Paris Bible", *The Early Medieval Bible. Its Production, Decoration, and Use* (ed. R. Gameson; Cambridge: Cambridge UP 1994) 155–76. See also Smalley, Study (1983) 334 f.

[93] Light, Versions (1984) 90. The standard discussions of the *correctoria* include H. DENIFLE, "Die Handschriften der Bibelkorrektorien des 13. Jahrhunderts", *ALKMA* 4 (1888) 263–311 and 471–601; E. MANGENOT, "Correctoires de la Bible", DB 2 (1926) 1022–26.

[94] See F. VAN STEENBERGHEN, *Aristotle in the West: the Origins of Latin Aristotelianism* (Louvain: Nauwelaerts 1955); idem, *The Philosophical Movement in the Thirteenth Century* (Edinburgh: Nel-

triumph of neo-Platonism and its reception into Christian thought in late Antiquity had rendered large parts of his philosophy useless: his pragmatic interpretation of the material world; his cosmology, anthropology, and ethics. What remained of interest was the neutral realm of methodology which Aristotle himself had considered a tool, not a part of philosophy. Aristotle was known as *the* logician in the earlier Middle Ages. Boethius' partial translation of the *Organon* (Categories and Perihermeneias) together with Porphyry's Isagoge and Boethius' own commentaries became the main textbook for the study of *dialectica*, the medieval form of logic, from ca. AD 1000 on. When the full *Organon* became available in Latin during the twelfth century, the Aristotelian *logica antiqua* nourished the rationalism current among theologians such as Abelard and John of Salisbury, but especially among the masters of the new faculty of arts at Paris.

At that time, through newly opened channels of communication with the Greek East and the Arab world, more and more of Aristotle's writings became known, initially through and with their Arab commentators, after 1230 through translations from the Greek originals as well. *De anima* and the Metaphysics were translated by 1140, the cosmological writings (Physics, *De caelo*, On Generation and Corruption, and the *Meteorologica*) by 1190. Robert Grosseteste provided a translation of the Nicomachean Ethics together with excerpts from Greek commentators in 1246/47. By the time of Thomas Aquinas' arrival in Paris, the entire corpus of Aristotelian writings was available for study and use by Western scholars. Availability alone, however, did not guarantee reception. In some cases, it took decades until a particular work was cited in the scholarly debates. Moreover, ecclesiastical authorities and monastic writers continued to harbor deep suspicions, at first of the dialecticians who embraced the *logica antiqua*, but soon of the entire corpus and its author. Absalon of St. Victor, Abbot of Springiersbach in the Rhineland, put it bluntly: "The spirit of Christ does not rule where the spirit of Aristotle dominates".[95] The center of the reception of Aristotle and his Arab commentators was the arts faculty at Paris. In the early decades of the thirteenth century, an enthusiastic generation of young *artistes* introduced ever new Aristotelian writings as texts for their instruction. The ecclesiastical reaction was swift and severe. In 1210, a Paris synod prohibited lecturing on the books of natural philosophy, a prohibition which the statutes of Robert of Courçon repeated in 1215. It proved impossible, however, to stem the tide. During the university strike of 1229/31, the new university of Toulouse tried to attract students with an advertisement that "those who wish to scrutinize the bosom of nature to the inmost can hear here the books of Aristotle which were forbidden at Paris",[96]

son 1955); B. G. Dod, "Aristoteles Latinus", *The Cambridge History of Later Medieval Philosophy: From the Rediscovery of Aristotle to the Disintegration of Scholasticism, 1100–1600* (ed. N. Kretzmann / A. J. P. Kenny / J. Pinborg; New York: Cambridge UP 1982) 45–79; W. Kluxen, "Aristoteles / Aristotelismus, V. 1. Abendländischer Aristotelismus", TRE 3 (1978) 782–89.

[95] *Sermo 4 in Adventu Domini* (PL 211, 37 D).

[96] L. Thorndike, *University Records and Life in the Middle Ages* (Records of Civilization 38; New York: Columbia UP 1944), 34.

and by 1255 the entire Aristotelian corpus was integrated into the liberal arts curriculum at Paris as well.

The reception was slower and much more hesitant among the theologians, many of whom regarded Aristotle's teaching on central philosophical issues as "godless". Four points were especially offensive: the alleged theory of the eternity of matter, and thus of the world, which seemed to contradict the Christian doctrine of creation; the limitation of divine providence to the sublunary sphere; the understanding of the soul as the form of the body which threatened the belief in the immortality of the soul; and the system of a natural ethics which seemed to undermine the values of Christian spirituality. Where theologians used Aristotle, they did so under the Augustinian license of "carrying away the gold of Egypt",[97] that is, of utilizing pagan learning as an aid to interpreting the Bible and explaining the doctrines of the Christian faith. In the first part of the thirteenth century, this use was highly eclectic. Pieces of Aristotelian philosophy were adapted to the attempt of building a rational synthesis of Christian doctrines, and observations of the natural world were integrated into the interpretation of the literal sense of the Bible. Philip the Chancellor seems to have been one of the first to use the Aristotelian *libri naturales* in biblical exegesis during his teaching in Paris (1206–18), despite his negative evaluation of Aristotle as a philosopher. His popular Moralities on the Psalms (RBMA 6952) drew on Aristotle's *De animalibus* for useful sermon illustrations. Roland of Cremona, the first Dominican master in the university of Paris, wrote a commentary on Job (RBMA 7514) in which he rejected Aristotle on the eternity of the world but eloquently defended the usefulness of the *libri naturales.*[98] As so many other theologians, he owed his exposure to Aristotle and the Arabic philosophers to years of teaching in a faculty of arts.

In the course of the century, the gap between theologians and artists widened. The thoroughgoing Aristotelianism of a Siger of Brabant no longer attempted to reconcile the philosopher's teaching with the tenets of the Christian faith. The specter of a "double truth" appeared on the horizon. Theologians everywhere resisted this trend, but there can be little doubt that the reception of Aristotle was altering the general climate of the theological discussion. It led to a rigorous questioning of basic assumptions, wide-spread scepticism toward traditional solutions, and new efforts at a rational defense of the faith. The biblical commentaries reflect the changing climate. Interest in the literal exposition of the text intensified even more with the availability of natural explanations of many details. There were attempts to dismiss challenges to biblical truths, but more frequently the effort was aimed at demonstrating the concordance of biblical text and scientific knowledge, or allowing the latter to enrich the interpretation of a particular passage. Smalley reports an example from the Daniel commentary of John of La Rochelle (RBMA 4896) where the author considers various natural explanations of the report that the three Hebrew youths retained their physical strength despite their prolonged fast

[97] Augustine, *De doctrina Christiana* II. 40–42.
[98] Smalley, Study (1983) 310–11.

(Dan 1:15), describing a complicated interplay of physiological, psychological, medical, and spiritual factors.[99]

Beyond creating a different general climate for theological inquiry, the new science had an enormous impact on the specific methods of biblical interpretation. Aristotelian logic suggested new procedures of subdividing biblical books and chapters. The interpreter could begin by giving a summary of the *argumentum*, following the rules of rhetorical analysis, and he could settle contradictory statements by verbal distinctions. Questions could now be raised in the course of the exposition, and the masters felt free to discuss philosophical issues as part of their commentary. Around the middle of the century, a significant change took place in regard to the structure of the *accessus*, the general introduction to a biblical book.[100] The older form treated authorial intention, subject matter, literary procedure, usefulness, and the specific part of philosophy to which the writing contributed. The new form employed the Aristotelian four causes and discussed material cause (subject matter), efficient cause (author), formal cause (literary style and genre), and final cause (the role of the particular biblical book in leading the reader to salvation).[101] The thematic difference may not seem great, but the outlook on the literary issues posed by each biblical book was changing dramatically. Biblical writings were no longer seen as repositories of divine mysteries only but could also be appreciated as works of an (inspired) human mind to be analyzed like other literature. The focus of interpretation shifted to the human author, and the new definition of the literal sense was "that which the author intended". For the Old Testament, it seems that Guerric of St. Quentin, the successor of Hugh of St. Cher in the second Dominican chair at Paris, was one of the first to use the four causes in his prologues, first in his commentary on Wisdom (RBMA 2672), and even more clearly in the Isaiah commentary of 1230/35 which otherwise followed the Dominican Postill quite closely (RBMA 2675).[102] When speaking of the *causa efficiens* of the book, Guerric distinguished two aspects: Isaiah was the "operative", the Holy Spirit the "moving" cause.

5. Old Testament Interpretation and the New Science: Some Paradigms

General works: M.-D. Chenu, *La théologie comme science au XIIIe siècle* (3rd ed.; BiblThom 33; Paris: Vrin 1957); J. Chydenius, *Medieval Institutions and the Old Testament* (Societas Scientiarum Fennica. Commentationes humanarum litterarum 37:2; Helsinki 1965); G. R. Evans /

[99] Smalley, Study (1983) 314 f.

[100] A. J. Minnis, "Henry of Ghent on the Transmission and Reception of Theology", *Ad Litteram: Authoritative Texts and their Medieval Readers* (ed. M. Jordan / K. Emery; Notre Dame UP 1992) 275–326, here 276. See also Minnis, Medieval Theory of Authorship (1988), and the article by Quain cited in n. 14 above.

[101] A. J. Minnis, "Discussions of 'Authorial Role' and 'Literary Form' in Late-Medieval Scriptural Exegesis", BGDS (T) 99 (1977) 37–65; here 41 f.

[102] Smalley, Study (1983) 296–98; eadem, "A Commentary on Isaiah by Guerric of St. Quentin OP", *Miscellanea Giovanni Mercati* 2: *Letteratura Medioevale* (Studi e Testi 122; Rome: Vatican Library 1946) 383–97.

A. E. McGrath / A. D. Galloway, *The Science of Theology* (The History of Christian Theology 1; Grand Rapids, MI: Eerdmans 1986); G. R. Evans, *Philosophy and Theology in the Middle Ages* (London / New York: Routledge 1993); U. Köpf, *Die Anfänge der theologischen Wissenschaftstheorie im 13. Jahrhundert* (BHTh 49; Tübingen: Mohr-Siebeck 1974); *Medieval Exegesis of Wisdom Literature: Essays by Beryl Smalley* (ed. R. E. Murphy; Atlanta: Scholars Press 1986).

5.1. *Prophecy*

Due to a variety of biblical texts which tell of failed prophecies such as Jonah's announcement of the destruction of Nineveh (Jonah 3) or Isaiah's prediction of King Hezekiah's death (Isa 38:1), the problem of biblical prophets as fallible human authors had been an important subject of reflection for a long time. Discussing Paul's rapture into third heaven (2 Cor 12:2) in Book 12 of *De Genesi ad litteram*, Augustine not only distinguished between corporeal, spiritual, and intellectual visions but also between kinds of prophets: those who only see images, such as Pharaoh (Gen 41:1–8) or King Belshazzar (Dan 3:5–9); those who have the interpretation, such as Joseph; and those who are given both, such as Daniel or John, the author of the Book of Revelation – the true prophets. Prophecy, he held, is an activity of the human mind aided by the help of God. Cassiodorus, who provided the classical definition of biblical prophecy,[103] already observed that a distinction must be made between divine and merely human word in the prophetic message. The gift of prophecy is not always present. The prophet Nathan first encouraged David to pursue the building of the temple but then had to correct himself (2 Sam 7:1–17).[104]

The thirteenth century saw the emergence of a theological treatise *De prophetia* which addressed the many problems surrounding this topic in a systematic fashion. It did not appear as an excursus in biblical commentaries but had its place in the *summae* and the collections of *quaestiones.*[105] Philip the Chancellor's *Summa de bono* contains a full treatise on prophecy which discusses questions such as: which power of the soul is the seat of prophecy? Do angels have the gift? Is a prophecy the cause of its object or vice versa? In what sense was Caiaphas a prophet (John 11:50–51)? Can the gift be lost or forfeited?[106] Qu. 18 of Alexander of Hales' Disputed Questions is entitled, *De prophetia.*[107] The first part discusses prophetic knowledge, the second the prophetic utterance. While the Augustinian heritage determines the substance, the

[103] "Prophecy is the divine breath which proclaims with unshakable truth the outcome of events through the deeds or words of certain persons", Cassiodorus, *Explanation of the Psalms* 1 (tr. P. G. Walsh; ACW 51; New York: Paulist Press 1990) 27–28.

[104] Gregory the Great, *Hom. in Ezek. I. 1* (PL 76, 793 C–94 A).

[105] B. Decker, *Die Entwicklung der Lehre von der prophetischen Offenbarung von Wilhelm von Auxerre bis zu Thomas von Aquin* (Studien zur historischen Theologie NF 7; Breslau: Müller und Seifert 1940); J.-P. Torrell, *Recherches sur la théorie de la prophétie au moyen-âge, XIIe–XIVe siècles* (Dokimion, Nouveaux suppléments à la *FZPhTh* 13; Fribourg: Editions universitaires 1992).

[106] *Philippi Cancellarii Parisiensis Summa de bono* (ed. N. Wicki; Bern: Francke 1985); Decker, Entwicklung (1940) 60–73.

[107] *Magistri Alexandri de Hales Quaestiones disputatae antequam esset frater* 1 (Quaracchi: Collegium S. Bonaventurae 1960) 294–337.

new Aristotelian science clearly informs the argumentation. The objects of prophetic proclamation are future contingents; since the Holy Spirit is the moving cause, their necessity must be affirmed, but it is a necessity *per accidens*, and inferior causes can lead to seemingly false prophecies. Albert the Great, in a *Quaestio Disputata* on prophecy, analyzes Cassiodorus' definition according to Aristotle's four causes: the material cause is the event predicted, the formal its inspiration, the efficient the divine mover, and the final the content of the proclamation. Albert follows Aristotle in allowing for a natural explanation of many dream phenomena, but he distinguishes inspired scriptural prophecy with its christological content from that "of which the philosophers speak".[108] Avicenna, Averroes, and Maimonides had developed theories which emphasized the psychological and moral predisposition of the prophetic personality exemplified by Muhammad and Moses.[109] It was this explanation of prophecy from "natural" causes which Christian theologians rejected. Giles of Rome listed it for Avicenna, Alkindi, and Maimonides among the "errors of the philosophers".[110]

Thomas Aquinas was the theologian who took the dialogue with these partners most seriously trying to integrate the thought of the philosophers into his system rather than refuting them. A full treatise on prophecy appears twice in his works; an earlier form as q. 12 of his *Quaestiones de veritate*,[111] and a mature form in *Summa theologiae* IIaIIae q. 171–74. Like Philip the Chancellor, Aquinas discusses prophecy as a charism, under the rubric of *gratia gratis data.* In the *Summa*, it is the key concept among the charisms of knowledge, and the scriptural prophets, including Moses and David, are the author's main focus. Thomas acknowledges the natural phenomenon of prophecy but, like Albert, he seeks to distinguish it from the activity of the scriptural prophets who were granted a measure of inspiration and revelation. Even in their case, however, the proclamation must be understood as a personal decision involving the prophet's natural faculties as well as human courage and discernment. The acquisition of prophetic knowledge itself is transient and limited in scope. Prophets can err, failing to distinguish properly between God's word and their own thoughts. In q. 173 a. 4, Thomas poses the question whether the biblical prophets were always aware of what they prophesied. His answer speaks of the prophet's mind as a "deficient" instrument of the primary agent, the Holy Spirit. True prophets know what they are saying, but their knowledge goes through the filter of their personality. It is incumbent on the expositor to seek

---

[108] Decker, Entwicklung (1940) 95; J.-P. TORRELL, "La question disputée De Prophetia de Saint Albert le Grand: Edition critique et commentaire", Recherches (1992) 119–204; here 129 and 175; B. ROEST, "Divination, Visions, and Prophecy According to Albert the Great", *Media Latinitas* (FS L. J. Engels; ed. R. I. A. Nip et al.; IP 28; Turnhout: Brepols 1996) 323–28.

[109] Decker, Entwicklung (1940) 15–38.

[110] "Tractatus de erroribus philosophorum Aristotelis, Averrois, Avicennae, Algazelis, Alkindi et Rabbi Moysis", *Siger de Brabant et l'Averroïsme latin au XIIIe siècle.* IIe Partie: Textes inédits (2nd ed.; ed. P. Mandonnet; PhBelg VII; Louvain: Institut Supérieur de Philosophie de l'Université 1908) 13 no. 16; 16 no. 15; 23 no. 8.

[111] *Truth, St. Thomas Aquinas* 2. Questions X–XX (tr. J. V. McGlyn; Chicago: Henry Regnery 1953) 102–79.

out their human intention. Seeking the divine meaning, however, and expounding the spiritual senses remains the higher task.[112]

5.2. Creation

The dialogue with the philosophers informed the discussion of other major topics in Old Testament interpretation as well. One of them was the exegesis of the six-days' creation in Genesis 1. The early Church knew the genre of "hexaëmeral" sermons which discussed the creation account in dialogue with contemporary philosophy.[113] Basil of Caesarea, the author of the most influential *Hexaëmeron* of the Greek tradition, opened his first homily with an apologetic discussion of several philosophical approaches to cosmogony: "Let us allow them to refute each other".[114] In the schools of the twelfth century, we find a renewed interest in looking at Genesis 1 in the light of philosophical theories. Thierry of Chartres who wrote a treatise "On the Works of the Six Days" states his intention of giving the reader a scientific account of creation "according to physics and the letter".[115] The work attempts to harmonize the biblical story with a speculative physics derived from Plato's *Timaeus* and Aristotle of whom Thierry already knew more than the logical writings. For him, Moses was a "scientist" who explained the origin of the world in terms of both, the synergism of the four elements and the necessity of the four causes. Robert Grosseteste wrote his Hexaëmeron as a biblical commentary on Gen 1:1–2:15, beginning with glosses on the standard Jeromian prologues.[116] In the actual commentary, he presents a flood of alternative explanations for all significant details but makes it clear that he regards Genesis 1 as part of any systematic discourse about God and God's relation to the world. This assumption calls for dialogue with the philosophers and their theories of cosmogony. For Grosseteste, however, the matter is settled from the outset. "In the use of this single word, 'in the beginning', Moses overthrows the error of the philosophers who said that the world has no beginning in time".[117] While this kind of polemic remained part of the Genesis commentaries, a more serious debate was conducted in the theological *summae*. There, the irreconcilable difference between

[112] Decker, Entwicklung (1940) 165–208; P. Synave / P. Benoit, *Prophecy and Inspiration: A Commentary on the Summa theologica II–II, questions 171–78* (New York: Desclee Co. 1961).

[113] See J. C. M. Van Winden, "Hexaëmeron", RAC 14 (1988) 1250–69. For this section see also: Centre d'études des religions du livre: *In principio: Interprétations des premiers versets de la Genèse* (Paris: Etudes Augustiniennes 1973); S. Jaki, *Genesis 1 through the Ages* (London: Thomas More Press 1992), chaps. 3 and 4, pp. 70–145.

[114] Saint Basil, *Exegetical Homilies* (tr. Sister A. C. Way; FC 46; Washington, DC: Catholic UP 1963) Hom. 1–9, pp. 3–150; here 3–19. A new critical edition of the Greek text has been prepared by E. Amand de Mendieta and S. Y. Rudberg, *Basilius von Caesarea: Homilien zum Hexaemeron* (GCS NF 2; Berlin: Akademie-Verlag 1997).

[115] The text is printed in B. Hauréau, *Notices et extraits de quelques manuscrits latins de la Bibliothèque Nationale* I (Paris: Klinksieck 1890) 52–70; here 52. For the context, see J. M. Parent, *La doctrine de la création dans l'Ecole de Chartres: Etudes et textes* (PIEMO 8; Paris: Vrin 1938).

[116] See R. C. Dales / S. Gieben, "The Prooemium to Robert Grosseteste's Hexaemeron", *Spec.* 43 (1968) 451–61.

[117] *Hexaemeron* I. 8. 1 (Martin, 56).

a creation out of nothing and the eternity of the world was regularly noted, but the arguments of the *libri naturales* were carefully reported, scrutinized and weighed. In the *Summa Fratris Alexandri*, the first major work of this genre, the treatise on the Hexaëmeron is an integral part of the discussion of God and creation, and the new science plays a significant role in it; it not only suggests the organization of the argument but helps with the details. It is Aristotle who explains the shape of heaven and the firmament. The traditional distinction between the *opus divisionis* (day 1–3) and the *opus ornatus* (day 4–6) is interpreted in terms of potentiality and form, and the questions raised are largely over issues of natural philosophy.[118] Albert the Great went even farther in trying to accommodate the cosmogonic theories of Aristotle and his commentators to the teaching of Genesis 1. He freely drew on the complete Aristotle, having commented on many of his writings himself. The Hexaëmeron is treated in twenty-four *quaestiones* of his *Summa Theologiae*.[119] Aristotle's *De coelo et mundo* provides the substance of the definition of heaven and earth in the first question already, and the *Meteorologica*, the Physics, and *De Animalibus* are used in the responses. On major issues such as the creation of light, Albert reports on different opinions among patristic authors as well as the philosophers. His own position stays well within the Christian tradition, but he often finds new formulations suggested by the philosophical discussion because "the saints say nothing certain in common" on so many points.[120]

The seriousness of the dialogue reached a new height with Thomas Aquinas. Posing the question, "whether the world is eternal", in his Sentences Commentary, Thomas adduced fourteen arguments for and nine against.[121] He argued that neither side can prove its position; any answer is at best probable. In the *Summa Theologiae*, he is less equivocal; the question, "whether it is an article of faith that the world has a beginning", is answered in the affirmative because Genesis 1 and the first article of the Nicene Creed say so.[122] In the short treatise "On the Eternity of the World", however, Thomas changed the question: Is it a contradiction to say that the world in all its substance was created by God and, at the same time, that its duration does not have a beginning?[123] The answer here was No, and with this solution, Thomas gave the other side the maximum of what could be conceded: Neither the eternity of the world nor its

---

[118] Part I, Book II, Inquis. 3, Tract. 2: "De rerum corporalium distinctione et ornatu seu de opere sex dierum"; *Alexandri de Hales Summa theologica* 2 (Quaracchi: Collegium S. Bonaventurae 1928) 319–66. Alexander of Hales is not the only author of this work; it seems to be a compilation from the circle of his friends and colleagues.

[119] Pars II, tract. XI, quaest. 43–67; *Alberti Magni Opera Omnia* 32 (ed. S. C. A. Borgnet; Paris: L. Vivès 1895) 507–626.

[120] Quaest. 52 sol.; *Opera Omnia* 32 (ed. Borgnet) 551.

[121] II Sent. dist. 1 q. 1 a. 5; *S. Thomae Aquinatis Opera Omnia* 1. *In Quattuor Libros Sententiarum* (ed. R. Busa; Indicis Thomistici Supplementum; Stuttgart: Frommann-Holzboog 1980) 125.

[122] *Summa Theologiae* I a quaest. 46 art. 2.

[123] *In hoc ergo tota consistit quaestio, utrum esse creatum a Deo secundum totam substantiam, et non habere durationis principium, repugnent ad invicem, an non*; Opusculum XXIII; *Thomae Aquinatis ... Opera Omnia* 27 (ed. S. E. Fretté; Paris: L. Vivès 1875) 450–53; here 451 a. A useful collection in English is the volume, *St. Thomas Aquinas, Siger of Brabant, St. Bonaventure On the Eternity of the World* (ed. C. Vollert et al.; MPTT 16; Milwaukee: Marquette UP 1964).

non-eternity can be proved by reason. Faith alone must decide. Thomas' treatise on the Hexaëmeron in Quest. 65–74 of the First Part of the *Summa Theologiae* makes the same point: Everything that is has been created by God instantaneously and *ex nihilo* – Christian faith holds this as a matter of revealed truth. But Genesis 1 is not a scientific account; it is retrospective prophecy, highly metaphorical, and in need of the kind of rational explication which the writings of the philosophers provide.

5.3. The Old Law

Thomas conceded far less in the debate over another issue of great importance for the dialogue with Jewish scholars: the observance of the Old Testament law. His mature reflections on the "Old Law" form part of the comprehensive treatise *De lege* in the *Summa Theologiae*, IaIIae qq. 90–108.[124] Discussing natural and human law, Thomas draws heavily on Aristotle, including the ethical writings. When he comes to the Old Law, however, quotations from Aristotle are almost totally absent. The Old Law is divided into three categories: moral, ceremonial, and judicial precepts. Moral law provides the bridge to the earlier discussion. It is exemplified by the Ten Commandments and coextensive with the substance of the natural law. The center of the section is the treatment of the precepts of the ceremonial law of which the judicial law is a subcategory. Like many of his contemporaries, Thomas showed great interest in, and considerable sympathy for, the observance of the Mosaic law which was taken so seriously in the life of ancient Israel and of contemporary Jews. The Old Testament law, Thomas held, is good in all its parts, given by God to the people of Israel in an act of gratuitous election as a help for the righteous and a warning for the wayward and weak. Though imperfect compared to the New Law that was to come, the Old Law was more perfect than the natural law – perfectly suited for its time, salutary, and binding in its function of regulating worship of God and service to neighbor in Israelite society.

It is all the more surprising that Thomas showed himself unyielding at two points. First, he insisted that the Old Law never justified; it promoted justice, but it did not have the power of cleansing from sin.[125] This position forced him into some awkward reasoning when it came to explaining how Old Testament saints were saved when faith in Christ was required. Second, he declared that keeping the ceremonial law after it was abolished was a mortal sin.[126] Modern Jewish scholars still are puzzled by this latter position; it seems to them illogical and unwarranted.[127] Why this severity and inflexibility? For

[124] A concise analysis of qq. 98–105 is found in JOHN Y. B. HOOD, *Aquinas and the Jews* (Philadelphia: University of Pennsylvania Press 1995) 38–61. See also ULRICH KÜHN: *Via Caritatis: Theologie des Gesetzes bei Thomas von Aquin* (KiKonf 9; Göttingen: Vandenhoeck & Ruprecht 1965) 163–91.

[125] *Summa theologiae* Q. 103 a. 2 corp.; cf. Q. 100 a. 12 corp.

[126] *Summa theologiae* Q. 103 a. 4.

[127] See M. WYSCHOGROD, "A Jewish Reading of St. Thomas Aquinas on the Old Law", *Understanding Scripture: Explorations of Jewish and Christian Traditions of Interpretation* (ed. C. Thoma /

Thomas, it was dictated by the normative evidence of the New Testament, especially the Epistles of the Apostle Paul. Verses from Romans, Galatians, and Hebrews appear at crucial points of his argument in all its parts. In Thomas' eyes, Paul was the first systematic theologian, and the system he taught can be read from the very sequence of his letters: After Romans, which establishes justification by faith in Christ, 1 Corinthians treats of the sacraments of the New Law, 2 Corinthians of its ministers; "there should necessarily follow the epistle to the Galatians, treating of the termination of the sacraments of the Old Testament".[128] Aquinas' stance is his honest synthesis of two unreconciled strands in Paul's own thinking: the positive evaluation of the Jewish law and its rejection in the situation of the Christian mission to the Gentile world.[129]

While they are hardly mentioned in the section on the Old Law, the new sciences provided the methodological framework for the application of the biblical texts to the issue at hand. Laws, Aristotle said, are given for an end. This principle encouraged Aquinas to inquire into the causes of specific laws. The longest articles are reserved for the causes of ceremonial precepts in the Old Testament (qq. 102 and 105), and the most engaging discussions take place in the responses to the specific objections raised. Following his reading of Paul, Thomas distinguished two basic causes: the ordering of the worship of God in Israel, and the foreshadowing of this worship's fulfillment in the coming of Christ. He called these causes "literal" and "figurative", leaving no doubt that, with the entire Christian tradition, he regarded the second as the more important one; for Christians, the ceremonies of the Mosaic law have their value as prefigurations: "omnia in figuram contingebant illis" (1 Cor 10:11). In an age of renewed appreciation for literal sense and rational argument, however, the investigation of the "literal" causes proved to be far more interesting. Origen had denied a literal sense to many precepts of the Tora. Ralph of Flaix, on the other hand, whose twelfth century commentary on Leviticus was the standard tool for the interpretation of this book in the thirteenth century,[130] inquired with utmost care into possible rational explanations of the text, always asking whether a precept "will stand according to the letter", even though his goal was to prove the need for allegorical interpretation because in his opinion most of the precepts in their literal sense were irrational or impractical.

M. Wyschogrod; New York: Paulist Press 1987) 125–37; and the cautious conclusions of E. A. Synan, "Some Medieval Perceptions of the Controversy on Jewish Law", ibid., 102–24.

[128] Ad Gal. c. 1 lect. 1 "Epistola ad Galatas", *Thomae Aquinatis ... Opera Omnia* 21 (ed. S. E. Fretté; Paris: L. Vivès 1876) 174 b–75 a. English translation: *Commentary on Saint Paul's Epistle to the Galatians* (tr. F. R. Larcher; Aquinas Scripture Series 1; Albany: Magi Books 1966) p. 3. On Paul as teacher of systematic theology, see O. H. Pesch, "Paul as Professor of Theology: The Image of the Apostle in St. Thomas' Theology", *The Thomist* 38 (1974) 584–605.

[129] See the article by Synan cited above, n. 127. Synan also discusses Robert Grosseteste who sympathized with the position of the observant Jewish Christians in Antioch (Gal 2:11–21) but concluded, similar to Thomas, that the Pauline argument made the continuing observance impossible, even for Jewish Christians. On Grosseteste's argument, see also Smalley, The Biblical Scholar, Robert Grosseteste (1956; above, n. 77) 81 f.

[130] Smalley, Ralph of Flaix (see above, n. 53); see also her article "An Early Twelfth Century Commentator on the Literal Sense of Leviticus", *RThAM* 35 (1969) 78–99.

The difficulty of establishing the precise meaning of many *mitzvot* was, of course, an even greater problem for Jews who were convinced of the permanent validity of their laws. Maimonides wrote his *Guide of the Perplexed* for contemporaries baffled by the apparent pointlessness of many of their religious precepts. His solution was not spiritualization but rationalization. Moses was not only the ideal prophet; he was also the wisest lawgiver. Whatever the details of his legislation (they do reflect the circumstances of an ancient culture), his precepts had two aims: to promote ethical values such as justice, kindness, mercy, and pity among a simple people, and to teach the worship of the true God against the temptation of idolatry. Both aims are prominent also in Thomas Aquinas' argumentation. His quest for literal causes, not just the literal sense, of the ceremonial precepts of the Old Law profited greatly by Maimonides' rational explanations. "Rabbi Moses" is repeatedly quoted, especially on the issue of sacrifices which he had declared to be legislated for the express purpose of discouraging idolatry.[131] SMALLEY has suggested that, in utilizing Maimonides, Thomas was following the lead of William of Auvergne through the intermediary of John of La Rochelle's *Tractatus de praeceptis et legibus* which he knew as part of the *Summa fratris Alexandri.*[132] William was one of the first to use the newly available Latin translation of the "Guide" which appeared soon after 1220. He was impressed and found the argument quite convincing that seemingly irrational precepts had just and reasonable causes – so much so, that he enlarged the scope of the inquiry and added reasons of his own.[133] SMALLEY showed how William was led by his defense of the law's literal sense to a fundamental critique of the spiritual senses in biblical interpretation which was unusual at the time: Allegory and tropology, he held, can become imposition instead of exposition when the literal explanation is slighted. This observation in turn led her to surmise that Thomas' hermeneutical theory, often praised as a breakthrough for the literal sense, was in reality a defense of the spiritual senses in reaction to William's attack. In her eyes, William of Auvergne was the true innovator, not Thomas Aquinas.

5.4. *The Books of Solomon*

To her many insights concerning the impact of the new science SMALLEY added an observation about changing preferences among biblical books. The Psalms and the Pauline Epistles were favorites of earlier monastic interpreters, joined in the twelfth century by Genesis and the Gospels. In an age of world chroni-

---

[131] A famous example is Exod 23:19: "You shall not boil a kid in the milk of its dam". In Q. 102 a. 6 ad 4, Thomas cites concern over cruelty, the reason suggested by Maimonides, and adds one of his own: "the reason could be that the gentiles, in their idolatrous feasts, used to cook the kid's flesh in this way". See Smalley, Study (1983) 303–06, where the history of the exegesis of this verse is sketched.

[132] See her seminal article: "William of Auvergne, John of La Rochelle, and St. Thomas Aquinas on the Old Law", in eadem, Studies in Medieval Thought and Learning (1981) 121–81. In the Preface to the third edition of her *Study of the Bible* (1983) xv–xvi, she underscores once more the importance of her discovery.

[133] William of Auvergne (1981) 135 f.

cles the interest in the historical books of the Old Testament burgeoned, and the curriculum of the schools encouraged the coverage of ever more diverse elements of the biblical tradition in the exegetical lectures of the masters. In the thirteenth century, SMALLEY noted, an important shift occurred. The masters paid increased attention to the Wisdom literature of the Old Testament – Job, Proverbs, Qoheleth / Ecclesiastes, Canticum / Song of Songs and Sirach. Commentaries on some of these books multiplied, and a number of exegetes left interpretations of nothing but one or more of the sapiential books.[134] One group among them enjoyed particular favor: the "three books of Solomon", Proverbs, Ecclesiastes, and the Song of Songs. It was assumed that King Solomon "the Wise" wrote them in order to teach central aspects of the spiritual life. The Dominican Postill gives the traditional definitions of Solomon's intention: "In the first (Proverbia), he educates beginners; in the second (Qoheleth), he admonishes the advanced; in the third (Canticum), he addresses the perfect … In the first, he teaches to live in the world, in the second to despise the world, in the third to love God and seek delight in him only".[135] This coherent approach goes back via Jerome to Origen who also drew a parallel to the system of sciences: Proverbs teaches ethics or moral philosophy, Qoheleth physics or natural philosophy, and Canticum "visionary" or "inspective" philosophy.[136]

We discussed earlier the intense interest in Song of Songs among monastic exegetes of the twelfth and thirteenth century. There was interest in Ecclesiastes as well. Gregory the Great had introduced the idea that the entire book was a dialogue: the "Preacher" reports the voices of many different people, answering their doubts and questions in one final verse: "The end of the matter. All have been heard. Fear God and keep his commandments" (12:13).[137] In the twelfth century, the literal sense of Ecclesiastes was emphasized. Hugh of St. Victor denied the need to explore a spiritual sense; the author, he suggested, wants to move his readers' hearts to detachment from the things of this world "by the clear truth of reasons and plain argument".[138] Andrew of St. Victor contributed greatly to the understanding of individual "words and phrases".[139] A real shift in the exegetical treatment of the "Books of Solomon", however, occurred with the reception of the *libri naturales* into the arts curri-

---

[134] See Smalley, Study (1983) 361, and *Medieval Exegesis of Wisdom Literature: Essays by Beryl Smalley* (ed. R. E. Murphy; Atlanta: Scholars Press 1986). R. BERNDT, "Skizze zur Auslegungsgeschichte der Bücher Prouerbia und Ecclesiastes in der abendländischen Kirche", *SacEr* 34 (1994) 5–34, lists the extant commentaries on Proverbs and Ecclesiastes.

[135] Smalley, Medieval Exegesis (1986) 42.

[136] Berndt, Skizze (1994) 10–13. For Jerome's adaptation, see PL 23, 1012 f. S. HOLM-NIELSEN, "The Book of Ecclesiastes and the Interpretation of it in Jewish and Christian Theology", ASTI 10 (1976) 38–96, discusses Jerome and possible Jewish parallels but fails to take into account the Origenistic background.

[137] Gregory the Great, *Dial.* IV.4 (PL 77, 324 A). The text is quoted as the second protheme to the Book of Qoheleth in the Glossa ordinaria (RBMA 11803:2).

[138] *Homiliae in Ecclesiasten*, Prol. (PL 175, 115 AB). Hugh's commentary covers only Qoh 1:1–4:8; it became nevertheless a classic quickly.

[139] *Andreas de S. Victore, Expositiones historicae in Libros Salomonis* (ed. R. Berndt; CCCM 53B; Turnhout: Brepols 1991).

culum in the first decades of the thirteenth century which stirred theologians and exegetes to a new interest in the scientific aspects of biblical teaching. The interpretation of Ecclesiastes, which was concerned with the "nature of the things of this world", was bound to reflect this trend. William of Auvergne left commentaries on all three books, Proverbs, Ecclesiastes, and the Song of Songs. In his exegesis of Ecclesiastes he did draw on some Aristotelian texts but still insisted that the "Preacher" did not teach natural philosophy; he rather demonstrated its vanity. This was not the last word, however. The Dominican Postill already quoted a wide array of *libri naturales*, and Bonaventure's full commentary used the entire Aristotelian corpus freely.[140] The development may be illustrated by considering Qoh 1:7 which speaks of the recycling of the earth's water supply: "All the rivers run into the sea, yet the sea does not overflow: unto the place from whence the rivers come, they return, to flow again."[141] Hugh of St. Victor treated the verse as scientific information, drawing a parallel to the circulation of the body's blood supply. William of Auvergne quoted Aristotle's *Meteorologica*, noting with satisfaction that the verse "confirms Aristotle's opinion". He was cited by the Dominican Postill which added a verse from the poet Lucan. Against the objection that ocean water is salty but river water sweet Bonaventure pitted Aristotle's remark that all water is sweet by nature as the experiment of filtering sea water proves. It was only when William of Moerbeke's new translation of the *Meteorologica* became available in the 1260s that the matter was clarified. Siger of Brabant pointed out that the real Aristotle did not support, but clearly contradicted the recycling theory of Qoh 1:7.

The new interest in the sapiential literature is easy to understand. Its content was closer than that of other biblical books to the secular sciences being explored at that time. The questions which the literal sense of the Solomonic books raised often paralleled the philosophical material taught in the arts faculties. Yet, theologians tried to discuss these questions in the framework of their own "science". The interpretation of Ecclesiastes demonstrates the point. The interpreters drew on the new resources eagerly, but they were more interested in harmonizing the biblical teaching on the nature of things with the new sciences rather than allowing contradictions to stand. Thus, the thirteenth century interpretation of Ecclesiastes did not discard the older exegetical tradition. It enriched it by making room for the discussion of a wider range of issues.

6. The Great Masters: Albert, Thomas, Bonaventure

It is generally recognized today that the contribution of the three great scholastic theologians of the thirteenth century to Christian thought and culture was not only important for the fields of philosophy and systematic theology,

---

140 *Opera Omnia* VI (1893) 3–99. See below, pp. 551–52.

141 Smalley used this verse as one of her test cases in comparing various commentaries on Qoheleth. See *Medieval Interpretations*, pp. 14, 26–28, 44, 70, 84, 109.

but that they were significant biblical interpreters as well. All three were friars – Albert and Thomas Dominicans, Bonaventure a Franciscan. We have noted the central place occupied by biblical studies in the academic formation of the mendicants throughout the century. All three studied at Paris during their formative years and taught there in the context of their order's *studium* as well as at the university. For the Dominicans during the first three decades of their existence, Paris functioned as the *studium generale* where the lectors for all other *studia* received their final education. The Dominican presence had its center at the convent of Saint-Jacques which was not only a residence facility for masters and students, but a place of intensive and stimulating life together, both intellectually and spiritually. Recent studies have established the probability that much of the scholarly work originating at Saint-Jacques during the thirteenth century was the result of team work rather than the achievement of individuals. This applies to the production of the *Postilla in totam Bibliam* and the great Biblical Concordance which were assembled as a cooperative venture under the supervision of Hugh of St. Cher as well as to the widely used *Correctorium Bibliae* and the monumental *Speculum Maius* which goes under the name of Vincent of Beauvais.[142]

6.1. Albert the Great

Sources: RBMA 2 (1950) 972–1004; Schneyer 1 (1969) 92–114; *Beati Alberti Magni ... Opera Omnia, ex editione Lugdunensi [1651] religiose castigata* 1–38 (ed. A. Borgnet; Paris: Vivès 1890–99); *Sancti Doctoris Ecclesiae Alberti Magni ... Opera Omnia* (Cologne Edition) 1–15 (ed. B. Geyer / W. Kübel; Münster: Aschendorff 1951–93); M. Weiss (ed.), *B. Alberti Magni ... Commentarii in Iob ... primum ex V codicibus manuscriptis editi* (Freiburg i. B. 1904).

Bibliographies: F. J. Catania, "A Bibliography of St. Albert the Great", *MSM* 37 (1959/60) 11–28; cf. 38 (1960/61) 61–64; W. Fauser, *Die Werke des Albertus Magnus in ihrer handschriftlichen Überlieferung*, Teil I. *Die echten Werke* (Münster i. W.: Aschendorff 1982); M. H. Laurent / Y. Congar, "Essai de bibliographie albertienne", *RThom* 36 (1931) 422–68; J. Schöpfer, "Bibliographie der Albertliteratur von 1960 bis 1980", *Albertus Magnus, doctor universalis, 1280–1980* (ed. G. Meyer / A. Zimmermann; WSAMA. P 6; Mainz: Matthias-Grünewald-Verlag 1980) 495–508.

General works: *Albertus Magnus and the Sciences. Commemorative Essays* (ed. J. A. Weisheipl; STPIMS 49; Toronto: PIMS 1980) 13–51; *Albertus Magnus, sein Leben und seine Bedeutung* (ed. M. Entrich; Graz: Styria Verlag 1982); *Studia Albertina* (FS für Bernhard Geyer; ed. H. Ostlender; BGPhMA, Suppl. 4; Münster i. W.: Aschendorff 1952); S. Tugwell, "The Life and Works of Albert", *Albert and Thomas: Selected Writings* (CWS; New York, NY: Paulist Press 1988) 3–38, 96–116; J. M. Vosté, *S. Albertus Magnus Sacrae Paginae Magister*, II. *In Vetus Testamentum* (Rome: Collegio Angelico 1933).

With all his personal stature as a scholar and writer, Friar Albertus de Alemania, or "Albert of Lauingen" as he called himself, is an eloquent witness to this Dominican team spirit.[143] Albert's writings contain frequent references to his

[142] See above, p. 512 f. The Correctorium of Saint-Jacques is represented by Denifle's group A and B. For Vincent of Beauvais, see the contributions in *Lector et Compilator: Vincent de Beauvais, frère prêcheur, un intellectuel et son milieu au XIIIe siècle* (ed. S. Lusignan and M. Paulmier-Foucart; coll. M. Chr. Duchenne; Rencontres à Royaumont 9; Nancy: ARTEM CNRS 1997).

[143] On Albert's life, see J. A. Weisheipl, "The Life and Works of St. Albert the Great", *Albertus Magnus and the Sciences* (ed. J. A. Weisheipl; 1980) 13–51; Tugwell, The Life and Works of Albert, *Albert and Thomas, Selected Writings* (1988) 3–38, 96–116. The list of his works for the critical Co-

"colleagues" (*socii*) who provided him with requests for textbooks and assistance in their production. Doubts about the authenticity of his eucharistic writings and parts of his *Summa* may reflect the massive contribution to these works of Albert's *socius*, Gottfried of Duisburg.[144] In the conclusion of his Commentary on Aristotle's *Politics*, Albert defended himself vigorously against the criticism of lazy, grouchy traditionalists who would poison the atmosphere of common endeavor and would not allow their brothers "to seek the truth in sweet collegiality".[145]

Albert spent only a few years in Paris. Born toward the end of the twelfth century, he was recruited for the Dominican order by Jordan of Saxony, Dominic's successor, while he studied the liberal arts at Padua in the 1220s. Jordan sent him to the priory at Cologne for further study. Soon Albert served as lector in several German priories including Strassburg from where he was sent to Paris as *sententiarius* in the early 1240s. He received his license in 1245 and lectured for three years as regent master, succeeding Guerric of Saint-Quentin in the second Dominican chair at the university. Thomas Aquinas who arrived in Paris during this time heard him there and followed him to Cologne in 1248 where Albert was sent to organize a new regional *studium generale* in accordance with the decision of the General Chapter that same year. Cologne remained his favorite city. He finally settled there in 1269/70 after an immensely active life in the service of his order, the papacy, and the Church in Germany including a two year term as bishop of Ratisbon in 1260–62. It was at the *studium* in Cologne that he taught his last courses before old age forced him to quit, and he died at the Dominican cloister on November 15, 1280, having survived Thomas Aquinas and Bonaventure by almost six years.

Contemporaries already called Albert "the Great". He was a devout churchman, a conscientious administrator, a skilled diplomat, and a blunt, forthright pastor. His true passion was the education of his younger confreres and his own scholarly pursuits on their behalf. Characteristic of Albert was his indomitable curiosity. A keen observer of nature, he was interested in all kinds of phenomena from animal behavior to astronomical irregularities, always trying to find an explanation. His constant travels, on foot according to the requirements of his order, afforded opportunities to observe, collect, inquire, and note down material for his wide-ranging investigations. He was convinced that "the whole world is *theologia* for human beings because the heavens proclaim the glory of God and the firmament announces the works of his hands".[146] It cannot come as a surprise that Albert was vitally interested in the writings of Aristotle, especially the treatises on natural philosophy. His first acquaintance with them dated to his student days in Italy and his years in Paris where the *libri naturales* were already being read and taught. In the course of his long life,

logne Edition has been drawn up by W. Fauser, *Die Werke des Albertus Magnus* (1982). The older Paris edition is A. Borgnet, *Sancti Alberti Magni Opera Omnia*, 38 vols. (1890–99).

[144] P. Simon, "Albert der Grosse", TRE 2 (1978) 177–84; here 181.

[145] Y. Congar, "In dulcedine societatis quaerere veritatem", *Albertus Magnus, Doctor Universalis 1280–1980* (ed. G. Meyer / A. Zimmermann; 1980) 47–57; here 57.

[146] *Opera Omnia* (Cologne Edition) 21/1 (ed. B. Schmidt; Münster: Aschendorff 1987) 412:35–37.

Albert wrote commentaries on all of Aristotle's books of which he knew, just as he commented on the entire Pseudo-Dionysian corpus in his younger years. Through his enthusiasm and the example of his untiring scholarship, he probably did more than anyone else to assure the full Aristotle a permanent place in the studies prescribed in his order and beyond. When Pope Alexander IV consulted him in 1255 about a response to the new curriculum of the arts faculty at Paris which was squarely based on the books of Aristotle, Albert apparently advised against a condemnation. He was of the opinion that the philosophers must be debated on their own ground.[147]

While Albert assiduously promoted the study of Aristotle, he rarely taught him; his commentaries did not grow out of lectures but were composed independently as aids to the studies of his confreres. The biblical commentaries reflect a different situation. Lecturing on the Bible was the primary duty of a Dominican lector, and Albert performed this task through many years. The claim that he expounded the entire Bible is probably exaggerated. Attested and at least partially extant are commentaries on the four Gospels and on a number of Old Testament books: Isaiah, Jeremiah with Lamentations and Baruch, Ezekiel, Daniel, the Twelve Minor Prophets, and Job (RBMA 972, 974–94).[148] Commentaries under Albert's name on the Song of Songs, the Psalms, and Prov 31:10–31 (*De muliere forti*) are generally considered inauthentic.[149] It seems clear today that the authentic scriptural commentaries must all be dated in the final years of Albert's active life, i.e., the decade from ca. 1264 to 1274. They were revisions and expansions of lectures given earlier or at that time. Albert, it seems, returned to the biblical materials deliberately after he had completed his other interpretations and treatises. Somewhat surprisingly, their influence was not significant, judging from the manuscript evidence.[150] A. Fries has established the probable sequence: First came the Gospel commentaries, then Isaiah, Jeremiah, Lamentations, Baruch, Ezekiel, Daniel, and finally Job.[151] All of these demonstrate how deeply Albert was steeped in the language of the Bible on which he could draw freely and which he quoted incessantly.

Albert's hermeneutics were fully in tune with contemporary scholarship. One of his major methodological procedures was the logical division of textual units, including numbered chapters; his exegetical exploration focused deliber-

---

[147] Tugwell, Life and Works (1988) 14.

[148] Fauser, Die Werke (1982) 211–37 [no. 42–54]. The Isaiah Commentary and the fragments on Jeremiah and Ezekiel have been published in vol. 19 of the Cologne Edition (ed. F. Siepmann / H. Ostlender; 1952). The commentary on Job was published by M. Weiss, *B. Alberti Magni … Commentarii in Iob* (1904). Lamentations, Baruch, Daniel, and the Minor Prophets are only accessible in the Paris edition of the *Opera Omnia*, vols. 18–19.

[149] B. Geyer, "Albertus Magnus: Umstrittene Bibelkommentare unter dem Namen des Albertus Magnus", *Scholastik* 33 (1958) 558–66, arguing on Psalms against A. Fries, "Zum Daniel- und Psalmenkommentar Alberts des Großen", *RThAM* 19 (1952) 337–42.

[150] O. Grönemann, "Das Werk Alberts des Grossen und die Kölner Ausgabe der Opera Omnia", *RThAM* 59 (1992) 125–54, here 145; B. Geyer, "Die handschriftliche Verbreitung der Werke Alberts des Grossen als Maßstab seines Einflusses", *Studia Mediaevalia in honorem R. I. Martin O. P.* (Brugge 1948) 25.

[151] A. Fries, "Die Entstehungszeit der Bibelkommentare Alberts des Grossen", *Albertus Magnus, Doctor Universalis* (1980) 119–39.

ately on the literal sense.[152] This did not mean, however, that he rejected the traditional fourfold sense. The beginning of his *Summa Theologiae* of 1268 contains a chapter, "On the four modes of interpreting Scripture", which raises thirteen problems relating to issues under debate at that time. The first two concern the statement that metaphors such as Jotham's parable in Judg 9:7–15 say "false" things, and the third questions the literal truth of Isa 37:29: "I will put a ring in your nose and a bit between your lips". Albert determines that "what counts in the literal sense is not what is being said but the cause of what is being said", which means that "the intention of the speaker expressed in the letter is the literal sense".[153] Other problems focus on the relation of the literal to the spiritual senses and of the spiritual senses to one another.

Despite his concentration on the literal interpretation, however, Albert shows little interest in Jewish exegesis. The main reason is his notion of Old and New Testament together as a strictly Christian book given to the Church as God's gracious gift. The New Testament alone is the key to the Old. Albert developed his view of the biblical canon already in his academic *principium* of 1245 which is preserved.[154] In the Jewish tradition, the tripartite canon of Tora, Nebiim and Ketubim reflected grades of authority. The Tora ranked first, with Prophets and Writings far behind. Wisdom, Sirach, Judith, Tobit, and 1–2 Maccabees had no canonical standing; they were only "to be read". Albert did not distinguish grades of authority.[155] A particular book may have been regarded as apocryphal at one time. But when the Church accepted it into its canon, it was discerned as being inspired. God is at the origin of the canon, and the Holy Spirit is the primary author of all its parts. Human authors are involved, but their role can only be of secondary importance. Since the Western Church had accepted the six deutero-canonical books excluded from the Jewish canon, the medieval consensus reckoned with forty-five rather than thirty-nine books of he Old Testament. The twelfth century saw serious challenges to this number. Like most scholars, however, Albert reaffirmed the full canon of forty-five books against Jerome's criticism. He also included the Septuagintal additions to Esther and Daniel (Bel, Susanna, Prayer of Azariah), Baruch and Epistle of Jeremiah as parts of Jeremiah, and the Prayer of Manasseh, and quoted all of them as "scripture".

Albert shared the high regard of his contemporaries for the biblical Wisdom literature, especially the book of Jesus Sirach. Together with Wisdom, he counted Sirach among the group of five Solomonic books without attributing them to Solomon directly. The Church added them because they were "taken

---

[152] A. VACCARI, "S. Alberto Magno e l'esegesi medievale", *Bib.* 13 (1932) 257–72, 369–84; J. M. VOSTÉ, *S. Albertus Magnus Sacrae Paginae Magister*, II. *In Vetus Testamentum* (Rome: Collegio Angelico 1933); Smalley, Study (1983) 299.

[153] Tract. I qu. 5 cap. 4; *Opera Omnia* (Cologne Edition), vol. 34/1 (ed. D. Siedler 1978) 20–22; here 21:62–65.

[154] It was discovered and published by A. FRIES, "Principium Biblicum Alberti Magni", *Studia Albertina* (1952) 128–47. See also A. FRIES, "Eine Vorlesung Alberts des Großen über den biblischen Kanon", *Divus Thomas* 28 (Fribourg 1950) 195–213.

[155] The following section summarizes material presented by A. FRIES, "Der Schriftkanon bei Albert dem Großen", *Divus Thomas* 28 (Fribourg 1950) 195–213.

from the words of Solomon".[156] The opening biblical mottoes for several of his writings are borrowed from Jesus Sirach: Sir 24:5–6 opens the Prologue to his Sentences commentary; Sir 48:22–27 the Prologue to Isaiah; Sir 24:44 to Daniel; Sir 49:12 to the Minor Prophets.[157] The motto for the *principium*, Albert's opening lecture as a master at Paris, comes from Sirach as well: Sir 24:33 – a verse of which he was particularly fond:[158] "Moses commanded a law in the precepts of righteousness, and an inheritance to the house of Jacob, and the promises to Israel". Taking his cue from these words, the new master unfolded with great dialectical skill the content of the entire Bible as the system of a revelatory canon.[159] The leading concept is the understanding of Scripture as law. The three parts of the verse translate easily into the description of a tripartite law in Scripture: 1) God's law as given (the Pentateuch, the five Solomonic and the five prophetic books, and the Psalter); 2) God's law as received (the historical books of the Old Testament); 3) God's law as fulfilled (the New Testament).

The first division is the most interesting one: God's law in its substance. Albert subdivides it into three blocks of material. According to its plain content, this law is contained in the five books of Moses. According to its relation to moral goodness, it is spelled out in three of the Solomonic books: Proverbs teaches the right middle, Ecclesiastes the right means, the Song of Songs the right goal; Wisdom and Sirach encourage the necessary disposition for the good life. Finally, according to its relation to reward and punishment, it is found in two forms of prophecy: first, in the future prophecies of the five prophetic books: Isaiah, Jeremiah, Ezekiel, Daniel, and the Minor Prophets. Daniel with its additions is a special case. The author does not announce punishment to the people but only comfort; liberation from the exile, from the devil, and from the Antichrist of the endtime; he is a historian and also a prophet of Christ's work. Second, in the form of the petition for the fulfillment of the prophetic predictions characteristic of the Psalms. With Augustine and Cassiodorus, Albert regarded the Psalter strictly as a prophetic book and David as "the greatest among prophets and kings" who constantly prayed for deliverance as well as for the coming of Christ and his Church.

The second division of the canon describes God's law as received. The historical books of the Old Testament describe Israel's response to God's commands as paradigmatic of human history wavering between faithfulness and unfaithfulness yet always returning to the promise of restoration. Albert again distinguishes three groups: Joshua, 1–3 Kingdoms (to 2 Kgs 10) tell of Israel's standing firm; in the second group, Judges and Ruth speak of Israel's wavering but regaining its stand, 3 Kingdoms 11 through 4 Kingdoms of wavering and sinking ever more deeply into apostasy while Chronicles describes a mixture of both. The books of the third group describe Israel's return after its defection:

---

156 "Principium" (ed. A. Fries 1952) 133: 27 f.

157 Langton used the same verse as the motto for his commentary on the Minor Prophets. For a comparison with Albert, see Smalley, Study (1983) 299.

158 Fries, Eine Vorlesung (1950) 201 n. 3.

159 See the tabulation of the system in Fries, Eine Vorlesung (1950) 198.

1–2 Maccabees report the final victory; Ezra and Nehemiah the retaking of the heritage. Finally, the story of Israel's corporate response is paralleled by four books demonstrating God's support of exemplary individuals so that they could stand firm against internal doubts (Judit and Esther) and external temptations (Job and Tobit).

The elaborate analytical scheme is completely artificial. Nevertheless, the ingenuity with which the pieces are fitted together into a coherent whole is amazing. Albert's skill in the art of the logical division of textual units is in evidence in all his commentaries. It is to his credit that his analysis always takes the plain text seriously. In the commentary on Lamentations, he first reviews earlier spiritual interpretations which relate the book's four parts to the four elements or the four seasons. His own classification is different. According to him, the prophet successively laments the loss of temporal goods which support life (*bonum utile*) and of psychological goods which enhance life (*bonum gloriosum*), then his present misery, and finally the contrast of present misery to happy past – the worst form of unhappiness according to Boethius.[160] While firmly anchored in the investigation of the letter, proceeding by a discussion of the meaning of words, context, logical sequence, and questions about *realia*, Albert's explanation always includes doctrine, moral exhortation, and edifying application for which he adduces a host of authorities. His commentaries teem with quotations of Bible verses; these often seem to be inserted for no other reason than external similitude or verbal assonance. A wide range of Christian authors is cited, including medieval theologians (Haymo of Auxerre, Anselm of Canterbury, Bernard of Clairvaux, Gilbert of Poitiers) and Eastern Fathers, especially John Chrysostom and John of Damascus. The modern editor of Albert's Isaiah Commentary states that Albert had Jerome's commentary before him as one of his main sources.[161] A. Vosté, however, has convincingly argued that all excerpts from Jerome here and elsewhere were taken from the *Glossa ordinaria*, even when Albert attributes them to "Hieronymus in originali".[162]

That the *Glossa ordinaria* and the Dominican *Postilla* were Albert's primary source for the Christian exegetical tradition seems clear. They are supplemented, however, by frequent references to less obvious materials, including non-Christian literature. Albert's commentary on the prophet's vision in Isaiah 6 cites Gregory of Nyssa, Pseudo-Dionysius, John of Damascus, and Bernard, but also Democritus, works of Aristotle, and Ptolemaeus' Almagest.[163] Commenting on the Seraphim's "Holy, Holy, Holy" (v. 3), he quotes and rejects the interpretation of "the Jews" that "Holy" is repeated three times because of the princes, the priests, and the people, but also a Christian explanation according to which it represents the three persons of the trinity while "Lord God" denotes the one essence of the deity.[164] Again, in v. 4, he argues against

[160] *Opera Omnia* (Paris Edition), 18 (ed. Borgnet) 250.
[161] *Opera Omnia* (Cologne Edition) 19 (ed. F. Siepmann; Münster i. W. 1952) IX a.
[162] Vosté, *S. Albertus Magnus* II (1933) 8–11.
[163] *Opera Omnia* (Cologne Edition) 19 (ed. Siepmann) 85–100.
[164] Ibid. 92:20–31.

an unnamed *Hebraeus* who, "following the fables of the Talmud", interprets the smoke as a result of the sacrifice which the angels have lit on the golden altar before God.[165] While not truly innovative and pace-setting, Albert the Great's interpretation of the Old Testament exhibits the best of late thirteenth century scholarship in the rich context of traditional biblical studies, and it adds to it the personal imprint of the "Doctor Universalis" for whom the Bible teaches all truth.

6.2. Thomas Aquinas

Sources: RBMA 5 (1974) 8019–43 (OT); Schneyer 5 (1974) 579–627; *S. Thomae Aquinatis Opera Omnia ut sunt in Indice Thomistico, additis 61 scriptis ex aliis medii aevi auctoribus* 1–7 (Index Thomisticus, Suppl.; ed. R. Busa; Stuttgart: Frommann and Holzboog 1980); *Sancti Thomae Aquinatis Opera Omnia, jussu impensaque Leonis XIII, P. M., edita* (Rome: Commissio Leonina; 1882 ff [Leonine Edition]), *Sancti Thomae Aquinatis Opera Omnia* 1–25 (Parma: Fiaccadori 1852–73; New York, NY: Musurgia 1948–50 [Parma Edition]); *Doctoris Angelici Divi Thomae Aquinatis Opera Omnia* 1–34 (ed. P. Fretté / E. Maré; Paris: Louis Vivès 1871–82 [Paris Edition]), M. D. Jaffe / A. Damico, *Thomas Aquinas. The Literal Exposition on Job: A Scriptural Commentary Concerning Providence* (CRSS 7; Atlanta: Scholars Press 1989); *St. Thomas Aquinas, Summa Theologiae. Latin Text and English Translation* 1–61 (ed. T. Gilby et al.; New York: McGraw Hill 1964–81 [Blackfriars Edition]); *Saint Thomas Aquinas: On the Truth of the Catholic Faith* (4 vols. in 5; tr. by A. Pegis et al.; Garden City, NY: Doubleday Image Books 1955–57; repr. as *Saint Thomas Aquinas: The Summa contra Gentiles*; Notre Dame, IN: Notre Dame UP 1975); *Thomas d'Aquin. Commentaire sur les psaumes* (tr. and ed. J.-E. Stroobant de Saint-Eloy; Paris: Cerf 1996).

Bibliographies: V. J. Bourke, *Thomistic Bibliography 1920–1940* (MSM, Supplement to vol. 21; St. Louis, MO 1945); *Bulletin Thomiste* 1–12 (1924–65); continued by *Rassegna di Letteratura Tomistica* 1–29 (Roma: Pontificia Università S. Tommaso d'Aquino 1966–93); H. F. Dondaine / H. V. Shooner, *Codices manuscripti operum Thomae de Aquino* 1–2 (Rome: Commissio Leonina 1967–73), 3 (Paris / Montreal: J. Vrin / Presses de l'université 1985); P. Mandonnet / J. Destrez, *Bibliographie Thomiste* (2nd ed.; Bibliothèque Thomiste 1; Paris: Vrin 1960); T. L. Miethe / V. J. Bourke, *Thomistic Bibliography 1940–1978* (Westport, CT: Greenwood Press 1980).

Concordance: R. Busa, *Index Thomisticus* 1–49 (Stuttgart: Frommann and Holzboog 1974–80).

General works: M. Aillet, *Lire la Bible avec S. Thomas: le passage de la littera à la res dans la Somme théologique* (SF NS 80; Fribourg: Editions Universitaires 1993); M. Arias Reyero, *Thomas von Aquin als Exeget.* Die Prinzipien seiner Schriftdeutung und seine Lehre von den Schriftsinnen (SlgHor 3; Einsiedeln: Johannes-Verlag 1971); E. Benz, "Joachim-Studien, III. Thomas von Aquin und Joachim von Fiore. Die katholische Antwort auf die spiritualistische Kirchen- und Geschichtsauffassung", *ZKG* 53 (1934) 52-116; M. D. Chenu, *Toward Understanding St. Thomas* (Chicago: Henry Regnery 1964); M. Corbin, *Le chemin de la théologie chez Thomas d'Aquin* (BArPh NS 16; Paris: Beauchesne 1974); P. Glorieux, "Essai sur les commentaires scripturaires de saint Thomas et leur chronologie", *RThAM* 17 (1950) 237–66; P. Mandonnet, "Chronologie des écrits scripturaires de saint Thomas d'Aquin", *RThom* 33 (1928) and 34 (1929); P. E. Persson, *Sacra Doctrina: Reason and Revelation in Aquinas* (Philadelphia: Fortress Press 1970); C. Spicq, "Saint Thomas d'Aquin exégète", DThC 15 (1946) 694–738; M. Seckler, *Das Heil in der Geschichte. Geschichtstheologisches Denken bei Thomas von Aquin* (München: Kösel-Verlag 1964); Th. Torrance, "Scientific Hermeneutics According to St. Thomas Aquinas", *JTS* 13 (1962) 259–89; J.-P. Torrell, *Initiation à saint Thomas d'Aquin, sa personne et son œuvre* (Paris: Cerf / Fribourg: Editions universitaires 1993); English tr.: *Saint Thomas Aquinas* 1. *The Person and His Work* (Washington DC: The Catholic University of America Press 1996–); J.-P. Torrell / D. Bouthilier, "Quand S. Thomas méditait sur Isaïe", *RThom* 98 (1990) 5–47; J. A. Weisheipl, *Friar Thomas d'Aquino, His Life, Thought, and Work* (rev. ed.; Washington DC: Catholic UP 1983).

[165] Ibid. 93:6–8.

The Dominican contribution to theology in the schools of the thirteenth century reached its climax in the work of Thomas Aquinas. Despite considerable controversy surrounding specific tenets of his teaching at the time of his death among university masters and even within his order, the Dominican leadership realized the great value of his achievements and tried to capitalize on the wide respect which their confrere enjoyed. In 1309, the General Chapter admonished all lectors in the order to follow the teaching of Thomas, and several works of his were soon used as tools of instruction in the Dominican houses of study.[166] But Thomas did not introduce any revolutionary breakthrough. His *Summa theologiae* did not replace Peter Lombard's *Sentences* as the standard textbook in theology until the late fifteenth century; his commentary on the *Sentences*, together with his commentation of Boethius, Pseudo-Dionysius, and especially Aristotle, was far more influential among his contemporaries. Nevertheless, the impact of his keen mind in the defense of the faith was felt in all branches of Christian learning for generations to come. Thomas' apologetic zeal which was part of his Dominican heritage motivated him to clarify traditional concepts and methodologies in such a way that the bridge between theology and the new sciences remained visible and passable. His strength was the synthesis of traditional and innovative thinking, not the replacement of one by the other. This strength certainly characterizes his endeavors in the field of biblical interpretation.

Born ca. 1225/26 as a son of a count of Aquino in central Italy, Thomas joined the Dominican friars against the wishes of his family at the age of sixteen or seventeen while he was a student of the *artes* at the university of Naples.[167] The priory of San Domenico at Naples was his home convent. His superiors sent him to Paris for further study, probably in 1246 when Albert the Great was there. He accompanied Albert to the new *studium generale* at Cologne in 1248 and was sent back to Paris in 1251 in order to prepare for the master's course of study. His graduate years in Paris turned out to be a time of serious crisis for his order's relationship with the university. Nevertheless, with the active support of the new pope, Alexander IV, a friend of the mendicants, Thomas received his license and incepted as master of theology in the spring of 1256. He began his first Paris regency in the fall of that same year in the second Dominican chair, residing at Saint Jacques. In 1259 he relinquished the position, probably to make room for another Dominican graduate. His provincial chapter in Italy named him a preacher general, and it seems that he was also assigned to teach at one or more *studia* of his province, especially at Orvieto where Pope Urban IV and his curia were residing for some time (1262–64). From 1265–67, we find him in Rome where he was asked to reorganize theological and philosophical studies at the priory of Santa Sabina. The project of writing his *Summa theologiae* was part of this attempt at educational re-

[166] Tugwell, Albert and Thomas (1988) 236–43.

[167] For the current discussion on the details of Thomas' life, see especially Weisheipl, Friar Thomas d'Aquino (1984); and Tugwell: "Thomas Aquinas, Introduction", Albert and Thomas (1988) 201–360.

form, conceived and begun at that time.[168] In 1268, he was asked to go to Paris for a second regency during a period of renewed tension over the mendicant presence in the university. After four years he returned to Naples to establish a new regional *studium* at his home convent of San Domenico in 1272. On December 6, 1273, he abruptly ceased all work, reportedly in reaction to a visionary experience during mass, and died three months later, on March 7, 1274, at the Cistercian Abbey of Fossanova near Priverno on his way to the Council of Lyon which Pope Gregory X had asked him to attend.

Albert the Great noticed the extraordinary gifts of his student early on. A *reportatio* of his own lectures on Pseudo-Dionysius, begun in Paris and finished in Cologne, is preserved in Thomas' "illegible" hand. Albert made use of the young scholar's skills in disputations and nominated him for the master's course in Paris. It seems that Thomas shared Albert's respect for Aristotle, but not his enthusiasm. His first acquaintance with the *libri naturales* probably goes back to his days at Naples, an early center of Aristotelian studies. In Paris, he may have listened to lectures on Aristotle's Ethics and the *De Anima* in the arts faculty, and he probably read what was available in Latin translation at that time. Knowledge of Aristotle, however, was for him an aid to theological study, an auxiliary enterprise, not a prerequisite for the knowledge of truth. MARK JORDAN has warned recently against speaking too confidently of Aquinas' "Aristotelianism".[169] Thomas tried honestly to understand Aristotle. His commentaries on many writings of "the philosopher" were close readings of the text, explaining as precisely as possible what was being said but not deducing from it, let alone defending, an Aristotelian system of truth. Thomas regarded Aristotle as an authority, undoubtedly the foremost philosophical authority, but "the philosophers", including Aristotle, were by definition non-Christians in his eyes. They were discussion partners teaching natural truths which reason alone can grasp, but these truths were at best stepping stones on the way to the truth of the Catholic Faith.[170] Already in his *principium* as a master of theology Thomas expressed himself unambiguously about his priorities as a scholar.[171] Taking as his motto Ps 104:13, "Watering the mountains from your higher places", he defined the role of a teacher of theology as that of the mediator of God's revelation. Rain from the sky reaches first the mountains, which signify the teachers in their elevated state, and distributes itself from there in streams and rivers to fertilize the earth. While apologetics for his "order of preachers" are part of this rhetoric, the teachers' central responsibility of interpreting the biblical word through lecturing, disputing, and preaching is spelled out in no uncertain terms.

As a Paris master and a Dominican lector, Thomas was obliged to lecture regularly on individual biblical books after having taught the introductory

---

[168] See L. E. BOYLE, *The Setting of the Summa Theologiae of St. Thomas* (Toronto: PIMS 1982).

[169] M. JORDAN, *The Alleged Aristotelianism of Thomas Aquinas* (Etienne Gilson Series 15; Toronto: PIMS 1992).

[170] *Liber de veritate catholicae fidei contra errores infidelium* is the title of the *Summa contra Gentiles* in a number of manuscripts: Weisheipl, Friar Thomas (1983) 359.

[171] P. MANDONNET, *Opuscula omnia genuina* 4 (Paris: Lethielleux 1927) 481–90; English tr.: Tugwell, Albert and Thomas (1988) 355–65.

courses as a *cursor biblicus* during his years as a graduate student. MANDONNET suggested that, since Thomas held disputations twice weekly during his Paris residencies, his biblical lectures were severely curtailed at those times. At the Dominican *studia* in Italy, disputations were less frequent, and during his last years in Naples Thomas did not dispute at all but lectured five times a week and preached regularly.[172] It seems that Thomas, like most of his colleagues, alternated between explaining Old Testament and New Testament books. The biographical and bibliographical traditions mention lectures on Matthew, John, and the Pauline Epistles from the New Testament; Isaiah, Jeremiah, Lamentations, Psalms, Job and Song of Songs from the Old. With the exception of a commentary on Song of Songs, which has left no trace, the textual tradition bears out these reports.

Aquinas' most extensive Old Testament commentary is the *Expositio in Job ad litteram* (RBMA 8027). The published text, extant in fifty-nine manuscripts, is an *ordinatio*, the carefully edited form of lectures given at Orvieto between 1261 and 1264.[173] BERYL SMALLEY has pointed out that Thomas' interpretation deviates significantly from the tradition which concentrated almost exclusively on the spiritual meaning of the person of Job as a Christ-like model of patience in suffering.[174] The difference lies not only in the concentration on the literal sense of Job; Roland of Cremona's earlier commentary on Job took the literal sense seriously.[175] Rather, Thomas begins with a different understanding of the book's nature and its place in the canon. In the prologue, he lays out the framework in philosophical terms. A major problem in any explanation of nature and morality, he says, is the question of providence versus chance or fate. Doubts about the reality of God and his providence arise from a variety of human experiences. Such doubts, however, are pernicious. Most seriously, lack of faith in God undermines moral responsibility. Therefore, after Tora and Prophets, the biblical *hagiographa*, books which teach wisdom, have made it their primary concern to combat this error. The Book of Job holds first place among them. Its entire intention "turns on showing by plausible arguments that human affairs are ruled by divine providence."[176] The author, whoever he may be, demonstrates his thesis as part of the broader supposition that all natural development is governed in this way; he argues it out specifically in light of the contrary evidence of the suffering of the righteous.

This unified vision of the Book of Job as a coherent argument for God's providence is the key to Aquinas' interpretation. He shares this understanding with Moses Maimonides whose precedent he follows.[177] It allows him to sub-

[172] P. Mandonnet, Chronologie des écrits scripturaires (1929) 53–69; 132–45.

[173] Weisheipl, Friar Thomas (1983) 368. The text is available in the Leonine edition, *Sancti Thomae Aquinatis Opera Omnia*; vol. 26 (1965). An English translation with introduction has been published by A. DAMICO / M. D. YAFFE, Thomas Aquinas, The Literal Exposition on Job (1989).

[174] Smalley, Study (1983) 301 f.

[175] A. DONDAINE, "Un commentaire scripturaire de Roland de Crémone, 'Le Livre de Job'", *AFP* 11 (1941) 109–37; here 124. Cf. also Smalley, Study (1983) 310 f.

[176] Damico / Yaffe, Thomas Aquinas (1989) 68.

[177] Moses Maimonides, The Guide of the Perplexed III. 22–23; see M. D. YAFFE, "Providence in Medieval Aristotelianism: Moses Maimonides and Thomas Aquinas on the Book of Job", *Hebrew Studies* 19–20 (1980/81) 62–74; J. S. LEVINGER, "Maimonides' Exegesis of the Book of Job",

ject the entire text to a rigorous rhetorical analysis. Each speech, each significant clause or phrase is explained as a component of the overall argument the logic of which the exegete tries to reconstruct in minute detail. It also allows him to bypass the historical questions: Was there a historical Job? What time is presupposed? What circumstances? Most importantly, it allows him to disregard the spiritual senses; Gregory the Great, he says, has treated them with sufficient subtlety and clarity already. He boldly proposes "to expound according to the literal sense". Literal sense here does not mean the explanation of words and grammar but the analysis of the logic of an argument and thus is defined as the intention of the author. For Thomas, this was "scientific" exegesis in the strictest Aristotelian sense. Science is *cognitio per causas.* His goal was to uncover the reason for every turn of the phrase in the book.

The interpretation of the literal sense as the intention of an author's rhetoric also dominates Aquinas' commentaries on several prophetic books of the Old Testament: Isaiah, Jeremiah, and Lamentations. The commentary on Isaiah (RBMA 8027) has come down to us in sixteen manuscripts; of one fourth (34:1–50:1), we even have the autograph.[178] The transcription of the whole from Thomas' illegible hand was provided by Jacobinus of Asti at the end of the thirteenth century. Jacobinus gave the work the title, "Sententia et expositio ad litteram super Ysaiam". After a traditional *accessus* (treating author, genre, subject matter, utility) and the exposition of a Jeromian prologue, the interpretation moves by chapters. At the beginning of each unit, Thomas provides a "division" of the argument tracing the exact logical progression of the prophet's supposed intention, and then proceeds verse by verse, stressing definitions and biblical parallels. For Isaiah 1–11, the comments are fairly full. They include some theological excursions and questions in which the lecturer raises a *sed contra* that is resolved by making distinctions. On Isa 6:1 ("I saw the Lord"), it is objected that no one can see God (Exod 33:20; John 1:18); Thomas answers that the truth of the phrase depends on the kind of vision that is described. From Isaiah 12 on, there are only short explanations which look like rapid notes taken down in preparation for lectures. The tradition does not say under what circumstances the lectures were delivered; they have been variously dated. Today the general consensus is that they constitute a survey course of the *cursor biblicus* given at Paris or Cologne in 1252–53.[179] Few sources are quoted. Thomas seems to have used the standard tools on which the *biblicus* was expected to draw: the *Glossa ordinaria* and the Dominican Postill. That he had a wider range of sources at his disposal is clear from the first chapters. In the section on Isaiah 6, e.g., he refers several times to Pseudo-Dionysius, to Gregory the Great, Augustine, and once to Chrysostom. In the margin, Thomas regularly added "collationes" in the manner of biblical

---

Creative Biblical Exegesis: Christian and Jewish Hermeneutics Through the Centuries (ed. B. Uffenheimer / H. Graf Reventlow; JSOT, Suppl. 59; Sheffield: Sheffield Academic Press 1988) 81–88. Albert the Great whose commentary was written after Thomas', makes the same assumption. As for Maimonides see also Chap. 31.3, sect. 5, above (S. Klein-Braslavy).

[178] MS Vat. lat. 9850, fol. 105–14. See the introduction to *Opera Omnia* (Leonine Edition), 28 (1974) 1*–64*, and Weisheipl, Friar Thomas (1983) 479–81.

[179] *Opera Omnia* (Leonine Edition), 28 (1974) 19*–20*; Weisheipl, ibid., 480 f.

distinctiones, catchwords from the text paired with one or more Scripture verses. In Jacobinus' transcription they are introduced by "Nota super illo verbo". They may have been notes for exegetical expansion during the lectures.[180]

The incomplete commentary on Jeremiah (RBMA 8040), which covers Jer 1:1–42:1 and was transcribed by Peter of Andria, exists in five manuscripts.[181] As in the Isaiah commentary, there is a traditional *accessus* and a brief exposition of a prologue of Jerome. Then the text is explained by chapters, each introduced by a general theme ("Here he shows ...") and its subdivisions which analyze the logic of the prophet's intention. In the first chapter, Thomas includes some formal discussion of theological issues, e.g., on the prophet's sanctification in the womb (1:5). Throughout the commentary, he adds cross-references to other passages in Jeremiah and elsewhere. The *Glossa ordinaria* is quoted, but no other sources seem to be identified. As in the Isaiah commentary, "collationes" are regularly added at the end of chapter units, introduced by "Nota quod". Thomas apparently regarded Jeremiah, Lamentations, and Baruch as one work in three parts. On Jer 2:1 he remarks: "Here begins Jeremiah's own message ... It has three parts: In the first, he predicts the future captivity; in the second, he laments it after the fact in Lamentations; in the third, he moves the captives to penitence in the book of Baruch".[182] For the Aquinas commentary on Lamentations (RBMA 8041), only two manuscripts are extant.[183] The prooemium, expanding Ezek 2:9–10 as its motto, notes the challenge of the poetic language and explains "lamentations, song, and woe" (Ezek 2:10) as the threefold sense in which the book is expounded in the Gloss: the historical which refers to the lament over the captivity, the mystical which looks to the Church, and the "typical, tropological, or moral" which concerns the soul. In the commentary, Thomas at first gives for each section all three explanations, historical, allegorical, and moral, followed by the interpretation of the Hebrew title letter. From the sixth section on (Lam 1:6), only the literal interpretation is given because "the expositions of the [Hebrew] letters, the rhetorical placement, and the mystical sense are sufficiently laid out in the Glosses".[184] While many scholars date the commentaries on Jeremiah and Lamentations to Aquinas' years in Italy, all this evidence as well as the similarities to the Isaiah commentary suggest that they rather belong to Thomas' teaching as *cursor biblicus* at the beginning of his career.

A commentary on the first third of the Psalter (Psalms 1–54) which we have as a *reportatio* in five manuscripts may also date from this early period.[185] It is normally assigned to Thomas' final teaching in Naples, the abrupt ending at Ps 54:10 being attributed to the event of December 6, 1273.[186] But the style of

---

[180] See *Opera Omnia* (Leonine Edition), 28, 16f*; P.-M. Gils, "Les 'Collationes' marginales dans l'autographe du commentaire de saint Thomas sur Isaïe", *RSPT* 42 (1958) 254–64.

[181] Weisheipl, Friar Thomas (1983) 370, 481. The text is available in the Paris edition, *Opera Omnia* 19 (1876) 66–198.

[182] *Opera Omnia* (Paris Edition) 19 (1876) 74 b f.

[183] The text is printed ibid. 198–225; Weisheipl, Friar Thomas (1983) 370.

[184] Ibid. 207 a.

[185] Tugwell, Albert and Thomas (1988) 248, 332 f, n. 475.

[186] Weisheipl, Friar Thomas (1983) 302–07, 368 f.

the interpretation has much in common with Isaiah, Jeremiah, and Lamentations. The traditional *accessus* is very conservative, praising the Psalter as the one book which "does not treat a special topic but the general subject matter of all theology" and "contains the whole of Sripture". With the Augustinian tradition, Thomas defends the Davidic authorship and the nature of the Psalms as prophecy which allows him to extend the literal sense, the one which he says he will expound, to Christ and his body, the Church. The commentary often proceeds on two levels, acknowledging both a sense relating to Christ or the Church and to the circumstances of David's story. Biblical parallels are amply adduced, but references to outside sources except the Gloss seem rare, though Aristotle is occasionally quoted. The Psalter was often chosen as the first object of lectures by a *baccalaureus biblicus*.

Compared with Aquinas' major theological works and even his exegetical works on the New Testament, the volume of scholarship on his Old Testament commentaries has been slight. The distribution of manuscripts suggests that they did not have a wide circulation and little impact on the history of interpretation. The exception is the Job commentary which was often copied and encouraged consideration of the literal sense of the book. In the early fourteenth century, Dominic Grima of Toulouse planned a "Lectura super Bibliam", an exegetical collection on the complete Bible, of which he finished at least one volume on the Pentateuch and the historical books.[187] The preface mentions a special feature. After the literal, rhetorical, and spiritual interpretation of each section, there would be "at least two questions" concerning the text which would be solved by references to the works of Aquinas – the systematic works, of course, not the exegetical. Thomas' *Summae*, Treatises, and Disputed Questions are themselves constantly referring to Bible verses as *auctoritates* and need to be taken into account in the consideration of his interpretation of the Old Testament. We have done this when we considered the topics of prophecy, creation, the Old Law, and the Solomonic Books in an earlier section. The speculative works, however, also influenced the theory of biblical interpretation in a significant way. Thomas did not write a special treatise on biblical hermeneutics, but a number of texts have been cited and analyzed in this context time and again.[188]

The earliest one, *Quodlibetum* VII q. 6 a. 14–16, probably dates from the time of Thomas' inception in the spring of 1256.[189] It addresses three issues raised by a senior master and commented upon by the *inceptor*: "Do the same words of Holy Scripture conceal several senses? Should one distinguish four senses of Holy Scripture? Should these senses be distinguished in other writ-

187 See *Histoire littéraire de la France* 36 (Paris: Imprimerie Nationale 1927) 238–60.

188 The most comprehensive study in this area is Arias Reyero, Thomas von Aquin als Exeget (1971). The book features an appendix (263–73) in which the major texts are reprinted from the critical editions. See also Torrance, Scientific Hermeneutics (1962) 259–89. All substantive treatments of *Summa theologiae* I a q. 1 in the vast literature on the nature of theology discuss the subject.

189 Weisheipl, Friar Thomas (1983) 104–07. Art. 14–16 contain the first of two regular disputed questions which are appended to the Quodlibet in many manuscripts without any relation to its topic. Their provenance is not indicated.

ings?" The second, *Super Epistolam ad Galatas Lectura c. IV lectio 7*, belongs to the Italian period; it explains Gal 4:24 and discusses the difference between literal sense and spiritual senses. The third and most important one forms part of the first question of the *Summa theologiae*, Ia q. 1 a. 9–10. Article 9 discusses "whether Holy Scripture should use metaphor"; article 10 "whether in Holy Scripture one word may have several senses". These texts demonstrate once more that Thomas was no innovationist in biblical hermeneutics but brought greater conceptual clarity to the theory. Scholars have sometimes praised him as the creator, or at least the principal advocate, of the literal sense in the thirteenth century.[190] This praise is clearly misplaced. Admittedly, however, the key to Thomas' hermeneutics must be sought in his understanding of the literal sense. In an Aristotelian environment, Thomas embraced fully its new definition as authorial intention. This meant first of all serious systematic attention being given to the human writers as instrumental authors of Scripture. It prompted Thomas to analyze the Book of Job and the prophets in terms of their argument. Secondly, it meant a reconsideration of the Bible's human language in terms of its multivalence as well as its univocity. Augustine had described language as a human convention of signs pointing to things. Hugh of St. Victor had honed this theory, insisting on the univocity of language signs in their primary meaning: one word means first one thing, and one thing only. In the exposition of a text, not only verbal sign (*littera*) and deeper meaning (*sententia*) must be considered, but also the primary meaning of the words (*sensus*) as an intermediate step; the literal sense consists of *littera* and *sensus* together. Thomas stood in this tradition and fitted it into the framework of the new science. "The task of a good interpreter is not to consider the words (*verba*) but the sense (*sensus*)".[191] *Sensus*, however, must include authorial intention in order to be the proper sense of anything spoken or written, according to Aristotle.[192] The literal sense as the full intention of an author does not reside in words but in the mind.

From these premises, Thomas drew several conclusions. (1) The literal sense is the only basis from which an argument over biblical interpretation can proceed. In *Summa theologiae* Ia q. 1 a. 6, he had concluded that sacred doctrine is a science; in a. 8, that as such it is "argumentative", using reason, causality, and rational proof in defense of the faith. This kind of discourse would have no chance if it left the solid ground of established linguistic convention. (2) The literal sense includes metaphor, parable, and intentional figuration. Thomas was quite aware that all theological talk must be metaphorical or symbolical because human reason grasps spiritual truths by the similitude of sensible things only. But even plain human speech reckons with metaphor and parable being part of an author's intention. Here, Thomas went clearly beyond the Au-

---

[190] See Arias Reyero, Thomas von Aquin als Exeget (1971) 146, 153 f.

[191] In Matthaeum C. XXVII c. 1, *Opera Omnia* (Paris Edition) 19 (ed. Fretté) 644 b.

[192] "Whatever sense is drawn from the words of anything written but is not intended by the author, is not a proper sense. This is because through one written phrase an author can understand one thing only, since it does not happen that several things are understood at one and the same time, according to the Philsopher", Quodl. VII q. 6 a. 14 ob. 5; *Opera Omnia* (Paris Edition) 15 (ed. Fretté) 513 a.

gustinian tradition which, without reflecting on authorial intention, declared all figuration in the Bible to be part of the spiritual sense. (3) The literal sense is the only sense which any book other than the Bible can ever have. All language used, all books written by human authors, reflect the authors' intentions, nothing else. Human books do not and cannot have a spiritual sense.[193]

The third point demonstrates most vividly that the literal sense in hermeneutics is not Thomas' main preoccupation. He is not interested in literature but in the Bible. None of his hermeneutical texts has the literal sense as its topic; all of them focus on the fourfold sense of Scripture, clarifications concerning literal sense being incidental to that discussion. The reason is the double authorship of the Bible. The principal author is God, whose intention not only includes the signification of words but also of the things to which they point in the context of his universal *scientia* and the history of salvation which he discloses in the biblical texts. In the Bible, and only in the Bible, the author's intention can and does include both literal sense and spiritual senses.

The concentration on the deeper meaning of Scripture, on the spiritual senses as the final goal based on the literal sense, freed Thomas from any narrow literalism in biblical interpretation. Discussing the failure of Jer 1:2 to mention Jehoahaz and Jehoiachin among the kings of Judah between Josiah and Zedekiah (2 Kgs 23:30–35; 24:6–15), he remarked: "Holy Scripture is not concerned about minor details".[194] And in an extended discussion of various interpretations of Gen 1:2, he concluded: "Every truth that can be adapted to the sacred text without prejudice to the letter, is the sense of Holy Scripture".[195] Here the Origenistic-Augustinian hermeneutical dynamic becomes visible again: Scripture has been given for a purpose; it leads the human soul upward from letter to spirit, from the world of sense experience to the world of saving truth. Aquinas wholeheartedly endorsed this tradition. We mentioned earlier that, after working on William of Auvergne, Beryl Smalley revised her earlier impression of the intention of Thomas' hermeneutical theory. Rather than fighting for the literal sense of Scripture, Thomas came to the defense of the spiritual senses at a time when enthusiasm for the former seemed to sweep some colleagues off their feet. He was "the enlightened conservative on the four senses".[196]

6.3. Bonaventure

Sources: RBMA 2 (1950) 1770–82; Schneyer 1 (1969) 592–657; Schneyer, "Die Universitätspredigten Bonaventuras. Versuch einer Zusammenstellung", FSt 56 (1974) 179–90; *Collationes in Hexaemeron et Bonaventuriana quaedam selecta* (ed. F. Delorme; BSFMA 8; Quaracchi: Collegium S. Bo-

[193] On the reception history of these points, see A. J. Minnis, "Fifteenth Century Versions of Thomistic Literalism: Girolamo Savonarola and Alfonso de Madrigal", in: Lerner, Neue Richtungen (1994) 163–80.

[194] "sacra scriptura non curat minutias", *Opera Omnia* (Paris Edition) 19 (ed. Fretté) 70 a.

[195] *De Potentia* II q. 4 a. 1 Resp., *Opera Omnia* (Paris Edition) 13 (ed. Fretté) 119 a. English: *On the Power of God* (tr. English Dominican Fathers; Westminster, MD: Newman Press 1952) II. 9.

[196] See sect. 5.3. above. The phrase occurs in the Preface to the third edition of Smalley, Study (1983) xvi.

naventurae 1934); *Doctoris Seraphici S. Bonaventurae ... Opera omnia* 1–10 (Ad Claras Aquas: Ex typographia Collegii S. Bonaventurae 1882–1902); B. Distelbrink, *Bonaventurae scripta authentica, dubia vel spuria critice recensita* (Rome: Istituto Storico Cappuccini 1975); *Saint Bonaventure* (tr. and ed. E. Cousins; CWS; New York, NY: Paulist Press 1978); *St. Bonaventure's Collations on the Ten Commandments* (tr. P. J. Spaeth; St. Bonaventure, NY: Franciscan Institute of St. Bonaventure University 1995); *Saint Bonaventure. Les six jours de la Création* (tr. M. Ozilou; Paris: Cerf 1991); *Saint Bonaventure. Les dix commandements* (tr. M. Ozilou; Paris: Cerf 1992); *The Works of Bonaventure*, III. *The Breviloquium* (tr. J. de Vinck; Paterson, NJ: St. Anthony Guild Press 1963).

Bibliography: J. G. Bougerol, *Bibliographia Bonaventuriana (c. 1850–1973)*, *S. Bonaventura 1274–1974*, 5 (Grottaferrata: Collegio San Bonaventura 1974).

Concordance: *Thesaurus Bonaventurianus* (ed. C. Wenin; Louvain: Publications du Cetedoc de l'Université catholique de Louvain 1972–79).

General works: *S. Bonaventura 1274–1974*, 4. *Theologica* (Grottaferrata: Collegio San Bonaventura 1974; cf. n. 197 below); J. G. Bougerol, *Introduction to the Works of Bonaventure* (Paterson, NJ: St. Anthony Guild Press 1964); idem, *Lexique Saint Bonaventure* (Paris: Etudes Franciscains 1969); W. Hellmann, "Scripture: The Dawn of Contemplation in the Collationes in Hexaemeron", *MF* 75 (1975) 563–70; H. Mercker, *Schriftauslegung als Weltauslegung. Untersuchungen zur Stellung der Schrift in der Theologie Bonaventuras* (München: F. Schöningh 1971); J. Ratzinger, *The Theology of History in St. Bonaventure* (Chicago: Franciscan Herald Press 1971); T. Reist, *Saint Bonaventure as a Biblical Commentator: A Translation and Analysis of His Commentary on Luke XVIII, 34–XIX, 42* (Lanham, MD: UP of America 1985); C. Vermeij: "Geschiedenis der exegetische werken van den hl. Bonaventura", CFN 2 (1931) 261-90; T. Zweerman, "Prolegomena zur Lektüre von Texten Bonaventuras über das Buch der Schöpfung", *FS* 71 (1989) 29–41.

If Thomas Aquinas can be called "conservative" in his biblical hermeneutics, this judgment seems to apply even more to his older contemporary, Bonaventure.[197] Born around 1217 at Bagnoregio near Viterbo in central Italy, Johannes Fidanza was enrolled as a student of the *artes* at the university of Paris from 1234–43, probably finishing his course of studies as a master.[198] In 1243, he became a Franciscan, took up residence at the new Parisian Friary between the gates of Saint-Germain and Saint-Michel, and began to study theology. His early schooling at the friary of his home town was probably a factor in this decision as was the recollection of a miraculous healing in his early teens, attributed to Saint Francis whom his mother had invoked during a serious illness. "Bonaventure" was the name he took as a friar. Among his first teachers in theology were Alexander of Hales and John of La Rochelle. From 1248 to 1250, Bonaventure lectured as a biblical bachelor, 1250–52 as *sententiarius.* He incepted as a master of theology between 1253 and 1255 during the height of the crisis over the mendicant chairs in the university and may have replaced William of Melitona in the remaining Franciscan chair,[199] although his accep-

---

197 On his life and work, see Bougerol, Introduction (1964); idem, *Saint Bonaventure* (tr. and ed. E. Cousins; 1978) 16–68. The year 1974 saw the publication of several essay volumes in honor of Bonaventure, most importantly five volumes under the general title, *S. Bonaventura 1274–1974* (Grottaferrata: Collegio San Bonaventura); vol. 1 contains the *Bibliographia Bonaventuriana (c. 1850–1973)* by J. G. Bougerol, vol. 4 the *Theologica.* The standard edition of Bonaventure's works is the Quaracchi edition: *Doctoris Seraphici S. Bonaventurae ... Opera omnia* 1–10 (1882–1902). On authentic and inauthentic works, see B. Distelbrink, *Bonaventurae scripta: authentica, dubia vel spuria critice recensita* (1975).

198 The date of birth used to be given as 1221. Recent scholarship makes a strong case for the earlier date. See J. F. Quinn, "Chronology of St. Bonaventure (1217–57)", *FSt* 32 (1972) 168–86; T. Crowley, "St. Bonaventure Chronology Reappraisal", *FS* 56 (1974) 310–22.

199 Quinn, Chronology (1972) 181–86.

tance by the secular masters was not yet assured. His regency was cut short by his election as Minister General of the Order in February, 1257. Bonaventure stopped teaching but continued to preach and write despite a heavy administrative workload. Almost all of his spiritual treatises were composed during those important years. They included the official Life of Saint Francis (*Vita seu Legenda Maior* and *Minor*), which the General Chapter at Narbonne in 1260 commissioned him to write.

As Minister General, Bonaventure was at the Grand Couvent des Cordeliers in Paris frequently, heavily involved in the second phase of the mendicant controversy at the university, and deeply concerned over what he perceived as a new "paganism", the Latin Averroïsm taught by masters in the arts faculty.[200] The polemic against this philosophical current was the major agenda behind the famous three series of public addresses or "collations" which he delivered at that time and which expressed his mature theological position: "On the Ten Commandments", "On the Seven Gifts of the Holy Spirit", and "On the Hexaëmeron". The titles suggest that they are biblical expositions; in reality they are topical essays under biblical headings.[201] "On the Ten Commandments" is a *reportatio* of Sunday sermons preached at the university during Lent, 1267, which discuss the ethical foundations of the Christian life. "On the Seven Gifts" records nine sermons preached to the clergy of Paris in the spring of the following year, 1268; they interpret the seven gifts of the Spirit (Isa 11:2–3) in terms of the essential elements of Christian spirituality which Bonaventure characterizes as a theology of grace. The third series, "On the Hexaëmeron", consists of twenty-three public lectures delivered to large crowds at the Grand Couvent between April 9 and May 23, 1273.[202] For the last time in his life, Bonaventure displayed here his powerful spiritual rhetoric, using the framework of the seven days of creation to elucidate the 'illuminations' of correlation between God's creative and redemptive action. The series remained incomplete. It ended in the middle of the fourth 'illumination' when the author was raised to the position of cardinal by Pope Gregory X and charged with the preparation of the Second Council of Lyon in 1274 during which he died.

For Bonaventure as a Franciscan, the Bible was the Book of Books, comprising all knowledge necessary for salvation. This conviction did not exclude other knowledge such as that attainable by natural reason, but it set clear prio-

---

[200] See D. L. Douie, "St. Bonaventure's Part in the Conflict Between Seculars and Mendicants at Paris", *S. Bonaventura 1274–1974* 2 (1974) 585–612; eadem, *The Conflict between the Seculars and the Mendicants at the University of Paris in the Thirteenth Century* (Aquinas Papers 23; London: Blackfriars 1954).

[201] The texts may be found in *Opera Omnia* V, 329–532. An English translation is available for the first series only: *St. Bonaventure's Collations on the Ten Commandments* (1995). For a recent translation of the Hexaëmeron into French, see: *Saint Bonaventure. Les six jours de la Création* (1991).

[202] The text is extant in two independent *reportationes* one of which the Quaracchi editors considered to be an official version and printed in *Opera Omnia* V, 329–449. More recently, both have been judged to be private transcriptions, of which the one published in 1934 by Delorme (*Collationes in Hexaemeron et Bonaventuriana quaedam selecta*) may be more faithful to Bonaventure's oral presentation. See D. Hattrup, *Ekstatik der Geschichte: Die Entwicklung der christologischen Erkenntnistheorie Bonaventuras* (Paderborn: Ferdinand Schöningh 1993) 269–304.

rities. "Let the person who wants to learn seek knowledge at the source, that is, in sacred scripture, since with the philosophers there is no knowledge which would grant forgiveness of sins".[203] In the final analysis, only this saving knowledge can matter to a human being. Salvation, however, is through Christ, and therefore Christ alone is the center of all knowledge and wisdom.[204] Seeking this wisdom involves an ascent, a spiritual journey. Thus, the spiritual senses must be the goal of biblical interpretation with anagogy as their epitome. Bonaventure practiced an unabashedly Christian exegesis of both the Old and New Testaments. For him, understanding the Bible begins with the Christian faith, not with the propaedeutics of philosophy. Philosophy is not a first step, but an added assurance for the believer. "Philosophy adds to the reasoning of truth and authority the reasoning of probability". Or, as he puts it in the sermon, '*Christus unus omnium magister*': "The order [in theologizing] is this: that we begin with the firmness of faith and proceed through the serenity of reason so as to arrive at the sweetness of contemplation. This is the order which Christ implied when he said: 'I am the Way, the Truth, and the Life'".[205] This does not mean that philosophy is dispensable. Bonaventure is quite clear on this point. Scripture is not easy to understand. We need the writings of the Church fathers as a necessary help. But they are often difficult and must be supplemented by the *summae* of the masters who deal with these difficulties and quote the writings of the philosophers. Therefore, there is a need to know and presuppose the latter.[206] In a way, Bonaventure does support a 'modern' curriculum for theologians. But he also insists that the goal must be the education of preachers and pastors, not of teachers. By the standards of the later thirteenth century, his approach to biblical interpretation looks quite old-fashioned – staunchly Augustinian, Gregorian, monastic, even Victorine. In a terse explanation of the three spiritual senses from his early years, he names Augustine as the master teacher of allegory, Gregory the Great of tropology, Pseudo-Dionysius of anagogy, and continues: "Anselm follows Augustine, Bernard follows Gregory, Richard of St. Victor follows Dionysius … for Anselm excels in reasoning, Bernard in preaching, Richard in contemplation, but Hugh [of St. Victor] in all three".[207]

It has often been pointed out that there is the progressive side also. Along with the emphasis on the spiritual senses, Bonaventure could strongly urge the importance of the literal sense. Moreover, he was an accomplished dialectician, using a disputational style in most of his works and handling logical dis-

---

[203] Hexaëmeron XIX. 7; *Opera Omnia* V, 421 a.

[204] See the sermon, "Christus unus omnium magister", *Opera Omnia* V, 567–74; English trl.: *What Manner of Man? Sermons on Christ by St. Bonaventure* (tr. Z. Hayes; Chicago: Franciscan Herald Press 1974) 21–55.

[205] Commentary on the Sentences I q. 1 ad 5.6; *Opera Omnia* I, 8 b; Sermon "Christus unus"; *Opera Omnia* V, 571 b; English: *What Manner of Man?* (above, n. 204) 34 f.

[206] Hexaëmeron XIX. 10; *Opera Omnia* V, 421 b. For the context of this argument, see below, p. 550.

[207] *Saint Bonaventure's De Reductione Artium ad Theologiam: A Commentary with an Introduction and Translation* (ed. E. T. Healey; St. Bonaventure, NY: St. Bonaventure College 1940) 46. On the Victorine relation: G. Zinn, "Book and Word: The Victorine Background of Bonaventure's Use of Symbols", *S. Bonaventura 1274–1974* 2 (1974) 143–69.

tinctions and subdivisions with ease. The books of Aristotle were familiar to him; references to the entire corpus are present in his writings, and he knew the arguments of his philosophical colleagues in the arts faculty with precision. This picture, however, is somewhat deceptive. BOUGEROL has observed that, however widely the student of the *artes* may have been exposed to Aristotelian writings, Aristotle was not read or expounded in the Franciscan *studia*, at least in Paris. In fact, from the time Bonaventure taught, his main source for references to Aristotle seems to have been a florilegium, the *Auctoritates Aristotelis.*[208] He was not really interested in "the philosopher". He used the arsenal of the new science in his work, but these techniques did not mean much to him. "Believe me, a time will come when the gold and silver vessels, I mean [rational] arguments, will not be worth anything".[209]

The situation is similar when it comes to Bonaventure's attitude toward the literal sense.[210] It is clear that one needs to learn the basics first when trying to understand a language. No one can interpret scripture and its spiritual content who does not constantly read, memorize, and keep in mind the biblical text "as the words sound outwardly". A reflection on John 2:7 drives home this sequence even more forcefully: "The Holy Spirit does not give spiritual understanding unless a person fills the jar, that is, his or her capacity, with water, that is, awareness of the literal sense, and then God turns the water of the literal sense into the wine of spiritual understanding".[211] The admonition sounds strong, but it only echoes Gregory the Great. Bonaventure cautions that one is not to seek allegories everywhere, but this warning, he says himself, was issued by Augustine who formulated the rule so basic to Franciscan literalism: "When the words directly signify matters of faith or charity, there is no need to seek a symbolic meaning also". Clearly Bonaventure did not share the general enthusiasm for the literal sense. He was not interested in Jewish exegesis. On the contrary, he repeated the cliché of the Jew "who is always bent on the literal sense", and then told the horror story of a Jewish lecturer in Paris who wanted to expound Isaiah 53 before an audience of Christian clerics but, since he read it only according to the letter, could not make sense of the passage and threw the book to the ground.[212] Bonaventure was interested in the upward dynamics of the scriptural senses, not in the literal sense as their foundation. "Scripture is like a lyre. The lower cord does not sound the harmony by itself; it does it with the others".

---

[208] J. G. BOUGEROL, "Dossier pour l'étude des rapports entre Saint Bonaventure et Aristote", *AHDL* 40 (1973) 135–222. The florilegium has been critically edited by J. HAMESSE: *Les Auctoritates Aristotelis. Un florilège médiéval. Etude historique et édition critique* (Philosophes medievaux 17; Louvain: Publications universitaires / Paris: Nauwelaerts 1974).

[209] Hexaëmeron XVII. 28; *Opera Omnia* V, 414 b.

[210] H. RIEDLINGER, "Zur buchstäblichen und mystischen Schriftauslegung Bonaventuras", *Grundfragen christlicher Mystik* (ed. H. Schmidt / D. Bauer; Stuttgart: Frommann, Holzboog 1985) 139–56.

[211] Hexaëmeron XIX. 8; *Opera Omnia* V, 421 b.

[212] *Hexaëm.* XIX. 9 in the version published by Delorme (above, n. 202) 215. The text in *Opera Omnia* V, 421 b is less specific about the occasion but more graphic in describing the outcome: "He threw down the book, calling on God to confound Isaiah because what he said, it seemed to him, could not be maintained".

Some of the writings of Bonaventure's academic period are clearly related to his lecturing on particular biblical books as a master. We have three authentic biblical commentaries under his name, two on the Gospels (Luke: RBMA 1176; John: RBMA 1178), and one on an Old Testament book, Qoheleth (RBMA 1173).[213] Medieval sources suggest that Bonaventure also lectured on Wisdom, but the commentary ascribed to him in the first edition of 1574 and printed in the *Opera Omnia* cannot be verified as being his.[214] The selection of sapiential books for Old Testament lectures was a general trend in the thirteenth century, as we have seen. Bonaventure not only accepted the Solomonic authorship of Ecclesiastes but also the tradition about its purpose: here, the wise king teaches to despise the world. His prologue used the modern form of the *accessus*, discussing the four causes of the book. It also added a peculiar feature. The discussion of each cause is followed by two or three *quaestiones* which deal with possible objections. Such questions also appear in the commentary itself. As a rule, Bonaventure first expounds the literal meaning verse by verse, paying attention to biblical parallels, distinctions to be made, natural explanations, and alternative interpretations for which the Dominican Postill is the major source; he also quotes Augustine, Jerome, Pseudo-Dionysius, John of Damascus, Hugh of St. Victor and, of course, Aristotle. In many cases, he adds an application *spiritualiter*. At the end of a section we regularly encounter *quaestiones* in which random objections are raised and formally answered; they are mostly peripheral. On Qoh 2:7–11, the question is asked concerning v. 8 why enjoying the performance of singers should be a sin, and if so, of what kind. On 3:2–8, the only problem raised is the apparent inadequacy of the list; it seems to be either too short or too long. Bonaventure's true originality appears in the outline he extracts from the text. Like Thomas Aquinas on Job, he interprets the entire book as a coherent and closely structured argument.[215] According to him, practically everything after the prooemium (1:1) is part of a logical treatise (*tractatus*), first formulating the proposition ("All is vanity", 1:2), then unfolding the proof in three steps (1:3–12:7), and finally drawing the conclusion (12:8). Bonaventure's own preface places the book under the motto of Ps 40:4, identifying its message as the spiritual opposition of *caritas* and *libido*, love of God and love of the world. The questions raised about the four causes inquire how the author can teach contempt of the world when the world is God's good creation. Bonaventure's *determinatio* refers to Hugh of St. Victor's analogy of the engagement ring: God gave the world to humans as a reminder of his love, not as an object to be loved for its own sake.[216]

---

[213] On the Qoheleth Commentary, see Distelbrink, *Bonaventurae Scripta* (1975) 14–18; Bougerol, Introduction (1964) 94–98; Smalley, Medieval Exegesis (1986) 39–46. The text is found in *Opera Omnia* VI, 3–99.

[214] *Opera Omnia* VI, 107–233. Distelbrink, *Bonaventurae Scripta* (1975) 18–19; I. Brady, "The Opera Omnia of St. Bonaventura Revisited", *Proceedings of the Seventh Centenary Celebration of the Death of Saint Bonaventure, St. Bonaventure University, St. Bonaventure, N. Y., July 12–15, 1974* (St. Bonaventure, NY: Franciscan Institute 1975) 47–59; here 53 f.

[215] See the schema reproduced graphically in *Opera Omnia* VI, 100–03.

[216] *De arrha animae* 4 (PL 176, 954 f); English tr.: *Hugh of St. Victor. Soliloquy on the Earnest Money of the Soul* (tr. K. Herbert; Milwaukee: Marquette UP 1956) 16–18.

Wrong love must be countered by right contempt. Werner Dettloff has shown how major themes of Bonaventure's later polemical stance are present in this early commentary already. He points especially to the strong criticism of *curiositas*, which the author interprets as the pursuit of philosophical knowledge for its own sake.[217] Like Bonaventure's other biblical commentaries, the rich and clear exposition of Ecclesiastes quickly became a classic. Smalley reports that all later commentaries used it as a source. The almost universal imitation of the practice to add questions to each section lends support to her observation.[218]

While Thomas Aquinas did not write a separate treatise on biblical hermeneutics, Bonaventure wrote his *Breviloquium*. Having lectured on Peter Lombard's Sentences, he composed the work at the request of his confreres as a "brief summary of true theology". The bulk consists of a summary of seven theological topics, but the prologue explicitly considers the principles of biblical interpretation. M.-D. Chenu has called this text "the most beautiful program of biblical hermeneutics which the thirteenth century has offered".[219] Other texts of importance are the prologue to the Commentary on Luke, and Collations XIII–XIX of the Hexaëmeron. Bonaventure opens the *Breviloquium* by discussing the four dimensions of Scripture according to Eph 3:14–19: breadth, length, height, and depth. Scripture's *breadth* is the full range of books in a harmonious canon of Old and New Testament which, like a stream of water swelled from humble beginnings in the legal books to become a mighty river through the confluence of the historical and sapiential books, the prophets, the gospels, and the apostolic writings and visions. Its *length* is the well-ordered history of the world in its three phases and seven ages which, like a beautiful poem, reflect its own creation and the natural stages of human life. Its *height* is the divine order in the Church, the angelic world, and the inner mysteries of the deity, Christ being the 'one hierarch' in all of them – another vision of beauty. Finally, in the discussion of the *depth* of Scripture, Bonaventure describes the three spiritual senses rising above the literal sense as the supremely fitting expression of the nature and purpose of Scripture. Scripture does not want to persuade our reason but to lift our heart. This anagogical hermeneutic is as Franciscan as it is Augustinian. Augustine's 'On Christian Doctrine' is the obvious source when it comes to suggesting procedures of interpretation to weary beginners.

The argument of the prologue makes it clear that Bonaventure did not regard biblical hermeneutics as a matter of teachable rules or curricular struc-

---

[217] W. Dettloff, "Weltverachtung und Heil. Eine Interpretation der allgemeinen Einleitung Bonaventuras zu seinem Qohelethkommentar", *S. Bonaventura 1274–1974* 4 (1974) 21–55.

[218] Smalley, Study (1983) 274; Medieval Exegesis (1986) 39 f.

[219] *La théologie comme science au XIIIe siècle* (3rd ed.; Paris: Vrin 1957) 54. The text of the Breviloquium is found in *Opera Omnia* V, 201–91; English tr. by J. De Vinck, *The Works of Bonaventure,* II. *The Breviloquium* (Paterson NJ: St. Anthony Guild Press 1963). Most treatments of Bonaventure's hermeneutics focus on the analysis of this Prooemium. See Bougerol, Introduction (1964) 88–94, 108–12; H. J. Klauck, "Theorie der Exegese bei Bonaventura", *S. Bonaventura 1274–1974* 4 (1974) 71–128; Riedlinger (above, n. 210); T. Reist, Saint Bonaventure as a Biblical Commentator (1985) 29–65.

tures but as part of a total vision of reality both as created nature and as history. In a first reflection, he applied the four dimensions of Eph 3:18 to the entire universe, its content, its course from the beginning, its end of final glory and ultimate rejection for souls saved and condemned.[220] Scripture is not just a literary document to be studied; being God's revelation, it is itself part of God's universal history with the world.[221] In a bold move, Bonaventure expressed this action and interaction between God and the world through the imagery of 'the book'. In the Augustinian tradition he found the concept of God's two books, the created world and the biblical record of salvation, both of which point back to God, their author. Bonaventure adapted and deepened the image as a perfect expression of his comprehensive theology of history.[222] 'Book' means an abiding witness to something full and complete. God himself is the primal book, reading and being read in his creation. Before the Fall, humans made in the image of God could read this book. This ability was lost, and now they need help in their effort to read. Scripture provides this help. It teaches humans to read again the book of God's created reality as image and parabolic truth.

This understanding of the restorative role of the Bible has consequences for the relation between theology and philosophy. Like his contemporaries, Bonaventure still identified theology with the biblical witness. He did not, however, give it the name of *sacra pagina* or *sacra doctrina* but called it consistently *sacra scriptura*, the one book which allows the other to be read again. The notion of restoration is crucial here. Philosophy, the natural knowledge which human reason can attain on its own even after the Fall, may well be regarded in a curricular context as the handmaid of theology, serving the queen of sciences as an auxiliary enterprise. On a deeper level, however, it is itself served by theology. In a very real sense, Scripture acts as the handmaid of philosophy, freeing reason to see the world as it really is, in its dependence on God and its directedness toward his future, with Christ being the mediator in both directions.[223] Despite his respect for human knowledge and the achievements of the human mind in the great philosophers, Bonaventure's theological thinking seems to be marked by a deep suspicion, an underlying anti-Aristotelian and even anti-philosophical bias. This was not a slowly growing prejudice.[224] It was present from the beginning, but found its focus in the polemic against the dangers of the new philosophical secularism during his final years, a polemic which makes his creative mind appear far less progressive than it was. Bonaventure was not a backward-looking traditionalist. He was not against right philosophy, the *philosophia Christi*, which would live by the forgiveness of sins. He was, however, suspicious of the human delusion of self-sufficiency, of the innately sinful

---

[220] *Opera Omnia* V, 201 b f; De Vinck, p. 2 f.

[221] Ratzinger, The Theology of History in St. Bonaventure (1971).

[222] W. Rauch, *Das Buch Gottes: Eine systematische Untersuchung des Buchbegriffes bei Bonaventura* (MThS. S 20; München: Max Hueber Verlag 1961).

[223] Dettloff, Weltverachtung (1974) 46. Mercker, Schriftauslegung als Weltauslegung (1971).

[224] W. Dettloff, "Die franziskanische Vorentscheidung im theologischen Denken des heiligen Bonaventura", *MTZ* 13 (1962) 107–15; following up on suggestions by Ratzinger, Theology of History.

curiosity of reason, and thus, in the last analysis, of the destructive potential of human pride. He could reconcile the Franciscan ethos of humility with a rational approach to the Bible and a full academic curriculum to support it, but not with an emancipated secular science for which the Bible would be a book just like others, used and studied to the greater glory of the human mind rather than to the glory of God.

7. Conclusion: Old Testament Scholarship at the End of the Thirteenth Century

Sources: Roger Bacon, *Compendium studii theologiae* (ed. and tr. T. S. Maloney; STGMA 20; Leiden: Brill 1988); *Opus Maius* 1–3 (ed. J. H. Bridges; Oxford: Clarendon 1897–1900); Roger Bacon, *Moralis Philosophia. Baconis Operis Maioris Pars Septima* (ed. E. Massa / F. Delorme; Bibliotheca scriptorum latinorum mediae et recentioris aetatis; Zürich: Thesaurus Mundi 1953); R. B. Burke, *Roger Bacon. The Opus Maius. A Translation* (Philadelphia, PA: University of Pennsylvania Press 1928); *Fr. Rogeri Bacon Opera Quaedam Hactenus Inedita* I (ed. J. S. Brewer; London: Longman, Green 1859).

General works: *Roger Bacon and the Sciences. Commemorative Essays* (ed. J. Hacket; STGMA 57; Leiden: Brill 1997); E. R. Daniel, "Roger Bacon and the De seminibus scripturarum", *MS* 34 (1972) 462–67; R. C. Petry, "Reforming Critiques of Robert Grosseteste, Roger Bacon, and Ramon Lull and Their Related Impact Upon Medieval Society: Historical Studies in the Critical Temper and the Practice of Tradition", *The Impact of the Church Upon its Culture. Reappraisals of the History of Christianity* (ed. J. C. Brauer; Essays in Divinity 2; Chicago, IL: Chicago UP 1968) 95–120; M. A. Schmidt, "Roger Bacons Verteidigung der 'biblischen' gegen die 'systematische' Lehrweise in der Theologie", *ThZ* 28 (1971) 32–42.

When the thirteenth century opened, a major turning point in the history of biblical interpretation had occurred already: the monastic *lectio divina* had been replaced by the theological curriculum of the schools as the primary setting for biblical exegesis. John van Engen described this exchange as a major cultural shift.[225] Rather than serving as the anchor of the ascetic triangle of reading, prayer, and contemplation, the Bible had become a textbook of instruction in an educational setting of much wider scope. According to van Engen, a second major shift took place between 1225 and 1275 when the application of biblical knowledge to contemporary issues moved to the forefront. In the Paris faculty of theology, this shift came at the end of the twelfth century already when the masters redefined the task of biblical instruction in light of a new professional goal, preaching. Both developments were not movements on a one-way road away from an edifying *lectio divina* to a detached investigation of the text by objective scholars. We saw how deeply the piety of the new mendicant orders which were organized around preaching and pastoral work as their tasks, influenced the schools, and how, in turn, the schools, especially Paris and Oxford, shaped the intellectual life not only of the mendicants but in all monastic orders and among the secular clergy as well.

---

[225] Van Engen, Studying Scripture, *Neue Richtungen* (1994) 17–38.

The new framework of biblical studies certainly meant progress on many fronts. The thirteenth century turned out to be an age of tools. By the end of the century, the biblical research tools were perfected: a relatively unified Vulgate text; standard chapter divisions, prologues and *accessus* materials; the verbal concordance; preachers' access to the interpretive tradition through the Dominican Postill and the collections of *distinctiones*. The reception of Aristotle led to dramatic changes in the approach to biblical texts, first and foremost the redefinition of the literal sense as the intention of the (human) author with its potential of encouraging the treatment of the Bible as literature, but also changes in the theological and ethical system built upon the Bible via its allegorical and tropological senses. It seems much more difficult to assess the progress in hermeneutical terms. Rather than making room for new directions, the principle of a multiple interpretation of the Bible, specifically the tradition of its fourfold sense, continued as strong as ever. In the next two centuries, new forms of mystical spirituality in the existing religious orders and in new semi-monastic communities emphasized the centrality of biblical anagogy at the very time when the understanding of the literal sense was heading toward chaos.[226]

Beryl Smalley equated the progress of medieval biblical scholarship with the growing interest in the literal sense of the Old Testament, and therefore with the mastery of Hebrew language among Christian exegetes. As she saw it, Christian Hebrew scholarship peaked with Andrew of St. Victor and Herbert of Bosham in the late twelfth century already. In comparison, the thirteenth century was disappointing. While the awareness and knowledge of Hebrew was becoming more common, the friars' contribution marked a plateau without reaching new heights. A recent assessment is even more negative. A. Saltman speaks of "a tendency of late to exaggerate Christian-Jewish contacts and Christian knowledge of Hebrew in the Middle Ages"; he doubts that even Nicholas of Lyra, "the most 'Jewish' of the medieval Christian exegetes", could have passed an examination in elementary Hebrew.[227] It seems that looking at progress in terms of Smalley's definition of "biblical scholarship" is of little help in understanding the advance of Old Testament interpretation in the thirteenth century. If we consider the broader issues of biblical hermeneutics, we observe the attempt throughout the century to find a proper balance between the four scriptural senses in the face of the lure of the new sciences on the one hand, and the struggle for the integration of these sciences into a broad theological program on the other. Such a program would take its start from a careful investigation of the literal sense, but it was expected to provide spiritual nourishment for the life of faith, opening up the path to meditation, contemplation, and the final vision of endtime and heavenly home.

---

[226] See K. Froehlich, "'Always to Keep the Literal Sense in Holy Scripture Means to Kill One's Soul': The State of Biblical Hermeneutics at the Beginning of the Fifteenth Century", *Literary Uses of Typology from the Late Middle Ages to the Present* (ed. E. Miner; Princeton NJ: Princeton UP 1977) 20–48.

[227] Saltman, Stephen Langton (1978) 30 (cf. n. 40 above).

The work of Roger Bacon, one of the most fascinating minds of the century, allows us to catch a rare glimpse of the complex dynamics of this struggle.[228] Born ca. 1214/15, Bacon studied the *artes* in Oxford and taught them at Oxford and Paris. After 1247, he apparently relinquished his regency but, using Paris as a home base and visiting England periodically, engaged in all kinds of unconventional scientific research. He joined the Franciscan order around 1256 but never held a public office. He never taught theology and left no biblical commentaries, but he was an astute observer of the contemporary scene. Of great importance were his contacts to cardinal Guy Foulques who, as Pope Clement IV, asked him in 1266 to write down his ideas on the reform of academic studies. In answer, Bacon sent several writings, including his *Opus Maius*, the *Opus Minus*, and probably the *Opus tertium*.[229] In these treatises, while criticizing present academic conditions, he developed a grand vision of university studies built around Aristotelian science as philosophical propaedeutics for a theology which would include proficiency in languages, morality, and natural and experimental science. The works may not have reached the pope; Clement IV died in 1268. Bacon was formally censured by his superiors and kept under house arrest. For his last years, he stayed at the Oxford friary where he wrote his late polemical works, the *Compendium studii philosophiae* (1271/72) and the *Compendium studii theologiae* (1292).[230]

His critique of contemporary intellectual life is often caustic, unjust, and grossly exaggerated, but quite specific. Among the indications of a general decline of culture and society the *Compendium studii philosophiae* names the long papal interregnum after Clement IV; the conflict between mendicants and seculars at the university of Paris and among the two orders; the machinations of the legal profession, and most importantly the loss of quality education for theologians. For the last forty years, Bacon laments, young mendicants have been preaching and teaching without the solid liberal arts background required for Bible study.[231] This complaint echoes a passage in the *Opus Minus* where he draws up a list of "seven errors in theology".[232] The list is most interesting. (1) In academic practice, Bacon suggests, philosophy dominates the work of theologians. This reverses the proper order of things. Revelation preceded the philosophers. Theologians ought to use philosophy rather than al-

---

[228] An excellent introduction to modern Bacon scholarship is the volume: *Roger Bacon and the Sciences. Commemorative Essays* (ed. J. Hackett; 1997). On Bacon's life, see Hackett's essay: "Roger Bacon, His Life, Career, and Works", ibid. 9–22. On Bacon and the Bible, see Smalley, Study (1983) 279f; 329–35.

[229] The bulk of these texts must still be consulted in older editions: *Opus Maius* 1–3 (ed. J. H. Bridges; Oxford: Clarendon 1897–1900); *Opus Minus* and *Opus Tertium* in: *Fr. Rogeri Bacon Opera Quaedam Hactenus Inedita* I (ed. J. S. Brewer; London: Longman, Green 1859). English tr. of the *Opus Maius*: R. B. Burke, *Roger Bacon. The Opus Maius. A Translation* (Philadelphia: University of Pennsylvania Press 1928).

[230] For the *Compendium studii philosophiae*, see *Opera Quaedam* (ed. Brewer; 1859) 393–519; for the *Compendium studii theologiae*: *Roger Bacon, Compendium studii theologiae* (ed. and tr. T. S. Maloney; 1988).

[231] Cf. *Compendium studii philosophiae* (ed. Brewer) 418–30.

[232] *Opus Minus* (ed. Brewer) 322–59 (the manuscript text breaks off before reaching the seventh error).

lowing it to dictate their agenda.[233] (2) Theologians neglect the "major sciences". In Bacon's system, these are mathematics, *perspectiva*, moral and experimental science, and alchemy. They deal with nature, a central interest of the empiricist who defends even magic as a curricular option.[234] (3) Knowledge of the few sciences used by theologians is inadequate because their sources remain unknown. The "sapiential languages" (Greek, Hebrew, Aramaic, Arabic) are not studied; translations are far too few and mostly faulty. Teachers like Alexander of Hales and Albert are regarded as authorities, but their knowledge of languages and scientific subject matter does not measure up.[235] (4) In the theological faculty, the lectures on the *Sentences* are scheduled at the best hours while the biblical lecturers must beg for slots, and Peter Comestor's *Histories* are not even taught any more. (5) The text of the Paris Vulgate is hopelessly flawed. The so-called "correctories" have made things worse; their "correctors" are "corruptors". Bacon made the point about the need for a revised Vulgate time and again.[236] (6) The worst problem is the deplorable condition of the literal sense of the Bible; due to the other errors, truth cannot be ascertained from it. This must affect the spiritual senses. How can they be known when the basis is unsafe?

Bacon's polemic, while provocative, reveals the dilemma of biblical studies at the end of the century. On the one hand, his critique reflects the new situation of academic theology with its scientific presuppositions, broadened linguistic requirements, and wide-ranging philosophical concerns. On the other hand, when he develops his own vision of true theology, Bacon's ideal turns out to be traditional. His heroes are the Oxford "biblical theologians" of the previous generation: Robert Grosseteste, Adam Marsh, William of Sherwood. He has high praise for Hugh of St. Victor and calls on Augustine's *De doctrina Christiana* to provide the rationale for the study of languages and *realia*. The goal of his vision of a theological education with the Bible as its text and the new sciences as its presupposition is the cultivation of the spiritual life which was at the heart of the mendicant ethos. At the beginning of the century, Peter the Chanter articulated the new framework for Bible study in the schools: preaching was to be the "roof" completing the building of a scientific theological curriculum. At the end of the century, Roger Bacon painted an unflattering picture of the progress made. He concluded that contemporary academic theology, setting false priorities, was unhelpful for the central task of preaching the biblical message. "We know for sure and see it everywhere that a simple friar who has not listened to scores of lectures on theology or, if he has, does

---

[233] On the priority of biblical revelation: *Opus Tertium*, c. 24 (ed. Brewer) 79–81; *Opus Maius* (ed. Bridges) 29. See also J. Hackett, "Philosophy and Theology in Roger Bacon's *Opus Maius*", *Philosophy and the God of Abraham. Essays in Memory of James A. Weisheipl* (ed. R. J. Long; Papers in Medieval Studies; Toronto: PIMS 1991) 55–69.

[234] See J. Hackett, "Roger Bacon on the Classification of the Sciences", *Roger Bacon and the Sciences* (1997) 49–65.

[235] Cf. *Compendium studii philosophiae* c. 6–8 (ed. Brewer) 432–95. On Bacon's opinion of Albert the Great, see J. Hackett, "The Attitude of Roger Bacon to the *scientia* of Albertus Magnus", *Albertus Magnus and the Sciences* (1980) 53–72.

[236] For an assessment of his criticism, see Light, Versions et révisions (BTT 4; 1984) 76–78.

not care, preaches incomparably better than the greatest masters in theology. Plainly, preaching does not depend on the study of theology but on the church's doctrine known to everyone, on an understanding of vices and virtues, penalties and rewards and salutary teachings of this sort, the knowledge of which is written in the hearts through the Church's liturgical practice. Preaching precedes the study of theology – which does not mean, of course, that a good theologian should not be a better preacher".[237]

[237] *Compendium studii philosophiae* c. 5 (ed. Brewer) 427 f.

Chapter Thirty-six

Development of Biblical Interpretation in the Syrian Churches of the Middle Ages

By Lucas Van Rompay, Leiden

General works: [see vol. I/1, ch. 17 as well as:] S. Brock, *A Brief Outline of Syriac Literature* (Kottayam 1997); D. D. Bundy, "The Peshitta of Isaiah 53:9 and the Syrian Commentators", *OrChr* 62 (1978) 158–65; M. Goréa-Autexier, "La Bible des Syriens à la lumière des citations de *Job*", *RB* 106 (1999) 481–510; T. Jansma, "Investigations into the Early Syrian Fathers on Genesis. An Approach to the Exegesis of the Nestorian Church and to the Comparison of Nestorian and Jewish Exegesis", OTS 12 (1958) 69–181; L. Van Rompay, "La littérature exégètique syriaque et le rapprochement des traditions syrienne-occidentale et syrienne-orientale", *Parole de l'Orient* 20 (1995) 221–35.

Bibliographies: [see vol. I/1, ch. 17 as well as:] S. P. Brock, *Syriac Studies. A Classified Bibliography (1960–1990)* (Kaslik 1996); idem, "Syriac Studies. A Classified Bibliography (1991–1995)", *Parole de l'Orient* 23 (1998) 241–350; B. Chiesa, "Gen 2, 15–3, 24 nella più antica esegesi giudeo-araba", *Atti della VI Settimana di Studi «Sangue e antropologia nella teologia» Roma, 23–28 novembre 1987* (Rome 1989) esp. 1072–78 ("Nota bibliografica sulla letteratura esegetica siriaca").

1. Introduction

In the thirties of the seventh century the political map of the Middle East was drastically altered as a result of the expansion of Islam. The West-Syrian Christians, living mainly in Syria and Northern Mesopotamia, exchanged Byzantine for Arab occupation, while the East Syrians, after the fall of the Sassanid Empire, likewise came under Arab rule. Both Monophysites and Nestorians were freed from the harassment of the Chalcedonian authorities, and contacts between the various groups were intensified. In the first period of Arab rule Christians were not hampered in the practice of their religion or in their cultural and literary activities. In fact, the seventh century was a very productive period and saw the emergence of a number of outstanding figures in Syriac literature, among both West and East Syrians.

However, after a time the steady process of arabization and islamization began to weaken the Christian communities, who were forced to create a new self-image and to reflect on their position as minority groups within the Muslim world. This reflection contributed to the need to define their cultural patrimony and to reformulate it in such a way that it could easily be transmitted to posterity. In the field of exegesis a number of works emerged which, in addition to their importance as witnesses of contemporary exegetical activity, reproduce and summarise earlier literary products.

In many respects, Syriac successfully resisted the process of arabization, in its literary as well as its spoken language forms. However, in some areas Christians adopted Arabic – either alongside or in place of Syriac – as their language of daily communication. As a means to safeguard the faithful transmission of traditional texts, notably of the Bible, the classical language became the subject of special study. Two important fields are worthy of mention here. One concerns the establishing of the correct orthography, vocalisation, and pronunciation of the biblical text, which resulted in the so-called masoretic manuscripts.[1] The other field is that of lexicography, which deals with the more difficult words in the Bible. Although very little is known about the earliest specimens of this genre, much lexicographical material has been preserved, not only in the later compendia,[2] but also in exegetical commentaries, particularly in those of Išoʿdad of Merv [see 3.5] and Barhebraeus [see 5].

Along with these deliberate attempts to maintain Syriac as their prime literary language, Christian authors also started writing in Arabic. In this way, an important part of Syriac literary tradition found its way into Arab culture. Since Syrian Christians always had worked in bilingual or multilingual contexts, they were able not only to survive in this new situation, but also to take advantage of some of the achievements of their Muslim neighbours, to which their new language gave them access.

2. West-Syrian Works of the Early Islamic Period

2.1. *Jacob of Edessa*

Editions and translations: I.-B. Chabot, *Iacobi Edesseni Hexaemeron seu in opus creationis libri septem* (CSCO 92/Syr. 44; Louvain 1928; Syriac); A. Vaschalde, *Iacobi Edesseni Hexaemeron seu in opus creationis libri septem* (CSCO 97/Syr. 48; Louvain 1932; Latin transl.); G. Phillips, *Scholia on Passages of the Old Testament by Mar Jacob, Bishop of Edessa* (London 1864; Syriac and English transl.); W. Wright, "Two Epistles of Mar Jacob, Bishop of Edessa", *Journal of Sacred Literature* NS 10 (1867) 430–61 (Syriac); F. Nau, "Traduction des lettres XII et XIII de Jacques d'Édesse (Exégèse biblique)", *Revue de l'Orient Chrétien* 10 (1905) 197–208, 258–82 (French transl.).

Studies: W. Adler, "Jacob of Edessa and the Jewish Pseudepigrapha in Syriac Chronography", *Tracing the Treads. Studies in the Vitality of Jewish Pseudepigrapha* (ed. J. C. Reeves; SBL, Early Judaism and Its Literature 6; Atlanta 1994) 143–71; S. P. Brock, "Abraham and the Ravens: A Syriac Counterpart to Jubilees 11–12 and Its Implications", *JSJ* 9 (1978) 135–52; H. J. W. Drijvers, "Jakob von Edessa", TRE 16 (1987) 468–70, with further references; D. Kruisheer, "Reconstructing Jacob of Edessa's Scholia", *The Book of Genesis in Jewish and Oriental Christian Interpretation. A Collection of Essays* (ed. J. Frishman / L. Van Rompay; Traditio Exegetica Graeca 5; Louvain 1997) 187–96; idem, "Ephrem, Jacob of Edessa, and the Monk Severus. An Analysis of Ms. Vat. Syr. 103, ff. 1–72", *Symposium Syriacum VII* (ed. R. Lavenant; OCA 256; Rome 1998) 599–605.

[1] J. P. P. Martin, "Tradition karkaphienne, ou la Massore chez les Syriens", *Journal asiatique*, Sixième série 14 (1869) 245–379.

[2] The most important is that of Bar Bahlul (2nd half of the 10th century), see R. Duval, *Lexicon Syriacum auctore Hassano Bar Bahlule* 1–3 (Paris 1901).

In the West-Syrian area the transmission of culture and knowledge was for many centuries situated in influential monasteries. Jacob of Edessa, the first great Syrian scholar of the Muslim period, spent most of his life in monasteries, in those of Qennešre, Kaisum, Eusebona and Tell ʿAdda, interrupted by a few – not very successful – years as bishop of Edessa (684–88 and again in the first half of 708, during the last months of his life).

Jacob's interest in biblical studies manifests itself in his revision of the Syriac Old Testament, which was completed around 705. This work, of which only part has been preserved, is mainly based on the Peshitta text, while incorporating much material from the Syro-Hexapla as well as from Greek biblical manuscripts available to Jacob.[3] It did not enjoy great popularity.[4] Another extensive work is his *Hexaemeron*, the completion of which was prevented by his death. Despite its title, this work is not devoted primarily to biblical exegesis but – within the framework of the biblical account of creation – deals with physics, geography, astronomy, and the natural sciences.

Recent investigation has brought to light that ms. Vat. Syr. 103, known as the main witness of the *Catena* of the monk Severus [see 2.3], contains, among other things, a running commentary by Jacob on the Octateuch (the Pentateuch with Job, Joshua, Judges). This independent work was, in all probability, added to Severus's work only at a later stage of the latter's transmission. It still awaits publication and study.[5]

Distinct from this running commentary is a "Book of *Scholia*" dealing with problems of biblical text and interpretation. Although this has not come down to us in its entirety, selections and excerpts may be found in Severus's compilation as well as in some other manuscripts. Only a few of these *Scholia* have been published.[6]

A further important source for the study of Jacob's views on the biblical text are his letters, which have still not been published in full.[7] In those which are devoted to biblical matters he discusses, among other things, biblical chronology, questions concerning the authorship of Job (for which he defends Moses' authorship) and Psalms (not all Psalms should be ascribed to David), the question of the first language (for which he accepts Eusebius of Emesa's opinion that this was Hebrew, against many Syrian exegetes who argued that it was Syriac). With regard to Job 3:8 (where MT and Peshitta read "Leviathan", whereas Septuagint has "the big dragon"), Jacob says that factually (*suʿrānāʾit*) the expression points to the big dragon in the seas, whereas spiritually (*ruḥānāʾit*) and "in a higher manner" (*metʿallyānāʾit*, cp. the terms used by Daniel

[3] There are two important recent publications: R. J. Saley, *The Samuel Manuscript of Jacob of Edessa. A Study in Its Underlying Textual Traditions* (Monographs of the Peshitta Institute Leiden 9; Leiden 1998) and A. Salvesen, *The Books of Samuel in the Syriac Version of Jacob of Edessa* (Monographs of the Peshitta Institute Leiden 10; Leiden 1999; Syriac and English transl.).

[4] For Jacob's activities in connection with the Syriac Masorah, see Martin, Tradition karkaphienne (1869).

[5] Kruisheer, Ephrem, Jacob of Edessa, and the Monk Severus (1998). An edition and translation of the commentary, by Dirk Kruisheer, are in preparation.

[6] Phillips, Scholia (1864); Salvesen, The Books of Samuel (1999) xxi–xxv.

[7] An edition, translation and study of the letters are being prepared by Dr. Jan van Ginkel.

of Ṣalaḥ [see vol. I/1, ch. 17, 6.2]) it applies in *theoria* to the big dragon Satan, who will grasp and kill Christ.

Jacob reveals himself in his works as an erudite biblical philologist who possessed a thorough knowledge of both Syriac and Greek literature. Moreover, he must have had some knowledge of Hebrew and was able to avail himself of the aid of Jewish scholars. A full study of his sources and his working method remains a desideratum. Jacob's acquaintance with apocryphal and pseudepigraphical works (among them *Jubilees* or a work very similar to it) deserves special mention.

Jacob's exegetical works became authoritative in the later tradition. All subsequent exegetes of the West-Syrian tradition refer to him, whereas echoes of his work are also found in the East-Syrian commentary by Išoʿdad of Merv [see 3.5]. In addition, excerpts from either his commentary or the Scholia have been incorporated in an Armenian commentary attributed to Ephrem.[8]

2.2. Moses bar Kepa

Editions and translations: B. CHIESA, "Gen 2, 15–3, 24 nella più antica esegesi giudeo-araba", *Atti della VI Settimana di Studi «Sangue e antropologia nella teologia» Roma, 23–28 novembre 1987* (Rome 1989) esp. 1079–95 ("Gen 2, 15–3, 24 nel commento di Moshe bar Kepha"; Italian transl.); G. DIETTRICH, *Eine jakobitische Einleitung in den Psalter in Verbindung mit zwei Homilien aus dem grossen Psalmenkommentar des Daniel von Ṣalaḥ* (BZAW V; Giessen 1901) 1–127 (Syriac and German transl.); L. SCHLIMME, *Der Hexaemeronkommentar des Moses Bar Kepha* 1–2 (GOF I, 14; Wiesbaden 1977; German transl.).

Study: J.-M. VOSTÉ, "L'introduction de Moše bar Kepa aux Psaumes de David", *RB* 38 (1929) 214–28.

A monk, like Jacob of Edessa, Moses bar Kepa received his education in the West-Syrian monastery of Mar Sergius near Balad, on the river Tigris. In 863 he became bishop of Mosul, a position which he apparently held until his death in 903.

Moses bar Kepa was the first Syrian exegete to become known in Europe,[9] but only parts of his work, which must have comprised commentaries on almost the entire Old Testament and New Testament, have come down to us. As regards the Old Testament, his main works to have survived include a *Commentary on the Hexaemeron* (unpublished, but accessible in a German translation) and a *Commentary on the Psalms*, of which only the preface has so far been published.

One of Moses' main sources in his *Commentary on the Hexaemeron* (especially in Books III–V) is Jacob of Edessa's *Hexaemeron*, and this reveals an im-

[8] Cf. E. G. MATHEWS, "The Armenian Commentary on Genesis Attributed to Ephrem the Syrian", *The Book of Genesis in Jewish and Oriental Christian Interpretation. A Collection of Essays* (ed. J. Frishman / L. Van Rompay; Traditio Exegetica Graeca 5; Louvain 1997) 143–61; idem, *The Armenian Commentary on Genesis Attributed to Ephrem the Syrian* (CSCO 572–73/Arm. 24–25; Louvain 1998; Armenian and English transl.).

[9] In 1569 Andreas Masius published a Latin translation of Moses' *On Paradise*, based on a Syriac manuscript offered to him by the Syrian priest Moses of Mardin. Masius's translation was later reprinted in Migne's PG 111, 481–608. The Syriac text has remained unpublished.

portant characteristic of his work, which like Jacob's, gives considerable attention to secular sciences. However, Moses adds to this theology, exegesis and biblical philology. Among the general questions treated in the introduction (Book I), there is a survey of the translations of the Old Testament (from Hebrew into Greek as well as from Greek into Syriac), based mainly on Epiphanius of Salamis's *On Measures and Weights*, in which Moses, on the authority of Philoxenus of Mabbog, gives priority to the Septuagint over the Peshitta. In another chapter Moses argues that the Old Testament should not only be interpreted literally ("corporally and factually"), but also spiritually and allegorically.[10]

In Book II of the *Commentary on the Hexaemeron*, which is a running commentary on Gen 1:1–2:7, Moses unfolds a broad panorama of exegesis. In addition to historical exegesis (which takes an important place), this includes all kinds of non-literal explanation. Greek patristic writers are quoted, such as Basil of Caesarea, Gregory of Nazianzus, Gregory of Nyssa, John Chrysostom, Athanasius and Cyril of Alexandria, and Severus of Antioch. The Syriac writers referred to are Ephrem (whose *Commentary on Genesis* is often quoted), Jacob of Serug, Jacob of Edessa, Zenobius (of Gzirta?), Philoxenus of Mabbog, and Severus Sebokt. Some remarks deal with Septuagint readings, the readings of Symmachus and Theodotion, or specific features of the Hebrew language. Of particular interest are a few references to "Theodore the Nestorian", i.e., Theodore of Mopsuestia, whose historical exegesis, known to Moses either directly or through contemporary East-Syrian sources, was not always incompatible with Moses' general approach to the Bible.

In the introduction to the *Commentary on the Psalms*, Moses, basing himself on Athanasius (*Letter to Marcellinus*) and Epiphanius (*On Measures and Weights*), deals with the various *theoriae* that can be detected in the Psalter. He also discusses various literary problems. Among other things, he refutes the opinion of "Theodore the Nestorian and others" that all Psalms should be ascribed to David. Like Athanasius, Irenaeus of Lyon, Hippolytus of Rome, Origen and Jacob of Edessa, all of whom he explicitly mentions, Moses is of the opinion that David is the author of only part of the Psalms (73 as is later specified). Apart from remarks on the singing and musical accompaniment of the Psalms, he briefly discusses the questions of the different subscriptions in Hebrew, Greek and Syriac and the divergences in the division and numbering of the Psalms. And finally, this introduction contains some sections which are identical to those found in the introduction to the *Hexaemeron* (on the various translations of the Old Testament as well as on its literal and spiritual interpretation).

[10] The corresponding Syriac terms can be found in Moses' introduction to the *Commentary on the Psalms* (see below): corporally = *gušmānā'it*; factually = *suʿrānā'it*; spiritually = *ruḥānā'it*; allegorically = *pel(')etānā'it.*

2.3. *Two Exegetical "Catenae"*

Studies: C. Bravo, "Un Comentario de Jacobo de Edesa al Gen 1, 1–7, atribuído a S. Efrén", *Bib.* 31 (1950) 390–401; T. Jansma, "The Provenance of the Last Sections in the Roman Edition of Ephrem's Commentary on Exodus", *Le Muséon* 85 (1972) 155–69; Kruisheer, Ephrem, Jacob of Edessa, and the Monk Severus (1998) [see 2.1].

Only a few sections of the two works mentioned here have been published. The first work is preserved in a ms. from the eighth or ninth century and consists of extracts from various writers, forming a commentary on a great part of the Old Testament and New Testament.[11] Greek authors predominate in this collection, and they include all the names referred to in connection with the preceding works. In addition, mention should be made of Olympiodorus, deacon of Alexandria, who is quoted for Job and Qohelet, as well as of two authors from whom the anonymous compiler has borrowed explanations of the Song of Songs: Symmachus[12] and John bar Aptonaya.[13] A further characteristic of this *catena* is that quotations are sometimes given according to the Syro-Hexapla [see vol. I/1, ch. 17, 1.2.1], while some biblical books (Ezra, Nehemiah, 1–2 Chronicles) appear only in the form of well-chosen extracts from the Syro-Hexapla.[14]

The second *catena* is the work of the monk Severus, completed in a monastery near Edessa in 861. The Old Testament portion of this work originally consisted of extracts from Ephrem and Jacob of Edessa. In its later transmission the work was expanded with a commentary on the Octateuch by Jacob of Edessa[15] as well as with quotations from various other authors, both Greek (e. g., Hippolytus of Rome, Isidore of Pelusium, Gregory of Nyssa, and Symmachus[16]) and Syriac (e. g., Daniel of Ṣalaḥ and George, bishop of the Arabs).

3. East-Syrian Works

3.1. *East-Syrian Exegesis in the Seventh Century*

As we have seen [see vol. I/1, ch. 17, 5.4], the crisis around Ḥenana of Adiabene (ca. 600) demonstrates that Theodore of Mopsuestia's authority did not remain completely unshaken in the School of Nisibis.[17] In the second half of the

---

[11] Ms. London, British Library, Add. 12.168. Cf. W. Wright, *A Catalogue of Syriac Manuscripts in the British Museum Acquired since the year 1838* II (London 1871) 904–08.

[12] Cf. C. Van den Eynde, *La version syriaque du Commentaire de Grégoire de Nysse sur le Cantique des Cantiques* (Bibliothèque du Muséon 10; Louvain 1939) 46–49, 90–95 (Syriac); 117–20 (Latin transl.).

[13] P. Krüger, "Johannes bar Aphtonājā und die syrische Übersetzung seines Kommentars zum Hohen Liede", *OrChr* 50 (1966) 61–71; R. Köbert, "Syrische Fragmente eines griechischen Kommentars zum Hohen Lied", *Bib.* 48 (1967) 111–14.

[14] W. Baars, *New Syro-Hexaplaric Texts* (Leiden 1968) 20–21.

[15] Cf. Kruisheer, Ephrem, Jacob of Edessa and the Monk Severus (1998).

[16] Cf. Van den Eynde, La version syriaque (1939) 49–59; 121–26 (Latin transl.).

[17] Cf. also G. J. Reinink, "‹Edessa Grew Dim and Nisibis Shone Forth›: The School of Nisibis at the Transition of the Sixth-Seventh Century", *Centres of Learning. Learning and Location in Pre-Modern Europe and the Near East* (ed. J. W. Drijvers / A. A. MacDonald; Leiden 1995) 77–89.

seventh century we again hear voices, from the monks this time, which very subtly express their dissatisfaction with the current teaching of exegesis in the East-Syrian Church.[18] Dadišoʿ Qaṭraya, in his *Commentary on the Asceticon of Abba Isaiah*, makes a distinction between three exegetical approaches to the Book of Psalms: the historical (*tašʿitānāyā*), the homiletic (*mtargmānāyā*), and the spiritual interpretation (*ruḥānāyā*). The historical interpretation, which Dadišoʿ immediately links with the name of Theodore, is said to be appropriate to scholars (*ʾeskolāyē* "those of the schools"), whereas the homiletic interpretation, with which the names of Basil and John Chrysostom are connected, is said to be of use to the laity. The spiritual interpretation is being practised by the solitaries and holy men during their singing of the psalms. Dadišoʿ strongly defends the monks against those who despise them for practising spiritual exegesis. Although historical interpretation is always the first step, one should also learn from Scripture how to know and glorify God and keep his commandments. In order to attain this, one should not confine oneself to the literal text, but try to understand the "hint" (*remzā*) of hidden and spiritual things, which is contained in the text and to which solitaries and holy men are particularly sensitive. Dadišoʿ further argues that this approach is not foreign to Theodore's exegesis. In fact, Theodore himself – though knowing that those who achieve purity of heart and are worthy of divine revelations are few – had recommended the use of Scripture as a means of instruction towards virtuous life.

In Dadišoʿ's time a complex tradition of ascetic and monastic literature had developed, which was to a large extent based on the works of the fourth-century Origenist monk Evagrius of Pontus.[19] Dadišoʿ apparently tries to bring about some kind of reconciliation between Theodore and Evagrius. A similar attempt to accomodate Evagrian ideas to Theodore's exegesis may be found in the section "On the revelations and powers which happen to the saints in images" of Isaac of Nineveh's *Mystic Treatises*.[20] In this section Theodore's exegetical works are explicitly referred to on more than one occasion.

Since very little of Theodore's ascetic works is preserved, we cannot ascertain the exact position taken by Theodore in this regard. It should be noted, however, that both Dadišoʿ and Isaac (who were contemporaries), while slightly distancing themselves from scholarly exegesis as practised in their day, explicitly claimed to have Theodore's approval.

---

[18] Cf. R. Macina, "L'homme à l'école de Dieu. D'Antioche à Nisibe. Profil herméneutique, théologique et kérygmatique du mouvement scoliaste nestorien. Monographie programmatique", *Proche-Orient Chrétien* 32 (1982) 56–72; P. Bettiolo, "Esegesi e purezza di cuore. La testimonianza di Dadišoʿ Qaṭraya (VII sec.), nestoriano e solitario", *Annali di Storia dell'Esegesi* 3 (1986) 201–13; C. Molenberg, "The Silence of the Sources: The Sixth Century and East-Syrian 'Antiochene' Exegesis", *The Sixth Century: End or Beginning?* (ed. P. Allen / E. Jeffreys; Byzantina Australiensia 10; Brisbane 1996) 145–62.

[19] On Evagrius and his influence in the Syriac world, see A. Guillaumont, "Evagrius Ponticus", TRE 10 (1982) 565–70, with further references. Some remarks on Evagrius's exegesis will be found in P. Géhin, *Évagre le Pontique. Scholies aux Proverbes* (SC 340; Paris 1987) 26–32.

[20] A. J. Wensinck, *Mystic Treatises by Isaac of Nineveh* (Verhandelingen der Koninklijke Akademie van Wetenschappen te Amsterdam, Afdeeling Letterkunde, Nieuwe Reeks, 23, 1; Amsterdam 1923; English transl.) 105–09.

3.2. Theodore bar Koni's "Scholion"

Edition and translation: A. Scher, *Theodorus bar Kōnī. Liber Scholiorum* (CSCO 55, 69/Syr. 19, 26; Paris – Leipzig 1910–12; Syriac); R. Hespel / R. Draguet, *Théodore bar Koni. Livre des scolies (recension de Séert)* (CSCO 431–32/Syr. 187–88; Louvain 1981/82; French transl.).

Study: S. Griffith, "Theodore bar Kônî's *Scholion*: A Nestorian *Summa contra Gentiles* from the First Abbasid Century", *East of Byzantium. Syria and Armenia in the Formative Period* (ed. N. G. Garsoïan / T. F. Mathews / R. W. Thomson; Washington 1982) 53–72.

This voluminous work was in all probability completed at the end of the eighth century (around 791/792). It consists of 11 books (*mēmrē*), nine of which deal with exegesis. Books 1–5 are devoted to the Old Testament. Theodore does not provide a running commentary, but explains select problems in a series of questions and answers. After having dealt with one biblical book or a number of books taken together (e.g., the Pentateuch, the Twelve Prophets), he provides a list of difficult words found in those books, along with short explanations.

Bar Koni proves himself to be a faithful pupil of Theodore of Mopsuestia, whose ideas he often repeats and whom he respectfully quotes. His purpose was not to create an original work, but to instruct people and to elucidate the meaning of Scripture "in view of the modest knowledge of those who have only recently embarked on studying and reading the commentaries of the Blessed Interpreter" (Introduction of *Mēmrā* 10). Bar Koni's work may, therefore, be seen as a handbook, to be used along with the writings of Theodore of Mopsuestia, of which he must have had a first-hand knowledge.

Among the questions on Psalms, Bar Koni devotes a section to the difference between historical and allegorical interpretation, in which the latter is explicitly rejected. Moreover, while viewing the Song of Songs as one of the books of Solomon (along with Proverbs and Qohelet), he regards it as Solomon's defence of Pharaoh's daughter, whom he had married and on whose account he was blamed by his people. Bar Koni sees no profit in the book, since it does not contain the name of "Lord" or "God" and for this reason he refrains from further comment. In taking this position, Bar Koni is one of the very few who strictly adhered to Theodore of Mopsuestia's view on the Song of Songs. A slightly different attitude *vis-à-vis* the "Interpreter", however, can be found in the commentary on the Twelve Prophets, where Bar Koni discusses the problem of the discrepancies between the Syriac and Greek biblical versions and tries to mitigate Theodore of Mopsuestia's negative assessment of the Syriac version of these biblical books.

In many places Bar Koni's text shows a very striking agreement with other East-Syrian works, in particular the *Commentary* of Išoʿdad [see 3.5] and, to a lesser extent, the *Anonymous Commentary* [see 3.4]. The exact nature of this relationship has not yet been satisfactorily explained.

3.3. Išoʿ bar Nun's Selected Questions

Editions and translations: E. G. Clarke, *The Selected Questions of Ishō bar Nūn on the Pentateuch. Edited and Translated from Ms Cambridge Add. 2017. With a Study of the Relationship of Ishōʿdadh of Merv, Theodore bar Kōnī and Ishō bar Nūn on Genesis* (SPB 5; Leiden 1962; Syriac and English transl.); D. Bundy, "The Questions and Answers on Isaiah by Išoʿ bar Nūn", *Orientalia Lovaniensia Periodica* 16 (1985) 167–78 (Syriac and English transl.).

Studies: C. Molenberg, *The Interpreter Interpreted. Išoʿ bar Nun's Selected Questions on the Old Testament* (Ph. D. thesis; Groningen 1990); eadem, "Išo^c bar Nun and Išoʿdad of Merv on the Book of Genesis: A Study of Their Interrelationship", *The Book of Genesis in Jewish and Oriental Christian Interpretation. A Collection of Essays* (ed. J. Frishman / L. Van Rompay; Traditio Exegetica Graeca 5; Louvain 1997) 197–228.

Išoʿ bar Nun was Catholicos-Patriarch of the East-Syrian Church from 823 until his death in 828. His "Selected Questions" may, however, date from an earlier period in his life, when he was a teacher, first in the Great Convent of Mount Izla, to the northeast of Nisibis, and later in Mosul. His work may, therefore, belong to the end of the eighth century.

Like Bar Koni's "Scholion", Išoʿ bar Nun's work deals with both the Old and New Testament in a series of questions and answers. The work as it is presently known, exists in one manuscript and may represent only part of the original collection. The author appears to have reworked and reshaped his sources to such an extent that the works on which he drew are not easily recognizable. His independent nature also reveals itself in the way he deals with East-Syrian exegetical tradition. Although he often reproduces traditional interpretations and respectfully quotes Theodore of Mopsuestia, on some occasions he deliberately presents a spiritual, not to say allegorical, explanation.[21] With regard to the composition of Psalm 119 (LXX 118), which contains an alphabetical acrostic with eight verses for each of the 22 letters, Išoʿ bar Nun adduces spiritual or allegorical interpretations that may be traced back to Gregory of Nazianzus and Origen, possibly through the intermediacy of Evagrius of Pontus. As for the number of 300 men, fighting with Gideon against the Midianites (Judges 7), Išoʿ bar Nun juxtaposes a historical explanation with a *theoria* concerning the Holy Trinity, the latter again echoing Origen's interpretation.

One is reminded here of the discussion on historical and spiritual exegesis in Dadišoʿ's work [see 3.1], where the influence of Origen and Evagrius did indeed play an important role. In addition, broadening Theodore of Mopsuestia's concept of historical and typological exegesis and elaborating his own ideas of *theoria* in Scripture (which for him was clearly distinct from allegory), Išoʿ bar Nun may have been guided by the works of Chrysostom and the Cappadocians, which had for centuries circulated among East-Syrian scholars.

---

[21] Molenberg, The Interpreter Interpreted (1990) esp. 264–71, 274–80; eadem, The Silence of the Sources (1996) 156–62, where much attention is given to the possible influence of John Chrysostom's writings on Išoʿ bar Nun.

3.4. *The Commentary on Gen-Exod 9:32 of ms. (olim) Diyarbakir 22 and the Anonymous Commentary on the Old Testament*

Editions and translations: L. Van Rompay, *Le commentaire sur Genèse-Exode 9,32 du manuscrit (olim) Diyarbakir 22* (CSCO 483–84/Syr. 205–06; Louvain 1986; Syriac and French transl.); A. Levene, *The Early Syrian Fathers on Genesis. From a Syriac Ms. on the Pentateuch in the Mingana Collection. The First Eighteen Chapters of the Ms. Edited with Introduction, Translation and Notes; and Including a Study in Comparative Exegesis* (London 1951; Syriac and English transl.).

Study: Jansma, Investigations (1958).

Three separate but interrelated texts must be distinguished here: 1) an anonymous commentary on Gen-Exod 9:32, preserved only in ms. (olim) Diyarbakir 22; 2) an anonymous commentary on the Pentateuch (published in part by Levene), preserved in a number of manuscripts; 3) the continuation of the preceding commentary, covering the remaining books of the Old Testament (in two mss.) or the entire Old Testament and New Testament (in one ms., i.e., ms. Diyarbakir 22).

The oldest stage of this hybrid material is found in the *Diyarbakir Commentary on Gen-Exod 9:32.* This running commentary, which in the only extant manuscript is acephalous and truncated at the end, is to a large extent based on Theodore of Mopsuestia's commentaries and interpretations,[22] to which the opinions of a few other Greek writers and a number of Syrian exegetes have been added. Among the latter, the most prominent place is occupied by Rabban Gabriel Qaṭraya, in all likelihood a teacher at the School of Seleucia in the seventh century. More frequently than Theodore bar Koni and Išoʿ bar Nun, the author of the *Diyarbakir Commentary* quotes readings from "the Greek" and "the Hebrew". In all probability, the former have their origin in the Greek translations of Theodore of Mopsuestia's commentaries, while the latter can be explained as isolated pieces of Jewish tradition [see vol. I/1, ch. 17, 1.2.1]. This commentary is further characterized by the transliteration of words from Persian as well as from the language of Bet-Qaṭraye (the region situated to the west of the Arab-Persian Gulf) used to explain Syriac words in the Bible. Various indications point to the eighth century as the time of composition of this commentary.

The *Anonymous Commentary on the Pentateuch* in the title is presented as "a commentary, or elucidation of difficult words in the Pentateuch, which is drawn from the Commentary of saintly Mar Theodore and from the traditions of the Syrians: Mar Ephrem and John and Abraham of Bet-Rabban and Mar Michael and other teachers". As far as we can judge from the section on Gen-Exod 9:32, the *Anonymous Commentary* is an abridged version of the *Diyarbakir Commentary.* Apart from abridging and slightly reworking his main source, the redactor also added a few quotations from other sources, notably

---

[22] On this work as a possible source for our knowledge of Theodore's *Commentary on Genesis* (which is not preserved in the direct tradition), see F. Petit, "Les fragments grecs d'Eusèbe d'Émèse et de Théodore de Mopsueste. L'apport de Procope de Gaza", *Le Muséon* 104 (1991) 352–53.

from Išoʿdad of Merv [see 3.5]. Since he also has introduced some additional words from the language of Bet-Qaṭraye, it may be assumed that, like the author of the *Diyarbakir Commentary*, he had a special relationship to the Christian community in that region. He may have been active at the end of the ninth or the beginning of the tenth century.

It remains unknown whether the *Anonymous Commentary* was originally restricted to the Pentateuch and was expanded in the later tradition, or whether it originally included the entire Old Testament (or even the Old Testament with the New Testament) and was only partly copied in most manuscripts.

3.5. Išoʿdad of Merv's Commentary on the Old Testament

Editions and translations: J.-M. Vosté / C. Van den Eynde, *Išoʿdad de Merv. Commentaire sur l'Ancien Testament*, I. *Genèse* (CSCO 126/Syr. 67; Louvain 1950; Syriac); C. Van den Eynde, *Išoʿdad de Merv. Commentaire sur l'Ancien Testament*, I. *Genèse* (CSCO 156/Syr. 75; Louvain 1955; French transl.); II. *Exode-Deutéronome* (CSCO 176, 179/Syr. 80–81; Louvain 1958); III. *Livre des Sessions* (CSCO 229–30/Syr. 96–97; Louvain 1962/63); IV. *Isaïe et les Douze* (CSCO 303–04/Syr. 128–29; Louvain 1969); V. *Jérémie, Ézéchiel, Daniel* (CSCO 328–29/Syr. 146–47; Louvain 1972); VI. *Psaumes* (CSCO 433–34/Syr. 185–86; Louvain 1981; Syriac and French transl.).

Studies: M. Albert, "Les commentaires syriens sur les Psaumes. Un exemple: le Psaume 45", *Le Psautier chez les Pères* (Cahiers de Biblia Patristica 4; Strasbourg 1994) 255–70; G. Diettrich, *Išôʿdâdh's Stellung in der Auslegungsgeschichte des Alten Testamentes an seinen Commentaren zu Hosea, Joel, Jona, Sacharja 9–14 und einigen angehängten Psalmen veranschaulicht* (BZAW VI; Giessen 1902); C. Leonhard, *Ishodad of Merv's Exegesis of the Psalms 119, 139–47. A Study of His Interpretation in the Light of the Syriac Translation of Theodore of Mopsuestia's Commentary* (Ph. D. thesis Vienna 1999); idem, "Išoʿdad's Commentary on Psalm 141, 2. A Quotation of Theodore of Mopsuestia's Lost Commentary", StPatr (ed. E. J. Yarnold; Leuven, forthcoming); C. Molenberg, *The Commentary on the Books of the Holy Prophets in a Manuscript in Leningrad. An Epitome of Išoʿdad of Merv* (CSCO 494/Subs. 77; Louvain 1987); eadem, Išoʿ bar Nun and Išoʿdad of Merv on the Book of Genesis (1997) [see 3.3] 197–228; A. Salvesen, "Hexaplaric Readings in Išoʿdad of Merv's Commentary on Genesis", *The Book of Genesis in Jewish and Oriental Christian Interpretation. A Collection of Essays* (ed. J. Frishman / L. Van Rompay; Traditio Exegetica Graeca 5; Louvain 1997) 229–52.

The work of Išoʿdad (ca. 850), which also comprises a *Commentary on the New Testament*, represents one of the most expansive forms of the East-Syrian exegetical tradition. Apart from its significance for our knowledge of East-Syrian exegesis in the ninth century, its value also consists in its having incorporated so many fragments of exegesis from earlier times, which are otherwise not or only imperfectly known to us. Both the theological concepts and the exegetical principles largely reflect the ideas of Theodore of Mopsuestia as they were transmitted in Išoʿdad's time. Works of other authors, however, were also part of the East-Syrian exegetical tradition, especially those of Ephrem, Basil of Caesarea and the Cappadocians, and Chrysostom, as well as exegetical works by various teachers of the schools of Nisibis and Seleucia (among them Narsai, Mar Aba Catholicos, and Ḥenana [see vol. I/1, ch. 17, 5.3]).

Recent research has pointed out that Išoʿdad used both Išoʿ bar Nun's *Selected Questions* [see 3.3] and the *Diyarbakir Commentary* [see 3.4] (the latter in a recension which may not have been completely identical to the one preserved in the only extant manuscript) as direct sources, and copied large sections from these works, adapting and rearranging them according to his own editorial principles.

Išoʿdad did not confine himself to collecting and reproducing what was transmitted to him by previous generations. It appears that from time to time he consulted directly the original works of such authors as Ephrem and Theodore of Mopsuestia. In addition, he had access to works which were not commonly used among East-Syrian exegetes. One example is Paul of Tella's Syro-Hexaplaric version of the Old Testament, from which Išoʿdad was the first East-Syrian exegete to borrow *Yawnāyā* quotations [see vol. I/1, ch. 17, 1.2.1], which he did not distinguish from the "Greek" quotations drawn from other sources.[23] Eusebius of Emesa's *Commentary on the Octateuch* [see vol. I/1, ch. 17, 3.3, with n. 37] is another work which Išoʿdad was the first to use, while it had remained unknown to his East-Syrian predecessors.[24]

The number and nature of the sources explicitly mentioned by Išoʿdad provide direct insights into literary life in ninth century East-Syrian monasteries and schools. Even if the introduction of so many different sources into his *Commentary* may be due primarily to the personal initiative of the learned compiler, the majority of the works quoted must have circulated and been used and discussed among scholars and exegetes. The broad panorama which unfolds in this *Commentary* shows to what extent East-Syrian exegesis, while always acknowledging Theodore of Mopsuestia as its main authority, had in the course of centuries adopted a much more varied approach to the biblical text.

Among the many authors on whom Išoʿdad drew, the following may be singled out: John the Solitary (used in the *Commentary* on Qohelet [see vol. I/1, ch. 17, 4.3]), Evagrius of Pontus (Qohelet and Job), Philo of Alexandria (twice quoted on Exodus), Gregory of Nyssa (Song of Songs), Cyril of Alexandria (Isaiah and Daniel; the quotations probably derive from marginal notes in a Syro-Hexaplaric manuscript), Theodoret of Cyrrus (Jeremiah and Daniel), Jacob of Edessa (Job [see 2.1]). In particular in the case of those biblical books on which Theodore of Mopsuestia had expressed himself categorically, Išoʿdad, along with other East-Syrian exegetes, subtly introduced other authorities to counterbalance Theodore's views. This is the case for the Song of Songs (where Išoʿdad's view diverges from Bar Koni's judgement [see 3.2]), Job (where both Chrysostom and Ḥenana are amply used), and to a lesser extent for Psalms and the Twelve Prophets (where he sees, more often than Theodore, a prophecy with a double signification).

---

[23] For the use of the Syro-Hexapla among East-Syrians from the beginning of the ninth century onwards, see R. B. TER HAAR ROMENY, "Biblical Studies in the Church of the East: The Case of Catholicos Timothy I", StPatr (ed. E. J. Yarnold; Leuven, forthcoming).

[24] Cf. R. B. TER HAAR ROMENY, *A Syrian in Greek Dress. The Use of Greek, Hebrew, and Syriac Biblical Texts in Eusebius of Emesa's Commentary on Genesis* (Traditio Exegetica Graeca 6; Louvain 1997) 28 and pass.

3.6. *The Garden of Delights* (Gannat Bussāmē)

Edition and translation: G. J. Reinink, *Gannat Bussame*, I. *Die Adventssonntage* (CSCO 501–02/Syr. 211–12; Louvain 1988; Syriac and German transl.).

Study: G. J. Reinink, *Studien zur Quellen- und Traditionsgeschichte des Evangelienkommentars der Gannat Bussame* (CSCO 414/Subs. 57; Louvain 1979).

This work, which may be dated to the tenth century, contains commentaries on the biblical pericopes (both OT and NT) read during liturgical services. It is arranged according to the Sundays and feasts of the liturgical year. Within the framework of the East-Syrian lectionary, the compiler has brought together interpretations culled from commentaries as well as from other works of exegetical content, especially homilies.

The works which in the Old Testament sections of the *Gannat Bussāmē* have been used as direct sources include: 1) a source which was closely related to Išoʿdad's *Commentary* [see 3.5] as well as to the *Anonymous Commentary* [see 3.4]; 2) a source which was nearly identical to the *Diyarbakir Commentary* [see 3.4]; 3) exegetical homilies by Mar Aba II of Kaškar. The quotations from the homilies (*mēmrē* or *turgāmē*) of the latter, which appear in the commentaries on Genesis, Numbers, and Isaiah (to which many quotations in the Gospel commentaries should be added), constitute the main source of our knowledge of this author. Before becoming Catholicos-Patriarch of the East-Syrian Church (probably in 741), Mar Aba studied at the School of Seleucia in the second half of the seventh century. While familiar with the works and ideas of Theodore of Mopsuestia as they were transmitted and developed in the schools of his day, Mar Aba also displays the marked influence of John Chrysostom in his writings.[25] The passages incorporated into the *Gannat Bussāmē*, therefore, are able to shed some light on the formation of the earlier East-Syrian exegetical tradition.

3.7. *Other East-Syrian Exegetical Works*

In addition to the commentaries which have just been mentioned and which in recent years have been studied by scholars, other works are still awaiting further investigation.

A collection of *Questions on the (Divine) Economy*, dealing mainly with exegesis of both Old and New Testament, has sometimes been ascribed to Ḥenanišoʿ bar Serošway, who probably lived in the second half of the ninth century. It appears, however, that the end of the twelfth century is a *terminus post quem* for its composition.[26] Two short works, published by G. Hoffmann, the first of which is a biblical glossary, while the second contains extracts from a commentary, are of an unknown date.[27]

---

[25] On the style of Mar Aba's homilies, see G. J. Reinink, "Rhetorik in der Homilie zu Jes 52,13–53,12 des Katholikos Mar Aba II. von Kaškar", *IV Symposium Syriacum 1984* (ed. H. J. W. Drijvers / R. Lavenant / C. Molenberg / G. J. Reinink; OCA 229; Rome 1987) 307–16.

[26] Reinink, Gannat Bussame I (CSCO 502/Syr. 212; 1988) XLVIII–XLIX [see 3.6].

[27] G. Hoffmann, *Opuscula Nestoriana* (Kiel etc. 1880; Syriac); cf. Reinink, Gannat Bussame (CSCO 502/Syr. 212; 1988) XLVI–XLVII.

Two *Commentaries on Psalms* are as yet unpublished.[28] The first is anonymous and has been preserved in one manuscript (ms. Sachau 215); it consists largely of the exegesis of Theodore of Mopsuestia. The second, an expanded version of the preceding, is ascribed to Denḥa-Grigor and may date to the ninth century.[29] Most manuscripts containing the Denḥa-Grigor *Commentary* also include extracts from other works dealing with the Psalms. Along with passages taken from Theodore bar Koni [see 3.2], the anonymous *Explanation of Liturgical Services* (Ps.-George of Arbela), John bar Penkaye's *World History* (end of the 7th century), and John bar Zoʿbi's *Well-woven Fabric* (*Zqorā mlaḥḥmā*, ca. 1200) – all equally known in direct tradition – introductions to the Psalms are quoted that are otherwise unknown to us and are ascribed to Aḥob Qaṭraya (6th century?) and Natniel of Širzor (ca. 600).[30]

Two metrical works are representatives of the school tradition of the tenth century: Elias of Anbar's *Book of Instruction* (*Ktābā d-durrāšā*, 1st half of the 10th century) contains many sections in which Old Testament events are typologically or even allegorically interpreted,[31] whereas Emmanuel bar Šahhare's *Hexaemeron* (ca. 950), consisting of 28 *mēmrē*, betrays on the one hand the influence of Narsai's *Homilies* [see vol. I/1, ch. 17, 5.3], and on the other hand reflects the later developments of Syriac Hexaemeron literature.[32] A comprehensive prose treatment of the entire history of salvation, with a great deal of exegetical material, is found in Solomon of Basra's *Book of the Bee* (1st half of the 13th century).[33] The same wide scope is adopted in Isaac Ešbadnaya's *Poem on the Divine Economy* (mid 15th century), to which the author himself added a prose commentary containing many quotations from earlier exegetical literature.[34]

One of the first East-Syrian exegetes writing in Arabic was Ibn aṭ-Ṭayyib (d. 1043). His work *Paradise of Christendom* (*Firdaws al-Naṣrāniyya*) contains commentaries on most of the books of the Bible, while he explains the Psalms in a separate *Commentary*.[35] As far as can be judged from the *Commentary on Genesis* (which is part of the *Paradise*), Ibn aṭ-Ṭayyib used Īšoʿdad of Merv

[28] Cf. Van den Eynde, Commentaire d'Īšoʿdad VI (CSCO 434/Syr. 186; 1981) XXXIII–XXXIV and XXXVI–XXXVII [see 3.5].

[29] Extracts have been published by B. Vandenhoff, *Exegesis psalmorum imprimis messianicorum apud Syros Nestorianos* (Rheine 1899; Syriac and Latin transl.).

[30] L. Van Rompay, *Théodore de Mopsueste. Fragments syriaques du Commentaire des Psaumes (Psaume 118 et Psaumes 138–48)* (CSCO 436/Syr. 190; Louvain 1982) IX–XIV.

[31] Cf. A. K. Juckel, *Der Ktābā d-Durrāšā (Ktābā d-Maʾwātā) des Elijā von Anbār. Mēmrā I–III* (CSCO 559–60/Syr. 226–27; Louvain 1996); idem, "Typologie und Angelologie im Ktābā d-Durrāšā des Ostsyrers Elījā von Anbār", *V Symposium Syriacum 1988* (ed. R. Lavenant; OCA 236; Rome 1990) 173–79.

[32] Cf. E. ten Napel, "The Textual Tradition of Emmanuel bar Shahhare's Hexaemeron in the Light of the Monastic School-Tradition", StPatr 18, 4 (ed. E. A. Livingstone; Kalamazoo / Leuven 1990) 289–95, with further references.

[33] E. A. W. Budge, *The Book of the Bee* (Anecdota Oxoniensia, Semitic Series 1, 2; Oxford 1886; Syriac and English transl.).

[34] Cf. Reinink, Studien (1979) 49–60.

[35] Cf. R. Köbert, "Ibn aṭ-Ṭaiyib's Erklärung von Psalm 44", *Bib.* 43 (1962) 338–48 (German transl.).

[see 3.5] as his main source.[36] Through Ibn aṭ-Ṭayyib's work, part of East-Syrian exegesis was transmitted to the Christian-Arabic world, whenceforth it found its way to the Ethiopian exegetical tradition.[37]

4. Dionysius bar Ṣalibi's Commentary on the Old Testament

Editions and translations: T. Fish, "The Literal Commentary on the Book of Joel the Prophet by Dionysius Bar Ṣalībi († 1171)", *Journal of the Manchester University Egyptian and Oriental Society* 24 (1942–45) 22–27 (English transl.); Schlimme, Der Hexaemeronkommentar II (1977) 756–861 [see 2.2] (German transl. of the commentary on Gen 1–2:7); W. Strothmann, *Syrische Katenen aus dem Ecclesiastes-Kommentar des Theodor von Mopsuestia* (GOF I, 29; Wiesbaden 1988; Syriac text of the factual commentary on Qohelet); idem, *Kohelet-Kommentar des Dionysius bar Ṣalībī. Auslegung des Septuaginta-Textes* (GOF I, 31; Wiesbaden 1988; Syriac text of the spriritual commentary on Qohelet); A. de Halleux, "Une version syriaque révisée du commentaire d'Hippolyte sur Suzanne", *Le Muséon* 101 (1988) 297–341 (Syriac and French transl.).

Studies: G. G. Blum, "Dionysius bar Ṣalībī", TRE 9 (1982) 6–9, with further references; A. de Halleux, "Hippolyte en version syriaque", *Le Muséon* 102 (1989) 19–42; D. Bundy, "The Genesis Commentary of Dionysius Bar Salibi", StPatr 25 (ed. E. A. Livingstone; Leuven 1993) 244–52.

The literary heritage of this bishop and prolific author of the West-Syrian Church (d. 1171) includes a commentary on the entire Bible, written in the last years of the author's life. This work is for the most part as yet unpublished. For most of the Old Testament books there is a double commentary: one factual (*suʿrānāyā*) and one spiritual (*ruḥānāyā*). For a number of books (Psalms, Proverbs, Qohelet, Song of Songs, Jeremiah and Daniel) Bar Ṣalibi based the factual commentary on the Peshitta and the spiritual on the Septuagint, known to him in the version of the Syro-Hexapla [see vol. I/1, ch. 17, 1.2.1].[38] The situation with regard to the various commentaries is rather complicated. While nearly all the books are provided with a factual commentary, the second commentary is not always purely spiritual, but in some cases of a mixed nature (factual and spiritual). For Jeremiah there is even a third commentary.

In the introduction, the author presents his work as a compilation of various older sources. It appears, however, that in general he did not work with very many sources at the same time; rather for each book (or parts of it) he copied large sections from a single source or a limited number of sources. In the factual commentary on the first chapters of Genesis, Moses bar Kepa was his

[36] Cf. J. C. J. Sanders, *Ibn aṭ-Ṭaiyib. Commentaire sur la Genèse* (CSCO 274–75/Arab. 24–25; Louvain 1967).

[37] Cf. R. W. Cowley, *Ethiopian Biblical Interpretation. A Study in Exegetical Tradition and Hermeneutics* (Cambridge 1988). This extremely rich work shows examples of Christian exegetical tradition as it developed throughout Syriac, Christian Arabic, and Ethiopic literature. With regard to Psalms mention should be made of K. Stoffregen Pedersen, *Traditional Ethiopian Exegesis of the Book of Psalms* (Äthiopistische Forschungen 36; Wiesbaden 1995; Amharic with English transl.) esp. 294, where the links with East-Syrian exegesis and the possible role of Ibn aṭ-Ṭayyib's Psalm Commentary are discussed. A further illustration of the presence of originally Syriac theological and exegetical motifs in Ethiopic literature may be found in Getatchew Haile / Misrak Amare, *Beauty of Creation* (JSSMon 16; Manchester 1991).

[38] On the commentary on Isaiah, see S. Khalil, "Le Commentaire d'Isaïe de Denys bar Ṣalībī. Notes Bibliographiques", *OrChr* 62 (1978) 158–65; Bundy, The Peshitta of Isaiah 53:9 (1983) 41–42 [see General Works].

model [see 2.2]. The factual commentary of Qohelet consists of excerpts from Theodore of Mopsuestia's *Commentary* [see vol. I/1, ch. 17, 5.2], with some additions from that of John the Solitary [see vol. I/1, ch. 17, 4.3]. To his commentary on Daniel, Bar Ṣalibi added a Syriac version of Hippolytus's *Commentary on Susanna.* This version, datable to the early sixth century and not otherwise known to us, had been slightly revised (perhaps by Bar Ṣalibi himself) and interspersed with a few scholia by Jacob of Edessa [see 2.1].

In the factual commentary, the author aims at reconstructing the original meaning of the text as well as explaining the historical context of the biblical story. As can clearly be seen in the commentaries on Qohelet and Joel, Bar Ṣalibi went much further than Bar Kepa in adopting and incorporating interpretations which originally belonged to the East-Syrian tradition and even stemmed from Theodore of Mopsuestia himself. Bar Ṣalibi's dependence, for many parts of his commentary, on Išoʿdad of Merv should be viewed in the same light. The spiritual commentary, which in general is more concise than the factual, offers an interpretation of an allegorical type. West-Syrian antecedents for this approach may be found in Daniel of Ṣalaḥ [see vol. I/1, ch. 17, 6.2] and Jacob of Edessa [see 2.1]. However, when, e.g., the daughters of Lot are seen as "types of the *theoretikos* and the *praktikos*" and the intoxication of Lot as "a type of the intoxication of the mind (*nous*) by the *pneumatikos*", this betrays a more direct dependence on the writings of Evagrius of Pontus and the ascetical-monastic literature which evolved from them.[39]

Further research will be needed in order to assess fully the importance of this commentary, both as a repository of earlier exegetical tradition and as a testimony to Syriac culture in a period which has been described as the "Syriac Renaissance".[40]

5. Barhebraeus's Storehouse of Mysteries (*'Auṣar Rāzē*)

Editions and translations: M. Sprengling / W. C. Graham, *Barhebraeus' Scholia on the Old Testament*, I. *Genesis – II Samuel* (Oriental Institute Publications 13; Chicago 1931; Syriac and English transl.); cf. J.-M. Fiey, "Esquisse d'une bibliographie de Bar Hébraeus († 1286)", *Parole de l'Orient* 13 (1986) 279–312 (with a list of the partial editions of the *Storehouse* on p. 284–88).

Studies: J. Göttsberger, *Barhebräus und seine Scholien zur Heiligen Schrift* (Biblische Studien 5, 4–5; Freiburg i. B. 1900); T. Jansma, "Barhebraeus' Scholion on the Words 'Let there be Light' (Gen I, 3) as Presented in his 'Storehouse of Mysteries'. Some Observations on the Vicissitudes of the Exposition of a Biblical Passage", *Abr Nahrain* 13 (1972/73) 100–14; W. Hage, "Gregor Barhebräus", TRE 14 (1985) 158–64, with further references.

Barhebraeus (d. 1286), who for 22 years held the highest position in the West-Syrian Church in the former Persian territory, assembled in one volume (*Storehouse of Mysteries*, probably written in 1277/78) commentaries on all the books of the Bible, both Old and New Testament.

While Barhebraeus's personal contribution to the field of exegesis was fairly

[39] Cf. Bundy, The Genesis Commentary (1993) 251–52.

[40] P. Kawerau, *Die Jakobitische Kirche im Zeitalter der syrischen Renaissance* (Berlin 1955).

modest, the *Storehouse*, which takes the form of a biblical handbook, is a remarkable achievement. Without attempting to shape his commentaries into a coherent structure, the author included remarks pertaining to many different fields: textual criticism, exegesis, chronology, lexicography, and "masoretic" remarks on the phonology and pronunciation of biblical words (with special attention devoted to the differences between East and West Syriac). Most of these fields are touched upon by Barhebraeus in his other works and these, together with his biblical commentaries, bear witness to his immense erudition, which encompasses nearly all aspects of Syriac literary culture, in which the Bible and biblical studies occupy a prominent place. This comprehensive concept of biblical commentary is not new – in the West-Syrian tradition it may be traced back to Jacob of Edessa [see 2.1]) – but Barhebraeus pursued it much further than any of the previous exegetes had done.

In the field of textual criticism Barhebraeus juxtaposes to the Peshitta many quotations of "the Greek", which he culled from his sources or drew from a Syro-Hexapla manuscript available to him. Not unlike some of his predecessors, in cases of discrepancies he was inclined to give priority to the rendering of the Syro-Hexapla rather than to that of the Peshitta. In addition to the "Greek" quotations (and references to the other columns of the Hexapla, i. e., Aquila, Symmachus, and Theodotion, as well as Jacob of Edessa's revision of the biblical text), Barhebraeus has included, notably in his commentary on Psalms, a number of readings taken from the Armenian and from the Coptic biblical versions.[41] However, the latter have no real impact on his understanding of the biblical text. Not only do they add to the learned nature of the commentary, they also give some inkling of the horizon of the author's intellectual world. He must have realized that other Christian communities in the Middle East, like the Armenians and the Copts, did in fact preserve within their own traditions the same Christian heritage as the Syrians. Barhebraeus's remarks on the phonology and pronunciation of biblical words build upon the Syrian 'masoretic' tradition; the earlier phase of this tradition is known to us mainly through the work of the monks of Qarqapta, who are explicitly mentioned by Barhebraeus, particularly in his commentary on Psalms.[42]

As an exegete Barhebraeus depended largely on Dionysius bar Ṣalibi [see 4], without however maintaining the division between factual and spiritual commentaries. From Bar Ṣalibi he excerpted many sections of East-Syrian provenance, especially from Išoʿdad of Merv.[43] However, he does not confine himself to the "corporeal", the "factual or historical" meaning of Scripture, but in many cases interprets the Bible in a "spiritual" sense, here again echoing the position taken by Jacob of Edessa, Moses bar Kepa and Dionysius bar Ṣalibi. In some instances, Barhebraeus's explanations are based on his personal experiences, referring to customs or practices found among the Mongols, the Armenians, the Arabs, the Indians, the Greeks, and the Franks.

---

[41] Göttsberger, Barhebräus und seine Scholien (1900) 147, has counted 159 quotations from the Armenian and 45 from the Coptic Bible.

[42] For some examples, see Martin, Tradition karkaphienne (1869) 261–67.

[43] Cf. Diettrich, Išôʿdâdh's Stellung (1902) XXXIV–XLII.

With regard to the sources which Barhebraeus quotes explicitly, it is not always possible, at the present stage of the research, to distinguish between those sources to which he had direct access, and those of which he had only a second-hand knowledge. Dionysius bar Ṣalibi is not mentioned explicitly, but the names of Jacob of Edessa and Daniel of Ṣalaḥ regularly appear, the latter in the commentary on Psalms.

6. Epilogue

The works of Dionysius bar Ṣalibi and Barhebraeus in the West-Syrian area and Isaac Ešbadnaya in the East-Syrian area, bring to close Syriac exegetical literature, which covers more than one millennium. In the present chapter, a great number of works and authors have been surveyed, representing a broad panorama of Syriac Old Testament exegesis. Some exegetes made personal and original contributions to the field; others, especially in the later period, were led mainly by their predecessors' works, and recycled older material or drew upon the anonymous exegetical school tradition. They illustrate the patterns of development of Syriac exegesis, which throughout the centuries continued to occupy a prominent place in Syriac learning and education, adapting to the changing historical circumstances within the Syrian Christian communities.

As in our treatment of the Syriac exegetical literature of the pre-Islamic period [see vol. I/1, ch. 17], this survey of the Islamic period has been largely restricted to purely exegetical works. Other genres that could also shed light on the way Syrian Christians understood and used their Bible have been excluded. One such genre is that of the homiletic literature.[44] Another field which has been mentioned only incidentally is that of ascetic literature. As we have seen, important new trends in biblical interpretation originated among the monks, who were familiar with the works of Evagrius of Pontus, one of the followers of Origen. This new approach, which placed great emphasis on spiritual and even allegorical interpretation, found its way into the exegetical commentaries, such as those of Išoʿ bar Nun, Išoʿdad of Merv, and Dionysius bar Ṣalibi. A more systematic study of ascetic and monastic literature from the viewpoint of biblical interpretation is clearly needed.

Evagrius's influence affected both West- and East-Syrian commentators. In a more general sense, it may be said that the two main branches of Syrian exegetes gradually allowed more scope for views which differed from those to which they originally adhered, and therefore came much closer to each other. West-Syrian exegetes were more openly adopting interpretations of Antiochene or East-Syrian origin, and ultimately Dionysius bar Ṣalibi, followed by Barhebraeus, even included whole sections of the East-Syrian commentary of Išoʿdad of Merv in his own work. At the same time, East-Syrian exegetes gradually felt free to make more extensive use of typology and spiritual exegesis than Theodore of Mopsuestia would have allowed.

---

44 See vol. I/1, ch. 17, 7 with n. 56.

The importance of Syriac exegesis is not restricted to the cultural area of Syriac Christianity as outlined above. Throughout history Syrian Christians have maintained close contacts with Christians in neighbouring regions, especially in Armenia, Egypt, and Ethiopia. Exegetical texts and traditions of Syrian origin have had an impact on the exegetical literature in Armenian, Christian Arabic (written both in Syria and in Egypt), and Ethiopic. Further comparative study of the exegetical literature in those languages and in Syriac may yield interesting insights into the broader literary and historical contexts of Syriac exegesis.

As for the Syrian Christians themselves, even today they continue to read and study their classical biblical commentaries. Although very little new material has been added to the exegetical tradition since the fifteenth century,[45] the great achievements of the past are fostered within the Syrian communities and play an important role in preserving the Syrian Christian identity in our day.

---

[45] For some remarks on the literary activity in modern times, see Baumstark, Geschichte (1922) 329–35; R. Macuch, *Geschichte der spät- und neusyrischen Literatur* (Berlin 1976); S. Brock, "Some Observations on the Use of Classical Syriac in the Twentieth Century", *JJS* 34 (1989) 363–75. For Neo-Syriac literature, which started being written in the seventeenth century, see also A. Mengozzi, "The Neo-Aramaic Manuscripts of the British Library: Notes on the Study of the Durikyāṯā as a Neo-Syriac Genre", *Le Muséon* 112 (1999) 459–94.

Chapter Thirty-seven

Elements of Biblical Interpretation in Medieval Jewish-Christian Disputation

By Günter Stemberger, Vienna

Bibliographies: J. Rosenthal, "Anti-Christian Polemics from its Beginnings to the End of 18th Century", Areshet 2 (1959/60) 130–79; 3 (1960/61) 433–39; H. Schreckenberg, *Die christlichen Adversus-Judaeos-Texte und ihr literarisches und historisches Umfeld* (1.–11. Jh.: EHS. T 172, Frankfurt/M.: P. Lang [3]1995; 11.–13. Jh.: EHS. T 335, [2]1991; 13.–20. Jh.: EHS. T 497, 1994).

General works: A. S. Abulafia, *Christians and Jews in the Twelfth-Century Renaissance* (London: Routledge 1995); G. Dahan, *Les intellectuels chrétiens et les juifs au moyen âge* (Patrimoines Judaïsme; Paris: Cerf 1990); A. Grossman, "The Jewish-Christian Polemic and Jewish Biblical Exegesis in Twelfth-Century France" (Hebr.), *Zion* 51 (1986) 29–60; O. Limor / G. Stroumsa (eds.), *Contra Iudaeos. Ancient and Medieval Polemics between Christians and Jews* (TSMJ 10; Tübingen: Mohr 1996); J. E. Rembaum, "The Development of a Jewish Exegetical Tradition regarding Isaiah 53", *HTR* 75 (1982) 289–311; E. I. J. Rosenthal, "Anti-Christian polemic in medieval Bible commentaries", *JJS* 11 (1960) 115–35; G. Stemberger, "Die Messiasfrage in den christlich-jüdischen Disputationen des Mittelalters", JBTh 8 (1993) 239–50; E. Touitou, "Rashbam's exegetical method and the historical reality of his time" (Hebr.), in: *Studies in Rabbinic Literature, Bible and Jewish History* (FS E. Z. Melammed; ed. Y. D. Gilat / Ch. Levine / Z. M. Rabinowitz; Ramat-Gan 1982) 48–74; H. Trautner-Kromann, *Shield and Sword. Jewish Polemics against Christianity and the Christians in France and Spain from 1100–1500* (TSMJ 8; Tübingen: Mohr 1993).

1. Antecedents

From the very beginnings of Christianity and its separation from Judaism, one of the main issues was the correct interpretation of the Bible and the consequences to be drawn from it. Most of the biblical texts important in later controversy are to be found already in the New Testament or Justin Martyr. Initially, the Christian understanding of these texts was fully within the broad range of possibilities present in first-century Judaism in Palestine and the diaspora. Two factors contributed to rendering the Christian interpretation of crucial biblical texts unacceptable to mainstream Judaism: the first and most important reason was the Christian insistence that its way of reading these texts as fulfilled in Christ was the only legitimate interpretation, and the (doctrinal and practical) consequences to which this position led. The second factor which enforced the split and contributed to making a fruitful discussion of the common biblical texts impossible, was the narrowing of the Jewish spectrum of legitimate interpretation after 70 when interpretative traditions like that of Qumran or of different apocalyptic currents disappeared and, most important, the Alexandrian school of interpretation (Philo) was no longer continued and appreciated. Christian-Jewish disputations such as, most notably, that between Justin and Trypho, soon proved to lead nowhere; the basic assumptions underlying the interpretation of the Bible were too different. Individual discussions between Christians and Jews about the correct understanding of certain biblical texts never stopped completely; but in general both sides found it more useful to present their own followers with the right interpretation of the texts. Jews normally ignored, at least at the very surface of their interpretations, or barely alluded to Christian ways of understanding biblical texts. Christians, on the other side, preferred purely literary 'disputations' in order to reject the Jewish readings and to defend the Christian interpretation. These writings were no longer intended to convince the other side, but only to confirm the Christian reader in the correctness of the Christian position. But even this literary effort almost stopped at the end of the patristic period, when the same arguments had already been repeated too many times.

2. Renewal of the Disputations in the Middle Ages

Leaving aside a few earlier Christian authors, as Agobard of Lyon who engaged in disputations with Jews, the real revival of Jewish-Christian disputations started in the twelfth century and reached its apogee in the thirteenth, with a few later examples in the fourteenth century.

What distinguished this renewal from earlier efforts, was mainly a much greater awareness of the traditions of the other side: Jewish participants in the debate now knew the Gospels or even other parts of the New Testament, and also the main Christian dogmas; they translated essential parts of the Gospels into Hebrew and tried to coin Hebrew terms for Christian beliefs. Somewhat later, at first mediated by Jewish converts to Christianity, Christians became acquainted with Talmud and Midrash which they first attacked and condemned (mainly at Paris in 1240–42), then tried to exploit for their christological interpretation (Barcelona 1263; Tortosa 1413–14). By far the most important Christian expert in talmudic literature was Raymund Martini who wrote his main works in the wake of the disputation of Barcelona.

Another point, too, distinguished this new stage in the history of Christian-Jewish debate and disputations and is most important in our context: although most of the biblical texts which were discussed, were the classical ones known from the first centuries of the Christian era, there was now a new consciousness of general hermeneutical questions with regard to biblical interpretation.

Before entering into a more detailed discussion, the main texts which witness to this phase of debate should be mentioned. The Jewish side is represented by Joseph Qimhi's *Sefer ha-Berit* and Jacob ben Reuben's *Milḥamot ha-Shem* (12th c.), Naḥmanides' account of the disputation of Barcelona, the recently re-discovered Hebrew account of the second disputation of Paris, a polemical work by Joseph ha-Meqanne (= R. Joseph b. R. Nathan Official) and the *Sefer Niẓẓaḥon Vetus* (late 13th c.). Polemical anti-Christian interpretations to be found in many Jewish Bible commentaries of this period (e. g. those of Rashi and Rashbam) supplement these texts. The Christian side is represented by the account of the disputation of Ceuta and G. Crispin's *Disputatio Iudei et Christiani* (12th c.), the Latin accounts of the disputations of Paris and Barcelona, the works of Raymund Martini and Inghetto Contardo's account of the disputation of Mallorca (13th c.). It is not important how correctly each text portrays the arguments of the other side, since we use Christian and Jewish texts taking each group mainly for its own side and the awareness of the other side.

3. A Common Biblical Text

In the early period of Jewish-Christian disputation the question of the correct biblical text was still hotly debated; Christians frequently accused the Jews of having corrupted the biblical text, and Jews reciprocated by pointing to "biblical quotations" which either were not to be found in the Hebrew or had there a different meaning. In the Middle Ages, the Christian disputants were in general aware of the differences between the Jewish and the Christian canons and tried to stick in disputations to the common biblical ground. Peter the Venerable insists that Jews and Christians have the same Bible:

> Quis enim nostrorum aliquid unquam addidit ad uerbum legis tuae, quis aliquid dempsit? Immo seruamus libros intactos, seruamus incorruptos et sicut per Moysen scripti et per fidos interpretes ad uniuersarum gentium linguas de Hebraica translati peruenerunt ... Habeo ego Latinus, habet Graecus, habet barbarus de libris illis quicquid, tu Iudee, habes. Scribimus quod scribis, legimus quod legis ... [1]

The Latin account of the disputation of Barcelona states programmatically that Paulus Christiani was to prove his theses *per scripturas comunes et autenticas apud Iudeos.*[2] Raymund Martini writes shortly after the disputation of Barcelona and still impressed by it his *Capistrum Iudaeorum*; there he states at the very beginning:

> Duobus autem modis Iudaei circa textum veritatem impugnant ... vel dicendo non sic haberi in Hebraeo, sumpta occasione ex hoc quod beatus Hieronymus saepius sensum ex sensu, quam verbum e verbo transtulerit, vel si forte textum concesserint, dicendo non sic debere intelligi, vel exponi. Auctoritates igitur istas, cum Dei auxilio, verbum ex verbo transferam, et concordias quandoque atque verborum expositionem rabinorum suorum ponam interius, vel exterius, in margine contra primum. Contra secundum vero, collegi in Talmud, et ex aliis libris authenticis apud eos, quaedam dicta magistrorum suorum antiquorum inducentium vel exponentium auctoritates huiusmodi, et alia verba prophetarum.[3]

Raymund thus strove for a more literal translation of the Hebrew Bible than that of the Vulgate and tried to demonstrate that the Christian interpretation may be found in Jewish texts. Occasionally he tried his hand at textual criticism, as, e.g., in *Capistrum* I.6.17 (p.264) with regard to Hag 2:7:

---

[1] Petri Venerabilis *Adversus Iudeorum Inveteratum Duritiem* 4 (CCCM LVIII) p.99.

[2] Latin account of the disputation (ed. F. I. Baer), *Tarbiz* 2,2 (1931) 185–87; 185.

[3] A. Robles Sierra, *Raimundi Martini Capistrum Iudaeorum. Texto crítico y traducción* 1–2 (Würzburger Forschungen zur Missions- und Religionswissenschaft, I. Corpus Islamo-Christianum 3; Würzburg: Echter 1990/1993) I, 54.

> Sciendum est autem hic, quod, ubi nos habemus: "*veniet desiderium omnium gentium*" [Vg: *et veniet desideratus cunctis gentibus*] in Hebraeo est "venient", nisi in paucis valde libris, et referunt ad seipsos. Quod absque dubio constat fuisse mutatum, tum quia in libris aliquibus invenitur adhuc "*et veniet*"; tum quia sic nobis olim tam a LXX quam ab aliis interpretibus translatum est.

He then proceeds to accuse the Jews of falsifying the biblical text,

> pervertentes verba viventis Dei, tiqqun soferim, id est aptationem scribarum vel computantium illud vocantes, tam in dictionibus perfectis, quam in litteris, quam in vocalibus, sive punctis.

The accusation was not new and Martini himself was to return to it much more extensively in his *Pugio Fidei.* But, as J. COHEN remarks, no earlier author

> had developed the idea as succinctly or extensively as Martini did, nor did it figure in their polemics in so crucial a fashion. To my knowledge, Martini was the first Christian Hebraist to air this charge and the first to link it with *tiqqun soferim.*[4]

For most authors, of course, the text of the Vulgate remained authoritative and its use could even be attributed to the Jewish participant in the debate (frequently, but not always, in Inghetto Contardo and in Gilbert Crispin).[5]

4. General Hermeneutical Issues

Participants in the debate on both sides were aware of the fact that Jews and Christians were separated not simply by different interpretations of individual biblical texts, but by their general hermeneutical principles. The understanding of *prophecy* was an important, but not main difference. The dispute cannot be reduced to the point that according to the Christian side, biblical texts have been fulfilled in Christ whereas, according to Jewish understanding, they speak of something which is still to come or are not at all related to the future. Not only Christian tradition (e.g. Matt 11:13) regards the whole Bible as prophecy. This idea can be found in medieval Judaism too: authors like Saadiah and Maimonides, but also Joseph Kara and others may call the whole Bible, including the Torah, "prophets". But for them, this terminology means something different from what the Christian side associates with it: prophecy is not primarily the prediction of the future, but the inspired word of God mediated by his chosen messengers and intended first of all to guide the present daily life of the Jewish people. The Christian idea that large parts of the Bible – mainly the laws – are of only temporary importance and may be done away with once the biblical prophecies are fulfilled, is vehemently contradicted by the Jewish position that God's word lasts forever. The continued controversy whether the "ceremonial laws" of the Bible are still to be observed after the advent of

---

[4] J. COHEN, *The Friars and the Jews. The Evolution of Medieval Anti-Judaism* (Ithaca: Cornell 1982) 148, n. 37.

[5] Gilbert even cites the Jew quoting Deut 27:26 in the version of Gal 3:10: Abulafia, Christians and Jews (1995) 98. The Jews of Mallorca depicted by Inghetto seem not to know Hebrew, as is clear from the assertion *uos habetis pronomina masculini et feminini et neutri generis, sicut et nos*: Inghetto Contardo, *Disputatio contra Iudaeos* (ed. G. Dahan; Collection Auteurs Latins du Moyen ge; Paris: Les Belles Lettres 1993) 204; = *Die Disputationen zu Ceuta (1179) und Mallorca (1286)* (ed. O. Limor; MGH.QG 15; München: MGH 1994) 240. See Dahan, Les intellectuels (1990) 30–32.

Christ – a point we are to return to in the next paragraph – is closely bound up with this Christian view of biblical prophecy.

The hermeneutical differences between the two groups are, however, much more general; they may be reduced to the problem of the legitimate use of allegorical interpretation. On the Christian side, one might quote Bartholomew of Exeter († 1184) who attributes Jewish blindness above all to the fact

> quod illi omnem ueteris instrumenti scripturam, in qua literalem possunt sensum inuenire, ad literam semper accipiunt, nisi manifestum perhibeat Christo testimonium. ... Nos uero non solum scripturam sanctam sed res factas et facta ipsa mistice interpretamur, ita tamen ut nec in rebus gestis historia, nec in scripturis competiens intelligentia per allegorie libertatem aliquatenus euacuetur.[6]

On the Jewish side, many interpreters of the Bible were also very conscious of the hermeneutical differences between their own and earlier Jewish, but also Christian exegesis. The growing tendency of Jewish medieval exegesis to abandon popular midrashic interpretations in favour of the *peshat* is due to several reasons, not the least important one being the renewed Jewish-Christian disputation. When Christians started using midrashic texts for their own purposes, they frequently had to realize that their Jewish counterpart no longer interpreted the biblical text in the same way as the traditional sources.[7]

As to the Jewish view of Christian exegesis, Abraham ibn Ezra's introduction to his Torah commentary is a good contemporary example. In the earlier version of this introduction Christian exegesis is only the third method from which Ibn Ezra intends to distinguish himself. The later version, written in Christian surroundings, advances the Christian exegesis to the first place and is more explicit:

> The first way is that of the scholars of the uncircumcised who say that the whole Torah consists of mysteries and allegories – thus everything said in the book of Genesis and equally all the precepts and straightforward commandments. Everyone according to his insight either adds or takes away, once for the better, once for the worse ... But the truth is to interpret every commandment and matter and word just as they are written wherever they are intelligible.[8]

Ibn Ezra concedes that some words of the Bible contain mysteries, as, e.g., the story of the garden of Eden and the tree of knowledge. Here both the literal

---

[6] Bartholomew of Exeter, *Disputatio contra Judeos*, quoted by G. Dahan, Les intellectuels (1990) 473, n. 1. A more traditional formulation of the contrast is used by Peter the Venerable (CCCM LVIII p. 99): "Sequeris tu quandoque in illis litteram mortificantem, sequor ego semper in illis spiritum uiuificantem. Rodis tu corticem, edo ego medullam". This image of the nut the shell of which must be broken to get to the eatable kernel, the true interior meaning of Scripture, is also traditional and repeated by many authors (see, e.g., Inghetto, ed. Dahan, 174; ed. Limor, 221 and n. 145), including Jews who turn it against the Christian interpretation.

[7] Anthropomorphisms were, e.g., no real problem in the popular way of speaking of the Midrash although the Rabbis were perfectly aware that such expressions were not to be understood literally. Beginning with Saadiah and Jewish philosophy, however, the correct interpretation of these ways of speaking became an important topic. It is therefore nothing but polemic when Peter the Venerable says that even in these cases "nec metaphoram nec allegoriam ... per quos omnia ista digne Deo adaptantur, Iudei suscipere uelint, sed solam in hiis litteram occidentem intelligant", *Adv. Iudeorum Inv. Duritiem* 5, 153.

[8] Text translated from the *Torat Chaim Chumash, Bereshit* I (ed. M. L. Katzenellenbogen; Jerusalem: Harav Kook 1986) 299. A much more sweeping accusation of Christian interpretation as arbitrary, choosing according to one's wishes what is to be read literally or allegorically, is attributed to the Jew quoted by Gilbert Crispin (ed. B. Blumenkranz; Utrecht / Antwerpen 1956, 72).

and the allegorical interpretations are correct and the interpreter has to listen to the wisdom of his heart and to that of the fathers. The Christian interpreters with their allegories are blind and dumb. Comparing the approximation to the true interpretation to a point within a circle, Ibn Ezra concludes that the Christian interpreters are completely outside the circle.

Another contemporary who also moved from Islamic Spain to the Christian world (Narbonne) was Joseph Qimhi. In his *Sefer ha-Berit* he thus confronts Jewish and Christian interpretation:

> The *min* (heretic, Christian) said: You understand most of the Torah literally while we understand it figuratively. Your whole reading of the Bible is erroneous for you resemble him who gnaws at the bone, while we [suck at] the marrow within. You are like the beast that eats the chaff, while we [eat] the wheat.
>
> The *ma'amin* (believer) said: Tell me. When the Holy One, blessed be He, gave the Torah to Moses who taught it to Israel, did he understand it figuratively or not? If you say that he did not understand it figuratively but literally and taught it so to Israel, then Israel is not to be held accountable in this matter. How is it that the Creator did not teach it to Moses figuratively so that he might have taught it [so] to Israel?[9]

Qimhi concedes that the Torah is not to be taken altogether literally or altogether figuratively and some commandments may be understood in both ways. But the obviously figurative understanding of the circumcision of the heart (Jer 4:4) does not do away with the literal fulfilment of the circumcision of the flesh (Gen 17:12). It is also unacceptable to say that the laws were meant to be understood literally for a limited time only until Jesus came and taught them figuratively, since God's word will not depart from Israel's mouths (Isa 59:21).

The opposition of literal versus allegorical interpretation was frequently exaggerated in the disputation; the real differences were, of course, not so clearcut. Both sides accepted the existence of several meanings of the biblical text at the same time (the Christian doctrine of the four senses of Scripture having its counterpart in the Jewish thesis of the *Pardes* – although formulated later and hardly ever applied in practice; but the presence of multiple meanings of the Bible is an old Jewish tradition). For the purposes of polemic, however, the finer shades were frequently neglected and only the main differences were emphasized and contrasted.

5. The Question of the Biblical Law

The text by Qimhi quoted above takes up a problem which from the very beginnings of Jewish-Christian disputation was a main point of contention: the understanding of the biblical commandments. Were they to be observed literally or to be understood as allegories of a higher reality? Or – to introduce a temporal factor into the problem – were they to be observed literally only in a first stage of history and then to be abrogated with the advent of the Messiah after which they continued to function only as symbols and allegories?

---

[9] Ed. F. Talmage (Jerusalem 1974) 38. Translation quoted: F. TALMAGE, *The Book of the Covenant of Joseph Kimḥi* (Toronto: Pontifical Institute of Mediaeval Studies 1972) 46 f.

The general Christian position that the Law of Moses was abrogated with the coming of Christ and his new covenant, was primarily based on Jer 31:31 ff. This passage was therefore frequently discussed between Christians and Jews. The Jewish side insisted that the text speaks of a renewed covenant and not of a new Torah; 31:33 explicitly says: "I will put my law in their inward parts", which implies that the Torah which God had already given and which the people had forgotten, would be written on their hearts, and not a new one.[10]

Another objection against the Christian understanding is raised in the second disputation of Paris where one of the points the Christian speaker wanted to prove was that "the same Messiah who is God, rejected and annulled the whole Torah of Moses and all who hold fast to it".[11] The Christian claim that Mal 3:1: "and suddenly the Lord whom you seek shall enter his temple, and the messenger of the covenant in whom you delight", refers to the Christian Messiah is rejected by the Jew who points out that the Hebrew *pit'om* does not mean 'soon', as the Christian maintains, but 'suddenly' which might also happen in the distant future. But then, for the purpose of the argument, he seems to accept the Christian argumentation only to turn it against the Christian idea that Christ abrogated the law:

> Following your words, it is difficult to see how Malachi prophesied the birth of Jesus and the renewal of the covenant and the new law which Jesus introduced. Does he not say at the end of his words: "Remember the law of Moses my servant which I commanded him on Horeb" (3:22)? If it was to end, why did he exhort them thus at the end of all his words?[12]

This argument is a strong attack against the Christian habit of taking single phrases out of their context in order to support their messianic interpretation. Such a use of proof-texts had been common practice even in rabbinic Midrash, but was no longer acceptable in the Middle Ages with the growing awareness of the literal meaning and the historical context of biblical texts, especially if they were to be used for polemical purposes.

Against the Christian claim that all commandments except the rational ones have been annulled, the Jewish speaker objects:

> Even according to your words many commandments in the Torah have remained that have not been renewed, namely the rational laws. But then this is not a new covenant. And more, Jesus did not abolish the former laws as they were written. For if you say that they were abolished, why do you [not] interpret the commandments of the Torah of Moses as "a proverb and a byword" (Deut 28:37)...?[13]

This is a general objection to Christian selectivity with regard to biblical commandments some of which were maintained whereas others were deemed to be no longer in force. The criteria for such a differentiation were never made suf-

---

[10] See e.g. *Niẓẓaḥon Vetus* (ed. D. Berger, *The Jewish-Christian Debate in the High Middle Ages*; Judaica Texts and Translations 4; Philadelphia: Jewish Publication Society 1979) § 71 (English 89 f, Hebrew 47); the text played an important role in the second disputation of Paris; see J. Shatzmiller, *La deuxième controverse de Paris* (Collection de la *REJ*; Paris: E. Peeters 1994) 55 (Hebr.), 73 f (French tr.), 81 f (Sentencia lata per illustrem regem Francorum).

[11] Ed. Shatzmiller, 48.

[12] Ed. Shatzmiller, 50.

[13] Ed. Shatzmiller 55. The negation 'not' has been inserted by the editor; the continuation of the text seems to be corrupt, cf. Shatzmiller, 74 n. 114 to the French translation.

ficiently clear and were therefore always open to attack. As an example, we may quote Meir ben Simeon of Narbonne. In his *Milḥemet Miẓvah* he wrote polemically against his Christian counterpart who accused the Jews of transgressing the biblical law by taking interest:

> Furthermore, you have shouted endlessly with your mouth about the matter of interest-taking ... What greater crime have you found in this than [breaking] the prohibition of the eating of swine, and forbidden animals, and corpses, and fish without fins and scales, since you turn all this into *mashal*, which is called figura, so you can eat them? Why do you not interpret the prohibition against taking interest in the same way, as allegory ... and allow even members of your own people to take interest?[14]

The Christian answers by distinguishing between commandments which reason acknowledges, including commandments of justness and charity as, e.g., the prohibition of taking interest: they have to be accepted in their literal meaning whereas others have to be interpreted allegorically.

It is, of course, not so easy to distinguish the precepts according to their rationality. The Jewish disputant accepts the necessity of interpreting commandments allegorically which taken literally would be impossible (e.g., the circumcision of the heart). But there is a wide field of commandments which are not against reason although their reason remains unknown. In these cases the Jewish side insisted on the mere fact that God had commanded it, to test Israel's obedience and love. A typical example is to be found in the book of Joseph ha-Meqanne. A certain priest, having in front of him a cutlet of roast pork, asked him what the God of the Jews would lose if they ate pork. Joseph answers with a story about a man who gives his wife several orders which she does not understand, but obeys all the same, thus demonstrating her love for him:

> Thus, when our God and Lord, our Beloved, commanded us: You shall not murder, you shall not commit adultery, you shall not steal and the like, and we keep these commandments, it is only reasonable. It would not make known our love toward our creator. But when he commanded us not to eat pork (Deut 14:8) and similar commandments which make man wonder at us, saying: What is its advantage, – by keeping them our love toward our creator becomes known, and therefore it is said: "The Lord tries the righteous" (Ps 11:5).[15]

The Christian argument that many biblical laws (and other texts) contradict each other and therefore have to be understood allegorically is countered by the Jewish insistence that these texts only seem to be contradictory. God may forbid or allow something according to the circumstances:

> he [the Christian] will ask you: Who permitted Moses to make the copper serpent that he fashioned in the desert? Does it not say: "You shall not make for yourself a sculptured image or any likeness ..." (Exod 20:4)? Answer him: The mouth which prohibited is the same mouth that permitted ... Thus, one should not scrutinize the commandments of the Creator, blessed be he, on the basis of human reason; rather, what he prohibited is prohibited and what he permitted is permitted ... "You shall not make for yourself" (Exod 20:4), i.e., on your own authority, but on my authority you may.[16]

In many cases traditional interpretation teaches how to reconcile apparent contradictions:

---

14 Text and translation: H. Trautner-Kromann, Shield and Sword (1993) 77 f.
15 *Sepher Joseph Hamekane* (ed. J. Rosenthal; Jerusalem: Mekize Nirdamim 1970) § 47 (p. 60).
16 *Nizzaḥon Vetus* § 48, 73; Hebr. text 32 f.

> Nobody could resolve the biblical contradictions, were it not for the Talmud which decides between them; and all is given from Sinai, even if one permits and another forbids, one declares clean and another declares unclean. In this regard is it written "to follow the majority" (Exod 23:2). And the halakhah is forever according to the majority.
> And were it not for the Talmud, nobody could learn a commandment correctly and understand its essence. For the laws of the Sabbath are written in the Bible in five places, here a little and there a little, and before one reaches the second, one has forgotten the first. But in the Talmud all the laws of the Torah are brought together and easy to learn. There are also laws written in the book which one could not understand without tradition ... and he who does not learn Talmud, will not be able to understand the Bible. He is like a man who has been given the inner keys, but not the outer keys. How will he enter?[17]

The appeal to tradition for the correct understanding of the Bible was something the Christian side should have understood; but uttered by a Jew it could become dangerous, Judaism being tolerated by the Catholic Church only because it was considered a witness to biblical religion. The Latin protocol of the disputation thus summarizes the confession of R. Judas:

> Item dixit, quod due sunt leges et una non potuit fieri nisi per verba sapiencium, et illa est talmud, et continetur in ea quod verba sapiencium magis debent servari et maius peccatum est illa transgredi quam legem scriptam, in lege enim scriptum est "facere et non facere" et non meretur mortem in illis, qui autem transgreditur verba sapiencium, meretur mortem.[18]

This insistence that the Talmud was even more important than the Bible was one of the reasons for the condemnation of the Talmud at Paris. But only a few years later, Pope Innocent IV himself accepted the Jewish position that in order to practice their religion they absolutely needed the Talmud:

> Sane magistris Iudeorum regni tui nuper proponentibus coram nobis et fratribus nostris, quod sine illo libro qui Hebraice Talamut dicitur, Bibliam et alia statuta sue legis secundum fidem ipsorum intelligere nequeunt, nos qui iuxta mandatum divinum in eadem lege ipsos tolerare tenemur, dignum eis duximus respondendum, quod sicut eos ipsa lege sic perconsequens suis libris nolumus iniuste privare.[19]

6. Christological versus Historical Interpretation

The christological interpretation of the Bible had such a long tradition that hardly any innovation might be expected in the Middle Ages. There are only very few texts which have not been used time and again, and rejected by Jews from time immemorial. One of these not so traditional prooftexts was Lev 12:2: "When a woman produces (or: receives) seed[20] and bears a male ...".

---

[17] The Hebrew account of the Paris disputation (1240) by R. Yeḥiel, in: J. D. Eisenstein, *Oẓar Wikuḥim* (New York 1928) 82 f.

[18] Ch. Merchavia, *The Church versus Talmudic and Midrashic Literature [500–1248]* (Jerusalem: Bialik Institute 1970; Hebr.) 454 f; text also in I. Loeb, "La controverse de 1240 sur le Talmud", *REJ* 3 (1881) 55–57.

[19] S. Simonsohn, *The Apostolic See and the Jews. Documents: 492–1404* (STPIMS 94; Toronto 1988) 197.

[20] This is the traditional understanding of *tazriʿa*. For a modern philological interpretation see J. Milgrom, *Leviticus 1–16* (AB 3; New York: Doubleday 1991) 743 f. He translates: "when a woman at childbirth bears a male ...".

The text is understood as announcing the virgin birth of the Messiah at the disputation of Ceuta and again at Mallorca. Inghetto quotes it to reinforce his understanding of the most traditional text Isa 7:11–14 as referring not to a son of Ahaz, but to the Messiah:

> Audite Moysen in precepto quod dedit, ut mulieres omnes, que suscepto semine et masculum pepererint, per XL dies inmundas eas esse precepit. Cur ergo preceptum istud cum conditione posuit, quando dixit: Mulieres que suscepto semine? Quia sciebat virginem sine semine parituram ... Quare hoc apertum est, quod in beata Maria impleta fuit illa prophetia.[21]

This interpretation, not common even in medieval disputations, may have become known via the Glossa ordinaria. That Jews knew the Christian allegorical interpretation of the text in the twelfth century, may be learnt from the later version of Abraham Ibn Ezra's introduction to his Torah commentary where he says that Christians regard the word "when she receives seed" as a hint to the "house of their frivolity" (*tiflatam*), i.e. to their doctrines. Clearer is Josef ha-Meqanne (§ 33) who writes:

> I heard a heretic (*apiqoros*) who behaved irreverently and said: It is written "A woman – if she receives seed and bears a male" (Lev 12:2). Who was this woman who received seed and bore a male, and no man is mentioned here? The opponent asked him: And who was it? He said to him: It was Mary.[22] He answered him: But it is also written: 'and if she bears a female' (12:5). Thus, the Hanged One [Jesus] had a sister.

The text ends with a note of irony typical for these writings. The context of the verse used as Christian allegory contradicts Christian teachings.

The most important change in the disputations of the Middle Ages with regard to messianic or christological proof-texts brought forward by the Christian side is the growing insistence of the Jews that these texts have to be understood in their historical context. Typical was the interpretation of Isa 7:14 quoted above as referring to Hezekiah, son of Ahaz, whose birth is a sign that God will save Jerusalem from Rezin and Pekah; the birth of Jesus, having taken place centuries later, would not have been a sign for Ahaz. Less frequent, but on the same line, is the explanation which refers the text to Isaiah's young wife who bore a son after his intercourse with her (Isa 8:3).[23] The child of Isa 9:5, the prince of peace, is then again Hezekiah. Joseph Qimhi notes that Jerome in the Vulgate wrongly translated "vocabitur" (*yiqqare*) instead of the reading of MT "he shall call" (*yiqra*), and then continues:

> "The Wonderful Counsellor, Mighty God, Everlasting Father shall call his name the prince of peace". This is Hezekiah the righteous whom God called prince of peace. Sects, wars, and dissensions had proliferated in the time of his father Ahaz, for Pekah the son of Remaliah and Rezin, king of Aram, warred against him, defeated him, and destroyed his land. The prophet Isaiah announced to him that a child had been born, upon whose shoulder would rest the dominion of the House of David. We have found it stated explicitly in Chronicles [2 Chr 29:1]

---

[21] Ed. Limor, 196. The parallel argument at Ceuta ibid. 140. Dahan, Inghetto (1993) 134, n. 50, refers to the Glossa ord. (interlin.) in Lev 12:2 and to Nicholas of Lyra, where the same interpretation is to be found.

[22] The text reads *ḥrbh*, but a manuscript reads *mri'h*; see J. Rosenthal, *Sepher* (1970) 55, in the note to his text.

[23] See e.g. *Niẓẓaḥon Vetus* §§ 84–87, ed. D. Berger 55–60 (Hebr.), 100–06 (tr.), and 274–77 (commentary with reference to earlier texts).

that Hezekiah had already been born. These names were mentioned according to the circumstances: *Wonderful*, for He brought wonders with him; *Counsellor*, for He counselled him to walk in the ways of the Lord, for his father was wicked; *Mighty God*, for He caused him to grow mighty over his enemies; *Everlasting Father*, for He added fifteen years to his life [2 Kgs 20:6].[24]

The use of 1 Chr 3:24 as a messianic text is an interesting case because it is based on Jewish tradition. It is used in the second disputation of Paris by the convert Paul (most probably Pablo Christiani):

See, you have it written in Bereshit Rabbati: A certain man, the Messiah, Anani is his name, as it is said: "and behold, one like the Son of man came with the clouds [*ʿanane*] of heaven" (Dan 7:13); and we find that fourteen generations from Zerubbabel Anani is born, as is written there: "And the sons of Elioenai: Hodaviah ..." until "Anani, seven" (1 Chr 3:24), and after Anani there is no further genealogy. Therefore, this Anani is born in the time of the second Temple and is Jesus.

The Rabbi answered: Anani was the seventh generation from Zerubbabel. How can you say that seven generations lasted until the end of the second Temple, until Jesus? ... If they understood what you said they would stone you! For how is it possible that Anani is Jesus, since Anani had father and mother, a grandfather and six brothers, as it is explicitly said there![25]

The rabbinic tradition that Anani is the Messiah, is abandoned by the Jewish disputant not only because it has been taken over by the Christian side for its purposes, but mainly because it would not fit a historic reading of the text. That this new literal reading serves the purposes of the polemic, is of course most welcome.

One of the most traditional christological prooftexts was Gen 49:10: "The scepter shall not depart from Judah nor the ruler's staff from between his feet, until comes to whom it belongs [*Shilo*]". Also in Jewish tradition, this text was normally interpreted as referring to the Messiah. But the Christian insistence that rulers from Judah had long since ceased and that, therefore, the Messiah must already have come, led Jewish interpreters to a new 'historical' reading of the text. A classical Jewish argument against referring the verse to Jesus is summarized, after many other texts, in the *Sefer Nizzaḥon Vetus* § 28:

How can one maintain that the kingdom of Judah did not cease until Jesus? There was, after all, no king in Israel from the time of Zedekiah, for even in the days of the second Temple there was no king in Israel but only governors subordinate to the kings of Media, Persia, or Rome. Now, a long time passed between Zedekiah and the birth of Jesus, and so how can the verse say that the kingdom would not depart from Judah until Jesus comes? Furthermore, what relationship is there between "Shiloh" and Jesus' name?[26]

Many historical facts are brought forward in the discussion (e.g. at Barcelona) at what time kingdom and rulership ceased among the Jews and whether patriarchs and exilarchs are to be counted like kings, what really constitutes a ces-

---

[24] Talmage, The Book of the Covenant (1972) 29.

[25] Ed. Shatzmiller, 52; transl. 68 f. The same argument, but without the Jewish objection, is found in Raymund Martini's *Capistrum* I.5.9 (ed. A. Robles, 208–10; here too *Bereshit Rabba* is quoted where such a text cannot be found. But the rabbinic tradition exists, e.g. in *Tanḥuma Buber Toldot* 20 (70 a–b) and *Aggadat Bereshit* 44 (ed. Buber, 89 f). The Targum to 1 Chr 3:24 is explicit: "... and Anani – he is the king Messiah who will be revealed – in all, seven".

[26] Ed. D. Berger, 21 (text), 60 (transl.), 249 f (comm.).

sation (and not just an interruption) of Jewish kingship and the like. A more radical historical reading understands the text in the framework of biblical history; Jacob promises Judah that his tribe will be dominant until David arises to whom the kingdom belongs (*shilo* read as *shello*, "which is his"). This is the interpretation of, among others, Yosef Qimhi in his *Sefer ha-Berit*, and his son David Qimhi in his commentary to Gen 49:10. Others regard Shilo as the name of the biblical city, as Ibn Ezra writes in his commentary on Gen 49:10:

> *Shilo.* Some follow the Targum and understand *shello.* Others derive from the root of *u-veshilyatah* (Deut 28:57: "the *afterbirth* which comes out from between her feet"). Again others derive it from the word *shalil* ('embryo'). And there is one who explains it from the town Shilo and interprets [the verb *ba*, 'to come'] in the expression *yavo* ("will come") as having the same meaning as in *u-va ha-shemesh* (Lev 22:7: "the sun has set"), i.e. "until the end of Shilo comes". For thus is it written: "He forsook his dwelling at Shilo" (Ps 78:60), and afterwards: "and he chose David his servant" (Ps 78:70).[27]

According to this interpretation, the promise contained in Gen 49:10 is that the tribe of Judah will be preeminent in Israel until the sanctuary of Shilo comes to an end and David as the one to whom the kingdom belongs, will become king.

Other examples of this historical approach of Jewish disputants may be found in the interpretation of Psalms, as e.g. in the Disputation of Mallorca where a whole series of verses applied by Inghetto to Jesus are stereotypically referred to Solomon by the Jewish speaker: "'In Salomone impletum fuit hoc, quod fuit rex post David' (Ps 132:11; Ps 72:1); 'hoc totum impletum fuit in Salomone, quia reges Tharsis et Arabum et Sabba adoraverunt et munera Salomoni obtulerunt' (Ps 72:10); 'hoc totum contingit in tempore Salomonis, quia numquam Israel pacem habuit nisi in tempore eius' (Ps 72:2–3)".[28]

Perhaps even more interesting is the interpretation of Isa 61:1 f ("The spirit of the Lord God is upon me, because the Lord has anointed me to bring good tidings to the afflicted ..."); this text, in Qumran already understood of a messianic figure and referred to Jesus in the NT and ever since in Christian tradition, is commented upon by the Jew in the disputation of Mallorca: "Hoc totum dixit Ysayas populo Iudeorum quando erant in captivitate Babilonis, quia sicut scitis in diebus illis prophetavit Ysayas". Inghetto objects that the text goes on to promise the restoration of abandoned cities which cannot be applied to the Jews who even now are in exile; it therefore has to be applied to Jesus. The Jew counters: "Magistri nostri et sapientes doctores nostri glosaverunt sicut dixi, et ipsi credendi sunt"; to Inghetto who asks: "Cui melius credendum est: an magistris vestris an prophete", the Jew answers: "Magistris, quia ipsi postea fuerunt, et viderunt que transacta erant, et sciebant que esset veritatis causa".[29] Inghetto naively implies that he relies on the text of the prophet alone and not on external tradition; against this, the Jewish speaker confesses clearly to rely on authoritative tradition. Even more remarkable is the thesis

---

27 *Josef ha-Meqanne* § 22 (ed. Rosenthal, 44) takes up this interpretation quoted by Ibn Ezra and expands it.

28 Ed. Limor, 220 f; ed. Dahan, 174–76.

29 Ed. Limor, 298 f; ed. Dahan, 294.

that Isaiah 61 was spoken in the Babylonian exile. This idea which adumbrates the theory of a "Deutero-Isaiah", was not original to the Mallorcan Jew; Abraham Ibn Ezra writes his commentary on Isa 40:1:

> These first comforting promises, with which the second part of the book of Isaiah begins, refer, as R. Moses Hakkohen believes, to the restoration of the temple by Zerubbabel; according to my opinion to the coming redemption from our present exile; prophecies concerning the Babylonian exile are introduced only as an illustration ... About the last section of the book there is no doubt, that it refers to a period yet to come.[30]

Although Ibn Ezra rejects the position that part of Isaiah was written in a later period and does not doubt that the last chapters of the book deal with the future, the thesis here attributed to Moses Hakkohen seems to have been more widely known and accepted. It perfectly suited the needs of disputation with Christians to read the purportedly messianic texts in the context of biblical history. The historical criticism of the Bible is still far away; this is clear from, among other facts, the continued messianic calculations based on Daniel which led Naḥmanides and other contemporaries to expect the coming of the Messiah in the not too distant future.[31] But there is no doubt that disputations with Christians helped prepare its way.

[30] *The Commentary of Ibn Ezra on Isaiah, ed. from MSS. and translated* ... by M. Friedländer, I. Translation (London 1873; repr. New York: Ph. Feldheim s. a.) 170.

[31] R. Chazan, *Barcelona and Beyond. The Disputation of 1263 and its Aftermath* (Berkeley: University of California 1990) 172–94.

Supplement to Chapter Five

Ben Sira and the Wisdom of Solomon: Their Interpretative Significance

5.3. Canon and Scripture in the Book of Ben Sira (Jesus Sirach / Ecclesiasticus)

By Pancratius C. Beentjes, Utrecht

Sources: P. C. Beentjes, *The Book of Ben Sira in Hebrew: A Text Edition of all Extant Hebrew Manuscripts & A Synopsis of all parallel Hebrew Ben Sira Texts* (VTSup 68; Leiden: Brill 1997); *Facsimiles of the Fragments Hitherto Recovered of the Book of Ecclesiasticus in Hebrew* (Oxford / Cambridge: Oxford and Cambridge University 1901); *The Book of Ben Sira: Text, Concordance and An Analysis of the Vocabulary* (ed. Z. Ben-Ḥayyim; The Historical Dictionary of the Hebrew Language; Jerusalem: Keter Press 1973); S. Schechter / C. Taylor, *The Wisdom of Ben Sira: Portions of the Book of Ecclesiasticus from Hebrew Manuscripts in the Cairo Genizah Collection* (Cambridge: Cambridge University 1899); M. H. Segal, *Seper ben-Sira' haššalem* (Jerusalem: Bialik 1933; [2]1958); F. Vattioni, *Ecclesiastico: Testo ebraico con apparato critico e versioni greca, latina e siriaca* (Testi 1; Napels: Istituto Orientale di Napoli 1968); Y. Yadin, *The Ben Sira Scroll from Masada* (Jerusalem: The Israel Exploration Society and The Shrine of the Book 1965); J. Ziegler, *Sapientia Iesu Filii Sirach* (Septuaginta XII, 2; Göttingen: Vandenhoeck & Ruprecht 1965).

Bibliography: F. V. Reiterer (ed.), *Bibliographie zu Ben Sira* (BZAW 266; Berlin: de Gruyter 1998).

Studies: R. A. Argall, *1 Enoch and Sirach: A Comparative Literary and Conceptual Analysis of the Themes of Revelation, Creation and Judgment* (SBL Early Judaism and Its Literature 8; Atlanta, GA: Scholars Press 1995); E. G. Bauckmann, "Die Proverbien und die Sprüche des Jesus Sirach. Eine Untersuchung zum Strukturwandel der israelitischen Weisheitslehre", *ZAW* 72 (1960) 33–63; J. B. Bauer, "Sir 15, 14 et Gen 1, 1", *VD* 41 (1963) 243–44; idem, "Der priesterliche Schöpfungshymnus in Gen. 1 [Sir 15:14]", *TZ* 20 (1964) 1–9; P. C. Beentjes, *Jesus Sirach en Tenach: Een onderzoek naar en een classificatie van parallellen, met bijzondere aandacht voor hun functie in Sirach 45:6–26* (Nieuwegein: Selbstverlag 1981); idem, "Discovering a New Path of Intertextuality: Inverted Quotations and Their Dynamics", *Literary Structure and Rhetorical Strategies in the Hebrew Bible* (ed. L. J. de Regt / J. de Waard / J. P. Fokkelman; Assen: Van Gorcum 1996) 31–50; idem, "Relations between Ben Sira and the Book of Isaiah", *The Book of Isaiah. Le Livre d'Isaïe* (ed. J. Vermeylen; BETL 81; Louvain: Peeters 1989) 155–59; idem, "«The Countries Marvelled at You»: King Solomon in Ben Sira 47:12–22", *BTFT* 45 (1984) 6–14; idem, "Hezekiah and Isaiah. A Study on Ben Sira 48:15–25", *New Avenues in the Study of the Old Testament* (ed. A. S. van der Woude; OTS 25; Leiden: Brill 1989) 77–88; idem, "«Sweet is His Memory, Like Honey to the Palate»: King Josiah in Ben Sira 49, 1–4", *BZ* 34 (1990) 262–66; C. Begg, "Ben Sirach's Non-mention of Ezra", *BN* 42 (1988) 14–18; A. Bentzen, "Sirach, der Chronist, und Nehemiah", *StTh* 3 (1951) 158–61; G. B. Caird, "Ben Sira and the Dating of the Septuagint", SE VII [= TU 126] (Berlin 1982) 95–100; N. Calduch-Benages, "Ben Sira y el Canon de las Escrituras", *Greg* 78 (1997) 359–70; J. Carmignac, "Les rapports entre l'Ecclésiastique et Qumran", *RevQ* 3 (1961) 209–18; A. Chester, "Citing the Old Testament", *It is Written: Scripture Citing Scripture; Essays in Honour of Barnabas Lindars* (ed. D.A. Carson / H.G.M. Williamson; Cambridge: Cambridge UP 1988) 141–69; P.R. Davies, *Scribes and Schools. The Canonization of the Hebrew Scriptures* (Library of Ancient Israel; London 1998); A.A. Di Lella, "Conservative and Progressive Theology: Sirach and Wisdom", *CBQ* 28 (1966) 139–54; D. Dimant, "Use and Interpretation of Mikra in the Apocrypha and Pseudepigrapha", *Mikra. Text, Translation, Reading and Interpretation of the Hebrew Bible in Ancient Judaism and Early Christianity* (ed. M. Mulder; CRINT II, 1; Assen: Van Gorcum 1988) 379–419; J.W. Doeve, "Jezus Sirach en Daniël", *Rondom het Woord* 11 (1969) 58–74; A. Eberharter, *Der Kanon des Alten Testaments zur Zeit des Ben Sira* (ATA III, 3; Münster: Aschendorf 1911); R. Egger-Wenzel / I. Krammer (eds.), *Der Einzelne und seine Gemeinschaft bei Ben Sira* (BZAW 270; Berlin: de Gruyter 1998); D.E. Fox, "Ben Sira on OT Canon again: The Date of Daniel", *WTJ* 49 (1987) 335–50; J.K. Gasser, *Die Bedeutung der Sprüche Jesu Ben Sira für die Datierung des althebräischen Spruchbuches* (BFChrT VIII, 2–3; Gütersloh: Bertelsmann 1904); M. Gilbert, "Wisdom Literature", *Jewish Writings of the Second Temple Period: Apocrypha, Pseudepigrapha, Qumran Sectarian Writings, Philo, Josephus* (ed. M.E. Stone; CRINT II, 2; Assen: Van Gorcum 1984) 283–324; idem, "Siracide", DBSup XII (Paris: Letouzey & Ané 1996) 1389–1437; idem, "Jesus Sirach", RAC XVII (ed. E. Dassmann a.o.; Stuttgart: Anton Herseman 1997) 878–906; M. Haran, "Some Problems of Canonization of Scripture", *Tarbiz* 25 (1956) 245–71 (repr. in: S.Z. Leiman (ed.), *The Canon and Masorah of the Hebrew Bible* [New York 1974] 224–53); M. Hengel, "Die Septuaginta als 'christliche Schriftensammlung' und das Problem ihres Kanons", *Verbindliches Zeugnis* I. *Kanon-Schrift-Tradition* (ed. W. Pannenberg / Th. Schneider; DiKi 7, Freiburg-Göttingen 1992) 34–127; idem, "«Schriftauslegung» und «Schriftverwendung» in der Zeit des Zweiten Tempels", *Schriftauslegung im antiken Judentum und in Urchristentum* (ed. M. Hengel / H. Löhr; WUNT 73; Tübingen: Mohr 1994) 1–71; P. Höffken, "Warum schwieg Jesus Sirach über Esra?", *ZAW* 87 (1975) 184–201; W. Horbury, "Jewish Inscriptions and Jewish Literature in Egypt, with Special Reference to Ecclesiasticus", *Studies in Early Jewish Epigraphy* (ed. J.W. van Henten / P.W. van der Horst; AGJU; Leiden: Brill 1994) 9–43; E. Jacob, "L'Histoire d'Israel vue par Ben Sira", *Mélanges bibliques André Robert* (Paris: Bloud et Gay 1957) 288–94; E. Janssen, *Das Gottesvolk und seine Geschichte. Geschichtsbild und Selbstverständnis im palästinischen Schrifttum von Jesus Sirach bis Jehuda ha-Nasi* (Neukirchen-Vluyn: Neukirchener Verlag 1971); O. Kaiser, "Judentum und Hellenismus. Ein Beitrag zur Frage nach dem hellenistischen Einfluß auf Kohelet und Jesus Sirach", *Der Mensch unter dem Schicksal* (ed. O. Kaiser; BZAW 161; Berlin: W. de Gruyter 1985) 135–53; H.-V. Kieweler, *Ben Sira zwischen Judentum und Hellenismus. Eine kritische Auseinandersetzung mit Th. Middendorp* (BEATAJ 30; Frankfurt a.M.: Peter Lang 1992); idem, "Abraham und der Preis der Väter bei Ben Sira", *Amt und Gemeinde* 37 (1986) 70–72; J.L. Koole, "Die Bibel des Ben-Sira", OTS 14 (1965) 374–96; J.L. Kugel, "On Hidden Hatred and Open Reproach: Early Exegesis of Leviticus 19:17 [Sir 19:13–17]", *HTR* 80 (1987) 43–61; J.C.H. Lebram, "Aspekte der alttestamentlichen Kanonbildung", *VT* 18 (1968) 173–89; M.R. Lehmann, "11QPsa and Ben Sira", *RevQ* 11 (1983) 239–51; idem, "Ben Sira and the Qumran Literature", *RevQ* 3 (1961) 117–24; J. Lévêque, "Le Portrait d'Élie dans l'Éloge des Pères", *Ce Dieu qui vient. Mélanges offerts à Bernard Renaud* (LD 159; Paris: Cerf 1995) 215–29; J.R. Levison, *Portraits of Adam in Early Judaism. From Sirach to 2 Baruch* (JSPSup 1; Sheffield: Sheffield Academic Press 1988); B.L. Mack, *Wisdom and the Hebrew Epic. Ben Sira's Hymn in Praise of the Fathers* (Chicago: Chicago Press 1985); R.A.F. MacKenzie, "Ben Sira as Historian", *Trinification of the World* (FS F.E. Crowe, ed. T.A. Dumme / J.-M. Laporte; Toronto 1978) 313–27; J. Marböck, "Sir 38, 24–39, 11: Der schriftgelehrte Weise. Ein Beitrag zu Gestalt und Werk ben Siras", *La Sagesse de l'Ancien Testament* (ed. M. Gilbert; BETL 51; Louvain: Peeters 1979) 293–316 [= J. Marböck, *Gottes Weisheit unter uns. Zur Theologie des Buches Sirach* (ed. I. Fischer; HBS 6; Freiburg: Herder 1995) 25–51]; idem, "Die 'Geschichte Israels' als 'Bundesgeschichte' nach dem Sirachbuch", *Der Neue Bund im Alten. Studien zur Bundestheologie der beiden Testamente* (ed. E. Zenger; QD 146; Freiburg: Herder 1993) 177–97 [= J. Marböck, *Gottes Weisheit*, 103–23]; idem, "Henoch-Adam-der Thronwagen: Zur frühjüdischen pseudepigraphischen Tradition bei ben Sira", *BZ* 25 (1981) 103–11 [= J. Marböck, *Gottes Weisheit*, 133–43]; J.D. Martin, "Ben Sira's Hymn to the Fathers. A Messianic Perspective", *Crises and Perspectives. Studies in Ancient Near Eastern Polytheism, Biblical Theology, Palestinian Archaeology and Intertestamental Literature*, OTS 24 (1986) 107–23; idem, "Ben Sira – A Child of His Time", *A Word in Season. Essays in Honor of William McKane* (JSOTSup 42; Sheffield: Sheffield Academic Press 1986) 141–61; J.C. Matthes, "Das Buch Sirach und Kohelet in ihrem gegenseitigen Verhältnis. Die Prioritätsfrage", *Vierteljahresschrift für Bibelkunde*

2 (1904/05) 158–263; TH. MIDDENDORP, *Die Stellung Jesu ben Sira zwischen Judentum und Hellenismus* (Leiden: Brill 1973); A. MINNISALE, *La Versione Greca del Siracide. Confronto con il Testo Ebraico alla luce dell'attrivita midrascica e del metodo targumico* (AnBib 133; Rome 1995); D. PATTE, *Early Jewish Hermeneutic in Palestine* (SBLDS 22; Missoula, MT 1975); V. PETERCA, "Das Porträt Salomos bei Ben Sirach (47,12–22): ein Beitrag zu der Midraschexegese", *»Wünschet Jerusalem Frieden«* (ed. M. Augustin / K. D. Schunek; BEATAJ 13; Frankfurt: Peter Lang 1988) 457–63; F. V. REITERER, "Das Verhältnis Ijobs und Ben Siras", *The Book of Job* (ed. W. A. M. Beuken; BETL 114; Louvain: Peeters 1994) 405–29; H.-P. RÜGER, "Le Siracide: un livre à la frontière du canon", *Le Canon de l'Ancien Testament. Sa formation et son histoire* (ed. J.-D. Kaestli/O. Wermelinger; Geneva: Labor et Fides 1984) 47–69; idem, "Zum Text von Sir 40,10 und Ex 10,21", *ZAW* 80 (1970) 103–09; J. T. SANDERS, *Ben Sira and Demotic Wisdom* (SBLMS 28; Chico: Scholars Press 1983); J. SCHILDENBERGER, "Die Bedeutung von Sir 48,24 f für die Verfasserfrage von Is 40–66", *AT Studien. Festschrift Nötscher* (BBB 1; Bonn: Hanstein 1950) 188–204; E. J. SCHNABEL, *Law and Wisdom from Ben Sira to Paul: A Traditional Historical Enquiry into the Relation of Law* (WUNT 2. Reihe, Bd. 16; Tübingen: Mohr 1985); G. T. SHEPPARD, *Wisdom as a Hermeneutical Construct* (BZAW 151; Berlin: W. de Gruyter 1980); P. W. SKEHAN / A. A. DI LELLA, *The Wisdom of Ben Sira* (AB 39; New York: Doubleday 1987); J. G. SNAITH, "Biblical Quotations in the Hebrew of Ecclesiasticus", *JTS* 18 (1967) 1–12; idem, "Ben Sira's Supposed Love of Liturgy", *VT* 25 (1975) 167–74; H. STADELMANN, *Ben Sira als Schriftgelehrter: Eine Untersuchung zum Berufsbild des vor-Makkabäischen Sofer unter Berücksichtigung seines Verhältnisses zu Priester-, Propheten-, und Weisheitslehrertum* (WUNT 2. Reihe, Bd. 6; Tübingen: Mohr 1980); O. H. STECK, "Externe Indizien aus dem hebräischen Sirachbuch", *Der Abschluß der Prophetie im Alten Testament. Ein Versuch zur Frage der Vorgeschichte des Kanons* (BThSt 17; Neukirchen-Vluyn: Neukirchener Verlag 1991) 136–44; B. G. WRIGHT, *No Small Difference. Sirach's Relationship to its Hebrew Parent Text* (SBLSCS 26; Atlanta, GA: Scholars Press 1989).

1. Introduction

The Book of Ben Sira is one of the few Old Testament books that provides information on its author and its place of origin as well: "Training in wise conduct, and smooth-running proverbs of Simeon ben Jeshua ben Eliezer ben Sira,[1] who poured them out from his understanding heart" (Sir 50:27). Also the date of publication of the book can be established quite accurately, namely between 200 and 180 BCE. For in Chapter 50 of his book, Ben Sira is praising the big efforts of Simon, the High Priest, who renovated the Temple and fortified the walls of Jerusalem (Sir 50:1–3). These building activities are also described by Josephus (*Ant. Jud.* 12.3), who sets these constructions during the reign of the Seleucid king Antiochus III (224–187 BCE). Precisely during this period, viz. from 220–195 BCE, Simon, son of Onias II, officiated as High Priest. The exuberant, sometimes even fanatic praise of Simon, who is characterized as "the glory of his people" (Sir 50:1), justifies the supposition that Ben Sira knew this High Priest and composed this paean immediately after his death. The most plausible inference, then, is that this happened around 190 BCE.

---

[1] Only in Greek, one finds here an additional: "from Jerusalem".

2. Ben Sira and the 'Canon'

In 132 BCE, being the 38th year of king Euergetes' reign, Ben Sira's grandson came to Egypt and started translating his grandfather's book into Greek because of the large Jewish community in Egypt. The grandson opens the *Prologos* ('Preface') to his Greek translation as follows: "A legacy of great value has come down to us through the law, the prophets, and the others who followed in their steps, and Israel deserves recognition for its traditions of learning and wisdom" (Prol. 1–3; REB). Here we meet a tripartite division of the Old Testament (Law, Prophets, Writings) that is very familiar to us.[2] However we should not rush to a conclusion from this. For the fact that Ben Sira's grandson deals with a tripartite division of what is called the Old Testament, does not necessarily mean that such a tripartite division was already in vogue in his grandfather's time (ca. 190–80 BCE). The question should be posed therefore whether in Ben Sira's time there was something in existence that can be compared to what we have called the 'Palestinian canon' and what Biblical books were reckoned among it.[3] It therefore goes without saying that in this contribution the *Hebrew* text(s) of the Book of Ben Sira will be the basis to work on, since the Greek translation represents a further stage in the growth of the biblical canon.

In the Hebrew portions of the Book of Ben Sira that have been recovered between 1896 and 1982, the word *torah* occurs twelve times, nearly all referring to the *lex revelata*, the Sinaitic revelation of the Mosaic law embodied in the Pentateuch.[4] This use comes close to the technical term 'Torah' that in our days is being used to indicate the Five Books of Moses, or Pentateuch, as such.

As far as the section of the Prophets is concerned, the description of Joshua in Sir 46:1 ("the successor of Moses in the prophetic office") is strong evidence that in Ben Sira's time the later terminology of reckoning the Books of Joshua, Judges, Samuel, and Kings to the 'Former Prophets' was already in the air. Chapters 46–49 in the Book of Ben Sira are structured as a continuous story of prophets: Joshua (46:1), Samuel (46:13), Nathan (47:1), Elijah (48:1), Elisha (48, 12).[5] The three 'major prophets' are treated by Ben Sira in just that (canonical) order in which their books have been handed over to us: Isaiah (48:20), Jeremiah (49:6), and Ezekiel (49:8).[6] And, moreover, they are characterized by allusions and quotations from their 'own' books.[7] The fact that Sir 49:10

---

[2] There are two further instances in the Prologue of the grandson that contain similar formulae: "the law, the prophets, and the other writings of our ancestors" (Prol. 8–10); "the law itself, as well as the prophets and the other writings" (Prol. 24–25).

[3] Since Lebram in respect of this question only quotes the first part of Sir 39:1–3, he arrives at a wrong conclusion. For the content of Sir 39:2–3 is resisting to consider 39:1 as proof for a kind of tripartite division of the Hebrew Bible. Lebram, Aspekte der alttestamentlichen Kanonbildung (1968) 180.

[4] E.g., Sir 32:15–18, 23; 41:18; 45:5; 49:4. See Middendorp, Die Stellung Jesu ben Siras (1973) 162–64; Schnabel, Law and Wisdom (1985) 31–34.

[5] Mack, Wisdom and the Hebrew Epic (1985) 37–41.

[6] See Beentjes, Hezekiah and Isaiah (1989).

[7] Steck, Externe Indizien (1991) 137.

speaks about "the twelve prophets" is documentary evidence that already Ben Sira was familiar with this technical term to indicate that collection of prophetic books.[8] That he mentions "the Twelve Prophets" almost immediately after Ezekiel, just as in the later 'Palestinian canon', is an important supplementary datum. The Hebrew text has a further interesting detail; for between the mention of Ezekiel (Sir 49:8) and the Twelve prophets (49:10) Ben Sira makes reference to Job (49:9). I think it possible that some traces of ink at the caesura after the word 'Job' in MS B. yield the word *nabi'* ('prophet'). According to some Rabbis, Job was considered a prophet; Josephus too listed Job among the Prophets (*Contra Apion* 1.8).[9]

Nowhere in his book, does Ben Sira point to a third collection of holy scriptures, identical to the later *Ketubîm*, as the collection of 'Writings' that concludes the Hebrew canon. Though not *defined* as a separate collection of books, one can find in the Book of Ben Sira traces of writings that in later time were reckoned among the *Ketubîm*.

It is beyond any doubt that Ben Sira harked back to the Book of Proverbs: "Ben Sira's dependence on Proverbs can be detected in almost every portion of his book".[10] That Ben Sira knew the Book of Psalms can be gathered from a number of instances in his book. In Sir 14:20, and Sir 50:28 – thus forming a kind of *inclusio* – the reader is reminded of Psalm 1. And the words of Sir 51:12° ("He also exalteth the horn of his people"; KJV) is a strict quotation from Ps 148:14. In other instances in his work, Ben Sira is also citing from or alluding to Psalms.[11] This can serve as a small piece of evidence that Ben Sira knew the Book of Psalms already as a whole. The first chapter of the Book of Lamentations has been adopted and reworked by Ben Sira to describe God as a resource to the widow, being the oppressed people of Israel (Sir 35:13–17 [Gr 32, 16–22]).[12]

Whether Ben Sira already knew and made use of the Book of Chronicles is hard to decide. On the basis of some *hapax legomena* from 2 Chronicles appearing in the Book of Ben Sira ('the good LORD' [Sir 45:25 c/ 2 Chron 30:18]; 'to leave the Torah of YHWH' [Sir 49:4 c/2 Chron 12:1), one might infer that Ben Sira indeed used the Book of Chronicles.[13]

There is consensus of opinion that Ben Sira does not mention, nor quote from, the books of Esther, Ruth, Daniel, Song of Songs, and the Book of Ezra. That there is no reference to Ezra in "The Praise of the Fathers" (Chapters 44–50) is very amazing, and there are widely divergent views for this non-mention of Ezra.[14] It is my conviction that the non-mention of Ezra is caused

---

[8] After 49:10, the noun 'prophet' or 'prophecy' is no longer used in the Book of Ben Sira.

[9] The Greek translation apparently misread the Hebrew word *'iyyôb* ('Job') as *'ôyeb* ('enemy'). I do not agree with KOOLE that the mentioning of Job in Sir 49:9 is suspicious ('verdächtig'); Koole, Die Bibel des Ben Sira (1965) 379, n. 1.

[10] Skehan / Di Lella, The Wisdom of Ben Sira (1987) 43.

[11] E.g. Sir 14:15/Ps 49:11; Sir 45:15 d/Ps 89:30; Sir 45:12/Ps 21:4.

[12] See Beentjes, Jesus Sirach en Tenach (1981) 24–26.

[13] Rüger, Le Siracide (1984) 61–63.

[14] See, e.g., the articles by BEGG and HÖFFKEN; Koole, Die Bibel des Ben Sira (1965) 383; Stadelmann, Ben Sira als Schriftgelehrter (1980) 163, n. 1.

by Ben Sira's presentation of Aaron as the one who was chosen by God "out of all mankind" and was authorized "to teach the precepts to his people, and the norms to the descendants of Israel" (Sir 45:17), a wording that seems to be adopted from Ezra 7:10! In other words, although Ezra in biblical tradition is presented as a descendant of Aaron (Ezra 7:5), he did not fit into Ben Sira's concept, since it is the extreme and absolute emphasis on High Priesthood that structures the Hymn in Praise of the Famous (Aaron: Sir 45:6–22; Simon: Sir 50:1–24).[15]

Almost for a century, there is an ungoing and animate discussion whether Ben Sira has made use of the Book of Qoheleth. Whereas N. PETERS at the turn of this century catalogued a hugh number of parallels between the Book of Ben Sira and Qoheleth, after a thorough investigation F. J. BACKHAUS recently came to the conclusion that there is no indication whatsoever for *direct* literary affinity between Qoheleth and Ben Sira.[16] Discussing this kind of problem, an important role is reserved for *methodological* questions. They will be paid attention to in the next section.

3. Ben Sira Citing Scripture

In what way precisely does Ben Sira quote from those Hebrew books that already in his days were more or less reckoned among 'Holy Scripture'? To begin with, let me stipulate that I disagree with ROBERT A. KRAFT, who in an earlier contribution to this project maintained: "The body of the book of *Sirach*, however, gives no explicit references to scriptural passages ...".[17] In the following paragraphs his point of view will be disproved.

3.1. Introductory Formulae

In several instances, Ben Sira makes use of words or phrases that can be considered as 'markers' indicating that what follows is a reference to Scripture.

1) Seven times in the Hebrew text of the Book of Ben Sira, *halô'* occurs as an introduction to a rhetorical question: Sir 14:15; 31[34]:19; 35[32]:15; 37:2; 38:5; 42:22; 46:4. In four of these occurrences, *halô'* functions explicitly as referring to a special passage of the Hebrew Bible:

– Sir 14:15 ("Will you not leave your riches to others ...?") is a clear allusion to Ps 49:11; not only since both texts have three Hebrew words in common, but also as both passages have other interesting parallel wordings, such as 'Sheol', 'death', and the identical verbal root *blh* ('to be exhausted').

---

[15] See Beentjes, Jesus Sirach en Tenach (1981) 175–96.

[16] N. PETERS, "Ekklesiastes und Ekklesiastikus", *BZ* 1 (1903) 47–54, 129–50; F. J. BACKHAUS, "Qohelet und Sirach", *BN* 69 (1993) 32–55.

[17] R. A. KRAFT, "Scripture and Canon in Jewish Apocrypha and Pseudepigrapha", *Hebrew Bible / Old Testament*, (HBOT I/1) (ed. M. Saebø; Göttingen: Vandenhoeck & Ruprecht 1996) 199–216 (211).

- Sir 38:5 ("Was not water sweetened by a log ...?") undoubtedly reminds of Exod 15:25. This connexion is confirmed by Sir 38:9b: "Pray to the LORD and He will heal you".[18]

- Sir 46, 4 ("Was it not through him that the sun stood still ...?") is a straight reference to Josh 10, 13b. This reference to Scripture is prepared by Sir 46, 1 e ("Wreaking vengeance on the enemy") that is a plain adoption from Josh 10, 13 a ("Until the nation had taken vengeance on its enemies").

- Sir 35:15 [Gr 32:18–19] ("Do not the tears that stream down her cheek cry out against the one that causes them to fall ?") bears a striking resemblance to Lam 1:2 a. In both passages this phrase is connected with the noun 'widow' (Sir 35:14/Lam 1:1), that both times is used in an *allegoric* sense.[19]

2) In some instances, the Hebrew conjunction *kî* functions as an introduction to a biblical quotation.[20] So in Sir 5, 1–8, the author with the help of five *'mr*-utterances has created a *rhetorical* pattern in order to attribute to the reader's address certain thoughts or remarks, which as a matter of fact may or may not be produced by the addressed. Their literary function is to offer the author an opportunity to react to a number of misconceptions which, in fact, have been created by himself! The Hebrew verb *'mr* in this passage is most adequately rendered by 'to think'.

Among the literary devices of this pericope, further attention is demanded by a number of *kî*-clauses (Sir 5:3 b, 4 b, 6 c, 7 c, 8 b). Together with their preceding prohibitives (Sir 5:3 a, 4 a, 5 a, 7 a, 8 a) they belong to the chain of rhetorical moments which provides a deeper understanding of the passage as a whole. At first sight, the function of the *kî*-clauses seems to be identical to all of its five appearances: with the help of the *kî*-clause the author is trying to present convincing arguments in order to persuade the reader to desist from a well-defined action, thought or utterance: "Do not say / do not think ..., for ...".[21] It hardly can be accidental, that precisely in the final *kî*-clause of this pericope, namely in Sir 5:8 b ("Do not rely on ill-gotten gains [*kî*] they will not avail on the day of wrath"), a definite reference to Prov 11:4 has been adopted ("Wealth avails naught in the day of wrath"). The particle *kî* in Sir 5:8 b is not only to be considered to function as the (grammatical) opening of the motivation, it also marks the transition to a saying that has been adopted from tradition, viz. Prov 11:4. It is very significant that with the help of an *explicit biblical quotation*, Ben Sira has brought to a conclusion this crucial passage in his book of wisdom. Many times Ben Sira uses a biblical quotation to conclude a paragraph.

3) Only once, namely in 48:10c, Ben Sira uses *hakkatûb* ('it is written') as an introductory formula. It is followed by a quotation from Mal 3:23 b–24 a. Both

---

18 I also like to point to MS B's marginal variant reading *bmhlh* (Sir 38:9), since this rare term is also showing up in Exod 15:26 b.

19 For more points of resemblance see Beentjes, Jesus Sirach en Tenach (1981) 24–26.

20 In the Book of Qoheleth, it is the author's most favourite way to introduce quotations.

21 An extensive analysis of Sir 5:1–8 is offered by P. C. Beentjes, "Ben Sira 5, 1–8: A Literary and Rhetorical Analysis", *The Literary Analysis of Hebrew Texts: Papers Read at a Symposium held at the Juda Palache Institute* (ed. E. G. L. Schrijver / N. A. van Uchelen / I. E. Zwiep; Amsterdam: University of Amsterdam 1992) 45–59.

passages refer to Elijah's task in the future. It can hardly be accidental that Ben Sira's passage devoted to Elijah (Sir 48:1–12) not only at the end, viz. in 48:10c, contains this explicit parallel quotation from Mal 3:23b–24a, but also at the opening has an expression ("his words blazed like a torch"; Sir 48:1b) that has been adopted from Mal 3:19, where the same words have been used in a *reversed order* to indicate the Day of the Lord to come.[22]

Before we shall pay attention in a moment to the phenomenon of the inverted quotation as a literary device and a stylistic pattern of quotation, we first should draw an important conclusion from the examples offered so far. It appears that Ben Sira in all those cases where he quotes Scripture, not only adopted the biblical wording as such, but also added a *contextual clue* that supports his use of Scripture. This is a major methodological observation that is important for people who like to discuss intertextuality in the Book of Ben Sira.[23] If such an additional contextual clue is not fixed in advance, we become caught up in a very unwanted situation, as was the case in Ben Sira research at the beginning of this century. Enormous synopses were published in which almost every Hebrew word and sentence from the Book of Ben Sira was traced back to the Hebrew Bible.[24] It is striking, however, to ascertain that those lists to a high degree are completely different from each other, since the compilers did not give the matter due consideration with respect to methodological points of reference.[25]

3.2. Inverted Quotations

In the previous paragraph dealing with Sir 48:1b and Mal 3:19, the term 'inverted quotation' was introduced. My first encounter with this stylistic feature was caused by examining a small text in Ben Sira's famous 'Hymn in Praise of the Fathers' (Ben Sira 44–50) relating to Samuel. The description of Samuel (Sir 46:13–20) has completely been set in the *third* person singular. The only exception, however, is the third bicolon of verse 19, in which suddenly the *first* person is used: "Ransom and sandals, from whom did I take?" Here Ben Sira refers to 1 Sam 12:3, where it says: "From whom did I take ransom and sandals?". The issue now is not the famous text critical question relating to the

[22] Further details: P. C. Beentjes, "Het portret van Elia bij Jesus Sirach", *Amsterdamse Cahiers voor Exegese en Bijbelse Theologie* 5 (1984) 147–55.

[23] "Detailed study is the criterion, and the detailed study ought to respect the context and not be limited to juxtaposing mere excerpts. Two passages may sound the same in splendid isolation, but when seen in context reflect difference rather than similarity", S. Sandmel, "Parallelomania", *JBL* 81 (1962) 2. "For it is not only through such study of contextual information in both occurrences that we can hope to discover something (if any) we may see in his quotations. Our aim is to discover something of what Ben Sira meant by his quotations and references rather than to assess how many there are or to show how wide their range", Snaith, Biblical Quotations (1967) 4.

[24] Schechter-Taylor, The Wisdom of Ben Sira (1899) 12–38; Eberharter, Der Kanon des Alten Testaments (1911) 6–52; Gasser, Die Bedeutung der Sprüche Jesu (1904) 203–53. See also Middendorp, Die Stellung Jesu ben Siras (1973) 49–91.

[25] As an example, this has been investigated in respect of Sir 36:1–17 by Beentjes, Jesus Sirach en Tenach (1981) 5–19.

Hebrew verbal form *w*^{e}*'a'lîm* ('I turned a blind eye'). It is sufficiently known that in 1 Sam 12:3 the Septuagint did not translate that Hebrew verbal form, but a substantive (*hupodèma*). This justifies the supposition that, in the Hebrew text, it found the word *na'alîm* ('sandals'). And it is precisely this textual form which one meets with in the Hebrew as well as in the Greek text of Sir 46:19 c.[26]

Much more interesting than this text critical matter, however, is the question how Ben Sira in his text (46:19 c) has remodelled the phrase from 1 Sam 12:3. For he did not just simply copy these words from Samuel's valedictory address, but he introduced an interesting change in the sequence. As a matter of fact, he took them over in precisely the *reversed* sequence:

Sir 46:19 c "Ransom and sandals, from whom did I take?"
1 Sam 12:3 "From whom did I take ransom and sandals?"

A current term for this remarkable literary phenomenon does not exist. In view of the most striking characteristic of this stylistic figure, the notion *inverted quotation* would be the most suitable name for it.

After having discovered such a striking intertextual relationship, the first question to be answered would be whether this phenomenon appears more often in the Book of Ben Sira. A closer examination brings to light that indeed a number of such 'reversed quotations' can be established. Most of them are found within Chapters 44–50, being the 'Hymn in Praise of the Famous'. This should not be surprising, since in this particular section of his book Ben Sira is offering a portrayal of biblical heroes, who of course to a high degree are described with the help of biblical vocabulary. In the previous paragraph, we already mentioned Sir 48:1 b. There can be no doubt that Ben Sira adopted the rare expression "his words blazed like a torch" from Mal 3:19, where the same words have been used in a *reversed* order. Although all commentators of course mention Ben Sira's use of Scripture here, no one however has ever drawn attention to the fact that this use of Scripture, being a reversed quotation, should be marked off from a so called *parallel* quotation, as in Sir 48:10, where Mal 3:23 b–24 a is cited.

Sir 48:19 ("they were in anguish like a woman in labour") must in the same way be considered an inverted quotation from Isa 13:8 ("like a woman in labour they will be in anguish").

In Sir 45:15 ab, the ordination of Aaron is described with the help of an inversion of the vocabulary of Exod 28:41. As the word-pair 'anoint / install' everywhere in the Old Testament is presented in that fixed order, the reversed order in Sir 45:15 points to a deliberate use of inverted quotation by Ben Sira.[27]

---

[26] So apparently in very early days, already *two* Hebrew text forms of 1 Sam 12:3 were in circulation. The Masoretes preferred the reading *w*^{e}*'a'lîm 'êney bô* ('and I did blind my eyes with it') to the textual form with *na'alîm* ('sandals') that has been handed down in the Septuagint version of 1 Sam 12:3 and also in the Hebrew and Greek text of Sir 46:19 c. In the three latter cases, the combination *'ênay bô* is understood as *'anah bô* ('to answer').

[27] This observation is on firm ground, as Sir 45:6–14 has been modelled upon Exodus 28 as a kind of 'structural use of Scripture', that will be described in the next paragraph.

Other instances in the Book of Ben Sira where Scripture has been quoted in a reversed order are:

Sir 7:11/1 Sam 2:7; Ps 75:8
Sir 9:5 a/Job 31:1 b
Sir 18:32/Prov 23:20–21
Sir 20:4/Prov 17:28
Sir 32[35]:23/Prov 19:16[28]

3.3. Structural Use of Scripture

In his stimulating doctoral thesis, D. Patte investigated a literary device that he coined 'structural use of Scripture (or structural style)'.[29] It is a phenomenon to the effect that a passage in a (non-canonical Jewish) writing to a high degree is structured by elements from *one* or *two* biblical texts. As an example Patte mentions *Sibylline Oracles* 3:8–45, in which one can clearly recognize the pattern of Isa 40:18–28, whereas *Sibylline Oracles* 3:62–91 should be read in the light of Deuteronomy 13.[30] He also analyzed, for example, *1 Enoch*, and Qumran literature, such as *The Rule of the Community* (1 QS) and *The Hodayot Scroll* (1 QH).[31] Patte discovered the application of 'structural use of Scripture' just in Jewish writings that can be dated to about the second century BCE, being the same period in which Ben Sira composed his book.

In a recent article on Sir 6:5–17, I was sceptical about the possibility whether this passage displays a structural use of Scripture from 1 Samuel 25:

Sir 6:4 b/1 Sam 25:5 b	'to give greetings'
Sir 6:9 b/1 Sam 25:39	'to punish for an insult'
Sir 6:16 a/1 Sam 25:29	'the bundle of life'
Sir 6:17 a/1 Sam 25:25	'as his name is, so are his words/so is he'[32]

Since the vocabulary used here is quite unique, such a striking resemblance can hardly be a coincidence. I therefore have changed my mind; so I am tempted now to think that in Sir 6:5–17 we have the first occurrence of structural use of Scripture in the Book of Ben Sira.

Would it be coincidence that Ben Sira precisely in the most crucial part of his book, namely the extensive description of Aaron (Sir 45:6–22), as well as in the subsequent pericope dealing with Phinehas (Sir 45:23–25) utilized this

[28] See also Sir 24:15 a (LXX)/Exod 30:23 (LXX); Sir 24:15 b (LXX)/Exod 30:34 (LXX). Further examples of inverted quotations, both in Hebrew and in Greek biblical texts, in Qumran literature, in New Testament texts, in Greek and Latin literature, are reviewed in Beentjes, Discovering a new path of intertextuality (1996) 34–49.

[29] Patte, Early Jewish hermeneutic (1975) 171, 189.

[30] Patte, Early Jewish hermeneutic, 186–89.

[31] Patte, Early Jewish hermeneutic, 189–96, 266–77.

[32] P. C. Beentjes, "«Ein Mensch ohne Freund ist wie eine linke Hand ohne die Rechte»", *Freundschaft bei Ben Sira: Beiträge des Symposions zu Ben Sira Salzburg 1995* (ed. F. V. Reiterer; BZAW 244; Berlin: De Gruyter 1996) 1–18 (esp. 14–15). Sir 6:5–17 is the first of *seven* passages in Ben Sira's book dealing with friendship.

structural use of Scripture in a rather creative way? Sir 45:6–26 is no less than a key text, both to the structure and to the theology of the 'Hymn in praise of the Famous'. With the section on Aaron and Phinehas, Ben Sira wants to 'prove' that the succession of the Davidic dynasty has been transferred to the High Priestly dynasty of Aaron and his descendants. That is why Ben Sira not only pays so much attention to Aaron (Sir 45, 6–22), but also to Simon (Sir 50:1–24), the High Priest of his own days. Both texts on these two High Priests are expressely interrelated.[33]

Ben Sira's extensive description of Aaron (Sir 45:6–22) is characterized by a twofold 'structural use of Scripture':[34]

1) Sir 45:6–14 has been structured by references to Exodus 28. This observation is reinforced by the fact that in Sir 45:6–14 there are no parallels whatsoever to the other two biblical narratives (Exodus 39; Leviticus 8) in which the same subject is treated as in Exodus 28.

– Only in Sir 45:10 c and Exod 28:15, 29–30 one finds the quite rare word-combination 'the breastpiece for decision'.

– The 'rustle of bells' (Sir 45:8 c–9) is found in Exod 28:35, be it that Ben Sira has replaced the strange motivation for it as given in Exod 28:35 ("and so he will not die") by the reason as given in Exod 28:12 ("as reminders of the sons of Israel").

– We already mentioned the combination of the verbs 'to anoint' and 'to install' (Sir 45:15) that are used in a reversed order as compared with Exod 28:41. It hardly can be coincidence that such an inverted quotation is found at a crucial point in the passage on Aaron, namely at the transition from one subject ('the Holy One') to another ('Moses') and precisely before a second structural use of Scripture (Numbers 16–18) shows up.

2) The mention of Moses in Sir 45:15 a plays an important role within the section of Sir 45:15–22. In the first place, from here on the Ben Sira report is in keeping with Exodus 28, where Moses is the agent all the time, whereas in Sir 45:6 ff it is at least suggested that 'the Holy One' is the subject of investing Aaron. Second, Moses plays a crucial role relating to the legitimation of Aaron's other duties. For it is Moses who in Sir 45:17 hands over to Aaron exactly the same tasks as in Sir 45:5 had been handed down to him by God. In this way, Ben Sira has firmly anchored the High Priest's legitimation: Aaron has received it directly from Moses (45:17), and the latter directly from God himself (45:5).[35]

Against this background, one can explain why Ben Sira in 45:18ff reverts to Numbers 16, the 'classic' narrative about Korah, son of Levi, who contested Aaron's election by God claiming those priestly functions for himself. The death of Korah and his supporters by fire makes undoubtedly clear that YHWH has destined the High Priesthood for Aaron. The salutary intercession

[33] More details are to be found in Beentjes, Jesus Sirach en Tenach (1981) 175–99.

[34] This term has to be preferred to the notion 'anthological style', as the latter could suggest a certain degree of arbitrariness, that is absolutely incorrect. See e.g. Snaith, Ben Sira's supposed love of liturgy (1975) 172–73.

[35] This must be the reason why Sir 45:4 b and 45:16 a bear such a striking resemblance.

by Aaron as reported in Num 17:6–15 (REB 16:41–50) and the narrative on his budding rod (Num 17:16–26 [REB 17:1–10]) have the same intention. Though Ben Sira does not explicitly mention these two stories, there is consensus of opinion that he summarized them in the first half of 45:20 ("he increased the glory of Aaron").

Sir 45:20 bc–21 is a very special interpretation of Num 18:8–19. For since in the Pentateuch this instruction on special offerings has no relation whatsoever with the narratives in Numbers 16 and 17, in Sir 45:20 bc–21, however, it is emphatically brought to the fore as an *extra argument* in favour of Aaron's special position. It therefore can be no accident that Ben Sira's description of Aaron is concluded in 45:22 with an extensive quotation from Num 18:20, being in fact the *most extensive biblical parallel* to be found in the Book of Ben Sira.

3) There can be no doubt that the passage on Phinehas (Sir 45:23–24) depends on Num 25:11–13. This is self-evident, not only because of the literal parallel between Sir 45:23 f and Num 25:13 b ("he made expiation for the Israelites"), but equally from the vocabulary in Sir 45:23–24 that has been adopted from Num 25:11–13 ('to show zeal'; 'covenant of peace'; 'priesthood for ever').[36]

Sir 45:23–24 unfolds a rather remarkable pattern. Each of its five bicola namely alternately consists of half a verse with vocabulary adopted from Num 25:11–13, followed by half a verse with Ben Sira's own idiom. Here we met with a special kind of structural use of Scripture:

(a)	Sir 45:23 a	Num 25:11 a
	Sir 45:23 b	----------------
(b)	Sir 45:23 c	Num 25:11 + 13 b
	Sir 45:23 d	----------------
(c)	Sir 45:23 e	----------------
	Sir 45:23 f	Num 25:13 b
(d)	Sir 45:24 a	----------------
	Sir 45:24 b	Num 25:12
(e)	Sir 45:24 c	----------------
	Sir 45:24 d	Num 25:13 a

3.4. Unique Word Combinations in Ben Sira and Their Parallels in the Hebrew Bible

Discussing this type of Ben Sira's use of Scripture, some preliminary remarks are in order. An expression or formula consisting of at least two words that is found only once both in the Book of Ben Sira and in the Hebrew Bible, can easily create the impression that there *must* be a direct dependence between Ben Sira and his Hebrew Bible. It is quite possible, however, that despite a striking resemblance, an unique combination in the Book of Ben Sira has nothing to do with an identical expression to be found in the Hebrew Bible. Therefore it

[36] Sir 45:24 d: 'the *High* Priesthood for ever'.

must be the *context* that adduces further evidence Ben Sira purposely adopted such unique word combinations from holy scriptures of his day.

When in Sir 40:1 d the rare expression "mother of all living beings" is used, people at first glance are apt to think that Ben Sira quotes Gen 3:20. However, Ben Sira is using this rare expression as a metaphor to describe the *earth*, whereas the same expression in Genesis in a popular way seeks to explain the name of Eve. The conclusion therefore must be, that there is no direct relationship between this unique expression in Sir 40:1 and Gen 3:20, since their context is totally different.

The unique expression 'precious stones' occurring in Sir 45:11 and 50:9, by a large number of Ben Sira commentators is immediately related to Isa 54:12 being the only occurrence of this formula in the entire Hebrew Bible. Strikingly, nobody emphasized that the context is quite different. In the Isaian passage, the wording 'precious stones' has a bearing on the rebuilding of the New Jerusalem, whereas in the Book of Ben Sira these words function as a description of the High Priestly vestments of Aaron and Simon. The completely different use of this identical word-combination does not favour a direct link between Isa 54:12 and the two occurrences in the Book of Ben Sira. This is confirmed by the observation that the expression 'precious stones' occurs no less than four times in the *War Scroll* from Qumran (1QM 5:6, 9, 14; 12:13), "which suggests that the phrase may well have been a customary way of saying 'precious stones'. Thus the additional evidence of the Dead Sea Scrolls increases our knowledge of postbiblical Hebrew usages and in this case increases in our minds a very reasonable doubt that Ben Sira 'copied' the phrase from Isaiah!".[37] This is solid proof that Ben Sira in his book uses contemporary idiom rather than being directly dependent on identical phraseology from the Hebrew Bible.

It was the discovery of the Ben Sira Scroll from Masada in 1964 that has further refined the question of interrelationship between the Book of Ben Sira and the Hebrew Bible. The Masada Scroll, containing the Hebrew text of Sir 39:27–44:17, has been dated 100–75 BCE, whereas the Hebrew manuscripts that were recovered from the Cairo Genizah originate in the Middle Ages (eleventh or twelfth century). A comparison between these two types of text proves without any doubt that one has to be very cautious in establishing direct interrelationship between the Book of Ben Sira and the Hebrew Bible.

The Hebrew text of Sir 40:15 b in the mediaeval MS B has the wording *ʿal šen selaʿ* ('on sheer rock'). It therefore seems a parallel to Job 39:28 b, where the same expression shows up. Though the text of Sir 40:15 b is heavily damaged in the Masada Scroll, the final word of this colon has fortunately been preserved: *ṣûr*. This synonym of *selaʿ* seems to represent the older textual form and is transmitted also as the marginal variant reading in MS B itself: *ʿal šen ṣûr*. It looks as though somebody altered the original expression *ʿal šen ṣûr* into *ʿal šen selaʿ* in MS B to *create* a close parallel to the biblical wording of Job 39:28 b. However the copyist of MS B drew attention to another textual

37 Snaith, Biblical Quotations (1967) 6.

form, which seems closer to the original reading, in the margin of the manuscript. The margin of MS B often provides a textual form that coincides with the Masada text.[38]

A similar example is in Sir 42:15b. The Hebrew text completely coincides with the text of Job 15:17b. In both texts the formula *w^e zeh ḥazîtî wa'asperâh* functions as an introductory call to attention ('Lehreröffnungsformel'). The reader could easily be misled to assume that Sir 42:15b was a deliberate parallel to the Book of Job. In the Masada Scroll, however, the final word is written as *w'šnnh.* With the very rare verb *šnn* II (only Deut 6:7), the Masada text again represents the older textual form. In MS B, it was probably a copyist's familiarity with the scriptural passage of Job 15:17b that caused alternation of the original Ben Sira text to a more common synonym.

The examples mentioned above are clear evidence that we should be very reluctant in rashly assigning rare expressions in the Book of Ben Sira to adoptions from identical formulae found in the Hebrew Bible.

In my doctoral thesis, there is given an extensive inventory of all unique word combinations to be found in the Hebrew Ben Sira.[39] Put to the test with the criterion of contextual similarity, it appeared that only ten of these unique word-combinations in the Book of Ben Sira with certainty can be considered a parallel of biblical texts. It is rather striking to ascertain how these occurrences have been spread throughout the Book of Ben Sira.

Two unique word combinations are found in the prayer for Israel's delivery:

(1) 'the leaders of Moab' (Sir 36:10 [Gr 12]/Num 24:17e);
(2) 'Jacob's tribes' (Sir 36:11/Isa 49:6).[40]

Two such unique formulae are in the 'Hymn on God's Work in Creation' (Sir 42:15–43:33):

(1) 'Heaven itself manifests its glory' (Sir 43:1/Exod 24:10);[41]
(2) 'With renewed strength' (Sir 43:30/Isa 40:31).

Six parallels to unique expressions can be established between the 'Hymn in Praise of the Famous' (Sir 44–50) and the Hebrew Bible:

(1) 'Father of many nations' (Sir 44:17/Gen 17:4–5);
(2) 'to approach the cloud' (Sir 45:5/Exod 20:2);
(3) 'to eat the food-offerings of YHWH' (Sir 45:21/Deut 18:1);
(4) 'to anoint to be prophet in your place' (Sir 48:8/1 Kgs 19:16);
(5) 'trumpets of beaten metal' (Sir 50:16/Num 10:2).[42]
(6) 'to console the mourners of Zion' (Sir 48:24/Isa 61:3).

This sixth parallel is strong evidence that this Isaian formula, being a famous gloss, already at the end of the second century BCE was reckoned among the

[38] See Beentjes, A Text Edition (1997) 68–78.
[39] Beentjes, Jesus Sirach en Tenach (1981) 107–73.
[40] Beentjes, Jesus Sirach en Tenach (1981) 127–31.
[41] There is also a kind of inverted quotation between these two texts!
[42] One could even say that Sir 50:16 is a kind of 'structural use of Scripture'. See Beentjes, Jesus Sirach en Tenach (1981) 120–21.

established Hebrew text of the Book of Isaiah. The appearance of this Isaian gloss in Sir 48:24, however, is not only of great importance as far as canonical history of the Hebrew Bible is concerned, but is also solid proof that Ben Sira *identified* the messenger from Isaiah 61 with the prophet himself, just as Ben Sira makes *Isaiah* strike the camp of the Assyrians instead of the angel of the LORD as in the biblical narrative.[43]

No less than 43 unique word combinations to be found in the Hebrew text of Ben Sira must be disqualified as being no parallels of identical biblical wordings, since both (con)texts have nothing in common but the Hebrew characters.[44] This means that Ben Sira loses the usual image of being merely a copyist or imitator of biblical phrases and expressions. After careful investigation, it seems likely that he turns out to be a very careful author who in a very selective and conscientious way adopted and elaborated the Holy scriptures of his day into his own book.

---

[43] Schildenberger, Die Bedeutung (1950); Beentjes, Relations (1989).
[44] An inventory of these 43 occurrences by Beentjes, Jesus Sirach en Tenach (1981) 133–73.

5.4 Wisdom of Solomon and Scripture

By MAURICE GILBERT, Rome

Sources: J. ZIEGLER (ed.), *Sapientia Salomonis* (Septuaginta Vetus Testamentum Graecum XII, 1; Göttingen: Vandenhoeck & Ruprecht 1962, ^{2}1980).

Commentaries: D. WILSON, *The Wisdom of Solomon* (AB XLIII; New York: Doubleday 1979); C. LARCHER, *Le Livre de la Sagesse ou la Sagesse de Salomon* (Ebib 1, 3, 5; Paris: Gabalda 1983–85); A. SCHMITT, *Das Buch der Weisheit. Ein Kommentar* (Würzburg: Echter 1986); J. VÍLCHEZ LINDEZ, *Sabiduría* (Nueva Biblia Española, Sapientiales V; Estella, Navarra: Verbo Divino 1990); G. SCARPAT, *Libro della Sapienza* (Biblica, Testi e Studi 1, 3, 6; Brescia: Paideia 1989, 1996, 1999).

Bibliographies: M. GILBERT, «Bibliographie générale sur *Sag.*», in: C. LARCHER, *Le Livre de la Sagesse ou la Sagesse de Salomon* (Ebib 1; Paris: Gabalda 1983) 11–48; C. DOGNIEZ, *Bibliography of the Septuagint – Bibliographie de la Septante (1970–93)* (VTSup LX; Leiden: Brill 1995) 221–30.

General works: J. FICHTNER, «Der AT-Text der Sapientia Salomonis», *ZAW* 57 (1939) 155–92; C. LARCHER, *Etudes sur le livre de la Sagesse* (Ebib; Paris: Gabalda 1969) 85–103.

1. Introduction

Among the Jewish Apocrypha the Wisdom of Solomon deserves special attention. Indeed this book is full of biblical reminiscences: anyone who is familiar with the Bible will easily identify them. However, precise analysis is more difficult to make. Wisdom is a poetical work, or in a certain sense a rhythmic prose composition. It does not explicitly offer direct exegesis of the biblical texts, nor give any explicit quotation. The anonymity is almost complete; not only is the author unknown, but he makes no reference to any name, biblical or otherwise; the Red Sea is the only location mentioned (10:18; 19:7), besides the prophets generally (7:27), the Law (18:4), or the precept of the Law (16:6; allusion to Gen 2:17?).

The book antedates the fixing of the Jewish canon, but it cannot antedate the reign of the emperor Augustus, as this work by a single author includes terms particular to the Augustan era[1]. It thus belongs to an earlier period of biblical interpretation and it is impossible to determine the "authoritative" character of the biblical author refers.

If Wisdom is not really a commentary on the biblical texts, neither is it a cento. It is an original work, firmly rooted in Jewish tradition. This originality appears in the intrinsic links the author makes between the biblical traditions on the one hand and strictly Jewish traditions and Hellenistic culture on the other. In this he has certain similarities with Philo, but he is different from him on account of a more eclectic philosophy, lack of use of allegory and through references to a number of biblical texts, not only those belonging to the Pentateuch.

The impact of Hellenism on Wisdom is important. The book was written in Greek, that is certain. The literary genre is not a biblical one, but Greek, as it

---

[1] Cf. Gilbert, Critique des dieux (1973) 172.

refers to epideictic argument and, more particularly, to the *encomium*, or praise formula, as set out in the treatises on rhetoric developed by Aristotle and Cicero among others. Philo also sometimes used the principles of these (cf. *Quod omnis probus* and *De Virtutibus: De Nobilitate*). Besides this general background, Wisdom refers to Hellenism repeatedly by criticising its preferences, as well as by adopting some theses, after having adapted them for his purpose. It criticises excessive hedonism based on materialism (1:16–2:21); it stigmatizes the mystery cults (14:15–29); it borrows from the Isis cult some characteristics of the goddess which it applies to Wisdom, and it fills out this figure by giving her characteristics of the Stoic *pneuma*. It mentions the *philanthropia* of the righteous as well as of God in the Greek manner (12:19) and Greek philosophy allows the author the possibility of disproving the error of cults devoted to elements of the cosmos (13:1–9).

In other respects the author of Wisdom belongs within the movement of Jewish tradition. From this point of view his retelling of the events of the biblical exodus is significant (16–19). We can without doubt consider these chapters as a midrashic rereading. A number of recent studies stress both the roots of these chapters in Jewish tradition and the author's originality.[2] Some of his interpretations of the biblical text are found in rabbinic tradition, but others are peculiar to him. This is true, for example, of the meaning which is given to the manna (16:20–29), to the darkness which encompasses the wicked (17:2–6) and to the intercession of Aaron (18:20–25). These few data allow us to understand the difficulty with which the interpreter, trying to specify the place and role of the biblical texts in Wisdom, is confronted. Not only does the author give his own message, often making use of biblical texts, but at the same time he actualizes them, seeing his contemporaries as the Egyptians of the exodus, or rereading the old texts of the biblical tradition through Jewish interpretations of his time.

In the following pages we will successively use two working methods. First we will follow the author according to the thread of his discourse, noting its structure.[3] In a second stage we will summarize the data, following the classical order of biblical texts.[4]

2. Wisdom under the Influence of Hebrew Bible

2.1. Opposed Theses Concerning the Righteous and the Wicked in Life and Death

Special studies: M. Kolarcik, *The Ambiguity of Death in the Book of Wisdom 1–6* (AnBib 127; Roma: Pontificio Istituto Biblico 1991) esp. 114–31, 135–46; G. W. E. Nickelsburg, Jr., *Resurrection, Immortality, and Eternal Life in Intertestamental Judaism* (HTS 26; Cambridge, MA: Harvard

---

[2] Maneschg, Erzählung (1981); idem, Gott (1984); Priotto, Prima Pasqua (1987); Dumoulin, Entre la Manne (1994); Mazzinghi, Notte (1995).

[3] Cf. Fichtner, Der AT-Text (1939).

[4] Cf. Larcher, Etudes (1969).

1972) esp. 48–92; J. Schaberg, «Major Midrashic Traditions in Wisdom 1, 1–6, 25», *JSJ* 13 (1982) 75–101; A. Schmitt, «Komposition, Tradition und zeitgeschichtlicher Hintergrund in Weish 1, 16–2, 24 und 4, 20–5, 23», *Text, Methode und Grammatik. Wolfgang Richter zum 65. Geburtstag* (ed. W. Gross / H. Irsigler / T. Seidl; St Ottilien: EOS 1991) 404–21; A. Sisti, «La morte prematura in *Sap.* 4, 7–17», *RivB* 31 (1983) 129–46; M. J. Suggs, «Wisdom of Solomon 2, 10–5: A Homily Based on the Fourth Servant Song», *JBL* 76 (1957) 26–33; J. P. Weisengoff, «The Impious of Wisdom 2», *CBQ* 11 (1949) 40–65, esp. 53–60.

It is now generally agreed that Wis 1:1–6:21 forms the first part of the book. It extends as far as the exordium of the epideictic argument. Structured concentrically it can be summarised in the following manner: addressing the princes, the author asserts that Wisdom does not reveal herself to the wicked and he reminds the reader not to forget that there will be a divine judgment (1:1–12). The fate of the wicked is then introduced by the thesis according to which creation implies immortality, while the wicked are on the side of death. What these latter say disregards everything beyond this world and this, in their opinion, justifies the frantic search for pleasure; since the righteous present a challenge to them they plot against them. But they do not know that God created humanity for incorruptibility (1:13–2:24). Then three forms of paradox concerning the fate of the righteous and of those who oppose them are described: some of the righteous die in pain, have no offspring or die early, while some of the wicked attain prosperity, have children and enjoy a long life. The former will be rewarded in the life that is to come, while the latter will encounter failure (3–4). The author then describes the confrontation in the world to come between the wicked and the righteous. The wicked have to recognize the triumph of the righteous and the folly of their own choices. This second speech of the wicked is then complemented by the description of the joy of the righteous and the final cosmic battle led by God against the wicked (5). Returning to exhortation the author reaches a conclusion in which he invites the princes not to forget the divine judgment waiting form them. They should receive Wisdom who reveals herself to all who look for her; she is guarantee of immortality (6).

This first part of the book is the one where it is most difficult to define references to the Hebrew Bible and where scholars in the past have sometimes been wrong. The beginning of the first speech of the wicked (2:1–9), lauding extreme indulgence in pleasure, is not a critical allusion to Qohelet who advocates contentment with the simple pleasures of life.[5] However some allusions to other texts are easily identified. Both the exhortations to the princes hark back to Ps 2:10–12 (Wis 1:1; 6:1, 9, 11). The "murmuring" (Wis 1:10–11) of the wicked is reminiscent of the accounts of the starving Hebrews in the desert (especially Exodus 16).

The similarity between Wis 2:12a und Isa 3:10 Lxx especially raises a problem of textual criticism of the prophetic verse in the Greek version. On the other hand Wis 4:10, describing the righteous who are prematurely "taken away" harks back to the figure of Enoch in Gen 5:24 Lxx. The welcome of the eunuch in the temple (Wis 3:14) recalls Isa 56:2, 4–5. The armour God wears

[5] Cf. Weisengoff, Impious (1949) 53–60.

for the final cosmic battle (Wis 5:17–20) is inspired by Isa 59:16–17. In this way we can note several detailed links. Two others are even more important since they reflect the author's fundamental theses.

He claims that "God did not create death" (Wis 1:13), but that it entered the world "by the envy of the devil" (Wis 2:24), and that "God created the universe for it to endure" (Wis 1:14) and that he "created human beings for incorruptibility" and made mankind "an image of his own nature" (Wis 2:23). The radical contrast with the purpose of the wicked is clearly based on Genesis 1–3. If, as scholars usually think, the devil is the snake of Genesis 3, this brings it closer to the theme of God's image, which harks back to Gen 1:26–27. So the author offers interpretations of both stories of creation, complementing the one with the other.[6]

The second case concerns the sources of the main theme of Wisdom 1–6: the persecution and triumph of the reighteous, a theme which is underlined by speeches concerning the fate of the wicked. It seems that the theme originates in Isa 52:13–53:12, filled out with some elements of Isaiah 13–14. It may have been enlarged by allusion to the ancient Jewish tradition concerning Enoch, and it is in Daniel 7–12 that it is given its apocalyptic dimension. It then receives in Wisdom 1–6, where all these traditions meet together, a sapiential dimension, in which however messianism is lacking.[7]

2.2. *Wisdom and the Wise*

Special studies: M. Gilbert, «La structure de la prière de Salomon (Sg 9)», *Bib.* 51 (1970) 301–31, esp. 321–26; idem, «Volonté de Dieu et don de la Sagesse (Sg 9,17 s.)», *NRT* 93 (1971) 145–66; idem, «La figure de Salomon en Sg 7–9», *Etudes sur le judaïsme hellénistique* (ed. R. Kuntzmann / J. Schlosser; LD 119; Paris: Cerf 1984) 225–49; D. McLain Carr, *From D to Q: A Study of Early Jewish Interpretations of Solomon's Dream at Gibeon* (SBLMS 44; Atlanta, GA: Scholars Press 1991) esp. 145–64.

The encomium or praise itself, explicitly announced in Wis 6:22, covers Wisdom 7–8, with Wisdom 9, which stands at the centre of the book, offering a prayer for the gift of Wisdom. In the continuation of Wisdom 6 the author discloses his identity, hiding his name under the figure of Solomon, the paragon of the wise. It is Solomon at the height of his glory, recalling in his mature years how he obtained Wisdom during his youth. It also explains what Wisdom is and what he received from her. For this the author first evokes his origin common to every human being who may receive Wisdom. Solomon, however, attained her because he requested her through prayer, preferring her to any other virtue appropriate to royalty. He received her and she brought him all those good things besides the gift of understanding (7:1–22 a). He then continues with the praise of Wisdom herself: her nature is so beneficially pure

[6] On the meaning of death, compare Gilbert, Relecture (1987) 324–28, and Kolarcik, Ambiguity (1991) 135–48.

[7] Cf. Suggs, Wisdom (1957); Nickelsburg, Resurrection (1972); Schaberg, Major Midrashic (1982).

that she enters everything without blemish; because she finds her source in God, she radiates perfection. Her effect is then to govern the universe with kindness and to make saints into friends of God and prophets (7:22–8:1). Returning to the experience of Solomon, the author recalls that, in desiring her as a wife, he sought from her the gifts of a noble personality and the status of a great king. That is why he requested her through prayer, conscious that, despite his own natural gifts, he could only receive her from God (8:2–21).

This encomium or praise, once again structured in a concentric fashion, shows the nature, origin and activity of Wisdom for Solomon. It quite properly reaches its climax in the prayer (7:7; 8:21). This is then developed further in Wisdom 9, which is also similarly structured. The author, conscious of his frail humanity and concerned with his vocation, requests Wisdom first of all. Only Wisdom can help him fulfil his royal task. Finally, once again stressing human frailty, he insists on the necessity of this gift of Wisdom, which he requests and which he compares to the holy spirit. Thanks to this gift the ancestors could make straight their paths, learn what was pleasing to God and finally achieve salvation.[8]

The figure of Solomon, as it is evoked in Wisdom 7–9, reflects the stories of 1 Kings 3 und 2 Chronicles 1 concerning the prayer of the young king at Gibeon and the mention in 1 Kgs 5:13 of his great learning. There is only a slight allusion in Wis 9:8 to the building and consecration of the temple. The book mentions nothing concerning the juridical insight of Solomon, the visit of the Queen of Sheba, the administrative organization of the state, or the king's marriages and their idolatrous consequences. His rule over the neighbouring kingdoms is merely evoked in Wis 8:14. Wisdom 7–9 mentions only the prayer of Gibeon, first recalled in Wis 7:7–12 with the king's desire for Wisdom, rather than for the possessions which ususally form the privileged acquisition of royal persons. The granting of these latter was made because of the king's choice of Wisdom. In Wisdom 7–9 however Solomon is not said to have entered a sanctuary and, in distinction from 1 Kings 3, there is no mention of a dream which has, in any case, already been dropped in 2 Chronicles 1. In Wisdom 9, in a paraphrase of the prayer of Gibeon, there is a new literary structure, even though some of the original elements are retained: the praise of David in 1 Kgs 3:6 serves to clarify Wis 9:3 concerning the lot of every human being. The gift of right judgment of 1 Kgs 3:9 reappears in Wis 9:12. It is chiefly the argument based on Solomon's prayer which is the same.[9]

As for the figure of Wisdom, even if Wisdom 7–9 continues the development from Proverbs 8 and Sirach 24, which are basic texts on this issue, the author nevertheless goes his own way. The concept of Wisdom which he describes shows in fact some degree of influence from the Stoic doctrine concerning the cosmic *pneuma*. In comparing Wisdom with the holy spirit (Wis 9:17), he continues on from Ezek 36:27.[10] However the debate continues whether the

---

[8] Gilbert, Structure (1970).

[9] Gilbert, Structure (1970) 321–26; idem, Figure de Salomon (1984) 229–33; McLain Carr, From D (1991) 145–64.

[10] Gilbert, Volonté (1971) 157–62.

words *genetis* (Wis 7:12) and *technitis* (7:21; 8:6) may not be fresh interpretations of the famous *'mwn* of Prov 8:30.[11] The idea of marriage to Wisdom becomes more sharply focused: Prov 4:6b Lxx offers an invitation to love her; the same verbal root is found in Wis 8:2c; cf. also Sir 15:2b. There is however no clear reference to Song of Songs.

As becomes evident, far more than is the case with Wisdom 1-6, these later chapters show important connections with texts of the Hebrew Bible which evoke Wisdom. Such texts, however, are used freely.

2.3. The Wisdom and the Heroes of Genesis-Exodus

Special studies: P. Beauchamp, «Le salut corporel des justes et la conclusion du livre de la Sagesse», *Bib.* 45 (1964) 491–526; P. C. Beentjes, «"You Have Given a Road in the Sea": What is Wisdom 14,3 Talking about?», *ETL* 68 (1992) 137–41; S. Cheon, *The Exodus Story in the Wisdom of Solomon. A Study in Biblical Interpretation* (JSPSup 23; Sheffield Academic Press 1997); P. Dumoulin, *Entre la Manne et l'Eucharistie. Etude de Sg 16,15–17,1a* (AnBib 132; Roma: Pontificio Istituto Biblico 1994) esp. 41–153; P. Enns, «A Retelling of the Song at the Sea in Wis 10:20–21», *Bib.* 76 (1995) 1–24; idem, *Exodus Retold. Ancient Exegesis of the Departure from Egypt in Wis 10:15–21 and 19:1–9* (HSM 57; Atlanta, GA: Scholars Press 1997); M. Gilbert, *La critique des dieux dans le Livre de la Sagesse (Sg 13–15)* (AnBib 53; Rome: Biblical Institute 1973); H. Maneschg, *Die Erzählung von der ehernen Schlange (Num 21,4–9) in der Auslegung der frühen jüdischen Literatur. Eine traditionsgeschichtliche Studie* (Europäische Hochschulschriften XXIII, 157; Frankfurt a. M / Bern: Lang 1981) esp. 101–91; idem, «Gott Erzieher, Retter und Heiland seines Volkes zur Reinterpretation von Num 21,4–9 in Weish 16,5–14», *BZ* 28 (1984) 214–29; L. Mazzinghi, *Notte di paura e di luce. Esegesi di Sap 17,1–18,4* (AnBib 134; Roma: Pontificio Istituto Biblico 1995); M. Priotto, *La prima Pasqua in Sap 18,5–25* (Supplementi alla *RivB* 15; Bologna: Dehoniane 1987); idem, «Il significato del confronto Egitto-Sodoma in Sap. 19,13–17», *RivB* 32 (1984) 369–94; U. Schwenk-Bressler, *Sapientia Salomonis als ein Beispiel frühjüdischer Textauslegung. Die Auslegung des Buches Genesis, Exodus 1–15 und Teilen der Wüstentradition in Sap 10–19* (BEATAJ 32; Frankfurt a. M / Berlin / Bern: Lang 1993).

Continuing on from the prayer of Wisdom 9, and in particular its concluding verse 9:18, chapters 10–19 take the form of hymnic *anamnesis*.[12] In order to link Wisdom 9 with a recollection of the events of the exodus, the author inserts Wisdom 10 where he successively evokes Adam, Cain and Abel, Noah, Abraham, Lot, Jacob, Joseph and, finally, the Hebrew people led by Moses, without however naming them. All these, apart from Cain, received the benefits of Wisdom which preserved them, kept them, rescued them from danger and saved them. These heroes were confronted by adversity, oppression, and even their own sin, as for example Adam. So the contrast between the righteous and the wicked, which forms the basis of Wisdom 1–6, reappears and is maintained right until the end of the book.

This second half of the book develops a rereading of the events of Israel's foundation and, from a literary point of view, confirms through well known historical examples the main theses that the author expounds in the preceding chapters.

---

[11] Cf. Gilbert, Figure de Salomon (1984) 234 f.
[12] Cf. Schwenk-Bressler, Sapientia (1993).

This short survey offered by Wisdom 10 centers on the ancestral heroes, but it is Wisdom which leads them and ensures their success; in this the author goes beyond the reading of history proposed in Sirach 44–49. The action of Wisdom is in line with the affirmations of Wis 7:27cd that it is an inward personal activity. However Wis 10:17cd compares the cloud of the desert with Wisdom. Incidents recounted in Genesis-Exodus are hardly mentioned here, but are just sufficiently present to be recognised. Some details however come from Jewish non-biblical traditions. Among these, for example, we find the conversion of Adam after his fall and also his mastery of the universe (Wis 10:1–2), which goes beyond Gen 1:26, 28.

2.4. Divine Mercy and Cultic Errors

In reality the aim of the author is to develop an confrontation, a *synkrisis*, between the misfortune the Egyptians suffered and the blessings the Hebrews received during the exodus. However, after setting over against each other the water of the Nile in the plague stories which had become unfit to drink and the water of the rock which slaked the thirst of the Israelites (Wis 11:1–14), he affirms that the plague was provoked by the worship of reptiles and worthless insects (Wis 11:15). He thereby introduces two digressions, analysed here, before presenting the whole *synkrisis*.

The aim of the first digression (Wis 11:15–12:27) is to explain why the Lord punished the Egyptians with such leniency, and later even the Canaanites. To the latter he sent hornets (Wis 12:8; cf. Exod 23:28), while the former were infested with insects, frogs and serpents. Acting in this way, the Lord was not lacking in power, but gave space for repentance to the guilty Egyptians, because he loves his creatures and he is present in them with his incorruptible spirit (Wis 11:21–12:2). Towards the Canaanites, accustomed to evil practices like those of the Greek mysteries (Wis 12:3–7), he shows his graciousness (*philanthropia*), that the righteous should imitate (Wis 12:19–22).

Once more the stories of the Pentateuch and of Joshua are used freely through a method which resembles that of Midrash. However some of the Wisdom texts are inspired more directly from parts of the Hebrew Bible. For example Wis 11:22 harks back to Isa 40:15 in a form which remains difficult to define, and Wis 12:12 may have been inspired by Job 9:12, 19 or Jer 27:44 Lxx (50:44 MT); Wis 11:17 may be a Hellenistic paraphrase of Gen 1:1–2. The author of Wisdom seeks to explain those events of the exodus story which affected the Egyptians by reference to the act of creation.

The second degression (Wisdom 13–15) justifies the punishment of the Egyptians because they practised zoolatry (cf. Exod 8:22), so that it is the folly of the ancient religions which is condemned. The author of Wisdom first shows it by criticising the worship of heavenly bodies and cosmic elements as argued by philosophers, and then condemns idolatry of which he describes the practices, origin and consequences.

The criticism of the cult of natural powers makes an implicit allusion to Genesis 1 (Wis 13:2c, 3c, 5b) and the name of God of Israel (Exod 3:14) is mentioned in accordance with Lxx. The portrait of the idolatrous woodcutter (Wis 13:11–19) is partly inspired by Isa 44:9–20. Wis 14:25 is inspired by Hos 4:2 Lxx, with reference to the Decalogue. Wis 15:10a quotes Isa 44:20 Lxx and Wis 15:11 refers to Gen 2:7. Wis 15:15 recalls Ps 113:1–16 Lxx. In opposition to the attitude of the idolater, the author refers to the case of Noah who had taken refuge "on a frail barque" (Wis 14:6) and the renewed faithfulness of Israel to the God of Sinai (Wis 15:1; cf. Exod 34:6). The threefold scheme itself which criticises the pagan religions adapts the biblical tradition to the situation of author's time(cf. Deut 4:16–19; Ezek 8; Bel and the Dragon Lxx).[13]

2.5. Punishment for the Wicked – Blessing for the Righteous

From the beginning of ch. 11 the author introduces a *synkrisis*, or confrontation, between the righteous and the wicked at the time of the exodus of Israel from Egypt. Seven diptychs follow each other, with the second and the third as the two final examples introduced together. After having introduced the second and the third, the author inserts two digressions which we have explained above, in sect. 2.4. We now return to the whole *synkrisis*. For each hardship affecting the Egyptians of Pharaoh the author sets up an opposition to the blessing granted to Israel during the exodus. Besides these, there is a link made between hardship-punishment and blessing; this forms part of the working of the cosmos which inflicts harm on some and helps others; the principle is affirmed in Wis 11:5. Moreover the victims are punished by the same means which enabled them to commit the misdeed. This is another principle affirmed in Wis 11:16. In brief the seven diptychs are arranged in the following way:

1: water of the Nile – water of the rock (11:1–14)
2: frogs – quails (16:1–4)
3: horseflies and grasshoppers – bronze snake (16:5–14)
4: harvest destroyed by hail – manna (16:15–29)
5: darkness – light (17:1–18:4)
6: death of the first-born – the sparing of Israel (18:5–25)
7: the Egyptians engulfed by the Red Sea – the liberation of Israel (19:1–9)

The unity of this *synkrisis* is marked by an allusion to the psalm of Exodus 15 in Wis 10:20 and 19:9.[14] In the series of seven diptychs the first and the last show the action of the same cosmic element, water. Finally it is in the central diptych, the fourth, that the author explains his principal thesis that, under the hand of God, the creation is at the service of the righteous (16:24–26). This thesis is mentioned again at the end of the book (19:10–12, 18–21).

In order to set out this *synkrisis*, the author certainly refers to the stories of the Pentateuch. At the same time this development also brings answers to further questions. He aims to encourage the Jewish community of his time and

[13] Cf. Gilbert, Critique des dieux (1973).
[14] Cf. Enns, Retelling (1995), and Exodus Retold (1997).

so he makes centemporary allusions in a number of instances (cf. Wis 18:8–9), using Jewish tradition to interpret biblical texts. In the final analysis he displays a tendency to identify the Egyptians of Pharaoh's time with the Hellenized pagans who practised the Greek mystery cults.

In our author's opinion the religious heritage of Israel is the only one which offers light, food and a long life. Indeed the eschatological dimension of the *synkrisis* has been noted by a number of recent studies, especially in regard to Wis 11:9–10; 16:13–14, 26; 17:14; 18:4, 7, 14–16, 24. The originality of our author lies in the fact that for him eschatological time is prefigured, and even anticipated, in the events that brought about the exodus. The cosmic powers, which were so active during the exodus that they were regarded as constituting a "new creation" (19:6), are also seen as significant for his conception of eschatology.[15] At the same time, Wisdom 1–6 receives further illumination, thanks to the reflection back on the exodus, which the author never fully explains: the eschatological age implies a renewal of the cosmos. Is the author thinking here about the resurrection of the body?[16]

The texts of Exodus describe the ten plagues of Egypt. The number, but not the order, is retained by Ezekiel the Tragedian (Eusebius, *Praep. evang.* 9.29.12 [GCS 43, 1, 532]) and by Philo (*De vita Mosis* 1.94–146). On the other hand, Wis 11:1–14 + 16:1–19:9 only mentions six of them, to which is added the drowning of the Egyptians in the Red Sea. In this interpretation, the number 7 is the one of Pss 78:44–51; 105:28–36 keep for the plagues themselves. Each text presents a different order for them. For instance, compared to Exodus 7–12, Wisdom does not take into account the plague of mosquitos, the plague upon the cattle and the ulcers; the plagues inflicted by the horseflies and the grasshoppers are brought together in a panel of the same diptych (16:9). In this way the author of Wisdom retains the freedom which is evident in both biblical and non-biblical traditions. The *synkrisis* as a whole, however, has no biblical antecedent. Ps 78:3–28 mentions only four blessings granted to Israel: the crossing of the Red Sea, the water from the rock, the manna and the quails. Similarly Ps 105:39–41 refers only to the cloud, the quails, the manna and the water from the rock. In this Wisdom retains its originality.

The author meditates on the corresponding texts of Exodus and Numbers, but he also uses some other passages of the Hebrew Bible. So, for example, Wis 16:13b may have been influenced by Tob 13:2 in order to assert the supreme power of God over Hades. Wis 16:26 interprets Deut 8:3 Lxx regarding the Word that provides food. In Wisdom 17 the fear of the Egyptians is possibly reported under the influence of texts such as Job 4:12–16; 7:13–15; 33:15. Does Wis 18:9c make an allusion to the singing of the Hallel Psalms (Psalms 113–118) during the paschal meal? Opinions diverge on this point.[17] Wis 19:6–21 seems to be a rereading of the events of the exodus based on Gen 1:1–2:4a; it is really the thesis of the author that *the exodus was already a new act of creation*.

---

[15] Cf. above, n. 2.

[16] Cf. Beauchamp, Salut corporel (1964).

[17] Compare Priotto, Prima Pasqua (1987) 87–89, and Larcher, Livre (1985) 1006–08.

3. Hebrew Bible in Wisdom

Special studies: R. T. CLIFFORD, «Proverbs as a Source for Wisdom of Solomon», *Treasures of Wisdom* (ed. N. Calduch-Benages and J. Vermeylen; BETL 143; Leuven: University Press - Peeters 1999) 255–63; V. D'ALARIO, «La réflexion sur le sens de la vie en Sg 1–6. Une réponse aux questions de Job et de Qohélet», *Treasures of Wisdom*, 313–29; M. GILBERT, «La relecture de Gn 1–3 dans le Livre de la Sagesse», *La création dans l'Orient ancien* (ed. L. Derousseaux; LD 127; Paris: Cerf 1987) 323–44; P. W. SKEHAN, *Studies in Israelite Poetry and Wisdom* (CBQMS I; Washington D. C.: The Catholic Biblical Association of America 1971) esp. 149–236.

After this overall glance at Wisdom, we can begin the search again from a different perspective. In this we will follow the biblical order of the books. Several questions require to be raised. Does the author of Wisdom resort to the Hebrew Bible? Does he use the Septuagint? Does he know one or other of the apocryphal or deuterocanonical books?

Both stories of the creation (Gen 1–3) are among those to which the author of Wisdom refers throughout his book. For him the aim of creation was life and not death (Wis 1:13–14; 2:23–24); the creation was achieved by Wisdom (Wis 9:1); it was a work of love (Wis 11:24); but the creation was misunderstood by philosophers (Wis 13:3, 5), and degraded by idolaters (Wis 13:13; 15:8, 11); until finally it was renewed during the exodus (Wis 19:6 ff).[18]

On the other hand the remainder of Genesis is only used in order to introduce Wis 10:1–14, or, in Wis 19:13–17, to offer a final repudiation of the Egyptians who are identified with the Sodomites (Gen 19:11).[19] In all these texts the author appears to be using Septuagint, but possibly in Wis 10:3 he resorts to the Hebrew Bible of Gen 4:5–6 concerning the anger of Cain.[20]

All the developments of Wisdom 10–19 concerning the exodus depend on the stories of the books of Exodus and Numbers, even though the author of Wisdom retains his own freedom of approach and though he also rereads them in conjunction with Jewish interpretations of his own time. Some scholars have noted that he uses the language of the Septuagint "when the Hebrew text is obscure or difficult".[21]

If it is difficult to show any clear allusion the book of Leviticus, yet Deuteronomy is certainly present: Wis 6:7ab is inspired by Deut 1:17 Lxx and Wis 16:26 reworks Deut 8:3 Lxx from the distinctive viewpoint of our author. 1 Kings 3 and its parallel 2 Chronicles 1 form the basis in Wisdom 7–9 of the descriptions of the wise and the formulation of the prayer. In particular the alternation *phronêsis/ sophia* follows the Septuagint of 1 Kgs 3:14; 5:9, while 2 Chronicles 1 prefers *sophia kai synesis*. Wis 1:1 ("heartfelt simplicity") was put together from 1 Chron 29:17 Lxx. The warrior figure of the Logos in Wis 18:15 is drawn from the angel of 1 Chron 21:16.

The prophetical corpus is present almost everywhere in Wisdom, but it does not form part of the structure of the book, save for the theme of persecution

[18] Cf. Gilbert, Relecture (1987).
[19] Cf. Priotto, Significato (1984).
[20] Larcher, Etudes (1969) 87.
[21] Larcher, Etudes (1969) 88.

followed by exaltation in Wis 2:4–5, where the author could have been influenced by the tradition of Isaiah 13–14; 52–53, apart also from the description of the idolatrous woodcutter in Wis 13:11–19 and the judgment of the potter in Wis 15:10. Both these latter are drawn from Isa 44:9–20 Lxx. Possible references to Isaiah, Septuagint or Hebrew Bible, are found throughout the book, but they are transposed by the author of Wisdom into a context of his own and treated very freely. Of the entire book of Isaiah, Wisdom appears to make special use of Isaiah 40–66.[22] Of the other prophetical books: Jeremiah, Ezekiel and the Twelve, references in Wisdom appear only piecemeal and such allusions are less frequent and less significant, apart from Wis 9:17.[23]

The Psalms are another source of Wisdom, as important as Isaiah but, except for Psalm 2 which is referred to in Wisdom 1 and 6 and Psalms 78 (77) and 105 (104) which evoke the exodus event to which the author refers, the Psalter does not contribute to the overall structure of the book. Reference to Psalms is sporadic and shows the author's general familiarity with them which he knows in Septuagint, although knowledge of the Hebrew text is not to be excluded.[24]

Our author also refers from time to time to Job; he appears to have access to the Hebrew text of the book, but his use of the Septuagint is a matter of controversy, as, for example, Job 9:12b, 19b in Wis 12:12.

Concerning the book of Proverbs[25] a curious feature is evident in Prov 9:6a Lxx: in the great unical mss, a text from Wis 6:21b has been added. Wis 3:11a cites almost verbatim Prov 1:7d Lxx. Similarly Wis 9:9b, 11c concerning the presence of Wisdom close to the Creator, and to the wise, may have been inspired by Prov 8:27a (*symparousa/ symparêmen*). We have already mentioned above the problem raised by the word *'mwn* of Prov 8:30a (Hebrew text) and the terms used in Wis 7:12b, 22a and 8:6b. The author clearly had access to the Septuagint of Proverbs but reference to the Hebrew text is not to be excluded.

It is rather surprising to find, on the other hand, that Wisdom does not appear to make any allusion to either Song of Songs or Qohelet. Throughout the relationship between the wise and Wisdom (especially in Wisdom 8) is the reverse of that of Song of Songs between the lover and the beloved.[26] As regards Wis 2:1–9 it is impossible to demonstrate any allusion to Qohelet, even though the message of Wisdom concerning immortality offers an answer to both the fears of Qohelet and the anxiety of Job.[27]

Among the missing books of the Hebrew Bible which are present in the Septuagint, Tobit Lxx seems to be known by the author of Wisdom, and Wisdom has some similarities of language and thought with 2 Maccabees.[28] The Greek version of Sirach could have been used by the author of Wisdom: in Wis 8:21a

---

22 Cf. Shehan, Studies (1971) 163–71.
23 Cf. above, n. 10.
24 Cf. Skehan, Studies (1971) 149–62.
25 However, on themes, cf. Clifford, Proverbs (1999).
26 Cf. Gilbert, Figure de Salomon (1984) 236–38.
27 Cf. D'Alario, Réflexion (1999).
28 Cf. Larcher, Etudes (1969) 90.

the meaning of "owner" given to *egkratês* can be read in Sir 6:27a. In a similar context (Sir 6:27a H is inspired form Prov 4:13a); in Wis 2:5b the term *anapodismos* could refer to Sir 48:23a; other features may be explained in the same way: the same judgment is passed on the wicked and their offspring, the same sapiential interest in the history of Israel appears and Wisdom's role as a female figures is presented. Nevertheless all these features are, in the final analysis, not really convincing.

That Wisdom has been influenced by the book of Daniel is mainly demonstrated by the use of certain expressions, such as the "brilliance" of the righteous (Dan 12:3 and Wis 3:7a), "the intelligence of the truth" (Dan 9:13 and Wis 3:9a). Nor should we forget that the scheme of persecution followed by exaltation of Wisdom 2, 4–5 is in direct line with Daniel 7–12. The closeness to Theodotion's version is puzzling.

It is clear that Wisdom shows that its author uses extensively the Hebrew Bible. Because of the themes chosen some texts of the Hebrew Bible were an obvious source. The constant references to Genesis 1–3 may be explained by the sapiential perspective which favoured reflection on creation and which endeavours to understand history on the basis of creation. On the other hand it seems impossible to deny that the author of Wisdom has retained the freedom to make use of the Hebrew biblical text, even though he more often uses the Septuagint. Finally, among the apocryphal and deuterocanonical writings, the use of Tobit, of 2 Maccabees, and perhaps of Sirach is not really surprising when we realise that the author also uses non-biblical Jewish sources, as well as Greek source materials. It is thus impossible to draw a conclusion regarding the contents of his Bible. On the other side the absence of Qohelet and Song of Songs is surprising.

4. Conclusion

The author of Wisdom does not explicitly cite any biblical text. Nevertheless his book is full of implicit references. He also uses an anthological style, following well-known examples such as Proverbs 1–9, Nehemiah 9, and Sirach. Beyond the biblical texts he necessarily refers to, lots of other texts, often woven together, appear in his writing on account of the subjects he deals with. He expresses his own thought using biblical words and expressions, even though he also uses other sources, either Jewish or Greek. So his familiarity with the Bible, and even more his consciousness of a deep unity that underlies the Bible, is used to create a truly unified work. Such an attitude implies prolonged meditation on the biblical texts, so that he uses them in an unconstrained and natural way. This also implies a consciousness that a substantial continuity connects the former texts with his own work. He does not deny his people's heritage. Nor is his exegesis servile or contrived in any way. He developes what he has read in the older texts in accord with his own thought and originality, shaping them also to the opportunities of his own day. His exegesis becomes actualizing to his contemporaries and the unexpected relationships between different biblical texts give rise to a new message which is his own.

Contributors

Abbreviations

Indexes

Names/Topics/References

Contributors

Pancratius C. Beentjes (b. 1946), Professor of Old Testament and Hebrew, Catholic Theological University Utrecht (KTU). Selected publ.: *Jesus Sirach en Tenach,* Nieuwegein 1981; *Jesus, zoon van Sirach,* Averbode 1982; *The Book of Ben Sira in Hebrew. A Text Edition of all Extant Hebrew Manuscripts, and a Synopsis of all Parallel Hebrew Ben Sira Texts* (VTS 68), Leiden 1997; *The Book of Ben Sira in Modern Research. Proceedings of the First International Ben Sira Conference* (Soesterberg, 28–31 July 1996) (BZAW 255), Berlin 1997; *Wijsheid van Salomo,* Boxtel / Brugge 1987.

Rainer Berndt (b. 1951), Professor of Medieval History of Philosophy and Theology, Philosophisch-Theologische Hochschule Sankt Georgen, Frankfurt am Main, Director of the Hugo von Sankt Viktor-Institut. Selected publ.: *André de Saint-Victor († 1175). Exégète et théologien* (Bibliotheca Victorina 2), Turnhout 1991; "Überlegungen zum Verhältnis von Exegese und Theologie in 'De sacramentis christiane fidei' Hugos von St. Viktor", in: *Neue Richtungen in der hoch- und spätmittelalterlichen Bibelexegese* (hg. von R. Lerner), München 1996, 65–78; (ed.) *Das Frankfurter Konzil von 794. Kristallisationspunkt karolingischer Kultur* (Quellen und Abhandlungen zur mittelrheinischen Kirchengeschichte 80), Mainz 1997; (ed.) *Petrus Canisius (1521–1597). Humanist und Europäer* (Erudiri Sapientia 1), Berlin 2000.

Robert Brody (b. 1955), Professor of Talmud, the Hebrew University of Jerusalem. Selected publ.: *Teshuvot Rav Natronai bar Hilai Gaon,* Jerusalem / Cleveland 1994 [Hebrew]; *The Geonim of Babylonia and the Shaping of Medieval Jewish Culture,* New Haven, CT 1998.

Mordechai Cohen (b. 1964), Associate Professor of Bible, Yeshiva University, New York. Selected publ.: "'The Best of Poetry…': Literary Approaches to the Bible in the Spanish Peshat Tradition", *Torah U-Madda Journal* 6 (1995/96) 15–57; "*Hesed:* Divine or Human? The Syntactic Ambiguity of Ruth 2:20", *Hazon Nahum: Essays in Honor of Dr. Norman Lamm* (ed. Y. Elman and J. Gurock), New York 1997, 11–38; "Moses Ibn Ezra vs. Maimonides: Argument for a Poetic Definition of Metaphor (*Isti'ārā*)", *Edebiyât: Journal of Middle Eastern and Comparative Literature* (2000); "Radak vs. Ibn Ezra and Maimonides: A New Approach to *Derekh Mashal* in the Bible" [Hebrew], *Proceedings of the Twelfth World Congress of Jewish Studies, Division A: The Bible and Its World* (ed. R. Margolin), Jerusalem 1999, 27–41; *Three Approaches to Biblical Metaphor: Radak and His Predecessors, Abraham Ibn Ezra and Maimonides* [forthcoming].

Gilbert Dahan (b. 1943), Directeur de recherche au Centre national de la recherche scientifique (CNRS), Directeur d'études à l'Ecole pratique des hautes études (Sciences religieuses). Selected publ.: *Guillaume de Bourges. Livre des Guerres du Seigneur et deux homélies* (Sources chrétiennes 288), Paris 1981; *Les intellectuels chrétiens et les juifs au moyen âge,* Paris 1990; *Inghetto Contardo. Disputatio contra Iudeos,* Paris 1993; *L'exégèse chrétienne de la Bible en Occident médiéval, XIIe–XIVe s.,* Paris 1999.

Yaakov Elman (b. 1943), Associate Professor of Judaic Studies, Yeshiva University, New York. Selected publ.: *Authority and Tradition: Toseftan Baraitot in Talmudic Babylonia,* New York 1994; (ed., with J. Gurock), *Hazon Nahum: Studies in Jewish*

Law, Thought and History (N. Lamm-FS), New York 1997; (ed., with I. Gershoni), *Transmitting Jewish Tradition: Orality and Cultural Diffusion,* New Haven, CT 2000; *Dream Interpretation from Classical Jewish Sources,* by Rabbi Solomon Almoli, translated and annotated by Y. Elman, Hoboken, NJ 1998; "Progressive *Derash* and Retrospective *Peshat*: Non-Halakhic Considerations in Talmud Torah", in: S. Carmy (ed.), *Modern Scholarship in the Study of Torah: Contributions and Limitations,* Northvale, NJ 1996, 189–287.

G. R. Evans (b. 1944), PhD., Litt.D., D.Litt., FRHistS, FRSA, Faculty of History, University of Cambridge. Selected publ.: *The language and logic of the Bible*, 1–2, Cambridge 1983/84; *Augustine on Evil,* Cambridge 1983; *Problems of Authority in the Reformation Debates,* Cambridge 1994; *The Church and the Churches,* Cambridge 1994; *Method in Ecumenical Theology,* Cambridge 1996.

Paul B. Fenton (b. 1951), Professor of Hebrew and Jewish Studies, Université de Paris IV-Sorbonne. Selected publ.: *Obadyah Maimonides' Treatise of the Pool,* London 1981, [2]1995; David Maimonides, *Doctor ad Solitudinem,* Jerusalem 1987; *Deux traités de mystique juive,* Lagrasse 1987; *Published Material from Cambridge Genizah Collections,* Cambridge 1989; *Une Bibliographie de l'œuvre de Georges Vajda,* Paris 1991; *A Judeo-Arabic Commentary on the Pirqey Rabbi Eliʿezer by Judah Ibn Malka,* Jerusalem 1991; Ibn Arabi, *La Production des cercles,* Paris 1995; *Philosophie et exégèse dans le Jardin de la métaphore,* Leiden 1997; Joseph Ibn Waqâr, *Fundamentals of the Qabbalah,* Jerusalem 2000.

Daniel Frank (b. 1955), Ph.D. Harvard; Assistant Professor of Near Eastern Languages and Cultures, The Ohio State University, Columbus, OH. Selected publ.: (ed.), *The Jews of Medieval Islam: Community, Society, and Identity,* Leiden 1995.

Karlfried Froehlich (b. 1930), Benjamin B. Warfield Professor of Ecclesiastical History, Princeton Theological Seminary. Selected publ.: (with H. C. Kee and F. W. Young), *Understanding the New Testament,* Englewood Cliffs, NJ [3]1965 (also in German: *Das Geschehen Ohnegleichen. Panorama des Neuen Testaments,* Stuttgart 1967); *Biblical Interpretation in the Early Church,* Philadelphia 1984; (with M. T. Gibson), *Biblia Latina cum Glossa Ordinaria: Facsimile Reprint of the Editio Princeps, Adolf Rusch of Strassburg, 1480/81,* I–IV, Turnhout 1992; (with T. E. Fretheim), *The Bible as Word of God in a Postmodern Age,* Minneapolis 1998.

Stephen Garfinkel (b. 1949), Assistant Professor of Bible and Dean of the Graduate School, Jewish Theological Seminary, New York. Selected publ.: "Of Thistles and Thorns: A New Approach to Ezekiel ii 6", VT 37 (1987) 421–37; "Another Model for Ezekiel's Abnormalities", *JANES* 19 (1989) 39–50; "Applied Peshat: Historical-Critical Method and Religious Meaning", *JANES* 22 (1993) 19–28.

Maurice Gilbert (b. 1934), Professor of Old Testament Exegesis, Pontifical Biblical Institute, Rome. Selected publ.: *La critique des dieux dans le livre de la Sagesse* (AnBib 53), Rome 1973; *Les louanges du Seigneur,* Paris 1991; *La Sapienza di Salomone,* Rome 1995; *Il a parlé par les prophètes,* Namur / Bruxelles 1998.

Aryeh Grabois (b. 1930), Professor Emeritus of Medieval History, University of Haifa. Selected publ.: "The Bible in the Middle Ages", *Dictionary of the Middle Ages*, II, New York 1983, 210–17; "L'exégèse rabbinique", *Le Moyen Age et la Bible,* (BTT 4; éd. P. Riché / G. Lobrichon), Paris 1984, 233–60; *Les sources hébraïques du Moyen Age (Typologie des sources du moyen âge occidental)*, 1–2, *Turnhout 1988–93; Le pèlerin occidental en Terre sainte au Moyen Age, Louvain-La-Neuve 1998.*

Frederick E. Greenspahn (b. 1946), Professor of Judaic Studies, University of Denver, CO. Selected publ: *Hapax Legomena in Biblical Hebrew,* Chico, CA 1984; *Essential Papers on Israel and the Ancient Near East,* New York 1991; *When Brothers Dwell To-*

gether, The Preeminence of Younger Siblings in the Hebrew Bible, New York 1994; *An Introduction to Aramaic,* Atlanta 1999.

AVRAHAM GROSSMAN (b. 1936), Professor of Jewish History, The Hebrew University of Jerusalem. Selected publ.: *The Babylonian Exilarchate in the Gaonic Period,* Jerusalem 1984; *The Early Sages of Ashkenaz*, Jerusalem 1988; *The Early Sages of France,* Jerusalem 1995; *The Jewish Woman in Europe in the High Middle Ages,* Jerusalem [in print].

MOSHE IDEL (b. 1947), Max Cooper Professor of Jewish Thought, The Hebrew University of Jerusalem. Selected publ.: *Kabbalah: New Perspectives,* New Haven, CT 1988; *Perakim be-kabbalah nevuit,* Jerusalem 1990; *Golem: Magical and Mystical Traditions on the Artificial Anthropoid,* Albany 1990; *Hasidism: Between Ecstasy and Magic,* Albany 1995; *Messianic Mystics,* New Haven, CT 1998.

STEPHAN CH. KESSSLER (b. 1959), Lecturer of the Early Church and Patristics, Albert-Ludwigs-Universität, Freiburg i. Br. Selected publ.: *Gregor der Große als Exeget,* Innsbruck / Wien 1995; "Das Menschenbild der 'Regula Magistri': Mönchtum als Erziehung zur Erlösung", *Il monachesimo occidentale dalle origini alla 'Regula Magistri'* (Studia Ephemeridis Augustinianum 62), Roma 1998, 107–17; "Le mariage du prophète Osée (Os 1,2) dans la littérature patristique", *Revue des Sciences Religieuses* 73 (1999) 223–28; *Les Douze Prophètes: Osée* (ed. E. Bons / J. Joosten / S. C. Kessler; La Bible d'Alexandrie 23.1), Paris 2000.

SARA KLEIN-BRASLAVY (b. 1942), Professor of Jewish Medieval Philosophy, Tel Aviv University. Selected publ.: *Maimonides' Interpretation of the Story of Creation,* Jerusalem ^{2}1978 [Hebrew]; *Maimonides' Interpretation of the Adam Stories in Genesis – a Study in Maimonides' Anthropology,* Jerusalem 1986 [Hebrew]; *King Solomon and Philosophical Esotericism in the Thought of Maimonides,* Jerusalem 1996 [Hebrew].

ULRICH KÖPF (b. 1941), Professor of Church History and Director of the Institut für Spätmittelalter und Reformation, University of Tübingen. Selected publ.: *Die Anfänge der theologischen Wissenschaftstheorie im 13. Jahrhundert* (BHTh 49), Tübingen 1974; *Religiöse Erfahrung in der Theologie Bernards von Clairvaux* (BHTh 61), Tübingen 1980; (Ed. and author), *Historisch-kritische Geschichtsbetrachtung. Ferdinand Christian Baur und seine Schüler* (Contubernium 40), Sigmaringen 1994.

CLAUDIO LEONARDI (b. 1926), Professor of Latin Medieval Literature, University of Florence. Selected publ.: (with G. Pozzi), *Scrittrici mistiche italiane,* Genova 1988; (ed.), *Il Cristo,* III. *Testi teologici e spirituali in lingua latina da Agostino ad Anselmo di Canterbury,* Milano 1989; (ed.), *Il Cristo,* IV. *Testi teologici e spirituali in lingua latina da Abelardo a San Bernardo,* Milano 1991; (ed.), *Il Cristo,* V. *Testi teologici e spirituali da Riccardo di san Vittore a Caterina da Siena,* Milano 1992; (ed.), *Girolamo Savonarola, Verità della profezia. De veritate prophetica dyalogus,* Firenze 1997.

AHARON MAMAN (b. 1947), Professor of Hebrew Language, The Hebrew University of Jerusalem. Selected publ.: *The Comparative Study of the Hebrew Lexicon with Arabic and Aramaic in the Linguistic Literature of the Jews from Rav Saadia Gaon (10th cent.) to Ibn Barun (12th cent.),* Jerusalem 1986 [Hebrew, large English Summary]; "The Lexical Element in David Alfasi's Dictionary Definitions", *Genizah Research after Ninety Years: The Case of Judeo-Arabic* (eds. J. Blau / S. C. Reif), Cambridge 1992, 119–25; "Peshat and Derash in Medieval Hebrew lexicons", *Israel Oriental Studies* 19 (1999) 343–57; "Karaites and Mishnaic Hebrew: Quotations and Usage", *Studies in Mishnaic Hebrew* (eds. M. Bar-Asher / S. E. Fassberg), Scripta Hierosolymitana 37 (1998) 264–83.

JOHN REVELL (b. 1934), Professor in the Department of Near and Middle Eastern Civilizations, University of Toronto. Selected publ.: "Hebrew Accents and Greek Ekphonetic Neumes", *Studies in Eastern Chant IV, Crestwood,* NY 1979, 140–70; *Nesiga (retraction of word stress) in Tiberian Hebrew* (Textos y Estudios "Cardenal Cisneros" 39), Madrid 1987; *The Designation of the Individual: Expressive Usage in Biblical Narrative* (Contributions to Biblical Exegesis and Theology 14), Kampen 1996; "The Leningrad Codex as a Representative of the Masoretic Text", *The Leningrad Codex: A facsimile edition,* Grand Rapids 1998, xxix–xlvi.

Lucas Van Rompay (b. 1949), Professor of Aramaic Language and Literature, University of Leiden, (from Oct. 2000) Professor of Eastern Christianity, Department of Religion, Duke University, NC. Selected publ.: *Théodore de Mopsueste. Fragments syriaques du Commentaire des Psaumes (Psaume 118 et Psaumes 138–148),* Leuven 1982; *Le commentaire sur Genèse-Exode 9,32 du manuscrit (olim) Diyarbakir 22,* Leuven 1986; (with J. Frishman), *The Book of Genesis in Jewish and Oriental Christian Interpretation. A Collection of Essays* (Traditio Exegetica Graeca 5), Leuven 1997.

Magne Sæbø (b. 1929), Professor Emeritus of Old Testament Theology, The Norwegian Lutheran School of Theology (formerly: Free Faculty of Theology), Oslo. Selected publ.: *Sacharja 9–14. Untersuchungen von Text und Form* (WMANT 34), Neukirchen-Vluyn 1969; *Ordene og Ordet. Gammeltestamentlige studier,* Oslo 1979; *Salomos ordspråk, Forkynneren, Høysangen, Klagesangene* [Commentary], Oslo 1986; *On the Way to Canon. Creative Tradition History in the Old Testament* (JSOTSup 191), Sheffield 1998; (ed.) *Librum Esther (Biblia Hebraica quinta editione, 16. Megilloth),* Stuttgart [forthcoming].

Angel Sáenz-Badillos (b. 1940), Professor of Hebrew Language and Literature, Universidad Complutense, Madrid. Selected publ.: *Las Tešubot de Dunaš ben Labraṭ. Edición crítica y traducción española,* Granada 1980; *Menaḥem ben Saruq, Maḥberet. Edición crítica*, Granada 1986; (with J. Targarona), *Gramáticos hebreos de al-Andalus (ss. X–XII),* Filología y Biblia, Córdoba 1988; *A History of the Hebrew Language,* Cambridge 1993; (with J. Targarona), *Los judíos de Sefarad ante la Biblia. La interpretación de la Biblia en el Medievo,* Córdoba 1997.

Uriel Simon (b. 1929), Professor Emeritus of Bible, Bar-Ilan University. Selected publ.: *Reading Prophetic Narratives,* Bloomington / Indianapolis 1977; *Abraham Ibn Ezra's two Commentaries on the Minor Prophets – An Annotated Critical Edition,* Ramat Gan 1989 [Hebrew]; *Four Approaches to the Book of Psalms – From Saadiah Gaon to Abraham Ibn Ezra,* Albany 1991; *The Book of Jonah,* Philadelphia 1999.

Günter Stemberger (b. 1940), Professor of Jewish Studies, University of Vienna. Selected publ.: *Juden und Christen im Heiligen Land. Palästina unter Konstantin und Theodosius,* München 1987 (Eng. rev. ed., Edinburgh 2000); *Midrasch. Vom Umgang der Rabbinen mit der Bibel. Einführung, Texte, Erläuterungen,* München 1989; *Pharisäer, Sadduzäer, Essener* (SBS 144), Stuttgart 1991 (Eng. ed., Minneapolis 1995); *Einleitung in Talmud und Midrash,* München ^{8}1992 (Eng. rev. ed., Edinburgh 1996); (with Chr. Dohmen), *Hermeneutik der Jüdischen Bibel und des Alten Testaments,* Stuttgart 1996.

Abbreviations

As for the system of references to and abbreviations of Biblical, Apocryphical and Pseudepigraphical books, Classical and Patristic works, Dead Sea Scroll texts, Targums, Mishnaic and other rabbinic material a general reference may be made to the rules and abbreviations listed in "*JBL* Instructions for Contributors" (*SBL Membership Directory and Handbook*, Decatur, GA 1994, 223-30).

1. General and Non-literary Abbreviations

AAJR	American Acedemy for Jewish Research
ad loc.	ad locum
AJS	The Association for Jewish Studies
Akk.	Akkadian
ann.	annotated
Arab.	Arabic
Aram.	Aramaic
Assyr.	Assyrian
b.	ben/bar; babli
Bab.	Babylonian
BCE	Before Common Era
BH	Biblia Hebraica
B/bk(s).	B/book(s)
B.M.	British Museum
BN	Bibliothèque Nationale
ch./chap(s).	chapter(s)
ca.	circa
Can.	Canaanite
CE	Common Era
cf.	confer, compare
CNRS	Centre National de la Recherche Scientifique
col(s).	column(s)
Copt.	Coptic
cr.	copyright
CSIC	Consejo Superior de Investigaciones Cientificas
DSS	Dead Sea Scrolls
ed(s).	editor(s) / edited by
Eg.	Egyptian
Eng.	English
ep(s).	epistle(s)
ET	English translation
et al.	et alii
Eth.	Ethiopic
f(f).	following unit(s) [the point is left out before another punctuation mark]
fig(s).	figure(s)
fol(s).	folio
frg(s).	fragment(s)
FS	Festschrift
G	Greek version
HB	Hebrew Bible
Heb.	Hebrew
i. a.	inter alia
i. e.	id est
ibid.	ibidem
j.	jeruschalmi (cf. y.)
JPS(A)	Jewish Publication Society (of America)
Lat.	Latin
LXX	Septuagint
MA	Middle Ages/Mittelalter/ Moyen Age
MS/s(S/s)	Manuscript(s)
MT	Mas(s)oretic Text
NE	New Edition
NF	Neue Folge
ni.	nifʾal
n(n).	note(s)
no(s).	number(s)
NS	New Series
NT	New Testament

obv.	obverse
OG	Old Greek
OS	Old Series
OT	Old Testament
P	Peshitta
p(p).	page(s)
Pal.	Palestinian
pass.	passim
Pers.	Persian
Phoen.	Phoenician
pi.	pi'el
Pl(s).	plate(s)
pl.	plural
Q	Qumran
q. v.	quod vide
RV	Revised Version
s. a.	sine anno
Sam.	Samaritan
SBL	The Society of Biblical Literature
sect.	section(s)
sg.	singular
s. v.	sub voce
Syr.	Syriac
TaNaK	*T*ora *N*ebi'im, *K*etubim ('Law, Prophets, Writings'), acronym for Hebrew Bible
Tg(s).	Targum(s)
tr./trans.	translated/translation
UP	University Press
v(v).	verse(s)
var.	variant
Vg	Vulgate
VL	Vetus Latina
vs.	versus
y.	yerushalmi

2. Abbreviations of Periodicals, Yearbooks, Reference Works and Series

Only abbreviations of periodicals are in *italics*

AASF	Annales Academiae Scientiarum Fennicae
AB	Anchor Bible
ABD	*Anchor Bible Dictionary*
ABMA	Auctores Britannici Medii Aevi
ACar	Analecta Cartusiana
ACi	Analecta Cisterciensia
ACW	Ancient Christian Writers. The Works of the Fathers in Translation (ed. J. Quaten / J. C. Plumpe)
AFH	*Archivum Franciscanum Historicum*
AFP	*Archivum Fratrum Praedicatorum*
AfR	*Archiv für Reformationsgeschichte*
AGPh	*Archiv für Geschichte der Philosophie (und Soziologie)*
AGJU	Arbeiten zur Geschichte des antiken Judentums und des Urchristentums
AGPh	*Archiv für Geschichte der Philosophie (und Soziologie)*
AGWG	Abhandlungen der Gesellschaft der Wissenschaften zu Göttingen
AHDL	*Archives d'histoire doctrinale et littéraire du moyen âge*
AHR	*American Historical Review*
AJSL	*American Journal of Semitic Languages and Literatures*
AJu	*Archives Juives*
AKG	Arbeiten zur Kirchengeschichte
ALBO	Analecta Lovaniensia Biblica et Orientalia
ALGHJ	Arbeiten zur Literatur und Geschichte des Hellenistischen Judentums
ALK(G)MA	*Archiv für Literatur- und Kirchengeschichte des Mittelalters*
ALW	*Archiv für Liturgiewissenschaft*
AnBib	Analecta Biblica

ANF	The Ante-Nicene Fathers. Translation of the Writings of the Fathers down to A.D. 325
Ang.	*Angelicum*
AnOr	Analecta Orientalia
ANRW	*Aufstieg und Niedergang der Römischen Welt* (II, ed. W. Haase / H. Temporini)
Ant.	*Antiquitates (Judaicae)*
Anton.	*Antonianum*
APOT	*Apocrypha and Pseudepigrapha of the Old Testament* (ed. R. H. Charles)
ASOC	*Analecta Sacri Ordinis Cisterciensis*
ASP	American Studies in Papyrology
ASTI	Annual of the Swedish Theological Institute (of Jerusalem)
ATA	Alttestamentliche Abhandlungen
ATANT	Abhandlungen zur Theologie des Alten und Neuen Testaments
ATD	Das Alte Testament Deutsch
ATR	*Anglican Theological Review*
AuA	Antike und Abendland
AuC	Antike und Christentum
AUG	Acta Universitatis Gothoburgensis
Aug	*Augustinianum*
AzTh	Arbeiten zur Theologie
AV	Authorized Version
BA	*Biblical Archaeologist*
BArPh(NS)	Bibliothèque des Archives de philosophie
BAug	Bibliothèque Augustinienne
BBB	Bonner biblische Beiträge
BEATAJ	Beiträge zur Erforschung des Alten Testaments und des antiken Judentums
Ben.	*Benedictina*
BetM	*Beth Mikra*
BETL	Bibliotheca Ephemeridum Theologicarum Lovaniensium
BEvT	Beiträge zur evangelischen Theologie
BFChrT	Beiträge zur Förderung christlicher Theologie
BFSMA	Bibliotheca Franciscana Scholastica Medii Aevi
BGBE	Beiträge zur Geschichte der biblischen Exegese
BGBH	Beiträge zur Geschichte der biblischen Hermeneutik
BGDS(T)	Beiträge zur Geschichte der deutschen Sprache und Literatur (Ausgabe Tübingen)
BGPhMA	Beiträge zur Geschichte der Philosophie und Theologie des Mittelalters
BHEAT	*Bulletin d'histoire et d'exégèse de l'Ancien Testament*
BHT	Beiträge zur historischen Theologie
Bib.	*Biblica*
BiblThom	Bibliothèque Thomiste
BibOr	Biblica et orientalia
BICS	*Bulletin of the Institute of Classical Studies*
Bijdragen	*Bijdragen. Tijdschrift voor Filosofie en Theologie* (cf. *BTFT*)
BJRL	*Bulletin of the John Rylands University Library of Manchester*
BKV	Bibliothek der Kirchenväter
BLE	*Bulletin de littérature ecclésiastique*
BNs	*Biblische Notizen*

BP	Biblia Patristica
BPhM	*Bulletin de philosophie médiévale*
BPSup	Biblia Patristica. Supplément
BRHE	Bibliothèque de la Revue d'histoire ecclésiastique
BTB	*Biblical Theology Bulletin*
BTFT	*Bijdragen. Tijdschrift voor Filosofie en Theologie* (cf. *Bijdragen*)
BThSt	Biblisch-Theologische Studien
BTT	*Bible de tous les temps* (I-VIII)
BWANT	Beiträge zur Wissenschaft vom Alten und Neuen Testament
BZ	*Biblische Zeitschrift*
BZAW	Beiheft zur *ZAW*
BZNW	Beiheft zur *ZNW*
CA	Confessio Augustana
CAG	Commentaria in Aristotelem Graeca
CAH	*Cambridge Ancient History*
CBQ	*The Catholic Biblical Quarterly*
CBQMS	CBQ Monograph Series
CCat	Corpus Catholicorum
CCCM	Corpus Christianorum. Continuatio mediaevalis [= CChr.CM]
CCG	Corpus Christianorum, series graeca [= CChr.SG]
CChr.CM	see CCCM
CChr.SG	see CCG
CChr.SL	see CCL
CCL	Corpus Christianorum, series latina [= CChr.SL]
CCM	*Cahiers de civilisation médiévale X^{e}–XIIe siècles*
CFN	Collectanea Franciscana Neerlandica
CH	*Church History*
CHB	*The Cambridge History of the Bible* (I-III)
CiFS	Cistercian Fathers Series
CIL	Corpus inscriptionum Latinarum
Cîteaux	*Cîteaux - Commentarii Cistercienses*
Cîteaux.SD	Cîteaux - Commentarii Cistercienses. Studia et documenta
CJ	*Classical Journal*
COCR	*Collectanea Ordinis Cisterciensium Reformatorum*
COD	*Conciliorum Oecumenicorum Decreta*
CP	*Classical Philology*
CPG	Clavis Patrum Graecorum
CPL	Clavis Patrum Latinorum
CR	Corpus reformatorum
CRINT	Compendia rerum Iudaicarum ad Novum Testamentum
CRSS	Classics in Religious Studies
CS	*Cahiers sioniens*
CSCO	Corpus scriptorum christianorum Orientalium
CSEL	Corpus scriptorum ecclesiasticorum Latinorum
CUP	*Chartularium Universitatis Parisiensis*
CWS	*The Classics of Western Spirituality* (ed. R.J. Payne / J. Farina)
DB	*Dictionnaire de la Bible*
DBI	*A Dictionary of Biblical Interpretation* (ed. R.J. Coggins / J.L. Houlden)

DBSup	Dictionnaire de la Bible. Supplément
DHGE	*Dictionnaire d'histoire et de géographie ecclésiastique*
DictS	*Dictionnaire de spiritualité ascétique et mystique*
DiKi	Dialog der Kirchen
DJD	*Discoveries in the Judaean Desert*
DMA	Dictionary of the Middle Ages
DS	*Enchiridion symbolorum* (ed. A. Denzinger / A. Schönmetzer)
DTC	*Dictionnaire de théologie catholique*
EA	Erlanger Ausgabe der Werke M. Luthers
Ebib	Etudes bibliques
EDB	*Encyclopedic Dictionary of the Bible* (ed. L. F. Hartman)
EdF	Erträge der Forschung
EHR	*English Historical Review*
EHS	Europäische Hochschulschriften
EJM	Etudes sur le Judaïsme Médiéval
EncJud	*Encyclopaedia Judaica* (Jerusalem 1972)
EKL	*Evangelisches Kirchenlexikon*
EncBibl	*Encyclopaedia Biblica* (Jerusalem)
EncRel	*Encyclopaedia of Religion* (ed. M. Eliade)
EPhM	Etudes de philosophie médiévale
EPRO	Etudes préliminaires aux religions orientales dans l'Empire Romain
ERE	*Encyclopaedia of Religion and Ethics*
ErIsr	Eretz Israel
EstBib	*Estudios bíblicos*
ETH	Etudes de théologie historique
ETL	*Ephemerides Theologicae Lovanienses*
EvTh	*Evangelische Theologie*
FB	Forschung zur Bibel
FC	*Fathers of the Church*
FChLDG	Forschungen zur christlichen Literatur- und Dogmengeschichte
FKDG	Forschungen zur Kirchen- und Dogmengeschichte
FontC	Fontes Christiani. Zweisprachige Neuausgabe christlicher Quellentexte aus Altertum und Mittelalter
FRLANT	Forschungen zur Religion und Literatur des Alten und Neuen Testaments
FS	Franziskanische Studien
FSt	Franciscan Studies
FTS	Freiburger theologische Studien
FZPhTh	*Freiburger Zeitschrift für Philosophie und Theologie*
GCS	Die Griechischen christlichen Schriftsteller der ersten drei Jahrhunderte
GOF	Göttinger Orientforschungen
GOTR	*Greek Orthodox Theological Review*
GRBS	*Greek, Roman, and Byzantine Studies*
GRM	*Germanisch-romanische Monatsschrift*
Greg	*Gregorianum*
GTA	Göttinger theologische Arbeiten
GTB	Van Gorcum's theologische bibliotheek
GuG	*Geschichte und Gesellschaft*

HAR	Hebrew Annual Review
HAW	*Handbuch der Altertumswissenschaften*
HBOT	*Hebrew Bible / Old Testament. The History of Its Interpretation* (ed. M. Sæbø)
HBS	Herders biblische Studien
HDG	*Handbuch der Dogmengeschichte* (ed. M. Schmaus / J. Geiselmann / H. Rahner)
HDTG	*Handbuch der Dogmen- und Theologiegeschichte* (ed. C. Andresen)
HE	Histoire de l'Eglise
Hen	*Henoch*
HKG	*Handbuch der Kirchengeschichte* (ed. G. Krüger)
HSM	Harvard Semitic Monographs
HTR	*Harvard Theological Review*
HTS	Harvard Theological Studies
HUCA	Hebrew Union College Annual
HZ	*Historische Zeitschrift*
IDB	*Interpreter's Dictionary of the Bible*
IKZ	*Internationale Kirchliche Zeitschrift*
Int	*Interpretation*
IP	Instrumenta Patristica
IRT	Issues in Religion and Theology
ITQ	*Irish Theological Quarterly*
JA	*Journal Asiatique*
JAAR	*Journal of the American Academy of Religion*
JAC	Jahrbuch für Antike und Christentum
JANES(CU)	*Journal of the Ancient Near Eastern Society of Columbia University*
JAOS	*Journal of the American Oriental Society*
JB	*Jerusalem Bible* [cf. SBJ]
JBL	*Journal of Biblical Literature*
JBR	*Journal of Bible and Religion*
JBTh	Jahrbuch für Biblische Theologie
JEH	*Journal of Ecclesiastical History*
JHI	*Journal of the History of Ideas*
JHS	*Journal of Hellenic Studies*
JJS	*Journal of Jewish Studies*
JNES	*Journal of Near Eastern Studies*
JPSV	Jewish Publication Society Version
JQR	*Jewish Quarterly Review*
JR	*Journal of Religion*
JRAS	*Journal of the Royal Asiatic Society*
JSJ	*Journal for the Study of Judaism in the Persian, Hellenistic and Roman Periods*
JSOT	*Journal for the Study of the Old Testament*
JSOTSup	Journal for the Study of the Old Testament. Supplement Series
JSP	*Journal for the Study of Pseudepigrapha*
JSPSup	JSP.Supplement Series
JSS	*Journal of Semitic Studies*
JSSMon	JSS.Monograph
JTC	*Journal for Theology and the Church*
JTS	*Journal of Theological Studies*

Kairos	*Kairos. Zeitschrift für Religionswissenschaft und Theologie*
KiKonf	Kirche und Konfession
KJV	King James Version
KuD	*Kerygma und Dogma*
LCC	Library of Christian Classics
LCL	Loeb Classical Library
LD	Lectio Divina
Leshonenu	*Leshonenu. A Journal for the Study of the Hebrew Language and Cognate Subjects*
LM	*Lexikon des Mittelalters*
LPGL	*Patristic Greek Lexicon* (G. W. H. Lampe)
LTK	Lexikon für Theologie und Kirche
MA	*Moyen-âge. Revue d'histoire et de philologie*
MBM	Münchener Beiträge zur Mediävistik und Renaissance-Forschung
MeH	*Medievalia et Humanistica*
MF	*Miscellanea francescana*
MGH	Monumenta Germaniae historica inde ab a. C. 500 usque ad a. 1500
MGH.AA	MGH. Auctores antiquissimi
MGH.Cap	MGH. Capitularia regnum Francorum
MGH.QG	MGH. Quellen zur Geistesgeschichte des Mittelalters
MGI	Mitteilungen des Grabmann-Instituts
MGWJ	*Monatsschrift für Geschichte und Wissenschaft des Judentums*
MH	Museum Helveticum
MHUC	Monographs of the Hebrew Union College
Mikra	*Mikra. Text, Translation, Reading and Interpretation of the Hebrew Bible in Ancient Judaism and Early Christianity* (CRINT II/1, ed. M. J. Mulder)
MPTT	Mediaeval Philosophical Texts in Translation
MRTS	Medieval and Renaissance Texts and Studies
MS	*Medieval Studies (Toronto)*
MSM	*Modern Schoolman*
MSR	*Mélanges de science religieuse*
MThSt	Marburger theologische Studien
MThS.S	Münchener theologische Studien. Systematische Abteilung
MTZ	*Münchener Theologische Zeitschrift für das Gesamtgebiet der katholischen Theologie*
NAB	New American Bible
NEB	New English Bible
NechtB	Neue Echter Bibel
NedTT	*Nederlands Theologisch Tijdschrift*
NAWG.PH	Nachrichten der Akademie der Wissenschaften in Göttingen, I. Philologisch-historische Klasse
NIV	New International Version
NJB	New Jerusalem Bible
NKZ	*Neue Kirchliche Zeitschrift*
NPNF	Nicene and Post-Nicene Fathers
NRSV	New Revised Standard Version
NRT	*Nouvelle revue théologique*
NSchol	*New Scholasticism*

OBL	Orientalia et Biblica Lovaniensia
OBO	Orbis Biblicus et Orientalis
OCA	Orientalia Christiana Analecta
OCD	*Oxford Classical Dictionary*
OLD	*Oxford Latin Dictionary*
OrAnt	*Oriens antiquus*
OrChr	*Oriens christianus*
OTP	*The Old Testament Pseudepigrapha* (ed. J. H. Charlesworth)
OTS	Oudtestamentische Studiën
PAAJR	Proceedings of the American Academy for Jewish Research
PBA	Proceedings of the British Academy
PG	Patrologiae cursus completus. Series Graeca (ed. J.-P. Migne)
PhBelg	Philosophes Belges
PIEM	Publications de l'Institut d'études médiévales
PIEMO	Publications de l'Institut d'études médiévales d'Ottawa
PL	Patrologiae cursus completus. Series Latina (ed. J.-P. Migne)
PLSup	Patrologiae Latinae supplementum
PrJ	Preussische Jahrbücher
PTA	Papyrologische Texte und Abhandlungen
PVTG	Pseudepigrapha Veteris Testamenti graece
PW	Real-Encyclopädie der classischen Altertumswissenschaft (Pauly-Wissowa)
PWSup	Supplements to PW
QD	Quaestiones disputatae
RAC	*Reallexikon für Antike und Christentum*
RAug	*Recherches Augustiniennes*
RB	*Revue biblique*
RBén	*Revue bénédictine; de critique, d'histoire et de littérature religieuses*
RBMA	Repertorium biblicum medii aevi
RBPH	*Revue Belge de philologie et d'histoire*
REAug	*Revue des études augustiniennes*
REB	*The Revised English Bible*
RechBib	Recherches bibliques
REJ	*Revue des études juives*
REL	*Revue des études latines*
RelSt	*Religious Studies*
RFNS	*Rivista di filosofia neo-scolastica*
ResQ	*Restoration Quarterly*
RevQ	*Revue de Qumran*
RGG^3	*Religion in Geschichte und Gegenwart* (3rd ed.)
RHE	*Revue d'histoire ecclésiastique*
RHPR	*Revue d'histoire et de philosophie religieuses*
RHSp	*Revue d'histoire de la spiritualité*
RivB	*Rivista biblica*
RMAL	*Revue du moyen-âge latin*
RMab	*Revue Mabillon*
RNord	*Revue du Nord*
RöHM	Römische Historische Mitteilungen

RQ — *Römische Quartalschrift für christliche Altertumskunde und Kirchengeschichte*
RQSuppl — RQ Supplement
RSLR — Rivista di storia e letteratura religiosa
RSPT — *Revue des sciences philosophiques et théologiques*
RSR — *Recherches de science religieuse*
RSV — *Revised Standard Version*
RSyn — *Revue de synthèse*
RT(h)AM — *Recherches de théologie ancienne et médiévale*
RThom — *Revue Thomiste*
RTL — *Revue théologique de Lovain*
RVV — Religionsgeschichtliche Versuche und Vorarbeiten

SacEr — *Sacris erudiri*
Saec. — *Saeculum*
SANT — Studien zum Alten und Neuen Testament
SAQ — Sammlung ausgewählter kirchen- und dogmengeschichtlicher Quellenschriften
SB — Sources bibliques
SBJ — *La Sainte Bible de Jérusalem* (cf. JB)
SBLDS — SBL Dissertation Series
SBLMS — SBL Monograph Series
SBLSCS — SBL Septuagint and Cognate Studies (cf. SCS)
SC — Sources chrétiennes
ScrHier — Scripta Hierosolymitana
SCS — Septuagint and Cognate Studies (cf. SBLSCS)
SEAug — Studia ephemerides "Augustinianum"
Sef. — *Sefarad*
SF — Studia Friburgensia
SGLG — Studia Graeca et Latina Gothoburgensia
SHT — Studies in Historical Theology
SJ — Studia Judaica
SJLA — Studies in Judaism in Late Antiquity
SJT — *Scottish Journal of Theology*
SMGH — Schriften der Monumenta Germaniae historica
SMRH — Studies in Medieval and Renaissance History
SOTSMS — The Society for Old Testament Study Monograph Series
SPB — Studia postbiblica
Spec. — *Speculum. A Journal of Mediaeval Studies*
SpicBon — Spicilegium Bonaventurianum
SR — *Studies in Religion / Sciences religieues*
SSAM — Settimane di studio del centro italiano di studi sull'alto medioevo (Settimane di Spoleto)
SSL — Spicilegium sacrum Lovaniense
StAns — Studia Anselmiana
STGMA — Studien und Texte zur Geistesgeschichte des Mittelalters
StIsl — *Studia Islamica*
StPatr — Studia patristica
STPIMS — Studies and Texts. Pontifical Institute of Mediaeval Studies (St. Michael's College, Univ. of Toronto)
StTh — *Studia Theologica*

TAPhS — Transactions of the American Philosophical Society
TaS — Texts and Studies

ThBü	Theologische Bücherei
ThLZ	*Theologische Literaturzeitung*
ThPh	*Theologie und Philosophie*
ThR	*Theologische Rundschau*
THS	Transactions of the Royal Historical Society
ThW	Theologische Wissenschaft (Stuttgart)
TJHSE	Transactions. Jewish Historical Society of England
TQ	*Theologische Quartalschrift*
TRE	*Theologische Realenzyklopädie*
TS	*Theological Studies*
TSMAO	Typologie des sources du moyen âge occidental
TSMJ	Texts and Studies in Medieval and Early Modern Judaism
TU	Texte und Untersuchungen zur Geschichte der altchristlichen Literatur
TZ	*Theologische Zeitschrift*
VD	*Verbum Domini*
VF	*Verkündigung und Forschung*
VGI	Veröffentlichungen des Grabmann-Instituts
VivPen	*Vivre et penser*
VT	*Vetus Testamentum*
VTSup	Supplements to VT
WA	Weimarer Ausgabe (M. Luther, Werke. Kritische Gesamtausgabe)
WDB	*Westminster Dictionary of the Bible*
WdF	Wege der Forschung
WSAMA.P	Walberger Studien der Albertus-Magnus-Akademie - Philosophische Reihe
WTJ	*Westminster Theological Journal*
WUNT	Wissenschaftliche Untersuchungen zum Neuen Testament
YJS	Yale Judaica Series
ZAW	*Zeitschrift für die alttestamentliche Wissenschaft*
ZHB	*Zeitschrift für hebräische Bibliographie*
ZHT	*Zeitschrift für historische Theologie*
ZKG	*Zeitschrift für Kirchengeschichte*
ZKT	*Zeitschrift für katholische Theologie*
ZNW	*Zeitschrift für die Neutestamentliche Wissenschaft*
ZPE	*Zeitschrift für Papyrologie und Epigraphik*
ZTK	*Zeitschrift für Theologie und Kirche*
ZWJ	*Zeitschrift für Wissenschaft des Judentums*

Indexes

Names/Topics/References

Names

1. Biblical and Classical Names

There may be minor differences in the spelling of the names

2. Modern Authors

From about 1650

Topics

Arabic, Aramaic, Hebrew, Syriac as well as Greek titles and terms
are presented in transcription

References

The references are divided into the following groups: 1. Hebrew Bible / Old Testament (687); 2. Hellenistic-Jewish Literature (702); 3. Apocrypha and Pseudepigrapha (702); 4. Qumran (705); 5. New Testament (706); 6. Targum (706); 7. Mishnah (706); 8. Midrash and Related Works (707); 9. The Palestinian Talmud (707); 10. The Babylonian Talmud (707); 11. Greek and Latin Authors (709); 12. Early Christian Writings (709); 13. Christian Medieval Writings (710); 14. Jewish Medieval Writings (721); 15. Arabic Medieval Writings (729); 16. Various (729) – Due to the usage of the individual contributors there are minor variants in the writing of some titles, and there may be shift of traditional Latin and modern English names of Classical and Medieval works. – As for references with Septuagint deviations square brackets are used.

1. Hebrew Bible / Old Testament

Genesis 116, 123, 134, 178, 183, 185–186, 188–193, 201–202, 204, 208–210, 216, 229, 240, 246, 248, 254–256, 277, 309, 363, 367, 371, 378, 380, 396, 420, 435, 488, 499, 507, 514, 515, 529, 562, 568, 570–571, 573–574, 611–612, 615

1–3 318, 609, 615, 617
1 83, 118, 525–527, 612
1:1 61, 201, 223
1:1–2 612
1:1–2:4a 614
1:1–2:7 563
1:1–2:15 525
1:1–21:10 187
1:2 546
1:3 305, 391, 399
1:4 226
1:5 252, 432
1:8 226, 252
1:9–10 226
1:11 226
1:12 226
1:14–19 85, 226
1:16 226
1:21 229
1:22 70, 435
1:26 85, 250, 612
1:26–27 609
1:28 612
2–3 78
2:1 398
2:3 186
2:7 613
2:7–5:1 396, 398
2:10–14 402
2:11 380
2:15 83
2:17 606
2:19–20 233
2:20 58
2:21 399, 435, 471, 609
3:1 305, 385
3:2 186
3:7 57, 221, 252, 335
3:12 70
3:20 80, 603
3:21 229
3:22 250
3:32 381
4–5 318
4:1–17 207, 217
4:5–6 615
4:7 254
4:13 59
4:15 229

28:12–13	316
28:20	440
29:1	403
29:20	437
29:63	440
30:1	432
30:15	432
30:30	399, 432
31:7	436
31:43	94
32:4	411
32:7	403
32:8	402
32:11	440
32:14	411
32:26	409, 452
34:25	403
34:31	409
35:22	385
36:2	382
36:12	427
36:24	393
36:31	430
36:31–36	383
37:1	336
37:2	57, 324
37:4	448
37:12	409
37:31	70
37:34–35	403
38:1	386
38:9	92
39:7	411
39:8	72
39:8–9	427
41:1–8	523
41:6	406
41:49	86
41:54	81
41:56	84
41:57	81, 401
42:9	403
42:29–34	59
44:15	305
44:21	69
44:25	69
46:2	422
46:15	128, 393
46:18–19	427
46:26–27	72
47:31	86
48:3	445
48:8	81
48:10	81, 411
48:17–20	427
49	122, 404
49:6	385
49:9	394, 404
49:10	438, 588–589
49:17	404
49:19	380
49:22	296

Exodus

	122, 184, 186, 216, 255, 277, 359, 367, 371, 378, 420–421, 423, 435, 503, 570, 611–612, 614–615
1:1	122
1:7	286, 379
1:15–16	422
2:5	108
2:15	360
3	471
3:5	453
3:14	310, 612
3:15	382
3:22	362
4:9	422
4:20	423
6:3	380, 445
7–12	614
7:1	219
7:20	219
7:24	380
8:22	612
9:6	401
9:10	380
9:23 ff	108
9:32	568
10:21	288
11:4	384
12:1	384
12:4	265
12:9	107, 130
13:9	381
13:16	431
14:2	436
14:19	386
15	122, 613
15:1–19	253
15:1 ff	294
15:5	265

2. Hellenistic–Jewish Literature

3. Apocrypha and Pseudepigrapha

4. Qumran

5. New Testament

6. Targum

7. Mishnah

8. Midrash and Related Works

Genesis Rabba
8:9 62
28:9 425
30:8 409
39:7 422
53:15 133
59:11 400
60:8 428
68:12 318
70:8 403
76:2 402
84:21 403
91:5 84

Exodus Rabba
9:1 62
14:1 288

Numeri Rabba
13:15 57

Bereshit Rabba
588

Aggadat Bereshit
44 588

Mekilta Shirata
285

Mekilta Baḥodesh
5 61

Midraš ha-neʿelam
450

Midrash Pirqê de Rabbi ʾEliʿezer
13 317

Midrash Rabbah
481, 488, 507

Pesikta Rabbati
3:2 62

Seder ʿOlam
488

Tanḥuma Buber Toldot
20 (70a–b) 588

Yalqut Shimʿoni
750 273

9. The Palestinian Talmud

Berakot
4:3(8a) 89

Demai
5:2(24c) 89

Ketubot
8:11(32c) 419

Qiddushin
27b 89

Šabbat
15:2(15c) 89

10. The Babylonian Talmud

ʿAboda Zara
58b 62

Baba Batra
10a 393
15a 62, 394, 408
16a 318
119b 432
123b 393

Berakot
4a 61

11. Greek and Latin Authors

12. Early Christian Writings

13. Christian Medieval Writings

Commentary on Luke
552

Vita (of St. Francis)
548

Bullarium Fransiscanum
168

Capitula de examinandis ecclesiasticis
802 156

Capitulare missorum
803 156

Cassiodorus
Expositio
503

Explanation of the Psalms
1 523

Institutiones
204

Claudius of Turin
Quaestiones super libros Regum
222

Conciliorum Oecumenicorum Decreta (COD)
139f Can.2 156
220 Can.18 157
240 Const.11 157
326f 169

Codex Theodosianus
XVI.8.4 49

Commentary on the Pentateuch (anon.)
566, 568–569, 571

Constitutiones fratrum predicatorum (1228)
dist.1 c.4 166
dist.2 c.16 166
dist.2 c.23 166
dist.2 c.29 166, 173
dist.2 c.31 165
dist.2 c.36 166

Constitutiones fratrum predicatorum (1238–40)
dist.2 c.1 166
dist.2 c.14 166

Chartularium Universitatis Parisiensis (CUP)
1,113 no.57. 173
1,175f no.133. 164
1,183f no.146. 164
1,226 176
1,226f no.200. 168
1,251 no. 227. 164
1,253 no.230. 174
1,290f no.254. 164
1,319–26 no.280–82. 169
1,362 no.314. 169
1,385f 173
1,389 no.340. 164
1,405f no.358. 169
1,409f no.360. 169
1,410f no.361. 164
1,418f no.370. 164
1,530–32 no.461. 174
1,59–61 no.1. 162
1,78–80 no.20. 162, 174–175
1,85 no.27. 174
1,90–93 no.32. 163
2,554–56 no.1096. 173
2,672–686 no.1185. 174
2,683 no.1185. 177
2,691–697 no.1188. 175
2,692 176
2,697–704 no.1189. 176
2,698 no.1189. 170
2,700 176

Dadišoʿ Qaṭraya
Commentary on the Asceticon of Abba Isaiah
565

Denḥa-Grigor
Commentary on Psalms
572

Dionysius bar Ṣalibi
Commentary on the Old Testament
573

Diyarbakir Commentary on Gen–Exod 9:32
568–569, 571

Dominic Grima of Toulouse
Lectura super Bibliam
544

14. Jewish Medieval Writings

15. Arabic Medieval Writings

16. Various

Kultureller Wandel im Mittelalter

Wolfgang Hage

Das Christentum im frühen Mittelalter (476–1054)

Vom Ende des weströmischen Reiches bis zum west-östlichen Schisma.
Zugänge zur Kirchengeschichte, Band 4 / Kleine Vandenhoeck-Reihe, Band 1567.
1993. 192 Seiten, 11 Karten, kartoniert
ISBN 3-525-33590-3

Diese Darstellung behandelt die kirchengeschichtliche Entwicklung im Abendland und darüber hinaus auch die Geschichte der Christenheit in Byzanz und im vor- und frühislamischen Orient und sprengt damit den traditionellen eurozentrischen Rahmen.

Otto Brunner

Sozialgeschichte Europas im Mittelalter

Kleine Vandenhoeck-Reihe, Band 1442.
2. Auflage 1984. 104 Seiten, kartoniert
ISBN 3-525-33422-2

Klar zusammenfassend und mit begrifflicher Präzision beschreibt Otto Brunner die innere Struktur von Staat und Gesellschaft im Mittelalter, die Tatsachen des menschlichen Zusammenlebens und dessen Ordnungen im mittelalterlichen Europa.

Horst Fuhrmann

Deutsche Geschichte im hohen Mittelalter

Deutsche Geschichte, Band 2 / Kleine Vandenhoeck-Reihe, Band 1438.
3., durchgesehene und bibliographisch ergänzte Auflage 1993. 277 Seiten, kartoniert
ISBN 3-525-33589-X

Die chronologische Darstellung beschreibt den tiefgreifenden politischen und sozialen, wirtschaftlichen und kulturellen Wandel, der sich zwischen der Mitte des 11. und dem Beginn des 13. Jh. vollzog.

Herbert Grundmann

Ketzergeschichte des Mittelalters

Die Kirche in ihrer Geschichte, Band 2, Lieferung G/1.
3., durchgesehene Auflage 1978.
IV, 67 Seiten, kartoniert
ISBN 3-525-52327-0

Inhalt: Häresien im Fränkischen Reich / Die ersten Ketzergruppen im Abendland / Ketzerei im Zeitalter der Kirchenreform und des Investiturstreits / Häretische Wanderprediger und Sektierer in der ersten Hälfte des 12. Jh. / Ketzerprozesse gegen Theologen im 12. Jh. / Die Katharer / Waldenser und Humiliaten / Kirchliche Maßnahmen gegen Ketzerei – Entstehung der Inquisition / Spiritualistische und philosophische Häresien im 13. Jh. / Häretische Beginen und Begarden im 14. Jh. / Politik und Ketzerei bis zu den Hussitenkriegen.

„... Herbert Grundmanns knappe Darstellung ist immer klar geprägt und äußerst objektiv gehalten. Sie ist mit einer gut ausgewählten, oft von kurzen, kritischen Stellungnahmen begleiteten Bibliographie versehen. Grundmann vermeidet es, geschichtsphilosophische Deutungsprinzipien anzuwenden, und grenzt sich sehr bestimmt gegen zu einseitige marxistische Auffassungen und Deutungen ab.“

Historische Zeitschrift

V&R
Vandenhoeck & Ruprecht